MW01146626

H. L. MENCKEN

Six Book Collection

The American Credo

The American Language

The Philosophy Of Friedrich Nietzsche

A Book Of Burlesques

A Book Of Prefaces

Damn! A Book Of Calumny

CONTENTS

BOOK ONE. THE AMERICAN CREDO

PREFACE

THE AMERICAN CREDO

BOOK TWO. THE AMERICAN LANGUAGE

PREFACE

I. By Way of Introduction

FOOTNOTES:

II. The Beginnings of American

FOOTNOTES:

III. The Period of Growth

FOOTNOTES:

IV. American and English Today

FOOTNOTES:

V. Tendencies in American

FOOTNOTES:

VI. The Common Speech

FOOTNOTES:

VII. Differences in Spelling

FOOTNOTES:

VIII. Proper Names in America

FOOTNOTES:

IX. Miscellanea

FOOTNOTES:

Bibliography

List of Words and Phrases

BOOK THREE. THE PHILOSOPHY OF FRIEDRICH NIETZSCHE

PREFACE TO THE THIRD EDITION

PART ONE. NIETZSCHE THE MAN

I. BOYHOOD AND YOUTH

II. THE BEGINNINGS OF THE PHILOSOPHER

III. BLAZING A NEW PATH

IV. THE PROPHET OF THE SUPERMAN

V. THE PHILOSOPHER AND THE MAN

PART TWO. NIETZSCHE THE PHILOSOPHER

I. DIONYSUS VERSUS APOLLO

II. THE ORIGIN OF MORALITY

III. BEYOND GOOD AND EVIL

IV. THE SUPERMAN

V. ETERNAL RECURRENCE

VI. CHRISTIANITY

VII. TRUTH

VIII. CIVILIZATION

IX. WOMEN AND MARRIAGE

X. GOVERNMENT

XI. CRIME AND PUNISHMENT

XII. EDUCATION

XIII. SUNDRY IDEAS

XIV. NIETZSCHE VS. WAGNER

PART THREE. NIETZSCHE THE PROPHET

I. NIETZSCHE'S ORIGINS

II. NIETZSCHE AND HIS CRITICS

HOW TO STUDY NIETZSCHE

BOOK FOUR. A BOOK OF BURLESQUES

I.—DEATH I.—Death. A Philosophical Discussion

II.—FROM THE PROGRAMME OF A CONCERT

III.—The Wedding. A Stage Direction

IV.—The Visionary

V.—The Artist. A Drama Without Words

VI.—Seeing The World

VII.—From the Memoirs of the Devil

VIII.—Litanies for the Overlooked

IX.—Asepsis. A Deduction in Scherzo Form

X.—Tales of the Moral and Pathological

XI. The Jazz Webster

XII.—The Old Subject

XIII.—Panoramas of People

XIV.—Homeopathics

XV.—Vers Libre

BOOK FIVE. A BOOK OF PREFACES

PREFACE TO THE FOURTH EDITION

I. JOSEPH CONRAD

II. THEODORE DREISER

III. JAMES HUNEKER

IV. PURITANISM AS A LITERARY FORCE

DAMN! A BOOK OF CALUMNY

I. PATER PATRLÆ

II. THE REWARD OF THE ARTIST

III. THE HEROIC CONSIDERED

IV. THE BURDEN OF HUMOR

V. THE SAVING GRACE

VI. MORAL INDIGNATION

VII. STABLE-NAMES

VIII. THE JEWS

IX. THE COMSTOCKIAN PREMISS

X. THE LABIAL INFAMY

XI. A TRUE ASCETIC   .

XII. ON LYING

XIII. HISTORY

XIV. THE CURSE OF CIVILIZATION

XV. EUGENICS

XVI. THE JOCOSE GODS

XVII. WAR

XVIII. MORALIST AND ARTIST

XIX. ACTORS

XX. THE CROWD

XXI. AN AMERICAN PHILOSOPHER

XXII. CLUBS

XXIII. FIDELIS AD URNUM

XXIV. A THEOLOGICAL MYSTERY

XXV. THE TEST OF TRUTH

XXVI. LITERARY INDECENCIES

XXVII. VIRTUOUS VANDALISM

XXVIII. A FOOTNOTE ON THE DUEL OF SEX

XXIX. ALCOHOL

XXX. THOUGHTS ON THE VOLUPTUOUS

XXXI. THE HOLY ESTATE

XXXII. DICHTUNG UND WAHRHEIT

XXXIII. WILD SHOTS

XXXIV. BEETHOVEN

XXXV. THE TONE ART

XXXVI. ZOOS

XXXVII. ON HEARING MOZART

XXXVIII. THE ROAD TO DOUBT

XXXIX. A NEW USE FOR CHURCHES

XL. THE ROOT OF RELIGION

XLI. FREE WILL

XLII. QUID EST VERITAS?

XLIII. THE DOUBTER'S REWARD

XLIV. BEFORE THE ALTAR

XLV. THE MASK

XLVI. PIA VENEZIANI, POI CRISTIANI

XLVII. OFF AGAIN, ON AGAIN

XLVIII. THEOLOGY

XLIX. EXEMPLI GRATIA

BOOK ONE.
THE AMERICAN CREDO

A Contribution Toward the Interpretation of the National Mind
WITH GEORGE JEAN NATHAN

PREFACE

I

The superficial, no doubt, will mistake this little book for a somewhat laborious attempt at jocosity. Because, incidentally to its main purpose, it unveils occasional ideas of so inordinate an erroneousness that they verge upon the ludicrous, it will be set down a piece of spoofing, and perhaps denounced as in bad taste. But all the while that main purpose will remain clear enough to the judicious. It is, in brief, the purpose of clarifying the current exchange of rhetorical gas bombs upon the subject of American ideals and the American character, so copious, so cocksure and withal so ill-informed and inconclusive, by putting into plain propositions some of the notions that lie at the heart of those ideals and enter into the very substance of that character. "For as he thinketh in his heart, " said Solomon, "so *is* he." It is a saying, obviously, that one may easily fill with fantastic meanings, as the prevailing gabble of the mental healers, New Thoughters, efficiency engineers, professors of scientific salesmanship and other such mountebanks demonstrates, but nevertheless it is one grounded, at bottom, upon an indubitable fact. Deep down in every man there is a body of congenital attitudes, a corpus of ineradicable doctrines and ways of thinking, that determines his reactions to his ideational environment as surely as his physical activity is determined by the length of his *tibiæ* and the capacity of his lungs. These primary attitudes, in fact, constitute the essential man. It is by recognition of them that one arrives at an accurate understanding of his place and function as a member of human society; it is by a shrewd reckoning and balancing of them, one against another, that one forecasts his probable behaviour in the face of unaccustomed stimuli.

All the arts and sciences that have to do with the management of men in the mass are founded upon a proficient practice of that sort of reckoning. The practical politician, as every connoisseur of ochlocracy knows, is not a man who seeks to inoculate the innumerable caravan of voters with new ideas; he is a man who seeks to search out and prick into energy the basic ideas that are already in them, and to turn the resultant effervescence of emotion to his own uses. And so with the religious teacher, the social and economic reformer, and every other variety of popular educator, down to and including the humblest press-agent of a fifth assistant Secretary of State, moving-picture actor, or Y.M.C.A. boob-squeezing committee. Such adept professors of conviction and enthusiasm, in the true sense, never actually teach anything new; all they do is to give new forms to beliefs already in being, to arrange the bits of glass, onyx, horn, ivory, porphyry and corundum in the mental kaleidoscope of the populace into novel permutations. To change the figure, they may give the medulla oblongata, the cerebral organ of the great masses of simple men, a powerful diuretic or emetic, but they seldom, if ever, add anything to its primary supply of fats, proteids and carbohydrates.

One speaks of the great masses of simple men, and it is of them, of course, that the ensuing treatise chiefly has to say. The higher and more delicately organized tribes and sects of men are susceptible to no such ready anatomizing, for the body of beliefs upon which their ratiocination grounds itself is not fixed but changing, and not artless and crystal-clear but excessively complex and obscure. It is, indeed, the chief mark of a man emerged from the general that he has lost most of his original certainties, and is full of a scepticism which plays like a spray of acid upon all the ideas that come within his purview, including especially his own. One does not become surer as one advances in knowledge, but less sure. No article of faith is proof against the disintegrating effects of increasing information; one might almost describe the acquirement of knowledge as a process of disillusion. But among the humbler ranks of men who make up the great bulk of every civilized people the increase of information is so slow and so arduous that this effect is scarcely to be discerned. If, in the course of long years, they gradually lose their old faiths, it is only to fill the gaps with new faiths that restate the old ones in new terms. Nothing, in fact, could be more commonplace than the observation that the crazes which periodically ravage the proletariat today are, in the main, no more than distorted echoes of delusions cherished centuries ago. The fundamental religious ideas of the lower orders of Christendom have not changed materially in two thousand years, and they were old when they were first borrowed from the heathen of northern Africa and Asia Minor. The Iowa Methodist of today, imagining him competent to understand them at all, would be able to accept the tenets of Augustine without changing more than a few accents and punctuation marks. Every Sunday his raucous ecclesiastics batter his ears with diluted and debased filches from *De Civitate Dei*, and almost every article of his practical ethics may be found clearly stated in the eminent bishop's Ninety-third Epistle. And so in politics. The Bolsheviki of the present not only poll-parrot the balderdash of the French demagogues of 1789; they also mouth what was gospel to every *bête blonde* in the Teutonic forest of the fifth century. Truth shifts and changes like a cataract of diamonds; its aspect is never precisely the same at two successive instants. But error flows down the channel of history like some great stream of lava or infinitely lethargic glacier. It is the one relatively fixed thing in a world of chaos. It is, perhaps, the one thing that gives human society the small stability that it needs, amid all the oscillation of a gelatinous cosmos, to save it from the wreck that ever menaces. Without their dreams men would have fallen upon and devoured one another long ago—and yet every dream is an illusion, and every illusion is a lie.

Nevertheless, this immutability of popular ideas is not quite perfect. The main current, no doubt, goes on unbrokenly, but there are many eddies along the edges and many small tempests on the surface. Thus the aspect changes, if not the substance. What men believe in one century is apparently abandoned in some other century, and perhaps supplanted by something quite to the contrary. Or, at all events, to the contrary in appearance. Off goes the head of the king, and tyranny gives way to freedom. The change seems abysmal. Then, bit by bit, the face of freedom hardens, and by and by it is the old face of tyranny. Then another cycle, and another. But under the play of all these opposites there is something fundamental and permanent—the basic delusion that men may be governed and yet be free. It is only on the surface that there are transformations—and these we must study and make the most of, for of what is underneath men are mainly unconscious. The thing that colours the upper levels is largely the instinctive functioning of race and nationality, the ineradicable rivalry of tribe and tribe, the primary struggle for existence. At bottom, no doubt, the plain men of the whole world are almost indistinguishably alike; a learned anthropologist, Prof. Dr. Boas, has written a book to prove it. But, collected into herds, they gather delusions that are special to herds. Beside the underlying mass thinking there is a superimposed group thinking—a sort of unintelligent class consciousness. This we may prod into. This, in the case of the *Homo americanus*, is what is prodded into in the present work. We perform, it seems to us, a useful pioneering.

Incomplete though our data may be, it is at least grounded upon a resolute avoidance of *a priori* methods, an absolutely open-minded effort to get at the facts. We pounce upon them as they bob up, convinced that even the most inconsiderable of them may have its profound significance—that the essential may be hidden in the trivial. All we aim at is a first marshalling of materials, an initial running of lines. We are not architects, but furnishers of bricks, nails and laths. But it is our hope that what we thus rake up and pile into a rough heap may yet serve the purposes of an organizer, and so help toward the establishment of the dim and vacillating truth, and rid the scene of, at all events, the worst and most obvious of its present accumulation of errors.

II

In the case of the American of the multitude that accumulation of errors is of astounding bulk and consequence. His ideas are not only grossly misapprehended by all foreigners; they are often misapprehended by his own countrymen of superior education, and even by himself.

This last, at first blush, may seem a mere effort at paradox, but its literal truth becomes patent on brief inspection. Ask the average American what is the salient passion in his emotional armamentarium—what is the idea that lies at the bottom of all his other ideas—and it is very probable that, nine times out of ten, he will nominate his hot and unquenchable rage for liberty. He regards himself, indeed, as the chief exponent of liberty in the whole world, and all its other advocates as no more than his followers, half timorous and half envious. To question his ardour is to insult him as grievously as if one questioned the honour of the republic or the chastity of his wife. And yet it must be plain to any dispassionate observer that this ardour, in the course of a century and a half, has lost a large part of its old burning reality and descended to the estate of a mere phosphorescent superstition. The American of today, in fact, probably enjoys less personal liberty than any other man of Christendom, and even his political liberty is fast succumbing to the new dogma that certain theories of government are virtuous and lawful and others abhorrent and felonious. Laws limiting the radius of his free activity multiply year by year: it is now practically impossible for him to exhibit anything describable as genuine individuality, either in action or in thought, without running afoul of some harsh and unintelligible penalty. It would surprise no impartial observer if the motto, *In God we trust,* were one day expunged from the coins of the republic by the Junkers at Washington, and the far more appropriate word, *Verboten*, substituted. Nor would it astound any save the most romantic if, at the same time, the goddess of liberty were taken off the silver dollars to make room for a bas relief of a policeman in a spiked helmet.

Moreover, this gradual (and, of late, rapidly progressive) decay of freedom goes almost without challenge; the American has grown so accustomed to the denial of his constitutional rights and to the minute regulation of his conduct by swarms of spies, letter-openers, informers and *agents provocateurs* that he no longer makes any serious protest. It is surely a significant fact that, in the face of the late almost incredible proceedings under the so-called Espionage Act and other such laws, the only objections heard of came either from the persons directly affected—nine-tenths of them Socialists, pacifists, or citizens accused of German sympathies, and hence without any rights whatever in American law and equity—or from a small group of professional libertarians, chiefly naturalized aliens. The American people, as a people, acquiesced docilely in all these tyrannies, both during the war and after the war, just as they acquiesced in the invasion of their common rights by the Prohibition Amendment. Worse, they not only acquiesced docilely; they approved actively; they were quite as hotly against the few protestants as they were against the original victims, and gave their hearty approbation to every proposal that the former be punished too. The really startling phenomenon of the war, indeed, was not the grotesque abolition of liberty in the name of liberty, but the failure of that usurpation to arouse anything approaching public indignation. It is impossible to imagine the men of Jackson's army or even of Grant's army submitting to any such absolutism without a furious struggle, but in these latter days it is viewed with the utmost complacency. The descendants of the Americans who punished John Adams so melodramatically for the Alien and Seditions Acts of 1789 failed to raise a voice against the far more drastic legislation of 1917. What is more, they failed to raise a voice against its execution upon the innocent as well as upon the guilty, in gross violation of the most elemental principles of justice and rules of law.

Thus the Americano, put to the test, gave the lie to what is probably his proudest boast, and revealed the chronic human incapacity for accurate self-analysis. But if he thereby misjudged and misjudges himself, he may find some consolation for his error in the lavishness with which even worse misjudgment is heaped upon him by foreigners. To this day, despite the intimate contact of five long years of joint war, the French and the English are ignorant of his true character, and show it in their every discussion of him, particularly when they discuss him in camera. It is the secret but general view of the French, we are informed by confidential agents, that he is a fellow of loose life and not to be trusted with either a wine-pot, a virgin or a domestic fowl—an absurdly inaccurate generalization from the aberrations of soldiers in a far land, cut off from the moral repressions that lie upon them and colour all their acts at home. It is the view of the English, so we hear upon equally reliable authority, that he is an earnest but extremely inefficient oaf, incapable of either the finer technic of war or of its machine-like discipline—another thumping error, for the American is actually extraordinarily adept and ingenious in the very arts that modern war chiefly makes use of, and there is, since the revolt of the Prussian, no other such rigidly regimented man in the world. He has, indeed, reached such a pass in the latter department that it has become almost impossible for him to think of himself save as an obedient member of some vast, powerful and unintelligibly despotic organization—a church, a trades-union, a political party, a tin-pot fraternal order, or what not—, and often he is a member of more than one, and impartially faithful to all. Moreover, as we have seen, he lives under laws which dictate almost every detail of his public and private conduct, and punish every sign of bad discipline with the most appalling rigour; and these laws are enforced by police who supply the chance gaps in them extempore, and exercise that authority in the best manner of prison guards, animal trainers and drill sergeants.

The English and the French, beside these special errors, have a full share in an error that is also embraced by practically every other foreign people. This is the error of assuming, almost as an axiom beyond question, that the Americans are a sordid, money-grubbing people, with no thought above the dollar. You will find it prevailing everywhere on the Continent of Europe. To the German the United States is Dollarica, and the salient American personality, next to the policeman who takes bribes and the snuffling moralist in office, is the Dollarprinzessin. To the Italian the country is a sort of savage wilderness in which everything else, from religion to beauty and from decent repose to human life, is sacrificed to profit. Italians cross the ocean in much the same spirit that our runaway school-boys used to go off to fight the Indians. Some, lucky, return home in a few years with fortunes and gaudy tales; others, succumbing to the natives, are butchered at their labour and buried beneath the cinders of hideous and God-forsaken mining towns. All carry the thought of escape from beginning to end; every Italian hopes to get away with his takings as soon as possible, to enjoy them on some hillside where life and property are reasonably safe from greed. So with the Russian, the Scandinavian, the Balkan hillman, even the Greek and Armenian. The picture of America that they conjure up is a picture of a titanic and merciless struggle for gold, with the stakes high and the contestants correspondingly ferocious. They see the American as one to whom nothing under the sun has any value save the dollar—not truth, or beauty, or philosophical ease, or the common decencies between man and man.

This view, of course, is full of distortion and misunderstanding, despite the fact that even Americans, by hearing it stated so often, have come to allow it a good deal of soundness. The American's concept of himself, as we have seen, is sometimes anything but accurate; in this case he errs almost as greatly as when he venerates himself as the prince of freemen, with gyveless wrists and flashing eyes. As for the foreigner, what he falls into is the typically Freudian blunder of projecting his own worst weakness into another. The fact is that it is he, and not the native American, who is the incorrigible and unimaginative money-grubber. He comes to the United States in search of money, and in search of money alone, and pursuing that single purpose without deviation he makes the mistake of assuming that the American is at the same business, and in the same fanatical manner. From all the complex and colourful life of the country, save only the one enterprise of money-making, he is shut off almost hermetically, and so he concludes that that one enterprise embraces the whole show. Here the unreliable promptings of his sub-conscious passion are helped out by observations that are more logical. Unfamiliar with the language, excluded from all free social intercourse with the native, and regarded as, if actually human at all, then at least a distinctly inferior member of the species, he is forced into the harshest and most ill-paid labour, and so he inevitably sees the American as a pitiless task-master and ascribes the exploitation he is made a victim of to a fabulous exaggeration of his own avarice.

Moreover, the greater success and higher position of the native seem to bear out this notion. In a struggle that is free for all and to the death, the native grabs all the shiniest stakes. *Ergo*, he must love money even more than the immigrant. This logic we do not defend, but there is—and out of it grows the prevailing foreign view of America and the Americans, for the foreigner who stays at home does not derive his ideas from the glittering, lascivious phrases of Dr. Wilson or from the passionate idealism of such superior Americans as Otto H. Kahn, Adolph S. Ochs, S. Stanwood Menken, Jacob H. Schiff, Marcus Loew, Henry Morgenthau, Abram Elkus, Samuel Goldfish, Louis D. Brandeis, Julius Rosenwald, Paul Warburg, Judge Otto Rosalsky, Adolph Zukor, the Hon. Julius Kahn, Simon Guggenheim, Stephen S. Wise and Barney Baruch, but from the hair-raising tales of returned "Americans, " *i.e.*, fellow peasants who, having braved the dragons, have come back to the fatherland to enjoy their booty and exhibit their wounds.

The native, as we say, has been so far influenced by this error that he cherishes it himself, or, more accurately, entertains it with shame. Most of his windy idealism is no more than a reaction against it—an evidence of an effort to confute it and live it down. He is never more sweetly flattered than when some politician eager for votes or some evangelist itching for a good plate tells him that he is actually a soaring altruist, and the only real one in the world. This is the surest way to fetch him; he never fails to swell out his chest when he hears that buncombe. In point of fact, of course, he is no more an altruist than any other healthy mammal. His ideals, one and all, are grounded upon self-interest, or upon the fear that is at the bottom of it; his benevolence always has a string tied to it; he could no more formulate a course of action to his certain disadvantage than an Englishman could, or a Frenchman, or an Italian, or a German. But to say that the advantage he pursues is always, or even usually, a monetary one—to argue that he is avaricious, or even, in these later years, a sharp trader—is to spit directly into the eye of the truth. There is probably, indeed, no country in the world in which mere money is held in less esteem than in these United States. Even more than the Russian Bolshevik the American democrat regards wealth with suspicion, and its too eager amassment with a bilious eye. Here alone, west of the Dvina, rich men are *ipso facto* scoundrels and *feræ naturæ*, with no rights that any slanderer is bound to respect. Here alone, the possession of a fortune puts a man automatically upon the defensive, and exposes him to special legislation of a rough and inquisitorial character and to the special animosity of judges, district attorneys and juries. It would be a literal impossibility for an Englishman worth $100, 000, 000 to avoid public office and public honour; it would be equally impossible for an American worth $100, 000, 000 to obtain either.

Americans, true enough, enjoy an average of prosperity that is above that witnessed in any other country. Their land, with less labour, yields a greater usufruct than other land; they get more money for their industry; they jingle more coin in their pockets than other peoples. But it is a grievous error to mistake that superior opulence for a sign of money-hunger, for they actually hold money very lightly, and spend a great deal more of it than any other race of men and with far less thought of values. The normal French family, it is often said, could live very comfortably for a week upon what the normal American family wastes in a week. There is, among Americans, not the slightest sign of the unanimous French habit of biting every franc, of calculating the cost of every luxury to five places of decimals, of utilizing every scrap, of sleeping with the bankbook under the pillow. Whatever is showy gets their dollars, whether they need it or not, even whether they can afford it or not. They are, so to speak, constantly on a bust, their eyes alert for chances to get rid of their small change.

Consider, for example, the amazing readiness with which they succumb to the imbecile bait of advertising! An American manufacturer, finding himself with a stock of unsalable goods or encountering otherwise a demand that is less than his production, does not have to look, like his English or German colleague, for foreign dumping grounds. He simply packs his surplus in gaudy packages, sends for an advertising agent, joins an Honest-Advertising club, fills the newspapers and magazines with lying advertisements, and sits down in peace while his countrymen fight their way to his counters. That they will come is almost absolutely sure; no matter how valueless the goods, they will leap to the advertisements; their one desire seems to be to get rid of their money. As a consequence of this almost pathological eagerness, the advertising bill of the American people is greater than that of all other peoples taken together. There is scarcely an article within the range of their desires that does not carry a heavy load of advertising; they actually pay out millions every year to be sold such commonplace necessities as sugar, towels, collars, lead-pencils and corn-meal. The business of thus bamboozling them and picking their pockets enlists thousands and thousands of artists, writers, printers, sign-painters and other such parasites. Their towns are bedaubed with chromatic eye-sores and made hideous with flashing lights; their countryside is polluted; their newspapers and magazines become mere advertising sheets; idiotic slogans and apothegms are invented to enchant them; in some cities they are actually taxed to advertise the local makers of wooden nutmegs. Multitudes of swindlers are naturally induced to adopt advertising as a trade, and some of them make great fortunes at it. Like all other men who live by their wits, they regard themselves as superior fellows, and every year they hold great conventions, bore each other with learned papers upon the psychology of their victims, speak of one another as men of genius, have themselves photographed by the photographers of newspapers eager to curry favour with them, denounce the government for not spending the public funds for advertising, and summon United States Senators, eminent chautauquans and distinguished vaudeville stars to entertain them. For all this the plain people pay the bill, and never a protest comes out of them.

As a matter of fact, the only genuinely thrifty folks among us, in the sense that a Frenchman, a Scot or an Italian is thrifty, are the immigrants of the most recent invasions. That is why they oust the native wherever the two come into contact—say in New England and in the Middle West. They acquire, bit by bit, the best lands, the best stock, the best barns, not because they have the secret of *making* more money, but because they have the resolution to *spend* less. As soon as they become thoroughly Americanized they begin to show the national prodigality. The old folks wear home-made clothes and stick to the farm; the native-born children order their garments from mail-order tailors and expose themselves in the chautauquas and at the great orgies of Calvinism and Wesleyanism. The old folks put every dollar they can wring from a reluctant environment into real property or the banks; the young folks put their inheritance into phonographs, Fords, boiled shirts, yellow shoes, cuckoo clocks, lithographs of the current mountebanks, oil stock, automatic pianos and the works of Harold Bell Wright, Gerald Stanley Lee and O. Henry.

III

But what, then, is the character that actually marks the American— that is, in chief? If he is not the exalted monopolist of liberty that he thinks he is nor the noble altruist and idealist he slaps upon the chest when he is full of rhetoric, nor the degraded dollar-chaser of European legend, then what is he? We offer an answer in all humility, for the problem is complex and there is but little illumination of it in the literature; nevertheless, we offer it in the firm conviction, born of twenty years' incessant meditation, that it is substantially correct. It is, in brief, this: that the thing which sets off the American from all other men, and gives a peculiar colour not only to the pattern of his daily life but also to the play of his inner ideas, is what, for want of a more exact term, may be called social aspiration. That is to say, his dominant passion is a passion to lift himself by at least a step or two in the society that he is a part of—a passion to improve his position, to break down some shadowy barrier of caste, to achieve the countenance of what, for all his talk of equality, he recognizes and accepts as his betters. The American is a pusher. His eyes are ever fixed upon some round of the ladder that is just beyond his reach, and all his secret ambitions, all his extraordinary energies, group themselves about the yearning to grasp it. Here we have an explanation of the curious restlessness that educated foreigners, as opposed to mere immigrants, always make a note of in the country; it is half aspiration and half impatience, with overtones of dread and timorousness. The American is violently eager to get on, and thoroughly convinced that his merits entitle him to try and to succeed, but by the same token he is sickeningly fearful of slipping back, and out of the second fact, as we shall see, spring some of his most characteristic traits. He is a man vexed, at one and the same time, by delusions of grandeur and an inferiority complex; he is both egotistical and subservient, assertive and politic, blatant and shy. Most of the errors about him are made by seeing one side of him and being blind to the other.

Such a thing as a secure position is practically unknown among us. There is no American who cannot hope to lift himself another notch or two, if he is good; there is absolutely no hard and fast impediment to his progress. But neither is there any American who doesn't have to keep on fighting for whatever position he has; no wall of caste is there to protect him if he slips. One observes every day the movement of individuals, families, whole groups, in both directions. All of our cities are full of brummagem aristocrats—aristocrats, at all events, in the view of their neighbours—whose grandfathers, or even fathers, were day labourers; and working for them, supported by them, heavily patronized by them, are clerks whose grandfathers were lords of the soil. The older societies of Europe, as every one knows, protect their caste lines a great deal more resolutely. It is as impossible for a wealthy pork packer or company promoter to enter the *noblesse* of Austria, even today, as it would be for him to enter the boudoir of a queen; he is barred out absolutely and even his grandchildren are under the ban. And in precisely the same way it is as impossible for a count of the old Holy Roman Empire to lose caste as it would be for the Dalai Lama; he may sink to unutterable depths within his order, but he cannot get himself out of it, nor can he lose the peculiar advantages that go with membership; he is still a *Graf*, and, as such, above the herd. Once, in a Madrid café, the two of us encountered a Spanish marquis who wore celluloid cuffs, suffered from pediculosis and had been drunk for sixteen years. Yet he remained a marquis in good standing, and all lesser Spaniards, including Socialists, envied him and deferred to him;

none would have dreamed of slapping him on the back. Knowing that he was quite as safe within his ancient order as a dog among the *canidæ*, he gave no thought to appearances. But in the same way he knew that he had reached his limit—that no conceivable effort could lift him higher. He was a grandee of Spain and that was all; above glimmered royalty and the hierarchy of the saints, and both royalty and the hierarchy of the saints were as much beyond him as grandeeism was beyond the polite and well-educated head-waiter who laved him with ice-water, when he had *mania-a-potu*.

No American is ever so securely lodged. There is always something just ahead of him, beckoning him and tantalizing him, and there is always something just behind him, menacing him and causing him to sweat. Even when he attains to what may seem to be security, that security is very fragile. The English soap-boiler, brewer, shyster attorney or stock-jobber, once he has got into the House of Lords, is reasonably safe, and his children after him; the possession of a peerage connotes a definite rank, and it is as permanent as anything can be in this world. But in America there is no such harbour; the ship is eternally at sea. Money vanishes, official dignity is forgotten, caste lines are as full of gaps as an ill-kept hedge. The grandfather of the Vanderbilts was a bounder; the last of the Washingtons is a petty employé in the Library of Congress.

It is this constant possibility of rising, this constant risk of falling, that gives a barbaric picturesqueness to the panorama of what is called fashionable society in America. The chief character of that society is to be found in its shameless self-assertion, its almost obscene display of its importance and of the shadowy privileges and acceptances on which that importance is based. It is assertive for the simple reason that, immediately it ceased to be assertive, it would cease to exist. Structurally, it is composed in every town of a nucleus of those who have laboriously arrived and a chaotic mass of those who are straining every effort to get on. The effort must be made against great odds. Those who have arrived are eager to keep down the competition of newcomers; on their exclusiveness, as the phrase is, rests the whole of their social advantage. Thus the candidate from below, before horning in at last, must put up with an infinity of rebuff and humiliation; he must sacrifice his self-respect today in order to gain the hope of destroying the self-respect of other aspirants tomorrow. The result is that the whole edifice is based upon fears and abasements, and that every device which promises to protect the individual against them is seized upon eagerly. Fashionable society in America therefore has no room for intelligence; within its fold an original idea is dangerous; it carries regimentation, in dress, in social customs and in political and even religious doctrines, to the last degree. In the American cities the fashionable man or woman must not only maintain the decorum seen among civilized folks everywhere; he or she must also be interested in precisely the right sports, theatrical shows and opera singers, show the right political credulities and indignations, and have some sort of connection with the right church. Nearly always, because of the apeing of English custom that prevails everywhere in America, it must be the so-called Protestant Episcopal Church, a sort of outhouse of the Church of England, with ecclesiastics who imitate the English sacerdotal manner much as small boys imitate the manner of eminent baseball players. Every fashionable Protestant Episcopal congregation in the land is full of ex-Baptists and ex-Methodists who have shed Calvinism, total immersion and the hallelujah hymns on their way up the ladder. The same impulse leads the Jews, whenever the possibility of invading the citadel of the Christians begins to bemuse them (as happened during the late war, for example, when patriotism temporarily adjourned the usual taboos), to embrace Christian Science—as a sort of halfway station, so to speak, more medical than Christian, and hence secure against ordinary derisions. And it is an impulse but little different which lies at the bottom of the much-discussed title-hunt.

A title, however paltry, is of genuine social value, more especially in America; it represents a status that cannot be changed overnight by the rise of rivals, or by personal dereliction, or by mere accident. It is a policy of insurance against dangers that are not to be countered as effectively in any other manner. Miss G——, the daughter of an enormously wealthy scoundrel, may be accepted everywhere, but all the while she is insecure. Her father may lose his fortune tomorrow, or be jailed by newspaper outcry, or marry a prostitute and so commit social suicide himself and murder his daughter, or she herself may fall a victim to some rival's superior machinations, or stoop to fornication of some forbidden variety, or otherwise get herself under the ban. But once she is a duchess, she is safe. No catastrophe short of divorce can take away her coronet, and even divorce will leave the purple marks of it upon her brow. Most valuable boon of all, she is now free to be herself, —a rare, rare experience for an American. She may, if she likes, go about in a Mother Hubbard, or join the Seventh Day Adventists, or declare for the Bolsheviki, or wash her own lingerie, or have her hair bobbed, and still she will remain a duchess, and, as a duchess, irremovably superior to the gaping herd of her political equals.

This social aspiration, of course, is most vividly violent and idiotic on its higher and more gaudy levels, but it is scarcely less earnest below. Every American, however obscure, has formulated within his secret recesses some concept of advancement, however meagre; if he doesn't aspire to be what is called fashionable, then he at least aspires to lift himself in some less gorgeous way. There is not a social organization in this land of innumerable associations that hasn't its waiting list of candidates who are eager to get in, but have not yet demonstrated their fitness for the honour. One can scarcely go low enough to find that pressure absent. Even the tin-pot fraternal orders, which are constantly cadging for members and seem to accept any one not a downright felon, are exclusive in their fantastic way, and no doubt there are hundreds of thousands of proud American freemen, the heirs of Washington and Jefferson, their liberty safeguarded by a million guns, who pine in secret because they are ineligible to membership in the Masons, the Odd Fellows or even the Knights of Pythias. On the distaff side, the thing is too obvious to need exposition. The patriotic societies among women are all machines for the resuscitation of lost superiorities. The plutocracy has shouldered out the old gentry from actual social leadership—that gentry, indeed, presents a prodigious clinical picture of the insecurity of social rank in America—but there remains at least the possibility of insisting upon a dignity which plutocrats cannot boast and may not even buy. Thus the county judge's wife in Smithville or the Methodist pastor's daughter in Jonestown consoles herself for the lack of an opera box with the thought (constantly asserted by badge and resolution) that she had a nobler grandfather, or, at all events, a decenter one, than the Astors, the Vanderbilts and the Goulds.

IV

It seems to us that the genuine characters of the normal American, the characters which set him off most saliently from the men of other nations, are the fruits of all this risk of and capacity for change in status that we have described, and of the dreads and hesitations that go therewith. The American is marked, in fact, by precisely the habits of mind and act that one would look for in a man insatiably ambitious and yet incurably fearful, to wit, the habits, on the one hand, of unpleasant assertiveness, of somewhat boisterous braggardism, of incessant pushing, and, on the other hand, of conformity, caution and subservience. He is forever talking of his rights as if he stood ready to defend them with his last drop of blood, and forever yielding them up at the first demand. Under both the pretension and the fact is the common motive of fear—in brief, the common motive of the insecure and uncertain man, the *average* man, at all times and everywhere, but especially the motive of the average man in a social system so crude and unstable as ours.

"More than any other people, " said Wendell Phillips one blue day, "we Americans are afraid of one another." The saying seems harsh. It goes counter to the national delusion of uncompromising courage and limitless truculence. It wars upon the national vanity. But all the same there is truth in it. Here, more than anywhere else on earth, the status of an individual is determined by the general consent of the general body of his fellows; here, as we have seen, there are no artificial barriers to protect him against their disapproval, or even against their envy. And here, more than anywhere else, the general consent of that general body of men is coloured by the ideas and prejudices of the inferior majority; here, there is the nearest approach to genuine democracy, the most direct and accurate response to mob emotions. Facing that infinitely powerful but inevitably ignorant and cruel corpus of opinion, the individual must needs adopt caution and fall into timorousness. The desire within him may be bold and forthright, but its satisfaction demands discretion, prudence, a politic and ingratiating habit. The walls are not to be stormed; they must be wooed to a sort of Jerichoan fall. Success thus takes the form of a series of waves of protective colouration; failure is a succession of unmaskings. The aspirant must first learn to imitate exactly the aspect and behaviour of the group he seeks to penetrate. There follows notice. There follows toleration. There follows acceptance.

Thus the hog-murderer's wife picks her way into the society of Chicago, the proud aristocracy of the abbatoir. And thus, no less, the former whiskey drummer insinuates himself into the Elks, and the rising retailer wins the *imprimatur* of wholesalers, and the rich peasant becomes a planter and the father of doctors of philosophy, and the servant girl enters the movies and acquires the status of a princess of the blood, and the petty attorney becomes a legislator and statesman, and Schmidt turns into Smith, and the newspaper reporter becomes a *littérateur* on the staff of the *Saturday Evening Post*, and all of us Yankees creep up, up, up. The business is never to be accomplished by headlong assault. It must be done circumspectly, insidiously, a bit apologetically, *pianissimo*; there must be no flaunting of unusual ideas, no bold prancing of an unaccustomed personality. Above all, it must be done without exciting fear, lest the portcullis fall and the whole enterprise go to pot. Above all, the manner of a Jenkins must be got into it.

That manner, of course, is not incompatible with a certain superficial boldness, nor even with an appearance of truculence. But what lies beneath the boldness is not really an independent spirit, but merely a talent for crying with the pack. When the American is most dashingly assertive it is a sure sign that he feels the pack behind him, and hears its comforting baying, and is well aware that his doctrine is approved. He is not a joiner for nothing. He joins something, whether it be a political party, a church, a fraternal order or one of the idiotic movements that incessantly ravage the land, because joining gives him a feeling of security, because it makes him a part of something larger and safer than he is himself, because it gives him a chance to work off steam without running any risk. The whole thinking of the country thus runs down the channel of mob emotion; there is no actual conflict of ideas, but only a succession of crazes. It is inconvenient to stand aloof from these crazes, and it is dangerous to oppose them. In no other country in the world is there so ferocious a short way with dissenters; in none other is it socially so costly to heed the inner voice and to be one's own man.

Thus encircled by taboos, the American shows an extraordinary timorousness in all his dealings with fundamentals, and the fact that many of these taboos are self-imposed only adds to their rigour. What every observant foreigner first notices, canvassing the intellectual life of the land, is the shy and gingery manner in which all the larger problems of existence are dealt with. We have, for example, positive laws which make it practically impossible to discuss the sex question with anything approaching honesty. The literature of the subject is enormous, and the general notion of its importance is thereby made manifest, but all save a very small part of that literature is produced by quacks and addressed to an audience that is afraid to hear the truth. So in politics. Almost alone among the civilized nations of the world, the United States pursues critics of the dominant political theory with mediaeval ferocity, condemning them to interminable periods in prison, proceeding against them by clamour and perjury, treating them worse than common blacklegs, and at times conniving at their actual murder by the police. And so, above all, in religion. This is the only country of Christendom in which there is no anti-clerical party, and hence no constant and effective criticism of clerical pretension and corruption. The result is that all of the churches reach out for tyranny among us, and that most of them that show any numerical strength already exercise it. In half a dozen of our largest cities the Catholic Church is actually a good deal more powerful than it is in Spain, or even in Austria. Its acts are wholly above public discussion; it makes and breaks public officials; it holds the newspapers in terror; it influences the police and the courts; it is strong enough to destroy and silence any man who objects to its polity. But this is not all. The Catholic Church, at worst, is an organization largely devoted to perfectly legitimate and even laudable purposes, and it is controlled by a class of men who are largely above popular passion, and intelligent enough to see beyond the immediate advantage. More important still, its international character gives it a detached and superior point of view, and so makes it stand aloof from some of the common weaknesses of the native mob. This is constantly revealed by its opposition to Prohibition, vice-crusading and other such crazes of the disinherited and unhappy. The rank and file of its members are ignorant and emotional and are thus almost ideal cannon-fodder for the bogus reformers who operate upon the proletariat, but they are held back by their clergy, to whose superior interest in genuine religion is added a centuries-old heritage of worldly wisdom. Thus the Church of Rome, in America at least, is a civilizing agency, and we may well overlook its cynical alliance with political corruption in view of its steady enmity to that greater corruption which destroys the very elements of liberty, peace and human dignity. It may be a bit too intelligently selfish and harshly realistic, but it is assuredly not swinish.

This adjective, however, fits the opposition as snugly as a coat of varnish—and by the opposition we mean the group of Protestant churches commonly called evangelical, to wit, the Methodist, the Baptist, the Presbyterian and their attendant imitators and inferiors. It is out of this group that the dominating religious attitude of the American people arises, and, in particular is from this group that we get our doctrine that religious activity is not to be challenged, however flagrantly it may stand in opposition to common honesty and common sense. Under cover of that artificial toleration—the product, not of a genuine liberalism, but simply of a mob distrust of dissent—there goes on a tyranny that it would be difficult to match in modern history. Save in a few large cities, every American community lies under a sacerdotal despotism whose devices are disingenuous and dishonourable, and whose power was magnificently displayed in the campaign for Prohibition—a despotism exercised by a body of ignorant, superstitious, self-seeking and thoroughly dishonest men. One may, without prejudice, reasonably defend the Catholic clergy. They are men who, at worst, pursue an intelligible ideal and dignify it with a real sacrifice. But in the presence of the Methodist clergy it is difficult to avoid giving way to the weakness of indignation. What one observes is a horde of uneducated and inflammatory dunderheads, eager for power, intolerant of opposition and full of a childish vanity—a mob of holy clerks but little raised, in intelligence and dignity, above the forlorn half-wits whose souls they chronically rack. In the whole United States there is scarcely one among them who stands forth as a man of sense and information. Illiterate in all save the elementals, untouched by the larger currents of thought, drunk with their power over dolts, crazed by their immunity to challenge by their betters, they carry over into the professional class of the country the spirit of the most stupid peasantry, and degrade religion to the estate of an idiotic phobia. There is not a village in America in which some such preposterous jackass is not in eruption. Worse, he is commonly the leader of its opinion—its pattern in reason, morals and good taste. Yet worse, he is ruler as well as pattern. Wrapped in his sacerdotal cloak, he stands above any effective criticism. To question his imbecile ideas is to stand in contumacy of the revelation of God.

A number of years ago, while engaged in journalism in a large American city, one of us violated all journalistic precedents by printing an article denouncing the local evangelical clergy as, with few exceptions, a pack of scoundrels, and offered in proof their brisk and constant trade in contraband marriages, especially the marriages of girls under the age of consent. He showed that the offer of a two dollar fee was sufficient to induce the majority of these ambassadors of Christ to marry a girl of fourteen or fifteen to a boy a few years older. There followed a great outcry from the accused, with the usual demands that the offending paper print a retraction and discharge the guilty writer from its staff. He thereupon engaged a clipping bureau to furnish him with clippings from the newspapers of the whole country, showing the common activities of the evangelical clergy elsewhere. The result was that he received and reprinted an amazing mass of putrid scandal, greatly to the joy of that moral community. It appeared that these eminent Christian leaders were steadily engaged, North, East, South and West, in doings that would have disgraced so many ward heelers or oyster-shuckers—shady financial transactions, gross sexual irregularities, all sorts of minor crimes. The publication of this evidence from day to day gave the chronicler the advantage of the offensive, and so got him out of a tight place. In the end, as if tickled by his assault, the hierarchy of heaven came to his aid. That is to say, the Lord God

Jehovah arranged it that one of the leading Methodist clergymen of the city—in fact, the chronicler's chief opponent—should be taken in an unmentionable sexual perversion at the headquarters of the Young Men's Christian Association, and so be forced to leave town between days. This catastrophe, as we say, the chronicler ascribes to divine intervention. It was entirely unexpected; he knew that the fellow was a liar and a rogue, but he had never suspected that he was also a hog. The episode demoralized the defence to such an extent that it was impossible, in decency, to go on with the war. The chronicler was at once, in fact, forced into hypocritical efforts to prevent the fugitive ecclesiastic's pursuit, extradition, trial and imprisonment, and these efforts, despite their disingenuous character, succeeded. Under another name, he now preaches Christ and Him crucified in the far West, and is, we daresay, a leading advocate of Prohibition, vice-crusading and the other Methodist reforms.

But here we depart from the point. It is not that an eminent Wesleyan should be taken in crim. con. with a member of the Y.M.C.A.; it is that the whole Wesleyan scheme of things, despite the enormous multiplication of such incidents, should still stand above all direct and devastating criticism in America. It is an ignorant and dishonest cult of ignorant and dishonest men, and yet no one has ever had at it from the front. All the newspaper clippings that we have mentioned were extraordinarily discreet. Every offence of a clergyman was presented as if it were an isolated phenomenon, and of no general significance; there was never any challenge of an ecclesiastical organization which bred and sheltered such men, and carried over their curious ethics into its social and political activities. That careful avoidance of the main issue is always observable in These States. Prohibition was saddled upon the country, against the expressed wish of at least two-thirds of the people, by the political chicanery of the same organization, and yet no one, during the long fight, thought to attack it directly; to have done so would have been to violate the taboo described. So when the returning soldiers began to reveal the astounding chicaneries of the Young Men's Christian Association, it was marvelled at for a few weeks, as Americans always marvel at successful pocket-squeezings, but no one sought the cause in the character of the pious brethren primarily responsible. And so, again, when what is called liberal opinion began to revolt against the foreign politics of Dr. Wilson, and in particular, against his apparent repudiation of his most solemn engagements, and his complete insensibility, in the presence of a moral passion, to the most elementary principles of private and public honour. A thousand critics, friendly and unfriendly, sought to account for his amazing shifts and evasions on unintelligible logical grounds, but no one, so far as we know, ventured to point out that his course could be accounted for in every detail, and without any mauling of the facts whatsoever, upon the simple ground that he was a Presbyterian.

We sincerely hope that no one will mistake us here for anarchists who seek to hold the Presbyterian code of ethics, or the Presbyterians themselves, up to derision. We confess frankly that, as private individuals, we are inclined against that code and that all our prejudices run against those who subscribe to it—which is to say, in the direction of toleration, of open dealing, and even of a certain mild snobbishness. We are both opposed to moral enthusiasm, and never drink with a moral man if it can be avoided. The taboos that we personally subscribe to are taboos upon the very things that Presbyterians hold most dear—for example, moral certainty, the proselyting appetite, and what may be described as the passion of the policeman. But we are surely not fatuous enough to cherish our ideas to the point of fondness. In the long run, we freely grant, it may turn out that the Presbyterians are right and we are wrong—in brief, that God loves a moral man more than he loves an amiable and honourable one. Stranger things, indeed, have happened; one might even argue without absurdity that God is actually a Presbyterian Himself. Whether He is or is not we do not presume to say; we simply record the fact that it is our present impression that He is not—and then straightway admit that our view is worth no more than that of any other pair of men.

Meanwhile, however, it is certainly not going too far to notice the circumstance that there is an irreconcilable antithesis between the two sorts of men that we have described—that a great moral passion is fatal to the gentler and more caressing amenities of life, and *vice versa*. The man of morals has a certain character, and the man of honour has a quite different character. No one not an idiot fails to differentiate between the two, or to order his intercourse with them upon an assumption of their disparity. What we know in the United States as a Presbyterian is pre-eminently of the moral type. Perhaps more than any other man among us he regulates his life, and the lives of all who fall under his influence, upon a purely moral plan. In the main, he gets the principles underlying that plan from the Old Testament; if he is to be described succinctly, it is as one who carries over into modern life, with its superior complexity of sin, the simple and rigid ethical concepts of the ancient Jews. And in particular, he subscribes to their theory that it is virtuous to make things hot for the sinner, by which word he designates any person whose conduct violates the ordinances of God as he himself is aware of them and interprets them. Sin is to the Presbyterian the salient phenomenon of this wobbling and nefarious world, and the pursuit and chastisement of sinners the one avocation that is permanently worth while. The product of that simple doctrine is a character of no little vigour and austerity, and one much esteemed by the great masses of men, who are always uneasily conscious of their own weakness in the face of temptation and thus have a sneaking veneration for the man apparently firm, and who are always ready to believe, furthermore, that any man who seems to be having a pleasant time is a rascal and deserving of the fire.

The Presbyterian likewise harbours this latter suspicion. More, he commonly erects it into a certainty. Every single human act, he holds, must be either right or wrong—and the overwhelming majority of them are wrong. He knows exactly what these wrong ones are; he recognizes them instantly and infallibly, by a sort of inspired intuition; and he believes that they should all be punished automatically and with the utmost severity. No one ever heard of a Presbyterian overlooking a fault, or pleading for mercy for the erring. He would regard such an act as the weakness of one ridden by the Devil. From such harsh judgments and retributions, it must be added in fairness, he does not except himself. He detects his own aberration almost as quickly as he detects the aberration of the other fellow, and though he may sometimes seek— being, after all, only human—to escape its consequences, he by no means condones it. Nothing, indeed, could exceed the mental anguish of a Presbyterian who has been betrayed, by the foul arts of some lascivious wench, into any form of adultery, or, by the treason of his senses in some other way, into a voluptuous yielding to the lure of the other *beaux arts*. It has been our fortune, at various times, to be in the confidence of Presbyterians thus seduced from their native virtue, and we bear willing testimony to their sincere horror. Even the least pious of them was as greatly shaken up by what to us, on our lower plane, seemed a mere peccadillo, perhaps in bad taste but certainly not worth getting into a sweat about, as we ourselves would have been by a gross breach of faith.

But, as has been before remarked, the bitter must go with the sweet. In the face of so exalted a moral passion it would be absurd to look for that urbane habit which seeks the well-being of one's self and the other fellow, not in exact obedience to harsh statutes, but in ease, dignity and the more delicate sort of self-respect. That is to say, it would be absurd to ask a thoroughly moral man to be also a man of honour. The two, in

26

fact, are eternal enemies; their endless struggle achieves that happy mean of philosophies which we call civilization. The man of morals keeps order in the world, regimenting its lawless hordes and organizing its governments; the man of honour mellows and embellishes what is thus achieved, giving to duty the aspect of a privilege and making human intercourse a thing of fine faiths and understandings. We trust the former to do what is righteous; we trust the latter to do what is seemly. It is seldom that a man can do both. The man of honour inevitably exalts the punctilio above the law of God; one may trust him, if he has eaten one's salt, to respect one's daughter as he would his own, but if he happens to be under no such special obligation it may be hazardous to trust him with even one's charwoman or one's mother-in-law. And the man of morals, confronted by a moral situation, is usually wholly without honour. Put him on the stand to testify against a woman, and he will tell all he knows about her, even including what he has learned in the purple privacy of her boudoir. More, he will not tell it reluctantly, shame-facedly, apologetically, but proudly and willingly, in response to his high sense of moral duty. It is simply impossible for such a man to lie like a gentleman. He lies, of course, like all of us, and perhaps more often than most of us on the other side, but he does it, not to protect sinners from the moral law, but to make their punishment under the moral law more certain, swift, facile and spectacular.

By this long route we get at our *apologia* for Dr. Wilson, a man from whom we both differ in politics, in theology, in ethics and in epistemology, but one whose great gifts, particularly for moral endeavour in the grand manner, excite our sincere admiration. Both his foes and his friends, it seems to us, do him a good deal of injustice. The former, carried away by that sense of unlikeness which lies at the bottom of most of the prejudices of uncritical men, denounce him out of hand because he is not as they are. A good many of these foes, of course, are not actually men of honour themselves; some of them, in fact, belong to sects and professions—for example, that of intellectual Socialist and that of member of Congress—in which no authentic man of honour could imaginably have a place. But it may be accurately said of them, nevertheless, that if actual honour is not in them, then at least they have something of the manner of honour—that they are moving in the direction of honour, though not yet arrived. Few men, indeed, may be said to belong certainly and irrevocably in either category, that of the men of honour or that of the men of morals. Dr. Wilson, perhaps, is one such man. He is as palpably and exclusively a man of morals as, say, George Washington was a man of honour. He is, in the one category, a great beacon, burning almost blindingly; he is, in the other, no more than a tallow dip, guttering asthmatically. But the majority of men occupy a sort of twilight zone, and the most that may be said of them is that their faces turn this way or that. Such is the case with Dr. Wilson's chief foes. Their eyes are upon honour, as upon some new and superlatively sweet enchantment, and, bemused to starboard, they view the scene to port with somewhat extravagant biliousness. Thus, when they contemplate His Excellency's long and perhaps unmatchable series of violations of his troth—in the matter of "keeping us out of the war, " in the matter of his solemn promises to China, in the matter of his statement of war aims and purposes, in the matter of his shifty dealing with the Russian question, in the matter of his repudiation of the armistice terms offered to the Germans, in the matter of his stupendous lying to the Senate committee on foreign relations, and so on, *ad infinitum*—when they contemplate all that series of evasions, dodgings, hypocrisies, double-dealings and plain mendacities, they succumb to an indignation that is still more than half moral, and denounce him bitterly as a Pecksniff, a Tartuffe and a Pinto. In that judgment, as we shall show, there is naught save a stupid incapacity to understand an unlike man—in brief, no more than the dunderheadedness which makes a German regard every Englishman as a snuffling poltroon, hiding behind his vassals, and causes an Englishman to look upon every German as a fiend in human form, up to his hips in blood.

But one expects a man's foes to misjudge him, and even to libel him deliberately; a good deal of their enmity, in fact, is often no more than a product of their uneasy consciousness that they have dealt unfairly with him; one is always most bitter, not toward the author of one's wrongs, but toward the victim of one's wrongs. Unluckily, Dr. Wilson's friends have had at him even more cruelly. When, seeking to defend what they regard as his honour, they account for his incessant violation of his pledges—to the voters in 1916, to the soldiers drafted for the war, to the Chinese on their entrance, to the Austrians when he sought to get them out, to the Germans when he offered them his fourteen points, to the country in the matter of secret diplomacy—when his friends attempt to explain his cavalier repudiation of all these pledges on the ground that he could not have kept them without violating later pledges, they achieve, of course, only an imbecility, obvious and damning, for it must be plain that no man is permitted, in honour, to make antagonistic engagements, or to urge his private tranquillity or even the public welfare as an excuse for changing their terms without the consent of the parties of the second part. A man of honour is one who simply does whatever he says he will do, provided the other party holds to the compact too. One cannot imagine him shifting, trimming and making excuses; it is his peculiar mark that he never makes excuses—that the need of making them would fill him with unbearable humiliation. The moment a man of honour faces the question of his honour, he is done for; it can no more stand investigation than the chastity of a woman can stand investigation. In such a character, Dr. Wilson would have been bound irrevocably by all his long series of solemn engagements, from the first to the last, without the slightest possibility of dotting an "i" or of cutting off the tail of a comma. It would have been as impossible for him to have repudiated a single one of them at the desire of his friends or in the interest of his idealistic enterprises as it would have been for him to have repudiated it to his own private profit.

But here is where both foes and friends go aground; both attempt to inject concepts of honour into transactions predominatingly, and perhaps exclusively, coloured by concepts of morals. The two things are quite distinct, as the two sorts of men are quite distinct. Beside the obligation of honour there is the obligation of morals, entirely independent and often directly antagonistic. And beside the man who yields to the punctilio—the man of honour, the man who keeps his word—there is the man who submits himself, regardless of his personal engagements and the penalties that go therewith, to the clarion call of the moral law. Dr. Wilson is such a man. He is, as has been remarked, a Presbyterian, a Calvinist, a militant moralist. In that rôle, devoted to that high cause, clad in that white garment, he was purged of all obligations of honour to any merely earthly power. His one obligation was to the moral law—in brief, to the ordinance of God, as determined by Christian pastors. Under that moral law, specifically, he was charged to search out and determine its violations by the accused in the dock, to wit, by the German nation, according to the teaching of those pastors and the light within, and to fix and execute a punishment that should be swift, terrible and overwhelming.

To this business, it must be granted by even his most extravagant opponents, he addressed himself with the loftiest resolution and singleness of purpose, excluding all puerile questions of ways and means. He was, by the moral law, no more bound to take into account the process whereby the accused was brought to book and the weight of retribution brought to bear than a detective is bound to remember how any ordinary prisoner is snared for the mill of justice. The detective himself may have been an important factor in that process; he may have taken the prisoner by some stratagem involving the most gross false pretences; he may have even played the *agent provocateur* and so actually suggested, planned and supervised the crime. But surely that would be a ridiculous critic who would argue thereby that the detective should forthwith forget the law violated and the punishment justly provided for it, and go over to the side of the defence on the ground that his dealings with the prisoner involved him in obligations of honour. The world would laugh at such a moral moron, if it did not actually destroy him as an enemy of society. It recognizes the two codes that we have described, and it knows that they are antagonistic. It expects a man sworn to the service of morality to discharge his duty at any cost to his honour, just as it expects a man publicly devoted to honour to keep his word at any cost to his or to the public morals. Moreover, it inclines, when there is a conflict, toward the side of morals; the overwhelming majority of men are men of morals, not men of honour. They believe that it is vastly more important that the guilty should be detected, taken into custody and exposed to the rigour of the law than that the honour of this or that man should be preserved. In truth, there are frequent circumstances under which they positively esteem a man who thus sacrifices his honour, or even their own honour. The man of *dis*honour may actually take on the character of a public hero. Thus, in 1903, when the late Major General Roosevelt, then President, tore up the treaty of 1846, whereby the United States guaranteed the sovereignty of Columbia in the Isthmus of Panama, the great masses of the American plain people not only at once condoned this grave breach of honour, but actually applauded Dr. Roosevelt because his act furthered the great moral enterprise of digging the canal.

These distinctions, of course, are familiar to all men who devote themselves to the study of the human psyche; that morals and honour are not one and the same thing, but two very distinct and even antithetical things, is surely no news to the judicious. But what is thus merely an axiom of ethics, politics or psychology is often kept strangely secret in the United States. We have acquired the habit of evading all the facts of life save those that are most superficial; by long disuse we have almost lost the capacity for thinking analytically and accurately. A thing may be universally known among us, and yet never get itself so much as mentioned. Around scores of elementary platitudes there hangs a shuddering silence as complete as that which hedges in the sacred name of a Polynesian chief. At every election time, in our large cities, most of the fundamental issues are concealed, particularly when they happen to take on a theological colour, which is very often. It is, for example, the timorous public theory, born of this fear of the forthright fact, that when a man sets up as a candidate for, say, a judgeship, the question of his private religious faith is of no practical importance—that it makes no difference whether he is a Catholic or a Methodist. The truth is, of course, that his faith is often of the very first importance—that it will colour his conduct of the forensic combats before him even more than his politics, his capacity to digest proteids or the social aspirations of his wife. One constantly notes, in American jurisprudence, the effects of theological prejudices on the bench; there are at least a dozen controlling decisions, covering especially the new moral legislation, which might almost be mistaken by a layman for sermons by the Rev. Dr. Billy Sunday. The Prohibitionists, during their long and very adroit campaign, shrewdly recognized the importance of controlling the judiciary; in particular, they threw all their power against the election of candidates who were known to be Catholics, or Jews, or free-thinkers. As a result they packed the bench of nearly every state with Methodist, Baptist and Presbyterian judges, and these gentlemen at once upheld all their maze of outrageous statutes. That they would do so if elected was known in advance, and yet, so far as the record shows, it was a rare thing for any one to attack them on the ground of their religion, and rarer still for any such attack to influence many votes. The taboo was working. The majority of voters were eager to avoid that issue. They felt, in some vague and unintelligible way, that it was improper to raise it.

So with all other primary issues. There is surely no country in the world in which the marriage relation is discussed more copiously than in the United States, and yet there is no country in which its essentials are more diligently avoided. Some years ago, seeking to let some sagacity into the prevailing exchange of platitudes, one of us wrote a book upon the subject, grounding it upon the obvious doctrine that women have much more to gain by marriage than men, and that the majority of men are aware of it, and would never marry at all if it were not for women's relentless effort to bring them to it. This banality the writer supported, by dint of great painstaking, in a somewhat novel way. That is to say, he put upon himself the limitation of employing no theory, statement of fact or argument in the book that was not already embodied in a common proverb in some civilized language. Now and then it was a bit hard to find the proverb, but in most cases it was very easy, and in some cases he found, not one, but dozens. Well, this laborious *pastiche* of the obvious made such a sensation that it sold better than any other book that the author had ever written—and the reviews unanimously described it, either with praise or with blame, as an extraordinary collection of heresies, most of them almost too acrid to be bruited about. In other words, this mass of platitudes took Americans by surprise, and somehow shocked them. What was commonplace to even the peasants of the European Continent was so unfamiliar to even the literate minority over here that the book acquired a sort of sinister repute, and the writer himself came to be discussed as a fellow with the habit of arising in decorous society and indelicately blowing his nose.

There is, of course, something of the same shrinking from the elemental facts of life in England; it seems to run with the Anglo-Saxon. This accounts for the shuddering attitude of the English to such platitude-monging foreigners as George Bernard Shaw, the Scotsman disguised as an Irishman, and G. K. Chesterton, who shows all the physical and mental stigmata of a Bavarian. Shaw's plays, which once had all England by the ears, were set down as compendiums of the self-evident by the French, a realistic and plain-spoken people, and were sniffed at in Germany by all save the middle classes, who correspond to the *intelligentsia* of Anglo-Saxondom. But in America, even more than in England, they were viewed as genuinely satanic. We shall never forget, indeed, the tremulous manner in which American audiences first listened to the feeble rattling of the palpable in such pieces as "Man and Superman" and "You Never Can Tell." It was precisely the manner of an old maid devouring "What Every Girl of Forty-Five Should Know" behind the door. As for Chesterton, his banal arguments in favour of alcohol shocked the country so greatly that his previous high services to religious superstition were forgotten, and today he is seldom mentioned by respectable Americans.

V

It is necessary to repeat that we rehearse all these facts, not in indignation, nor indeed in any spirit of carping whatever, but in perfect serenity and simply as descriptive sociologists. This attitude of mind is but little comprehended in America, where the emotions dominate all human reactions, and even such dismal sciences as paleontology, pathology and comparative philology are gaudily coloured by patriotic and other passions. The typical American learned man suffers horribly from the national disease; he is eternally afraid of something. If it is not that some cheese-monger among his trustees will have him cashiered for receiving a picture post-card from Prof. Dr. Scott Nearing, it is that some sweating and scoundrelly German or Frenchman will discover and denounce his cribs, and if it is not that the foreigner will have at him, it is that he will be robbed of his step from associate to full professor by some rival whose wife is more amiable to the president of the university, or who is himself more popular with the college athletes. Thus surrounded by fears, he translates them, by a familiar psychological process, into indignations. He announces what he has to say in terms of raucous dudgeon, as a negro, having to go past a medical college at night, intones some bellicose gospel-hymn. He is, in brief, vociferously correct. During the late war, at a time of unusual suspicions and hence of unusual hazards, this eagerness to prove orthodoxy by choler was copiously on exhibition. Thus one of the leading American zoölogists printed a work in which, after starting off by denouncing the German naming of new species as ignorant, dishonest and against God, he gradually worked himself up to the doctrine that any American who put a tooth into a slab of *Rinderbrust mit Meerrettig*, or peeped at *Simplicissimus* with the blinds down, or bought his children German-made jumping-jacks, was a traitor to the Constitution and a secret agent of the Wilhelmstrasse. And thus there were American pathologists and bacteriologists who denounced Prof. Dr. Paul Ehrlich as little better than a quack hired by the Krupps to poison Americans, and who displayed their pious horror of the late Prof. Dr. Robert Koch by omitting all acknowledgment of obligation to him from their monographs. And finally there was the posse of "two thousand American Historians" assembled by Mr. Creel to instruct the plain people in the new theory of American history, whereby the Revolution was represented as a lamentable row in an otherwise happy family, deliberately instigated by German intrigue—a posse which reached its greatest height of correct indignation in its approval of the celebrated Sisson documents, to the obscene delight of the British authors thereof.

As we say, we are devoid of all such lofty passions, and hence must present our observations in the flat, unimaginative, unemotional manner of a dentist pulling a tooth. It would not be going too far, in fact, to call us emotional idiots. What ails us is a constitutional suspicion that the other fellow, after all, may be right, or, in any event, partly right. In the present case we by no means reprehend the avoidance of issues that we have described; we merely record it. The fact is that it has certain very obvious uses, and is probably inevitable in a democratic society. It is commonly argued that free speech is necessary to the prosperity of a democracy, but in this doctrine we take no stock. On the contrary, there are plain reasons for holding that free speech is more dangerous to a democracy than to any other form of government, and no doubt these reasons, if only unconsciously, were at the bottom of the extraordinary body of repressive legislation put upon the books during the late war. The essential thing about a democracy is that the men at the head of the state are wholly dependent, for a continuance of their power, upon the good opinion of the popular majority. While they are actually in office, true enough, they are theoretically almost completely irresponsible, but their terms of office are usually so short that they must give constant thought to the imminent canvassing of their acts, and this threat of being judged and turned out commonly greatly conditions their exercise of their power, even while they hold it to the full. Of late, indeed, there has actually arisen the doctrine that they are responsible at all times and must respond to every shift in public sentiment, regardless of their own inclinations, and there has even grown up the custom of subjecting them to formal discipline, as by what is called the recall. The net result is that a public officer under a democracy is bound to regard the popular will during the whole of his term in office, and cannot hope to carry out any intelligible plan of his own if the mob has been set against it.

Now, the trouble with this scheme is that the mob reaches its conclusions, not by logical steps but by emotional steps, and that its information upon all save a very small minority of the questions publicly at issue is always scant and inaccurate. It is thus constantly liable to inflammation by adroit demagogues, or rabble-rousers, and inasmuch as these rabble-rousers are animated as a sole motive by the hope of turning out the existing officers of state and getting the offices for themselves, the man in office must inevitably regard them as his enemies and the doctrines they preach as subversive of good government. This view is not altogether selfish. There is, in fact, sound logic in it, for it is a peculiarity of the mob mind that it always takes in most hospitably what is intrinsically most idiotic—that between two antagonistic leaders it always follows the one who is longest on vague and brilliant words and shortest on sense. Thus the man in office, if he would be free to carry on his duties in anything approaching freedom and comfort, must adopt measures against that tendency to run amuck.

Three devices at once present themselves. One is to take steps against the rabble-rousers by seeking to make it appear that they are traitors, and so arousing the mob against them—in brief, to deny them their constitutional right to free speech under colour of criminal statutes. The second is to combine this plan with that of flooding the country with official news by a corps of press-agents, chautauquans and other such professors of deception. The third is to meet the rabble-rousers on their own ground, matching their appeals to the emotions with appeals even more powerful, and out-doing their vague and soothing words with words even more vague and soothing. All three plans have been in operation since the first days of the republic; the early Federalists employed the first two with such assiduity that the mob of that time finally revolted. All three have been brought to the highest conceivable point of perfection by Dr. Wilson, a man whose resolute fidelity to his moral ideas is matched only by his magnificent skill at playing upon every prejudice and weakness of the plain people.

But men of such exalted and varied gifts are not common. The average head of a democratic state is not *ipso facto* the best rabble-rouser within that state, but merely one of the best. He may be able, on fair terms, to meet any individual rival, but it is rare for him to be able to meet the whole pack, or even any considerable group. To relieve him from that difficulty, and so prevent the incessant running amuck of the populace, it is necessary to handicap all the remaining rabble-rousers, and this is most effectively done by limitations upon free speech which originate as statutes and gradually take on the form and potency of national customs. Such limitations arose in the United States by precisely that process. They began in the first years of the republic as definite laws. Some of those laws were afterward abandoned, but what was fundamentally sound in them remained in force as custom.

It must be obvious that even Dr. Wilson, despite his tremendous gift for the third of the devices that we have named, would have been in sore case during his second administration if it had not been for his employment of the other two. Imagine the United States during the Summer of 1917 with absolute free speech the order of the day! The mails would have been flooded with Socialist and pacifist documents, every street-corner would have had its screaming soap-box orator, the newspapers would have shaken the very heavens with colossal alarms, and conscientious objection would have taken on the proportions of a national frenzy. In the face of such an avalanche of fears and balderdash, there would have been no work at all for the German propagandists; in fact, it is likely that a great many of them, under suspicion on account of their relative moderation, would have been lynched as agents of the American munitions patriots. For the mob, it must be remembered, infallibly inclines, not to the side of the soundest logic and loftiest purpose, but to the side of the loudest noise, and without the artificial aid of a large and complex organization of press-agents and the power to jail any especially effective opponent forthwith, even a President of the United States would be unable to bawl down the whole fraternity. That it is matter of the utmost importance, in time of war, to avoid any such internal reign of terror must be obvious to even the most fanatical advocate of free speech. There must be, in such emergencies, a resolute pursuit of coherent policies, and that would be obviously impossible with the populace turning distractedly to one bogus messiah after another, and always seeking to force its latest craze upon the government. Thus, while one may perchance drop a tear or two upon the Socialists jailed by a sort of lynch law for trying to exercise their plain constitutional rights, and upon the pacifists tarred and feathered by mobs led by government agents, and upon the conscientious objectors starved and clubbed to death in military dungeons, it must still be plain that such barbarous penalties were essentially necessary. The victims, in the main, were half-wits suffering from the martyr complex; it was their admitted desire to sacrifice themselves for the Larger Good. This desire was gratified—not in the way they hoped for, of course, but nevertheless in a way that must have given any impartial observer a feeling of profound, if discreditable, satisfaction.

What a republic has to fear especially is the rabble-rouser who advocates giving an objective reality to the gaudy theories which lie at the foundations of the prevailing scheme of government. He is far more dangerous than a genuine revolutionist, for the latter comes with ideas that are actually new, or, at all events, new to the mob, and so he has to overcome its congenital hostility to novelty. But the reformer who, under a democracy, bases his case upon the principles upon which democracy is founded has an easy road, for the populace is familiar with those principles and eager to see them put into practical effect. The late Cecil Chesterton, in his penetrating "History of the United States, " showed how Andrew Jackson came to power by that route. Jackson, he said, was simply a man so naïve that he accepted the lofty doctrines of the Declaration of Independence without any critical questioning whatever, and "really acted as if they were true." The appearance of such a man, he goes on, was "appalling" to the political aristocrats of 1825. They themselves, of course, enunciated those doctrines daily and based their whole politics upon them—but not to the point of really executing them. So when Jackson came down from the mountains with the same sonorous words upon his lips, but with the addition of a solemn promise to carry them out—when he thus descended upon them, he stole their thunder and spiked their guns, and after a brief struggle he had disposed of them. The Socialists, free-speech fanatics, anti-conscriptionists, anti-militarists and other such democratic maximalists of 1917 and 1918 were, in essence, nothing but a new and formidable horde of Jacksons. Their case rested upon principles held to be true by all good Americans, and constantly reaffirmed by the highest officers of state. It was thus extremely likely that, if they were permitted to woo the public ear, they would quickly amass a majority of suffrages, and so get the conduct of things into their own hands. So it became necessary, in order that the great enterprises then under way might be pushed to a successful issue, that all these marplots be silenced, and it was accordingly done. This proceeding, of course, was theoretically violative of their common rights, and hence theoretically un-American. All the theory, in fact, was on the side of the victims. But war time is no time for theories, and a man with war powers in his hands is not one to parley with them.

As we have said, the menace presented by such unintelligent literalists is probably a good deal more dangerous to a democracy than to a government of any other form. Under an aristocracy, for example, such as prevailed, in one form or another, in England, Germany, Italy and France before the war, it is possible to give doctrinaires a relatively free rein, for even if they succeed in converting the mob to their whim-wham, there remain insuperable impediments to its adoption and execution as law. In England, as every one knows, the impediment was a ruling caste highly skilled in the governmental function and generally trusted by a majority of the populace—a ruling caste firmly intrenched in the House of Lords and scarcely less powerful in the House of Commons. In France it was a bureaucracy so securely protected by law and custom that nothing short of a political cataclysm could shake it. In Germany and Italy it was an aristocracy buttressed by laws cunningly designed to nullify the numerical superiority of the mob, and by a monarchical theory that set up a heavy counterweight to public opinion.

In the face of such adroit checks and balances it is a matter of relative indifference whether the mob blows scalding hot or freezing cold. Whatever the extravagance of its crazes, there remains effective machinery for holding them in check until they spend themselves, which is usually soon enough. Thus the English government, though theoretically as much opposed to anarchists as the American government, gave them cheerful asylum before the war and permitted them to preach their lamentable notions almost without check, whereas in America they early aroused great fears and were presently put under such disabilities that their propaganda became almost impossible. Even in France, where they had many converts and were frequently in eruption, there was far more hospitality in the Germany of Bismarck's day, the Socialists, after a brief and aberrant attempt to suppress them, were allowed to run free, despite the fact that their doctrine was quite as abhorrent to German official doctrine as anarchism was to American official doctrine. The German ruling caste of those days was sheltered behind laws and customs which enabled it to pull the teeth of Socialism, even in the face of enormous Socialist majorities. But under a democracy it is difficult, and often downright impossible, to oppose the popular craze of the moment with any effect, and so there must be artificial means of disciplining the jake-fetchers who seek to set such enthusiasms in motion. The shivering fear of Bolshevism, visible of late among the capitalists of America, is based upon a real danger. These capitalists have passed through the burning fires of Rooseveltian trust-busting and Bryanistic populism, and they know very well that half a dozen Lenines and Trotskis, turned loose upon the plain people, would quickly recruit a majority of them for a holy war upon capital, and that they have the political power to make such a holy war devastating.

The amateur of popular psychology may wonder why it is that the mob, in the face of the repressions constantly practised in the United States, does not occasionally rise in revolt, and so get back its right to be wooed and ravished by all sorts of mountebanks. Theoretically it has that right, and what is more, it has the means of regaining it; nothing could resist it if it made absolute free speech an issue in a national campaign and voted for the candidate advocating it. But something is overlooked here, and that is the fact that the mob has no liking for free speech *per se*. Some of the grounds of its animosity we have rehearsed. Others are not far to seek. One of them lies in the mob's chronic suspicion of all advocates of ideas, born of its distaste for ideas themselves. The mob-man cannot imagine himself throwing up his job and deserting his home, his lodge and his speakeasy to carry a new gospel to his fellows, and so he is inclined to examine the motives of any other man who does so. The one motive that is intelligible to him is the desire for profit, and he commonly concludes at once that this is what moves the propagandist before him. His reasoning is defective, but his conclusion is usually not far from wrong. In point of fact, idealism is not a passion in America, but a trade; all the salient idealists make a living at it, and some of them, for example, Dr. Bryan and the Rev. Dr. Sunday, are commonly believed to have amassed large fortunes. For an American to advocate a cause without any hope of private usufruct is almost unheard of; it would be difficult to find such a man who was not plainly insane. The most eloquent and impassioned of American idealists are candidates for public office; on the lower levels idealism is no more than a hand-maiden of business, like advertising or belonging to the Men and Religion Forward Movement.

Another and very important cause of the proletarian's failure to whoop for free speech is to be found in his barbarous delight in persecution, regardless of the merits of the cause. The spectacle of a man exercising the right of free speech yields, intrinsically, no joy, for there is seldom anything dramatic about it. But the spectacle of a man being mobbed, jailed, beaten and perhaps murdered for trying to exercise it is a good show like any other good show, and the populace is thus not only eager to witness it but even willing to help it along. It is therefore quite easy to set the mob upon, say, the Bolsheviki, despite the fact that the Bolsheviki have the professed aim of doing the mob an incomparable service. During the late high jinks of the Postoffice and the Department of Justice, popular opinion was always on the side of the raiding parties. It applauded every descent upon a Socialist or pacifist meeting, not because it was very hotly in favour of war—in fact, it was lukewarm about war, and resisted all efforts to heat it up until overwhelming swarms of yokel-yankers were turned upon it—but because it was in favour of a safe and stimulating form of rough-house, with the police helping instead of hindering. It never stopped to inquire about the merits of the matter. All it asked for was a melodramatic raid, followed by a noisy trial of the accused in the newspapers, and the daily publication of sensational (and usually bogus) evidence about the discovery of compromising literature in his wife's stockings, including records of his receipt of $100, 000 from von Bernstorff, Carranza or some other transient hobgoblin. The celebrated O'Leary trial was typical. After months of blood-curdling charges in the press, it turned out when the accused got before a court that the evidence against him, on which it was sought to convict him of a capital offence, was so feeble that it would have scarcely sufficed to convict him of an ordinary misdemeanor, and that most of this feeble testimony was palpably perjured. Nevertheless, public opinion was nearly unanimously against him from first to last, and the jury which acquitted him was almost apologetic about its inability to give the populace the crowning happiness of a state hanging.

Under cover of the war, of course, the business of providing such shows prospered extraordinarily, but it is very active even in time of peace. The surest way to get on in politics in America is to play the leading part in a prosecution which attracts public notice. The list of statesmen who have risen in that fashion includes the names of many of the highest dignity, *e.g.*, Hughes, Folk, Whitman, Heney, Baker and Palmer. Every district attorney in America prays nightly that God will deliver into his hands some Thaw, or Becker, or O'Leary, that he may get upon the front pages and so become a governor, a United States senator, or a justice of the Supreme Court of the United States. The late crusade against W. R. Hearst, which appeared to the public as a great patriotic movement, was actually chiefly managed by a subordinate prosecuting officer who hoped to get high office out of it.

This last aspirant failed in his enterprise largely because he had tackled a man who was himself of superb talents as a rouser of the proletariat, but nine times out of ten the thing succeeds. Its success is due almost entirely to the factor that we have mentioned, to wit, to the circumstance that the sympathy of the public is always on the side of the prosecution. This sympathy goes so far that it is ready to condone the most outrageous conduct in judges and prosecuting officers, providing only they give good shows. During the late war upon Socialists, pacifists, anti-conscriptionists and other such heretics, judges theoretically employed to insure fair trials engaged in the most amazing attacks upon prisoners before them, denouncing them without hearing them, shutting out evidence on their side and making stump speeches to the jury against them. That conduct aroused no public indignation; on the contrary, such judges were frequently praised in the newspapers and a good many of them were promoted to higher courts. Even in time of peace there is no general antipathy to that sort of thing. At least two-thirds of our judges, federal, state and municipal, colour their decisions with the newspaper gabble of the moment; even the Supreme Court has shown itself delicately responsive to the successive manias of the Uplift, which is, at bottom, no more than an organized scheme for inventing new crimes and making noisy pursuit of new categories of criminals. Some time ago an intelligent Mexican, after studying our courts, told us that he was surprised that, in a land ostensibly of liberty, so few of the notorious newspaper-wooers and blacklegs upon the bench were assassinated. It is, in fact, rather curious. The thing happens very seldom, and then it is usually in the South, where the motive is not altruistic but political. That is to say, the assassin merely desires to remove one blackleg in order to make a place for some other blackleg. He has no objection to systematized injustice; all he desires is that it be dispensed in favour of his own side.

VI

The mob delight in melodramatic and cruel spectacles, thus constantly fed and fostered by the judicial arm in the United States, is also at the bottom of another familiar American phenomenon, to wit, lynching. A good part of the enormous literature of lynching is devoted to a discussion of its causes, but most of that discussion is ignorant and some of it is deliberately mendacious. The majority of Southern commentators argue that the motive of the lynchers is a laudable yearning to "protect Southern womanhood, " despite the plain fact that only a very small proportion of the blackamoors hanged and burned are even so much as accused of molesting Southern womanhood. On the other hand, some of the negro intellectuals of the North ascribe the recurrent butcheries to the Southern white man's economic jealousy of the Southern black, who is fast acquiring property and reaching out for the prerogatives that go therewith. Finally, certain white Northerners seek a cause in mere political animosity, arguing that the Southern white hates the negro because the latter is his theoretical equal at the polls, though actually not permitted to vote.

All of these notions seem to us to be fanciful. Lynching is popular in the South simply because the Southern populace, like any other populace, delights in thrilling shows, and because no other sort of show is provided by the backward culture of the region. The introduction of prize-fighting down there, or baseball on a large scale, or amusement places like Coney Island, or amateur athletic contests, or picnics like those held by the more truculent Irish fraternal organizations, or any other such wholesale devices for shocking and diverting the proletariat would undoubtedly cause a great decline in lynching. The art is practised, in the overwhelming main, in remote and God-forsaken regions, in which the only rival entertainment is offered by one-sided political campaigns, third-rate chautauquas and Methodist revivals. When it is imitated in the North, it is always in some drab factory or mining town. Genuine race riots, of course, sometimes occur in the larger cities, but these are always economic in origin, and have nothing to do with lynching, properly so-called. One could not imagine an actual lynching at, say, Atlantic City, with ten or fifteen bands playing, blind pigs in operation up every alley, a theatre in every block or two, and the boardwalk swarming with ladies of joy. Even a Mississippian, transported to such scenes, succumbs to the atmosphere of pleasure, and so has no seizures of moral rage against the poor darkey. Lynching, in brief, is a phenomenon of isolated and stupid communities, a mark of imperfect civilization; it follows the hookworm and malaria belt; it shows itself in inverse proportion to the number of shoot-the-chutes, symphony orchestras, roof gardens, theatres, horse races, yellow journals and automatic pianos. No one ever heard of a lynching in Paris, at Newport, or in London. But there are incessant lynchings in the remoter parts of Russia, in the backwoods of Serbia, Bulgaria and Herzegovina, in Mexico and Nicaragua, and in such barbarous American states as Alabama, Georgia and South Carolina.

The notion that lynching in the South is countenanced by the gentry or that they take an actual hand in it is libelous and idiotic. The well-born and well-bred Southerner is no more a savage than any other man of condition. He may live among savages, but that no more makes him a savage than an English gentleman is made one by having a place in Wales, or a Russian by living on his estate in the Ukraine. What Northern observers mistake for the gentry of the South, when they report the participation of "leading citizens" in a lynching, is simply the office-holding and commercial bourgeoisie—the offspring of the poor white trash who skulked at home during the Civil War, robbing the widows and orphans of the soldiers at the front, and so laying the foundations of the present "industrial prosperity" of the section, *i.e.*, its conversion from a region of large landed estates and urbane life into a region of stinking factories, filthy mining and oil towns, child-killing cotton mills, vociferous chambers of commerce and other such swineries. It is, of course, a fact that the average lynching party in Mississippi or Alabama is led by the mayor and that the town judge climbs down from his bench to give it his official support, but it is surely not a fact that these persons are of the line of such earlier public functionaries as Pickens, Troup and Pettus. On the contrary, they correspond to the lesser sort of Tammany office-holders and to the vermin who monopolize the public functions in such cities as Boston and Philadelphia. The gentry, with few exceptions, have been forced out of the public service everywhere south of the Potomac, if not out of politics. The Democratic victory in 1912 flooded all the governmental posts at Washington with Southerners, and they remain in power to this day, and some of them are among the chief officers of the nation. But in the whole vast corps there are, we believe, but ten who would be accepted as gentlemen by Southern standards, and only three of these are in posts of any importance. In the two houses of Congress there is but one.

It is thus absurd to drag the gentry of the South—the Bourbons of New England legend—into a discussion of the lynching problem. They represent, in fact, what remains of the only genuine aristocracy ever visible in the United States, and lynching, on the theoretical side, is far too moral a matter ever to engage an aristocracy. The true lynchers are the plain people, and at the bottom of the sport there is nothing more noble than the mob man's chronic and ineradicable poltroonery. Cruel by nature, delighting in sanguinary spectacles, and here brought to hatred of the negro by the latter's increasing industrial, (*not* political, capitalistic or social) rivalry, he naturally diverts himself in his moments of musing with visions of what he would do to this or that Moor if he had the courage. Unluckily, he hasn't, and so he is unable to execute his dream *a cappella*. If, inflamed by liquor, he attempts it, the Moor commonly gives him a beating, or even murders him. But what thus lies beyond his talents as an individual at once becomes feasible when he joins himself with other men in a like situation. This is the genesis of a mob of lynchers. It is composed primarily of a few men with definite grievances, sometimes against the negro lynched but often against quite different negroes. It is composed secondarily of a large number of fifth-rate men eager for a thrilling show, involving no personal danger. It is composed in the third place of a few rabble-rousers and politicians, all of them hot to exhibit themselves before the populace at a moment of public excitement and in an attitude of leadership. It is the second element that gives life to the general impulse. Without its ardent appetite for a rough and shocking spectacle there would be no lynching. Its influence is plainly shown by the frequent unintelligibility of the whole proceeding; all its indignation over the crime alleged to be punished is an afterthought; any crime will answer, once its blood is up. Thus the most characteristic lynchings in the South are not those in which a confessed criminal is done to death for a definite crime, but those in which, in sheer high spirits, some convenient African is taken at random and lynched, as the newspapers say, "on general principles." That sort of lynching is the most honest and normal, and we are also inclined to think that it is also the most enjoyable, for the other sort brings moral indignation with it, and moral indignation is disagreeable. No man can be both indignant and happy.

But here, seeking to throw a feeble beam or two of light into the mental processes of the American proletarian, we find ourselves entering upon a discussion that grows narrow and perhaps also dull. Lynching, after all, is not an American institution, but a peculiarly Southern institution, and even in the South it will die out as other more seemly recreations are introduced. It would be quite easy, we believe, for any Southern community to get rid of it by establishing a good brass band and having concerts every evening. It would be even easier to get rid of it by borrowing a few professional scoundrels from the Department of Justice, having them raid the "study" of the local Methodist archdeacon, and forthwith trying him publicly—with a candidate for governor as prosecuting officer—for seduction under promise of salvation. The trouble down there is not a special viciousness. The Southern poor white, taking him by and large, is probably no worse and no better than the anthropoid proletarian of the North. What ails the whole region is Philistinism. It has lost its old aristocracy of the soil and has not yet developed an aristocracy of money. The result is that its cultural ideas are set by stupid and unimaginative men—Southern equivalents of the retired Iowa steer staffers and grain sharks who pollute Los Angeles, American equivalents of the rich English nonconformists. These men, though they have accumulated wealth, have not yet acquired the capacity to enjoy civilized recreations. Worse, most of them are still so barbarous that they regard such recreations as immoral. The dominating opinion of the South is thus against most of the devices that would diminish lynching by providing substitutes for it. In every Southern town some noisy clown of a Methodist or Presbyterian clergyman exercises a local tyranny. These men are firmly against all the divertissements of more cultured regions. They oppose prize-fighting, horse-racing, Sunday baseball and games of chance. They are bitter prohibitionists. By their incessant vice-crusades they reduce the romance of sex to furtiveness and piggishness. They know nothing of music or the drama, and view a public library merely as something to be rigorously censored. We are convinced that their ignorant moral enthusiasm is largely to blame for the prevalence of lynching. No doubt they themselves are sneakingly conscious of the fact, or at least aware of it subconsciously, for lynching is the only public amusement that they never denounce.

Their influence reveals strikingly the readiness of the inferior American to accept ready-made opinions. He seems to be pathetically eager to be told what to think, and he is apparently willing to accept any instructor who takes the trouble to tackle him. This, also, was brilliantly revealed during the late war. The powers which controlled the press during that fevered time swayed the populace as they pleased. So long as the course of Dr. Wilson was satisfactory to them he was depicted as a second Lincoln, and the plain people accepted the estimate without question. To help reinforce it the country was actually flooded with lithographs showing Lincoln and Wilson wreathed by the same branch of laurel, and copies of the print got into millions of humble homes. But immediately Dr. Wilson gave offence to his superiors, he began to be depicted as an idiot and a scoundrel, and this judgment promptly displaced the other one in the popular mind. The late Major General Roosevelt was often a victim of that sort of boob-bumping. A man of mercurial temperament, constantly shifting his position on all large public questions, he alternately gave great joy and great alarm to the little group of sagaciously wilful men which exercises genuine sovereignty over the country, and this alternation of emotions showed itself, by way of the newspapers and other such bawdy agencies, in the vacillation of public opinion. The fundamental platitudes of the nation were used both for him and against him, and always with immense effect. One year he was the last living defender of the liberties fought for by the Fathers; the next year he was an anarchist. Roosevelt himself was much annoyed by this unreliability of the mob. Now and then he sought to overcome it by direct appeals, but in the long run he was usually beaten. Toward the end of his life he resigned himself to a policy of great discretion, and so withheld his voice until he was sure what hymn was being lined out.

The newspapers and press associations, of course, do not impart the official doctrine of the moment in terms of forthright instructions; they get it over, as the phrase is, in the form of delicate suggestions, most of them under cover of the fundamental platitudes aforesaid. Their job is not to inspire and inform public discussion, but simply to colour it, and the task most frequently before them is that of giving a patriotic and virtuous appearance to whatever the proletariat is to believe. They do this, of course, to the tune of deafening protestations of their own honesty and altruism. But there is really no such thing as an honest newspaper in America; if it were set up tomorrow it would perish within a month. Every journal, however rich and powerful, is the trembling slave of higher powers, some financial, some religious and some political. It faces a multitude of censorships, all of them very potent. It is censored by the Postoffice, by the Jewish advertisers, by the Catholic Church, by the Methodists, by the Prohibitionists, by the banking oligarchy of its town, and often by even more astounding authorities, including the Sinn Fein. Now and then a newspaper makes a valiant gesture of revolt, but it is only a gesture. There is not a single daily in the United States that would dare to discuss the problem of Jewish immigration honestly. Nine tenths of them, under the lash of snobbish Jewish advertisers, are even afraid to call a Jew a Jew; their orders are to call him a Hebrew, which is regarded as sweeter. During the height of the Bolshevist scare not one American paper ventured to direct attention to the plain and obtrusive fact that the majority of Bolshevists in Russia and Germany and at least two-thirds of those taken in the United States were of the faith of Moses, Mendelssohn and Gimbel. But the Jews are perhaps not the worst. The Methodists, in all save a few big cities, exercise a control over the press that is far more rigid and baleful. In the Anti-Saloon League they have developed a machine for terrorizing office-holders and the newspapers that is remarkably effective, and they employed it during the long fight for Prohibition to throttle all opposition save the most formal.

In this last case, of course, the idealists who thus forced the speakeasy upon the country had an easy task, for all of the prevailing assumptions and prejudices of the mob were in their favour. No doubt it is true, as has been alleged, that a majority of the voters of the country were against Prohibition and would have defeated it at a plebiscite, but equally without doubt a majority of them were against the politicians so brutally clubbed by the Anti-Saloon League, and ready to believe anything evil of them, and eager to see them manhandled. Moreover, the League had another thing in its favour: it was operated by strictly moral men, oblivious to any notion of honour. Thus it advocated and procured the abolition of legalized liquor selling without the slightest compensation to the men who had invested their money in the business under cover of and even at the invitation of the law—a form of repudiation and confiscation unheard of in any other civilized country. Again, it got through the constitutional amendment by promising the liquor men to give them one year to dispose of their lawfully accumulated stocks—and then broke its promise under cover of alleged war necessity, despite the fact that the war was actually over. Both proceedings, so abhorrent to any man of honour, failed to arouse any indignation among the plain people. On the contrary the plain people viewed them as, in some vague way, smart and creditable, and as, in any case, thoroughly justified by the superior moral obligation that we have hitherto discussed.

Thus the *Boobus americanus* is lead and watched over by zealous men, all of them highly skilled at training him in the way that he should think and act. The Constitution of his country guarantees that he shall be a free man and assumes that he is intelligent, but the laws and customs that have grown up under that Constitution give the lie to both the guarantee and the assumption. It is the fundamental theory of all the more recent American law, in fact, that the average citizen is half-witted, and hence not to be trusted to either his own devices or his own thoughts. If there were not regulations against the saloon (it seems to say) he would get drunk every day, dissipate his means, undermine his health and beggar his family. If there were not postal regulations as to his reading matter, he would divide his time between Bolshevist literature and pornographic literature and so become at once an anarchist and a guinea pig. If he were not forbidden under heavy penalties to cross a state line with a wench, he would be chronically unfaithful to his wife. Worse, if his daughter were not protected by statutes of the most draconian severity, she would succumb to the first Italian she encountered, yield up her person to him, enroll herself upon his staff and go upon the streets. So runs the course of legislation in this land of freemen. We could pile up example upon example, but will defer the business for the present. Perhaps it may be resumed in a work one of us is now engaged upon—a full length study of the popular mind under the republic. But that work will take years....

VII

No doubt we should apologize for writing, even so, so long a preface to so succinct a book. The one excuse we can think of is that, having read it, one need not read the book. That book, as we have said, may strike the superficial as jocular, but in actual fact it is a very serious and even profound composition, not addressed to the casual reader, but to the scholar. Its preparation involved a great diligence, and its study is not to be undertaken lightly. What the psychologist will find to admire in it, however, is not its learning and painstaking, its laborious erudition, but its compression. It establishes, we believe, a new and clearer method for a science long run to turgidity and flatulence. Perhaps it may be even said to set up an entirely new science, to wit, that of descriptive sociological psychology. We believe that this field will attract many men of inquiring mind hereafter and yield a valuable crop of important facts. The experimental method, intrinsically so sound and useful, has been much abused by orthodox psychologists; it inevitably leads them into a trackless maze of meaningless tables and diagrams; they keep their eyes so resolutely upon the intellectual process that they pay no heed to the primary intellectual materials.

Nevertheless, it must be obvious that the conclusions that a man comes to, the emotions that he harbours and the crazes that sway him are of much less significance than the fundamental assumptions upon which they are all based.

There has been, indeed, some discussion of those fundamental assumptions of late. We have heard, for example, many acute discourses upon the effects produced upon the whole thinking of the German people, peasants and professors alike, by the underlying German assumption that the late Kaiser was anointed of God and hence above all ordinary human responsibility. We have heard talk, too, of the curious Irish axiom that there is a mysterious something in the nature of things, giving the Irish people an indefeasible right to govern Ireland as they please, regardless of the safety of their next-door neighbours. And we have heard many outlandish principles of the same sort from political theorists, *e.g.*, regarding the inalienable right of democracy to prevail over all other forms of government and the inalienable right of all national groups, however small, to self-determination. Well, here is an attempt to assemble in convenient form, without comment or interpretation, some of the fundamental beliefs of the largest body of human beings now under one flag in Christendom. It is but a beginning. The field is barely platted. It must be explored to the last furlong and all its fantastic and fascinating treasures unearthed and examined before ever there can be any accurate understanding of the mind of the American people.

GEORGE   JEAN   NATHAN
H.   L.   MENCKEN
New   *York,*   *1920.*

THE AMERICAN CREDO

§1. That the philoprogenitive instinct in rabbits is so intense that the alliance of two normally assiduous rabbits is productive of 265 offspring in one year.

§2. That there are hundreds of letters in the Dead Letter Office whose failure to arrive at their intended destinations was instrumental in separating as many lovers.

§3. That the Italian who sells bananas on a push-cart always takes the bananas home at night and sleeps with them under his bed.

§4. That a man's stability in the community and reliability in business may be measured by the number of children he has.

§5. That in Japan an American can buy a beautiful geisha for two dollars and that, upon being bought, she will promptly fall madly in love with him and will run his house for him in a scrupulously clean manner.

§6. That all sailors are gifted with an extraordinary propensity for amour, but that on their first night of shore leave they hang around the water-front saloons and are given knock-out drops.

§7. That when a comedian, just before the rise of the curtain, is handed a telegram announcing the death of his mother or only child, he goes out on the stage and gives a more comic performance than ever.

§8. That the lions in the cage which a lion-tamer enters are always sixty years old and have had all their teeth pulled.

§9. That the Siamese Twins were joined together by gutta percha moulded and painted to look like a shoulder blade.

§10. That if a woman about to become a mother plays the piano every day, her baby will be born a Victor Herbert.

§11. That all excursion boats are so old that if they ran into a drifting beer-keg they would sink.

§12. That a doctor knows so much about women that he can no longer fall in love with one of them.

§13. That when one takes one's best girl to see the monkeys in the zoo, the monkeys invariably do something that is very embarrassing.

§14. That firemen, awakened suddenly in the middle of the night, go to fires in their stocking feet.

§15. That something mysterious goes on in the rooms back of chop suey restaurants.

§16. That oil of pennyroyal will drive away mosquitoes.

§17. That the old ladies on summer hotel verandas devote themselves entirely to the discussion of scandals.

§18. That a bachelor, expecting a feminine visitor, by way of subtle preliminary strategy smells up his rooms with Japanese punk.

§19. That all one has to do to gather a large crowd in New York is to stand on the curb a few moments and gaze intently at the sky.

§20. That one can get an excellent bottle of wine in France for a franc.

§21. That it is dangerous to drink out of a garden hose, since if one does one is likely to swallow a snake.

§22. That all male negroes can sing.

§23. That when a girl enters a hospital as a nurse, her primary object is always to catch one of the doctors.

§24. That the postmasters in small towns read all the postcards.

§25. That a young girl ought to devote herself sedulously to her piano lessons since, when she is married, her playing will be a great comfort to her husband.

§26. That all theater box-office employés are very impolite and hate to sell a prospective patron a ticket.

§27. That all great men have illegible signatures.

§28. That all iron-moulders and steam-fitters, back in the days of freedom, used to get drunk every Saturday night.

§29. That if a man takes a cold bath regularly every morning of his life he will never be ill.

§30. That ginger snaps are made of the sweepings of the floor in the bakery.

§31. That every circus clown's heart is breaking for one reason or another.

§32. That a bull-fighter always has so many women in love with him that he doesn't know what to do.

§33. That George M. Cohan spends all his time hanging around Broadway cafés and street-corners making flip remarks.

§34. That one can never tell accurately what the public wants.

§35. That every time one sat upon an old-fashioned horse-hair sofa one of the protruding sharp hairs would stab one through the union suit.

§36. That when an ocean vessel collides with another vessel or hits an iceberg and starts to sink, the ship's band promptly rushes up to the top deck and begins playing "Nearer, My God, to Thee."

§37. That in no town in America where it has played has "Uncle Tom's Cabin" ever failed to make money. ,

§38. That the tenement districts are the unhealthy places they are because the dwellers hang their bed-clothing out on the fire-escapes.

§39. That, in small town hotels, the tap marked "hot water" always gives forth cold water and that the tap marked "cold" always gives forth hot.

§40. That every lieutenant in the American army who went to France had an affair with a French comtesse.

§41. That when cousins marry, their children are born blind, deformed, or imbecile.

§42. That a cat falling from the twentieth story of the Singer Building will land upon the pavement below on its feet, uninjured and as frisky as ever.

§43. That the accumulation of great wealth always brings with it great unhappiness.

§44. That it is unlucky to count the carriages in a funeral.

§45. That the roulette wheel at Monte Carlo is controlled by a wire as thin as a hair which is controlled in turn by a button hidden beneath the rug near the operator's great toe.

§46. That Polish women are so little human that one of them can have a baby at 8 A.M. and cook her husband's dinner at noon.

§47. That Henry James never wrote a short sentence.

§48. That it is bad luck to kill a spider.

§49. That German peasants are possessed of a profound knowledge of music.

§50. That every coloured cook has a lover who never works, and that she feeds him by stealing the best part of every dish she cooks.

§51. That George Bernard Shaw doesn't really believe anything he writes.

§52. That the music of Richard Wagner is all played *fortissimo*, and by cornets.

§53. That the Masonic order goes back to the days of King Solomon.

§54. That swearing is forbidden by the Bible.

§55. That all newspaper reporters carry notebooks.

§56. That whiskey is good for snake-bite.

§57. That surgeons often kill patients for the sheer pleasure of it.

§58. That ten drops of camphor in half a glass of water will prevent a cold.

§59. That the first thing a country jake does when he comes to New York is to make a bee line for Grant's Tomb and the Aquarium.

§60. That if one's nose tickles it is a sign that one is going to meet a stranger or kiss a fool.

§61. That if one's right ear burns, it is a sign that some one is saying nice things about one.

§62. That if one's left ear burns, it is a sign that some one is saying mean things about one.

§63. That French women use great quantities of perfume in lieu of taking a bath.

§64. That a six-footer is invariably a virtuoso of amour superior to a man of, say, five feet seven.

§65. That a soubrette is always fifteen or twenty years older than she looks.

§66. That what impels most men to have their finger-nails manicured is a vanity for having manicured finger-nails.

§67. That water rots the hair and thus causes baldness.

§68. That when one twin dies, the other twin becomes exceedingly melancholy and soon also dies.

§69. That one may always successfully get a cinder out of the eye by not touching the eye, but by rolling it in an outward direction and simultaneously blowing the nose.

§70. That if one wears light weight underwear winter and summer the year 'round, one will never catch a cold.

§71. That a drunken man is invariably more bellicose than a sober man.

§72. That all prize-fighters and baseball players have their hair cut round in the back.

§73. That the work of a detective calls for exceptionally high sagacity and cunning.

§74. That on the first day of the season in the pleasure parks many persons, owing to insufficiently tested apparatus, are regularly killed on the roller-coasters.

§75. That a play, a novel, or a short story with a happy ending is necessarily a commercialized and inartistic piece of work.

§76. That a person who follows up a cucumber salad with a dish of ice-cream will inevitably be the victim of cholera morbus.

§77. That a Sunday School superintendent is always carrying on an intrigue with one of the girls in the choir.

§78. That it is one of the marks of a gentleman that he never speaks evil of a woman.

§79. That a member of the Masons cannot be hanged.

§80. That a policeman can eat *gratis* as much fruit and as many peanuts off the street-corner stands as he wants.

§81. That the real President of the United States is J. P. Morgan.

§82. That onion breath may be promptly removed by drinking a little milk.

§83. That onion breath may be promptly removed by eating a little parsley.

§84. That Catholic priests conduct their private conversations in Latin.

§85. That John Drew is a great society man.

§86. That all Swedes are stupid fellows, and have very thick skulls.

§87. That all the posthumously printed stories of David Graham Phillips and Jack London have been written by hacks hired by the magazine editors and publishers.

§88. That a man like Charles Schwab, who has made a great success of the steel business, could in the same way easily have become a great composer like Bach or Mozart had he been minded thus to devote his talents.

§89. That the man who doesn't hop promptly to his feet when the orchestra plays "The Star Spangled Banner" as an overture to Hurtig and Seamon's "Hurly-Burly Girlies" must have either rheumatism or pro-German sympathies.

§90. That every workman in Henry Ford's factory owns a pretty house in the suburbs and has a rose-garden in the back-yard.

§91. That all circus people are very pure and lead domestic lives.

§92. That if a spark hits a celluloid collar, the collar will explode.

§93. That when a bachelor who has hated children for twenty years gets married and discovers he is about to become a father, he is delighted.

§94. That drinking three drinks of whiskey a day will prevent pneumonia.

§95. That every negro who went to France with the army had a liaison with a white woman and won't look at a nigger wench any more.

§96. That all Russians have unpronounceable names.

§97. That awnings keep rooms cool.

§98. That it is very difficult to decipher a railroad time-table.

§99. That gamblers may always be identified by their habit of wearing large diamonds.

§100. That when a man embarks in a canoe with a girl, the chances are two to one that the girl will move around when the boat is in mid-stream and upset it.

§101. That German babies are brought up on beer in place of milk.

§102. That a man with two shots of cocaine in him could lick Jack Dempsey.

§103. That fully one half the repertoire of physical ailments is due to uric acid.

§104. That a woman, when buying a cravat for a man, always picks out one of green and purple with red polka-dots.

§105. That a negro's vote may always be readily bought for a dollar.

§106. That cripples always have very sunny dispositions.

§107. That if one drops a crust of bread into one's glass of champagne, one can drink indefinitely without getting drunk.

§108. That a brass band always makes one feel like marching.

§109. That, when shaving on a railway train, a man invariably cuts himself.

§110. That the male Spaniard is generally a handsome, flashing-eyed fellow, possessed of fiery temper.

§111. That after drinking a glass of absinthe one has peculiar hallucinations and nightmares.

§112. That since the Indians were never bald, baldness comes from wearing tight hats.

§113. That all wine-agents are very loose men.

§114. That the editor of a woman's magazine is always a lizzie.

§115. That what is contained in the pitcher on the speakers' platform is always ice-water.

§116. That all Senators from Texas wear sombreros, chew tobacco, expectorate profusely, and frequently employ the word "maverick."

§117. That the meters on taxicabs are covertly manipulated by the chauffeurs by means of wires hidden under the latters' seats.

§118. That Lillian Russell is as beautiful today as she was thirty-five years ago.

§119. That if a young woman can hold a lighted match in her fingers until it completely burns up, it is a sign that her young man really loves her.

§120. That if a young woman accidentally puts on her lingerie wrong side out, it is a sign that she will be married before the end of the year.

§121. That if a bride wears an old garter with her new finery, she will have a happy married life.

§122. That a sudden chill is a sign that somebody is walking over one's grave.

§123. That some ignoble Italian is at the bottom of every Dorothy Arnold *fugax*.

§124. That a tarantula will not crawl over a piece of rope.

§125. That millionaires always go to sleep at the opera.

§126. That Paderewski can get all the pianos he wants for nothing.

§127. That a bloodhound never makes a mistake.

§128. That celery is good for the nerves.

§129. That the jokes in *Punch* are never funny.

§130. That the Mohammedans are heathens.

§131. That a sudden shock may cause the hair to turn grey over night.

§132. That the farmer is an honest man, and greatly imposed upon.

§133. That all the antique furniture sold in America is made in Grand Rapids, Mich., and that the holes testifying to its age are made either with gimlets or by trained worms.

§134. That if a dog is fond of a man it is an infallible sign that the man is a good sort, and one to be trusted.

§135. That blondes are flightier than brunettes.

§136. That a nurse, however ugly, always looks beautiful to the sick man.

§137. That book-keepers are always round-shouldered.

§138. That if one touches a hop-toad, one will get warts.

§139. That a collar-button that drops to the floor when one is dressing invariably rolls into an obscure and inaccessible spot and eludes the explorations of its owner.

§140. That an American ambassador has the French, German, Italian, Spanish, Portuguese, Russian and Japanese languages at his finger tips, and is chummy with royalty.

§141. That the ready-made mail order blue serge suits for men are put together with mucilage, and turn green after they have been in the sunlight for a day or two.

§142. That if one has only three matches left, the first two will invariably go out, but that the third and last will remain lighted.

§143. That all Chinamen smoke opium.

§144. That every country girl who falls has been seduced by a man from the city.

§145. That an intelligent prize-fighter always triumphs over an ignorant prize-fighter, however superior the latter in agility and strength.

§146. That a doctor's family never gets sick.

§147. That nature designed a horse's tail primarily as a flicker-off of flies.

§148. That nicotine keeps the teeth in a sound condition.

§149. That when an Odd Fellow dies he is always given a magnificent funeral by his lodge, including a band and a parade.

§150. That the man who is elected president of the Senior Class in a college is always the most popular man in his class.

§151. That a minor actress in a theatrical company always considers the leading man a superb creature, and loves him at a distance.

§152. That a Southern levee is a gay place.

§153. That when a dog whines in the middle of the night, it is a sure sign that some one is going to die.

§154. That the stenographer in a business house is always coveted by her employer, who invites her to luncheon frequently, gradually worms his way into her confidence, keeps her after office hours one day, accomplishes her ruin, and then sets her up in a magnificently furnished apartment in Riverside Drive and appeases her old mother by paying the latter's expenses for a summer holiday with her daughter at the seashore.

§155. That the extinction of the Indian has been a deplorable thing.

§156. That everybody has a stomach-ache after Thanksgiving dinner.

§157. That, in summer, tan shoes are much cooler on the feet than black shoes.

§158. That every man who calls himself Redmond is a Jew whose real name is Rosenberg.

§159. That General Grant never directed a battle save with a cigar in his mouth.

§160. That there is something slightly peculiar about a man who wears spats.

§161. That the more modest a young girl is, the more innocent she is.

§162. That what a woman admires above everything else in a man is an upright character.

§163. That seafaring men drink nothing but rum.

§164. That no family in the slums has less than six children.

§165. That a piece of camphor worn on a string around the neck will ward off disease.

§166. That a saloon with a sign reading "Family Entrance" on its side door invariably has a bawdy house upstairs.

§167. That the wife of a rich man always wistfully looks back into the past and wishes she had married a poor man.

§168. That all persons prominent in smart society are very dull.

§169. That when ordering a drink of whiskey at a bar, a man always used to instruct the bartender as to the size of the drink he desired by saying "two fingers" or "three fingers."

§170. That all the wine formerly served in Italian restaurants was made in the cellar, and was artificially coloured with some sort of dye that was very harmful to the stomach.

§171. That bootblacks whistle because they are so happy.

§172. That stokers on ocean liners are from long service so used to the heat of the furnaces that they don't notice it.

§173. That what draws men to horse races is love of the sport.

§174. That tarantulas often come from the tropics in bunches of bananas, and that when one of them stings a negro on the wharf he swells up, turns green and dies within three hours.

§175. That a man will do anything for the woman he loves.

§176. That the reason William Gillette, who has been acting for over forty years, always smokes cigars in the parts he plays is because he is very nervous when on the stage.

§177. That the doughnut is an exceptionally indigestible article.

§178. That one captive balloon in every two containing persons on pleasure bent breaks away from its moorings, and drifts out to sea.

§179. That a workingman always eats what is in his dinnerpail with great relish.

§180. That children were much better behaved twenty years ago than they are today.

§181. That the cashier of a restaurant in adding up a customer's cheque always adds a dollar which is subsequently split between himself and the waiter.

§182. That it is impossible to pronounce the word "statistics" without stuttering.

§183. That the profession of white slaving, in 1900 controlled exclusively by Chinamen, has since passed entirely under the control of Italians.

§184. That every person in the Riviera lives in a "villa."

§185. That the chief form of headgear among the Swiss is the Alpine hat.

§186. That each year a man volunteers to take his children to the circus merely as a subterfuge to go himself.

§187. That all marriages with actresses turn out badly.

§188. That San Francisco is a very gay place, and full of opium joints.

§189. That an elevator operator never succeeds in stopping his car on a level with the floor.

§190. That they don't make any pianos today as good as the old square ones.

§191. That a man who habitually clears his throat before he speaks is generally a self-important hypocrite and a bluffer.

§192. That Maurice Maeterlinck, the Belgian Dr. Frank Crane, leads a monastic life.

§193. That whenever a vaudeville comedian quotes a familiar commercial slogan, such as "His Master's Voice, " or "Eventually, why not now?", he is paid $50 a performance for doing so.

§194. That all Asiatic idols have large precious rubies in their foreheads.

§195. That when the foe beheld Joan of Arc leading the French army against them, a look of terror froze their features and that, casting their arms from them, they broke into a frenzied and precipitate flight.

§196. That the late King Edward VII as Prince of Wales easily got every girl he wanted.

§197. That the penitentiaries of the United States contain a great number of hapless prisoners possessed of a genuine gift for poetry.

§198. That if a cat gets into a room where a baby is sleeping, the cat will suck the baby's breath and kill it.

§199. That all men named Clarence, Claude or Percy are sissies.

§200. That a street car conductor steals every fifth nickel.

§201. That the security of a bank is to be estimated in proportion to the solidity of the bank building.

§202. That seventy-five per cent of all taxicab drivers have at one time or another been in Sing Sing.

§203. That one can buy a fine suit of clothes in London for twelve dollars.

§204. That the chicken salad served in restaurants is always made of veal.

§205. That a play without a bed in it never makes any money in Paris.

§206. That Conan Doyle would have made a wonderful detective.

§207. That an oyster-shucker every month or so discovers a pearl which he goes out and sells for five hundred dollars.

§208. That a napkin is always wrapped around a champagne bottle for the purpose of hiding the label, and that the quality of the champagne may be judged by the amount of noise the cork makes when it is popped.

§209. That because a married woman remains loyal to her husband she loves him.

§210. That every time one blows oneself to a particularly expensive cigar and leans back to enjoy oneself with a good smoke after a hearty and satisfying dinner, the cigar proceeds to burn down the side.

§211. That when a police captain goes on a holiday he always gets boilingly drunk.

§212. That an Italian puts garlic in everything he eats, including coffee.

§213. That if one hits a negro on the head with a cobblestone, the cobblestone will break.

§214. That all nuns have entered convents because of unfortunate love affairs.

§215. That, being surrounded by alcoholic beverages and believing the temptation would be irresistible once he began, a bartender in the old days never took a drink.

§216. That all millionaires are born in small ramshackle houses situated near railroad tracks.

§217. That farmers afford particularly easy prey for book-agents and are the largest purchasers of cheap sets of Guy de Maupassant, Rudyard Kipling and O. Henry.

§218. That George Washington never told a lie.

§219. That a dark cigar is always a strong one.

§220. That the night air is poisonous.

§221. That a hair from a horse's tail, if put into a bottle of water, will turn into a snake.

§222. That champagne is the best of all wines.

§223. That it snowed every Christmas down to fifteen years ago.

§224. That if a young woman finds a piece of tea leaf floating around the top of her tea cup, it is a sign that she will be married before the end of the year.

§225. That if, after one lusty blow, a girl's birthday cake reveals nine candles still burning, it is a sign that it will be nine years before she gets married.

§226. That if, while promenading, a girl and her escort walk on either side of a water hydrant or other obstruction instead of both walking 'round it on the same side, they will have a misunderstanding before the month is over.

§227. That it is unlikely that a man and woman who enter a hotel without baggage after 10 P.M. and register are man and wife.

§228. That all country girls have clear, fresh, rosy complexions.

§229. That chorus girls spend the time during the entr'-actes sitting around naked in their dressing-rooms telling naughty stories.

§230. That many soldiers' lives have been saved in battle by bullets lodging in Bibles which they have carried in their breast pockets.

§231. That each year the Fourth of July exodus to the bathing beaches on the part of persons from the city establishes a new record.

§232. That women with red hair or wide nostrils are possessed of especially passionate natures.

§233. That three-fourths of the inhabitants of Denver are lungers who have gone there for the mountain air.

§234. That, when sojourning in Italy, one always feels very lazy.

§235. That the people of Johnstown, Pa., still talk of nothing but the flood.

§236. That there is no finer smell in the world than that of burning autumn leaves.

§237. That Jules Verne anticipated all the great modern inventions.

§238. That a man is always a much heartier eater than a woman.

§239. That all the girls in Mr. Ziegfeld's "Follies" are extraordinarily seductive, and that at least 40 head of bank cashiers are annually guilty of tapping the till in order to buy them diamonds and Russian sables.

§240. That a college sophomore is always a complete ignoramus.

§241. That rubbers in wet weather are a preventive of colds.

§242. That if one eats oysters in a month not containing an "r, " one is certain to get ptomaine poisoning.

§243. That a woman with a 7½-C foot always tries to squeeze it into a 4½-A shoe.

§244. That no shop girl ever reads anything but Laura Jean Libbey and the cheap sex magazines.

§245. That there is something peculiar about a man who wears a red tie.

§246. That all Bolsheviki and Anarchists have whiskers.

§247. That all the millionaires of Pittsburgh are very loud fellows, and raise merry hell with the chorus girls every time they go to New York.

§248. That a man of fifty-five is always more experienced than a man of thirty-five.

§249. That new Bermuda potatoes come from Bermuda.

§250. That the boy who regularly stands at the foot of his class in school always turns out in later life to be very successful.

§251. That the ornamental daggers fashioned out of one hundred dollars' worth of Chinese coins strung together, which one buys in Pekin or Hong Kong for three dollars and a quarter, are fashioned out of one hundred dollars' worth of Chinese coins.

§252. That it is hard to find any one in Hoboken, N.J., who can speak English.

§253. That the head-waiter in a fashionable restaurant has better manners than any other man in the place.

§254. That a girl always likes best the man who is possessed of a cavalier politeness.

§255. That the most comfortable room conceivable is one containing a great big open fireplace.

§256. That brunettes are more likely to grow stout in later years than blondes.

§257. That a sepia photograph of the Coliseum, framed, is a work of art.

§258. That every time one crosses the English Channel one encounters rough weather and is very sea-sick.

§259. That the Navajo blankets sold to trans-continental tourists by the Indians on the station platform at Albuquerque, New Mexico, are made by the Elite Novelty M'f'g. Co. of Passaic, N.J., and are bought by the Indians in lots of 1, 000.

§260. That appendicitis is an ailment invented by surgeons twelve years ago for money-making purposes and that, in the century before that time, no one was ever troubled with it.

§261. That a theatrical matinée performance is always inferior to an evening performance, the star being always eager to hurry up the show in order to get a longer period for rest before the night performance.

§262. That John D. Rockefeller would give his whole fortune for a digestion good enough to digest a cruller.

§263. That a clergyman leads an easy and lazy life, and spends most of his time visiting women parishioners while their husbands are at work.

§264. That it is almost sure death to eat cucumbers and drink milk at the same meal.

§265. That all bank cashiers, soon or late, tap the till.

§266. That the members of fashionable church choirs, during the sermon, engage in kissing and hugging behind the pipe-organ.

§267. That women who are in society never pay any attention to their children, and wish that they would die.

§268. That if one gets one's feet wet, one is sure to catch cold.

§269. That all French women are very passionate, and will sacrifice everything to love.

§270. That when a drunken man falls he never hurts himself.

§271. That all Chinese laundrymen sprinkle their laundry by taking a mouthful of water and squirting it out at their wash in a fine spray; and that, whatever the cost of living to a white man, the Chinese laundryman always lives on eight cents a day.

§272. That if one fixes a savage beast with one's eye, the beast will remain rooted to the spot and presently slink away.

§273. That if one eats cucumbers and then goes in swimming, one will be seized with a cramp.

§274. That hiccoughs may be stopped by counting slowly up to one hundred.

§275. That newspaper reporters hear, every day, a great many thumping scandals that they fail to print, and that they refrain through considerations of honour.

§276. That the young East Side fellow who plays violin solos at the moving-picture theatre around the corner is so talented that, if he had the money to go to Europe to study, he would be a rival to Kreisler within three years.

§277. That Paderewski, during the piano-playing days, wore a wig, and was actually as bald as a coot.

§278. That lightning never strikes twice in the same place.

§279. That when a doctor finds there is nothing the matter with a man who has come to consult him, he never frankly tells the man there's nothing wrong with him, but always gives him bread pills.

§280. That, in a family crisis, the son always sticks to the mother and the daughter to the father.

§281. That beer is very fattening.

§282. That no man of first-rate mental attainments ever goes in for dancing.

§283. That a woman can't sharpen a lead pencil.

§284. That on every trans-Atlantic steamer there are two smooth gamblers who, the moment the ship docks, sneak over the side with the large sum of money they have won from the passengers.

§285. That if one gets out of bed on the left side in the morning, one has a mean disposition for the rest of the day.

§286. That a woman who has led a loose life is so grateful for the respect shown her by the man who asks her to marry him that she makes the best kind of wife.

§287. That fish is a brain food.

§288. That street-corner beggars have a great deal of money hidden away at home under the kitchen floor.

§289. That it is advisable for a young woman who takes gas when having a tooth pulled to be accompanied by some one, by way of precaution against the dentist.

§290. That all girls educated in convents turn out in later life to be hell-raisers.

§291. That a young girl may always safely be trusted with the kind of man who speaks of his mother.

§292. That a nine-year-old boy who likes to play with toy steam engines is probably a born mechanical genius and should be educated to be an engineer.

§293. That all celebrated professional humourists are in private life heavy and witless fellows.

§294. That when one stands close to the edge of a dizzy altitude, one is seized peculiarly with an impulse to jump off.

§295. That if one eats an apple every night before retiring, one will never be ill.

§296. That all negroes born south of the Potomac can play the banjo and are excellent dancers.

§297. That whenever a negro is educated he refuses to work and becomes a criminal.

§298. That whenever an Italian begins to dress like an American and to drive a Dodge car, it is a sign he has taken to black-handing or has acquired an interest in the white-slave trust.

§299. That, in the days when there were breweries, the men who drove beer-wagons drank 65 glasses of beer a head a day, and that it didn't hurt them because it came direct from the wood.

§300. That, until the time of American intervention, the people of the Philippines were all cannibals, and displayed the heads of their fallen enemies on poles in front of their houses.

§301. That whenever a crowd of boys goes camping in summer two or three of them are drowned, and the rest come home suffering from poison ivy.

§302. That whenever a will case gets into the courts, the lawyers gobble all the money, and the heirs come out penniless.

§303. That every female moving-picture star carries on an intrigue with her leading man, and will marry him as soon as he can get rid of his poor first wife, who took in washing in order to pay for his education in the art of acting.

§304. That all theatrical managers are Jews, and that most of them can scarcely speak English.

§305. That a great many of women's serious diseases are due to high French heels.

§306. That if one does not scratch a mosquito bite, it will stop itching.

§307. That when a girl gives a man a pen-knife for a present, their friendship will come to an unhappy end unless he exercises the precaution to ward off bad luck by giving her a penny.

§308. That whenever one takes an umbrella with one, it doesn't rain.

§309. That the cloth used in suits made in England is so good that it never wears out.

§310. That cinnamon drops are coloured red with a dye-stuff manufactured out of the dried bodies of cochineal insects.

§311. That the missionaries in China and Africa make fortunes robbing the natives they are sent out to convert.

§312. That there is a revolution in Central America every morning before breakfast, and that the sole object of all the revolutionary chiefs is to seize the money in the public treasury and make off to Paris.

§313. That whenever there is a funeral in an Irish family the mourners all get drunk and proceed to assault one another with clubs.

§314. That all immigrants come to America in search of liberty, and that when they attempt to exercise it they should be immediately sent back.

§315. That whenever a rich American girl marries a foreign nobleman, he at once gets hold of all her money, then beats her and then runs away with an actress.

§316. That if one begins eating peanuts one cannot stop.

§317. That a bachelor never has any one to sew the buttons on his clothes.

§318. That whenever a dog wags his tail it is a sign that he is particularly happy.

§319. That an Italian street labourer can do a hard day's work on one large plate of spaghetti a day.

§320. That if one breaks a mirror one will have bad luck for seven years.

§321. That two men seldom agree that the same girl is good-looking.

§322. That in the infinitesimal space of time between the springing of the trap-door and his dropping through it, a hanged man sees his entire life pass in panorama before him.

§323. That when Washington crossed the Delaware, he stood up in the bow of the boat holding aloft a large American flag.

§324. That whereas a man always hopes his first child will be a boy, his wife always hopes that it will be a girl.

§325. That the first time a boy smokes a cigar he always becomes deathly sick.

§326. That a woman always makes a practice of being deliberately late in keeping an appointment with a man.

§327. That if, encountering a savage beast in the jungle, one falls upon the ground, lies still and pretends that one is dead, the savage beast will promptly make off and not hurt one.

§328. That if one sits in front of the Café de la Paix, in Paris, one will soon or late see everybody in the world that one knows.

§329. That it is always twice as hard to get rid of a summer cold as to get rid of a winter cold.

§330. That a soft speaking voice is the invariable mark of a well-bred man.

§331. That the persons who most vociferously applaud the playing of "Dixie" in restaurants are all Northerners who have never been further South than Allentown, Pa.

§332. That the larger the dog, the safer he is for children.

§333. That Catholic priests never solicit money from their parishioners, but merely assess them so much a head, and make them pay up instantly.

§334. That nine times in ten when one is in pain, and a doctor assures one that he is squirting morphine into one's arm, what he is really squirting in is only warm water.

§335. That a German civilian, before the war, had to get off the sidewalk whenever an army lieutenant approached him on the street, and that, if he failed to do so instantly, the lieutenant was free to run him through with his sword.

§336. That while it may be possible, in every individual case of spiritualist communication with the dead, to prove fraud by the medium, the accumulated effect of such communications is to demonstrate the immortality of the soul.

§337. That an Italian who earns and saves $1, 000 in America can take the money home, invest it in an estate, and live like a rich man thereafter.

§338. That all Mormons, despite the laws against it, still practise polygamy, and that they have agents all over the world recruiting cuties for their harems.

§339. That when a man goes to a photographer's to have his picture taken, the knowledge that he is having his picture taken always makes him very self-conscious, thus causing him to assume an expression which results in the photograph being an inaccurate likeness.

§340. That if the lower line on the palm of one's hand is a long one, it is a sign that one is going to live to a ripe old age.

§341. That Italian counts, before the war, always used to make their expenses when they came to America by acting as wine agents.

§342. That a Russian peasant, in the days of the czar, drank two quarts of vodka a day.

§343. That a German farmer can raise more produce on one acre of land than an American can raise on a hundred.

§344. That a boil on the neck purifies the blood and is worth $1,000.

§345. That whenever a Frenchman comes home unexpectedly, some friend of the family makes a quick sneak out of the back door.

§346. That every negro servant girl spends at least half of her wages on preparations for taking the kink out of her hair.

§347. That the licorice candy sold in cheap candy stores is made of old rubber boots.

§348. That if a boy is given all he wants to drink at home he will not drink when he is away from home.

§349. That the second-class passengers on a trans-Atlantic steamship always have more fun than the first-class passengers.

§350. That a drunken man always pronounces every "s" as "sh."

§351. That champagne will prevent seasickness.

§352. That thin wrists and slender ankles are unmistakable signs of aristocratic breeding.

§353. That when one asks a girl to go canoeing she always brings along a bright red or yellow sofa cushion.

§354. That when a woman buys cigars for a man she always judges the quality of the cigars by the magnificence of the cigar-bands.

§355. That candle light makes a woman forty-five years old look fifteen years younger.

§356. That the winters in the United States are a good deal less cold than they used to be, and that the change has been caused by the Gulf Stream.

§357. That the Thursday matinées given by Chauncey Olcott are attended only by Irish servant girls.

§358. That the reason the British authorities didn't lock up Bernard Shaw during the war was because they were afraid of his mind.

§359. That Professor Garner is able to carry on long and intimate conversations with monkeys in their own language.

§360. That oysters are a great aphrodisiac.

§361. That if one sleeps with one's head on a high pillow one will be round-shouldered.

§362. That coal miners get so dirty that they have to wash so often that they are the cleanest working-men in the world.

§363. That the average French housewife can make such a soup out of the contents of a garbage-can that the eater will think he is at the Ritz.

§364. That such authors as Dr. Frank Crane and Herbert Kaufman do not really believe what they write, but print it simply for the money that is in it.

§365. That the average newspaper cartoonist makes $100, 000 a year.

§366. That when a play is given in an insane asylum the inmates always laugh at the tragic moments and cry at the humorous moments.

§367. That if a girl takes the last cake off a plate she will die an old maid.

§368. That men high in public affairs always read detective stories for diversion.

§369. That the wireless news bulletins posted daily on ocean liners are made up on board.

§370. That the Swiss, when they sing, always yodel.

§371. That all German housewives are very frugal.

§372. That if one holds a buttercup under a person's chin and a yellow light is reflected upon that person's chin, it is a sign that he likes butter.

§373. That all penny-in-the-slot weighing machines make a fat woman lighter and a thin woman heavier.

§374. That in the period just before a woman's baby is born the woman's face takes on a peculiar spiritual and holy look.

§375. That when a Chinese laundryman hands one a slip for one's laundry, the Chinese letters which he writes on the slip have nothing to do with the laundry but are in reality a derogatory description of the owner.

§376. That an old woman with rheumatism in her leg can infallibly predict when it is going to rain.

§377. That Philadelphia is a very sleepy town.

§378. That it is impossible for a man to learn how to thread a needle.

§379. That there is something unmanly about a grown man playing the piano, save only when he plays it in a bordello.

§380. That a couple of quinine pills, with a chaser of rye whiskey, will cure a cold.

§381. That all Congressmen who voted for Prohibition are secret lushers and have heavy stocks of all sorts of liquors in their cellars.

§382. That a certain Exalted Personage in Washington is a gay dog with the ladies and used to cut up with a stock company actress.

§383. That all the best cooks are men.

§384. That all Japanese butlers are lieutenants in the Japanese Navy and that they read and copy all letters received by the folks they work for.

§385. That the best way to stop nose-bleed is to drop a door-key down the patient's back.

§386. That a thunder-storm will cause milk to turn sour.

§387. That if a man drinks three glasses of buttermilk every day he will never be ill.

§388. That whenever two Indians meet they greet each other with the word "How!"

§389. That the Justices of the Supreme Court of the United States all chew tobacco while hearing cases, but that they are very serious men otherwise, and never laugh, or look at a pretty girl, or get tight.

§390. That all negro prize-fighters marry white women, and that they afterward beat them.

§391. That New Orleans is a very gay town and full of beautiful French creoles.

§392. That gin is good for the kidneys.

§393. That the English lower classes are so servile that they say "Thank you, sir, " if one kicks them in the pantaloons.

§394. That the gipsies who go about the country are all horse-thieves, and that they will put a spell upon the cattle of any farmer who has them arrested for stealing his mare.

§395. That every bachelor of easy means has an illicit affair with a grass widow in a near-by city and is the father of several illegitimate children.

§396. That a country editor receives so many presents of potatoes, corn, rutabagas, asparagus, country ham, carrots, turnips, etc., that he never has to buy any food.

§397. That whenever news reached him of another Federal disaster Abraham Lincoln would laugh it off with a very funny and often somewhat smutty story, made up on the spot.

§398. That George Washington died of a heavy cold brought on by swimming the Potomac in the heart of winter to visit a yellow girl on the Maryland shore.

§399. That all negroes who show any intelligence whatever are actually two-thirds white, and the sons of United States Senators.

§400. That the late King Leopold of Belgium left 350 illegitimate children.

§401. That Senator Henry Cabot Lodge is a very brainy man, though somewhat stuck up.

§402. That if one eats ice-cream after lobster one will be doubled up by belly-ache.

§403. That Quakers, for all their religion, are always very sharp traders and have a great deal of money hidden away in banks.

§404. That old baseball players always take to booze, and so end their days either as panhandlers, as night watchmen or as janitors of Odd Fellows' halls.

§405. That the object of the players, in college football, is to gouge out one another's eyes and pull off one another's ears.

§406. That the sort of woman who carries around a Pomeranian dog, if she should ever have a child inadvertently, would give the midwife $500 to make away with it.

§407. That a woman likes to go to a bargain sale, fight her way to the counter, and have pins stuck into her and her feet mashed by other women.

§408. That, if one swallows an ounce of olive oil before going to a banquet, one will not get drunk.

§409. That a mud-turtle is so tenacious of life that if one cuts off his head a new one will grow in its place.

§410. That the only things farmers read are government documents and patent-medicine almanacs.

§411. That if one's ear itches it is a sign that some one is talking of one.

§412. That Italian children, immediately they leave the cradle, are sewed into their underclothes, and that they never get a bath thereafter until they are confirmed.

§413. That all Catholic priests are very hearty eaters, and have good wine cellars.

§414. That politics in America would be improved by turning all the public offices over to business men.

§415. That department store sales are always fakes, and that they mark down a few things to attract the women and then swindle them by lifting the prices on things they actually want.

§416. That 100, 000 abortions are performed in Chicago every year.

§417. That John D. Rockefeller has a great mind, and would make a fine President if it were not for his craze for money.

§418. That all the Jews who were drafted during the late war were put into the Quartermaster's Department on account of their extraordinary business acumen.

§419. That a jury never convicts a pretty woman.

§420. That chorus girls in the old days got so tired of drinking champagne that the sound of a cork popping made them shudder.

§421. That the Massachusetts troops, after the first battle of Bull Run, didn't stop running until they reached Harrisburg, Pa.

§422. That General Grant was always soused during a battle, and that on the few occasions when he was sober he got licked.

§423. That the late King Edward used to carry on in Paris at such a gait that he shocked even the Parisians.

§424. That it takes an Englishman two days to see a joke, and that he always gets it backward even then.

§425. That headwaiters in fashionable hotels make $100 a day.

§426. That if a bat flies into a woman's hair, the hair must be cut off to get it out.

§427. That all the women in Chicago have very large feet.

§428. That on cold nights policemen always sneak into stables on their beats and go to sleep.

§429. That all the school-boys in Boston have bulged brows, wear large spectacles and can read Greek.

§430. That all dachshunds come from Germany.

§431. That nine out of every ten Frenchmen have syphilis.

§432. That the frankfurters sold at circuses and pleasure parks are made of dog meat.

§433. That all the cheaper brands of cigarettes are sophisticated with drugs, and in time cause those who smoke them to get softening of the brain.

§434. That rock-and-rye will cure a cold.

§435. That a country boy armed with a bent pin can catch more fish than a city angler with the latest and most expensive tackle.

§436. That red-haired girls are especially virulent.

§437. That all gamblers eventually go broke.

§438. That the worst actress in the company is always the manager's wife.

§439. That an elephant in a circus never forgets a person who gives him a chew of tobacco or a rotten peanut, but will single him out from a crowd years afterward and bash in his head with one colossal blow.

§440. That it is unlucky to put your hat on a bed.

§441. That an old sock makes the best wrapping for a sore throat.

§442. That lighting three cigarettes with one match will bring some terrible calamity upon one or other of the three smokers.

§443. That milking a cow is an operation demanding a special talent that is possessed only by yokels, and that a person born in a large city can never hope to acquire it.

§444. That whenever there is a rough-house during a strike, it is caused by foreign anarchists who are trying to knock out American idealism.

§445. That, whatever the demerits of Jews otherwise, they are always very kind to their old parents.

§446. That the Swiss army, though small, is so strong that not even the German army in its palmy days could have invaded Switzerland, and that it is strong because all Swiss are patriots to the death.

§447. That when two Frenchmen fight a duel, whether with pistols or with swords, neither of them is ever hurt half so much as he would have been had he fought an honest American wearing boxing-gloves.

§448. That whenever Prohibition is enforced in a region populated by negroes, they take to morphine, heroin and other powerful drugs, and begin murdering all of the white inhabitants.

§449. That all the great writers of the world now use typewriters.

§450. That all Presidents of the United States get many hot tips on the stock-market, but that they are too honourable to play them, and so turn them over to their wives, who make fortunes out of them.

§451. That Elihu Root is an intellectual giant, and that it is a pity the suspicion of him among farmers makes it impossible to elect him President.

§452. That no man not a sissy can ever learn to thread a needle or darn a sock.

§453. That all glass blowers soon or late die of consumption.

§454. That all women who go in bathing at the French seaside resorts affect very naughty one-piece bathing suits.

§455. That George M. Cohan and Irving Berlin can only play the piano with one finger.

§456. That farmers always go into gold mine swindles because of the magnificently embossed stock certificates.

§457. That the Germans eat six regular meals a day, and between times stave off their appetite with numerous Schweitzer cheese sandwiches, blutwurst and beer.

§458. That David Belasco teaches his actresses how to express emotion by knocking them down and pulling them around the stage by the hair.

§459. That only Americans travel in the first class carriages of foreign railway trains, and that fashionable Englishmen always travel third class.

§460. That the whiskey sold in blind pigs contains wood alcohol and causes those who drink it to go blind.

§461. That wealthy society women never wear their pearl necklaces in public, but always keep them at home in safes and wear indistinguishable imitations instead.

§462. That the late Charles Yerkes had no less than twenty girls, for each of whom he provided a Fifth Avenue mansion and a yearly income of $50, 000.

§463. That when one goes to a railroad station to meet some one, the train is never on time.

§464. That the theatregoers in the Scandinavian countries care for nothing but Ibsen and Strindberg.

§465. That all doctors write prescriptions illegibly.

§466. That Englishwomen are very cold.

§467. That when the weather man predicts rain it always turns out fair, and that when he predicts fair it always rains.

§468. That lemon juice will remove freckles.

§469. That if a woman wears a string of amber beads she will never get a sore throat.

§470. That no well-bred person ever chews gum.

§471. That all actors sleep till noon, and spend the afternoon calling on women.

§472. That the men who make sauerkraut press it into barrels by jumping on it with their bare feet.

§473. That the moment a nigger gets eight dollars, he goes to a dentist and has one of his front teeth filled with gold.

§474. That one never sees a Frenchman drunk, all the souses whom one sees in Paris being Americans.

§475. That a daughter is always a much greater comfort to a mother in after life than a son.

§476. That a man with a weak, receding chin is always a nincompoop.

§477. That English butlers always look down on their American employers, and frequently have to leave the room to keep from laughing out loud.

§478. That the most faithful and loving of all dogs is the Newfoundland.

§479. That a man always dislikes his mother-in-law, and goes half-crazy every time she visits him.

§480. That if one doesn't scratch a mosquito bite it will stop itching.

§481. That all the men in the moving picture business were formerly cloak and suit merchants, and that they are now all millionaires.

§482. That the accumulation of money makes a man hard, and robs him of all his finer qualities.

§483. That, in an elevator, it is always a man who usurps the looking-glass.

§484. That it is very unlucky to wear an opal.

§485. That if a man's eyebrows meet, it is a sign that he has a very unpleasant nature.

§486. That a negro ball always ends up in a grand free-for-all fight, in which several coons are mortally slashed with razors.

§487. That if Houdini were locked up in Sing Sing, he would manage to make his get-away in less than half an hour's time.

§488. That Bob Ingersoll is in hell.

THE END

BOOK TWO.
THE AMERICAN LANGUAGE

A Preliminary Inquiry into the Development of English in the United States

PREFACE

The aim of this book is best exhibited by describing its origin. I am, and have been since early manhood, an editor of newspapers, magazines and books, and a critic of the last named. These occupations have forced me into a pretty wide familiarity with current literature, both periodical and within covers, and in particular into a familiarity with the current literature of England and America. It was part of my daily work, for a good many years, to read the principal English newspapers and reviews; it has been part of my work, all the time, to read the more important English novels, essays, poetry and criticism. An American born and bred, I early noted, as everyone else in like case must note, certain salient differences between the English of England and the English of America as practically spoken and written— differences in vocabulary, in syntax, in the shades and habits of idiom, and even, coming to the common speech, in grammar. And I noted too, of course, partly during visits to England but more largely by a somewhat wide and intimate intercourse with English people in the United States, the obvious differences between English and American pronunciation and intonation.

Greatly interested in these differences—some of them so great that they led me to seek exchanges of light with Englishmen—I looked for some work that would describe and account for them with a show of completeness, and perhaps depict the process of their origin. I soon found that no such work existed, either in England or in America—that the whole literature of the subject was astonishingly meagre and unsatisfactory. There were several dictionaries of Americanisms, true enough, but only one of them made any pretension to scientific method, and even that one was woefully narrow and incomplete. The one more general treatise, the work of a man foreign to both England and America in race and education, was more than 40 years old, and full of palpable errors. For the rest, there was only a fugitive and inconsequential literature—an almost useless mass of notes and essays, chiefly by the minor sort of pedagogues, seldom illuminating, save in small details, and often incredibly ignorant and inaccurate. On the large and important subject of American pronunciation, for example, I could find nothing save a few casual essays. On American spelling, with its wide and constantly visible divergences from English usages, there was little more. On American grammar there was nothing whatever. Worse, an important part of the poor literature that I unearthed was devoted to absurd efforts to prove that no such thing as an American variety of English existed—that the differences I constantly encountered in English and that my English friends encountered in American were chiefly imaginary, and to be explained away by denying them.

Still intrigued by the subject, and in despair of getting any illumination from such theoretical masters of it, I began a collection of materials for my own information, and gradually it took on a rather formidable bulk. My interest in it being made known by various articles in the newspapers and magazines, I began also to receive contributions from other persons of the same fancy, both English and American, and gradually my collection fell into a certain order, and I saw the workings of general laws in what, at first, had appeared to be mere chaos. The present book then began to take form—its preparation a sort of recreation from other and far different labor. It is anything but an exhaustive treatise upon the subject; it is not even an exhaustive examination of the materials. All it pretends to do is to articulate some of those materials—to get some approach to order and coherence into them, and so pave the way for a better work by some more competent man. That work calls for the equipment of a first-rate philologist, which I am surely not. All I have done here is to stake out the field, sometimes borrowing suggestions from other inquirers and sometimes, as in the case of American grammar, attempting to run the lines myself.

That it should be regarded as an anti-social act to examine and exhibit the constantly growing differences between English and American, as certain American pedants argue sharply—this doctrine is quite beyond my understanding. All it indicates, stripped of sophistry, is a somewhat childish effort to gain the approval of Englishmen—a belated efflorescence of the colonial spirit, often commingled with fashionable aspiration. The plain fact is that the English themselves are not deceived, nor do they grant the approval so ardently sought for. On the contrary, they are keenly aware of the differences between the two dialects, and often discuss them, as the following pages show. Perhaps one dialect, in the long run, will defeat and absorb the other; if the two nations continue to be partners in great adventures it may very well happen. But even in that case, something may be accomplished by examining the differences which exist today. In some ways, as in intonation, English usage is plainly better than American. In others, as in spelling, American usage is as plainly better than English. But in order to develop usages that the people of both nations will accept it is obviously necessary to study the differences now visible. This study thus shows a certain utility. But its chief excuse is its human interest, for it prods deeply into national idiosyncrasies and ways of mind, and that sort of prodding is always entertaining.

I am thus neither teacher, nor prophet, nor reformer, but merely inquirer. The exigencies of my vocation make me almost completely bilingual; I can write English, as in this clause, quite as readily as American, as in this here one. Moreover, I have a hand for a compromise dialect which embodies the common materials of both, and is thus free from offense on both sides of the water—as befits the editor of a magazine published in both countries. But that compromise dialect is the living speech of neither. What I have tried to do here is to make a first sketch of the living speech of These States. The work is confessedly incomplete, and in places very painfully so, but in such enterprises a man must put an arbitrary term to his labors, lest some mischance, after years of diligence, take him from them too suddenly for them to be closed, and his laborious accumulations, as Ernest Walker says in his book on English surnames, be "doomed to the waste-basket by harassed executors."

If the opportunity offers in future I shall undoubtedly return to the subject. For one thing, I am eager to attempt a more scientific examination of the grammar of the American vulgar speech, here discussed briefly in Chapter VI. For another thing, I hope to make further inquiries into the subject of American surnames of non-English origin. Various other fields invite. No historical study of American pronunciation exists; the influence of German, Irish-English, Yiddish and other such immigrant dialects upon American has never been investigated; there is no adequate treatise on American geographical names. Contributions of materials and suggestions for a possible revised edition of the present book will reach me if addressed to me in care of the publisher at 220 West Forty-second Street, New York. I shall also be very grateful for the correction of errors, some perhaps typographical but others due to faulty information or mistaken judgment.

In conclusion I borrow a plea in confession and avoidance from Ben Jonson's pioneer grammar of English, published in incomplete form after his death. "We have set down, " he said, "that that in our judgment agreeth best with reason and good order. Which notwithstanding, if it seem to any to be too rough hewed, let him plane it out more smoothly, and I shall not only not envy it, but in the behalf of my country most heartily thank him for so great a benefit; hoping that I shall be thought sufficiently to have done my part if in tolling this bell I may draw others to a deeper consideration of the matter; for, touching myself, I must needs confess that after much painful churning this only would come which here we have devised."

Mencken.

Baltimore, January 1, 1919.

I. By Way of Introduction

§ 1. The Diverging Streams

—Thomas Jefferson, with his usual prevision, saw clearly more than a century ago that the American people, as they increased in numbers and in the diversity of their national interests and racial strains, would make changes in their mother tongue, as they had already made changes in the political institutions of their inheritance. "The new circumstances under which we are placed, " he wrote to John Waldo from Monticello on August 16, 1813, "call for new words, new phrases, and for the transfer of old words to new objects. An American dialect will therefore be formed."

Nearly a quarter of a century before this, another great American, and one with an expertness in the matter that the too versatile Jefferson could not muster, had ventured upon a prophecy even more bold and specific. He was Noah Webster, then at the beginning of his stormy career as a lexicographer. In his little volume of "Dissertations on the English Language, " printed in 1789 and dedicated to "His Excellency, Benjamin Franklin, Esq., LL.D., F.R.S., late President of the Commonwealth of Pennsylvania, " Webster argued that the time for regarding English usage and submitting to English authority had already passed, and that "a future separation of the American tongue from the English" was "necessary and unavoidable." "Numerous local causes, " he continued, "such as a new country, new associations of people, new combinations of ideas in arts and sciences, and some intercourse with tribes wholly unknown in Europe, will introduce new words into the American tongue. These causes will produce, in a course of time, a language in North America as different from the future language of England as the modern Dutch, Danish and Swedish are from the German, or from one another."(Pp. 22-23)

Neither Jefferson nor Webster put a term upon his prophecy. They may have been thinking, one or both, of a remote era, not yet come to dawn, or they may have been thinking, with the facile imagination of those days, of a period even earlier than our own. In the latter case, they allowed far too little (and particularly Webster) for factors that have worked powerfully against the influences they saw so clearly in operation about them. One of these factors, obviously, has been the vast improvement in communications across the ocean, a change scarcely in vision a century ago. It has brought New York relatively nearer to London today than it was to Boston, or even to Philadelphia, during Jefferson's presidency, and that greater proximity has produced a steady interchange of ideas, opinions, news and mere gossip. We latter-day Americans know a great deal more about the everyday affairs of England than the early Americans, for we read more English books, and have more about the English in our newspapers, and meet more Englishmen, and go to England much oftener. The effects of this ceaseless traffic in ideas and impressions, so plainly visible in politics, in ethics and aesthetics, and even in the minutae of social intercourse, are also to be seen in the language. On the one hand there is a swift exchange of new inventions on both sides, so that much of our American slang quickly passes to London and the latest English fashions in pronunciation are almost instantaneously imitated, at least by a minority, in New York; and on the other hand the English, by so constantly having the floor, force upon us, out of their firmer resolution and certitude, a somewhat sneaking respect for their own greater conservatism of speech, so that our professors of the language, in the overwhelming main, combat all signs of differentiation with the utmost diligence, and safeguard the doctrine that the standards of English are the only reputable standards of American.

This doctrine, of course, is not supported by the known laws of language, nor has it prevented the large divergences that we shall presently examine, but all the same it has worked steadily toward a highly artificial formalism, and as steadily against the investigation of the actual national speech. Such grammar, so-called, as is taught in our schools and colleges, is a grammar standing four-legged upon the theorizings and false inferences of English Latinists, eager only to break the wild tongue of Shakespeare to a rule; and its frank aim is to create in us a high respect for a book language which few of us ever actually speak and not many of us even learn to write. That language, heavily artificial though it may be, undoubtedly has notable merits. It shows a sonority and a stateliness that you must go to the Latin of the Golden Age to match; its "highly charged and heavy-shotted" periods, in Matthew Arnold's phrase, serve admirably the obscurantist purposes of American pedagogy and of English parliamentary oratory and leader-writing; it is something for the literary artists of both countries to prove their skill upon by flouting it. But to the average American, bent upon expressing his ideas, not stupendously but merely clearly, it must always remain something vague and remote, like Greek history or the properties of the parabola, for he never speaks it or hears it spoken, and seldom encounters it in his everyday reading. If he learns to write it, which is not often, it is with a rather depressing sense of its artificiality. He may master it as a Korean, bred in the colloquial Onmun, may master the literary Korean-Chinese, but he never thinks in it or quite feels it.

This fact, I daresay, is largely responsible for the notorious failure of our schools to turn out students who can put their ideas into words with simplicity and intelligibility. What their professors try to teach is not their mother-tongue at all, but a dialect that stands quite outside their common experience, and into which they have to translate their thoughts, consciously and painfully. Bad writing consists in making the attempt, and failing through lack of practise. Good writing consists, as in the case of Howells, in deliberately throwing overboard the principles so elaborately inculcated, or, as in the case of Lincoln, in standing unaware of them. Thus the study of the language he is supposed to use, to the average American, takes on a sort of bilingual character. On the one hand, he is grounded abominably in a grammar and syntax that have always been largely artificial, even in the country where they are supposed to prevail, and on the other hand he has to pick up the essentials of his actual speech as best he may. "Literary English, " says Van Wyck Brooks, [1]"with us is a tradition, just as Anglo-Saxon law with us is a tradition. They persist, not as the normal expressions of a race, ... but through prestige and precedent and the will and habit of a dominating class largely out of touch with a national fabric unconsciously taking form out of school." What thus goes on out

---

[1] America's Coming of Age; New York, 1915, p. 15. See also the preface to Every-Day English, by Richard Grant White; Boston, 1881, p. xviii.

of school does not interest the guardians of our linguistic morals. No attempt to deduce the principles of American grammar, or even of American syntax, from the everyday speech of decently spoken Americans has ever been made. There is no scientific study, general and comprehensive in scope, of the American vocabulary, or of the influences lying at the root of American word-formation. No American philologist, so far as I know, has ever deigned to give the same sober attention to the *sermo plebeius* of his country that he habitually gives to the mythical objective case in theoretical English, or to the pronunciation of Latin, or to the irregular verbs in French.

§ 2. The Academic Attitude

—This neglect of the vulgate by those professionally trained to investigate it, and its disdainful dismissal when it is considered at all, are among the strangest phenomena of American scholarship. In all other countries the everyday speech of the people, and even the speech of the illiterate, have the constant attention of philologists, and the laws of their growth and variation are elaborately studied. In France, to name but one agency, there is the Société des Parlers de France, with its diligent inquiries into changing forms; moreover, the Académie itself is endlessly concerned with the subject, and is at great pains to observe and note every fluctuation in usage.[2] In Germany, amid many other such works, there are the admirable grammars of the spoken speech by Dr. Otto Bremer. In Sweden there are several journals devoted to the study of the vulgate, and the government has recently granted a subvention of 7500 *kronen* a year to an organization of scholars called the Undersökningen av Svenska Folkmaal, formed to investigate it systematically. [3] In Norway there is a widespread movement to overthrow the official Dano-Norwegian, and substitute a

---

[2] The common notion that the Académie combats changes is quite erroneous. In the preface to the first edition of its dictionary (1694) it disclaimed any purpose "to make new words and to reject others at its pleasure." In the preface to the second edition (1718) it confessed that "ignorance and corruption often introduce manners of writing" and that "convenience establishes them." In the preface to the third edition (1740) it admitted that it was "forced to admit changes which the public has made." And so on. Says D. M. Robertson, in A History of the French Academy (London, 1910): "The Academy repudiates any assumption of authority over the language with which the public in its own practise has not first clothed it. So much, indeed, does it confine itself to an interpretation merely of the laws of language that its decisions are sometimes contrary to its own judgment of what is either desirable or expedient."

[3] Cf. *Scandinavian Studies and Notes*, vol. iv, no. 3, Aug. 1917, p. 258.

national language based upon the speech of the peasants.[4] In Spain the Academia is constantly at work upon its great Diccionario, Ortografía and Gramática, and revises them at frequent intervals (the last time in 1914), taking in all new words as they appear and all new forms of old ones. And in Latin-America, to come nearer to our own case, the native philologists have produced a copious literature on the matter closest at hand, and one finds in it very excellent works upon the Portuguese dialect of Brazil, and the variations of Spanish in Mexico, the Argentine, Chile, Peru, Ecuador, Uruguay and even Honduras and Costa Rica. [5]But in the United States the business has attracted little attention, and less talent. The only existing formal treatise upon the subject[6] was written by a Swede trained in Germany and is heavy with errors and omissions. And the only usable dictionary of Americanisms [7]was written in England, and is the work of an expatriated lawyer. Not a single volume by a native philologist, familiar with the language by daily contact and professionally equipped for the business, is to be found in the meagre bibliography.

I am not forgetting, of course, the early explorations of Noah Webster, of which much more anon, nor the labors of our later dictionary makers, nor the inquiries of the American Dialect Society, [8]nor even the occasional illuminations of such writers as Richard Grant White, Thomas S. Lounsbury and Brander Matthews. But all this preliminary work has left the main field almost uncharted. Webster, as we shall see, was far more a reformer of the American dialect than a student of it. He introduced radical changes into its spelling and

---

[4] This movement won official recognition so long ago as 1885, when the Storting passed the first of a series of acts designed to put the two languages on equal footing. Four years later, after a campaign going back to 1874, provision was made for teaching the *landsmaal* in the schools for the training of primary teachers. In 1899 a professorship of the *landsmaal* was established in the University of Christiania. The school boards in the case of primary schools, and the pupils in the case of middle and high schools are now permitted to choose between the two languages, and the *landsmaal* has been given official status by the State Church. The chief impediment to its wider acceptance lies in the fact that it is not, as it stands, a natural language, but an artificial amalgamation of peasant dialects. It was devised in 1848-50 by Ivar Aasen. *Vide* The Language Question, *London Times* Norwegian Supplement, May 18, 1914.

[5] A few such works are listed in the bibliography. More of them are mentioned in Americanismos, by Miguel de Toro y Gisbert; Paris, n. d.

[6] Maximilian Schele de Vere: Americanisms: The English of the New World; New York, 1872.

[7] Richard H. Thornton: An American Glossary ..., 2 vols.; Phila. and London, 1912.

[8] Organized Feb. 19, 1889, with Dr. J. J. Child, of Harvard, as its first president.

pronunciation, but he showed little understanding of its direction and genius. One always sees in him, indeed, the teacher rather than the scientific inquirer; the ardor of his desire to expound and instruct was only matched by his infinite capacity for observing inaccurately, and his profound ignorance of elementary philological principles. In the preface to the first edition of his American Dictionary, published in 1828—the first in which he added the qualifying adjective to the title— he argued eloquently for the right of Americans to shape their own speech without regard to English precedents, but only a year before this he had told Captain Basil Hall [Author of Travels in North America; London, 1829] that he knew of but fifty genuine Americanisms—a truly staggering proof of his defective observation. Webster was the first American professional scholar, and despite his frequent engrossment in public concerns and his endless public controversies, there was always something sequestered and almost medieval about him. The American language that he described and argued for was seldom the actual tongue of the folks about him, but often a sort of Volapük made up of one part faulty reporting and nine parts academic theorizing. In only one department did he exert any lasting influence, and that was in the department of orthography. The fact that our spelling is simpler and usually more logical than the English we chiefly owe to him. But it is not to be forgotten that the majority of his innovations, even here, were not adopted, but rejected, nor is it to be forgotten that spelling is the least of all the factors that shape and condition a language.

The same caveat lies against the work of the later makers of dictionaries; they have gone ahead of common usage in the matter of orthography, but they have hung back in the far more important matter of vocabulary, and have neglected the most important matter of idiom altogether. The defect in the work of the Dialect Society lies in a somewhat similar circumscription of activity. Its constitution, adopted in 1889, says that "its object is the investigation of the spoken English of the United States and Canada, " but that investigation, so far, has got little beyond the accumulation of vocabularies of local dialects, such as they are. Even in this department its work is very far from finished, and the Dialect Dictionary announced years ago has not yet appeared. Until its collections are completed and synchronized, it will be impossible for its members to make any profitable inquiry into the general laws underlying the development of American, or even to attempt a classification of the materials common to the whole speech. The meagreness of the materials accumulated in the five slow-moving volumes of *Dialect Notes* shows clearly, indeed, how little the American philologist is interested in the language that falls upon his ears every hour of the day. And in *Modern Language Notes* that impression is reinforced, for its bulky volumes contain exhaustive studies of all the other living languages and dialects, but only an occasional essay upon American.

Now add to this general indifference a persistent and often violent effort to oppose any formal differentiation of English and American, initiated by English purists but heartily supported by various Americans, and you come, perhaps, to some understanding of the unsatisfactory state of the literature of the subject. The pioneer dictionary of Americanisms, published in 1816 by John Pickering, a Massachusetts lawyer, [9] was not only criticized unkindly; it was roundly denounced as something subtly impertinent and corrupting, and even Noah Webster took a formidable fling at it. [10] Most of the American philologists of the early days—Witherspoon, Worcester, Fowler, Cobb and their like—were uncompromising advocates of conformity, and combatted every indication of a national independence in speech with the utmost vigilance. One of their company, true enough, stood out against the rest. He was George Perkins Marsh, and in his "Lectures on the English Language"[11] he argued that "in point of naked syntactical accuracy, the English of America is not at all inferior to that of England." But even Marsh expressed the hope that Americans would not, "with malice prepense, go about to republicanize our orthography and our syntax, our grammars and our dictionaries, our nursery hymns (*sic*) and our Bibles" to the point of actual separation. [12] Moreover, he was a philologist only by courtesy; the regularly ordained school-masters were all against him. The fear voiced by William C. Fowler, professor of rhetoric at Amherst, that Americans might "break loose from the laws of the English language" [13]altogether, was echoed by the whole fraternity, and so the corrective bastinado was laid on.

---

[9] A Vocabulary or Collection of Words and Phrases which Have Been Supposed to be Peculiar to the United States of America; Boston, 1816.

[10] A Letter to the Hon. John Pickering on the Subject of His Vocabulary; Boston, 1817.

[11] 4th ed., New York, 1870, p. 669.

[12] *Op. cit.* p. 676

[13] The English Language; New York 1850; rev. ed., 1855. This was the first American text-book of English for use in colleges. Before its publication, according to Fowler himself (rev. ed., p. xi), the language was studied only "superficially" and "in the primary schools." He goes on: "Afterward, when older, in the academy, during their

It remained, however, for two professors of a later day to launch the doctrine that the independent growth of American was not only immoral, but a sheer illusion. They were Richard Grant White, for long the leading American writer upon language questions, at least in popular esteem, and Thomas S. Lounsbury, for thirty-five years professor of the English language and literature in the Sheffield Scientific School at Yale, and an indefatigable controversialist. Both men were of the utmost industry in research, and both had wide audiences. White's "Words and Their Uses, " published in 1872, was a mine of erudition, and his "Everyday English, " following eight years later, was another. True enough, Fitzedward Hall, the Anglo-Indian-American philologist, disposed of many of his etymologies and otherwise did execution upon him, [14]but in the main his contentions held water. Lounsbury was also an adept and favorite expositor. His attacks upon certain familiar pedantries of the grammarians were penetrating and effective, and his two books, "The Standard of Usage in English" and "The Standard of Pronunciation in English, " not to mention his excellent "History of the English Language" and his numerous magazine articles, showed a profound knowledge of the early development of the language, and an admirable spirit of free inquiry. But both of these laborious scholars, when they turned from English proper to American English, displayed an unaccountable desire to deny its existence altogether, and to the support of that denial they brought a critical method that was anything but unprejudiced. White devoted not less than eight long articles in the *Atlantic Monthly*[15] to a review of the fourth edition of John Russell Bartlett's American Glossary, [16] and when he came to the end he had disposed of nine-tenths of Bartlett's specimens and called into question the authenticity of at least half of what remained. And no wonder, for his method was simply that of erecting tests so difficult and so arbitrary that only the exceptional word or phrase could pass them, and then only by a sort of chance. "To stamp a word or a phrase as an Americanism, " he said, "it is necessary to show that (1) it is of so-called 'American' origin—that is,

---

preparation for college, our pupils perhaps despised it, in comparison with the Latin and the Greek; and in the college they do not systematically study the language after they come to maturity."

[14] In Recent Exemplifications of False Philology; London, 1872.

[15] Americanisms, parts I-VIII, April, May, July, Sept., Nov., 1878; Jan., March, May, 1879.

[16] A Glossary of Words and Phrases Usually Regarded as Peculiar to the United States, 4th ed.; Boston, 1877.

that it first came into use in the United States of North America, or that (2) it has been adopted in those States from some language other than English, or has been kept in use there while it has **wholly** passed out of use in England." Going further, he argued that unless "the simple words in compound names" were used in America "in a sense different from that in which they are used in England" the compound itself could not be regarded as an Americanism. The absurdity of all this is apparent when it is remembered that one of his rules would bar out such obvious Americanisms as the use of *sick* in place of *ill*, of *molasses* for *treacle*, and of *fall* for *autumn*, for all of these words, while archaic in England, are by no means wholly extinct; and that another would dispose of that vast category of compounds which includes such unmistakably characteristic Americanisms as *joy-ride, rake-off, show-down, up-lift, out-house, rubber-neck, chair-warmer, fire-eater* and *back-talk.*

Lounsbury went even further. In the course of a series of articles in *Harper's Magazine*, in 1913, [17] he laid down the dogma that "cultivated speech ... affords the only legitimate basis of comparison between the language as used in England and in America, " and then went on:

In the only really proper sense of the term, an Americanism is a word or phrase naturally used by an educated American which under similar conditions would not be used by an educated Englishman. The emphasis, it will be seen, lies in the word "educated."

This curious criterion, fantastic as it must have seemed to European philologists, was presently reinforced, for in his fourth article Lounsbury announced that his discussion was "restricted to the **written** speech of educated men." The result, of course, was a wholesale slaughter of Americanisms. If it was not impossible to reject a word, like White, on the ground that some stray English poet or other had once used it, it was almost always possible to reject it on the ground that it was not admitted into the vocabulary of a college professor when he sat down to compose formal book-English. What remained was a small company, indeed—and almost the whole field of American idiom and American grammar, so full of interest for the less austere explorer, was closed without even a peek into it.

White and Lounsbury dominated the arena and fixed the fashion. The later national experts upon the national language, with a few somewhat timorous exceptions, pass over its peculiarities without

---

[17] Feb., March, June, July, Sept.

noticing them. So far as I can discover, there is not a single treatise in type upon one of its most salient characters—the wide departure of some of its vowel sounds from those of orthodox English. Marsh, C. H. Grandgent and Robert J. Menner have printed a number of valuable essays upon the subject, but there is no work that co-ordinates their inquiries or that attempts otherwise to·cover the field. When, in preparing materials for the following chapters, I sought to determine the history of the *a*-sound in America, I found it necessary to plow through scores of ancient spelling-books, and to make deductions, perhaps sometimes rather rash, from the works of Franklin, Webster and Cobb. Of late the National Council of Teachers of English has appointed a Committee on American Speech and sought to let some light into the matter, but as yet its labors are barely begun and the publications of its members get little beyond preliminaries. Such an inquiry involves a laboriousness which should have intrigued Lounsbury: he once counted the number of times the word *female* appears in "Vanity Fair." But you will find only a feeble dealing with the question in his book on pronunciation. Nor is there any adequate work (for Schele de Vere's is full of errors and omissions) upon the influences felt by American through contact with the languages of our millions of immigrants, nor upon our peculiarly rich and characteristic slang. There are several excellent dictionaries of English slang, and many more of French slang, but I have been able to find but one devoted exclusively to American slang, and that one is a very bad one.

§ 3. The View of Writing Men

—But though the native *Gelehrten* thus neglect the vernacular, or even oppose its study, it has been the object of earnest lay attention since an early day, and that attention has borne fruit in a considerable accumulation of materials, if not in any very accurate working out of its origins and principles. The English, too, have given attention to it— often, alas, satirically, or even indignantly. For a long while, as we shall see, they sought to stem its differentiation by heavy denunciations of its vagaries, and so late as the period of the Civil War they attached to it that quality of abhorrent barbarism which they saw as the chief mark of the American people. But in later years they have viewed it with a greater showing of scientific calm, and its definite separation from correct English, at least as a spoken tongue, is now quite frankly admitted. The Cambridge History of English Literature, for example, says that English and American are now "notably dissimilar" in vocabulary, and that the latter is splitting off into a distinct dialect.[18] The Eleventh Edition of the Encyclopaedia Britannica, going further, says that the two languages are already so far apart that "it is not uncommon to meet with [American] newspaper articles of which an untravelled Englishman would hardly be able to understand a sentence."[19] A great many other academic authorities, including A. H. Sayce and H. W. and F. G. Fowler, bear testimony to the same effect.

On turning to the men actually engaged in writing English, and particularly to those aspiring to an American audience, one finds nearly all of them adverting, at some time or other, to the growing difficulties of intercommunication. William Archer, Arnold Bennett, H. G. Wells, Sidney Low, the Chestertons and Kipling are some of those who have dealt with the matter at length. Low, in an article in the *Westminster Gazette*[20] ironically headed "Ought American to be Taught in our Schools?" has described how the latter-day British business man is "puzzled by his ignorance of colloquial American" and "painfully hampered" thereby in his handling of American trade. He continues:

In the United States of North America the study of the English tongue forms part of the educational scheme. I gather this because I find that they have professors of the English language and literature in the Universities there, and I note that in the schools there are certain hours alloted for "English" under instructors who specialize in that subject. This is quite right. English is still far from being a dead language, and our American kinsfolk are good enough to appreciate the fact.

But I think we should return the compliment. We ought to learn the American language in our schools and colleges. At present it is strangely neglected by the educational authorities. They pay attention to linguistic attainments of many other kinds, but not to this. How many thousands of youths are at this moment engaged in puzzling their brains over Latin and Greek grammar only Whitehall knows. Every well-conducted seminary has some instructor who is under the delusion that he is teaching English boys and girls to speak French with a good Parisian accent. We teach German, Italian, even Spanish, Russian, modern Greek, Arabic, Hindustani. For a moderate fee you can acquire a passing acquaintance with any of these tongues at the Berlitz Institute and the Gouin Schools. But even in these polyglot

---

[18] Vol. xiv, pp. 484-5; Cambridge, 1917.
[19] Vol. xxv, p. 209.
[20] July 18, 1913.

establishments there is nobody to teach you American. I have never seen a grammar of it or a dictionary. I have searched in vain at the book-sellers for "How to Learn American in Three Weeks" or some similar compendium. Nothing of the sort exists. The native speech of one hundred millions of civilized people is as grossly neglected by the publishers as it is by the schoolmasters. You can find means to learn Hausa or Swahili or Cape Dutch in London more easily than the expressive, if difficult, tongue which is spoken in the office, the bar-room, the tram-car, from the snows of Alaska to the mouths of the Mississippi, and is enshrined in a literature that is growing in volume and favor every day.

Low then quotes an extract from an American novel appearing serially in an English magazine—an extract including such Americanisms as *side-stepper*, *saltwater-taffy*, *Prince-Albert*(coat), *boob*, *bartender* and *kidding*, and many characteristically American extravagances of metaphor. It might be well argued, he goes on, that this strange dialect is as near to "the tongue that Shakespeare spoke" as "the dialect of Bayswater or Brixton, " but that philological fact does not help to its understanding. "You might almost as well expect him [the British business man] to converse freely with a Portuguese railway porter because he tried to stumble through Caesar when he was in the Upper Fourth at school."

In the *London Daily Mail*, W. G. Faulkner lately launched this proposed campaign of education by undertaking to explain various terms appearing in American moving-pictures to English spectators. Mr. Faulkner assumed that most of his readers would understand *sombrero*, *sidewalk*, *candy-store*, *freight-car*, *boost*, *elevator*, *boss*, *crook* and *fall* (for *autumn*) without help, but he found it necessary to define such commonplace Americanisms as *hoodlum*, *hobo*, *bunco-steerer*, *rubber-neck*, *drummer*, *sucker*, *dive* (in the sense of a thieves' resort), *clean-up*, *graft* and *to feature*. Curiously enough, he proved the reality of the difficulties he essayed to level by falling into error as to the meanings of some of the terms he listed, among them *dead-beat*, *flume*, *dub* and *stag*. Another English expositor, apparently following him, thought it necessary to add definitions of *hold-up*, *quitter*, *rube*, *shack*, *road-agent*, *cinch, live-wire* and *scab,* [21] but he, too, mistook the meaning of *dead-beat*, and in addition he misdefined *band-wagon* and substituted *get-out*, seemingly an invention of his own, for *get-away*. Faulkner, somewhat belated in his animosity, seized the opportunity to read a homily upon the vulgarity and extravagance of the American language, and argued that the introduction of its coinages through the moving-picture theatre (*Anglais, cinema*) "cannot be regarded without serious misgivings, if only because it generates and encourages mental indiscipline so far as the choice of expressions is concerned." In other words, the greater pliability and resourcefulness of American is a fault to be corrected by the English tendency to hold to that which is established.

Cecil Chesterton, in the *New Witness*, recently called attention to the increasing difficulty of intercommunication, not only verbally, but in writing. The American newspapers, he said, even the best of them, admit more and more locutions that puzzle and dismay an English reader. After quoting a characteristic headline he went on:

I defy any ordinary Englishman to say that that is the English language or that he can find any intelligible meaning in it. Even a dictionary will be of no use to him. He must know the language colloquially or not at all.... No doubt it is easier for an Englishman to understand American than it would be for a Frenchman to do the same, just as it is easier for a German to understand Dutch than it would be for a Spaniard. But it does not make the American language identical with the English. [22]

Chesterton, however, refrained from denouncing this lack of identity; on the contrary, he allowed certain merits to American. "I do not want anybody to suppose, " he said, "that the American language is in any way inferior to ours. In some ways it has improved upon it in vigor and raciness. In other ways it adheres more closely to the English of the best period." Testimony to the same end was furnished before this by William Archer. "New words, " he said, "are begotten by new conditions of life; and as American life is far more fertile of new conditions than ours, the tendency toward neologism cannot but be

---

[21] Of the words cited as still unfamiliar in England, Thornton has traced *hobo* to 1891, *hold-up* and *bunco* to 1887, *dive* to 1882, *dead-beat* to 1877, *hoodlum* to 1872, *road-agent* to 1866, *stag* to 1856, *drummer* to 1836 and *flume* to 1792. All of them are probably older than these references indicate.

[22] Summarized in *Literary Digest*, June 19, 1915.

stronger in America than in England. America has enormously enriched the language, not only with new words, but (since the American mind is, on the whole, quicker and wittier than the English) with apt and luminous colloquial metaphors."[23]

The list of such quotations might be indefinitely prolonged. There is scarcely an English book upon the United States which does not offer some discussion, more or less profound, of American peculiarities of speech, both as they are revealed in spoken discourse (particularly pronunciation and intonation) and as they show themselves in popular literature and in the newspapers, and to this discussion protest is often added, as it very often is by the reviews and newspapers. "The Americans, " says a typical critic, "have so far progressed with their self-appointed task of creating an American language that much of their conversation is now incomprehensible to English people."[24] On our own side there is almost equal evidence of a sense of difference, despite the fact that the educated American is presumably trained in orthodox English, and can at least read it without much feeling of strangeness. "The American, " says George Ade, in his book of travel, "In Pastures New," (1906, p.6) "must go to England in order to learn for a dead certainty that he does not speak the English language.... This pitiful fact comes home to every American when he arrives in London—that there are two languages, the English and the American. One is correct; the other is incorrect. One is a pure and limpid stream; the other is a stagnant pool, swarming with bacilli." This was written in 1906. Twenty-five years earlier Mark Twain had made the same observation. "When I speak my native tongue in its utmost purity in England, " he said, "an Englishman can't understand me at all."[25] The languages, continued Mark, "were identical several generations ago, but our changed conditions and the spread of our people far to the south and far to the west have made many alterations in our pronunciation, and have introduced new words among us and changed the meanings of old ones." Even before this the great humorist had marked and hailed these differences. Already in "Roughing It", (Hartford, 1872, p. 45) he was celebrating "the vigorous new vernacular of the occidental plains and mountains, " and in all his writings, even the most serious, he

---

[23] America Today, *Scribner's*, Feb. 1899, p. 218.

[24] *London Court Journal*, Aug. 28, 1892.

[25] Concerning the American Language, in The Stolen White Elephant; Boston, 1882. A footnote says that the essay is "part of a chapter crowded out of A Tramp Abroad." (Hartford, 1880.)

deliberately engrafted its greater liberty and more fluent idiom upon the stem of English, and so lent the dignity of his high achievement to a dialect that was as unmistakably American as the point of view underlying it.

The same tendency is plainly visible in William Dean Howells. His novels are mines of American idiom, and his style shows an undeniable revolt against the trammels of English grammarians. In 1886 he made a plea in *Harper's* for a concerted effort to put American on its own legs. "If we bother ourselves, " he said, "to write what the critics imagine to be 'English, ' we shall be priggish and artificial, and still more so if we make our Americans talk 'English.' ... On our lips our continental English will differ more and more from the insular English, and we believe that this is not deplorable but desirable."[26] Howells then proceeded to discuss the nature of the difference, and described it accurately as determined by the greater rigidity and formality of the English of modern England. In American, he said, there was to be seen that easy looseness of phrase and gait which characterized the English of the Elizabethan era, and particularly the Elizabethan hospitality to changed meanings and bold metaphors. American, he argued, made new words much faster than English, and they were, in the main, words of much greater daring and savor.

The difference between the two tongues, thus noted by the writers of both, was made disconcertingly apparent to the American troops when they first got to France and came into contact with the English. Fraternizing was made difficult by the wide divergence in vocabulary and pronunciation—a divergence interpreted by each side as a sign of uncouthness. The Y. M. C. A. made a characteristic effort to turn the resultant feeling of strangeness and homesickness among the Americans to account. In the *Chicago Tribune's* Paris edition of July 7, 1917, I find a large advertisement inviting them to make use of the Y. M. C. A. clubhouse in the Avenue Montaigue, "where **American** is spoken." Earlier in the war the *Illinoiser Staats Zeitung*, no doubt seeking to keep the sense of difference alive, advertised that it would "publish articles daily in the **American** language."

§ 4. Foreign Observers

—What English and American laymen have thus observed has not escaped the notice of continental philologists. The first edition of

---

[26] The Editor's Study, *Harper's Magazine*, Jan. 1886.

Bartlett, published in 1848, brought forth a long and critical review in the *Archiv für das Studium der neueren Sprachen und Literaturen* by Prof. Felix Flügel, [27] and in the successive volumes of the *Archiv*, down to our own day, there have been many valuable essays upon Americanisms, by such men as Herrig, Koehler and Koeppel. Various Dutch philologists, among them Barentz, Keijzer and Van der Voort, have also discussed the subject, and a work in French has been published by G. A. Barringer. [28] That, even to the lay Continental, American and English now differ considerably, is demonstrated by the fact that many of the popular German *Sprachführer* appear in separate editions, *Amerikanisch* and *Englisch*. This is true of the "Metoula Sprachführer" published by Prof. F. Lanenscheidt [29] and of the "Polyglott Kuntz" books.[30] The American edition of the latter starts off with the doctrine that "*Jeder, der nach Nord-Amerika oder Australien will, muss Englisch können,* " but a great many of the words and phrases that appear in its examples would be unintelligible to many Englishmen—*e. g., free-lunch, real-estate agent, buckwheat, corn* (for *maize*), *conductor, pop-corn* and *drug-store*—and a number of others would suggest false meanings or otherwise puzzle—*e. g., napkin, saloon, wash-stand, water-pitcher* and *apple-pie.* [31] To these pedagogical examples must be added that of Baedeker, of guide-book celebrity. In his guide-book to the United States, prepared for Englishmen, he is at pains to explain the meaning of various American words and phrases.

A philologist of Scandinavian extraction, Elias Molee, has gone so far as to argue that the acquisition of correct English, to a people grown so mongrel in blood as the Americans, has become a useless burden. In

---

[27] Die englische Sprache in Nordamerika, band iv, heft i; Braunschweig, 1848.

[28] Étude sur l'Anglais Parlé aux Etats Unis (la Langue Américaine), *Actes de la Société Philologique de Paris*, March, 1874.

[29] Metoula-Sprachführer.... Englisch von Karl Blattner; Ausgabe für Amerika; Berlin-Schöneberg, 1912.

[30] Polyglott Kuntze; Schnellste Erlernung jeder Sprache ohne Lehrer; Amerikanisch; Bonn a. Rh., n. d.

[31] Like the English expositors of American slang, this German falls into several errors. For example, he gives *cock* for *rooster, boots* for *shoes, braces* for *suspenders* and *postman* for *letter-carrier*, and lists *iron-monger, joiner* and *linen-draper* as American terms. He also spells *wagon* in the English manner, with two *g*'s, and translates *Schweinefüsse* as *pork-feet*. But he spells such words as *color* in the American manner and gives the pronunciation of *clerk* as the American *klörk*, not as the English *klark*.

place of it he proposes a mixed tongue, based on English, but admitting various elements from the other Germanic languages. His grammar, however, is so much more complex than that of English that most Americans would probably find his artificial "American" very difficult of acquirement. At all events it has made no progress.[32]

§ 5. The Characters of American

—The characters chiefly noted in American speech by all who have discussed it are, first, its general uniformity throughout the country, so that, dialects, properly speaking, are confined to recent immigrants, to the native whites of a few isolated areas and to the negroes of the South; and, secondly, its impatient disdain of rule and precedent, and hence its large capacity (distinctly greater than that of the English of England) for taking in new words and phrases and for manufacturing new locutions out of its own materials. The first of these characters has struck every observer, native and foreign. In place of the local dialects of other countries we have a general *Volkssprache* for the whole nation, and if it is conditioned at all it is only by minor differences in pronunciation and by the linguistic struggles of various groups of newcomers. "The speech of the United States, " said Gilbert M. Tucker, "is quite unlike that of Great Britain in the important particular that here we have no dialects." [33] "We all, " said Mr. Taft during his presidency, "speak the same language and have the same ideas." "Manners, morals and political views, " said the *New York World*, (Oct. 1, 1909) commenting upon this dictum, "have all undergone a standardization which is one of the remarkable aspects of American evolution. Perhaps it is in the uniformity of language that this development has been most noteworthy. Outside of the Tennessee mountains and the back country of New England there is no true dialect." "While we have or have had single counties as large as Great Britain, " says another American observer, "and in some of our states England could be lost, there is practically no difference between the American spoken in our 4, 039, 000 square miles of territory, except as spoken by foreigners. We, assembled here, would be perfectly understood by delegates from Texas, Maine, Minnesota, Louisiana, or

---

[32] Molee's notions are set forth in Plea for an American Language ...; Chicago, 1888; and Tutonish; Chicago, 1902. He announced the preparation of A Dictionary of the American Language in 1888, but so far as I know it has not been published. He was born in Wisconsin, of Norwegian parents, in 1845, and pursued linguistic studies at the University of Wisconsin, where he seems to have taken a Ph. B.

[33] American English, *North American Review*, Jan. 1883.

Alaska, or from whatever walk of life they might come. We can go to any of the 75, 000 postoffices in this country and be entirely sure we will be understood, whether we want to buy a stamp or borrow a match."34 "From Portland, Maine, to Portland, Oregon, " agrees an English critic, "no trace of a distinct dialect is to be found. The man from Maine, even though he may be of inferior education and limited capacity, can completely understand the man from Oregon."35

No other country can show such linguistic solidarity, nor any approach to it—not even Canada, for there a large part of the population resists learning English altogether. The Little Russian of the Ukraine is unintelligible to the citizen of Petrograd; the Northern Italian can scarcely follow a conversation in Sicilian; the Low German from Hamburg is a foreigner in Munich; the Breton flounders in Gascony. Even in the United Kingdom there are wide divergences.36 "When we remember, " says the New International Encyclopaedia[Art. Americanisms, 2nd ed.] "that the dialects of the countries (sic) in England have marked differences—so marked, indeed that it may be doubted whether a Lancashire miner and a Lincolnshire farmer could understand each other—we may well be proud that our vast country has, strictly speaking, only one language." This uniformity was noted by the earliest observers; Pickering called attention to it in the preface to his Vocabulary and ascribed it, no doubt accurately, to the restlessness of the Americans, their inheritance of the immigrant spirit, "the frequent removals of people from one part of our country to another." It is especially marked in vocabulary and grammatical forms—the foundation stones of a living speech. There may be slight differences in pronunciation and intonation—a Southern softness, a Yankee drawl, a Western burr—but in the words they use and the way they use them all Americans, even the least tutored, follow the same line. One observes, of course, a polite speech and a common speech, but the common speech is everywhere the same, and its uniform vagaries take the place of the dialectic variations of other lands. A Boston street-car conductor could go to work in Chicago, San Francisco or New Orleans without running the slightest risk of misunderstanding

---

34 J. F. Healy, general manager of the Davis Colliery Co. at Elkins, W. Va., in a speech before the West Virginia Coal Mining Institute, at Wheeling, Dec. 1910; reprinted as The American Language; Pittsburgh, 1911.

35 *Westminster Review*, July, 1888, p. 35.

36 W. W. Skeat distinguishes no less than 9 dialects in Scotland, 3 in Ireland and 30 in England and Wales. *Vide*English Dialects From the Eighth Century to the Present Day; Cambridge, 1911, p. 107 *et seq.*.

his new fares. Once he had picked up half a dozen localisms, he would be, to all linguistic intents and purposes, fully naturalized.

Of the intrinsic differences that separate American from English the chief have their roots in the obvious disparity between the environment and traditions of the American people since the seventeenth century and those of the English. The latter have lived under a stable social order, and it has impressed upon their souls their characteristic respect for what is customary and of good report. Until the war brought chaos to their institutions, their whole lives were regulated, perhaps more than those of any other people save the Spaniards, by a regard for precedent. The Americans, though largely of the same blood, have felt no such restraint, and acquired no such habit of conformity. On the contrary, they have plunged to the other extreme, for the conditions of life in their new country have put a high value upon the precisely opposite qualities of curiosity and daring, and so they have acquired that character of restlessness, that impatience of forms, that disdain of the dead hand, which now broadly marks them. From the first, says a recent literary historian, they have been "less phlegmatic, less conservative than the English. There were climatic influences, it may be; there was surely a spirit of intensity everywhere that made for short effort."[37] Thus, in the arts, and thus in business, in politics, in daily intercourse, in habits of mind and speech. The American is not, in truth, lacking in a capacity for discipline; he has it highly developed; he submits to leadership readily, and even to tyranny. But, by a curious twist, it is not the leadership that is old and decorous that fetches him, but the leadership that is new and extravagant. He will resist dictation out of the past, but he will follow a new messiah with almost Russian willingness, and into the wildest vagaries of economics, religion, morals and speech. A new fallacy in politics spreads faster in the United States than anywhere else on earth, and so does a new fashion in hats, or a new revelation of God, or a new means of killing time, or a new metaphor or piece of slang.

Thus the American, on his linguistic side, likes to make his language as he goes along, and not all the hard work of his grammar teachers can hold the business back. A novelty loses nothing by the fact that it is a novelty; it rather gains something, and particularly if it meet the national fancy for the terse, the vivid, and, above all, the bold and imaginative. The characteristic American habit of reducing complex concepts to the starkest abbreviations was already noticeable in

---

[37] F. L. Pattee: A History of American Literature Since 1870; New York, 1916.

colonial times, and such highly typical Americanisms as *O. K., N. G.,* and *P. D. Q.,* have been traced back to the first days of the republic. Nor are the influences that shaped these early tendencies invisible today, for the country is still in process of growth, and no settled social order has yet descended upon it. Institution-making is still going on, and so is language-making. In so modest an operation as that which has evolved *bunco* from *buncombe* and *bunk* from *bunco* there is evidence of a phenomenon which the philologist recognizes as belonging to the most primitive and lusty stages of speech. The American vulgate is not only constantly making new words, it is also deducing roots from them, and so giving proof, as Prof. Sayce says, that "the creative powers of language are even now not extinct."[38]

But of more importance than its sheer inventions, if only because much more numerous, are its extensions of the vocabulary, both absolutely and in ready workableness, by the devices of rhetoric. The American, from the beginning, has been the most ardent of recorded rhetoricians. His politics bristles with pungent epithets; his whole history has been bedizened with tall talk; his fundamental institutions rest as much upon brilliant phrases as upon logical ideas. And in small things as in large he exercises continually an incomparable capacity for projecting hidden and often fantastic relationships into arresting parts of speech. Such a term as *rubber-neck* is almost a complete treatise on American psychology; it reveals the national habit of mind more clearly than any labored inquiry could ever reveal it. It has in it precisely the boldness and disdain of ordered forms that are so characteristically American, and it has too the grotesque humor of the country, and the delight in devastating opprobriums, and the acute feeling for the succinct and savory. The same qualities are in *rough-house, water-wagon, near-silk, has-been, lame-duck* and a thousand other such racy substantives, and in all the great stock of native verbs and adjectives. There is, indeed, but a shadowy boundary in these new coinages between the various parts of speech. *Corral,* borrowed from the Spanish, immediately becomes a verb and the father of an adjective. *Bust,* carved out of *burst,* erects itself into a noun. *Bum,* coming by way of an earlier *bummer* from the German *bummler,* becomes noun, adjective, verb and adverb. Verbs are

---

[38] A. H. Sayce: Introduction to the Science of Language, 2 vols.; London, 1900. See especially vol. ii, ch. vi.

fashioned out of substantives by the simple process of prefixing the preposition: *to engineer, to chink, to stump, to hog.* Others grow out of an intermediate adjective, as *to boom.* Others are made by torturing nouns with harsh affixes, as *to burglarize* and *to itemize,* or by groping for the root, as *to resurrect.* Yet others are changed from intransitive to transitive: a sleeping-car *sleeps* thirty passengers. So with the adjectives. They are made of substantives unchanged: *codfish, jitney.* Or by bold combinations: *down-and-out, up-state, flat-footed.* Or by shading down suffixes to a barbaric simplicity: *scary, classy, tasty.* Or by working over adverbs until they tremble on the brink between adverb and adjective: *right* and *near* are examples.

All of these processes, of course, are also to be observed in the English of England; in the days of its great Elizabethan growth they were in the lustiest possible being. They are, indeed, common to all languages; they keep language alive. But if you will put the English of today beside the American of today you will see at once how much more forcibly they are in operation in the latter than in the former. English has been arrested in its growth by its purists and grammarians. It shows no living change in structure and syntax since the days of Anne, and very little modification in either pronunciation or vocabulary. Its tendency is to conserve that which is established; to say the new thing, as nearly as possible, in the old way; to combat all that expansive gusto which made for its pliancy and resilience in the days of Shakespeare. In place of the old loose-footedness there is set up a preciosity which, in one direction, takes the form of unyielding affectations in the spoken language, and in another form shows itself in the heavy Johnsonese of current English writing—the Jargon denounced by Sir Arthur Quiller-Couch in his Cambridge lectures. This "infirmity of speech" Quiller-Couch finds "in parliamentary debates and in the newspapers"; ... "it has become the medium through which Boards of Government, County Councils, Syndicates, Committees, Commercial Firms, express the processes as well as the conclusions of their thought, and so voice the reason of their being." Distinct from journalese, the two yet overlap, "and have a knack of assimilating each other's vices."[39]

---

[39] *Cf.* the chapter, Interlude: On Jargon, in Quiller-Couch's On the Art of Writing; New York, 1916. Curiously enough, large parts of the learned critic's book are written in the very Jargon he attacks.

American, despite the gallant efforts of the professors, has so far escaped any such suffocating formalization. We, too, of course, have our occasional practitioners of the authentic English Jargon; in the late Grover Cleveland we produced an acknowledged master of it. But in the main our faults in writing lie in precisely the opposite direction. That is to say, we incline toward a directness of statement which, at its greatest, lacks restraint and urbanity altogether, and toward a hospitality which often admits novelties for the mere sake of their novelty, and is quite uncritical of the difference between a genuine improvement in succinctness and clarity, and mere extravagant raciness. "The tendency, " says one English observer, "is ... to consider the speech of any man, as any man himself, as good as any other."[40] "All beauty and distinction, " says another, [41] "are ruthlessly sacrificed to force." Moreover, this strong revolt against conventional bonds is by no means confined to the folk-speech, nor even to the loose conversational English of the upper classes; it also gets into more studied discourse, both spoken and written. I glance through the speeches of Dr. Woodrow Wilson, surely a purist if we have one at all, and find, in a few moments, half a dozen locutions that an Englishman in like position would never dream of using, among them *we must get a move on*, [42] *hog* as a verb, [43] *gum-shoe* as an adjective with verbal overtones, [44] *onery* in place of *ordinary*, [45] and *that is going some*.[46] From the earliest days, indeed, English critics have found this gipsy tendency in our most careful writing. They denounced it in Marshall, Cooper, Mark Twain, Poe, Lossing, Lowell and Holmes, and even in Hawthorne and Thoreau; and it was no less academic a work than W. C. Brownell's "French Traits" which brought forth, in a London literary journal, the dictum that "the language most depressing to the cultured Englishman is the language of the cultured American." Even "educated American English, " agrees the chief of modern English grammarians, "is now almost entirely independent of British influence,

---

[40] Alexander Francis: Americans: an Impression; New York, 1900.

[41] G. Lowes Dickinson, in the *English Review*, quoted by *Current Literature*, April, 1910.

[42] Speech before the Chamber of Commerce Convention, Washington, Feb. 19, 1916.

[43] Speech at workingman's dinner, New York, Sept. 4, 1912.

[44] Wit and Wisdom of Woodrow Wilson, comp. by Richard Linthicum; New York, 1916, p. 54.

[45] Speech at Ridgewood, N. J., April 22, 1910.

[46] Wit and Wisdom ..., p. 56.

and differs from it considerably, though as yet not enough to make the two dialects—American English and British English—mutually unintelligible."[47]

American thus shows its character in a constant experimentation, a wide hospitality to novelty, a steady reaching out for new and vivid forms. No other tongue of modern times admits foreign words and phrases more readily; none is more careless of precedents; none shows a greater fecundity and originality of fancy. It is producing new words every day, by trope, by agglutination, by the shedding of inflections, by the merging of parts of speech, and by sheer brilliance of imagination. It is full of what Bret Harte called the "sabre-cuts of Saxon"; it meets Montaigne's ideal of "a succulent and nervous speech, short and compact, not as much delicated and combed out as vehement and brusque, rather arbitrary than monotonous, not pedantic but soldierly, as Suetonius called Caesar's Latin." One pictures the common materials of English dumped into a pot, exotic flavorings added, and the bubblings assiduously and expectantly skimmed. What is old and respected is already in decay the moment it comes into contact with what is new and vivid. Let American confront a novel problem alongside English, and immediately its superior imaginativeness and resourcefulness become obvious. *Movie* is better than *cinema*; it is not only better American, it is better English. *Bill-board* is better than *hoarding*. *Office-holder* is more honest, more picturesque, more thoroughly Anglo-Saxon that *public-servant*. *Stem-winder* somehow has more life in it, more fancy and vividness, than the literal *keyless-watch*. Turn to the terminology of railroading (itself, by the way, an Americanism): its creation fell upon the two peoples equally, but they tackled the job independently. The English, seeking a figure to denominate the wedge-shaped fender in front of a locomotive, called it a *plough*; the Americans, characteristically, gave it the far more pungent name of *cow-catcher*. So with the casting where two rails join. The English called it a *crossing-plate*. The Americans, more responsive to the suggestion in its shape, called it a *frog*.

This boldness of conceit, of course, makes for vulgarity. Unrestrained by any critical sense—and the critical sense of the professors counts for little, for they cry wolf too often—it flowers in

---

[47] Henry Sweet: A New English Grammar, Logical and Historical, 2 parts; Oxford, 1900-03, part i, p. 224.

such barbaric inventions as *tasty, alright, no-account, pants, go-aheadativeness, tony, semi-occasional, to fellowship* and *to doxologize*. Let it be admitted: American is not infrequently vulgar; the Americans, too, are vulgar (Bayard Taylor called them "Anglo-Saxons relapsed into semi-barbarism"); America itself is unutterably vulgar. But vulgarity, after all, means no more than a yielding to natural impulses in the face of conventional inhibitions, and that yielding to natural impulses is at the heart of all healthy language-making. The history of English, like the history of American and every other living tongue, is a history of vulgarisms that, by their accurate meeting of real needs, have forced their way into sound usage, and even into the lifeless catalogues of the grammarians. The colonial pedants denounced *to advocate* as bitterly as they ever denounced *to compromit* or *to happify*, and all the English authorities gave them aid, but it forced itself into the American language despite them, and today it is even accepted as English and has got into the Oxford Dictionary. *To donate*, so late as 1870, was dismissed by Richard Grant White as ignorant and abominable and to this day the English will have none of it, but there is not an American dictionary that doesn't accept it, and surely no American writer would hesitate to use it. [48] *Reliable, gubernatorial, standpoint* and *scientist* have survived opposition of equal ferocity. The last-named was coined by William Whewell, an Englishman, in 1840, but was first adopted in America. Despite the fact that Fitzedward Hall and other eminent philologists used it and defended it, it aroused almost incredible opposition in England. So recently as 1890 it was denounced by the *London Daily News* as "an ignoble Americanism, " and according to William Archer it was finally accepted by the English only "at the point of the bayonet."[49]

The purist performs a useful office in enforcing a certain logical regularity upon the process, and in our own case the omnipresent

---

[48] Despite this fact an academic and ineffective opposition to it still goes on. On the Style Sheet of the *Century Magazine* it is listed among the "words and phrases to be avoided." It was prohibited by the famous *Index Expurgatorius* prepared by William Cullen Bryant for the *New York Evening Post*, and his prohibition is still theoretically in force, but the word is now actually permitted by the *Post*. The *Chicago Daily News* Style Book, dated July 1, 1908, also bans it.

[49] *Scientist* is now in the Oxford Dictionary. So are *reliable, standpoint* and *gubernatorial*. But the *Century Magazine* still bans *standpoint* and the *Evening Post* (at least in theory) bans both *standpoint* and *reliable*. The *Chicago Daily News* accepts *standpoint*, but bans *reliable* and *gubernatorial*. All of these words, of course, are now quite as good as *ox* or *and*.

example of the greater conservatism of the English corrects our native tendency to go too fast, but the process itself is as inexorable in its workings as the precession of the equinoxes, and if we yield to it more eagerly than the English it is only a proof, perhaps, that the future of what was once the Anglo-Saxon tongue lies on this side of the water. "The story of English grammar, " says Murison, "is a story of simplification, of dispensing with grammatical forms."[50] And of the most copious and persistent enlargement of vocabulary and mutation of idiom ever recorded, perhaps, by descriptive philology. English now has the brakes on, but American continues to leap in the dark, and the prodigality of its movement is all the indication that is needed of its intrinsic health, its capacity to meet the ever-changing needs of a restless and iconoclastic people, constantly fluent in racial composition, and disdainful of hampering traditions. "Language, " says Sayce, "is no artificial product, contained in books and dictionaries and governed by the strict rules of impersonal grammarians. It is the living expression of the mind and spirit of a people, ever changing and shifting, whose sole standard of correctness is custom and the common usage of the community.... The first lesson to be learned is that there is no intrinsic right or wrong in the use of language, no fixed rules such as are the delight of the teacher of Latin prose. What is right now will be wrong hereafter, what language rejected yesterday she accepts today."[51]

§ 6. The Materials of American

—One familiar with the habits of pedagogues need not be told that, in their grudging discussions of American, they have spent most of their energies upon vain attempts to classify its materials. White and Lounsbury, as I have shown, carried the business to the limits of the preposterous; when they had finished identifying and cataloguing Americanisms there were no more Americanisms left to study. The ladies and gentlemen of the American Dialect Society, though praiseworthy for their somewhat deliberate industry, fall into a similar

---

[50] *Art.* Changes in the Language Since Shakespeare's Time, Cambridge History of English Literature, vol. xiv. p. 491.

[57]

[58] *Op. cit.*, pp. 119-28.

[59] Alfred L. Elwyn, M. D.: Glossary of Supposed Americanisms ...; Phila., 1859.

[51] Introduction to the Science of Language, vol. ii, pp. 333-4.

fault, for they are so eager to establish minute dialectic variations that they forget the general language almost altogether.

Among investigators of less learning there is a more spacious view of the problem, and the labored categories of White and Lounsbury are much extended. Pickering, the first to attempt a list of Americanisms, rehearsed their origin under the following headings:

1. "We have formed some new words."

2. "To some old ones, that are still in use in England, we have affixed new significations."

3. "Others, which have long been obsolete in England, are still retained in common use among us."

Bartlett, in the second edition of his dictionary, dated 1859, increased these classes to nine;

1. Archaisms, *i. e.*, old English words, obsolete, or nearly so, in England, but retained in use in this country.

2. English words used in a different sense from what they are in England. These include many names of natural objects differently applied.

3. Words which have retained their original meaning in the United States, though not in England.

4. English provincialisms adopted into general use in America.

5. Newly coined words, which owe their origin to the productions or to the circumstances of the country.

6. Words borrowed from European languages, especially the French, Spanish, Dutch and German.

7. Indian words.

8. Negroisms.

9. Peculiarities of pronunciation.

Some time before this, but after the publication of Bartlett's first edition in 1848, William C. Fowler, professor of rhetoric at Amherst, devoted a brief chapter to "American Dialects" in his well-known work on English[58] and in it one finds the following formidable classification of Americanisms:

1. Words borrowed from other languages.

a. Indian, as *Kennebec, Ohio, Tombigbee*; *sagamore, quahaug, succotash.*

b. Dutch, as *boss, kruller, stoop.*

c. German, as *spuke* (?), *sauerkraut*.

d. French, as *bayou, cache, chute, crevasse, levee*.

e. Spanish, as *calaboose, chapparal, hacienda, rancho, ranchero*.

f. Negro, as *buckra*.

2. Words "introduced from the necessity of our situation, in order to express new ideas."

a. Words "connected with and flowing from our political institutions, " as *selectman, presidential, congressional, caucus, mass-meeting, lynch-law, help* (for *servants*).

b. Words "connected with our ecclesiastical institutions, " as *associational, consociational, to fellowship, to missionate*.

c. Words "connected with a new country, " as *lot, diggings, betterments, squatter*.

3. Miscellaneous Americanisms.

a. Words and phrases become obsolete in England, as *talented, offset* (for *set-off*), *back and forth* (for *backward and forward*).

b. Old words and phrases "which are now merely provincial in England, " as *hub, whap* (?), *to wilt*.

c. Nouns formed from verbs by adding the French suffix *-ment*, as *publishment, releasement, requirement*.

d. Forms of words "which fill the gap or vacancy between two words which are approved, " as *obligate* (between *oblige* and *obligation*) and *variate* (between *vary* and *variation*).

e. "Certain compound terms for which the English have different compounds, " as *bank-bill, (bank-note), book-store (bookseller's shop), bottom-land (interval land), clapboard (pale), sea-board (sea-shore), side-hill (hill-side)*.

f. "Certain colloquial phrases, apparently idiomatic, and very expressive, " as *to cave in, to flare up, to flunk out, to fork over, to hold on, to let on, to stave off, to take on*.

g. Intensives, "often a matter of mere temporary fashion, " as *dreadful, mighty, plaguy, powerful*.

h. "Certain verbs expressing one's state of mind, but partially or timidly, " as *to allot upon* (for *to count upon*), *to calculate, to expect* (*to think* or *believe*), *to guess, to reckon*.

i. "Certain adjectives, expressing not only quality, but one's subjective feelings in regard to it, " as *clever, grand, green, likely, smart, ugly*.

j. Abridgments, as *stage* (for *stage-coach*), *turnpike* (for *turnpike-road*), *spry* (for *sprightly*), *to conduct* (for *to conduct one's self*).

k. "Quaint or burlesque terms, " as to *tote, to yank; humbug, loafer, muss, plunder* (for *baggage*), *rock* (for *stone*).

l. "Low expressions, mostly political, " as *slangwhanger, loco foco, hunker; to get the hang of*.

m. "Ungrammatical expressions, disapproved by all, " as *do don't, used to could, can't come it, Universal preacher* (for *Universalist*), *there's no two ways about it*.

Elwyn, in 1859, attempted no classification.[59] He confined his glossary to archaic English words surviving in America, and sought only to prove that they had come down "from our remotest ancestry" and were thus undeserving of the reviling lavished upon them by English critics. Schele de Vere, in 1872, followed Bartlett, and devoted himself largely to words borrowed from the Indian dialects, and from the French, Spanish and Dutch. But John S. Farmer, in 1889, (Americanisms Old and New) ventured upon a new classification, prefacing it with the following definition:

An Americanism may be defined as a word or phrase, old or new, employed by general or respectable usage in America in a way not sanctioned by the best standards of the English language. As a matter of fact, however, the term has come to possess a wider meaning, and it is now applied not only to words and phrases which can be so described, but also to the new and legitimately born words adapted to the general needs and usages, to the survivals of an older form of English than that now current in the mother country, and to the racy, pungent vernacular of Western life.

He then proceeded to classify his materials thus:

1. Words and phrases of purely American derivation, embracing words originating in:

a. Indian and aboriginal life.

b. Pioneer and frontier life.

c. The church.

d. Politics.

e. Trades of all kinds.

f. Travel, afloat and ashore.

2. Words brought by colonists, including:

a. The German element.

b. The French.

c. The Spanish.

d. The Dutch.

e. The negro.

f. The Chinese.

3. Names of American things, embracing:

a. Natural products.

b. Manufactured articles.

4. Perverted English words.

5. Obsolete English words still in good use in America.

6. English words, American by inflection and modification.

7. Odd and ignorant popular phrases, proverbs, vulgarisms, and colloquialisms, cant and slang.

8. Individualisms.

9. Doubtful and miscellaneous.

Sylvia Clapin, in 1902, (A New Dictionary of Americanisms, Being a Glossary of Words Supposed to be Peculiar to the United States and the Dominion of Canada; New York) reduced these categories to four:

1. Genuine English words, obsolete or provincial in England, and universally used in the United States.

2. English words conveying, in the United States, a different meaning from that attached to them in England.

3. Words introduced from other languages than the English:— French, Dutch, Spanish, German, Indian, etc.

4. Americanisms proper, *i. e.*, words coined in the country, either representing some new idea or peculiar product.

Thornton, in 1912, substituted the following:

1. Forms of speech now obsolete or provincial in England, which survive in the United States, such as *allow, bureau, fall, gotten, guess, likely, professor, shoat.*

2. Words and phrases of distinctly American origin, such as *belittle, lengthy, lightning-rod, to darken one's doors, to bark up the wrong tree, to come out at the little end of the horn, blind tiger, cold snap, gay Quaker, gone coon, long sauce, pay dirt, small potatoes, some pumpkins.*

3. Nouns which indicate quadrupeds, birds, trees, articles of food, etc., that are distinctively American, such as *ground-hog, hang-bird, hominy, live-oak, locust, opossum, persimmon, pone, succotash, wampum, wigwam.*

4. Names of persons and classes of persons, and of places, such as *Buckeye, Cracker, Greaser, Hoosier, Old Bullion, Old Hickory,* the *Little Giant, Dixie, Gotham,* the *Bay State,* the *Monumental City.*

5. Words which have assumed a new meaning, such as *card, clever, fork, help, penny, plunder, raise, rock, sack, ticket, windfall.*

In addition, Thornton added a provisional class of "words and phrases of which I have found earlier examples in American than in English writers; ... with the *caveat* that further research may reverse the claim"—a class offering specimens in *alarmist, capitalize, eruptiveness, horse of another colour* (*sic!*), *the jig's up, nameable, omnibus bill, propaganda* and *whitewash.*

No more than a brief glance at these classifications is needed to show that they hamper the inquiry by limiting its scope—not so much, to be sure, as the ridiculous limitations of White and Lounsbury, but still very seriously. They meet the ends of purely descriptive lexicography, but largely leave out of account some of the most salient characters of a living language, for example, pronunciation and idiom. Only Bartlett and Farmer establish a separate category of Americanisms produced by changes in pronunciation, though even Thornton, of course, is obliged to take notice of such forms as *bust* and *bile.* None of them, however, goes into the matter at any length, nor even into the matter of etymology. Bartlett's etymologies are scanty and often inaccurate; Schele de Vere's are sometimes quite fanciful;

Thornton offers scarcely any at all. The best of these collections of Americanisms, and by long odds, is Thornton's. It presents an enormous mass of quotations, and they are all very carefully dated, and it corrects most of the more obvious errors in the work of earlier inquirers. But its very dependence upon quotations limits it chiefly to the written language, and so the enormously richer materials of the spoken language are passed over, and particularly the materials evolved during the past twenty years. One searches the two fat volumes in vain for such highly characteristic forms as *would of*, *near-accident*, and *buttinski*, the use of *sure* as an adverb, and the employment of *well* as a sort of general equivalent of the German *also*.

These grammatical and syntactical tendencies are beyond the scope of Thornton's investigation, but it is plain that they must be prime concerns of any future student who essays to get at the inner spirit of the language. Its difference from standard English is not merely a difference in vocabulary, to be disposed of in an alphabetical list; it is, above all, a difference in pronunciation, in intonation, in conjugation and declension, in metaphor and idiom, in the whole fashion of using words. A page from one of Ring W. Lardner's baseball stories contains few words that are not in the English vocabulary, and yet the thoroughly American color of it cannot fail to escape anyone who actually listens to the tongue spoken around him. Some of the elements which enter into that color will be considered in the following pages. The American vocabulary, of course, must be given first attention, for in it the earliest American divergences are embalmed and it tends to grow richer and freer year after year, but attention will also be paid to materials and ways of speech that are less obvious, and in particular to certain definite tendencies of the grammar of spoken American, hitherto wholly neglected.

II. The Beginnings of American

§ 1. In Colonial Days

—William Gifford, the first editor of the *Quarterly Review*, is authority for the tale that some of the Puritan clergy of New England, during the Revolution, proposed that English be formally abandoned as the national language of America, and Hebrew adopted in its place. An American chronicler, Charles Astor Bristed, makes the proposed tongue Greek, and reports that the change was rejected on the ground that "it would be more convenient for us to keep the language as it is, and make the English speak Greek."[1] The story, though it has the support of the editors of the Cambridge History of American Literature, [2] has an apocryphal smack; one suspects that the savagely anti-American Gifford invented it. But, true or false, it well indicates the temper of those times. The passion for complete political independence of England bred a general hostility to all English authority, whatever its character, and that hostility, in the direction of present concern to us, culminated in the revolutionary attitude of Noah Webster's "Dissertations on the English Language, " printed in 1789. Webster harbored no fantastic notion of abandoning English altogether, but he was eager to set up American as a distinct and independent dialect. "Let us, " he said, "seize the present moment, and establish a national language as well as a national government.... As an independent nation our honor requires us to have a system of our own, in language as well as government."

Long before this the challenge had been flung. Scarcely two years after the Declaration of Independence Franklin was instructed by Congress, on his appointment as minister to France, to employ "the language of the United States, " not simply English, in all his "replies or answers" to the communications of the ministry of Louis XVI. And eight years before the Declaration Franklin himself had drawn up a characteristically American scheme of spelling reform, and had offered plenty of proof in it, perhaps unconsciously, that the standards of spelling and pronunciation in the New World had already diverged noticeably from those accepted on the other side of the ocean.[3] In acknowledging the dedication of Webster's "Dissertations" Franklin endorsed both his revolt against English domination and his forecast of widening differences in future, though protesting at the same time against certain Americanisms that have since come into good usage, and even migrated to England.[4]

This protest was marked by Franklin's habitual mildness, but in other quarters dissent was voiced with far less urbanity. The growing independence of the colonial dialect, not only in its spoken form, but also in its most dignified written form, had begun, indeed, to attract the attention of purists in both England and America, and they sought to dispose of it in its infancy by *force majeure*. One of the first and most vigorous of the attacks upon it was delivered by John Witherspoon, a Scotch clergyman who came out in 1769 to be president of Princeton *in partibus infidelium*. This Witherspoon brought a Scotch hatred of the English with him, and at once became a leader of the party of independence; he signed the Declaration to the tune of much rhetoric, and was the only clergyman to sit in the Continental Congress. But in matters of learning he was orthodox to the point of hunkerousness, and the strange locutions that he encountered on all sides aroused his pedagogic ire. "I have heard in this country, " he wrote in 1781, "in the senate, at the bar, and from the pulpit, and see daily in dissertations from the press, errors in grammar, improprieties and vulgarisms which hardly any person of the same class in point of rank and literature would have fallen into in Great Britain."[5] It was Witherspoon who coined the word *Americanism*—and at once the English guardians of the sacred vessels began employing it as a general synonym for vulgarism and barbarism. Another learned immigrant, the Rev. Jonathan Boucher, soon joined him. This Boucher was a friend of Washington, but was driven back to England by his Loyalist sentiments. He took revenge by printing various charges against the Americans, among them that of "making all the haste they can to rid themselves of the [English] language."

After the opening of the new century all the British reviews maintained an eager watchfulness for these abhorrent inventions, and denounced them, when found, with the utmost vehemence. The *Edinburgh*, which led the charge, opened its attack in October, 1804, and the appearance of the five volumes of Chief Justice Marshall's "Life of George Washington, " during the three years following, gave the signal for corrective articles in the *British Critic*, the *Critical Review*, the *Annual*, the *Monthly* and the *Eclectic*. The *British Critic*, in April, 1808, admitted somewhat despairingly that the damage was already done—that "the common speech of the United States has departed very considerably from the standard adopted in England." The others, however, sought to stay the flood by invective against Marshall and, later, against his rival biographer, the Rev. Aaron Bancroft. The *Annual*, in 1808, pronounced its high curse and anathema upon "that torrent of barbarous phraseology" which was pouring across the Atlantic, and which threatened "to destroy the purity of the English language."[6] In Bancroft's "Life of George Washington" (1808), according to the *British Critic*, there were gross Americanisms, inordinately offensive to Englishmen, "at almost every page."

The Rev. Jeremy Belknap, long anticipating Elwyn, White and Lounsbury, tried to obtain a respite from this abuse by pointing out the obvious fact that many of the Americanisms under fire were merely survivors of an English that had become archaic in England, but this effort counted for little, for on the one hand the British purists enjoyed the chase too much to give it up, and on the other hand there began to dawn in America a new spirit of nationality, at first very faint, which viewed the differences objected to, not with shame, but with a fierce sort of pride. In the first volume of the *North American Review* William Ellery Channing spoke out boldly for "the American language and literature, "[7] and a year later Pickering published his defiant dictionary of "words and phrases which have been supposed to be peculiar to the United States." This thin collection of 500 specimens set off a dispute which yet rages on both sides of the Atlantic. Pickering, however, was undismayed. He had begun to notice the growing difference between the English and American vocabulary and pronunciation, he said, while living in London from 1799 to 1801, and he had made his collections with the utmost care, and after taking counsel with various prudent authorities, both English and American. Already in the first year of the century, he continued, the English had accused the people of the new republic of a deliberate "design to effect an entire change in the language" and while no such design was actually harbored, the facts were the facts, and he cited the current newspapers, the speeches from pulpit and rostrum, and Webster himself in support of them. This debate over Pickering's list, as I say, still continues. Lounsbury, entrenched behind his grotesque categories, once charged that four-fifths of the words in it had "no business to be there, " and Gilbert M. Tucker[8] has argued that only 70 of them were genuine Americanisms. But a careful study of the list, in comparison with the early quotations recently collected by Thornton, seems to indicate that both of these judgments, and many others no less, have done injustice to Pickering. He made the usual errors of the pioneer, but his sound contributions to the subject were anything but inconsiderable, and it is impossible to forget his diligence and his constant shrewdness. He established firmly the native origin of a number of words now in universal use in America—*e. g.*, *backwoodsman*, *breadstuffs*, *caucus*, *clapboard*, *sleigh* and *squatter*—and of such familiar derivatives as *gubernatorial* and *dutiable*, and he worked out the genesis of not a few loan-words, including *prairie*, *scow*, *rapids*, *hominy* and *barbecue*. It was not until 1848, when the first edition of Bartlett appeared, that his work was supplanted.

§ 2. Sources of Early Americanisms

—The first genuine Americanisms were undoubtedly words borrowed bodily from the Indian dialects—words, in the main, indicating natural objects that had no counterparts in England. We find *opossum*, for example, in the form of *opasum*, in Captain John Smith's "Map of Virginia" (1612), and, in the form of *apossoun*, in a Virginia document two years older. *Moose* is almost as old. The word is borrowed from the Algonquin *musa*, and must have become familiar to the Pilgrim Fathers soon after their landing in 1620, for the woods of Massachusetts then swarmed with the huge quadrupeds and there was no English name to designate them. Again, there are *skunk* (from the Abenaki Indian *seganku*), *hickory*, *squash*, *paw-paw*, *raccoon*, *chinkapin*, *porgy*, *chipmunk*, *pemmican*, *terrapin*, *menhaden*, *catalpa*, *persimmon* and*cougar*. Of these, *hickory* and *terrapin* are to be found in Robert Beverley's "History and Present State of Virginia" (1705), and *squash*, *chinkapin* and *persimmon* are in documents of the preceding century. Many of these words, of course, were shortened or otherwise modified on being taken into colonial English. Thus *chinkapin* was originally *checkinqumin*, and *squash* appears in early documents as *isquontersquash*, *askutasquash*, *isquonkersquash* and *squantersquash*. But William Penn, in a letter dated August 16, 1683, used the latter in its present form. Its variations show a familiar effort to bring a new and strange word into harmony with the language—an effort arising from what philologists call the law of Hobson-Jobson. This name was given to it by Col. Henry Yule and A. C. Burnell, compilers of a standard dictionary of Anglo-Indian terms. They found that the British soldiers in India, hearing strange words from the lips of the natives, often converted them into English words of similar sound, though of widely different meaning. Thus the words *Hassan* and *Hosein*, frequently used by the Mohammedans of the country in their devotions, were turned into *Hobson-Jobson*. The same process is constantly in operation elsewhere. By it the French *route de roi* has become *Rotten Row* in English, *écrevisse* has become *crayfish*, and the English *bowsprit* has become *beau pré* (=*beautiful meadow*) in French. The word *pigeon*, in *Pigeon English*, offers another example; it has no connection with the bird, but merely represents a Chinaman's attempt to pronounce the word *business*. No doubt *squash* originated in the same way. That *woodchuck* did so is practically certain. Its origin is to be sought, not in *wood* and *chuck*, but in the Cree word *otchock*, used by the Indians to designate the animal.

In addition to the names of natural objects, the early colonists, of course, took over a great many Indian place-names, and a number of words to designate Indian relations and artificial objects in Indian use. To the last division belong *hominy, pone, toboggan, canoe, tapioca, moccasin, pow-wow, papoose, tomahawk, wigwam, succotash* and *squaw*, all of which were in common circulation by the beginning of the eighteenth century. Finally, new words were made during the period by translating Indian terms, for example, *war-path, war-paint, pale-face, medicine-man, pipe-of-peace* and *fire-water*. The total number of such borrowings, direct and indirect, was a good deal larger than now appears, for with the disappearance of the red man the use of loan-words from his dialects has decreased. In our own time such words as *papoose, sachem, tepee, wigwam* and *wampum* have begun to drop out of everyday use;[9] at an earlier period the language sloughed off *ocelot, manitee, calumet, supawn, samp* and *quahaug*, or began to degrade them to the estate of provincialisms.[10] A curious phenomenon is presented by the case of *maize*, which came into the colonial speech from some West Indian dialect, went over into orthodox English, and from English into French, German and other continental languages, and was then abandoned by the colonists. We shall see other examples of that process later on.

Whether or not *Yankee* comes from an Indian dialect is still disputed. An early authority, John G. E. Heckwelder, argued that it was derived from an Indian mispronunciation of the word *English*.[11]Certain later etymologists hold that it originated more probably in an Indian mishandling of the French word *Anglais*. Yet others derive it from the Scotch *yankie*, meaning a gigantic falsehood. A fourth party derive it from the Dutch, and cite an alleged Dutch model for "Yankee Doodle, " beginning "*Yanker* didee doodle down."[12] Of these theories that of Heckwelder is the most plausible. But here, as in other directions, the investigation of American etymology remains sadly incomplete. An elaborate dictionary of words derived from the Indian languages, compiled by the late W. R. Gerard, is in the possession of the Smithsonian Institution, but on account of a shortage of funds it remains in manuscript.

From the very earliest days of English colonization the language of the colonists also received accretions from the languages of the other colonizing nations. The French word *portage*, for example, was already in common use before the end of the seventeenth century, and soon after came *chowder, cache, caribou, voyageur*, and various words that, like the last-named, have since become localisms or disappeared altogether. Before 1750 *bureau*, [13] *gopher, batteau, bogus*, and *prairie* were added, and *caboose*, a word of Dutch origin, seems to have come in through the French. *Carry-all* is also French in origin, despite its English quality. It comes, by the law of Hobson-Jobson, from the French *carriole*. The contributions of the Dutch during the half century of their conflicts with the English included *cruller, cold-slaw, dominie* (for *parson*), *cookey, stoop, span* (of horses), *pit* (as in *peach-pit*), *waffle, hook* (a point of land), *scow, boss, smearcase* and *Santa Claus*.[14] Schele de Vere credits them with *hay-barrack*, a corruption of *hooiberg*. That they established the use of *bush* as a designation for back-country is very probable; the word has also got into South African English. In American it has produced a number of familiar derivatives, *e. g., bush-whacker* and *bush-league*. Barrère and Leland also credit the Dutch with *dander*, which is commonly assumed to be an American corruption of *dandruff*. They say that it is from the Dutch word *donder* (=*thunder*). *Op donderen*, in Dutch, means to burst into a sudden rage. The chief Spanish contributions to American were to come after the War of 1812, with the opening of the West, but *creole, calaboose, palmetto, peewee, key* (a small island), *quadroon, octoroon, barbecue, pickaninny* and *stampede* had already entered the language in colonial days. *Jerked beef* came from the Spanish *charqui* by the law of Hobson-Jobson. The Germans who arrived in Pennsylvania in 1682 also undoubtedly gave a few words to the language, though it is often difficult to distinguish their contributions from those of the Dutch. It seems very likely, however, that *sauerkraut*[15] and *noodle* are to be credited to them. Finally, the negro slaves brought in *gumbo, goober, juba* and *voodoo* (usually corrupted to *hoodoo*), and probably helped to corrupt a number of other loan-words, for example *banjo* and *breakdown*. *Banjo* seems to be derived from *bandore* or *bandurria*, modern French and

Spanish forms of *tambour*, respectively. It may, however, be an actual negro word; there is a term of like meaning, *bania*, in Senegambian. Ware says that *breakdown*, designating a riotous negro dance, is a corruption of the French *rigadon*. The word is not in the Oxford Dictionary. Bartlett listed it as an Americanism, but Thornton rejected it, apparently because, in the sense of a collapse, it has come into colloquial use in England. Its etymology is not given in the American dictionaries.

§ 3. New Words of English Material

—But of far more importance than these borrowings was the great stock of new words that the colonists coined in English metal—words primarily demanded by the "new circumstances under which they were placed, " but also indicative, in more than one case, of a delight in the business for its own sake. The American, even in the early eighteenth century, already showed many of the characteristics that were to set him off from the Englishman later on—his bold and somewhat grotesque imagination, his contempt for authority, his lack of aesthetic sensitiveness, his extravagant humor. Among the first colonists there were many men of education, culture and gentle birth, but they were soon swamped by hordes of the ignorant and illiterate, and the latter, cut off from the corrective influence of books, soon laid their hands upon the language. It is impossible to imagine the austere Puritan divines of Massachusetts inventing such verbs as *to cowhide* and *to logroll*, or such adjectives as *no-account* and *stumped*, or such adverbs as *no-how* and *lickety-split*, or such substantives as *bull-frog*, *hog-wallow* and *hoe-cake*; but under their eyes there arose a contumacious proletariat which was quite capable of the business, and very eager for it. In Boston, so early as 1628, there was a definite class of blackguard roisterers, chiefly made up of sailors and artisans; in Virginia, nearly a decade earlier, John Pory, secretary to Governor Yeardley, lamented that "in these five moneths of my continuance here there have come at one time or another eleven sails of ships into this river, but fraighted more with ignorance than with any other marchansize." In particular, the generation born in the New World was uncouth and iconoclastic;[16]the only world it knew was a rough world, and the virtues that environment engendered were not those of niceness, but those of enterprise and resourcefulness.

Upon men of this sort fell the task of bringing the wilderness to the ax and the plow, and with it went the task of inventing a vocabulary for the special needs of the great adventure. Out of their loutish ingenuity came a great number of picturesque names for natural objects, chiefly boldly descriptive compounds: *bull-frog, canvas-back, lightning-bug, mud-hen, cat-bird, razor-back, garter-snake, ground-hog* and so on. And out of an inventiveness somewhat more urbane came such coinages as *live-oak, potato-bug, turkey-gobbler, poke-weed, copper-head, eel-grass, reed-bird, egg-plant, blue-grass, pea-nut, pitch-pine, cling-stone* (peach), *moccasin-snake, June-bug*and *butter-nut. Live-oak* appears in a document of 1610; *bull-frog* was familiar to Beverley in 1705; so was *James-Town weed* (later reduced to *Jimson weed*, as the English *hurtleberry* or *whortleberry* was reduced to *huckleberry*). These early Americans were not botanists. They were often ignorant of the names of the plants they encountered, even when those plants already had English names, and so they exercised their fancy upon new ones. So arose *Johnny-jump-up* for the *Viola tricolor*, and *basswood* for the common European *linden* or *lime-tree* (*Tilia*), and *locust* for the *Robinia pseudacacia* and its allies. The *Jimson weed* itself was anything but a novelty, but the pioneers apparently did not recognize it, and so we find them ascribing all sorts of absurd medicinal powers to it, and even Beverley solemnly reporting that "some Soldiers, eating it in a Salad, turn'd natural Fools upon it for several Days." The grosser features of the landscape got a lavish renaming, partly to distinguish new forms and partly out of an obvious desire to attain a more literal descriptiveness. I have mentioned *key* and *hook*, the one borrowed from the Spanish and the other from the Dutch. With them came *run, branch, fork, bluff,* (noun), *neck, barrens, bottoms, underbrush, bottom-land, clearing, notch, divide, knob, riffle, gap, rolling-country* and *rapids*, [17]and the extension of *pond* from artificial pools to small natural lakes, and of *creek* from small arms of the sea to shallow feeders of rivers. Such common English geographical terms as *downs, weald, wold, fen, bog, fell, chase, combe, dell, heath* and *moor* disappeared from the colonial tongue, save as fossilized in a few proper names. So did *bracken.*

With the new landscape came an entirely new mode of life—new foods, new forms of habitation, new methods of agriculture, new kinds of hunting. A great swarm of neologisms thus arose, and, as in the previous case, they were chiefly compounds. *Back-country, back-*

woods, back-woodsman, back-settlers, back-settlements: all these were in common use early in the eighteenth century. *Back-log* was used by Increase Mather in 1684. *Log-house* appears in the Maryland Archives for 1669.[18] *Hoe-cake, Johnny-cake, pan-fish, corn-dodger, roasting-ear, corn-crib, corn-cob* and *pop-corn* were all familiar before the Revolution. So were *pine-knot, snow-plow, cold-snap, land-slide, salt-lick, prickly-heat, shell-road* and *cane-brake. Shingle* was a novelty in 1705, but one S. Symonds wrote to John Winthrop, of Ipswich, about a *clapboarded* house in 1637. *Frame-house* seems to have come in with *shingle. Trail, half-breed, Indian-summer* and *Indian-file* were obviously suggested by the Red Men. *State-house* was borrowed, perhaps, from the Dutch. *Selectman* is first heard of in 1685, displacing the English *alderman. Mush* had displaced *porridge* by 1671. Soon afterward *hay-stack* took the place of the English *hay-cock*, and such common English terms as *byre, mews, weir,* and *wain* began to disappear. *Hired-man* is to be found in the Plymouth town records of 1737, and *hired-girl* followed soon after. So early as 1758, as we find by the diary of Nathaniel Ames, the second-year students at Harvard were already called *sophomores*, though for a while the spelling was often made *sophimores. Camp-meeting* was later; it did not appear until 1799. But *land-office* was familiar before 1700, and *side-walk, spelling-bee, bee-line, moss-back, crazy-quilt, mud-scow, stamping-ground* and a hundred and one other such compounds were in daily use before the Revolution. After that great upheaval the new money of the confederation brought in a number of new words. In 1782 Gouverneur Morris proposed to the Continental Congress that the coins of the republic be called, in ascending order, *unit, penny-bill, dollar* and *crown*. Later Morris invented the word *cent*, substituting it for the English *penny*.[19] In 1785 Jefferson proposed *mill, cent, dime, dollar* and *eagle*, and this nomenclature was adopted.

Various nautical terms peculiar to America, or taken into English from American sources, came in during the eighteenth century, among them, *schooner, cat-boat* and *pungy*, not to recall *batteau* and *canoe*. According to a recent historian of the American merchant marine, [20] the first schooner ever seen was launched at Gloucester, Mass., in 1713. The word, it appears, was originally spelled *scooner*.

To scoon was a verb borrowed by the New Englanders from some Scotch dialect, and meant to skim or skip across the water like a flat stone. As the first schooner left the ways and glided out into Gloucester harbor, an enraptured spectator shouted: "Oh, see how she scoons!" "A *scooner* let her be!" replied Captain Andrew Robinson, her builder— and all boats of her peculiar and novel fore-and-aft rig took the name thereafter. The Dutch mariners borrowed the term and changed the spelling, and this change was soon accepted in America. The Scotch root came from the Norse *skunna*, to hasten, and there are analogues in Icelandic, Anglo-Saxon and Old High German. The origin of *cat-boat* and *pungy* I have been unable to determine. Perhaps the latter is related in some way to *pung*, a one-horse sled or wagon. *Pung* was once widely used in the United States, but of late it has sunk to the estate of a New England provincialism. Longfellow used it, and in 1857 a writer in the *Knickerbocker Magazine* reported that *pungs* filled Broadway, in New York, after a snow-storm.

Most of these new words, of course, produced derivatives, for example, *to stack hay*, *to shingle*, *to shuck* (i. e., corn), *to trail* and *to caucus*. *Backwoods* immediately begat *backwoodsman* and was itself turned into a common adjective. The colonists, indeed, showed a beautiful disregard of linguistic nicety. At an early date they shortened the English law-phrase, *to convey by deed*, to the simple verb, *to deed*. Pickering protested against this as a barbarism, and argued that no self-respecting law-writer would employ it, but all the same it was firmly entrenched in the common speech and it has remained there to this day. *To table*, for *to lay on the table*, came in at the same time, and so did various forms represented by *bindery*, for *bookbinder's shop*. *To tomahawk* appeared before 1650, and *to scalp* must have followed soon after. Within the next century and a half they were reinforced by many other such new verbs, and by such adjectives made of nouns as *no-account* and *one-horse*, and such nouns made of verbs as *carry-all* and *goner*, and such adverbs as *no-how*. In particular, the manufacture of new verbs went on at a rapid pace. In his letter to Webster in 1789, Franklin denounced *to advocate*, *to progress*, and *to oppose*—a vain enterprise, for all of them are now in perfectly good usage. *To advocate*, indeed, was used by Thomas Nashe in 1589, and by John Milton half a century later, but it seems to have been reinvented in America. In 1822 and again in 1838

Robert Southey, then poet laureate, led two belated attacks upon it, as a barbarous Americanism, but its obvious usefulness preserved it, and it remains in good usage on both sides of the Atlantic today—one of the earliest of the English borrowings from America. In the end, indeed, even so ardent a purist as Richard Grant White adopted it, as he did *to placate*.[21]

Webster, though he agreed with Franklin in opposing *to advocate*, gave his *imprimatur* to *to appreciate* (*i. e.*, to rise in value), and is credited by Sir Charles Lyell[22] with having himself invented *to demoralize*. He also approved *to obligate*. *To antagonize* seems to have been given currency by John Quincy Adams, *to immigrate* by John Marshall, *to eventuate* by Gouverneur Morris, and *to derange* by George Washington. Jefferson, always hospitable to new words, used *to belittle* in his "Notes on Virginia, " and Thornton thinks that he coined it. Many new verbs were made by the simple process of prefixing the preposition to common nouns, *e. g.*, *to clerk*, *to dicker*, *to dump*, *to blow*, (*i. e.*, to bluster or boast), *to cord* (*i. e.*, wood) *to stump*, *to room* and *to shin*. Others were made by transforming verbs in the orthodox vocabulary, *e. g.*, *to cavort* from *to curvet*, and *to snoop* from *to snook*. Others arose as metaphors, *e. g.*, *to whitewash* (figuratively) and *to squat* (on unoccupied land). Others were made by hitching suffixes to nouns, *e. g.*, *to negative*, *to deputize*, *to locate*, *to legislate*, *to infract*, *to compromit* and *to happify*. Yet others seem to have been produced by onomatopoeia, *e. g.*, *to fizzle*, or to have arisen by some other such spontaneous process, so far unintelligible, *e. g.*, *to tote*. With them came an endless series of verb-phrases, *e. g.*, *to draw a bead*, *to face the music*, *to darken one's doors*, *to take to the woods*, *to fly off the handle*, *to go on the war-path* and *to saw wood*—all obvious products of frontier life. Many coinages of the pre-Revolutionary era later disappeared. Jefferson used *to ambition* but it dropped out nevertheless, and so did *to compromit*, (*i. e.*, to compromise), *to homologize*, and *to happify*. Fierce battles raged 'round some of these words, and they were all violently derided in England. Even so useful a verb as *to locate*, now in perfectly good usage, was denounced in the third volume of the *North American Review*, and other purists of the times tried to put down *to legislate*.

The young and tender adjectives had quite as hard a row to hoe, particularly *lengthy*. The *British Critic* attacked it in November, 1793, and it also had enemies at home, but John Adams had used it in his diary in 1759 and the authority of Jefferson and Hamilton was behind it, and so it survived. Years later James Russell Lowell spoke of it as "the excellent adjective, "[23] and boasted that American had given it to English. *Dutiable* also met with opposition, and moreover, it had a rival, *customable*; but Marshall wrote it into his historic decisions, and thus it took root. The same anonymous watchman of the *North American Review* who protested against *to locate* pronounced his anathema upon "such barbarous terms as *presidential* and *congressional*, " but the plain need for them kept them in the language. *Gubernatorial* had come in long before this, and is to be found in the New Jersey Archives of 1734. *Influential* was denounced by the Rev. Jonathan Boucher and by George Canning, who argued that *influent* was better, but it was ardently defended by William Pinkney, of Maryland, and gradually made its way. *Handy, kinky, law-abiding, chunky, solid* (in the sense of well-to-do), *evincive, complected, judgmatical, underpinned, blooded* and *cute* were also already secure in revolutionary days. So with many nouns. Jefferson used *breadstuffs* in his Report of the Secretary of State on Commercial Restrictions, December 16, 1793. *Balance*, in the sense of remainder, got into the debates of the First Congress. *Mileage* was used by Franklin in 1754, and is now sound English. *Elevator*, in the sense of a storage house for grain, was used by Jefferson and by others before him. *Draw*, for *drawbridge*, comes down from Revolutionary days. So does *slip*, in the sense of a berth for vessels. So does *addition*, in the sense of a suburb. So, finally, does *darkey*.

The history of many of these Americanisms shows how vain is the effort of grammarians to combat the normal processes of language development. I have mentioned the early opposition to *dutiable, influential, presidential, lengthy, to locate, to oppose, to advocate, to legislate* and *to progress. Bogus, reliable* and *standpoint* were attacked with the same academic ferocity. All of them are to be found in Bryant's *Index Expurgatorius*[24] (*circa* 1870), and *reliable* was denounced by Bishop Coxe as "that abominable barbarism" so late as 1886.[25] Edward S. Gould, another uncompromising purist, said of *standpoint* that it was "the bright particular star ... of solemn philological blundering" and "the very counterpart of Dogberry's *non-com*."[26] Gould also protested against *to jeopardize, leniency* and *to demean*, and Richard Grant White joined him in an onslaught upon *to donate*. But all of these words are in good use in the United States today, and some of them have gone over into English.[27]

§ 4. Changed Meanings

—A number of the foregoing contributions to the American vocabulary, of course, were simply common English words with changed meanings. *To squat*, in the sense of *to crouch*, had been sound English for centuries; what the colonists did was to attach a figurative meaning to it, and then bring that figurative meaning into wider usage than the literal meaning. In a somewhat similar manner they changed the significance of *pond*, as I have pointed out. So, too, with *creek*. In English it designated (and still designates) a small inlet or arm of a large river or of the sea; in American, so early as 1674, it designated any small stream. Many other such changed meanings crept into American in the early days. A typical one was the use of *lot* to designate a *parcel* of land. Thornton says, perhaps inaccurately, that it originated in the fact that the land in New England was distributed by lot. Whatever the truth, *lot*, to this day, is in almost universal use in the United States, though rare in England. Our conveyancers, in describing real property, always speak of "all that *lot* or *parcel* of land."[28] Other examples of the application of old words to new purposes are afforded by *freshet, barn* and *team*. A *freshet*, in eighteenth century English, meant any stream of fresh water; the colonists made it signify an inundation. A *barn* was a house or shed for storing crops; in the colonies the word came to mean a place for keeping cattle also. A *team*, in English, was a pair of draft horses; in the colonies it came to mean both horses and vehicle.

The process is even more clearly shown in the history of such words as *corn* and *shoe*. *Corn*, in orthodox English, means grain for human consumption, and especially wheat, *e. g.*, the *Corn* Laws. The earliest settlers, following this usage, gave the name of *Indian corn* to what the Spaniards, following the Indians themselves, had called *maíz*. But gradually the adjective fell off, and by the middle of the eighteenth century *maize* was called simply *corn*, and grains in general were called *breadstuffs*. Thomas Hutchinson, discoursing to George III in 1774, used *corn* in this restricted sense, speaking of "rye and *corn* mixed." "What *corn*?" asked George. "*Indian corn*, " explained Hutchinson, "or, as it is called in authors, *maize*."[29] So with *shoe*. In English it meant (and still means) a topless article of foot-wear, but the colonists extended its meaning to varieties covering the ankle, thus displacing the English *boot*, which they reserved for foot coverings reaching at least to the knee. To designate the English *shoe* they began to use the word *slipper*. This distinction between English and American usage still prevails, despite the affectation which has lately sought to revive *boot*, and with it its derivatives, *boot-shop* and *bootmaker*.

Store, shop, lumber, pie, dry-goods, cracker, rock and *partridge* among nouns and *to haul, to jew, to notify* and *to heft* among verbs offer further examples of changed meanings. Down to the middle of the eighteenth century *shop* continued to designate a retail establishment in America, as it does in England to this day. *Store* was applied only to a large establishment—one showing, in some measure, the character of a warehouse. But in 1774 a Boston young man was advertising in the *Massachusetts Spy* for "a *place* as a *clerk* in a *store*" (three Americanisms in a row!). Soon afterward *shop* began to acquire its special American meaning as a factory, *e. g.*, *machine-shop*. Meanwhile *store* completely displaced *shop* in the English sense, and it remained for a late flowering of Anglomania, as in the case of *boot* and *shoe*, to restore, in a measure, the *status quo ante*. *Lumber*, in eighteenth century English, meant disused furniture, and this is its common meaning in England today. But the colonists early employed it to designate timber, and that use of it is now universal in America. Its familiar derivatives, *e. g.*, *lumber-yard, lumberman, lumberjack*, greatly reinforce this usage. *Pie*, in English, means a meat-pie; in American it means a fruit-pie. The English call a fruit-pie a *tart*; the Americans call a meat-pie a *pot-pie*. *Dry-goods*, in England, means "non-liquid goods, as corn" (*i. e.*, wheat); in the United States the term means "textile fabrics or wares."[30] The difference had appeared before 1725. *Rock*, in English, always means a large mass; in America it may mean a small stone, as in *rock-pile* and *to throw a rock*. The Puritans were putting *rocks* into the foundations of their meeting-houses so early as 1712.[31] *Cracker* began to be used for *biscuit* before the Revolution. *Tavern* displaced *inn* at the same time. As for*partridge*, it is cited by a late authority[32] as a salient example of changed meaning, along with *corn*and *store*. In England the term is applied only to the true partridge (*Perdix perdix*) and its nearly related varieties, but in the United States it is also used to designate the ruffed grouse (*Bonasa umbellus*), the common quail (*Colinus virginianus*) and various other tetraonoid birds. This confusion goes back to colonial times. So with *rabbit*. Properly speaking, there are no native rabbits in the United States; they are all hares. But the early colonists, for some unknown reason, dropped the word *hare* out of their vocabulary, and it is rarely heard in American speech to this day. When it appears it is almost always applied to the so-called Belgian hare, which, curiously enough, is not a hare at all, but a true rabbit.

To haul, in English, means to move by force or violence; in the colonies it came to mean to transport in a vehicle, and this meaning survives in sound American. *To jew*, in English, means to cheat; the colonists made it mean to haggle, and devised *to jew down* to indicate an effort to work a reduction in price. *To heft*, in English, means to lift; the early Americans made it mean to weigh by lifting, and kept the idea of weighing in its derivatives, *e. g.*, *hefty*. Finally, there is the familiar American misuse of *Miss* or *Mis'* for *Mrs.*. It was so widespread by 1790 that on November 17 of that year Webster solemnly denounced it in the *American Mercury*.

§ 5. Archaic English Words

—Most of the colonists who lived along the American seaboard in 1750 were the descendants of immigrants who had come in fully a century before; after the first settlements there had been much less fresh immigration than many latter-day writers have assumed. According to Prescott F. Hall, "the population of New England ... at the date of the Revolutionary War ... was produced out of an immigration of about 20, 000 persons **who arrived before 1640**, "[33]and we have Franklin's authority for the statement that the total population of the colonies in 1751, then about 1, 000, 000, had been produced from an original immigration of less than 80, 000.[34]Even at that early day, indeed, the colonists had begun to feel that they were distinctly separated, in culture and customs, from the mother-country, [35] and there were signs of the rise of a new native aristocracy, entirely distinct from the older aristocracy of the royal governors' courts.[36] The enormous difficulties of communication with England helped to foster this sense of separation. The round trip across the ocean occupied the better part of a year, and was hazardous and expensive; a colonist who had made it was a marked man, —as Hawthorne said, "the *petit-maître* of the colonies." Nor was there any very extensive exchange of ideas, for though most of the books read in the colonies came from England, the great majority of the colonists, down to the middle of the century, seem to have read little save the Bible and biblical commentaries, and in the native literature of the time one seldom comes upon any reference to the English authors who were glorifying the period of the Restoration and the reign of Anne. Moreover, after 1760 the colonial eyes were upon France rather than upon England, and Rousseau, Montesquieu, Voltaire and the Encyclopedists began to be familiar names to thousands who were scarcely aware of Addison and Steele, or even of the great Elizabethans.[37]

The result of this isolation, on the one hand, was that proliferation of the colonial speech which I have briefly reviewed, and on the other hand, the preservation of many words and phrases that gradually became obsolete in England. The Pilgrims of 1620 brought over with them the English of James I and the Revised Version, and their descendants of a century later, inheriting it, allowed its fundamentals to be little changed by the academic overhauling that the mother tongue was put to during the early part of the eighteenth century. In part they were ignorant of this overhauling, and in part they were indifferent to it. Whenever the new usage differed from that of the Bible they were inclined to remain faithful to the Bible, not only because of its pious authority but also because of the superior pull of its imminent and constant presence. Thus when an artificial prudery in English ordered the abandonment of the Anglo-Saxon *sick* for the Gothic *ill*, the colonies refused to follow, for *sick* was in both the Old Testament and the New;[38] and that refusal remains in force to this day.

A very large number of words and phrases, many of them now exclusively American, are similar survivals from the English of the seventeenth century, long since obsolete or merely provincial in England. Among nouns Thornton notes *fox-fire, flap-jack, jeans, molasses, beef* (to designate the live animal), *chinch, cord-wood, homespun, ice-cream, julep* and *swingle-tree*; Halliwell[39] adds *andiron, bay-window, cesspool, clodhopper, cross-purposes, greenhorn, loophole, ragamuffin, riff-raff, rigmarole* and *trash*; and other authorities cite *stock* (for cattle), *fall* (for autumn), *offal, din, underpinning* and *adze. Bub*, used in addressing a boy, is very old English, but survives only in Américan. *Flap-jack* goes back to Piers Plowman, but has been obsolete in England for two centuries. *Muss*, in the sense of a row, is also obsolete over there, but it is to be found in "Anthony and Cleopatra." *Char*, as a noun, disappeared from English a long time ago, but it survives in American as *chore*. Among the adjectives similarly preserved are *to whittle, to wilt* and *to approbate. To guess*, in the American sense of *to suppose*, is to be found in "Henry VI":

Not all together; better far, I *guess*,

That we do make our entrance several ways.

In "Measure for Measure" Escalus says "I *guess* not" to Angelo. The New English Dictionary offers examples much older—from Chaucer, Wyclif and Gower. *To interview* is in Dekker. *To loan*, in the American sense of to lend, is in 34 and 35 Henry VIII, but it dropped out of use in England early in the eighteenth century, and all the leading dictionaries, both English and American, now call it an Americanism.[40] *To fellowship*, once in good American use but now reduced to a provincialism, is in Chaucer. Even *to hustle*, it appears, is ancient. Among adjectives, *homely*, which means only homelike or unadorned in England, was used in its American sense of plain-featured by both Shakespeare and Milton. Other such survivors are *burly, catty-cornered, likely, deft, copious, scant* and *ornate*. Perhaps *clever* also belongs to this category, that is, in the American sense of amiable.

"Our ancestors, " said James Russell Lowell, "unhappily could bring over no English better than Shakespeare's." Shakespeare died in 1616; the Pilgrims landed four years later; Jamestown was founded in 1607. As we have seen, the colonists, saving a few superior leaders, were men of small sensitiveness to the refinements of life and speech: soldiers of fortune, amateur theologians, younger sons, neighborhood "advanced thinkers, " bankrupts, jobless workmen, decayed gentry, and other such fugitives from culture—in brief, Philistines of the sort who join tin-pot fraternal orders today, and march in parades, and whoop for the latest mountebanks in politics. There was thus a touch of rhetoric in Lowell's saying that they spoke the English of Shakespeare; as well argue that the London grocers of 1885 spoke the English of Pater. But in a larger sense he said truly, for these men at least brought with them the vocabulary of Shakespeare—or a part of it, —even if the uses he made of it were beyond their comprehension, and they also brought with them that sense of ease in the language, that fine disdain for formality, that bold experimentalizing in words, which was so peculiarly Elizabethan. There were no grammarians in that day; there were no purists that anyone listened to; it was a case of saying your say in the easiest and most satisfying way. In remote parts of the United States there are still direct and almost pure-blooded descendants of those seventeenth century colonists. Go among them, and you will hear more words from the Shakespearean vocabulary, still alive and in common service, than anywhere else in the world, and more of the loose and brilliant syntax of that time, and more of its gipsy phrases.[41]

§ 6. Colonial Pronunciation

—The debate that long raged over the pronunciation of classical Latin exhibits the difficulty of determining with exactness the shades of sound in the speech of a people long departed from earth. The American colonists, of course, are much nearer to us than the Romans, and so we should have relatively little difficulty in determining just how they pronounced this or that word, but against the fact of their nearness stands the neglect of our philologists, or, perhaps more accurately, our lack of philologists. What Sweet did to clear up the history of English pronunciation, [42] and what Wilhelm Corssen did for Latin, no American professor has yet thought to attempt for American. The literature is almost, if not quite a blank. But here and there we may get a hint of the facts, and though the sum of them is not large, they at least serve to set at rest a number of popular errors.

One of these errors, chiefly prevalent in New England, is that the so-called Boston pronunciation, with its broad *a*'s (making *last, path* and *aunt* almost assonant with *bar*) comes down unbrokenly from the day of the first settlements, and that it is in consequence superior in authority to the pronunciation of the rest of the country, with its flat *a*'s (making the same words assonant with *ban*). A glance through Webster's "Dissertations" is sufficient to show that the flat *a* was in use in New England in 1789, for the pronunciation of such words as *wrath*, *bath* and *path*, as given by him, makes them rhyme with *hath*.[43] Moreover, he gives *aunt* the same *a*-sound. From other sources come indications that the *a* was likewise flattened in such words as *plant*, *basket*, *branch*, *dance*, *blast*, *command* and *castle*, and even in *balm* and *calm*. Changes in the sound of the letter have been going on in English ever since the Middle English period, [44] and according to Lounsbury[45] they have moved toward the disappearance of the Continental *a*, "the fundamental vowel-tone of the human voice." Grandgent, another authority, [46] says that it became flattened "by the sixteenth century" and that "until 1780 or thereabouts the standard language had no broad *a*." Even in such words as *father*, *car* and *ask* the flat *a* was universally used. Sheridan, in the dictionary he published in 1780, [47] actually gave no *ah*-sound in his list of vowels. This habit of flatting the *a* had been brought over, of course, by the early colonists, and was as general in America, in the third quarter of the eighteenth century, as in England. Benjamin Franklin, when he wrote his "Scheme for a New Alphabet and a Reformed Mode of Spelling, " in 1768, apparently had no suspicion that any other *a* was possible. But between 1780 and 1790, according to Grandgent, a sudden fashion for the broad *a* (not the *aw*-sound, as in *fall*, but the Continental sound as in *far*) arose in England, [48] and this fashion soon found servile imitation in Boston. But it was as much an affectation in those days as it is today, and Webster indicated the fact pretty plainly in his "Dissertations." How, despite his opposition, the broad *a* prevailed East of the Connecticut river, and how, in the end, he himself yielded to it, and even tried to force it upon the whole nation—this will be rehearsed in the next chapter.

The colonists remained faithful much longer than the English to various other vowel-sounds that were facing change in the eighteenth century, for example, the long *e*-sound in *heard*. Webster says that the custom of rhyming *heard* with *bird* instead of with *feared* came in at the beginning of the Revolution. "To most people in this country, " he adds, "the English pronunciation appears like affectation." He also argues for rhyming *deaf* with *leaf*, and protests against inserting a *y*-sound before the *u* in such words as *nature*. Franklin's authority stands behind *git* for *get*. This pronunciation, according to Menner, [49] was correct in seventeenth century England, and perhaps down to the middle of the next century. So was the use of the Continental *i*-

sound in *oblige*, making it *obleege*. It is probable that the colonists clung to these disappearing usages much longer than the English. The latter, according to Webster, were unduly responsive to illogical fashions set by the exquisites of the court and by popular actors. He blames Garrick, in particular, for many extravagant innovations, most of them not followed in the colonies. But Garrick was surely not responsible for the use of a long *i*-sound in such words as *motive*, nor for the corruption of *mercy* to *marcy*. Webster denounced both of these barbarisms. The second he ascribed somewhat lamely to the fact that the letter *r* is called *ar*, and proposed to dispose of it by changing the *ar* to *er*.

As for the consonants, the colonists seem to have resisted valiantly that tendency to slide over them which arose in England after the Restoration. Franklin, in 1768, still retained the sound of *l* in such words as *would* and *should*, a usage not met with in England after the year 1700. In the same way, according to Menner, the *w* in *sword* was sounded in America "for some time after Englishmen had abandoned it." The sensitive ear of Henry James detected an unpleasant *r*-sound in the speech of Americans, long ago got rid of by the English, so late as 1905; he even charged that it was inserted gratuitously in innocent words.[50] The obvious slurring of the consonants by Southerners is explained by a recent investigator[51] on the ground that it began in England during the reign of Charles II, and that most of the Southern colonists came to the New World at that time. The court of Charles, it is argued, was under French influence, due to the king's long residence in France and his marriage to Henrietta Marie. Charles "objected to the inharmonious contractions *will'nt* (or *wolln't*) and *wasn't* and *weren't* ... and set the fashion of using the softly euphonious *won't* and *wan't*, which are used in speaking to this day by the best class of Southerners." A more direct French influence upon Southern pronunciation is also pointed out. "With full knowledge of his *g's* and his *r's*, ... [the Southerner] sees fit to glide over them, ... and he carries over the consonant ending one word to the vowel beginning the next, just as the Frenchman does." The political importance of the South, in the years between the Mecklenburg Declaration and the adoption of the Constitution, tended to force its provincialisms upon the common language. Many of the acknowledged leaders of the nascent nation were Southerners, and their pronunciation, as well as their phrases, must have become familiar everywhere. Pickering gives us a hint, indeed, at the process whereby their usage influenced that of the rest of the people.[52]

The Americans early dropped the *h*-sound in such words as *when* and *where*, but so far as I can determine they never elided it at the beginning of words, save in the case of *herb*, and a few others. This elision is commonly spoken of as a cockney vulgarism, but it has extended to the orthodox English speech. In *ostler* the initial *h* is openly left off; in *hotel* and *hospital* it is seldom sounded, even by the most careful Englishmen. Certain English words in *h*, in which the *h* is now sounded, betray its former silence by the fact that not *a* but *an* is still put before them. It is still good English usage to write *an hotel* and *an historical*; it is the American usage to write *a hotel* and *a historical*.

The great authority of Webster was sufficient to establish the American pronunciation of *schedule*. In England the *sch* is always given the soft sound, but Webster decided for the hard sound, as in *scheme*. The variance persists to this day. The name of the last letter of the alphabet, which is always *zed* in English, is usually made *zee* in the United States. Thornton shows that this Americanism arose in the eighteenth century.

FOOTNOTES:

[1] Bristed was a grandson of John Jacob Astor and was educated at Cambridge. He contributed an extremely sagacious essay on The English Language in America to a volume of Cambridge Essays published by a group of young Cambridge men; London, 1855.

[2] Vol. i, p. vi.

[3] Scheme for a New Alphabet and a Reformed Mode of Spelling; Philadelphia, 1768.

[4] Dec. 26, 1789. The Works of B. Franklin, ed. by A. F. Smyth; New York, 1905, vol. i, p. 40.

[5] *The Druid*, No. 5; reprinted in Witherspoon's Collected Works, edited by Ashbel Green, vol. iv; New York, 1800-1.

[6] *Vide*, in addition to the citations in the text, the *British Critic*, Nov. 1793; Feb. 1810; the *Critical Review*, July 1807; Sept. 1809; the *Monthly Review*, May 1808; the *Eclectic Review*, Aug. 1813.

[7] 1815, pp. 307-14; reprinted in his Remarks on National Literature, Boston, 1823.

[8] American English, *North American Review*, April, 1883.

[9] A number of such Indian words are preserved in the nomenclature of Tammany Hall and in that of the Improved Order of Red Men, an organization with more than 500, 000 members. The Red Men, borrowing from the Indians, thus name the months, in order: *Cold Moon, Snow, Worm, Plant, Flower, Hot, Buck, Sturgeon, Corn, Travelers', Beaver* and *Hunting*. They call their officers *incohonee, sachem, wampum-keeper*, etc. But such terms, of course, are not in general use.

[10] A long list of such obsolete Americanisms is given by Clapin in his Dictionary.

[11] An Account of the History, Manners and Customs of the Indian Nations....; Phila., 1818.

[12] *Cf.* Hans Brinker, by Mary Maples Dodge; New York, 1891.

[13] (*a*) A chest of drawers, (*b*) a government office. In both senses the word is rare in English, though its use by the French is familiar. In the United States its use in (*b*) has been extended, *e. g.*, in *employment-bureau.*

[14] From *Sint-Klaas—Saint Nicholas. Santa Claus* has also become familiar to the English, but the Oxford Dictionary still calls the name an Americanism.

[15] The spelling is variously *sauerkraut, saurkraut, sourkraut* and *sourkrout.*

[16] *Cf.* The Cambridge History of American Literature, vol. i, pp. 14 and 22.

[17] The American origin of this last word has been disputed, but the weight of evidence seems to show that it was borrowed from the *rapides* of the French Canadians. It is familiar in the United States and Canada, but seldom met with in England.

[18] *Log-cabin* came in later. Thornton's first quotation is dated 1818. The *Log-Cabin* campaign was in 1840.

[19] Theo. Roosevelt: Gouverneur Morris; Boston, 1888, p. 104.

[20] William Brown Meloney: The Heritage of Tyre; New York, 1916, p. 15.

[21] *Vide* his preface to Every-Day English, pp. xxi and xv, respectively.

[22] *Vide* Lyell's Travels in North America; London, 1845.

[23] Pref. to the Biglow Papers, 2nd series, 1866.

[24] Reprinted in Helpful Hints in Writing and Reading, comp. by Grenville Kleiser; New York, 1911, pp. 15-17.

[25] A. Cleveland Coxe: Americanisms in England, *Forum*, Oct., 1886.

[26] Edwin S. Gould: Good English, or, Popular Errors in Language: New York, 1867; pp. 25-27.

[27] *Cf.* Ch. I, § 5, and Ch. V, § 1.

[28] *Lott* appears in the Connecticut Code of 1650. *Vide* the edition of Andrus; Hartford, 1822. On page 35 is "their landes, *lotts* and accommodations." On page 46 is "meadow and home *lotts*."

[29] *Vide* Hutchinson's Diary, vol. i, p. 171; London, 1883-6.

[30] The definitions are from the Concise Oxford Dictionary of Current English (1914) and the Standard Dictionary (1906), respectively.

[31] S. Sewall: Diary, April 14, 1712: "I lay'd a *Rock* in the North-east corner of the Foundation of the Meeting-house."

[32] The Americana, ... *art.* Americanisms: New York, 1903-6.

[33] Immigration, 2nd ed.; New York, 1913, p. 4. Sir J. R. Seeley says, in The Expansion of England (2nd ed.; London, 1895, p. 84) that the emigration from England to New England, after the meeting of the Long Parliament (1640), was so slight for a full century that it barely balanced "the counter-movement of colonists quitting the colony." Richard Hildreth, in his History of the United States, vol. i, p. 267, says that the departures actually exceeded the arrivals.

[34] Works, ed. by Sparks: vol. ii, p. 319.

[35] *Cf.* Pehr Kalm: Travels into N. America, tr. by J. R. Forster, 3 vols.; London, 1770-71.

[36] Sydney George Fisher: The True Story of the American Revolution; Phila. and London, 1902, p. 27. See also John T. Morse's Life of Thomas Jefferson in the American Statesmen series (Boston and New York, 1898), p. 2. Morse points out that Washington, Jefferson and Madison belonged to this new aristocracy, not to the old one.

[37] *Cf.* the Cambridge History of American Literature, vol. i, p. 119. Francis Jeffrey, writing on Franklin in the*Edinburgh Review* for July, 1806, hailed him as a prodigy who had arisen "in a society where there was no relish and no encouragement for literature."

[38] Examples of its use in the American sense, considered vulgar and even indecent in England, are to be found in Gen. xlviii, 1; II Kings viii, 7; John xi, 1, and Acts ix, 37.

[39] J. O. Halliwell (Phillips): A Dictionary of Archaisms and Provincialisms, Containing Words now Obsolete in England All of Which are Familiar and in Common Use in America, 2nd ed.; London, 1850.

[40] An interesting discussion of this verb appeared in the *New York Sun*, Nov. 27, 1914.

[41] *Cf.* J. H. Combs: Old, Early and Elizabethan English in the Southern Mountains, *Dialect Notes*, vol. iv, pt. iv, pp. 283-97.

[42] Henry Sweet: A History of English Sounds; London, 1876; Oxford, 1888.

[43] P. 124.

[44] *Cf. Art.* Changes in the Language Since Shakespeare's Time, by W. Murison, in The Cambridge History of English Literature, vol. xiv, p. 485.

[45] English Spelling and Spelling Reform; New York, 1909.

[46] C. H. Grandgent: Fashion and the Broad *A*, *Nation*, Jan. 7, 1915.

[47] Thomas Sheridan: A Complete Dictionary of the English Language; London, 1780.

[48] It first appeared in Robert Nares' Elements of Orthography; London, 1784. In 1791 it received full approbation in John Walker's Critical Pronouncing Dictionary.

[49] Robert J. Menner; The Pronunciation of English in America, *Atlantic Monthly*, March, 1915.

[50] The Question of Our Speech; Boston and New York, 1906, pp. 27-29.

[51] Elizabeth H. Hancock: Southern Speech, *Neale's Monthly*, Nov., 1913, pp. 606-7.

[52] *Vide* his remarks on *balance* in his Vocabulary. See also Marsh, p. 671.

III. The Period of Growth

§ 1. The New Nation

—The American language thus began to be recognizably differentiated from English in both vocabulary and pronunciation by the opening of the nineteenth century, but as yet its growth was hampered by two factors, the first being the lack of a national literature of any pretentions and the second being an internal political disharmony which greatly conditioned and enfeebled the national consciousness. During the actual Revolution common aims and common dangers forced the Americans to show a united front, but once they had achieved political independence they developed conflicting interests, and out of those conflicting interests came suspicions and hatreds which came near wrecking the new confederation more than once. Politically, their worst weakness, perhaps, was an inability to detach themselves wholly from the struggle for domination still going on in Europe. The surviving Loyalists of the revolutionary era— estimated by some authorities to have constituted fully a third of the total population in 1776—were ardently in favor of England, and such patriots as Jefferson were as ardently in favor of France. This engrossment in the quarrels of foreign nations was what Washington warned against in his Farewell Address. It was at the bottom of such bitter animosities as that between Jefferson and Hamilton. It inspired and perhaps excused the pessimism of such men as Burr. Its net effect was to make it difficult for the people of the new nation to think of themselves, politically, as Americans. Their state of mind, vacillating, uncertain, alternately timorous and pugnacious, has been well described by Henry Cabot Lodge in his essay on "Colonialism in America."[1] Soon after the Treaty of Paris was signed, someone referred to the late struggle, in Franklin's hearing, as the War for Independence. "Say, rather, the War of the Revolution, " said Franklin. "The War for Independence is yet to be fought."

"That struggle, " adds Lossing, "occurred, and that independence was won, by the Americans in the War of 1812."[2] In the interval the new republic had passed through a period of *Sturm und Drang* whose gigantic perils and passions we have begun to forget—a period in which disaster ever menaced, and the foes within were no less bold and pertinacious than the foes without. Jefferson, perhaps, carried his fear of "monocrats" to the point of monomania, but under it there was undoubtedly a body of sound fact. The poor debtor class (including probably a majority of the veterans of the Revolution) had been fired by the facile doctrines of the French Revolution to demands which threatened the country with bankruptcy and anarchy, and the class of property-owners, in reaction, went far to the other extreme. On all sides, indeed, there flourished a strong British party, and particularly in New England, where the so-called codfish aristocracy (by no means extinct, even today) exhibited an undisguised Anglomania, and looked forward confidently to a *rapprochement* with the mother country.[3] This Anglomania showed itself, not only in ceaseless political agitation, but also in an elaborate imitation of English manners. We have already seen, on Noah Webster's authority, how it even extended to the pronunciation of the language.

The first sign of the dawn of a new national order came with the election of Thomas Jefferson to the Presidency in 1800. The issue in the campaign was a highly complex one, but under it lay a plain conflict between democratic independence and the old doctrine of dependence and authority; and with the Alien and Sedition Laws about his neck, so vividly reminiscent of the issues of the Revolution itself, Adams went down to defeat. Jefferson was violently anti-British and pro-French; he saw all the schemes of his political opponents, indeed, as English plots; he was the man who introduced the bugaboo into American politics. His first acts after his inauguration were to abolish all ceremonial at the court of the republic, and to abandon spoken discourses to Congress for written messages. That ceremonial, which grew up under Washington, was an imitation, he believed, of the formality of the abhorrent Court of St. James; as for the speeches to Congress, they were palpably modelled upon the speeches from the throne of the English kings. Both reforms met with wide approval; the exactions of the English, particularly on the high seas, were beginning to break up the British party. But confidence in the solidarity and security of the new nation was still anything but universal. The surviving doubts, indeed, were strong enough to delay the ratification of the Twelfth Amendment to the Constitution, providing for more direct elections of President and Vice-President, until the end of 1804, and even then three of the five New England states rejected it, [4] and have never ratified it, in fact, to this day. Democracy was still experimental, doubtful, full of gunpowder. In so far as it had actually come into being, it had come as a boon conferred from above. Jefferson, its protagonist, was the hero of the populace, but he was not of the populace himself, nor did he ever quite trust it.

It was reserved for Andrew Jackson, a man genuinely of the people, to lead and visualize the rise of the lower orders. Jackson, in his way, was the archetype of the new American—ignorant, pushful, impatient of restraint and precedent, an iconoclast, a Philistine, an Anglophobe in every fibre. He came from the extreme backwoods and his youth was passed amid surroundings but little removed from downright savagery.[5] Thousands of other young Americans like him were growing up at the same time—youngsters filled with a vast impatience of all precedent and authority, revilers of all that had come down from an elder day, incorrigible libertarians. They swarmed across the mountains and down the great rivers, wrestling with the naked wilderness and setting up a casual, impromptu sort of civilization where the Indian still menaced. Schools were few and rudimentary; there was not the remotest approach to a cultivated society; any effort to mimic the amenities of the East, or of the mother country, in manner or even in speech, met with instant derision. It was in these surroundings and at this time that the thorough-going American of tradition was born: blatant, illogical, elate, "greeting the embarrassed gods" uproariously and matching "with Destiny for beers." Jackson was unmistakably of that company in his every instinct and idea, and it was his fate to give a new and unshakable confidence to its aspiration at the Battle of New Orleans. Thereafter all doubts began to die out; the new republic was turning out a success. And with success came a vast increase in the national egoism. The hordes of pioneers rolled down the western valleys and on to the great plains.[6] America began to stand for something quite new in the world—in government, in law, in public and private morals, in customs and habits of mind, in the minutia of social intercourse. And simultaneously the voice of America began to take on its characteristic twang, and the speech of America began to differentiate itself boldly and unmistakably from the speech of England. The average Philadelphian or Bostonian of 1790 had not the slightest difficulty in making himself understood by a visiting Englishman. But the average Ohio boatman of 1810 or plainsman of 1815 was already speaking a dialect that the Englishman would have shrunk from as barbarous and unintelligible, and before long it began to leave its mark upon and to get direction and support from a distinctively national literature.

That literature, however, was very slow in coming to a dignified, confident and autonomous estate. Down to Jefferson's day it was almost wholly polemical, and hence lacking in the finer values; he himself, an insatiable propagandist and controversialist, was one of its chief ornaments. "The novelists and the historians, the essayists and the poets, whose names come to mind when American literature is mentioned, " says a recent literary historian, "have all flourished since 1800."[7] Pickering, so late as 1816, said that "in this country we can hardly be said to have any authors by profession." It was a true saying, though the new day was about to dawn; Bryant had already written "Thanatopsis" and was destined to publish it the year following. Difficulties of communication hampered the circulation of the few native books that were written; it was easier for a man in the South to get books from London than to get them from Boston or New York, and the lack of a copyright treaty with England flooded the country with cheap English editions. "It is much to be regretted, " wrote Dr. David Ramsay, of Charleston, S. C., to Noah Webster in 1806, "that there is so little intercourse in a literary way between the states. As soon as a book of general utility comes out in any state it should be for sale in all of them." Ramsay asked for little; the most he could imagine was a sale of 2, 000 copies for an American work in America. But even that was far beyond the possibilities of the time.

An external influence of great potency helped to keep the national literature scant and timorous during those early and perilous days. It was the extraordinary animosity of the English critics, then at the zenith of their pontifical authority, to all books of American origin or flavor. This animosity, culminating in Sydney Smith's famous sneer, [8] was but part of a larger hostility to all things American, from political theories to table manners. The American, after the war of 1812, became the pet abomination of the English, and the chief butt of the incomparable English talent for moral indignation. There was scarcely an issue of the *Quarterly Review*, the *Edinburgh*, the *Foreign Quarterly*, the *British Review* or *Blackwood's*, for a generation following 1814, in which he was not stupendously assaulted. Gifford, Sydney Smith and the poet Southey became specialists in this business; it took on the character of a holy war; even such mild men as Wordsworth were recruited for it. It was argued that the Americans were rogues and swindlers, that they lived in filth and squalor, that they were boors in social intercourse, that they were poltroons and savages in war, that they were depraved and criminal, that they were wholly devoid of the remotest notion of decency or honor. The *Foreign*

Quarterly, summing up in January, 1844, pronounced them "horn-handed and pig-headed, hard, persevering, unscrupulous, carnivorous, with a genius for lying." Various Americans went to the defense of their countrymen, among them, Irving, Cooper, Timothy Dwight, J. K. Paulding, John Neal, Edward Everett and Robert Walsh. Paulding, in "John Bull in America, or, the New Munchausen, " published in 1825, attempted satire. Even an Englishman, James Sterling, warned his fellow-Britons that, if they continued their intolerant abuse, they would "turn into bitterness the last drops of good-will toward England that exist in the United States." But the avalanche of denunciation kept up, and even down to a few years ago it was very uncommon for an Englishman to write of American politics, or manners, or literature without betraying his dislike. Not, indeed, until the Prussian began monopolizing the whole British talent for horror and invective did the Yankee escape the lash.[9]

This gigantic pummelling, in the long run, was destined to encourage an independent spirit in the national literature, if only by a process of mingled resentment and despair, but for some time its chief effect was to make American writers of a more delicate aspiration extremely self-conscious and diffident. The educated classes, even against their will, were influenced by the torrent of abuse; they could not help finding in it an occasional reasonableness, an accidental true hit. The result, despite the efforts of Channing, Knapp and other such valiant defenders of the native author, was uncertainty and skepticism in native criticism. "The first step of an American entering upon a literary career, " says Lodge, writing of the first quarter of the century, "was to pretend to be an Englishman in order that he might win the approval, not of Englishmen, but of his own countrymen." Cooper, in his first novel, "Precaution, " chose an English scene, imitated English models, and obviously hoped to placate the critics thereby. Irving, too, in his earliest work, showed a considerable discretion, and his "History of New York, " as everyone knows, was first published anonymously. But this puerile spirit did not last long. The English onslaughts were altogether too vicious to be received lying down; their very fury demanded that they be met with a united and courageous front. Cooper, in his second novel, "The Spy, " boldly chose an American setting and American characters, and though the influence of his wife, who came of a Loyalist family, caused him to avoid any direct attack upon the English, he attacked them indirectly, and with great effect, by opposing an immediate and honorable success to their derisions. "The Spy" ran through three editions in four months; it was followed by his long line of thoroughly American novels; in 1834 he formally apologized to his countrymen for his early truancy in "Precaution." Irving, too, soon adopted a bolder tone, and despite his English predilections, he refused an offer of a hundred guineas for an article for the *Quarterly Review*, made by Gifford in 1828, on the ground that "the *Review* has been so persistently hostile to our country that I cannot draw a pen in its service."

The same year saw the publication of the first edition of Webster's American Dictionary of the English language, and a year later followed Samuel L. Knapp's "Lectures on American Literature, " the first history of the national letters ever attempted. Knapp, in his preface, thought it necessary to prove, first of all, that an American literature actually existed, and Webster, in his introduction, was properly apologetic, but there was no real need for timorousness in either case, for the American attitude toward the attack of the English was now definitely changing from uneasiness to defiance. The English critics, in fact, had overdone the thing, and though their clatter was to keep up for many years more, they no longer spread terror or had much influence. Of a sudden, as if in answer to them, doubts turned to confidence, and then into the wildest sort of optimism, not only in politics and business, but also in what passed for the arts. Knapp boldly defied the English to produce a "tuneful sister" surpassing Mrs. Sigourney; more, he argued that the New World, if only by reason of its superior scenic grandeur, would eventually hatch a poetry surpassing even that of Greece and Rome. "What are the Tibers and Scamanders, " he demanded, "measured by the Missouri and the Amazon? Or what the loveliness of Illysus or Avon by the Connecticut or the Potomack?"

In brief, the national feeling, long delayed at birth, finally leaped into being in amazing vigor. "One can get an idea of the strength of that feeling, " says R. O. Williams, "by glancing at almost any book taken at random from the American publications of the period. Belief in the grand future of the United States is the key-note of everything said and done. All things American are to be grand—our territory, population, products, wealth, science, art—but especially our political institutions and literature. The unbounded confidence in the material development of the country which now characterizes the extreme northwest of the United States prevailed as strongly throughout the eastern part of the Union during the first thirty years of the century; and over and above a belief in, and concern for, materialistic progress, there were enthusiastic anticipations of achievements in all the moral and intellectual fields of national greatness."[10] Nor was that vast optimism wholly without warrant. An American literature was actually coming into being, and with a wall of hatred and contempt shutting in England, the new American writers were beginning to turn to the Continent for inspiration and encouragement. Irving had already drunk at Spanish springs; Emerson and Bayard Taylor were to receive powerful impulses from Germany, following Ticknor, Bancroft and Everett before them; Bryant was destined to go back to the classics. Moreover, Cooper and John P. Kennedy had shown the way to native sources of literary material, and Longfellow was making ready to follow them; novels in imitation of English models were no longer heard of; the ground was preparing for "Uncle Tom's Cabin." Finally, Webster himself, as Williams demonstrated, worked better than he knew. His American Dictionary was not only thoroughly American: it was superior to any of the current dictionaries of the English, so much so that for a good many years it remained "a sort of mine for British lexicography to exploit."

Thus all hesitations disappeared, and there arose a national consciousness so soaring and so blatant that it began to dismiss all British usage and opinion as puerile and idiotic. William L. Marcy, when Secretary of State under Pierce (1853-57), issued a circular to all American diplomatic and consular officers, loftily bidding them employ only "the American language" in communicating with him. The Legislature of Indiana, in an act approved February 15, 1838, establishing the state university at Bloomington, [11] provided that it should instruct the youth of the new commonwealth (it had been admitted to the Union in 1816) "in the American, learned and foreign languages ... and literature." Such grandiose pronunciamentos well indicate and explain the temper of the era.[12]It was a time of expansion and braggadocia. The new republic would not only produce a civilization and a literature of its own; it would show the way for all other civilizations and literatures. Rufus Wilmot Griswold, the enemy of Poe, rose from his decorous Baptist pew to protest that so much patriotism amounted to insularity and absurdity, but there seems to have been no one to second the motion. It took, indeed, the vast shock of the Civil War to unhorse the optimists. While the Jackson influence survived, it was the almost unanimous national conviction that "he who dallies is a dastard, and he who doubts is damned."

§ 2. The Language in the Making

—All this jingoistic bombast, however, was directed toward defending, not so much the national vernacular as the national beautiful letters. True enough, an English attack upon a definite American locution always brought out certain critical minute-men, but in the main they were anything but hospitable to the racy neologisms that kept crowding up from below, and most of them were eager to be accepted as masters of orthodox English and very sensitive to the charge that their writing was bestrewn with Americanisms. A glance through the native criticism of the time will show how ardently even the most uncompromising patriots imitated the Johnsonian jargon then fashionable in England. Fowler and Griswold followed pantingly in the footsteps of Macaulay; their prose is extraordinarily ornate and self-conscious, and one searches it in vain for any concession to colloquialism. Poe, the master of them all, achieved a style so elephantine that many an English leader-writer must have studied it with envy. A few bolder spirits, as we have seen, spoke out for national freedom in language as well as in letters—among them, Channing—but in the main the Brahmins of the time were conservatives in that department, and it is difficult to imagine Emerson or Irving or Bryant sanctioning the innovations later adopted so easily by Howells. Lowell and Walt Whitman, in fact, were the first men of letters, properly so called, to give specific assent to the great changes that were firmly fixed in the national speech during the half century between the War of 1812 and the Civil War. Lowell did so in his preface to the second series of "The Biglow Papers." Whitman made his declaration in "An American Primer." In discussing his own poetry, he said: "It is an attempt to give the spirit, the body and the man, new words, new potentialities of speech—an American, a cosmopolitan (for the best of America is the best cosmopolitanism) range of self-expression." And then: "The Americans are going to be the most fluent and melodious-voiced people in the world—and the most perfect users of words. The new times, the new people, the new vistas need a new tongue according— yes, and what is more, they will have such a new tongue." To which, as everyone knows, Whitman himself forthwith contributed many daring (and still undigested) novelties, *e. g., camerado, romanza, Adamic* and *These States.*

Meanwhile, in strong contrast to the lingering conservatism above there was a wild and lawless development of the language below, and in the end it forced itself into recognition, and profited by the literary declaration of independence of its very opponents. "The *jus et norma loquendi,* " says W. R. Morfill, the English philologist, "do not depend upon scholars." Particularly in a country where scholarship is still new and wholly cloistered, and the overwhelming majority of the people are engaged upon novel and highly exhilarating tasks, far away from schools and with a gigantic cockiness in their hearts. The remnants of the Puritan civilization had been wiped out by the rise of the proletariat under Jackson, and whatever was fine and sensitive in it had died with it. What remained of an urbane habit of mind and utterance began to be confined to the narrowing feudal areas of the south, and to the still narrower refuge of the Boston Brahmins, now, for the first time, a definitely recognized caste of *intelligentsia*, self-charged with carrying the torch of culture through a new Dark Age. The typical American, in Paulding's satirical phrase, became "a bundling, gouging, impious" fellow, without either "morals, literature, religion or refinement." Next to the savage struggle for land and dollars, party politics was the chief concern of the people, and with the disappearance of the old leaders and the entrance of pushing upstarts from the backwoods, political controversy sank to an incredibly low level. Bartlett, in the introduction to the second edition of his Glossary, describes the effect upon the language. First the enfranchised mob, whether in the city wards or along the western rivers, invented fantastic slang-words and turns of phrase; then they were "seized upon by stump-speakers at political meetings"; then they were heard in Congress; then they got into the newspapers; and finally they came into more or less good usage. Much contemporary evidence is to the same effect. Fowler, in listing "low expressions" in 1850, described them as "chiefly political." "The vernacular tongue of the country, " said Daniel Webster, "has become greatly vitiated, depraved and corrupted by the style of the congressional debates." Thornton, in the appendix to his Glossary, gives some astounding specimens of congressional oratory between the 20's and 60's, and many more will reward the explorer who braves the files of the *Congressional Globe*. This flood of racy and unprecedented words and phrases beat upon and finally penetrated the retreat of the *literati*, but the purity of speech cultivated there had little compensatory influence upon the vulgate. The newspaper was now enthroned, and *belles lettres* were cultivated almost in private, and as a mystery. It is probable, indeed, that "Uncle Tom's Cabin" and "Ten Nights in a Bar-room, " both published in the early 50's, were the first contemporary native books, after Cooper's day, that the American people, as a people, ever read. Nor did the pulpit, now fast falling from its old high estate, lift a corrective voice. On the contrary, it joined the crowd, and Bartlett denounces it specifically for its bad example, and cites, among its crimes against the language, such inventions as *to doxologize* and *to funeralize.* To these novelties, apparently without any thought of their uncouthness, Fowler adds to *missionate* and *consociational.*

As I say, the pressure from below broke down the defenses of the purists, and literally forced a new national idiom upon them. Pen in hand, they might still achieve laborious imitations of Johnson and Macaulay, but their mouths began to betray them. "When it comes to talking, " wrote Charles Astor Bristed for Englishmen in 1855, "the most refined and best educated American, who has habitually resided in his own country, the very man who would write, on some serious topic, volumes in which no peculiarity could be detected, will, in half a dozen sentences, use at least as many words that cannot fail to strike the inexperienced Englishman who hears them for the first time." Bristed gave a specimen of the American of that time, calculated to flabbergast his inexperienced Englishman; you will find it in the volume of Cambridge Essays, already cited. His aim was to explain and defend Americanisms, and so shut off the storm of English reviling, and he succeeded in producing one of the most thoughtful and persuasive essays on the subject ever written. But his purpose failed and the attack kept up, and eight years afterward the Very Rev. Henry Alford, D.D., dean of Canterbury, led a famous assault. "Look at those phrases, " he said, "which so amuse us in their speech and books; at their reckless exaggeration and contempt for congruity; and then compare the character and history of the nation—its blunted sense of moral obligation and duty to man; its open disregard of conventional right where aggrandizement is to be obtained; and I may now say, its reckless and fruitless maintenance of the most cruel and unprincipled war in the history of the world."[13] In his American edition of 1866 Dr. Alford withdrew this reference to the Civil War and somewhat ameliorated his indignation otherwise, but he clung to the main counts in his indictment, and most Englishmen, I daresay, still give them a certain support. The American is no longer a "vain, egotistical, insolent, rodomontade sort of fellow"; America is no longer the "brigand confederation" of the *Foreign Quarterly* or "the loathsome creature, ... maimed and lame, full of sores and ulcers" of Dickens; but the Americanism is yet regarded with a bilious eye, and pounced upon viciously when found. Even the friendliest English critics seem to be daunted by the gargantuan copiousness of American inventions in speech. Their position, perhaps, was well stated by Capt. Basil Hall, author of the celebrated "Travels in North America, " in 1827. When he argued that "surely such innovations are to be deprecated, " an American asked him this question: "If a word becomes universally current in America, why should it not take its station in the language?" "Because, " replied Hall in all seriousness, "there are words enough in our language already."

§ 3. The Expanding Vocabulary

—A glance at some of the characteristic coinages of the time, as they are revealed in the *Congressional Globe*, in contemporary newspapers and political tracts, and in that grotesque small literature of humor which began with Judge Thomas C. Haliburton's "Sam Slick" in 1835, is almost enough to make one sympathize with Dean Alford. Bartlett quotes *to doxologize* from the *Christian Disciple*, a quite reputable religious paper of the 40's. *To citizenize* was used and explained by Senator Young, of Illinois, in the Senate on February 1, 1841, and he gave Noah Webster as authority for it. *To funeralize* and *to missionate*, along with *consociational*, were contributions of the backwoods pulpit; perhaps it also produced *hell-roaring* and *hellion*, the latter of which was a favorite of the Mormons and even got into a sermon by Henry Ward Beecher. *To deacon*, a verb of decent mien in colonial days, signifying to read a hymn line by line, responded to the rough humor of the time, and began to mean to swindle or adulterate, *e. g.*, to put the largest berries at the top of the box, to extend one's fences *sub rosa*, or to mix sand with sugar. A great rage for extending the vocabulary by the use of suffixes seized upon the corn-fed etymologists, and they produced a formidable new vocabulary in -*ize, -ate, -ify, -acy, -ous* and -*ment*. Such inventions as *to obligate, to concertize, to questionize, retiracy, savagerous, coatee* (a sort of diminutive for coat) and *citified* appeared in the popular vocabulary, and even got into more or less good usage. Fowler, in 1850, cited *publishment* and *releasement* with no apparent thought that they were uncouth. And at the same time many verbs were made by the simple process of back formation, as, *to resurrect, to excurt, to resolute, to burgle*[14] and *to enthuse.*[15]

Some of these inventions, after flourishing for a generation or more, were retired with blushes during the period of aesthetic consciousness following the Civil War, but a large number have survived to our own day, and are in good usage. Not even the most bilious purist would think of objecting to *to affiliate, to itemize, to resurrect* or *to Americanize* today, and yet all of them gave grief to the judicious when they first appeared in the debates of Congress, brought there by statesmen from the backwoods. Nor to such simpler verbs of the period as *to corner* (*i. e.*, the market), *to boss* and *to lynch*.[16] Nor perhaps to *to boom, to boost, to kick* (in the sense of to protest), *to coast* (on a sled), *to engineer, to collide, to chink* (*i. e.*, logs), *to feaze, to splurge, to aggravate* (in the sense of to anger), *to yank* and *to crawfish*. These verbs have entered into the very fibre of the American vulgate, and so have many nouns derived from them, *e. g., boomer, boom-town, bouncer, kicker, kick, splurge, roller-coaster*. A few of them, *e. g., to collide* and *to feaze*, were archaic English terms brought to new birth; a few others, *e. g., to holler*[17] and *to muss*, were obviously mere corruptions. But a good many others, *e. g., to bulldoze, to hornswoggle* and *to scoot*, were genuine inventions, and redolent of the soil.

With the new verbs came a great swarm of verb-phrases, some of them short and pithy and others extraordinarily elaborate, but all showing the true national talent for condensing a complex thought, and often a whole series of thoughts, into a vivid and arresting image. Of the first class are *to fill the bill, to fizzle out, to make tracks, to peter out, to plank down, to go back on, to keep tab, to light out* and *to back water*. Side by side with them we have inherited such common coins of speech as *to make the fur fly, to cut a swath, to know him like a book, to keep a stiff upper lip, to cap the climax, to handle without gloves, to freeze on to, to go it blind, to pull wool over his eyes, to know the ropes, to get solid with, to spread one's self, to run into the ground, to dodge the issue, to paint the town red, to take a back seat* and *to get ahead of.* These are so familiar that we use them and hear them without thought; they seem as authentically parts of the English idiom as *to be left at the post.* And yet, as the labors of Thornton have demonstrated, all of them are of American nativity, and the circumstances surrounding the origin of some of them have been accurately determined. Many others are palpably the products of the great movement toward the West, for example, *to pan out, to strike it rich, to jump* or *enter a claim, to pull up stakes, to rope in, to die with one's boots on, to get the deadwood on, to get the drop, to back and fill* (a steamboat phrase used figuratively) and *to get the bulge on*. And in many others the authentic American is no less plain, for example, in *to kick the bucket, to put a bug in his ear, to see the elephant, to crack up, to do up brown, to bark up the wrong tree, to jump on with both feet, to go the whole hog, to make a kick, to buck the tiger, to let it slide* and *to come out at the little end of the horn. To play possum* belongs to this list. To it Thornton adds *to knock into a cocked hat*, despite its English sound, and *to have an ax to grind. To go for*, both in the sense of belligerency and in that of partisanship, is also American, and so is *to go through* (*i. e.*, to plunder).

Of adjectives the list is scarcely less long. Among the coinages of the first half of the century that are in good use today are *non-committal, highfalutin, well-posted, down-town, played-out, flat-footed, whole-souled* and *true-blue*. The first appears in a Senate debate of 1841; *highfalutin* in a political speech of the same decade. Both are useful words; it is impossible, not employing them, to convey the ideas behind them without circumlocution. The use of *slim* in the sense of meagre, as in *slim chance, slim attendance* and *slim support*, goes back still further. The English use *small* in place of it. Other, and less respectable contributions of the time are *brash, brainy, peart, locoed, pesky, picayune, scary, well-heeled, hardshell* (e. g., Baptist), *low-flung, codfish* (to indicate opprobrium) and *go-to-meeting*. The use of *plumb* as an adjective, as in *plumb crazy*, is an English archaism that was revived in the United States in the early years of the century. In the more orthodox adverbial form of *plump* it still survives, for example, in "she fell *plump* into his arms." But this last is also good English.

The characteristic American substitution of *mad* for *angry* goes back to the eighteenth century, and perhaps denotes the survival of an English provincialism. Witherspoon noticed it and denounced it in 1781, and in 1816 Pickering called it "low" and said that it was not used "except in very familiar conversation." But it got into much better odor soon afterward, and by 1840 it passed unchallenged. Its use is one of the peculiarities that Englishmen most quickly notice in American colloquial speech today. In formal written discourse it is less often encountered, probably because the English marking of it has so conspicuously singled it out. But it is constantly met with in the newspapers and in the *Congressional Record*, and it is not infrequently used by such writers as Howells and Dreiser. In the familiar simile, *as mad as a hornet*, it is used in the American sense. But *as mad as a March hare* is English, and connotes insanity, not mere anger. The English meaning of the word is preserved in *mad-house* and *mad-dog*, but I have often noticed that American rustics, employing the latter term, derive from it a vague notion, not that the dog is demented, but that it is in a simple fury. From this notion, perhaps, comes the popular belief that dogs may be thrown into hydrophobia by teasing and badgering them.

It was not, however, among the verbs and adjectives that the American word-coiners of the first half of the century achieved their gaudiest innovations, but among the substantives. Here they had temptation and excuse in plenty, for innumerable new objects and relations demanded names, and here they exercised their fancy without restraint. Setting aside loan words, which will be considered later, three main varieties of new nouns were thus produced. The first consisted of English words rescued from obsolescence or changed in meaning, the second of compounds manufactured of the common materials of the mother tongue, and the third of entirely new inventions. Of the first class, good specimens are *deck* (of cards), *gulch*, *gully* and *billion*, the first three old English words restored to usage in America and the last a sound English word changed in meaning. Of the second class, examples are offered by *gum-shoe*, *mortgage-shark*, *dug-out*, *shot-gun*, *stag-party*, *wheat-pit*, *horse-sense*, *chipped-beef*, *oyster-supper*, *buzz-saw*, *chain-gang* and *hell-box*. And of the third there are instances in *buncombe*, *greaser*, *conniption*, *bloomer*, *campus*, *galoot*, *maverick*, *roustabout*, *bugaboo* and *blizzard*.

Of these coinages, perhaps those of the second class are most numerous and characteristic. In them American exhibits one of its most marked tendencies: a habit of achieving short cuts in speech by a process of agglutination. Why explain laboriously, as an Englishman might, that the notes of a new bank (in a day of innumerable new banks) are insufficiently secure? Call them *wild-cat* notes and have done! Why describe a gigantic rain storm with the lame adjectives of everyday? Call it a *cloud-burst* and immediately a vivid picture of it is conjured up. *Rough-neck* is a capital word; it is more apposite and savory than the English *navvy*, and it is overwhelmingly more American.[18]*Square-meal* is another. *Fire-eater* is yet another. And the same instinct for the terse, the eloquent and the picturesque is in *boiled-shirt, blow-out, big-bug, claim-jumper, spread-eagle, come-down, back-number, claw-hammer* (coat), *bottom-dollar, poppy-cock, cold-snap, back-talk, back-taxes, calamity-howler, cut-off, fire-bug, grab-bag, grip-sack, grub-stake, pay-dirt, tender-foot, stocking-feet, ticket-scalper, store-clothes, small-potatoes, cake-walk, prairie-schooner, round-up, snake-fence, flat-boat, under-the-weather, on-the-hoof,* and *jumping-off-place.* These compounds (there must be thousands of them) have been largely responsible for giving the language its characteristic tang and color. Such specimens as *bell-hop, semi-occasional, chair-warmer* and *down-and-out* are as distinctively American as baseball or the quick-lunch.

The spirit of the language appears scarcely less clearly in some of the coinages of the other classes. There are, for example, the English words that have been extended or restricted in meaning, *e. g., docket* (for court calendar), *betterment* (for improvement to property), *collateral* (for security), *crank* (for fanatic), *jumper* (for tunic), *tickler* (for memorandum or reminder), [19]*carnival* (in such phrases as *carnival of crime*), *scrape* (for fight or difficulty), [20] *flurry* (of snow, or in the market), *suspenders, diggings* (for habitation) and *range.* Again, there are the new assemblings of English materials, *e. g., doggery, rowdy, teetotaler, goatee, tony* and *cussedness.* Yet again, there are the purely artificial words, *e. g., sockdolager, hunkydory, scalawag, guyascutis, spondulix, slumgullion, rambunctious, scrumptious, to skedaddle, to absquatulate* and *to exfluncticate.*[21] In the use of the last-named coinages fashions change. In the 40's *to absquatulate* was in good usage, but it has since disappeared. Most of the other inventions of the time, however, have to some extent survived, and it would be difficult to find an American of today who did not know the meaning of *scalawag* and *rambunctious* and who did not occasionally use them. A whole series of artificial American words groups itself around the prefix *ker,* for example, *ker-flop, ker-splash, ker-thump, ker-bang, ker-plunk, ker-slam* and *ker-flummux.* This prefix and its onomatopoeic daughters have been borrowed by the English, but Thornton and Ware agree that it is American. Its origin has not been determined. As Sayce says, "the native instinct of language breaks out wherever it has the chance, and coins words which can be traced back to no ancestors."

In the first chapter I mentioned the superior imaginativeness revealed by Americans in meeting linguistic emergencies, whereby, for example, in seeking names for new objects introduced by the building of railroads, they surpassed the English *plough* and *crossing-plate* with *cow-catcher* and *frog*. That was in the 30's. Already at that early day the two languages were so differentiated that they produced wholly distinct railroad nomenclatures. Such commonplace American terms as *box-car, caboose, air-line* and *ticket-agent* are still quite unknown in England. So are *freight-car, flagman, towerman, switch, switching-engine, switch-yard, switchman, track-walker, engineer, baggage-room, baggage-check, baggage-smasher, accommodation-train, baggage-master, conductor, express-car, flat-car, hand-car, way-bill, expressman, express-office, fast-freight, wrecking-crew, jerk-water, commutation-ticket, commuter, round-trip, mileage-book, ticket-scalper, depot, limited, hot-box,* iron-horse, *stop-over, tie, rail, fish-plate, run, train-boy, chair-car, club-car, diner, sleeper, bumpers, mail-clerk, passenger-coach, day-coach, excursionist, excursion-train, railroad-man, ticket-office, truck* and *right-of-way*, not to mention the verbs, *to flag, to derail, to express, to dead-head, to side-swipe, to stop-over, to fire* (i. e., a locomotive), *to switch, to side-track, to railroad, to commute, to telescope* and *to clear the track*. These terms are in constant use in America; their meaning is familiar to all Americans; many of them have given the language everyday figures of speech.[22] But the majority of them would puzzle an Englishman, just as the English *luggage-van, permanent-way, goods-waggon, guard, carrier, booking-office, return-ticket, railway-rug, R. S. O.* (railway sub-office), *tripper, line, points, shunt, metals* and *bogie* would puzzle the average untravelled American.

In two other familiar fields very considerable differences between English and American are visible; in both fields they go back to the era before the Civil War. They are politics and that department of social intercourse which has to do with drinking. Many characteristic American political terms originated in revolutionary days, and have passed over into English. Of such sort are *caucus* and *mileage*. But the majority of those in common use today were coined during the extraordinarily exciting campaigns following the defeat of Adams by Jefferson. Charles Ledyard Norton has devoted a whole book to their etymology and meaning;[23] the number is far too large for a list of them to be attempted here. But a few characteristic specimens may be recalled, for example, the simple agglutinates: *omnibus-bill, banner-state, favorite-son, anxious-bench, gag-rule, office-seeker* and *straight-ticket*; the humorous metaphors: *pork-barrel, pie-counter, wire-puller, land-slide, carpet-bagger, lame-duck* and *on the fence*; the old words put to new uses: *plank, platform, machine, precinct, slate, primary, floater, repeater, bolter, stalwart, filibuster, regular* and *fences*; the new coinages: *gerrymander, heeler, buncombe, roorback, mugwump* and *to bulldoze*; the new derivatives: *abolitionist, candidacy, boss-rule, per-diem, to lobby* and *boodler*; and the almost innumerable verbs and verb-phrases: *to knife, to split a ticket, to go up Salt River, to bolt, to eat crow, to boodle, to divvy, to grab* and *to run*. An English candidate never *runs*; he *stands*. To *run*, according to Thornton, was already used in America in 1789; it was universal by 1820. *Platform* came in at the same time. *Machine* was first applied to a political organization by Aaron Burr. The use of *mugwump* is commonly thought to have originated in the Blaine campaign of 1884, but it really goes back to the 30's. *Anxious-bench* (or *anxious-seat*) at first designated only the place occupied by the penitent at revivals, but was used in its present political sense in Congress so early as 1842. *Banner-state* appears in *Niles' Register* for December 5, 1840. *Favorite-son* appears in an ode addressed to Washington on his visit to Portsmouth, N. H., in 1789, but it did not acquire its present ironical sense until it was applied to Martin Van Buren. Thornton has traced *bolter* to 1812, *filibuster* to 1863, *roorback* to 1844, and *split-ticket* to 1842. *Regularity* was an issue in Tammany Hall in 1822.[24] There were *primaries* in New York city in 1827, and hundreds of *repeaters* voted. In 1829 there were *lobby-agents* at Albany, and they soon became *lobbyists*; in 1832 *lobbying* had already extended to Washington. All of these terms are now as firmly imbedded in the American vocabulary as *election* or *congressman*.

In the department of conviviality the imaginativeness of Americans has been shown in both the invention and the naming of new and often highly complex beverages. So vast has been the production of novelties, in fact, that England has borrowed many of them, and their names with them. And not only England: one buys *cocktails* and *gin-fizzes* in "American bars" that stretch from Paris to Yokohama. *Cocktail, stone-fence* and *sherry-cobbler* were mentioned by Irving in 1809;[25] by Thackeray's day they were already well-known in England. Thornton traces the *sling* to 1788, and the *stinkibus* and *anti-fogmatic*, both now extinct, to the same year. The origin of the *rickey, fizz, sour, cooler, skin, shrub* and *smash*, and of such curious American drinks as the *horse's neck, Mamie Taylor, Tom-and-Jerry, Tom-Collins, John-Collins, bishop, stone-wall, gin-fix, brandy-champarelle, golden-slipper, hari-kari, locomotive, whiskey-daisy, blue-blazer, black-stripe, white-plush* and *brandy-crusta* is quite unknown; the historians of alcoholism, like the philologists, have neglected them.[26] But the essentially American character of most of them is obvious, despite the fact that a number have gone over into English. The English, in naming their drinks, commonly display a far more limited imagination. Seeking a name, for example, for a mixture of whiskey and soda-water, the best they could achieve was *whiskey-and-soda*. The Americans, introduced to the same drink, at once gave it the far more original name of *high-ball*. So with *ginger-ale* and *ginger-pop*. So with *minerals* and *soft-drinks*. Other characteristic Americanisms (a few of them borrowed by the English) are *red-eye, corn-juice, eye-opener, forty-rod, squirrel-whiskey, phlegm-cutter, moon-shine, hard-cider, apple-jack* and *corpse-reviver*, and the auxiliary drinking terms, *speak-easy, sample-room, blind-pig, barrel-house, bouncer, bung-starter, dive, doggery, schooner, shell, stick, duck, straight, saloon, finger, pony* and *chaser*. Thornton shows that *jag, bust, bat* and *to crook the elbow* are also Americanisms. So are *bartender* and *saloon-keeper*. To them might be added a long list of common American synonyms for *drunk*, for example, *piffled, pifflicated, awry-eyed, tanked, snooted, stewed, ossified, slopped, fiddled, edged, loaded, het-up, frazzled, jugged, soused, jiggered, corned, jagged* and *bunned*. Farmer and Henley list *corned* and *jagged* among English synonyms, but the former is obviously an Americanism derived from *corn-whiskey* or *corn-juice*, and Thornton says that the latter originated on this side of the Atlantic also.

§ 4. Loan-Words

—The Indians of the new West, it would seem, had little to add to the contributions already made to the American vocabulary by the Algonquins of the Northeast. The American people, by the beginning of the second quarter of the nineteenth century, knew almost all they were destined to know of the aborigine, and they had names for all the new objects that he had brought to their notice and for most of his peculiar implements and ceremonies. A few translated Indian terms, *e. g., squaw-man, big-chief, great-white-father* and *happy-hunting ground*, represent the meagre fresh stock that the western pioneers got from him. Of more importance was the suggestive and indirect effect of his polysynthetic dialects, and particularly of his vivid proper names, *e. g., Rain-in-the-Face, Young-Man-Afraid-of-His-Wife* and *Voice-Like-Thunder*. These names, and other word-phrases like them, made an instant appeal to American humor, and were extensively imitated in popular slang. One of the surviving coinages of that era is *Old-Stick-in-the-Mud*, which Farmer and Henley note as having reached England by 1823.

Contact with the French in Louisiana and along the Canadian border, and with the Spanish in Texas and further West, brought many more new words. From the Canadian French, as we have already seen, *prairie, batteau, portage* and *rapids* had been borrowed during colonial days; to these French contributions *bayou, picayune, levee, chute, butte, crevasse*, and *lagniappe* were now added, and probably also *shanty* and *canuck*. The use of *brave* to designate an Indian warrior, almost universal until the close of the Indian wars, was also of French origin.

From the Spanish, once the Mississippi was crossed, and particularly after the Mexican war, in 1846, there came a swarm of novelties, many of which have remained firmly imbedded in the language. Among them were numerous names of strange objects:

lariat, lasso, ranch, loco (weed), *mustang, sombrero, canyon, desperado, poncho, chapparel, corral, broncho, plaza, peon, cayuse, burro, mesa, tornado, sierra* and *adobe.* To them, as soon as gold was discovered, were added *bonanza, eldorado, placer* and *vigilante. Cinch* was borrowed from the Spanish *cincha* in the early Texas days, though its figurative use did not come in until much later. *Ante,* the poker term, though the etymologists point out its obvious origin in the Latin, probably came into American from the Spanish. Thornton's first example of its use in its current sense is dated 1857, but Bartlett reported it in the form of *anti* in 1848. *Coyote* came from the Mexican dialect of Spanish; its first parent was the Aztec *coyotl. Tamale* had a similar origin, and so did *frijole* and *tomato.* None of these is good Spanish.[27] As usual, derivatives quickly followed the new-comers, among them *peonage, broncho-buster, ranchman* and *ranch-house,* and the verbs *to ranch, to lasso, to corral, to ante up,* and *to cinch. To vamose* (from the Spanish *vamos,* let us go), came in at the same time. So did *sabe.* So did *gazabo.*

This was also the period of the first great immigrations, and the American people now came into contact, on a large scale, with peoples of divergent race, particularly Germans, Irish Catholics from the South of Ireland (the Irish of colonial days "were descendants of Cromwell's army, and came from the North of Ireland"), [28] and, on the Pacific Coast, Chinese. So early as the 20's the immigration to the United States reached 25, 000 in a year; in 1824 the Legislature of New York, in alarm, passed a restrictive act.[29] The Know-Nothing movement of the 50's need not concern us here. Suffice it to recall that the immigration of 1845 passed the 100, 000 mark, and that that of 1854 came within sight of 500, 000. These new Americans, most of them Germans and Irish, did not all remain in the East; a great many spread through the West and Southwest with the other pioneers. Their effect upon the language was not large, perhaps, but it was still very palpable, and not only in the vocabulary. Of words of German origin, *saurkraut* and *noodle,* as we have seen, had come in during the colonial period, apparently through the so-called Pennsylvania Dutch, *i. e.,* a mixture, much debased, of the German dialects of Switzerland, Suabia and the Palatinate. The new immigrants now contributed *pretzel, pumpernickel, hausfrau, lager-beer, pinocle, wienerwurst, dumb* (for stupid), *frankfurter, bock-beer, schnitzel, leberwurst, blutwurst, rathskeller, schweizer* (cheese), *delicatessen, hamburger* (*i. e.,* steak), *kindergarten* and *katzenjammer*.[30]From them, in all probability, there also came two very familiar Americanisms, *loafer* and *bum*. The former, according to the Standard Dictionary, is derived from the German *laufen*; another authority says that it originated in a German mispronounciation of *lover, i. e.,* as *lofer*.[31] Thornton shows that the word was already in common use in 1835. *Bum* was originally *bummer*, and apparently derives from the German *bummler*.[32] Both words have produced derivatives: *loaf*(noun), *to loaf, corner-loafer, common-loafer, to bum, bum* (adj.) and *bummery*, not to mention *on the bum. Loafer* has migrated in England, but *bum* is still unknown there in the American sense. In English, indeed, *bum* is used to designate an unmentionable part of the body and is thus not employed in polite discourse.

Another example of debased German is offered by the American *Kriss Kringle*. It is from *Christkindlein*, or *Christkind'l*, and properly designates, of course, not the patron saint of Christmas, but the child in the manger. A German friend tells me that the form *Kriss Kringle*, which is that given in the Standard Dictionary, and the form *Krisking'l*, which is that most commonly used in the United States, are both quite unknown in Germany. Here, obviously, we have an example of a loan-word in decay. Whole phrases have gone through the same process, for example, *nix come erous* (from *nichts kommt heraus*) and *'rous mit 'im* (from *heraus mit ihm*). These phrases, like *wie geht's* and *ganz gut*, are familiar to practically all Americans, no matter how complete their ignorance of correct German. Most of them know, too, the meaning of *gesundheit, kümmel, seidel, wanderlust, stein, speck, maennerchor, schützenfest, sängerfest, turnverein, hoch, yodel, zwieback,* and *zwei* (as in *zwei bier*). I have found *snitz* (=*schnitz*) in *Town Topics*.[33] *Prosit* is in all American dictionaries.[34] *Bower*, as used in cards, is an Americanism derived from the German *bauer*, meaning the jack. The exclamation, *ouch!* is classed as an Americanism by Thornton, and he gives an example dated 1837. The New English Dictionary refers it to the German*autsch*, and Thornton says that "it may have come across with the Dunkers or the Mennonites."*Ouch* is not heard in English, save in the sense of a clasp or buckle set with precious stones (=OF *nouche*), and even in that sense it is archaic. *Shyster* is very probably German also; Thornton has traced it back to the 50's.[35] *Rum-dumb* is grounded upon the meaning of *dumb* borrowed from the German; it is not listed in the English slang dictionaries.[36] Bristed says that the American meaning of *wagon*, which indicates almost any four-wheeled, horse-drawn vehicle in this country but only the very heaviest in England, was probably influenced by the German *wagen*. He also says that the American use of *hold on* for *stop* was suggested by the German *halt an*, and White says that the substitution of *standpoint* for *point of view*, long opposed by all purists, was first made by an American professor who sought "an Anglicized form" of the German *standpunkt*. The same German influence may be behind the general facility with which American forms compound nouns. In most other languages, for example, Latin and French, the process is rare, and even English lags far behind American. But in German it is almost unrestricted. "It is, " says L. P. Smith, "a great step in advance toward that ideal language in which meaning is expressed, not by terminations, but by the simple method of word position."

The immigrants from the South of Ireland, during the period under review, exerted an influence upon the language that was vastly greater than that of the Germans, both directly and indirectly, but their contributions to the actual vocabulary were probably less. They gave American, indeed, relatively few new words; perhaps *shillelah*, *colleen*, *spalpeen*, *smithereens* and *poteen* exhaust the unmistakably Gaelic list. *Lallapalooza* is also probably an Irish loan-word, though it is not Gaelic. It apparently comes from *allay-foozee*, a Mayo provincialism, signifying a sturdy fellow. *Allay-foozee*, in its turn, comes from the French *Allez-fusil*, meaning "Forward the muskets!"—a memory, according to P. W. Joyce, [37] of the French landing at Killala in 1798. Such phrases as *Erin go bragh* and such expletives as *begob* and *begorry* may perhaps be added: they have got into American, though they are surely not distinctive Americanisms. But of far more importance than these few contributions to the vocabulary were certain speech habits that the Irish brought with them—habits of pronunciation, of syntax and even of grammar. These habits were, in part, the fruit of efforts to translate the idioms of Gaelic into English, and in part borrowings from the English of the age of James I. The latter, preserved by Irish conservatism in speech, [38] came into contact in America with habits surviving, with more or less change, from the same time, and so gave those American habits an unmistakable reinforcement. The Yankees, so to speak, had lived down such Jacobean pronunciations as *tay* for *tea* and *desave* for *deceive*, and these forms, on Irish lips, struck them as uncouth and absurd, but they still clung, in their common speech, to such forms as *h'ist* for *hoist*, *bile* for *boil*, *chaw* for *chew*, *jine* for *join*, [39] *sass* for *sauce*, *heighth* for *height* and *rench* for *rinse* and *lep* for *leap*, and the employment of precisely the same forms by the thousands of Irish immigrants who spread through the country undoubtedly gave them a certain support, and so protected them, in a measure, from the assault of the purists. And the same support was given to *drownded* for *drowned*, *oncet* for *once*, *ketch* for *catch*, *ag'in* for *against* and *onery* for *ordinary*.

Certain usages of Gaelic, carried over into the English of Ireland, fell upon fertile soil in America. One was the employment of the definite article before nouns, as in French and German. An Irishman does not say "I am good at Latin, " but "I am good at *the* Latin." In the same way an American does not say "I had measles, " but "I had *the* measles." There is, again, the use of the prefix *a* before various adjectives and gerunds, as in *a-going* and *a-riding*. This usage, of course, is native to English, as *aboard* and *afoot* demonstrate, but it is much more common in the Irish dialect, on account of the influence of the parallel Gaelic form, as in *a-n-aice=a-near*, and it is also much more common in American. There is, yet again, a use of intensifying suffixes, often set down as characteristically American, which was probably borrowed from the Irish. Examples are *no-siree* and *yes-indeedy*, and the later *kiddo* and *skiddoo*. As Joyce shows, such suffixes, in Irish-English, tend to become whole phrases. The Irishman is almost incapable of saying plain yes or no; he must always add some extra and gratuitous asseveration.[40] The American is in like case. His speech bristles with intensives: *bet your life, not on your life, well I guess, and no mistake*, and so on. The Irish extravagance of speech struck a responsive chord in the American heart. The American borrowed, not only occasional words, but whole phrases, and some of them have become thoroughly naturalized. Joyce, indeed, shows the

Irish origin of scores of locutions that are now often mistaken for native Americanisms, for example, *great shakes*, *dead* (as an intensive), *thank you kindly*, *to split one's sides* (i. e., laughing), and *the tune the old cow died of*, not to mention many familiar similes and proverbs. Certain Irish pronunciations, Gaelic rather than archaic English, got into American during the nineteenth century. Among them, one recalls *bhoy*, which entered our political slang in the middle 40's and survived into our own time. Again, there is the very characteristic American word *ballyhoo*, signifying the harangue of a *ballyhoo-man*, or *spieler* (that is, barker) before a cheap show, or, by metaphor, any noisy speech. It is from *Ballyhooly*, the name of a village in Cork, once notorious for its brawls. Finally, there is *shebang*. Schele de Vere derives it from the French *cabane*, but it seems rather more likely that it is from the Irish *shebeen*.

The propagation of Irishisms in the United States was helped, during many years, by the enormous popularity of various dramas of Irish peasant life, particularly those of Dion Boucicault. So recently as 1910 an investigation made by the *Dramatic Mirror* showed that some of his pieces, notably "Kathleen Mavourneen, " "The Colleen Bawn" and "The Shaugraun, " were still among the favorites of popular audiences. Such plays, at one time, were presented by dozens of companies, and a number of Irish actors, among them Andrew Mack, Chauncey Olcott and Boucicault himself, made fortunes appearing in them. An influence also to be taken into account is that of Irish songs, once in great vogue. But such influences, like the larger matter of American borrowings from Anglo-Irish, remain to be investigated. So far as I have been able to discover, there is not a single article in print upon the subject. Here, as elsewhere, our philologists have wholly neglected a very interesting field of inquiry.

From other languages the borrowings during the period of growth were naturally less. Down to the last decades of the nineteenth century, the overwhelming majority of immigrants were either Germans or Irish; the Jews, Italians and Slavs were yet to come. But the first Chinese appeared in 1848, and soon their speech began to contribute its inevitable loan-words. These words, of course, were first adopted by the miners of the Pacific Coast, and a great many of them have remained California localisms, among them such verbs as *to yen* (to desire strongly, as a Chinaman desires opium) and *to flop-flop* (to lie down), and such nouns as *fun*, a measure of weight. But a number of others have got into the common speech of the whole country, *e. g.*, *fan-tan, kow-tow, chop-suey, ginseng, joss, yok-a-mi* and *tong*. Contrary to the popular opinion, *dope* and *hop* are not from the Chinese. Neither, in fact, is an Americanism, though the former has one meaning that is specially American, *i. e.*, that of information or formula, as in *racing-dope* and *to dope out*. Most etymologists derive the word from the Dutch *doop*, a sauce. In English, as in American, it signifies a thick liquid, and hence the viscous cooked opium. *Hop* is simply the common name of the *Humuluslupulus*. The belief that hops have a soporific effect is very ancient, and hop-pillows were brought to America by the first English colonists.

The derivation of *poker*, which came into American from California in the days of the gold rush, has puzzled etymologists. It is commonly derived from *primero*, the name of a somewhat similar game, popular in England in the sixteenth century, but the relation seems rather fanciful. It may possibly come, indirectly, from the Danish word *pokker*, signifying the devil. *Pokerish*, in the sense of alarming, was a common adjective in the United States before the Civil War; Thornton gives an example dated 1827. Schele de Vere says that *poker*, in the sense of a hobgoblin, was still in use in 1871, but he derives the name of the game from the French *poche* (=*pouche*, *pocket*). He seems to believe that the bank or pool, in the early days, was called the *poke*. Barrère and Leland, rejecting all these guesses, derive *poker* from the Yiddish *pochger*, which comes in turn from the verb *pochgen*, signifying to conceal winnings or losses. This *pochgen* is obviously related to the German *pocher* (=*boaster, braggart*). There were a good many German Jews in California in the early days, and they were ardent gamblers. If Barrère and Leland are correct, then *poker* enjoys the honor of being the first loan-word taken into American from the Yiddish.

§ 5. Pronunciation

—Noah Webster, as we saw in the last chapter, sneered at the broad *a*, in 1789, as an Anglomaniac affectation. In the course of the next 25 years, however, he seems to have suffered a radical change of mind, for in "The American Spelling Book, " published in 1817, he ordained it in *ask, last, mass, aunt, grant, glass* and their analogues, and in his 1829 revision he clung to this pronunciation, beside adding *master*, *pastor, amass, quaff, laugh, craft*, etc., and even *massive*. There is some difficulty, however, in determining just what sound he proposed to give the *a*, for there are several *a*-sounds that pass as broad, and the two main ones differ considerably. One appears in *all*, and may be called the *aw*-sound. The other is in *art*, and may be called the *ah*-sound. A quarter of a century later Richard Grant White distinguished between the two, and denounced the former as "a British peculiarity." Frank H. Vizetelly, writing in 1917, still noted the difference, particularly in such words as *daunt, saunter* and *laundry*. It is probable that Webster, in most cases, intended to advocate the *ah*-sound, as in *father*, for this pronunciation now prevails in New England. Even there, however, the *a* often drops to a point midway between *ah* and *aa*, though never actually descending to the flat *aa*, as in *an, at* and *anatomy*.

But the imprimatur of the Yankee Johnson was not potent enough to stay the course of nature, and, save in New England, the flat *a* swept the country. He himself allowed it in *stamp* and *vase*. His successor and rival, Lyman Cobb, decided for it in *pass, draft, stamp* and *dance*, though he kept to the *ah*-sound in *laugh, path, daunt* and *saunter*. By 1850 the flat *a* was dominant everywhere West of the Berkshires and South of New Haven, and had even got into such proper names as *Lafayette* and *Nevada*.[41]

Webster failed in a number of his other attempts to influence American pronunciation. His advocacy of *deef* for *deaf* had popular support while he lived, and he dredged up authority for it out of Chaucer and Sir William Temple, but the present pronunciation gradually prevailed, though *deef* remains familiar in the common speech. Joseph E. Worcester and other rival lexicographers stood against many of his pronunciations, and he took the field against them in the prefaces to the successive editions of his spelling-books. Thus, in that to "The Elementary Spelling Book, " dated 1829, he denounced the "affectation" of inserting a *y*-sound before the *u* in such words as *gradual* and *nature*, with its compensatory change of *d* into a French *j* and of *t* into *ch*. The English lexicographer, John Walker, had argued for this "affectation" in 1791, but Webster's prestige, while he lived, remained so high in some quarters that he carried the day, and the older professors at Yale, it is said, continued to use *natur* down to

1839.[42] He favored the pronunciation of *either* and *neither* as *ee-ther* and *nee-ther*, and so did most of the English authorities of his time. The original pronunciation of the first syllable, in England, probably made it rhyme with *bay*, but the *ee*-sound was firmly established by the end of the eighteenth century. Toward the middle of the following century, however, there arose a fashion of an *ai*-sound, and this affectation was borrowed by certain Americans. Gould, in the 50's, put the question, "Why do you say *i*-ther and *ni*-ther?" to various Americans. The reply he got was: "The words are so pronounced by the best-educated people in England." This imitation still prevails in the cities of the East. "All of us, " says Lounsbury, "are privileged in these latter days frequently to witness painful struggles put forth to give to the first syllable of these words the sound of *i* by those who have been brought up to give it the sound of *e*. There is apparently an impression on the part of some that such a pronunciation establishes on a firm foundation an otherwise doubtful social standing."[43] But the vast majority of Americans continue to say *ee-ther* and not *eye-ther*. White and Vizetelly, like Lounsbury, argue that they are quite correct in so doing. The use of *eye-ther*, says White, is no more than "a copy of a second-rate British affectation."

FOOTNOTES:

[1] In Studies in History; Boston, 1884.

[2] Benson J. Lossing: Our Country....; New York, 1879.

[3] The thing went, indeed, far beyond mere hope. In 1812 a conspiracy was unearthed to separate New England from the republic and make it an English colony. The chief conspirator was one John Henry, who acted under the instructions of Sir John Craig, Governor-General of Canada.

[4] Maine was not separated from Massachusetts until 1820.

[5] *Vide* Andrew Jackson...., by William Graham Sumner; Boston, 1883, pp. 2-10.

[6] Indiana and Illinois were erected into territories during Jefferson's first term, and Michigan during his second term. Kentucky was admitted to the union in 1792, Tennessee in 1796, Ohio in 1803. Lewis and Clark set out for the Pacific in 1804. The Louisiana Purchase was ratified in 1803, and Louisiana became a state in 1812.

[7] Barrett Wendell: A Literary History of America; New York, 1900.

[8] "In the four quarters of the globe, who reads an American book? or goes to an American play? or looks at an American picture or statue?" *Edinburgh Review*, Jan., 1820.

[9] *Cf.* As Others See Us, by John Graham Brooks; New York, 1908, ch. vii. Also, The Cambridge History of American Literature, vol. i, pp. 205-8.

[10] Our Dictionaries and Other English Language Topics; New York, 1890, pp. 30-31.

[11] It is curious to note that the center of population of the United States, according to the last census, is now "in southern Indiana, in the western part of Bloomington city, Monroe county." Can it be that this early declaration of literary independence laid the foundation for Indiana's recent pre-eminence in letters? *Cf.* The Language We Use, by Alfred Z. Reed, *New York Sun*, March 13, 1918.

[12] Support also came from abroad. Czar Nicholas I, of Russia, smarting under his defeat in the Crimea, issued an order that his own state papers should be prepared in Russian and American—not English.

[13] A Plea for the Queen's English; London, 1863; 2nd ed., 1864; American ed., New York, 1866.

[14] J. R. Ware, in Passing English of the Victorian Era, says that *to burgle* was introduced to London by W. S. Gilbert in The Pirates of Penzance (April 3, 1880). It was used in America 30 years before.

[15] This process, of course, is philologically respectable, however uncouth its occasional products may be. By it we have acquired many everyday words, among them, *to accept* (from *acceptum*), *to exact* (from *exactum*), *to darkle* (from *darkling*), and *pea* (from *pease=pois*).

[16] All authorities save one seem to agree that this verb is a pure Americanism, and that it is derived from the name of Charles Lynch, a Virginia justice of the peace, who jailed many Loyalists in 1780 without warrant in law. The dissentient, Bristed, says that *to linch* is in various northern English dialects, and means to beat or maltreat.

[17] The correct form of this appears to be *halloo* or *holloa*, but in America it is pronounced *holler* and usually represented in print by *hollo* or *hollow*. I have often encountered *holloed* in the past tense. But the Public Printer frankly accepts *holler*. *Vide* the *Congressional Record*, May 12, 1917, p. 2309. The word, in the form of *hollering*, is here credited to "Hon." John L. Burnett, of Alabama. There can be no doubt that the hon. gentleman said *hollering*, and not *holloaing*, or *holloeing*, or *hollowing*, or *hallooing*. *Hello* is apparently a variation of the same word.

[18] *Rough-neck* is often cited, in discussions of slang, as a latter-day invention, but Thornton shows that it was used in Texas in 1836.

[19] This use goes back to 1839.

[20] Thornton gives an example dated 1812. Of late the word has lost its final *e* and shortened its vowel, becoming *scrap*.

[21] *Cf.* Terms of Approbation and Eulogy.... by Elise L. Warnock, *Dialect Notes*, vol. iv, part 1, 1913. Among the curious recent coinages cited by Miss Warnock are *scallywampus, supergobosnoptious, hyperfirmatious, scrumdifferous* and *swellellegous*.

[22] *E. g., single-track mind, to jump the rails, to collide head-on, broad-gauge man, to walk the ties, blind-baggage, underground-railroad, tank-town.*

[23] Political Americanisms....; New York and London, 1890.

[24] Gustavus Myers: The History of Tammany Hall; 2nd ed.; New York, 1917, ch. viii.

[25] Knickerbocker's History of New York; New York, 1809, p. 241.

[26] Extensive lists of such drinks, with their ingredients, are to be found in the Hoffman House Bartender's Guide, by Charles Mahoney, 4th ed.; New York, 1916; in The Up-to-date Bartenders' Guide, by Harry Montague; Baltimore, 1913; and in Wehman Brothers' Bartenders' Guide; New York, 1912. An early list, from the *Lancaster (Pa.) Journal* of Jan. 26, 1821, is quoted by Thornton, vol. ii, p. 985.

[27] Many such words are listed in Félix Ramos y Duarte's Diccionaro de Mejicanismos, 2nd ed. Mexico City, 1898; and in Miguel de Toro y Gisbert's Americanismos; Paris, n. d.

[28] Prescott F. Hall: Immigration.... New York, 1913, p. 5.

[29] Most of the provisions of this act, however, were later declared unconstitutional. Several subsequent acts met the same fate.

[30] The majority of these words, it will be noted, relate to eating and drinking. They mirror the profound effect of German immigration upon American drinking habits and the American cuisine. It is a curious fact that loan-words seldom represent the higher aspirations of the creditor nation. French and German have borrowed from English, not words of lofty significance, but such terms as *beefsteak, roast-beef, pudding, grog, jockey, tourist, sport, five-o'clock-tea, cocktail* and *sweepstakes*. "The contributions of England to European civilization, as tested by the English words in Continental languages," says L. P. Smith, "are not, generally, of a kind to cause much national self-congratulation." Nor would a German, I daresay, be very proud of the German contributions to American.

[31] *Vide* a paragraph in *Notes and Queries*, quoted by Thornton, vol. i, p. 248.

[32] Thornton offers examples of this form ranging from 1856 to 1885. During the Civil War the word acquired the special meaning of looter. The Southerners thus applied it to Sherman's men. *Vide* Southern Historical

Society Papers, vol. xii, p. 428; Richmond, 1884. Here is a popular rhyme that survived until the early 90's:

Isidor, psht, psht!

Vatch de shtore, psht, psht!

Vhile I ketch de *bummer*

Vhat shtole de suit of clothes!

Bummel-zug is common German slang for slow train.

[33] Jan. 24, 1918, p. 4.

[34] Nevertheless, when I once put it into a night-letter a Western Union office refused to accept it, the rules requiring all night-letters to be in "plain English." Meanwhile, the English have borrowed it from American, and it is actually in the Oxford Dictionary.

[35] The word is not in the Oxford Dictionary, but Cassell gives it and says that it is German and an Americanism. The Standard Dictionary does not give its etymology. Thornton's first example, dated 1856, shows a variant spelling, *shuyster*, thus indicating that it was then recent. All subsequent examples show the present spelling. It is to be noted that the suffix *-ster* is not uncommon in English, and that it usually carries a deprecatory significance, as in *trickster*, *punster*, *gamester*, etc.

[36] The use of *dumb* for stupid is widespread in the United States. *Dumb-head*, obviously from the German *dummkopf*, appears in a list of Kansas words collected by Judge J. C. Ruppenthal, of Russell, Kansas. (*Dialect Notes*, vol. iv, pt. v, 1916, p. 322.) It is also noted in Nebraska and the Western Reserve, and is very common in Pennsylvania. *Uhrgucker* (=*uhr-gucken*) is also on the Kansas list of Judge Ruppenthal.

[37] English As We Speak It in Ireland, 2nd ed.; London and Dublin, 1910, pp. 179-180.

[38] "Our people, " says Dr. Joyce, "are very conservative in retaining old customs and forms of speech. Many words accordingly that are discarded as old-fashioned—or dead and gone—in England, are still flourishing—alive and well, in Ireland. [They represent] ... the classical English of Shakespeare's time, " pp. 6-7.

[39] Pope rhymed *join* with *mine*, *divine* and *line*; Dryden rhymed *toil* with *smile*. William Kenrick, in 1773, seems to have been the first English lexicographer to denounce this pronunciation. *Tay* survived in England until the second half of the eighteenth century. Then it fell into disrepute, and certain purists, among them Lord Chesterfield, attempted to change the *ea*-sound to *ee* in all words, including even *great*. *Cf.* the remarks under *boil* in A Desk-Book of Twenty-Five Thousand Words Frequently Mispronounced, by Frank H. Vizetelly; New York, 1917. Also, The Standard of Pronunciation in English, by T. S. Lounsbury; New York, 1904, pp. 98-103.

[40] Amusing examples are to be found in Donlevy's Irish Catechism. To the question, "Is the Son God?" the answer is not simply "Yes, " but "Yes, certainly He is." And to the question, "Will God reward the good and punish the wicked?", the answer is "Certainly; there is no doubt He will."

[41] Richard Meade Bache denounced it, in *Lafayette*, during the 60's. *Vide* his Vulgarisms and Other Errors of Speech, 2nd ed., Philadelphia, 1869, p. 65.

[42] R. J. Menner: The Pronunciation of English in America, *Atlantic Monthly*, March, 1915, p. 361.

[43] The Standard of Pronunciation in English, pp. 109-112.

IV. American and English Today

§ 1. The Two Vocabularies

—By way of preliminary to an examination of the American of today I offer a brief list of terms in common use that differ in American and English. Here are 200 of them, all chosen from the simplest colloquial vocabularies and without any attempt at plan or completeness:

American	English
ash-can	dust-bin
baby-carriage	pram
backyard	garden
baggage	luggage
baggage-car	luggage-van
ballast (railroad)	metals
bath-tub	bath
beet	beet-root
bid (noun)	tender
bill-board	hoarding
boarder	paying-guest
boardwalk (seaside)	promenade
bond (finance)	debenture
boot	Blucher, or Wellington

brakeman	brakesman
bucket	pail
bumper (car)	buffer
bureau	chest of drawers
calendar (court)	cause-list
campaign (political)	canvass
can (noun)	tin
candy	sweets
cane	stick
canned-goods	tinned-goods
car (railroad)	carriage, van or waggon
checkers (game)	draughts
chicken-yard	fowl-run
chief-clerk	head-clerk
city-editor	chief-reporter
city-ordinance	by-law
clipping (newspaper)	cutting
coal-oil	paraffin
coal-scuttle	coal-hod
commission-merchant	factor
conductor (of a train)	guard
corn	maize, or Indian corn
corner (of a street)	crossing
corset	stays
counterfeiter	coiner
cow-catcher	plough
cracker	biscuit
cross-tie	sleeper
delicatessen-store	Italian-warehouse

department-store	stores
Derby (hat)	bowler
dime-novel	shilling-shocker
druggist	chemist
drug-store	chemist's-shop
drummer	bagman
dry-goods-store	draper's-shop
editorial	leader, or leading-article
elevator	lift
elevator-boy	lift-man
excursionist	tripper
express-company	carrier
filing-cabinet	nest-of-drawers
fire-department	fire-brigade
fish-dealer	fishmonger
floor-walker	shop-walker
fraternal-order	friendly-society
freight	goods
freight-agent	goods-manager
freight-car	goods-waggon
frog (railway)	crossing-plate
garters (men's)	sock-suspenders
gasoline	petrol
grade (railroad)	gradient
grain	corn
grain-broker	corn-factor
grip	hold-all
groceries	stores
hardware-dealer	ironmonger

haystack	haycock
headliner	topliner
hod-carrier	hodman
hog-pen	piggery
hospital (private)	nursing-home
huckster	coster (monger)
hunting	shooting
Indian	Red Indian
Indian Summer	St. Martin's Summer
instalment-business	credit-trade
instalment-plan	hire-purchase plan
janitor	caretaker
legal-holiday	bank-holiday
letter-box	pillar-box
letter-carrier	postman
livery-stable	mews[1]
locomotive engineer	engine-driver
lumber	deals
mad	angry
Methodist	Wesleyan
molasses	treacle
monkey-wrench	spanner
moving-picture-theatre	cinema
napkin (dinner)	serviette
necktie	tie, or cravat
news-dealer	news-agent
newspaper-man	pressman, or journalist
oatmeal	porridge
officeholder	public-servant

orchestra (seats in a theatre)	stalls
overcoat	great-coat
package	parcel
parlor	drawing-room
parlor-car	saloon-carriage
patrolman (police)	constable
pay-day	wage-day
peanut	monkey-nut
pie (fruit)	tart
pitcher	jug
poorhouse	workhouse
post-paid	post-free
potpie	pie
prepaid	carriage-paid
press (printing)	machine
program (of a meeting)	agenda
proof-reader	corrector-of-the-press
public-school	board-school
quotation-marks	inverted-commas
railroad	railway
railroad-man	railway-servant
rails	line
rare (of meat)	underdone
receipts (in business)	takings
Rhine-wine	Hock
road-bed (railroad)	permanent-way
road-repairer	road-mender
roast	joint
roll-call	division

rooster	cock
round-trip-ticket	return-ticket
rutabaga	mangel-wurzel
saleswoman	shop-assistant
saloon	public-house
scarf-pin	tie-pin
scow	lighter
sewer	drain
shirtwaist	blouse
shoe	boot
shoemaker	bootmaker
shoestring	bootlace
shoe-tree	boot-form
sick	ill
sidewalk	pavement
silver (collectively)	plate
sled	sledge
sleigh	sledge
soft-drinks	minerals
spigot	tap
squash	vegetable-marrow
stem-winder	keyless-watch
stockholder	shareholder
stocks	shares
store-fixtures	shop-fittings
street-cleaner	crossing-sweeper
street-railway	tramway
subway	tube, or underground
suspenders (men's)	braces

sweater	jersey
switch (noun, railway)	points
switch (verb, railway)	shunt
taxes (municipal)	rates
taxpayer (local)	ratepayer
tenderloin (of beef)	under-cut
ten-pins	nine-pins
thumb-tack	drawing-pin
ticket-office	booking-office
tinner	tinker
tin-roof	leads
track (railroad)	line
trained-nurse	hospital-nurse
transom (of door)	fanlight
trolley-car	tramcar
truck (vehicle)	lorry
truck (of a railroad car)	bogie
trunk	box
typewriter (operator)	typist
typhoid-fever	enteric
undershirt	vest
vaudeville-theatre	music-hall
vegetables	greens
vest	waistcoat
warden (of a prison)	governor
warehouse	stores
wash-rag	face-cloth
wash-stand	wash-hand-stand
wash-wringer	mangle

waste-basket	waste-paper-basket
whipple-tree[2]	splinter-bar
witness-stand	witness-box
wood-alcohol	methylated-spirits

§ 2. Differences in Usage

—The differences here listed, most of them between words in everyday employment, are but examples of a divergence in usage which extends to every department of daily life. In his business, in his journeys from his home to his office, in his dealings with his family and servants, in his sports and amusements, in his politics and even in his religion the American uses, not only words and phrases, but whole syntactical constructions, that are unintelligible to the Englishman, or intelligible only after laborious consideration. A familiar anecdote offers an example in miniature. It concerns a young American woman living in a region of prolific orchards who is asked by a visiting Englishman what the residents do with so much fruit. Her reply is a pun: "We eat all we can, and what we can't we can." This answer would mystify nine Englishmen out of ten, for in the first place it involves the use of the flat American *a* in *can't* and in the second place it applies an unfamiliar name to the vessel that every Englishman knows as a *tin*, and then adds to the confusion by deriving a verb from the substantive. There are no such things as *canned-goods* in England; over there they are *tinned*. The *can* that holds them is a *tin*; *to can* them is *to tin* them.... And they are counted, not as *groceries*, but as *stores*, and advertised, not on *bill-boards* but on *hoardings*.[3] And the cook who prepares them for the table is not *Nora* or *Maggie*, but *Cook*, and if she does other work in addition she is not a *girl for general housework*, but a *cook-general*, and not *help*, but a *servant*. And the boarder who eats them is not a *boarder* at all, but a *paying-guest*, though he is said *to board*. And the grave of the tin, once it is emptied, is not the *ash-can*, but the *dust-bin*, and the man who carries it away is not the *garbage-man* or the *ash-man* or the *white-wings*, but the *dustman*.

An Englishman, entering his home, does not walk in upon the *first floor*, but upon the *ground floor*. What he calls the *first floor* (or, more commonly, *first storey*, not forgetting the penultimate *e*!) is what we call the *second floor*, and so on up to the roof—which is covered not with *tin*, but with *slate, tiles* or *leads*. He does not *take* a paper; he *takes in* a paper. He does not ask his servant, "is there any *mail* for me?" but, "are there any *letters* for me?" for *mail*, in the American sense, is a word that he seldom uses, save in such compounds as *mail-van* and *mail-train*. He always speaks of it as *the post*. The man who brings it is not a *letter-carrier*, but a *postman*. It is *posted*, not *mailed*, at a *pillar-box*, not at a *mail-box*. It never includes *postal-cards*, but only *post-cards*; never *money-orders*, but only *postal-orders*. The Englishman dictates his answers, not to a *typewriter*, but to a *typist*; a *typewriter* is merely the machine. If he desires the recipient to call him by telephone he doesn't say, "*phone me* at a quarter *of* eight, *" but "*ring me up* at a quarter *to* eight." And when the call comes he says "*are you there?*" When he gets home, he doesn't find his wife waiting for him in the *parlor* or *living-room*, [4] but in the *drawing-room* or in her *sitting-room*, and the tale of domestic disaster that she has to tell does not concern the *hired-girl* but the *slavey* and the *scullery-maid*. He doesn't bring her a box of *candy*, but a box of *sweets*. He doesn't leave a *derby* hat in the hall, but a *bowler*. His wife doesn't wear *shirtwaists* but *blouses*. When she buys one she doesn't say "*charge it*" but "*put it down*." When she orders a *tailor-made suit*, she calls it a *coat-and-skirt*. When she wants a *spool of thread* she asks for a *reel of cotton*. Such things are bought, not in the *department-stores*, but at the *stores*, which are substantially the same thing. In these stores *calico* means a plain cotton cloth; in the United States it means a printed cotton cloth. Things bought on the instalment plan in England are said to be bought on the *hire-purchase* plan or system; the instalment business itself is the *credit-trade*. Goods ordered by *post*(not mail) on which the dealer pays the cost of transportation are said to be sent, not *postpaid* or *prepaid*, but *post-free* or *carriage-paid*.

An Englishman does not wear *suspenders* and *neckties*, but *braces* and *cravats*. *Suspenders* are his wife's garters; his own are *sock-suspenders*. The family does not seek sustenance in a *rare tenderloin* and *squash*, but in *underdone under-cut* and *vegetable marrow*. It does not eat *beets*, but *beet-roots*. The wine on the table, if miraculously German, is not *Rhine wine*, but *Hock*.... The maid who laces the stays of the mistress of the house is not *Maggie* but *Robinson*. The nurse-maid is not *Lizzie* but *Nurse*. So, by the way, is a trained nurse in a hospital, whose full style is not *Miss Jones*, but *Nurse Jones*. And the hospital itself, if private, is not a hospital at all, but a *nursing-home*, and its trained nurses are plain *nurses*, or *hospital nurses*, or maybe *nursing sisters*. And the white-clad young gentlemen who make love to them are not *studying medicine* but *walking the hospitals*. Similarly, an English law student does not study law, but *the* law.

If an English boy goes to a *public school*, it is not a sign that he is getting his education free, but that his father is paying a good round sum for it and is accepted as a gentleman. A *public school* over there corresponds to our *prep school*; it is a place maintained chiefly by endowments, wherein boys of the upper classes are prepared for the universities. What we know as a *public school* is called a *board school* in England, not because the pupils are boarded but because it is managed by a school board. English school-boys are divided, not into *classes*, or *grades*, but into *forms*, which are numbered, the lowest being the *first form*. The benches they sit on are also called *forms*. The principal of an English school is a *head-master* or *head-mistress*; the lower pedagogues used to be *ushers*, but are now *assistant masters* (or *mistresses*). The head of a university is a *chancellor*. He is always some eminent public man, and a *vice-chancellor* performs his duties. The head of a mere college may be a *president, principal, rector, dean* or *provost*. At the universities the students are not divided into *freshmen, sophomores, juniors* and *seniors*, as with us, but are simply *first-year men, second-year men*, and so on. Such distinctions, however, are not as important in England as in America; members of the university (they are called *members*, not *students*) do not flock together according to seniority. An English university man does not *study*; he *reads*. He knows nothing of *frats, class-days, senior-proms* and such things; save at Cambridge and Dublin he does not even have a *commencement*. On the other hand his daily speech is full of terms unintelligible to an

American student, for example, *wrangler, tripos, head, pass-degree* and *don*.

The upkeep of board-schools in England comes out of the *rates*, which are local taxes levied upon householders. For that reason an English municipal taxpayer is called a *ratepayer*. The functionaries who collect and spend his money are not *office-holders* but *public-servants*. The head of the local police is not a *chief of police*, but a *chief constable*. The fire *department* is the fire *brigade*. The *street-cleaner* is a *crossing-sweeper*. The parish *poorhouse* is a *workhouse*. If it is maintained by two or more parishes jointly it becomes a *union*. A pauper who accepts its hospitality is said to be *on the rates*. A policeman is a *bobby* familiarly and *constable* officially. He is commonly mentioned in the newspapers, not by his surname, but as *P. C. 643a*—i. e., Police Constable No. 643a. The *fire laddie*, the *ward executive*, the *roundsman*, the *strong-arm squad* and other such objects of American devotion are unknown in England. An English saloon-keeper is officially a licensed *victualler*. His saloon is a *public house*, or, colloquially, a *pub*. He does not sell beer by the *bucket* or *can* or *growler* or *schooner*, but by the *pint*. He and his brethren, taken together, are the *licensed trade*. His back-room is a *parlor*. If he has a few upholstered benches in his place he usually calls it a *lounge*. He employs no *bartenders* or *mixologists*. *Barmaids* do the work, with maybe a *barman* to help.

The American language, as we have seen, has begun to take in the English *boot* and *shop*, and it is showing hospitality to *head-master, haberdasher* and *week-end*, but *subaltern, civil servant, porridge, moor, draper, treacle, tram* and *mufti* are still strangers in the United States, as *bleachers, picayune, air-line, campus, chore, scoot, stogie* and *hoodoo* are in England. A *subaltern* is a commissioned officer in the army, under the rank of captain. A *civil servant* is a public servant in the national civil service; if he is of high rank, he is usually called a *permanent official*. *Porridge, moor, scullery, draper, treacle* and *tram*, though unfamiliar, still need no explanation. *Mufti* means ordinary male clothing; an army officer out of uniform is said to be in *mufti*. To this officer a sack-suit or business-suit is a *lounge-suit*. He carries his clothes, not in a *trunk* or *grip* or *suit-case*, but in a *box*. He does not *miss* a train; he *loses* it. He does not ask for a *round-trip* ticket, but for a *return* ticket. If he proposes to go to the theatre he does not *reserve* or *engage* seats; he *books* them, and not at the *box-office*, but at the *booking-office*. If he sits downstairs, it is not in the *orchestra*, but in the *stalls*. If he likes vaudeville, he goes to a *music-hall*, where the *head-liners* are *top-liners*. If he has to stand in line, he does it, not in a *line*, but in a *queue*.

In England a corporation is a *public company* or *limited liability company*. The term *corporation*, over there, is applied to the mayor, aldermen and sheriffs of a city, as in *the London corporation*. An Englishman writes *Ltd.* after the name of an incorporated bank or trading company as we write *Inc*. He calls its president its *chairman* or *managing director*. Its stockholders are its *shareholders*, and hold *shares* instead of *stock* in it. Its bonds are *debentures*. The place wherein such companies are floated and looted—the Wall Street of England—is called the *City*, with a capital *C*. Bankers, stock-jobbers, promoters, directors and other such leaders of its business are called *City* men. The financial editor of a newspaper is its *City* editor. Government bonds are *consols*, or *stocks*, or the *funds*.[5] To have *money in the stocks* is to own such bonds. Promissory notes are *bills*. An Englishman hasn't a *bank-account*, but a *banking-account*. He draws *cheques*(not *checks*), not on his *bank*, but on his *bankers*.[6] In England there is a rigid distinction between a *broker* and a *stock-broker*. A *broker* means, not a dealer in securities, as in our *Wall Street broker*, but a dealer in second-hand furniture. *To have the brokers*[7] *in the house* means to be bankrupt, with one's very household goods in the hands of one's creditors.

Tariff reform, in England, does not mean a movement toward free trade, but one toward protection. The word *Government*, meaning what we call the administration, is always capitalized and plural, e. g., "The Government *are* considering the advisability, etc." *Vestry, committee, council, ministry* and even *company* are also plural, though sometimes not capitalized. A member of Parliament does not *run* for office; he *stands*.[8] He does not make a *campaign*,

175

but a *canvass*. He does not represent a *district*, but a *division* or *constituency*. He never makes a *stumping trip*, but always a *speaking tour*. When he looks after his fences he calls it *nursing the constituency*. At a political meeting (they are often rough in England) the *bouncers* are called *stewards*; the suffragettes used to delight in stabbing them with hatpins. A member of Parliament is not afflicted by the numerous bugaboos that menace an American congressman. He knows nothing of *lame ducks, pork barrels, gag-rule, junkets, gerrymanders, omnibus bills, snakes, niggers in the woodpile, Salt river, crow, bosses, ward heelers, men higher up, silk-stockings, repeaters, ballot-box stuffers* and *straight* and *split tickets* (he always calls them *ballots* or *voting papers*). He has never heard of *direct primaries*, the *recall* or the *initiative and referendum*. A *roll-call* in Parliament is a *division*. A member speaking is said to be *up* or *on his legs*. When the house adjourns it is said to *rise*. A member referring to another in the course of a debate does not say "the gentleman from Manchester, " but "the *honorable* gentleman" (written *hon. gentleman*) or, if he happens to be a privy councillor, "the *right honorable* gentleman, " or, if he is a member for one of the universities, "the *honorable and learned* gentleman." If the speaker chooses to be intimate or facetious, he may say "my honorable *friend*."

In the United States a *pressman* is a man who runs a printing press; in England he is a newspaper reporter, or, as the English usually say, a *journalist*.[9] This journalist works, not at *space* rates, but at *lineage* rates. A printing press is a *machine*. An editorial in a newspaper is a *leading article* or *leader*. An editorial paragraph is a *leaderette*. A newspaper clipping is a *cutting*. A proof-reader is a *corrector of the press*. A pass to the theatre is an *order*. The room-clerk of a hotel is the *secretary*. A real-estate agent or dealer is an *estate-agent*. The English keep up most of the old distinctions between physicians and surgeons, barristers and solicitors. A surgeon is often plain *Mr.*, and not *Dr.* Neither he nor a doctor has an *office*, but always a *surgery* or *consulting room*. A barrister is greatly superior to a solicitor. He alone can address the higher courts and the parliamentary committees; a solicitor must keep to office work and the courts of first instance. A man with a grievance goes first to his solicitor, who then *instructs* or *briefs* a barrister for him. If that barrister, in the course of the trial, wants certain evidence removed from the record, he moves that it be *struck out*, not *stricken out*, as an American lawyer would say. Only barristers may become judges. An English barrister, like his American brother, takes a *retainer* when he is engaged. But the rest of his fee does not wait upon the termination of the case: he expects and receives a *refresher* from time to time. A barrister is never admitted to the bar, but is always *called.* If he becomes a *King's Counsel*, or *K. C.* (a purely honorary appointment), he is said to have *taken silk.*

The common objects and phenomena of nature are often differently named in English and American. As we saw in a previous chapter, such Americanisms as *creek* and *run*, for small streams, are practically unknown in England, and the English *moor* and *downs* early disappeared from American. The Englishman knows the meaning of *sound* (*e. g.*, Long Island *Sound*), but he nearly always uses *channel* in place of it. In the same way the American knows the meaning of the English *bog*, but rejects the English distinction between it and *swamp*, and almost always uses *swamp*, or *marsh* (often elided to *ma'sh*). The Englishman seldom, if ever, describes a severe storm as a *hurricane*, a *cyclone*, a *tornado* or a *blizzard*. He never uses *cold-snap*, *cloudburst* or *under the weather*. He does not say that the temperature is *29 degrees* (Fahrenheit) or that the thermometer or the mercury is at 29 degrees, but that there are *three degrees of frost*. He calls ice water *iced-water*. He knows nothing of *blue-grass* country or of *pennyr'yal*. What we call the *mining regions* he knows as the *black country*. He never, of course, uses *down-East* or *up-State*. Many of our names for common fauna and flora are unknown to him save as strange Americanisms, *e. g.*, *terrapin*, *moose*, *persimmon*, *gumbo*, *egg-plant*, *alfalfa*, *sweet-corn*, *sweet-potato* and *yam*. Until lately he called the *grapefruit* a *shaddock*. He still calls the *beet* a *beet-root* and the *rutabaga* a *mangel-wurzel*. He is familiar with many fish that we seldom see, *e. g.*, the *turbot*. He also knows the *hare*, which is seldom heard of in America. But he knows nothing of *devilled-crabs*, *crab-cocktails*, *clam-chowder* or *oyster-stews*, and he never goes to *oyster-suppers*, *clam-bakes* or *burgoo-picnics*. He doesn't buy *peanuts* when he goes to the circus. He calls them *monkey-nuts*, and to eat them publicly is *infra dig*. The common American use of *peanut* as an adjective of disparagement, as in *peanut politics*, is incomprehensible to him.

In England a *hack* is not a public coach, but a horse let out at hire, or one of similar quality. A life insurance policy is usually not an insurance policy at all, but an *assurance* policy. What we call the normal income tax is the *ordinary* tax; what we call the surtax is the *supertax*.[10] An Englishman never lives *on* a street, but always *in* it. He never lives in a *block* of houses, but in a *row*; it is never in a *section* of the city, but always in a *district*. Going home by train he always takes the *down-train*, no matter whether he be proceeding southward to Wimbleton, westward to Shepherd's Bush, northward to Tottenham or eastward to Noak's Hill. A train headed toward London is always an *up-train*, and the track it runs on is the *up-line*. *Eastbound* and *westbound* tracks and trains are unknown in England. When an Englishman boards a bus it is not at a *street-corner*, but at a *crossing*, though he is familiar with such forms as Hyde Park *Corner*. The place he is bound for is not three *squares* or *blocks* away, but three *turnings*. *Square*, in England, always means a small park. A backyard is a *garden*. A subway is always a *tube*, or the *underground*, or the *Metro*. But an underground passage for pedestrians is a *subway*. English streets have no *sidewalks*; they always call them *pavements* or *footways*. An automobile is always a *motor-car* or *motor*. *Auto* is almost unknown, and with it the verb *to auto*. So is *machine*. So is *joy-ride*.

An Englishman always calls russet, yellow or tan shoes *brown* shoes (or, if they cover the ankle, *boots*). He calls a pocketbook a *purse*, and gives the name of *pocketbook* to what we call a *memorandum-book*. His walking-stick is always a *stick*, never a *cane*. By *cord* he means something strong, almost what we call *twine*; a thin cord he always calls a *string*; his *twine* is the lightest sort of *string*. When he applies the adjective *homely* to a woman he means that she is simple and home-loving, not necessarily that she is plain. He uses *dessert*, not to indicate the whole last course at dinner, but to designate the fruit only; the rest is *ices* or *sweets*. He uses *vest*, not in place of *waistcoat*, but in place of *undershirt*. Similarly, he applies *pants*, not to his trousers, but to his drawers. An Englishman who inhabits bachelor quarters is said to live in *chambers*; if he has a flat he calls it a *flat*, and not an *apartment*;[11] *flat-houses* are often *mansions*. The janitor or superintendent thereof is a *care-taker*. The scoundrels who snoop around in search of divorce evidence are not *private detectives*, but *private enquiry agents*.

The Englishman is naturally unfamiliar with baseball, and in consequence his language is bare of the countless phrases and metaphors that it has supplied to American. Many of these phrases and metaphors are in daily use among us, for example, *fan, rooter, bleachers, batting-average, double-header, pennant-winner, gate-money, busher, minor-leaguer, glass-arm, to strike out, to foul, to be shut out, to coach, to play ball, on the bench, on to his curves* and *three strikes and out*. The national game of draw-poker has also greatly enriched American with terms that are either quite unknown to the Englishman, or known to him only as somewhat dubious Americanisms, among them *cold-deck, kitty, full-house, divvy, a card up his sleeve, three-of-a-kind, to ante up, to pony up, to hold out, to cash in, to go it one better, to chip in* and *for keeps*. But the Englishman uses many more racing terms and metaphors than we do, and he has got a good many phrases from other games, particularly cricket. The word *cricket* itself has a definite figurative meaning. It indicates, in general, good sportsmanship. To take unfair advantage of an opponent is not *cricket*. The sport of boating, so popular on the Thames, has also given colloquial English some familiar terms, almost unknown in the United States, *e. g., punt* and *weir*. Contrariwise, *pungy, batteau* and *scow* are unheard of in England, and *canoe* is not long emerged from the estate of an Americanism.[12] The game known as *ten-pins* in America is called *nine-pins* in England, and once had that name over here. The Puritans forbade it, and its devotees changed its name in order to evade the prohibition.[13] Finally, there is *soccer*, a form of football quite unknown in the United States. What we call simply football is *Rugby* or *Rugger* to the Englishman. The word *soccer* is derived from *association*; the rules of the game were established by the London Football Association. *Soccer* is one of the relatively few English experiments in ellipsis. Another is to be found in *Bakerloo*, the name of one of the London underground lines, from *Baker-street* and *Waterloo*, its termini.

The English have an ecclesiastical vocabulary with which we are almost unacquainted, and it is in daily use, for the church bulks large in public affairs over there. Such terms as *vicar, canon, verger, prebendary, primate, curate, non-conformist, dissenter, convocation, minster, chapter, crypt, living, presentation, glebe, benefice, locum tenens, suffragan, almoner, dean* and *pluralist* are to be met with in the English newspapers constantly, but on this side of the water they are seldom encountered. Nor do we hear much of *matins, lauds, lay-readers, ritualism* and the *liturgy*. The English use of *holy orders* is also strange to us. They do not say that a young man is *studying for the ministry*, but that he is *reading for holy orders*. They do not say that he is *ordained*, but that he *takes orders*. Save he be in the United Free Church of Scotland, he is never a *minister*; save he be a nonconformist, he is never a *pastor*; a clergyman of the Establishment is always either a *rector*, a *vicar* or a *curate*, and colloquially a *parson*.

In American *chapel* simply means a small church, usually the branch of some larger one; in English it has the special sense of a place of worship unconnected with the establishment. Though three-fourths of the people of Ireland are Catholics (in Munster and Connaught, more than nine-tenths), and the Protestant Church of Ireland has been disestablished since 1871, a Catholic place of worship in the country is still a *chapel* and not a *church*.[14] So is a Methodist wailing-place in England, however large it may be, though now and then *tabernacle* is substituted. In the same way the English Catholics sometimes vary *chapel* with *oratory*, as in *Brompton Oratory*. A Methodist, in Great Britain, is not a *Methodist*, but a *Wesleyan*. Contrariwise, what the English call simply a *churchman* is an *Episcopalian* in the United States, what they call the *Church* (always capitalized!) is the *Protestant Episcopal* Church, [15] what they call a *Roman Catholic* is simply a *Catholic*, and what they call a *Jew* is usually softened (if he happens to be an advertiser) to a *Hebrew*. The English Jews have no such idiotic fear of the plain name as that which afflicts the more pushing and obnoxious of the race in America.[16] "News of

Jewry" is a common head-line in the *London Daily Telegraph*, which is owned by Lord Burnham, a Jew, and has had many Jews on its staff, including Judah P. Benjamin, the American. The American language, of course, knows nothing of *dissenters*. Nor of such gladiators of dissent as the *Plymouth Brethren*, nor of the *nonconformist conscience*, though the United States suffers from it even more damnably than England. The English, to make it even, get on without *circuit-riders*, *holy-rollers*, *Dunkards*, *Seventh Day Adventists* and other such American *ferae naturae*, and are born, live, die and go to heaven without the aid of either the *uplift* or the *chautauqua*.

In music the English cling to an archaic and unintelligible nomenclature, long since abandoned in America. Thus they call a double whole note a *breve*, a whole note a *semibreve*, a half note a *minim*, a quarter note a *crotchet*, an eighth note a *quaver*, a sixteenth note a *semi-quaver*, a thirty-second note a *demisemiquaver*, and a sixty-fourth note a *hemidemisemiquaver*, or *semidemisemiquaver*. If, by any chance, an English musician should write a one-hundred-and-twenty-eighth note he probably wouldn't know what to call it. This clumsy terminology goes back to the days of plain chant, with its *longa*, *brevis*, *semi-brevis*, *minima* and *semiminima*. The French and Italians cling to a system almost as confusing, but the Germans use *ganze*, *halbe*, *viertel*, *achtel*, etc. I have been unable to discover the beginnings of the American system, but it would seem to be borrowed from the German. Since the earliest times the majority of music teachers in the United States have been Germans, and most of the rest have had German training.

In the same way the English hold fast to a clumsy and inaccurate method of designating the sizes of printers' types. In America the simple point system makes the business easy; a line of *14-point* type occupies exactly the vertical space of two lines of *7-point*. But the English still indicate differences in size by such arbitrary and confusing names as *brilliant*, *diamond*, *small pearl*, *pearl*, *ruby*, *ruby-nonpareil*, *nonpareil*, *minion-nonpareil*, *emerald*, *minion*, *brevier*, *bourgeois*, *long primer*, *small pica*, *pica*, *English*, *great primer* and *double pica*. They also cling to a fossil system of numerals in stating ages. Thus, an Englishman will say that he is *seven-and-forty*, not that he is *forty-seven*. This is probably a direct survival, preserved by more than a thousand years of English conservatism, of the Anglo-Saxon *seofan-and-feowertig*. He will also say that he weighs eleven *stone* instead of 154 pounds. A *stone* is 14 pounds, and it is always used in stating the heft of a man. Finally, he employs such designations of time as *fortnight* and *twelvemonth* a great deal more than we do, and has certain special terms of which we know nothing, for example, *quarter-day, bank holiday, long vacation, Lady Day* and *Michaelmas. Per contra*, he knows nothing whatever of our *Thanksgiving, Arbor, Labor* and *Decoration Days*, or of *legal holidays*, or of *Yom Kippur*.

In English usage, to proceed, the word *directly* is always used to signify *immediately*; in American a contingency gets into it, and it may mean no more than *soon*. In England *quite* means "completely, wholly, entirely, altogether, to the utmost extent, nothing short of, in the fullest sense, positively, absolutely"; in America it is conditional, and means only nearly, approximately, substantially, as in "he sings *quite* well." An Englishman does not say "I will pay you *up*" for an injury, but "I will pay you *back*." He doesn't look *up* a definition in a dictionary; he looks it *out*. He doesn't say, being ill, "I am *getting* on well," but "I am *going* on well." He doesn't use the American "different *from*" or "different *than*"; he uses "different *to*." He never adds the pronoun in such locutions as "it hurts *me,*" but says simply "it hurts." He never "catches *up with you*" on the street; he "catches *you up.*" He never says "are you through?" but "have you finished?" He never uses *to notify* as a transitive verb; an official act may be *notified*, but not a person. He never uses *gotten* as the perfect participle of *get*; he always uses plain *got*.[17] An English servant never washes the *dishes*; she always washes the *dinner* or *tea things*. She doesn't *live out*, but *goes into service*. She smashes, not the *mirror*, but the *looking-glass*. Her beau is not her *fellow*, but her *young man*. She does not *keep company* with him but *walks out* with him.

That an Englishman always calls out "*I* say!", and not simply "say!" when he desires to attract a friend's attention or register a protestation of incredulity—this perhaps is too familiar to need notice. His "*hear, hear!*" and "*oh, oh!*" are also well known. He is much less prodigal with *good-bye* than the American; he uses *good-day* and *good-*

afternoon far more often. A shop-assistant would never say *good-bye* to a customer. To an Englishman it would have a subtly offensive smack; *good-afternoon* would be more respectful. Another word that makes him flinch is *dirt*. He never uses it, as we do, to describe the soil in the garden; he always says *earth*. Various very common American phrases are quite unknown to him, for example, *over his signature*, *on time* and *planted to corn*. The first-named he never uses, and he has no equivalent for it; an Englishman who issues a signed statement simply makes it *in writing*. He knows nothing of our common terms of disparagement, such as *kike*, *wop*, *yap* and *rube*. His pet-name for a tiller of the soil is not *Rube* or *Cy*, but *Hodge*. When he goes gunning he does not call it *hunting*, but *shooting*; *hunting* is reserved for the chase of the fox.

An intelligent Englishwoman, coming to America to live, told me that the two things which most impeded her first communications with untravelled Americans, even above the gross differences between England and American pronunciation and intonation, were the complete absence of the general utility adjective *jolly* from the American vocabulary, and the puzzling omnipresence and versatility of the American verb *to fix*. In English colloquial usage *jolly* means almost anything; it intensifies all other adjectives, even including *miserable* and *homesick*. An Englishman is *jolly* tired, *jolly* hungry or *jolly well* tired; his wife is *jolly* sensible; his dog is *jolly* keen; the prices he pays for things are *jolly dear* (never *steep* or *stiff* or *high*: all Americanisms). But he has no noun to match the American *proposition*, meaning proposal, business, affair, case, consideration, plan, theory, solution and what not: only the German *zug* can be ranged beside it.[18] And he has no verb in such wide practise as *to fix*. In his speech it means only to make fast or to determine. In American it may mean to repair, as in "the plumber *fixed* the pipe"; to dress, as in "Mary *fixed* her hair"; to prepare, as in "the cook is *fixing* the gravy"; to bribe, as in "the judge was *fixed*"; to settle, as in "the quarrel was *fixed* up"; to heal, as in "the doctor *fixed* his boil"; to finish, as in "Murphy *fixed* Sweeney in the third round"; to be well-to-do, as in "John is well-*fixed*"; to arrange, as in "I *fixed* up the quarrel"; to be drunk, as in "the whiskey *fixed* him"; to punish, as in "I'll *fix* him"; and to correct, as in "he *fixed* my bad Latin." Moreover, it is used in all its

English senses. An Englishman never goes to a dentist to have his teeth *fixed*. He does not *fix* the fire; he *makes it up*, or *mends* it. He is never *well-fixed*, either in money or by liquor.[19]

The English use *quite* a great deal more than we do, and, as we have seen, in a different sense. *Quite rich*, in American, means tolerably rich, richer than most; *quite so*, in English, is identical in meaning with *exactly so*. In American *just* is almost equivalent to the English *quite*, as in *just lovely*. Thornton shows that this use of *just* goes back to 1794. The word is also used in place of *exactly* in other ways, as in *just in time*, *just how many* and *just what do you mean?*

§ 3. Honorifics

—Among the honorifics and euphemisms in everyday use one finds many notable divergences between the two languages. On the one hand the English are almost as diligent as the Germans in bestowing titles of honor upon their men of mark, and on the other hand they are very careful to withhold such titles from men who do not legally bear them. In America every practitioner of any branch of the healing art, even a chiropodist or an osteopath, is a doctor *ipso facto*, but in England, as we have seen, a good many surgeons lack the title and it is not common in the lesser ranks. Even graduate physicians may not have it, but here there is a yielding of the usual meticulous exactness, and it is customary to address a physician in the second person as *Doctor*, though his card may show that he is only *Medicinae Baccalaureus*, a degree quite unknown in America. Thus an Englishman, when he is ill, always sends for the *doctor*, as we do. But a surgeon is usually plain *Mr.*[20] An English veterinarian or dentist or druggist or masseur is never *Dr.*

Nor *Professor*. In all save a few large cities of America every male pedagogue is a professor, and so is every band leader, dancing master and medical consultant. But in England the title is very rigidly restricted to men who hold chairs in the universities, a necessarily small body. Even here a superior title always takes precedence. Thus, it used to be *Professor* Almroth Wright, but now it is always *Sir* Almroth Wright. Huxley was always called *Professor* Huxley until he was appointed to the Privy Council. This appointment gave him the right to have *Right Honourable* put before his name, and thereafter it was customary to call him simply *Mr.* Huxley, with the *Right*

Honourable, so to speak, floating in the air. The combination, to an Englishman, was more flattering than *Professor*, for the English always esteem political dignities far more than the dignities of learning. This explains, perhaps, why their universities distribute so few honorary degrees. In the United States every respectable Protestant clergyman is a D.D., and it is almost impossible for a man to get into the papers without becoming an LL.D., [21] but in England such honors are granted only grudgingly. So with military titles. To promote a war veteran from sergeant to colonel by acclamation, as is often done in the United States, is unknown over there. The English have nothing equivalent to the gaudy tin soldiers of our governors' staffs, nor to the bespangled colonels and generals of the Knights Templar and Patriarchs Militant, nor to the nondescript captains and majors of our country towns. An English railroad conductor (*railway guard*) is never *Captain*, as he always is in the United States. Nor are military titles used by the police. Nor is it the custom to make every newspaper editor a colonel, as is done south of the Potomac. Nor is an attorney-general or postmaster-general called *General*. Nor are the glories of public office, after they have officially come to an end, embalmed in such clumsy quasi-titles as *ex-United States Senator*, *ex-Judge of the Circuit Court of Appeals*, *ex-Federal Trade Commissioner* and *former Chief of the Fire Department*.

But perhaps the greatest difference between English and American usage is presented by *the Honorable*. In the United States the title is applied loosely to all public officials of apparent respectability, from senators and ambassadors to the mayors of fifth-rate cities and the members of state legislatures, and with some show of official sanction to many of them, especially congressmen. But it is questionable whether this application has any actual legal standing, save perhaps in the case of certain judges. Even the President of the United States, by law, is not *the Honorable*, but simply *the President*. In the First Congress the matter of his title was exhaustively debated; some members wanted to call him *the Honorable* and others proposed *His Excellency* and even *His Highness*. But the two Houses finally decided that it was "not proper to annex any style or title other than that expressed by the Constitution." Congressmen themselves are not *Honorables*. True enough, the *Congressional Record*, in printing a set speech, calls it "Speech of *Hon.* John Jones" (without the *the* before the *Hon.*—a characteristic Americanism), but in reporting the ordinary remarks of a member it always calls him plain *Mr.* Nevertheless, a country congressman would be offended if his partisans, in announcing his appearance on the stump, did not prefix *Hon.*to his name. So would a state senator. So would a mayor or governor. I have seen the sergeant-at-arms of the United States Senate referred to as *Hon.* in the records of that body.[22] More, the prefix is actually usurped by the Superintendent of State Prisons of New York.[23]

In England the thing is more carefully ordered, and bogus *Hons.* are unknown. The prefix is applied to both sexes and belongs by law, *inter alia*, to all present or past maids of honor, to all justices of the High Court during their terms of office, to the Scotch Lords of Session, to the sons and daughters of viscounts and barons, to the younger sons and all daughters of earls, and to the members of the legislative and executive councils of the colonies. But *not* to members of Parliament, though each is, in debate, an *hon. gentleman.* Even a member of the cabinet is not an*Hon.*, though he is a *Right Hon.* by virtue of membership in the Privy Council, of which the Cabinet is legally merely a committee. This last honorific belongs, not only to privy councillors, but also to all peers lower than marquesses (those above are *Most Hon.*), to Lord Mayors during their terms of office, to the Lord Advocate and to the Lord Provosts of Edinburgh and Glasgow. Moreover, a peeress whose husband is a *Right Hon.* is a *Right Hon.* herself.

The British colonies follow the jealous usage of the mother-country. Even in Canada the lawless American example is not imitated. I have before me a "Table of Titles to be Used in Canada, " laid down by royal warrant, which lists those who are *Hons.* and those who are not *Hons.* in the utmost detail. Only privy councillors of Canada (not to be confused with imperial privy councillors) are permitted to retain the prefix after going out of office, though ancients who were legislative councillors at the time of the union, July 1, 1867, may still use it by a sort of courtesy, and former speakers of the Dominion Senate and House of Commons and various retired judges may do so on application to the King, countersigned by the governor-general. The following are lawfully *the Hon.*, but only during their tenure of office: the solicitor-general, the speaker of the House of Commons, the presidents and speakers of the provincial legislatures, members of the executive councils of the provinces, the chief justice, the judges of the

Supreme and Exchequer Courts, the judges of the Supreme Courts of Ontario, Nova Scotia, New Brunswick, British Columbia, Prince Edward Island, Saskatchewan and Alberta, the judges of the Courts of Appeal of Manitoba and British Columbia, the Chancery Court of Prince Edward Island, and the Circuit Court of Montreal—these, and no more. A lieutenant-governor of a province is not *the Hon.*, but *His Honor*. The governor-general is *His Excellency*, and so is his wife, but in practise they usually have superior honorifics, and do not forget to demand their use.

But though an Englishman, and, following him, a colonial, is thus very careful to restrict *the Hon.* to proper uses, he always insists, when he serves without pay as an officer of any organization, to indicate his volunteer character by writing *Hon.* before the name of his office. If he leaves it off it is a sign that he is a hireling. Thus, the agent of the New Zealand government in London, a paid officer, is simply the *agent*, but the agents at Brisbane and Adelaide, in Australia, who serve for the glory of it, are *hon. agents*. In writing to a Briton one must be careful to put *Esq.*, behind his name, and not *Mr.*, before it. The English make a clear distinction between the two forms. *Mr.*, on an envelope, indicates that the sender holds the receiver to be his inferior; one writes to *Mr.* John Jackson, one's green-grocer, but to James Thompson, *Esq.*, one's neighbor. Any man who is entitled to the *Esq.* is a *gentleman*, by which an Englishman means a man of sound connections and dignified occupation—in brief, of ponderable social position. Thus a dentist, a shop-keeper or a clerk can never be a gentleman in England, even by courtesy, and the qualifications of an author, a musical conductor, a physician, or even a member of Parliament have to be established. But though he is thus enormously watchful of masculine dignity, an Englishman is quite careless in the use of *lady*. He speaks glibly of *lady-clerks, lady-typists, lady-doctors* and *lady-inspectors*. In America there is a strong disposition to use the word less and less, as is revealed by the substitution of *saleswoman* and *salesgirl* for the *saleslady* of yesteryear. But in England *lady* is still invariably used instead of woman in such compounds as *lady-golfer, lady-secretary* and *lady-champion*. The *women's singles*, in England tennis, are always *ladies' singles; women's wear*, in English shops, is always *ladies' wear*. Perhaps the cause of this distinction between *lady* and *gentleman* has been explained by Price Collier in "England and the English." In England, according to Collier, the male is always first. His comfort goes before his wife's comfort, and maybe his dignity also. *Gentleman-clerk* or *gentleman-author* would make an Englishman howl, though he uses *gentleman-rider*. So would the growing American custom of designating the successive heirs of a private family by the numerals proper to royalty. John Smith *3rd* and William Simpson *IV* are gravely received at Harvard; at Oxford they would be ragged unmercifully.

An Englishman, in speaking or writing of public officials, avoids those long and clumsy combinations of title and name which figure so copiously in American newspapers. Such locutions as *Assistant Secretary of the Interior* Jones, *Fourth Assistant Postmaster-General* Brown, *Inspector of Boilers* Smith, *Judge of the Appeal Tax Court* Robinson, *Chief Clerk of the Treasury* Williams and *Collaborating Epidermologist* White[24] are quite unknown to him. When he mentions a high official, such as the Secretary for Foreign Affairs, he does not think it necessary to add the man's name; he simply says "the Secretary for Foreign Affairs" or "the Foreign Secretary." And so with the Lord Chancellor, the Chief Justice, the Prime Minister, the Bishop of Carlisle, the Chief Rabbi, the First Lord (of the Admiralty), the Master of Pembroke (College), the Italian Ambassador, and so on. Certain ecclesiastical titles are sometimes coupled to surnames in the American manner, as in *Dean Stanley*, and *Canon Wilberforce*, but *Prime Minister Lloyd-George* would seem heavy and absurd. But in other directions the Englishman has certain clumsinesses of his own. Thus, in writing a letter to a relative stranger, he sometimes begins it, not *My dear Mr. Jones* but *My dear John Joseph Jones*. He may even use such a form as *My dear Secretary for War* in place of the American *My dear Mr. Secretary*. In English usage, incidentally, *My dear* is more formal than simply *Dear*. In America, of course, this distinction is lost, and such forms as *My dear John Joseph Jones* appear only as conscious imitations of English usage.

I have spoken of the American custom of dropping the definite article before *Hon.* It extends to *Rev.* and the like, and has the authority of very respectable usage behind it. The opening sentence of the *Congressional Record* is always: "The Chaplain, *Rev.————,*

D.D., offered the following prayer." When chaplains for the army or navy are confirmed by the Senate they always appear in the *Record* as *Revs.*, never as *the Revs.* I also find the honorific without the article in the New International Encyclopaedia, in the *World* Almanac, and in a widely-popular American grammar-book.[25] So long ago as 1867, Gould protested against this elision as barbarous and idiotic, and drew up the following *reductio ad absurdum*:

At last annual meeting of Black Book Society, honorable John Smith took the chair, assisted by reverend John Brown and venerable John White. The office of secretary would have been filled by late John Green, but for his decease, which rendered him ineligible. His place was supplied by inevitable John Black. In the course of the evening eulogiums were pronounced on distinguished John Gray and notorious Joseph Brown. Marked compliment was also paid to able historian Joseph White, discriminating philosopher Joseph Green, and learned professor Joseph Black. But conspicuous speech of the evening was witty Joseph Gray's apostrophe to eminent astronomer Jacob Brown, subtle logician Jacob White, etc., etc.[26]

Richard Grant White, a year or two later, joined the attack in the New York *Galaxy*, and William Cullen Bryant included the omission of the article in his *Index Expurgatorius*, but these anathemas were as ineffective as Gould's irony. The more careful American journals, of course, incline to the *the*, and I note that it is specifically ordained on the Style-sheet of the *Century Magazine*, but the overwhelming majority of American newspapers get along without it, and I have often noticed its omission on the sign-boards at church entrances.[27] In England it is never omitted.

§ 4. Euphemisms and Forbidden Words

—But such euphemisms as *lady-clerk* are, after all, much rarer in English than in American usage. The Englishman seldom tries to gloss menial occupations with sonorous names; on the contrary, he seems to delight in keeping their menial character plain. He says *servants*, not *help*. Even his railways and banks have *servants*; the chief trades-union of the English railroad men is the Amalgamated Society of Railway *Servants*. He uses *employé* in place of *clerk*, *workman* or *laborer* much less often than we do. True enough he calls a boarder a *paying-guest*, but that is probably because even a boarder may be a gentleman. Just as he avoids calling a fast train the *limited*, the *flier* or the *cannon-ball*, so he never calls an *undertaker* a *funeral director* or *mortician*, [28] or a *dentist* a *dental surgeon* or *ontologist*, or an *optician* an *optometrist*, or a *barber shop* (he always makes it *barber's shop*) a *tonsorial parlor*, or a common public-house a *café*, a *restaurant*, an *exchange*, a *buffet* or a *hotel*, or a tradesman a *storekeeper* or *merchant*, or a fresh-water college a *university*. A *university*, in England, always means a collection of colleges.[29] He avoids displacing terms of a disparaging or disagreeable significance with others less brutal, or thought to be less brutal, *e. g.*, *ready-to-wear* or *ready-tailored* for *ready-made*, *used* or *slightly-used* for *second-hand*, *mahoganized* for *imitation-mahogany*, *aisle manager* for *floor-walker* (he makes it *shop-walker*), *loan-office* for *pawn-shop*. Also, he is careful not to use such words as *rector*, *deacon* and *baccalaureate* in merely rhetorical senses.[30]

When we come to words, that, either intrinsically or by usage, are improper, a great many curious differences between English and American reveal themselves. The Englishman, on the whole, is more plain-spoken than the American, and such terms as *bitch*, *mare* and *in foal* do not commonly daunt him, largely, perhaps, because of his greater familiarity with country life; but he has a formidable index of his own, and it includes such essentially harmless words as *sick*, *stomach*, *bum* and *bug*. The English use of *ill* for *sick* I have already noticed, and the reasons for the English avoidance of *bum*. *Sick*, over there, means nauseated, and when an Englishman says that he was *sick* he means that he vomited, or, as an American would say, was *sick at the stomach*. The older (and still American) usage, however, survives in various compounds. *Sick-list*, for example, is official in the Navy, [31] and *sick-leave* is known in the Army, though it is more common to say of a soldier that he is *invalided home*. *Sick-room* and *sick-bed* are also in common use, and *sick-flag* is used in place of the American *quarantine-flag*. But an Englishman hesitates to mention his stomach in the presence of ladies, though he discourses freely about his liver. To avoid the necessity he employs such euphemisms as *Little Mary*. As for *bug*, he restricts its use very rigidly to the *Cimex lectularius*, or common bed-bug, and hence the word has a highly impolite connotation. All other crawling things he calls *insects*. An American of my acquaintance once greatly offended an English friend by using *bug* for *insect*. The two were playing billiards one summer evening in the Englishman's house, and various flying things came through the window and alighted on the cloth. The American, essaying a shot, remarked that he had killed a *bug* with his cue. To the Englishman this seemed a slanderous reflection upon the cleanliness of his house.[32]

The Victorian era saw a great growth of absurd euphemisms in England, including *second wing* for the leg of a fowl, but it was in America that the thing was carried farthest. Bartlett hints that *rooster* came into use in place of *cock* as a matter of delicacy, the latter word having acquired an indecent significance, and tells us that, at one time, even *bull* was banned as too vulgar for refined ears. In place of it the early purists used *cow-creature*, *male-cow* and even *gentleman-cow*.[33]*Bitch*, *ram*, *buck* and *sow* went the same way, and there was a day when even *mare* was prohibited. Bache tells us that *pismire* was also banned, *antmire* being substituted for it. In 1847 the word *chair* was actually barred out and *seat* was adopted in its place.[34] These were the palmy days of euphemism. The delicate *female* was guarded from all knowledge, and even from all suspicion, of evil. "To utter aloud in her presence the word *shirt*, " says one historian, "was an open insult."[35]Mrs. Trollope, writing in 1832, tells of "a young German gentleman of perfectly good manners" who "offended one of the principal families ... by having pronounced the word *corset* before the ladies of it."[36] The word *woman*, in those sensitive days, became a term of reproach, comparable to the German *mensch*; the uncouth *female* took its place.[37] In the same way the legs of the fair became *limbs* and their breasts *bosoms*, and *lady* was substituted for *wife*. *Stomach*, under the ban in England, was transformed, by some unfathomable magic, into a euphemism denoting the whole region from the nipples to the pelvic arch. It was during this time that the newspapers invented such locutions as *interesting* (or *delicate*) *condition*, *criminal operation*, *house of ill* (or *questionable*) *repute*, *disorderly-house*, *sporting-house*, *statutory offense*, *fallen woman* and *criminal assault*. Servant girls ceased to be seduced, and began to be *betrayed*. Various French terms, *enceinte* and *accouchement* among them, were imported to conceal the fact that lawful wives occasionally became pregnant and had lyings-in.

White, between 1867 and 1870, launched various attacks upon these ludicrous gossamers of speech, and particularly upon *enceinte*, *limb* and *female*, but only *female* succumbed. The passage of the notorious Comstock Postal Act, in 1873, greatly stimulated the search for euphemisms. Once that act was upon the statute-books and Comstock himself was given the amazingly inquisitorial powers of a post-office inspector, it became positively dangerous to print certain ancient and essentially decent English words. To this day the effects of that old reign of terror are still visible. We yet use *toilet* and *public comfort station* in place of better terms, [38] and such idiotic forms as *red-light district*, *disorderly-house*, *blood-poison*, *social-evil*, *social disease* and *white slave* ostensibly conceal what every flapper is talking about. The word *cadet*, having a foreign smack and an innocent native meaning, is preferred to the more accurate *procurer*; even prostitutes shrink from the forthright *pimp*, and employ a characteristic American abbreviation, *P. I.*—a curious brother to *S. O. B.* and *2 o'clock*. Nevertheless, a movement toward honesty is getting on its legs. The vice crusaders, if they have accomplished nothing else, have at least forced the newspapers to use the honest terms, *syphilis*, *prostitute*, *brothel* and *venereal disease*, albeit somewhat gingerly. It is, perhaps, significant of the change going on that the *New York Evening Post* recently authorized its reporters to use *street-walker*.[39] But in certain quarters the change is viewed with alarm, and curious traces of the old prudery still survive. The Department of Health of New York City, in April, 1914, announced that its efforts to diminish venereal disease were much handicapped because "in most newspaper offices the words *syphilis* and *gonorrhea* are still tabooed, and without the use of these terms it is almost impossible to correctly state the problem." The Army Medical Corps, in the early part of 1918, encountered the same difficulty: most newspapers refused to print its bulletins regarding venereal disease in the army. One of the newspaper trade journals thereupon sought the opinions of editors upon the subject, and all of them save one declared against the use of the two words. One editor put the blame upon the Postoffice, which still cherishes the Comstock tradition. Another reported that "at a recent conference of the Scripps Northwest League editors" it was decided that "the use of such terms as *gonorrhea*, *syphilis*, and even *venereal diseases* would not add to the tone of the papers, and that the term *vice diseases* can be readily substituted."[40] The Scripps papers are otherwise anything but distinguished for their "tone, " but in this department they yield to the Puritan habit. An even more curious instance of prudery came to my notice in Philadelphia several years ago. A one-act play of mine, "The Artist, " was presented at the Little Theatre there, and during its run, on February 26, 1916, the *Public Ledger* reprinted some of the dialogue. One of the characters in the piece is *A Virgin*. At every occurrence a change was made to *A Young Girl*. Apparently, even *virgin* is still regarded as too frank in Philadelphia.[41] Fifty years ago the very word *decent* was indecent in the South: no respectable woman was supposed to have any notion of the difference between *decent* and *indecent*.

In their vocabularies of opprobrium and profanity English and Americans diverge sharply. The English *rotter* and *blighter* are practically unknown in America, and there are various American equivalents that are never heard in England. A *guy*, in the American vulgate, simply signifies a man; there is not necessarily any disparaging significance. But in English, high or low, it means one who is making a spectacle of himself. The derivative verb, *to guy*, is unknown in English; its nearest equivalent is *to spoof*, which is unknown in American. The average American, I believe, has a larger vocabulary of profanity than the average Englishman, and swears a good deal more, but he attempts an amelioration of many of his oaths by softening them to forms with no apparent meaning. *Darn(=dern=durn)* for *damn* is apparently of English origin, but it is heard ten thousand times in America to once in England. So is *dog-gone*. Such euphemistic written forms as *damphool* and *damfino* are also far more common in this country. *All-fired* for *hell-fired, gee-whiz* for *Jesus, tarnal* for *eternal, tarnation* for *damnation, cuss* for *curse, goldarned* for *God-damned, by gosh* for *by God* and *great Scott* for *great God* are all Americanisms; Thornton has traced *all-fired* to 1835, *tarnation* to 1801 and *tarnal* to 1790. *By golly* has been found in English literature so early as 1843, but it probably originated in America; down to the Civil War it was the characteristic oath of the negro slaves. Such terms as *bonehead, pinhead* and *boob* have been invented, perhaps, to take the place of the English *ass*, which has a flavor of impropriety in America on account of its identity in sound with the American pronunciation of *arse*.[42] At an earlier day *ass* was always differentiated by making it *jackass*. Another word that is improper in America but not in England is *tart*. To an Englishman the word connotes sweetness, and so, if he be of the lower orders, he may apply it to his sweetheart. But to the American it signifies a prostitute, or, at all events, a woman of too ready an amiability.

But the most curious disparity between the profane vocabulary of the two tongues is presented by *bloody*. This word is entirely without improper significance in America, but in England it is regarded as the vilest of indecencies. The sensation produced in London when George Bernard Shaw put it into the mouth of a woman character in his play, "Pygmalion, " will be remembered. "The interest in the first English performance, " said the *New York Times*, [43] "centered in the heroine's utterance of this banned word. It was waited for with trembling, heard shudderingly, and presumably, when the shock subsided, interest dwindled." But in New York, of course, it failed to cause any stir. Just why it is regarded as profane and indecent by the English is one of the mysteries of the language. The theory that it has some blasphemous reference to the blood of Christ is disputed by many etymologists. It came in during the latter half of the seventeenth century, and at the start it apparently meant no more than "in the manner of a blood, " *i. e.*, a rich young roisterer of the time. Thus, *bloody drunk* was synonymous with as *drunk as a lord*. The adjective remained innocuous for 200 years. Then it suddenly acquired its present abhorrent significance. It is regarded with such aversion by the English that even the lower orders often substitute *bleeding* as a euphemism.

So far no work devoted wholly to the improper terms of English and American has been published, but this lack may be soon remedied by a compilation made by a Chicago journalist. It is entitled "The Slang of Venery and Its Analogues, " and runs to two large volumes. A small edition, mimeographed for private circulation, was issued in 1916. I have examined this work and found it of great value. If the influence of comstockery is sufficient to prevent its publication in the United States, as seems likely, it will be printed in Switzerland.

FOOTNOTES:

[1] It should be noted that *mews* is used only in the larger cities. In the small towns *livery-stable* is commoner. *Mews* is quite unknown in America save as an occasional archaism.

[2] Sometimes *whiffle-tree.*

[3] The latter has crept into American of late. I find it on p. 58 of The United States at War, a pamphlet issued by the Library of Congress, 1917. The compiler of this pamphlet is a savant bearing the fine old British name of Herman H. B. Meyer.

[4] *Living-room,* however, is gradually making its way in England. It was apparently suggested, in America, by the German *wohnzimmer.*

[5] This form survives in the American term *city-stock,* meaning the bonds of a municipality. But government securities are always called *bonds.*

[6] *Cf.* A Glossary of Colloquial Slang and Technical Terms in Use in the Stock Exchange and in the Money Market, by A. J. Wilson, London, 1895.

[7] Or *bailiffs.*

[8] But he is *run* by his party organization. *Cf.* The Government of England, by A. Lawrence Lowell; New York, 1910, vol. ii, p. 29.

[9] Until very recently no self-respecting American newspaper reporter would call himself a *journalist.* He always used *newspaper man,* and referred to his vocation, not as a profession, but as the newspaper *business.* This old prejudice, however, now seems to be breaking down. *Cf.* Don't Shy at Journalist, *The Editor and Publisher and Journalist,* June 27, 1914.

[10] *Cf.* a speech of Senator La Follette, *Congressional Record,* Aug. 27, 1917, p. 6992.

[11] According to the New International Encyclopedia, 2nd ed. (*Art.* Apartment House), the term *flat* "is usually in the United States restricted to apartments in houses having no elevator or hall service." In New York such apartments are commonly called *walk-up apartments.* Even with the qualification, *apartment* is better than *flat.*

[12] Canoeing was introduced into England by John MacGregor in 1866, and there is now a Royal Canoe Club. In America the canoe has been familiar from the earliest times, and in Mme. Sarah Kemble Knight's diary (1704) there is much mention of *cannoos.* The word itself is from an Indian dialect, probably the Haitian, and came into American through the Spanish, in which it survives as *canoa.*

[13] "An act was passed to prohibit playing *nine-pins*; as soon as the law was put in force, it was notified everywhere, '*Ten-pins* played here.'"—Capt. Marryat: Diary in America, vol. iii, p. 195.

[14] "The term *chapel,* " says Joyce, in English as We Speak It in Ireland, "has so ingrained itself in my mind that to this hour the word instinctively

springs to my lips when I am about to mention a Catholic place of worship; and I always feel some sort of hesitation or reluctance in substituting the word *church*. I positively could not bring myself to say, 'Come, it is time now to set out for *church*' It must be either *mass* or chapel."

[15] Certain dissenters, of late, show a disposition to borrow the American usage. Thus the *Christian World*, organ of the English Congregationalists, uses *Episcopal* to designate the Church of England.

[16] So long ago as the 70's certain Jews petitioned the publishers of Webster's and Worcester's dictionaries to omit their definitions of the verb *to jew*, and according to Richard Grant White, the publisher of Worcester's complied. Such a request, in England, would be greeted with derision.

[17] But nevertheless he uses *begotten*, not *begot*.

[18] This specimen is from the *Congressional Record* of Dec. 11, 1917: "I do not like to be butting into this *proposition*, but I look upon this postoffice business as a purely business *proposition*." The speaker was "Hon" Homer P. Snyder, of New York. In the *Record* of Jan. 12, 1918, p. 8294, *proposition* is used as a synonym for state of affairs.

[19] Already in 1855 Bristed was protesting that *to fix* was having "more than its legitimate share of work all over the Union." "In English conversation, " he said, "the panegyrical adjective of all work is *nice*; in America it is *fine*." This was before the adoption of *jolly* and its analogues, *ripping*, *stunning*, *rattling*, etc.

[20] In the Appendix to the Final Report of the Royal Commission on Venereal Diseases, London, 1916, p. iv., I find the following: "*Mr.* C. J. Symonds, F.R.C.S., M.D.; *Mr.* F. J. McCann, F.R.C.S., M.D.; *Mr.* A. F. Evans, F.R.C.S". *Mr.* Symonds is consulting surgeon to Guy's Hospital, *Mr.* McCann is an eminent London gynecologist, and *Mr.* Evans is a general surgeon in large practise. All would be called *Doctor* in the United States.

[21] Among the curious recipients of this degree have been Gumshoe Bill Stone, Uncle Joe Cannon and Josephus Daniels. Billy Sunday, the evangelist, is a D.D.

[22] *Congressional Record*, May 16, 1918, p. 7147.

[23] *Vide* his annual reports, printed at Sing Sing Prison.

[24] I encountered this gem in *Public Health Reports*, a government publication, for April 26, 1918, p. 619.

[25] For the *Record* see the issue of Dec. 14, 1917, p. 309. For the New International Encyclopaedia see the article on Brotherhood of Andrew and Philip. For the *World* Almanac see the article on Young People's Society of Christian Endeavor, ed. of 1914. The grammar-book is Longman's Briefer Grammar; New York, 1908, p. 160. The editor is George J. Smith, a member of the board of examiners of the New York City Department of Education.

[26] Edwin S. Gould: Good English; New York, 1867, pp. 56-57.

[27] Despite the example of Congress, however, the Department of State inserts the *the*. *Vide* the *Congressional Record*, May 4, 1918, p. 6552. But the War Department, the Treasury and the Post Office omit it. *Vide* the *Congressional Record*, May 11, 1918, p. 6895 and p. 6914 and May 14, p. 7004, respectively. So, it appears, does the White House. *Vide* the *Congressional Record*, May 10, 1918, p. 6838, and June 12, 1918, p. 8293.

[28] In the 60's an undertaker was often called an *embalming surgeon* in America.

[29] In a list of American "universites" I find the Christian of Canton, Mo., with 125 students; the Lincoln, of Pennsylvania, with 184; the Southwestern Presbyterian, of Clarksville, Tenn., with 86; and the Newton Theological, with 77. Most of these, of course, are merely country high-schools.

[30] The Rev. John C. Stephenson in the *New York Sun*, July 10, 1914: ... "that empty courtesy of addressing every clergyman as *Doctor*.... And let us abolish the abuse of ... *baccalaureate* sermons for sermons before graduating classes of high schools and the like."

[31] *Cf.* Dardanelles Commission Report; London, 1916, p. 58, § 47.

[32] Edgar Allan Poe's "The Gold *Bug*" is called "The Golden *Beetle*" in England. Twenty-five years ago an Englishman named *Buggey*, laboring under the odium attached to the name, had it changed to *Norfolk-Howard*, a compound made up of the title and family name of the Duke of Norfolk. The wits of London at once doubled his misery by adopting *Norfolk-Howard* as a euphemism for *bed-bug*.

[33] A recent example of the use of *male-cow* was quoted in the *Journal* of the American Medical Association, Nov. 17, 1917, advertising page 24.

[34] *New York Organ* (a "*family journal* devoted to temperance, morality, education and general literature"), May 29, 1847. One of the editors of this delicate journal was T. S. Arthur, author of Ten Nights in a Bar-room.

[35] John Graham Brooks: As Others See Us; New York, 1908, p. 11.

[36] Domestic Manners of the Americans, 2 vols.; London, 1832; vol. i, p. 132.

[37] *Female*, of course, was epidemic in England too, but White says that it was "not a Briticism, " and so early as 1839 the Legislature of Maryland expunged it from the title of a bill "to protect the reputation of unmarried *females*, " substituting *women*, on the ground that *female* "was an Americanism in that application."

[38] The French *pissoir*, for instance, is still regarded as indecent in America, and is seldom used in England, but it has gone into most of the Continental languages. It is curious to note, however, that these languages also have their pruderies. Most of them, for example, use *W. C.*, an abbreviation of the English *water-closet*, as a euphemism. The whole subject of national pruderies, in both act and speech, remains to be investigated.

[39] Even the *Springfield Republican*, the last stronghold of Puritan *Kultur*, printed the word on Oct. 11, 1917, in a review of New Adventures, by Michael Monahan.

[40] *Pep*, July, 1918, p. 8.

[41] Perhaps the Quaker influence is to blame. At all events, Philadelphia is the most pecksniffian of American cities, and thus probably leads the world. Early in 1918, when a patriotic moving-picture entitled "To Hell with the Kaiser" was sent on tour under government patronage, the word *hell* was carefully toned down, on the Philadelphia billboards, to *h*——.

[42] *Cf.* R. M. Bache: Vulgarisms and Other Errors of Speech; Phila., 1869, p. 34 *et seq.*.

[43] April 14, 1914.

V. Tendencies in American

§ 1. International Exchanges

—More than once, during the preceding chapters, we encountered Americanisms that had gone over into English, and English locutions that had begun to get a foothold in the United States. Such exchanges are made very frequently and often very quickly, and though the guardians of English still attack every new Americanism vigorously, even when, as in the case of *scientist*, it is obviously sound and useful, they are often routed by public pressure, and have to submit in the end with the best grace possible. For example, consider *caucus*. It originated in Boston at some indeterminate time before 1750, and remained so peculiarly American for more than a century following that most of the English visitors before the Civil War remarked its use. But, according to J. Redding Ware, [1] it began to creep into English political slang about 1870, and in the 80's it was lifted to good usage by the late Joseph Chamberlain. Ware, writing in the first years of the present century, said that the word had become "very important" in England, but was "not admitted into dictionaries." But in the Concise Oxford Dictionary, dated 1914, it is given as a sound English word, though its American origin is noted. The English, however, use it in a sense that has become archaic in America, thus preserving an abandoned American meaning in the same way that many abandoned British meanings have been preserved on this side. In the United States the word means, and has meant for years, a meeting of some division, large or small, of a political or legislative body for the purpose of agreeing upon a united course of action in the main assembly. In

England it means the managing committee of a party or fraction—something corresponding to our national committee, or state central committee, or steering committee, or to the half-forgotten congressional caucuses of the 20's. It has a disparaging significance over there, almost equal to that of our words *organization* and *machine*. Moreover, it has given birth to two derivatives of like quality, both unknown in America—*caucusdom*, meaning machine control, and *caucuser*, meaning a machine politician.[2]

A good many other such Americanisms have got into good usage in England, and new ones are being exported constantly. Farmer describes the process of their introduction, and assimilation. American books, newspapers and magazines, especially the last, circulate in England in large number, and some of their characteristic locutions pass into colloquial speech. Then they get into print, and begin to take on respectability. "The phrase, 'as the Americans say, '" he continues, "might in some cases be ordered from the type foundry as a logotype, so frequently does it do introduction duty."[3] Ware shows another means of ingress: the argot of sailors. Many of the Americanisms he notes as having become naturalized in England, *e. g., boodle, boost* and *walk-out*, are credited to Liverpool as a sort of half-way station. Travel brings in still more: England swarms with Americans, and Englishmen themselves, visiting America, bring home new and racy phrases. Bishop Coxe says[4] that Dickens, in his "American Notes, " gave English currency to *reliable, influential, talented* and *lengthy*. Bristed, writing in 1855, said that *talented* was already firmly fixed in the English vocabulary by that time. All four words are in the Concise Oxford Dictionary, and only *lengthy* is noted as "originally an Americanism." Finally, there is the influence of the moving pictures. Hundreds of American films are shown in England every week, and the American words and phrases appearing in their titles, sub-titles and other explanatory legends thus become familiar to the English. "The patron of the picture palace, " says W. G. Faulkner, in an article in the *London Daily Mail*, "learns to think of his railway station as a *depot*; he has alternatives to one of our newest words, *hooligan*, in *hoodlum* and *tough*; he watches a *dive*, which is a thieves' kitchen or a room in which bad characters meet, and whether the villain talks of *dough* or *sugar* he knows it is money to which he is referring. The musical ring of the word *tramp* gives way to the stodgy *hobo* or *dead-beat*. It may be that the plot reveals an attempt to deceive some simple-minded person. If it does, the innocent one is spoken of as a *sucker*, a *come-on*, a *boob*, or a *lobster* if he is stupid into the bargain."

Mr. Faulkner goes on to say that a great many other Americanisms are constantly employed by Englishmen "who have not been affected by the avalanche ... which has come upon us through the picture palace." "Thus today, " he says, "we hear people speak of the *fall* of the year, a *stunt* they have in hand, their desire to *boost* a particular business, a *peach* when they mean a pretty girl, a *scab*—a common term among strikers, —the *glad-eye*, *junk* when they mean worthless material, their efforts *to make good*, the *elevator* in the hotel or office, the *boss* or manager, the *crook* or swindler; and they will tell you that they have the *goods*—that is, they possess the requisite qualities for a given position." The venerable Frederic Harrison, writing in the *Fortnightly Review* in the Spring of 1918, denounced this tendency with a vigor recalling the classical anathemas of Dean Alford and Sydney Smith.[5] "Stale American phrases, ..." he said, "are infecting even our higher journalism and our parliamentary and platform oratory.... A statesman is now *out* for victory; he is *up against* pacificism.... He has a *card up his sleeve*, by which the enemy are at last to be *euchred*. Then a fierce fight in which hundreds of noble fellows are mangled or drowned is a *scrap*.... To criticise a politician is to call for his *scalp*.... The other fellow is beaten to a *frazzle*." And so on. "Bolshevism, " concluded Harrison sadly, "is ruining language as well as society."

But though there are still many such alarms by constables of the national speech, the majority of Englishmen continue to make borrowings from the tempting and ever-widening American vocabulary. What is more, some of these loan-words take root, and are presently accepted as sound English, even by the most watchful. The two Fowlers, in "The King's English, " separate Americanisms from other current vulgarisms, but many of the latter on their list are actually American in origin, though they do not seem to know it—for example, *to demean* and *to transpire*. More remarkable still, the Cambridge History of English Literature lists *backwoodsman, know-nothing* and *yellow-back* as English compounds, apparently in forgetfulness of their American origin, and adds *skunk, squaw* and *toboggan* as direct importations from the Indian tongues, without noting that they came through American, and remained definite Americanisms for a long while.[6] It even adds *musquash*, a popular name for the *Fiber zibethicus*, borrowed from the Algonquin *muskwessu* but long since degenerated to *musk-rat* in America. *Musquash* has been in disuse in this country, indeed, since the middle of the last century, save as a stray localism, but the English have preserved it, and it appears in the Oxford Dictionary.[7]

A few weeks in London or a month's study of the London newspapers will show a great many other American pollutions of the well of English. The argot of politics is full of them. Many beside *caucus* were introduced by Joseph Chamberlain, a politician skilled in American campaign methods and with an American wife to prompt him. He gave the English their first taste of *to belittle*, one of the inventions of Thomas Jefferson. *Graft* and *to graft* crossed the ocean in their nonage. *To bluff* has been well understood in England for 30 years. It is in Cassell's and the Oxford Dictionaries, and has been used by no less a magnifico than Sir Almroth Wright.[8] *To stump*, in the form of *stump-oratory*, is in Carlyle's "Latter-Day Pamphlets, " *circa* 1850, and *caucus* appears in his "Frederick the Great;"[9] though, as we have seen on the authority of Ware, it did not come into general use in England until ten years later. *Buncombe* (usually spelled *bunkum*) is in all the later English dictionaries. In the London stock market and among English railroad men various characteristic Americanisms have got a foothold. The meaning of *bucket-shop* and *to water*, for example, is familiar to every London broker's clerk. English trains are now *telescoped* and carry *dead-heads*, and in 1913 a rival to the Amalgamated Order of Railway *Servants* was organized under the name of the National Union of *Railway Men*. The beginnings of a movement against the use of *servant* are visible in other directions, and the American *help* threatens to be substituted; at all events, *Help Wanted* advertisements are now occasionally encountered in English newspapers. But it is American verbs that seem to find the way into English least difficult, particularly those compounded with prepositions and adverbs, such as *to pan out* and *to swear off*. Most of them, true enough, are still used as conscious Americanisms, but used they are, and with increasing frequency. The highly typical American verb *to loaf* is now naturalized, and Ware says that *The Loaferies* is one of the common nicknames of the Whitechapel workhouse.

It is curious, reading the fulminations of American purists of the last generation, to note how many of the Americanisms they denounced have not only got into perfectly good usage at home but even broken down all guards across the ocean. *To placate* and *to antagonize* are examples. The Oxford Dictionary distinguishes between the English and American meanings of the latter: in England a man may antagonize only another man, in America he may antagonize a mere idea or thing. But, as the brothers Fowler show, even the English meaning is of American origin, and no doubt a few more years will see the verb completely naturalized in Britain. *To placate*, attacked vigorously by all native grammarians down to (but excepting) White, now has the authority of the *Spectator*, and is accepted by Cassell. *To donate* is still under the ban, but *to transpire* has been used by the *London Times*. Other old bugaboos that have been embraced are *gubernatorial, presidential* and *standpoint*. White labored long and valiantly to convince Americans that the adjective derived from *president* should be without the *i* in its last syllable, following the example of *incidental, regimental, monumental, governmental, oriental, experimental* and so on; but in vain, for *presidential* is now perfectly good English. *To demean* is still questioned, but English authors of the first rank have used it, and it will probably lose its dubious character very soon.

The flow of loan-words in the opposite direction meets with little impediment, for social distinction in America is still largely dependent upon English recognition, and so there is an eager imitation of the latest English fashions in speech. This emulation is most noticeable in the large cities of the East, and particularly in what Schele de Vere called "Boston and the Boston dependencies." New York is but little behind. The small stores there, if they are of any pretentions, are now almost invariably called *shops*. Shoes for the well-to-do are no longer *shoes*, but *boots*, and they are sold in *bootshops*. One encounters, too, in the side-streets off Fifth avenue, a multitude of *gift-shops, tea-shops* and *haberdashery-shops*. In Fifth avenue itself there are several *luggage-shops*. In August, 1917, signs appeared in the New York surface cars in which the conductors were referred to as *guards*. This effort to be English and correct was exhibited over the sign manual of Theodore P. Shonts, president of the Interborough, a gentleman of Teutonic name, but evidently a faithful protector of the king's English. On the same cars, however, painted notices, surviving from some earlier régime, mentioned the guards as *conductors*. *To Let* signs are now as common in all our cities as *For Rent* signs. We all know the *charwoman*, and have begun to forget our native modification of *char*, to wit, *chore*. Every apartment-house has a *tradesmen's-entrance*. In Charles street, in Baltimore, some time ago, the proprietor of a fashionable stationery store directed me, not to the elevator, but to the *lift*.

Occasionally, some uncompromising patriot raises his voice against these importations, but he seldom shows the vigorous indignation of the English purists, and he seldom prevails. White, in 1870, warned Americans against the figurative use of *nasty* as a synonym for *disagreeable*.[10] This use of the word was then relatively new in England, though, according to White, the *Saturday Review* and the *Spectator* had already succumbed. His objections to it were unavailing; *nasty* quickly got into American and has been there ever since. In 1883 Gilbert M. Tucker protested against *good-form*, *traffic* (in the sense of travel), *to bargain* and *to tub* as Briticisms that we might well do without, but all of them took root and are perfectly sound American today. There is, indeed, no intelligible reason why such English inventions and improvements should not be taken in, even though the motive behind the welcome to them may occasionally cause a smile. English, after all, is the mother of American, and the child, until lately, was still at nurse. The English, confronted by some of our fantastic innovations, may well regard them as impudences to be put down, but what they offer in return often fits into our vocabulary without offering it any outrage. American, indeed, is full of lingering Briticisms, all maintaining a successful competition with native forms. If we take back *shop* it is merely taking back something that *store* has never been able to rid us of: we use *shop-worn*, *shoplifter*, *shopping*, *shopper*, *shop-girl* and *to shop* every day. In the same way the word *penny* has survived among us, despite the fact that there has been no American coin of that name for more than 125 years. We have *nickel-in-the-slot* machines, but when they take a cent we call them *penny-in-the-slot* machines. We have *penny-arcades* and *penny-whistles*. We do not play *cent*-ante, but *penny*-ante. We still "turn an honest *penny*" and say "a *penny* for your thoughts." The pound and the shilling became extinct a century ago, but the penny still binds us to the mother tongue.

§ 2. Points of Difference

—These exchanges and coalescences, however, though they invigorate each language with the blood of the other and are often very striking in detail, are neither numerous enough nor general enough to counteract the centrifugal force which pulls them apart. The simple fact is that the spirit of English and the spirit of American have been at odds for nearly a century, and that the way of one is not the way of the other. The loan-words that fly to and fro, when examined closely, are found to be few in number both relatively and absolutely: they do not greatly affect the larger movements of the two languages. Many of them, indeed, are little more than temporary borrowings; they are not genuinely adopted, but merely momentarily fashionable. The class of Englishmen which affects American phrases is perhaps but little larger, taking one year with another, than the class of Americans which affects English phrases. This last class, it must be plain, is very small. Leave the large cities and you will have difficulty finding any members of it. It is circumscribed, not because there is any very formidable prejudice against English locutions as such, but simply because recognizably English locutions, in a good many cases, do not fit into the American language. The American thinks in American and the Englishman in English, and it requires a definite effort, usually but defectively successful, for either to put his thoughts into the actual idiom of the other.

The difficulties of this enterprise are well exhibited, though quite unconsciously, by W. L. George in a chapter entitled "Litany of the Novelist" in his book of criticism, "Literary Chapters."[11] This chapter, it is plain by internal evidence, was written, not for Englishmen, but for Americans. A good part of it, in fact, is in the second person—we are addressed and argued with directly. And throughout there is an obvious endeavor to help out comprehension by a studied use of purely American phrases and examples. One hears, not of the *East End*, but of the *East Side*; not of the *City*, but of *Wall Street*; not of *Belgravia* or the *West End*, but of *Fifth avenue*; not of *bowler* hats, but of *Derbys*; not of idlers in *pubs*, but of *saloon loafers*; not of *pounds*, *shillings* and *pence*, but of *dollars* and *cents*. In brief, a gallant attempt upon a strange tongue, and by a writer of the utmost skill—but a hopeless failure none the less. In the midst of his best American, George drops into Briticism after Briticism, some of them quite as unintelligible to the average American reader as so many Gallicisms. On page after page they display the practical impossibility of the enterprise: *back-garden* for *back-yard*, *perambulator* for *baby-carriage*, *corn*-market for *grain*-market, coal-*owner* for coal-*operator*, *post* for *mail*, and so on. And to top them there are English terms that have no American equivalents at all, for example, *kitchen-fender*.

The same failure, perhaps usually worse, is displayed every time an English novelist or dramatist essays to put an American into a novel or a play, and to make him speak American. However painstakingly it is done, the Englishman invariably falls into capital blunders, and the result is derided by Americans as Mark Twain derided the miners' lingo of Bret Harte, and for the same reason. The thing lies deeper than vocabulary and even than pronunciation and intonation; the divergences show themselves in habits of speech that are fundamental and almost indefinable. And when the transoceanic gesture is from the other direction they become even plainer. An Englishman, in an American play, seldom shows the actual speech habit of the Sassenach; what he shows is the speech habit of an American actor trying to imitate George Alexander. "There are not five playwrights in America, " said Channing Pollock one day, "who can write English"—that is, the English of familiar discourse. "Why should there be?" replied Louis Sherwin. "There are not five thousand people in America who can *speak* English."[12]

The elements that enter into the special character of American have been rehearsed in the first chapter: a general impatience of rule and restraint, a democratic enmity to all authority, an extravagant and often grotesque humor, an extraordinary capacity for metaphor[13]— in brief, all the natural marks of what Van Wyck Brooks calls "a popular life which bubbles with energy and spreads and grows and slips away ever more and more from the control of tested ideas, a popular life with the lid off."[14] This is the spirit of America, and from it the American language is nourished. Brooks, perhaps, generalizes a bit too lavishly. Below the surface there is also a curious conservatism, even a sort of timorousness; in a land of manumitted peasants the primary trait of the peasant is bound to show itself now and then; as Wendell Phillips once said, "more than any other people, we Americans are afraid of one another"—that is, afraid of opposition, of derision, of all the consequences of singularity. But in the field of language, as in that of politics, this suspicion of the new is often transformed into a suspicion of the merely unfamiliar, and so its natural tendency toward conservatism is overcome. It is of the essence of democracy that it remain a government by amateurs, and under a government by amateurs it is precisely the expert who is most questioned—and it is the expert who commonly stresses the experience of the past. And in a democratic society it is not the iconoclast who seems most revolutionary, but the purist. The derisive designation of *high-brow* is thoroughly American in more ways than one. It is a word put together in an unmistakably American fashion, it reflects an habitual American attitude of mind, and its potency in debate is peculiarly national too.

I daresay it is largely a fear of the weapon in it—and there are many others of like effect in the arsenal—which accounts for the far greater prevalence of idioms from below in the formal speech of America than in the formal speech of England. There is surely no English novelist of equal rank whose prose shows so much of colloquial looseness and ease as one finds in the prose of Howells: to find a match for it one must go to the prose of the neo-Celts, professedly modelled upon the speech of peasants, and almost proudly defiant of English grammar and syntax, and to the prose of the English themselves before the Restoration. Nor is it imaginable that an Englishman of comparable education and position would ever employ such locutions as those I have hitherto quoted from the public addresses of Dr. Wilson—that is, innocently, seriously, as a matter of course. The Englishman, when he makes use of coinages of that sort, does so in conscious relaxation, and usually with a somewhat heavy sense of doggishness. They are proper to the paddock or even to the dinner table, but scarcely to serious scenes and occasions. But in the United States their use is the rule rather than the exception; it is not the man who uses them, but the man who doesn't use them, who is marked off. Their employment, if high example counts for anything, is a standard habit of the language, as their diligent avoidance is a standard habit of English.

A glance through the *Congressional Record* is sufficient to show how small is the minority of purists among the chosen leaders of the nation. Within half an hour, turning the pages at random, I find scores of locutions that would paralyze the stenographers in the House of Commons, and they are in the speeches, not of wild mavericks from the West, but of some of the chief men of the two Houses. Surely no Senator occupied a more conspicuous position, during the first year of the war, than Lee S. Overman, of North Carolina, chairman of the Committee on Rules, and commander of the administration forces on the floor. Well, I find Senator Overman using *to enthuse* in a speech of the utmost seriousness and importance, and not once, but over and over again.[15] I turn back a few pages and encounter it again—this time in the mouth of General Sherwood, of Ohio. A few more, and I find a fit match for it, to wit, *to biograph.*[16] The speaker here is Senator L. Y. Sherman, of Illinois. In the same speech he uses *to resolute.* A few more, and various other characteristic verbs are unearthed: *to demagogue,* [17] *to dope out*[18] *to fall down*[19](in the sense of to fail), *to jack up,* [20] *to phone,* [21] *to peeve,* [22] *to come across,* [23] *to hike, to butt in,* [24] *to back pedal, to get solid with, to hooverize, to trustify, to feature, to insurge, to haze, to reminisce, to camouflage, to play for a sucker,* and so on, almost *ad infinitum.* And with them, a large number of highly American nouns, chiefly compounds, all pressing upward for recognition: *tin-Lizzie, brain-storm, come-down, pin-head, trustification, pork-barrel, buck-private, dough-boy, cow-country.* And adjectives: *jitney, bush* (for rural), *balled-up,* [25] *dolled-up, phoney, tax-paid.*[26] And phrases: *dollars to doughnuts, on the job, that gets me, one best bet.* And back-formations: *ad, movie, photo.* And various substitutions and Americanized inflections: *over*for *more than, gotten* for *got* in the present perfect, [27] *rile* for *roil, bust* for *burst.* This last, in truth, has come into a dignity that even grammarians will soon hesitate to question. Who, in America, would dare to speak of *bursting* a broncho, or of a *trust-burster?*[28]

§ 3. Lost Distinctions

—This general iconoclasm reveals itself especially in a disdain for most of the niceties of modern English. The American, like the Elizabethan Englishman, is usually quite unconscious of them and even when they have been instilled into him by the hard labor of pedagogues he commonly pays little heed to them in his ordinary discourse. The English distinction between *will* and *shall* offers a salient case in point. This distinction, it may be said at once, is far more a confection of the grammarians than a product of the natural forces shaping the language. It has, indeed, little etymological basis, and is but imperfectly justified logically. One finds it disregarded in the

Authorized Version of the Bible, in all the plays of Shakespeare, in the essays of the reign of Anne, and in some of the best examples of modern English literature. The theory behind it is so inordinately abstruse that the Fowlers, in "The King's English, "[29] require 20 pages to explain it, and even then they come to the resigned conclusion that the task is hopeless. "The idiomatic use [of the two auxiliaries], " they say, "is so complicated that those who are not to the manner born can hardly acquire it."[30] Well, even those who are to the manner born seem to find it difficult, for at once the learned authors cite blunder in the writings of Richardson, Stevenson, Gladstone, Jowett, Oscar Wilde, and even Henry Sweet, author of the best existing grammar of the English language. In American the distinction is almost lost. No ordinary American, save after the most laborious reflection, would detect anything wrong in this sentence from the *London Times*, denounced as corrupt by the Fowlers: "We must reconcile what we would like to do with what we can do." Nor in this by W. B. Yeats: "The character who delights us may commit murder like Macbeth ... and yet we will rejoice in every happiness that comes to him." Half a century ago, impatient of the effort to fasten the English distinction upon American, George P. Marsh attacked it as of "no logical value or significance whatever, " and predicted that "at no very distant day this verbal quibble will disappear, and one of the auxiliaries will be employed, with all persons of the nominative, exclusively as the sign of the future, and the other only as an expression of purpose or authority."[31] This prophecy has been substantially verified. *Will* is sound American "with all persons of the nominative, " and *shall* is almost invariably an "expression of purpose or authority."[32]

And so, though perhaps not to the same extent, with *who* and *whom*. Now and then there arises a sort of panicky feeling that *whom* is being neglected, and so it is trotted out, [33] but in the main the American language tends to dispense with it, at least in its least graceful situations. Noah Webster, always the pragmatic reformer, denounced it so long ago as 1783. Common sense, he argued, was on the side of "*who* did he marry?" Today such a form as "*whom* are you talking to?" would seem somewhat affected in ordinary discourse in America; "*who* are you talking to?" is heard a thousand times oftener—and is doubly American, for it substitutes *who* for *whom* and puts a preposition at the end of a sentence: two crimes that most English purists would seek to avoid. It is among the pronouns that the only remaining case inflections in English are to be found, if we forget the possessive, and even here these survivors of an earlier day begin to grow insecure. Lounsbury's defense of "it is *me,* "[34] as we shall see in the next chapter, has support in the history and natural movement of the language, and that movement is also against the preservation of the distinction between *who* and *whom.* The common speech plays hob with both of the orthodox inflections, despite the protests of grammarians, and in the long run, no doubt, they will be forced to yield to its pressure, as they have always yielded in the past. Between the dative and accusative on the one side and the nominative on the other there has been war in the English language for centuries, and it has always tended to become a war of extermination. Our now universal use of *you* for *ye* in the nominative shows the dative and accusative swallowing the nominative, and the practical disappearance of *hither, thither* and *whither,* whose place is now taken by *here, there* and *where,* shows a contrary process. In such wars a *posse comitatus* marches ahead of the disciplined army. American stands to English in the relation of that posse to that army. It is incomparably more enterprising, more contemptuous of precedent and authority, more impatient of rule.

A shadowy line often separates what is currently coming into sound usage from what is still regarded as barbarous. No self-respecting American, I daresay, would defend *ain't* as a substitute for *isn't,* say in "he *ain't* the man, " and yet *ain't* is already tolerably respectable in the first person, where English countenances the even more clumsy *aren't. Aren't* has never got a foothold in the American first person; when it is used at all, which is very rarely, it is always as a conscious Briticism. Facing the alternative of employing the unwieldy "am I not in this?" the American turns boldly to "*ain't* I in this?" It still grates a bit, perhaps, but *aren't* grates even more. Here, as always, the popular speech is pulling the exacter speech along, and no one familiar with its successes in the past can have much doubt that it will succeed again, soon or late. In the same way it is breaking down the inflectional distinction between adverb and adjective, so that "I feel *bad*" begins to take on the dignity of a national idiom, and *sure, to go big* and *run slow*[35] become almost respectable. When, on the entrance of the United States into the war, the Marine Corps chose "treat 'em *rough*" as its motto, no one thought to raise a grammatical objection, and the clipped adverb was printed upon hundreds of thousands of posters and displayed in every town in the country, always with the imprimatur of the national government. So, again, American, in its spoken form, tends to obliterate the distinction between nearly related adjectives, *e. g.*, *healthful* and *healthy*, *tasteful* and *tasty*. And to challenge the somewhat absurd text-book prohibition of terminal prepositions, so that "where are we *at*?" loses its old raciness. And to dally with the double negative, as in "I have no doubt *but* that."[36]

But these tendencies, or at least the more extravagant of them, belong to the next chapter. How much influence they exert, even indirectly, is shown by the American disdain of the English precision in the use of the indefinite pronoun. I turn to the *Saturday Evening Post*, and in two minutes find: "*one* feels like an atom when *he* begins to review *his* own life and deeds."[37] The error is very rare in English; the Fowlers, seeking examples of it, could get them only from the writings of a third-rate woman novelist, Scotch to boot. But it is so common in American that it scarcely attracts notice. Neither does the appearance of a redundant *s* in such words as *towards*, *downwards*, *afterwards* and *heavenwards*. In England this *s* is used relatively seldom, and then it usually marks a distinction in meaning, as it does on both sides of the ocean between *beside* and *besides*. "In modern standard English, " says Smith, [38] "though not in the English of the United States, a distinction which we feel, but many of us could not define, is made between *forward* and *forwards*; *forwards* being used in definite contrast to any other direction, as 'if you move at all, you can only move *forwards*, ' while *forward* is used where no such contrast is implied, as in the common phrase 'to bring a matter forward.'"[39] This specific distinction, despite Smith, probably retains some force in the United States too, but in general our usage allows the *s* in cases where English usage would certainly be against it. Gould, in the 50's, noted its appearance at the end of such words as *somewhere* and *anyway*, and denounced it as vulgar and illogical. Thornton has traced *anyways* back to 1842 and shown that it is an archaism, and to be found in the Book of Common Prayer (*circa* 1560); perhaps it has been preserved by analogy with *sideways*. Henry James, in "The Question of Our Speech, " attacked "such forms of impunity as *somewheres else* and *nowheres else*, *a good ways on* and *a good ways off*" as "vulgarisms with what a great deal of general credit for what we good-naturedly call 'refinement' appears so able to coexist."[40] *Towards* and *afterwards*, though frowned upon in

England, are now quite sound in American. I find the former in the title of an article in *Dialect Notes*, which plainly gives it scholastic authority.[41] More (and with no little humor), I find it in the deed of a fund given to the American Academy of Arts and Letters to enable the gifted philologs of that sanhedrin "to consider its duty *towards* the conservation of the English language in its beauty and purity."[42] Both *towards* and *afterwards*, finally, are included in the *New York Evening Post's* list of "words no longer disapproved when in their proper places, " along with *over* for *more than*, and *during* for *in the course of*.

In the last chapter we glanced at several salient differences between the common coin of English and the common coin of American—that is, the verbs and adjectives in constant colloquial use—the rubber-stamps, so to speak, of the two languages. America has two adverbs that belong to the same category. They are *right* and *good*. Neither holds the same place in English. Thornton shows that the use of *right*, as in *right away, right good* and *right now*, was already widespread in the United States early in the last century; his first example is dated 1818. He believes that the locution was "possibly imported from the southwest of Ireland." Whatever its origin, it quickly attracted the attention of English visitors. Dickens noted *right away* as an almost universal Americanism during his first American tour, in 1842, and poked fun at it in the second chapter of "American Notes." *Right* is used as a synonym for *directly*, as in *right away, right off, right now* and *right on time*; for *moderately*, as in *right well, right smart, right good* and *right often*, and in place of *precisely*, as in *right there*. Some time ago, in an article on Americanisms, an English critic called it "that most distinctively American word, " and concocted the following dialogue to instruct the English in its use:

How do I get to——?

Go *right* along, and take the first turning (*sic*) on the *right*, and you are *right* there.

Right?

Right.

Right! [43]

Like W. L. George, this Englishman failed in his attempt to write correct American despite his fine pedagogical passion. No American would ever say "take the first turning"; he would say "turn at the first corner." As for *right away*, R. O. Williams argues that "so far as analogy can make good English, it is as good as one could choose."[44] Nevertheless, the Oxford Dictionary admits it only as an Americanism, and avoids all mention of the other American uses of *right* as an adverb. *Good* is almost as protean. It is not only used as a general synonym for all adjectives and adverbs connoting satisfaction, as in *to feel good, to be treated good, to sleep good*, but also as a reinforcement to other adjectives and adverbs, as in "I hit him *good* and hard" and "I am *good* and tired." Of late *some* has come into wide use as an adjective-adverb of all work, indicating special excellence or high degree, as in *some girl, some sick, going some*, etc. It is still below the salt, but threatens to reach a more respectable position. One encounters it in the newspapers constantly and in the *Congressional Record*, and not long ago a writer in the *Atlantic Monthly*[45] hymned it ecstatically as "*some* word—a true super-word, in fact" and argued that it could be used "in a sense for which there is absolutely no synonym in the dictionary." Basically, it appears to be an adjective, but in many of its common situations the grammarians would probably call it an adverb. It gives no little support to the growing tendency, already noticed, to break down the barrier between the two parts of speech.

§ 4. Foreign Influences Today

—No other great nation of today supports so large a foreign population as the United States, either relatively or absolutely; none other contains so many foreigners forced to an effort, often ignorant and ineffective, to master the national language. Since 1820 nearly 35, 000, 000 immigrants have come into the country, and of them probably not 10, 000, 000 brought any preliminary acquaintance with English with them. The census of 1910 showed that nearly 1, 500, 000 persons then living permanently on American soil could not speak it at all; that more than 13, 000, 000 had been born in other countries, chiefly of different language; and that nearly 20, 000, 000 were the children of such immigrants, and hence under the influence of their speech habits. Altogether, there were probably at least 25, 000, 000 whose house language was not the vulgate, and who thus spoke it in competition with some other language. No other country houses so many aliens. In Great Britain the alien population, for a century past, has never been more than 2 per cent of the total population, and since the passage of the Alien Act of 1905 it has tended to decline steadily. In

Germany, in 1910, there were but 1, 259, 873 aliens in a population of more than 60, 000, 000, and of these nearly a half were German-speaking Austrians and Swiss. In France, in 1906, there were 1, 000, 000 foreigners in a population of 39, 000, 000 and a third of them were French-speaking Belgians, Luxembourgeois and Swiss. In Italy, in 1911, there were but 350, 000 in a population of 35, 000, 000.

This large and constantly reinforced admixture of foreigners has naturally exerted a constant pressure upon the national language, for the majority of them, at least in the first generation, have found it quite impossible to acquire it in any purity, and even their children have grown up with speech habits differing radically from those of correct English. The effects of this pressure are obviously two-fold; on the one hand the foreigner, struggling with a strange and difficult tongue, makes efforts to simplify it as much as possible, and so strengthens the native tendency to disregard all niceties and complexities, and on the other hand he corrupts it with words and locutions from the language he has brought with him, and sometimes with whole idioms and grammatical forms. We have seen, in earlier chapters, how the Dutch and French of colonial days enriched the vocabulary of the colonists, how the German immigrants of the first half of the nineteenth century enriched it still further, and how the Irish of the same period influenced its everyday usages. The same process is still going on. The Italians, the Slavs, and, above all, the Russian Jews, make steady contributions to the American vocabulary and idiom, and though these contributions are often concealed by quick and complete naturalization their foreignness to English remains none the less obvious. *I should worry*, [46] in its way, is correct English, but in essence it is as completely Yiddish as *kosher, ganof, schadchen, oi-yoi, matzoh* or *mazuma*.[47] *Black-hand*, too, is English in form, but it is nevertheless as plainly an Italian loan-word as *spaghetti, mafia* or *padrone*.

The extent of such influences upon American, and particularly upon spoken American, remains to be studied; in the whole literature I can find but one formal article upon the subject. That article[48]deals specifically with the suffix *-fest*, which came into American from the German and was probably suggested by familiarity with *sängerfest*. There is no mention of it in any of the dictionaries of Americanisms, and yet, in such forms as *talk-fest* and *gabfest* it is met with almost daily. So with *-heimer, -inski* and *-bund*. Several years ago *-heimer* had a great vogue in slang, and was rapidly done to death. But *wiseheimer* remains in colloquial use as a facetious synonym for *smart-aleck*, and after awhile it may gradually acquire dignity. Far lowlier words, in fact, have worked their way in. *Buttinski*, perhaps, is going the same route. As for the words in *-bund*, many of them are already almost accepted. *Plunder-bund* is now at least as good as *pork-barrel* and *slush-fund*, and *money-bund* is frequently heard in Congress.[49] Such locutions creep in stealthily, and are secure before they are suspected. Current slang, out of which the more decorous language dredges a large part of its raw materials, is full of them. *Nix* and *nixy*, for *no*, are debased forms of the German *nichts*; *aber nit*, once as popular as *camouflage*, is obviously *aber nicht*. And a steady flow of nouns, all needed to designate objects introduced by immigrants, enriches the vocabulary. The Hungarians not only brought their national condiment with them; they also brought its name, *paprika*, and that name is now thoroughly American.[50] In the same way the Italians brought in *camorra, padrone, spaghetti* and a score of other substantives, and the Jews made contributions from Yiddish and Hebrew and greatly reinforced certain old borrowings from German. Once such a loan-word gets in it takes firm root. During the first year of American participation in the World War an effort was made, on patriotic grounds, to substitute *liberty-cabbage* for *sour-kraut*, but it quickly failed, for the name had become as completely Americanized as the thing itself, and so *liberty-cabbage* seemed affected and absurd. In the same way a great many other German words survived the passions of the time. Nor could all the influence of the professional patriots obliterate that German influence which has fastened upon the American *yes* something of the quality of *ja*.

Constant familiarity with such contributions from foreign languages and with the general speech habits of foreign peoples has made American a good deal more hospitable to loan-words than English, even in the absence of special pressure. Let the same word knock at the gates of the two languages, and American will admit it more readily, and give it at once a wider and more intimate currency. Examples are afforded by *café, vaudeville, employé, boulevard, cabaret, toilette, exposé, kindergarten, dépôt, fête* and *menu*. *Café*, in American, is a word of much larger and more varied meaning than in English and is used much more frequently, and by many more persons. So is *employé*, in the naturalized form of *employee*. So is *toilet*: we have even seen it as a euphemism for native terms that otherwise would be in daily use. So is *kindergarten*: I read lately of a *kindergarten* for the elementary instruction of conscripts. Such words are not unknown to the Englishman, but when he uses them it is with a plain sense of their foreignness. In American they are completely naturalized, as is shown by the spelling and pronunciation of most of them. An American would no more think of attempting the French pronunciation of *depot* or of putting the French accents upon it than he would think of spelling *toilet* with the final *te* or of essaying to pronounce *Anheuser* in the German manner. Often curious battles go on between such loan-words and their English equivalents, and with varying fortunes. In 1895 Weber and Fields tried to establish *music-hall* in New York, but it quickly succumbed to *vaudeville-theatre*, as *variety* had succumbed to *vaudeville* before it. In the same way *lawn-fete* (without the circumflex accent, and commonly pronounced *feet*) has elbowed out the English *garden-party*. But now and then, when the competing loan-word happens to violate American speech habits, a native term ousts it. The French *crèche* offers an example; it has been entirely displaced by *day-nursery*.

The English, in this matter, display their greater conservatism very plainly. Even when a loan-word enters both English and American simultaneously a sense of foreignness lingers about it on the other side of the Atlantic much longer than on this side, and it is used with far more self-consciousness. The word *matinée* offers a convenient example. To this day the English commonly print it in italics, give it its French accent, and pronounce it with some attempt at the French manner. But in America it is entirely naturalized, and the most ignorant man uses it without any feeling that it is strange. The same lack of any sense of linguistic integrity is to be noticed in many other directions—for example, in the freedom with which the Latin *per* is used with native nouns. One constantly sees *per day*, *per dozen*, *per hundred*, *per mile*, etc., in American newspapers, even the most careful, but in England the more seemly *a* is almost always used, or the noun itself is made Latin, as in *per diem*. *Per*, in fact, is fast becoming an everyday American word. Such phrases as "as *per* your letter (or order) of the 15th inst." are incessantly met with in business correspondence. The same greater hospitality is shown by the readiness with which various un-English prefixes and affixes come into fashion, for example, *super-* and *-itis*. The English accept them gingerly; the Americans take them in with enthusiasm, and naturalize them instanter.[51]

The same deficiency in reserve is to be noted in nearly all other colonialized dialects. The Latin-American variants of Spanish, for example, have adopted a great many words which appear in true Castilian only as occasional guests. Thus in Argentina *matinée, menu, début, toilette* and *femme de chambre* are perfectly good Argentine, and in Mexico *sandwich* and *club* have been thoroughly naturalized. The same thing is to be noted in the French of Haiti, in the Portuguese of Brazil, and even in the Danish of Norway. Once a language spreads beyond the country of its origin and begins to be used by people born, in the German phrase, to a different *Sprachgefühl,* the sense of loyalty to its vocabulary is lost, along with the instinctive feeling for its idiomatic habits. How far this destruction of its forms may go in the absence of strong contrary influences is exhibited by the rise of the Romance languages from the vulgar Latin of the Roman provinces, and, here at home, by the decay of foreign languages in competition with English. The Yiddish that the Jews from Russia bring in is German debased with Russian, Polish and Hebrew; in America, it quickly absorbs hundreds of words and idioms from the speech of the streets. Various conflicting German dialects, among the so-called Pennsylvania Dutch and in the German areas of the Northwest, combine in a patois that, in its end forms, shows almost as much English as German. Classical examples of it are "es giebt gar kein *use,* " "Ich kann es nicht *ständen*" and "mein *stallion* hat über die *fenz gescheumpt* und dem nachbar sein *whiet* abscheulich *gedämätscht.*"[52] The use of *gleiche* for *to like*, by false analogy from *gleich* (=*like, similar*) is characteristic. In the same way the Scandinavians in the Northwest corrupt their native Swedish and Dano-Norwegian. Thus, American-Norwegian is heavy with such forms as *strit-kar, reit-evé, nekk-töi* and *staits-pruessen*, for *street-car, right away, necktie* and *states-prison*, and admits such phrases as "det *meka* ingen *difrens.*"[53]

The changes that Yiddish has undergone in America, though rather foreign to the present inquiry, are interesting enough to be noticed. First of all, it has admitted into its vocabulary a large number of everyday substantives, among them *boy, chair, window, carpet, floor, dress, hat, watch, ceiling, consumption, property, trouble, bother, match, change, party, birthday, picture, paper*(only in the sense of *newspaper*), *gambler, show, hall, kitchen, store, bedroom, key, mantelpiece, closet, lounge, broom, tablecloth, paint, landlord, fellow, tenant, shop, wages, foreman, sleeve, collar, cuff, button, cotton, thimble, needle, pocket, bargain, sale, remnant, sample, haircut, razor, waist, basket, school, scholar, teacher, baby, mustache, butcher, grocery, dinner, street* and *walk*. And with them many characteristic Americanisms, for example, *bluffer, faker, boodler, grafter, gangster, crook, guy, kike, piker, squealer, bum, cadet, boom, bunch, pants, vest, loafer, jumper, stoop, saleslady, ice-box* and *raise*, with their attendant verbs and adjectives. These words are used constantly; many of them have quite crowded out the corresponding Yiddish words. For example, *ingel*, meaning *boy* (it is a Slavic loan-word in Yiddish), has been obliterated by the English word. A Jewish immigrant almost invariably refers to his son as his *boy*, though strangely enough he calls his daughter his *meidel*. "Die *boys* mit die *meidlach* haben a good time" is excellent American Yiddish. In the same way *fenster* has been completely displaced by *window*, though *tür* (=*door*) has been left intact. *Tisch* (=*table*) also remains, but *chair* is always used, probably because few of the Jews had chairs in the old country. There the *beinkel*, a bench without a back, was in use; chairs were only for the well-to-do. *Floor*has apparently prevailed because no invariable corresponding word was employed at home: in various parts of Russia and Poland a floor is a *dill*, a *podlogé*, or a *bricke*. So with *ceiling*. There were six different words for it.

Yiddish inflections have been fastened upon most of these loan-words. Thus, "er hat ihm *abgefaked*" is "he cheated him, " *zubumt* is the American *gone to the bad, fix'n* is to *fix, usen* is *to use*, and so on. The feminine and diminutive suffix -*ké* is often added to nouns. Thus *bluffer* gives rise to *blufferké* (=*hypocrite*), and one also notes *dresské, hatké, watchké* and *bummerké*. "Oi! is sie a *blufferké*!" is good American Yiddish for "isn't she a hypocrite!" The suffix -*nick*, signifying agency, is also freely applied. *Allrightnick* means an upstart, an offensive boaster, one of whom his fellows would say "He is all right" with a sneer. Similarly, *consumptionick* means a victim of tuberculosis. Other suffixes are *-chick* and *-ige*, the first exemplified in *boychick*, a diminutive of *boy*, and the second in *next-doorige*, meaning the woman next-door, an important person in ghetto social life. Some of the loan-words, of course, undergo changes on Yiddish-speaking lips. Thus, *landlord* becomes *lendler, lounge* becomes *lunch, tenant* becomes *tenner*, and *whiskers* loses its final *s*. "Wie gefällt dir sein *whisker*?" (=how do you like his beard?) is good Yiddish, ironically intended. *Fellow*, of course, changes to the American *feller*, as in "Rosie hat schon a *feller*" (=Rosie has got a *feller, i. e.*, a sweetheart). *Show*, in the sense of *chance*, is used constantly, as in "git ihm a *show*" (=give him a chance). *Bad boy* is adopted bodily, as in "er is a *bad boy*." To *shut up* is inflected as one word, as in "er hat nit gewolt *shutup'n*" (=he wouldn't shut up). *To catch* is used in the sense of to obtain, as in "*catch'n* a gmilath chesed" (=to raise a loan). Here, by the way, *gmilath chesed* is excellent Biblical Hebrew. *To bluff*, unchanged in form, takes on the new meaning of to lie: a *bluffer* is a liar. Scores of American phrases are in constant use, among them, *all right, never mind, I bet you, no sir* and *I'll fix you*. It is curious to note that *sure Mike*, borrowed by the American vulgate from Irish English, has gone over into American Yiddish. Finally, to make an end, here are two complete and characteristic American Yiddish sentences: "Sie wet *clean'n* die *rooms, scrub'n* dem *floor, wash'n* die *windows, dress'n* dem *boy* und gehn in *butcher-store* und in *grocery*. Dernoch vet sie machen *dinner* und gehn in *street* für a *walk*."[54]

American itself, in the Philippines, and to a lesser extent in Puerto Rico and on the Isthmus, has undergone similar changes under the influence of Spanish and the native dialects. Maurice P. Dunlap[55] offers the following specimen of a conversation between two Americans long resident in Manila:

Hola, amigo.

Komusta kayo.

Porque were you hablaing with ese señorita?

She wanted a job as lavandera.

Cuanto?

Ten cents, conant, a piece, so I told her no kerry.

Have you had chow? Well, spera till I sign this chit and I'll take a paseo with you.

Here we have an example of Philippine American that shows all the tendencies of American Yiddish. It retains the general forms of American, but in the short conversation, embracing but 41 different words, there are eight loan-words from the Spanish (*hola, amigo, porque, ese, señorita, lavandera, cuanto* and *paseo*), two Spanish locutions in a debased form (*spera* for *espera* and *no kerry* for *no quiro*), two loan-words from the Taglog (*komusta* and *kayo*), two from Pigeon English (*chow* and *chit*), one Philippine-American localism (*conant*), and a Spanish verb with an English inflection (*hablaing*).

The immigrant in the midst of a large native population, of course, exerts no such pressure upon the national language as that exerted upon an immigrant language by the native, but nevertheless his linguistic habits and limitations have to be reckoned with in dealing with him, and the concessions thus made necessary have a very ponderable influence upon the general speech. In the usual sense, as we have seen, there are no dialects in American; two natives, however widely their birthplaces may be separated, never have any practical difficulty understanding each other. But there are at least quasi-dialects among the immigrants—the Irish, the German, the Scandinavian, the Italian, the Jewish, and so on—and these quasi-dialects undoubtedly leave occasional marks, not only upon the national vocabulary, but also upon the general speech habits of the country, as in the case, for example, of the pronunciation of *yes*, already mentioned, and in that of the substitution of the diphthong *oi* for the *ur*-sound in such words as *world*, *journal* and *burn*—a Yiddishism now almost universal among the lower classes of New York, and threatening to spread.[56] More important, however, is the support given to a native tendency by the foreigner's incapacity for employing (or even comprehending) syntax of any complexity, or words not of the simplest. This is the tendency toward succinctness and clarity, at whatever sacrifice of grace. One English observer, Sidney Low, puts the chief blame for the general explosiveness of American upon the immigrant, who must be communicated with in the plainest words available, and is not socially worthy of the suavity of circumlocution anyhow.[57] In his turn the immigrant seizes upon these plainest words as upon a sort of convenient Lingua Franca—his quick adoption of *damn* as a universal adjective is traditional—and throws his influence upon the side of the underlying speech habit when he gets on in the vulgate. Many characteristic Americanisms of the sort to stagger lexicographers—for example, *near-silk*—have come from the Jews, whose progress in business is a good deal faster than their progress in English. Others, as we have seen, have come from the German immigrants of half a century ago, from the so-called Pennsylvania Dutch (who are notoriously ignorant and uncouth), and from the Irish, who brought with them a form of English already very corrupt. The same and similar elements greatly reinforce the congenital tendencies of the dialect—toward the facile manufacture of compounds, toward a disregard of the distinctions between parts of speech, and, above all, toward the throwing off of all etymological restraints.

§ 5. Processes of Word Formation

—Some of these tendencies, it has been pointed out, go back to the period of the first growth of American, and were inherited from the English of the time. They are the products of a movement which, reaching its height in the English of Elizabeth, was dammed up at home, so to speak, by the rise of linguistic self-consciousness toward the end of the reign of Anne, but continued almost unobstructed in the colonies. For example, there is what philologists call the habit of back-formation—a sort of instinctive search, etymologically unsound, for short roots in long words. This habit, in Restoration days, precipitated a quasi-English word, *mobile*, from the Latin *mobile vulgus*, and in the days of William and Mary it went a step further by precipitating *mob* from *mobile*. *Mob* is now sound English, but in the eighteenth century it was violently attacked by the new sect of purists, [58] and though it survived their onslaught they undoubtedly greatly impeded the formation and adoption of other words of the same category. But in the colonies the process went on unimpeded, save for the feeble protests of such stray pedants as Witherspoon and Boucher. *Rattler* for *rattlesnake, pike* for *turnpike, draw* for *drawbridge, coon* for *raccoon, possum* for *opossum, cuss* for *customer, cute* for *acute, squash* for *askutasquash*—these American back-formations are already antique; *Sabbaday* for *Sabbath-day* has actually reached the dignity of an archaism. To this day they are formed in great numbers; scarcely a new substantive of more than two syllables comes in without bringing one in its wake. We have thus witnessed, within the past two years, the genesis of scores now in wide use and fast taking on respectability; *phone* for *telephone, gas* for *gasoline, co-ed* for *co-educational, pop* for *populist, frat* for *fraternity, gym* for *gymnasium, movie* for *moving-picture, prep-school* for *preparatory-school, auto* for *automobile, aero* for *aeroplane.* Some linger on the edge of vulgarity: *pep* for *pepper, flu* for *influenza, plute* for *plutocrat, pen* for *penitentiary, con* for *confidence* (as in *con-man, con-game* and *to con*), *convict* and *consumption, defi* for *defiance, beaut* for *beauty, rep* for *reputation, stenog* for *stenographer, ambish* for *ambition, vag* for *vagrant, champ* for *champion, pard* for *partner, coke* for *cocaine, simp* for *simpleton, diff* for *difference.* Others are already in perfectly good usage: *smoker* for *smoking-car, diner* for *dining-car, sleeper* for *sleeping-car, oleo* for *oleomargarine, hypo* for *hyposulphite of soda, Yank* for *Yankee, confab* for *confabulation, memo* for *memorandum, pop-concert* for *popular-concert. Ad* for *advertisement* is struggling hard for recognition; some of its compounds, *e. g., ad-writer, want-ad, display-ad, ad-card, ad-rate, column-ad* and *ad-man,* are already accepted in technical terminology. *Boob* for *booby* promises to become sound American in a few years; its synonyms are no more respectable than it is. At its heels is *bo* for *hobo,* an altogether fit successor to *bum* for *bummer.*[59]

A parallel movement shows itself in the great multiplication of common abbreviations. "Americans, as a rule, " says Farmer, "employ abbreviations to an extent unknown in Europe.... This trait of the American character is discernible in every department of the national life and thought."[60] *O. K., C. O. D., N. G., G. O. P.* (get out and push) and *P. D. Q.,* are almost national hall-marks; the immigrant learns them immediately after *damn* and *go to hell.* Thornton traces *N. G.* to 1840; *C. O. D.* and *P. D. Q.* are probably as old. As for *O. K.,* it was in use so early as 1790, but it apparently did not acquire its present significance until the 20's; originally it seems to have meant "ordered recorded."[11] During the presidential campaign of 1828 Jackson's enemies, seeking to prove his illiteracy, alleged that he used it for "oll korrect." Of late the theory has been put forward that it is derived from an Indian word, *okeh*, signifying "so be it, " and Dr. Woodrow Wilson is said to support this theory and to use *okeh* in endorsing government papers, but I am unaware of the authority upon which the etymology is based. Bartlett says that the figurative use of *A No. 1*, as in *an A No. 1 man*, also originated in America, but this may not be true. There can be little doubt, however, about *T. B.* (for *tuberculosis*), *G. B.* (for *grand bounce*), *23, on the Q. T.*, and *D. & D.* (*drunk and disorderly*). The language breeds such short forms of speech prodigiously; every trade and profession has a host of them; they are innumerable in the slang of sport.[61]

What one sees under all this, account for it as one will, is a double habit, the which is, at bottom, sufficient explanation of the gap which begins to yawn between English and American, particularly on the spoken plane. On the one hand it is a habit of verbal economy—a jealous disinclination to waste two words on what can be put into one, a natural taste for the brilliant and succinct, a disdain of all grammatical and lexicographical daintiness, born partly, perhaps, of ignorance, but also in part of a sound sense of their imbecility. And on the other hand there is a high relish and talent for metaphor—in Brander Matthews' phrase, "a figurative vigor that the Elizabethans would have realized and understood." Just as the American rebels instinctively against such parliamentary circumlocutions as "I am not prepared to say" and "so much by way of being, "[62] just as he would fret under the forms of English journalism, with its reporting empty of drama, its third-person smothering of speeches and its complex and unintelligible jargon, [63] just so, in his daily speech and writing he chooses terseness and vividness whenever there is any choice, and seeks to make one when it doesn't exist. There is more than mere humorous contrast between the famous placard in the wash-room of the British Museum: "These Basins Are For Casual Ablutions Only, " and the familiar sign at American railroad-crossings: "Stop! Look! Listen!" Between the two lies an abyss separating two cultures, two habits of mind, two diverging tongues. It is almost unimaginable that Englishmen, journeying up and down in elevators, would ever have stricken the teens out of their speech, turning *sixteenth* into simple *six* and *twenty-fourth* into *four*; the clipping is almost as far from their way of doing things as the climbing so high in the air. Nor have they the brilliant facility of Americans for making new words of grotesque but penetrating tropes, as in *corn-fed*, *tight-wad*, *bone-head*, *bleachers* and *juice* (for *electricity*); when they attempt such things the result is often lugubrious; two hundred years of schoolmastering has dried up their inspiration. Nor have they the fine American hand for devising new verbs; *to maffick* and *to limehouse* are their best specimens in twenty years, and both have an almost pathetic flatness. Their business with the language, indeed, is not in this department. They are not charged with its raids and scoutings, but with the organization of its conquests and the guarding of its accumulated stores.

For the student interested in the biology of language, as opposed to its paleontology, there is endless material in the racy neologisms of American, and particularly in its new compounds and novel verbs. Nothing could exceed the brilliancy of such inventions as *joy-ride*, *high-brow*, *road-louse*, *sob-sister*, *nature-faker*, *stand-patter*, *lounge-lizard*, *hash-foundry*, *buzz-wagon*, *has-been*, *end-seat-hog*, *shoot-the-chutes* and *grape-juice-diplomacy*. They are bold; they are vivid; they have humor; they meet genuine needs. *Joy-ride*, I note, is already going over into English, and no wonder. There is absolutely no synonym for it; to convey its idea in orthodox English would take a whole sentence. And so, too, with certain single words of metaphorical origin: *barrel* for large and illicit wealth, *pork* for unnecessary and dishonest appropriations of public money, *joint* for illegal liquor-house, *tenderloin* for gay and dubious neighborhood.[64] Most of these, and of the new compounds with them, belong to the vocabulary of disparagement. Here an essential character of the American shows itself: his tendency to combat the disagreeable with irony, to heap ridicule upon what he is suspicious of or doesn't understand.

The rapidity with which new verbs are made in the United States is really quite amazing. Two days after the first regulations of the Food Administration were announced, *to hooverize* appeared spontaneously in scores of newspapers, and a week later it was employed without any visible sense of its novelty in the debates of Congress and had taken on a respectability equal to that of *to bryanize*, *to fletcherize* and *to oslerize*. *To electrocute* appeared inevitably in the first public discussion of capital punishment by electricity; *to taxi* came in with the first taxi-cabs; *to commute* no doubt accompanied the first commutation ticket; *to insurge* attended the birth of the Progressive balderdash. Of late the old affix *-ize*, once fecund of such monsters as *to funeralize*, has come into favor again, and I note, among its other products, *to belgiumize, to vacationize, to picturize* and *to scenarioize*. In a newspaper headline I even find *to s o s*, in the form of its gerund.[65] Many characteristic American verbs are compounds of common verbs and prepositions or adverbs, with new meanings imposed. Compare, for example, *to give* and *to give out, to go back* and *to go back on, to beat* and *to beat it, to light* and *to light out, to butt* and *to butt in, to turn* and *to turn down, to show* and *to show up, to put* and *to put over, to wind* and *to wind up*. Sometimes, however, the addition seems to be merely rhetorical, as in *to start off, to finish up, to open up* and *to hurry up*. *To hurry up* is so commonplace in America that everyone uses it and no one notices it, but it remains rare in England. *Up* seems to be essential to many of these latter-day verbs, e. g., *to pony up, to doll up, to ball up*; without it they are without significance. Nearly all of them are attended by derivative adjectives or nouns; *cut-up, show-down, kick-in, come-down, hang-out, start-off, run-in, balled-up, dolled-up, wind-up, bang-up, turn-down, jump-off*.

In many directions the same prodigal fancy shows itself—for example, in the free interchange of parts of speech, in the bold inflection of words not inflected in sound English, and in the invention of wholly artificial words. The first phenomenon has already concerned us. Would an English literary critic of any pretensions employ such a locution as "all by her *lonesome*"? I have a doubt of it—and yet I find that phrase in a serious book by the critic of the *New Republic*.[66] Would an English M. P. use "he has another *think* coming" in debate? Again I doubt it—but even more anarchistic dedications of verbs and adjectives to substantival use are to be found in the *Congressional Record* every day. *Jitney* is an old American substantive lately revived; a month after its revival it was also an adjective, and before long it may also be a verb and even an adverb. *To lift up* was turned tail first and made a substantive, and is now also an adjective and a verb. *Joy-ride* became a verb the day after it was born as a noun. And what of *livest*? An astounding inflection, indeed—but with quite sound American usage behind it. The *Metropolitan Magazine*, of which Col. Roosevelt is an editor, announces on its letter paper that it is "the *livest* magazine in America, " and *Poetry*, the organ of the new poetry movement, prints at the head of its contents page the following encomium from the *New York Tribune*: "the *livest* art in America today is poetry, and the *livest* expression of that art is in this little Chicago monthly."

Now and then the spirit of American shows a transient faltering, and its inventiveness is displaced by a banal extension of meaning, so that a single noun comes to signify discrete things. Thus *laundry*, meaning originally a place where linen is washed, has come to mean also the linen itself. So, again, *gun* has come to mean fire-arms of all sorts, and has entered into such compounds as *gun-man* and *gun-play*. And in the same way *party* has been borrowed from the terminology of the law and made to do colloquial duty as a synonym for *person*. But such evidences of poverty are rare and abnormal; the whole movement of the language is toward the multiplication of substantives. A new object gets a new name, and that new name enters into the common vocabulary at once. *Sundae* and *hokum* are late examples; their origin is dubious and disputed, but they met genuine needs and so they seem to be secure. A great many more such substantives are deliberate inventions, for example, *kodak, protectograph, conductorette, bevo, klaxon, vaseline, jap-a-lac, resinol, autocar, postum, crisco, electrolier, addressograph, alabastine, orangeade, pianola, victrola, dictagraph, kitchenette, crispette, cellarette, uneeda, triscuit* and *peptomint*. Some of these indicate attempts at description: *oleomargarine, phonograph* and *gasoline* are older examples of that class. Others represent efforts to devise designations that will meet the conditions of advertising psychology and the trade-marks law, to wit, that they be (*a*) new, (*b*) easily remembered, and (*c*) not directly descriptive. Probably the most successful invention of this sort is *kodak*, which was devised by George Eastman, inventor of the portable camera so called. *Kodak* has so far won acceptance as a common noun that Eastman is often forced to assert his proprietary right to it.[67] *Vaseline* is in the same position. The annual crop of such inventions in the United States is enormous.[68] The majority die, but a hearty few always survive.

Of analogous character are artificial words of the *scalawag* and *rambunctious* class, the formation of which constantly goes on. Some of them are shortened compounds: *grandificent* (from*grand* and *magnificent*), *sodalicious* (from *soda* and *delicious*) and *warphan(age)* (from *war* and *orphan(age)*).[69] Others are made up of common roots and grotesque affixes: *swelldoodle*, *splendiferous* and *peacharino*. Yet others are mere extravagant inventions: *scallywampus*, *supergobsloptious* and *floozy*. Most of these are devised by advertisement writers or college students, and belong properly to slang, but there is a steady movement of selected specimens into the common vocabulary. The words in -*doodle* hint at German influences, and those in -*ino* owe something to Italian, or at least to popular burlesques of what is conceived to be Italian.

§ 6. Pronunciation

—"Language, " said Sayce, in 1879, "does not consist of letters, but of sounds, and until this fact has been brought home to us our study of it will be little better than an exercise of memory."[70] The theory, at that time, was somewhat strange to English grammarians and etymologists, despite the investigations of A. J. Ellis and the massive lesson of Grimm's law; their labors were largely wasted upon deductions from the written word. But since then, chiefly under the influence of Continental philologists, and particularly of the Dane, J. O. H. Jespersen, they have turned from orthographical futilities to the actual sounds of the tongue, and the latest and best grammar of it, that of Sweet, is frankly based upon the spoken English of educated Englishmen—not, remember, of conscious purists, but of the general body of cultivated folk. Unluckily, this new method also has its disadvantages. The men of a given race and time usually write a good deal alike, or, at all events, attempt to write alike, but in their oral speech there are wide variations. "No two persons, " says a leading contemporary authority upon English phonetics, [71] "pronounce exactly alike." Moreover, "even the best speaker commonly uses more than one style." The result is that it is extremely difficult to determine the prevailing pronunciation of a given combination of letters at any time and place. The persons whose speech is studied pronounce it with minute shades of difference, and admit other differences according as they are conversing naturally or endeavoring to exhibit their pronunciation. Worse, it is impossible to represent a great many of these shades in print. Sweet, trying to do it, [72] found himself, in the end, with a preposterous alphabet of 125 letters. Prince L.-L. Bonaparte more than doubled this number, and Ellis brought it to 390.[73] Other phonologists, English and Continental, have gone floundering into the same bog. The dictionary-makers, forced to a far greater economy of means, are brought into obscurity. The difficulties of the enterprise, in fact, are probably unsurmountable. It is, as White says, "almost impossible for one person to express to another by signs the sound of any word." "Only the voice, " he goes on, "is capable of that; for the moment a sign is used the question arises, What is the value of that sign? The sounds of words are the most delicate, fleeting and inapprehensible things in nature.... Moreover, the question arises as to the capability to apprehend and distinguish sounds on the part of the person whose evidence is given."[74] Certain German orthoepists, despairing of the printed page, have turned to the phonograph, and there is a Deutsche Grammophon-Gesellschaft in Berlin which offers records of specimen speeches in a great many languages and dialects, including English. The phonograph has also been put to successful use in language teaching by various American correspondence schools.

In view of all this it would be hopeless to attempt to exhibit in print the numerous small differences between English and American pronunciation, for many of them are extremely delicate and subtle, and only their aggregation makes them plain. According to a recent and very careful observer, [75] the most important of them do not lie in pronunciation at all, properly so called, but in intonation. In this direction, he says, one must look for the true characters "of the English accent." I incline to agree with White, [76] that the pitch of the English voice is somewhat higher than that of the American, and that it is thus more penetrating. The nasal twang which Englishmen observe in the *vox Americana*, though it has high overtones, is itself not high pitched, but rather low pitched, as all constrained and muffled tones are apt to be. The causes of that twang have long engaged phonologists, and in the main they agree that there is a physical basis for it—that our generally dry climate and rapid changes of temperature produce an actual thickening of the membranes concerned in the production of sound.[77] We are, in brief, a somewhat snuffling people, and much more given to catarrhs and coryzas than the inhabitants of damp Britain. Perhaps this general impediment to free and easy utterance, subconsciously apprehended, is responsible for the American tendency to pronounce the separate syllables of a word with much more care than an Englishman bestows upon them; the American, in giving *extraordinary* six distinct syllables instead of the Englishman's grudging four, may be seeking to make up for his natural disability. Marsh, in his "Lectures on the English Language, "[78] sought two other explanations of the fact. On the one hand, he argued that the Americans of his day read a great deal more than the English, and were thus much more influenced by the spelling of words, and on the other hand he pointed out that "our flora shows that the climate of even our Northern States belongs ... to a more Southern type than that of England, " and that "in Southern latitudes ... articulation is generally much more distinct than in Northern regions." In support of the latter proposition he cited the pronunciation of Spanish, Italian and Turkish, as compared with that of English, Danish and German—rather unfortunate examples, for the pronunciation of German is at least as clear as that of Italian. Swedish would have supported his case far better: the Swedes debase their vowels and slide over their consonants even more markedly than the English. Marsh believed that there was a tendency among Southern peoples to throw the accent back, and that this helped to "bring out all the syllables." One finds a certain support for this notion in various American peculiarities of stress. *Advertisement* offers an example. The prevailing American pronunciation, despite incessant pedagogical counterblasts, puts the accent on the penult, whereas the English pronunciation stresses the second syllable. *Paresis* illustrates the same tendency. The English accent the first syllable, but, as Krapp says, American usage clings to the accent on the second syllable.[79] There are, again, *pianist*, *primarily* and *telegrapher*. The English accent the first syllable of each; we commonly accent the second. In *temporarily* they also accent the first; we accent the third. Various other examples might be cited. But when one had marshalled them their significance would be at once set at naught by four very familiar words, *mamma*, *papa*, *inquiry* and *ally*. Americans almost invariably accent each on the first syllable; Englishmen stress the second. For months, during 1918, the publishers of the Standard Dictionary, advertising that work in the street-cars, explained that *ally* should be accented on the second syllable, and pointed out that owners of their dictionary were safeguarded against the vulgarism of accenting it on the first. Nevertheless, this free and highly public instruction did not suffice to exterminate *al´ly*. I made note of the pronunciations overheard, with the word constantly on all lips. But one man of my acquaintance regularly accented the second syllable, and he was an eminent scholar, professionally devoted to the study of language.

Thus it is unsafe, here as elsewhere, to generalize too facilely, and particularly unsafe to exhibit causes with too much assurance. "Man frage nicht warum, " says Philipp Karl Buttmann. "Der Sprachgebrauch lässt sich nur beobachten."[80] But the greater distinctness of American utterance, whatever its genesis and machinery, is palpable enough in many familiar situations. "The typical American accent, " says Vizetelly, "is often harsh and unmusical, but it sounds all of the letters to be sounded, and slurs, but does not distort, the rest."[81] An American, for example, almost always sounds the first *l* in *fulfill*; an Englishman makes the first syllable *foo*. An American sounds every syllable in *extraordinary, literary, military, secretary* and the other words of the *-ary*-group; an Englishman never pronounces the *a* of the penultimate syllable. *Kindness*, with the *d* silent, would attract notice in the United States; in England, according to Jones, [82] the *d* is "very commonly, if not usually" omitted. *Often*, in America, commonly retains a full *t*; in England it is actually and officially *offen*. Let an American and an Englishman pronounce *program* (*me*). Though the Englishman retains the long form of the last syllable in writing, he reduces it in speaking to a thick triple consonant, *grm*; the American enunciates it clearly, rhyming it with *damn*. Or try the two with any word ending in *-g*, say *sporting* or *ripping*. Or with any word having *r* before a consonant, say *card, harbor, lord* or *preferred*. "The majority of Englishmen, " says Menner, "certainly do not pronounce the *r* ...; just as certainly the majority of educated Americans pronounce it distinctly."[83]Henry James, visiting the United States after many years of residence in England, was much harassed by this persistent *r*-sound, which seemed to him to resemble "a sort of morose grinding of the back teeth."[84] So sensitive to it did he become that he began to hear where it was actually non-existent, save as an occasional barbarism, for example, in *Cuba-r, vanilla-r* and *California-r*. He put the blame for it, and for various other departures from the strict canon of contemporary English, upon "the American common school, the American newspaper, and the American Dutchman and Dago." Unluckily for his case, the full voicing of the *r* came into American long before the appearance of any of these influences. The early colonists, in fact, brought it with them from England, and it still prevailed there in Dr. Johnson's day, for he protested publicly against the "rough snarling sound" and led the movement which finally resulted in its extinction.[85] Today, extinct, it is mourned by English purists, and the Poet Laureate denounces the clergy of the Established Church for saying "the *sawed* of the *Laud*" instead of "the sword of the Lord."[86]

But even in the matter of elided consonants American is not always the conservator. We cling to the *r*, we preserve the final *g*, we give *nephew* a clear *f*-sound instead of the clouded Englishυ-sound, and we boldly nationalize *trait* and pronounce its final *t*, but we drop the second *p* from *pumpkin* and change the *m* to *n*, we change the *ph*(=*f*)-sound to plain *p* in *diphtheria, diphthong* and *naphtha*, [87] we relieve *rind* of its final *d*, and, in the complete sentence, we slaughter consonants by assimilation. I have heard Englishmen say *brand-new*, but on American lips it is almost invariably *bran-new*. So nearly universal is this nasalization in the United States that certain American lexicographers have sought to found the term upon *bran* and not upon *brand*. Here the national speech is powerfully influenced by Southern dialectical variations, which in turn probably derive partly from French example and partly from the linguistic limitations of the negro. The latter, even after two hundred years, has great difficulties with our consonants, and often drops them. A familiar anecdote well illustrates his speech habit. On a train stopping at a small station in Georgia a darkey threw up a window and yelled "Wah ee?" The reply from a black on the platform was "Wah oo?" A Northerner aboard the train, puzzled by this inarticulate dialogue, sought light from a Southern passenger, who promptly translated the first question as "Where is he?" and the second as "Where is who?" A recent viewer with alarm[88] argues that this conspiracy against the consonants is spreading, and that English printed words no longer represent the actual sounds of the American language. "Like the French, " he says, "we have a marked *liaison*—the borrowing of a letter from the preceding word. We invite one another to 'c'meer' (=come here) ... 'Hoo-zat?' (=who is that?) has as good a *liaison* as the French *vois avez*." This critic believes that American tends to abandon *t* for *d*, as in *Sadd'y* (=Saturday) and *siddup* (=sit up), and to get rid of *h*, as in "ware-zee?" (=where is he?). But here we invade the vulgar speech, which belongs to the next chapter.

Among the vowels the most salient difference between English and American pronunciation, of course, is marked off by the flat American *a*. This flat *a*, as we have seen, has been under attack at home for nearly a century. The New Englanders, very sensitive to English example, substitute a broad *a* that is even broader than the English, and an *a* of the same sort survives in the South in a few words, *e. g., master, tomato* and *tassel*, but everywhere else in the country the flat *a* prevails. Fashion and the example of the stage oppose it, [89] and it is under the ban of an active wing of schoolmasters, but it will not down. To the average American, indeed, the broad *a* is a banner of affectation, and he associates it unpleasantly with spats, Harvard, male tea-drinking, wrist watches and all the other objects of his social suspicion. He gets the flat sound, not only into such words as *last, calf, dance* and *pastor*, but even into *piano* and *drama. Drama* is sometimes *drayma* west of Connecticut, but almost never *drahma* or *drawma. Tomato* with the *a* of *bat*, may sometimes borrow the *a* of *plate*, but *tomahto* is confined to New England and the South. *Hurrah*, in American, has also borrowed the *a* of *plate*; one hears *hurray* much oftener than *hurraw*. Even *amen* frequently shows that *a*, though not when sung. Curiously enough, it is displaced in *patent* by the true flat *a*. The English rhyme the first syllable of the word with *rate*; in America it always rhymes with *rat*.

The broad *a* is not only almost extinct outside of New England; it begins to show signs of decay even there. At all events, it has gradually disappeared from many words, and is measurably less sonorous in those in which it survives than it used to be. A century ago it appeared, not only in *dance, aunt, glass, past*, etc., but also in *Daniel, imagine, rational* and *travel*.[90] And in 1857 Oliver Wendell Holmes reported it in *matter, handsome, caterpillar, apple* and *satisfaction*. It has been displaced in virtually all of these, even in the most remote reaches of the back country, by the national flat *a*. Grandgent[91] says that the broad *a* is now restricted in New England to the following situations:

1. when followed by *s* or *ns*, as in *last* and *dance*.

2. when followed by *r* preceding another consonant, as in *cart*.

3. when followed by *lm*, as in *calm*.

4. when followed by *f, s* or *th*, as in *laugh, pass* and *path*.

The *u*-sound also shows certain differences between English and American usage. The English reduce the last syllable of *figure* to *ger*;

the educated American preserves the *u*-sound as in *nature*. The English make the first syllable of *courteous* rhyme with *fort*; the American standard rhymes it with *hurt*. The English give an *oo*-sound to the *u* of *brusque*; in America the word commonly rhymes with *tusk*. A *u*-sound, as everyone knows, gets into the American pronunciation of *clerk*, by analogy with *insert*; the English cling to a broad *a*-sound, by analogy with *hearth*. Even the latter, in the United States, is often pronounced to rhyme with *dearth*. The American, in general, is much less careful than the Englishman to preserve the shadowy *y*-sound before *u* in words of the *duke*-class. He retains it in *few*, but surely not in *new*. Nor in *duke, blue, stew, due, duty* and *true*. Nor even in *Tuesday*. Purists often attack the simple *oo*-sound. In 1912, for example, the Department of Education of New York City warned all the municipal high-school teachers to combat it.[92] But it is doubtful that one pupil in a hundred was thereby induced to insert the *y* in *induced*. Finally there is *lieutenant*. The Englishman pronounces the first syllable *left*; the American invariably makes it *loot*. White says that the prevailing American pronunciation is relatively recent. "I never heard it, " he reports, "in my boyhood."[93] He was born in New York in 1821.

The *i*-sound presents several curious differences. The English make it long in all words of the *hostile*-class; in America it is commonly short, even in *puerile*. The English also lengthen it in *sliver*; in America the word usually rhymes with *liver*. The short *i*, in England, is almost universally substituted for the *e* in *pretty*, and this pronunciation is also inculcated in most American schools, but I often hear an unmistakable *e*-sound in the United States, making the first syllable rhyme with *bet*. Contrariwise, most Americans put the short *i* into *been*, making it rhyme with *sin*. In England it shows a long *e*-sound, as in *seen*. A recent poem by an English poet makes the word rhyme with *submarine, queen* and *unseen*.[94] The *o*-sound, in American, tends to convert itself into an *aw*-sound. *Cog* still retains a pure *o*, but one seldom hears it in *log* or *dog*. Henry James denounces this "flatly-drawling group" in "The Question of Our Speech, "[95] and cites *gawd, dawg, sawft, lawft, gawne, lawst* and *frawst* as horrible examples. But the English themselves are not guiltless of the same fault. Many of the accusations that James levels at American, in truth, are echoed by Robert Bridges in "A Tract on the Present State of English Pronunciation." Both spend themselves upon opposing what, at bottom, are probably natural and inevitable movements—for example, the gradual decay of all the vowels to one of neutral color, represented by the *e* of *danger*, the *u* of *suggest*, the second *o* of *common* and the *a* of *prevalent*. This decay shows itself in many languages. In both English and High German, during their middle periods, all the terminal vowels degenerated to *e*—now sunk to the aforesaid neutral vowel in many German words, and expunged from English altogether. The same sound is encountered in languages so widely differing otherwise as Arabic, French and Swedish. "Its existence, " says Sayce, "is a sign of age and decay; meaning has become more important than outward form, and the educated intelligence no longer demands a clear pronunciation in order to understand what is said."[96]

All these differences between English and American pronunciation, separately considered, seem slight, but in the aggregate they are sufficient to place serious impediments between mutual comprehension. Let an Englishman and an American (not of New England) speak a quite ordinary sentence, "My aunt can't answer for my dancing the lancers even passably, " and at once the gap separating the two pronunciations will be manifest. Here only the *a* is involved. Add a dozen everyday words—*military*, *schedule*, *trait*, *hostile*, *been*, *lieutenant*, *patent*, *nephew*, *secretary*, *advertisement*, and so on—and the strangeness of one to the other is augmented. "Every Englishman visiting the States for the first time, " said an English dramatist some time ago, "has a difficulty in making himself understood. He often has to repeat a remark or a request two or three times to make his meaning clear, especially on railroads, in hotels and at bars. The American visiting England for the first time has the same trouble."[97] Despite the fact that American actors imitate English pronunciation to the best of their skill, this visiting Englishman asserted that the average American audience is incapable of understanding a genuinely English company, at least "when the speeches are rattled off in conversational style." When he presented one of his own plays with an English company, he said, many American acquaintances, after witnessing the performance, asked him to lend them the manuscript, "that they might visit it again with some understanding of the dialogue."[98]

FOOTNOTES:

[1] In Passing English of the Victorian Era; London, n. d., p. 68.

[2] The Oxford Dictionary, following the late J. H. Trumbull, the well-known authority on Indian languages, derives the word from the Algonquin *cau-cau-as-u*, one who advises. But most other authorities, following Pickering, derive it from *caulkers*. The first caucuses, it would appear, were held in a caulkers' shop in Boston, and were called *caulkers' meetings*. The Rev. William Gordon, in his History of the Rise and Independence of the United States, Including the Late War, published in London in 1788, said that "more than fifty years ago Mr. Samuel Adams' father and twenty others, one or two from the north end of the town [Boston], where the ship business is carried on, used to meet, make a *caucus*, and lay their plans for introducing certain persons into places of trust and power."

[3] Americanisms Old and New; p. vii.

[4] A. Cleveland Coxe: Americanisms in England, *Forum*, Oct. 1886.

[5] Reprinted, in part, in the *New York Sun*, May 12, 1918.

[6] Vol. xiv. pp. 507, 512.

[7] In this connection it is curious to note that, though the raccoon is an animal quite unknown in England, there was, until lately, a destroyer called the *Raccoon* in the British Navy. This ship was lost with all hands off the Irish coast, Jan. 9, 1918.

[8] The Unexpurgated Case Against Woman Suffrage; London, 1913, p. 9. *To bluff* has also gone into other languages, notably the Spanish. During the Cuban revolution of March, 1917, the newspapers of Havana, objecting to the dispatches sent out by American correspondents, denounced the latter as *los blofistas*. Meanwhile, *to bluff* has been shouldered out in the country of its origin, at least temporarily, by a verb borrowed from the French, *to camouflage*. This first appeared in the Spring of 1917.

[9] Book iv, ch. iii. The first of the six volumes was published in 1858 and the last in 1865.

[10] Words and Their Use, new ed.; New York, 1876, p. 198.

[11] Boston, 1918, pp. 1-43.

[12] *Green Book Magazine*, Nov., 1913, p. 768.

[13] An interesting note on this characteristic is in College Words and Phrases, by Eugene H. Babbitt, *Dialect Notes*, vol. ii, pt. i, p. 11.

[14] America's Coming of Age; p. 15.

[15] March 26, 1918, pp. 4376-7.

[16] Jan. 14, 1918, p. 903.

[17] Mr. Campbell, of Kansas, in the House, Jan. 19, 1918, p. 1134.

[18] Mr. Hamlin, of Missouri, in the House, Jan. 19, 1918, p. 1154.

[19] Mr. Kirby, of Arkansas, in the Senate, Jan. 24, 1918, p. 1291; Mr. Lewis, of Illinois, in the Senate, June 6, 1918, p. 8024.

[20] Mr. Weeks of Massachusetts, in the Senate, Jan. 17, 1918, p. 988.

[21] Mr. Smith, of South Carolina, in the Senate, Jan. 17, 1918, p. 991.

[22] Mr. Borland, of Missouri, in the House, Jan. 29, 1918, p. 1501.

[23] May 4, 1917, p. 1853.

[24] Mr. Snyder, of New York, Dec. 11, 1917.

[25] *Balled-up* and its verb, *to ball up*, were originally somewhat improper, no doubt on account of the slang significance of *ball*, but of late they have made steady progress toward polite acceptance.

[26] After the passage of the first War Revenue Act cigar-boxes began to bear this inscription: "The contents of this box have been *taxed paid* as cigars of Class B as indicated by the Internal Revenue stamp affixed." Even *tax-paid*, which was later substituted, is obviously better than this clumsy double inflection.

[27] Mr. Bankhead, of Alabama, in the Senate, May 14, 1918, p. 6995.

[28] *Bust* seems to be driving out *burst* completely when used figuratively. Even in a literal sense it creeps into more or less respectable usage. Thus I find "a *busted* tire" in a speech by Gen. Sherwood, of Ohio, in the House, Jan. 24, 1918. The familiar American derivative, *buster*, as in *Buster Brown*, is unknown to the English.

[29] Pp. 133-154.

[30] L. Pearsall Smith, in The English Language, p. 29, says that "the differentiation is ... so complicated that it can hardly be mastered by those born in parts of the British Islands in which it has not yet been established"— *e. g.*, all of Ireland and most of Scotland.

[31] Quoted by White, in Words and Their Uses, pp. 264-5. White, however, dissented vigorously and devoted 10 pages to explaining the difference between the two auxiliaries. Most of the other authorities of the time were also against Marsh—for example, Richard Meade Bache (See his Vulgarisms and Other Errors of Speech, p. 92 *et seq.*). Sir Edmund Head, governor-general of Canada from 1854 to 1861, wrote a whole book upon the subject: *Shall* and *Will*, or Two Chapters on Future Auxiliary Verbs; London, 1856.

[32] The probable influence of Irish immigration upon the American usage is not to be overlooked. Joyce says flatly (English As We Speak It in Ireland, p. 77) that, "like many another Irish idiom this is also found in American society chiefly through the influence of the Irish." At all events, the Irish example must have reinforced it. In Ireland "*Will* I light the fire, ma'am?" is colloquially sound.

[33] Often with such amusing results as "*whom* is your father?" and "*whom* spoke to me?" The exposure of excesses of that sort always attracts the wits, especially Franklin P. Adams.

[34] "It is *I*" is quite as unsound historically. The correct form would be "it *am* I" or "I am it." Compare the German: "ich *bin* es, " not, "es *ist* ich."

[35] A common direction to motormen and locomotive engineers. The English form is "slow down." I note, however, that "drive slow*ly*" is in the taxicab shed at the Pennsylvania Station, in New York.

[36] I quote from a speech made by Senator Sherman, of Illinois, in the United States Senate on June 20, 1918. *Vide Congressional Record* for that day, p. 8743. Two days later, "There is no question *but* that" appeared in a letter by John Lee Coulter, A.M., Ph.D., dean of West Virginia University. It was read into the *Record* of June 22 by Mr. Ashwell, one of the Louisiana representatives. Even the pedantic Senator Henry Cabot Lodge, oozing Harvard from every pore, uses *but that. Vide* the *Record* for May 14, 1918, p. 6996.

[37] June 15, 1918, p. 62.

[38] The English Language, p. 79.

[39] This phrase, of course, is a Briticism, and seldom used in America. The American form is "to take a matter up."

[40] P. 30.

[41] A Contribution *Towards*, etc., by Prof. H. Tallichet, vol. 1, pt. iv.

[42] *Yale Review*, April, 1918, p. 545.

[43] I Speak United States, *Saturday Review*, Sept. 22, 1894.

[44] Our Dictionaries, pp. 84-86.

[45] Should Language Be Abolished? by Harold Goddard, *Atlantic Monthly*, July, 1918, p. 63.

[46] In Yiddish, *ish ka bibble*. The origin and meaning of the phrase have been variously explained. The prevailing notion seems to be that it is a Yiddish corruption of the German *nicht gefiedelt* (=*not fiddled*=*not flustered*). But this seems to me to be fanciful. To the Jews *ish* is obviously the first personal pronoun and*kaa* probably corruption of *kann*. As for *bibble* I suspect that it is the offspring of *bedibbert*(=*embarrassed, intimidated*). The phrase thus has an ironical meaning, *I should be embarrassed*, almost precisely equivalent to *I should worry*.

[47] All of which, of course, are coming into American, along with many other Yiddish words. These words tend to spread far beyond the areas actually settled by Jews. Thus I find *mazuma* in A Word-List from Kansas, from the collectanea of Judge J. C. Ruppenthal, of Russell, Kansas, *Dialect Notes*, vol. iv. pt. v, 1916, p. 322.

[48] Louise Pound: Domestication of the Suffix -*fest*, *Dialect Notes*, vol. iv, pt. v, 1916. Dr. Pound, it should be mentioned, has also printed a brief note on -*inski*. Her observation of American is peculiarly alert and accurate.

[49] For example, see the *Congressional Record* for April 3, 1918, p. 4928.

[50] *Paprika* is in the Standard Dictionary, but I have been unable to find it in any English dictionary. Another such word is *kimono*, from the Japanese.

[51] *Cf.* Vogue Affixes in Present-Day Word-Coinage, by Louise Pound, *Dialect Notes*, vol. v, pt. i, 1918. Dr. Pound ascribes the vogue of *super-* to German influences, and is inclined to think that -*dom* may be helped by the German -*thum*.

[52] *Vide* Pennsylvania Dutch, by S. S. Haldeman; Philadelphia, 1872. Also, The Pennsylvania German Dialect, by M. D. Learned; Baltimore, 1889. Also Die Zukunft deutscher Bildung in Amerika, by O. E. Lessing, *Monatshefte für deutsche Sprache und Pedagogik*, Dec., 1916. Also, Where Do You Stand? by Herman Hagedorn; New York, 1918, pp. 106-7. Also, On the German Dialect Spoken in the Valley of Virginia, by H. M. Hays, *Dialect Notes*, vol. iii, pt. iv, 1908, pp. 263-78.

[53] *Vide* Notes on American-Norwegian, by Nils Flaten, *Dialect Notes*, vol. ii, 1900. Also, for similar corruptions, The Jersey Dutch Dialect, by J. Dyneley Prince, *ibid.*, vol. iii, pt. vi, 1910, pp. 461-84. Also, see under Hempl, Flom, Bibaud, Buies and A. M. Elliott in the bibliography.

[54] For all these examples of American Yiddish I am indebted to the kindness of Abraham Cahan, editor of the *Jewish Daily Forward*. Mr. Cahan is not only editor of the chief Yiddish newspaper of the United States, but also an extraordinarily competent writer of English, as his novel, The Rise of David Levinsky, demonstrates.

[55] What Americans Talk in the Philippines, *American Review of Reviews*, Aug., 1913.

[56] *Cf.* The English of the Lower Classes in New York City and Vicinity, *Dialect Notes*, vol. i, pt. ix, 1896. It is curious to note that the same corruption occurs in the Spanish spoken in Santo Domingo. The Dominicans thus change *porque* into *poique*. Cf. Santo Domingo, by Otto Schoenrich; New York, 1918, p. 172. See also High School Circular No. 17, Dept. of Education, City of New York, June 19, 1912, p. 6.

[57] The American People, 2 vols.; New York, 1909-11, vol. ii, pp. 449-50. For a discussion of this effect of contact with foreigners upon a language see also Beach-la-Mar, by William Churchill; Washington, 1911, p. 11 *et seq.*

[58] *Vide* Lounsbury: The Standard of Usage in English, pp. 65-7.

[59] For an exhaustive discussion of these formations *cf.* Clipped Words, by Elizabeth Wittman, *Dialect Notes*, vol. iv, pt. ii, 1914.

[60] Americanisms Old and New, p. 1.

[61] *Cf.* Semi-Secret Abbreviations, by Percy W. Long, *Dialect Notes*, vol. iv, pt. iii, 1915.

[62] The classical example is in a parliamentary announcement by Sir Robert Peel: "When that question is made to me in a proper time, in a proper place, under proper qualifications, and with proper motives, I will hesitate long before I will refuse to take it into consideration."

[63] *Cf.* On the Art of Writing, by Sir Arthur Quiller-Couch; p. 100 *et seq.*

[64] This use of *tenderloin* is ascribed to Alexander (alias "Clubber") Williams, a New York police captain. *Vide* the *New York Sun*, July 11, 1913. Williams, in 1876, was transferred from an obscure precinct to West Thirtieth Street. "I've been having chuck steak ever since I've been on the force, " he said, "and now I'm going to have a bit of tenderloin." "The name, " says the *Sun*, "has endured more than a generation, moving with the changed amusement geography of the city, and has been adopted in all parts of the country."

[65] *New York Evening Mail*, Feb. 2, 1918, p. 1.

[66] Horizons, by Francis Hackett; New York, 1918, p. 53.

[67] It has even got into the Continental languages. In October, 1917, the Verband Deutscher Amateurphotographen-Vereine was moved to issue the following warning: "Es gibt kein deutschen *Kodaks.Kodak*, als Sammelname für photographische Erzeugnisse ist falsch und bezeichnet nur die Fabrikate der Eastman-*Kodak*-Company. Wer von einem *Kodak* spricht und nur allgemein eine photographische Kamera meint, bedenkt nicht, dass er mit der Weiterverbreitung dieses Wortes die deutsche Industrie zugunsten der amerikanisch-englischen schädigt."

[68] *Cf.* Word-Coinage and Modern Trade Names, by Louise Pound, *Dialect Notes*, vol. iv, pt. i, 1913, pp. 29-41. Most of these coinages produce derivatives, *e. g.*, *bevo-officer, to kodak, kodaker.*

[69] This conscious shortening, of course, is to be distinguished from the shortening that goes on in words by gradual decay, as in *Christmas* (from *Christ's mass*) and *daisy* (from *day's eye*).

[70] The Science of Language, vol. ii, p. 339.

[71] Daniel Jones: The Pronunciation of English, 2nd ed.; Cambridge, 1914, p. 1. Jones is lecturer in phonetics at University College, London.

[72] *Vide* his Handbook of Phonetics, p. xv, *et seq.*

[73] It is given in Ellis' Early English Pronunciation, p. 1293 *et seq.* and in Sayce's The Science of Language, vol. i, p. 353 *et seq.*

[74] Every-Day English, p. 29.

[75] Robert J. Menner: The Pronunciation of English in America, *Atlantic Monthly*, March, 1915, p. 366.

[76] Words and Their Uses, p. 58.

[77] The following passage from Kipling's American Notes, ch. i, will be recalled: "Oliver Wendell Holmes says that the Yankee schoolmarm, the cider and the salt codfish of the Eastern states are responsible for what he calls a nasal accent. I know better. They stole books from across the water without paying for 'em, and the snort of delight was fixed in their nostrils for ever by a just Providence. That is why they talk a foreign tongue today."

[78] Lecture xxx. The English Language in America.

[79] Modern English, p. 166. *Cf.* A Desk-Book of 25, 000 Words Frequently Mispronounced, by Frank H. Vizetelly, p. 652.

[80] Lexilogus, 2nd ed.; Berlin, 1860, p. 239. An English translation was published in London in 1846.

[81] A Desk-Book of 25, 000 Words Frequently Mispronounced, p. xvi.

[82] The Pronunciation of English, p. 17.

[83] The Pronunciation of English in America, *op. cit.*, p. 362.

[84] The Question of Our Speech, p. 29 *et seq.*

[85] *Cf.* The Cambridge History of English Literature, vol. xiv, p. 487.

[86] Robert Bridges: A Tract on the Present State of English Pronunciation; Oxford, 1913.

[87] An interesting discussion of this peculiarity is in Some Variant Pronunciations in the New South, by William A. Read, *Dialect Notes*, vol. iii, pt. vii, 1911, p. 504 *et seq.*

[88] Hugh Mearns: Our Own, Our Native Speech, *McClure's Magazine*, Oct., 1916.

[89] The American actor imitates, not only English pronunciation in all its details, but also English dress and bearing. His struggles with such words as *extraordinary* are often very amusing.

[90] *Cf.* Duncan Mackintosh: Essai Raisonné sur la Grammaire et la Pronunciation Anglais; Boston, 1797.

[91] Fashion and the Broad *A*, *Nation*, Jan 7, 1915.

[92] High School Circular No. 17, June 19, 1912.

[93] Every-Day English, p. 243.

[94] Open Boats, by Alfred Noyes, New York, 1917, pp. 89-91.

[95] P. 30.

[96] The Science of Language, vol. i, p. 259.

[97] B. MacDonald Hastings, *New York Tribune*, Jan. 19, 1913.

[98] Various minor differences between English and American pronunciation, not noted here, are discussed in British and American Pronunciation, by Louise Pound, *School Review*, vol. xxiii, no. 6, June, 1915.

VI. The Common Speech

§ 1. Grammarians and Their Ways

—So far, in the main, the language examined has been of a relatively pretentious and self-conscious variety—the speech, if not always of formal discourse, then at least of literate men. Most of the examples of its vocabulary and idiom, in fact, have been drawn from written documents or from written reports of more or less careful utterances, for example, the speeches of members of Congress and of other public men. The whole of Thornton's excellent material is of this character. In his dictionary there is scarcely a locution that is not supported by printed examples.

It must be obvious that such materials, however lavishly set forth, cannot exhibit the methods and tendencies of a living speech with anything approaching completeness, nor even with accuracy. What men put into writing and what they say when they take sober thought are very far from what they utter in everyday conversation. All of us, no matter how careful our speech habits, loosen the belt a bit, so to speak, when we speak familiarly to our fellows, and pay a good deal less heed to precedents and proprieties, perhaps, than we ought to. It was a sure instinct that made Ibsen put "bad grammar" into the mouth of Nora Helmar in "A Doll's House." She is a general's daughter and the wife of a professor, but even professor's wives are not above occasional bogglings of the cases of pronouns and the conjugations of verbs. The professors themselves, in truth, must have the same habit, for sometimes they show plain signs of it in print. More than once, plowing through profound and interminable treatises of grammar and syntax in preparation for the present work, I have encountered the cheering spectacle of one grammarian exposing, with contagious joy, the grammatical lapses of some other grammarian. And nine times out of ten, a few pages further on, I have found the enchanted purist erring himself.[1] The most funereal of the sciences is saved from utter horror by such displays of human malice and fallibility. Speech itself, indeed, would become almost impossible if the grammarians could follow their own rules unfailingly, and were always right.

But here we are among the learned; and their sins, when detected and exposed, are at least punished by conscience. What are of more importance, to those interested in language as a living thing, are the offendings of the millions who are not conscious of any wrong. It is among these millions, ignorant of regulation and eager only to express their ideas clearly and forcefully, that language undergoes its great changes and constantly renews its vitality. These are the genuine makers of grammar, marching miles ahead of the formal grammarians. Like the Emperor Sigismund, each man among them may well say: "*Ego sum ... super grammaticam.*" It is competent for any individual to offer his contribution—his new word, his better idiom, his novel figure of speech, his short cut in grammar or syntax—and it is by the general vote of the whole body, not by the verdict of a small school, that the fate of the innovation is decided. As Brander Matthews says, there is not even representative government in the matter; the *posse comitatus* decides directly, and despite the sternest protest, finally. The ignorant, the rebellious and the daring come forward with their brilliant barbarisms; the learned and conservative bring up their objections. "And when both sides have been heard, there is a show of hands; and by this the irrevocable decision of the community itself is rendered."[2] Thus it was that the Romance languages were fashioned out of the wreck of Latin, the vast influence of the literate minority to the contrary notwithstanding. Thus it was, too, that English lost its case inflections and many of its old conjugations, and that our *yes* came to be substituted for the *gea-se* (=*so be it*) of an earlier day, and that we got rid of *whom* after *man* in *the man I saw*, and that our stark pronoun of the first person was precipitated from the German *ich*. And thus it is that, in our own day, the language faces forces in America which, not content with overhauling and greatly enriching its materials, now threaten to work changes in its very structure.

Where these tendencies run strongest, of course, is on the plane of the vulgar spoken language. Among all classes the everyday speech departs very far from orthodox English, and even very far from any recognizable spoken English, but among those lower classes which make up the great body of the people it gets so far from orthodox English that it gives promise, soon or late, of throwing off its old bonds altogether, or, at any rate, all save the loosest of them. Behind it is the gigantic impulse that I have described in earlier chapters: the impulse of an egoistic and iconoclastic people, facing a new order of life in highly self-conscious freedom, to break a relatively stable language, long since emerged from its period of growth, to their novel and multitudinous needs, and, above all, to their experimental and impatient spirit. This impulse, it must be plain, would war fiercely upon any attempt at formal regulation, however prudent and elastic; it is often rebellious for the mere sake of rebellion. But what it comes into conflict with, in America, is nothing so politic, and hence nothing so likely to keep the brakes upon it. What it actually encounters here is a formalism that is artificial, illogical and almost unintelligible—a formalism borrowed from English grammarians, and by them brought into English, against all fact and reason, from the Latin. "In most of our grammars, perhaps in all of those issued earlier than the opening of the twentieth century, " says Matthews, "we find linguistic laws laid down which are in blank contradiction with the genius of the language."[3] In brief, the American school-boy, hauled before a pedagogue to be instructed in the structure and organization of the tongue he speaks, is actually instructed in the structure and organization of a tongue that he never hears at all, and seldom reads, and that, in more than one of the characters thus set before him, does not even exist.

The effects of this are two-fold. On the one hand he conceives an antipathy to a subject so lacking in intelligibility and utility. As one teacher puts it, "pupils tire of it; often they see nothing in it, because there *is* nothing in it."[4] And on the other hand, the school-boy goes entirely without sympathetic guidance in the living language that he actually speaks, in and out of the classroom, and that he will probably speak all the rest of his life. All he hears in relation to it is a series of sneers and prohibitions, most of them grounded, not upon principles deduced from its own nature, but upon its divergences from the theoretical language that he is so unsuccessfully taught. The net result is that all the instruction he receives passes for naught. It is not sufficient to make him a master of orthodox English and it is not sufficient to rid him of the speech-habits of his home and daily life. Thus he is thrown back upon these speech-habits without any helpful restraint or guidance, and they make him a willing ally of the radical and often extravagant tendencies which show themselves in the vulgar tongue. In other words, the very effort to teach him an excessively tight and formal English promotes his use of a loose and rebellious English. And so the grammarians, with the traditional fatuity of their order, labor for the destruction of the grammar they defend, and for the decay of all those refinements of speech that go with it.

The folly of this system, of course, has not failed to attract the attention of the more intelligent teachers, nor have they failed to observe the causes of its failure. "Much of the fruitlessness of the study of English grammar, " says Wilcox, [5] "and many of the obstacles encountered in its study are due to 'the difficulties created by the grammarians.' These difficulties arise chiefly from three sources—

excessive classification, multiplication of terms for a single conception, and the attempt to treat the English language as if it were highly inflected." So long ago as the 60's Richard Grant White began an onslaught upon all such punditic stupidities. He saw clearly that "the attempt to treat English as if it were highly inflected" was making its intelligent study almost impossible, and proposed boldly that all English grammar-books be burned.[6] Of late his ideas have begun to gain a certain acceptance, and as the literature of denunciation has grown[7] the grammarians have been constrained to overhaul their texts. When I was a school-boy, during the penultimate decade of the last century, the chief American grammar was "A Practical Grammar of the English Language, " by Thomas W. Harvey.[8] This formidable work was almost purely synthetical: it began with a long series of definitions, wholly unintelligible to a child, and proceeded into a maddening maze of pedagogical distinctions, puzzling even to an adult. The latter-day grammars, at least those for the elementary schools, are far more analytical and logical. For example, there is "Longmans' Briefer Grammar, " by George J. Smith, [9] a text now in very wide use. This book starts off, not with page after page of abstractions, but with a well-devised examination of the complete sentence, and the characters and relations of the parts of speech are very simply and clearly developed. But before the end the author begins to succumb to precedent, and on page 114 I find paragraph after paragraph of such dull, flyblown pedantry as this:

Some Intransitive Verbs are used to link the Subject and some Adjective or Noun. These Verbs are called Copulative Verbs, and the Adjective or Noun is called the Attribute.

The Attribute always describes or denotes the person or thing denoted by the Subject.

Verbals are words that are derived from Verbs and express action or being without asserting it. Infinitives and Participles are Verbals.

And so on. Smith, in his preface, says that his book is intended, "not so much to 'cover' the subject of grammar as to *teach* it, " and calls attention to the fact, somewhat proudly, that he has omitted "the rather hard subject of gerunds, " all mention of conjunctive adverbs, and even the conjugation of verbs. Nevertheless, he immerses himself in the mythical objective case of nouns on page 108, and does not emerge until the end.[10] "The New-Webster-Cooley Course in English, "[11]another popular text, carries reform a step further. The subject of case is approached through the personal pronouns, where it retains its only surviving intelligibility, and the more lucid **object form** is used in place of **objective case**. Moreover, the pupil is plainly informed, later on, that "a noun has in reality but two case-forms: a possessive and a common case-form." This is the best concession to the facts yet made by a text-book grammarian. But no one familiar with the habits of the pedagogical mind need be told that its interior pull is against even such mild and obvious reforms. Defenders of the old order are by no means silent; a fear seems to prevail that grammar, robbed of its imbecile classifications, may collapse entirely. Wilcox records how the Council of English Teachers of New Jersey, but a few years ago, spoke out boldly for the recognition of no less than five cases in English. "Why five?" asks Wilcox. "Why not eight, or ten, or even thirteen? Undoubtedly because there are five cases in Latin."[12] Most of the current efforts at improvement, in fact, tend toward a mere revision and multiplication of classifications; the pedant is eternally convinced that pigeon-holing and relabelling are contributions to knowledge. A curious proof in point is offered by a pamphlet entitled "Reorganization of English in Secondary Schools, " compiled by James Fleming Hosic and issued by the National Bureau of Education.[13] The aim of this pamphlet is to rid the teaching of English, including grammar, of its accumulated formalism and ineffectiveness—to make it genuine instruction instead of a pedantic and meaningless routine. And how is this revolutionary aim set forth? By a meticulous and merciless splitting of hairs, a gigantic manufacture of classifications and sub-classifications, a colossal display of professorial bombast and flatulence.

I could cite many other examples. Perhaps, after all, the disease is incurable. What such laborious stupidity shows at bottom is simply this: that the sort of man who is willing to devote his life to teaching grammar to children, or to training school-marms to do it, is not often the sort of man who is intelligent enough to do it competently. In particular, he is not often intelligent enough to grapple with the fluent and ever-amazing permutations of a living and rebellious speech. The only way he can grapple with it at all is by first reducing it to a fixed and formal organization—in brief, by first killing it and embalming it. The difference in the resultant proceedings is not unlike that between a gross dissection and a surgical operation. The difficulties of the former are quickly mastered by any student of normal sense, but even the most casual of laparotomies calls for a man of special skill and address. Thus the elementary study of the national language, at least in America, is almost monopolized by dullards. Children are taught it by men and women who observe it inaccurately and expound it ignorantly. In most other fields the pedagogue meets a certain corrective competition and criticism. The teacher of any branch of applied mathematics, for example, has practical engineers at his elbow and they quickly expose and denounce his defects; the college teacher of chemistry, however limited his equipment, at least has the aid of text-books written by actual chemists. But English, even in its most formal shapes, is chiefly taught by those who cannot write it decently and who get no aid from those who can. One wades through treatise after treatise on English style by pedagogues whose own style is atrocious. A Huxley or a Stevenson might have written one of high merit and utility—but Huxley and Stevenson had other fish to fry, and so the business was left to Prof. Balderdash. Consider the standard texts on prosody—vast piles of meaningless words—hollow babble about spondees, iambics, trochees and so on—idiotic borrowings from dead languages. Two poets, Poe and Lanier, blew blasts of fresh air through that fog, but they had no successors, and it has apparently closed in again. In the department of prose it lies wholly unbroken; no first-rate writer of English prose has ever written a text-book upon the art of writing it.

§ 2. Spoken American As It Is

—But here I wander afield. The art of prose has little to do with the stiff and pedantic English taught in grammar-schools and a great deal less to do with the loose and lively English spoken by the average American in his daily traffic. The thing of importance is that the two differ from each other even more than they differ from the English of a Huxley or a Stevenson. The school-marm, directed by grammarians, labors heroically, but all her effort goes for naught. The young American, like the youngster of any other race, inclines irresistibly toward the dialect that he hears at home, and that dialect, with its piquant neologisms, its high disdain of precedent, its complete lack of self-consciousness, is almost the antithesis of the hard and stiff speech that is expounded out of books. It derives its principles, not from the subtle logic of learned and stupid men, but from the rough-and-ready logic of every day. It has a vocabulary of its own, a syntax of its own, even a grammar of its own. Its verbs are conjugated in a way that defies all the injunctions of the grammar books; it has its contumacious rules of tense, number and case; it has boldly re-established the double negative, once sound in English; it admits double comparatives, confusions in person, clipped infinitives; it lays hands on the vowels, changing them to fit its obscure but powerful spirit; it disdains all the finer distinctions between the parts of speech.

This highly virile and defiant dialect, and not the fossilized English of the school-marm and her books, is the speech of the Middle American of Joseph Jacobs' composite picture—the mill-hand in a small city of Indiana, with his five years of common schooling behind him, his diligent reading of newspapers, and his proud membership in the Order of Foresters and the Knights of the Maccabees.[14] Go into any part of the country, North, East, South or West, and you will find multitudes of his brothers—car conductors in Philadelphia, immigrants of the second generation in the East Side of New York, iron-workers in the Pittsburgh region, corner grocers in St. Louis, holders of petty political jobs in Atlanta and New Orleans, small farmers in Kansas or Kentucky, house carpenters in Ohio, tinners and plumbers in Chicago, —genuine Americans all, hot for the home team, marchers in parades, readers of the yellow newspapers, fathers of families, sheep on election day, undistinguished norms of the *Homo Americanus.* Such typical Americans, after a fashion, know English. They can read it—all save the "hard" words, *i. e.,* all save about 90 per cent of the words of Greek and Latin origin.[15] They can understand perhaps two-thirds of it as it comes from the lips of a political orator or clergyman. They have a feeling that it is, in some recondite sense, superior to the common speech of their kind. They recognize a fluent command of it as the salient mark of a "smart" and "educated" man, one with "the gift of gab." But they themselves never speak it or try to speak it, nor do they look with approbation on efforts in that direction by their fellows.

In no other way, indeed, is the failure of popular education made more vividly manifest. Despite a gigantic effort to enforce certain speech habits, universally in operation from end to end of the country, the masses of the people turn almost unanimously to very different speech habits, nowhere advocated and seldom so much as even accurately observed. The literary critic, Francis Hackett, somewhere speaks of "the enormous gap between the literate and unliterate American." He is apparently the first to call attention to it. It is the national assumption that no such gap exists—that all Americans, at least if they be white, are so outfitted with sagacity in the public schools that they are competent to consider any public question intelligently and to follow its discussion with understanding. But the truth is, of course, that the public school accomplishes no such magic. The inferior man, in America as elsewhere, remains an inferior man despite the hard effort made to improve him, and his thoughts seldom if ever rise above the most elemental concerns. What lies above not only does not interest him; it actually excites his derision, and he has coined a unique word, *high-brow*, to express his view of it. Especially in speech is he suspicious of superior pretension. The school-boy of the lower orders would bring down ridicule upon himself, and perhaps criticism still more devastating, if he essayed to speak what his teachers conceive to be correct English, or even correct American, outside the school-room. On the one hand his companions would laugh at him as a prig, and on the other hand his parents would probably cane him as an impertinent critic of their own speech. Once he has made his farewell to the school-marm, all her diligence in this department goes for nothing.[16] The boys with whom he plays baseball speak a tongue that is not the one taught in school, and so do the youths with whom he will begin learning a trade tomorrow, and the girl he will marry later on, and the saloon-keepers, star pitchers, vaudeville comedians, business sharpers and political mountebanks he will look up to and try to imitate all the rest of his life.

So far as I can discover, there has been but one attempt by a competent authority to determine the special characters of this general tongue of the *mobile vulgus*. That authority is Dr. W. W. Charters, now head of the School of Education at the University of Illinois. In 1914 Dr. Charters was dean of the faculty of education and professor of the theory of teaching in the University of Missouri, and one of the problems he was engaged upon was that of the teaching of grammar. In the course of this study he encountered the theory that such instruction should be confined to the rules habitually violated—that the one aim of teaching grammar was to correct the speech of the pupils, and that it was useless to harass them with principles which they already instinctively observed. Apparently inclining to this somewhat dubious notion, Dr. Charters applied to the School Board of Kansas City for permission to undertake an examination of the language actually used by the children in the elementary schools of that city, and this permission was granted. The materials thereupon gathered were of two classes. First, the teachers of grades III to VII inclusive in all the Kansas City public-schools were instructed to turn over to Dr. Charters all the written work of their pupils, "ordinarily done in the regular order of school work" during a period of four weeks. Secondly, the teachers of grades II to VII inclusive were instructed to make note of "all oral errors in grammar made in the school-room and around the school-building" during the five school-days of one week, by children of any age, and to dispatch these notes to Dr. Charters also. The result was an accumulation of material so huge that it was unworkable with the means at hand, and so the investigator and his assistants reduced it. Of the oral reports, two studies were made, the first of those from grades III and VII and the second of those from grades VI and VII. Of the written reports, only those from grades VI and VII of twelve typical schools were examined.

The ages thus covered ran from nine or ten to fourteen or fifteen, and perhaps five-sixths of the material studied came from children above twelve. Its examination threw a brilliant light upon the speech actually employed by children near the end of their schooling in a typical American city, and, *per corollary*, upon the speech employed by their parents and other older associates. If anything, the grammatical and syntactical habits revealed were a bit less loose than those of the authentic *Volkssprache*, for practically all of the written evidence was gathered under conditions which naturally caused the writers to try to write what they conceived to be correct English, and even the oral evidence was conditioned by the admonitory presence of the teachers. Moreover, it must be obvious that a child of the lower classes, during the period of its actual study of grammar, probably speaks better English than at any time before or afterward, for it is only then that any positive pressure is exerted upon it to that end. But even so, the departures from standard usage that were unearthed were numerous and striking, and their tendency to accumulate in definite groups showed plainly the working of general laws.[17]

Thus, no less than 57 per cent of the oral errors reported by the teachers of grades III and VII involved the use of the verb, and nearly half of these, or 24 per cent, of the total, involved a confusion of the past tense form and the perfect participle. Again, double negatives constituted 11 per cent of the errors, and the misuse of adjectives or of adjectival forms for adverbs ran to 4 per cent. Finally, the difficulties of the objective case among the pronouns, the last stronghold of that case in English, were responsible for 7 per cent, thus demonstrating a clear tendency to get rid of it altogether. Now compare the errors of these children, half of whom, as I have just said, were in grade III, and hence wholly uninstructed in formal grammar, with the errors made by children of the second oral group—that is, children of grades VI and VII, in both of which grammar is studied. Dr. Charters' tabulations show scarcely any difference in the character and relative rank of the errors discovered. Those in the use of the verb drop from 57 per cent of the total to 52 per cent, but the double negatives remain at 7 per cent and the errors in the case of pronouns at 11 per cent.

In the written work of grades VI and VII, however, certain changes appear, no doubt because of the special pedagogical effort against the more salient oral errors. The child, pen in hand, has in mind the cautions oftenest heard, and so reveals something of that greater exactness which all of us show when we do any writing that must bear critical inspection. Thus, the relative frequency of confusions between the past tense forms of verbs and the perfect participles drops from 24 per cent to 5 per cent, and errors based on double negatives drop to 1 per cent. But this improvement in one direction merely serves to unearth new barbarisms in other directions, concealed in the oral tables by the flood of errors now remedied. It is among the verbs that they are still most numerous; altogether, the errors here amount to exactly 50 per cent of the total. Such locutions as *I had went* and *he seen* diminish relatively and absolutely, but in all other situations the verb is treated with the lavish freedom that is so characteristic of the American common speech. Confusions of the past and present tenses jump from 2 per cent to 19 per cent, thus eloquently demonstrating the tenacity of the error. And mistakes in the forms of nouns and pronouns increase from 2 per cent to 16: a shining proof of a shakiness which follows the slightest effort to augment the vocabulary of everyday.

The materials collected by Dr. Charters and his associates are not, of course, presented in full, but his numerous specimens must strike familiar chords in every ear that is alert to the sounds and ways of the *sermo vulgus*. What he gathered in Kansas City might have been gathered just as well in San Francisco, or New Orleans, or Chicago, or New York, or in Youngstown, O., or Little Rock, Ark., or Waterloo, Iowa. In each of these places, large or small, a few localisms might have been noted—*oi* substituted for ur in New York, *you-all* in the South, a few Germanisms in Pennsylvania and in the upper Mississippi Valley, a few Spanish locutions in the Southwest, certain peculiar vowel-forms in New England—but in the main the report would have been identical with the report he makes. That vast uniformity which marks the people of the United States, in political doctrine, in social habit, in general information, in reaction to ideas, in prejudices and enthusiasms, in the veriest details of domestic custom and dress, is nowhere more marked than in language. The incessant neologisms of the national speech sweep the whole country almost instantly, and the iconoclastic changes which its popular spoken form are undergoing show themselves from coast to coast. "He hurt *his* self, " cited by Dr. Charters, is surely anything but a Missouri localism; one hears it everywhere. And so, too, one hears "she invited *him* and *I*, " and "it hurt *terrible*, " and "I *set* there, " and "this *here* man, " and "no, I *never, neither*", and "he *ain't* here, " and "where is he *at*?" and "it seems *like* I remember, " and "if I *was* you, " and "*us* fellows, " and "he *give* her hell." And "he *taken* and kissed her, " and "he *loaned* me a dollar, " and "the man was *found* two dollars, " and "the bee *stang* him, " and "I *wouldda* thought, " and "*can* I have one?" and "he got *hisn*, " and "the boss *left* him off, " and "the baby *et* the soap, " and "*them* are the kind I like, " and "he *don't* care, " and "no one has *their* ticket, " and "how *is* the folks?" and "if you would *of gotten* in the car you could *of rode* down."

Curiously enough, this widely dispersed and highly savory dialect—already, as I shall show, come to a certain grammatical regularity—has attracted the professional writers of the country almost as little as it has attracted the philologists. There are foreshadowings of it in "Huckleberry Finn, " in "The Biglow Papers" and even in the rough humor of the period that began with J. C. Neal and company and ended with Artemus Ward and Josh Billings, but in those early days it had not yet come to full flower; it wanted the influence of the later immigrations to take on its present character. The enormous dialect literature of twenty years ago left it almost untouched. Localisms were explored diligently, but the general dialect went virtually unobserved. It is not in "Chimmie Fadden"; it is not in "David Harum"; it is not even in the pre-fable stories of George Ade, perhaps the most acute observer of average, undistinguished American types, urban and rustic, that American literature has yet produced. The business of reducing it to print had to wait for Ring W. Lardner, a Chicago newspaper reporter. In his grotesque tales of base-ball players, so immediately and so deservedly successful and now so widely imitated, [18] Lardner reports the common speech not only with humor, but also with the utmost accuracy. The observations of Charters and his associates are here reinforced by the sharp ear of one specially competent, and the result is a mine of authentic American.

In a single story by Lardner, in truth, it is usually possible to discover examples of almost every logical and grammatical peculiarity of the emerging language, and he always resists very stoutly the temptation to overdo the thing. Here, for example, are a few typical sentences from "The Busher's Honeymoon":[19]

I and Florrie *was* married the day before yesterday just *like* I told you we *was* going to be.... You *was* wise to get married in Bedford, where *not nothing* is nearly half so dear.... The sum of what I have *wrote* down is $29.40.... Allen told me I *should ought* to give the priest $5.... I never *seen* him before.... I didn't used to eat *no* lunch in the playing season except when I *knowed* I was not going to work.... I guess the meals *has* cost me all together about $1.50, and I have *eat* very little myself....

I was willing to tell her all about *them* two poor girls.... They must not be *no* mistake about who is the boss in my house. Some men *lets* their *wife* run all over them.... Allen has *went* to a college football game. One of the reporters *give* him a pass.... He called up and said he *hadn't* only the one pass, but he was not hurting my feelings *none*.... The flat across the hall from this *here* one is for rent.... If we should *of boughten* furniture it would cost us in the neighborhood of $100, even without *no* piano.... I consider myself lucky to *of* found out about this before it was too late and somebody else had *of* gotten the tip.... It will always be *ourn*, even when we move away.... Maybe you could *of did* better if you had *of went* at it in a different way.... Both *her* and you *is* welcome at my house.... I never *seen* so much wine *drank* in my life....

Here are specimens to fit into most of Charters' categories—verbs confused as to tense, pronouns confused as to case, double and even triple negatives, nouns and verbs disagreeing in number, *have* softened to *of*, *n* marking the possessive instead of *s*, *like* used in place of *as*, and the personal pronoun substituted for the demonstrative adjective. A study of the whole story would probably unearth all the remaining errors noted in Kansas City. Lardner's baseball player, though he has pen in hand and is on his guard, and is thus very careful to write *would not* instead of *wouldn't* and even *am not* instead of *ain't*, offers a comprehensive and highly instructive panorama of popular speech habits. To him the forms of the subjunctive mood have no existence, and *will* and *shall* are identical, and adjectives and adverbs are indistinguishable, and the objective case is merely a variorum form of the nominative. His past tense is, more often than not, the orthodox present tense. All fine distinctions are obliterated in his speech. He uses invariably the word that is simplest, the grammatical form that is handiest. And so he moves toward the philological millennium dreamed of by George T. Lanigan, when "the singular verb shall lie down with the plural noun, and a little conjugation shall lead them."

§ 3. The Verb

—A study of the materials amassed by Charters and Lardner, if it be reinforced by observation of what is heard on the streets every day, will show that the chief grammatical peculiarities of spoken American lie among the verbs and pronouns. The nouns in common use, in the overwhelming main, are quite sound in form. Very often, of course, they do not belong to the vocabulary of English, but they at least belong to the vocabulary of American: the proletariat, setting aside transient slang, calls things by their proper names, and pronounces those names more or less correctly. The adjectives, too, are treated rather politely, and the adverbs, though commonly transformed into adjectives, are not further mutilated. But the verbs and pronouns undergo changes which set off the common speech very sharply from both correct English and correct American. Their grammatical relationships are thoroughly overhauled and sometimes they are radically modified in form.

This process is natural and inevitable, for it is among the verbs and pronouns, as we have seen, that the only remaining grammatical inflections in English, at least of any force or consequence, are to be found, and so they must bear the chief pressure of the influences that have been warring upon all inflections since the earliest days. The primitive Indo-European language, it is probable, had eight cases of the noun; the oldest known Teutonic dialect reduced them to six; in Anglo-Saxon they fell to four, with a weak and moribund instrumental hanging in the air; in Middle English the dative and accusative began to decay; in Modern English they have disappeared altogether, save as ghosts to haunt grammarians. But we still have two plainly defined conjugations of the verb, and we still inflect it for number, and, in part, at least, for person. And we yet retain an objective case of the pronoun, and inflect it for person, number and gender.

Some of the more familiar conjugations of verbs in the American common speech, as recorded by Charters or Lardner or derived from my own collectanea, are here set down:

Present	*Preterite*	*Perfect Participle*
Am	was	bin (or ben)[20]
Attack	attackted	attackted
(Be)[21]	was	bin (or ben) [20]
Beat	beaten	Beat
Become[22]	become	became
Begin	begun	Began
Bend	bent	Bent
Bet	bet	Bet
Bind	bound	Bound
Bite	bitten	Bit
Bleed	bled	Bled
Blow	blowed (or blew)	blowed (or blew)
Break	broken	Broke
Bring	brought (or brung, or brang)	Brung
Broke (passive)	broke	Broke
Build	built	Built
Burn	burnt[23]	Burnt
Burst[24]	——	——
Bust	busted	Busted
Buy	bought (or boughten)	bought (or boughten)
Can	could	could'a

Catch	caught[25]	Caught
Choose	chose	Choose
Climb	clum	Clum
Cling (to hold fast) clung	clung	
Cling (to ring)	clang	Clang
Come	come	Came
Creep	crep (or crope)	Crep
Crow	crew	Crew
Cut	cut	Cut
Dare	dared	Dared
Deal	dole	Dealt
Dig	dug	Dug
Dive	dove	Dived
Do	done	done (or did)
Drag	drug	dragged
Draw	drawed[26]	drawed (or drew)
Dream	dreampt	dreampt
Drink	drank (or drunk)	Drank
Drive	drove	Drove
Drown	drownded	drownded
Eat	et (or eat)	Ate
Fall	fell (or fallen)	Fell
Feed	fed	Fed
Feel	felt	Felt
Fetch	fetched[27]	Fetch
Fight	fought[28]	Fought
Find	found	Found

Fine	found	Found
Fling	flang	Flung
Flow	flew	Flowed
Fly	flew	Flew
Forget	forgotten	forgotten
Forsake	forsaken	Forsook
Freeze	frozen (or friz)	Frozen
Get	got (or gotten)	Gotten
Give	give	Give
Glide	glode[29]	Glode
Go	went	Went
Grow	growed	Growed
Hang	hung[30]	Hung
Have	had	had (or hadden)
Hear	heerd	heerd (or heern)
Heat	het[31]	Het
Heave	hove	Hove
Hide	hidden	Hid
H'ist[32]	h'isted	h'isted
Hit	hit	Hit
Hold	helt	held (or helt)
Holler	hollered	hollered
Hurt	hurt	Hurt
Keep	kep	Kep
Kneel	knelt	Knelt
Know	knowed	Knew
Lay	laid (or lain)	Laid

Lead	led	Led
Lean	lent	Lent
Leap	lep	Lep
Learn	learnt	Learnt
Lend	loaned[33]	Loaned
Lie (to falsify)	lied	Lied
Lie (to recline)	laid (or lain)	Laid
Light	lit	Lit
Lose	lost	Lost
Make	made	Made
May	——	might'a
Mean	meant	Meant
Meet	met	Met
Mow	mown	Mowed
Pay	paid	Paid
Plead	pled	Pled
Prove	proved (or proven)	Proven
Put	put	Put
Quit	quit	Quit
Raise	raised	Raised
Read	read	Read
Rench[34]	renched	renched
Rid	rid	Rid
Ride	ridden	Rode
Rile[35]	riled	Riled
Ring	rung	Rang
Rise	riz (or rose)	Riz
Run	run	Ran

Say	sez	Said
See	seen	Saw
Sell	sold	Sold
Send	sent	Sent
Set	set[36]	Sat
Shake	shaken (or shuck)	Shook
Shave	shaved	Shaved
Shed	shed	Shed
Shine (to polish)	shined	Shined
Shoe	shoed	Shoed
Shoot	shot	Shot
Show	shown	showed
Sing	sung	Sang
Sink	sunk	Sank
Sit[37]	——	——
Skin	skun	Skun
Sleep	slep	Slep
Slide	slid	Slid
Sling	slang	Slung
Slit	slitted	Slitted
Smell	smelt	Smelt
Sneak	snuck	Snuck
Speed	speeded	speeded
Spell	spelt	Spelt
Spill	spilt	Spilt
Spin	span	Span
Spit	spit	Spit
Spoil	spoilt	Spoilt
Spring	sprung	Sprang

Steal	stole	Stole
Sting	stang	Stang
Stink	stank	Stank
Strike	struck	Struck
Swear	swore	Swore
Sweep	swep	Swep
Swell	swole	swollen
Swim	swum	Swam
Swing	swang	Swung
Take	taken	Took
Teach	taught	Taught
Tear	tore	Torn
Tell	tole	Tole
Think	thought[38]	thought
Thrive	throve	Throve
Throw	throwed	Threw
Tread	tread	Tread
Wake	woke	Woken
Wear	wore	Wore
Weep	wep	Wep
Wet	wet	Wet
Win	won (or wan)[39]	won (or wan)
Wind	wound	Wound
Wish (wisht)	wisht	Wisht
Wring	wrung	Wrang
Write	written	Wrote

A glance at these conjugations is sufficient to show several general tendencies, some of them going back, in their essence, to the earliest days of the English language. The most obvious is that leading to the transfer of verbs from the so-called strong conjugation to the weak—a change already in operation before the Norman Conquest, and very marked during the Middle English period. Chaucer used *growed* for *grew* in the prologue to "The Wife of Bath's Tale, " and *rised* for *rose* and *smited* for *smote* are in John Purvey's edition of the Bible, *circa* 1385.[40] Many of these transformations were afterward abandoned, but a large number survived, for example, *climbed* for *clomb* as the preterite of *to climb*, and *melted* for *molt* as the preterite of *to melt*. Others showed themselves during the early part of the Modern English period. *Comed* as the perfect participle of *to come* and *digged* as the preterite of *to dig* are both in Shakespeare, and the latter is also in Milton and in the Authorized Version of the Bible. This tendency went furthest, of course, in the vulgar speech, and it has been embalmed in the English dialects. *I seen* and *I knowed*, for example, are common to many of them. But during the seventeenth century it seems to have been arrested, and even to have given way to a contrary tendency—that is, toward strong conjugations. The English of Ireland, which preserves many seventeenth century forms, shows this plainly. *Ped* for *paid*, *gother* for *gathered*, and *ruz* for *raised* are still in use there, and Joyce says flatly that the Irish, "retaining the old English custom [*i. e.*, the custom of the period of Cromwell's invasion, *circa* 1650], have a leaning toward the strong inflection."[41] Certain verb forms of the American colonial period, now reduced to the estate of localisms, are also probably survivors of the seventeenth century.

"The three great causes of change in language, " says Sayce, "may be briefly described as (1) imitation or analogy, (2) a wish to be clear and emphatic, and (3) laziness. Indeed, if we choose to go deep enough we might reduce all three causes to the general one of laziness, since it is easier to imitate than to say something new."[42] This tendency to take well-worn paths, paradoxically enough, is responsible both for the transfer of verbs from the strong to the weak declension, and for the transfer of certain others from the weak to the strong. A verb in everyday use tends almost inevitably to pull less familiar verbs with it, whether it be strong or weak. Thus *fed* as the preterite of *to feed* and *led* as the preterite of *to lead* paved the way for *pled* as the preterite of *to plead*, and *rode* as plainly performed the same office for *glode*, and *rung* for *brung*, and *drove* for *dove* and *hove*, and *stole* for *dole*, and *won* for *skun*. Moreover, a familiar verb, itself acquiring a faulty inflection, may fasten a similar inflection upon another verb of like sound. Thus *het*, as the preterite of *to heat*, no doubt owes its existence to the example of *et*, the vulgar preterite of *to eat*. So far the irregular verbs. The same combination of laziness and imitativeness works toward the regularization of certain verbs that are historically irregular. In addition, of course, there is the fact that regularization is itself intrinsically simplification—that it makes the language easier. One sees the antagonistic pull of the two influences in the case of verbs ending in *-ow*. The analogy of *knew* suggests *snew* as the preterite of *to snow*, and it is sometimes encountered in the American vulgate. But the analogy of *snowed* also suggests *knowed*, and the superior regularity of the form is enough to overcome the greater influence of *knew* as a more familiar word than *snowed*. Thus *snew* grows rare and is in decay, but *knowed* shows vigor, and so do *growed* and *throwed*. The substitution of *heerd* for *heard* also presents a case of logic and convenience supporting analogy. The form is suggested by *steered*, *feared* and *cheered*, but its main advantage lies in the fact that it gets rid of a vowel change, always an impediment to easy speech. Here, as in the contrary direction, one barbarism breeds another. Thus *taken*, as the preterite of *to take*, has undoubtedly helped to make preterites of two other perfects, *shaken* and *forsaken*.

But in the presence of two exactly contrary tendencies, the one in accordance with the general movement of the language since the Norman Conquest and the other opposed to it, it is unsafe, of course, to attempt any very positive generalizations. All one may exhibit with safety is a general habit of treating the verb conveniently. Now and then, disregarding grammatical tendencies, it is possible to discern what appear to be logical causes for verb phenomena. That *lit* is preferred to *lighted* and *hung* to *hanged* is probably the result of an aversion to fine distinctions, and perhaps, more fundamentally, to the passive. Again, the use of *found* as the preterite of *to fine* is obviously due to an ignorant confusion of *fine* and *find*, due to the wearing off of *-d* in *find*, and that of *lit* as the preterite of *to alight* to a confusion of *alight* and *light*. Yet again, the use of *tread* as its own preterite in place of *trod* is probably the consequence of a vague feeling that a verb ending with *d* is already of preterite form. *Shed* exhibits the same process. Both are given a logical standing by such preterites as *bled*, *fed*, *fled*, *led*, *read*, *dead* and *spread*. But here, once more, it is hazardous to lay down laws, for *shredded*, *headed*, *dreaded*, *threaded* and *breaded* at once come to mind. In other cases it is still more difficult to account for preterites in common use. *Drug* is wholly illogical, and so are *clum* and *friz*. Neither, fortunately, has yet supplanted the more intelligible form of its verb, and so it is not necessary to speculate about them. As for *crew*, it is archaic English surviving in American, and it was formed, perhaps, by analogy with *knew*, which has succumbed in American to *knowed*.

Some of the verbs of the vulgate show the end products of language movements that go back to the Anglo-Saxon period, and even beyond. There is, for example, the disappearance of the final *t* in such words as *crep, slep, lep, swep* and *wep*. Most of these, in Anglo-Saxon, were strong verbs. The preterite of *to sleep (slâepan)*, for example, was *slēp*, and that of *to weep* was *weop*. But in the course of time both *to sleep* and *to weep* acquired weak preterite endings, the first becoming *slâepte* and the second *wepte*. This weak conjugation was itself degenerated. Originally, the inflectional suffix had been *-de* or *-ede* and in some cases *-ode*, and the vowels were always pronounced. The wearing down process that set in in the twelfth century disposed of the finale, but in certain words the other vowel survived for a good while, and we still observe it in such archaisms as *belovéd*. Finally, however, it became silent in other preterites, and *loved*, for example, began to be pronounced (and often written) as a word of one syllable: *lov'd*.[43] This final *d*-sound now fell upon difficulties of its own. After certain consonants it was hard to pronounce clearly, and so the sonant was changed into the easier surd, and such words as *pushed* and *clipped* became, in ordinary conversation, *pusht* and *clipt*. In other verbs the *t*-sound had come in long before, with the degenerated weak ending, and when the final *e* was dropped their stem vowels tended to change. Thus arose such forms as *slept*. In vulgar American another step is taken, and the suffix is dropped altogether. Thus, by a circuitous route, verbs originally strong, and for many centuries hovering between the two conjugations, have eventually become strong again.

The case of *helt* is probably an example of change by false analogy. During the thirteenth century, according to Sweet, [44] "*d* was changed to *t* in the weak preterites of verbs [ending] in *rd, ld* and *nd*." Before that time the preterite of *sende (send)* had been *sende*; now it became *sente*. It survives in our modern *sent*, and the same process is also revealed in *built, girt, lent, rent* and *bent*. The popular speech, disregarding the fact that *to hold* is a strong verb, arrives at *helt* by imitation. In the case of *tole*, which I almost always hear in place of *told*, there is a leaping of steps. The *d* is got rid of without any transitional use of *t*. So also, perhaps, in *swole*, which is fast displacing *swelled*. *Attackted* and *drownded* seem to be examples of an effort to dispose of harsh combinations by a contrary process. Both are very old in English. *Boughten* and *dreampt* present greater difficulties. Lounsbury says that *boughten* probably originated in the Northern [*i. e.*, Lowland Scotch] dialect of English, "which ... inclined to retain the full form of the past participle, " and even to add its termination "to words to which it did not properly belong."[45] I record *dreampt* without attempting to account for it. I have repeatedly heard a distinct *p*-sound in the word.

The general tendency toward regularization is well exhibited by the new verbs that come into the language constantly. Practically all of them show the weak conjugation, for example, *to phone, to bluff, to rubber-neck, to ante, to bunt, to wireless, to insurge* and *to loop-the-loop*. Even when a compound has as its last member a verb ordinarily strong, it remains weak itself. Thus the preterite of *to joy-ride* is not *joy-rode*, nor even *joy-ridden*, but *joy-rided*. And thus *bust*, from *burst*, is regular and its preterite is *busted*, though *burst* is irregular and its preterite is the verb itself unchanged. The same tendency toward regularity is shown by the verbs of the *kneel*-class. They are strong in English, but tend to become weak in colloquial American. Thus the preterite of *to kneel*, despite the example of *to sleep* and its analogues, is not *knel'*, nor even *knelt*, but *kneeled*. I have even heard *feeled* as the preterite of *to feel*, as in "I *feeled* my way, " though here *felt* still persists. *To spread* also tends to become weak, as in "he *spreaded* a piece of bread." And *to peep* remains so, despite the example of *to leap*. The confusion between the inflections of *to lie* and those of *to lay* extends to the higher reaches of spoken American, and so does that between *lend* and *loan*. The proper inflections of *to lend* are often given to *to loan*, and so *leaned* becomes *lent*, as in "I *lent* on the counter." In the same way *to set* has almost completely superseded *to sit*, and the preterite of the former, *set*, is used in place of *sat*. But the perfect participle (which is also the disused preterite) of *to sit* has survived, as in "I have *sat* there." *To speed* and *to shoe* have become regular, not only because of the general tendency toward the weak conjugation, but also for logical reasons. The prevalence of speed contests of various sorts, always to the intense interest of the proletariat, has brought such words as *speeder, speeding, speed-mania, speed-maniac* and *speed-limit* into daily use, and *speeded* harmonizes with them better than the stronger *sped*. As for *shoed*, it merely reveals the virtual disappearance of the verb in its passive form. An American would never say that his wife was well *shod*; he would say that she wore good shoes. *To shoe* suggests to him only the shoeing of animals, and so, by way of *shoeing* and *horse-shoer*, he comes to *shoed*. His misuse of *to learn* for *to teach* is common to most of the English dialects. More peculiar to his speech is the use of *to leave* for *to let*. Charters records it in "Washington *left* them have it, " and there are many examples of it in Lardner. *Spit*, in American, has become invariable; the old preterite, *spat*, has completely disappeared. But *slit*, which is now invariable in English (though it was strong in Old English and had both strong and weak preterites in Middle English), has become regular in American, as in "she *slitted* her skirt."

In studying the American verb, of course, it is necessary to remember always that it is in a state of transition, and that in many cases the manner of using it is not yet fixed. "The history of language, " says Lounsbury, "when looked at from the purely grammatical point of view, is little else than the history of corruptions." What we have before us is a series of corruptions in active process, and while some of them have gone very far, others are just beginning. Thus it is not uncommon to find corrupt forms side by side with orthodox forms, or even two corrupt forms battling with each other. Lardner, in the case of *to throw*, hears "if he had *throwed*"; my own observation is that *threw* is more often used in that situation. Again, he uses "the rottenest I ever seen *gave*"; my own belief is that *give* is far more commonly used. The conjugation of *to give*, however, is yet very uncertain, and so Lardner may report accurately. I have heard "I *given*" and "I would of *gave*, " but "I *give*" seems to be prevailing, and "I would of *give*" with it, thus reducing *to give* to one invariable form, like those of *to cut, to hit, to put, to cost, to hurt* and *to spit*. My table of verbs shows various other uncertainties and confusions. The preterite of *to hear* is *heerd*;

the perfect may be either *heerd* or *heern*. That of *to do* may be either *done* or *did*, with the latter apparently prevailing; that of *to draw* is *drew* if the verb indicates to attract or to abstract and *drawed* if it indicates to draw with a pencil. Similarly, the preterite of *to blow* may be either *blowed* or *blew*, and that of *to drink* oscillates between *drank* and *drunk*, and that of *to fall* is still usually *fell*, though *fallen* has appeared, and that of *to shake* may be either *shaken* or *shuck*. The conjugation of *to win* is yet far from fixed. The correct English preterite, *won*, is still in use, but against it are arrayed *wan* and *winned*. *Wan* seems to show some kinship, by ignorant analogy, with *ran* and *began*. It is often used as the perfect participle, as in "I have *wan* $4."

The misuse of the perfect participle for the preterite, now almost the invariable rule in vulgar American, is common to many other dialects of English, and seems to be a symptom of a general decay of the perfect tenses. That decay has been going on for a long time, and in American, the most vigorous and advanced of all the dialects of the language, it is particularly well marked. Even in the most pretentious written American it shows itself. The English, in their writing, still use the future perfect, albeit somewhat laboriously and self-consciously, but in America it has virtually disappeared: one often reads whole books without encountering a single example of it. Even the present perfect and the past perfect seem to be instinctively avoided. The Englishman says "I *have* dined, " but the American says "I *am through* dinner"; the Englishman says "I *had* slept, " but the American often says "I *was done* sleeping." Thus the perfect tenses are forsaken for the simple present and the past. In the vulgate a further step is taken, and "I *have been* there" becomes "I *been* there." Even in such phrases as "he *hasn't* been here, " *ain't* (=*am not*) is commonly substituted for *have not*, thus giving the present perfect a flavor of the simple present. The step from "I *have taken*" to "*I taken*" was therefore neither difficult nor unnatural, and once it had been made the resulting locution was supported by the greater apparent regularity of its verb. Moreover, this perfect participle, thus put in place of the preterite, was further reinforced by the fact that it was the adjectival form of the verb, and hence collaterally familiar. Finally, it was also the authentic preterite in the passive voice, and although this influence, in view of the decay of the passive, may not have been of much consequence, nevertheless it is not to be dismissed as of no consequence at all.

The contrary substitution of the preterite for the perfect participle, as in "I have *went*" and "he has *did*, " apparently has a double influence behind it. In the first place, there is the effect of the confused and blundering effort, by an ignorant and unanalytical speaker, to give the perfect some grammatical differentiation when he finds himself getting into it—an excursion not infrequently made necessary by logical exigencies, despite his inclination to keep out. The nearest indicator at hand is the disused preterite, and so it is put to use. Sometimes a sense of its uncouthness seems to linger, and there is a tendency to give it an *en*-suffix, thus bringing it into greater harmony with its tense. I find that *boughten*, just discussed, is used much oftener in the perfect than in the simple past tense;[46] for the latter *bought* usually suffices. The quick ear of Lardner detects various other coinages of the same sort, among them *tooken*, as in "little Al might of *tooken* sick."[47] *Hadden* is also met with, as in "I would of *hadden*." But the majority of preterites remain unchanged. Lardner's baseball player never writes "I have *written*" or "I have *wroten*, " but always "I have *wrote*." And in the same way he always writes, "I have *did*, *ate*, *went*, *drank*, *rode*, *ran*, *saw*, *sang*, *woke* and *stole*." Sometimes the simple form of the verb persists through all tenses. This is usually the case, for example, with *to give*. I have noted "I *give*" both as present and as preterite, and "I have *give*, " and even "I had *give*." But even here "I have *gave*" offers rivalry to "I have *give*, " and usage is not settled. So, too, with *to come*. "I have *come*" and "I have *came*" seem to be almost equally favored, with the former supported by pedagogical admonition and the latter by the spirit of the language.

Whatever the true cause of the substitution of the preterite for the perfect participle, it seems to be a tendency inherent in English, and during the age of Elizabeth it showed itself even in the most formal speech. An examination of any play of Shakespeare's will show many such forms as "I have *wrote*, " "I am *mistook*" and "he has *rode*." In several cases this transfer of the preterite has survived. "I have *stood*, " for example, is now perfectly correct English, but before 1550 the form was "I have *stonden*." *To hold* and *to sit* belong to the same class; their original perfect participles were not *held* and *sat*, but *holden* and *sitten*. These survived the movement toward the formalization of the language which began with the eighteenth century, but scores of other such misplaced preterites were driven out. One of the last to go was *wrote*, which persisted until near the end of the century.[48] Paradoxically enough, the very purists who performed the purging showed a preference for *got* (though not for *forgot*), and it survives in correct English today in the preterite-present form, as in "I have *got*, " whereas in American, both vulgar and polite, the elder and more regular *gotten* is often used. In the polite speech *gotten* indicates a distinction between a completed action and a continuing action, —between obtaining and possessing. "I have *gotten* what I came for" is correct, and so is "I have *got* the measles." In the vulgar speech, much the same distinction exists, but the perfect becomes a sort of simple tense by the elision of *have*. Thus the two sentences change to "I *gotten* what I come for" and "I *got* the measles, " the latter being understood, not as past, but as present.

In "I have *got* the measles" *got* is historically a sort of auxiliary of *have*, and in colloquial American, as we have seen in the examples just given, the auxiliary has obliterated the verb. *To have*, as an auxiliary, probably because of its intimate relationship with the perfect tenses, is under heavy pressure, and promises to disappear from the situations in which it is still used. I have heard *was* used in place of it, as in "before the Elks *was* come here."[49] Sometimes it is confused ignorantly with a distinct *of*, as in "she would *of* drove, " and "I would *of* gave." More often it is shaded to a sort of particle, attached to the verb as an inflection, as in "he would 'a tole you, " and "who could 'a took it?" But this is not all. Having degenerated to such forms, it is now employed as a sort of auxiliary to itself, in the subjunctive, as in "if you had *of* went, " "if it had *of* been hard, " and "if I had *of* had."[50] I have encountered some rather astonishing examples of this doubling of the auxiliary: one appears in "I wouldn't had 'a went." Here, however, the *a* may belong partly to *had* and partly to *went*; such forms as *a-going* are very common in American. But in the other cases, and in such forms as "I had 'a wanted, " it clearly belongs to *had*. Sometimes for syntactical reasons, the degenerated form of *have* is put before *had* instead of after it, as in "I could *of* had her if I had *of* wanted to."[51] Meanwhile, *to have*, ceasing to be an auxiliary, becomes a general verb indicating compulsion. Here it promises to displace *must*. The

American seldom says "I *must* go"; he almost invariably says "I *have* to go, " or "I *have got* to go, " in which last case, as we have seen, *got* is the auxiliary.

The most common inflections of the verb for mode and voice are shown in the following paradigm of *to bite*:

Active Voice
Indicative Mode

Present	I bite	*Past Perfect*	I had of bit
Present Perfect	I have bit	*Future*	I will bite
Past	I bitten	*Future Perfect*	(wanting)

Subjunctive Mode

Present	If I bite	*Past Perfect*	If I had of bit
Past	If I bitten		

Potential Mode

Present	I can bite	*Past*	I could bite
Present Perfect	(wanting)	*Past Perfect*	I could of bit

Imperative (or Optative) Mode

Future	I shall (or will) bite

Infinitive Mode

(wanting)

Passive Voice
Indicative Mode

Present	I am bit	*Past Perfect*	I had been bit
Present Perfect	I been bit	*Future*	I will be bit
Past	I was bit	*Future Perfect*	(wanting)

Subjunctive Mode

Present	If I am bit	*Past Perfect*	If I had of been bit
Past	If I was bit		

Potential Mode

| **Present** | I can be bit | **Past** | I could be bit |
| **Present Perfect** | (wanting) | **Past Perfect** | I could of been bit |

Imperative Mode

(wanting)

Infinitive Mode

(wanting)

A study of this paradigm reveals several plain tendencies. One has just been discussed: the addition of a degenerated form of *have* to the preterite of the auxiliary, and its use in place of the auxiliary itself. Another is the use of *will* instead of *shall* in the first person future. *Shall* is confined to a sort of optative, indicating much more than mere intention, and even here it is yielding to *will*. Yet another is the consistent use of the transferred preterite in the passive. Here the rule in correct English is followed faithfully, though the perfect participle employed is not the English participle. "I am *broke*" is a good example. Finally, there is the substitution of *was* for *were* and of *am* for *be* in the past and present of the subjunctive. In this last case American is in accord with the general movement of English, though somewhat more advanced. *Be*, in the Shakespearean form of "where *be* thy brothers?" was expelled from the present indicative two hundred years ago, and survives today only in dialect. And as it thus yielded to *are* in the indicative, it now seems destined to yield to *am* and *is* in the subjunctive. It remains, of course, in the future indicative: "I will *be*." In American its conjugation coalesces with that of *am* in the following manner:

Present	I am	**Past Perfect**	I had of ben
Present Perfect	I bin (or ben)	**Future**	I will be
Past	I was	**Future** **Perfect**	(wanting)

And in the subjunction:

| **Present** | If I am | **Past Perfect** | If I had of ben |

Past   If I was

All signs of the subjunctive, indeed, seem to be disappearing from vulgar American. One never hears "if I *were* you, " but always "if I *was* you." In the third person the *-s* is not dropped from the verb. One hears, not "if she *go*, " but "if she *goes*." "If he *be* the man" is never heard; it is always "if he *is*." This war upon the forms of the subjunctive, of course, extends to the most formal English. "In Old English, " says Bradley, [52] "the subjunctive played as important a part as in modern German, and was used in much the same way. Its inflection differed in several respects from that of the indicative. But the only formal trace of the old subjunctive still remaining, except the use of *be* and *were*, is the omission of the final *s* in the third person singular. And even this is rapidly dropping out of use.... Perhaps in another generation the subjunctive forms will have ceased to exist except in the single instance of *were*, which serves a useful function, although we manage to dispense with a corresponding form in other verbs." Here, as elsewhere, unlettered American usage simply proceeds in advance of the general movement. *Be* and the omitted *s* are already dispensed with, and even *were* has been discarded.

In the same way the distinction between *will* and *shall*, preserved in correct English but already breaking down in the most correct American, has been lost entirely in the American common speech. *Will* has displaced *shall* completely, save in the imperative. This preference extends to the inflections of both. *Sha'n't* is very seldom heard; almost always *won't* is used instead. As for *should*, it is displaced by *ought to* (degenerated to *oughter* or *ought'a*), and in its negative form by *hadn't ought'a*, as in "he *hadn't oughter* said that, " reported by Charters. Lardner gives various redundant combinations of *should* and *ought*, as in "I don't feel as if I *should ought to* leave" and "they *should not ought to* of had." I have encountered the same form, but I don't think it is as common as the simple *ought'a*-forms. In the main, *should* is avoided, sometimes at considerable pains. Often its place is taken by the more positive *don't*. Thus "I *don't* mind" is used instead of "I *shouldn't* mind." *Don't* has also completely displaced *doesn't*, which is very seldom heard. "He *don't*" and "they *don't*" are practically universal. In the same way *ain't* has displaced *is not, am not, isn't* and *aren't*, and even *have not* and *haven't*. One recalls a famous

269

speech in a naval melodrama of twenty years ago: "We *ain't* got no manners, but we can fight like hell." Such forms as "he *ain't* here, " "I *ain't* the man, " "them *ain't* what I want" and "I *ain't* heerd of it" are common.

This extensive use of *ain't*, of course, is merely a single symptom of a general disregard of number, obvious throughout the verbs, and also among the pronouns, as we shall see. Charters gives many examples, among them, "how *is* Uncle Wallace and Aunt Clara?" "you *was*, " "there *is* six" and the incomparable "it *ain't* right to say, 'He *ain't* here today.'" In Lardner there are many more, for instance, "them Giants is not such rotten hitters, *is* they?" "the people *has* all wanted to shake hands with Matthewson and I" and "some of the men *has* brung their wife along." *Sez*(=*says*), used as the preterite of *to say*, shows the same confusion. One observes it again in such forms as "then I *goes* up to him." Here the decay of number helps in what threatens to become a decay of tense. Examples of it are not hard to find. The average race-track follower of the humbler sort seldom says "I *won* $2, " or even "I *wan* $2, " but almost always "I *win* $2." And in the same way he says "I *see* him come in, " not "I *saw* him" or "*seen* him." Charters' materials offers other specimens, among them "we *help* distributed the fruit, " "she *recognize*, hug, and *kiss* him" and "her father *ask* her if she intended doing what he *ask*." Perhaps the occasional use of *eat* as the preterite of *to eat*, as in "I *eat* breakfast as soon as I got up, " is an example of the same flattening out of distinctions. Lardner has many specimens, among them "if Weaver and them had not of *begin* kicking" and "they would of *knock* down the fence." I notice that *used*, in *used to be*, is almost always reduced to simple *use*, as in "it *use* to be the rule." One seldom, if ever, hears a clear *d* at the end. Here, of course, the elision of the *d* is due primarily to assimilation with the *t* of *to*—a second example of one form of decay aiding another form. But the tenses apparently tend to crumble without help. I frequently hear whole narratives in a sort of debased present: "I *says* to him.... Then he *ups* and *says*.... I *land* him one on the ear.... He *goes* down and out, ..." and so on.[53] Still under the spell of our disintegrating inflections, we are prone to regard the tense inflections of the verb as absolutely essential, but there are plenty of languages that get on without them, and even in our own language children and foreigners often reduce them to a few simple forms. Some time ago an Italian contractor said to me "I have *go* there often." Here one of our few surviving inflections was displaced by an analytical devise, and yet the man's meaning was quite clear, and it would be absurd to say that his sentence violated the inner spirit of English. That inner spirit, in fact, has inclined steadily toward "I have *go*" for a thousand years.

§ 4. The Pronoun

—The following paradigm shows the inflections of the personal pronoun in the American common speech:

First Person
Common Gender

	Singular	*Plural*
Nominative	I	we
Possessive Conjoint	my	our
Possessive Absolute	mine	ourn
Objective	me	us

Second Person
Common Gender

	Singular	
Nominative	you	yous
Possessive Conjoint	your	your
Possessive Absolute	yourn	yourn
Objective	you	yous

Third Person
Masculine Gender

Nominative	he	They
Possessive Conjoint	his	Their
Possessive Absolute	hisn	Theirn
Objective	him	Them

Feminine Gender

Nominative	she	They
Possessive Conjoint	her	Their
Possessive Absolute	hern	theirn
Objective	her	Them

Neuter Gender

Nominative	it	They
Possessive Conjoint	its	Theirn
Possessive Absolute	its	Their
Objective	it	Them

These inflections, as we shall see, are often disregarded in use, but nevertheless it is profitable to glance at them as they stand. The only variations that they show from standard English are the substitution of *n* for *s* as the distinguishing mark of the absolute form of the possessive, and the attempt to differentiate between the logical and the merely polite plurals in the second person by adding the usual sign of the plural to the former. The use of *n* in place of *s* is not an American innovation. It is found in many of the dialects of English, and is, in fact, historically quite as sound as the use of *s*. In John Wiclif's translation of the Bible (*circa* 1380) the first sentence of the Sermon on the Mount (Mark v, 3) is made: "Blessed be the pore in spirit, for the kyngdam in hevenes is *heren*." And in his version of Luke xxiv, 24, is this: "And some of *ouren* wentin to the grave." Here *heren*, (or *herun*) represents, of course, not the modern *hers*, but *theirs*. In Anglo-Saxon the word was *heora*, and down to Chaucer's day a modified form of it, *here*, was still used in the possessive plural in place of the modern *their*, though *they* had already displaced *hie* in the nominative.[54] But in John Purvey's revision of the Wiclif Bible, made a few years later, *hern* actually occurs in II Kings viii, 6, thus: "Restore thou to hir alle things that ben *hern*." In Anglo-Saxon there had been no distinction between the conjoint and absolute forms of the possessive pronouns; the simple genitive sufficed for both uses. But with the decay of that language the surviving remnants of its grammar began to be put to service somewhat recklessly, and so there arose a genitive inflection of this genitive—a true double inflection. In the Northern dialects of English that inflection was made by simply adding *s*, the sign of the possessive. In the Southern dialects the old *n*-declension was applied, and so there arose such forms as *minum* and *eowrum*(=*mine* and *yours*), from *min* and *eower* (=*my* and *your*).[55] Meanwhile, the original simple genitive, now become *youre*, also survived, and so the literature of the fourteenth century shows the three forms flourishing side by side: *youre, youres* and *youren*. All of them are in Chaucer.

Thus, *yourn, hern, hisn, ourn* and *theirn*, whatever their present offense to grammarians, are of a genealogy quite as respectable as that of *yours, hers, his, ours* and *theirs*. Both forms represent a doubling of inflections, and hence grammatical debasement. On the side of the *yours*-form is the standard usage of the past five hundred years, but on the side of the *yourn*-form there is no little force of analogy and logic, as appears on turning to *mine* and *thine*. In Anglo-Saxon, as we have seen, *my* was *min*; in the same way *thy* was *thin*. During the decadence of the language the final *n* was dropped in both cases before nouns—that is, in the conjoint form—but it was retained in the absolute form. This usage survives to our own day. One says "*my* book, " but "the book is *mine*"; "*thy* faith, " but "I am *thine*."[56] Also, one says "*no* matter, " but "I have *none*." Without question this retention of the *n* in these pronouns had something to do with the appearance of the *n*-declension in the treatment of *your, her, his* and *our*, and, after *their* had displaced *here* in the third person plural, in *their*. And equally without question it supports the vulgar American usage today. What that usage shows is simply the strong popular tendency to make language as simple and as regular as possible—to abolish subtleties and exceptions. The difference between "*his* book" and "the book is *his'n*" is exactly that between *my* and *mine, thy* and *thine*, in the examples just given. "Perhaps it would have been better, " says Bradley, "if the literary language had accepted *hisn*, but from some cause it did not do so."[57]

As for the addition of *s* to *you* in the nominative and objective of the second person plural, it exhibits no more than an effort to give clarity to the logical difference between the true plural and the mere polite plural. In several other dialects of English the same desire has given rise to cognate forms, and there are even secondary devices in American. In the South, for example, the true plural is commonly indicated by *you-all*, which, despite a Northern belief to the contrary, is never used in the singular by any save the most ignorant.[58] *You-all*, like *yous*, simply means *you-jointly* as opposed to the *you* that means *thou*. Again, there is the form observed in "you can *all of you* go to hell"—another plain effort to differentiate between singular and plural. The substitution of *you* for *thou* goes back to the end of the thirteenth century. It appeared in late Latin and in the other continental languages as well as in English, and at about the same time. In these languages the true singular survives alongside the transplanted plural, but English has dropped it entirely, save in its poetical and liturgical forms and in a few dialects. It passed out of ordinary polite speech before Elizabeth's day. By that time, indeed, its use had acquired an air of the offensive, such as it has today, save between intimates or to children, in Germany. Thus, at the trial of Sir Walter Raleigh in 1603, Sir Edward Coke, then attorney-general, displayed his animosity to Raleigh by addressing him as *thou*, and finally burst into the contemptuous "I *thou* thee, *thou* traitor!" And in "Twelfth Night" Sir Toby Belch urges Sir Andrew Aguecheek to provoke the disguised Viola to combat by *thouing* her. In our own time, with thou passed out entirely, even as a pronoun of contempt, the confusion between *you* in the plural and *you* in the singular presents plain difficulties to a man of limited linguistic resources. He gets around them by setting up a distinction that is well supported by logic and analogy. "I seen *yous*" is clearly separated from "I seen *you*.". And in the conjoint position "*yous* guys" is separated from "*you* liar."

So much for the personal pronouns. As we shall see, they are used in such a manner that the distinction between the nominative and the objective forms, though still existing grammatically, has begun to break down. But first it may be well to glance at the demonstrative and relative pronouns. Of the former there are but two in English, *this* and *that*, with their plural forms, *these* and *those*. To them, American adds a third, *them*, which is also the personal pronoun of the third person, objective case.[59] In addition it has adopted certain adverbial pronouns, *this-here*, *these-here*, *that-there*, *those-there* and *them-there*, and set up inflections of the original demonstratives by analogy with *mine*, *hisn* and *yourn*, to wit, *thisn*, *thesen*, *thatn* and *thosen*. I present some examples of everyday use:

Them are the kind I like.

Them men all work here.

Who is *this-here* Smith I hear about?

These-here are mine.

That-there medicine ain't no good.

Those-there wops has all took to the woods.

I wisht I had one of *them-there* Fords.

Thisn is better'n *thatn*.

I like *thesen* better'n *thosen*.

The origin of the demonstratives of the *thisn*-group is plain: they are degenerate forms of *this-one*, *that-one*, etc., just as *none* is a degenerate composition form of *no(t)-one*. In every case of their use that I have observed the simple demonstratives might have been set free and *one* actually substituted for the terminal *n*. But it must be equally obvious that they have been reinforced very greatly by the absolutes of the *hisn*-group, for in their relation to the original demonstratives they play the part of just such absolutes and are never used conjointly. Thus, one says, in American, "I take *thisn*" or "*thisn* is mine, " but one never says "I take *thisn* hat" or "*thisn* dog is mine." In this conjoint situation plain *this* is always used, and the same rule applies to *these*, *those* and *that.Them*, being a newcomer among the demonstratives, has not yet acquired an inflection in the absolute. I have never heard *them'n*, and it will probably never come in, for it is forbiddingly clumsy. One says, in American, both "*them* are mine" and "*them* collars are mine."

This-here, *these-here*, *that-there*, *those-there* and *them-there* are plainly combinations of pronouns and adverbs, and their function is to support the distinction between proximity, as embodied in *this* and *these*, and remoteness, as embodied in *that*, *those* and *them*. "*This-here* coat is mine" simply means "this coat, *here*, or this *present* coat, is mine." But the adverb promises to coalesce with the pronoun so completely as to obliterate all sense of its distinct existence, even as a false noun or adjective. As commonly pronounced, *this-here* becomes a single word, somewhat like *thish-yur*, and *these-here* becomes *these-yur*, and *that-there* and *them-there* become *that-ere* and *them-ere*. *Those-there*, if I observed accurately, is still pronounced more distinctly, but it, too, may succumb to composition in time. The adverb will then sink to the estate of a mere inflectional particle, as *one* has done in the absolutes of the *thisn*-group. *Them*, as a personal pronoun in the absolute, of course, is commonly pronounced *em*, as in "I seen *em*, " and sometimes its vowel is almost lost, but this is also the case in all save the most exact spoken English. Sweet and Lounsbury, following the German grammarians, argue that this *em* is not really a debased form of *them*, but the offspring of *hem*, which survived as the regular plural of the third person in the objective case down to the beginning of the fifteenth century. But in American *them* is clearly pronounced as a demonstrative. I have never heard "*em* men" or "*em* are the kind I like, " but always "*them* men" and "*them* are the kind I like."

The relative pronouns, so far as I have been able to make out, are declined as follows:

Nominative	who	which	what	that
Possessive Conjoint	whose	whose		
Possessive Absolute	whosen	whosen		
Objective	who	which	what	that

Two things will be noted in this paradigm. First there is the disappearance of *whom* as the objective form of *who*, and secondly there is the appearance of an inflected form of *whose* in the absolute, by analogy with *mine, hisn* and *thesen*. *Whom*, as we have seen, is fast disappearing from standard spoken American;[60] in the vulgar language it is already virtually extinct. Not only is *who* used in such constructions as "*who* did you find there?" where even standard spoken English would tolerate it, but also in such constructions as "the man *who* I saw, " "them *who* I trust in" and "to *who*?" Krapp explains this use of *who* on the ground that there is a "general feeling, " due to the normal word-order in English, that "the word which precedes the verb is the subject word, or at least the subject form."[61] But this explanation is probably fanciful. Among the plain people no such "general feeling" for case exists. Their only "general feeling" is a prejudice against case inflections in any form whatsoever. They use *who* in place of *whom* simply because they can discern no logical difference between the significance of the one and the significance of the other.

Whosen is obviously the offspring of the other absolutes in *n*. In the conjoint relation plain *whose* is always used, as in "*whose* hat is that?" and "the man *whose* dog bit me." But in the absolute *whosen* is often substituted, as in "if it ain't *hisn*, then *whosen* is it?" The imitation is obvious. There is an analogous form of *which*, to wit, *whichn*, resting heavily on *which one*. Thus, "*whichn* do you like?" and "I didn't say *whichn*" are plainly variations of "*which one* do you like?" and "I didn't say *which one*." That, as we have seen, has a like form, *thatn*, but never, of course, in the relative situation. "I like *thatn*, " is familiar, but "the one *thatn* I like" is never heard. If *that*, as a relative, could be used absolutely, I have no doubt that it would change to *thatn*, as it does as a demonstrative. So with *what*. As things stand, it is sometimes substituted for *that*, as in "them's the kind *what* I like." Joined to *but* it can also take the place of *that* in other situations, as in "I don't know *but what*."

The substitution of *who* for *whom* in the objective case, just noticed, is typical of a general movement toward breaking down all case distinctions among the pronouns, where they make their last stand in English and its dialects. This movement, of course, is not peculiar to vulgar American; nor is it of recent beginning. So long ago as the fifteenth century the old clear distinction between *ye*, nominative, and *you*, objective, disappeared, and today the latter is used in both cases. Sweet says that the phonetic similarity between *ye* and *thee*, the objective form of the true second singular, was responsible for this confusion.[62] At the start *ye* actually went over to the objective case, and the usage thus established shows itself in such survivors of the period as *harkee* (*hark ye*) and *look ye*. In modern spoken English, indeed, *you* in the objective often has a sound far more like that of *ye* than like that of *you*, as, for example, in "how do y' do?" and in American its vowel takes the neutral form of the *e* in the definite article, and the word becomes a sort of shortened *yuh*. But whenever emphasis is laid upon it, *you* becomes quite distinct, even in American. In "I mean *you*, " for example, there is never any chance of mistaking it for *ye*.

In Shakespeare's time the other personal pronouns of the objective case threatened to follow *you* into the nominative, and there was a compensatory movement of the nominative pronouns toward the objective. Lounsbury has collected many examples.[63] Marlowe used "is it *him* you seek?" "'tis *her* I esteem" and "nor *thee* nor *them*, shall want"; Fletcher used "'tis *her* I admire"; Shakespeare himself used "that's *me*." Contrariwise, Webster used "what difference is between the duke and *I*?" and Greene used "nor earth nor heaven shall part my love and *I*." Krapp has unearthed many similar examples from the Restoration dramatists.[64] Etheredge used "'tis *them*, " "it may be *him*, " "let you and *I*" and "nor is it *me*"; Matthew Prior, in a famous couplet, achieved this:

For thou art a girl as much brighter than *her*.

As he was a poet sublimer than *me*.

The free exchange continued, in fact, until the eighteenth century was well advanced; there are examples of it in Addison. Moreover, it survived, at least in part, even the attack that was then made upon it by the professors of the new-born science of English grammar, and to this day "it is *me*" is still in more or less good colloquial use. Sweet thinks that it is supported in such use, though not, of course, grammatically, by the analogy of the correct "it is *he*" and "it is *she*." Lounsbury, following Dean Alford, says it came into English in imitation of the French *c'est moi*, and defends it as at least as good as "it is *I*."[65] The contrary form, "between you and *I*, " has no defenders, and is apparently going out. But in the shape of "between my wife and *I*" it is seldom challenged, at least in spoken English.

All these liberties with the personal pronouns, however, fade to insignificance when put beside the thoroughgoing confusion of the case forms in vulgar American. "*Us* fellers" is so far established in the language that "*we* fellers, " from the mouth of a car conductor, would seem almost an affectation. So, too, is "*me* and *her* are friends." So, again, are "I seen you and *her*, " "*her* and I set down together, " "*him* and his wife, " and "I knowed it was *her*." Here are some other characteristic examples of the use of the objective forms in the nominative from Charters and Lardner:

Me and *her* was both late.

His brother is taller than *him*.

That little boy was *me*.

Us girls went home.

They were John and *him*.

Her and little Al is to stay here.

She says she thinks *us* and the Allens.

If Weaver and *them* had not of begin kicking.

But not *me*.

Him and I are friends.

Me and *them* are friends.

Less numerous, but still varied and plentiful, are the substitutions of nominative forms for objective forms:

She gave it to mother and *I*.

She took all of *we* children.

I want you to meet *he* and I at 29th street.

He gave *he* and I both some.

It is going to cost me $6 a week for a room for *she* and the baby.

Anything she has is O. K. for *I* and Florrie.

Here are some grotesque confusions, indeed. Perhaps the best way to get at the principles underlying them is to examine first, not the cases of their occurrence, but the cases of their non-occurrence. Let us begin with the transfer of the objective form to the nominative in the subject relation. "*Me* and *her* was both late" is obviously sound American; one hears it, or something like it, on the streets every day. But one never hears "*me* was late" or "*her* was late" or "*us* was late" or "*him* was late" or "*them* was late." Again, one hears "*us* girls was there" but never "*us* was there." Yet again, one hears "*her* and John was married, " but never "*her* was married." The distinction here set up should be immediately plain. It exactly parallels that between *her* and *hern*, *our* and *ourn*, *their* and *theirn*: the tendency, as Sweet says, is "to merge the distinction of nominative and objective in that of conjoint and absolute."[66] The nominative, in the subject relation, takes the usual nominative form only when it is in immediate contact with its verb. If it be separated from its verb by a conjunction or any other part of speech, even including another pronoun, it takes the objective form. Thus "*me* went home" would strike even the most ignorant shopgirl as "bad grammar, " but she would use "*me* and my friend went, " or "*me* and *him*, " or "*he* and *her*, " or "*me* and *them*" without the slightest hesitation. What is more, if the separation be effected by a conjunction and another pronoun, the other pronoun also changes to the objective form, even though its contact with the verb may be immediate. Thus one hears "*me* and *her* was there, " not "*me* and *she*"; *her* and "*him* kissed, " not "*her* and *he*." Still more, this second pronoun commonly undergoes the same inflection even when the first member of the group is not another pronoun, but a noun. Thus one hears "John and *her* were married, " not "John and *she*." To this rule there is but one exception, and that is in the case of the first person pronoun, especially in the singular. "*Him* and *me* are friends" is heard often, but "*him* and *I* are friends" is also heard. *I* seems to suggest the subject very powerfully; it is actually the subject of perhaps a majority of the sentences uttered by an ignorant man. At all events, it resists the rule, at least partially, and may even do so when actually separated from the verb by another pronoun, itself in the objective form, as for example, in "*I* and *him* were there."

In the predicate relation the pronouns respond to a more complex regulation. When they follow any form of the simple verb of being they take the objective form, as in "it's *me*, " "it ain't *him*, " and "I am *him*, " probably because the transitiveness of this verb exerts a greater pull than its function as a mere copula, and perhaps, too, because the passive naturally tends to put the speaker in the place of the object. "I seen *he*" or "he kissed *she*" or "he struck *I*" would seem as ridiculous to an ignorant American as to the Archbishop of Canterbury, and his instinct for simplicity and regularity naturally tends to make him reduce all similar expressions, or what seem to him to be similar expressions, to coincidence with the more seemly "I seen *him*." After all, the verb of being is fundamentally transitive, and, in some ways, the most transitive of all verbs, and so it is not illogical to bring its powers over the pronoun into accord with the powers exerted by the others. I incline to think that it is some such subconscious logic, and not the analogy of "it is *he*, " as Sweet argues, that has brought "it is *me*" to conversational respectability, even among rather careful speakers of English.[67]

But against this use of the objective form in the nominative position after the verb of being there also occurs in American a use of the nominative form in the objective position, as in "she gave it to mother and *I*" and "she took all of *we* children." What lies at the bottom of it seems to be a feeling somewhat resembling that which causes the use of the objective form before the verb, but exactly contrary in its effects. That is to say, the nominative form is used when the pronoun is separated from its governing verb, whether by a noun, a noun-phrase or another pronoun, as in "she gave it to mother and *I*, " "she took all of *we* children" and "he paid her and *I*" respectively. But here usage is far from fixed, and one observes variations in both directions—that is, toward using the correct objective when the pronoun is detached from the verb, and toward using the nominative even when it directly follows the verb. "She gave it to mother and *me*, " "she took all of *us* children" and "he paid her and *me*" would probably sound quite as correct, to a Knight of Pythias, as the forms just given. And at the other end Charters and Lardner report such forms as "I want you to meet *he* and *I*" and "it is going to cost me $6 a week for a room for *she* and the baby." I have noticed, however, that, in the overwhelming main, the use of the nominative is confined to the pronoun of the first person, and particularly to its singular. Here again we have an example of the powerful way in which *I* asserts itself. And superimposed upon that influence is a cause mentioned by Sweet in discussing "between you and *I*."[68] It is a sort of by-product of the pedagogical war upon "it is *me*." "As such expressions, " he says, "are still denounced by the grammars, many people try to avoid them in speech as well as in writing. The result of this reaction is that the *me* in such constructions as 'between John and *me*' and 'he saw John and *me*' sounds vulgar and ungrammatical, and is consequently corrected into *I*." Here the pedagogues, seeking to impose an inelastic and illogical grammar upon a living speech, succeed only in corrupting it still more.

Following *than* and *as* the American uses the objective form of the pronoun, as in "he is taller than *me*" and "such as *her*." He also uses it following *like*, but not when, as often happens, he uses the word in place of *as* or *as if*. Thus he says "do it like *him*, " but "do it like *he* does" and "she looks like *she* was sick." What appears here is an instinctive feeling that these words, followed by a pronoun only, are not adverbs, but prepositions, and that they should have the same power to put the pronoun into an oblique case that other prepositions have. Just as "the taller of *we*" would sound absurd to all of us, so "taller than *he*, " to the unschooled American, sounds absurd. This feeling has a good deal of respectable support. "As *her*" was used by Swift, "than *me*" by Burke, and "than *whom*" by Milton. The brothers Fowler show that, in some cases, "than *him*, " is grammatically correct and logically necessary.[69] For example, compare "I love you more than *him*" and "I love you more than *he*." The first means "I love you more than (I love) *him*"; the second, "I love you more than *he* (loves you)." In the first *him* does not refer to *I*, which is nominative, but to *you*, which is objective, and so it is properly objective also. But the American, of course, uses *him* even when the preceding noun is in the nominative, save only when another verb follows the pronoun. Thus, he says, "I love you better than *him*, " but "I love you better than *he* does."

In the matter of the reflexive pronouns the American vulgate exhibits forms which plainly show that it is the spirit of the language to regard *self*, not as an adjective, which it is historically, but as a noun. This confusion goes back to Anglo-Saxon days; it originated at a time when both the adjectives and the nouns were losing their old inflections. Such forms as *Petrussylf* (=*Peter's self*), *Cristsylf* (=*Christ's self*) and *Icsylf* (=*I, self*) then came into use, and along with them came combinations of *self* and the genitive, still surviving in *hisself* and *theirselves* (or *theirself*). Down to the sixteenth century these forms remained in perfectly good usage. "Each for *hisself*, " for example, was written by Sir Philip Sidney, and is to be found in the dramatists of the time, though modern editors always change it to *himself.* How the dative pronoun got itself fastened upon*self* in the third person masculine and neuter is one of the mysteries of language, but there it is, and so, against all logic, history and grammatical regularity, *himself, themselves* and *itself* (not *its-self*) are in favor today. But the American, as usual, inclines against these illogical exceptions to the rule set by *myself.* I constantly hear *hisself* and *theirselves*, as in "he done it *hisself*" and "they don't know *theirselves.*" Sometimes *theirself* is substituted for theirselves, as in "they all seen it *theirself.*" Also, the emphatic *own* is often inserted between the pronoun and the noun, as in "let every man save his *own* self."

The American pronoun does not necessarily agree with its noun in number. I find "I can tell each one what *they* make, " "each fellow put *their* foot on the line, " "nobody can do what *they* like" and "she was one of *these* kind of people" in Charters, and "I am not the kind of man that is always thinking about *their* record, " "if he was to hit a man in the head ... *they* would think *their* nose tickled" in Lardner. At the bottom of this error there is a real difficulty: the lack of a pronoun of the true common gender in English, corresponding to the French *soi* and *son*. *His*, after a noun or pronoun connoting both sexes, often sounds inept, and *his-or-her* is intolerably clumsy. Thus the inaccurate plural is often substituted. The brothers Fowler have discovered "anybody else who have only *themselves* in view" in Richardson and "everybody is discontented with *their* lot" in Disraeli, and Ruskin once wrote "if a customer wishes you to injure *their* foot." In spoken American, even the most careful, *they* and *their* often appear; I turn to the *Congressional Record* at random and in two minutes find "if anyone will look at the bank statements *they* will see."[70] In the lower reaches of the language the plural seems to get into every sentence of any complexity, even when the preceding noun or pronoun is plainly singular.

§ 5. The Adverb

—All the adverbial endings in English, save *-ly*, have gradually fallen into decay; it is the only one that is ever used to form new adverbs. At earlier stages of the language various other endings were used, and some of them survive in a few old words, though they are no longer employed in making new words. The Anglo-Saxon endings were *-e* and *-lice*. The latter was, at first, merely an *-e*-ending to adjectives in *-lic*, but after a time it attained to independence and was attached to adjectives not ending in *-lic*. In early Middle English this *-lice* changes to *-like*, and later on to *-li* and *-ly*. Meanwhile, the *-e*-ending, following the *-e*-endings of the nouns, adjectives and verbs, ceased to be pronounced, and so it gradually fell away. Thus a good many adverbs came to be indistinguishable from their ancestral adjectives, for example, *hard* in to *pull hard, loud* in *to speak loud*, and *deep* in *to bury deep* (=Anglo-Saxon, *dĕop-e*). Worse, not a few adverbs actually became adjectives, for example, *wide*, which was originally the Anglo-Saxon adjective *wid* (=*wide*) with the adverbial *-e*-ending, and *late*, which was originally the Anglo-Saxon adjective *laet* (=*slow*) with the same ending.

The result of this movement toward identity in form was a confusion between the two classes of words, and from the time of

Chaucer down to the eighteenth century one finds innumerable instances of the use of the simple adjective as an adverb. "He will answer *trewe*" is in Sir Thomas More; "and *soft* unto himself he sayd" in Chaucer; "the singers sang *loud*" in the Revised Version of the Bible (Nehemiah xii, 42), and "*indifferent* well" in Shakespeare. Even after the purists of the eighteenth century began their corrective work this confusion continued. Thus, one finds, "the people are *miserable* poor" in Hume, "how *unworthy* you treated mankind" in *The Spectator*, and "*wonderful* silly" in Joseph Butler. To this day the grammarians battle with the barbarism, still without complete success; every new volume of rules and regulations for those who would speak by the book is full of warnings against it. Among the great masses of the plain people, it goes without saying, it flourishes unimpeded. The cautions of the school-marm, in a matter so subtle and so plainly lacking in logic or necessity, are forgotten as quickly as her prohibition of the double negative, and thereafter the adjective and the adverb tend more and more to coalesce in a part of speech which serves the purposes of both, and is simple and intelligible and satisfying.

Charters gives a number of characteristic examples of its use: "wounded very *bad*, " "I *sure* was stiff, " "drank out of a cup *easy*, " "he looked up *quick*." Many more are in Lardner: "a chance to see me work *regular*, " "I am glad I was lucky enough to marry *happy*, " "I beat them *easy*, " and so on. And others fall upon the ear every day: "he done it *proper*, " "he done himself *proud*, " "she was dressed *neat*, " "she was *awful* ugly, " "the horse ran *O. K.*, " "it *near* finished him, " "it sells *quick*, " "I like it *fine*, " "he et *hoggish*, " "she acted *mean*, " "they keep company *steady*." The bob-tailed adverb, indeed, enters into a large number of the commonest coins of vulgar speech. *Near-silk*, I daresay, is properly *nearly-silk*. The grammarians protest that "run *slow*" should be "run *slowly*." But *near-silk* and "run *slow*" remain, and so do "to be in *bad*, " "to play it up *strong*" and their brothers. What we have here is simply an incapacity to distinguish any ponderable difference between adverb and adjective, and beneath it, perhaps, is the incapacity, already noticed in dealing with "it is *me*, " to distinguish between the common verb of being and any other verb. If "it *is* bad" is correct, then why should "it *leaks* bad" be incorrect? It is just this disdain of purely grammatical reasons that is at the bottom of most of the phenomena visible in vulgar American, and the same impulse is observable in all other languages during periods of inflectional decay. During the highly inflected stage of a language the parts of speech are sharply distinct, but when inflections fall off they tend to disappear. The adverb, being at best the step-child of grammar—as the old Latin grammarians used to say, "*Omnis pars orationis migrat in adverbium*"—is one of the chief victims of this anarchy. John Horne Tooke, despairing of bringing it to any order, even in the most careful English, called it, in his "Epea Ptercenta, " "the common sink and repository of all heterogeneous and unknown corruptions."

Where an obvious logical or lexical distinction has grown up between an adverb and its primary adjective the unschooled American is very careful to give it its terminal *-ly*. For example, he seldom confuses *hard* and *hardly*, *scarce* and *scarcely*, *real* and *really*. These words convey different ideas. *Hard* means unyielding; *hardly* means barely. *Scarce* means present only in small numbers; *scarcely* is substantially synonymous with *hardly*. *Real* means genuine; *really* is an assurance of veracity. So, again, with *late* and *lately*. Thus, an American says "I don't know, *scarcely*, " not "I don't know, *scarce*"; "he died *lately*, " not "he died *late*." But in nearly all such cases syntax is the preservative, not grammar. These adverbs seem to keep their tails largely because they are commonly put before and not after verbs, as in, for example, "I *hardly* (or *scarcely*) know, " and "I *really* mean it." Many other adverbs that take that position habitually are saved as well, for example, *generally*, *usually*, *surely*, *certainly*. But when they follow verbs they often succumb, as in "I'll do it *sure*" and "I seen him *recent*." And when they modify adjectives they sometimes succumb, too, as in "it was *sure* hot." Practically all the adverbs made of adjectives in *-y* lose the terminal *-ly* and thus become identical with their adjectives. I have never heard *mightily* used; it is always *mighty*, as in "he hit him *mighty* hard." So with *filthy*, *dirty*, *nasty*, *lowly*, *naughty* and their cognates. One hears "he acted *dirty*, " "he spoke *nasty*, " "the child behaved *naughty*, " and so on. Here even standard English has had to make concessions to euphony. *Cleanlily* is seldom used; *cleanly* nearly always takes its place. And the use of *illy* is confined to pedants.

Vulgar American, like all the higher forms of American and all save the most precise form of written English, has abandoned the old inflections of *here*, *there* and *where*, to wit, *hither* and *hence*, *thither* and *thence*, *whither* and *whence*. These fossil remains of dead cases are fast disappearing from the language. In the case of *hither* (=*to here*) even the preposition has been abandoned. One says, not "I came *to here*, " but simply "I came *here*." In the case of *hence*, however, *from here* is still used, and so with *from there* and *from where*. Finally, it goes without saying that the common American tendency to add *-s* to such adverbs as *towards* is carried to full length in the vulgar language. One constantly hears, not only *somewheres* and *forwards*, but even *noways* and *anyways*. Here we have but one more example of the movement toward uniformity and simplicity. *Anyways* is obviously fully supported by *sideways* and *always*.

§ 6. The Noun and Adjective

—The only inflections of the noun remaining in English are those for number and for the genitive, and so it is in these two regions that the few variations to be noted in vulgar American occur. The rule that, in forming the plurals of compound nouns or noun-phrases, the *-s* shall be attached to the principal noun is commonly disregarded, and it goes at the end. Thus, "I have two *sons-in-law*" is never heard; one always hears "I have two *son-in-laws*." So with the genitive. I once overheard this: "that umbrella is *the young lady I go with's*." Often a false singular is formed from a singular ending in *s*, the latter being mistaken for a plural. *Chinee*, *Portugee* and *Japanee* are familiar; I have also noted *trapee*, *tactic* and *summon* (from *trapeze*, *tactics* and *summons*). Paradoxically, the word *incidence* is commonly misused for *incident*, as in "he told an *incidence*." Here *incidence* (or *incident*) seems to be regarded as a synonym, not for *happening*, but for *story*. I have never heard "he told *of* an incidence." The *of* is always omitted. The general disregard of number often shows itself when the noun is used as object. I have already quoted Lardner's "some of the men has brung their *wife* along"; in a popular magazine I lately encountered "those book ethnologists ... can't see what is before their *nose*." Many similar examples might be brought forward.

The adjectives are inflected only for comparison, and the American commonly uses them correctly, with now and then a double comparative or superlative to ease his soul. *More better* is the commonest of these. It has a good deal of support in logic. A sick man is reported today to be *better*. Tomorrow he is further improved. Is he to be reported *better* again, or *best*? The standard language gets around the difficulty by using *still better*. The American vulgate boldly employs *more better*. In the case of *worse*, *worser* is used, as Charters shows. He also reports *baddest*, *more queerer* and *beautifulest*. *Littler*, which he notes, is still outlawed from standard English, but it has, with *littlest*, a respectable place in American. The late Richard Harding Davis wrote a play called "The *Littlest* Girl." The American freely compares adjectives that are incapable of the inflection logically. Charters reports *most principal*, and I myself have heard *uniquer* and even *more uniquer*, as in "I have never saw nothing *more uniquer*." I have also heard *more ultra*, *more worse*, *idealer*, *liver* (that is, *more alive*), and *wellest*, as in "he was the *wellest* man you ever seen." In general, the *-er* and *-est* terminations are used instead of the *more* and *most* prefixes, as in *beautiful*, *beautifuller*, *beautifullest*. The fact that the comparative relates to two and the superlative to more than two is almost always forgotten. I have never heard "the *better* of the two, " but always "the *best* of the two." Charters also reports "the *hardest* of the two" and "my brother and I measured and he was the *tallest*." I have frequently heard "it ain't so *worse*, " but here a humorous effect seems to have been intended.

Adjectives are made much less rapidly in American than either substantives or verbs. The only suffix that seems to be in general use for that purpose is *-y*, as in *tony*, *classy*, *daffy*, *nutty*, *dinky*, *leery*, etc. The use of the adjectival prefix *super-* is confined to the more sophisticated classes; the plain people seem to be unaware of it.[71] This relative paucity of adjectives appears to be common to the more primitive varieties of speech. E. J. Hills, in his elaborate study of the vocabulary of a child of two, [72] found that it contained but 23 descriptive adjectives, of which six were the names of colors, as against 59 verbs and 173 common nouns. Moreover, most of the 23 minus six were adjectives of all work, such as *nasty*, *funny* and *nice*. Colloquial American uses the same rubber-stamps of speech. *Funny* connotes the whole range of the unusual; *hard* indicates every shade of difficulty;

nice is everything satisfactory; *bully* is a superlative of almost limitless scope.

The decay of *one* to a vague *n*-sound, as in *this'n*, is matched by a decay of *than* after comparatives. *Earlier than* is seldom if ever heard; composition reduces the two words to *earlier'n*. So with *better'n, faster'n, hotter'n, deader'n*, etc. Once I overheard the following dialogue: "I like a belt *more looser'n* what this one is." "Well, then, why don't you unloosen it *more'n* you got it unloosened?"

§ 7. The Double Negative

—Syntactically, perhaps the chief characteristic of vulgar American is its sturdy fidelity to the double negative. So freely is it used, indeed, that the simple negative appears to be almost abandoned. Such phrases as "I see nobody" or "I know nothing about it" are heard so seldom that they appear to be affectations when encountered; the well-nigh universal forms are "I *don't* see nobody" and "I *don't* know nothing about it." Charters lists some very typical examples, among them, "he ain't *never* coming back *no* more, " "you *don't* care for nobody but yourself, " "couldn't be *no* more happier" and "I *can't* see nothing." In Lardner there are innumerable examples: "they was *not* no team, " "I have *not* never thought of that, " "I can't write *no* more, " "no chance to get *no* money from *nowhere*, " "we *can't* have nothing to do, " and so on. Some of his specimens show a considerable complexity, for example, "Matthewson was *not* only going as far as the coast, " meaning, as the context shows, that he was going as far as the coast and no further. *Only* gets into many other examples, *e. g.*, "he hadn't *only* the one pass" and "I don't work nights no more, *only* except Sunday nights." This latter I got from a car conductor. Many other curious specimens are in my collectanea, among them: "one swaller don't make *no* summer, " "I *never* seen nothing I would of rather saw, " and "once a child gets burnt once it *won't* never stick its hand in *no* fire *no* more, " and so on. The last embodies a triple negative. In "the more faster you go, the sooner you *don't* get there" there is an elaborate muddling of negatives that is very characteristic.

Like most other examples of "bad grammar" encountered in American the compound negative is of great antiquity and was once quite respectable. The student of Anglo-Saxon encounters it constantly. In that language the negative of the verb was formed by prefixing a particle, *ne*. Thus, *singan* (=*to sing*) became *ne singan* (=*not to sing*). In case the verb began with a vowel the *ne*dropped its *e* and was combined with the verb, as in *naefre* (never), from *ne-aefre* (=*not ever*). In case the verb began with an *h* or a *w* followed by a vowel, the *h* or *w* of the verb and the *e* of *ne* were both dropped, as in *naefth* (=*has not*), from *ne-haefth* (=*not has*), and *nolde* (=*would not*), from *ne-wolde*. Finally, in case the vowel following a *w* was an *i*, it changed to *y*, as in *nyste*(=*knew not*), from *ne-wiste*. But inasmuch as Anglo-Saxon was a fully inflected language the inflections for the negative did not stop with the verbs; the indefinite article, the indefinite pronoun and even some of the nouns were also inflected, and survivors of those forms appear to this day in such words as *none* and *nothing*. Moreover, when an actual inflection was impossible it was the practise to insert this *ne* before a word, in the sense of our *no* or *not*. Still more, it came to be the practise to reinforce *ne*, before a vowel, with *nā* (=*not*) or *naht* (=*nothing*), which later degenerated to *nat* and *not*. As a result, there were fearful and wonderful combinations of negatives, some of them fully matching the best efforts of Lardner's baseball player. Sweet gives several curious examples.[73] "Nān ne dorste nān thing āscian, " translated literally, becomes "*no* one dares *not* ask *nothing*." "Thaet hus nā ne feoll" becomes "the house did *not* fall *not*." As for the Middle English "he *never* nadde *nothing*, " it has too modern and familiar a ring to need translating at all. Chaucer, at the beginning of the period of transition to Modern English, used the double negative with the utmost freedom. In "The Knight's Tale" is this:

He *nevere* yet *no* vileynye *ne* sayde

In al his lyf unto *no* maner wight.

By the time of Shakespeare this license was already much restricted, but a good many double negatives are nevertheless to be found in his plays, and he was particularly shaky in the use of *nor*. In "Richard III" one finds "I never was *nor never* will be"; in "Measure for Measure, " "harp not on that *nor* do *not* banish treason, " and in "Romeo and Juliet, " "thou expectedst not, *nor* I looked not for." This misuse of *nor* is still very frequent. In other directions, too, the older forms show a tendency to survive all the assaults of grammarians. "*No* it *doesn't*, " heard every day and by no means from the ignorant only, is a sort of double negative. The insertion of *but* before that, as in "I doubt *but* that" and "there is no question *but* that, " makes a double negative that is probably full-blown. Nevertheless, as we have seen, it is heard on the floor of Congress every day, and the Fowlers show that it is also common in England.[74] Even worse forms get into the *Congressional Record*. Not long ago, for example, I encountered "without *hardly* an exception" in a public paper of the utmost importance.[75] There are, indeed, situations in which the double negative leaps to the lips or from the pen almost irresistibly; even such careful writers as Huxley, Robert Louis Stevenson and Leslie Stephen have occasionally dallied with it.[76] It is perfectly allowable in the Romance languages, and, as we have seen, is almost the rule in the American vulgate. Now and then some anarchistic student of the language boldly defends and even advocates it. "The double negative, " said a writer in the *London Review* a long time ago, [77] "has been abandoned to the great injury of strength of expression." Surely "I won't take nothing" is stronger than either "I will take nothing" or "I won't take anything."

"Language begins, " says Sayce, "with sentences, not with single words." In a speech in process of rapid development, unrestrained by critical analysis, the tendency to sacrifice the integrity of words to the needs of the complete sentence is especially marked. One finds it clearly in American. Already we have examined various assimilation and composition forms: *that'n, use' to, would'a, them 'ere* and so on. Many others are observable. *Off'n* is a good example; it comes from *off of* and shows a preposition decaying to the form of a mere inflectional particle. One constantly hears "I bought it *off'n* John." *Sort'a, kind'a* and their like follow in the footsteps of *would'a*. *Usen't* follows the analogy of *don't* and *wouldn't*. *Would 've* and *should 've* are widely used; Lardner commonly hears them as *would of* and *should of*. The neutral *a*-particle also appears in other situations, especially before *way*, as in *that'a way* and *this'a way*. It is found again in *a tall*, a liaison form of *at all*.[78]

§ 8. Pronunciation

—Before anything approaching a thorough and profitable study of the sounds of the American common speech is possible, there must be a careful assembling of the materials, and this, unfortunately, still awaits a philologist of sufficient enterprise and equipment. Dr. William

A. Read, of the State University of Louisiana, has made some excellent examinations of vowel and consonant sounds in the South, Dr. Louise Pound has done capital work of the same sort in the Middle West, [79] and there have been other regional studies of merit. But most of these become misleading by reason of their lack of scope; forms practically universal in the nation are discussed as dialectical variations. This is the central defect in the work of the American Dialect Society, otherwise very industrious and meritorious. It is essaying to study localisms before having first platted the characteristics of the general speech. The dictionaries of Americanisms deal with pronunciation only casually, and often very inaccurately; the remaining literature is meagre and unsatisfactory.[80] Until the matter is gone into at length it will be impossible to discuss any phase of it with exactness. No single investigator can examine the speech of the whole country; for that business a pooling of forces is necessary. But meanwhile it may be of interest to set forth a few provisional ideas.

At the start two streams of influence upon American pronunciation may be noted, the one an inheritance from the English of the colonists and the other arising spontaneously within the country, and apparently much colored by immigration. The first influence, it goes without saying, is gradually dying out. Consider, for example, the pronunciation of the diphthong *oi*. In Middle English it was as in *boy*, but during the early Modern English period it was assimilated with that of the *i* in *wine*, and this usage prevailed at the time of the settlement of America. The colonists thus brought it with them, and at the same time it lodged in Ireland, where it still prevails. But in England, during the pedantic eighteenth century, this *i*-sound was displaced by the original *oi*-sound, not by historical research but by mere deduction from the spelling, and the new pronunciation soon extended to the polite speech of America. In the common speech, however, the *i*-sound persisted, and down to the time of the Civil War it was constantly heard in such words as *boil, hoist, oil, join, poison* and *roil*, which thus became *bile, hist, ile, jine, pisen* and *rile*. Since then the school-marm has combatted it with such vigor that it has begun to disappear, and such forms as *pisen, jine, bile* and *ile* are now very seldom heard, save as dialectic variations. But in certain other words, perhaps supported by Irish influence, the *i*-sound still persists. Chief among them are *hoist* and *roil*. An unlearned American, wishing to say that he was enraged, never says that he was *roiled*, but always that he was *riled.* Desiring to examine the hoof of his horse, he never orders the animal to *hoist* but always to *hist.* In the form of *booze-hister*, the latter is almost in good usage. I have seen *booze-hister* thus spelled and obviously to be thus pronounced, in an editorial article in the *American Issue*, organ of the Anti-Saloon League of America.[81]

Various similar misplaced vowels were brought from England by the colonists and have persisted in America, while dying out of good England usage. There is, for example, short *i* in place of long *e*, as in *critter* for *creature. Critter* is common to almost all the dialects of English, but American has embedded the vowel in a word that is met with nowhere else and has thus become characteristic, to wit, *crick* for *creek.* Nor does any other dialect make such extensive use of *slick* for *sleek.* Again, there is the substitution of the flat *a* for the broad *a* in *sauce.* England has gone back to the broad *a*, but in America the flat *a* persists, and many Americans who use *sassy* every day would scarcely recognize *saucy* if they heard it. Yet again, there is *quoit.* Originally, the English pronounced it *quate*, but now they pronounce the diphthong as in *doily.* In the United States the *quate* pronunciation remains. Finally, there is *deaf.* Its proper pronunciation, in the England that the colonists left, was *deef*, but it now rhymes with *Jeff.* That new pronunciation has been adopted by polite American, despite the protests of Noah Webster, but in the common speech the word is still always *deef.*

However, a good many of the vowels of the early days have succumbed to pedagogy. The American proletarian may still use *skeer* for *scare*, but in most of the other words of that class he now uses the vowel approved by correct English usage. Thus he seldom permits himself such old forms as *dreen* for *drain, keer* for *care, skeerce* for *scarce* or even *cheer* for *chair.* The Irish influence supported them for a while, but now they are fast going out. So, too, are *kivver* for *cover, crap* for *crop*, and *chist* for *chest.* But *kittle* for *kettle* still shows a certain vitality, *rench* is still used in place of *rinse*, and *squinch* in place of *squint*, and a flat *a* continues to displace various *e*-sounds in such words as *rare* for *rear* (e. g., as a horse) and *wrassle* for *wrestle.* Contrariwise, *e* displaces *a* in *catch* and *radish*, which are commonly pronounced *ketch* and *reddish.* This *e*-sound was once accepted in standard English; when it got into spoken

American it was perfectly sound; one still hears it from the most pedantic lips in *any*.[82] There are also certain other ancients that show equally unbroken vitality among us, for example, *stomp* for *stamp*, [83] *snoot* for *snout*, *guardeen* for *guardian*, and *champeen* for *champion*.

But all these vowels, whether approved or disapproved, have been under the pressure, for the past century, of a movement toward a general vowel neutralization, and in the long run it promises to dispose of many of them. The same movement also affects standard English, as appears by Robert Bridges' "Tract on the Present State of English Pronunciation, " but I believe that it is stronger in America, and will go farther, at least with the common speech, if only because of our unparalleled immigration. Standard English has 19 separate vowel sounds. No other living tongue of Europe, save Portuguese, has so many; most of the others have a good many less; Modern Greek has but five. The immigrant, facing all these vowels, finds some of them quite impossible; the Russian Jew, as we have seen, cannot manage *ur*. As a result, he tends to employ a neutralized vowel in all the situations which present difficulties, and this neutralized vowel, supported by the slip-shod speech-habits of the native proletariat, makes steady progress. It appears in many of the forms that we have been examining—in the final *a* of *would'a*, vaguely before the *n* in *this'n* and *off'n*, in place of the original *d* in *use' to*, and in the common pronunciation of such words as *been*, *come* and *have*, particularly when they are sacrificed to sentence exigencies, as in "I *b'n* thinking, " "*c'm 'ere*, " and "he would *'ve* saw you."

Here we are upon a wearing down process that shows many other symptoms. One finds, not only vowels disorganized, but also consonants. Some are displaced by other consonants, measurably more facile; others are dropped altogether. *D* becomes *t*, as in *holt*, or is dropped, as in *tole*, *han'kerchief*, *bran-new* and *fine* (for *find*). In *ast* (for *ask*) *t* replaces *k*: when the same word is used in place of *asked*, as often happens, e. g., in "I *ast* him his name, " it shoulders out *ked*. It is itself lopped off in *bankrup*, *quan'ity*, *crep*, *slep*, *wep*, *kep*, *gris'-mill* and *les* (=*let's* = *let us*), and is replaced by *d* in *kindergarden* and *pardner*. *L* disappears, as in *a'ready* and *gent'man*. *S* becomes *tsh*, as in *pincers*. The same *tsh* replaces *c*, as in *pitcher* for *picture*, and *t*, as in *amachoor*. *G* disappears from the ends of words, and sometimes, too, in the middle, as in *stren'th* and *reco'nize.R*, though it is better preserved in American than in English, is also under pressure, as appears by *bust, stuck on* (for *struck on*), *cuss* (for *curse*), *yestiddy, sa's'parella, pa'tridge, ca'tridge, they is*(for *there is*) and *Sadd'y* (for *Saturday*). An excrescent *t* survives in a number of words, e. g., *onc't, twic't, clos't, wisht* (for *wish*) and *chanc't*; it is an heirloom from the English of two centuries ago. So is the final *h* in *heighth*. An excrescent *b*, as in *chimbley* and *fambly*, seems to be native. Whole syllables are dropped out of words, paralleling the English butchery of*extraordinary*; for example, in *bound'ry, hist'ry, lib'ry* and *prob'ly. Ordinary*, like *extraordinary*, is commonly enunciated clearly, but it has bred a degenerated form, *onry* or *onery*, differentiated in meaning. Consonants are misplaced by metathesis, as in *prespiration, hunderd, brethern, childern, interduce, apern, calvary, govrenment, modren* and *wosterd* (for *worsted*). *Ow* is changed to *er*, as in*feller, swaller, yeller, beller, umbreller* and *holler*; *ice* is changed to *ers* in*jaunders*. Words are given new syllables, as in *ellum, mischievious* and *municipial*.

In the complete sentence, assimilation makes this disorganization much more obvious. Mearns, in a brief article[84] gives many examples of the extent to which it is carried. He hears "wah zee say?" for "what does he say?" "ware zee?" for "where is he?" "ast 'er in" for "ask her in, " "itt'm owd" for "hit them out, " "sry" for "that is right, " and "c'meer" for "come here." He believes that *t* is gradually succumbing to *d*, and cites "ass bedder" (for "that's better"), "wen juh ged din?" (for "when did you get in?"), and "siddup" (for "sit up"). One hears countless other such decayed forms on the street every day. *Have to* is almost invariably made *hafta*, with the neutral vowel where I have put the second *a. Let's*, already noticed, is *le' 's*. The neutral vowel replaces the *oo* of *good* in *g'by*. "What did you say" reduces itself to "wuz ay?" *Maybe* is *mebby, perhaps* is *p'raps, so long* is *s'long, excuse me* is *skus me*; the common salutation, "How are you?" is so dismembered that it finally emerges as a word almost indistinguishable from *high*. Here there is room for inquiry, and that inquiry deserves the best effort of American phonologists, for the language is undergoing rapid changes under their very eyes, or, perhaps more accurately, under their very ears, and a study of those changes should yield a great deal of interesting matter. How did the word *stint*, on American lips, first convert itself into *stent* and then into *stunt*? By what process was *baulk* changed into *buck*? Both *stunt* and *buck* are among the commonest words in the everyday American vocabulary, and yet no one, so far, has investigated them scientifically.

A by-way that is yet to be so much as entered is that of naturalized loan-words in the common speech. A very characteristic word of that sort is *sashay*. Its relationship to the French *chasse* seems to be plain, and yet it has acquired meanings in American that differ very widely from the meaning of *chassé*. How widely it is dispersed may be seen by the fact that it is reported in popular use, as a verb signifying to prance or to walk consciously, in Southeastern Missouri, Nebraska, Northwestern Arkansas, Eastern Alabama and Western Indiana, and, with slightly different meaning, on Cape Cod. The travels of *café* in America would repay investigation; particularly its variations in pronunciation. I believe that it is fast becoming *kaif*. *Plaza*, *boulevard*, *vaudeville*, *menu* and *rathskeller* have entered into the common speech of the land, and are pronounced as American words. Such words, when they come in verbally, by actual contact with immigrants, commonly retain some measure of their correct native pronunciation. *Spiel*, *kosher*, *ganof* and *matzoh* are examples; their vowels remain un-American. But words that come in visually, say through street-signs and the newspapers, are immediately overhauled and have thoroughly Americanized vowels and consonants thereafter. School-teachers have been trying to establish various pseudo-French pronunciations of *vase* for fifty years past, but it still rhymes with *face* in the vulgate. *Vaudeville* is *vawd-vill*; *boulevard* has a hard *d* at the end; *plaza* has two flat *a*'s; the first syllable of *menu* rhymes with *bee*; the first of *rathskeller* with *cats*; *fiancée* is *fy-ancé-y*; *née* rhymes with *see*; *décolleté* is *de-coll-ty*; *hofbräu* is *huffbrow*; the German *w* has lost its *v*-sound and becomes an American *w*. I have, in my day, heard *proteege* for *protégé*, *habichoo* for *habitué*, *connisoor* for *connisseur*, *shirtso* for *scherzo*, *premeer* for *première*, *eetood* for *étude* and *prelood* for *prelude*. *Divorcée* is *divorcey*, and has all the rakishness of the adjectives in *-y*. The first syllable of *mayonnaise* rhymes with *hay*. *Crème de menthe* is *cream de mint*. *Schweizer* is *swite-ser*. *Rochefort* is *roke-fort*. I have heard *début* with the last syllable rhyming with *nut*. I have heard *minoot* for *minuet*. I have heard *tchef doover* for *chef d'œuvre*. And who doesn't remember

As I walked along the *Boys Boo-long*

With an independent air

and

Say *aw re-vore*,

But not good-by!

Charles James Fox, it is said, called the red wine of France *Bordox* to the end of his days. He had an American heart; his great speeches for the revolting colonies were more than mere oratory.

FOOTNOTES:

[1] Sweet, perhaps the abbot of the order, makes almost indecent haste to sin. See the second paragraph on the very first page of vol. i of his New English Grammar.

[2] *Yale Review*, April, 1918, p. 548.

[3] *Yale Review*, *op. cit.*, p. 560.

[4] The Difficulties Created by Grammarians Are to be Ignored, by W. H. Wilcox, *Atlantic Educational Journal*, Nov., 1912, p. 8. The title of this article is quoted from ministerial instructions of 1909 to the teachers of French *lyceés*.

[5] *Op cit.* p. 7. Mr. Wilcox is an instructor in the Maryland State Normal School.

[6] See especially chapters ix and x of Words and Their Uses and chapters xvii, xviii and xix of Every-Day English; also the preface to the latter, p. xi *et seq.* The study of other languages has been made difficult by the same attempt to force the characters of Greek and Latin grammar upon them. One finds a protest against the process, for example, in E. H. Palmer's Grammar of Hindustani, Persian and Arabic; London, 1906. In all ages, indeed, grammarians appear to have been fatuous. The learned will remember Aristophanes' ridicule of them in The Clouds, 660-690.

[7] The case is well summarized in Simpler English Grammar, by Patterson Wardlaw, *Bull. of the University of S. Carolina*, No. 38, pt. iii, July, 1914.

[8] Cincinnati, 1868; rev. ed., 1878.

[9] New York, 1903; rev. ed., 1915.

[10] Even Sweet, though he bases his New English Grammar upon the spoken language and thus sets the purists at defiance, quickly succumbs to the labelling mania. Thus his classification of tenses includes such fabulous

monsters as these: continuous, recurrent, neutral, definite, indefinite, secondary, incomplete, inchoate, short and long.

[11] By W. F. Webster and Alice Woodworth Cooley; Boston, 1903; rev. eds., 1905 and 1909. The authors are Minneapolis teachers.

[12] *Op. cit.* p. 8.

[13] Bulletin No. 2; Washington, 1917.

[14] The Middle American, *American Magazine*, March, 1907.

[15] *Cf.* White: Every-Day English, p. 367 *et seq.*

[16] *Cf.* Sweet: New English Grammar, vol. i, p. 5.

[17] Dr. Charters' report appears as Vol. XVI, No. 2, *University of Missouri Bulletin*, Education Series No. 9, Jan., 1915. He was aided in his inquiry by Edith Miller, teacher of English in one of the St. Louis high-schools.

[18] You Know Me Al: New York, 1916.

[19] *Saturday Evening Post*, July 11, 1914.

[20] *Bin* is the correct American pronunciation. *Bean*, as we have seen, is the English. But I have often found *ben*, rhyming with *pen*, in such phrases as "I *ben* there."

[21] See p. 209.

[22] Seldom used. *Get* is used in the place of it, as in "I am *getting* old" and "he *got* sick."

[23] *Burned*, with a distinct *d*-sound, is almost unknown in American. See p. 201.

[24] Not used.

[25] *Cotched* is heard only in the South, and mainly among the negroes. *Catch*, of course, is always pronounced *ketch*.

[26] But "I *drew* three jacks, " in poker.

[27] *Fotch* is also heard, but it is not general.

[28] *Fit* and *fitten*, unless my observation errs, are heard only in dialect. *Fit* is archaic English. *Cf.* Thornton, vol. i, p. 322.

[29] *Glode* once enjoyed a certain respectability in America. It occurs in the *Knickerbocker Magazine* for April, 1856.

[30] *Hanged* is never heard.

[31] *Het* is incomplete without the addition of *up*. "He was *het up*" is always heard, not "he was *het*."

[32] Always so pronounced. See p. 236.

[33] See pp. 57 and 202.

[34] Always used in place of *rinse*.

[35] Always used in place of *roil*.

[36] *Sot* is heard as a localism only.

[37] See *set*, which is used almost invariably in place of *sit*.

[38] *Thunk* is never used seriously; it always shows humorous intent.

[39] See pp. 201 and 211.

[40] *Cf.* Lounsbury: History of the English Language, pp. 309-10.

[41] English As We Speak It In Ireland, p. 77.

[42] The Science of Language, vol. i, p. 166.

[43] The last stand of the distinct *-ed* was made in Addison's day. He was in favor of retaining it, and in the *Spectator* for Aug. 4, 1711, he protested against obliterating the syllable in the termination "of our praeter perfect tense, as in these words, *drown'd, walk'd, arriv'd,* for *drowned, walked, arrived,* which has very much disfigured the tongue, and turned a tenth part of our smoothest words into so many clusters of consonants."

[44] A New English Grammar, pt. i, p. 380.

[45] History of the English Language, p. 398.

[46] And still more often as an adjective, as in "it was a *boughten* dress."

[47] You Know Me Al, p. 180; see also p. 122.

[48] *Cf.* Lounsbury: History of the English Language, pp. 393 *et seq.*

[49] Remark of a policeman talking to another. What he actually said was "before the Elks was *c'm 'ere.*" *Come* and *here* were one word, approximately *cmear*. The context showed that he meant to use the past perfect tense.

[50] These examples are from Lardner's story, A New Busher Breaks In, in You Know Me Al, pp. 122 *et seq.*

[51] You Know Me Al, *op. cit.*, p. 124.

[52] The Making of English, p. 53.

[53] *Cf. Dialect Notes*, vol. iii, pt. i, p. 59; *ibid.*, vol. III, pt. iv, p. 283.

[54] Henry Bradley, in The Making of English, pp. 54-5: "In the parts of England which were largely inhabited by Danes the native pronouns (*i. e., heo, his, heom* and *heora*) were supplanted by the Scandinavian pronouns which are represented by the modern *she, they, them* and *their.*" This substitution, at first dialectical, gradually spread to the whole language.

[55] *Cf.* Sweet: A New English Grammar, pt. i, p. 344, par. 1096.

[56] Before a noun beginning with a vowel *thine* and *mine* are commonly substituted for *thy* and *my,* as in "*thine* eyes" and "*mine* infirmity." But this is solely for the sake of euphony. There is no compensatory use of *my* and *thy* in the absolute.

[57] The Making of English, p. 58.

[58] *Cf.* The Dialect of Southeastern Missouri, by D. S. Crumb, *Dialect Notes*, vol. ii, pt. iv, 1903, p. 337.

[59] It occurs, too, of course, in other dialects of English, though by no means in all. The Irish influence probably had something to do with its

prosperity in vulgar American. At all events, the Irish use it in the American manner. Joyce, in English As We Speak It in Ireland, pp. 34-5, argues that this usage was suggested by Gaelic. In Gaelic the accusative pronouns, *e*, *i* and *iad* (=*him*, *her* and *them*) are often used in place of the nominatives, *sé*, *si* and *siad* (=*he*, *she* and *they*), as in "is *iad* sin na buachaillidhe" (=*them* are the boys). This is "good grammar" in Gaelic, and the Irish, when they began to learn English, translated the locution literally. The familiar Irish "John is dead and *him* always so hearty" shows the same influence.

[60] Pp. 144-50.

[61] Modern English, p. 300.

[62] A New English Grammar, pt. i, p. 339.

[63] History of the English Language, pp. 274-5.

[64] Modern English, p. 288-9.

[65] *Cf.* p. 145n.

[66] A New English Grammar, pt. i, p. 341.

[67] It may be worth noting here that the misuse of *me* for *my*, as in "I lit *me* pipe" is quite unknown in American, either standard or vulgar. Even "*me* own" is seldom heard. This boggling of the cases is very common in spoken English.

[68] A New English Grammar, pt. i, p. 341.

[69] The King's English, p. 63.

[70] "Hon." Edward E. Browne, of Wisconsin, in the House of Representatives, July 18, 1918, p. 9965.

[71] *Cf.* Vogue Affixes in Present-Day Word-Coinage, by Louise Pound, *Dialect Notes*, vol. v, pt. i, 1918.

[72] The Speech of a Child Two Years of Age, *Dialect Notes*, vol. iv, pt. ii, 1914.

[73] A New English Grammar, pt. i, pp. 437-8.

[74] The King's English, p. 322. See especially the quotation from Frederick Greenwood, the distinguished English journalist.

[75] Report of Edward J. Brundage, attorney-general of Illinois, on the East St. Louis massacre, *Congressional Record*, Jan. 7, 1918, p. 661.

[76] The King's English, *op. cit.*

[77] Oct. 1, 1864.

[78] *At all*, by the way, is often displaced by *any* or *none*, as in "he don't lover her *any*" and "it didn't hurt me *none*."

[79] See the bibliography for the publication of Drs. Read and Pound.

[80] The only book that I can find definitely devoted to American sounds is A Handbook of American Speech, by Calvin L. Lewis; Chicago, 1916. It has

many demerits. For example, the author gives a *z*-sound to the *s* in *venison* (p. 52). This is surely not American.

[81] Maryland edition, July 18, 1914, p. 1.

[82] *Cf.* Lounsbury: The Standard of Pronunciation in English, p. 172 *et seq.*

[83] *Stomp* is used only in the sense of to stamp with the foot. One always *stamps* a letter. An analogue of *stomp*, accepted in correct English, is *strop* (*e. g., razor-strop*), from *strap*.

[84] Our Own, Our Native Speech, *McClure's Magazine*, Oct., 1916.

VII. Differences in Spelling

§ 1. Typical Forms

—Some of the salient differences between American and English spelling are shown in the following list of common words:

American	*English*
Anemia	anaemia
aneurism	aneurysm
annex (noun)	annexe
arbor	arbour
armor	armour
asphalt	asphalte
ataxia	ataxy
ax	axe
balk (verb)	baulk
baritone	barytone
bark (ship)	barque
behavior	behaviour
behoove	behove
buncombe	bunkum
burden (ship's)	burthen
cachexia	cachexy

caliber	calibre
candor	candour
center	centre
check (bank)	cheque
checkered	chequered
cider	cyder
clamor	clamour
clangor	clangour
cloture	closure[1]
color	colour
connection	connexion
councilor	councillor
counselor	counsellor
cozy	cosy
curb	kerb
cyclopedia	cyclopaedia
defense	defence
demeanor	demeanour
diarrhea	diarrhoea
draft (ship's)	draught
dreadnaught	dreadnought
dryly	drily
ecology	oecology
ecumenical	oecumenical
edema	oedema
encyclopedia	encyclopaedia
endeavor	endeavour
eon	aeon
epaulet	epaulette

esophagus	oesophagus
fagot	faggot
favor	favour
favorite	favourite
fervor	fervour
flavor	flavour
font (printer's)	fount
foregather	forgather
forego	forgo
form (printer's)	forme
fuse	fuze
gantlet (to run the—)	gauntlet
glamor	glamour
good-by	good-bye
gram	gramme
gray	grey
harbor	harbour
honor	honour
hostler	ostler
humor	humour
inclose	enclose
indorse	endorse
inflection	inflexion
inquiry	enquiry
jail	gaol
jewelry	jewellery
jimmy (burglar's)	jemmy
labor	labour
laborer	labourer

liter	litre
maneuver	manoeuvre
medieval	mediaeval
meter	metre
misdemeanor	misdemeanour
mold	mould
mollusk	mollusc
molt	moult
mustache	moustache
neighbor	neighbour
neighborhood	neighbourhood
net (adj.)	nett
odor	odour
offense	offence
pajamas	pyjamas
parlor	parlour
peas (plu. of pea)	pease
picket (military)	piquet
plow	plough
pretense	pretence
program	programme
pudgy	podgy
pygmy	pigmy
rancor	rancour
rigor	rigour
rumor	rumour
savory	savoury
scimitar	scimetar
septicemia	septicaemia

show (verb)	shew
siphon	syphon
siren	syren
skeptic	sceptic
slug (verb)	slog
slush	slosh
splendor	splendour
stanch	staunch
story (of a house)	storey
succor	succour
taffy	toffy
tire (noun)	tyre
toilet	toilette
traveler	traveller
tumor	tumour
valor	valour
vapor	vapour
veranda	verandah
vial	phial
vigor	vigour
vise (a tool)	vice
wagon	waggon
woolen	woollen

§ 2. General Tendencies

—This list is by no means exhaustive. According to a recent writer upon the subject, "there are 812 words in which the prevailing American spelling differs from the English."[2] But enough examples are given to reveal a number of definite tendencies. American, in general, moves toward simplified forms of spelling more rapidly than English, and has got much further along the road. Redundant and unnecessary letters have been dropped from whole groups of words—the *u* from the group of nouns in *-our*, with the sole exception of *Saviour*, and from such words as *mould* and *baulk*; the *e* from *annexe, asphalte, axe, forme, pease, storey*, etc.; the duplicate consonant from *waggon, nett, faggot, woollen, jeweller, councillor*, etc., and the silent foreign suffixes from *toilette, epaulette, programme, verandah*, etc. In addition, simple vowels have been substituted for degenerated diphthongs in such words as *anaemia, oesophagus, diarrhoea* and *mediaeval*, most of them from the Greek.

Further attempts in the same direction are to be seen in the substitution of simple consonants for compound consonants, as in *plow, bark, check, vial* and *draft*; in the substitution of *i* for *y* to bring words into harmony with analogues, as in *tire, cider* and *baritone* (*cf. wire, rider, merriment*), and in the general tendency to get rid of the somewhat uneuphonious *y*, as in *ataxia* and *pajamas*. Clarity and simplicity are also served by substituting *ct* for *x* in such words as *connection* and *inflection*, and *s* for *c* in words of the *defense* group. The superiority of *jail* to *gaol* is made manifest by the common mispronunciation of the latter, making it rhyme with *coal*. The substitution of *i* for *e* in such words as *indorse, inclose* and *jimmy* is of less patent utility, but even here there is probably a slight gain in euphony. Of more obscure origin is what seems to be a tendency to avoid the *o*-sound, so that the English *slog* becomes *slug, podgy* becomes *pudgy, nought* becomes *naught, slosh* becomes *slush, toffy* becomes *taffy*, and so on. Other changes carry their own justification. *Hostler* is obviously better American than *ostler*, though it may be worse English. *Show* is more logical than *shew*.[3] *Cozy* is more nearly phonetic than *cosy. Curb* has analogues in *curtain, curdle, curfew, curl, currant, curry, curve, curtsey, curse, currency, cursory, curtail, cur, curt* and many other common words: *kerb* has very few, and of them only *kerchief* and *kernel*are in general use. Moreover, the English themselves use *curb* as a verb and in all noun senses save that shown in *kerbstone*.

But a number of anomalies remain. The American substitution of *a* for *e* in *gray* is not easily explained, nor is the substitution of *k* for *c* in *skeptic* and *mollusk*, nor the retention of *e* in *forego*, nor the unphonetic substitution of *s* for *z* in *fuse*, nor the persistence of the first *y* in *pygmy*. Here we have plain vagaries, surviving in spite of attack by orthographers. Webster, in one of his earlier books, denounced the *k* in *skeptic* as "a mere pedantry, " but later on he adopted it. In the same way *pygmy*, *gray* and *mollusk* have been attacked, but they still remain sound American. The English themselves have many more such illogical forms to account for. In the midst of the *our*-words they cling to a small number in *or*, among them, *stupor*. Moreover, they drop the *u* in many derivatives, for example, in *arboreal*, *armory*, *clamorously*, *clangorous*, *odoriferous*, *humorist*, *laborious* and *rigorism*. If it were dropped in all derivatives the rule would be easy to remember, but it is retained in some of them, for example, *colourable*, *favourite*, *misdemeanour*, *coloured*and *labourer*. The derivatives of *honour* exhibit the confusion clearly. *Honorary*, *honorarium* and *honorific* drop the *u*, but *honourable* retains it. Furthermore, the English make a distinction between two senses of *rigor*. When used in its pathological sense (not only in the Latin form of *rigor mortis*, but as an English word) it drops the *u*; in all other senses it retains the *u*. The one American anomaly in this field is *Saviour*. In its theological sense it retains the *u*; but in that sense only. A sailor who saves his ship is its *savior*, not its *saviour*.

§ 3. The Influence of Webster

—At the time of the first settlement of America the rules of English orthography were beautifully vague, and so we find the early documents full of spellings that would give an English lexicographer much pain today. Now and then a curious foreshadowing of later American usage is encountered. On July 4, 1631, for example, John Winthrop wrote in his journal that "the governour built a *bark* at Mistick, which was launched this day." But during the eighteenth century, and especially after the publication of Johnson's dictionary, there was a general movement in England toward a more inflexible orthography, and many hard and fast rules, still surviving, were then laid down. It was Johnson himself who established the position of the *u* in the *our* words. Bailey, Dyche and the other lexicographers before him were divided and uncertain; Johnson declared for the *u*, and though his reasons were very shaky[4] and he often neglected his own precept, his authority was sufficient to set up a usage which still defies attack in England. Even in America this usage was not often brought into question until the last quarter of the eighteenth century. True enough, *honor* appears in the Declaration of Independence, but it seems to have got there rather by accident than by design. In Jefferson's original draft it is spelled *honour*. So early as 1768 Benjamin Franklin had published his "Scheme for a New Alphabet and a Reformed Mode of Spelling, with Remarks and Examples Concerning the Same, and an Enquiry Into its Uses" and induced a Philadelphia typefounder to cut type for it, but this scheme was too extravagant to be adopted anywhere, or to have any appreciable influence upon spelling.[5]

It was Noah Webster who finally achieved the divorce between English example and American practise. He struck the first blow in his "Grammatical Institute of the English Language, " published at Hartford in 1783. Attached to this work was an appendix bearing the formidable title of "An Essay on the Necessity, Advantages and Practicability of Reforming the Mode of Spelling, and of Rendering the Orthography of Words Correspondent to the Pronunciation, " and during the same year, at Boston, he set forth his ideas a second time in the first edition of his "American Spelling Book." The influence of this spelling book was immediate and profound. It took the place in the schools of Dilworth's "Aby-sel-pha, " the favorite of the generation preceding, and maintained its authority for fully a century. Until Lyman Cobb entered the lists with his "New Spelling Book, " in 1842, its innumerable editions scarcely had any rivalry, and even then it held its own. I have a New York edition, dated 1848, which contains an advertisement stating that the annual sale at that time was more than a million copies, and that more than 30, 000, 000 copies had been sold since 1783. In the late 40's the publishers, George F. Cooledge & Bro., devoted the whole capacity of the fastest steam press in the United States to the printing of it. This press turned out 525 copies an hour, or 5, 250 a day. It was "constructed expressly for printing Webster's Elementary Spelling Book [the name had been changed in 1829] at an expense of $5, 000." Down to 1889, 62, 000, 000 copies of the book had been sold.

The appearance of Webster's first dictionary, in 1806, greatly strengthened his influence. The best dictionary available to Americans before this was Johnson's in its various incarnations, but against Johnson's stood a good deal of animosity to its compiler, whose implacable hatred of all things American was well known to the citizens of the new republic. John Walker's dictionary, issued in London in 1791, was also in use, but not extensively. A home-made school dictionary, issued at New Haven in 1798 or 1799 by one Samuel Johnson, Jr.—apparently no relative of the great Sam—and a larger work published a year later by Johnson and the Rev. John Elliott, pastor in East Guilford, Conn., seem to have made no impression, despite the fact that the latter was commended by Simeon Baldwin, Chauncey Goodrich and other magnificoes of the time and place, and even by Webster himself. The field was thus open to the laborious and truculent Noah. He was already the acknowledged magister of lexicography in America, and there was an active public demand for a dictionary that should be wholly American. The appearance of his first duodecimo, according to Williams, [6] thereby took on something of the character of a national event. It was received, not critically, but patriotically, and its imperfections were swallowed as eagerly as its merits. Later on Webster had to meet formidable critics, at home as well as abroad, but for nearly a quarter of a century he reigned almost unchallenged. Edition after edition of his dictionary was published, each new one showing additions and improvements. Finally, in 1828, he printed his great "*American* Dictionary of the English Language, " in two large octavo volumes. It held the field for half a century, not only against Worcester and the other American lexicographers who followed him, but also against the best dictionaries produced in England. Until very lately, indeed, America remained ahead of England in practical dictionary making.

Webster had declared boldly for simpler spellings in his early spelling books; in his dictionary of 1806 he made an assault at all arms upon some of the dearest prejudices of English lexicographers. Grounding his wholesale reforms upon a saying by Franklin, that "those people spell best who do not know how to spell"—*i. e.*, who spell phonetically and logically—he made an almost complete sweep of whole classes of silent letters—the *u* in the *-our* words, the final *e* in *determine* and *requisite*, the silent *a* in *thread, feather* and *steady*, the silent *b* in *thumb*, the *s* in *island*, the *o* in *leopard*, and the redundant consonants in *traveler, wagon, jeweler*, etc. (English: *traveller, waggon, jeweller*). More, he lopped the final *k* from *frolick, physick* and their analogues. Yet more, he transposed the *e* and the *r* in all words ending in *re*, such as *theatre, lustre, centre* and *calibre*. Yet more, he changed the *c* in all words of the *defence* class to *s*. Yet more, he changed *ph* to *f* in words of the *phantom* class, *ou* to *oo* in words of the *group* class, *ow* to *ou* in *crowd*, *porpoise* to *porpess*, *acre* to *aker*, *sew* to *soe*, *woe* to *wo*, *soot* to *sut*, *gaol* to *jail*, and *plough* to *plow*. Finally, he antedated the simplified spellers by inventing a long list of boldly phonetic spellings, ranging from *tung* for *tongue* to *wimmen* for *women*, and from *hainous* for *heinous* to *cag* for *keg*.

A good many of these new spellings, of course, were not actually Webster's inventions. For example, the change from *-our* to *-or* in words of the *honor* class was a mere echo of an earlier English usage, or, more accurately, of an earlier English uncertainty. In the first three folios of Shakespeare, 1623, 1632 and 1663-6, *honor* and *honour* were used indiscriminately and in almost equal proportions; English spelling was still fluid, and the *-our*-form was not consistently adopted until the fourth folio of 1685. Moreover, John Wesley, the founder of Methodism, is authority for the statement that the *-or*-form was "a fashionable impropriety" in England in 1791. But the great authority of Johnson stood against it, and Webster was surely not one to imitate fashionable improprieties. He deleted the *u* for purely etymological reasons, going back to the Latin *honor*, *favor* and *odor* without taking account of the intermediate French *honneur*, *faveur* and *odeur*. And where no etymological reasons presented themselves, he made his changes by analogy and for the sake of uniformity, or for euphony or simplicity, or because it pleased him, one guesses, to stir up the academic animals. Webster, in fact, delighted in controversy, and was anything but free from the national yearning to make a sensation.

A great many of his innovations, of course, failed to take root, and in the course of time he abandoned some of them himself. In his early "Essay on the Necessity, Advantage and Practicability of Reforming the Mode of Spelling" he advocated reforms which were already discarded by the time he published the first edition of his dictionary. Among them were the dropping of the silent letter in such words as *head*, *give*, *built* and *realm*, making them *hed*, *giv*, *bilt* and *relm*; the substitution of doubled vowels for decayed diphthongs in such words as *mean*, *zeal* and *near*, making them *meen*, *zeel* and *neer*; and the substitution of *sh* for *ch* in such French loan-words as *machine* and *chevalier*, making them *masheen* and *shevaleer*. He also declared for *stile* in place of *style*, and for many other such changes, and then quietly abandoned them. The successive editions of his dictionary show still further concessions. *Croud, fether, groop, gillotin, iland, insted, leperd, soe, sut, steddy, thret, thred, thum* and *wimmen* appear only in the 1806 edition. In 1828 he went back to *crowd, feather, group, island, instead, leopard, sew, soot, steady, thread, threat, thumb* and *women*, and changed *gillotin* to *guillotin*. In addition, he restored the final *e* in *determine, discipline, requisite, imagine*, etc. In 1838, revising his dictionary, he abandoned a good many spellings that had appeared in either the 1806 or the 1828 edition, notably *maiz* for *maize, suveran* for *sovereign* and *guillotin* for *guillotine*. But he stuck manfully to a number that were quite as revolutionary—for example, *aker* for *acre, cag* for *keg, grotesk* for *grotesque, heinous* for *heinous, porpess* for *porpoise* and *tung* for *tongue*—and they did not begin to disappear until the edition of 1854, issued by other hands and eleven years after his death. Three of his favorites, *chimist* for *chemist, neger* for *negro* and *zeber* for *zebra*, are incidentally interesting as showing changes in American pronunciation. He abandoned *zeber* in 1828, but remained faithful to *chimist* and *neger* to the last.

But though he was thus forced to give occasional ground, and in more than one case held out in vain, Webster lived to see the majority of his reforms adopted by his countrymen. He left the ending in *-or* triumphant over the ending in *-our*, he shook the security of the ending in *-re*, he rid American spelling of a great many doubled consonants, he established the *s* in words of the *defense* group, and he gave currency to many characteristic American spellings, notably *jail, wagon, plow, mold* and *ax*. These spellings still survive, and are practically universal in the United States today; their use constitutes one of the most obvious differences between written English and written American. Moreover, they have founded a general tendency, the effects of which reach far beyond the field actually traversed by Webster himself. New words, and particularly loan-words, are simplified, and hence naturalized in American much more quickly than in English. *Employé* has long since become *employee* in our newspapers, and *asphalte* has lost its final *e*, and *manoeuvre* has become *maneuver*, and *pyjamas* has become *pajamas*. Even the terminology of science is simplified and Americanized. In medicine, for example, the highest American usage countenances many forms which would seem barbarisms to an English medical man if he encountered them in the *Lancet*. In derivatives of the Greek *haima* it is the almost invariable American custom to spell the root syllable *hem*, but the more conservative English make it *haem*—e. g., in *haemorrhage* and *haemiplegia*. In an exhaustive list of diseases issued by the United States Public Health Service[7] the *haem*-form does not appear once. In the same way American usage prefers*esophagus*, *diarrhea* and *gonorrhea* to the English *oesophagus*, *diarrhoea* and *gonorrhoea*. In the style-book of the *Journal* of the American Medical Association[8] I find many other spellings that would shock an English medical author, among them *curet* for *curette*, *cocain* for *cocaine*, *gage* for *gauge*, *intern* for *interne*, *lacrimal* for *lachrymal*, and a whole group of words ending in *−er* instead of in *-re*.

Webster's reforms, it goes without saying, have not passed unchallenged by the guardians of tradition. A glance at the literature of the first years of the nineteenth century shows that most of the serious authors of the time ignored his new spellings, though they were quickly adopted by the newspapers. Bancroft's "Life of Washington" contains *-our* endings in all such words as *honor*, *ardor* and *favor*. Washington Irving also threw his influence against the *-or* ending, and so did Bryant and most of the other literary big-wigs of that day. After the appearance of "An American Dictionary of the English Language, " in 1828, a formal battle was joined, with Lyman Cobb and Joseph E. Worcester as the chief opponents of the reformer. Cobb and Worcester, in the end, accepted the *-or* ending and so surrendered on the main issue, but various other champions arose to carry on the war. Edward S. Gould, in a once famous essay, [9] denounced the whole Websterian orthography with the utmost fury, and Bryant, reprinting this philippic in the *Evening Post*, said that on account of Webster "the English language has been undergoing a process of corruption for the last quarter of a century, " and offered to contribute to a fund to have Gould's denunciation "read twice a year in every school-house in the United States, until every trace of Websterian spelling disappears from the land." But Bryant was forced to admit that, even in 1856, the chief novelties of the Connecticut school-master "who taught millions to read but not one to sin" were "adopted and propagated by the largest publishing house, through the columns of the most widely circulated monthly magazine, and through one of the ablest and most widely circulated newspapers in the United States"—which is to say, the *Tribune* under Greeley. The last academic attack was delivered by Bishop Coxe in 1886, and he contented himself with the resigned statement that "Webster has corrupted our spelling sadly." Lounsbury, with his active interest in spelling reform, ranged himself on the side of Webster, and effectively disposed of the controversy by showing that the great majority of his spellings were supported by precedents quite as respectable as those behind the fashionable English spellings. In Lounsbury's opinion, a good deal of the opposition to them was no more than a symptom of antipathy to all things American among certain Englishmen and of subservience to all things English among certain Americans.[10]

Webster's inconsistency gave his opponents a formidable weapon for use against him—until it began to be noticed that the orthodox English spelling was quite as inconsistent. He sought to change *acre* to *aker*, but left *lucre* unchanged. He removed the final *f* from *bailiff*, *mastiff*, *plaintiff* and *pontiff*, but left it in *distaff*. He changed *c* to *s* in words of the *offense* class, but left the *c* in *fence*. He changed the *ck* in *frolick*, *physick*, etc., into a simple *c*, but restored it in such derivatives as *frolicksome*. He deleted the silent *u* in *mould*, but left it in *court*. These slips were made the most of by Cobb in a pamphlet printed in 1831.[11] He also detected Webster in the frequent *faux pas* of using spellings in his definitions and explanations that conflicted with the spellings he advocated. Various other purists joined in the attack, and it was renewed with great fury after the appearance of Worcester's dictionary, in 1846. Worcester, who had begun his lexicographical labors by editing Johnson's dictionary, was a good deal more conservative than Webster, and so the partisans of conformity rallied around him, and for a while the controversy took on all the rancor of a personal quarrel. Even the editions of Webster printed after his death, though they gave way on many points, were violently arraigned. Gould, in 1867, belabored the editions of 1854 and 1866, [12] and complained that "for the past twenty-five years the Websterian replies have uniformly been bitter in tone, and very free in the imputation of personal motives, or interested or improper motives, on the part of opposing critics." At this time Webster himself had been dead for twenty-two years. Schele de Vere, during the same year, denounced the publishers of the Webster dictionaries for applying "immense capital and a large stock of energy and perseverance" to the propagation of his "new and arbitrarily imposed orthography."[13]

§ 4. Exchanges

—As in vocabulary and in idiom, there are constant exchanges between English and American in the department of orthography. Here the influence of English usage is almost uniformly toward conservatism, and that of American usage is as steadily in the other direction. The logical superiority of American spelling is well exhibited by its persistent advance in the face of the utmost hostility. The English objection to our simplifications, as Brander Matthews points out, is not wholly or even chiefly etymological; its roots lie, to borrow James Russell Lowell's phrase, in an esthetic hatred burning "with as fierce a flame as ever did theological hatred." There is something inordinately offensive to English purists in the very thought of taking lessons from this side of the water, particularly in the mother tongue. The opposition, transcending the academic, takes on the character of the patriotic. "Any American, " continues Matthews, "who chances to note the force and the fervor and the frequency of the objurgations against American spelling in the columns of the *Saturday Review*, for example, and of the *Athenaeum*, may find himself wondering as to the date of the papal bull which declared the infallibility of contemporary British orthography, and as to the place where the council of the Church was held at which it was made an article of faith."[14] This was written more than a quarter of a century ago. Since then there has been a lessening of violence, but the opposition still continues. No self-respecting English author would yield up the *-our* ending for an instant, or write *check* for *cheque*, or transpose the last letters in the *-re* words.

Nevertheless, American spelling makes constant gains across the water, and they more than offset the occasional fashions for English spellings on this side. Schele de Vere, in 1867, consoled himself for Webster's "arbitrarily imposed orthography" by predicting that it could be "only temporary"—that, in the long run, "North America depends exclusively on the mother-country for its models of literature." But the event has blasted this prophecy and confidence, for the English, despite their furious reluctance, have succumbed to Webster more than once. The New English Dictionary, a monumental work, shows many silent concessions, and quite as many open yieldings—for example, in the case of *ax*, which is admitted to be "better than *axe* on every ground."

Moreover, English usage tends to march ahead of it, outstripping the liberalism of its editor, Sir James A. H. Murray. In 1914, for example, Sir James was still protesting against dropping the first *e* from *judgement*, a characteristic Americanism, but during the same year the Fowlers, in their Concise Oxford Dictionary, put *judgment* ahead of *judgement*; and two years earlier the Authors' and Printers' Dictionary, edited by Horace Hart, [15] had dropped *judgement* altogether. Hart is Controller of the Oxford University Press, and the Authors' and Printers' Dictionary is an authority accepted by nearly all of the great English book publishers and newspapers. Its last edition shows a great many American spellings. For example, it recommends the use of *jail* and *jailer* in place of the English *gaol* and *gaoler*, says that *ax* is better than *axe*, drops the final *e* from *asphalte* and *forme*, changes the *y* to *i* in *cyder*, *cypher* and *syren* and advocates the same change in *tyre*, drops the redundant *t* from *nett*, changes *burthen* to *burden*, spells *wagon* with one *g*, prefers *fuse* to *fuze*, and takes the *e* out of *storey*. "Rules for Compositors and Readers at the University Press, Oxford, " also edited by Hart (with the advice of Sir James Murray and Dr. Henry Bradley), is another very influential English authority.[16] It gives its imprimatur to *bark* (a ship), *cipher*, *siren*, *jail*, *story*, *tire* and *wagon*, and even advocates *kilogram* and *omelet*. Finally, there is Cassell's English Dictionary.[17] It clings to the *-our* and *-re* endings and to *annexe*, *waggon* and *cheque*, but it prefers *jail* to *gaol*, *net* to *nett*, *asphalt* to *asphalte* and *story* to *storey*, and comes out flatly for *judgment*, *fuse* and *siren*.

Current English spelling, like our own, shows a number of uncertainties and inconsistencies, and some of them are undoubtedly the result of American influences that have not yet become fully effective. The lack of harmony in the *-our* words, leading to such discrepancies as *honorary* and *honourable*, I have already mentioned. The British Board of Trade, in attempting to fix the spelling of various scientific terms, has often come to grief. Thus it detaches the final *-me* from *gramme* in such compounds as *kilogram* and *milligram*, but insists upon *gramme* when the word stands alone. In American usage *gram* is now common, and scarcely challenged. All the English authorities that I have consulted prefer *metre* and *calibre* to the American *meter* and *caliber*.[18] They also support the *ae* in such words as *aetiology, aesthetics, mediaeval* and *anaemia*, and the *oe* in *oesophagus, manoeuvre* and *diarrhoea*. They also cling to such forms as *mollusc, kerb, pyjamas* and *ostler*, and to the use of *x* instead of *ct* in *connexion* and *inflexion*. The Authors' and Printers' Dictionary admits the American *curb*, but says that the English *kerb* is more common. It gives *barque, plough* and *fount*, but grants that *bark, plow* and *font* are good in America. As between *inquiry* and *enquiry*, it prefers the American *inquiry* to the English *enquiry*, but it rejects the American *inclose* and *indorse* in favor of the English *enclose* and *endorse*.[19] Here American spelling has driven in a salient, but has yet to take the whole position. A number of spellings, nearly all American, are trembling on the brink of acceptance in both countries. Among them is *rime* (for *rhyme*). This spelling was correct in England until about 1530, but its recent revival was of American origin. It is accepted by the Oxford Dictionary and by the editors of the Cambridge History of English Literature, but it seldom appears in an English journal. The same may be said of *grewsome*. It has got a footing in both countries, but the weight of English opinion is still against it. *Develop* (instead of *develope*) has gone further in both countries. So has *engulf*, for *engulph*. So has *gipsy* for *gypsy*.

American imitation of English orthography has two impulses behind it. First, there is the colonial spirit, the desire to pass as English—in brief, mere affectation. Secondly, there is the wish among printers, chiefly of books and periodicals, to reach a compromise spelling acceptable in both countries, thus avoiding expensive revisions in case of republication in England.[20] The first influence need not detain us. It is chiefly visible among folk of fashionable pretensions, and is not widespread. At Bar Harbor, in Maine, some of the summer residents are at great pains to put *harbour* instead of *harbor* on their stationery, but the local postmaster still continues to stamp all mail *Bar Harbor*, the legal name of the place. In the same way American haberdashers sometimes advertise *pyjamas* instead of *pajamas*, just as they advertise *braces* instead of *suspenders* and *vests* instead of *undershirts*. But this benign folly does not go very far. Beyond occasionally clinging to the *-re* ending in words of the *theatre* group, all American newspapers and magazines employ the native orthography, and it would be quite as startling to encounter *honour* or *jewellery* in one of them as it would be to encounter *gaol* or *waggon*. Even the most fashionable jewelers in Fifth avenue still deal in *jewelry*, not in *jewellery*.

The second influence is of more effect and importance. In the days before the copyright treaty between England and the United States, one of the standing arguments against it among the English was based upon the fear that it would flood England with books set up in America, and so work a corruption of English spelling.[21] This fear, as we have seen, had a certain plausibility; there is not the slightest doubt that American books and American magazines have done valiant missionary service for American orthography. But English conservatism still holds out stoutly enough to force American printers to certain compromises. When a book is designed for circulation in both countries it is common for the publisher to instruct the printer to employ "English spelling." This English spelling, at the Riverside Press, [22] embraces all the *-our* endings and the following further forms:

cheque

chequered

connexion

dreamt

faggot

forgather

forgo

grey

inflexion

jewellery

leapt

premises (in logic)

waggon

It will be noted that *gaol, tyre, storey, kerb, asphalte, annexe, ostler, mollusc* and *pyjamas* are not listed, nor are the words ending in *-re*. These and their like constitute the English contribution to the compromise. Two other great American book presses, that of the Macmillan Company[23] and that of the J. S. Cushing Company, [24] add *gaol* and *storey* to the list, and also *behove, briar, drily, enquire, gaiety, gipsy, instal, judgement, lacquey, moustache, nought, pigmy, postillion, reflexion, shily, slily, staunch* and *verandah.* Here they go too far, for, as we have seen, the English themselves have begun to abandon *briar, enquire* and *judgement.* Moreover, *lacquey* is going out over there, and *gipsy* is not English, but American. The Riverside Press, even in books intended only for America, prefers certain English forms, among them, *anaemia, axe, mediaeval, mould, plough, programme* and *quartette,* but in compensation it stands by such typical Americanisms as *caliber, calk, center, cozy, defense, foregather, gray, hemorrhage, luster, maneuver, mustache, theater* and *woolen.* The Government Printing Office at Washington follows Webster's New International Dictionary, [25] which supports most of the innovations of Webster himself. This dictionary is the authority in perhaps a majority of American printing offices, with the Standard and the Century supporting it. The latter two also follow Webster, notably in his *-er* endings and in his substitution of *s* for *c* in words of the *defense* class. The Worcester Dictionary is the sole exponent of English spelling in general circulation in the United States. It remains faithful to most of the *-re* endings, and to *manoeuvre, gramme, plough, sceptic, woollen, axe* and many other English forms. But even Worcester favors such characteristic American spellings as *behoove, brier, caliber, checkered, dryly, jail* and *wagon.*

§ 5. Simplified Spelling

—The current movement toward a general reform of English-American spelling is of American origin, and its chief supporters are Americans today. Its actual father was Webster, for it was the long controversy over his simplified spellings that brought the dons of the American Philological Association to a serious investigation of the subject. In 1875 they appointed a committee to inquire into the possibility of reform, and in 1876 this committee reported favorably. During the same year there was an International Convention for the Amendment of English Orthography at Philadelphia, with several delegates from England present, and out of it grew the Spelling Reform Association.[26] In 1878 a committee of American philologists began preparing a list of proposed new spellings, and two years later the Philological Society of England joined in the work. In 1883 a joint manifesto was issued, recommending various general simplifications. In 1886 the American Philological Association issued independently a list of recommendations affecting about 3, 500 words, and falling under ten headings. Practically all of the changes proposed had been put forward 80 years before by Webster, and some of them had entered into unquestioned American usage in the meantime, *e. g.*, the deletion of the *u* from the *-our* words, the substitution of *er* for *re* at the end of words, the reduction of *traveller* to *traveler*, and the substitution of *z* for *s* wherever phonetically demanded, as in *advertize* and *cozy*.

The trouble with the others was that they were either too uncouth to be adopted without a struggle or likely to cause errors in pronunciation. To the first class belonged *tung* for *tongue*, *ruf* for *rough*, *batl* for *battle* and *abuv* for *above*, and to the second such forms as *cach* for *catch* and *troble* for *trouble*. The result was that the whole reform received a set-back: the public dismissed the industrious professors as a pack of dreamers. Twelve years later the National Education Association revived the movement with a proposal that a beginning be made with a very short list of reformed spellings, and nominated the following by way of experiment: *tho, altho, thru, thruout, thoro, thoroly, thorofare, program, prolog, catalog, pedagog* and *decalog*. This scheme of gradual changes was sound in principle, and in a short time at least two of the recommended spellings, *program* and *catalog*, were in general use. Then, in 1906, came the organization of the Simplified Spelling Board, with an endowment of $15, 000 a year from Andrew Carnegie, and a formidable membership of pundits. The board at once issued a list of 300 revised spellings, new and old, and in August, 1906, President Roosevelt ordered their adoption by the Government Printing Office. But this unwise effort to hasten matters, combined with the buffoonery characteristically thrown about the matter by Roosevelt, served only to raise up enemies, and since then, though it has prudently gone back to more discreet endeavors and now lays main stress upon the original 12 words of the National Education Association, the Board has not made a great deal of progress.[27] From time to time it issues impressive lists of newspapers and periodicals that are using some, at least, of its revised spellings and of colleges that have made them optional, but an inspection of these lists shows that very few publications of any importance have been converted[28] and that most of the great universities still hesitate. It has, however, greatly reinforced the authority behind many of Webster's spellings, and it has done much to reform scientific orthography. Such forms as *gram, cocain, chlorid, anemia* and *anilin* are the products of its influence.

Despite the large admixture of failure in this success there is good reason to believe that at least two of the spellings on the National Education Association list, *tho* and *thru*, are making not a little quiet progress. I read a great many manuscripts by American authors, and find in them an increasing use of both forms, with the occasional addition of *altho*, *thoro* and *thoroly*. The spirit of American spelling is on their side. They promise to come in as *honor*, *bark*, *check*, *wagon* and *story* came in many years ago, as *tire*, [29] *esophagus* and *theater* came in later on, as *program*, *catalog* and *cyclopedia* came in only yesterday, and as *airplane* (for *aëroplane*)[30] is coming in today. A constant tendency toward logic and simplicity is visible; if the spelling of English and American does not grow farther and farther apart it is only because American drags English along. There is incessant experimentalization. New forms appear, are tested, and then either gain general acceptance or disappear. One such, now struggling for recognition, is *alright*, a compound of *all* and *right*, made by analogy with *already* and *almost*. I find it in American manuscripts every day, and it not infrequently gets into print.[31] So far no dictionary supports it, but it has already migrated to England.[32] Meanwhile, one often encounters, in American advertising matter, such experimental forms as *burlesk*, *foto*, *fonograph*, *kandy*, *kar*, *holsum*, *kumfort* and *Q-room*, not to mention *sulfur*. *Segar* has been more or less in use for half a century, and at one time it threatened to displace *cigar*. At least one American professor of English predicts that such forms will eventually prevail. Even *fosfate* and *fotograph*, he says, "are bound to be the spellings of the future."[33]

§ 6. Minor Differences

—Various minor differences remain to be noticed. One is a divergence in orthography due to differences in pronunciation. *Specialty*, *aluminum* and *alarm* offer examples. In English they are *speciality*, *aluminium* and *alarum*, though *alarm* is also an alternative form. *Specialty*, in America, is always accented on the first syllable; *speciality*, in England, on the third. The result is two distinct words, though their meaning is identical. How *aluminium*, in America, lost its fourth syllable I have been unable to determine, but all American authorities now make it *aluminum* and all English authorities stick to *aluminium.*

Another difference in usage is revealed in the spelling and pluralization of foreign words. Such words, when they appear in an English publication, even a newspaper, almost invariably bear the correct accents, but in the United States it is almost as invariably the rule to omit these accents, save in publications of considerable pretensions. This is notably the case with *café crêpe, début, débutante, portière, levée, éclat, fête, régime, rôle, soirée, protégé, élite, mêlée, tête-à-tête* and *répertoire.* It is rare to encounter any of them with its proper accents in an American newspaper; it is rare to encounter them unaccented in an English newspaper. This slaughter of the accents, it must be obvious, greatly aids the rapid naturalization of a newcomer. It loses much of its foreignness at once, and is thus easier to absorb. *Dépôt* would have been a long time working its way into American had it remained *dépôt,* but immediately it became plain *depot* it got in. The process is constantly going on. I often encounter *naïveté* without its accents, and even *déshabille, hofbräu, señor* and *résumé. Cañon* was changed to *canyon* years ago, and the cases of *exposé, divorcée, schmierkäse, employé* and *matinée* are familiar. At least one American dignitary of learning, Brander Matthews, has openly defended and even advocated this clipping of accents. In speaking of *naïf* and *naïveté,* which he welcomes because "we have no exact equivalent for either word, " he says: "But they will need to shed their accents and to adapt themselves somehow to the traditions of our orthography."[34] He goes on: "After we have decided that the foreign word we find knocking at the doors of English [he really means American, as the context shows] is likely to be useful, we must fit it for naturalization by insisting that it shall shed its accents, if it has any; that it shall change its spelling, if this is necessary; that it shall modify its pronunciation, if this is not easy for us to compass; and that it shall conform to all our speech-habits, especially in the formation of the plural."[35]

In this formation of the plural, as elsewhere, English regards the precedents and American makes new ones. All the English authorities that I have had access to advocate retaining the foreign plurals of most of the foreign words in daily use, *e. g.*, *sanatoria, appendices, virtuosi, formulae* and *libretti.* But American usage favors plurals of native cut, and the *Journal* of the American Medical Association goes so far as to approve *curriculums* and *septums. Banditti,* in place of *bandits,* would seem an affectation in America, and so would *soprani* for *sopranos* and *soli* for *solos.*[36] The last two are common in England. Both English and American labor under the lack of native plurals for the two everyday titles, *Mister* and *Missus.* In the written speech, and in the more exact forms of the spoken speech, the French plurals, *Messieurs* and *Mesdames,* are used, but in the ordinary spoken speech, at least in America, they are avoided by circumlocution. When *Messieurs* has to be spoken it is almost invariably pronounced *messers,* and in the same way *Mesdame* sbecomes *mez-dames,* with the first syllable rhyming with *sez* and the second, which bears the accent, with *games.* In place of *Mesdames* a more natural form, *Madames,* seems to be gaining ground in America. Thus, I lately found *Dames du Sacré Coeur* translated as *Madames of the Sacred Heart* in a Catholic paper of wide circulation, [37] and the form is apparently used by American members of the community.

In capitalization the English are a good deal more conservative than we are. They invariably capitalize such terms as *Government, Prime Minister* and *Society,* when used as proper nouns; they capitalize *Press, Pulpit, Bar,* etc., almost as often. In America a movement against this use of capitals appeared during the latter part of the eighteenth century. In Jefferson's first draft of the Declaration of Independence *nature* and *creator,* and even *god* are in lower case.[38] During the 20's and 30's of the succeeding century, probably as a result of French influence, the disdain of capitals went so far that the days of the week were often spelled with small initial letters, and even *Mr.*became *mr.* Curiously enough, the most striking exhibition of this tendency of late years is offered by an English work of the highest scholarship, the Cambridge History of English Literature. It uses the lower case for all titles, even *baron* and *colonel* before proper names, and also avoids capitals in such words as *presbyterian, catholic* and *christian,* and in the second parts of such terms as Westminster *abbey* and Atlantic *ocean.*

Finally, there are certain differences in punctuation. The English, as everyone knows, put a comma after the street number of a house, making it, for example, *34, St. James street.* They usually insert a comma instead of a period after the hour when giving the time in figures, *e. g.*, *9, 27*, and omit the *0* when indicating less than 10 minutes, *e. g.*, *8, 7* instead of *8.07*. They do not use the period as the mark of the decimal, but employ a dot at the level of the upper dot of a colon, as in *3·1416*. They cling to the hyphen in such words as *to-day* and *to-night*; it begins to disappear in America. They use *an* before *hotel* and *historical*; Kipling has even used it before *hydraulic*;[39]American usage prefers *a*. But these small differences need not be pursued further.

FOOTNOTES:

[1] Fowler & Fowler, in The King's English, p. 23, say that "when it was proposed to borrow from France what we [*i. e.*, the English] now know as the *closure*, it seemed certain for some time that with the thing we should borrow the name, *clôture*; a press campaign resulted in *closure*." But in the *Congressional Record* it is still*cloture*, though with the loss of the circumflex accent, and this form is generally retained by American newspapers.

[2] Richard P. Read: The American Language, *New York Sun*, March 7, 1918.

[3] *To shew* has completely disappeared from American, but it still survives in English usage. *Cf.* The *Shewing*-Up of Blanco Posnet, by George Bernard Shaw. The word, of course, is pronounced *show*, not *shoe*. *Shrew*, a cognate word, still retains the early pronunciation of *shrow* in English, but is now phonetic in American.

[4] *Cf.* Lounsbury; English Spelling and Spelling Reform; p. 209 *et seq.* Johnson even advocated *translatour, emperour, oratour* and *horrour*. But, like most other lexicographers, he was often inconsistent, and the conflict between *interiour* and *exterior*, and *anteriour* and *posterior*, in his dictionary, laid him open to much mocking criticism.

[5] In a letter to Miss Stephenson, Sept. 20, 1768, he exhibited the use of his new alphabet. The letter is to be found in most editions of his writings.

[6] R. C. Williams: Our Dictionaries; New York, 1890, p. 30.

[7] Nomenclature of Diseases and Condition, prepared by direction of the Surgeon General; Washington, 1916.

[8] American Medical Association Style Book; Chicago, 1915.

[9] *Democratic Review*, March, 1856.

[10] *Vide* English Spelling and Spelling Reform, p. 229.

[11] A Critical Review of the Orthography of Dr. Webster's Series of Books ...; New York, 1831.

[12] Good English; p. 137 *et seq.*

[13] Studies in English; pp. 64-5.

[14] Americanisms and Briticisms; New York, 1892, p. 37.

[15] Authors' & Printers' Dictionary ... an attempt to codify the best typographical practices of the present day, by F. Howard Collins; 4th ed., revised by Horace Hart; London, 1912.

[16] Horace Hart: Rules for Compositors and Readers at the University Press, Oxford: 23rd ed.; London, 1914. I am informed by Mr. Humphrey Davy, of the *London Times*, that, with one or two minor exceptions, the *Times* observes the rules laid down in this book.

[17] Cassell's English Dictionary, ed. by John Williams, 37th thousand: London, 1908. This work is based upon the larger Encyclopaedic Dictionary, also edited by Williams.

[18] *Caliber* is now the official spelling of the United States Army. *Cf.* Description and Rules for the Management of the U. S. Rifle, *Caliber* .30 Model of 1903; Washington, 1915. But *calibre* is still official in England as appears by the Field Service Pocket-Book used in the European war (London, 1914, p. viii.)

[19] Even worse inconsistencies are often encountered. Thus *enquiry* appears on p. 3 of the Dardanelles Commission's First Report; London, 1917; but *inquiring* is on p. 1.

[20] Mere stupid copying may perhaps be added. An example of it appears on a map printed with a pamphlet entitled Conquest and Kultur, compiled by two college professors and issued by the Creel press bureau (Washington, 1918). On this map, borrowed from an English periodical called *New Europe* without correction, *annex* is spelled *annexe*. In the same way English spellings often appear in paragraphs reprinted from the English newspapers. As compensation in the case of *annexe* I find *annex* on pages 11 and 23 of A Report on the Treatment by the Enemy of British Prisoners of War Behind the Firing Lines in France and Belgium; Miscellaneous No. 7 (1918). When used as a verb the English always spell the word *annex.Annexe* is only the noun form.

[21] *Vide* Matthews: Americanisms and Briticisms, pp. 33-34.

[22] Handbook of Style in Use at the Riverside Press, Cambridge, Mass.; Boston, 1913.

[23] Notes for the Guidance of Authors; New York, 1918.

[24] Preparation of Manuscript, Proof Reading, and Office Style at J. S. Cushing Company's; Norwood, Mass., n. d.

[25] Style Book, a Compilation of Rules Governing Executive, Congressional and Departmental Printing, Including the *Congressional Record*, ed. of Feb., 1917; Washington, 1917. A copy of this style book is in the proof-room of nearly every American daily newspaper and its rules are generally observed.

[26] Accounts of earlier proposals of reform in English spelling are to be found in Sayce's Introduction to the Science of Language, vol. i, p. 330 *et seq.*, and White's Everyday English, p. 152 *et seq.* The best general treatment of the subject is in Lounsbury's English Spelling and Spelling Reform; New York, 1909.

[27] Its second list was published on January 28, 1908, its third on January 25, 1909, and its fourth on March 24, 1913, and since then there have been several others. But most of its literature is devoted to the 12 words and to certain reformed spellings of Webster, already in general use.

[28] The *Literary Digest* is perhaps the most important. Its usage is shown by the Funk & Wagnalls Company Style Card; New York, 1914.

[29] *Tyre* was still in use in America in the 70's. It will be found on p. 150 of Mark Twain's Roughing It; Hartford, 1872.

[30] *Vide* the *Congressional Record* for March 26, 1918, p. 4374. It is curious to note that the French themselves are having difficulties with this and the cognate words. The final *e* has been dropped from *biplan, monoplane* and *hydroplan*, but they seem to be unable to dispense with it in *aéroplane*.

[31] For example, in Teepee Neighbors, by Grace Coolidge; Boston, 1917, p. 220; Duty and Other Irish Comedies, by Seumas O'Brien; New York, 1916, p. 52; Salt, by Charles G. Norris; New York, 1918, p. 135, and The Ideal Guest, by Wyndham Lewis, *Little Review*, May, 1918, p. 3. O'Brien is an Irishman and Lewis an Englishman, but the printer in each case was American. I find *allright*, as one word but with two *ll's*, in Diplomatic Correspondence With Belligerent Governments, etc., European War, No. 4; Washington, 1918, p. 214.

[32] *Vide* How to Lengthen Our Ears, by Viscount Harberton; London, 1917, p. 28.

[33] Krapp: Modern English, p. 181.

[34] Why Not Speak Your Own Language? in *Delineator*, Nov., 1917, p. 12.

[35] I once noted an extreme form of this naturalization in a leading Southern newspaper, the *Baltimore Sun*. In an announcement of the death of an American artist it reported that he had studied at the *Bozart* in Paris. In New York I have also encountered *chaufer*.

[36] Now and then, of course, a contrary tendency asserts itself. For example, the plural of *medium*, in the sense of advertising medium, is sometimes made *media* by advertising men. *Vide* the *Editor and Publisher*, May 11, 1918.

[37] *Irish World*, June 26, 1918.

[38] *Vide* The Declaration of Independence, by Herbert Friedenwald, New York, 1904, p. 262 *et seq.*

[39] Now and then the English flirt with the American usage. Hart says, for example, that "originally the cover of the large Oxford Dictionary had '*a* historical.'" But "*an* historical" now appears there.

VIII. Proper Names in America

§ 1. Surnames

—A glance at any American city directory is sufficient to show that, despite the continued political and cultural preponderance of the original English strain, the American people have quite ceased to be authentically English in race, or even authentically British. The blood in their arteries is inordinately various and inextricably mixed, but yet not mixed enough to run a clear stream. A touch of foreignness still lingers about millions of them, even in the country of their birth. They show their alien origin in their speech, in their domestic customs, in their habits of mind, and in their very names. Just as the Scotch and the Welsh have invaded England, elbowing out the actual English to make room for themselves, so the Irish, the Germans, the Italians, the Scandinavians and the Jews of Eastern Europe, and in some areas, the French, the Slavs and the hybrid-Spaniards have elbowed out the descendants of the first colonists. It is not exaggerating, indeed, to say that wherever the old stock comes into direct and unrestrained conflict with one of these new stocks, it tends to succumb, or, at all events, to give up the battle. The Irish, in the big cities of the East, attained to a truly impressive political power long before the first native-born generation of them had grown up.[1] The Germans, following the limestone belt of the Alleghany foothills, pre-empted the best lands East of the mountains before the new republic was born.[2]And so, in our own time, we have seen the Swedes and Norwegians shouldering the native from the wheat lands of the Northwest, and the Italians driving the decadent New Englanders from their farms, and the Jews gobbling New York, and the Slavs getting a firm foothold in the mining regions, and the French Canadians penetrating New Hampshire and Vermont, and the Japanese and Portuguese menacing Hawaii, and the awakened negroes gradually ousting the whites from the farms of the South.[3] The birth-rate among all these foreign stocks is enormously greater than among the older stock, and though the death-rate is also high, the net increase remains relatively formidable. Even without the aid of immigration it is probable that they would continue to rise in numbers faster than the original English and so-called Scotch-Irish.[4]

Turn to the letter *z* in the New York telephone directory and you will find a truly astonishing array of foreign names, some of them in process of anglicization, but many of them still arrestingly outlandish. The only Anglo-Saxon surname beginning with *z* is *Zacharias*, [5] and even that was originally borrowed from the Greek. To this the Norman invasion seems to have added only *Zouchy*. But in Manhattan and the Bronx, even among the necessarily limited class of telephone subscribers, there are nearly 1500 persons whose names begin with the letter, and among them one finds fully 150 different surnames. The German *Zimmermann*, with either one *n* or two, is naturally the most numerous single name, and following close upon it are its derivatives, *Zimmer* and *Zimmern*. With them are many more German names: *Zahn, Zechendorf, Zeffert, Zeitler, Zeller, Zellner, Zeltmacher, Zepp, Ziegfeld, Zabel, Zucker, Zuckermann, Ziegler, Zillman, Zinser* and so on. They are all represented heavily, but they indicate neither the earliest nor the most formidable accretion, for underlying them are many Dutch names, *e. g.*, *Zeeman* and *Zuurmond*, and over them are a large number of Slavic, Italian and Jewish names. Among the first I note *Zabludosky, Zabriskie, Zachczynski, Zapinkow, Zaretsky, Zechnowitz, Zenzalsky* and *Zywachevsky*; among the second, *Zaccardi, Zaccarini, Zaccaro, Zapparano, Zanelli, Zicarelli* and *Zucca*; among the third, *Zukor, Zipkin* and *Ziskind*. There are, too, various Spanish names: *Zelaya, Zingaro*, etc. And Greek: *Zapeion, Zervakos* and *Zouvelekis*. And Armenian: *Zaloom, Zaron* and *Zatmajian*. And Hungarian: *Zadek, Zagor* and *Zichy*. And Swedish: *Zetterholm* and *Zetterlund*. And a number that defy placing: *Zrike, Zvan, Zwipf, Zula, Zur* and *Zeve*.

Any other American telephone directory will show the same extraordinary multiplication of exotic patronymics. I choose, at random, that of Pittsburgh, and confine myself to the saloon-keepers and clergymen. Among the former I find a great many German names: *Artz, Bartels, Blum, Gaertner, Dittmer, Hahn, Pfeil, Schuman, Schlegel, von Hedemann, Weiss* and so on. And Slavic names: *Blaszkiewicz, Bukosky, Puwalowski, Krzykolski, Tuladziecke* and *Stratkiewicz*. And Greek and Italian names: *Markopoulos, Martinelli, Foglia, Gigliotti* and *Karabinos*. And names beyond my determination: *Tyburski, Volongiatica, Herisko* and *Hajduk*. Very few Anglo-Saxon names are on the list; the continental foreigner seems to be driving out the native, and even the Irishman, from the saloon business. Among the clerics, naturally enough, there are more men of English surname, but even here I find such strange names as *Auroroff, Ashinsky, Bourajanis, Duic, Cillo, Mazure, Przvblski, Pniak, Bazilevich, Smelsz* and *Vrhunec*. But Pittsburgh and New York, it may be argued, are scarcely American; unrestricted immigration has swamped them; the newcomers crowd into the cities. Well, examine the roster of the national House of Representatives, which surely represents the whole country. On it I find *Bacharach, Dupré, Esch, Estopinal, Focht, Heintz, Kahn, Kiess, Kreider, La Guardia, Kraus, Lazaro, Lehbach, Romjue, Siegel* and *Zihlman*, not to mention the insular delegates, *Kalanianole, de Veyra, Davila* and *Yangko*, and enough Irishmen to organize a parliament at Dublin.

In the New York city directory the fourth most common name is now *Murphy*, an Irish name, and the fifth most common is *Meyer*, which is German and chiefly Jewish. The *Meyers* are the *Smiths* of Austria, and of most of Germany. They outnumber all other clans. After them come the *Schultzes* and *Krauses*, just as the *Joneses* and *Williamses* follow the *Smiths* in Great Britain. *Schultze* and *Kraus* do not seem to be very common names in New York, but *Schmidt, Muller, Schneider* and *Klein* appear among the fifty commonest.[6] *Cohen* and *Levy* rank eighth and ninth, and are both ahead of *Jones*, which is second in England, and *Williams*, which is third. *Taylor*, a highly typical British name, ranking fourth in England and Wales, is twenty-third in New York. Ahead of it, beside *Murphy, Meyer, Cohen* and *Levy*, are *Schmidt, Ryan, O'Brien, Kelly* and *Sullivan. Robinson*, which is twelfth in England, is thirty-ninth in New York; even *Schneider* and *Muller* are ahead of it. In Chicago *Olson, Schmidt, Meyer, Hansen* and *Larsen* are ahead of *Taylor*, and *Hoffman* and *Becker* are ahead of *Ward*; in Boston *Sullivan* and *Murphy* are ahead of any English name save *Smith*; in Philadelphia *Myers* is just below *Robinson*. Nor, as I have said, is this large proliferation of foreign surnames confined to the large cities. There are whole regions in the Southwest in which *López* and

Gonzales are far commoner names than *Smith*, *Brown* or *Jones*, and whole regions in the Middle West wherein *Olson* is commoner than either *Taylor* or *Williams*, and places both North and South where *Duval* is at least as common as *Brown*.

Moreover, the true proportions of this admixture of foreign blood are partly concealed by a wholesale anglicization of surnames, sometimes deliberate and sometimes the fruit of mere confusion. That *Smith*, *Brown* and *Miller* remain in first, second and third places among the surnames of New York is surely no sound evidence of Anglo-Saxon survival. The German and Scandinavian *Schmidt* has undoubtedly contributed many a *Smith*, and *Braun* many a *Brown*, and *Müller* many a *Miller*. In the same way *Johnson*, which holds first place among Chicago surnames, and *Anderson*, which holds third, are plainly reinforced from Scandinavian sources, and the former may also owe something to the Russian *Ivanof*. *Miller* is a relatively rare name in England; it is not among the fifty most common. But it stands thirtieth in Boston, fourth in New York and Baltimore, and second in Philadelphia.[7] In the last-named city the influence of *Müller*, probably borrowed from the Pennsylvania Dutch, is plainly indicated, and in Chicago it is likely that there are also contributions from the Scandinavian *Möller*, the Polish *Jannszewski* and the Bohemian *Mlinár*. *Myers*, as we have seen, is a common surname in Philadelphia. So are *Fox* and *Snyder*. In some part, at least, they have been reinforced by the Pennsylvania Dutch *Meyer*, *Fuchs* and *Schneider*. Sometimes *Müller* changes to *Miller*, sometimes to *Muller*, and sometimes it remains unchanged, but with the spelling made *Mueller*. *Muller* and *Mueller* do not appear among the commoner names in Philadelphia; all the *Müllers* seem to have become *Millers*, thus putting *Miller* in second place. But in Chicago, with *Miller* in fourth place, there is also *Mueller* in thirty-first place, and in New York, with *Miller* in third place, there is also *Muller* in twenty-fourth place.

Such changes, chiefly based upon transliterations, are met with in all countries. The name of *Taaffe*, familiar in Austrian history, had an Irish prototype, probably *Taft*. General *Demikof*, one of the Russian commanders at the battle of Zorndorf, in 1758, was a Swede born *Themicoud*. Franz Maria von *Thugut*, the Austrian diplomatist, was a member of an Italian Tyrolese family named *Tunicotto*. This became *Thunichgut* (=*do no good*) in Austria, and was changed to *Thugut* (=*do good*) to bring it into greater accord with its possessor's deserts.[8] In *Bonaparte* the Italian *buon(o)* became the French *bon*. Many English surnames are decayed forms of Norman-French names, for example, *Sidney* from *St. Denis*, *Divver* from *De Vere*, *Bridgewater* from *Burgh de Walter*, *Montgomery* from *de Mungumeri*, *Garnett* from *Guarinot*, and *Seymour* from *Saint-Maure*. A large number of so-called Irish names are the products of rough-and-ready transliterations of Gaelic patronymics, for example, *Findlay* from *Fionnlagh*, *Dermott* from *Diarmuid*, and*McLane* from *Mac Illeathiain*. In the same way the name of *Phoenix* Park, in Dublin, came from*Fion Uisg* (=*fine water*). Of late some of the more ardent Irish authors and politicians have sought to return to the originals. Thus, *O'Sullivan* has become *O Suilleabháin*, *Pearse* has become*Piarais*, *Mac Sweeney* has become *Mac Suibhne*, and *Patrick* has suffered a widespread transformation to *Padraic*. But in America, with a language of peculiar vowel-sounds and even consonant-sounds struggling against a foreign invasion unmatched for strength and variety, such changes have been far more numerous than across the ocean, and the legal rule of *idem sonans* is of much wider utility than anywhere else in the world. If it were not for that rule there would be endless difficulties for the *Wises* whose grandfathers were *Weisses*, and the *Leonards* born *Leonhards*, *Leonhardts* or *Lehnerts*, and the *Manneys* who descend and inherit from *Le Maines*.

"A crude popular etymology, " says a leading authority on surnames, [9] "often begins to play upon a name that is no longer significant to the many. So the *Thurgods* have become *Thoroughgoods*, and the *Todenackers* have become the Pennsylvania Dutch *Toothakers*, much as *asparagus* has become *sparrow-grass*." So, too, the *Wittnachts* of Boyle county, Kentucky, descendants of a Hollander, have become *Whitenecks*, and the *Lehns* of lower Pennsylvania, descendants of some far-off German, have become *Lanes*.[10] Edgar Allan *Poe* was a member of a family long settled in Western Maryland, the founder being one *Poh* or *Pfau*, a native of the Palatinate. Major George *Armistead*, who defended Fort

McHenry in 1814, when Francis Scott Key wrote "The Star-Spangled Banner, " was the descendant of an *Armstädt* who came to Virginia from Hesse-Darmstadt. General George A. *Custer*, the Indian fighter, was the great-grandson of one *Küster*, a Hessian soldier paroled after Burgoyne's surrender. William *Wirt*, anti-Masonic candidate for the presidency in 1832, was the son of one *Wörth*. William *Paca*, a signer of the Declaration of Independence, was the great-grandson of a Bohemian named *Paka*. General W. S. *Rosecrans* was really a *Rosenkrantz*. Even the surname of Abraham *Lincoln*, according to some authorities, was an anglicized form of *Linkhorn*.[11]

Such changes, in fact, are almost innumerable; every work upon American genealogy is full of examples. The first foreign names to undergo the process were Dutch and French. Among the former, *Reiger* was debased to *Riker*, *Van de Veer* to *Vandiver*, *Van Huys* to *Vannice*, *Van Siegel* to *Van Sickle*, *Van Arsdale* to *Vannersdale*, and *Haerlen* (or *Haerlem*) to *Harlan*;[12] among the latter, *Petit* became *Poteet*, *Caillé* changed to *Kyle*, *De la Haye* to *Dillehay*, *Dejean* to *Deshong*, *Guizot* to *Gossett*, *Guereant* to *Caron*, *Soule* to *Sewell*, *Gervaise* to *Jarvis*, *Bayle* to *Bailey*, *Fontaine* to *Fountain*, *Denis* to *Denny*, *Pebaudière* to *Peabody*, *Bon Pas* to *Bumpus* and *de l'Hôtel* to *Doolittle*. "Frenchmen and French Canadians who came to New England, " says Schele de Vere, "had to pay for such hospitality as they there received by the sacrifice of their names. The brave *Bon Coeur*, Captain Marryatt tells us in his Diary, became Mr. *Bunker*, and gave his name to Bunker's Hill."[13] But it was the German immigration that provoked the first really wholesale slaughter. A number of characteristic German sounds—for example, that of *ü* and the guttural in *ch* and *g*—are almost impossible to the Anglo-Saxon pharynx, and so they had to go. Thus, *Bloch* was changed to *Block* or *Black*, *Ochs* to *Oakes*, *Hock* to *Hoke*, *Fischbach* to *Fishback*, *Albrecht* to *Albert* or *Albright*, and *Steinweg* to *Steinway*, and the *Grundwort*, *bach*, was almost universally changed to *baugh*, as in *Brumbaugh*. The *ü* met the same fate: *Grün* was changed to *Green*, *Führ* to *Fear* or *Fuhr*, *Wärner* to *Warner*, *Düring* to *Deering*, and *Schnäbele* to *Snavely*, *Snabely* or *Snively*. In many other cases there were changes in spelling to preserve vowel sounds differently represented in German and English.

Thus, *Blum* was changed to *Bloom*, [14], *Reuss* to *Royce*, *Koester* to *Kester*, *Kuehle* to *Keeley*, *Schroeder* to *Schrader*, *Stehli* to *Staley*, *Weymann* to *Wayman*, *Friedmann* to *Freedman*, *Bauman* to *Bowman*, and *Lang* (as the best compromise possible) to *Long*. The change of *Oehm* to *Ames* belongs to the same category; the addition of the final *s* represents a typical effort to substitute the nearest related Anglo-Saxon name. Other examples of that effort are to be found in *Michaels* for *Michaelis*, *Bowers* for *Bauer*, *Johnson* for *Johannsen*, *Ford* for *Furth*, *Hines* for *Heintz*, *Kemp* for *Kempf*, *Foreman* for *Fuhrmann*, *Kuhns* or *Coons* for *Kuntz*, *Hoover* for *Huber*, *Levering* for *Liebering*, *Jones* for *Jonas*, *Swope* for *Schwab*, *Hite* or *Hyde* for *Heid*, *Andrews* for *André*, *Young* for *Jung*, and *Pence* for *Pentz*.[15]

The American antipathy to accented letters, mentioned in the chapter on spelling, is particularly noticeable among surnames. An immigrant named *Fürst* inevitably becomes plain *Furst* in the United States, and if not the man, then surely his son. *Löwe*, in the same way, is transformed into *Lowe* (pro. *low*), [16] *Lürmann* into *Lurman*, *Schön* into *Schon*, *Suplée* into *Suplee* or *Supplee*, *Lüders* into *Luders* and *Brühl* into *Brill*. Even when no accent betrays it, the foreign diphthong is under hard pressure. Thus the German *oe* disappears, and *Loeb* is changed to *Lobe* or *Laib*, *Oehler* to *Ohler*, *Loeser* to *Leser*, and *Schoen* to *Schon* or *Shane*. In the same way the *au* in such names as *Rosenau* changes to *aw*. So too, the French *oi*-sound is disposed of, and *Dubois* is pronounced *Doo-bóys*, and *Boileau* acquires a first syllable rhyming with *toil*. So with the *kn* in the German names of the *Knapp* class; they are all pronounced, probably by analogy with *Knight*, as if they began with *n*. So with *sch*; *Schneider* becomes *Snyder*, *Schlegel* becomes *Slagel*, and *Schluter* becomes *Sluter*. If a foreigner clings to the original spelling of his name he must usually expect to hear it mispronounced. *Roth*, in American, quickly becomes *Rawth*; *Frémont*, losing both accent and the French *e*, become *Freemont*; *Blum* begins to rhyme with *dumb*; *Mann* rhymes with *van*, and *Lang* with *hang*; *Krantz*, *Lantz* and their cognates with *chance*; *Kurtz* with *shirts*; the first syllable of *Gutmann* with *but*; the first of *Kahler* with *bay*; the first of *Werner* with *turn*; the first of *Wagner* with *nag*. *Uhler*, in America, is always *Youler*. *Berg* loses its German *e*-sound for an English *u*-sound, and its German hard *g* for an English *g*; it becomes identical with the *berg* of *iceberg*. The same change in the vowel occurs in *Erdmann*. In *König* the German diphthong succumbs to a long *o*, and the hard *g* becomes *k*; the common pronunciation is *Cone-ik*. Often, in *Berger*, the *g* becomes soft, and the name rhymes with *verger*. It becomes soft, too, in *Bittinger*. In *Wilstach* and *Welsbach* the *ch* becomes a *k*. In *Anheuser* the *eu* changes to a long *i*. The final *e*, important in German, is nearly always silenced; *Dohme* rhymes with *foam*; *Kühne* becomes *Keen*.

In addition to these transliterations, there are constant translations of foreign proper names. "Many a Pennsylvania *Carpenter*, " says Dr. Oliphant, [17] "bearing a surname that is English, from the French, from the Latin, and there a Celtic loan-word in origin, is neither English, nor French, nor Latin, nor Celt, but an original German *Zimmermann*."[18] A great many other such translations are under everyday observation. *Pfund* becomes *Pound*; *Becker, Baker*; *Schumacher, Shoemaker*; *König, King*; *Weisberg, Whitehill*; *Koch, Cook*;[19] *Neuman, Newman*; *Schaefer, Shepherd* or *Sheppard*; *Gutmann, Goodman*; *Goldschmidt, Goldsmith*; *Edelstein, Noblestone*; *Steiner, Stoner*; *Meister, Master(s)*; *Schwartz, Black*; *Weiss, White*; *Weber, Weaver*; *Bucher, Booker*; *Vogelgesang, Birdsong*; *Sontag, Sunday*, and so on. Partial translations are also encountered, *e. g.*, *Studebaker* from *Studebecker*, and *Reindollar* from *Rheinthaler*. By the same process, among the newer immigrants, the Polish *Wilkiewicz* becomes *Wilson*, the Bohemian *Bohumil* becomes *Godfrey*, and the Bohemian *Kovár* and the Russian *Kuznetzov* become *Smith*. Some curious examples are occasionally encountered. Thus Henry *Woodhouse*, a gentleman prominent in aeronautical affairs, came to the United States from Italy as Mario Terenzio Enrico *Casalegno*; his new surname is simply a translation of his old one. And the *Belmonts*, the bankers, unable to find a euphonious English equivalent for their German-Jewish patronymic of *Schönberg*, chose a French one that Americans could pronounce.

In part, as I say, these changes in surname are enforced by the sheer inability of Americans to pronounce certain Continental consonants, and their disinclination to remember the Continental vowel sounds. Many an immigrant, finding his name constantly mispronounced, changes its vowels or drops some of its consonants; many another shortens it, or translates it, or changes it entirely for the same reason. Just as a well-known Graeco-French poet changed his Greek name of *Papadiamantopoulos* to *Moréas* because *Papadiamantopoulos* was too much for Frenchmen, and as an eminent Polish-English novelist changed his Polish name of *Korzeniowski* to *Conrad* because few Englishmen could pronounce *owski* correctly, so the Italian or Greek or Slav immigrant, coming up for naturalization, very often sheds his family name with his old allegiance, and emerges as *Taylor*, *Jackson* or *Wilson*. I once encountered a firm of Polish Jews, showing the name of *Robinson & Jones* on its sign-board, whose partners were born *Rubinowitz* and *Jonas*. I lately heard of a German named *Knoche*—a name doubly difficult to Americans, what with the *kn* and the *ch*—who changed it boldly to *Knox* to avoid being called *Nokky*. A Greek named *Zoyiopoulous*, *Kolokotronis*, *Mavrokerdatos* or *Constantinopolous* would find it practically impossible to carry on amicable business with Americans; his name would arouse their mirth, if not their downright ire. And the same burden would lie upon a Hungarian named *Beniczkyné* or *Gyalui*, or *Szilagyi*, or *Vezercsillagok*. Or a Finn named *Kyyhkysen*, or *Jääskelainen*, or *Tuulensuu*, or *Uotinen*, —all honorable Finnish patronymics. Or a Swede named *Sjogren*, or *Schjtt*, or *Leijonhufvud*. Or a Bohemian named *Srb*, or *Hrubka*. Or, for that matter, a German named *Kannengiesser*, or *Schnapaupf*, or *Pfannenbecker*.

But more important than this purely linguistic hostility, there is a deeper social enmity, and it urges the immigrant to change his name with even greater force. For a hundred years past all the heaviest and most degrading labor of the United States has been done by successive armies of foreigners, and so a concept of inferiority has come to be attached to mere foreignness. In addition, these newcomers, pressing upward steadily in the manner already described, have offered the native a formidable, and considering their lower standards of living, what has appeared to him to be an unfair competition on his own plane, and as a result a hatred born of disastrous rivalry has been added to his disdain. Our unmatchable vocabulary of derisive names for foreigners reveals the national attitude. The French *boche*, the German *hunyadi* (for Hungarian), [20] and the old English *froggy* (for Frenchman) seem lone and feeble beside our great repertoire: *dago, wop, guinea, kike, goose, mick, harp,* [21] *bohick, bohunk, square-head, greaser, canuck, spiggoty,* [22] *chink, polack, dutchie, scowegian, hunkie* and *yellow-belly*. This disdain tends to pursue an immigrant with extraordinary rancor when he bears a name that is unmistakably foreign and hence difficult to the native, and open to his crude burlesque. Moreover, the general feeling penetrates the man himself, particularly if he be ignorant, and he comes to believe that his name is not only a handicap, but also intrinsically discreditable—that it wars subtly upon his worth and integrity.[23] This feeling, perhaps, accounted for a good many changes of surnames among Germans upon the entrance of the United States into the war. But in the majority of cases, of course, the changes so copiously reported—*e. g.*, from *Bielefelder* to *Benson*, and from *Pulvermacher* to *Pullman*—were merely efforts at protective coloration. The immigrant, in a time of extraordinary suspicion and difficulty, tried to get rid of at least one handicap.[24]

This motive constantly appears among the Jews, who face an anti-Semitism that is imperfectly concealed and may be expected to grow stronger hereafter. Once they have lost the faith of their fathers, a phenomenon almost inevitable in the first native-born generation, they shrink from all the disadvantages that go with Jewishness, and seek to conceal their origin, or, at all events, to avoid making it unnecessarily noticeable.[25] To this end they modify the spelling of the more familiar Jewish surnames, turning *Levy* into *Lewy, Lewyt, Levitt, Levin, Levine, Levey, Levie*[26] and even *Lever, Cohen* into *Cohn, Cahn, Kahn, Kann, Coyne* and *Conn, Aarons* into *Arens* and *Ahrens* and *Solomon* into *Salmon, Salomon* and *Solmson*. In the same way they shorten their long names, changing *Wolfsheimer* to *Wolf, Goldschmidt* to *Gold*, and *Rosenblatt, Rosenthal, Rosenbaum, Rosenau, Rosenberg, Rosenbusch, Rosenblum, Rosenstein, Rosenheim* and *Rosenfeldt* to *Rose*. Like the Germans, they also seek refuge in translations more or less literal. Thus, on the East Side of New York, *Blumenthal* is often changed to *Bloomingdale*,

Schneider to *Taylor*, *Reichman* to *Richman*, and *Schlachtfeld* to *Warfield*. *Fiddler*, a common Jewish name, becomes *Harper*; so does *Pikler*, which is Yiddish for *drummer*. *Stolar*, which is a Yiddish word borrowed from the Russian, signifying *carpenter*, is often changed to *Carpenter*. *Lichtman* and *Lichtenstein* become *Chandler*. *Meilach*, which is Hebrew for *king*, becomes *King*, and so does *Meilachson*. The strong tendency to seek English-sounding equivalents for names of noticeably foreign origin changes *Sher* into *Sherman*, *Michel* into *Mitchell*, *Rogowsky* into *Rogers*, *Kolinsky* into *Collins*, *Rabinovitch* into *Robbins*, *Davidovitch* into *Davis*, *Moiseyev* into *Macy* or *Mason*, and *Jacobson*, *Jacobovitch* and *Jacobovsky* into *Jackson*. This last change proceeds by way of a transient change to *Jake* or *Jack* as a nickname. *Jacob* is always abbreviated to one or the other on the East Side. *Yankelevitch* also becomes *Jackson*, for *Yankel* is Yiddish for *Jacob*.[27]

Among the immigrants of other stocks some extraordinarily radical changes in name are to be observed. Greek names of five, and even eight syllables shrink to *Smith*; Hungarian names that seem to be all consonants are reborn in such euphonious forms as *Martin* and *Lacy*. I have encountered a *Gregory* who was born *Grgurevich* in Serbia; a *Uhler* who was born *Uhlyarik*; a *Graves* who descends from the fine old Dutch family of *'s Gravenhage*. I once knew a man named *Lawton* whose grandfather had been a *Lautenberger*. First he shed the *berger* and then he changed the spelling of *Lauten* to make it fit the inevitable American mispronunciation. There is, again, a family of *Dicks*in the South whose ancestor was a *Schwettendieck*—apparently a Dutch or Low German name. There is, yet again, a celebrated American artist, of the Bohemian patronymic of *Hrubka*, who has abandoned it for a surname which is common to all the Teutonic languages, and is hence easy for Americans. The Italians, probably because of the relations established by the Catholic church, often take Irish names, as they marry Irish girls; it is common to hear of an Italian pugilist or politician named *Kelly* or *O'Brien*. The process of change is often informal, but even legally it is quite facile. The Naturalization Act of June 29, 1906, authorizes the court, as a part of the naturalization of any alien, to make an order changing his name.

This is frequently done when he receives his last papers; sometimes, if the newspapers are to be believed, without his solicitation, and even against his protest. If the matter is overlooked at the time, he may change his name later on, like any other citizen, by simple application to a court of record.

Among names of Anglo-Saxon origin and names naturalized long before the earliest colonization, one notes certain American peculiarities, setting off the nomenclature of the United States from that of the mother country. The relative infrequency of hyphenated names in America is familiar; when they appear at all it is almost always in response to direct English influences.[28] Again, a number of English family names have undergone modification in the New World. *Venable* may serve as a specimen. The form in England is almost invariably *Venables*, but in America the final *s* has been lost, and every example of the name that I have been able to find in the leading American reference-books is without it. And where spellings have remained unchanged, pronunciations have been frequently modified. This is particularly noticeable in the South. *Callowhill*, down there, is commonly pronounced *Carrol*; *Crenshawe* is *Granger*; *Hawthorne*, *Horton*; *Heyward*, *Howard*;*Norsworthy*, *Nazary*; *Ironmonger*, *Munger*; *Farinholt*, *Fernall*; *Camp*, *Kemp*; *Buchanan*, *Bohannan*; *Drewry*, *Droit*; *Enroughty*, *Darby*; and *Taliaferro*, *Tolliver*.[29] The English *Crowninshields* pronounce every syllable of their name; the American *Crowninshields* commonly make it *Crunshel*. *Van Schaick*, an old New York name, is pronounced *Von Scoik*. A good many American Jews, aiming at a somewhat laborious refinement, change the pronunciation of the terminal *stein* in their names so that it rhymes, not with *line*, but with *bean*. Thus, in fashionable Jewish circles, there are no longer any *Epsteins*, *Goldsteins* and *Hammersteins* but only *Epsteens*, *Goldsteens* and *Hammersteens*. The American Jews differ further from the English in pronouncing *Levy* to make the first syllable rhyme with *tea*; the English Jews always make the name *Lev-vy*. To match such American prodigies as *Darby* for *Enroughty*, the English themselves have *Hools*for *Howells*, *Sillinger* for *St. Leger*, *Sinjin* for *St. John*, *Pool* for *Powell*, *Weems* for *Wemyss*, *Kerduggen* for *Cadogen*, *Mobrer* for *Marlborough*, *Key* for *Cains*, *Marchbanks* for *Marjoribanks*,

Beecham for *Beauchamp*, *Chumley* for *Cholmondeley*, *Trosley* for *Trotterscliffe*, and *Darby* for *Derby*, not to mention *Maudlin* for *Magdalen*.

§ 2. Given Names

—The non-Anglo Saxon American's willingness to anglicize his patronymic is far exceeded by his eagerness to give "American" baptismal names to his children. The favorite given names of the old country almost disappear in the first native-born generation. The Irish immigrants quickly dropped such names as *Terence*, *Dennis* and *Patrick*, and adopted in their places the less conspicuous *John*, *George* and *William*. The Germans, in the same way, abandoned *Otto*, *August*, *Hermann*, *Ludwig*, *Heinrich*, *Wolfgang*, *Albrecht*, *Wilhelm*, *Kurt*, *Hans*, *Rudolf*, *Gottlieb*, *Johann*and *Franz*. For some of these they substituted the English equivalents: *Charles*, *Lewis*, *Henry*, *William*, *John*, *Frank* and so on. In the room of others they began afflicting their offspring with more fanciful native names: *Milton* and *Raymond* were their chief favorites thirty or forty years ago.[30] The Jews carry the thing to great lengths. At present they seem to take most delight in *Sidney*, *Irving*, *Milton*, *Roy*, *Stanley* and *Monroe*, but they also call their sons *John*, *Charles*, *Henry*, *Harold*, *William*, *Richard*, *James*, *Albert*, *Edward*, *Alfred*, *Frederick*, *Thomas*, and even *Mark*, *Luke* and *Matthew*, and their daughters *Mary*, *Gertrude*, *Estelle*, *Pauline*, *Alice* and *Edith*. As a boy I went to school with many Jewish boys. The commonest given names among them were *Isadore*, *Samuel*, *Jonas*, *Isaac* and *Israel*. These are seldom bestowed by the rabbis of today. In the same school were a good many German pupils, boy and girl. Some of the girls bore such fine old German given names as *Katharina*, *Wilhelmina*, *Elsa*, *Lotta*, *Ermentrude* and *Frankziska*. All these have begun to disappear.

The newer immigrants, indeed, do not wait for the birth of children to demonstrate their naturalization; they change their own given names immediately they land. I am told by Abraham Cahan that this is done almost universally on the East Side of New York. "Even the most old-fashioned Jews immigrating to this country, " he says, "change *Yosel* to *Joseph*, *Yankel* to *Jacob*, *Liebel* to *Louis*, *Feivel* to *Philip*, *Itzik* to *Isaac*, *Ruven* to *Robert*, and *Moise* or *Motel* to

Morris." Moreover, the spelling of *Morris*, as the position of its bearer improves, commonly changes to *Maurice*, though the pronunciation may remain *Mawruss*, as in the case of Mr. Perlmutter. The immigrants of other stocks follow the same habit. Every Bohemian *Vaclav* or *Vojtěch* becomes a *William*, every *Jaroslav* becomes a *Jerry*, every *Bronislav* a *Barney*, and every *Stanislav* a *Stanley*. The Italians run to *Frank* and *Joe*; so do the Hungarians and the Balkan peoples; the Russians quickly drop their national system of nomenclature and give their children names according to the American plan. Even the Chinese laundrymen of the big cities become *John*, *George*, *Charlie* and *Frank*; I once encountered one boasting the name of *Emil*.

The Puritan influence, in names as in ideas, has remained a good deal more potent in American than in England. The given name of the celebrated *Praise-God* Barebones marked a fashion which died out in England very quickly, but one still finds traces of it in America, *e. g.*, in such women's names as *Faith, Hope, Prudence, Charity* and *Mercy*, and in such men's names as *Peregrine*.[31]The religious obsession of the New England colonists is also kept in mind by the persistence of Biblical names: *Ezra, Hiram, Ezekial, Zachariah, Elijah, Elihu*, and so on. These names excite the derision of the English; an American comic character, in an English play or novel, always bears one of them. Again, the fashion of using surnames as given names is far more widespread in America than in England. In this country, indeed, it takes on the character of a national habit; fully three out of four eldest sons, in families of any consideration, bear their mothers' surnames as middle names. This fashion arose in England during the seventeenth century, and one of its fruits was the adoption of such well-known surnames as *Stanley, Cecil, Howard, Douglas* and *Duncan*as common given names.[32] It died out over there during the eighteenth century, and today the great majority of Englishmen bear such simple given names as *John, Charles* and *William*—often four or five of them—but in America it has persisted. A glance at a roster of the Presidents of the United States will show how firmly it has taken root. Of the ten that have had middle names at all, six have had middle names that were family surnames, and two of the six have dropped their other given names and used these surnames. This custom, perhaps, has paved the way for another: that of making given names of any proper nouns that happen to strike the fancy. Thus General Sherman was named after an Indian chief, *Tecumseh*, and a Chicago judge was baptized *Kenesaw Mountain*[33] in memory of the battle that General Sherman fought there. A late candidate for governor of New York had the curious given name of *D-Cady*.[34] Various familiar American given names, originally surnames, are almost unknown in England, among them, *Washington*, *Jefferson*, *Jackson*, *Lincoln*, *Columbus* and *Lee*. *Chauncey* forms a curious addition to the list. It was the surname of the second president of Harvard College, and was bestowed upon their offspring by numbers of his graduates. It then got into general use and acquired a typically American pronunciation, with the *a* of the first syllable flat. It is never encountered in England.

In the pronunciation of various given names, as in that of many surnames, English and American usages differ. *Evelyn*, in England, is given two syllables instead of three, and the first is made to rhyme with *leave*. *Irene* is given two syllables, making it *Irene-y*. *Ralph* is pronounced *Rafe*. *Jerome* is accented on the first syllable; in America it is always accented on the second.[35]

§ 3. Geographical Names

—"There is no part of the world, " said Robert Louis Stevenson, "where nomenclature is so rich, poetical, humorous and picturesque as in the United States of America." A glance at the latest United States Official Postal Guide[36] or report of the United States Geographic Board[37] quite bears out this opinion. The map of the country is besprinkled with place names from at least half a hundred languages, living and dead, and among them one finds examples of the most daring and elaborate fancy. There are Spanish, French and Indian names as melodious and charming as running water; there are names out of the histories and mythologies of all the great races of man; there are names grotesque and names almost sublime. No other country can match them for interest and variety. When there arises among us a philologist who will study them as thoroughly and intelligently as the Swiss, Johann Jakob Egli, studied the place names of Central Europe, his work will be an invaluable contribution to the history of the nation, and no less to an understanding of the psychology of its people.

The original English settlers, it would appear, displayed little imagination in naming the new settlements and natural features of the land that they came to. Their almost invariable tendency, at the start, was to make use of names familiar at home, or to invent banal compounds. *Plymouth Rock* at the North and *Jamestown* at the South are examples of their poverty of fancy; they filled the narrow tract along the coast with new *Bostons, Cambridges, Bristols* and *Londons,* and often used the adjective as a prefix. But this was only in the days of beginning. Once they had begun to move back from the coast and to come into contact with the aborigines and with the widely dispersed settlers of other races, they encountered rivers, mountains, lakes and even towns that bore far more engaging names, and these, after some resistance, they perforce adopted. The native names of such rivers as the *James,* the *York* and the *Charles* succumbed, but those of the *Potomac,* the *Patapsco,* the *Merrimack* and the *Penobscot* survived, and they were gradually reinforced as the country was penetrated. Most of these Indian names, in getting upon the early maps, suffered somewhat severe simplifications. *Potowánmeac* was reduced to *Potomack* and then to *Potomac; Unéaukara* became *Niagara; Reckawackes,* by the law of Hobson-Jobson, was turned into *Rockaway,* and *Pentapang* into *Port Tobacco.*[38] But, despite such elisions and transformations, the charm of thousands of them remained, and today they are responsible for much of the characteristic color of American geographical nomenclature. Such names as *Tallahassee, Susquehanna, Mississippi, Allegheny, Chicago, Kennebec, Patuxent* and *Arkansas* give a barbaric brilliancy to the American map. Only the map of Australia, with its mellifluous Maori names, can match it.

The settlement of the American continent, once the eastern coast ranges were crossed, proceeded with unparalleled speed, and so the naming of the new rivers, lakes, peaks and valleys, and of the new towns and districts no less, strained the inventiveness of the pioneers. The result is the vast duplication of names that shows itself in the Postal Guide. No less than eighteen imitative *Bostons* and *New Bostons* still appear, and there are nineteen *Bristols,* twenty-eight *Newports,* and twenty-two *Londons* and *New Londons.* Argonauts starting out from an older settlement on the coast would take its name with them, and so we find *Philadelphias* in Illinois, Mississippi, Missouri and Tennessee, *Richmonds* in Iowa, Kansas and nine other western states, and *Princetons*in fifteen. Even when a new name was hit upon it seems to have been hit upon simultaneously by scores of scattered bands of settlers; thus we find the whole land bespattered with *Washingtons, Lafayettes, Jeffersons* and *Jacksons*, and with names suggested by common and obvious natural objects, *e. g.,* *Bear Creek, Bald Knob* and *Buffalo.* The Geographic Board, in its last report, made a belated protest against this excessive duplication. "The names *Elk, Beaver, Cottonwood* and *Bald,* " it said, "are altogether too numerous."[39] Of postoffices alone there are fully a hundred embodying *Elk;* counting in rivers, lakes, creeks, mountains and valleys, the map of the United States probably shows at least twice as many such names.

A study of American geographical and place names reveals eight general classes, as follows: (*a*) those embodying personal names, chiefly the surnames of pioneers or of national heroes; (*b*) those transferred from other and older places, either in the eastern states or in Europe; (*c*) Indian names; (*d*) Dutch, Spanish and French names; (*e*) Biblical and mythological names; (*f*) names descriptive of localities; (*g*) names suggested by the local flora, fauna or geology; (*h*) purely fanciful names. The names of the first class are perhaps the most numerous. Some consist of surnames standing alone, as *Washington, Cleveland, Bismarck, Lafayette, Taylor* and *Randolph*; others consist of surnames in combination with various old and new *Grundwörter*, as *Pittsburgh, Knoxville, Bailey's Switch, Hagerstown, Franklinton, Dodge City, Fort Riley, Wayne Junction* and *McKeesport*; and yet others are contrived of given names, either alone or in combination, as *Louisville, St. Paul, Elizabeth, Johnstown, Charlotte, Williamsburg* and *Marysville.* The number of towns in the United States bearing women's given names is enormous. I find, for example, eleven postoffices called *Charlotte*, ten called *Ada* and no less than nineteen called *Alma.* Most of these places are small, but there is an *Elizabeth* with 75, 000 population, an *Elmira* with 40, 000, and an *Augusta* with nearly 45, 000.

The names of the second class we have already briefly observed. They are betrayed in many cases by the prefix *New*; more than 600 such postoffices are recorded, ranging from *New Albany* to *New Windsor.* Others bear such prefixes as *West, North* and *South,* or various distinguishing affixes, *e. g., Bostonia, Pittsburgh Landing,*

Yorktown and *Hartford City*. One often finds eastern county names applied to western towns and eastern town names applied to western rivers and mountains. Thus, *Cambria*, which is the name of a county but not of a postoffice in Pennsylvania, is a town name in seven western states; *Baltimore* is the name of a glacier in Alaska, and *Princeton* is the name of a peak in Colorado. In the same way the names of the more easterly states often reappear in the west, *e. g.*, in *Mount Ohio*, Colo., *Delaware*, Okla., and *Virginia City*, Nev. The tendency to name small American towns after the great capitals of antiquity has excited the derision of the English since the earliest days; there is scarcely an English book upon the states without some fling at it. Of late it has fallen into abeyance, though sixteen *Athenses* still remain, and there are yet many *Carthages*, *Uticas*, *Syracuses*, *Romes*, *Alexandrias*, *Ninevahs* and *Troys*. The third city of the nation, *Philadelphia*, got its name from the ancient stronghold of Philadelphus of Pergamun. To make up for the falling off of this old and flamboyant custom, the more recent immigrants have brought with them the names of the capitals and other great cities of their fatherlands. Thus the American map bristles with *Berlins*, *Bremens*, *Hamburgs*, *Warsaws* and *Leipzigs*, and is beginning to show *Stockholms*, *Venices*, *Belgrades* and *Christianias*.

The influence of Indian names upon American nomenclature is quickly shown by a glance at the map. No less than 26 of the states have names borrowed from the aborigines, and the same thing is true of most of our rivers and mountains. There was an effort, at one time, to get rid of these Indian names. Thus the early Virginians changed the name of the *Powhatan* to the *James*, and the first settlers in New York changed the name of *Horicon* to *Lake George*. In the same way the present name of the *White Mountains* displaced *Agiochook*, and *New Amsterdam*, and later *New York*, displaced *Manhattan*, which has been recently revived. The law of Hobson-Jobson made changes in other Indian names, sometimes complete and sometimes only partial. Thus, *Mauwauwaming* became *Wyoming*, *Maucwachoong* became *Mauch Chunk*, *Ouabache* became *Wabash*, *Asingsing* became *Sing-Sing*, and *Machihiganing* became *Michigan*. But this vandalism did not go far enough to take away the brilliant color of the aboriginal nomenclature. The second city of the United States bears an Indian name, and so do the largest

American river, and the greatest American water-fall, and four of the five great Lakes, and the scene of the most important military decision ever reached on American soil.

The Dutch place-names of the United States are chiefly confined to the vicinity of New York, and a good many of them have become greatly corrupted. *Brooklyn*, *Wallabout* and *Gramercy* offer examples. The first-named was originally *Breuckelen*, the second was *Waale Bobht*, and the third was *De Kromme Zee*. *Hell-Gate* is a crude translation of the Dutch *Helle-Gat*. During the early part of the last century the more delicate New Yorkers transformed the term into *Hurlgate*, but the change was vigorously opposed by Washington Irving, and so *Hell-Gate* was revived. The law of Hobson-Jobson early converted the Dutch *hoek* into *hook*, and it survives in various place-names, *e. g.*, *Kinderhook* and *Sandy Hook*. The Dutch *kill* is a *Grundwort* in many other names, *e. g.*, *Catskill*, *Schuylkill*, *Peekskill*, *Fishkill* and *Kill van Kull*; it is the equivalent of the American *creek*. Many other Dutch place-names will come familiarly to mind: *Harlem*, *Staten*, *Flushing*, *Cortlandt*, *Calver Plaat*, *Nassau*, *Coenties*, *Spuyten Duyvel*, *Yonkers*, *Hoboken* and *Bowery* (from *Bouvery*).[40] *Block* Island was originally *Blok*, and Cape *May*, according to Schele de Vere, was *Mey*, both Dutch. A large number of New York street and neighborhood names come down from Knickerbocker days, often greatly changed in pronunciation. *Desbrosses* offers an example. The Dutch called it *de Broose*, but in New York today it is commonly spoken of as *Dez-bros-sez*.

French place-names have suffered almost as severely. Few persons would recognize *Smackover*, the name of a small town in Arkansas, as French, and yet in its original form it was *Chemin Couvert*. Schele de Vere, in 1871, recorded the degeneration of the name to *Smack Cover*; the Postoffice, always eager to shorten and simplify names, has since made one word of it and got rid of the redundant *c*. In the same way *Bob Ruly*, a Missouri name, descends from *Bois Brulé*. "The American tongue, " says W. W. Crane, "seems to lend itself reluctantly to the words of alien languages."[41] This is shown plainly by the history of French place-names among us. A large number of them, *e. g.*, *Lac Superieur*, were translated into English at an early day, and most of those that remain are now pronounced as if they were English.

Thus *Des Moines* is *dee-moyns*, *Terre Haute* is *terry-hut*, *Beaufort* is *byu-fort*, *New Orleans* is *or-leens*, *Lafayette* has a flat *a*, *Havre de Grace* has another, and *Versailles* is *ver-sales*. The pronunciation of *sault*, as in *Sault Ste. Marie*, is commonly more or less correct; the Minneapolis, St. Paul and Sault Ste. Marie Railroad is popularly called the *Soo*. This may be due to Canadian example, or to some confusion between *Sault* and *Sioux*. The French *Louis*, in *St. Louis* and *Louisville*, is usually pronounced correctly. So is the *rouge* in *Baton Rouge*, though the *baton* is commonly boggled. It is possible that familiarity with *St. Louis* influenced the local pronunciation of *Illinois*, which is *Illinoy*, but this may be a mere attempt to improve upon the vulgar *Illin-i*.[42]

For a number of years the Geographic Board has been seeking vainly to reestablish the correct pronunciation of the name of the *Purgatoire* river in Colorado. Originally named the *Rio de las Animas* by the Spaniards, it was renamed the *Rivière du Purgatoire* by their French successors. The American pioneers changed this to *Picketwire*, and that remains the local name of the stream to this day, despite the effort of the Geographic Board to compromise on *Purgatoire* river. Many other French names are being anglicized with its aid and consent. Already half a dozen *Bellevues* have been changed to *Belleviews* and *Bellviews*, and the spelling of nearly all the *Belvédères* has been changed to *Belvidere*. *Belair*, La., represents the end-product of a process of decay which began with *Belle Aire*, and then proceeded to *Bellaire* and *Bellair*. All these forms are still to be found, together with *Bel Air*. The Geographic Board's antipathy to accented letters and to names of more than one word[43] has converted *Isle Ste. Thérèse*, in the St. Lawrence river, to *Isle Ste. Therese*, a truly abominable barbarism, and *La Cygne*, in Kansas, to *Lacygne*, which is even worse. *Lamoine*, *Labelle*, *Lagrange* and *Lamonte* are among its other improvements; *Lafayette*, for *La Fayette*, long antedates the beginning of its labors.

The Spanish names of the Southwest are undergoing a like process of corruption, though without official aid. *San Antonio* has been changed to *San Antone* in popular pronunciation and seems likely to go to *San Tone*; *El Paso* has acquired a flat American *a* and a *z*-sound in place of the Spanish *s*; *Los Angeles* presents such difficulties that no two of its inhabitants agree upon the proper pronunciation, and many compromise on simple *Los*, as the folks of *Jacksonville* commonly call their town *Jax*. Some of the most mellifluous of American place-names are in the areas once held by the Spaniards. It would be hard to match the beauty of *Santa Margarita, San Anselmo, Alamogordo, Terra Amarilla, Sabinoso, Las Palomas, Ensenada, Nogales, San Patricio* and *Bernalillo*. But they are under a severe and double assault. Not only do the present lords of the soil debase them in speaking them; in many cases they are formally displaced by native names of the utmost harshness and banality. Thus, one finds in New Mexico such absurdly-named towns as *Sugarite, Shoemaker, Newhope, Lordsburg, Eastview* and *Central*; in Arizona such places as *Old Glory, Springerville, Wickenburg* and *Congress Junction*, and even in California such abominations as *Oakhurst, Ben Hur, Drytown, Skidoo, Susanville, Uno* and *Ono*.

The early Spaniards were prodigal with place-names testifying to their piety, but these names, in the overwhelming main, were those of saints. Add *Salvador, Trinidad* and *Concepcion*, and their repertoire is almost exhausted. If they ever named a town *Jesus* the name has been obliterated by Anglo-Saxon prudery; even their use of the name as a personal appellation violates American notions of the fitting. The names of the Jewish patriarchs and those of the holy places in Palestine do not appear among their place-names; their Christianity seems to have been exclusively of the New Testament. But the Americans who displaced them were intimately familiar with both books of the Bible, and one finds copious proofs of it on the map of the United States. There are no less than seven *Bethlehems* in the Postal Guide, and the name is also applied to various mountains, and to one of the reaches of the Ohio river. I find thirteen *Bethanys*, seventeen *Bethels*, eleven *Beulahs*, nine *Canaans*, eleven *Jordans* and twenty-one *Sharons*. *Adam* is sponsor for a town in West Virginia and an island in the Chesapeake, and *Eve* for a village in Kentucky. There are five postoffices named *Aaron*, two named *Abraham*, two named *Job*, and a town and a lake named *Moses*. Most of the *St. Pauls* and *St. Josephs* of the country were inherited from the French, but the two *St. Patricks* show a later influence. Eight *Wesleys* and

Wesleyvilles, eight *Asburys* and twelve names embodying *Luther* indicate the general theological trend of the plain people. There is a village in Maryland, too small to have a postoffice, named *Gott*, and I find *Gotts Island* in Maine and *Gottville* in California, but no doubt these were named after German settlers of that awful name, and not after the Lord God directly. There are four *Trinities*, to say nothing of the inherited Spanish*Trinidads*.

Names wholly or partly descriptive of localities are very numerous throughout the country, and among the *Grundwörter* embodied in them are terms highly characteristic of America and almost unknown to the English vocabulary. *Bald Knob* would puzzle an Englishman, but the name is so common in the United States that the Geographic Board has had to take measures against it. Others of that sort are *Council Bluffs, Patapsco Neck, Delaware Water Gap, Curtis Creek, Walden Pond, Sandy Hook, Key West, Bull Run, Portage, French Lick, Jones Gulch, Watkins Gully, Cedar Bayou, Keams Canyon, Parker Notch, Sucker Branch, Fraziers Bottom* and *Eagle Pass.Butte Creek*, in *Montana*, is a name made up of two Americanisms. There are thirty-five postoffices whose names embody the word *prairie*, several of them, e. g., *Prairie du Chien*, Wis., inherited from the French. There are seven *Divides*, eight *Buttes*, eight town-names embodying the word *burnt*, innumerable names embodying *grove, barren, plain, fork, center, cross-roads, courthouse, cove* and *ferry*, and a great swarm of *Cold Springs, Coldwaters, Summits, Middletowns* and *Highlands*. The flora and fauna of the land are enormously represented. There are twenty-two *Buffalos* beside the city in New York, and scores of *Buffalo Creeks, Ridges, Springs*and *Wallows*. The *Elks*, in various forms, are still more numerous, and there are dozens of towns, mountains, lakes, creeks and country districts named after the *beaver, martin, coyote, moose* and*otter*, and as many more named after such characteristic flora as the *paw-paw*, the *sycamore*, the *cottonwood*, the *locust* and the *sunflower*. There is an *Alligator* in Mississippi, a *Crawfish* in Kentucky and a *Rat Lake* on the Canadian border of Minnesota. The endless search for mineral wealth has besprinkled the map with such names as *Bromide, Oil*

City, Anthracite, Chrome, Chloride, Coal Run, Goldfield, Telluride, Leadville and *Cement*.

There was a time, particularly during the gold rush to California, when the rough humor of the country showed itself in the invention of extravagant and often highly felicitous place-names, but with the growth of population and the rise of civic spirit they have tended to be replaced with more seemly coinages. *Catfish* creek, in Wisconsin, is now the *Yahara* river; the *Bulldog* mountains, in Arizona, have become the *Harosomas*; the *Picketwire* river, as we have seen, has resumed its old French name of *Purgatoire*. As with natural features of the landscape, so with towns. Nearly all the old *Boozevilles*, *Jackass Flats, Three Fingers, Hell-For-Sartains, Undershirt Hills, Razzle-Dazzles, Cow-Tails, Yellow Dogs, Jim-Jamses, Jump-Offs, Poker Citys* and *Skunktowns* have yielded to the growth of delicacy, but *Tombstone* still stands in Arizona, *Goose Bill* remains a postoffice in Montana, and the Geographic Board gives its imprimatur to the *Horsethief* trail in Colorado, to *Burning Bear* creek in the same state, and to *Pig Eye* lake in Minnesota. Various other survivors of a more lively and innocent day linger on the map:*Blue Ball*, Ark., *Cowhide*, W. Va., *Dollarville*, Mich., *Oven Fork*, Ky., *Social Circle*, Ga., *Sleepy Eye*, Minn., *Bubble*, Ark., *Shy Beaver*, Pa., *Shin Pond*, Me., *Rough-and-Ready*, Calif., *Non Intervention*, Va., *Noodle*, Tex., *Nursery*, Mo., *Number Four*, N. Y., *Oblong*, Ill., *Stock Yards*, Neb., *Stout*, Iowa, and so on. West Virginia, the wildest of the eastern states, is full of such place-names. Among them I find *Affinity, Annamoriah* (*Anna Maria?*), *Bee, Bias, Big Chimney, Billie, Blue Jay, Bulltown, Caress, Cinderella, Cyclone, Czar, Cornstalk, Duck, Halcyon, Jingo, Left Hand, Ravens Eye, Six, Skull Run, Three Churches, Uneeda, Wide Mouth, War Eagle* and *Stumptown*. The Postal Guide shows two *Ben Hurs*, five *St. Elmos* and ten *Ivanhoes*, but only one *Middlemarch*. There are seventeen *Roosevelts*, six *Codys* and six *Barnums*, but no *Shakespeare*. *Washington*, of course, is the most popular of American place-names. But among names of postoffices it is hard pushed by *Clinton, Centerville, Liberty, Canton, Marion* and *Madison*, and even by *Springfield, Warren* and *Bismarck*.

The Geographic Board, in its laudable effort to simplify American nomenclature, has played ducks and drakes with some of the most picturesque names on the national map. Now and then, as in the case of *Purgatoire*, it has temporarily departed from this policy, but in the main its influence has been thrown against the fine old French and Spanish names, and against the more piquant native names no less. Thus, I find it deciding against *Portage des Flacons* and in favor of the hideous *Bottle portage*, against *Cañada del Burro* and in favor of *Burro canyon* against *Canos y Ylas de la Cruz* and in favor of the barbarous *Cruz island*. In *Bougére landing* and *Cañon City* it has deleted the accents. The name of the *De Grasse river* it has changed to *Grass*. *De Laux* it has changed to the intolerable *Dlo*. And, as we have seen, it has steadily amalgamated French and Spanish articles with their nouns, thus achieving such forms as *Duchesne*, *Eldorado*, *Deleon* and *Laharpe*. But here its policy is fortunately inconsistent, and so a number of fine old names has escaped. Thus, it has decided in favor of *Bon Secours* and against *Bonsecours*, and in favor of *De Soto*, *La Crosse* and *La Moure*, and against *Desoto*, *Lacrosse* and *Lamoure*. Here its decisions are confused and often unintelligible. Why *Laporte*, Pa., and *La Porte*, Iowa? Why *Lagrange*, Ind., and *La Grange*, Ky.? Here it would seem to be yielding a great deal too much to local usage.

The Board proceeds to the shortening and simplification of native names by various devices. It deletes such suffixes as *town*, *city* and *courthouse*; it removes the apostrophe and often the genitives from such names as *St. Mary's*; it shortens *burgh* to *burg* and *borough* to *boro*; and it combines separate and often highly discreet words. The last habit often produces grotesque forms, *e. g.*, *Newberlin*, *Boxelder*, *Sabbathday lake*, *Fallentimber*, *Bluemountain*, *Westtown*, *Threepines* and*Missionhill*. It apparently cherishes a hope of eventually regularizing the spelling of *Allegany*. This is now *Allegany* for the Maryland county, the Pennsylvania township and the New York and Oregon towns, *Alleghany* for the mountains, the Colorado town and the Virginia town and springs, and *Allegheny* for the Pittsburgh borough and the Pennsylvania county, college and river. The Board inclines to *Allegheny* for both river and mountains. Other Indian names give it constant concern. Its struggles to set up

Chemquasabamticook as the name of a Maine lake in place ofChemquasabamtic and *Chemquassabamticook*, and *Chatahospee* as the name of an Alabama creek in place of *Chattahospee, Hoolethlocco, Hoolethloces, Hoolethloco* and *Hootethlocco* are worthy of its learning and authority.[44]

The American tendency to pronounce all the syllables of a word more distinctly than the English shows itself in geographical names. White, in 1880, [45] recorded the increasing habit of giving full value to the syllables of such borrowed English names as *Worcester* and *Warwick*. I have frequently noted the same thing. In Worcester county, Maryland, the name is usually pronounced *Wooster*, but on the Western Shore of the state one hears *Worcest-'r*.[46] *Norwich* is another such name; one hears *Nor-wich* quite as often as *Norrich*.[47] Yet another is *Delhi*; one often hears *Del-high*. White said that in his youth the name of the *Shawangunk* mountains, in New York, was pronounced *Shongo*, but that the custom of pronouncing it as spelled had arisen during his manhood. So with *Winnipiseogee*, the name of a lake; once *Winipisaukie*, it gradually came to be pronounced as spelled. There is frequently a considerable difference between the pronunciation of a name by natives of a place and its pronunciation by those who are familiar with it only in print. *Baltimore* offers an example. The natives always drop the medial *i* and so reduce the name to two syllables; the habit identifies them. *Anne Arundel*, the name of a county in Maryland, is usually pronounced *Ann 'ran'l* by its people. *Arkansas*, as everyone knows, is pronounced *Arkansaw* by the Arkansans, and the Nevadans give the name of their state a flat *a*. The local pronunciation of *Illinois* I have already noticed. *Iowa*, at home, is often *Ioway*.[48] Many American geographical names offer great difficulty to Englishmen. One of my English acquaintances tells me that he was taught at school to accent *Massachusetts* on the second syllable, to rhyme the second syllable of *Ohio* with *tea*, and to sound the first *c* in *Connecticut*. In Maryland the name of *Calvert* county is given a broad *a*, whereas the name of *Calvert* street, in Baltimore, has a flat *a*. This curious distinction is almost always kept up. A Scotchman, coming to America, would give the *ch* in such names as *Loch Raven* and *Lochvale* the guttural Scotch (and German) sound, but locally it is always pronounced as if it were *k*.

Finally, there is a curious difference between English and American usage in the use of the word *river*. The English invariably put it before the proper name, whereas we almost as invariably put it after. *The Thames river* would seem quite as strange to an Englishman as *the river Chicago* would seem to us. This difference arose more than a century ago and was noticed by Pickering. But in his day the American usage was still somewhat uncertain, and such forms as *the river Mississippi* were yet in use. Today *river* almost always goes after the proper name.

§ 4. Street Names

—"Such a locality as 'the *corner* of *Avenue H* and *Twenty-third* street, '" says W. W. Crane, "is about as distinctively American as Algonquin and Iroquois names like *Mississippi* and *Saratoga*."[49] Kipling, in his "American Notes, "[50] gives testimony to the strangeness with which the number-names, the phrase "the corner of, " and the custom of omitting *street* fall upon the ear of a Britisher. He quotes with amazement certain directions given to him on his arrival in San Francisco from India: "Go six blocks north to [the] corner of *Geary* and *Markey* [*Market?*]; then walk around till you strike [the] corner of *Gutter* and *Sixteenth*." The English always add the word *street* (or *road* or *place* or *avenue*) when speaking of a thoroughfare; such a phrase as "*Oxford* and *New Bond*" would strike them as incongruous. The American custom of numbering and lettering streets is almost always ascribed by English writers who discuss it, not to a desire to make finding them easy, but to sheer poverty of invention. The English apparently have an inexhaustible fund of names for streets; they often give one street more than one name. Thus, *Oxford* street, London, becomes the *Bayswater* road, *High* street, *Holland Park* avenue, *Goldhawke* road and finally the *Oxford* road to the westward, and *High Holborn*, *Holborn* viaduct, *Newgate* street, *Cheapside*, the *Poultry*, *Cornhill* and *Leadenhall* street to the eastward. The Strand, in the same way, becomes *Fleet* street, *Ludgate* hill and *Cannon* street. Nevertheless, there is a *First* avenue in *Queen's Park*, and parallel to it are *Second*, *Third*, *Fourth*, *Fifth* and *Sixth* avenues—all small streets leading northward from the Harrow road, just east of Kensal Green cemetery. I have observed that few Londoners have ever heard of them. There is also a *First* street in Chelsea—a very modest thoroughfare near Lennox gardens and not far from the Brompton Oratory.

Next to the numbering and lettering of streets, a fashion apparently set up by Major Pierre-Charles L'Enfant's plans for Washington, the most noticeable feature of American street nomenclature, as opposed to that of England, is the extensive use of such designations as *avenue, boulevard, drive* and *speedway. Avenue* is used in England, but only rather sparingly; it is seldom applied to a mean street, or to one in a warehouse district. In America the word is scarcely distinguished in meaning from *street.*[51] *Boulevard, drive* and *speedway* are almost unknown to the English, but they use *road* for urban thoroughfares, which is very seldom done in America, and they also make free use of *place, walk, passage, lane* and *circus*, all of which are obsolescent on this side of the ocean. Some of the older American cities, such as Boston and Baltimore, have surviving certain ancient English designations of streets, *e. g., Cheapside* and *Cornhill*; these are unknown in the newer American towns. *Broadway*, which is also English, is more common. Many American towns now have *plazas*, which are unknown in England. Nearly all have *City Hall parks, squares* or *places*; *City Hall* is also unknown over there. The principal street of a small town, in America, is almost always *Main street*; in England it is as invariably *High* street, usually with the definite article before *High*.

I have mentioned the corruption of old Dutch street and neighborhood names in New York. Spanish names are corrupted in the same way in the Southwest and French names in the Great Lakes region and in Louisiana. In New Orleans the street names, many of them strikingly beautiful, are pronounced so barbarously by the people that a Frenchman would have difficulty recognizing them. Thus, *Bourbon* has become *Bur-bun, Dauphine* is *Daw-fin, Foucher* is *Foosh'r, Enghien* is *En-gine*, and *Felicity* (originally *Félicité*) is *Fill-a-city.* The French, in their days, bestowed the names of the Muses upon certain of the city streets. They are now pronounced *Cal´-y-ope, Terp´-si-chore, Mel-po-mean´, You-terp´*, and so on. *Bon Enfants*, apparently too difficult for the native, has been translated into *Good Children*. Only *Esplanade* and *Bagatelle*, among the

French street names of the city, seem to be commonly pronounced with any approach to correctness.

FOOTNOTES:

[1] The great Irish famine, which launched the chief emigration to America, extended from 1845 to 1847. The Know Nothing movement, which was chiefly aimed at the Irish, extended from 1852 to 1860.

[2] A. B. Faust: The German Element in the United States, 2 vols.; Boston, 1909, vol. ii, pp. 34 *et seq.*

[3] Richard T. Ely: Outlines of Economics, 3rd rev. ed.; New York, 1916, p. 68.

[4] *Cf.* Seth K. Humphrey: Mankind; New York, 1917, p. 45.

[5] *Cf.* William G. Searle: Onomasticon Anglo-Saxonicum; Cambridge, 1897.

[6] *New York World* Almanac, 1914, p. 668.

[7] It was announced by the Bureau of War Risk Insurance on March 30, 1918, that there were then 15, 000*Millers* in the United States Army. On the same day there were 262 *John J. O'Briens*, of whom 50 had wives named *Mary*.

[8] *Cf.* Carlyle's Frederick the Great, bk. xxi, ch. vi.

[9] S. Grant Oliphant, in the *Baltimore Sun*, Dec. 2, 1906.

[10] Harriet *Lane* Johnston was of this family.

[11] *Cf.* Faust, *op. cit.*, vol. ii, pp. 183-4.

[12] A Tragedy of Surnames, by Fayette Dunlap, *Dialect Notes*, vol. iv, pt. 1, 1913, p. 7-8.

[13] Americanisms, p. 112.

[14] Henry Harrison, in his Dictionary of the Surnames of the United Kingdom; London, 1912, shows that such names as *Bloom*, *Cline*, etc., always represent transliterations of German names. They are unknown to genuinely British nomenclature.

[15] A great many more such transliterations and modifications are listed by Faust, *op. cit.*, particularly in his first volume. Others are in Pennsylvania Dutch, by S. S. Haldemann; London, 1872, p. 60 *et seq.*, and in The Origin of Pennsylvania Surnames, by L. Oscar Kuhns, *Lippincott's Magazine*, March, 1897, p. 395.

[16] I lately encountered the following sign in front of an automobile repair shop:

For   puncture   or   blow
Bring it to *Lowe*.

[17] *Baltimore Sun*, March 17, 1907.

[18] *Cf.* The Origin of Pennsylvania Surnames, *op. cit.*

[19] *Koch*, a common German name, has very hard sledding in America. Its correct pronunciation is almost impossible to Americans; at best it becomes *Coke*. Hence it is often changed, not only to *Cook*, but to *Cox*, *Koke* or even *Cockey*.

[20] This is army slang, but promises to survive. The Germans, during the war, had no opprobrious nicknames for their foes. The French were always *die Franzosen*, the English were *die Engländer*, and so on, even when most violently abused. Even *der Yankee* was rare.

[21] *Cf.* Some Current Substitutes for Irish, by W. A. McLaughlin, *Dialect Notes*, vol. iv, pt. ii.

[22] *Spiggoty*, originating at Panama, now means a native of any Latin-American region under American protection, and in general any Latin-American. It is navy slang, but has come into extensive civilian use. It is a derisive daughter of "No *spik* Inglese."

[23] *Cf.* Reaction to Personal Names, by Dr. C. P. Oberndorf, *Psychoanalytic Review*, vol. v, no. 1, January, 1918, p. 47 *et seq.* This, so far as I know, is the only article in English which deals with the psychological effects of surnames upon their bearers. Abraham, Silberer and other German psychoanalysts have made contributions to the subject. Dr. Oberndorf alludes, incidentally, to the positive social prestige which goes with an English air, and, to a smaller extent, with a French air in America. He tells of an Italian who changed his patronymic of *Dipucci* into *de Pucci* to make it more "aristocratic." And of a German bearing the genuinely aristocratic name of *von Landsschaffshausen* who changed it to "a typically English name" because the latter seemed more distinguished to his neighbors.

[24] The effects of race antagonism upon language are still to be investigated. The etymology of *slave* indicates that the inquiry might yield interesting results. The word *French*, in English, is largely used to suggest sexual perversion. In German anything *Russian* is barbarous, and *English* education hints at flagellation. The French, for many years, called a certain contraband appliance a *capote Anglaise*, but after the *entente cordiale* they changed the name to *capote Allemande*. The common English name to this day is *French letter*. *Cf.* The Criminal, by Havelock Ellis; London, 1910, p. 208.

[25] *Cf.* The Jews, by Maurice Fishberg; New York, 1911, ch. xxii, and especially p. 485 *et seq.*

[26] The English Jews usually change *Levy* to *Lewis*, a substitution almost unknown in America. They also change *Abraham* to *Braham* and *Moses* to *Moss*. *Vide* Surnames, Their Origin and Nationality, by L. B. McKenna; Quincy (Ill.), 1913, pp. 13-14.

[27] For these observations of name changes among the Jews I am indebted to Abraham Cahan.

[28] They arose in England through the custom of requiring an heir by the female line to adopt the family name on inheriting the family property. Formerly the heir dropped his own surname. Thus the ancestor of the present Duke of Northumberland, born *Smithson*, took the ancient name of *Percy* on succeeding to the underlying earldom in the eighteenth century. But about a hundred years ago, heirs in like case began to join the two names by hyphenation, and such names are now very common in the British peerage. Thus the surname of Lord Barrymore is *Smith-Barry*, that of Lord Vernon is *Venables-Vernon*, and that of the Earl of Wharncliffe is *Montagu-Stuart-Wortley-Mackenzie*.

[29] B. W. Green: Word-Book of Virginia Folk-Speech; Richmond, 1899, pp. 13-16.

[30] The one given name that they have clung to is *Karl*. This, in fact, has been adopted by Americans of other stocks, always, however, spelled *Carl*. Such combinations as *Carl* Gray, *Carl* Williams and even *Carl*Murphy are common. Here intermarriage has doubtless had its effect.

[31] *Cf.* Curiosities of Puritan Nomenclature, by Charles W. Bardsley; London, 1880.

[32] *Cf.* Bardsley, *op. cit.*, p. 205 *et seq.*

[33] The Geographic Board has lately decided that *Kenesaw* should be *Kennesaw*, but the learned jurist sticks to one *n*.

[34] Thornton reprints a paragraph from the *Congressional Globe* of June 15, 1854, alleging that in 1846, during the row over the Oregon boundary, when "Fifty-four forty or fight" was a political slogan, many "canal-boats, and even some of the babies, ... were christened *54° 40'*."

[35] The Irish present several curious variations. Thus, they divide *Charles* into two syllables. They also take liberties with various English surnames. *Bermingham*, for example, is pronounced *Brimmingham* in Ireland.

[36] Issued annually in July, with monthly supplements.

[37] The latest report is the fourth, covering the period 1890-1916; Washington, 1916.

[38] The authority here is River and Lake Names in the United States, by Edmund T. Ker; New York, 1911. Stephen G. Boyd, in Indian Local Names; York (Pa.), 1885, says that the original Indian name was*Pootuppag*.

[39] P. 17.

[40] *Cf.* Dutch Contributions to the Vocabulary of English in America, by W. H. Carpenter, *Modern Philology*, July, 1908.

[41] Our Naturalized Names, *Lippincott's Magazine*, April, 1899. It will be recalled how Pinaud, the French perfumer, was compelled to place advertisements in the street-cars, instructing the public in the proper pronunciation of his name.

[42] The same compromise is apparent in the pronunciation of *Iroquois*, which is *Iro-quoy* quite as often as it is *Iro-quoys*.

[43] *Vide* its Fourth Report (1890-1916), p. 15.

[44] The Geographic Board is composed of representatives of the Coast and Geodetic Survey, the Geological Survey, the General Land Office, the Post Office, the Forest Service, the Smithsonian Institution, the Biological Survey, the Government Printing Office, the Census and Lighthouse Bureaus, the General Staff of the Army, the Hydrographic Office, Library and War Records Office of the Navy, the Treasury and the Department of State. It was created by executive order Sept. 4, 1890, and its decisions are binding upon all federal officials. It has made, to date, about 15, 000 decisions. They are recorded in reports issued at irregular intervals and in more frequent bulletins.

[45] Every-Day English, p. 100.

[46] I have often noted that Americans, in speaking of the familiar *Worcestershire* sauce, commonly pronounce every syllable and enunciated *shire* distinctly. In England it is always *Woostersh'r*.

[47] The English have a great number of such decayed pronunciations, *e. g.*, *Maudlin* for *Magdalen College*, *Sister* for *Cirencester*, *Merrybone* for *Marylebone*. Their geographical nomenclature shows many corruptions due to faulty pronunciation and the law of Hobson-Jobson, *e. g.*, *Leighton Buzzard* for the Norman French *Leiton Beau Desart*.

[48] Curiously enough, Americans always use the broad *a* in the first syllable of *Albany*, whereas Englishmen rhyme the syllable with *pal*. The English also pronounce *Pall Mall* as if it were spelled *pal mal*. Americans commonly give it two broad *a*'s.

[49] Our Street Names, *Lippincott's Magazine*, Aug., 1897, p. 264.

[50] Ch. i.

[51] There are, of course, local exceptions. In Baltimore, for example, *avenue* used to be reserved for wide streets in the suburbs. Thus Charles *street*, on passing the old city boundary, became Charles *street-avenue*. Further out it became the Charles *street-avenue-road*—probably a unique triplication. But that was years ago. Of late many fifth-rate streets in Baltimore have been changed into avenues.

IX. Miscellanea

§ 1. Proverb and Platitude

—No people, save perhaps the Spaniards, have a richer store of proverbial wisdom than the Americans, and surely none other make more diligent and deliberate efforts to augment its riches. The American literature of "inspirational" platitude is enormous and almost unique. There are half a dozen authors, *e. g.*, Dr. Orison Swett Marden and Dr. Frank Crane, who devote themselves exclusively, and to vast profit, to the composition of arresting and uplifting apothegms, and the fruits of their fancy are not only sold in books but also displayed upon an infinite variety of calendars, banners and wall-cards. It is rarely that one enters the office of an American business man without encountering at least one of these wall-cards. It may, on the one hand, show nothing save a succinct caution that time is money, say, "Do It Now, " or "This Is My Busy Day"; on the other hand, it may embody a long and complex sentiment, ornately set forth. The taste for such canned sagacity seems to have arisen in America at a very early day. Benjamin Franklin's "Poor Richard's Almanac, " begun in 1732, remained a great success for twenty-five years, and the annual sales reached 10, 000. It had many imitators, and founded an aphoristic style of writing which culminated in the essays of Emerson, often mere strings of sonorous certainties, defectively articulated. The "Proverbial Philosophy" of Martin Farquhar Tupper, dawning upon the American public in the early 40's, was welcomed with enthusiasm; as Saintsbury says, [1] its success on this side of the Atlantic even exceeded its success on the other. But that was the last and perhaps the only importation of the sage and mellifluous in bulk. In late years the American production of such merchandise has grown so large that the balance of trade now flows in the other direction. Visiting Denmark, Germany, Switzerland, France and Spain in the spring of 1917, I found translations of the chief works of Dr. Marden on sale in all those countries, and with them the masterpieces of such other apostles of the New Thought as Ralph Waldo Trine and Elizabeth Towne. No other American books were half so well displayed.

The note of all such literature, and of the maxims that precipitate themselves from it, is optimism. They "inspire" by voicing and revoicing the New Thought doctrine that all things are possible to the man who thinks the right sort of thoughts—in the national phrase, to the *right-thinker*. This right-thinker is indistinguishable from the *forward-looker*, whose belief in the continuity and benignity of the evolutionary process takes on the virulence of a religious faith. Out of his confidence come the innumerable saws, axioms and *geflügelte Worte* in the national arsenal, ranging from the "It won't hurt none to try" of the great masses of the plain people to such exhilarating confections of the wall-card virtuosi as "The elevator to success is not running; take the stairs." Naturally enough, a grotesque humor plays about this literature of hope; the folk, though it moves them, prefer it with a dash of salt. "Smile, damn you, smile!" is a typical specimen of this seasoned optimism. Many examples of it go back to the early part of the last century, for instance, "Don't monkey with the buzz-saw" and "It will never get well if you pick it." Others are patently modern, *e. g.*, "The Lord is my shepherd; I should worry" and "Roll over; you're on your back." The national talent for extravagant and pungent humor is well displayed in many of these maxims. It would be difficult to match, in any other folk-literature, such examples as "I'd rather have them say 'There he goes' than 'Here he lies, '" or "Don't spit: remember the Johnstown flood, " or "Shoot it in the arm; your leg's full, " or "Cheer up; there ain't no hell, " or "If you want to cure homesickness, go back home." Many very popular phrases and proverbs are borrowings from above. "Few die and none resign" originated with Thomas Jefferson; Bret Harte, I believe, was the author of "No check-ee, no shirt-ee, " General W. T. Sherman is commonly credited with "War is hell, " and Mark Twain with "Life is one damn thing after another." An elaborate and highly characteristic proverb of the uplifting variety—"So live that you can look any man in the eye and tell him to go to hell"—was first given currency by one of the engineers of the Panama Canal, a gentleman later retired, it would seem, for attempting to execute his own counsel. From humor the transition to cynicism is easy, and so many of the current sayings are at war with the optimism of the majority. "Kick him again; he's down" is a depressing example. "What's the use?" a rough translation of the Latin "Cui bono?" is another. The same spirit is visible in "Tell your troubles to a policeman, " "How'd you like to be the ice-man?" "Some say she do and some say she don't, " "Nobody loves a fat man, " "I love my wife, but O you kid, " and "Would you for fifty cents?" The last originated in the ingenious mind of an advertisement writer and was immediately adopted. In the course of time it acquired a naughty significance, and helped to give a start to the amazing button craze of ten or twelve years ago—a saturnalia of proverb and phrase making which finally aroused the guardians of the public morals and was put down by the police.

That neglect which marks the study of the vulgate generally extends to the subject of popular proverb-making. The English publisher, Frank Palmer, prints an excellent series of little volumes presenting the favorite proverbs of all civilized races, including the Chinese and Japanese, but there is no American volume among them. Even such exhaustive collections as that of Robert Christy[2]contain no American specimens—not even "Don't monkey with the buzz-saw" or "Root, hog, or die."

§ 2. American Slang

—This neglect of the national proverbial philosophy extends to the national slang. There is but one work, so far as I can discover, formally devoted to it, [3] and that work is extremely superficial. Moreover, it has been long out of date, and hence is of little save historical value. There are at least a dozen careful treatises on French slang, [4] half as many on English slang, [5] and a good many on German slang, but American slang, which is probably quite as rich as that of France and a good deal richer than that of any other country, is yet to be studied at length. Nor is there much discussion of it, of any interest or value, in the general philological literature. Fowler and all the other early native students of the language dismissed it with lofty gestures; down to the time of Whitney it was scarcely regarded as a seemly subject for the notice of a man of learning. Lounsbury, less pedantic, viewed its phenomena more hospitably, and even defined it as "the source from which the decaying energies of speech are constantly refreshed, " and Brander Matthews, following him, has described its function as that of providing "substitutes for the good words and true which are worn out by hard service."[6] But that is about as far as the investigation has got. Krapp has some judicious paragraphs upon the matter in his "Modern English, "[7] there are a few scattered essays upon the underlying psychology, [8] and various uninforming magazine articles, but that is all. The practising authors of the country, like its philologians, have always shown a gingery and suspicious attitude. "The use of slang, " said Oliver Wendell Holmes, "is at once a sign and a cause of mental atrophy." "Slang, " said Ambrose Bierce fifty years later, "is the speech of him who robs the literary garbage carts on their way to the dumps." Literature in America, as we have seen, remains aloof from the vulgate. Despite the contrary examples of Mark Twain and Howells, all the more pretentious American authors try to write chastely and elegantly; the typical literary product of the country is still a refined essay in the *Atlantic Monthly*, perhaps gently jocose but never rough—by Emerson, so to speak, out of Charles Lamb—the sort of thing one might look to be done by a somewhat advanced English curate. George Ade, undoubtedly one of the most adept anatomists of the American character and painters of the American scene that the national literature has yet developed, is neglected because his work is grounded firmly upon the national speech—not that he reports it literally, like

Lardner and the hacks trailing after Lardner, but that he gets at and exhibits its very essence. It would stagger a candidate for a doctorate in philology, I daresay, to be told off by his professor to investigate the slang of Ade in the way that Bosson, [9] the Swede, has investigated that of Jerome K. Jerome, and yet, until something of the sort is undertaken, American philology will remain out of contact with the American language.

Most of the existing discussions of slang spend themselves upon efforts to define it, and, in particular, upon efforts to differentiate it from idiomatic neologisms of a more legitimate type. This effort is largely in vain; the border-line is too vague and wavering to be accurately mapped; words and phrases are constantly crossing it, and in both directions. There was a time, perhaps, when the familiar American counter-word, *proposition*, was slang; its use seems to have originated in the world of business, and it was soon afterward adopted by the sporting fraternity. But today it is employed without much feeling that it needs apology, and surely without any feeling that it is low. *Nice*, as an adjective of all work, was once in slang use only; today no one would question "a *nice* day, " or "a *nice* time" or "a *nice* hotel." *Awful* seems to be going the same route. "*Awful* sweet" and "*awfully* dear" still seem slangy and school-girlish, but "*awful* children, " "*awful* weather" and "an *awful* job" have entirely sound support, and no one save a pedant would hesitate to use them. Such insidious purifications and consecrations of slang are going on under our noses all the time. The use of *some* as a general adjective-adverb seems likely to make its way in the same manner. It is constantly forgotten by purists of defective philological equipment that a great many of our most respectable words and phrases originated in the plainest sort of slang. Thus, *quandary*, despite a fanciful etymology which would identify it with *wandreth* (=*evil*), is probably simply a composition form of the French phrase, *qu'en dirai-je?* Again, to turn to French itself, there is *tête*, a sound name for the human head for many centuries—though its origin was in the Latin *testa*(=*pot*), a favorite slang-word of the soldiers of the decaying empire, analogous to our own *block*, *nut* and *conch*. The word *slacker*, recently come into good usage in the United States as a designation for an unsuccessful shirker of conscription, is a substantive derived from the English verb *to slack*, which was born as university slang and remains so to this day. Brander Matthews, so recently as 1901, thought *to hold up* slang; it is now perfectly good American.

The contrary movement of words from the legitimate vocabulary into slang is constantly witnessed. Some one devises a new and intriguing trope or makes use of an old one under circumstances arresting the public attention, and at once it is adopted into slang, given a host of remote significances, and ding-donged *ad nauseam*. The Rooseveltian phrases, *muck-raker, Ananias Club, short and ugly word, nature-faker* and *big-stick*, offer examples. Not one of them was new and not one of them was of much pungency, but Roosevelt's vast talent for delighting the yokelry threw about them a charming air, and so they entered into current slang and were mouthed idiotically for months. Another example is to be found in *steam-roller*. It was first heard of in June, 1908, when it was applied by Oswald F. Schuette, of the *Chicago Inter-Ocean*, to the methods employed by the Roosevelt-Taft majority in the Republican National Committee in over-riding the protests against seating Taft delegates from Alabama and Arkansas. At once it struck the popular fancy and was soon heard on all sides. All the usual derivatives appeared, *to steam-roller, steam-rollered*, and so on. Since then, curiously enough, the term has gradually forced its way back from slang to good usage, and even gone over to England. In the early days of the Great War it actually appeared in the most solemn English reviews, and once or twice, I believe, in state papers.

Much of the discussion of slang by popular etymologists is devoted to proofs that this or that locution is not really slang at all—that it is to be found in Shakespeare, in Milton, or in the Revised Version. These scientists, of course, overlook the plain fact that slang, like the folk-song, is not the creation of people in the mass, but of definite individuals, and that its character *as* slang depends entirely upon its adoption by the ignorant, who use its novelties too assiduously and with too little imagination, and so debase them to the estate of worn-out coins, smooth and valueless. It is this error, often shared by philologists of sounder information, that lies under the doctrine that the plays of Shakespeare are full of slang, and that the Bard showed but a feeble taste in language. Nothing could be more absurd. The business of writing English, in his day, was unharassed by the proscriptions of purists, and so the vocabulary could be enriched more facilely than today, but though Shakespeare and his fellow-dramatists quickly adopted such neologisms as *to bustle, to huddle, bump, hubbub* and *pat*, it goes without saying that they exercised a sound discretion and that the slang of the Bankside was full of words and phrases which they were never tempted to use. In our own day the same discrimination is exercised by all writers of sound taste. On the one hand they disregard the senseless prohibitions of school-masters, and on the other hand they draw the line with more or less watchfulness, according as they are of conservative or liberal habit. I find *the best of the bunch* and *joke-smith* in Saintsbury;[10] one could scarcely imagine either in Walter Pater. But by the same token one could not imagine *chicken* (for young girl), [11] *aber nit, to come across* or *to camouflage* in Saintsbury.

What slang actually consists of doesn't depend, in truth, upon intrinsic qualities, but upon the surrounding circumstances. It is the user that determines the matter, and particularly the user's habitual way of thinking. If he chooses words carefully, with a full understanding of their meaning and savor, then no word that he uses seriously will belong to slang, but if his speech is made up chiefly of terms poll-parroted, and he has no sense of their shades and limitations, then slang will bulk largely in his vocabulary. In its origin it is nearly always respectable; it is devised not by the stupid populace, but by individuals of wit and ingenuity; as Whitney says, it is a product of an "exuberance of mental activity, and the natural delight of language-making." But when its inventions happen to strike the popular fancy and are adopted by the mob, they are soon worn threadbare and so lose all piquancy and significance, and, in Whitney's words, become "incapable of expressing anything that is real."[12] This is the history of such slang phrases, often interrogative, as "How'd you like to be the ice-man?" "How's your poor feet?" "Merci pour la langouste, " "Have a heart, " "This is the life, " "Where did you get that hat?" "Would you for fifty cents?" "Let her go, Gallegher, " "Shoo-fly, don't bother me, " "Don't wake him up" and "Let George do it." The last well exhibits the process. It originated in France, as "Laissez faire à Georges, " during the fifteenth century, and at the start had satirical reference to the multiform activities of Cardinal Georges d'Amboise, prime minister to Louis XII.[13] It later became common slang, was translated into English, had a revival during the early days of David Lloyd-George's meteoric career, was adopted into American without any comprehension of either its first or its latest significance, and enjoyed the brief popularity of a year.

Krapp attempts to distinguish between slang and sound idiom by setting up the doctrine that the former is "more expressive than the situation demands." "It is, " he says, "a kind of hyperesthesia in the use of language. *To laugh in your sleeve* is idiom because it arises out of a natural situation; it is a metaphor derived from the picture of one raising his sleeve to his face to hide a smile, a metaphor which arose naturally enough in early periods when sleeves were long and flowing; but *to talk through your hat* is slang, not only because it is new, but also because it is a grotesque exaggeration of the truth."[14] The theory, unluckily, is combated by many plain facts. *To hand it to him, to get away with it* and even *to hand him a lemon* are certainly not metaphors that transcend the practicable and probable, and yet all are undoubtedly slang. On the other hand, there is palpable exaggeration in such phrases as "he is not worth the powder it would take to kill him, " in such adjectives as *break-bone* (fever), and in such compounds as *fire-eater*, and yet it would be absurd to dismiss them as slang. Between *block-head* and *bone-head* there is little to choose, but the former is sound English, whereas the latter is American slang. So with many familiar similes, *e. g., like greased lightning, as scarce as hen's teeth*; they are grotesque hyperboles, but surely not slang.

The true distinction between slang and more seemly idiom, in so far as any distinction exists at all, is that indicated by Whitney. Slang originates in an effort, always by ingenious individuals, to make the language more vivid and expressive. When in the form of single words it may appear as new metaphors, *e. g., bird* and *peach*; as back formations, *e. g., beaut* and *flu*; as composition-forms, *e. g., whatdyecallem*; as picturesque compounds, *e. g., booze-foundry*; as onomatopes, *e. g., biff* and *zowie*; or in any other of the shapes that new terms take. If, by the chances that condition language-making, it acquires a special and limited meaning, not served by any existing locution, it enters into sound idiom and is presently wholly legitimatized; if, on the contrary, it is adopted by the populace as a counter-word and employed with such banal imitativeness that it soon loses any definite significance whatever, then it remains slang and is avoided by the finical. An example of the former process is afforded by *Tommy-rot*. It first appeared as English school-boy slang, but its obvious utility soon brought it into good usage. In one of Jerome K. Jerome's books, "Paul Kelver, " there is the following dialogue:

362

"The wonderful songs that nobody ever sings, the wonderful pictures that nobody ever paints, and all the rest of it. It's *Tommy-rot*!"

"I wish you wouldn't use slang."

"Well, you know what I mean. What is the proper word? Give it to me."

"I suppose you mean *cant*."

"No, I don't. *Cant* is something that you don't believe in yourself. It's *Tommy-rot*; there isn't any other word."

Nor was there any other word for *hubbub* and to *dwindle* in Shakespeare's time; he adopted and dignified them because they met genuine needs. Nor was there any other satisfactory word for *graft* when it came in, nor for *rowdy*, nor for *boom*, nor for *joy-ride*, nor for *omnibus-bill*, nor for *slacker*, nor for *trust-buster*. Such words often retain a humorous quality; they are used satirically and hence appear but seldom in wholly serious discourse. But they have standing in the language nevertheless, and only a prig would hesitate to use them as Saintsbury used *the best of the bunch* and *joke-smith*.

On the other hand, many an apt and ingenious neologism, by falling too quickly into the gaping maw of the proletariat, is spoiled forthwith. Once it becomes, in Oliver Wendell Holmes' phrase, "a cheap generic term, a substitute for differentiated specific expressions, " it quickly acquires such flatness that the fastidious flee it as a plague. One recalls many capital verb-phrases, thus ruined by unintelligent appreciation, *e. g.*, *to hand him a lemon, to freeze on to, to have the goods, to fall for it*, and *to get by*. One recalls, too, some excellent substantives, *e. g.*, *dope* and *dub*, and compounds, *e. g.*, *come-on* and *easy-mark*, and verbs, *e. g.*, *to vamp*. These are all quite as sound in structure as the great majority of our most familiar words, but their adoption by the ignorant and their endless use and misuse in all sorts of situations have left them tattered and obnoxious, and they will probably go the way, as Matthews says, of all the other "temporary phrases which spring up, one scarcely knows how, and flourish unaccountably for a few months, and then disappear forever, leaving no sign." Matthews is wrong in two particulars here. They do not arise by any mysterious parthenogenesis, but come from sources which, in many cases, may be determined. And they last, alas, a good deal more than a month. *Shoo-fly* afflicted the American people for at least two years, and "I *don't* think" and *aber nit* quite as long. Even "good-*night*" lasted a whole year.

A very large part of our current slang is propagated by the newspapers, and much of it is invented by newspaper writers. One needs but turn to the slang of baseball to find numerous examples. Such phrases as *to clout the sphere, the initial sack, to slam the pill* and *the dexter meadow* are obviously not of bleachers manufacture. There is not enough imagination in that depressing army to devise such things; more often than not, there is not even enough intelligence to comprehend them. The true place of their origin is the perch of the newspaper reporters, whose competence and compensation is largely estimated, at least on papers of wide circulation, by their capacity for inventing novelties. The supply is so large that connoisseurship has grown up; an extra-fecund slang-maker on the press has his following. During the summer of 1913 the *Chicago Record-Herald*, somewhat alarmed by the extravagant fancy of its baseball reporters, asked its readers if they would prefer a return to plain English. Such of them as were literate enough to send in their votes were almost unanimously against a change. As one of them said, "one is nearer the park when Schulte *slams the pill* than when he merely *hits the ball*." In all other fields the newspapers originate and propagate slang, particularly in politics. Most of our political slang-terms since the Civil War, from *pork-barrel* to *steam-roller*, have been their inventions. The English newspapers, with the exception of a few anomalies such as the *Pink-Un*, lean in the other direction; their fault is not slanginess, but an otiose ponderosity—in Dean Alford's words, "the insisting on calling common things by uncommon names; changing our ordinary short Saxon nouns and verbs for long words derived from the Latin."[15] The American newspapers, years ago, passed through such a stage of bombast, but since the invention of yellow journalism by the elder James Gordon Bennett—that is, the invention of journalism for the frankly ignorant and vulgar—they have gone to the other extreme. Edmund Clarence Stedman noted the change soon after the Civil War. "The whole country, " he wrote to Bayard Taylor in 1873, "owing to the contagion of our newspaper 'exchange' system, is flooded, deluged, swamped beneath a muddy tide of slang."[16] A thousand alarmed watchmen have sought to stay it since, but in vain. The great majority of our newspapers, including all those of large circulation, are chiefly written, as one observer says, "not in English, but in a strange jargon of words that would have made Addison or Milton shudder in despair."[17]

§ 3. The Future of the Language

—The great Jakob Grimm, the founder of comparative philology, hazarded the guess more than three-quarters of a century ago that English would one day become the chief language of the world, and perhaps crowd out several of the then principal idioms altogether. "In wealth, wisdom and strict economy, " he said, "none of the other living languages can vie with it." At that time the guess was bold, for English was still in fifth place, with not only French and German ahead of it, but also Spanish and Russian. In 1801, according to Michael George Mulhall, the relative standing of the five, in the number of persons using them, was as follows:

French	31, 450, 000
Russian	30, 770, 000
German	30, 320, 000
Spanish	26, 190, 000
English	20, 520, 000

The population of the United States was then but little more than 5, 000, 000, but in twenty years it had nearly doubled, and thereafter it increased steadily and enormously, and by 1860 it was greater than that of the United Kingdom. Since that time the majority of English-speaking persons in the world have lived on this side of the water; today there are nearly three times as many as in the United Kingdom and nearly twice as many as in the whole British Empire. This great increase in the American population, beginning with the great immigrations of the 30's and 40's, quickly lifted English to fourth place among the languages, and then to third, to second and to first. When it took the lead the attention of philologists was actively directed to the matter, and in 1868 one of them, a German named Brackebusch, first seriously raised the question whether English was destined to obliterate certain of the older tongues.[18] Brackebusch decided against on various philological grounds, none of them sound. His own figures, as the following table from his dissertation shows, [19] were against him:

English	60, 000, 000
German	52, 000, 000

Russian	45, 000, 000
French	45, 000, 000
Spanish	40, 000, 000

This in 1868. Before another generation had passed the lead of English, still because of the great growth of the United States, was yet more impressive, as the following figures for 1890 show:

English	111, 100, 000
German	75, 200, 000
Russian	75, 000, 000
French	51, 200, 000
Spanish	42, 800, 000
Italian	33, 400, 000
Portuguese	13, 000, 000[20]

Today the figures exceed even these. They show that English is now spoken by two and a half times as many persons as spoke it at the close of the American Civil War and by nearly eight times as many as spoke it at the beginning of the nineteenth century. No other language has spread in any such proportions. Even German, which is next on the list, shows but a four-fold gain since 1801, or just half that of English. The number of persons speaking Russian, despite the vast extension of the Russian empire during the last century of the czars, has little more than tripled, and the number speaking French has less than doubled. But here are the figures for 1911:

English	160, 000, 000
German	130, 000, 000
Russian	100, 000, 000
French	70, 000, 000
Spanish	50, 000, 000
Italian	50, 000, 000
Portuguese	25, 000, 000[21]

Japanese, perhaps, should follow French: it is spoken by 60, 000, 000 persons. But Chinese may be disregarded, for it is split into half a dozen mutually unintelligible dialects, and shows no sign of spreading beyond the limits of China. The same may be said of Hindustani, which is the language of 100, 000, 000 inhabitants of British India; it shows wide dialectical variations and the people who speak it are not likely to spread. But English is the possession of a race that is still pushing in all directions, and wherever that race settles the existing languages tend to succumb. Thus French, despite the passionate resistance of the French-Canadians, is gradually decaying in Canada; in all the newly-settled regions English is universal. And thus Spanish is dying out in our own Southwest, and promises to meet with severe competition in some of the nearer parts of Latin-America. The English control of the sea has likewise carried the language into far places. There is scarcely a merchant ship-captain on deep water, of whatever nationality, who does not find some acquaintance with it necessary, and it has become, in debased forms, the *lingua franca* of Oceanica and the Far East generally. "Three-fourths of the world's mail matter, " says E. H. Babbitt, "is now addressed in English, " and "more than half of the world's newspapers are printed in English."[22]

Brackebusch, in the speculative paper just mentioned, came to the conclusion that the future domination of English would be prevented by its unphonetic spelling, its grammatical decay and the general difficulties that a foreigner encounters in seeking to master it. "The simplification of its grammar, " he said, "is the commencement of dissolution, the beginning of the end, and its extraordinary tendency to degenerate into slang of every kind is the foreshadowing of its approaching dismemberment." But in the same breath he was forced to admit that "the greater development it has obtained" was the result of this very simplification of grammar, and an inspection of the rest of his reasoning quickly shows its unsoundness, even without an appeal to the plain facts. The spelling of a language, whether it be phonetic or not, has little to do with its spread. Very few men learn it by studying books; they learn it by hearing it spoken. As for grammatical decay, it is not a sign of dissolution, but a sign of active life and constantly renewed strength. To the professional philologist, perhaps, it may sometimes appear otherwise. He is apt to estimate languages by looking at their complexity; the Greek aorist elicits his admiration because it presents enormous difficulties and is inordinately subtle. But the object of language is not to bemuse grammarians, but to convey ideas, and the more simply it accomplishes that object the more effectively it meets the needs of an energetic and practical people and the larger its inherent vitality. The history of every language of Europe, since the earliest days of which we have record, is a history of simplifications. Even such languages as German, which still cling to a great many exasperating inflections, including the absurd inflection of the article for gender, are less highly inflected than they used to be, and are proceeding slowly but surely toward analysis. The fact that English has gone further along that road than any other civilized tongue is not a proof of its decrepitude, but a proof of its continued strength. Brought into free competition with another language, say German or French or Spanish, it is almost certain to prevail, if only because it is vastly easier—that is, as a spoken language—to learn. The foreigner essaying it, indeed, finds his chief difficulty, not in mastering its forms, but in grasping its lack of forms. He doesn't have to learn a new and complex grammar; what he has to do is to forget grammar.

Once he has done so, the rest is a mere matter of acquiring a vocabulary. He can make himself understood, given a few nouns, pronouns, verbs and numerals, without troubling himself in the slightest about accidence. "Me see she" is bad English, perhaps, but it would be absurd to say that it is obscure—and on some not too distant tomorrow it may be very fair American. Essaying an inflected language, the beginner must go into the matter far more deeply before he may hope to be understood. Bradley, in "The Making of English, "[23] shows clearly how German and English differ in this respect, and how great is the advantage of English. In the latter the verb *sing* has but eight forms, and of these three are entirely obsolete, one is obsolescent, and two more may be dropped out without damage to comprehension. In German the corresponding verb, *singen*, has no less than sixteen forms. How far English has proceeded toward the complete obliteration of inflections is shown by such barbarous forms of it as Pigeon English and Beach-la-Mar, in which the final step is taken without appreciable loss of clarity. The Pigeon English verb is identical in all tenses. *Go* stands for both *went* and *gone*; *makee* is both *make* and *made.* In the same way there is no declension of the pronoun for case. *My* is thus *I, me, mine* and our own *my*. "No belong *my*" is "it is not *mine*"—a crude construction, of course, but still clearly intelligible. Chinamen learn Pigeon English in a few months, and savages in the South Seas master Beach-la-Mar almost as quickly. And a white man, once he has accustomed himself to either, finds it strangely fluent and expressive. He cannot argue politics in it, nor dispute upon transubstantiation, but for all the business of every day it is perfectly satisfactory.

As we have seen in Chapters V and VI, the American dialect of English has gone further along the road thus opened ahead than the mother dialect, and is moving faster. For this reason, and because of the fact that it is already spoken by a far larger and more rapidly multiplying body of people than the latter, it seems to me very likely that it will determine the final form of the language. For the old control of English over American to be reasserted is now quite unthinkable; if the two dialects are not to drift apart entirely English must follow in American's tracks. This yielding seems to have begun; the exchanges from American into English grow steadily larger and more important than the exchanges from English into American. John Richard Green, the historian, discerning the inevitable half a century ago, expressed the opinion, amazing and unpalatable then, that the Americans were already "the main branch of the English people." It is not yet wholly true; a cultural timorousness yet shows itself; there is still a class which looks to England as the Romans long looked to Greece. But it is not the class that is shaping the national language, and it is not the class that is carrying it beyond the national borders. The Americanisms that flood the English of Canada are not borrowed from the dialects of New England Loyalists and fashionable New Yorkers, but from the common speech that has its sources in the native and immigrant proletariat and that displays its gaudiest freightage in the newspapers.

The impact of this flood is naturally most apparent in Canada, whose geographical proximity and common interests completely obliterate the effects of English political and social dominance. By an Order in Council, passed in 1890, the use of the redundant u in such words as *honor* and *labor* is official in Canada, but practically all the Canadian newspapers omit it. In the same way the American flat a has swept whole sections of the country, and American slang is everywhere used, and the American common speech prevails almost universally in the newer provinces. More remarkable is the influence that American has exerted upon the speech of Australia and upon the crude dialects of Oceanica and the Far East. One finds such obvious Americanisms as *tomahawk, boss, bush, canoe, go finish* (=*to die*) and *pickaninny* in Beach-la-Mar[24] and more of them in Pigeon English. And one observes a very large number of American words and phrases in the slang of Australia. The Australian common speech, in pronunciation and intonation, resembles Cockney English, and a great many Cockneyisms are in it, but despite the small number of Americans in the Antipodes it has adopted, of late, so many

Americanisms that a Cockney visitor must often find it difficult. Among them are the verb and verb-phrases, *to beef, to biff, to bluff, to boss, to break away, to chase one's self, to chew the rag, to chip in, to fade away, to get it in the neck, to back and fill, to plug along, to get sore, to turn down* and *to get wise*; the substantives, *dope, boss, fake, creek, knockout-drops* and *push* (in the sense of *crowd*); the adjectives, *hitched* (in the sense of *married*) and *tough* (as before *luck*), and the adverbial phrases, *for keeps* and *going strong*.[25]Here, in direct competition with English locutions, and with all the advantages on the side of the latter, American is making steady progress.

"This American language, " says a recent observer, "seems to be much more of a pusher than the English. For instance, after eight years' occupancy of the Philippines it was spoken by 800, 000, or 10 per cent, of the natives, while after an occupancy of 150 of India by the British, 3, 000, 000, or one per cent, of the natives speak English."[26] I do vouch for the figures. They may be inaccurate, in detail, but they at least state what seems to be a fact. Behind that fact are phenomena which certainly deserve careful study, and, above all, study divested of unintelligent prejudice. The attempt to make American uniform with English has failed ingloriously; the neglect of its investigation is an evidence of snobbishness that is a folly of the same sort. It is useless to dismiss the growing peculiarities of the American vocabulary and of grammar and syntax in the common speech as vulgarisms beneath serious notice. Such vulgarisms have a way of intrenching themselves, and gathering dignity as they grow familiar. "There are but few forms in use, " says Lounsbury, "which, judged by a standard previously existing, would not be regarded as gross barbarisms."[27] Each language, in such matters, is a law unto itself, and each vigorous dialect, particularly if it be spoken by millions, is a law no less. "It would be as wrong, " says Sayce, "to use *thou* for the nominative *thee* in the Somersetshire dialect as it is to say *thee art* instead of *you are* in the Queen's English." All the American dialect needs, in the long run, to make even pedagogues acutely aware of it, is a poet of genius to venture into it, as Chaucer ventured into the despised English of his day, and Dante into the Tuscan dialect, and Luther, in his translation of the Bible, into peasant German. Walt Whitman made a half attempt and then drew back; Lowell, perhaps, also heard the call, but too soon. The Irish dialect of English, vastly less important than the American, has already had its interpreters—Douglas Hyde, John Milington Synge and Augusta Gregory—and with what extraordinary results we all know. Here we have writing that is still indubitably English, but English rid of its artificial restraints and broken to the less self-conscious grammar and syntax of a simple and untutored folk. Synge, in his preface to "The Playboy of the Western World, "[28] tells us how he got his gypsy phrases "through a chink in the floor of the old Wicklow house where I was staying, that let me hear what was being said by the servant girls in the kitchen." There is no doubt, he goes on, that "in the happy ages of literature striking and beautiful phrases were as ready to the story-teller's or the playwright's hand as the rich cloaks and dresses of his time. It is probable that when the Elizabethan dramatist took his ink-horn and sat down to his work he used many phrases that he had just heard, as he sat at dinner, from his mother or his children."

The result, in the case of the neo-Celts, is a dialect that stands incomparably above the tight English of the grammarians—a dialect so naïf, so pliant, so expressive, and, adeptly managed, so beautiful that even purists have begun to succumb to it, and it promises to leave lasting marks upon English style. The American dialect has not yet come to that stage. In so far as it is apprehended at all it is only in the sense that Irish-English was apprehended a generation ago—that is, as something uncouth and comic. But that is the way that new dialects always come in—through a drum-fire of cackles. Given the poet, there may suddenly come a day when our *theirns* and *would'a hads* will take on the barbaric stateliness of the peasant locutions of old Maurya in "Riders to the Sea." They seem grotesque and absurd today because the folks who use them seem grotesque and absurd. But that is a too facile logic and under it is a false assumption. In all human beings, if only understanding be brought to the business, dignity will be found, and that dignity cannot fail to reveal itself, soon or late, in the words and phrases with which they make known their high hopes and aspirations and cry out against the intolerable meaninglessness of life.

FOOTNOTES:

[1] Cambridge History of English Literature, vol. xiii, p. 167.

[2] Proverbs, Maxims and Phrases of All Ages; New York, 1905. This work extends to 1267 pages and contains about 30, 000 proverbs, admirably arranged.

[3] James Maitland: The American Slang Dictionary; Chicago, 1891.

[4] For example, the works of Villatte, Virmaitre, Michel, Rigaud and Devau.

[5] The best of these, of course, is Farmer and Henley's monumental Slang and Its Analogues, in seven volumes.

[6] Matthews' essay, The Function of Slang, is reprinted in Clapin's Dictionary of Americanisms, pp. 565-581.

[7] P. 199 *et seq.*

[8] For example, The Psychology of Unconventional Language, by Frank K. Sechrist, *Pedagogical Seminary*, vol. xx, p. 413, Dec., 1913, and The Philosophy of Slang, by E. B. Taylor, reprinted in Clapin's Dictionary of Americanisms, pp. 541-563.

[9] Olaf E. Bosson: Slang and Cant in Jerome K. Jerome's Works; Cambridge, 1911.

[10] Cambridge History of English Literature, vol. xii, p. 144.

[11] Curiously enough, the American language, usually so fertile in words to express shades of meaning, has no respectable synonym for *chicken*. In English there is *flapper*, in French there is *ingénue*, and in German there is *backfisch*. Usually either the English or the French word is borrowed.

[12] The Life and Growth of Language, New York, 1897, p. 113.

[13] *Cf.* Two Children in Old Paris, by Gertrude Slaughter; New York, 1918, p. 233. Another American popular saying, once embodied in a coon song, may be traced to a sentence in the prayer of the Old Dessauer before the battle of Kesseldorf, Dec. 15, 1745: "Or if Thou wilt not help me, don't help those Hundvögte."

[14] Modern English, p. 211.

[15] A Plea for the Queen's English, p. 244.

[16] Life and Letters of E. C. Stedman, ed. by Laura Stedman and George M. Gould; New York, 1910, vol. i, p. 477.

[17] Governor M. R. Patterson, of Tennessee, in an address before the National Anti-Saloon League at Washington, Dec. 13, 1917.

[18] Long before this the general question of the relative superiority of various languages had been debated in Germany. In 1796 the Berlin Academy offered a prize for the best essay on The Ideal of a Perfect Language. It was won by one Jenisch with a treatise bearing the sonorous title of A Philosophico-Critical Comparison and Estimate of Fourteen of the Ancient and Modern Languages of Europe, viz., Greek, Latin, Italian, Spanish, Portuguese, French, German, Dutch, English, Danish, Swedish, Polish, Russian and Lithuanian.

[19] Is English Destined to Become the Universal Language?, by W. Brackebusch; Göttingen, 1868.

[20] I take these figures from A Modern English Grammar, by H. G. Buehler; New York, 1900, p. 3.

[21] *World Almanac*, 1914, p. 63.

[22] The Geography of Great Languages, *World's Work*, Feb., 1908, p. 9907. Babbitt predicts that by the year 2000 English will be spoken by 1, 100, 000, 000 persons, as against 500, 000, 000 speakers of Russian, 300, 000, 000 of Spanish, 160, 000, 000 of German and 60, 000, 000 of French.

[23] P. 5 *et seq.*

[24] *Cf.* Beach-la-Mar, by William Churchill, former United States consul-general in Samoa and Tonga. The pamphlet is published by the Carnegie Institution of Washington.

[25] A glossary of latter-day Australian slang is in Doreen and the Sentimental Bloke, by C. J. Dennis; New York, 1916.

[26] The American Language, by J. F. Healy; Pittsburgh, 1910, p. 6.

[27] History of the English Language, p. 476.

[28] Dublin, 1907. See also ch. ii of Ireland's Literary Renaissance, by Ernest A. Boyd; New York, 1916.

Bibliography

(With a few exceptions, this bibliography is restricted to books and articles consulted by the author in preparing the present work. It embraces all the literature that he has found useful.)

Abeille, Luciano: El idioma national de los argentinos; Paris, 1900.

Alford, Henry: A Plea for the Queen's English; London, 1863.

Allen, E. A.: The Origin in Literature of Vulgarisms, *Chautauquan*, Nov., 1890.

Allen, Grant: Americanisms (in Chambers' Encyclopaedia, new ed.; Phila., 1906, vol. i).

American Medical Association: Style-book; Chicago, 1915.

Anon.: *Art.* Americanisms, Everyman Encyclopaedia, ed. by Andrew Boyle; London, n. d.

---- *Art.* Americanisms, New International Encyclopaedia, 2nd ed., ed. by F. M. Colby and Talcott Williams; New York, 1917.

---- Americanisms, *London Academy*, March 2, 1889.

---- Americanisms, *Southern Literary Messenger*, Oct., 1848.

---- British Struggles With Our Speech, *Literary Digest*, June 19, 1915.

---- Don't Shy at *Journalist, Editor and Publisher*, June 27, 1914.

---- Good Form in England; New York, 1888.

---- I Speak United States, *London Saturday Review*, Sept. 22, 1894.

---- The King's English, *Paterson's Magazine*, Jan., 1817.

---- Our Strange New Language, *Literary Digest*, Sept. 16, 1916.

---- Polyglot Kuntze: schnellste Erlernung jeder Sprache ohne Lehrer: Amerikanisch; Bonn am Rhein, n. d.

---- Progress of Refinement, *New York Organ*, May 29, 1847.

---- Quick Lunch Lingo, *Literary Digest*, March 18, 1916.

---- They Spake With Diverse Tongues, *Atlantic Monthly*, July, 1909.

---- To Teach the American Tongue in Britain, *Literary Digest*, Aug. 9, 1913.

---- Word-Coining and Slang, *Living Age*, July 13, 1907.

Archer, William: America and the English Language, *Pall Mall Magazine*, Oct., 1898.

---- The American Language; New York, 1899.

Arona, Juan de: Diccionario de peruanismos; Lima, 1882.

Arthur, William: An Etymological Dictionary of Family and Christian Names; New York, 1857.

Ayres, Leonard P.: The Spelling Vocabularies of Personal and Business Letters (Circular E126, Division of Education, Russell Sage Foundation); New York, n. d.

Babbitt, Eugene H.: College Words and Phrases, *Dialect Notes*, vol. ii, pt. i, 1900.

---- The English of the Lower Classes in New York City and Vicinity, *Dialect Notes*, vol. i, pt. ix, 1896.

---- The Geography of the Great Languages, *World's Work*, Feb., 1908.

Bache, Richard Meade: Vulgarisms and Other Errors of Speech, 2nd ed.; Philadelphia, 1869.

Baker, Franklin T.: The Vernacular (in Munro's Principles of Secondary Education; New York, 1915, ch. ix).

Bardsley, Charles W.: Curiosities of Puritan Nomenclature; London, 1880.

Barentz, A. E.: Woordenboek der Engelsche spreektaal ... and Americanisms ...; Amsterdam, 1894.

Baring-Gould, S.: Family Names and Their Story; London, 1910.

Barker, Henry: British Family Names; London, 1894.

Barr, Robert: *Shall* and *Will*, *Bookman*, Dec., 1895.

Barrère, Albert (and Chas. G. Leland): A Dictionary of Slang, Jargon and Cant, 2 vols.; New York, 1889.

Barringer, G. A.: Étude sur l'Anglais parlé aux États Unis (la Langue Américaine), *Actes de la Société Philologique de Paris*, March, 1874.

Barthelmess, Harriet: Determining the Achievement of Pupils in Letter Writing, Bull. xvi, Dept. of Educational Investigation and Measurement, Boston Public Schools (School Document No. 6), 1918.

Bartlett, John Russell: A Glossary of Words and Phrases Usually Regarded as Peculiar to the United States; New York, 1848; 2nd ed. enlarged, Boston, 1859; 3rd ed., 1860; 4th ed., 1877.

Baumann, H.: Londinismen (Slang und Cant); 2nd ed.; Berlin, 1902.

Bean, C. Homer: How English Grammar Has Been Taught in America, *Education*, vol. xiv, no. 8, April, 1914.

Beauchamp, Wm. M.: Aboriginal Places Names of New York; Albany, 1907.

---- Indian Names in New York; Fayetteville (N. Y.), 1893.

Beck, T. Romeyn: Notes on Mr. Pickering's Vocabulary.... *Transactions of the Albany Institute*, vol. i, 1830.

Beidelman, William: The Story of the Pennsylvania Germans ... and Their Dialect; Easton (Pa.), 1898.

Bendelari, George: Curiosities of American Speech, *New York Sun*, Nov., 1895.

Benet, W. C.: Americanisms: English as Spoken and Written in the United States; Abbeville (S. C.), 1880.

Benton, Joel: The Webster Spelling-Book ..., *Magazine of American History*, Oct., 1883.

Bergström, G. A.: On Blendings of Synonyms or Cognate Expressions in English; Lund (Sweden), 1906.

Bibaud, Maximilien: Le Mémorial des Vicissitudes et des Progrès de la Langue Française en Canada; Montreal, 1879.

Blackmar, F. W.: Spanish-American Words, *Modern Language Notes*, vol. vi.

Blattner, Karl: Metoula-Sprachführer: Englisch; Ausgabe für Amerika; Berlin-Schöneberg, 1912.

Blue, Rupert, ed.: Nomenclature of Diseases and Conditions, U. S. Public Health Service, Misc. Pub. No. 16; Washington, 1916.

Bonnell, J. W.: Etymological Derivation of the Names of the States, *Journal of Education*, vol. xlvii, p. 378.

Bosson, Olaf E.: Slang and Cant in Jerome K. Jerome's Works; Cambridge, 1911.

Bowen, Edwin W.: Questions at Issue in Our English Speech; New York, 1914.

Boyd, Stephen G.: Indian Local Names; York (Pa.), 1885.

Brackebusch, W.: Is English Destined to Become the Universal Language of the World?; Göttingen, 1868.

Bradley, Henry: The Making of English; London, 1904.

Bradley, W. A.: In Shakespeare's America, *Harper's Magazine*, Aug., 1915.

Brandenburg, George C.: Psychological Aspects of Language, *Journal of Educational Psychology*, June, 1918.

Bridges, Robert: A Tract on the Present State of English Pronunciation; Oxford, 1913.

Bristed, Charles A.: The English Language in America (in Cambridge Essays; London, 1855).

Buck, Gertrude: Make-Believe Grammar, *School Review*, vol. xxii, Jan., 1909.

Buehler, H. G.: A Modern English Grammar; New York, 1900.

Buies, Arthur: Anglicismes et Canadianismes; Quebec, 1888.

Burch, G. J.: The Pronunciation of English by Foreigners; Oxford, 1911.

Burke, William: The Anglo-Irish Dialect, *Irish Ecclesiastical Record*, 1896.

Burton, Richard: American English, (in Literary Likings: Boston, 1899).

Buttmann, Philipp Karl: Lexilogus; London, 1846.

Carpenter, George R.: The Principles of English Grammar For the Use of Schools; New York, 1898.

Carpenter, W. H.: Dutch Contributions to the Vocabulary of English in America, *Modern Philology*, July, 1908.

Carter, Alice P.: American English, *Critic*, vol. xiii.

Century Magazine: Style-sheet; New York, 1915.

Channing, William Ellery: Essay on American Language and Literature, *North American Review*, Sept. 1815.

Chapin, Florence A.: Spanish Words That Have Become Westernisms, *Editor*, July 25, 1917.

Charters, W. W. (and Edith Miller): A Course of Study in Grammar Based Upon the Grammatical Errors of School Children of Kansas City, Mo., *University of Missouri Bulletin*, vol. xvi, no. 2, Jan., 1915.

Chesterton, Cecil: British Struggles With Our Speech (summary of art. in *New Witness*), *Literary Digest*, June 19, 1915.

Chicago Daily News: Style-book ...; Chicago, 1908.

Chicago, University of: Manual of Style ... 3rd ed.; Chicago, 1911.

Chubb, Percival: The Menace of Pedantry in the Teaching of English, *School Review*, vol. xx, Jan., 1912.

Churchill, William: Beach-la-mar: the Jargon or Trade Speech of the Western Pacific; Washington, 1911.

Clapin, Sylva: A New Dictionary of Americanisms ...; New York, (1902).

Clemens, Samuel L. (Mark Twain): Concerning the American Language (in The Stolen White Elephant: New York, 1888).

Cobb, Lyman: A Critical Review of the Orthography of Dr. Webster's Series of Books ...; New York, 1831.

---- New Spelling Book ...; New York, 1842.

Collins, F. Howard: Authors' & Printers' Dictionary, 4th ed., rev. by Horace Hart; London, 1912.

Combs, J. H.: Old, Early and Elizabethan English in the Southern Mountains, *Dialect Notes*, vol. iv, pt. iv, 1916.

Compton, A. G.: Some Common Errors of Speech; New York, 1898.

Coxe, A. Cleveland: Americanisms in England, *Forum*, Oct., 1886.

Crane, W. W.: The American Language, *Putnam's Monthly*, vol. xvi, p. 519.

---- Our Naturalized Names, *Lippincott's Magazine*, vol. lxiii, p. 575, April, 1899.

Crosland, T. W. H.: The Abounding American; London, 1907.

Cushing, J. S. Company: Preparation of Manuscript, Proof Reading, and Office Style at J. S. Cushing Company's; Norwood (Mass.), n. d.

Dana, Richard H., jun: A Dictionary of Sea Terms; London, 1841.

Dawson, A. H.: A Dictionary of English Slang and Colloquialisms; New York, 1913.

Dennis, C. J. Doreen and the Sentimental Bloke; New York, 1916.

Dialect Notes, vol. i, 1889-98; vol. ii, 1899-1904; vol. iii, 1905-12; vol. iv, 1913-16; vol. v, 1917-.

Douglas-Lithgow, R. A.: Dictionary of American Indian Place and Proper Names in New England; Salem (Mass.), 1909.

Dubbs, Joseph H.: A Study of Surnames; Lancaster (Pa.), 1886.

Dunlap, Fayette: A Tragedy of Surnames, *Dialect Notes*, vol. iv, pt. i, 1913.

Dunlap, Maurice P.: What Americans Talk in the Philippines, *American Review of Reviews*, Aug., 1913.

Dunn, Oscar: Glossaire Franco-Canadien; Quebec, 1880.

Dunstan, A. C.: Englische Phonetik; Berlin, 1912.

Earle, John: The Philology of the English Tongue; London, 1866; 5th ed., 1892.

---- A Simple Grammar of English Now in Use; London, 1898.

Eggleston, Edward: Wild Flowers of English Speech in America, *Century Magazine*, April, 1894.

Egli, Johann J.: Nomina Geographica, 2nd ed.; Zurich, 1893.

---- Der Völkergeist in den geographischen Namen; Zurich, 1894.

Elliott, A. M.: Speech-Mixture in French Canada: English and French, *American Journal of Philology*, vol. x, 1889, p. 133.

Elliott, John (and Samuel Johnson, Jr.): A Selected Pronouncing and Accented Dictionary ...; Suffield (Conn.), 1800.

Ellis, Alexander J.: On Early English Pronunciation, 4 vols.; London, 1869-89.

---- On Glosik, a Neu Sistem ov Inglish Spelling; London, 1870.

Elwyn, A. L.: A Glossary of Supposed Americanisms ...; Phila., 1859.

Emerson, Oliver Farrar: The Future of American Speech, *Dial*, vol. xiv.

---- A History of the English Language; New York, 1894.

English, Thomas Dunn: Irish in America, *New York Times*, Nov. 5, 1898.

Fallows, Samuel; Handbook of Briticisms, Americanisms, Colloquial and Provincial Words and Phrases; Chicago, 1883.

Farmer, John S.: Americanisms Old and New ...; London, 1889.

---- (and W. E. Henley): A Dictionary of Slang and Colloquial English; London, 1905.

---- (and W. E. Henley): Slang and its Analogues, 7 vols.; London, 1890-1904.

Ferguson, Robert: Surnames as a Science; London, 1883.

Fernald, F. A.: Ingglish az She iz Spelt; New York, 1885.

Ferraz, Juan Fernándes: Nahuatlismos de Costa Rica; San José de Costa Rica, 1892.

Field, Eugene: London letter in *Chicago News*, March 10, 1890.

Flaten, Nils: Notes on American-Norwegian, with a Vocabulary, *Dialect Notes*, vol. ii, pt. ii, 1900.

Flom, George T.: English Elements in Norse Dialects of Utica, Wisconsin, *Dialect Notes*, vol. ii, pt. iv, 1902.

Flügel, Felix: Die englische Philologie in Nordamerika, *Gersdorf's Repertorium*, 1852.

---- Die englische Sprache in Nordamerika, *Archiv für das Studium der neueren Sprachen und Literaturen*, band iv, heft i; Braunschweig, 1848.

Fowler, H. W. (and F. G. Fowler): The Concise Oxford Dictionary of Current English, 4th ed.; Oxford, 1914.

---- The King's English, 2nd ed.; Oxford, 1908.

Fowler, Wm. C.: The English Language ..., 2nd ed.; New York, 1855.

Franklin, Benjamin: Scheme for a New Alphabet and a Reformed Mode of Spelling; Phila., 1768.

Franzmeyer, F.: Studien über den Konsonantismus und Vokalismus der neuenglischen Dialekte; Strassburg, 1906.

Freeman, Edward A.: Some Points in American Speech and Customs, *Longman's Magazine*, Nov., 1882.

Funk & Wagnalls Company: Style-card; New York, 1914.

Geikie, A. S.: Canadian English, *Canadian Journal*, vol. ii, 1857, p. 344.

Gentry, Thomas G.: Family Names from the Irish, Anglo-Saxon, Anglo-Norman and Scotch; Phila., 1892.

Gerek, William (and others): Is There Really Such a Thing as the American Language?, *New York Sun*, March 10, 1918.

Giles, Richard: Slang and Vulgar Phrases; New York, 1913.

Gould, Edwin S.: Good English ...; New York, 1867.

Grade, P.: Das neger Englisch, *Anglia*, vol. xiv.

Graham, G. F.: A Book About Words; London, 1869.

Grandgent, C. H.: English in America, *Die Neueren Sprachen*, vol. ii, pp. 443 and 520.

----Fashion and the Broad *A*, *Nation*, Jan. 7, 1915.

----From Franklin to Lowell: a Century of New England Prounciation, *Publications of the Modern Language Association*, vol. ii.

---- Notes on American Pronouns, *Modern Language Notes*, vol. vi, p. 82; *ibid.*, p. 458.

de la Grasserie, Raoul: Étude scientifique sur l'argot et le parler populaire; Paris, 1907.

Green, B. W.: Word-book of Virginia Folk-speech; Richmond, 1899.

Greenough, James B. (and George L. Kittredge): Words and Their Ways in English Speech; New York, 1902.

Haldeman, S. S.: Pennsylvania Dutch ...; London, 1872.

Hale, Horatio: The Origin of Languages, *Proc. American Association for the Advancement of Science*, 1886.

Hale, W. G. (and others): Report of the Joint Committee on Grammatical Nomenclature Appointed by the National Education Association, the Modern Language Association of America, and the American Philological Association; Chicago, 1918.

[Hall, B. H.]: A Collection of College Words and Customs; Cambridge (Mass.), 1851; 2nd ed., 1856.

Hall, Fitzedward: English, Rational and Irrational, *Nineteenth Century*, Sept., 1880.

---- Modern English; New York, 1873.

---- Recent Exemplifications of False Philology; New York, 1872.

Halliwell (-Phillips), J. O.: A Dictionary of Archaic and Provincial Words, Obsolete Phrases, Proverbs and Ancient Customs ..., 2 vols.; London, 1847.

---- A Dictionary of Archaisms and Provincialisms, Containing Words Now Obsolete in England, All of Which are Familiar and in Common Use in America; 2nd ed., London, 1850.

Hancock, Elizabeth H.: Southern Speech, *Neale's Monthly*, Nov., 1913.

Hancock, T.: Newspaper English, *Academy*, Jan. 29, 1898.

Harrison, Henry: A Dictionary of the Surnames of the United Kingdom; London, 1912.

Harrison, James A.: Negro English, *Proc. American Philological Association*, 1885.

Hart, Horace: Rules for Compositors and Readers at the University Press, Oxford; 23rd ed.; London, 1914.

Hartt, Irene Widdemar: Americanisms, *Education*, vol. xiii.

Hastings, Basil MacDonald: More Americanisms (interview), *New York Tribune*, Jan. 19, 1913.

Hayden, Mary (and Marcus Hartog): The Irish Dialect of English: Its Origins and Vocabulary;*Fortnightly Review*, April and May, 1909.

Hays, H. M.: On the German Dialect Spoken in the Valley of Virginia, *Dialect Notes*, vol. iii, pt. iv, 1908.

Head, Edmund Walker: *Shall* and *Will*, or Two Chapters on Future Auxiliary Verbs; London, 1856.

Healy, J. F.: The American Language; Pittsburgh, 1910.

Helfenstein, James: A Comparative Grammar of the Teutonic Languages ...; London, 1870.

Hempl, George: Language Rivalry and Speech-Differentiation in the Case of Race-Mixture, *Tr. American Philological Assoc.*, vol. xxix, p. 31.

---- The Study of American English, *Chautauquan*, vol. xxii, p. 436.

Herrig, Ludwig: Die englische Sprache und Literatur in Nord-Amerika, *Der neueren Sprachen*, vol. xii, p. 24; vol. xiii, pp. 76 and 241; vol. xiv, p. 1.

Higginson, T. W.: American Flash Language in 1798, *Science*, May, 1885.

---- English and American Speech, *Harper's Bazar*, vol. xxx, p. 958.

Hill, Adams Sherman: Our English; New York, 1889.

Hodgins, Joseph L.: Our Common Speech, *New York Sun*, March 1, 1918.

Hoffman, C. F.: Philological Researches, *Literary World*, Aug. 21, 1847.

Holliday, Robert Cortes: Caun't Speak the Language (in Walking-Stick Papers; New York, 1918, p. 201).

Horn, W.: Historische neuenglische Grammatik; Strassburg, 1908.

---- Untersuchungen zur neuenglischen Lautgeschichte; Strassburg, 1905.

Hotten, John Camden: A Dictionary of Modern Slang, Cant and Vulgar Words ... London, 1859.

Howells, William Dean: The Editor's Study, *Harper's Magazine*, Jan., 1886.

Hurd, Seth T.: A Grammatical Corrector or Vocabulary of the Common Errors of Speech ...; Phila., 1847.

Inman, Thomas: On the Origin of Certain Christian and Other Names; Liverpool, 1866.

J. D. J.: American Conversation, *English Journal*, April, 1913.

James, Henry: The Question of Our Speech; Boston and New York, 1905.

Jespersen, Jens O. H.: The Growth and Structure of the English Language; Leipzig, 1905; 2nd ed., 1912.

---- A Modern Grammar on Historical Principles; 2 vols.; Heidelberg, 1909-14.

Johnson, Burges: The Everyday Profanity of Our Best People, *Century Magazine*, June, 1916.

Johnson, Samuel, Jr.: A School Dictionary ...; New Haven, (1798?).

Jones, Daniel: The Pronunciation of English; Cambridge, 1909.

Joyce, P. W.: English as We Speak It in Ireland, 2nd ed.; London, 1910.

Kaluza, Max: Historische Grammatik der englischen Sprache, 2 vols.; Berlin, 1900-1.

Keijzer, M.: Woordenboek van Americanismen ...; Gorinchem (Holland), 1854.

Kellner, Leon: Historical Outlines of English Syntax; London, 1892.

Kelton, Dwight H.: Indian Names of Places Near the Great Lakes; Detroit, 1888.

Ker, Edmund T.: River and Lake Names in the United States; New York, 1911.

Kleuz, H.: Schelten-Wörterbuch; Strassburg, 1910.

Knortz, Karl: Amerikanische Redensarten und Volksgebräuche, Leipzig, 1907.

Knox, Alexander: Glossary of Geographical and Topographical Terms; London, 1904.

Koehler, F.: Worterbuch der Amerikanismen ...; Leipzig, 1866.

Koeppel, Emil: Spelling-Pronunciation: Bemerkungen über den Einfluss des Schriftbildes auf den Laut in Englischen, *Quellen und Forschungen zur Sprach- und Culturgeschichte der Germanischen Völkes*, lxxxix; Strassburg, 1901.

Krapp, George Philip: Modern English; New York, 1910.

Krueger, G.: Was ist Slang, bezüglich Argot? (in Festschrift Adolf Taber; Braunschweig, 1905).

Kuhns, L. Oscar: The Origin of Pennsylvania Surnames, *Lippincott's Magazine*, vol. lix, p. 395, March, 1897.

Lacasse, R. P. Z.: Ces Jeunes-là, on ne les Comprend Plus (in Une Mine Produisant l'Or et l'Argent; Quebec, 1880, pp. 252-6).

Lang, Andrew: Americanisms, *London Academy*, March 2, 1895.

Lardner, Ring W.: You Know Me Al ... New York, 1916.

Latham, Edward: A Dictionary of Names, Nicknames and Surnames; London, 1904.

Latham, Robert G.: The English Language; London, 1841.

Learned, Marion D.: The Pennsylvania German Dialect, Part I; Baltimore, 1889.

Letzner, Karl: Worterbuch der englischen Volksprache Australiens und der englischen Mischsprachen; Halle, 1891.

Lewis, Calvin L.: A Handbook of American Speech; Chicago, 1916.

Lienemann, Oskar: Eigentümlichkeiten des Engl. d. Vereinigten Staaten nebst wenig bekannten Amerikanismen; Zittau, 1886.

Lighthall, W. D.: Canadian English, *Week* (Toronto), Aug. 16, 1889.

Littman, Enno: *23* and Other Numerical Expressions, *Open Court*, vol. xxii, 1908.

Lloyd, R. J.: Northern English; Leipzig, 1908.

Lodge, Henry Cabot: The Origin of Certain Americanisms, *Scribner's Magazine*, June, 1907.

---- Shakespeare's Americanisms (in Certain Accepted Heroes; New York, 1897).

Long, Charles M.: Virginia County Names; New York, 1908.

Long, Percy W.: Semi-Secret Abbreviations, *Dialect Notes*, vol. iv, pt. iii, 1915.

Lounsbury, Thomas R.: Americanisms Real or Reputed, *Harper's Magazine*, Sept. 1913.

---- Differences in English and American Usage, *Harper's Magazine*, July 1913.

---- The English Language in America, *International Review*, vol. viii, p. 472.

---- English Spelling and Spelling Reform; New York, 1909.

---- A History of the English Language, revised ed.; New York, 1907.

---- Linguistic Causes of Americanisms, *Harper's Magazine*, June, 1913.

---- Scotticisms and Americanisms, *Harper's Magazine*, Feb., 1913.

---- The Standard of Pronunciation in English; New York and London, 1904.

---- The Standard of Usage in English; New York and London, n. d.

---- What Americanisms Are Not, *Harper's Magazine*, March, 1913.

Low, Sidney: Ought American to be Taught in Our Schools?, *Westminster Gazette*, July 18, 1913.

Low, W. H.: The English Language; Baltimore, 1917.

Lowell, James Russell: prefaces to The Biglow Papers, 1st and 2nd series; Cambridge, 1848-66.

Lower, M. A.: Patronymica Brittanica; London, 1860.

Luick, K.: Studien zur englischen Lautgeschichte; Vienna, 1903.

Mackay, Charles: The Ascertainment of English, *Nineteenth Century*, Jan., 1890.

McKenna, L. B.: Surnames, Their Origin and Nationality; Quincy (Ill.), 1913.

Mackintosh, Duncan: Essai Raissoné sur la Grammaire et la Prononciation Anglais ...; Boston, 1797.

McLean, John: Western Americanisms (in The Indians: Their Manners and Customs; Toronto, 1889, pp. 197-201).

Macmillan Co.: Notes for the Guidance of Authors; New York, 1918.

Maitland, James: The American Slang Dictionary ...; Chicago, 1891.

March, Francis A.: Spelling Reform; Washington, 1893.

Marsh, George P.: Lectures on the English Language; New York, 1859; 4th ed., enlarged, 1870.

---- The Origin and History of the English Language; New York, 1862; rev. ed., 1885.

Maspero, J.: Singularidades del español de Buenos Ayres, *Memorias de la Sociedad de lingüistica de Paris*, tome ii.

Matthews, Brander: Americanisms and Britticisms ...; New York, 1892.

---- Is the English Language Decadent? *Yale Review*, April, 1918.

---- Outskirts of the English Language, *Munsey's Magazine*, Nov., 1913.

---- Parts of Speech; New York, 1901.

---- The Standard of Spoken English, *North American Review*, June, 1916.

---- Why Not Speak Your Own Language?, *Delineator*, Nov., 1917.

Mätzner, Eduard A. F.: Englische Grammatik, 2 vols.; Leipzig, 1860-65, 3rd ed., 1880-85; tr. by C. J. Grece, 3 vols., London, 1874.

Mead, Theo. H.: Our Mother Tongue; New York, 1890.

Mearns, Hugh: Our Own, Our Native Speech, *McClure's Magazine*, Oct., 1916; reprinted, *Literary Digest*, Sept. 30, 1916.

Melville, A. H.: An Investigation of the Function and Use of Slang, *Pedagogical Seminary*, vol. xix, 1912.

Membreño, Alberto: Hondureñismos; Tegucigalpa, 1895.

Mencken, H. L.: The American: His Language, *Smart Set*, Aug., 1913.

---- The American Language Again, *New York Evening Mail*, Nov. 22, 1917.

---- American Pronouns, *Baltimore Evening Sun*, Oct. 25, 1910.

---- The Curse of Spelling, *New York Evening Mail*, April 11, 1918.

---- England's English, *Baltimore Evening Sun*, Sept. 22, 1910.

---- How They Say It "Over There, " *New York Evening Mail*, Oct. 25, 1917.

---- More American, *Baltimore Evening Sun*, Oct. 20, 1910.

---- Moulding Our Speech, *Chicago Tribune*, Nov. 18, 1917.

---- The New Domesday Book, *New York Evening Mail*, April, 1918.

---- Nothing Dead About Language ..., *New York Evening Mail*, Sept. 28, 1917.

---- Notes on the American Language, *Baltimore Evening Sun*, Sept. 7, 1916.

---- Spoken American, *Baltimore Evening Sun*, Oct. 19, 1910.

---- The Two Englishes, *Baltimore Evening Sun*, Sept. 15, 1910.

Menner, Robert J.: Common Sense in Pronunciation, *Atlantic Monthly*, Aug., 1913.

---- The Pronunciation of English in America, *Atlantic Monthly*, March, 1915.

Molee, Elias: nu tutonish, an international union language; tacoma, 1906.(No capitals are used in the book. Even the title page is in lower case.)

---- Plea for an American Language ...; Chicago, 1888.

Molee, Elias: Pure Saxon English; or, Americans to the Front; Chicago, 1890.

---- Tutonish; Tacoma, (Wash.), n. d.

---- Tutonish, or, Anglo-German Union Tongue; Chicago, 1902.

Montgomery, M.: Types of Standard Spoken English; Strassburg, 1910.

Moon, G. Washington: The Dean's English, 7th ed.; New York, 1884.

Morris, Edward E.: Austral English ...; London, 1898.

Morris, Richard: Historical Outlines of English Accidence; London, 1872; 2nd ed. rev., 1895.

Murison, W.: Changes in the Language Since Shakespeare's Time, (in The Cambridge History of English Literature, vol. xiv.; New York, 1917).

Murray, James A. H.: A New English Dictionary ...; Oxford, 1888, etc.

Newcomen, George: Americanisms and Archaisms, *Academy*, vol. xlvii, p. 317.

Norton, Chas. Ledyard: Political Americanisms ...; New York and London, 1890.

Oliphant, Samuel Grant: The Clan of Fire and Forge, or, The Ancient and Honorable Smiths; Olivet (Mich.), 1910.

---- Surnames in Baltimore, *Baltimore Sunday Sun*, 62 weekly articles, Dec. 2, 1906-Jan. 26, 1908 inc.; index, Feb. 2, 9, 16, 23, 1908.

Oliphant, W. Kingston: The New English; London, 1886.

Onions, C. T.: Advanced English Syntax; London, 1894.

Palmer, A. Smythe: The Folk and Their Word-Lore; London, 1904.

Paul, C. K.: The American Language, *Month*, vol. xciv.

Paul, Hermann O. T.: Grundriss der germanischen Philologie, rev. ed., 3 vols.; Strassburg, 1901-1909.

---- Prinzipien der Sprachgeschichte; Halle, 1886; 4th ed., 1909; tr. as Principles of the History of Language by H. A. Strong; London, 1888; rev. ed., 1891.

Payne, James E. (and others): Style Book: a Compilation of Rules Governing Executive, Congressional, and Departmental Printing, Including the *Congressional Record*; Washington, 1917.

Pearson, T. R.: The Origin of Surnames, *Good Words*, June, 1897.

Pettman, Charles: Africanderisms: a Glossary of South African Colloquial Words and Phrases; London, 1913.

Phipson, Evascutes A.: British vs. American English, *Dialect Notes*, vol. i, pt. i, 1889.

Pickering, John: A Vocabulary or Collection of Words and Phrases Which Have Been Supposed to be Peculiar to the United States of America ...; Boston, 1816.

Pound, Louise: British and American Pronunciation, *School Review*, June, 1915.

---- Domestication of the Suffix *-fest*, *Dialect Notes*, vol. iv, pt. v, 1916.

---- Vogue Affixes in Present-Day Word-Coinage, *Dialect Notes*, vol. v, pt. i, 1918.

---- Word-Coinage and Modern Trade Names, *Dialect Notes*, vol. iv, pt. i, 1913.

Poutsma, H.: A Grammar of Late Modern English, 2 vols.; Groningen, 1904-5.

Prince, J. Dyneley: The Jersey Dutch Dialect, *Dialect Notes*, vol. iii, pt. vi, 1910.

Proctor, Richard A.: Americanisms, *Knowledge*, vol. viii.

---- English and American-English, *New York Tribune*, Aug. 14, 1881.

----"English as She is Spoke" in America, *Knowledge*, vol. vi.

Ralph, Julian: The Language of the Tenement-Folk, *Harper's Weekly*, vol. xli, p. 30.

Rambeau, A.: Amerikanisches, *Der neueren Sprachen*, vol. ii, p. 53.

Ramos y Duarte, Félis: Diccionario de mejicanismos ..., 2nd ed.; Mexico, 1898.

Read, Richard P.: The American Language, *New York Sun*, March 7, 1918.

---- The American Tongue, *New York Sun*, Feb. 26, 1918.

Read, William A.: The Southern *R*, *Louisiana State University Bull.*, Feb. 1910.

---- Variant Pronunciations in the New South, *Dialect Notes*, vol. iii, pt. vii, 1911.

Rippmann, W.: The Sounds of Spoken English; London, 1906.

Riverside Press: Handbook of Style in Use at the Riverside Press, Cambridge, Mass.; Boston and New York, 1913.

Root, E.: American and British Enunciation, *Lippincott's*, Sept., 1911.

Rupp, Israel D.: A Collection of ... Names of German, Swiss, Dutch, French and Other Immigrants in Pennsylvania from 1727 to 1776, 2nd rev. ed.; Phila., 1876.

Russell, T. Baron: Current Americanisms; London, 1893.

Salverte, Eusèbe: History of the Names of Men, Nations and Places, tr. by L. H. Mordacque, 2 vols.; London, 1862-4.

Sanchez, Jesus: Glosario de Voces Castellanas derivadas Nahüatl ó Mexicano; n. p., n. d.

Sanchez, Nellie van de Grift: Spanish and Indian Place Names of California; San Francisco, 1914.

Sanz, S. Monner: Notas al Castellano en America; Buenos Ayres, 1903.

Sayce, A. H.: Introduction to the Science of Language, 2 vols.; 4th ed., London, 1900.

Schele de Vere, M.: Americanisms: the English of the New World; New York, 1872.

---- Studies in English; New York, 1867.

Schulz, Carl B.: The King's English at Home, *New York Evening Mail*, Oct. 29, 1917.

Scott, Fred. N.: The Pronunciation of Spanish-American Words, *Modern Language Notes*, vol. vi.

---- Verbal Taboos, *School Review*, vol. xx, 1912, pp. 366-78.

Searle, William G.: Onomasticon Anglo-Saxonicum; Cambridge, 1897.

Sechrist, Frank K.: The Psychology of Unconventional Language, *Pedagogical Seminary*, vol. xx, Dec., 1913.

Seeman, B.: Die Volksnamen der amerikanischen Pflanzen; Hannover, 1851.

Shute, Samuel M.: A Manual of Anglo-Saxon; New York, 1867.

Skeat, W. W.: English Dialects From the Eighth Century to the Present Day; Cambridge, 1911.

---- An Etymological Dictionary of the English Language; Oxford, 1882; 4th ed., 1910.

---- A Primer of Classical and English Philology; Oxford, 1905.

Smalley, D. S.: American Phonetic Dictionary of the English Language; Cincinnati, 1855.

Smart, B. H.: A Practical Grammar of English Pronunciations; London, 1810.

Smith, Chas. Forster: Americanisms, *Southern Methodist Quarterly*, Jan., 1891.

---- On Southernisms, *Trans. American Philological Association*, 1883.

Soames, Laura: Introduction to English, French and German Phonetics; New York, 1899.

Sproull, Wm. O.: Hebrew and Rabbinical Words in Present Use, *Hebraica*, Oct., 1890.

Stearns, Edward J.: A Practical Guide to English Pronunciation for the Use of Schools; Boston, 1857.

Storm, J.: Englische Philologie; Leipzig, 1896.

Stratton, Clarence: Are You Uhmurican or American?, *New York Times*, July 22, 1917.

---- The New Emphasis of Oral English, *English Journal*, Sept., 1917.

Sunden, Karl: Contributions to the Study of Elliptical Words in Modern English; Upsala, 1904.

Sweet, Henry: A Handbook of Phonetics; London, 1877.

---- A History of English Sounds; London, 1876; Oxford, 1888.

---- The History of Language; London, 1900.

---- A New English Grammar, Logical and Historical, 2 vols.; Oxford, 1892-8; new ed., 1900-03.

---- The Practical Study of Languages; London, 1900.

---- A Primer of Spoken English; Oxford, 1900.

---- The Sounds of English; Oxford, 1908.

Swinton, William: Rambles Among Words; New York, n. d.

Tallichet, H.: A Contribution Towards a Vocabulary of Spanish and Mexican Words Used in Texas, *Dialect Notes*, vol. i, pt. iv.

Tamson, George J.: Word-Stress in English; Halle, 1898.

Tardivel, J. P.: L'Anglicisme: Voilà l'Ennemi; Quebec, 1880.

Taylor, Isaac: Words and Places, 3rd ed. rev.; London, 1873.

Thom, Wm. T.: Some Parallelisms Between Shakespeare's English and the Negro-English of the United States, *Shakespeariana*, vol. i, p. 129.

Thornton, Richard H.: An American Glossary ..., 2 vols.; Phila. and London, 1912.

Toller, T. N.: Outlines of the History of the English Language; Cambridge, 1900.

Tooker, William W.: Indian Names of Places in the Borough of Brooklyn; New York, 1901.

Toro y Gisbert, Miguel de: Americanismos; Paris, n. d.

Trench, Richard C.: English Past and Present; London, 1855; rev. ed., 1905.

---- On the Study of Words; London, 1851; rev. ed., 1904.

Trumbull, J. Hammond: The Composition of Indian Geographical Names, *Collection of the Conn. Historical Society*, vol. ii.

Tucker, Gilbert M.: American English: *North American Review*, April, 1883.

---- American English, a Paper Read Before the Albany Institute, July 6, 1882, With Revision and Additions; Albany, 1883.

---- Our Common Speech; New York, 1895.

Van der Voort, J. H.: Hedendaagsche Amerikanismen; Gouda (Holland), 1894.

Vizetelly, Frank H.: A Desk-book of 25, 000 Words Frequently Mispronounced; New York and London, 1917.

---- Essentials of English Speech, 2nd ed.; New York and London, (1917).

---- The Foreign Element in English, *New Age*, Oct., 1913.

Wagner, Leopold: Names and Their Meaning; London, 1892.

Walter, G. F.: Phillimore: Sporting Terms in Common Speech, *Monthly Review*, Nov., 1906.

Wardlaw, Patterson: Simpler English, *Bulletin of the University of South Carolina*, no. 38, pt. iii, July, 1914.

Ware, J. Redding: Passing English of the Victorian Era ...; London, n. d.

Warnock, Elsie L.: Terms of Approbation and Eulogy in American Dialect Speech, *Dialect Notes*, vol. iv, pt. i, 1913.

Warren, Arthur: Real Americanisms, *Boston Herald*, Nov. 20, 1892.

Watts, Harvey M.: Prof. Lounsbury and His Rout of the Dons on Americanisms, *Philadelphia Public Ledger*, April 16, 1915.

Webster, Noah: An American Dictionary of the English Language ... 2 vols.; New York, 1828.

---- The American Spelling Book ... Being the First Part of a Grammatical Institute of the English Language ... Boston, 1783.

---- The American Spelling Book ... revised ed.; Sandbornton (N. H.), 1835.

---- A Compendious Dictionary of the English Language; Hartford, 1806.

---- A Dictionary of the English Language Compiled for the Use of Common Schools in the United States; Boston, 1807.

---- A Dictionary of the English Language ... for Common Schools ...; Hartford, 1817.

---- Dissertations on the English Language ...; Boston, 1789.

---- The Elementary Spelling Book ... Phila., 1829.

---- The Elementary Spelling Book ... revised ed.; New York, 1848.

---- A Grammatical Institute of the English Language ... in Three Parts; Part 1, Containing a New and Accurate Standard of Pronunciation ...; Hartford, 1783.

---- A Letter to the Hon. John Pickering on the Subject of His Vocabulary; Boston, 1817.

---- The New American Spelling Book ...; New Haven, 1833.

Weekley, Ernest: Surnames; London, 1916.

Wetherill, Georgine N.: The American Language, *Anglo-Continental*, Jan., 1894.

Wheatley, Henry B.: Chronological Notices of the Dictionaries of the English Language, *Transactions of the Philological Society* (London), 1865.

White, D. S.: American Pronunciation, *Journal of Education*, July 13, 1916.

White, Richard Grant: Americanisms, parts i-viii, *Atlantic Monthly*, April, May, July, Sept., Nov., 1878; Jan., March, May, 1879.

---- British Americanisms, Atlantic Monthly, May, 1880.

---- Every-Day English ...; Boston, 1880.

---- Some Alleged Americanisms, *Atlantic Monthly*, Dec., 1883.

White, Richard Grant: Words and Their Uses, Past and Present; Boston, 1872; rev. ed., New York, 1876.

Whitman, Walt; Slang in America, *North American Review*, vol. cxli, p. 431.

Whitney, William D.: The Life and Growth of Language, New York, 1875.

---- Language and the Study of Language; New York, 1867.

Wilcox, W. H.: The Difficulties Created by the Grammarians are to be Ignored, *Atlantic Educational Journal*, Nov., 1912.

Williams, R. O.: Our Dictionaries; New York, 1890.

---- Some Questions of Good English; New York, 1897.

Wilson, A. J.: A Glossary of Colloquial Slang and Technical Terms in Use in the Stock Exchange and in the Money Market; London, 1895.

Wittmann, Elizabeth: Clipped Words, *Dialect Notes*, vol. iv, pt. ii, 1914.

Wright, Joseph: An English Dialect Dictionary, 6 vols.; London, 1896-1905.

---- The English Dialect Grammar; Oxford, 1905.

Wundt, W.: Die Sprache; Leipzig, 1900.

Wyld, H. C. K.: The Growth of English; London, 1907.

---- The Historical Study of the Mother Tongue; New York, 1906.

---- The Study of Living Popular Dialects and Its Place in the Modern Science of Language; London, 1904.

Yule, Henry (and A. C. Burnell). Hobson-Jobson: a Glossary of Anglo-Indian Words and Phrases, and of Kindred Terms, Etymological, Historical, Geographical and Discursive; new ed., ed. by Wm. Crooke; London, 1903.

List of Words and Phrases

The parts of speech are indicated only when it is desirable for clearness. The following abbreviations are used:

a. adjective	*pro.* pronoun
adv. adverb	*suf.* suffix
art. article	*v.* verb
n. noun	*vp.* verb-phrase.
pref. prefix	

THE END

BOOK THREE.
THE PHILOSOPHY OF FRIEDRICH NIETZSCHE

I shall be told, I suppose, that my philosophy is comfortless—because I speak the truth; and people prefer to believe that everything the Lord made is good. If you are one such, go to the priests, and leave philosophers in peace! *Arthur Schopenhauer.*

PREFACE TO THE THIRD EDITION

When this attempt to summarize and interpret the principal ideas of Friedrich Wilhelm Nietzsche was first published, in the early part of 1908, several of his most important books were yet to be translated into English and the existing commentaries were either fragmentary and confusing or frankly addressed to the specialist in philosophy. It was in an effort to make Nietzsche comprehensible to the general reader, at sea in German and unfamiliar with the technicalities of the seminaries, that the work was undertaken. It soon appeared that a considerable public had awaited that effort, for the first edition was quickly exhausted and there was an immediate demand for a special edition in England. The larger American edition which followed has since gone the way of its predecessor, and so the opportunity offers for a general revision, eliminating certain errors in the first draft and introducing facts and opinions brought forward by the publication of Dr. Oscar Levy's admirable complete edition of Nietzsche in English and by the appearance of several new and informative biographical studies, and a large number of discussions and criticisms. The whole of the section upon Nietzsche's intellectual origins has been rewritten, as has been the section on his critics, and new matter has been added to the biographical chapters. In addition, the middle portion of the book has been carefully revised, and a final chapter upon the study of Nietzsche, far more extensive than the original bibliographical note, has been appended. The effect of these changes, it is believed, has been to increase the usefulness of the book, not only to the reader who will go no further, but also to the reader who plans to proceed to Nietzsche's own writings and to the arguments of his principal critics and defenders.

That Nietzsche has been making progress of late goes without saying. No reader of current literature, nor even of current periodicals, can have failed to notice the increasing pressure of his ideas. When his name was first heard in England and America, toward the end of the nineties, he suffered much by the fact that few of his advocates had been at any pains to understand him. Thus misrepresented, he took on the aspect of an horrific intellectual hobgoblin, half Bakúnin and half Byron, a sacrilegious and sinister fellow, the father of all the wilder ribaldries of the day. In brief, like Ibsen before him, he had to bear many a burden that was not his. But in the course of time the truth about him gradually precipitated itself from this cloud of unordered enthusiasm, and his principal ideas began to show themselves clearly. Then the discovery was made that the report of them had been far more appalling than the substance. Some of them, indeed, had already slipped into respectable society in disguise, as the original inspirations of lesser sages, and others, on examination, turned out to be quite harmless, and even comforting. The worst that could be said of most of them was that they stood in somewhat violent opposition to the common platitudes, that they were a bit vociferous in denying this planet to be the best of all possible worlds. Heresy, of course, but falling, fortunately enough, upon ears fast growing attuned to heretical music. The old order now had fewer to defend it than in days gone by. The feeling that it must yield to something better, that contentment must give way to striving and struggle, that any change was better than no change at all— this feeling was abroad in the world. And if the program of change that Nietzsche offered was startling at first hearing, it was at least no more startling than the programs offered by other reformers. Thus he got his day in court at last and thus he won the serious attention of open-minded and reflective folk.

Not, of course, that Nietzsche threatens, today or in the near future, to make a grand conquest of Christendom, as Paul conquered, or the unknown Father of Republics. Far from it, indeed. Filtered through the comic sieve of a Shaw or sentimentalized by a Roosevelt, some of his ideas show a considerable popularity, but in their original state they are not likely to inflame millions. Broadly viewed, they stand in direct opposition to every dream that soothes the slumber of mankind in the mass, and therefore mankind in the mass must needs be suspicious of them, at least for years to come. They are pre-eminently for the man who is *not* of the mass, for the man whose head is lifted, however little, above the common level. They justify the success of that man, as Christianity justifies the failure of the man below. And so they give no promise of winning the race in general from its old idols, despite the fact that the pull of natural laws and of elemental appetites is on their side. But inasmuch as an idea, to make itself felt in the world, need not convert the many who serve and wait but only the few who rule, it must be manifest that the Nietzschean creed, in the long run, gives promise of exercising a very real influence upon human thought. Reduced to a single phrase, it may be called a counterblast to sentimentality—and it is precisely by breaking down sentimentality, with its fondness for moribund gods, that human progress is made. If

Nietzsche had left no other vital message to his time, he would have at least forced and deserved a hearing for his warning that Christianity is a theory for those who distrust and despair of their strength, and not for those who hope and fight on.

To plat his principal ideas for the reader puzzled by conflicting reports of them, to prepare the way for an orderly and profitable reading of his own books—such is the purpose of the present volume. The works of Nietzsche, as they have been done into English, fill eighteen volumes as large as this one, and the best available account of his life would make three or four more. But it is sincerely to be hoped that the student, once he has learned the main paths through this extensive country, will proceed to a diligent and thorough exploration. Of all modern philosophers Nietzsche is the least dull. He was undoubtedly the greatest German prose writer of his generation, and even when one reads him through the English veil it is impossible to escape the charm and color of his phrases and the pyrotechnic brilliance of his thinking.

MENCKEN.

BALTIMORE, November, 1913.

PART ONE. NIETZSCHE THE MAN

I. BOYHOOD AND YOUTH

Friedrich Nietzsche was a preacher's son, brought up in the fear of the Lord. It is the ideal training for sham-smashers and freethinkers. Let a boy of alert, restless intelligence come to early manhood in an atmosphere of strong faith, wherein doubts are blasphemies and inquiry is a crime, and rebellion is certain to appear with his beard. So long as his mind feels itself puny beside the overwhelming pomp and circumstance of parental authority, he will remain docile and even pious. But so soon as he begins to see authority as something ever finite, variable and all-too-human—when he begins to realize that his father and his mother, in the last analysis, are mere human beings, and fallible like himself—then he will fly precipitately toward the intellectual wailing places, to think his own thoughts in his own way and to worship his own gods beneath the open sky.

As a child Nietzsche was holy; as a man he was the symbol and embodiment of all unholiness. At nine he was already versed in the lore of the reverend doctors, and the pulpit, to his happy mother—a preacher's daughter as well as a preacher's wife—seemed his logical and lofty goal; at thirty he was chief among those who held that all pulpits should be torn down and fashioned into bludgeons, to beat out the silly brains of theologians.

The awakening came to him when he made his first venture away from the maternal apron-string and fireside: when, as a boy of ten, he learned that there were many, many men in the world and that these men were of many minds. With the clash of authority came the end of authority. If A. was right, B. was wrong—and B. had a disquieting habit of standing for one's mother, one's grandmother or the holy prophets. Here was the beginning of intelligence in the boy—the beginning of that weighing and choosing faculty which seems to give man at once his sense of mastery and his feeling of helplessness. The old notion that doubt was a crime crept away. There remained in its place the new notion that the only real crime in the world—the only unmanly, unspeakable and unforgivable offense against the race—was unreasoning belief. Thus the orthodoxy of the Nietzsche home turned upon and devoured itself.

The philosopher of the superman was born on October 15th, 1844, at Röcken, a small town in the Prussian province of Saxony. His father, Karl Ludwig Nietzsche, was a country pastor of the Lutheran Church and a man of eminence in the countryside. But he was more than a mere rural worthy, with an outlook limited by the fringe of trees on the horizon, for in his time he had seen something of the great world and had even played his humble part in it. Years before his son Friedrich was born he had been tutor to the children of the Duke of Altenburg. The duke was fond of him and took him, now and then, on memorable and eventful journeys to Berlin, where that turbulent monarch, King Friedrich Wilhelm IV, kept a tinsel court and made fast progress from imbecility to acute dementia. The king met the young tutor and found him a clever and agreeable person, with excellent opinions regarding all those things whereon monarchs are wont to differ with mobs. When the children of the duke became sufficiently saturated with learning, the work of Pastor Nietzsche at Altenburg was done and he journeyed to Berlin to face weary days in the anterooms of ecclesiastical magnates and jobbers of places. The king, hearing by chance of his presence and remembering him pleasantly, ordered that he be given without delay a vicarage worthy of his talents. So he was sent to Röcken, and there, when a son was born to him, he called the boy Friedrich Wilhelm, as a graceful compliment to his royal patron and admirer.

There were two other children in the house. One was a boy, Josef, who was named after the Duke of Altenburg, and died in infancy in 1850. The other was a girl, Therese Elisabeth Alexandra, who became in after years her brother's housekeeper, guardian angel and biographer. Her three names were those of the three noble children her father had grounded in the humanities. Elisabeth—who married toward middle age and is best known as Frau Förster-Nietzsche—tells us practically all that we know about the Nietzsche family and the private life of its distinguished son[52]. The clan came out of Poland, like so many other families of Eastern Germany, at the time of the sad, vain wars. Legend maintains that it was noble in its day and Nietzsche himself liked to think so. The name, says Elisabeth, was originally Nietzschy. "Germany is a great nation, " Nietzsche would say, "only because its people have so much Polish blood in their veins.... I am proud of my Polish descent. I remember that in former times a Polish noble, by his simple veto, could overturn the resolution of a popular assembly. There were giants in Poland in the time of my forefathers." He wrote a tract with the French title "*L'Origine de la famille de Nietzsche*" and presented the manuscript to his sister, as a document to be treasured and held sacred. She tells us that he was fond of maintaining that the Nietzsches had suffered greatly and fallen from vast grandeur for their opinions, religious and political. He had no proof of this, but it pleased him to think so.

Pastor Nietzsche was thrown from his horse in 1848 and died, after a lingering illness, on July 28th, 1849, when Friedrich was barely five years

---

[52] "D*as Leben Friedrich Nietzsche's,* " 3 vols. Leipsic, 1895-7-9.

old. Frau Nietzsche then moved her little family to Naumburg-on-the-Saale—"a Christian, conservative, loyal city." The household consisted of the mother, the two children, their paternal grandmother and two maiden aunts—the sisters of the dead pastor. The grandmother was something of a bluestocking and had been, in her day, a member of that queer circle of intellectuals and amateurs which raged and roared around Goethe at Weimar. But that was in the long ago, before she dreamed of becoming the wife of one preacher and the mother of another. In the year '50 she was well of all such youthful fancies and there was no doubt of the divine revelations beneath her pious roof. Prayers began the day and ended the day. It was a house of holy women, with something of a convent's placidity and quiet exaltation. Little Friedrich was the idol in the shrine. It was the hope of all that he would grow up into a man inimitably noble and impossibly good.

Pampered thus, the boy shrank from the touch of the world's rough hand. His sister tells us that he disliked the bad little boys of the neighborhood, who robbed bird's nests, raided orchards and played at soldiers. There appeared in him a quaint fastidiousness which went counter to the dearest ideals of the healthy young male. His school fellows, in derision, called him "the little pastor" and took delight in waylaying him and venting upon him their grotesque and barbarous humor. He liked flowers and books and music and when he went abroad it was for solitary walks. He could recite and sing and he knew the Bible so well that he was able to dispute about its mysteries. "As I think of him, " said an old school-mate years afterward, "I am forced irresistibly into a thought of the 12-year-old Jesus in the Temple." "The serious introspective child, with his dignified politeness, " says his sister, "seemed so strange to other boys that friendly advances from either side were out of the question."

There is a picture of the boy in all the glory of his first long-tailed coat. His trousers stop above his shoe-tops, his hair is long and his legs seem mere airy filaments. As one gazes upon the likeness one can almost smell the soap that scoured that high, shiny brow and those thin, white cheeks. The race of such seraphic boys has died out in the world. Gone are their slick, plastered locks and their translucent ears! Gone are their ruffled cuffs and their spouting of the golden text!

Nietzsche wrote verses before he was ten: pious, plaintive verses that scanned well and showed rhymes and metaphors made respectable by ages of honorable employment. His maiden effort, so far as we know, was an elegy entitled "The Grave of My Father." Later on he became aware of material things and sang the praises of rose and sunset. He played the piano, too, and knew his Beethoven well, from the snares for the left hand in "*Für Elise*" to the raging tumults of the C minor symphony. One

Sunday—it was Ascension day—he went to the village church and heard the choir sing the Hallelujah Chorus from "The Messiah." Here was music that benumbed the senses and soothed the soul and, boy as he was, he felt its supreme beauty. That night he covered pages of ruled paper with impossible pot-hooks. He, too, would write music!

Later on the difficulties of thorough-bass, as it was taught in the abysmal German text-books of the time, somewhat dampened his ardor, but more than once during his youth he thought seriously of becoming a musician. His first really ambitious composition was a piano *pièce* called "*Mondschein auf der Pussta*"—"Moonlight on the Pussta"—the pussta being the flat Bohemian prairie. The family circle was delighted with this maiden *opus*, and we may conjure up a picture of little Friedrich playing it of a quiet evening at home, while mother, grandmother, sister and aunts gathered round and marvelled at his genius. In later life he wrote songs and sonatas, and—if an enemy is to be believed—an opera in the grand manner. His sister, in her biography, prints some samples of his music. Candor compels the admission that it is even worse than it sounds.

Nietzsche, at this time, still seemed like piety on a monument, but as much as he revered his elders and as much as he relied upon their infallibility, there were yet problems which assailed him and gave him disquiet. When he did not walk and think alone, his sister was his companion, and to her he opened his heart, as one might to a sexless, impersonal confessor. In her presence, indeed, he really thought aloud, and this remained his habit until the end of his life. His mind, awakening, wandered beyond the little world hedged about by doting and complacent women. Until he entered the gymnasium—that great weighing place of German brains—he shrank from open revolt, and even from the thought of it, but he could not help dwelling upon the mysteries that rose before him. There were things upon which the scriptures, search them as he might, seemed to throw no light, and of which mothers and grandmothers and maiden aunts did not discourse. "One day, " says Elisabeth, "when he was yet very young, he said to me: 'You mustn't expect me to believe those silly stories about storks bringing babies. Man is a mammal and a mammal must get his own children for himself.'" Every child, perhaps, ponders such problems, but in the vast majority knowledge must wait until it may enter fortuitously and from without. Nietzsche did not belong to the majority. To him ideas were ever things to be sought out eagerly, to be weighed calmly, to be tried in the fire. For weal or for woe, the cornerstones of his faith were brought forth, with sweat and pain, from the quarry of his own mind.

Nietzsche went to various village schools—public and private—until he was ten, dutifully trudging away each morning with knapsack and lunch-basket. He kissed his mother at the gate when he departed and she was waiting for him, with another kiss, when he returned. As happiness goes, his was probably a happy childhood. The fierce joy of boyish combat—of fighting, of robbing, of slaying—was never his, but to a child so athirst for knowledge, each fresh discovery—about the sayings of Luther, the lions of Africa, the properties of an inverted fraction—must have brought its thrill. But as he came to the last year of his first decade, unanswerable questions brought their discontent and disquiet—as they do to all of us. There is a feeling of oppression and poignant pain in facing problems that defy solution and facts that refuse to fit into ordered chains. It is only when mastery follows that the fine stimulation of conscious efficiency drowns out all moody vapors.

When Nietzsche went to the gymnasium his whole world was overturned. Here boys were no longer mute and hollow vessels, to be stuffed with predigested learning, but human beings whose approach to separate entity was recognized. It was possible to ask questions and to argue moot points, and teaching became less the administration of a necessary medicine and more the sharing of a delightful meal. Your German school-master is commonly a martinet, and his birch is never idle, but he has the saving grace of loving his trade and of readily recognizing true diligence in his pupils. History does not record the name of the pedagogue who taught Nietzsche at the Naumburg gymnasium, but he must have been one who ill deserved his oblivion. He fed the eager, inquiring mind of his little student and made a new boy of him. The old unhealthy, uncanny embodiment of a fond household's impossible dreams became more likeable and more human. His exclusiveness and fastidiousness were native and ineradicable, perhaps, for they remained with him, in some degree, his whole life long, but his thirst for knowledge and yearning for disputation soon led him to the discovery that there were other boys worth cultivating: other boys whose thoughts, like his own, rose above misdemeanor and horse-play. With two such he formed a quick friendship, and they were destined to influence him greatly to the end of his youth. They organized a club for mutual culture, gave it the sonorous name of "*Der litterarischen Vereinigung Germania*" ("The German Literary Association") and drew up an elaborate scheme of study. Once a week there was a meeting, at which each of the three submitted an essay or a musical composition to the critical scrutiny of the others. They waded out into the deep water. One week they discussed "The Infancy of Nations, " and after that, "The Dæmonic Element in Music, " "Napoleon III" and "Fatalism in History." Despite its praiseworthy earnestness, this program causes a smile—and so does the transformation of the retiring and well-scrubbed little Nietzsche we have been observing into the long, gaunt Nietzsche of 14, with a yearning for the companionship of his fellows, and a voice beginning to growcomically harsh and deep, and a mind awhirl with unutterable things.

Nietzsche was a brilliant and spectacular pupil and soon won a scholarship at Pforta, a famous and ancient preparatory academy not far away. Pforta, in those days, was of a dignity comparable to Eton's or Harrow's. It was a great school, but tradition overpowered it. Violent combats between amateur sages were not encouraged: it was a place for gentlemen to acquire Euclid and the languages in a decent, gentlemanly way, and not an arena for gawky country philosophers to prance about in. But Nietzsche, by this time, had already become a frank rebel and delighted in elaborating and controverting the doctrines of the learned doctors. He drew up a series of epigrams under the head of "*Ideen*" and thought so well of them that he sent them home, to astonish and alarm his mother. Some of them exhibited a quite remarkable faculty for pithy utterance—as, for example, "War begets poverty and poverty begets peace"—while others were merely opaque renderings of thoughts half formed. He began to believe in his own mental cunning, with a sincerity which never left him, and, as a triumphant proof of it, he drew up a series of syllogisms designed to make homesickness wither and die. Thus he wrestled with life's problems as his boy's eyes saw them.

All this was good training for the philosopher, but to the Pforta professors it gave disquiet. Nietzsche became a bit too sure of himself and a bit too arrogant for discipline. It seemed to him a waste of time to wrestle with the studies that every oafish baron's son and future guardsman sought to master. He neglected mathematics and gave himself up to the hair-splitting of the Eleatics and the Pythagoreans, the Sophists and the Skeptics. He pronounced his high curse and anathema upon geography and would have none of it. The result was that when he went up for final examination he writhed and floundered miserably and came within an ace of being set down for further and more diligent labor with his books. Only his remarkable mastery of the German language and his vast knowledge of Christian doctrine—a legacy from his pious childhood—saved him. The old Nietzsche—the shrinking mother's darling of Naumburg—was now but a memory. The Nietzsche that went up to Bonn was a young man with a touch of cynicism and one not a little disposed to pit his sneer against the jurisprudence of the world: a young man with a swagger, a budding moustache and a head full of violently novel ideas about everything under the sun.

Nietzsche entered Bonn in October, 1864, when he was just 20 years old. He was enrolled as a student of philology and theology, but the latter was a mere concession to family faith and tradition, made grudgingly, and after the first semester, the reverend doctors of exegetics knew him no more. At the start he thought the university a delightful place and its people charming. The classrooms and beer gardens were full of young Germans like himself, who debated the doings of Bismarck, composed eulogies of Darwin, sang Rabelaisian songs in bad Latin, kept dogs, wore ribbons on their walking sticks, fought duels, and drank unlimited steins of pale beer. In the youth of every man there comes over him a sudden yearning to be a good fellow: to be "Bill" or "Jim" to multitudes, and to go down into legend with Sir John Falstaff and Tom Jones. This melancholy madness seized upon Nietzsche during his first year at Bonn. He frequented the theatres and posed as a connoisseur of opera *bouffe,* malt liquor and the female form divine. He went upon students' walking tours and carved his name upon the mutilated tables of country inns. He joined a student corps, bought him a little cap and set up shop as a devil of a fellow. His mother was not poor, but she could not afford the outlays that these ambitious enterprises required. Friedrich overdrew his allowance and the good woman, no doubt, wept about it, as mothers will, and wondered that learning came so dear.

But the inevitable reaction followed. Nietzsche was not designed by nature for a hero of pot-houses and duelling sheds. The old fastidiousness asserted itself—that queer, unhealthy fastidiousness which, in his childhood, had set him apart from other boys, and was destined, all his life long, to make him shrink from too intimate contact with his fellow-men. The touch of the crowd disgusted him: he had an almost insane fear of demeaning himself. All of this feeling had been obscured for awhile, by the strange charm of new delights and new companions, but in the end, the gloomy spinner of fancies triumphed over the university buck. Nietzsche resigned from his student corps, burned his walking sticks, foreswore smoking and roistering, and bade farewell to Johann Strauss and Offenbach forever. The days of his youth—of his carefree, merry gamboling—were over. Hereafter he was all solemnity and all seriousness.

"From these early experiences, " says his sister, "there remained with him a life-long aversion to smoking, beer-drinking and the whole *biergemüthlichkeit*. He maintained that people who drank beer and smoked pipes were absolutely incapable of understanding him. Such people, he thought, lacked the delicacy and clearness of perception necessary to grasp profound and subtle problems."

II. THE BEGINNINGS OF THE PHILOSOPHER

At Bonn Nietzsche became a student of Ritschl, the famous philologist, [1] and when Ritschl left Bonn for Leipsic, Nietzsche followed him. All traces of the good fellow had disappeared and the student that remained was not unlike those sophomores of medieval Toulouse who "rose from bed at 4 o'clock, and having prayed to God, went at 5 o'clock to their studies, their big books under their arms, their inkhorns and candles in their hands." Between teacher and pupil there grew up a bond of strong friendship. Nietzsche was taken, too, under the wing of motherly old Frau Ritschl, who invited him to her afternoons of coffee and cinnamon cake and to her evening soirées, where he met the great men of the university world and the eminent strangers who came and went. To Ritschl the future philosopher owed many things, indeed, including his sound knowledge of the ancients, his first (and last) university appointment and his meeting with Richard Wagner. Nietzsche always looked back upon these days with pleasure and there was ever a warm spot in his heart for the kindly old professor who led him up to grace.

Two years or more were thus spent, and then, in the latter part of 1867, Nietzsche began his term of compulsory military service in the fourth regiment of Prussian field artillery. He had hoped to escape because he was near-sighted and the only son of a widow, but a watchful *oberst-lieutenant* found loopholes in the law and so ensnared him. He seems to have been some sort of officer, for a photograph of the period shows him with epaulets and a sword. But lieutenant or sergeant, soldiering was scarcely his forte, and he cut a sorry figure on a horse. After a few months of unwilling service, in fact, he had a riding accident and came near dying as his father had died before him. As it was he wrenched his breast muscles so badly that he was condemned by a medical survey and discharged from the army.

During his long convalescence he busied himself with philological studies and began his first serious professional work—essays on the Theogony of Hesiod, the sources of Diogenes Laërtius and the eternal strife between Hesiod and Homer. He also made an index to an elaborate collection of German historical fragments and performed odd tasks of like sort for various professors. In October, 1868, he returned to Leipsic—not as an undergraduate, but as a special student. This change was advantageous, for it gave him greater freedom of action and protected him from that student *bonhomie* he had learned to despise. Again old Ritschl was his teacher and friend and again Frau Ritschl welcomed him to her *salon* and gave him of her good counsel and her excellent coffee.

Meanwhile there had occurred something that was destined to direct and color the whole stream of his life. This was his discovery of Arthur Schopenhauer. In the 60's, it would appear, the great pessimist was still scarcely more than a name in the German universities, which, for all their later heterodoxy, clung long to their ancient first causes. Nietzsche knew nothing of him, and in the seminaries of Leipsic not a soul maintained him.

Of Kant and of Hegel there was talk unlimited, and of Lotze and Fichte there were riotous disputations that roared and raged about the class-room of Fechner, then the university professor of philosophy. But of Schopenhauer nothing was heard, and so, when Nietzsche, rambling through an old Leipsic bookshop, happened upon a second-hand copy of "*Die Welt als Wille und Vorstellung*"[2] a new world came floating into his view. This was in 1865.

"I took the book to my lodgings, " he said years afterward, "and flung myself on a sofa and read and read and read. It seemed as if Schopenhauer were addressing me personally. I felt his enthusiasm and seemed to see him before me. Every line cried aloud for renunciation, denial, resignation!"

So much for the first flush of the ecstasy of discovery. That Nietzsche entirely agreed with everything in the book, even in his wildest transports of admiration, is rather doubtful. He was but 21—the age of great passions and great romance—and he was athirst for some writing that would solve the problems left unanswered by the accepted sages, but it is probable that when he shouted the Schopenhauer manifesto loudest he read into the text wild variations of his own. The premises of the pessimist gave credit and order to thoughts that had been rising up in his own mind; but the conclusions, if he subscribed to them at all, led him far afield. No doubt he was like one of those fantastic messiahs of new cults who search the scriptures for testimony—and find it. Late in life, when he was accused of inconsistency in first deifying Schopenhauer and then damning him, he made this defense, and despite the derisive sneers of his enemies, it seemed a fairly good one.

Schopenhauer's argument, to put it briefly, was that the will to exist—the primary instinct of life—was the eternal first cause of all human actions, motives and ideas. The old philosophers of Christendom had regarded intelligence as the superior of instinct. Some of them thought that an intelligent god ruled the universe and that nothing happened without his knowledge and desire. Others believed that man was a free agent, that whatever he did was the result of his own thought and choice, and that it was right, in consequence, to condemn him to hell for his sins and to exalt him to heaven for any goodness he might chance to show. Schopenhauer turned all this completely about. Intelligence, he said, was not the source of will, but its effect. When life first appeared upon earth, it had but one aim and object: that of perpetuating itself. This instinct, he said, was still at the bottom of every function of all living beings. Intelligence grew out of the fact that mankind, in the course of ages, began to notice that certain manifestations of the will to live were followed by certain invariable results. This capacity of perceiving was followed by a capacity for remembering, which in turn produced a capacity for anticipating. An intelligent man, said Schopenhauer, was merely one who remembered so many facts (the result either of personal experience or of the transmitted experience of others) that he could separate them into groups and observe their relationship, one to the other, and hazard a close guess as to their future effects: *i.e.* could reason about them.

Going further, Schopenhauer pointed out that this will to exist, this instinct to preserve and protect life, this old Adam, was to blame for the unpleasant things of life as well as for the good things—that it produced avarice, hatred and murder just as well as industry, resourcefulness and courage—that it led men to seek means of killing one another as well as means of tilling the earth and procuring food and raiment. He showed, yet further, that its bad effects were a great deal more numerous than its good effects and so accounted for the fact—which many men before him had observed—that life, at best, held more of sorrow than of joy.[3]

The will-to-live, argued Schopenhauer, was responsible for all this. Pain, he believed, would always outweigh pleasure in this sad old world until men ceased to want to live—until no one desired food or drink or house or wife or money. To put it more briefly, he held that true happiness would be impossible until mankind had killed will with will, which is to say, until the will-to-live was willed out of existence. Therefore the happiest man was the one who had come nearest this end—the man who had killed all the more obvious human desires, hopes and aspirations—the solitary ascetic—the monk in his cell—the soaring, starving poet—the cloud-enshrouded philosopher.

Nietzsche very soon diverged from this conclusion. He believed, with Schopenhauer, that human life, at best, was often an infliction and a torture, but in his very first book he showed that he admired, not the ascetic who tried to escape from the wear and tear of life altogether, but the proud, stiff-necked hero who held his balance in the face of both seductive pleasure and staggering pain; who cultivated within himself a sublime indifference, so that happiness and misery, to him, became mere words, and no catastrophe, human or superhuman, could affright or daunt him.[4]

It is obvious that there is a considerable difference between these ideas, for all their similarity in origin and for all Nietzsche's youthful worship of Schopenhauer. Nietzsche, in fact, was so enamoured by the honesty and originality of what may be called the data of Schopenhauer's philosophy that he took the philosophy itself rather on trust and did not begin to inquire into it closely or to compare it carefully with his own ideas until after he had committed himself in a most embarrassing fashion. The same phenomena is no curiosity in religion, science or politics.

Before a realization of these differences quite dawned upon Nietzsche he was busied with other affairs. In 1869, when he was barely 25, he was appointed, upon Ritschl's recommendation, to the chair of classical philology at the University of Basel, in Switzerland, an ancient stronghold of Lutheran theology. He had no degree, but the University of Leipsic promptly made him a doctor of philosophy, without thesis or examination, and on April 13th he left the old home at Naumburg to assume his duties. Thus passed that pious household. The grandmother had died long before—in 1856—and one of the maiden aunts had preceded her to the grave by a year. The other, long ill, had followed in 1867. But Nietzsche's mother lived until 1897, though gradually estranged from him by his opinions, and his sister, as we know, survived him.

Nietzsche was officially professor of philology, but he also became teacher of Greek in the pedagogium attached to the University. He worked like a Trojan and mixed Schopenhauer and Hesiod in his class-room discourses upon the origin of Greek verbs and other such dull subjects. But it is not recorded that he made a very profound impression, except upon a relatively small circle. His learning was abysmal, but he was far too impatient and unsympathetic to be a good teacher. His classes, in fact, were never large, except in the pedagogium. This, however, may have been partly due to the fact that in 1869, as in later years, there were comparatively few persons impractical enough to spend their days and nights in the study of philology.

In 1870 came the Franco-Prussian war and Nietzsche decided to go to the front. Despite his hatred of all the cant of cheap patriotism and his pious thankfulness that he was a Pole and not a German, he was at bottom a good citizen and perfectly willing to suffer and bleed for his country. But unluckily he had taken out Swiss naturalization papers in order to be able to accept his appointment at Basel, and so, as the subject of a neutral state, he had to go to the war, not as a warrior, but as a hospital steward.

Even as it was, Nietzsche came near giving his life to Germany. He was not strong physically—he had suffered from severe headaches as far back as 1862—and his hard work at Basel had further weakened him. On the battlefields of France he grew ill. Diphtheria and what seems to have been cholera morbus attacked him and when he finally reached home again he was a neurasthenic wreck. Ever thereafter his life was one long struggle against disease. He suffered from migraine, that most terrible disease of the nerves, and chronic catarrh of the stomach made him a dyspeptic. Unable to eat or sleep, he resorted to narcotics, and according to his sister, he continued their use throughout his life. "He wanted to get well quickly, " she says, "and so took double doses." Nietzsche, indeed, was a slave to drugs, and more than once in after life, long before insanity finally ended his career, he gave evidence of it.

Despite his illness he insisted upon resuming work, but during the following winter he was obliged to take a vacation in Italy. Meanwhile he had delivered lectures to his classes on the Greek drama and two of these he revised and published, in 1872, as his first book, "*Die Geburt der Tragödie*" ("The Birth of Tragedy"). Engelmann, the great Leipsic publisher, declined it, but Fritsch, of the same city, put it into type.[5] This book greatly pleased his friends, but the old-line philologists of the time thought it wild and extravagant, and it almost cost Nietzsche his professorship. Students were advised to keep away from him, and during the winter of 1872-3, it is said, he had no pupils at all.

Nevertheless the book, for all its iconoclasm, was an event. It sounded Nietzsche's first, faint battle-cry and put the question mark behind many tilings that seemed honorable and holy in philology. Most of the philologists of that time were German savants of the comic-paper sort, and their lives were spent in wondering why one Greek poet made the name of a certain plant masculine while another made it feminine. Nietzsche, passing over such scholastic futilities, burrowed down into the heart of Greek literature. Why, he asked himself, did the Greeks take pleasure in witnessing representations of bitter, hopeless conflicts, and how did this form of entertainment arise among them? Later on, his conclusions will be given at length, but in this place it may be well to sketch them in outline, because of the bearing they have upon his later work, and even upon the trend of his life.

In ancient Greece, he pointed out at the start, Apollo was the god of art—of life as it was recorded and interpreted—and Bacchus Dionysus was the god of life itself—of eating, drinking and making merry, of dancing and roistering, of everything that made men acutely conscious of the vitality and will within them. The difference between the things they represented has been well set forth in certain homely verses addressed by Rudyard Kipling to Admiral Robley D. Evans, U. S. N.:

Zogbaum draws with a pencil

And I do things with a pen,

But you sit up in a conning tower,

Bossing eight hundred men.

To him that hath shall be given

And that's why these books are sent

To the man who has *lived* more stories

Than Zogbaum or I could *invent.*

Here we have the plain distinction: Zogbaum and Kipling are apollonic, while Evans is dionysian. Epic poetry, sculpture, painting and story-telling are apollonic: they represent, not life itself, but some one man's visualized idea of life. But dancing, great deeds and, in some cases, music, are dionysian: they are part and parcel of life as some actual human being, or collection of human beings, is living it.

Nietzsche maintained that Greek art was at first apollonic, but that eventually there appeared a dionysian influence—the fruit, perhaps, of contact with primitive, barbarous peoples. Ever afterward there was constant conflict between them and this conflict was the essence of Greek tragedy. As Sarcey tells us, a play, to hold our attention, must depict some sort of battle, between man and man or idea and idea. In the melodrama of today the battle is between hero and villain; in the ancient Greek tragedy it was between Apollo and Dionysus, between the life contemplative and the life strenuous, between law and outlaw, between the devil and the seraphim.

Nietzsche, as we shall see, afterward applied this distinction in morals and life as well as in art. He called himself a dionysian and the crowning volume of his system of philosophy, which he had barely started when insanity overtook him, was to have been called "Dionysus."

---

[1]Friedrich Wilhelm Ritschl (1806-1876), the foremost philologist of modern times. He became a professor of classical literature and rhetoric in 1839 and founded the science of historical literary criticism, as we know it today.

[2]Arthur Schopenhauer (1788-1860) published this book, his *magnum opus*, at Leipsic in 1819. It has been translated into English as "The World as Will and Idea" and has appeared in many editions.

[3]Schopenhauer (*"Nachträge für Lehre vom Leiden der Welt"*) puts the argument thus: "Pleasure is never as pleasant as we expect it to be and pain is always more painful. The pain in the world always outweighs the pleasure. If you don't believe it, compare the respective feelings of two animals, one of which is eating the other."

[4]Later on, in "*Menschliches allzu Menschliches,* " II, Nietzsche argued that the ascetic was either a coward, who feared the temptations of pleasure and the agonies of pain, or an exhausted worldling who had become satiated with life.

[5]Begun in 1869, this maiden work was dedicated to Richard Wagner. At Wagner's suggestion Nietzsche eliminated a great deal of matter in the original draft. The full title was "The Birth of Tragedy from the Spirit of Music, " but this was changed, in 1886, when a third edition

was printed, to "The Birth of Tragedy, or Hellenism and Pessimism." Nietzsche then also added a long preface, entitled "An Attempt at Self-Criticism." The material originally excluded was published in 1896.

III. BLAZING A NEW PATH

Having given birth, in this theory of Greek tragedy, to an idea which, whatever its defects otherwise, was at least original, understandable and workable, Nietzsche began to be conscious, as it were, of his own intellect—or, in his sister's phrase, "to understand what a great man he was." During his first years at Basel he had cut quite a figure in academic society, for he was an excellent musician, he enjoyed dancing and he had plenty of pretty things to say to the ladies. But as his ideas clarified and he found himself more and more in conflict with the pundits about him, he withdrew within himself, and in the end he had few friends save Richard and Cosima Wagner, who lived at Tribschen, not far away. To one of his turn of mind, indeed, the atmosphere of the college town was bound to grow oppressive soon or late. Acutely aware of his own superiority, he showed no patience with the unctuous complacency of dons and dignitaries, and so he became embroiled in various conflicts, and even his admirers among his colleagues seldom ventured upon friendly advances.

There are critics who see in all this proof that Nietzsche showed signs of insanity from early manhood, but as a matter of fact it was his abnormally accurate vision and not a vision gone awry, that made him stand so aloof from his fellows. In the vast majority of those about him he saw the coarse metal of sham and pretense beneath the showy gilding of learning. He had before him, at close range, a good many of the great men of his time—the intellectuals whose word was law in the schools. He saw them on parade and he saw them in their shirt sleeves. What wonder that he lost all false reverence for them and began to estimate them in terms, not of their dignity and reputation, but of their actual credibility and worth? It was inevitable that he should compare his own ideas to theirs, and it was inevitable that he should perceive the difference between his own fanatical striving for the truth and the easy dependence upon precedent and formula which lay beneath their booming bombast. Thus there arose in him a fiery loathing for all authority, and a firm belief that his own opinion regarding any matter to which he had given thought was as sound, at the least, as any other man's. Thenceforth the assertive "*ich*" began to besprinkle his discourse and his pages. "I condemn Christianity. *I* have given to mankind.... *I* was never yet modest.... *I* think.... *I* say.... *I* do...." Thus he hurled his javelin at authority until the end.

To those about him, perhaps, Nietzsche seemed wild and impossible, but it is not recorded that any one ever looked upon him as ridiculous. His high brow, bared by the way in which he brushed his hair; his keen eyes, with their monstrous overhanging brows, and his immense, untrimmed moustache gave him an air of alarming earnestness. Beside the pedagogues about him—with their well-barbered, professorial beards, their bald heads and their learned spectacles—he seemed like some incomprehensible foreigner. The exotic air he bore delighted him and he cultivated it assiduously. He regarded himself as a Polish grandee set down by an unkind fate among German shopkeepers, and it gave him vast pleasure when the hotel porters and street beggars, deceived by his disorderly façade, called him "The Polack."

Thus he lived and had his being. The inquisitive boy of old Naumburg, the impudent youth of Pforta and the academic free lance of Bonn and Leipsic had become merged into a man sure of himself and contemptuous of all whose search for the truth was hampered or hedged about by any respect for statute or precedent. He saw that the philosophers and sages of the day, in many of their most gorgeous flights of logic, started from false premises, and he observed the fact that certain of the dominant moral, political and social maxims of the time were mere foolishness. It struck him, too, that all of this faulty ratiocination—all of this assumption of outworn doctrines and dependence upon exploded creeds—was not confined to the confessedly orthodox. There was fallacy no less disgusting in the other camp. The professed apostles of revolt were becoming as bad as the old crusaders and apologists.

Nietzsche harbored a fevered yearning to call all of these false prophets to book and to reduce their fine axioms to absurdity. Accordingly, he planned a series of twenty-four pamphlets and decided to call them "*Unzeitgemässe Betrachtungen*" which may be translated as "Inopportune Speculations, " or more clearly, "Essays in Sham-Smashing." In looking about for a head to smash in essay number one, his eye, naturally enough, alighted upon that of David Strauss, the favorite philosopher and fashionable iconoclast of the day. Strauss had been a preacher but had renounced the cloth and set up shop as a critic of Christianity.[1] He had labored with good intentions, no doubt, but the net result of all his smug agnosticism was that his disciples were as self-satisfied, bigoted and prejudiced in the garb of agnostics as they had been before as Christians. Nietzsche's clear eye saw this and in the first of his little pamphlets, "*David Strauss, der Bekenner und der Schriftsteller*" ("David Strauss, the Confessor and the Writer"), he bore down upon Strauss' *bourgeoise* pseudo-skepticism most savagely. This was in 1873.

"Strauss, " he said, "utterly evades the question, What is the meaning of life? He had an opportunity to show courage, to turn his back upon the Philistines, and to boldly deduce a new morality from that constant warfare which destroys all but the fittest, but to do this would have required a love of truth infinitely higher than that which spends itself in violent invectives against parsons, miracles and the historical humbug of the resurrection. Strauss had no such courage. Had he worked out the Darwinian doctrine to its last decimal he would have had the Philistines against him to a man. As it is, they are with him. He has wasted his time in combatting Christianity's nonessentials. For the idea at the bottom of it he has proposed no substitute. In consequence, his philosophy is stale."[2]

As a distinguished critic has pointed out, Nietzsche's attack was notable, not only for its keen analysis and ruthless honesty, but also for its courage. It required no little bravery, three years after Sedan, to tell the Germans that the new culture which constituted their pride was rotten, and that, unless it were purified in the fire of absolute truth, it might one day wreck their civilization.

In the year following Nietzsche returned to the attack with a criticism of history, which was then the fashionable science of the German universities, on account, chiefly, of its usefulness in exploding the myths of Christianity. He called his essay *"Vom Nutzen und Nachtheil der Historie für das Leben"* ("On the Good and Bad Effects of History upon Human Life") and in it he took issue with the reigning pedagogues and professors of the day. There was much hard thinking and no little good writing in this essay and it made its mark. The mere study of history, argued Nietzsche, unless some definite notion regarding the destiny of man were kept ever in mind, was misleading and confusing. There was great danger in assuming that everything which happened was part of some divine and mysterious plan for the ultimate attainment of perfection. As a matter of fact, many historical events were meaningless, and this was particularly true of those expressions of "governments, public opinion and majorities" which historians were prone to accentuate. To Nietzsche the ideas and doings of peoples seemed infinitely less important than the ideas and doings of exceptional individuals. To put it more simply, he believed that one man, Hannibal, was of vastly more importance to the world than all the other Carthaginians of his time taken together. Herein we have a reappearance of Dionysus and a foreshadowing of the *herrenmoral* and superman of later days.

Nietzsche's next essay was devoted to Schopenhauer and was printed in 1874. He called it *"Schopenhauer als Erzieher"* ("Schopenhauer as a Teacher") and in it he laid his burnt offering upon the altar of the great pessimist, who was destined to remain his hero, if no longer his god, until the end. Nietzsche was already beginning to read rebellious ideas of his own into "The World as Will and Idea, " but in two things—the theory of will and the impulse toward truth—he and Schopenhauer were ever as one. He preached a holy war upon all those influences which had made the apostle of pessimism, in his life-time, an unheard outcast. He raged against the narrowness of university schools of philosophy and denounced all governmental interference in speculation—whether it were expressed crudely, by inquisitorial laws and the *Index*, or softly and insidiously, by the bribery of comfortable berths and public honors.

"Experience teaches us, " he said, "that nothing stands so much in the way of developing great philosophers as the custom of supporting bad ones in state universities.... It is the popular theory that the posts given to the latter make them 'free' to do original work; as a matter of fact, the effect is quite the contrary.... No state would ever dare to patronize such men as Plato and Schopenhauer. And why? Because the state is always afraid of them.... It seems to me that there is need for a higher tribunal outside the universities to critically examine the doctrines they teach. As soon as philosophers are willing to resign their salaries, they will constitute such a tribunal. Without pay and without honors, it will be able to free itself from the prejudices of the age. Like Schopenhauer, it will be the judge of the so-called culture around it."[3]

Years later Nietzsche denied that, in this essay, he committed himself irretrievably to the whole philosophy of Schopenhauer and a fair reading bears him out. He was not defending Schopenhauer's doctrine of renunciation, but merely asking that he be given a hearing. He was pleading the case of foes as well as of friends: all he asked was that the forum be opened to every man who had something new to say.

Nietzsche regarded Schopenhauer as a king among philosophers because he shook himself entirely free of the dominant thought of his time. In an age marked, beyond everything, by humanity's rising reliance upon human reason, he sought to show that reason was a puny offshoot of an irresistible natural law—the law of self-preservation. Nietzsche admired the man's courage and agreed with him in his insistence that this law was at the bottom of all sentient activity, but he was never a subscriber to Schopenhauer's surrender and despair. From the very start, indeed, he was a prophet of defiance, and herein his divergence from Schopenhauer was infinite. As his knowledge broadened and his scope widened, he expanded and developed his philosophy, and often he found it necessary to modify it in detail. But that he ever turned upon himself in fundamentals is untrue. Nietzsche at 40 and Nietzsche at 25 were essentially the same. The germ of practically all his writings lies in his first book—nay, it is to be found further back: in the wild speculations of his youth.

The fourth of the "*Unzeitgemässe Betrachtungen*" (and the last, for the original design of the series was not carried out) was "Richard Wagner in Bayreuth."[4] This was published in 1876 and neither it nor the general subject of Nietzsche's relations with Wagner need be considered here. In a subsequent chapter the whole matter will be discussed. For the present, it is sufficient to say that Nietzsche met Wagner through the medium of Ritschl's wife; that they became fast friends; that Nietzsche hailed the composer as a hero sent to make the drama an epitome of the life unfettered and unbounded, of life defiant and joyful; that Wagner, after starting from the Schopenhauer base, travelled toward St. Francis rather than toward Dionysus, and that Nietzsche, after vain expostulations, read the author of "Parsifal" out of meeting and pronounced him anathema. It was all a case of misunderstanding. Wagner was an artist, and not a philosopher. Right or wrong, Christianity was beautiful, and as a thing of beauty it called aloud to him. To Nietzsche beauty seemed a mere phase of truth.

It was during this period of preliminary skirmishing that Nietzsche's ultimate philosophy began to formulate itself. He saw clearly that there was something radically wrong with the German culture of the day—that many things esteemed right and holy were, in reality, unspeakable, and that many things under the ban of church and state were far from wrong in themselves. He saw, too, that there had grown up a false logic and that its taint was upon the whole of contemporary thought. Men maintained propositions plainly erroneous and excused themselves by the plea that ideals were greater than actualities. The race was subscribing to one thing and practicing another. Christianity was official, but not a single real Christian was to be found in all Christendom. Thousands bowed down to men and ideas that they despised and denounced things that every sane man knew were necessary and inevitable. The result was a flavor of dishonesty and hypocrisy in all human affairs. In the abstract the laws—of the church, the state and society—were looked upon as impeccable, but every man, in so far as they bore upon him personally, tried his best to evade them.

Other philosophers, in Germany and elsewhere, had made the same observation and there was in progress a grand assault-at-arms upon old ideas. Huxley and Spencer, in England, were laboring hard in the vineyard planted by Darwin; Ibsen, in Norway, was preparing for his epoch-making life-work, and in far America Andrew D. White and others were battling to free education from the bonds of theology. Thus it will be seen that, at the start, Nietzsche was no more a pioneer than any one of a dozen other men. Some of these other men, indeed, were far better equipped for the fray than he, and their services, for a long while, seemed a great deal more important. But it was his good fortune, before his working days were over, to press the conflict much further afield than the others. Beginning where they ended, he fought his way into the very citadel of the enemy.

His attack upon Christianity, which is described at length later on, well exemplifies this uncompromising thoroughness. Nietzsche saw that the same plan would have to be pursued in examining all other concepts— religious, political or social. It would be necessary to pass over surface symptoms and go to the heart of things: to tunnel down deep into ideas; to trace out their history and seek out their origins. There were no willing hands to help him in this: it was, in a sense, a work new to the world. In consequence Nietzsche perceived that he would have to go slowly and that it would be needful to make every step plain. It was out of the question to expect encouragement: if the task attracted notice at all, this notice would probably take the form of blundering opposition. But Nietzsche began his clearing and his road cutting with a light heart. The men of his day might call him accursed, but in time his honesty would shame all denial. This was his attitude always: he felt that neglect and opprobrium were all in his day's work and he used to say that if ever the generality of men endorsed any idea that he had advanced he would be convinced at once that he had made an error.

In his preliminary path-finding Nietzsche concerned himself much with the history of specific ideas. He showed how the thing which was a sin in one age became the virtue of the next. He attacked hope, faith and charity in this way, and he made excursions into nearly every field of human thought—from art to primary education. All of this occupied the first half of the 70's. Nietzsche was in indifferent health and his labors tired him so greatly that he thought more than once of giving up his post at Basel, with its dull round of lecturing and quizzing. But his private means at this time were not great enough to enable him to surrender his salary and so he had to hold on. He thought, too, of going to Vienna to study the natural sciences so that he might attain the wide and certain knowledge possessed by Spencer, but the same considerations forced him to abandon the plan. He spent his winters teaching and investigating and his summers at various watering-places—from Tribschen, in Switzerland, where the Wagners were his hosts, to Sorrento, in Italy.

At Sorrento he happened to take lodgings in a house which also sheltered Dr. Paul Rée, the author of "Psychological Observations, " "The Origin of Moral Feelings, " and other metaphysical works. That Rée gave him great assistance he acknowledged himself in later years, but that his ideas were, in any sense, due to this chance meeting (as Max Nordau would have us believe) is out of the question, for, as we have seen, they were already pretty clear in his mind a long while before. But Rée widened his outlook a great deal, it is evident, and undoubtedly made him acquainted with the English naturalists who had sprung up as spores of Darwin, and with a number of great Frenchmen—Montaigne, Larochefoucauld, La Bruyère, Fontenelle, Vauvenargues and Chamfort.

Nietzsche had been setting down his thoughts and conclusions in the form of brief memoranda and as he grew better acquainted with the French philosophers, many of whom published their works as collections of aphorisms, he decided to employ that form himself. Thus he began to arrange the notes which were to be given to the world as "*Menschliches allzu Menschliches*" ("Human, All-too Human"). In 1876 he got leave from Basel and gave his whole time to the work. During the winter of 1876-7, with the aid of a disciple named Bernhard Cron (better known as Peter Gast) he prepared the first volume for the press. Nietzsche was well aware that it would make a sensation and while it was being set up his courage apparently forsook him and he suggested to his publisher that it be sent forth anonymously. But the latter would not hear of it and so the first part left the press in 1878.

As the author had expected, the book provoked a fine frenzy of horror among the pious. The first title chosen for it, "*Die Pflugschar*" ("The Plowshare"), and the one finally selected, "Human, All-too Human, " indicate that it was an attempt to examine the underside of human ideas. In it Nietzsche challenged the whole of current morality. He showed that moral ideas were not divine, but human, and that, like all things human, they were subject to change. He showed that good and evil were but relative terms, and that it was impossible to say, finally and absolutely, that a certain action was right and another wrong. He applied the acid of critical analysis to a hundred and one specific ideas, and his general conclusion, to put it briefly, was that no human being had a right, in any way or form, to judge or direct the actions of any other being. Herein we have, in a few words, that gospel of individualism which all our sages preach today.[5]

Nietzsche sent a copy of the book to Wagner and the great composer was so appalled that he was speechless. Even the author's devoted sister, who worshipped him as an intellectual god, was unable to follow him. Germany, in general, pronounced the work a conglomeration of crazy fantasies and wild absurdities—and Nietzsche smiled with satisfaction. In 1879 he published the second volume, to which he gave the sub-title of "*Vermischte Meinungen und Sprüche*" ("Miscellaneous Opinions and Aphorisms") and shortly thereafter he finally resigned his chair at Basel.

The third part of the book appeared in 1880 as "*Der Wanderer und sein Schatten*" ("The Wanderer and His Shadow"). The three volumes were published as two in 1886 as "*Menschliches allzu Menschliches*" with the explanatory sub-title, "*Ein Buch für Freie Geister*" ("A Book for Free Spirits").

———

[1]David Friedrich Strauss (1808-74) sprang into fame with his "*Das Leben Jesu,* " 1835 (Eng. tr. by George Eliot, 1846), but the book which served as Nietzsche's target was "*Der alte und der neue Glaube*" ("The Old Faith and the New"), 1872.

[2]"*David Strauss, der Bekenner und der Schriftsteller,* " § 7.

[3]"*Schopenhauer als Erzieher,* " § 8.

[4]According to Nietzsche's original plan the series was to have included pamphlets on "Literature and the Press, " "Art and Painters, " "The Higher Education, " "German and Counter-German, " "War and the Nation, " "The Teacher, " "Religion, " "Society and Trade, " "Society and Natural Science, " and "The City, " with an epilogue entitled "The Way to Freedom."

[5]It must be remembered, in considering all of Nietzsche's writings, that when he spoke of a human being, he meant a being of the higher sort— *i.e.* one capable of clear reasoning. He regarded the drudge class, which is obviously unable to think for itself, as unworthy of consideration. Its highest mission, he believed, was to serve and obey the master class. But he held that there should be no artificial barriers to the rise of an individual born to the drudge class who showed an accidental capacity for independent reasoning. Such an individual, he believed, should be admitted, *ipso facto*, to the master class. Naturally enough, he held to the converse too. *Vide* the chapter on "Civilization."

IV. THE PROPHET OF THE SUPERMAN

Nietzsche spent the winter of 1879-80 at Naumburg, his old home. During the ensuing year he was very ill, indeed, and for awhile he believed that he had but a short while to live. Like all such invalids he devoted a great deal of time to observing and discussing his condition. He became, indeed, a hypochondriac of the first water and began to take a sort of melancholy pleasure in his infirmities. He sought relief at all the baths and cures of Europe: he took hot baths, cold baths, salt-water baths and mud baths. Every new form of pseudo-therapy found him in its freshman class. To owners of sanatoria and to inventors of novel styles of massage, irrigation, sweating and feeding he was a joy unlimited. But he grew worse instead of better.

After 1880, his life was a wandering one. His sister, after her marriage, went to Paraguay for a while, and during her absence Nietzsche made his progress from the mountains to the sea, and then back to the mountains again. He gave up his professorship that he might spend his winters in Italy and his summers in the Engadine. In the face of all this suffering and travelling about, close application, of course, was out of the question. So he contented himself with working whenever and however his headaches, his doctors and the railway time-tables would permit—on hotel verandas, in cure-houses and in the woods. He would take long, solitary walks and struggle with his problems by the way. He swallowed more and more pills; he imbibed mineral waters by the gallon; he grew more and more moody and ungenial. One of his favorite haunts, in the winter time, was a verdant little neck of land that jutted out into Lake Maggiore. There he could think and dream undisturbed. One day, when he found that some one had placed a rustic bench on the diminutive peninsula, that passersby might rest, he was greatly incensed.

Nietzsche would make brief notes of his thoughts during his daylight rambles, and in the evenings would polish and expand them. As we have seen, his early books were sent to the printer as mere collections of aphorisms, without effort at continuity. Sometimes a dozen subjects are considered in two pages, and then again, there is occasionally a little essay of three or four pages. Nietzsche chose this form because it had been used by the French philosophers he admired, and because it well suited the methods of work that a pain-racked frame imposed upon him.

He was ever in great fear that some of his precious ideas would be lost to posterity—that death, the ever-threatening, would rob him of his rightful immortality and the world of his stupendous wisdom—and so he made efforts, several times, to engage an amanuensis capable of jotting down, after the fashion of Johnson's Boswell, the chance phrases that fell from his lips. His sister was too busy to undertake the task: whenever she was with him her whole time was employed in guarding him from lion-hunters, scrutinizing his daily fare and deftly inveigling him into answering his letters, brushing his clothes and getting his hair cut. Finally, Paul Rée and another friend, Fräulein von Meysenbug, brought to his notice a young Russian woman, Mlle. Lou Salomé, who professed vast interest in his work and offered to help him. But this arrangement quickly ended in disaster, for Nietzsche fell in love with the girl—she was only 20—and pursued her over half of Europe when she fled. To add to the humors of the situation Rée fell in love with her too, and the two friends thus became foes and there was even some talk of a duel. Mlle. Salomé, however, went to Rée, and with his aid she later wrote a book about

Nietzsche.[53] Frau Förster-Nietzsche sneers at that book, but the fact is not to be forgotten that she was very jealous of Mlle. Salomé, and gave constant proof of it by unfriendly word and act. In the end, the latter married one Prof. Andreas and settled down in Göttingen.

Early in 1881 Nietzsche published "*Morgenröte*" ("The Dawn of Day"). It was begun at Venice in 1880 and continued at Marienbad, Lago Maggiore and Genoa. It was, in a broad way, a continuation of "*Menschliches allzu Menschliches.*" It dealt with an infinite variety of subjects, from matrimony to Christianity, and from education to German patriotism. To all the test of fundamental truth was applied: of everything Nietzsche asked, not, Is it respectable or lawful? but, Is it essentially true? These early works, at best, were mere note-books. Nietzsche saw that the ground would have to be plowed, that people would have to grow accustomed to the idea of questioning high and holy things, before a new system of philosophy would be understandable or possible. In "*Menschliches allzu Menschliches*" and in "*Morgenröte*" he undertook this preparatory cultivation.

The book which followed, "*Die fröhliche Wissenschaft*" ("The Joyful Science") continued the same task. The first edition contained four parts and was published in 1882. In 1887 a fifth part was added. Nietzsche had now completed his plowing and was ready to sow his crop. He had demonstrated, by practical examples, that moral ideas were vulnerable, and that the Ten Commandments might be debated. Going further, he had adduced excellent historical evidence against the absolute truth of various current conceptions of right and wrong, and had traced a number of moral ideas back to decidedly lowly sources. His work so far had been entirely destructive and he had scarcely ventured to hint at his plans for a reconstruction of the scheme of things. As he himself says, he spent the four years between 1878 and 1882 in preparing the way for his later work.

"I descended, " he says, "into the lowest depths, I searched to the bottom, I examined and pried into an old faith on which, for thousands of years, philosophers had built as upon a secure foundation. The old structures came tumbling down about me. I undermined our old faith in morals." [54]

This labor accomplished, Nietzsche was ready to set forth his own notion of the end and aim of existence. He had shown that the old morality was like an apple rotten at the core—that the Christian ideal of humility made mankind weak and miserable; that many institutions regarded with superstitious reverence, as the direct result of commands from the creator

---

[53] "*Friedrich Nietzsche in seinen Werken;*" Vienna, 1894.
[54] Preface to "*Morgenröte,*" § 2; autumn, 1886.

(such, for instance, as the family, the church and the state), were mere products of man's "all-too-human" cupidity, cowardice, stupidity and yearning for ease. He had turned the searchlight of truth upon patriotism, charity and self-sacrifice. He had shown that many things held to be utterly and unquestionably good or bad by modern civilization were once given quite different values—that the ancient Greeks considered hope a sign of weakness, and mercy the attribute of a fool, and that the Jews, in their royal days, looked upon wrath, not as a sin, but as a virtue—and in general he had demonstrated, by countless instances and arguments, that all notions of good and evil were mutable and that no man could ever say, with utter certainty, that one thing was right and another wrong.

The ground was now cleared for the work of reconstruction and the first structure that Nietzsche reared was "*Also sprach Zarathustra*" ("Thus Spake Zoroaster"). This book, to which he gave the sub-title of "*Ein Buch für Alle und Keinen*" ("A book for all and none"), took the form of a fantastic, half-poetical half-philosophical rhapsody. Nietzsche had been delving into oriental mysticism and from the law-giver of the ancient Persians he borrowed the name of his hero—Zoroaster. But there was no further resemblance between the two, and no likeness whatever between Nietzsche's philosophy and that of the Persians.

The Zoroaster of the book is a sage who lives remote from mankind, and with no attendants but a snake and an eagle. The book is in four parts and all are made up of discourses by Zoroaster. These discourses are delivered to various audiences during the prophet's occasional wanderings and at the conferences he holds with various disciples in the cave that he calls home. They are decidedly oriental in form and recall the manner and phraseology of the biblical rhapsodists. Toward the end Nietzsche throws all restraint to the winds and indulges to his heart's content in the rare and exhilarating sport of blasphemy. There is a sort of parody of the last supper and Zoroaster's backsliding disciples engage in the grotesque and indecent worship of a jackass. Wagner and other enemies of the author appear, thinly veiled, as ridiculous buffoons.

In his discourses Zoroaster voices the Nietzschean idea of the superman—the idea that has come to be associated with Nietzsche more than any other. Later on, it will be set forth in detail. For the present, suffice it to say that it is the natural child of the notions put forward in Nietzsche's first book, "The Birth of Tragedy, " and that it binds his entire life work together into one consistent, harmonious whole. The first part of "*Also sprach Zarathustra*" was published in 1883, the second part following in the same year, and the third part was printed in 1884. The last part was privately circulated among the author's friends in 1885, but was not given to the public until 1892, when the entire work was printed in one volume. As showing Nietzsche's wandering life, it may be recorded that the book was conceived in the Engadine and written in Genoa, Sils Maria, Nice and Mentone.

"Jenseits von Gut und Böse" ("Beyond Good and Evil") appeared in 1886. In this book Nietzsche elaborated and systematized his criticism of morals, and undertook to show why he considered modern civilization degrading. Here he finally formulated his definitions of master-morality and slave-morality, and showed how Christianity was necessarily the idea of a race oppressed and helpless, and eager to escape the lash of its masters.

"Zur Genealogie der Moral" ("The Genealogy of Morals"), which appeared in 1887, developed these propositions still further. In it there was also a partial return to Nietzsche's earlier manner, with its merciless analysis of moral concepts. In 1888 Nietzsche published a most vitriolic attack upon Wagner, under the title of *"Der Fall Wagner"* ("The Case of Wagner"), the burden of which was the author's discovery that the composer, starting, with him, from Schopenhauer's premises, had ended, not with the superman, but with the Man on the cross. *"Götzendämmerung"* ("The Twilight of the Idols") a sort of parody of Wagner's *"Götterdämmerung"* ("The Twilight of the Gods") followed in 1889. *"Nietzsche contra Wagner"* ("Nietzsche versus Wagner") was printed the same year. It was made up of extracts from the philosopher's early works, and was designed to prove that, contrary to the allegations of his enemies, he had not veered completely about in his attitude toward Wagner.

Meanwhile, despite the fact that his health was fast declining and he was approaching the verge of insanity, Nietzsche made plans for a great four volume work that was to sum up his philosophy and stand forever as his *magnum opus*. The four volumes, as he planned them, were to bear the following titles:

1. *"Der Antichrist: Versuch einer Kritik des Christenthums"* ("The Anti-Christ: an Attempt at a Criticism of Christianity").

2. *"Der freie Geist: Kritik der Philosophie als einer nihilistischen Bewegung"* ("The Free Spirit: a Criticism of Philosophy as a Nihilistic Movement").

3. *"Der Immoralist: Kritik der verhängnissvollsten Art von Unwissenheit, der Moral"* ("The Immoralist: a Criticism of That Fatal Species of Ignorance, Morality").

4. *"Dionysus, Philosophie der ewigen Wiederkunft"* ("Dionysus, the Philosophy of Eternal Recurrence").

This work was to be published under the general title of "*Der Wille zur Macht: Versuch einer Umwerthung aller Werthe*" ("The Will to Power: an Attempt at a Transvaluation of all Values"), but Nietzsche got no further than the first book, "*Der Antichrist*" and a mass of rough notes for the others. "*Der Antichrist*" probably the most brilliant piece of writing that Germany had seen in half a century, was written at great speed between September 3rd and September 30th, 1888, but it was not published until 1895, six years after the philosopher had laid down his work forever.

During that same year C. G. Naumann, the Leipsic publisher, began the issue of a definite edition of all his writings, in fifteen volumes, under the editorial direction of Frau Förster-Nietzsche, Dr. Fritz Koegel, Peter Gast and E. von der Hellen. In this edition his notes for "*Der Wille zur Macht*" and his early philological essays were included. The notes are of great interest to the serious student of Nietzsche, for they show how some of his ideas changed with the years and point out the probable structure of his final system, but the general reader will find them chaotic, and often incomprehensible. In October, 1888, but three months before his breakdown, he began a critical autobiography with the title of "*Ecce Homo,*" and it was completed in three weeks. It is an extremely frank and entertaining book, with such chapter headings as "Why I am so Wise, " "Why I Write Such Excellent Books" and "Why I am a Fatality." In it Nietzsche sets forth his private convictions regarding a great many things, from cooking to climates, and discusses each of his books in detail. "*Ecce Homo*" was not printed until 1908, when it appeared at Leipsic in a limited edition of 1250 copies.

In January, 1889, at Turin, where he was living alone in very humble quarters, Nietzsche suddenly became hopelessly insane. His friends got news of it from his own hand. "I am Ferdinand de Lesseps, " he wrote to Prof. Burckhardt of Basel. To Cosima Wagner: "Ariadne, I love you!" To Georg Brandes, the Danish critic, he sent a telegram signed "The Crucified." Franz Overbeck, an old Basel friend, at once set out for Turin, and there he found Nietzsche thumping the piano with his elbows and singing wild songs. Overbeck brought him back to Basel and he was confined in a private asylum, where his general health greatly improved and hopes were entertained of his recovery. But he never got well enough to be left alone, and so his old mother, with whom he had been on bad terms for years, took him back to Naumburg. When, in 1893, his sister Elizabeth returned from Paraguay, where her husband had died, he was well enough to meet her at the railroad station. Four years later, when their mother died, Elizabeth removed him to Weimar, where she bought a villa called "*Silberblick*" (Silver View) in the suburbs. This villa had a garden overlooking the hills and the lazy river Ilm, and a wide, sheltered veranda for the invalid's couch. There he would sit day after day, receiving old friends but saying little. His mind never became clear enough for him to resume work, or even to read. He had to grope for words, slowly and painfully, and he retained only a cloudy memory of his own books. His chief delight was in music and he was always glad when someone came who could play the piano for him.

There is something poignantly pathetic in the picture of this valiant fighter—this arrogant *ja-sager*—this foe of men, gods and devils—being nursed and coddled like a little child. His old fierce pride and courage disappeared and he became docile and gentle. "You and I, my sister—we are happy!" he would say, and then his hand would slip out from his coverings and clasp that of the tender and faithful Lisbeth. Once she mentioned Wagner to him. "*Den habe ich sehr geliebt!*" he said. All his old fighting spirit was gone. He remembered only the glad days and the dreams of his youth.

Nietzsche died at Weimar on August 25, 1900, the immediate cause of death being pneumonia. His ashes are buried in the little village of Röcken, his birthplace.

V. THE PHILOSOPHER AND THE MAN

"My brother, " says Frau Förster-Nietzsche, in her biography, "was stockily and broadly built and was anything but thin. He had a rather dark, healthy, ruddy complexion. In all things he was tidy and orderly, in speech he was soft-spoken, and in general, he was inclined to be serene under all circumstances. All in all, he was the very antithesis of a nervous man.

"In the fall of 1888, he said of himself, in a reminiscent memorandum: 'My blood moves slowly. A doctor who treated me a long while for what was at first diagnosed as a nervous affection said: "No, your trouble cannot be in your nerves. I myself am much more nervous than you."'...

"My brother, both before and after his long illness seized him, was a believer in natural methods of healing. He took cold baths, rubbed down every morning and was quite faithful in continuing light, bed-room gymnastics."

At one time, she says, Nietzsche became a violent vegetarian and afflicted his friends with the ancient vegetarian horror of making a sarcophagus of one's stomach. It seems surprising that a man so quick to perceive errors, saw none in the silly argument that, because an ape's organs are designed for a vegetarian diet, a man's are so planned also. An acquaintance with elementary anatomy and physiology would have shown him the absurdity of this, but apparently he knew little about the human body, despite his uncanny skill at unearthing the secrets of the human mind. Nietzsche had read Emerson in his youth, and those Emersonian seeds which have come to full flower in the United States as the so-called New Thought movement—with Christian Science, osteopathy, mental telepathy, occultism, pseudo-psychology and that grand lodge of credulous *comiques*, the Society for Psychical Research, as its final blossoms—all of this probably made its mark on the philosopher of the superman, too.

Frau Förster-Nietzsche, in her biography, seeks to prove the impossible thesis that her brother, despite his constant illness, was ever well-balanced in mind. It is but fair to charge that her own evidence is against her. From his youth onward, Nietzsche was undoubtedly a neurasthenic, and after the Franco-Prussian war he was a constant sufferer from all sorts of terrible ills—some imaginary, no doubt, but others real enough. In many ways, his own account of his symptoms recalls vividly the long catalogue of aches and pains given by Herbert Spencer in his autobiography. Spencer had queer pains in his head and so did Nietzsche. Spencer roved about all his life in search of health and so did Nietzsche. Spencer's working hours were limited and so were Nietzsche's. The latter tells us himself that, in a single year, 1878, he was disabled 118 days by headaches and pains in the eyes.

Dr. Gould, the prophet of eye-strain, would have us believe that both of these great philosophers suffered because they had read too much during adolescence. It is more likely, however, that each was the victim of some definite organic malady, and perhaps of more than one. In Nietzsche's case things were constantly made worse by his fondness for self-medication, that vice of fools. Preparatory to his service as a hospital steward in 1870 he had attended a brief course of first-aid lectures at the military hospital at Erlangen, and thereafter he regarded himself as a finished pathologist and was forever taking his own doses. The amount of medicine he thus swallowed was truly appalling, and the only way he could break his appetite for one drug was by acquiring an appetite for another. Chloral, however, was his favorite, and toward the end he took it daily and in staggering quantities.

Meanwhile, his mental disturbances grew more and more visible. At times he would be highly excited and exalted, denouncing his foes, and proclaiming his own genius. This was his state when his friends were finally forced to put him under restraint. At other times he would show symptoms of melancholia—a feeling of isolation and friendlessness, a great sadness, a foreboding of death. The hostility with which his books were received gave sharpness and plausibility to this mood, and it pursued him through many a despairing day.

"An animal, when it is sick, " he wrote to Baron von Seydlitz, in 1888, "slinks away to some dark cavern, and so, too, does the *bête philosophe*. I am alone—absurdly alone—and in my unflinching and toilsome struggle against all that men have hitherto held sacred and venerable, I have become a sort of dark cavern myself—something hidden and mysterious, which is not to be explored...." But the mood vanished as the words were penned, and the defiant dionysian roared his challenge at his foes. "It is not impossible, " he said, "that I am the greatest philosopher of the century—perhaps even more than that! I may be the decisive and fateful link between two thousand centuries!"[55] Max Nordau[56] says that Nietzsche was crazy from birth, but the facts do not bear him out. It is much more reasonable to hold that the philosopher came into the world a sound and healthy animal, and that it remained for overstudy in his youth, over-work and over drugging later on, exposure on the battle field, functional disorders and constant and violent strife to undermine and eventually overthrow his intellect.

But if we admit the indisputable fact that Nietzsche died a madman and the equally indisputable fact that his insanity was not sudden, but progressive, we by no means read him out of court as a thinker. A man's reasoning is to be judged, not by his physical condition, but by its own ingenuity and accuracy. If a raving maniac says that twice two make four, it is just as true as it would be if Pope Pius X or any other undoubtedly sane man were to maintain it. Judged in this way Nietzsche's philosophy is very far from insane. Later on we shall consider it as a workable system, and point out its apparent truths and apparent errors, but in no place (saving, perhaps, one) is his argument to be dismissed as the phantasm of a lunatic.

Nietzsche's sister says that, in the practical affairs of life, the philosopher was absurdly impractical. He cared nothing for money and during the better part of his life had little need to do so. His mother, for a country pastor's widow, was well-to-do, and when he was twenty-five his professorship at Basel brought him 3, 000 francs a year. At Basel, in the late sixties, 3, 000 francs was the income of an independent, not to say opulent man. Nietzsche was a bachelor and lived very simply. It was only upon books and music and travel that he was extravagant.

After two years' service at Basel, the university authorities raised his wage to 4, 000 francs, and in 1879, when ill health forced him to resign, they gave him a pension of 3, 000 francs a year. Besides that, he inherited 30, 000 marks from one of his aunts, and so, altogether, he had an income

---

[55] Thomas Common: "Nietzsche as Critic, Philosopher, Poet and Prophet;" London, 1901, p. 54.

[56] "Degeneration;" Eng. tr.: New York, 1895; pp. 415-471.

of $900 or $1, 000 a year—the sum which Herbert Spencer regarded, all his life, as an insurance of perfect tranquillity and happiness.

Nietzsche's passion and dissipation, throughout his life, was music. In all his books musical terms and figures of speech are constantly encountered. He played the piano very well, indeed, and was especially fond of performing transcriptions of the Wagner opera scores. "My three solaces, " he wrote home from Leipsic, "are Schopenhauer's philosophy, Schumann's music and solitary walks." In his late youth, Wagner engrossed him, but his sympathies were broad enough to include Bach, Schubert and Mendelssohn. His admiration for the last named, in fact, helped to alienate him from Wagner, who regarded the Mendelssohn scheme of things as unspeakable.

Nietzsche's own compositions were decidedly heavy and scholastic. He was a skillful harmonist and contrapuntalist, but his musical ideas lacked life. Into the simplest songs he introduced harsh and far-fetched modulations. The music of Richard Strauss, who professes to be his disciple and has found inspiration in his "*Also sprach Zarathustra*" would have delighted him. Strauss has achieved the uncanny feat of writing in two keys at once. Such an effort would have enlisted Nietzsche's keen interest.

All the same, his music was not a mere creature of the study and of rules, and we have evidence that he was frequently inspired to composition by bursts of strong emotion. On his way to the Franco-Prussian war, he wrote a patriotic song, words and music, on the train. He called it "Adieu! I Must Go!" and arranged it for men's chorus, *a capella*. It would be worth while to hear a German *männerchor*, with its high, beery tenors, and ponderous basses, sing this curious composition. Certainly no more grotesque music was ever put on paper by mortal man.

Much has been written by various commentators about the strange charm of Nietzsche's prose style. He was, indeed, a master of the German language, but this mastery was not inborn. Like Spencer he made a deliberate effort, early in life, to acquire ease and force in writing. His success was far greater than Spencer's. Toward the end—in "*Der Antichrist,* " for instance—he attained a degree of powerful and convincing utterance almost comparable to Huxley's. But his style never exhibited quite that wonderful air of clearness, of utter certainty, of inevitableness which makes the "Lay Sermons" so tremendously impressive. Nietzsche was ever nearer to Carlyle than to Addison. "His style, " says a writer in the *Athenæum,* "is a shower of sparks, which scatter, like fireworks, all over the sky."

"My sense for form, " says Nietzsche himself, "awakened on my coming in contact with Sallust." Later on he studied the great French stylists, particularly Larochefoucauld, and learned much from them. He became a master of the aphorism and the epigram, and this skill, very naturally, led him to descend, now and then, to mere violence and invective. He called his opponents all sorts of harsh names—liar, swindler, counterfeiter, ox, ass, snake and thief. Whatever he had to say, he hammered in with gigantic blows, and to the accompaniment of fearsome bellowing and grimacing. "Nervous, vivid and picturesques, full of fire and a splendid vitality, " says one critic, "his style flashed and coruscated like a glowing flame, and had a sort of dithyrambic movement that at times recalls the swing of the Pindaric odes." Naturally, this very *abandon* made his poetry formless and grotesque. He scorned metres and rhymes and raged on in sheer savagery. Reading his verses one is forced irresistibly into the thought that they should be printed in varied fonts of type and in a dozen brilliant inks.

Nietzsche never married, but he was by no means a misogynist. His sister tells us, indeed, that he made a formal proposal of marriage to a young Dutch woman, Fräulein Tr——, at Geneva in 1876, and the story of his melodramatic affair with Mlle. Lou Salomé, six years later, was briefly rehearsed in the last chapter. There were also other women in his life, early and late, and certain scandal-mongers do not hesitate to accuse him of a passion for Cosima Wagner, apparently on the ground that he wrote to her, in his last mad days, "Ariadne, I love thee!" But his intentions were seldom serious. Even when he pursued Mlle. Salomé from Rome to Leipsic and quarrelled with his sister about her, and threatened poor Rée with fire-arms, there is good reason to believe that he shied at bell and book. His proposal, in brief, was rather one of a free union than one of marriage. For the rest, he kept safely to impossible flirtations. During all his wanderings he was much petted by the belles of pump room and hotel parlor, not only because he was a mysterious and romantic looking fellow, but also because his philosophy was thought to be blasphemous and indecent, particularly by those who knew nothing about it. But the fair admirers he singled out were either securely married or hopelessly antique. "For me to marry, " he soliloquized in 1887, "would probably be sheer asininity."

There are sentimental critics who hold that Nietzsche's utter lack of geniality was due to his lack of a wife. A good woman—alike beautiful and sensible—would have rescued him, they say, from his gloomy fancies. He would have expanded and mellowed in the sunshine of her smiles, and children would have civilized him. The defect in this theory lies in the fact that philosophers do not seem to flourish amid scenes of connubial joy. High thinking, it would appear, presupposes boarding house fare and hall bed-rooms. Spinoza, munching his solitary herring up his desolate backstairs, makes a picture that pains us, perhaps, but it must be admitted that it also satisfies our sense of eternal fitness. A married Spinoza, with two sons at college, another managing the family lens business, a daughter busy with her trousseau and a wife growing querulous and fat—the vision, alas, is preposterous, outrageous and impossible! We must think of philosophers as beings alone but not lonesome. A married Schopenhauer or Kant or Nietzsche would be unthinkable.

That a venture into matrimony might have somewhat modified Nietzsche's view of womankind is not at all improbable, but that this change would have been in the direction of greater accuracy does not follow. He would have been either a ridiculously henpecked slave or a violent domestic tyrant. As a bachelor he was comparatively well-to-do, but with a wife and children his thousand a year would have meant genteel beggary. His sister had her own income and her own affairs. When he needed her, she was ever at his side, but when his working fits were upon him—when he felt efficient and self-sufficient—she discreetly disappeared. A wife's constant presence, day in and day out, would have irritated him beyond measure or reduced him to a state of compliance and sloth. Nietzsche himself sought to show, in more than one place, that a man whose whole existence was colored by one woman would inevitably acquire some trace of her feminine outlook, and so lose his own sure vision. The ideal state for a philosopher, indeed, is celibacy tempered by polygamy. He must study women, but he must be free, when he pleases, to close his note book and go away and digest its contents with an open mind.

Toward the end of his life, when increasing illness made him helpless, Nietzsche's faithful sister took the place of wife and mother in his clouding world. She made a home for him and she sat by and watched him. They talked for hours—Nietzsche propped up with pillows, his old ruddiness faded into a deathly white, and his Niagara of a moustache showing dark against his pallid skin. They talked of Naumburg and the days of long ago and the fiery prophet of the superman became simple Brother Fritz. We are apt to forget that a great man is thus not only great, but also a man: that a philosopher, in a life time, spends less hours pondering the destiny of the race than he gives over to wondering if it will rain tomorrow and to meditating upon the toughness of steaks, the dustiness of roads, the stuffiness of railway coaches and the brigandage of gas companies.

Nietzsche's sister was the only human being that ever saw him intimately, as a wife might have seen him. Her affection for him was perfect and her influence over him perfect, too. Love and understanding, faith and gentleness—these are the things which make women the angels of joyous illusion. Lisbeth, the calm and trusting, had all in boundless richness. There was, indeed, something noble, and almost holy in the eagerness with which she sought her brother's comfort and peace of mind during his days of stress and storm, and magnified his virtues after he was gone.

PART TWO.
NIETZSCHE THE PHILOSOPHER

I. DIONYSUS VERSUS APOLLO

In one of the preceding chapters Nietzsche's theory of Greek tragedy was given in outline and its dependence upon the data of Schopenhauer's philosophy was indicated. It is now in order to examine this theory a bit more closely and to trace out its origin and development with greater dwelling upon detail. In itself it is of interest only as a step forward in the art of literary criticism, but in its influence upon Nietzsche's ultimate inquiries it has colored, to a measurable extent, the whole stream of modern thought.

Schopenhauer laid down, as his cardinal principle, it will be recalled, the idea that, in all the complex whirlpool of phenomena we call human life, the mere will to survive is at the bottom of everything, and that intelligence, despite its seeming kingship in civilization, is nothing more, after all, than a secondary manifestation of this primary will. In certain purely artificial situations, it may seem to us that reason stands alone (as when, for example, we essay to solve an abstract problem in mathematics), but in everything growing out of our relations as human beings, one to the other, the old instinct of race-and-self-preservation is plainly discernible. All of our acts, when they are not based obviously and directly upon our yearning to eat and take our ease and beget our kind, are founded upon our desire to appear superior, in some way or other, to our fellow men about us, and this desire for superiority, reduced to its lowest terms, is merely a desire to face the struggle for existence—to eat and beget—under more favorable conditions than those the world accords the average man. "Happiness is the feeling that power increases—that resistance is being overcome."(*"Der Antichrist,"* § 2.) Nietzsche went to Basel firmly convinced that these fundamental ideas of Schopenhauer were profoundly true, though he soon essayed to make an amendment to them. This amendment consisted in changing Schopenhauer's "will to live" into "will to power." That which does not live, he argued, cannot exercise a will to live, and when a thing is already in existence, how can it strive after existence? Nietzsche voiced the argument many times, but its vacuity is apparent upon brief inspection. He started out, in fact, with an incredibly clumsy misinterpretation of Schopenhauer's phrase. The philosopher of pessimism, when he said "will to live" obviously meant, not will to begin living, but will to continue living. Now, this will to continue living, if we are to accept words at their usual meaning, is plainly identical, in every respect, with Nietzsche's will to power. Therefore, Nietzsche's amendment was nothing more than the coinage of a new phrase to express an old idea. The unity of the two philosophers and the identity of the two phrases are proved a thousand times by Nietzsche's own discourses. Like Schopenhauer he believed that all human ideas were the direct products of the unconscious and unceasing effort of all living creatures to remain alive. Like Schopenhauer he believed that abstract ideas, in man, arose out of concrete ideas, and that the latter arose out of experience, which, in turn, was nothing more or less than an ordered remembrance of the results following an endless series of endeavors to meet the conditions of existence and so survive. Like Schopenhauer, he believed that the criminal laws, the poetry, the cookery and the religion of a race were alike expressions of this unconscious groping for the line of least resistance.

As a philologist, Nietzsche's interest, very naturally, was fixed upon the literature of Greece and Rome, and so it was but natural that his first tests of Schopenhauer's doctrines should be made in that field. Some time before this, he had asked himself (as many another man had asked before him) why it was that the ancient Greeks, who were an efficient and vigorous people, living in a green and sunny land, should so delight in gloomy tragedies. One would fancy that a Greek, when he set out to spend a pleasant afternoon, would seek entertainment that was frivolous and gay. But instead, he often preferred to see one of the plays of Thespis, Æschylus, Phrynichus or Pratinus, in which the heroes fought hopeless battles with fate and died miserably, in wretchedness and despair. Nietzsche concluded that the Greeks had this liking for tragedy because it seemed to them to set forth, truthfully and understandably, the conditions of life as they found it: that it appeared to them as a reasonable and accurate picture of human existence. The gods ordered the drama on the real stage of the world; the dramatist ordered the drama on the mimic stage of the theatre—and the latter attained credibility and verisimilitude in proportion as it approached an exact imitation or reproduction of the former. Nietzsche saw that this quality of realism was the essence of all stage plays. "Only insofar as the dramatist, " he said, "coalesces with the primordial dramatist of the world, does he reach the true function of his craft." ("*Die Geburt der Tragödie*, " § 5.) "Man posits himself as the standard.... A race cannot do otherwise than thus acquiesce in itself." (*Götzendämmerung*" ix, § 19) In other words, man is interested in nothing whatever that has no bearing upon his own fate: he himself is his own hero. Thus the ancient Greeks were fond of tragedy because it reflected their life in miniature. In the mighty warriors who stalked the boards and defied the gods each Greek recognized himself. In the conflicts on the stage he saw replicas of that titanic conflict which seemed to him to be the eternal essence of human existence.

But why did the Greeks regard life as a conflict? In seeking an answer to this Nietzsche studied the growth of their civilization and of their race ideas. These race ideas, as among all other peoples, were visualized and crystallized in the qualities, virtues and opinions attributed to the racial gods. Therefore, Nietzsche undertook an inquiry into the nature of the gods set up by the Greeks, and particularly into the nature of the two gods who controlled the general scheme of Greek life, and, in consequence, of Greek art, —for art, as we have seen, is nothing more or less than a race's view or opinion of itself, i.e. an expression of the things it sees and the conclusions it draws when it observes and considers itself. These gods were Apollo and Dionysus.

Apollo, according to the Greeks, was the inventor of music, poetry and oratory, and as such, became the god of all art. Under his beneficent sway the Greeks became a race of artists and acquired all the refinement and culture that this implies. But the art that he taught them was essentially contemplative and subjective. It depicted, not so much things as they were, as things as they had been. Thus it became a mere record, and as such, exhibited repose as its chief quality. Whether it were expressed as sculpture, architecture, painting or epic poetry, this element of repose, or of action translated into repose, was uppermost. A painting of a man running, no matter how vividly it suggests the vitality and activity of the runner, is itself a thing inert and lifeless. Architecture, no matter how much its curves suggest motion and its hard lines the strength which may be translated into energy, is itself a thing immovable. Poetry, so long as it takes the form of the epic and is thus merely a chronicle of past actions, is as lifeless, at bottom, as a tax list.

The Greeks, during Apollo's reign as god of art, thus turned art into a mere inert fossil or record—a record either of human life itself or of the emotions which the vicissitudes of life arouse in the spectator. This notion of art was reflected in their whole civilization. They became singers of songs and weavers of metaphysical webs rather than doers of deeds, and the man who could carve a flower was more honored among them than the man who could grow one. In brief, they began to degenerate and go stale. Great men and great ideas grew few. They were on the downward road.

What they needed, of course, was the shock of contact with some barbarous, primitive people—an infusion of good red blood from some race that was still fighting for its daily bread and had had no time to grow contemplative and retrospective and fat. This infusion of red blood came in good time, but instead of coming from without (as it did years afterward in Rome, when the Goths swooped down from the North), it came from within. That is to say, there was no actual invasion of barbarian hordes, but merely an auto-reversion to simpler and more primitive ideas, which fanned the dormant energy of the Greeks into flame and so allowed them to accomplish their own salvation. This impulse came in the form of a sudden craze for a new god—Bacchus Dionysus.

Bacchus was a rude, boisterous fellow and the very antithesis of the quiet, contemplative Apollo. We remember him today merely as the god of wine, but in his time he stood, not only for drinking and carousing, but also for a whole system of art and a whole notion of civilization. Apollo represented the life meditative; Bacchus Dionysus represented the life strenuous. The one favored those forms of art by which human existence is halted and embalmed in some lifeless medium—sculpture, architecture, painting or epic poetry. The other was the god of life in process of actual being, and so stood for those forms of art which are not mere records or reflections of past existence, but brief snatches of present existence itself—dancing, singing, music and the drama.

It will be seen that this barbarous invasion of the new god and his minions made a profound change in the whole of Greek culture. Instead of devoting their time to writing epics, praising the laws, splitting philosophical hairs and hewing dead marble, the Greeks began to question all things made and ordained and to indulge in riotous and gorgeous orgies, in which thousands of maidens danced and hundreds of poets chanted songs of love and war, and musicians vied with cooks and vintners to make a grand delirium of joy. The result was that the entire outlook of the Greeks, upon history, upon morality and upon human life, was changed. Once a people of lofty introspection and elegant repose, they became a race of violent activity and strong emotions. They began to devote themselves, not to writing down the praises of existence as they had found it, but to the task of improving life and of widening the scope of present and future human activity and the bounds of possible human happiness.[57]

But in time there came a reaction and Apollo once more triumphed. He reigned for awhile, unsteadily and uncertainly, and then, again, the pendulum swung to the other side. Thus the Greeks swayed from one god to the other. During Apollo's periods of ascendancy they were contemplative and imaginative, and man, to them, seemed to reach his loftiest heights when he was most the historian. But when Dionysus was their best-beloved, they bubbled over with the joy of life, and man seemed,

---

[57] "This enrichment of consciousness among the Greeks ... showed itself first in the development of lyric poetry, in which the gradual transition from the expression of universal religious and political feeling to that which is personal and individual formed a typical process." Dr. Wilhelm Windelband, "A History of Ancient Philosophy, " tr. by H. E. Cushman; p. 18; New York.

not an historian, but a maker of history—not an artist, but a work of art. In the end, they verged toward a safe middle ground and began to weigh, with cool and calm, the ideas represented by the two gods. When they had done so, they came to the conclusion that it was not well to give themselves unreservedly to either. To attain the highest happiness, they decided, humanity required a dash of both. There was need in the world for dionysians, to give vitality an outlet and life a purpose, and there was need, too, for apollonians, to build life's monuments and read its lessons. They found that true civilization meant constant conflict between the two—between the dreamer and the man of action, between the artist who builds temples and the soldier who burns them down, between the priest and policeman who insist upon the permanence of laws and customs as they are and the criminal and reformer and conqueror who insist that they be changed.

When they had learned this lesson, the Greeks began to soar to heights of culture and civilization that, in the past, had been utterly beyond them, and so long as they maintained the balance between Apollo and Dionysus they continued to advance. But now and again, one god or the other grew stronger, and then there was a halt. When Apollo had the upper hand, Greece became too contemplative and too placid. When Dionysus was the victor, Greece became wild and thoughtless and careless of the desires of others, and so turned a bit toward barbarism. This seesawing continued for a long while, but Apollo was the final victor—if victor he may be called. In the eternal struggle for existence Greece became a mere looker-on. Her highest honors went to Socrates, a man who tried to reduce all life to syllogisms. Her favorite sons were rhetoricians, dialecticians and philosophical cobweb-spinners. She placed ideas above deeds. And in the end, as all students of history know, the state that once ruled the world descended to senility and decay, and dionysians from without overran it, and it perished in anarchy and carnage.

But with this we have nothing to do.

Nietzsche noticed that tragedy was most popular in Greece during the best days of the country's culture, when Apollo and Dionysus were properly balanced, one against the other. This ideal balancing between the two gods was the result, he concluded, not of conscious, but of unconscious impulses. That is to say, the Greeks did not call parliaments and discuss the matter, as they might have discussed a question of taxes, but acted entirely in obedience to their racial instinct. This instinct—this will to live or desire for power—led them to feel, without putting it into words, or even, for awhile, into definite thoughts, that they were happiest and safest and most vigorous, and so best able to preserve their national existence, when they kept to the golden mean. They didn't reason it out; they merely felt it.

But as Schopenhauer shows us, instinct, long exercised, means experience, and the memory of experience, in the end, crystallizes into what we call intelligence or reason. Thus the unconscious Greek feeling that the golden mean best served the race, finally took the form of an idea: *i.e.* that human life was an endless conflict between two forces, or impulses. These, as the Greeks saw them, were the dionysian impulse to destroy, to burn the candle, to "use up" life; and the apollonian impulse to preserve. Seeing life in this light, it was but natural that the Greeks should try to exhibit it in the same light on their stage. And so their tragedies were invariably founded upon some deadly and unending conflict—usually between a human hero and the gods. In a word, they made their stage plays set forth life as they saw it and found it, for, like all other human beings, at all times and everywhere, they were more interested in life as they found it than in anything else on the earth below or in the vasty void above.

When Nietzsche had worked out this theory of Greek tragedy and of Greek life, he set out, at once, to apply it to modern civilization, to see if it could explain certain ideas of the present as satisfactorily as it had explained one great idea of the past. He found that it could: that men were still torn between the apollonian impulse to conform and moralize and the dionysian impulse to exploit and explore. He found that all mankind might be divided into two classes: the apollonians who stood for permanence and the dionysians who stood for change. It was the aim of the former to live in strict obedience to certain invariable rules, which found expression as religion, law and morality. It was the aim of the latter to live under the most favorable conditions possible; to adapt themselves to changing circumstances, and to avoid the snares of artificial, permanent rules.

Nietzsche believed that an ideal human society would be one in which these two classes of men were evenly balanced—in which a vast, inert, religious, moral slave class stood beneath a small, alert, iconoclastic, immoral, progressive master class. He held that this master class—this aristocracy of efficiency—should regard the slave class as all men now regard the tribe of domestic beasts: as an order of servitors to be exploited and turned to account. The aristocracy of Europe, though it sought to do this with respect to the workers of Europe, seemed to him to fail miserably, because it was itself lacking in true efficiency. Instead of practising a magnificent opportunism and so adapting itself to changing conditions, it stood for formalism and permanence. Its fetish was property in land and the worship of this fetish had got it into such a rut that it was becoming less and less fitted to survive, and was, indeed, fast sinking into helpless parasitism. Its whole color and complexion were essentially apollonic.[58]Therefore Nietzsche preached the gospel of Dionysus, that a new aristocracy of efficiency might take the place of this old aristocracy of memories and inherited glories. He believed that it was only in this way that mankind could hope to forge ahead. He believed that there was need in the world for a class freed from the handicap of law and morality, a class acutely adaptable and immoral; a class bent on achieving, not the equality of all men, but the production, at the top, of the superman.

II. THE ORIGIN OF MORALITY

It may be urged with some reason, by those who have read the preceding chapter carefully, that the Nietzschean argument, so far, has served only to bring us face to face with a serious contradiction. We have been asked to believe that all human impulses are merely expressions of the primary instinct to preserve life by meeting the changing conditions of existence, and in the same breath we have been asked to believe, too, that the apollonian idea—which, like all other ideas, must necessarily be a result of this instinct—destroys adaptability and so tends to make life extra hazardous and difficult and progress impossible. Here we have our contradiction: the will to live is achieving, not life, but death. How are we to explain it away? How are we to account for the fact that the apollonian idea at the bottom of Christian morality, for example, despite its origin in the will to live, has an obvious tendency to combat free progress? How are we to account for the fact that the church, which is based upon this Christian morality, is, always has been and ever will be a bitter and implacable foe of good health, intellectual freedom, self-defense and every other essential factor of efficiency?

Nietzsche answers this by pointing out that an idea, while undoubtedly an effect or expression of the primary life instinct, is by no means identical with it. The latter manifests itself in widely different acts as conditions change: it is necessarily opportunistic and variable. The former, on the contrary, has a tendency to survive unchanged, even after its truth is transformed into falsity. That is to say, an idea which arises from a true and healthy instinct may survive long after this instinct itself, in consequence of the changing conditions of existence, has disappeared and given place to an instinct diametrically opposite. This survival of ideas we call morality. By its operation the human race is frequently saddled with the notions of generations long dead and forgotten. Thus we modern Christians still subscribe to the apollonian morality of the ancient Jews— our moral forebears—despite the fact that their ideas were evolved under conditions vastly different from those which confront us today. Thus the expressions of the life instinct, by obtaining an artificial and unnatural

---

[58] *Vide* the chapter on "Civilization."

permanence, turn upon the instinct itself and defeat its beneficent purpose. Thus our contradiction is explained.

To make this rather complicated reasoning more clear it is necessary to follow Nietzsche through the devious twists and windings of his exhaustive inquiry into the origin of moral codes. In making this inquiry he tried to rid himself of all considerations of authority and reverence, just as a surgeon, in performing a difficult and painful operation, tries to rid himself of all sympathy and emotion. Adopting this plan, he found that a code of morals was nothing more than a system of customs, laws and ideas which had its origin in the instinctive desire of some definite race to live under conditions which best subserved its own welfare. The morality of the Egyptians, he found, was one thing, and the morality of the Goths was another. The reason for the difference lay in the fact that the environment of the Egyptians—the climate of their land, the nature of their food supply and the characteristics of the peoples surrounding them—differed from the environment of the Goths. The morality of each race was, in brief, its consensus of instinct, and once having formulated it and found it good, each sought to give it force and permanence. This was accomplished by putting it into the mouths of the gods. What was once a mere expression of instinct thus became the mandate of a divine law-giver. What was once a mere attempt to meet imminent—and usually temporary—conditions of existence, thus became a code of rules to be obeyed forever, no matter how much these conditions of existence might change. Wherefore, Nietzsche concluded that the chief characteristic of a moral system was its tendency to perpetuate itself unchanged, and to destroy all who questioned it or denied it.[1]

Nietzsche saw that practically all members of a given race, including the great majority of those who violated these rules, were influenced into believing them—or at least into professing to believe them—utterly and unchangeably correct, and that it was the main function of all religions to enforce and support them by making them appear as laws laid down, at the beginning of the world, by the lord of the universe himself, or at some later period, by his son, messiah or spokesman. "Morality, " he said, "not only commands innumerable terrible means for preventing critical hands being laid upon her: her security depends still more upon a sort of enchantment at which she is phenomenally skilled. That is to say, she knows how to *enrapture*. She appeals to the emotions; her glance paralyzes the reason and the will.... Ever since there has been talking and persuading on earth, she has been the supreme mistress of seduction."[2]Thus "a double wall is put up against the continued testing, selection and criticism of values. On one hand is revelation, and on the other, veneration and tradition. The authority of the law is based upon two assumptions—first, that God gave it, and secondly, that the wise men of the past obeyed it."[3] Nietzsche came to the conclusion that this universal tendency to submit to moral codes—this unreasonable, emotional faith in the invariable truth of moral regulations—was a curse to the human race and the chief cause of its degeneration, inefficiency and unhappiness. And then he threw down the gauntlet by denying that an ever-present deity had anything to do with framing such codes and by endeavoring to prove that, far from being eternally true, they commonly became false with the passing of the years. Starting out as expressions of the primary life-instinct's effort to adapt some individual or race to certain given conditions of existence, they took no account of the fact that these conditions were constantly changing, and that the thing which was advantageous at one time and to one race was frequently injurious at some other time and to another race.

This reduction of all morality to mere expressions of expedience engaged the philosopher during what he calls his "tunneling" period. To exhibit his precise method of "tunneling" let us examine, for example, a moral idea which is found in the code of every civilized country. This is the notion that there is something inherently and fundamentally wrong in the act of taking human life. We have good reason to believe that murder was as much a crime 5, 000 years ago as it is today and that it took rank at the head of all conceivable outrages against humankind at the very dawn of civilization. And why? Simply because the man who took his neighbor's life made the life of everyone else in his neighborhood precarious and uncomfortable. It was plain that what he had done once he could do again, and so the peace and security of the whole district were broken.

Now, it is apparent that the average human being desires peace and security beyond all things, because it is only when he has them that he may satisfy his will to live—by procuring food and shelter for himself and by becoming the father of children. He is ill-fitted to fight for his existence; the mere business of living and begetting his kind consumes all of his energies: "the world, as a world, " as Horace Greeley said, "barely makes a living." Therefore, it came to be recognized at the very beginning of civilization, that the man who killed other men was a foe to those conditions which the average man had to seek in order to exist—to peace and order and quiet and security. Out of this grew the doctrine that it was immoral to commit murder, and as soon as mankind became imaginative enough to invent personal gods, this doctrine was put into their mouths and so attained the force and authority of divine wisdom. In some such manner, said Nietzsche, the majority of our present moral concepts were evolved. At the start they were mere echoes of a protest against actions which made existence difficult and so outraged and opposed the will to live.

As a rule, said Nietzsche, such familiar protests as that against murder, which laid down the maxim that the community had rights superior to those of the individual, were voiced by the weak, who found it difficult to protect themselves, as individuals, against the strong. One strong man, perhaps, was more than a match, in the struggle for existence, for ten weak men and so the latter were at a disadvantage. But fortunately for them they could overcome this by combination, for they were always in an overwhelming majority, numerically, and in consequence they were stronger, taken together, than the phalanx of the strong. Thus it gradually became possible for them to enforce the rules that they laid down for their own protection—which rules always operated against the wishes—and, as an obvious corollary, against the best interests of—the strong.[4] When the time arrived for fashioning religious systems, these rules were credited to the gods, and again the weak triumphed. Thus the desire of the weak among the world's early races of men, to protect their crops and wives against the forays of the strong, by general laws and divine decrees instead of by each man fighting for his own, has come down to us in the form of the Christian commandments: "Thou shalt not steal.... Thou shalt not covet thy neighbor's house.... Thou shalt not covet thy neighbor's wife, nor his manservant, nor his maidservant, nor his ox, nor his ass, nor anything that is thy neighbor's."

Nietzsche shows that the device of putting man-made rules of morality into the mouths of the gods—a device practiced by every nation in history—has vastly increased the respectability and force of all moral ideas. This is well exhibited by the fact that, even today and among thinking men, offenses which happen to be included in the scope of the Ten Commandments, either actually or by interpretation, are regarded with a horror which seldom, if ever, attaches to offenses obviously defined and delimited by merely human agencies. Thus, theft is everywhere looked upon as dishonorable, but cheating at elections, which is fully as dangerous to the body politic, is commonly pardoned by public opinion as a normal consequence of enthusiasm, and in some quarters is even regarded as an evidence of courage, not to say of a high and noble sense of gratitude and honor.

Nietzsche does not deny that human beings have a right to construct moral codes for themselves, and neither does he deny that they are justified, from their immediate standpoint, at least, in giving these codes the authority and force of divine commands. But he points out that this procedure is bound to cause trouble in the long run, for the reason that divine commands are fixed and invariable, and do not change as fast as the instincts and needs of the race. Suppose, for instance, that all acts of Parliament and Congress were declared to be the will of God, and that, as a natural consequence, the power to repeal or modify them were abandoned. It is apparent that the world would outgrow them as fast as it does today, but it is also apparent that the notion that they were infallible would paralyze and block all efforts, by atheistic reformers, to overturn or amend them. As a result, the British and American people would be compelled to live in obedience to rules which, on their very face, would often seem illogical and absurd.

Yet the same thing happens to notions of morality. They are devised, at the start, as measures of expediency, and then given divine sanction in order to lend them authority. In the course of time, perhaps, the race outgrows them, but none the less, they continue in force—at least so long as the old gods are worshipped. Thus human laws become divine—and inhuman. Thus morality itself becomes immoral. Thus the old instinct whereby society differentiates between good things and bad, grows muddled and uncertain, and the fundamental purpose of morality—that of producing a workable scheme of living—is defeated. Thereafter it is next to impossible to distinguish between the laws that are still useful and those that have outlived their usefulness, and the man who makes the attempt— the philosopher who endeavors to show humanity how it is condemning as bad a thing that, in itself, is now good, or exalting as good a thing that, for all its former goodness, is now bad—this man is damned as a heretic and anarchist, and according as fortune serves him, is burned at the stake or merely read out of the human race.[5]

Nietzsche found that all existing moral ideas might be divided into two broad classes, corresponding to the two broad varieties of human beings— the masters and the slaves. Every man is either a master or a slave, and the same is true of every race. Either it rules some other race or it is itself ruled by some other race. It is impossible to think of a man or of a people as being utterly isolated, and even were this last possible, it is obvious that the community would be divided into those who ruled and those who obeyed. The masters are strong and are capable of doing as they please; the slaves are weak and must obtain whatever rights they crave by deceiving, cajoling or collectively intimidating their masters. Now, since all moral codes, as we have seen, are merely collections of the rules laid down by some definite group of human beings for their comfort and protection, it is evident that the morality of the master class has for its main object the preservation of the authority and kingship of that class, while the morality of the slave class seeks to make slavery as bearable as possible and to exalt and dignify those things in which the slave can hope to become the apparent equal or superior of his master.

The civilization which existed in Europe before the dawn of Christianity was a culture based upon master-morality, and so we find that the theologians and moralists of those days esteemed a certain action as right only when it plainly subserved the best interests of strong, resourceful men. The ideal man of that time was not a meek and lowly sufferer, bearing his cross uncomplainingly, but an alert, proud and combative being who knew his rights and dared maintain them. In consequence we find that in many ancient languages, the words "good" and "aristocratic" were synonymous. Whatever served to make a man a nobleman—cunning, wealth, physical strength, eagerness to resent and punish injuries—was considered virtuous, praiseworthy and moral, [6] and on the other hand, whatever tended to make a man sink to the level of the great masses—humility, lack of ambition, modest desires, lavish liberality and a spirit of ready forgiveness—was regarded as immoral and wrong.

"Among these master races, " says Nietzsche, "the antithesis 'good and bad' signified practically the same as 'noble and contemptible!' The despised ones were the cowards, the timid, the insignificant, the self-abasing—the dog-species of men who allowed themselves to be misused—the flatterers and, above all, the liars. It is a fundamental belief of all true aristocrats that the common people are deceitful. 'We true ones, ' the ancient Greek nobles called themselves.

"It is obvious that the designations of moral worth were at first applied to individual men, and not to actions or ideas in the abstract. The master type of man regards himself as a sufficient judge of worth. He does not seek approval: his own feelings determine his conduct. 'What is injurious to me, ' he reasons, 'is injurious in itself.' This type of man honors whatever qualities he recognizes in himself: his morality is self-glorification. He has a feeling of plentitude and power and the happiness of high tension. He helps the unfortunate, perhaps, but it is not out of sympathy. The impulse, when it comes at all, rises out of his superabundance of power—his thirst to function. He honors his own power, and he knows how to keep it in hand. He joyfully exercises strictness and severity over himself and he reverences all that is strict and severe. 'Wotan has put a hard heart in my breast, ' says an old Scandinavian saga. There could be no better expression of the spirit of a proud viking....

"The morality of the master class is irritating to the taste of the present day because of its fundamental principle that a man has obligations only to his equals; that he may act to all of lower rank and to all that are foreign as he pleases.... The man of the master class has a capacity for prolonged gratitude and prolonged revenge, but it is only among his equals. He has, too, great resourcefulness in retaliation; great capacity for friendship, and a strong need for enemies, that there may be an outlet for his envy, quarrelsomeness and arrogance, and that by spending these passions in this manner, he may be gentle towards his friends."[7]

By this ancient *herrenmoral*, or master-morality, Napoleon Bonaparte would have been esteemed a god and the Man of Sorrows an enemy to society. It was the ethical scheme, indeed, of peoples who were sure of themselves and who had no need to make terms with rivals or to seek the good will or forbearance of anyone. In its light, such things as mercy and charity seemed pernicious and immoral, because they meant a transfer of power from strong men, whose proper business it was to grow stronger and stronger, to weak men, whose proper business it was to serve the strong. In a word, this master-morality was the morality of peoples who knew, by experience, that it was pleasant to rule and be strong. They knew that the nobleman was to be envied and the slave to be despised, and so they came to believe that everything which helped to make a man noble was good and everything which helped to make him a slave was evil. The idea of nobility and the idea of good were expressed by the same word, and this verbal identity survives in the English language today, despite the fact that our present system of morality, as we shall see, differs vastly from that of the ancient master races.

In opposition to this master-morality of the strong, healthy nations there was the *sklavmoral*, or slave-morality, of the weak nations. The Jews of the four or five centuries preceding the birth of Christ belonged to the latter class. Compared to the races around them, they were weak and helpless. It was out of the question for them to conquer the Greeks or Romans and it was equally impossible for them to force their laws, their customs or their religion upon their neighbors on other sides. They were, indeed, in the position of an army surrounded by a horde of irresistible enemies. The general of such an army, with the instinct of self-preservation strong within him, does not attempt to cut his way out. Instead he tries to make the best terms he can, and if the leader of the enemy insists upon making him and his vanquished force prisoners, he endeavors to obtain concessions which will make this imprisonment as bearable as possible. The strong man's object is to take as much as he can from his victim; the weak man's is to save as much as he can from his conqueror.

The fruit of this yearning of weak nations to preserve as much of their national unity as possible is the thing Nietzsche calls slave-morality. Its first and foremost purpose is to discourage, and if possible, blot out, all those traits and actions which are apt to excite the ire, the envy, or the cupidity of the menacing enemies round about. Revenge, pride and ambition are condemned as evils. Humility, forgiveness, contentment and resignation are esteemed virtues. The moral man is the man who has lost all desire to triumph and exult over his fellow-men—the man of mercy, of charity, of self-sacrifice.

"The impotence which does not retaliate for injuries, " says Nietzsche, "is falsified into 'goodness;' timorous abjectness becomes 'humility;' subjection to those one hates is called 'obedience, ' and the one who desires and commands this impotence, abjectness and subjection is called God. The inoffensiveness of the weak, their cowardice (of which they have ample store); their standing at the door, their unavoidable time-serving and waiting—all these things get good names. The inability to get revenge is translated into an *unwillingness* to get revenge, and becomes forgiveness, a virtue.

"They are wretched—these mutterers and forgers—but they say that their wretchedness is of God's choosing and even call it a distinction that he confers upon them. The dogs which are liked best, they say, are beaten most. Their wretchedness is a test, a preparation, a schooling—something which will be paid for, one day, in happiness. They call that 'bliss.'"[8]

By the laws of this slave-morality the immoral man is he who seeks power and eminence and riches—the millionaire, the robber, the fighter, the schemer. The act of acquiring property by conquest—which is looked upon as a matter of course by master-morality—becomes a crime and is called theft. The act of mating in obedience to natural impulses, without considering the desire of others, becomes adultery; the quite natural act of destroying one's enemies becomes murder.

---

[1]II Thess. II, 15: "Hold the tradition which ye have been taught." Eusebius Pamphilus: "Those things which are written believe; those things which are not written, neither think upon nor inquire after." St. Austin: "Whatever ye hear from the holy scriptures let it favor well with you; whatever is without them refuse." See also St. Basil, Tertullian and every other professional moralist since, down to John Alexander Dowie and Emperor William of Germany.

[2]"*Morgenröte*, " preface, § 3.

[3]"*Der Antichrist*, " § 57.

[4]The fact that the state is founded, not upon a mysterious "social impulse" in man, but upon each individual's regard for his own interest, was first pointed out by Thomas Hobbes (1588-1679), in his argument against Aristotle and Grotius.

[5]The risk of such idol-smashing is well set forth at length by G. Bernard Shaw in the preface to "The Quintessence of Ibsenism;" London, 1904.

[6]Henry Bradley, in a lecture at the London Institution, in Jan 1907, showed that this was true of the ancient Britons, as is demonstrated by their liking for bestowing such names as Wolf and Bear upon themselves. It was true, also, of the North American Indians and of all primitive races conscious of their efficiency.

[7]"*Jenseits von Gut und Böse*, " § 260.

[8]"*Zur Genealogie der Moral*, " I, § 14.

III. BEYOND GOOD AND EVIL

Despite the divine authority which gives permanence to all moral codes, this permanence is constantly opposed by the changing conditions of existence, and very often the opposition is successful. The slave-morality of the ancient Jews has come down to us, with its outlines little changed, as ideal Christianity, but such tenacious persistence of a moral scheme is comparatively rare. As a general rule, in truth, races change their gods very much oftener than we have changed ours, and have less faith than we in the independence of intelligence. In consequence they constantly revamp and modify their moral concepts. The same process of evolution affects even our own code, despite the extraordinary tendency to permanence just noted. Our scheme of things, in its fundamentals, has persisted for 2, 500 years, but in matters of detail it is constantly in a state of flux. We still call ourselves Christians, but we have evolved many moral ideas that are not to be found in the scriptures and we have sometimes denied others that are plainly there. Indeed, as will be shown later on, the beatitudes would have wiped us from the face of the earth centuries ago had not our forefathers devised means of circumventing them without openly questioning them. Our progress has been made, not as a result of our moral code, but as a result of our success in dodging its inevitable blight.

All morality, in fact, is colored and modified by opportunism, even when its basic principles are held sacred and kept more or less intact. The thing that is a sin in one age becomes a virtue in the next. The ancient Persians, who were Zoroastrians, regarded murder and suicide, under any circumstances, as crimes. The modern Persians, who are Mohammedans, think that ferocity and foolhardiness are virtues. The ancient Japanese, to whom the state appeared more important than the man, threw themselves joyously upon the spears of the state's enemies. The modern Japanese, who are fledgling individualists, armor their ships with nickel steel and fight on land from behind bastions of earth and masonry. And in the same way the moral ideas that have grown out of Christianity, and even some of its important original doctrines, are being constantly modified and revised, despite the persistence of the fundamental notion of self-sacrifice at the bottom of them. In Dr. Andrew D. White's monumental treatise "On the Warfare of Science with Theology in Christendom" there are ten thousand proofs of it. Things that were crimes in the middle ages are quite respectable at present. Actions that are punishable by excommunication and ostracism in Catholic Spain today, are sufficient to make a man honorable in freethinking England. In France, where the church once stood above the king, it is now stripped of all rights not inherent in the most inconsequential social club. In Germany it is a penal offense to poke fun at the head of the state; in the United States it is looked upon by many as an evidence of independence and patriotism. In some of the American states a violation of the seventh commandment, in any form, is a felony; in Maryland, it is, in one form, a mere misdemeanor, and another form, no crime at all.

"Many lands did I see, " says Zarathustra, "and many peoples, and so I discovered the good and bad of many peoples.... Much that was regarded as good by one people was held in scorn and contempt by another. I found many things called bad here and adorned with purple honors there.... A catalogue of blessings is posted up for every people. Lo! it is the catalogue of their triumphs—the voice of their will to power!... Whatever enables them to rule and conquer and dazzle, to the dismay and envy of their neighbors, is regarded by them as the summit, the head, the standard of all things.... Verily, men have made for themselves all their good and bad. Verily they did not find it so: it did not come to them as a voice from heaven.... It is only through valuing that there comes value." (*Also sprach Zarathustra*" I.)

To proceed from the concrete to the general, and to risk a repetition, it is evident that all morality, as Nietzsche pointed out, is nothing more than an expression of expediency. [59] A thing is called wrong solely because a definite group of people, at some specific stage of their career, have found it injurious to them. The fact that they have discovered grounds for condemning it in some pronunciamento of their god signifies nothing, for the reason that the god of a people is never anything more than a reflection of their ideas for the time being. As Prof. Otto Pfleiderer has shown in his masterly treatise, "Christian Origins, "(tr. by David A. Huebsch: New York, 1906) Jesus Christ was a product of his age, mentally and spiritually as well as physically. Had there been no Jewish theology before him, he could not have sought or obtained recognition as a messiah, and the doctrines that he expressed—had he ever expressed them at all—would have fallen upon unheeding and uncomprehending ears.

Therefore it is plain that the Ten Commandments are no more immortal and immutable, in the last analysis, than the acts of Parliament. They have lasted longer, it is true, and they will probably continue in force for many years, but this permanence is only relative. Fundamentally they are merely expressions of expedience, like the rules of some great game, and it is easily conceivable that there may arise upon the earth, at some future day, a race to whom they will appear injurious, unreasonable and utterly immoral. "The time may come, indeed, when we will prefer the *Memorabilia* of Socrates to the Bible."("*Menschliches allzu Menschliches*" III.)

---

[59] The word *mos*, from signifying what is customary, has come to signify what is right." Sir Wm. Markby: "Elements of Law Considered with Reference to General Principles of Jurisprudence:" pp. 118, 5th ed., London, 1896.

Admitting this, we must admit the inevitable corollary that morality in the absolute sense has nothing to do with truth, and that it is, in fact, truth's exact antithesis. Absolute truth necessarily implies eternal truth. The statement that a man and a woman are unlike was true on the day the first man and woman walked the earth and it will be true so long as there are men and women. Such a statement approaches very near our ideal of an absolute truth. But the theory that humility is a virtue is not an absolute truth, for while it was undoubtedly true in ancient Judea, it was not true in ancient Greece and is debatable, to say the least, in modern Europe and America. The Western Catholic Church, despite its extraordinarily successful efforts at permanence, has given us innumerable proofs that laws, in the long run, always turn upon themselves. The popes were infallible when they held that the earth was flat and they were infallible when they decided that it was round—and so we reach a palpable absurdity. Therefore, we may lay it down as an axiom that morality, in itself, is the enemy of truth, and that, for at least half of the time, by the mathematical doctrine of probabilities, it is necessarily untrue.

If this is so, why should any man bother about moral rules and regulations? Why should any man conform to laws formulated by a people whose outlook on the universe probably differed diametrically from his own? Why should any man obey a regulation which is denounced, by his common-sense, as a hodge-podge of absurdities, and why should he model his whole life upon ideals invented to serve the temporary needs of a forgotten race of some past age? These questions Nietzsche asked himself. His conclusion was a complete rejection of all fixed codes of morality, and with them of all gods, messiahs, prophets, saints, popes, bishops, priests, and rulers.

The proper thing for a man to do, he decided, was to formulate his own morality as he progressed from lower to higher things. He should reject the old conceptions of good and evil and substitute for them the human valuations, good and bad. In a word, he should put behind him the morality invented by some dead race to make its own progress easy and pleasant, and credited to some man-made god to give it authority, and put in the place of this a workable personal morality based upon his own power of distinguishing between the things which benefit him and the things which injure him. He should (to make the idea clearer) judge a given action solely by its effect upon his own welfare; his own desire or will to live; and that of his children after him. All notions of sin and virtue should be banished from his mind. He should weigh everything in the scales of individual expedience.

Such a frank wielding of a razor-edged sword in the struggle for existence is frowned upon by our Jewish slave-morality. We are taught to believe that the only true happiness lies in self-effacement; that it is wrong to profit by the misfortune or weakness of another. But against this Nietzsche brings the undeniable answer that all life, no matter how much we idealize it, is, at bottom, nothing more or less than exploitation. The gain of one man is inevitably the loss of some other man. That the emperor may die of a surfeit the peasant must die of starvation. Among human beings, as well as among the bacilli in the hanging drop and the lions in the jungle, there is ever in progress this ancient struggle for existence. It is waged decently, perhaps, but it is none the less savage and unmerciful, and the devil always takes the hindmost.

"Life, " says Nietzsche, "is essentially the appropriation, the injury, the vanquishing of the unadapted and weak. Its object is to obtrude its own forms and insure its own unobstructed functioning. Even an organization whose individuals forbear in their dealings with one another (a healthy aristocracy, for example) must, if it would live and not die, act hostilely toward all other organizations. It must endeavor to gain ground, to obtain advantages, to acquire ascendancy. And this is not because it is *immoral*, but because it lives, and all life is will to power."(*Jenseits von Gut und Böse,* § 259) Nietzsche argues from this that it is absurd to put the stigma of evil upon the mere symptoms of the great struggle. "In itself, " he says, "an act of injury, violation, exploitation or annihilation cannot be wrong, for life operates, essentially and fundamentally, by injuring, violating, exploiting and annihilating, and cannot even be conceived of out of this character. One must admit, indeed, that, from the highest biological standpoint, conditions under which the so-called rights of others are recognized must ever be regarded as exceptional conditions—that is to say, as partial restrictions of the instinctive power-seeking will-to-live of the individual, made to satisfy the more powerful will-to-live of the mass. Thus small units of power are sacrificed to create large units of power. To regard the rights of others as being inherent in them, and not as mere compromises for the benefit of the mass-unit, would be to enunciate a principle hostile to life itself."(*"Zur Genealogie der Moral"* II,§11)

Nietzsche holds that the rights of an individual may be divided into two classes: those things he is able to do despite the opposition of his fellow men, and those things he is enabled to do by the grace and permission of his fellow men. The second class of rights may be divided again into two groups: those granted through fear and foresight, and those granted as free gifts. But how do fear and foresight operate to make one man concede rights to another man? It is easy enough to discern two ways. In the first place, the grantor may fear the risks of a combat with the grantee, and so give him what he wants without a struggle. In the second place, the grantor, while confident of his ability to overcome the grantee, may forbear because he sees in the struggle a certain diminution of strength on both sides, and in consequence, an impaired capacity for joining forces in effective opposition to some hostile third power.

And now for the rights obtained under the second head—by bestowal and concession. "In this case, " says Nietzsche, "one man or race has enough power, and more than enough, to be able to bestow some of it on another man or race." ("*Morgenröte,* " § 112) The king appoints one subject viceroy of a province, and so gives him almost regal power, and makes another cup-bearer and so gives him a perpetual right to bear the royal cup. When the power of the grantee, through his inefficiency, decreases, the grantor either restores it to him or takes it away from him altogether. When the power of the grantee, on the contrary, increases, the grantor, in alarm, commonly seeks to undermine it and encroach upon it. When the power of the grantee remains at a level for a considerable time, his rights become "vested" and he begins to believe that they are inherent in him— that they constitute a gift from the gods and are beyond the will and disposal of his fellow men. As Nietzsche points out, this last happens comparatively seldom. More often, the grantor himself begins to lose power and so comes into conflict with the grantee, and not infrequently they exchange places. "National rights, " says Nietzsche, "demonstrate this fact by their constant lapse and regenesis."(*Morgenröte,* § 112)

Nietzsche believed that a realization of all this would greatly benefit the human race, by ridding it of some of its most costly delusions. He held that so long as it sought to make the struggle for existence a parlor game, with rules laid down by some blundering god—that so long as it regarded its ideas of morality, its aspirations and its hopes as notions implanted by the creator in the mind of Father Adam—that so long as it insisted upon calling things by fanciful names and upon frowning down all effort to reach the ultimate verities—that just so long its progress would be fitful and slow. It was morality that burned the books of the ancient sages, and morality that halted the free inquiry of the Golden Age and substituted for it the credulous imbecility of the Age of Faith. It was a fixed moral code and a fixed theology which robbed the human race of a thousand years by wasting them upon alchemy, heretic-burning, witchcraft and sacerdotalism.

Nietzsche called himself an immoralist. He believed that all progress depended upon the truth and that the truth could not prevail while men yet enmeshed themselves in a web of gratuitous and senseless laws fashioned by their own hands. He was fond of picturing the ideal immoralist as "a magnificent blond beast"—innocent of "virtue" and "sin" and knowing only "good" and "bad." Instead of a god to guide him, with commandments and the fear of hell, this immoralist would have his own instincts and intelligence. Instead of doing a given thing because the church called it a virtue or the current moral code required it, he would do it because he knew that it would benefit him or his descendants after him. Instead of refraining from a given action because the church denounced it as a sin and the law as a crime, he would avoid it only if he were convinced that the action itself, or its consequences, might work him or his an injury.

Such a man, were he set down in the world today, would bear an outward resemblance, perhaps, to the most pious and virtuous of his fellow-citizens, but it is apparent that his life would have more of truth in it and less of hypocrisy and cant and pretense than theirs. He would obey the laws of the land frankly and solely because he was afraid of incurring their penalties, and for no other reason, and he would not try to delude his neighbors and himself into believing that he saw anything sacred in them. He would have no need of a god to teach him the difference between right and wrong and no need of priests to remind him of this god's teachings. He would look upon the woes and ills of life as inevitable and necessary results of life's conflict, and he would make no effort to read into them the wrath of a peevish and irrational deity at his own or his ancestors' sins. His mind would be absolutely free of thoughts of sin and hell, and in consequence, he would be vastly happier than the majority of persons about him. All in all, he would be a powerful influence for truth in his community, and as such, would occupy himself with the most noble and sublime task possible to mere human beings: the overthrow of superstition and unreasoning faith, with their long train of fears, horrors, doubts, frauds, injustice and suffering. [60] Under an ideal government—which Herbert Spencer defines as a government in which the number of laws has reached an irreducible minimum—such a man would prosper a great deal more than the priest-ridden, creed-barnacled masses about him. [61] In a state wherein communistic society, with its levelling usages and customs, had ceased to exist, and wherein each individual of the master class was permitted to live his life as much as possible in accordance with his own notions of good and bad, such a man would stand forth from the herd in proportion as his instincts were more nearly healthy and infallible than the instincts of the herd. Ideal anarchy, in brief, would insure the success of

---

[60] "It is my experience, " said Thomas H. Huxley, "that, aside from a few human affections, the only thing that gives lasting and untainted pleasure in the world, is the pursuit of truth and the destruction of error." See "The Life and Letters of T. H. Huxley, " by Leonard Huxley; London, 1900.

[61] "Read the suicide tables and see how many despairing men, hope less of keeping their homes together, pay with their lives the toil imposed upon them by squanderers of the public money." Helen Mathers in *P. T. O.*, Feb. 9 1907, p. 180. This is one of Tolstoi's chief arguments against all government.

those men who were wisest mentally and strongest physically, and the race would make rapid progress.

It is evident that the communistic and socialistic forms of government at present in fashion in the world oppose such a consummation as often as they facilitate it. Civilization, as we know it, makes more paupers than millionaires, and more cripples than Sandows. Its most conspicuous products, the church and the king, stand unalterably opposed to all progress. Like the frog of the fable, which essayed to climb out of a well, it slips back quite as often as it goes ahead.

And for these reasons Nietzsche was an anarchist—in the true meaning of that much-bespattered word—just as Herbert Spencer and Arthur Schopenhauer were anarchists before him.

IV. THE SUPERMAN

No doubt the reader who has followed the argument in the preceding chapters will have happened, before now, upon the thought that Nietzsche's chain of reasoning, so far, still has a gap in it. We have seen how he started by investigating Greek art in the light of the Schopenhauerean philosophy, how this led him to look into morality, how he revealed the origin of morality in transitory manifestations of the will to power, and how he came to the conclusion that it was best for a man to reject all ready-made moral ideas and to so order his life that his every action would be undertaken with some notion of making it subserve his own welfare or that of his children or children's children. But a gap remains and it may be expressed in the question: How is a man to define and determine his own welfare and that of the race after him?

Here, indeed, our dionysian immoralist is confronted by a very serious problem, and Nietzsche himself well understood its seriousness. Unless we have in mind some definite ideal of happiness and some definite goal of progress we had better sing the doxology and dismiss our congregation. Christianity has such an ideal and such a goal. The one is a Christ-like life on earth and the other is a place at the right hand of Jehovah in the hereafter. Mohammedanism, a tinsel form of Christianity, paints pictures of the same sort. Buddhism holds out the tempting bait of a race set free from the thrall of earthly desires, with an eternity of blissful nothingness.[1] The other oriental faiths lead in the same direction and Schopenhauer, in his philosophy, laid down the doctrine that humanity would attain perfect happiness only when it had overcome its instinct of self-preservation—that is to say, when it had ceased to desire to live. Even Christian Science—that most grotesque child of credulous faith and incredible denial—offers us the double ideal of a mortal life entirely free from mortal pain and a harp in the heavenly band for all eternity.

What had Nietzsche to offer in place of these things? By what standard was his immoralist to separate the good—or beneficial—things of the world from the bad—or damaging—things? And what was the goal that the philosopher had in mind for his immoralist? The answer to the first question is to be found in Nietzsche's definition of the terms "good" and "bad." "All that elevates the sense of power, the will to power, and power itself"—this is how he defined "good." "All that proceeds from weakness"— this is how he defined "bad." Happiness, he held, is "the feeling that power increases—that resistance is being overcome." "I preach not contentedness, " he said, "but more power; not peace, but war; not virtue, but efficiency. The weak and defective must go to the wall: that is the first principle of the dionysian charity. And we must help them to go."[2]

To put it more simply, Nietzsche offers the gospel of prudent and intelligent selfishness, of absolute and utter individualism. "One must learn, " sang Zarathustra, "how to love oneself, with a whole and hearty love, that one may find life with oneself endurable, and not go gadding about. This gadding about is familiar: it is called loving one's neighbor.'"[3] His ideal was an aristocracy which regarded the proletariat merely as a conglomeration of draft animals made to be driven, enslaved and exploited. "A good and healthy aristocracy, " he said, "must acquiesce, with a good conscience, in the sacrifice of a legion of individuals, who, for its benefit, must be reduced to slaves and tools. The masses have no right to exist on their own account: their sole excuse for living lies in their usefulness as a sort of superstructure or scaffolding, upon which a more select race of beings may be elevated."[4] Rejecting all permanent rules of good and evil and all notions of brotherhood, Nietzsche held that the aristocratic individualist—and it was to the aristocrat only that he gave, unreservedly, the name of human being—must seek every possible opportunity to increase and exalt his own sense of efficiency, of success, of mastery, of power. Whatever tended to impair him, or to decrease his efficiency, was bad. Whatever tended to increase it—at no matter what cost to others—was good. There must be a complete surrender to the law of natural selection—that invariable natural law which ordains that the fit shall survive and the unfit shall perish. All growth must occur at the top. The strong must grow stronger, and that they may do so, they must waste no strength in the vain task of trying to lift up the weak.

The reader may interrupt here with the question we encountered at the start: how is the dionysian individualist to know whether a given action will benefit him or injure him? The answer, of course, lies in the obvious fact that, in every healthy man, instinct supplies a very reliable guide, and that, when instinct fails or is uncertain, experiment must solve the problem. As a general thing, nothing is more patent than the feeling of power—the sense of efficiency, of capacity, of mastery. Every man is constantly and unconsciously measuring himself with his neighbors, and so becoming acutely aware of those things in which he is their superior. Let two men clash in the stock market and it becomes instantly apparent that one is richer, or more resourceful or more cunning than the other. Let two men run after an omnibus and it becomes instantly apparent that one is swifter than the other. Let two men come together as rivals in love, war, drinking or holiness, and one is bound to feel that he has bested the other. Such contests are infinite in variety and in number, and all life, in fact, is made up of them. Therefore, it is plain that every man is conscious of his power, and aware of it when this power is successfully exerted against some other man. In such exertions, argues Nietzsche, lies happiness, and so his prescription for happiness consists in unrestrained yielding to the will to power. That all men worth discussing so yield, despite the moral demand for humility, is so plain that it scarcely needs statement. It is the desire to attain and manifest efficiency and superiority which makes one man explore the wilds of Africa and another pile up vast wealth and another write books of philosophy and another submit to pain and mutilation in the prize ring. It is this yearning which makes men take chances and risk their lives and limbs for glory. Everybody knows, indeed, that in the absence of such a primordial and universal emulation the world would stand still and the race would die. Nietzsche asks nothing more than that the fact be openly recognized and admitted; that every man yield to the yearning unashamed, without hypocrisy and without wasteful efforts to feed and satisfy the yearning of other men at the expense of his own.

It is evident, of course, that the feeling of superiority has a complement in the feeling of inferiority. Every man, in other words, sees himself, in respect to some talent possessed in common by himself and a rival, in one of three ways: he knows that he is superior, he knows that he is inferior, or he is in doubt. In the first case, says Nietzsche, the thing for him to do is to make his superiority still greater by yielding to its stimulation: to make the gap between himself and his rival wider and wider. In the second case, the thing for him to do is to try to make the gap smaller: to lift himself up or to pull his rival down until they are equal or the old disproportion is reversed. In the third case, it is his duty to plunge into a contest and risk his all upon the cast of the die. "I do not exhort you to peace, " says Zarathustra, "but to victory!"[5] If victory comes not, let it be defeat, death and annihilation—but, in any event, let there be a fair fight. Without this constant strife—this constant testing—this constant elimination of the unfit—there can be no progress. "As the smaller surrenders himself to the greater, so the greater must surrender himself to the will to power and stake life upon the issue. It is the mission of the greatest to run risk and danger—to cast dice with death."[6] Power, in a word, is never infinite: it is always becoming.

Practically and in plain language, what does all this mean? Simply that Nietzsche preaches a mighty crusade against all those ethical ideas which teach a man to sacrifice himself for the theoretical good of his inferiors. A culture which tends to equalize, he says, is necessarily a culture which tends to rob the strong and so drag them down, for the strong cannot give of their strength to the weak without decreasing their store. There must be an unending effort to widen the gap; there must be a constant search for advantage, an infinite alertness. The strong man must rid himself of all idea that it is disgraceful to yield to his acute and ever present yearning for still more strength. There must be an abandonment of the old slave-morality and a transvaluation of moral values. The will to power must be emancipated from the bonds of that system of ethics which brands it with infamy, and so makes the one all-powerful instinct of every sentient creature loathsome and abominable.

It is only the under-dog, he says, that believes in equality. It is only the groveling and inefficient mob that seeks to reduce all humanity to one dead level, for it is only the mob that would gain by such leveling. "'There are no higher men, ' says the crowd in the market place. 'We are all equal; man is man; in the presence of God we are all equal!' In the presence of God, indeed! But I tell you that God is dead!" So thunders Zarathustra.[7] That is to say, our idea of brotherhood is part of the mob-morality of the ancient Jews, who evolved it out of their own helplessness and credited it to their god. We have inherited their morality with their god and so we find it difficult—in the mass—to rid ourselves of their point of view. Nietzsche himself rejected utterly the Judaic god and he believed that the great majority of intelligent men of his time were of his mind. That he was not far wrong in this assumption is evident to everyone. At the present time, indeed, it is next to impossible to find a sane man in all the world who believes in the actual existence of the deity described in the old testament. All theology is now an effort to explain away this god. Therefore, argues Nietzsche, it is useless to profess an insincere concurrence in a theistic idea at which our common sense revolts, and ridiculous to maintain the inviolability of an ethical scheme grounded upon this idea.

It may be urged here that, even if the god of Judea is dead, the idea of brotherhood still fives, and that, as a matter of fact, it is an idea inherent in the nature of man, and one that owes nothing to the rejected supernaturalism which once fortified and enforced it. That is to say, it may be argued that the impulse to self-sacrifice and mutual help is itself an instinct. The answer to this lies in the very patent fact that it is not. Nothing, indeed, is more apparent than the essential selfishness of man.

In so far as they are able to defy or evade the moral code without shame or damage, the strong always exploit the weak. The rich man puts up the price of the necessities of life and so makes himself richer and the poor poorer. The emperor combats democracy. The political boss opposes the will of the people for his own advantage. The inventor patents his inventions and so increases his relative superiority to the common run of men. The ecclesiastic leaves a small parish for a larger one—because the pay is better or "the field offers wider opportunities, " *i.e.* gives him a better chance to "save souls" and so increases his feeling of efficiency. The philanthropist gives away millions because the giving visualizes and makes evident to all men his virtue and power. It is ever the same in this weary old world: every slave would be a master if he could. Therefore, why deny it? Why make it a crime to do what every man's instincts prompt him to do? Why call it a sin to do what every man does, insofar as he can? The man who throws away his money or cripples himself with drink, or turns away from his opportunities—we call him a lunatic or a fool. And yet, wherein does he differ from the ideal holy man of our slave-morality—the holy man who tortures himself, neglects his body, starves his mind and reduces himself to parasitism, that the weak, the useless and unfit may have, through his ministrations, some measure of ease? Such is the argument of the dionysian philosophy. It is an argument for the actual facts of existence—however unrighteous and ugly those facts may be.

That the lifting up of the weak, in the long run, is an unprofitable and useless business is evident on very brief reflection. Philanthropy, considered largely, is inevitably a failure. Now and then we may transform an individual pauper or drunkard into a useful, producing citizen, but this happens very seldom. Nothing is more patent, indeed, than the fact that charity merely converts the unfit—who, in the course of nature, would soon die out and so cease to encumber the earth—into parasites—who live on indefinitely, a nuisance and a burden to their betters. The "reformed" drunkard always goes back to his cups: drunkardness, as every physician knows, is as essentially incurable as congenital insanity. And it is the same with poverty. We may help a pauper to survive by giving him food and drink, but we cannot thereby make an efficient man of him—we cannot rid him of the unfitness which made him a pauper. There are, of course, exceptions to this, as to other rules, but the validity of the rule itself will not be questioned by any observant man. It goes unquestioned, indeed, by those who preach the doctrine of charity the loudest. They know it would be absurd to argue that helping the unfit is profitable to the race, and so they fall back, soon or late, upon the argument that charity is ordained of God and that the impulse to it is implanted in every decent man. Nietzsche flatly denies this. Charity, he says, is a man-made idea, with which the gods have nothing to do. Its sole effect is to maintain the useless at the expense of the strong. In the mass, the helped can never hope to discharge in full their debt to the helpers. The result upon the race is thus retrogression.

And now for our second question. What was the goal Nietzsche had in mind for his immoralist? What was to be the final outcome of his overturning of all morality? Did he believe the human race would progress until men became gods and controlled the sun and stars as they now control the flow of great rivers? Or did he believe that the end of it all would be annihilation? After the publication of Nietzsche's earlier books, with their ruthless tearing down of the old morality, these questions were asked by critics innumerable in all the countries of Europe. The philosopher was laughed at as a crazy iconoclast who destroyed without rebuilding. He was called a visionary and a lunatic, and it was reported and believed that he had no answer: that his philosophy was doomed to bear itself to the earth, like an arch without a keystone. But in April, 1883, he began the publication of "*Also sprach Zarathustra*" and therein his reply was written large.

"I teach you, " cries Zarathustra, "the superman! Man is something that shall be surpassed. What, to man, is the ape? A joke or a shame. Man shall be the same to the superman: a joke or shame.... Man is a bridge connecting ape and superman.... The superman will be the final flower and ultimate expression of the earth. I conjure you to be faithful to the earth ... to cease looking beyond the stars for your hopes and rewards. You must sacrifice yourself to the earth that one day it may bring forth the superman."[8]

Here we hearken unto the materialist, the empiricist, the monist *par excellence.* And herein we perceive dimly the outlines of the superman. He will be rid of all delusions that hamper and oppress the will to power. He will be perfect in body and perfect in mind. He will know everything worth knowing and have strength and skill and cunning to defend himself against any conceivable foe. Because the prospect of victory will feed his will to power he will delight in combat, and his increasing capacity for combat will decrease his sensitiveness to pain. Conscious of his efficiency, he will be happy; having no illusions regarding a heaven and a hell, he will be content. He will see life as something pleasant—something to be faced gladly and with a laugh. He will say "yes" alike to its pleasures and to its ills. Rid of the notion that there is anything filthy in living—that the flesh is abominable[9] and life an affliction[10]—he will grow better and better fitted to meet the conditions of actual existence. He will be scornful, merciless and supremely fit. He will be set free from man's fear of gods and of laws, just as man has been set free from the ape's fear of lions and of open places.

To put it simply, the superman's thesis will be this: that he has been put into the world without his consent, that he must live in the world, that he owes nothing to the other people there, and that he knows nothing whatever of existence beyond the grave. Therefore, it will be his effort to attain the highest possible measure of satisfaction for the only unmistakable and genuinely healthy instinct within him: the yearning to live—to attain power—to meet and overcome the influences which would weaken or destroy him. "Keep yourselves up, my brethren, "cautions Zarathustra, "learn to keep yourselves up! The sea is stormy and many seek to keep afloat by your aid. The sea is stormy and all are overboard. Well, cheer up and save yourselves, ye old seamen!... What is your fatherland? The land wherein your children will dwell.... Thus does your love to these remote ones speak: 'Disregard your neighbors! Man is something to be surpassed!' Surpass yourself at the expense of your neighbor. What you cannot seize, let no man *give* you.... Let him who can command, obey!"[11] The idea, by this time, should be plain. The superman, in the struggle for existence, asks and gives no quarter. He believes that it is the destiny of sentient beings to progress upward, and he is willing to sacrifice himself that his race may do so. But his sacrifice must benefit, not his neighbor—not the man who should and must look out for himself—but the generations yet unborn.

It must be borne in mind that the superman will make a broad distinction between instinct and passion—that he will not mistake the complex thing we call love, with its costly and constant hurricanes of emotion, for the instinct of reproduction—that he will not mistake mere anger for war—that he will not mistake patriotism, with all its absurdities and illusions, for the homing instinct. The superman, in brief, will know how to renounce as well as how to possess, but his renunciation will be the child, not of faith or of charity, but of expediency. "Will nothing beyond your capacity, " says Zarathustra. "Demand nothing of yourself that is beyond achievement!... The higher a thing is, the less often does it succeed. Be of good cheer! What matter! Learn to laugh at yourselves!... Suppose you have failed? Has not the future gained by your failure?"[12] The superman, as Nietzsche was fond of putting it, must play at dice with death. He must have ever in mind no other goal but the good of the generations after him. He must be willing to battle with his fellows, as with illusions, that those who came after may not be afflicted by these enemies. He must be supremely unmoral and unscrupulous. His must be the gospel of eternal defiance.

Nietzsche, it will be observed, was unable to give any very definite picture of this proud, heaven-kissing superman. It is only in Zarathustra's preachments to "the higher man, " a sort of bridge between man and superman, that we may discern the philosophy of the latter. On one occasion Nietzsche penned a passage which seemed to compare the superman to "the great blond beasts" which ranged Europe in the days of the mammoth, and from this fact many commentators have drawn the conclusion that he had in mind a mere two-legged brute, with none of the higher traits that we now speak of as distinctly human. But, as a matter of fact, he harbored no such idea. In another place, wherein he speaks of three metamorphoses of the race, under the allegorical names of the camel, the lion and the child, he makes this plain. The camel, a hopeless beast of burden, is man. But when the camel goes into the solitary desert, it throws off its burden and becomes a lion. That is to say, the heavy and hampering load of artificial dead-weight called morality is cast aside and the instinct to live—or, as Nietzsche insists upon regarding it, the will to power—is given free rein. The lion is the "higher man"—the intermediate stage between man and superman. The latter appears neither as camel nor lion, but as a little child. He knows a little child's peace. He has a little child's calm. Like a babe *in utero* he is ideally adapted to his environment.

Zarathustra sees man "like a camel kneeling down to be heavy laden." What are his burdens? One is "to humiliate oneself." Another is "to love those who despise us." In the desert comes the first metamorphosis, and the "thou shalt" of the camel becomes the "I will" of the lion. And what is the mission of the lion? "To create for itself freedom for new creating." After the lion comes the child. It is "innocence and oblivion, a new starting, a play, a wheel rolling by itself, a prime motor, a holy asserting." The thought here is cast in the heightened language of mystic poetry, but its meaning, I take it, is not lost.[13]

Nietzsche, even more than Schopenhauer, recognized the fact that great mental progress—in the sense that mental progress means an increased capacity for grappling with the conditions of existence— necessarily has to depend upon physical efficiency. In exceptional cases a great mind may inhabit a diseased body, but it is obvious that this is not the rule. A nation in which the average man had but one hand and the duration of life was but 20 years could not hope to cope with even the weakest nation of modern Europe. So it is plain that the first step in the improvement of the race must be the improvement of the body. Jesus Christ gave expression to this need by healing the sick, and the chief end and aim of all modern science is that of making life more and more bearable. Every labor-saving machine ever invented by man has no other purpose than that of saving bodily wear and tear. Every religion aims to rescue man from the racking fear of hell and the strain of trying to solve the great problems of existence for himself. Every scheme of government that we know is, at bottom, a mere device for protecting human beings from injury and death.

Thus it will be seen that Nietzsche's program of progress does not differ from other programs quite so much as, at first sight, it may seem to do. He laid down the principle that, before anything else could be accomplished, we must have first looked to the human machine. As we have seen, the intellect is a mere symptom of the will to live. Therefore whatever removes obstacles to the free exercise of this will to live, necessarily promotes and increases intelligence. A race that was never incapacitated by illness would be better fitted than any other race for any conceivable intellectual pursuit: from making money to conjugating Greek verbs. Nietzsche merely states this obvious fact in an unaccustomed form.

His superman is to give his will to live—or will to power, as you please—perfect freedom. As a result, those individuals in whom this instinct most accurately meets the conditions of life on earth will survive, and in their offspring, by natural laws, the instinct itself will become more and more accurate. That is to say, there will appear in future generations individuals in whom this instinct will tend more and more to order the performance of acts of positive benefit and to forbid the performance of acts likely to result in injury. This injury, it is plain, may take the form of unsatisfied wants as well as of broken skulls. Therefore, the man—or superman—in whom the instinct reaches perfection will unconsciously steer clear of all the things which harass and batter mankind today—exhausting self-denials as well as exhausting passions. Whatever seems likely to benefit him, he will do; whatever seems likely to injure him he will avoid. When he is in doubt, he will dare—and accept defeat or victory with equal calm. His attitude, in brief, will be that of a being who faces life as he finds it, defiantly and unafraid—who knows how to fight and how to forbear—who sees things as they actually are, and not as they might or should be, and so wastes no energy yearning for the moon or in butting his head against stone walls. "This new table, O my brethren, I put over you: *Be hard!*"[14]

Such was the goal that Nietzsche held before the human race. Other philosophers before him had attempted the same thing. Schopenhauer had put forward his idea of a race that had found happiness in putting away its desire to live. Comte had seen a vision of a race whose every member sought the good of all. The humanitarians of all countries had drawn pictures of Utopias peopled by beings who had outgrown all human instincts—who had outgrown the *one* fundamental, unquenchable and eternal instinct of every living thing: the desire to conquer, to live, to remain alive. Nietzsche cast out all these fine ideals as essentially impossible. Man was of the earth, earthy, and his heavens and hells were creatures of his own vaporings. Only after he had ceased dreaming of them and thrown off his crushing burden of transcendental morality—only thus and then could he hope to rise out of the slough of despond in which he wallowed.

---

[1]"Nirvana is a cessation of striving for individual existence"—that is, after death. See "Dictionary of Philosophy and Psychology, " vol. II, pp. 178; New York, 1902.

[2]"Der Antichrist, " § 2.

[3]"*Also sprach Zarathustra, *" III.

[4]"*Jenseits von Gut und Böse, *" § 258.

[5]"*Also sprach Zarathustra, *" I.

[6]"*Also sprach Zarathustra, *" II.

[7]"*Also sprach Zarathustra, *" IV.

[8]"*Also sprach Zarathustra, *" I.

[9]Galatians V, 19, 20, 21.

[10]Job V, 7; XIV, 1; Ecclesiastes I, 1.

[11]"*Also sprach Zarathustra, *" I.

[12]"*Also sprach Zarathustra, *" IV.

[13]"*Also sprach Zarathustra, *" I.

[14]"*Also sprach Zarathustra, *" III.

V. ETERNAL RECURRENCE

In the superman Nietzsche showed the world a conceivable and possible goal for all human effort. But there still remained a problem and it was this: When the superman at last appears on earth, what then? Will there be another super-superman to follow and a super-supersuperman after that? In the end, will man become the equal of the creator of the universe, whoever or whatever He may be? Or will a period of decline come after, with a return down the long line, through the superman to man again, and then on to the anthropoid ape, to the lower mammals, to the asexual cell, and, finally, to mere inert matter, gas, ether and empty space?

Nietzsche answered these questions by offering the theory that the universe moves in regular cycles and that all which is now happening on earth, and in all the stars, to the uttermost, will be repeated, again and again, throughout eternity. In other words, he dreamed of a cosmic year, corresponding, in some fashion, to the terrestrial year. Man, who has sprung from the elements, will rise into superman, and perhaps infinitely beyond, and then, in the end, by catastrophe or slow decline, he will be resolved into the primary elements again, and the whole process will begin anew.

This notion, it must be admitted, was not original with Nietzsche and it would have been better for his philosophy and for his repute as an intelligent thinker had he never sought to elucidate it. In his early essay on history he first mentioned it and there he credited it to its probable inventors—the Pythagoreans.[1] It was their belief that, whenever the heavenly bodies all returned to certain fixed relative positions, the whole history of the universe began anew. The idea seemed to fascinate Nietzsche, in whom, despite his worship of the actual, there was an ever-evident strain of mysticism, and he referred to it often in his later books. The pure horror of it—of the notion that all the world's suffering would have to be repeated again and again, that men would have to die over and over again for all infinity, that there was no stopping place or final goal— the horror of all this appealed powerfully to his imagination. Frau Andreas-Salomé tells us that he "spoke of it only in a low voice and with every sign of the profoundest emotion" and there is reason to believe that, at one time, he thought there might be some confirmation of it in the atomic theory, and that his desire to go to Vienna to study the natural sciences was prompted by a wish to investigate this notion. Finally he became convinced that there was no ground for such a belief in any of the known facts of science, and after that, we are told, his shuddering horror left him.

It was then possible for him to deal with the doctrine of eternal recurrence as a mere philosophical speculation, without the uncomfortable reality of a demonstrated scientific fact, and thereafter he spent much time considering it. In "*Also sprach Zarathustra*" he puts it into the brain of his prophet-hero, and shows how it well-nigh drove the latter mad.

"I will come back, " muses Zarathustra, "with this sun, with this earth, with this eagle, with this serpent—*not* for a new life or a better life, but to the same life I am now leading. I will come back unto this same old life, in the greatest things and in the smallest, in order to teach once more the eternal recurrence of all things."[2]

In the end, Nietzsche turned this fantastic idea into a device for exalting his superman. The superman is one who realizes that all of his struggles will be in vain, and that, in future cycles, he will have to go through them over and over again. Yet he has attained such a superhuman immunity to all emotion—to all ideas of pleasure and pain—that the prospect does not daunt him. Despite its horror, he faces it unafraid. It is all a part of life, and in consequence it is good. He has learned to agree to everything that exists—even to the ghastly necessity for living again and again. In a word, he does not fear an endless series of lives, because life, to him, has lost all the terrors which a merely human man sees in it.

"Let us not only endure the inevitable, " says Nietzsche, "and still less hide it from ourselves: *let us love it!*"

As Vernon Lee (Miss Violet Paget)[3] has pointed out, this idea is scarcely to be distinguished from the fundamental tenet of stoicism. Miss Paget also says that it bears a close family resemblance to that denial of pain which forms the basis of Christian Science, but this is not true, for a vast difference exists between a mere denial of pain and a willingness to admit it, face it, and triumph over it. But the notion appears, in endless guises, in many philosophies and Goethe voiced it, after a fashion, in his maxim, "*Entbehren sollst du*" ("Man must do without"). The idea of eternal recurrence gives point, again, to a familiar anecdote. This concerns a joker who goes to an inn, eats his fill and then says to the innkeeper: "You and I will be here again in a million years: let me pay you then." "Very well, " replies the quick-witted innkeeper, "but first pay me for the beefsteak you ate the last time you were here—a million years ago."

Despite Nietzsche's conclusion that the known facts of existence do not bear it out, and the essential impossibility of discussing it to profit, the doctrine of eternal recurrence is by no means unthinkable. The celestial cycle put forward, as an hypothesis, by modern astronomy—the progression, that is, from gas to molten fluid, from fluid to solid, and from solid, by catastrophe, back to gas again—is easily conceivable, and it is easily conceivable, too, that the earth, which has passed through an uninhabitable state into a habitable state, may one day become uninhabitable again, and so keep seesawing back and forth through all eternity.

But what will be the effect of eternal recurrence upon the superman? The tragedy of it, as we have seen, will merely serve to make him heroic. He will defy the universe and say "yes" to life. Putting aside all thought of conscious existence beyond the grave, he will seek to live as nearly as possible in exact accordance with those laws laid down for the evolution of sentient beings on earth when the cosmos was first set spinning. But how will he know when he has attained this end? How will he avoid going mad with doubts about his own knowledge? Nietzsche gave much thought, first and last, to this epistemological problem, and at different times he leaned toward different schools, but his writing, taken as a whole, indicates that the fruit of his meditations was a thorough-going empiricism. The superman, indeed, is an empiricist who differs from Bacon only in the infinitely greater range of his observation and experiment. He learns by bitter experience and he generalizes from this knowledge. An utter and unquestioning materialist, he knows nothing of mind except as a function of body. To him speculation seems vain and foolish: his concern is ever with imminent affairs. That is to say, he believes a thing to be true when his eyes, his ears, his nose and his hands tell him it is true. And in this he will be at one with all those men who are admittedly above the mass today. Reject empiricism and you reject at one stroke, the whole sum of human knowledge.

When a man stubs his toe, for example, the facts that the injured member swells and that it hurts most frightfully appear to him as absolute certainties. If we deny that he actually knows these things and maintain that the spectacle of the swelling and the sensation of pain are mere creatures of his mind, we cast adrift from all order and common-sense in the universe and go sailing upon a stormy sea of crazy metaphysics and senseless contradictions. There are many things that we do not know, and in the nature of things, never can know. We do not know *why* phosphorus has a tendency to combine with oxygen, but the fact that it *has* we *do* know—and if we try to deny we *do* know it, we must deny that we are sentient beings, and in consequence, must regard life and the universe as mere illusions. No man with a sound mind makes any such denial. The things about us are real, just as our feeling that we are alive is real.[4]

From this it must be plain that the superman will have the same guides that we have, viz.: his instincts and senses. But in him they will be more accurate and more acute than in us, because the whole tendency of his scheme of things will be to fortify and develop them.[5] If any race of Europe devoted a century to exercising its right arms, its descendants, in the century following, would have right arms like piston-rods. In the same way, the superman, by subordinating everything else to his instinct to live, will make it evolve into something very accurate and efficient. His whole concern, in brief, will be to live as long as possible and so to avoid as much as possible all of those things which shorten life—by injuring the body from without or by using up energy within. As a result he will cease all effort to learn *why* the world exists and will devote himself to acquiring knowledge *how* it exists. This knowledge *how* will be within his capacity even more than it is within our capacity today. Our senses, as we have seen, have given us absolute knowledge that stubbing the toe results in swelling and pain. The superman's developed senses will give him absolute knowledge about everything that exists on earth. He will know exactly *how* a tubercle bacillus attacks the lung tissue, he will know exactly *how* the blood fights the bacillus, and he will know exactly *how* to interfere in this battle in such a manner that the blood shall be invariably victorious. In a word, he will be the possessor of exact and complete knowledge regarding the working of all the benign and malignant forces in the world about him, but he will not bother himself about insoluble problems. He will waste no time speculating as to *why* tubercle bacilli were sent into the world: his instinct to live will be satisfied by his success in stamping them out.

The ideal superman then is merely a man in whom instinct works without interference—a man who feels that it is right to live and that the only knowledge worth while is that which makes life longer and more bearable. The superman's instinct for life is so strong that its mere exercise satisfies him, and so makes him happy. He doesn't bother about the unknown void beyond the grave: it is sufficient for him to know that he is alive and that being alive is pleasant. He is, in the highest sense, a utilitarian, and he believes to the letter in Auguste Comte's[6] dictum that the only thing living beings can ever hope to accomplish on earth is to adapt themselves perfectly to the natural forces around them—to the winds and the rain, the hills and the sea, the thunderbolt and the germ of disease.

"I am a dionysian!" cries Nietzsche. "I am an immoralist!" He means simply that his ideal is a being capable of facing the horrors of life unafraid, of meeting great enemies and slaying them, of gazing down upon the earth in pride and scorn, of making his own way and bearing his own burdens. In the profane folk-philosophy of every healthy and vigorous people, we find some trace of this dionysian idea. "Let us so live day by day, " says a distinguished American statesman, "that we can look any man in the eye and tell him to go to hell!" We get a subtle sort of joy out of this saying because it voices our racial advance toward individualism and away from servility and oppression. We believe in freedom, in toleration, in moral anarchy. We have put this notion into innumerable homely forms.

Things   have   come   to   a   hell   of   a   pass
When a man can't wallop his own jackass!

So we phrase it. The superman, did he stalk the earth, would say the same thing.

---

[1]Pythagoras (B.C. 570?-500?) was a Greek who brought the doctrine of the transmigration of souls from Asia Minor to Greece. In Magna Graecia he founded a mystical brotherhood, half political party and half school of philosophy. It survived him for many years and its members revered him as the sage of sages. He was a bitter foe to democracy and took part in wars against its spread.

[2]"*Also sprach Zarathustra*, " III.

[3]*North American Review*, Dec., 1904.

[4]*Vide* the chapter on "Truth."

[5]It is very evident, I take it, that the principal function of all science is the widening of our perceptions. The chief argument for idealism used to be the axiom that our power of perception was necessarily limited and that it would be limited forever. This may be true still, but it is now apparent that these limits are being indefinitely extended, and may be extended, in future, almost infinitely. A thousand years ago, if any one had laid down the thesis that malaria was caused by minute animals, he would have been dismissed as a lunatic, because it was evident that no one could see these animals, and it was evident, too—that is to say, the scientists of that time held it to be evident—that this inability to see them would never be removed, because the human eye would always remain substantially as it was. But now we know that the microscope may increase the eye's power of perception a thousandfold. When we consider the fact that the spectroscope has enabled us to make a chemical analysis of the sun, that the telephone has enabled us to hear 2, 000 miles and that the x-rays have enabled us to see through flesh and bone, we must admit without reservation, that our power of perception, at some future day, may be infinite. And if we admit this we must admit the essential possibility of the superman.

[6]"*Cours de philosophie positive,* " tr. by Helen Martineau; London, 1853.

VI. CHRISTIANITY

Nietzsche's astonishingly keen and fearless criticism of Christianity has probably sent forth wider ripples than any other stone he ever heaved into the pool of philistine contentment. He opened his attack in "*Menschliches allzu Menschliches,* " the first book of his maturity, and he was still at it, in full fuming and fury, in "*Der Antichrist,* " the last thing he was destined to write. The closing chapter of "*Der Antichrist*"—his swan song—contains his famous phillipic, beginning "I condemn." It recalls Zola's "*j'accuse*" letter in the Dreyfus case, but it is infinitely more sweeping and infinitely more uproarious and daring.

"I condemn Christianity, " it begins. "I bring against it the most terrible of accusations that ever an accuser put into words. It is to me the greatest of all imaginable corruptions.... It has left nothing untouched by its depravity. It has made a worthlessness out of every value, a lie out of every truth, a sin out of everything straightforward, healthy and honest. Let anyone dare to speak to me of its humanitarian blessings! To do away with pain and woe is contrary to its principles. It lives by pain and woe: it has created pain and woe in order to perpetuate itself. It invented the idea of original sin.[1] It invented 'the equality of souls before God'—that cover for all the rancour of the useless and base.... It has bred the art of self-violation—repugnance and contempt for all good and cleanly instincts.... Parasitism is its praxis. It combats all good red-blood, all love and all hope for life, with its anæmic ideal of holiness. It sets up 'the other world' as a negation of every reality. The cross is the rallying post for a conspiracy against health, beauty, well-being, courage, intellect, benevolence— against life itself....

"This eternal accusation I shall write upon all walls: I call Christianity the one great curse, the one great intrinsic depravity, ... for which no expedient is sufficiently poisonous, secret, subterranean, mean! I call it the one immortal shame and blemish upon the human race!"[2]

So much for the philosopher's vociferous hurrah at the close of his argument. In the argument itself it is apparent that his indictment of Christianity contains two chief counts. The first is the allegation that it is essentially untrue and unreasonable, and the second is the theory that it is degrading. The first of these counts is not unfamiliar to the students of religious history. It was first voiced by that high priest who "rent his clothes" and cried "What need have we of any further witnesses? Ye have heard the blasphemy."[3] It was voiced again by the Romans who threw converts to the lions, and after the long silence of the middle ages, it was piped forth again by Voltaire, Hume, the encyclopedists and Paine. After the philosophers and scientists who culminated in Darwin had rescued reason for all time from the transcendental nonsense of the cobweb-spinners and metaphysicians, Huxley came to the front with his terrific heavy artillery and those who still maintained that Christianity was historically true—Gladstone and the rest of the forlorn hope—were mowed down. David Strauss, Lessing, Eichhorn, Michaelis, Bauer, Meyer, Ritschl, [4] Pfleiderer and a host of others joined in the chorus and in Nietzsche's early manhood the battle was practically won. By 1880 no reasonable man actually believed that there were devils in the swine, and it was already possible to deny the physical resurrection and still maintain a place in respectable society. Today a literal faith in the gospel narrative is confined to ecclesiastical reactionaries, pious old ladies and men about to be hanged.

Therefore, Nietzsche did not spend much time examining the historical credibility of Christianity. He did not try to prove, like Huxley, that the witnesses to the resurrection were superstitious peasants and hysterical women, nor did he seek to show, like Huxley again, that Christ might have been taken down from the cross before he was dead. He was intensely interested in all such inquiries, but he saw that, in the last analysis, they left a multitude of problems unsolved. The solution of these unsolved problems was the task that he took unto himself. Tunneling down, in his characteristic way, into the very foundations of the faith, he endeavored to prove that it was based upon contradictions and absurdities; that its dogmas were illogical and its precepts unworkable; and that its cardinal principles presupposed the acceptance of propositions which, to the normal human mind, were essentially unthinkable. This tunneling occupied much of Nietzsche's energy in "*Menschliches allzu Menschliches*, " and he returned to it again and again, in all of the other books that preceded "*Der Antichrist*." His method of working may be best exhibited by a few concrete examples.

Prayer, for instance, is an exceedingly important feature of Christian worship and any form of worship in which it had no place would be necessarily unchristian.[5] But upon what theory is prayer based? Examining the matter from all sides you will have to conclude that it is reasonable only upon two assumptions: first, that it is possible to change the infallible will and opinion of the deity, and secondly, that the petitioner is capable of judging what he needs. Now, Christianity maintains, as one of its main dogmas, that the deity is omniscient and all-wise, [6] and, as another fundamental doctrine, that human beings are absolutely unable to solve their problems without heavenly aid[7] *i.e.* that the deity necessarily knows what is best for any given man better than that man can ever hope to know it himself. Therefore, Christianity, in ordaining prayer, orders, as a condition of inclusion in its communion, an act which it holds to be useless. This contradiction, argues Nietzsche, cannot be explained away in terms comprehensible to the human intelligence.

Again Christianity holds that man is a mere creature of the deity's will, and yet insists that the individual be judged and punished for his acts. In other words, it tries to carry free will on one shoulder and determinism on the other, and its doctors and sages have themselves shown that they recognize the absurdity of this by their constant, but futile efforts to decide which of the two shall be abandoned. This contradiction is a legacy from Judaism, and Mohammedanism suffers from it, too. Those sects which have sought to remove it by an entire acceptance of determinism—under the name of predestination, fatalism, or what not—have become bogged in hopeless morasses of unreason and dogmatism. It is a cardinal doctrine of Presbyterianism, for instance, that "by the decree of God, for the manifestation of his glory, some men and angels are predestinated unto everlasting life and others foreordained to everlasting death ... without any foresight of faith or good works, or perseverance in either of them, or any other thing in the creature, as conditions...."[8] In other words, no matter how faithfully one man tries to follow in the footsteps of Christ, he may go to hell, and no matter how impiously another sins, he may be foreordained for heaven. That such a belief makes all religion, faith and morality absurd is apparent. That it is, at bottom, utterly unthinkable to a reasoning being is also plain.

Nietzsche devoted a great deal of time during his first period of activity to similar examinations of Christian ideas and he did a great deal to supplement the historical investigations of those English and German savants whose ruthless exposure of fictions and frauds gave birth to what we now call the higher criticism. But his chief service was neither in the field of historical criticism nor in that of the criticism of dogmas. Toward the end of his life he left the business of examining biblical sources to the archeologists and historians, whose equipment for the task was necessarily greater than his own, and the business of reducing Christian logic to contradiction and absurdity to the logicians. Thereafter, his own work took him a step further down and in the end he got to the very bottom of the subject. The answer of the theologians had been that, even if you denied the miracles, the gospels, the divinity of Christ and his very existence as an actual man, you would have to admit that Christianity itself was sufficient excuse for its own existence; that it had made the world better and that it provided a workable scheme of life by which men could live and die and rise to higher things. This answer, for awhile, staggered the agnostics and Huxley himself evidently came near being convinced that it was beyond rebuttal.[9] But it only made Nietzsche spring into the arena more confident than ever. "Very well, " he said, "we will argue it out. You say that Christianity has made the world better? I say that it has made it worse! You say that it is comforting and uplifting? I say that it is cruel and degrading! You say that it is the best religion mankind has ever invented? I say it is the most dangerous!"

Having thus thrown down the gage of battle, Nietzsche proceeded to fight like a Tartar, and it is but common fairness to say that, for a good while, he bore the weight of his opponents' onslaught almost unaided. The world was willing enough to abandon its belief in Christian supernaturalism and as far back as the early 80's the dignitaries of the Church of England—to employ a blunt but expressive metaphor—had begun to get in out of the wet. But the pietists still argued that Christianity remained the fairest flower of civilization and that it met a real and ever-present human want and made mankind better. To deny this took courage of a decidedly unusual sort—courage that was willing to face, not only ecclesiastical anathema and denunciation, but also the almost automatic opposition of every so-called respectable man. But Nietzsche, whatever his deficiencies otherwise, certainly was not lacking in assurance, and so, when he came to write "*Der Antichrist*" he made his denial thunderous and uncompromising beyond expression. No medieval bishop ever pronounced more appalling curses. No backwoods evangelist ever laid down the law with more violent eloquence. The book is the shortest he ever wrote, but it is by long odds the most compelling. Beginning *allegro*, it proceeds from *forte*, by an uninterrupted *crescendo* to *allegro con moltissimo molto fortissimo*. The sentences run into mazes of italics, dashes and asterisks. It is German that one cannot read aloud without roaring and waving one's arm.

Christianity, says Nietzsche, is the most dangerous system of slave-morality the world has ever known. "It has waged a deadly war against the highest type of man. It has put a ban on all his fundamental instincts. It has distilled evil out of these instincts. It makes the strong and efficient man its typical outcast man. It has taken the part of the weak and the low; it has made an ideal out of its antagonism to the very instincts which tend to preserve life and well-being.... It has taught men to regard their highest impulses as sinful—as temptations."[10] In a word, it tends to rob mankind of all those qualities which fit any living organism to survive in the struggle for existence.

As we shall see later on, civilization obscures and even opposes this struggle for existence, but it is in progress all the same, at all times and under all conditions. Every one knows, for instance, that one-third of the human beings born into the world every year die before they are five years old. The reason for this lies in the fact that they are, in some way or other, less fitted to meet the conditions of life on earth than the other two-thirds. The germ of cholera infantum is an enemy to the human race, and so long as it continues to exist upon earth it will devote all of its activity to attacking human infants and seeking to destroy them. It happens that some babies recover from cholera infantum, while others die of it. This is merely another way of saying that the former, having been born with a capacity for resisting the attack of the germ, or having been given the capacity artificially, are better fitted to survive, and that the latter, being incapable of making this resistance, are unfit.

All life upon earth is nothing more than a battle with the enemies of life. A germ is such an enemy, cold is such an enemy, lack of food is such an enemy, and others that may be mentioned are lack of water, ignorance of natural laws, armed foes and deficient physical strength. The man who is able to get all of the food he wants, and so can nourish his body until it becomes strong enough to combat the germs of disease; who gets enough to drink, who has shelter from the elements, who has devised means for protecting himself against the desires of other men—who yearn, perhaps, who take for themselves some of the things that he has acquired—such a man, it is obvious, is far better fitted to live than a man who has none of these things. He is far better fitted to survive, in a purely physical sense, because his body is nourished and protected, and he is far better fitted to attain happiness, because most of his powerful wants are satisfied.

Nietzsche maintains that Christianity urges a man to make no such efforts to insure his personal survival in the struggle for existence. The beatitudes require, he says, that, instead of trying to do so, the Christian shall devote his energies to helping others and shall give no thought to himself. Instead of exalting himself as much as possible above the common herd and thus raising his chances of surviving, and those of his children, above those of the average man, he is required to lift up this average man. Now, it is plain that every time he lifts up some one else, he must, at the same time, decrease his own store, because his own store is the only stock from which he can draw. Therefore, the tendency of the Christian philosophy of humility is to make men voluntarily throw away their own chances of surviving, which means their own sense of efficiency, which means their own "feeling of increasing power, " which means their own happiness. As a substitute for this natural happiness, Christianity offers the happiness derived from the belief that the deity will help those who make the sacrifice and so restore them to their old superiority. This belief, as Nietzsche shows, is no more borne out by known facts than the old belief in witches. It is, in fact, proved to be an utter absurdity by all human experience.

"I call an animal, a species, an individual, depraved, " he says, "when it loses its instincts, when it selects, when it *prefers* what is injurious to it.... Life itself is an instinct for growth, for continuance, for accumulation of forces, for *power:* where the will to power is wanting there is decline."[11] Christianity, he says, squarely opposes this will to power in the Golden Rule, the cornerstone of the faith. The man who confines his efforts to attain superiority over his fellow men to those acts which he would be willing to have them do toward him, obviously abandons all such efforts entirely. To put it in another form, a man can't make himself superior to the race in general without making every other man in the world, to that extent, his inferior. Now, if he follows the Golden Rule, he must necessarily abandon all efforts to make himself superior, because if he didn't he would be suffering all the time from the pain of seeing other men—whose standpoint the Rule requires him to assume—grow inferior. Thus his activity is restricted to one of two things: standing perfectly still or deliberately making himself inferior. The first is impossible, but Nietzsche shows that the latter is not, and that, in point of fact, it is but another way of describing the act of sympathy—one of the things ordered by the fundamental dogma of Christianity.

Sympathy, says Nietzsche, consists merely of a strong man giving up some of his strength to a weak man. The strong man, it is evident, is debilitated thereby, while the weak man, very often, is strengthened but little. If you go to a hanging and sympathize with the condemned, it is plain that your mental distress, without helping that gentleman, weakens, to a perceptible degree, your own mind and body, just as all other powerful emotions weaken them, by consuming energy, and so you are handicapped in the struggle for life to the extent of this weakness. You may get a practical proof of it an hour later by being overcome and killed by a foot-pad whom you might have been able to conquer, had you been feeling perfectly well, or by losing money to some financial rival for whom, under normal conditions, you would have been a match; and then again you may get no immediate or tangible proof of it at all. But your organism will have been weakened to some measurable extent, all the same, and at some time—perhaps on your death bed—this minute drain will make itself evident, though, of course, you may never know it.

"Sympathy, " says Nietzsche, "stands in direct antithesis to the tonic passions which elevate the energy of human beings and increase their feeling of efficiency and power. It is a depressant. One loses force by sympathizing and any loss of force which has been caused by other means—personal suffering, for example—is increased and multiplied by sympathy. Suffering itself becomes contagious through sympathy and under certain circumstances it may lead to a total loss of life. If a proof of that is desired, consider the case of the Nazarene, whose sympathy for his fellow men brought him, in the end, to the cross.

"Again, sympathy thwarts the law of development, of evolution, of the survival of the fittest. It preserves what is ripe for extinction, it works in favor of life's condemned ones, it gives to life itself a gloomy aspect by the number of the ill-constituted it *maintains* in life.... It is both a multiplier of misery and a conservator of misery. It is the principal tool for the advancement of decadence. It leads to nothingness, to the negation of all those instincts which are at the basis of life.... But one does not say 'nothingness;' one says instead 'the other world' or 'the better life.'... This innocent rhetoric, out of the domain of religio-moral fantasy, becomes far from innocent when one realizes what tendency it conceals: the tendency *hostile to life*."[12]

The foregoing makes it patent that Nietzsche was a thorough-going and uncompromising biological monist. That is to say, he believed that man, while superior to all other animals because of his greater development, was, after all, merely an animal, like the rest of them; that the struggle for existence went on among human beings exactly as it went on among the lions in the jungle and the protozoa in the sea ooze, and that the law of natural selection ruled all of animated nature—mind and matter—alike. Indeed, it is but just to credit him with being the pioneer among modern monists of this school, for he stated and defended the doctrine of morphological universality at a time when practically all the evolutionists doubted it, and had pretty well proved its truth some years before Haeckel wrote his "Monism" and "The Riddle of the Universe."

To understand all of this, it is necessary to go back to Darwin and his first statement of the law of natural selection. Darwin proved, in "The Origin of the Species, " that a great many more individuals of any given species of living being are born into the world each year than can possibly survive. Those that are best fitted to meet the condition of existence live on; those that are worst fitted die. The result is that, by the influence of heredity, the survivors beget a new generation in which there is a larger percentage of the fit. One might think that this would cause a greater number to survive, but inasmuch as the food and room on earth are limited, a large number must always die. But all the while the half or third, or whatever the percentage may be, which actually do survive become more and more fit. In consequence, a species, generation after generation, tends to become more and more adapted to meet life's vicissitudes, or, as the biologists say, more and more adapted to its environment.

Darwin proved that this law was true of all the lower animals and showed that it was responsible for the evolution of the lower apes into anthropoid apes, and that it could account, theoretically, for a possible evolution of anthropoid apes into man. But in "The Descent of Man" he argued that the law of natural selection ceased when man became an intelligent being. Thereafter, he said, man's own efforts worked against those of nature. Instead of letting the unfit of his race die, civilization began to protect and preserve them. The result was that nature's tendency to make all living beings more and more sturdy was set aside by man's own conviction that mere sturdiness was not the thing most to be desired. From this Darwin argued that if two tribes of human beings lived side by side, and if, in one of them, the unfit were permitted to perish, while in the other there were many "courageous, sympathetic and faithful members, who were always ready to warn each other of danger, and to aid and defend one another"—that in such a case, the latter tribe would make the most progress, despite its concerted effort to defy a law of nature.

Darwin's disciples agreed with him in this and some of them went to the length of asserting that civilization, in its essence, was nothing more or less than a successful defiance of this sort.[13] Herbert Spencer was much troubled by the resultant confusion and as one critic puts it, [14] the whole drift of his thought "appears to be inspired by the question: how to evade and veil the logical consequence of evolutionarism for human existence?" John Fiske, another Darwinian, accepted the situation without such disquieting doubt. "When humanity began to be evolved, " he said, "an entirely new chapter in the history of the universe was opened. Henceforth the life of the nascent soul came to be first in importance and the bodily life became subordinated to it."[15] Even Huxley believed that man would have to be excepted from the operation of the law of natural selection. "The ethical progress of society, " he said, "depends, not on imitating the cosmic process and still less on running away from it, but in combating it." He saw that it was audacious thus to pit man against nature, but he thought that man was sufficiently important to make such an attempt and hoped "that the enterprise might meet with a certain measure of success."[16] And the other Darwinians agreed with him.[17]

As all the best critics of philosophy have pointed out, [18] any philosophical system which admits such a great contradiction fails utterly to furnish workable standards of order in the universe, and so falls short of achieving philosophy's first aim. We must either believe with the scholastics that intelligence rules, or we must believe, with Haeckel, that all things happen in obedience to invariable natural laws. We cannot believe both. A great many men, toward the beginning of the 90's, began to notice this fatal defect in Darwin's idea of human progress. In 1891 one of them pointed out the conclusion toward which it inevitably led.[19] If we admitted, he said, that humanity had set at naught the law of natural selection, we must admit that civilization was working against nature's efforts to preserve the race, and that, in the end, humanity would perish. To put it more succinctly, man might defy the law of natural selection as much as he pleased, but he could never hope to set it aside. Soon or late, he would awaken to the fact that he remained a mere animal, like the rabbit and the worm, and that, if he permitted his body to degenerate into a thing entirely lacking in strength and virility, not all the intelligence conceivable could save him.

Nietzsche saw all this clearly as early as 1877.[20] He saw that what passed for civilization, as represented by Christianity, was making such an effort to defy and counteract the law of natural selection, and he came to the conclusion that the result would be disaster. Christianity, he said, ordered that the strong should give part of their strength to the weak, and so tended to weaken the whole race. Self-sacrifice, he said, was an open defiance of nature, and so were all the other Christian virtues, in varying degree. He proposed, then, that before it was too late, humanity should reject Christianity, as the "greatest of all imaginable corruptions, " and admit freely and fully that the law of natural selection was universal and that the only way to make real progress was to conform to it.

It may be asked here how Nietzsche accounted for the fact that humanity had survived so long—for the fact that the majority of men were still physically healthy and that the race, as a whole, was still fairly vigorous. He answered this in two ways. First, he denied that the race was maintaining to the full its old vigor. "The European of the present, " he said, "is far below the European of the Renaissance." It would be absurd, he pointed out, to allege that the average German of 1880 was as strong and as healthy—*i.e.* as well fitted to his environment—as the "blond beast" who roamed the Saxon lowlands in the days of the mammoth. It would be equally absurd to maintain that the highest product of modern civilization—the town-dweller—was as vigorous and as capable of becoming the father of healthy children as the intelligent farmer, whose life was spent in approximate accordance with all the more obvious laws of health.

Nietzsche's second answer was that humanity had escaped utter degeneration and destruction because, despite its dominance as a theory of action, few men actually practiced Christianity. It was next to impossible, he said, to find a single man who, literally and absolutely, obeyed the teachings of Christ.[21] There were plenty of men who thought they were doing so, but all of them were yielding in only a partial manner. Absolute Christianity meant absolute disregard of self. It was obvious that a man who reached this state of mind would be unable to follow any gainful occupation, and so would find it impossible to preserve his own life or the lives of his children. In brief, said Nietzsche, an actual and utter Christian would perish today just as Christ perished, and so, in his own fate, would provide a conclusive argument against Christianity.

Nietzsche pointed out further that everything which makes for the preservation of the human race is diametrically opposed to the Christian ideal. Thus Christianity becomes the foe of science. The one argues that man should sit still and let God reign; the other that man should battle against the tortures which fate inflicts upon him, and try to overcome them and grow strong. Thus all science is unchristian, because, in the last analysis, the whole purpose and effort of science is to arm man against loss of energy and death, and thus make him self-reliant and unmindful of any duty of propitiating the deity. That this antagonism between Christianity and the search, for truth really exists has been shown in a practical way time and again. Since the beginning of the Christian era the church has been the bitter and tireless enemy of all science, and this enmity has been due to the fact that every member of the priest class has realized that the more a man learned the more he came to depend upon his own efforts, and the less he was given to asking help from above. In the ages of faith men prayed to the saints when they were ill. Today they send for a doctor. In the ages of faith battles were begun with supplications, and it was often possible to witness the ridiculous spectacle of both sides praying to the same God. Today every sane person knows that the victory goes to the wisest generals and largest battalions.

Nietzsche thus showed, first, that Christianity (and all other ethical systems having self-sacrifice as their basis) tended to oppose the law of natural selection and so made the race weaker; and secondly, that the majority of men, consciously or unconsciously, were aware of this, and so made no effort to be absolute Christians. If Christianity were to become universal, he said, and every man in the world were to follow Christ's precepts to the letter in all the relations of daily life, the race would die out in a generation. This being true—and it may be observed inpassing that no one has ever successfully controverted it—there follows the converse: that the human race had best abandon the idea of self-sacrifice altogether and submit itself to the law of natural selection. If this is done, says Nietzsche, the result will be a race of supermen—of proud, strong dionysians—of men who will say "yes" to the world and will be ideally capable of meeting the conditions under which life must exist on earth.

In his efforts to account for the origin of Christianity, Nietzsche was less happy, and indeed came very near the border-line of the ridiculous. The faith of modern Europe, he said, was the result of a gigantic effort on the part of the ancient Jews to revenge themselves upon their masters. The Jews were helpless and inefficient and thus evolved a slave-morality. Naturally, as slaves, they hated their masters, while realizing, all the while, the unmanliness of the ideals they themselves had to hold to in order to survive. So they crucified Christ, who voiced these same ideals, and the result was that the outside world, which despised the Jews, accepted Christ as a martyr and prophet and thus swallowed the Jewish ideals without realizing it. In a word, the Jews detested the slave-morality which circumstances thrust upon them, and got their revenge by foisting it, in a sugar-coated pill, upon their masters.

It is obvious that this idea is sheer lunacy. That the Jews ever realized the degenerating effect of their own slave-morality is unlikely, and that they should take counsel together and plan such an elaborate and complicated revenge, is impossible. The reader of Nietzsche must expect to encounter such absurdities now and then. The mad German was ordinarily a most logical and orderly thinker, but sometimes the traditional German tendency to indulge in wild and imbecile flights of speculation cropped up in him.

---

[1]*Vide* the chapter on "Crime and Punishment."

[2]"*Der Antichrist*, " § 62.

[3]St. Mark XIV, 63, 64.

[4]Albrecht Ritschl (1822-89), who is not to be confused with Nietzsche's teacher at Bonn and Leipsic. Ritschl founded what is called the Ritschlian movement in theology. This has for its object the abandonment of supernaturalism and the defence of Christianity as a mere scheme of living. It admits that the miracle stories are fables and even concedes that Christ was not divine, but maintains that his teachings represent the best wisdom of the human race. See Denny: "Studies in Theology, " New York, 1894.

[5]Ph. IV, 6: "Be careful for nothing; but in everything by prayer and supplication, with thanksgiving, let your requests be made known to God."

[6]Deut. XXXII, 4: "He is the rock, his work is perfect." See also a hundred similar passages in the Old and New Testaments.

[7]Isaiah XLIV, 8: "Now, O Lord, thou art our Father; we are the clay and thou our potter; and we all are the work of thy hand."

[8]"The Constitution of the Presbyterian Church in the United States, " pp. 16 to 20: Philadelphia, 1841.

[9]To the end of his days Huxley believed that, to the average human being, even of the highest class, some sort of faith would always be necessary. "My work in the London hospitals, " he said, "taught me that the preacher often does as much good as the doctor." It would be interesting to show how this notion has been abandoned in recent years. The trained nurse, who was unknown in Huxley's hospital days, now takes the place of the confessor, and as Dr. Osler has shown us in "Science and Immortality, " men die just as comfortably as before.

[10]"*Der Antichrist,* " § 5.

[11]"*Der Antichrist,* " § 6.

[12]"*Der Antichrist,* " § 7.

[13]Alfred Russell Wallace: "Darwinism, " London, 1889.

[14]Alexander Tille, introduction to the Eng. tr. of "The Works of Friedrich Nietzsche, " vol. XI; New York, 1896.

[15]John Fiske: "The Destiny of Man;" London, 1884.

[16]Romanes Lecture on "Evolution and Ethics, " 1893.

[17]As a matter of fact this dualism still lives. Thus it was lately defended by a correspondent of the New York *Sun:* "If there can be such a thing as an essential difference there surely is one between the animal evolution discovered by Darwin and the self-culture, progress and spiritual aspiration of man." Many other writers on the subject take the same position.

[18]See the article on "Monism" in the New International Encyclopedia.

[19]A. J. Balfour: "Fragment on Progress;" London, 1891.

[20]He was a monist, indeed, as early as 1873, at which time he had apparently not yet noticed Darwin's notion that the human race could successfully defy the law of natural selection. "The absence of any cardinal distinction between man and beast, " he said, "is a doctrine which I consider true." ("*Unzeitgemässe Betrachtungen,*" I, 189.) Nevertheless, in a moment of sophistry, late in life, he undertook to criticize the law of natural selection and even to deny its effects (*vide* "Roving Expeditions of an Inopportune Philosopher, " § 14, in "The Twilight of the Idols"). It is sufficient to say, in answer, that the law itself is inassailable and that all of Nietzsche's work, saving this single unaccountable paragraph, helps support it. His frequent sneers at Darwin, in other places, need not be taken too seriously. Everything English, toward the close of his life, excited his ire, but the fact remains that he was a thorough Darwinian and that, without Darwin's work, his own philosophy would have been impossible.

[21]This observation is as old as Montaigne, who said: "After all, the stoics were actually stoical, but where in all Christendom will you find a Christian?"

VII. TRUTH

At the bottom of all philosophy, of all science and of all thinking, you will find the one all-inclusive question: How is man to tell truth from error? The ignorant man solves this problem in a very simple manner: he holds that whatever he believes, he *knows;* and that whatever he knows is true. This is the attitude of all amateur and professional theologians, politicians and other numbskulls of that sort. The pious old maid, for example, who believes in the doctrine of the immaculate conception looks upon her faith as proof, and holds that all who disagree with her will suffer torments in hell. Opposed to this childish theory of knowledge is the chronic doubt of the educated man. He sees daily evidence that many things held to be true by nine-tenths of all men are, in reality, false, and he is thereby apt to acquire a doubt of everything, including his own beliefs.

At different times in the history of man, various methods of solving or evading the riddle have been proposed. In the age of faith it was held that, by his own efforts alone, man was unable, even partly, to distinguish between truth and error, but that he could always go for enlightenment to an infallible encyclopedia: the word of god, as set forth, through the instrumentality of inspired scribes, in the holy scriptures. If these scriptures said that a certain proposition was true, it *was* true, and any man who doubted it was either a lunatic or a criminal.[1] This doctrine prevailed in Europe for many years and all who ventured to oppose it were in danger of being killed, but in the course of time the number of doubters grew so large that it was inconvenient or impossible to kill all of them, and so, in the end, they had to be permitted to voice their doubts unharmed.

The first man of this new era to inflict any real damage upon the ancient churchly idea of revealed wisdom was Nicolas of Cusa, a cardinal of the Roman Catholic Church, who lived in the early part of the fifteenth century.[2] Despite his office and his time, Nicolas was an independent and intelligent man, and it became apparent to him, after long reflection, that mere belief in a thing was by no means a proof of its truth. Man, he decided was prone to err, but in the worst of his errors, there was always some kernel of truth, else he would revolt against it as inconceivable. Therefore, he decided, the best thing for man to do was to hold all of his beliefs lightly and to reject them whenever they began to appear as errors. The real danger, he said, was not in making mistakes, but in clinging to them after they were known to be mistakes.

It seems well nigh impossible that a man of Nicolas' age and training should have reasoned so clearly, but the fact remains that he did, and that all of modern philosophy is built upon the foundations he laid. Since his time a great many other theories of knowledge have been put forward, but all have worked, in a sort of circle, back to Nicolas. It would be interesting, perhaps, to trace the course and history of these variations and denials, but such an enterprise is beyond the scope of the present inquiry. Nicolas by no means gave the world a complete and wholly credible system of philosophy. Until the day of his death scholasticism was dominant in the world that he knew, and it retained its old hold upon human thought, in fact, for nearly two hundred years thereafter. Not until Descartes, in 1619, made his famous resolution "to take nothing for the truth without clear knowledge that it is such, " did humanity in general begin to realize, as Huxley says, that there was sanctity in doubt. And even Descartes could not shake himself free of the supernaturalism and other balderdash which yet colored philosophy. He laid down, for all time, the emancipating doctrine that "the profession of belief in propositions, of the truth of which there is no sufficient evidence, is immoral"—a doctrine that might well be called the Magna Charta of human thought[3]—but it should not be forgotten that he also laid down other doctrines and that many of them were visionary and silly. The philosophers after him rid their minds of the old ideas but slowly and there were frequent reversions to the ancient delusion that a man's mind is a function of his soul—whatever that may be—and not of his body. It was common, indeed, for a philosopher to set out with sane, debatable, conceivable ideas—and then to go soaring into the idealistic clouds.[4] Only in our own time have men come to understand that the ego, for all its seeming independence, is nothing more than the sum of inherited race experience—that a man's soul, his conscience and his attitude of mind are things he has inherited from his ancestors, just as he has inherited his two eyes, his ten toes and his firm belief in signs, portents and immortality. Only in our own time have men ceased seeking a golden key to all riddles, and sat themselves down to solve one riddle at a time.

Those metaphysicians who fared farthest from the philosopher of Cusa evolved the doctrine that, in themselves, things have no existence at all, and that we can think of them only in terms of our impressions of them. The color green, for example, may be nothing but a delusion, for all we can possibly know of it is that, under certain conditions, our optic nerves experience a sensation of greenness. Whether this sensation of greenness is a mere figment of our imagination or the reflection of an actual physical state, is something that we cannot tell. It is impossible, in a word, to determine whether there are actual things around us, which produce real impressions upon us, or whether our idea of these things is the mere result of subjective impressions or conditions. We know that a blow on the eyes may cause us to see a flash of light which does not exist and that a nervous person may feel the touch of hands and hear noises which are purely imaginary. May it not be possible, also, that all other sensations have their rise within us instead of without, and that in saying that objects give us impressions we have been confusing cause and effect?

Such is the argument of those metaphysicians who doubt, not only the accuracy of human knowledge, but also the very capacity of human beings to acquire knowledge. It is apparent, on brief reflection, that this attitude, while theoretically admissible, is entirely impracticable, and that, as a matter of fact, it gives us no more substantial basis for intelligent speculation than the old device of referring all questions to revelation. To say that nothing exists save in the imagination of living beings is to say that this imagination itself does not exist. This, of course, is an absurdity, because every man is absolutely certain that he himself is a real thing and that his mind is a real thing, too, and capable of thought. In place of such cob-web spinning, modern philosophers—driven to it, it may be said, in parenthesis, by the scientists—have gone back to the doctrine that, inasmuch as we can know nothing of anything save through the impressions it makes upon us, these impressions must be accepted provisionally as accurate, so long as they are evidently normal and harmonize one with the other.

That is to say, our perceptions, corrected by our experience and our common sense, must serve as guides for us, and we must seize every opportunity to widen their range and increase their accuracy. For millions of years they have been steadily augmenting our store of knowledge. We know, for instance, that when fire touches us it causes an impression which we call pain and that this impression is invariably the same, and always leads to the same results, in all normal human beings. Therefore, we accept it as an axiom that fire causes pain. There are many other ideas that may be and have been established in the same manner: by the fact that they are universal among sane men. But there is also a multitude of things which produce different impressions upon different men, and here we encounter the problem of determining which of these impressions is right and which is wrong. One man, observing the rising and setting of the sun, concludes that it is a ball of fire revolving about the earth. Another man, in the face of the same phenomena, concludes that the earth revolves around the sun. How, then, are we to determine which of these men has drawn the proper conclusion?

As a matter of fact, it is impossible in such a case, to come to any decision which can be accepted as utterly and absolutely true. But all the same the scientific empiric method enables us to push the percentage of error nearer and nearer to the irreducible minimum. We can observe the phenomenon under examination from a multitude of sides and compare the impression it produces with the impressions produced by kindred phenomena regarding which we know more. Again, we can put this examination into the hands of men specially trained and fitted for such work—men whose conclusions we know, by previous experience, to be above the average of accuracy. And so, after a long time, we can formulate some idea of the thing under inspection which violates few or none of the other ideas held by us. When we have accomplished this, we have come as near to the absolute truth as it is possible for human beings to come.

I need not point out that this method does not contemplate a mere acceptance of the majority vote. Its actual effect, indeed, is quite the contrary, for it is only a small minority of human beings who may be said, with any truth, to be capable of thought. It is probable, for example, that nine-tenths of the people in Christendom today believe that Friday is an unlucky day, while only the remaining tenth hold that one day is exactly like another. But despite this, it is apparent that the idea of the latter will survive and that, by slow degrees, it will be forced upon the former. We know that it is true, not because it is accepted by all men or by the majority of men—for, as a matter of fact, we have seen that it isn't—but because we realize that the few who hold to it are best capable of distinguishing between actual impressions and mere delusions.

Again, the scientific method tends to increase our knowledge by the very fact that it discourages unreasoning faith. The scientist realizes that most of his so-called facts are probably errors and so he is willing to harbor doubts of their truth and to seek for something better. Like Socrates he boldly says "I know that I am ignorant." He realizes, in fact, that error, when it is constantly under fire, is bound to be resolved in the long run into something approximating the truth. As Nicolas pointed out 500 years ago, nothing is utterly and absolutely true and nothing is utterly and absolutely false. There is always a germ of truth in the worst error, and there is always a residuum of error in the soundest truth. Therefore, an error is fatal only when it is hidden from the white light of investigation. Herein lies the difference between the modern scientist and the moralist. The former holds nothing sacred, not even his own axioms; the latter lays things down as law and then makes it a crime to doubt them.

It is in this way—by submitting every idea to a searching, pitiless, unending examination—that the world is increasing its store of what may be called, for the sake of clearness, absolute knowledge. Error always precedes truth, and it is extremely probable that the vast majority of ideas held by men of today—even the sanest and wisest men—are delusions, but with the passing of the years our stock of truth grows larger and larger. "A conviction, " says Nietzsche, "always has its history—its previous forms, its tentative forms, its states of error. It becomes a conviction, indeed, only after having been *not* a conviction, and then *hardly* a conviction. No doubt falsehood is one of these embryonic forms of conviction. Sometimes only a change of persons is needed to transform one into the other. That which, in the son, is a conviction, was, in the father, still a falsehood."[5] The tendency of intelligent men, in a word, is to approach nearer and nearer the truth, by the processes of rejection, revision and invention. Many old ideas are rejected by each new generation, but there always remain a few that survive. We no longer believe with the cave-men that the thunder is the voice of an angry god and the lightning the flash of his sword, but we still believe, as they did, that wood floats upon water, that seeds sprout and give forth plants, that a roof keeps off the rain and that a child, if it lives long enough, will inevitably grow into a man or a woman. Such ideas may be called truths. If we deny them we must deny at once that the world exists and that we exist ourselves.

Nietzsche's discussion of these problems is so abstruse and so much complicated by changes in view that it would be impossible to make an understandable summary of it in the space available here. In his first important book, "*Menschliches allzu Menschliches*" he devoted himself, in the main, to pointing out errors made in the past, without laying down any very definite scheme of thought for the future. In the early stages of human progress, he said, men made the mistake of regarding everything that was momentarily pleasant or beneficial as absolutely and eternally true. Herein they manifested the very familiar human weakness for rash and hasty generalization, and the equally familiar tendency to render the ideas of a given time and place perpetual and permanent by erecting them into codes of morality and putting them into the mouths of gods. This, he pointed out, was harmful, for a thing might be beneficial to the men of today and fatal to the men of tomorrow. Therefore, he argued that while a certain idea's effect was a good criterion, humanly speaking, of its present or current truth, it was dangerous to assume that this effect would be always the same, and that, in consequence, the idea itself would remain true forever.

Not until the days of Socrates, said Nietzsche, did men begin to notice this difference between imminent truth and eternal truth. The notion that such a distinction existed made its way very slowly, even after great teachers began to teach it, but in the end it was accepted by enough men to give it genuine weight. Since that day philosophy and science, which were once merely different names for the same thing, have signified two separate things. It is the object of philosophy to analyze happiness, and by means of the knowledge thus gained, to devise means for safeguarding and increasing it. In consequence, it is necessary for philosophy to generalize— to assume that the thing which makes men happy today will make them happy tomorrow. Science, on the contrary, concerns itself, not with things of the uncertain future, but with things of the certain present. Its object is to examine the world as it exists today, to uncover as many of its secrets as possible, and to study their effect upon human happiness. In other words, philosophy first constructs a scheme of happiness and then tries to fit the world to it, while science studies the world with no other object in view than the increase of knowledge, and with full confidence that, in the long run, this increase of knowledge will increase efficiency and in consequence happiness.

It is evident, then, that science, for all its contempt for fixed schemes of happiness, will eventually accomplish with certainty what philosophy— which most commonly swims into the ken of the average man as morality—is now trying to do in a manner that is not only crude and unreasonable, but also necessarily unsuccessful. In a word, just so soon as man's store of knowledge grows so large that he becomes complete master of the natural forces which work toward his undoing, he will be perfectly happy. Now, Nietzsche believed, as we have seen in past chapters, that man's instinctive will to power had this same complete mastery over his environment as its ultimate object, and so he concluded that the will to power might be relied upon to lead man to the truth. That is to say, he believed that there was, in every man of the higher type (the only type he thought worth discussing) an instinctive tendency to seek the true as opposed to the false, that this instinct, as the race progressed, grew more and more accurate, and that its growing accuracy explained the fact that, despite the opposition of codes of morality and of the iron hand of authority, man constantly increased his store of knowledge. A thought, he said, arose in a man without his initiative or volition, and was nothing more or less than an expression of his innate will to obtain power over his environment by accurately observing and interpreting it. It was just as reasonable, he said, to say *It* thinks as to say *I* think, [6] because every intelligent person knew that a man couldn't control his thoughts. Therefore, the fact that these thoughts, in the long run and considering the human race as a whole, tended to uncover more and more truths proved that the will to power, despite the danger of generalizing from its manifestations, grew more and more accurate and so worked in the direction of absolute truth. Nietzsche believed that mankind was ever the slave of errors, but he held that the number of errors tended to decrease. When, at last, truth reigned supreme and there were no more errors, the superman would walk the earth.

Now it is impossible for any man to note the workings of the will to power save as it is manifested in his own instincts and thoughts, and therefore Nietzsche, in his later books, urges that every man should be willing, at all times, to pit his own feelings against the laws laid down by the majority. A man should steer clear of rash generalization from his own experience, but he should be doubly careful to steer clear of the generalizations of others. The greatest of all dangers lies in subscribing to a thesis without being certain of its truth. "This not-wishing-to-see what one sees ... is a primary requisite for membership in a party, in any sense whatsoever. Therefore, the party man becomes a liar by necessity." The proper attitude for a human being, indeed, is chronic dissent and skepticism. "Zarathustra is a skeptic.... Convictions are prisons.... The freedom from every kind of permanent conviction, the ability to search freely, belong to strength.... The need of a belief, of something that is unconditioned is a sign of weakness. The man of belief is necessarily a dependent man.... His instinct gives the highest honor to self-abnegation. He does not belong to himself, but to the author of the idea he believes."[7] It is only by skepticism, argues Nietzsche, that we can hope to make any progress. If all men accepted without question, the *dicta* of some one supreme sage, it is plain that there could be no further increase of knowledge. It is only by constant turmoil and conflict and exchange of views that the minute granules of truth can be separated from the vast muck heap of superstition and error. Fixed truths, in the long run, are probably more dangerous to intelligence than falsehoods.[8]

This argument, I take it, scarcely needs greater elucidation. Every intelligent man knows that if there had been no brave agnostics to defy the wrath of the church in the middle ages, the whole of Christendom would still wallow in the unspeakably foul morass of ignorance which had its center, during that black time, in an infallible sovereign of sovereigns. Authority, at all times and everywhere, means sloth and degeneration. It is only doubt that creates. It is only the minority that counts.

The fact that the great majority of human beings are utterly incapable of original thought, and so must, perforce, borrow their ideas or submit tamely to some authority, explains Nietzsche's violent loathing and contempt for the masses. The average, self-satisfied, conservative, orthodox, law-abiding citizen appeared to him to be a being but little raised above the cattle in the barn-yard. So violent was this feeling that every idea accepted by the majority excited, for that very reason, his suspicion and opposition. "What everybody believes, " he once said, "is never true." This may seem like a mere voicing of brobdingnagian egotism, but as a matter of fact, the same view is held by every man who has spent any time investigating the history of ideas. "Truth, " said Dr. Osler a while ago, "scarcely ever carries the struggle for acceptance at its first appearance." The masses are always a century or two behind. They have made a virtue of their obtuseness and call it by various fine names: conservatism, piety, respectability, faith. The nineteenth century witnessed greater human progress than all the centuries before it saw or even imagined, but the majority of white men of today still believe in ghosts, still fear the devil, still hold that the number 13 is unlucky and still picture the deity as a patriarch in a white beard, surrounded by a choir of resplendent amateur musicians. "We think a thing, " says Prof. Henry Sedgwick, "because all other people think so; or because, after all, we *do* think so; or because we are told so, and think we must think so; or because we once thought so, and think we still think so; or because, having thought so, we think we *will* think so."

Naturally enough, Nietzsche was an earnest opponent of the theological doctrine of free will. He held, as we have seen, that every human act was merely the effect of the will to power reacting against environment, and in consequence he had to reject absolutely the notion of volition and responsibility. A man, he argued, was not an object *in vacuo* and his acts, thoughts, impulses and motives could not be imagined without imagining some cause for them. If this cause came from without, it was clearly beyond his control, and if it came from within it was no less so, for his whole attitude of mind, his instinctive habits of thoughts, his very soul, so-called, were merely attributes that had been handed down to him, like the shape of his nose and the color of his eyes, from his ancestors. Nietzsche held that the idea of responsibility was the product and not the cause of the idea of punishment, and that the latter was nothing more than a manifestation of primitive man's will to power—to triumph over his fellows by making them suffer the handicap and humiliation of pain. "Men were called free, " he said, "in order that they might be condemned and punished.... When we immoralists try to cleanse psychology, history, nature and sociology of these notions, we find that our chief enemies are the theologians, who, with their preposterous idea of 'a moral order of the world, ' go on tainting the innocence of man's struggle upward with talk of punishment and guilt. Christianity is, indeed, a hangman's metaphysic."[9] As a necessary corollary of this, Nietzsche denied the existence of any plan in the cosmos. Like Haeckel, he believed that but two things existed— energy and matter; and that all the phenomena which made us conscious of the universe were nothing more than symptoms of the constant action of the one upon the other. Nothing ever happened without a cause, he said, and no cause was anything other than the effect of some previous cause. "The destiny of man, " he said, "cannot be disentangled from the destiny of everything else in existence, past, present and future.... We are a part of the whole, we exist in the whole.... There is nothing which could judge, measure or condemn our being, for that would be to judge, measure and condemn the whole.... But there is nothing outside of the whole.... The concept of God has hitherto made our existence a crime.... We deny God, we deny responsibility by denying God: it is only thereby that we save man."[10]

Herein, unluckily, Nietzsche fell into the trap which has snapped upon Haeckel and every other supporter of atheistic determinism. He denied that the human will was free and argued that every human action was inevitable, and yet he spent his whole life trying to convince his fellow men that they should do otherwise than as they did in fact. In a word, he held that they had no control whatever over their actions, and yet, like Moses, Mohammed and St. Francis, he thundered at them uproariously and urged them to turn from their errors and repent.

---

[1]J. W. Draper, "A History of the Conflict Between Religion and Science;" New York, 1874.

[2]Richard Falckenberg: "A History of Modern Philosophy, " tr. by A. C. Armstrong, Jr.; New York, 1897; Chap. I.

[3]T. H. Huxley: "Hume, " preface; London, 1879.

[4]Comte and Kant, for example.

[5]"*Der Antichrist*, " § 55.

[6]"*Jenseits von Gut und Böse*, " VII.

[7]"*Der Antichrist*, " § 54.

[8]"*Menschliches allzu Menschliches*, " § 483.

[9]"*Götzendämmerung*, " VI.

[10]"*Götzendämmerung*, " VI.

VIII. CIVILIZATION

On the surface, at least, the civilization of today seems to be moving slowly toward two goals. One is the eternal renunciation of war and the other is universal brotherhood: one is "peace on earth" and the other is "good will to men." Five hundred years ago a statesman's fame rested frankly and solely upon the victories of his armies; today we profess to measure him by his skill at keeping these armies in barracks. And in the internal economy of all civilized states we find today some pretence at unrestricted and equal suffrage. In times past it was the chief concern of all logicians and wiseacres to maintain the proposition that God reigned. At present, the dominant platitude of Christendom—the cornerstone of practically every political party and the stock-in-trade of every politician—is the proposition that the people rule.

Nietzsche opposed squarely both the demand for peace and the demand for equality, and his opposition was grounded upon two arguments. In the first place, he said, both demands were rhetorical and insincere and all intelligent men knew that neither would ever be fully satisfied. In the second place, he said, it would be ruinous to the race if they were. That is to say, he believed that war was not only necessary, but also beneficial, and that the natural system of castes was not only beneficent, but also inevitable. In the demand for universal peace he saw only the yearning of the weak and useless for protection against the righteous exploitation of the useful and strong. In the demand for equality he saw only the same thing. Both demands, he argued, controverted and combated that upward tendency which finds expression in the law of natural selection.

"The order of castes, " said Nietzsche, "is the dominating law of nature, against which no merely human agency may prevail. In every healthy society there are three broad classes, each of which has its own morality, its own work, its own notion of perfection and its own sense of mastery. The first class comprises those who are obviously superior to the mass intellectually; the second includes those whose eminence is chiefly muscular, and the third is made up of the mediocre. The third class, very naturally, is the most numerous, but the first is the most powerful.

"To this highest caste belongs the privilege of representing beauty, happiness and goodness on earth.... Its members accept the world as they find it and make the best of it.... They find their happiness in those things which, to lesser men, would spell ruin—in the labyrinth, in severity toward themselves and others, in effort. Their delight is self-governing: with them asceticism becomes naturalness, necessity, instinct. A difficult task is regarded by them as a privilege; to play with burdens which would crush others to death is their recreation. They are the most venerable species of men. They are the most cheerful, the most amiable. They rule because they are what they are. They are not at liberty to be second in rank.

"The second caste includes the guardians and keepers of order and security—the warriors, the nobles, the king—above all, as the highest types of warrior, the judges and defenders of the law. They execute the mandates of the first caste, relieving the latter of all that is coarse and menial in the work of ruling.

"At the bottom are the workers—the men of handicraft, trade, agriculture and the greater part of art and science. It is the law of nature that they should be public utilities—that they should be wheels and functions. The only kind of happiness of which they are capable makes intelligent machines of them. For the mediocre, it is happiness to be mediocre. In them the mastery of one thing—*i.e.* specialism—is an instinct.

"It is unworthy of a profound intellect to see in mediocrity itself an objection. It is, indeed, a necessity of human existence, for only in the presence of a horde of average men is the exceptional man a possibility....

"Whom do I hate most among the men of today? The socialist who undermines the workingman's healthy instincts, who takes from him his feeling of contentedness with his existence, who makes him envious, who teaches him revenge.... There is no wrong in unequal rights: it lies in the vain pretension to equal rights."[1]

It is obvious from this that Nietzsche was an ardent believer in aristocracy, but it is also obvious that he was not a believer in the thing which passes for aristocracy in the world today. The nobility of Europe belongs, not to his first class, but to his second class. It is essentially military and legal, for in themselves its members are puny and inefficient, and it is only the force of law that maintains them in their inheritance.

The fundamental doctrine of civilized law, as we know it today, is the proposition that what a man has once acquired shall belong to him and his heirs forever, without need on his part or theirs to defend it personally against predatory rivals. This transfer of the function of defense from the individual to the state naturally exalts the state's professional defenders— that is, her soldiers and judges—and so it is not unnatural to find the members of this class, and their parasites, in control of most of the world's governments and in possession of a large share of the world's wealth, power and honors.[2] To Nietzsche this seemed grotesquely illogical and unfair. He saw that this ruling class expended its entire energy in combating experiment and change and that the aristocracy it begot and protected—an aristocracy often identical, very naturally, with itself— tended to become more and more unfit and helpless and more and more a bar to the ready recognition and unrestrained functioning of the only true aristocracy—that of efficiency.

Nietzsche pointed out that one of the essential absurdities of a constitutional aristocracy was to be found in the fact that it hedged itself about with purely artificial barriers. Next only to its desire to maintain itself without actual personal effort was its jealous endeavor to prevent accessions to its ranks. Nothing, indeed, disgusts the traditional belted earl quite so much as the ennobling of some upstart brewer or iron-master. This exclusiveness, from Nietzsche's point of view, seemed ridiculous and pernicious, for a true aristocracy must be ever willing and eager to welcome to its ranks—and to enroll in fact, automatically—all who display those qualities which make a man extraordinarily fit and efficient. There should always be, he said, a free and constant interchange of individuals between the three natural castes of men. It should be always possible for an abnormally efficient man of the slave class to enter the master class, and, by the same token, accidental degeneration or incapacity in the master class should be followed by swift and merciless reduction to the ranks of slaves. Thus, those aristocracies which presented the incongruous spectacle of imbeciles being intrusted with the affairs of government seemed to him utterly abhorrent, and those schemes of caste which made a mean birth an offset to high intelligence seemed no less so.

So long as man's mastery of the forces of nature is incomplete, said Nietzsche, it will be necessary for the vast majority of human beings to spend their lives in either supplementing those natural forces which are partly under control or in opposing those which are still unleashed. The business of tilling the soil, for example, is still largely a matter of muscular exertion, despite the vast improvement in farm implements, and it will probably remain so for centuries to come. Since such labor is necessarily mere drudgery, and in consequence unpleasant, it is plain that it should be given over to men whose realization of its unpleasantness is least acute. Going further, it is plain that this work will be done with less and less revolt and less and less driving, as we evolve a class whose ambition to engage in more inviting pursuits grows smaller and smaller. In a word, the ideal ploughman is one who has no thought of anything higher and better than ploughing. Therefore, argued Nietzsche, the proper performance of the manual labor of the world makes it necessary that we have a laboring class, which means a class content to obey without fear or question.

This doctrine brought down upon Nietzsche's head the pious wrath of all the world's humanitarians, but empiric experiment has more than once proved its truth. The history of the hopelessly futile and fatuous effort to improve the negroes of the Southern United States by education affords one such proof. It is apparent, on brief reflection, that the negro, no matter how much he is educated, must remain, as a race, in a condition of subservience; that he must remain the inferior of the stronger and more intelligent white man so long as he retains racial differentiation. Therefore, the effort to educate him has awakened in his mind ambitions and aspirations which, in the very nature of things, must go unrealized, and so, while gaining nothing whatever materially, he has lost all his old contentment, peace of mind and happiness. Indeed, it is a commonplace of observation in the United States that the educated and refined negro is invariably a hopeless, melancholy, embittered and despairing man.

Nietzsche, to resume, regarded it as absolutely essential that there be a class of laborers or slaves—his "third caste"—and was of the opinion that such a class would exist upon earth so long as the human race survived. Its condition, compared to that of the ruling class, would vary but slightly, he thought, with the progress of the years. As man's mastery of nature increased, the laborer would find his task less and less painful, but he would always remain a fixed distance behind those who ruled him. Therefore, Nietzsche, in his philosophy, gave no thought to the desires and aspirations of the laboring class, because, as we have just seen, he held that a man could not properly belong to this class unless his desires and aspirations were so faint or so well under the control of the ruling class that they might be neglected. All of the Nietzschean doctrines and ideas apply only to the ruling class. It was at the top, he argued, that mankind grew. It was only in the ideas of those capable of original thought that progress had its source. William the Conqueror was of far more importance, though he was but a single man, than all the other Normans of his generation taken together.

Nietzsche was well aware that his "first caste" was necessarily small in numbers and that there was a strong tendency for its members to drop out of it and seek ease and peace in the castes lower down. "Life, " he said, "is always hardest toward the summit—the cold increases, the responsibility increases."[3] But to the truly efficient man these hardships are but spurs to effort. His joy is in combating and in overcoming—in pitting his will to power against the laws and desires of the rest of humanity. "I do not advise you to labor, " says Zarathustra, "but to fight. I do not advise you to compromise and make peace, but to conquer. Let your labor be fighting and your peace victory.... You say that a good cause will hallow even war? I tell you that a good war hallows every cause. War and courage have done more great things than charity. Not your pity, but your bravery lifts up those about you. Let the little girlies tell you that 'good' means 'sweet' and 'touching.' I tell you that 'good' means 'brave.'... The slave rebels against hardships and calls his rebellion superiority. Let your superiority be an acceptance of hardships. Let your commanding be an obeying.... Let your highest thought be: 'Man is something to be surpassed.'... I do not advise you to love your neighbor—the nearest human being. I advise you rather to flee from the nearest and love the furthest human being. Higher than love to your neighbor is love to the higher man that is to come in the future.... Propagate yourself upward. Thus live your life. What are many years worth? I do not spare you.... Die at the right time!"[4]

The average man, said Nietzsche, is almost entirely lacking in this gorgeous, fatalistic courage and sublime egotism. He is ever reluctant to pit his private convictions and yearnings against those of the mass of men. He is either afraid to risk the consequences of originality or fearful that, since the majority of his fellows disagree with him, he must be wrong. Therefore, no matter how strongly an unconventional idea may possess a man, he commonly seeks to combat it and throttle it, and the ability to do this with the least possible expenditure of effort we call self-control. The average man, said Nietzsche, has the power of self-control well developed, and in consequence he seldom contributes anything positive to the thought of his age and almost never attempts to oppose it.

We have seen in the preceding chapter that if every man, without exception, were of this sort, all human progress would cease, because the ideas of one generation would be handed down unchanged to the next and there would be no effort whatever to improve the conditions of existence by the only possible method—constant experiment with new ideas. Therefore, it follows that the world must depend for its advancement upon those revolutionists who, instead of overcoming their impulse to go counter to convention, give it free rein. Of such is Nietzsche's "first caste" composed. It is plain that among the two lower castes, courage of this sort is regarded, not as an evidence of strength, but as a proof of weakness. The man who outrages conventions is a man who lacks self-control, and the majority, by a process we have examined in our consideration of slave-morality, has exalted self-control, which, at bottom, is the antithesis of courage, into a place of honor higher than that belonging, by right, to courage itself.

But Nietzsche pointed out that the act of denying or combating accepted ideas is a thing which always tends to inspire other acts of the same sort. It is true enough that a revolutionary idea, so soon as it replaces an old convention and obtains the sanction of the majority, ceases to be revolutionary and becomes itself conventional, but all the same the mere fact that it has succeeded gives courage to those who harbor other revolutionary ideas and inspires them to give these ideas voice. Thus, it happens that courage breeds itself, and that, in times of great conflict, of no matter what sort, the world produces more than an average output of originality, or, as we more commonly denominate it, genius. In this manner Nietzsche accounted for a fact that had been noticed by many men before him: that such tremendous struggles as the French Revolution and the American Civil War are invariably followed by eras of diligent inquiry, of bold overturning of existing institutions and of marked progress. People become accustomed to unrestrained combat and so the desirability of self-control becomes less insistent.

Nietzsche had a vast contempt for what he called "the green-grazing happiness of the herd." Its strong morality and its insistence upon the doctrine that whatever is, is right—that "God's in his heaven; all's well with the world"—revolted him. He held that the so-called rights of the masses had no justifiable existence, since everything they asserted as a right was an assertion, more or less disguised, of the doctrine that the unfit should survive. "There are, " he said, "only three ways in which the masses appear to me to deserve a glance: first, as blurred copies of their betters, printed on bad paper and from worn out plates; secondly, as a necessary opposition to stimulate the master class, and thirdly, as instruments in the hands of the master class. Further than this I hand them over to statistics— and the devil."[5] Kant's proposal that the morality of every contemplated action be tested by the question, "Suppose everyone did as I propose to do?" seemed utterly ridiculous to Nietzsche because he saw that "everyone" always opposed the very things which meant progress; and Kant's corollary that the sense of duty contemplated in this dictum was "the obligation to act in reverence for law, " proved to Nietzsche merely that both duty and law were absurdities. "Contumely, " he said, "always falls upon those who break through some custom or convention. Such men, in fact, are called criminals. Everyone who overthrows an existing law is, at the start, regarded as a wicked man. Long afterward, when it is found that this law was bad and so cannot be re-established, the epithet is changed. All history treats almost exclusively of wicked men who, in the course of time, have come to be looked upon as good men. All progress is the result of successful crimes."[6]

Dr. Turck, [7] Miss Paget, M. Nordau and other critics see in all this good evidence that Nietzsche was a criminal at heart. At the bottom of all philosophies, says Miss Paget, [8] there is always one supreme idea. Sometimes it is a conception of nature, sometimes it is a religious faith and sometimes it is a theory of truth. In Nietzsche's case it is "my taste." He is always irritated: "*I* dislike, " "*I* hate, " "*I* want to get rid of" appear on every page of his writings. He delights in ruthlessness, his fellow men disgust him, his physical senses are acute, he has a sick ego. For that reason he likes singularity, the lonely Alps, classic literature and Bizet's "clear yellow" music. Turck argues that Nietzsche was a criminal because he got pleasure out of things which outraged the majority of his fellow men, and

Nordau, in supporting this idea, shows that it is possible for a man to experience and approve criminal impulses and still never act them: that there are criminals of the chair as well as of the dark lantern and sandbag. The answer to all of this, of course, is the fact that the same method of reasoning would convict every original thinker the world has ever known of black felony: that it would make Martin Luther a criminal as well as Jack Sheppard, John the Baptist as well as the Borgias, and Galileo as well as Judas Iscariot; that it would justify the execution of all the sublime company of heroes who have been done to death for their opinions, from Jesus Christ down the long line.

---

[1]*"Der Antichrist,"* § 57.

[2]In "The Governance of England, " (London: 1904) Sidney Low points out (chap. X) that, despite the rise of democracy, the government of Great Britain is still entirely in the hands of the landed gentry and nobility. The members of this class plainly owe their power to the military prowess of their ancestors, and their identity with the present military and judicial class is obvious. The typical M.P., in fact, also writes "J.P." after his name and "Capt." or "Col." before it. The examples of Russia, Germany, Japan, Austria, Italy, Spain and the Latin-American republics scarcely need be mentioned. In China the military, judicial and legislative-executive functions are always combined, and in the United States, while the military branch of the second caste is apparently impotent, it is plain that the balance of legislative power in every state and in the national legislature is held by lawyers, just as the final determination of all laws rests with judges.

[3]*"Der Antichrist,"* § 55.

[4]The quotations are from various chapters in the first part of *"Also sprach Zarathustra."*

[5]*"Vom Nutzen und Nachtheil der Historie für das Leben."*

[6]*"Morgenröte,"* § 20.

[7]*"Friedrich Nietzsche und seine philosophische Irrwege,"* Leipsic, 1891.

[8]*North American Review*, Dec., 1904.

IX. WOMEN AND MARRIAGE

Nietzsche's faithful sister, with almost comical and essentially feminine disgust, bewails the fact that, as a very young man, the philosopher became acquainted with the baleful truths set forth in Schopenhauer's immortal essay "On Women." That this daring work greatly influenced him is true, and that he subscribed to its chief arguments all the rest of his days is also true, but it is far from true to say that his view of the fair sex was borrowed bodily from Schopenhauer or that he would have written otherwise than as he did if Schopenhauer had never lived. Nietzsche's conclusions regarding women were the inevitable result, indeed, of his own philosophical system. It is impossible to conceive a man who held his opinions of morality and society laying down any other doctrines of femininity and matrimony than those he scattered through his books.

Nietzsche believed that there was a radical difference between the mind of man and the mind of woman and that the two sexes reacted in diametrically different ways to those stimuli which make up what might be called the clinical picture of human society. It is the function of man, he said, to wield a sword in humanity's battle with everything that makes life on earth painful or precarious. It is the function of woman, not to fight herself, but to provide fresh warriors for the fray. Thus the exercise of the will to exist is divided between the two: the man seeking the welfare of the race as he actually sees it and the woman seeking the welfare of generations yet unborn. Of course, it is obvious that this division is by no means clearly marked, because the man, in struggling for power over his environment, necessarily improves the conditions under which his children live, and the woman, working for her children, often benefits herself. But all the same the distinction is a good one and empiric observation bears it out. As everyone who has given a moment's thought to the subject well knows, a man's first concern in the world is to provide food and shelter for himself and his family, while a woman's foremost duty is to bear and rear children. "Thus, " said Nietzsche, "would I have man and woman: the one fit for warfare, the other fit for giving birth; and both fit for dancing with head and legs"[1]—that is to say: both capable of doing their share of the race's work, mental and physical, with conscious and superabundant efficiency.

Nietzsche points out that, in the racial economy, the place of woman may be compared to that of a slave-nation, while the position of man resembles that of a master-nation. We have seen how a weak nation, unable, on account of its weakness, to satisfy its will to survive and thirst for power by forcing its authority upon other nations, turns to the task of keeping these other nations, as much as possible, from enforcing their authority upon it. Realizing that it cannot rule, but must serve, it endeavors to make the conditions of its servitude as bearable as possible. This effort is commonly made in two ways: first by ostensibly renouncing its desire to rule, and secondly, by attempts to inoculate its powerful neighbors with its ideas in subterranean and round-about ways, so as to avoid arousing their suspicion and opposition. It becomes, in brief, humble and cunning, and with its humility as a cloak, it seeks to pit its cunning against the sheer might of those it fears.

The position of women in the world is much the same. The business of bearing and rearing children is destructive to their physical strength, and in consequence makes it impossible for them to prevail by force when their ideas and those of men happen to differ. To take away the sting of this incapacity, they make a virtue of it, and it becomes modesty, humility, self-sacrifice and fidelity; to win in spite of it they cultivate cunning, which commonly takes the form of hypocrisy, cajolery, dissimulation and more or less masked appeals to the masculine sexual instinct. All of this is so often observed in every-day life that it has become commonplace. A woman is physically unable to force a man to do as she desires, but her very inability to do so becomes a sentimental weapon against him, and her blandishments do the rest. The spectacle of a strong man ruled by a weak woman is no rare one certainly, and Samson was neither the first nor last giant to fall before a Delilah. There is scarcely a household in all the world, in truth, in which the familiar drama is not being acted and reacted day after day.

Now, it is plain from the foregoing that, though women's business in the world is of such a character that it inevitably leads to physical degeneration, her constant need to overcome the effects of this degeneration by cunning produces constant mental activity, which, by the law of exercise, should produce, in turn, great mental efficiency. This conclusion, in part, is perfectly correct, for women, as a sex, are shrewd, resourceful and acute; but the very fact that they are always concerned with imminent problems and that, in consequence, they are unaccustomed to dealing with the larger riddles of life, makes their mental attitude essentially petty. This explains the circumstance that despite their mental suppleness, they are not genuinely strong intellectually. Indeed, the very contrary is true. Women's constant thought is, not to lay down broad principles of right and wrong; not to place the whole world in harmony with some great scheme of justice; not to consider the future of nations; not to make two blades of grass grow where one grew before; but to deceive, influence, sway and please men. Normally, their weakness makes masculine protection necessary to their existence and to the exercise of their overpowering maternal instinct, and so their whole effort is to obtain this protection in the easiest way possible. The net result is that feminine morality is a morality of opportunism and imminent expediency, and that the normal woman has no respect for, and scarcely any conception of abstract truth. Thus is proved the fact noted by Schopenhauer and many other observers: that a woman seldom manifests any true sense of justice or of honor.

It is unnecessary to set forth this idea in greater detail, because everyone is familiar with it and proofs of its accuracy are supplied in infinite abundance by common observation. Nietzsche accepted it as demonstrated. When he set out to pursue the subject further, he rejected entirely the Schopenhauerean corollary that man should ever regard woman as his enemy, and should seek, by all means within his power, to escape her insidious influence. Such a notion naturally outraged the philosopher of the superman. He was never an advocate of running away: to all the facts of existence he said "yes." His ideal was not resignation or flight, but an intelligent defiance and opposition. Therefore, he argued that man should accept woman as a natural opponent arrayed against him for the benevolent purpose of stimulating him to constant efficiency. Opposition, he pointed out, was a necessary forerunner of function, and in consequence the fact that woman spent her entire effort in a ceaseless endeavor to undermine and change the will of man, merely served to make this will alert and strong, and so increased man's capacity for meeting and overcoming the enemies of his existence.

A man conscious of his strength, observes Nietzsche, need have no fear of women. It is only the man who finds himself utterly helpless in the face of feminine cajolery that must cry, "Get thee behind me, Satan!" and flee. "It is only the most sensual men, " he says, "who have to shun women and torture their bodies." The normal, healthy man, despite the strong appeal which women make to him by their subtle putting forward of the sexual idea—visually as dress, coquetry and what not—still keeps a level head. He is strong enough to weather the sexual storm. But the man who cannot do this, who experiences no normal reaction in the direction of guardedness and caution and reason, must either abandon himself utterly as a helpless slave to woman's instinct of race-preservation, and so become a bestial voluptuary, or avoid temptation altogether and so become a celibate.[2]

There is nothing essentially evil in woman's effort to combat and control man's will by constantly suggesting the sexual idea to him, because it is necessary, for the permanence of the race, that this idea be presented frequently and powerfully. Therefore, the conflict between masculine and feminine ideals is to be regarded, not as a lamentable battle, in which one side is right and the other wrong, but a convenient means of providing that stimulation-by-opposition without which all function, and in consequence all progress, would cease. "The man who regards women as an enemy to be avoided, " says Nietzsche, "betrays an unbridled lust which loathes not only itself, but also its means."[3]

There are, of course, occasions when the feminine influence, by its very subtlety, works harm to the higher sort of men. It is dangerous for a man to love too violently and it is dangerous, too, for him to be loved too much.'

"The natural inclination of women to a quiet, uniform and peaceful existence "—that is to say, to a slave-morality—"operates adversely to the heroic impulse of the masculine free spirit. Without being aware of it, women act like a person who would remove stones from the path of a mineralogist, lest his feet should come in contact with them—forgetting entirely that he is faring forth for the very purpose of coming in contact with them.... The wives of men with lofty aspirations cannot resign themselves to seeing their husbands suffering, impoverished and slighted, even though it is apparent that this suffering proves, not only that its victim has chosen his attitude aright, but also that his aims—some day, at least—will be realized. Women always intrigue in secret against the higher souls of their husbands. They seek to cheat the future for the sake of a painless and agreeable present."[4] In other words, the feminine vision is ever limited in range. Your typical woman cannot see far ahead; she cannot reason out the ultimate effect of a complicated series of causes; her eye is always upon the present or the very near future. Thus Nietzsche reaches, by a circuitous route, a conclusion supported by the almost unanimous verdict of the entire masculine sex, at all times and everywhere.

Nietzsche quite agrees with Schopenhauer (and with nearly everyone else who has given the matter thought) that the thing we call love is grounded upon physical desire, and that all of those arts of dress and manner in which women excel are mere devices for arousing this desire in man, but he points out, very justly, that a great many other considerations also enter into the matter. Love necessarily presupposes a yearning to mate, and mating is its logical consequence, but the human imagination has made it more than that. The man in love sees in his charmer, not only an attractive instrument for satisfying his comparatively rare and necessarily brief impulses to dalliance, but also a worthy companion, guide, counsellor and friend. The essence of love is confidence— confidence in the loved one's judgment, honesty and fidelity and in the persistence of her charm. So large do these considerations loom among the higher classes of men that they frequently obscure the fundamental sexual impulse entirely. It is a commonplace, indeed, that in the ecstasies of amorous idealization, the notion of the function itself becomes obnoxious. It may be impossible to imagine a man loving a woman without having had, at some time, conscious desire for her, but all the same it is undoubtedly true that the wish for marriage is very often a wish for close and constant association with the one respected, admired and trusted rather than a yearning for the satisfaction of desire.

All of this admiration, respect and trust, as we have seen, may be interpreted as confidence, which, in turn, is faith. Now, faith is essentially unreasonable, and in the great majority of cases, is the very antithesis of reason. Therefore, a man in love commonly endows the object of his affection with merits which, to the eye of a disinterested person, she obviously lacks. "Love ... has a secret craving to discover in the loved one as many beautiful qualities as possible and to raise her as high as possible." "Whoever idolizes a person tries to justify himself by idealizing; and thus becomes an artist (or self-deceiver) in order to have a clear conscience." Again there is a tendency to illogical generalization. "Everything which pleases me once, or several times, is pleasing of and in itself." The result of this, of course, is quick and painful disillusion. The loved one is necessarily merely human and when the ideal gives way to the real, reaction necessarily follows. "Many a married man awakens one morning to the consciousness that his wife is far from attractive."[5] And it is only fair to note that the same awakening is probably the bitter portion of most married women, too.

In addition, it is plain that the purely physical desire which lies at the bottom of all human love, no matter how much sentimental considerations may obscure it, is merely a passion and so, in the very nature of things, is intermittent and evanescent. There are moments when it is overpowering, but there are hours, days, weeks and months when it is dormant. Therefore, we must conclude with Nietzsche, that the thing we call love, whether considered from its physical or psychical aspect, is fragile and short-lived.

Now, inasmuch as marriage, in the majority of cases, is a permanent institution (as it is, according to the theory of our moral code, in *all* cases), it follows that, in order to make the relation bearable, something must arise to take the place of love. This something, as we know, is ordinarily tolerance, respect, *camaraderie*, or a common interest in the well-being of the matrimonial firm or in the offspring of the marriage. In other words, the discovery that many of the ideal qualities seen in the life-companion through the rosy glasses of love do not existis succeeded by a common-sense and unsentimental decision to make the best of those real ones which actually do exist.

From this it is apparent that a marriage is most apt to be successful when the qualities imagined in the beloved are all, or nearly all, real: that is to say, when the possibility of disillusion is at an irreducible minimum. This occurs sometimes by accident, but Nietzsche points out that such accidents are comparatively rare. A man in love, indeed, is the worst possible judge of his*inamorata's* possession of those traits which will make her a satisfactory wife, for, as we have noted, he observes her through an ideal haze and sees in her innumerable merits which, to the eye of an unprejudiced and accurate observer, she does not possess. Nietzsche, at different times, pointed out two remedies for this. His first plan proposed that marriages for love be discouraged, and that we endeavor to insure the permanence of the relation by putting the selection of mates into the hands of third persons likely to be dispassionate and far-seeing: a plan followed with great success, it may be recalled, by most ancient peoples and in vogue, in a more or less disguised form, in many European countries today. "It is impossible, " he said, "to found a permanent institution upon an idiosyncrasy. Marriage, if it is to stand as the bulwark of civilization, cannot be founded upon the temporary and unreasonable thing called love. To fulfil its mission, it must be founded upon the impulse to reproduction, or race permanence; the impulse to possess property (women and children are property); and the impulse to rule, which constantly organizes for itself the smallest unit of sovereignty, the family, and which needs children and heirs to maintain, by physical force, whatever measure of power, riches and influence it attains."

Nietzsche's second proposal was nothing more or less than the institution of trial marriage, which, when it was proposed years later by an American sociologist, [6] caused all the uproar which invariably rises in the United States whenever an attempt is made to seek absolute truth. "Give us a term, " said Zarathustra, "and a small marriage, that we may see whether we are fit for the great marriage."[7] The idea here, of course, is simply this: that, when a man and a woman find it utterly impossible to live in harmony, it is better for them to separate at once than to live on together, making a mock of the institution they profess to respect, and begetting children who, in Nietzsche's phrase, cannot be regarded other than as mere "scapegoats of matrimony." Nietzsche saw that this notion was so utterly opposed to all current ideals and hypocrisies that it would be useless to argue it, and so he veered toward his first proposal. The latter, despite its violation of one of the most sacred illusions of the Anglo-Saxon race, is by no means a mere fantasy of the chair. Marriages in which love is subordinated to mutual fitness and material considerations are the rule in many countries today, and have been so for thousands of years, and if it be urged that, in France, their fruit has been adultery, unfruitfulness and degeneration, it may be answered that, in Turkey, Japan and India, they have become the cornerstones of quite respectable civilizations.

Nietzsche believed that the ultimate mission and function of human marriage was the breeding of a race of supermen and he saw very clearly that fortuitous pairing would never bring this about. "Thou shalt not only propagate thyself, " said Zarathustra, "but propagate thyself upward. Marriage should be the will of two to create that which is greater than either. But that which the many call marriage—alas! what call I that? Alas I that soul-poverty of two! Alas! that soul-filth of two! Alas! that miserable dalliance of two! Marriage they call it—and they say that marriages are made in heaven. I like them not: these animals caught in heavenly nets.... Laugh not at such marriages! What child has not reason to weep over its parents?" It is the old argument against haphazard breeding. We select the sires and dams of our race-horses with most elaborate care, but the strains that mingle in our children's veins get there by chance. "Worthy and ripe for begetting the superman this man appeared to me, but when I saw his wife earth seemed a madhouse. Yea, I wish the earth would tremble in convulsions when such a saint and such a goose mate! This one fought for truth like a hero—and then took to heart a little dressed-up lie. He calls it his marriage. That one was reserved in intercourse and chose his associates fastidiously—and then spoiled his company forever. He calls it his marriage. A third sought for a servant with an angel's virtues. Now he is the servant of a woman. Even the most cunning buys his wife in a sack."[8]

As has been noted, Nietzsche was by no means a declaimer against women. A bachelor himself and constitutionally suspicious of all who walked in skirts, he nevertheless avoided the error of damning the whole sex as a dangerous and malignant excrescence upon the face of humanity. He saw that woman's mind was the natural complement of man's mind; that womanly guile was as useful, in its place, as masculine truth; that man, to retain those faculties which made him master of the earth, needed a persistent and resourceful opponent to stimulate them and so preserve and develop them. So long as the institution of the family remained a premise in every sociological syllogism, so long as mere fruitfulness remained as much a merit among intelligent human beings as it was among peasants and cattle—so long, he saw, it would be necessary for the stronger sex to submit to the parasitic opportunism of the weaker.

But he was far from exalting mere women into goddesses, after the sentimental fashion of those virtuosi of illusion who pass for law-givers in the United States, and particularly in the southern part thereof. Chivalry, with its ridiculous denial of obvious facts, seemed to him unspeakable and the good old sub-Potomac doctrines that a woman who loses her virtue is, *ipso facto*, a victim and not a criminal or *particeps criminis*, and that a "lady, " by virtue of being a "lady, " is necessarily a reluctant and helpless quarry in the hunt of love—these ancient and venerable fallacies would have made him laugh. He admitted the great and noble part that woman had to play in the world-drama, but he saw clearly that her methods were essentially deceptive, insincere and pernicious, and so he held that she should be confined to her proper role and that any effort she made to take a hand in other matters should be regarded with suspicion, and when necessary, violently opposed. Thus Nietzsche detested the idea of women's suffrage almost as much as he detested the idea of chivalry. The participation of women in large affairs, he argued, could lead to but one result: the contamination of the masculine ideals of justice, honor and truth by the feminine ideals of dissimulation, equivocation and intrigue. In women, he believed, there was an entire absence of that instinctive liking for a square deal and a fair fight which one finds in all men—even the worst.

Hence, Nietzsche believed that, in his dealings with women, man should be wary and cautious. "Let men fear women when she loveth: for she sacrificeth all for love and nothing else hath value to her.... Man is for woman a means: the end is always the child.... Two things are wanted by the true man: danger and play. Therefore he seeketh woman as the most dangerous toy within his reach.... Thou goest to women? *Don't forget thy whip!*"[9] This last sentence has helped to make Nietzsche a stench in the nostrils of the orthodox, but the context makes his argument far more than a mere effort at sensational epigram. He is pointing out the utter unscrupulousness which lies at the foundation of the maternal instinct: an unscrupulousness familiar to every observer of humanity.[10] Indeed, it is so potent a factor in the affairs of the world that we have, by our ancient device of labelling the inevitable the good, exalted it to the dignity and estate of a virtue. But all the same, we are instinctively conscious of its inherent opposition to truth and justice, and so our law books provide that a woman who commits a crime in her husband's presence is presumed to have been led to it by her desire to work what she regards as his good, which means her desire to retain his protection and good will. "Man's happiness is: 'I will.' Woman's happiness is: 'He will.'"[11]

Maternity, thought Nietzsche, was a thing even more sublime than paternity, because it produced a more keen sense of race responsibility. "Is there a state more blessed, " he asked, "than that of a woman with child?... Even worldly justice does not allow the judge and hangman to lay hold on her."[12] He saw, too, that woman's insincere masochism[13] spurred man to heroic efforts and gave vigor and direction to his work by the very fact that it bore the outward aspect of helplessness. He saw that the resultant stimulation of the will to power was responsible for many of the world's great deeds, and that, if woman served no other purpose, she would still take an honorable place as the most splendid reward—greater than honors or treasures—that humanity could bestow upon its victors. The winning of a beautiful and much-sought woman, indeed, will remain as great an incentive to endeavor as the conquest of a principality so long as humanity remains substantially as it is today.

It is unfortunate that Nietzsche left us no record of his notions regarding the probable future of matrimony as an institution. We have reason to believe that he agreed with Schopenhauer's analysis of the "lady,

" *i.e.* the woman elevated to splendid, but complete parasitism. Schopenhauer showed that this pitiful creature was the product of the monogamous ideal, just as the prostitute was the product of the monogamous actuality. In the United States and England, unfortunately, it is impossible to discuss such matters with frankness, or to apply to them the standards of absolute truth, on account of the absurd axiom that monogamy is ordained of God, —with which maxim there appears the equally absurd corollary: that the civilization of a people is to be measured by the degree of dependence of its women. Luckily for posterity this last revolting doctrine is fast dying, though its decadence is scarcely noticed and wholly misunderstood. We see about us that women are becoming more and more independent and self-sufficient and that, as individuals, they have less and less need to seek and retain the good will and protection of individual men, but we overlook the fact that this tendency is fast undermining the ancient theory that the family is a necessary and impeccable institution and that without it progress would be impossible. As a matter of fact, the idea of the family, as it exists today, is based entirely upon the idea of feminine helplessness. So soon as women are capable of making a living for themselves and their children, without the aid of the fathers of the latter, the old cornerstone of the family—the masculine defender and bread-winner—will find his occupation gone, and it will become ridiculous to force him, by law or custom, to discharge duties for which there is no longer need. Wipe out your masculine defender, and your feminine parasite-*haus-frau*—and where is your family?

This tendency is exhibited empirically by the rising revolt against those fetters which the family idea has imposed upon humanity: by the growing feeling that divorce should be a matter of individual expedience; by the successful war of cosmopolitanism upon insularity and clannishness and upon all other costly outgrowths of the old idea that because men are of the same blood they must necessarily love one another; and by the increasing reluctance among civilized human beings to become parents without some reason more logical than the notion that parenthood, in itself, is praiseworthy. It seems plain, in a word, that so soon as any considerable portion of the women of the world become capable of doing men's work and of thus earning a living for themselves and their children without the aid of men, there will be in full progress a dangerous, if unconscious, war upon the institution of marriage. It may be urged in reply that this will never happen, because of the fact that women are physically unequal to men, and that in consequence of their duty of child-bearing, they will ever remain so, but it may be answered to this that use will probably vastly increase their physical fitness; that science will rob child-bearing of most of its terrors within a comparatively few years; and that the woman who seeks to go it alone will have only herself and her child to maintain, whereas, the man of today has not only himself and his child, but also the woman. Again, it is plain that the economic handicap of child-bearing is greatly overestimated. At most, the business of maternity makes a woman utterly helpless for no longer than three months, and in the case of a woman who has three children, this means nine months in a life time. It is entirely probable that alcohol alone, not to speak of other enemies of efficiency, robs the average man of quite that much productive activity during his three score years and ten.

———

[1]"*Also sprach Zarathustra*, " III.

[2]Nietzsche saw, of course ("The Genealogy of Morals, " III), that temporary celibacy was frequently necessary to men with peculiarly difficult and vitiating tasks ahead of them. The philosopher who sought to solve world riddles, he said, had need to steer clear of women, for reasons which appealed, with equal force, to the athlete who sought to perform great feats of physical strength. It is obvious, however, that this desire to escape distraction and drain differs vastly from ethical celibacy.

[3]"*Morgenröte*, " § 346.

[4]"*Menschliches allzu Menschliches*, " § 431, 434.

[5]All of these quotations are from "*Morgenröte*."

[6]Elsie Clews Parsons: "The Family, " New York, 1906. Mrs. Parsons is a doctor of philosophy, a Hartley house fellow and was for six years a lecturer on sociology at Barnard College.

[7]"*Also sprach Zarathustra*, " III.

[8]"*Also sprach Zarathustra*, " I.

[9]"*Also sprach Zarathustra*, " I.

[10]Until quite recently it was considered indecent and indefensible to mention this fact, despite its obviousness. But it is now discussed freely enough and in Henry Arthur Jones' play, "The Hypocrites, " it is presented admirably in the character of the mother whose instinctive effort to protect her son makes her a scoundrel and the son a cad.

[11]"*Also sprach Zarathustra*, " I.

[12]"*Morgenröte*, " § 552.

[13]Prof. Dr. R. von Krafft Ebing: "Masochism is ... a peculiar perversion ... consisting in this, that the individual seized with it is dominated by the idea that he is wholly and unconditionally subjected to the will of a person of the opposite sex, who treats him imperiously and humiliates and maltreats him."

X. GOVERNMENT

Like Spencer before him, Nietzschebelieved, as we have seen, that the best possible system of government was that which least interfered with the desires and enterprises of the efficient and intelligent individual. That is to say, he held that it would be well to establish, among the members of his first caste of human beings, a sort of glorified anarchy. Each member of this caste should be at liberty to work out his own destiny for himself. There should be no laws regulating and circumscribing his relations to other members of his caste, except the easily-recognizable and often-changing laws of common interest, and above all, there should be no laws forcing him to submit to, or even to consider, the wishes and behests of the two lower castes. The higher man, in a word, should admit no responsibility whatever to the lower castes. The lowest of all he should look upon solely as a race of slaves bred to work his welfare in the most efficient and uncomplaining manner possible, and the military caste should seem to him a race designed only to carry out his orders and so prevent the slave caste marching against him.

It is plain from this that Nietzsche stood squarely opposed to both of the two schemes of government which, on the surface, at least, seem to prevail in the western world today. For the monarchial ideal and for the democratic ideal he had the same words of contempt. Under an absolute monarchy, he believed, the military or law-enforcing caste was unduly exalted, and so its natural tendency to permanence was increased and its natural opposition to all experiment and progress was made well nigh irresistible. Under a communistic democracy, on the other hand, the mistake was made of putting power into the hands of the great, inert herd, which was necessarily and inevitably ignorant, credulous, superstitious, corrupt and wrong. The natural tendency of this herd, said Nietzsche, was to combat change and progress as bitterly and as ceaselessly as the military-judicial caste, and when, by some accident, it rose out of its rut and attempted experiments, it nearly always made mistakes, both in its premises and its conclusions and so got hopelessly bogged in error and imbecility. Its feeling for truth seemed to him to be almost *nil*; its mind could never see beneath misleading exteriors. "In the market place, " said Zarathustra, "one convinces by gestures, but real reasons make the populace distrustful."[1]

That this natural incompetence of the masses is an actual fact was observed by a hundred philosophers before Nietzsche, and fresh proofs of it are spread copiously before the world every day. Wherever universal suffrage, or some close approach to it, is the primary axiom of government, the thing known in the United States as "freak legislation" is a constant evil. On the statute books of the great majority of American states there are laws so plainly opposed to all common-sense that they bear an air of almost pathetic humor. One state legislature, [2] in an effort to prevent the corrupt employment of insurance funds, passes laws so stringent that, in the face of them, it is utterly impossible for an insurance company to transact a profitable business. Another considers an act contravening rights guaranteed specifically by the state and national constitutions;[3] yet another[4] passes a law prohibiting divorce under any circumstances whatever. And the spectacle is by no means confined to the American states. In the Australian Commonwealth, mob-rule has burdened the statutes with regulations which make difficult, if not impossible, the natural development of the country's resources and trade. If, in England and Germany, the effect of universal suffrage has been less apparent, it is because in these countries the two upper castes have solved the problem of keeping the proletariat, despite its theoretical sovereignty, in proper leash and bounds.

The possibility of exercising this control seemed to Nietzsche to be the saving grace of all modern forms of government, just as their essential impossibility appeared as the saving grace alike of Christianity and of communistic civilization. In England, as we have seen, [5] the military-judicial caste, despite the Reform Act of 1867, has retained its old dominance, and in Germany, despite the occasional success of the socialists, it is always possible for the military aristocracy, by appealing to the vanity of the *bourgeoisie*, to win in a stand-up fight. In America, the proletariat, when it is not engaged in functioning in its own extraordinary manner, is commonly the tool, either of the first of Nietzsche's castes or of the second. That is to say, the average legislature has its price, and this price is often paid by those who believe that old laws, no matter how imperfect they may be, are better than harum-scarum new ones. Naturally enough, the most intelligent and efficient of Americans—members of the first caste—do not often go to a state capital with corruption funds and openly buy legislation, but nevertheless their influence is frequently felt. President Roosevelt, for one, has more than once forced his views upon a reluctant proletariat and even enlisted it under his banner—as in his advocacy of centralization, a truly dionysian idea, for example—and in the southern states the educated white class—which there represents, though in a melancholy fashion, the Nietzschean first caste—has found it easy to take from the black masses their very right to vote, despite the fact that they are everywhere in a great majority numerically, and so, by the theory of democracy, represent whatever power lies in the state. Thus it is apparent that Nietzsche's argument against democracy, like his argument against brotherhood, is based upon the thesis that both are rejected instinctively by all those men whose activity works for the progress of the human race.[6]

It is obvious, of course, that the sort of anarchy preached by Nietzsche differs vastly from the beery, collarless anarchy preached by Herr Most and his unwashed followers. The latter contemplates a suspension of all laws in order that the unfit may escape the natural and rightful exploitation of the fit, whereas the former reduces the unfit to *de facto* slavery and makes them subject to the laws of a master class, which, in so far as the relations of its own members, one to the other, are concerned, recognizes no law but that of natural selection. To the average American or Englishman the very name of anarchy causes a shudder, because it invariably conjures up a picture of a land terrorized by low-browed assassins with matted beards, carrying bombs in one hand and mugs of beer in the other. But as a matter of fact, there is no reason whatever to believe that, if all laws were abolished tomorrow, such swine would survive the day. They are incompetents under our present paternalism and they would be incompetents under dionysian anarchy. The only difference between the two states is that the former, by its laws, protects men of this sort, whereas the latter would work their speedy annihilation. In a word, the dionysian state would see the triumph, not of drunken loafers, but of the very men whose efforts are making for progress today: those strong, free, self-reliant, resourceful men whose capacities are so much greater than the mob's that they are often able to force their ideas upon it despite its theoretical right to rule them and its actual endeavor so to do. Nietzschean anarchy would create an aristocracy of efficiency. The strong man—which means the intelligent, ingenious and far-seeing man—would acknowledge no authority but his own will and no morality but his own advantage. As we have seen in previous chapters, this would re-establish the law of natural selection firmly upon its disputed throne, and so the strong would grow ever stronger and more efficient, and the weak would grow ever more obedient and tractile.

It may be well at this place to glance briefly at an objection that has been urged against Nietzsche's argument by many critics, and particularly by those in the socialistic camp. Led to it, no doubt, by their too literal acceptance of Marx's materialistic conception of history, they have assumed that Nietzsche's higher man must necessarily belong to the class denominated, by our after-dinner speakers and leader writers, "captains of industry, " and to this class alone. That is to say, they have regarded the higher man as identical with the pushing, grasping buccaneer of finance, because this buccaneer has seemed to them to be the only man of today who is truly "strong, free, self-reliant and resourceful" and the only one who actually "acknowledges no authority but his own will." As a matter of fact, all of these assumptions are in error. For one thing, the "captain of industry" is not uncommonly the reverse of a dionysian, and without the artificial aid of our permanent laws, he might often perish in the struggle for existence. For another thing, it is an obvious fact that the men who go most violently counter to the view of the herd, and who battle most strenuously to prevail against it—our true criminals and transvaluers and breakers of the law—are not such men as Rockefeller, but men such as Pasteur; not such men as Morgan and Hooley, but sham-smashers and truth-tellers and mob-fighters after the type of Huxley, Lincoln, Bismarck, Darwin, Virchow, Haeckel, Hobbes, Macchiavelli, Harvey and Jenner, the father of vaccination.

Jenner, to choose one from the long list, was a real dionysian, because he boldly pitted his own opinion against the practically unanimous opinion of all the rest of the human race. Among those members of the ruling class in England who came after him—those men, that is, who made vaccination compulsory—the dionysian spirit was still more apparent. The masses themselves did not want to be vaccinated, because they were too ignorant to understand the theory of inoculation and too stupid to be much impressed by its unvisualized and—for years, at least—impalpable benefits. Yet their rulers forced them, against their will, to bare their arms. And why was this done? Was it because the ruling class was possessed by a boundless love for humanity and so yearned to lavish upon it a wealth of Christian devotion? Not at all. The real motive of the law makers was to be found in two considerations. In the first place, a proletariat which suffered from epidemics of small-pox was a crippled mob whose capacity for serving its betters, in the fields and factories of England, was sadly decreased. In the second place experience proved that when smallpox raged in the slums, it had an unhappy habit of stretching out its arms in the direction of mansion and castle, too. Therefore, the proletariat was vaccinated and small-pox was stamped out—not because the ruling class loved the workers, but because it wanted to make them work for it as continuously as possible and to remove or reduce their constant menace to its life and welfare. In so far as it took the initiative in these proceedings, the military ruling-class of England raised itself to the eminence of Nietzsche's first caste. That Jenner himself, when he put forward his idea and led the military caste to carry it into execution, was an ideal member of the first caste, is plain. The goal before him was fame everlasting—and he gained it.

I have made this rather long digression because the opponents of Nietzsche have voiced their error a thousand times and have well-nigh convinced a great many persons of its truth. It is apparent enough, of course, that a great many men whose energy is devoted to the accumulation of money are truly dionysian in their methods and aims, but it is apparent, too, that a great many others are not. Nietzsche himself was well aware of the dangers which beset a race enthralled by commercialism, and he sounded his warning against them. Trade, being grounded upon security, tends to work for permanence in laws and customs, even after the actual utility of these laws and customs is openly questioned. This is shown by the persistence of free trade in England and of protectionism in the United States, despite the fact that the conditions of existence, in both countries, have materially changed since the two systems were adopted, and there is now good ground, in each, for demanding reform. So it is plain that Nietzsche did not cast his higher man in the mold of a mere millionaire. It is conceivable that a careful analysis might prove Mr. Morgan to be a dionysian, but it is certain that his character as such would not be grounded upon his well-known and oft-repeated plea that existing institutions be permitted to remain as they are.

Yet again, a great many critics of Nietzsche mistake his criticism of existing governmental institutions for an argument in favor of their immediate and violent abolition. When he inveighs against monarchy or democracy, for instance, it is concluded that he wants to assassinate all the existing rulers of the world, overturn all existing governments and put chaos, carnage, rapine and anarchy in their place. Such a conclusion, of course, is a grievous error. Nietzsche by no means believed that reforms could be instituted in a moment or that the characters and habits of thought of human beings could be altered by a lightning stroke. His whole philosophy, in truth, was based upon the idea of slow evolution, through infinitely laborious and infinitely protracted stages. All he attempted to do was to indicate the errors that were being made in his own time and to point out the probable character of the truths that would be accepted in the future. He believed that it was only by constant skepticism, criticism and opposition that progress could be made, and that the greatest of all dangers was inanition. Therefore, when he condemned all existing schemes of government, it meant no more than that he regarded them as based upon fundamental errors, and that he hoped and believed that, in the course of time, these errors would be observed, admitted and swept away, to make room for other errors measurably less dangerous, and in the end for truths. Such was his mission, as he conceived it: to attack error wherever he saw it and to proclaim truth whenever he found it. It is only by such iconoclasm and proselyting that humanity can be helped. It is only after a mistake is perceived and admitted that it can be rectified.

Nietzsche's argument for the "free spirit" by no means denies the efficacy of co-operation in the struggle upward, but neither does it support that blind fetishism which sees in co-operation the sole instrument of human progress. In one of his characteristic thumb-nail notes upon evolution he says: "The most important result of progress in the past is the fact that we no longer live in constant fear of wild beasts, barbarians, gods and our own dreams."[7] It may be argued, in reference to this, that organized government is to be thanked for our deliverance, but a moment's thought will show the error of the notion. Humanity's war upon wild beasts was fought and won by individualists, who had in mind no end but their personal safety and that of their children, and the subsequent war upon barbarians would have been impossible, or at least unsuccessful, had it not been for the weapons invented and employed during the older fight against beasts. Again, it is apparent that our emancipation from the race's old superstitions regarding gods and omens has been achieved, not by communal effort, but by individual effort. Knowledge and not government brought us the truth that made us free. Government, in its very essence, is opposed to all increase of knowledge. Its tendency is always toward permanence and against change. It is unthinkable without some accepted scheme of law or morality, and such schemes, as we have seen, stand in direct antithesis to every effort to find the absolute truth. Therefore, it is plain that the progress of humanity, far from being the result of government, has been made entirely without its aid and in the face of its constant and bitter opposition. The code of Hammurabi, the laws of the Medes and Persians, the Code Napoleon and the English common law have retarded the search for the ultimate verities almost as much, indeed, as the Ten Commandments.

Nietzsche denies absolutely that there is inherent in mankind a yearning to gather into communities. There is, he says, but one primal instinct in human beings (as there is in all other animals), and that is the desire to remain alive. All those systems of thought which assume the existence of a "natural morality" are wrong. Even the tendency to tell the truth, which seems to be inborn in every civilized white man, is not "natural, " for there have been—and are today—races in which it is, to all intents and purposes, entirely absent.[8] And so it is with the so-called social instinct. Man, say the communists, is a gregarious animal and can be happy only in company with his fellows, and in proof of it they cite the fact that loneliness is everywhere regarded as painful and that, even among the lower animals, there is an impulse toward association. The facts set forth in the last sentence are indisputable, but they by no means prove the existence of an elemental social feeling sufficiently strong to make its satisfaction an end in itself. In other words, while it is plain that men flock together, just as birds flock together, it is going too far to say that the mere joy of flocking—the mere desire to be with others—is at the bottom of the tendency. On the contrary, it is quite possible to show that men gather in communities for the same reason that deer gather in herds: because each individual realizes (unconsciously, perhaps) that such a combination materially aids him in the business of self-protection. One deer is no match for a lion, but fifty deer make him impotent.[9]

Nietzsche shows that, even after communities are formed, the strong desire of every individual to look out for himself, regardless of the desires of others, persists, and that, in every herd there are strong members and weak members. The former, whenever the occasion arises, sacrifice the latter: by forcing the heavy, killing drudgery of the community upon them or by putting them, in time of war, into the forefront of the fray. The result is that the weakest are being constantly weeded out and the strongest are always becoming stronger and stronger. "Hence, " says Nietzsche, "the first 'state' made its appearance in the form of a terrible tyranny, a violent and unpitying machine, which kept grinding away until the primary raw material, the man-ape, was kneaded and fashioned into alert, efficient man."

Now, when a given state becomes appreciably more efficient than the states about it, it invariably sets about enslaving them. Thus larger and larger states are formed, but always there is a ruling master-class and a serving slave-class. "This, " says Nietzsche, "is the origin of the state on earth, despite the fantastic theory which would found it upon some general agreement among its members. He who can command, he who is a master by nature, he who, in deed and gesture, behaves violently—what need has he for agreements? Such beings come as fate comes, without reason or pretext.... Their work is the instinctive creation of forms: they are the most unconscious of all artists; wherever they appear, something new is at once created—a governmental organism which lives; in which the individual parts and functions are differentiated and brought into correlation, and in which nothing at all is tolerable unless some utility with respect to the whole is implanted in it. They are innocent of guilt, of responsibility, of charity—these born rulers. They are ruled by that terrible art-egotism which knows itself to be justified by its work, as the mother knows herself to be justified by her child."

Nietzsche points out that, even after nations have attained some degree of permanence and have introduced ethical concepts into their relations with one another, they still give evidence of that same primary will to power which is responsible, at bottom, for every act of the individual man. "The masses, in any nation, " he says, "are ready to sacrifice their lives, their goods and chattels, their consciences and their virtue, to obtain that highest of pleasures: the feeling that they rule, either in reality or in imagination, over others. On these occasions they make virtues of their instinctive yearnings, and so they enable an ambitious or wisely provident prince to rush into a war with the good conscience of his people as his excuse. The great conquerors have always had the language of virtue on their lips: they have always had crowds of people around them who felt exalted and would not listen to any but the most exalted sentiments....

When man feels the sense of power, he feels and calls himself good, and at the same time those who have to endure the weight of his power call him evil. Such is the curious mutability of moral judgments!... Hesiod, in his fable of the world's ages, twice pictured the age of the Homeric heroes and made two out of one. To those whose ancestors were under the iron heel of the Homeric despots, it appeared evil; while to the grandchildren of these despots it appeared good. Hence the poet had no alternative but to do as he did: his audience was composed of the descendants of both classes."[10]

Nietzsche saw naught but decadence and illusion in humanitarianism and nationalism. To profess a love for the masses seemed to him to be ridiculous and to profess a love for one race or tribe of men, in preference to all others, seemed to him no less so. Thus he denied the validity of two ideals which lie at the base of all civilized systems of government, and constitute, in fact, the very conception of the state. He called himself, not a German, but "a good European."

"We good Europeans, " he said, "are not French enough to 'love mankind.' A man must be afflicted by an excess of Gallic eroticism to approach mankind with ardour. Mankind! Was there ever a more hideous old woman among all the old women? No, we do not love mankind!... On the other hand, we are not German enough to advocate nationalism and race-hatred, or to take delight in that national blood-poisoning which sets up quarantines between the nations of Europe. We are too unprejudiced for that—too perverse, too fastidious, too well-informed, too much travelled. We prefer to live on mountains—apart, unseasonable.... We are too diverse and mixed in race to be patriots. We are, in a word, good Europeans—the rich heirs of millenniums of European thought....

"We rejoice in everything, which like ourselves, loves danger, war and adventure—which does not make compromises, nor let itself be captured, conciliated or faced.... We ponder over the need of a new order of things—even of a new slavery, for the strengthening and elevation of the human race always involves the existence of slaves...."[11]

"The horizon is unobstructed.... Our ships can start on their voyage once more in the face of danger.... The sea—our sea!—lies before us!"[12]

---

[1]"*Also sprach Zarathustra,* " IV.

[2]That of Wisconsin at the 1907 session.

[3]This has been done, time and again, by the legislature of every state in the Union, and the overturning of such legislation occupies part of the time of all the state courts of final judicature year after year.

[4]That of South Carolina.

[5]*Vide* the chapter on "Civilization."

[6]Said the Chicago *Tribune*, "the best all-round newspaper in the United States, " in a leading article, June 10, 1907: "Jeremy Bentham speaks of 'an incoherent and undigested mass of law, shot down, as from a rubbish cart, upon the heads of the people.' This is a fairly accurate summary of the work of the average American legislature, from New York to Texas.... Bad, crude and unnecessary laws make up a large part of the output of every session.... Roughly speaking, the governor who vetoes the most bills is the best governor. When a governor vetoes none the legitimate presumption is, not that the work of the legislature was flawless, but that he was timid, not daring to oppose ignorant popular sentiment ... or that he had not sense enough to recognize a bad measure when he saw it."

[7]"*Morgenröte, "* § 5.

[8]"The word 'honesty' is not to be found in the code of either the Socratic or the Christian virtues. It represents a new virtue, not quite ripened, frequently misunderstood and hardly conscious of itself. It is yet something in embryo, which we are at liberty either to foster or to check."—"*Morgenröte, "* § 456.

[9]An excellent discussion of this subject, by Prof. Warner Fite, of Indiana University, appeared in *The Journal of Philosophy, Psychology and Scientific Methods* of July 18, 1907. Prof. Fite's article is called "The Exaggeration of the Social, " and is a keen and sound criticism of "the now popular tendency to regard the individual as the product of society." As he points out, "any consciousness of belonging to one group rather than another must involve some sense of individuality." In other words, gregariousness is nothing more than an instinctive yearning to profit personally by the possibility of putting others, to some measurable extent, in the attitude of slaves.

[10]"*Morgenröte, "* § 189.

[11]"*Die fröhliche Wissenschaft, "* § 377.

[12]"*Die fröhliche Wissenschaft, "* § 343.

XI. CRIME AND PUNISHMENT

Nietzsche says that the thing which best differentiates man from the other animals is his capacity for making and keeping a promise. That is to say, man has a trained and efficient memory and it enables him to project an impression of today into the future. Of the millions of impressions which impinge upon his consciousness every day, he is able to save a chosen number from the oblivion of forgetfulness. An animal lacks this capacity almost entirely. The things that it remembers are far from numerous and it is devoid of any means of reinforcing its memory. But man has such a means and it is commonly called conscience. At bottom it is based upon the principle that pain is always more enduring than pleasure. Therefore, "in order to make an idea stay it must be burned into the memory; only that which never ceases to hurt remains fixed."[1] Hence all the world's store of tortures and sacrifices. At one time they were nothing more than devices to make man remember his pledges to his gods. Today they survive in the form of legal punishments, which are nothing more, at bottom, than devices to make a man remember his pledges to his fellow men.

From all this Nietzsche argues that our modern law is the outgrowth of the primitive idea of barter—of the idea that everything has an equivalent and can be paid for—that when a man forgets or fails to discharge an obligation in one way he may wipe out his sin by discharging it in some other way. "The earliest relationship that ever existed, " he says, "was the relationship between buyer and seller, creditor and debtor. On this ground man first stood face to face with man. No stage of civilization, however inferior, is without the institution of bartering. To fix prices, to adjust values, to invent equivalents, to exchange things—all this has to such an extent preoccupied the first and earliest thought of man, that it may be said to constitute thinking itself. Out of it sagacity arose, and out of it, again, arose man's first pride—his first feeling of superiority over the animal world. Perhaps, our very word man (*manus*) expresses something of this.[2] Man calls himself the being who weighs and measures."[3]

Now besides the contract between man and man, there is also a contract between man and the community. The community agrees to give the individual protection and the individual promises to pay for it in labor and obedience. Whenever he fails to do so, he violates his promise, and the community regards the contract as broken. Then "the anger of the outraged creditor—or community—withdraws its protection from the debtor—or law-breaker—and he is laid open to all the dangers and disadvantages of life in a state of barbarism. Punishment, at this stage of civilization, is simply the image of a man's normal conduct toward a hated, disarmed and cast-down enemy, who has forfeited not only all claims to protection, but also all claims to mercy. This accounts for the fact that war (including the sacrificial cult of war) has furnished all the forms in which punishment appears in history."[4]

It will be observed that this theory grounds all ideas of justice and punishment upon ideas of expedience. The primeval creditor forced his debtor to pay because he knew that if the latter didn't pay he (the creditor) would suffer. In itself, the debtor's effort to get something for nothing was not wrong, because, as we have seen in previous chapters, this is the ceaseless and unconscious endeavor of every living being, and is, in fact, the most familiar of all manifestations of the primary will to live, or more understandably, of the will to acquire power over environment. But when the machinery of justice was placed in the hands of the state, there came a transvaluation of values. Things that were manifestly costly to the state were called wrong, and the old individualistic standards of good and bad— *i.e.* beneficial and harmful—became the standards of good and evil—*i.e.* right and wrong.

In this way, says Nietzsche, the original purpose of punishment has become obscured and forgotten. Starting out as a mere means of adjusting debts, it has become a machine for enforcing moral concepts. Moral ideas came into the world comparatively late, and it was not until man had begun to be a speculative being that he invented gods, commandments and beatitudes. But the institution of punishment was in existence from a much earlier day. Therefore, it is apparent that the moral idea, —the notion that there is such a thing as good and such a thing as evil, —far from being the inspiration of punishment, was engrafted upon it at a comparatively late period. Nietzsche says that man, in considering things as they are today, is very apt to make this mistake about their origins. He is apt to conclude, because the human eye is used for seeing, that it was created for that purpose, whereas it is obvious that it may have been created for some other purpose and that the function of seeing may have arisen later on. In the same way, man believes that punishment was invented for the purpose of enforcing moral ideas, whereas, as a matter of fact, it was originally an instrument of expediency only, and did not become a moral machine until a code of moral laws was evolved.[5]

To show that the institution of punishment itself is older than the ideas which now seem to lie at the base of it, Nietzsche cites the fact that these ideas themselves are constantly varying. That is to say, the aim and purpose of punishment are conceived differently by different races and individuals. One authority calls it a means of rendering the criminal helpless and harmless and so preventing further mischief in future. Another says that it is a means of inspiring others with fear of the law and its agents. Another says that it is a device for destroying the unfit. Another holds it to be a fee exacted by society from the evil-doer for protecting him against the excesses of private revenge. Still another looks upon it as society's declaration of war against its enemies. Yet another says that it is a scheme for making the criminal realize his guilt and repent. Nietzsche shows that all of these ideas, while true, perhaps, in some part, are fallacies at bottom. It is ridiculous, for instance, to believe that punishment makes the law-breaker acquire a feeling of guilt and sinfulness. He sees that he was indiscreet in committing his crime, but he sees, too, that society's method of punishing his indiscretion consists in committing a crime of the same sort against *him*. In other words, he cannot hold his own crime a sin without also holding his punishment a sin—which leads to an obvious absurdity. As a matter of fact, says Nietzsche, punishment really does nothing more than "augment fear, intensify prudence and subjugate the passions." And in so doing it *tames* man, but does not make him better. If he refrains from crime in future, it is because he has become more prudent and not because he has become more moral. If he regrets his crimes of the past, it is because his punishment, and not his so-called conscience, hurts him.

But what, then, is conscience? That there is such a thing every reasonable man knows. But what is its nature and what is its origin? If it is not the regret which follows punishment, what is it? Nietzsche answers that it is nothing more than the old will to power, turned inward. In the days of the cave men, a man gave his will to power free exercise. Any act which increased his power over his environment, no matter how much it damaged other men, seemed to him good. He knew nothing of morality. Things appeared to him, not as good or evil, but as good or bad—beneficial or harmful. But when civilization was born, there arose a necessity for controlling and regulating this will power. The individual had to submit to the desire of the majority and to conform to nascent codes of morality. The result was that his will to power, which once spent itself in battles with other individuals, had to be turned upon himself. Instead of torturing others, he began to torture his own body and mind. His ancient delight in cruelty and persecution (a characteristic of all healthy animals) remained, but he could not longer satisfy it upon his fellow men and so he turned it upon himself, and straightway became a prey to the feeling of guilt, of sinfulness, of wrong-doing—with all its attendant horrors.

Now, one of the first forms that this self-torture took was primitive man's accusation against himself that he was not properly grateful for the favors of his god. He saw that many natural phenomena benefited him, and he thought that these phenomena occurred in direct obedience to the deity's command. Therefore, he regarded himself as the debtor of the deity, and constantly accused himself of neglecting to discharge this debt, because he felt that, by so accusing, he would be most apt to discharge it in full, and thus escape the righteous consequences of insufficient payment. This led him to make sacrifices—to place food and drink upon his god's altar, and in the end, to sacrifice much more valuable things, such, for instance, as his first born child. The more vivid the idea of the deity became and the more terrible he appeared, the more man tried to satisfy and appease him. In the early days, it was sufficient to sacrifice a square meal or a baby. But when Christianity—with its elaborate and certain theology—arose, it became necessary for a man to sacrifice himself.

Thus arose the Christian idea of sin. Man began to feel that he was in debt to his creator hopelessly and irretrievably, and that, like a true bankrupt, he should offer all he had in partial payment. So he renounced everything that made life on earth bearable and desirable and built up an ideal of poverty and suffering. Sometimes he hid himself in a cave and lived like an outcast dog—and then he was called a saint. Sometimes he tortured himself with whips and poured vinegar into his wounds—and then he was a flagellant of the middle ages. Sometimes, he killed his sexual instinct and his inborn desire for property and power—and then he became a penniless celibate in a cloister.

Nietzsche shows that this idea of sin, which lies at the bottom of all religions, was and is an absurdity; that nothing, in itself, is sinful, and that no man is, or can be a sinner. If we could rid ourselves of the notion that there is a God in Heaven, to whom we owe a debt, we would rid ourselves of the idea of sin. Therefore, argues Nietzsche, it is evident that skepticism, while it makes no actual change in man, always makes him feel better. It makes him lose his fear of hell and his consciousness of sin. It rids him of that most horrible instrument of useless, senseless and costly torture—his conscience. "Atheism, " says Nietzsche, "will make a man innocent."

---

[1]"*Zur Genealogie der Moral,* " II, § 3.

[2]In the ancient Sanskrit the word from which "man" comes meant "to think, to weigh, to value, to reckon, to estimate."

[3]"*Zur Genealogie der Moral,* " II, § 8.

[4]"*Zur Genealogie der Moral,* " II, § 9.

[5]A familiar example of this superimposition of morality is afforded by the history of costume. It is commonly assumed that garments were originally designed to hide nakedness as much as to afford warmth and adorn the person, whereas, as a matter of fact, the idea of modesty probably did not appear until man had been clothed for ages.

XII. EDUCATION

Education, as everyone knows, has two main objects: to impart knowledge and to implant culture. It is the object of a teacher, first of all, to bring before his pupil as many concrete facts about the universe—the fruit of long ages of inquiry and experience—as the latter may be capable of absorbing in the time available. After that, it is the teacher's aim to make his pupil's habits of mind sane, healthy and manly, and his whole outlook upon life that of a being conscious of his efficiency and eager and able to solve new problems as they arise. The educated man, in a word, is one who knows a great deal more than the average man and is constantly increasing his area of knowledge, in a sensible, orderly logical fashion; one who is wary of sophistry and leans automatically and almost instinctively toward clear thinking.

Such is the purpose of education, in its ideal aspect. As we observe the science of teaching in actual practice, we find that it often fails utterly to attain this end. The concrete facts that a student learns at the average school are few and unconnected, and instead of being led into habits of independent thinking he is trained to accept authority. When he takes his degree it is usually no more than a sign that he has joined the herd. His opinion of Napoleon is merely a reflection of the opinion expressed in the books he has studied; his philosophy of life is simply the philosophy of his teacher—tinctured a bit, perhaps, by that of his particular youthful idols. He knows how to spell a great many long words and he is familiar with the table of logarithms, but in the readiness and accuracy of his mental processes he has made comparatively little progress. If he was illogical and credulous and a respecter of authority as a freshman he remains much the same as a graduate. In consequence, his usefulness to humanity has been increased but little, if at all, for, as we have seen in previous chapters, the only man whose life is appreciably more valuable than that of a good cow is the man who thinks for himself, clearly and logically, and lends some sort of hand, during his life-time, in the eternal search for the ultimate verities.

The cause for all this lies, no doubt, in the fact that school teachers, taking them by and large, are probably the most ignorant and stupid class of men in the whole group of mental workers. Imitativeness being the dominant impulse in youth, their pupils acquire some measure of their stupidity, and the result is that the influence of the whole teaching tribe is against everything included in genuine education and culture.

That this is true is evident on the surface and a moment's analysis furnishes a multitude of additional proofs. For one thing, a teacher, before he may begin work, must sacrifice whatever independence may survive within him upon the altar of authority. He becomes a cog in the school wheel and must teach only the things countenanced and approved by the powers above him, whether those powers be visible in the minister of education, as in Germany; in the traditions of the school, as in England, or in the private convictions of the millionaire who provides the cash, as in the United States. As Nietzsche points out, the schoolman's thirst for the truth is always conditioned by his yearning for food and drink and a comfortable bed. His archetype is the university philosopher, who accepts the state's pay[1] and so surrenders that liberty to inquire freely which alone makes philosophy worth while.

"No state, " says Nietzsche, "would ever dare to patronize such men as Plato and Schopenhauer. And why? Simply because the state is always afraid of them. They tell the truth.... Consequently, the man who submits to be a philosopher in the pay of the state must also submit to being looked upon by the state as one who has waived his claim to pursue the truth into all its fastnesses. So long as he holds his place, he must acknowledge something still higher than the truth—and that is the state....

"The sole criticism of a philosophy which is possible and the only one which proves anything—namely, an attempt to live according to it—is never put forward in the universities. There the only thing one hears of is a wordy criticism of words. And so the youthful mind, without much experience in life, is confronted by fifty verbal systems and fifty criticisms of them, thrown together and hopelessly jumbled. What demoralization! What a mockery of education! It is openly acknowledged, in fact, that the object of education is not the acquirement of learning, but the successful meeting of examinations. No wonder then, that the examined student says to himself 'Thank God, I am not a philosopher, but a Christian and a citizen!...'

"Therefore, I regard it as necessary to progress that we withdraw from philosophy all governmental and academic recognition and support.... Let philosophers spring up naturally, deny them every prospect of appointment, tickle them no longer with salaries—yea, persecute them! Then you will see marvels! They will then flee afar and seek a roof anywhere. Here a parsonage will open its doors; there a schoolhouse. One will appear upon the staff of a newspaper, another will write manuals for young ladies' schools. The most rational of them will put his hand to the plough and the vainest will seek favor at court. Thus we shall get rid of bad philosophers."[2]

The argument here is plain enough. The professional teacher must keep to his rut. The moment he combats the existing order of things he loses his place. Therefore he is wary, and his chief effort is to transmit the words of authority to his pupils unchanged. Whether he be a philosopher, properly so-called, or something else matters not. In a medical school wherein Chauveau's theory of immunity was still maintained it would be hazardous for a professor of pathology to teach the theory of Ehrlich. In a Methodist college in Indiana it would be foolhardy to dally with the doctrine of apostolic succession. Everywhere the teacher must fashion his teachings according to the creed and regulations of his school and he must even submit to authority in such matters as text books and pedagogic methods. Again, his very work itself makes him an unconscious partisan of authority, as against free inquiry. During the majority of his waking hours he is in close association with his pupils, who are admittedly his inferiors, and so he rapidly acquires the familiar, self-satisfied professorial attitude of mind. Other forces tend to push him in the same direction and the net result is that all his mental processes are based upon ideas of authority. He believes and teaches a thing, not because he is convinced by free reasoning that it is true, but because it is laid down as an axiom in some book or was laid down at some past time, by himself.

In all this, of course, I am speaking of the teacher properly so-called—of the teacher, that is, whose sole aim and function is teaching. The university professor whose main purpose in life is original research and whose pupils are confined to graduate students engaged in much the same work, is scarcely a professional teacher, in the customary meaning of the word. The man I have been discussing is he who spends all or the greater part of his time in actual instruction. Whether his work be done in a primary school, a secondary school or in the undergraduate department of a college or university does not matter In all that relates to it, he is essentially and almost invariably a mere perpetuator of doctrines. In some cases, naturally enough, these doctrines are truths, but in a great many other cases they are errors. An examination of the physiology, history and "English" books used in the public schools of America will convince anyone that the latter proposition is amply true.

Nietzsche's familiarity with these facts is demonstrated by numerous passages in his writings. "Never, " he says, "is either real proficiency or genuine ability the result of toilsome years at school." The study of the classics, he says, can never lead to more than a superficial acquaintance with them, because the very modes of thought of the ancients, in many cases, are unintelligible to men of today. But the student who has acquired what is looked upon in our colleges as a mastery of the humanities is acutely conscious of his knowledge, and so the things that he cannot understand are ascribed by him to the dulness, ignorance or imbecility of the ancient authors. As a result he harbors a sort of sub-conscious contempt for the learning they represent and concludes that learning cannot make real men happy, but is only fit for the futile enthusiasm of "honest, poor and foolish old book-worms."

Nietzsche's own notion of an ideal curriculum is substantially that of Spencer. He holds that before anything is put forward as a thing worth teaching it should be tested by two questions: Is it a fact? and, Is the presentation of it likely to make the pupil measurably more capable of discovering other facts? In consequences, he holds the old so-called "liberal" education in abomination, and argues in favor of a system of instruction based upon the inculcation of facts of imminent value and designed to instill into the pupil orderly and logical habits of mind and a clear and accurate view of the universe. The educated man, as he understands the term, is one who is above the mass, both in his thirst for knowledge and in his capacity for differentiating between truth and its reverse. It is obvious that a man who has studied biology and physics, with their insistent dwelling upon demonstrable facts, has proceeded further in this direction than the man who has studied Greek mythology and metaphysics, with their constant trend toward unsupported and gratuitous assumption and their essential foundation upon undebatable authority.

Nietzsche points out, in his early essay upon the study of history, that humanity is much too prone to consider itself historically. That is to say, there is too much tendency to consider man as he has seemed rather than man as he has been—to dwell upon creeds and manifestoes rather than upon individual and racial motives, characters and instincts.[3] The result is that history piles up misleading and useless records and draws erroneous conclusions from them. As a science in itself, it bears but three useful aspects—the monumental, the antiquarian and the critical. Its true monuments are not the constitutions and creeds of the past—for these, as we have seen, are always artificial and unnatural—but the great men of the past—those fearless free spirits who achieved immortality by their courage and success in pitting their own instincts against the morality of the majority. Such men, he says, are the only human beings whose existence is of interest to posterity. "They live together as timeless contemporaries:" they are the landmarks along the weary road the human race has traversed. In its antiquarian aspect, history affords us proof that the world is progressing, and so gives the men of the present a definite purpose and justifiable enthusiasm. In its critical aspect, history enables us to avoid the delusions of the past, and indicates to us the broad lines of evolution. Unless we have in mind some definite program of advancement, he says, all learning is useless. History, which merely accumulates records, without "an ideal of humanistic culture" always in mind, is mere pedantry and scholasticism.

All education, says Nietzsche, may be regarded as a continuation of the process of breeding.[4] The two have the same object: that of producing beings capable of surviving in the struggle for existence. A great many critics of Nietzsche have insisted that since the struggle for existence means a purely physical contest, he is in error, for education does not visibly increase a man's chest expansion or his capacity for lifting heavy weights. But it is obvious none the less that a man who sees things as they are, and properly estimates the world about him, is far better fitted to achieve some measure of mastery over his environment than the man who is a slave to delusions. Of two men, one of whom believes that the moon is made of green cheese and that it is possible to cure smallpox by merely denying that it exists, and the other of whom harbors no such superstitions, it is plain that the latter is more apt to live long and acquire power.

A further purpose of education is that of affording individuals a means of lifting themselves out of the slave class and into the master class. That this purpose is accomplished—except accidently—by the brand of education ladled out in the colleges of today is far from true. To transform a slave into a master we must make him intelligent, self-reliant, resourceful, independent and courageous. It is evident enough, I take it, that a college directed by an ecclesiastic and manned by a faculty of asses— a very fair, and even charitable, picture of the average small college in the United States—is not apt to accomplish this transformation very often. Indeed, it is a commonplace observation that a truly intelligent youth is aided but little by the average college education, and that a truly stupid one is made, not less, but more stupid. The fact that many graduates of such institutions exhibit dionysian qualities in later life merely proves that they are strong enough to weather the blight they have suffered. Every sane man knows that, after a youth leaves college, he must devote most of his energies during three or four years, to ridding himself of the fallacies, delusions and imbecilities inflicted upon him by messieurs, his professors.

The intelligent man, in the course of his life, nearly always acquires a vast store of learning, because his mind is constantly active and receptive, but intelligence and mere learning are by no means synonymous, despite the popular notion that they are. Disregarding the element of sheer good luck—which is necessarily a small factor—it is evident that the man who, in the struggle for wealth and power, seizes a million dollars for himself, is appreciably more intelligent than the man who starves. That this achievement, which is admittedly difficult, requires more intelligence again, than the achievement of mastering the Latin language, which presents so few difficulties that it is possible to any healthy human being with sufficient leisure and patience, is also evident. In a word, the illiterate contractor, who says, "I seen" and "I done" and yet manages to build great bridges and to acquire a great fortune, is immeasurably more vigorous intellectually, and immeasurably more efficient and respectable, as a man, than the college professor who laughs at him and presumes to look down upon him. A man's mental powers are to be judged, not by his ability to accomplish things that are possible to every man foolish enough to attempt them, but by his capacity for doing things beyond the power of other men. Education, as we commonly observe it today, works toward the former, rather than toward the latter end.

———

[1]Nietzsche is considering, of course, the condition of affairs in Germany, where all teaching is controlled by the state. But his arguments

apply to other countries as well and to teachers of other things besides philosophy.

[2]"*Schopenhauer als Erzieher,* " § 8.

[3]An excellent discussion of this error will be found in Dr. Alex. Tille's introduction to William Haussmann's translation of "*Zur Genealogie der Moral,* " pp. xi *et seq.*; London, 1907.

[4]"*Morgenröte,* " § 397.

XIII. SUNDRY IDEAS

Death.—It is Schopenhauer's argument in his essay "On Suicide, " that the possibility of easy and painless self-destruction is the only thing that constantly and considerably ameliorates the horror of human life. Suicide is a means of escape from the world and its tortures—and therefore it is good. It is an ever-present refuge for the weak, the weary and the hopeless. It is, in Pliny's phrase, "the greatest of all blessings which Nature gives to man, " and one which even God himself lacks, for "he could not compass his own death, if he willed to die." In all of this exaltation of surrender, of course, there is nothing whatever in common with the dionysian philosophy of defiance. Nietzsche's teaching is all in the other direction. He urges, not surrender, but battle; not flight, but war to the end. His curse falls upon those "preachers of death" who counsel "an abandonment of life"—whether this abandonment be partial, as in asceticism, or actual, as in suicide. And yet Zarathustra sings the song of "free death" and says that the higher man must learn "to die at the right time." Herein an inconsistency appears, but it is on the surface only. Schopenhauer regards suicide as a means of escape, Nietzsche sees in it a means of good riddance. It is time to die, says Zarathustra, when the purpose of life ceases to be attainable—when the fighter breaks his sword arm or falls into his enemy's hands. And it is time to die, too, when the purpose of life is attained—when the fighter triumphs and sees before him no more worlds to conquer. "He who hath a goal and an heir wisheth death to come at the right time for goal and heir." One who has "waxed too old for victories, " one who is "yellow and wrinkled, " one with a "toothless mouth"—for such an one a certain and speedy death. The earth has no room for cumberers and pensioners. For them the highest of duties is the payment of nature's debt, that there may be more room for those still able to wield a sword and bear a burden in the heat of the day. The best death is that which comes in battle "at the moment of victory;" the second best is death in battle in the hour of defeat. "Would that a storm came, " sings Zarathustra, "to shake from the tree of life all those apples that are putrid and gnawed by worms. It is cowardice that maketh them stick to their branches"—cowardice which makes them afraid to die. But there is another cowardice which makes men afraid to live, and this is the cowardice of the Schopenhauerean pessimist. Nietzsche has no patience with it. To him a too early death seems as abominable as a death postponed too long. "Too early died that Jew whom the preachers of slow death revere. Would that he had remained in the desert and far away from the good and just! Perhaps he would have learned how to live and how to love the earth—and even how to laugh. He died too early. He himself would have revoked his doctrine, had he reached mine age!"[1] Therefore Nietzsche pleads for an intelligent regulation of death. One must not die too soon and one must not die too late. "Natural death, " he says, "is destitute of rationality. It is really *ir*rational death, for the pitiable substance of the shell determines how long the kernel shall exist. The pining, sottish prison-warder decides the hour at which his noble prisoner is to die.... The enlightened regulation and control of death belongs to the morality of the future. At present religion makes it seem immoral, for religion presupposes that when the time for death comes, God gives the command."[2]

The Attitude at Death.—Nietzsche rejects entirely that pious belief in signs and portents which sees a significance in death-bed confessions and "dying words." The average man, he says, dies pretty much as he has lived, and in this Dr. Osler[3] and other unusually competent and accurate observers agree with him. When the dying man exhibits unusual emotions or expresses ideas out of tune with his known creed, the explanation is to be found in the fact that, toward the time of death the mind commonly gives way and the customary processes of thought are disordered. "The way in which a man thinks of death, in the full bloom of his life and strength, is certainly a good index of his general character and habits of mind, but at the hour of death itself his attitude is of little importance or significance. The exhaustion of the last hours—especially when an old man is dying—the irregular or insufficient nourishment of the brain, the occasional spasms of severe physical pain, the horror and novelty of the whole situation, the atavistic return of early impressions and superstitions, and the feeling that death is a thing unutterably vast and important and that bridges of an awful kind are about to be crossed—all of these things make it irrational to accept a man's attitude at death as an indication of his character during life. Moreover, it is not true that a dying man is more honest than a man in full vigor. On the contrary, almost every dying man is led, by the solemnity of those at his bedside, and by their restrained or flowing torrents of tears, to conscious or unconscious conceit and make-believe. He becomes, in brief, an actor in a comedy.... No doubt the seriousness with which every dying man is treated has given many a poor devil his only moment of real triumph and enjoyment. He is, *ipso facto*, the star of the play, and so he is indemnified for a life of privation and subservience."[4]

The Origin of Philosophy.—Nietzsche believed that introspection and self-analysis, as they were ordinarily manifested, were signs of disease, and that the higher man and superman would waste little time upon them. The first thinkers, he said, were necessarily sufferers, for it was only suffering that made a man think and only disability that gave him leisure to do so. "Under primitive conditions, " he said, "the individual, fully conscious of his power, is ever intent upon transforming it into action. Sometimes this action takes the form of hunting, robbery, ambuscade, maltreatment or murder, and at other times it appears as those feebler imitations of these things which alone are countenanced by the community. But when the individual's power declines—when he feels fatigued, ill, melancholy or satiated, and in consequence, temporarily lacks the yearning to function—he is a comparatively better and less dangerous man." That is to say, he contents himself with thinking instead of doing, and so puts into thought and words "his impressions and feelings regarding his companions, his wife or his gods." Naturally enough, since his efficiency is lowered and his mood is gloomy his judgments are evil ones. He finds fault and ponders revenges. He gloats over enemies or envies his friends. "In such a state of mind he turns prophet and so adds to his store of superstitions or devises new acts of devotion or prophesies the downfall of his enemies. Whatever he thinks, his thoughts reflect his state of mind: his fear and weariness are more than normal; his tendency to action and enjoyment are less than normal. Herein we see the genesis of the poetic, thoughtful, priestly mood. Evil thoughts must rule supreme therein.... In later stages of culture, there arose a caste of poets, thinkers, priests and medicine men who all acted the same as, in earlier years, individuals used to act in their comparatively rare hours of illness and depression. These persons led sad, inactive lives and judged maliciously.... The masses, perhaps, yearned to turn them out of the community, because they were parasites, but in this enterprise there was great risk, because these men were on terms of familiarity with the gods and so possessed vast and mysterious power. Thus the most ancient philosophers were viewed. The masses hearkened unto them in proportion to the amount of dread they inspired. In such a way contemplation made its appearance in the world, with an evil heart and a troubled head. It was both weak and terrible, and both secretly abhorred and openly worshipped.... *Pudenda origo!*"[5]

Priestcraft.—So long as man feels capable of taking care of himself he has no need of priests to intercede for him with the deity. Efficiency is proverbially identified with impiety: it is only when the devil is sick that the devil a monk would be. Therefore "the priest must be regarded as the saviour, shepherd and advocate of the sick.... It is his providence to rule over the sufferers...." In order that he may understand them and appeal to them he must be sick himself, and to attain this end there is the device of asceticism. The purpose of asceticism, as we have seen, is to make a man voluntarily destroy his own efficiency. But the priest must have a certain strength, nevertheless, for he must inspire both confidence and dread in his charges, and must be able to defend them—against whom? "Undoubtedly against the sound and strong.... He must be the natural adversary and despiser of all barbarous, impetuous, unbridled, fierce, violent, beast-of-prey healthiness and power."[6] Thus he must fashion himself into a new sort of fighter—"a new zoological terror, in which the polar bear, the nimble and cool tiger and the fox are blended into a unity as attractive as it is awe-inspiring." He appears in the midst of the strong as "the herald and mouthpiece of mysterious powers, with the determination to sow upon the soil, whenever and wherever possible, the seeds of suffering, dissension and contradiction.... Undoubtedly he brings balms and balsams with him, but he must first inflict the wound, before he may act as physician.... It is only the unpleasantness of disease that is combated by him—not the cause, not the disease itself!" He dispenses, not specifics, but narcotics. He brings surcease from sorrow, not by showing men how to attain the happiness of efficiency, but by teaching them that their sufferings have been laid upon them by a god who will one day repay them with bliss illimitable.

God.—"A god who is omniscient and omnipotent and yet neglects to make his wishes and intentions certainly known to his creatures—certainly this is not a god of goodness. One who for thousands of years has allowed the countless scruples and doubts of men to afflict them and yet holds out terrible consequences for involuntary errors—certainly this is not a god of justice. Is he not a cruel god if he knows the truth and yet looks down upon millions miserably searching for it? Perhaps he is good, but is unable to communicate with his creatures more intelligibly. Perhaps he is wanting in intelligence—or in eloquence. So much the worse! For, in that case, he may be mistaken in what he calls the truth. He may, indeed, be a brother to the 'poor, duped devils' below him. If so, must he not suffer agonies on seeing his creatures, in their struggle for knowledge of him, submit to tortures for all eternity? Must it not strike him with grief to realize that he cannot advise them or help them, except by uncertain and ambiguous signs?... All religions bear traces of the fact that they arose during the intellectual immaturity of the human race—before it had learned the obligation to speak the truth. Not one of them makes it the duty of its god to be truthful and understandable in his communications with man."["*Morgenröte,* " § 91.]

Self-Control.—Self-control, says Nietzsche, consists merely in combating a given desire with a stronger one. Thus the yearning to commit a murder may be combated and overcome by the yearning to escape the gallows and to retain the name and dignity of a law-abiding citizen. The second yearning is as much unconscious and instinctive as the first, and in the battle between them the intellect plays but a small part. In general there are but six ways in which a given craving may be overcome. First, we may avoid opportunities for its gratification and so, by a long disuse, weaken and destroy it. Secondly, we may regulate its gratification, and by thus encompassing its flux and reflux within fixed limits, gain intervals during which it is faint. Thirdly, we may intentionally give ourselves over to it and so wear it out by excess—provided we do not act like the rider who lets a runaway horse gallop itself to death and, in so doing, breaks his own neck, —which unluckily is the rule in this method. Fourthly, by an intellectual trick, we may associate gratification with an unpleasant idea, as we have associated sexual gratification, for example, with the idea of indecency. Fifthly, we may find a substitute in some other craving that is measurably less dangerous, Sixthly, we may find safety in a general war upon all cravings, good and bad alike, after the manner of the ascetic, who, in seeking to destroy his sensuality, at the same time destroys his physical strength, his reason and, not infrequently, his life.

The Beautiful.—Man's notion of beauty is the fruit of his delight in his own continued existence. Whatever makes this existence easy, or is associated, in any manner, with life or vigor, seems to him to be beautiful. "Man mirrors himself in things. He counts everything beautiful which reflects his likeness. The word 'beautiful' represents the conceit of his species.... Nothing is truly ugly except the degenerating man. But other things are called ugly, too, when they happen to weaken or trouble man. They remind him of impotence, deterioration and danger: in their presence he actually suffers a loss of power. Therefore he calls them ugly. Whenever man is at all depressed he has an intuition of the proximity of something 'ugly.' His sense of power, his will to power, his feeling of pride and efficiency—all sink with the ugly and rise with the beautiful. The ugly is instinctively understood to be a sign and symptom of degeneration. That which reminds one, in the remotest degree, of degeneracy seems ugly. Every indication of exhaustion, heaviness, age, or lassitude, every constraint—such as cramp or paralysis—and above all, every odor, color or counterfeit of decomposition—though it may be no more than a far-fetched symbol—calls forth the idea of ugliness. Aversion is thereby excited—man's aversion to the decline of his type." ["*Götzendämmerung,*" IX, § 19.]

The phrase "art for art's sake" voices a protest against subordinating art to morality—that is, against making it a device for preaching sermons—but as a matter of fact, all art must praise and glorify and so must lay down values. It is the function of the artist, indeed, to select, to choose, to bring into prominence. The very fact that he is able to do this makes us call him an artist. And when do we approve his choice? Only when it agrees with our fundamental instinct—only when it exhibits "the desirableness of life." "Therefore art is the great stimulus to life. We cannot conceive it as being purposeless or aimless. 'Art for art's sake' is a phrase without meaning." ["*Götzendämmerung,* " IX, § 24.]

Liberty.—The worth of a thing often lies, not in what one attains by it, but in the difficulty one experiences in getting it. The struggle for political liberty, for example, has done more than any other one thing to develop strength, courage and resourcefulness in the human race, and yet liberty itself, as we know it today, is nothing more or less than organized morality, and as such, is necessarily degrading and degenerating. "It undermines the will to power, it levels the racial mountains and valleys, it makes man small, cowardly and voluptuous. Under political liberty the herd-animal always triumphs." But the very fight to attain this burdensome equality develops the self-reliance and unconformity which stand opposed to it, and these qualities often persist. Warfare, in brief, makes men fit for real, as opposed to political freedom. "And what is freedom? The will to be responsible for one's self. The will to keep that distance which separates man from man. The will to become indifferent to hardship, severity, privation and even to life. The will to sacrifice men to one's cause and to sacrifice one's self, too.... The man who is truly free tramples under foot the contemptible species of well-being dreamt of by shop-keepers, Christians, cows, women, Englishmen and other democrats. The free man is a warrior.... How is freedom to be measured? By the resistance it has to overcome—by the effort required to maintain it. We must seek the highest type of freemen where the highest resistance must be constantly overcome: five paces from tyranny, close to the threshold of thraldom.... Those peoples who were worth something, who became worth something, never acquired their greatness under political liberty. Great danger made something of them—danger of that sort which first teaches us to know our resources, our virtues, our shields and swords, our genius—which compels us to be strong." ["*Götzendämmerung,* " IX, § 38.]

Science—The object of all science is to keep us from drawing wrong inferences—from jumping to conclusions. Thus it stands utterly opposed to all faith and is essentially iconoclastic and skeptical. "The wonderful in science is the reverse of the wonderful in juggling. The juggler tries to make us see a very simple relation between things which, in point of fact, have no relation at all. The scientist, on the contrary, compels us to abandon our belief in simple casualities and to see the enormous complexity of phenomena. The simplest things, indeed, are extremely complex—a fact which will never cease to make us wonder." The effect of science is to show the absurdity of attempting to reach perfect happiness and the impossibility of experiencing utter woe. "The gulf between the highest pitch of happiness and the lowest depth of misery has been created by imaginary things." ["*Morgenröte,* " § 6.]

That is to say, the heights of religious exaltation and the depths of religious fear and trembling are alike creatures of our own myth-making. There is no such thing as perfect and infinite bliss in heaven and there is no such thing as eternal damnation in hell. Hereafter our highest happiness must be less than that of the martyrs who saw the heavenly gates opening for them, and our worst woe must be less than that of those medieval sinners who died shrieking and trembling and with the scent of brimstone in their noses. "This space is being reduced further and further by science, just as through science we have learned to make the earth occupy less and less space in the universe, until it now seems infinitely small and our whole solar system appears as a mere point." ["*Morgenröte,* " § 7.]

The Jews.—For the Jewish slave-morality which prevails in the western world today, under the label of Christianity, Nietzsche had, as we know, the most violent aversion and contempt, but he saw very clearly that this same morality admirably served and fitted the Jews themselves; that it had preserved them through long ages and against powerful enemies, and that its very persistence proved alike its own ingenuity and the vitality of its inventors as a race. "The Jews, " said Nietzsche, "will either become the masters of Europe or lose Europe, as they once lost Egypt, And it seems to be improbable that they will lose again. In Europe, for eighteen centuries; they have passed through a school more terrible than that known to any other nation, and the experiences of this time of stress and storm have benefited the individual even more than the community. In consequence, the resourcefulness and alertness of the modern Jew are extraordinary.... In times of extremity, the people of Israel less often sought refuge in drink or suicide than any other race of Europe. Today, every Jew finds in the history of his forebears a voluminous record of coolness and perseverance in terrible predicaments—of artful cunning and clever fencing with chance and misfortune. The Jews have hid their bravery under the cloak of submissiveness; their heroism in facing contempt surpasses that of the saints. People tried to make them contemptible for twenty centuries by refusing them all honors and dignities and by pushing them down into the mean trades. The process did not make them cleaner, alas! but neither did it make them contemptible. They have never ceased to believe themselves qualified for the highest of activities. They have never failed to show the virtues of all suffering peoples. Their manner of honoring their parents and their children and the reasonableness of their marriage customs make them conspicuous among Europeans. Besides, they have learned how to derive a sense of power from the very trades forced upon them. We cannot help observing, in excuse for their usury, that without this pleasant means of inflicting torture upon their oppressors, they might have lost their self-respect ages ago, for self-respect depends upon being able to make reprisals. Moreover, their vengeance has never carried them too far, for they have that liberality which comes from frequent changes of place, climate, customs and neighbors. They have more experience of men than any other race and even in their passions there appears a caution born of this experience. They are so sure of themselves that, even in their bitterest straits, they never earn their bread by manual labor as common workmen, porters or peasants.... Their manners, it may be admitted, teach us that they have never been inspired by chivalrous, noble feelings, nor their bodies girt with beautiful arms: a certain vulgarity always alternates with their submissiveness. But now they are intermarrying with the gentlest blood of Europe, and in another hundred years they will have enough good manners to save them from making themselves ridiculous, as masters, in the sight of those they have subdued." It was Nietzsche's belief that the Jews would take the lead before long, in the intellectual progress of the world. He thought that their training, as a race, fitted them for this leadership. "Where, " he asked, "shall the accumulated wealth of great impressions which forms the history of every Jewish family—that great wealth of passions, virtues, resolutions, resignations, struggles and victories of all sorts—where shall it find an outlet, if not in great intellectual functioning?" The Jews, he thought, would be safe guides for mankind, once they were set free from their slave-morality and all need of it. "Then again, " he said, "the old God of the Jews may rejoice in Himself, in His creation and in His chosen people—and all of us will rejoice with Him."["*Morgenröte*, " § 205.]

The Gentleman.—A million sages and diagnosticians, in all ages of the world, have sought to define the gentleman, and their definitions have been as varied as their own minds. Nietzsche's definition is based upon the obvious fact that the gentleman is ever a man of more than average influence and power, and the further fact that this superiority is admitted by all. The vulgarian may boast of his bluff honesty, but at heart he looks up to the gentleman, who goes through life serene and imperturbable. There is in the flatter, in truth, an unmistakable air of fitness and efficiency, and it is this which makes it possible for him to be gentle and to regard those below him with tolerance. "The demeanor of high-born persons, " says Nietzsche, "shows plainly that in their minds the consciousness of power is ever-present. Above all things, they strive to avoid a show of weakness, whether it takes the form of inefficiency or of a too-easy yielding to passion or emotion. They never sink exhausted into a chair. On the train, when the vulgar try to make themselves comfortable, these higher folk avoid reclining. They do not seem to get tired after hours of standing at court. They do not furnish their houses in a comfortable, but in a spacious and dignified manner, as if they were the abodes of a greater and taller race of beings. To a provoking speech, they reply with politeness and self-possession—and not as if horrified, crushed, abashed, enraged or out of breath, after the manner of plebeians. The aristocrat knows how to preserve the appearance of ever-present physical strength, and he knows, too, how to convey the impression that his soul and intellect are a match to all dangers and surprises, by keeping up an unchanging serenity and civility, even under the most trying circumstances." ["*Morgenröte*, " § 201.]

Dreams.—Dreams are symptoms of the eternal law of compensation. In our waking hours we develop a countless horde of yearnings, cravings and desires, and by the very nature of things, the majority of them must go ungratified. The feeling that something is wanting, thus left within us, is met and satisfied by our imaginary functionings during sleep. That is to say, dreams represent the reaction of our yearnings upon the phenomena actually encountered during sleep—the motions of our blood and intestines, the pressure of the bedclothes, the sounds of church-bells, domestic animals, etc., and the state of the atmosphere. These phenomena are fairly constant, but our dreams vary widely on successive nights. Therefore, the variable factor is represented by the yearnings we harbor as we go to bed. Thus, the man who loves music and must go without it all day, hears celestial harmonies in his sleep. Thus the slave dreams of soaring like an eagle. Thus the prisoner dreams that he is free and the sailor that he is safely at home. Inasmuch as the number of our conscious and unconscious desires, each day, is infinite, there is an infinite variety in dreams. But always the relation set forth may be predicated.

———

[1]"*Also sprach Zarathustra*, " I.

[2]"*Menschliches allzu Menschliches*, " III, § 185.

[3]"*Science and Immortality*, " New York, 1904.

[4]"*Menschliches allzu Menschliches*, " II, § 88.

[5]"*Morgenröte*, " § 42.

[6]"*Zur Genealogie der Moral*, " III, 11 to 17.

XIV. NIETZSCHE VS. WAGNER

Nietzsche believed in heroes and, in his youth, was a hero worshipper. First Arthur Schopenhauer's bespectacled visage stared from his shrine and after that the place of sacredness and honor was held by Richard Wagner. When the Wagner of the philosopher's dreams turned into a Wagner of very prosaic flesh and blood, there came a time of doubt and stress and suffering for poor Nietzsche. But he had courage as well as loyalty, and in the end he dashed his idol to pieces and crunched the bits underfoot. Faith, doubt, anguish, disillusion—it is not a rare sequence in this pitiless and weary old world.

Those sapient critics who hold that Nietzsche discredited his own philosophy by constantly writing against himself, find their chief ammunition in his attitude toward the composer of "*Tristan und Isolde*" In the decade from 1869 to 1878 the philosopher was the king of German Wagnerians. In the decade from 1879 to 1889, he was the most bitter, the most violent, the most resourceful and the most effective of Wagner's enemies. On their face these things seem to indicate a complete change of front and a careful examination bears out the thought. Butthe same careful examination reveals another fact: that the change of front was made, not by Nietzsche, but by Wagner.

As we have seen, the philosopher was an ardent musician from boyhood and so it was not unnatural that he should be among the first to recognize Wagner's genius. The sheer musicianship of the man overwhelmed him and he tells us that from the moment the piano transcription of "*Tristan und Isolde*" was printed he was a Wagnerian. The music was bold and daring: it struck out into regions that the *süsslich* sentimentality of Donizetti and Bellini and the pallid classicism of Beethoven and Bach had never even approached. In Wagner Nietzsche saw a man of colossal originality and sublime courage, who thought for himself and had skill at making his ideas comprehensible to others. The opera of the past had been a mere *potpourri* of songs, strung together upon a filament of banal recitative. The opera of Wagner was a symmetrical and homogeneous whole, in which the music was unthinkable without the poetry and the poetry impossible without the music.

Nietzsche, at the time, was saturated with Schopenhauer's brand of individualism, and intensely eager to apply it to realities. In Wagner he saw a living, breathing individualist—a man who scorned the laws and customs of his craft and dared to work out his own salvation in his own way. And when fate made it possible for him to meet Wagner, he found the composer preaching as well as practising individualism. In a word, Wagner was well nigh as enthusiastic a Schopenhauerean as Nietzsche himself. His individualism almost touched the boundary of anarchy. He had invented a new art of music and he was engaged in the exciting task of smashing the old one to make room for it.

Nietzsche met Wagner in Leipsic and was invited to visit the composer at his home near Tribschen, a suburb of Lucerne. He accepted, and on May 15, 1869, got his first glimpse of that queer household in which the erratic Richard, the ingenious Cosima and little Siegfried lived and had their being. When he moved to Basel, he was not far from Tribschen and so he fell into the habit of going there often and staying long. He came, indeed, to occupy the position of an adopted son, and spent the Christmas of 1869 and that of 1870 under the Wagner rooftree. This last fact alone is sufficient to show the intimate footing upon which he stood. Christmas, among the Germans, is essentially a family festival and mere friends are seldom asked to share its joys.

Nietzsche and Wagner had long and riotous disputations at Tribschen, but in all things fundamental they agreed. Together they accepted Schopenhauer's data and together they began to diverge from his conclusions. Nietzsche saw in Wagner that old dionysian spirit which had saved Greek art. The music of the day was colorless and coldblooded. A too rigid formalism stood in the way of all expression of actual life. Wagner proposed to batter this formalism to pieces and Nietzsche was his prophet and *claque*.

It was this enthusiasm, indeed, which determined the plan of "*Die Geburt der Tragödie*". Nietzsche had conceived it as a mere treatise upon the philosophy of the Greek drama. His ardor as an apostle, his yearning to convert the stolid Germans, his wild desire to do something practical and effective for Wagner, made him turn it into a gospel of the new art. To him Wagner was Dionysus, and the whole of his argument against Apollo was nothing more than an argument against classicism and for the Wagnerian romanticism. It was a bomb-shell and its explosion made Germany stare, but another—perhaps many more—were needed to shake the foundations of philistinism. Nietzsche loaded the next one carefully and hurled it at him who stood at the very head of that self-satisfied conservatism which lay upon all Germany. This man was David Strauss. Strauss was the prophet of the good-enough. He taught that German art was sound, that German culture was perfect. Nietzsche saw in him the foe of Dionysus and made an example of him. In every word of that scintillating philippic there was a plea for the independence and individualism and outlawry that the philosopher saw in Wagner.[1]

Unluckily the disciple here ran ahead of the master and before long Nietzsche began to realize that he and Wagner were drifting apart. So long as they met upon the safe ground of Schopenhauer's data, the two agreed, but after Nietzsche began to work out his inevitable conclusions, Wagner abandoned him. To put it plainly, Wagner was the artist before he was the philosopher, and when philosophy began to grow ugly he turned from it without regret or qualm of conscience. Theoretically, he saw things as Nietzsche saw them, but as an artist he could not afford to be too literal. It was true enough, perhaps, that self-sacrifice was a medieval superstition, but all the same it made effective heroes on the stage.

Nietzsche was utterly unable, throughout his life, to acknowledge anything but hypocrisy or ignorance in those who descended to such compromises. When he wrote "*Richard Wagner in Bayreuth*" he was already the prey of doubts, but it is probable that he still saw the "ifs" and "buts" in Wagner's individualism but dimly. He could not realize, in brief, that a composer who fought beneath the banner of truth, against custom and convention, could ever turn aside from the battle. Wagner agreed with Nietzsche, perhaps, that European civilization and its child, the European art of the day, were founded upon lies, but he was artist enough to see that, without these lies, it would be impossible to make art understandable to the public. So in his librettos he employed all of the old fallacies—that love has the supernatural power of making a bad man good, that one man may save the soul of another, that humility is a virtue.[2]

It is obvious from this, that the apostate was not Nietzsche, but Wagner. Nietzsche started out in life as a seeker after truth, and he sought the truth his whole life long, without regarding for an instant the risks and dangers and consequences of the quest. Wagner, so long as it remained a mere matter of philosophical disputation, was equally radical and courageous, but he saw very clearly that it was necessary to compromise with tradition in his operas. He was an atheist and a mocker of the gods, but the mystery and beauty of the Roman Catholic ritual appealed to his artistic sense, and so, instead of penning an opera in which the hero spouted aphorisms by Huxley, he wrote "*Parsifal*" And in the same way, in his other music dramas, he made artistic use of all the ancient fallacies and devices in the lumber room of chivalry. He was, indeed, a philosopher in his hours of leisure only. When he was at work over his music paper, he saw that St. Ignatius was a far more effective and appealing figure than Herbert Spencer and that the conventional notion that marriage was a union of two immortal souls was far more picturesque than the Schopenhauer-Nietzschean idea that it was a mere symptom of the primary will to live.

In 1876 Nietzsche began to realize that he had left Wagner far behind and that thereafter he could expect no support from the composer. They had not met since 1874, but Nietzsche went to Bayreuth for the first opera season. A single conversation convinced him that his doubts were well-founded—that Wagner was a mere dionysian of the chair and had no intention of pushing the ideas they had discussed to their bitter and revolutionary conclusion. Most other men would have seen in this nothing more than an evidence of a common-sense decision to sacrifice the whole truth for half the truth, but Nietzsche was a rabid hater of compromise. To make terms with the philistines seemed to him to be even worse than joining their ranks. He saw in Wagner only a traitor who knew the truth and yet denied it.

Nietzsche was so much disgusted that he left Bayreuth and set out upon a walking tour, but before the end of the season he returned and heard some of the operas. But he was no longer a Wagnerian and the music of the "Ring" did not delight him. It was impossible, indeed, for him to separate the music from the philosophy set forth in the librettos. He believed, with Wagner, that the two were indissolubly welded, and so, after awhile, he came to condemn the whole fabric—harmonies and melodies as well as heroes and dramatic situations.

When Wagner passed out of his life Nietzsche sought to cure his loneliness by hard work and "*Menschliches allzu Menschliches*" was the result. He sent a copy of the first volume to Wagner and on the way it crossed a copy of "*Parsifal.*" In this circumstance is well exhibited the width of the breach between the two men. To Wagner "*Menschliches allzu Menschliches*" seemed impossibly and insanely radical; to Nietzsche "*Parsifal*", with all its exaltation of ritualism, was unspeakable. Neither deigned to write to the other, but we have it from reliable testimony that Wagner was disgusted and Nietzsche's sister tells us how much the music-drama of the grail enraged him.

A German, when indignation seizes him, rises straightway to make a loud and vociferous protest. And so, although Nietzsche retained, to the end of his life, a pleasant memory of the happy days he spent at Tribschen and almost his last words voiced his loyal love for Wagner the man, he conceived it to be his sacred duty to combat what he regarded as the treason of Wagner the philosopher. This notion was doubtlessly strengthened by his belief that he himself had done much to launch Wagner's bark. He had praised, and now it was his duty to blame. He had been enthusiastic at the first task, and he determined to be pitiless at the second.

But he hesitated for ten years, because, as has been said, he could not kill his affection for Wagner, the man. It takes courage to wound one's nearest and dearest, and Nietzsche, for all his lack of sentiment, was still no more than human. In the end, however, he brought himself to the heroic surgery that confronted him, and the result was "*Der Fall Wagner*". In this book all friendship and pleasant memories were put aside. Wagner was his friend of old? Very well: that was a reason for him to be all the more exact and all the more unpitying.

"What does a philosopher firstly and lastly require of himself?" he asks. "To overcome his age in himself; to become timeless! With what, then, has he to fight his hardest fight? With those characteristics and ideas which most plainly stamp him as the child of his age." Herein we perceive Nietzsche's fundamental error. Deceived by Wagner's enthusiasm for Schopenhauer and his early, amateurish dabbling in philosophy, he regarded; the composer as a philosopher. But Wagner, of course, was first of all an artist, and it is the function of an artist, not to reform humanity, but to depict it as he sees it, or as his age sees it—fallacies, delusions and all. George Bernard Shaw, in his famous criticism of Shakespeare, shows us how the Bard of Avon made just such a compromise with the prevailing opinion of his time. Shakespeare, he says, was too intelligent a man to regard Rosalind as a plausible woman, but the theatre-goers of his day so regarded her and he drew her to their taste.[3] An artist who failed to make such a concession to convention would be an artist without an audience. Wagner was no Christian, but he knew that the quest of the holy grail was an idea which made a powerful appeal to nine-tenths of civilized humanity, and so he turned it into a drama. This was not conscious lack of sincerity, but merely a manifestation of the sub-conscious artistic feeling for effectiveness.[4]

Therefore, it is plain that Nietzsche's whole case against Wagner is based upon a fallacy and that, in consequence, it is not to be taken too seriously. It is true enough that his book contains some remarkably acute and searching observations upon art, and that, granting his premises, his general conclusions would be correct, but we are by no means granting his premises. Wagner may have been a traitor to his philosophy, but if he had remained loyal to it, his art would have been impossible. And in view of the sublime beauty of that art we may well pardon him for not keeping the faith.

"*Der Fall Wagner*" caused a horde of stupid critics to maintain that Nietzsche, and not Wagner, was the apostate, and that the mad philosopher had begun to argue against himself. As an answer to this ridiculous charge, Nietzsche published a little book called "*Nietzsche contra Wagner.*" It was made up entirely of passages from his earlier books and these proved conclusively that, ever since his initial divergence from Schopenhauer's conclusions, he had hoed a straight row. He was a dionysian in "*Die Geburt der Tragödie*" and he was a dionysian still in "*Also Sprach Zarathustra.*"

---

[1]That Wagner gave Nietzsche good reason to credit him with these qualities is amply proved. "I have never read anything better than your book, " wrote the composer in 1872. "It is masterly." And Frau Cosima and Liszt, who were certainly familiar with Wagner's ideas, supported Nietzsche's assumption, too. "Oh, how fine is your book, " wrote the former, "how fine and how deep—how deep and how keen!" Liszt sent from Prague (Feb. 29, 1872) a pompous, patronizing letter. "I have read your book twice, " he said. In all of this correspondence there is no hint that Nietzsche had misunderstood Wagner's position or had laid down any propositions from which the composer dissented.

[2]There is an interesting discussion of this in James Huneker's book, "Mezzotints in Modern Music, " page 285 *et. seq.*, New York, 1899.

[3]See "George Bernard Shaw: His Plays;" page 102 *et seq.*, Boston, 1905.

[4]"Wagner's creative instinct gave the lie to his theoretical system:" R. A. Streatfield, "Modern Music and Musicians, " p. 272; New York, 1906.

PART THREE.
NIETZSCHE THE PROPHET

I. NIETZSCHE'S ORIGINS

The construction of philosophical family trees for Nietzsche has ever been one of the favorite pastimes of his critics and interpreters. Thus Dr. Oscar Levy, editor of the English translation of his works, makes him the heir of Goethe and Stendhal, and the culminating figure of the "Second Renaissance" launched by the latter, who was "the first man to cry halt to the Kantian philosophy which had flooded all Europe."[1] Dr. M. A. Mügge agrees with this genealogy so far as it goes, but points out that Nietzsche was also the intellectual descendant of certain pre-Socratic Greeks, particularly Heraclitus, and of Spinoza and Stirner.[2] Alfred Fouillée, the Frenchman, is another who gives him Greek blood, but in seeking his later forebears Fouillée passes over the four named by Levy and Mügge and puts Hobbes, Schopenhauer, Darwin, Rousseau and Diderot in place of them.[3] Again, Thomas Common says that "perhaps Nietzsche is most indebted to Chamfort and Schopenhauer, " but also allows a considerable influence to Hobbes, and endeavors to show how Nietzsche carried on, consciously and unconsciously, certain ideas originating with Darwin and developed by Huxley, Spencer and the other evolutionists.[4] Dr. Alexander Tille has written a whole volume upon this latter relationship.[5]Finally, Paul Elmer More, the American, taking the cue from Fouillée, finds the germs of many of Nietzsche's doctrines in Hobbes, and then proceeds to a somewhat elaborate discussion of the mutations of ethical theory during the past two centuries, showing how Hume superimposed the idea of sympathy as a motive upon Hobbes' idea of self-interest, and how this sympathy theory prevailed over that of self-interest, and degenerated into sentimentalism, and so opened the way for Socialism and other such delusions, and how Nietzsche instituted a sort of Hobbesian revival.[6] Many more speculations of that sort, some of them very ingenious and some merely ingenuous, might be rehearsed. By one critic or another Nietzsche has been accused of more or less frank borrowings from Xenophanes, Democritus, Pythagoras, Callicles, Parmenides, Arcelaus, Empedocles, Pyrrho, Hegesippus, the Eleatic Zeno, Machiavelli, Comte, Montaigne, Mandeville, La Bruyère, Fontenelle, Voltaire, Kant, La Rochefoucauld, Helvétius, Adam Smith, Malthus, Butler, Blake, Proudhon, Paul Rée, Flaubert, Taine, Gobineau, Renan, and even from Karl Marx!—a long catalogue of meaningless names, an exhaustive roster of pathfinders and protestants. A Frenchman, Jules de Gaultier, has devoted a whole book to the fascinating subject.[7]

But if we turn from this laborious and often irrelevant search for common ideas and parallel passages to the actual facts of Nietzsche's intellectual development, we shall find, perhaps, that his ancestry ran in two streams, the one coming down from the Greeks whom he studied as school-boy and undergraduate, and the other having its source in Schopenhauer, the great discovery of his early manhood and the most powerful single influence of his life. No need to argue the essentially Greek color of Nietzsche's apprentice thinking. It was, indeed, his interest in Greek literature and life that made him a philologist by profession, and the same interest that converted him from a philologist into a philosopher. The foundation of his system was laid when he arrived at his conception of the conflict between the Greek gods Apollo and Dionysus, and all that followed belonged naturally to the working out of that idea. But what he got from the Greeks of his early adoration was more than a single idea and more than the body of miscellaneous ideas listed by the commentators: it was the Greek outlook, the Greek spirit, the Greek attitude toward God and man. In brief, he ceased to be a German pastor's son, brought up in the fear of the Lord, and became a citizen of those gorgeous and enchanted isles, much as Shelley had before him. The sentimentality of Christianity dropped from him like an old garment; he stood forth, as it were, bare and unashamed, a pagan in the springtime of the world, a *ja-sager*. More than the reading of books, of course, was needed to work that transformation—the blood that leaped had to be blood capable of leaping—but it was out of books that the stimulus came, and the feeling of surety, and the beginnings of a workable philosophy of life. It is not a German that speaks in "The Antichrist, " nor even the Polish noble that Nietzsche liked to think himself, but a Greek of the brave days before Socrates, a spokesman of Hellenic innocence and youth.

No doubt it was the unmistakably Greek note in Schopenhauer—the delivery of instinct, so long condemned to the ethical dungeons—that engendered Nietzsche's first wild enthusiasm for the Frankfort sage. The atmosphere of Leipsic in 1865 was heavy with moral vapors, and the daring dissent of Schopenhauer must have seemed to blow through it like a sharp wind from the sea. And Nietzsche, being young and passionate, was carried away by the ecstasy of discovery, and so accepted the whole Schopenhauerean philosophy without examining it too critically—the bitter with the sweet, its pessimism no less than its rebellion. He, too, had to go through the green-sickness of youth, particularly of German youth. The Greek was yet but half way from Naumburg to Attica, and he now stopped a moment to look backward. "Every line, " he tells us somewhere, "cried out renunciation, denial, resignation.... Evidences of this sudden change are still to be found in the restless melancholy of the leaves of my diary at that period, with all their useless self-reproach and their desperate gazing upward for recovery and for the transformation of the whole spirit of mankind. By drawing all my qualities and my aspirations before the forum of gloomy self-contempt I became bitter, unjust and unbridled in my hatred of myself. I even practised bodily penance. For instance, I forced myself for a fortnight at a stretch to go to bed at two o'clock in the morning and to rise punctually at six." But not for long. The fortnight of self-accusing and hair-shirts was soon over. The green-sickness vanished.[8] The Greek emerged anew, more Hellenic than ever. And so, almost from the start, Nietzsche rejected quite as much of Schopenhauer as he accepted. The Schopenhauerean premise entered into his system—the will to live was destined to become the father, in a few years, of the will to power—but the Schopenhauerean conclusion held him no longer than it took him to inspect it calmly. Thus he gained doubly—first, by the acquisition of a definite theory of human conduct, one giving clarity to his own vague feelings, and secondly, by the reaction against an abject theory of human destiny, the very antithesis of that which rose within him.

And yet, for all his dissent, for all his instinctive revolt against the resignationism which overwhelmed him for an hour, Nietzsche nevertheless carried away with him, and kept throughout his life, some touch of Schopenhauer's distrust of the search for happiness. Nine years after his great discovery we find him quoting and approving his teacher's words: "A happy life is impossible; the highest thing that man can aspire to is a *heroic* life." And still later we find him thundering against "the green-grazing happiness of the herd." What is more, he gave his assent later on, though always more by fascination than by conviction, to the doctrine of eternal recurrence, the most hopeless idea, perhaps, ever formulated by man. But in all this a certain distinction is to be noted: Schopenhauer, despairing of the happy life, renounced even the heroic life, but Nietzsche never did anything of the sort. On the contrary, his whole philosophy is a protest against that very despair. The heroic life may not bring happiness, and it may even fail to bring good, but at all events it will shine gloriously in the light of its own heroism. In brief, high endeavor is an end in itself—nay, the noblest of all ends. The higher man does not work for a wage, not even for the wage of bliss: his reward is in the struggle, the danger, the aspiration. As for the happiness born of peace and love, of prosperity and tranquillity, that is for "shopkeepers, women, Englishmen and cows." The man who seeks it thereby confesses his incapacity for the loftier joys and hazards of the free spirit, and the man who wails because he cannot find it thereby confesses his unfitness to live in the world. "My formula for greatness, " said Nietzsche toward the end of his life, "is *amor fati* ... not only to bear up under necessity, but to *love* it." Thus, borrowing Schopenhauer's pessimism, he turned it, in the end, into a defiant and irreconcilable optimism—not the slave optimism of hope, with its vain courting of gods, but the master optimism of courage.

So much for the larger of the direct influences upon Nietzsche's thinking. Scarcely less was the influence of that great revolution in man's view of man, that genuine "transvaluation of all values, " set in motion by the publication of Charles Darwin's "The Origin of Species, " in 1859. In the chapter on Christianity I have sketched briefly the part that Nietzsche played in the matter, and have shown how it rested squarely upon the parts played by those who went before him. He himself was fond of attacking Darwin, whom he disliked as he disliked all Englishmen, and of denying that he had gotten anything of value out of Darwin's work, but it is not well to take such denunciations and denials too seriously. Like Ibsen, Nietzsche was often an unreliable witness as to his own intellectual obligations. So long as he dealt with ideas his thinking was frank and clear, but when he turned to the human beings behind them, and particularly when he discussed those who had presumed to approach the problems he undertook to solve himself, his incredible intolerance, jealousy, spitefulness and egomania, and his savage lust for bitter, useless and unmerciful strife, combined to make his statements dubious, and sometimes even absurd. Thus with his sneers at Darwin and the other evolutionists, especially Spencer. If he did not actually follow them, then he at least walked side by side with them, and every time they cleared another bit of the path he profited by it too. One thing, at all events, they gave to the world that entered into Nietzsche's final philosophy, and without which it would have stopped short of its ultimate development, and that was the conception of man as a mammal. Their great service to human knowledge was precisely this. They found man a loiterer at the gates of heaven, a courtier in the ante-chambers of gods. They brought him back to earth and bade him help himself.

Meanwhile, the reader who cares to go into the matter further will find Nietzsche elbowing other sages in a multitude of places. He himself has testified to his debt to Stendhal (Marie Henri Beyle), that great apologist for Napoleon Bonaparte and exponent of the Napoleonic philosophy. "Stendhal, " he says, "was one of the happiest accidents of my life.... He is quite priceless, with his penetrating psychologist's eye and his grip upon facts, recalling that of the greatest of all masters of facts (*ex ungue Napoleon—*); and last, but not least, as an *honest*atheist—one of a species rare and hard to find in France.... Maybe I myself am jealous of Stendhal? He took from me the best of atheistic jokes, that I might best have made: 'the only excuse for God is that He doesn't exist.'"[9] Of his debt to Max Stirner the evidence is less clear, but it has been frequently alleged, and, as Dr. Mügge says, "quite a literature has grown up around the question." Stirner's chief work, "*Der Einzige und sein Eigentum*, "[10] was first published in 1844, the year of Nietzsche's birth, and in its strong plea for the emancipation of the individual there are many ideas and even phrases that were later voiced by Nietzsche. Dr. Mügge quotes a few of them: "What is good and what is evil? I myself am my own rule, and I am neither good nor evil. Neither word means anything to me.... Between the two vicissitudes of victory and defeat swings the fate of the struggle—master or slave!... Egoism, not love, must decide." Others will greet the reader of Stirner's book: "As long as you believe in the truth, you do not believe in yourself; you are a servant, a religious man. You alone are the truth.... Whether what I think and do is Christian, what do I care? Whether it is human, liberal, humane, whether unhuman, illiberal, unhumane, what do I ask about that? If only it accomplishes what I want, if only I satisfy myself in it, then overlay it with predicates if you will: it is all one to me...." But, as Dr. J. L. Walker well says, in his introduction to Mr. Byington's English translation, there is a considerable gulf between Stirner and Nietzsche, even here. The former's plea is for absolute liberty for all men, great and small. The latter is for liberty only in the higher castes: the chandala he would keep in chains. Therefore, if Nietzsche actually got anything from Stirner, it certainly did not enter unchanged into the ultimate structure of his system.

The other attempts to convict him of appropriating ideas come to little more. Dr. Mügge, for example, quotes these pre-Nietzschean passages from Heracleitus: "War is universal and right, and by strife all things arise and are made use of ... Good and evil are the same.... To me, one is worth ten thousand, if he be the best." And Mr. More quotes this from Hobbes:

"In the first place, I put forth, for a general inclination of all mankind, a perpetual and restless desire of power after power, that ceaseth only with death"—to which the reader may add, "Whatsoever is the object of any man's appetite or desire, that is it which he for his part calleth good ... for these words of good, evil and contemptible are ever used with relation to the person that useth them; there being nothing simply and absolutely so; nor any common rule of good and evil, to be taken for the nature of objects themselves."[11] But all these passages prove no more than that men of past ages saw the mutability of criteria, and their origin in human aspiration and striving. Not only Heracleitus, but many other Greeks, voiced that ethical scepticism. It was for many years, indeed, one of the dominant influences in Greek philosophy, and so, if Nietzsche is accused of borrowing it, that is no more than saying what I have already said: that he ate Greek grapes in his youth and became, to all intellectual intents and purposes, a Greek himself. A man must needs have a point of view, a manner of approach to life, and that point of view is no less authentic when he reaches it through his reading and by the exercise of a certain degree of free choice than when he accepts it unthinkingly from the folk about him. The service of Heracleitus and the other Greeks to Nietzsche was not that they gave him his philosophy, but that they made him a philosopher. It was the questions they asked rather than the answers they made that interested and stimulated him, and if, at times, he answered much as they had done, that was only proof of his genuine kinship with them.

On the artistic, as opposed to the analytical side, Nietzsche's most influential teacher, perhaps, was Goethe, the noblest intellectual figure of modern Germany, the common *stammvater* of all the warring schools of today—in Nietzsche's own phrase, "not only a good and great man, but a culture itself." His writings are full of praises of his hero, whom he began to read as a boy of eight or ten years. His grandmother, Frau Erdmuthe Nietzsche, was a sister to Dr. Krause, professor of divinity at Weimar in Goethe's day, and she lived in the town while the poet held his court there, and undoubtedly came into contact with him. Her mother, Frau Pastor Krause, was probably the Muthgen of Goethe's diary. But despite all this, she thought that "Faust" and "Elective Affinities" were "not fit for little boys" and so it remained for Judge Pindar, the father of one of young Nietzsche's Naumburg playmates, to conduct the initiation.[12] Thirty years afterward, Nietzsche gratefully acknowledged his debt to Herr Pindar, and his vastly greater debt to Goethe—"a thorough-going realist in the midst of an unreal age.... He did not sever himself from life, but entered into it. Undaunted, he took as much as possible to himself.... What he sought was *totality*."[13]

Nietzsche was also an extravagant admirer of Heinrich Heine, and tried to imitate that poet's "sweet and passionate music." "People will say some day, " he declared, "that Heine and I were the greatest artists, by far, that ever wrote in German, and that we left the best any mere German[14] could do an incalculable distance behind us."[15] Another poet he greatly revered was Friedrich Hölderlin, a South German rhapsodist of the Goethe-Schiller period, who wrote odes in free rhythms and philosophical novels in gorgeous prose, and died the year before Nietzsche was born, after forty years of insanity. Karl Joel, [16] Dr. Mügge and other critics have sought to connect Nietzsche, through Hölderlin, with the romantic movement in Germany, but the truth is that both Nietzsche and Hölderlin, if they were romantics at all, were of the Greek school rather than the German. Certainly, nothing could be further from genuine German romanticism, with its sentimentality, its begging of questions and its booming patriotism, than the gospel of the superman. What Nietzsche undoubtedly got from the romantics was a feeling of ease in the German language, a disregard for the artificial bonds of the schools, a sense of hospitality to the gipsy phrase. In brief, they taught him how to write. But they certainly did not teach him what to write.

Even so, it is probable that he was as much influenced by certain Frenchmen as he ever was by Germans—particularly by Montaigne, La Bruyère, La Rochefoucauld, Fontenelle, Vauvenargues and Chamfort, his constant companions on his wanderings. He borrowed from them, not only the somewhat obvious device of putting his argument into the form of apothegms and epigrams, but also their conception of the dialectic as one of the fine arts—in other words, their striving after style. "It is to a small number of French authors, " he once said, "that I return again and again. I believe only in French culture, and regard all that is called culture elsewhere in Europe, especially in Germany, as mere misunderstanding.... The few persons of higher culture that I have met in Germany have had French training—above all, Frau Cosima Wagner, by long odds the best authority on questions of taste I ever heard of."[17]This preference carried him so far, indeed, that he usually wrote more like a Frenchman than like a German, toying with words, experimenting with their combinations, matching them as carefully as pearls for a necklace. "Nietzsche, " says one critic, [18] "whether for good or evil, introduced Romance (not romantic!) qualities of terseness and clearness into German prose; it was his endeavor to free it from those elements which he described as *deutsch und schwer*." (German and heavy.)

For the rest, he denounced Klopstock, Herder, Wieland, Lessing and Schiller, the remaining gods in Germany's literary valhalla, even more bitterly than he denounced Kant and Hegel, the giants of orthodox German philosophy.

---

[1]"The Revival of Aristocracy, " London, 1906, pp. 14-59.

[2]"Friedrich Nietzsche: His Life and Work, " New York, 1909, pp. 315-320.

[3]"*Nietzsche et l'Immoralisme*, " Paris, 1902, p. 294.

[4]"Nietzsche as Critic, Philosopher, Poet and Prophet, " London, 1901, pp. xi-xxiii.

[5]"*Von Darwin bis Nietzsche*, " Leipsic, 1895.

[6]"Nietzsche, " Boston, 1912, pp. 18-45.

[7]"*De Kant à Nietzsche,* " Paris, 1900.

[8]Nietzsche himself, in after years, viewed this attack humorously, and was wont to say that it was caused, not by Schopenhauer alone, but also (and chiefly) by the bad cooking of Leipsic. See "*Ecce Homo,* " II, i.

[9]"*Ecce Homo,* " II, 3.

[10]Eng. tr. by Steven T. Byington, "The Ego and His Own, " New York, 1907.

[11]The Leviathan, I, vi; London, 1651.

[12]Frau Förster-Nietzsche: "The Life of Nietzsche" (Eng. tr.), Vol. I, p. 31.

[13]"*Götzendämmerung,* " IX, 49.

[14]Heine was a Jew—and Nietzsche, as we know, liked to think himself a Pole.

[15]"*Ecce Homo,* " II, 4.

[16]"*Nietzsche und die Romantik,* " Jena, 1905.

[17]"*Ecce Homo,* " II, 3.

[18]J. G. Robertson: "A History of German Literature, " Edinburgh, 1902, pp. 611-615.

II. NIETZSCHE AND HIS CRITICS

Let us set aside at the start that great host of critics whose chief objection to Nietzsche is that he is blasphemous, that his philosophy and his manner outrage the piety and prudery of the world. Of such sort are the pale parsons who arise in suburban pulpits to dispose of him in the half hour between the first and second lessons, as their predecessors of the 70's and 80's disposed of Darwin, Huxley and Spencer. Let them read their indictments and bring in their verdicts and pronounce their bitter sentences! The student of Nietzsche must perceive at once the irrelevance of that sort of criticism. It was the deliberate effort of the philosopher, from the very start of what he calls his tunnelling period, to provoke and deserve the accusation of sacrilege. In framing his accusations against Christian morality he tried to make them, not only persuasive and just, but also as offensive as possible. No man ever had more belief in the propagandist value of a *succès de scandale*. He tried his best to shock the guardians of the sacred vessels, to force upon them the burdens of an active defense, to bring them out into the open, to attract attention to the combat by accentuating its mere fuming and fury. If he succeeded in the effort, if he really outraged Christendom, then it is certainly absurd to bring forward that deliberate achievement as an exhibit against itself.

The more pertinent and plausible criticisms of Nietzsche, launched against him in Europe and America by many industrious foes, may be reduced for convenience to five fundamental propositions, to wit:

(*a*) He was a decadent and a lunatic, and in consequence his philosophy is not worthy of attention.

(*b*) His writings are chaotic and contradictory and it is impossible to find in them any connected philosophical system.

(*c*) His argument that self-sacrifice costs more than it yields, and that it thus reduces the average fitness of a race practising it, is contradicted by human experience.

(*d*) The scheme of things proposed by him is opposed by ideas inherent in all civilized men.

(*e*) Even admitting that his criticism of Christian morality is well-founded, he offers nothing in place of it that would work as well.

It is scarcely worth while to linger over the first and second of these propositions. The first has been defended most speciously by Max Nordau, in "Degeneration, " a book which made as much noise, when it was first published in 1893, as any of Nietzsche's own. Nordau's argument is based upon a theory of degeneration borrowed quite frankly from Cesare Lombroso, an Italian quasi-scientist whose modest contributions to psychiatry were offset by many volumes of rubbish about spooks, table-tapping, mental telepathy, spirit photography and the alleged stigmata of criminals and men of genius. Degeneracy and decadence were terms that filled the public imagination in the 80's and 90's, and even Nietzsche himself seemed to think, at times, that they had definite meanings and that his own type of mind was degenerate. As Nordau defines degeneracy it is "a morbid deviation from the original type"—*i.e.* from the physical and mental norm of the species—and he lays stress upon the fact that by "morbid" he means "infirm" or "incapable of fulfilling normal functions." But straightway he begins to regard *any*deviation as morbid and degenerate, despite the obvious fact that it may be quite the reverse. He says, for example, that a man with web toes is a degenerate, and then proceeds to argue elaborately from that premise, entirely overlooking the fact that web toes, under easily imaginable circumstances, might be an advantage instead of a handicap, and that, under the ordinary conditions of life, we are unable to determine with any accuracy whether they are the one thing or the other. So with the symptoms of degeneracy that he discovers in Nietzsche. He shows that Nietzsche differed vastly from the average, every-day German of his time, and even from the average German of superior culture—that he thought differently, wrote differently, admired different heroes and believed in different gods—but he by no means proves thereby that Nietzsche's processes of thought were morbid or infirm, or that the conclusions he reached were invalid *a priori*. Since Nordau startled the world with his book, the Lombrosan theory of degeneracy has lost ground among psychologists and pathologists, but it is still launched against Nietzsche by an occasional critic, and so it deserves to be noticed.

Nordau's discussion of Nietzsche's insanity is rather more intelligent than his discussion of the philosopher's alleged degeneracy, if only because his facts are less open to dispute, but here, too, he forgets that the proof of an idea is not to be sought in the soundness of the man fathering it, but in the soundness of the idea itself. One asks of a pudding, not if the cook who offers it is a good woman, but if the pudding itself is good. Nordau, in attempting to dispose of Nietzsche's philosophy on the ground that the author died a madman, succeeds only in piling up a mass of uncontroverted but irrelevant accusations. He shows that Nietzsche was an utter believer in his own wisdom, that he had a fondness for repeating certain favorite arguments *ad nauseam*, that he was violently impatient of criticism, that he chronically underestimated the man opposed to him, that he sometimes indulged in blasphemy for the sheer joy of shocking folks, and that he was often hypnotized by the exuberance of his own verbosity, but it must be plain that this indictment has its effective answer in the fact that it might be found with equal justice against almost any revolutionary enthusiast one selected at random—for example, Savonarola, Tolstoi, Luther, Ibsen, Garrison, Phillips, Wilkes, Bakúnin, Marx, or Nordau himself. That Nietzsche died insane is undoubted, and that his insanity was not sudden in its onset is also plain, and one may even admit frankly that it is visible, here and there, in his writings, particularly those of his last year or two; but that his principal doctrines, the ideas upon which his fame are based, are the fantasies of a maniac is certainly wholly false. Had he sought to prove that cows had wings, it might be fair today to dismiss him as Nordau attempts to dismiss him. But when he essayed to prove that Christianity impeded progress, he laid down a proposition that, whatever its novelty and daring, was obviously not irrational, and neither was there anything irrational in the reasoning whereby he supported it. One need go no further for proof of this than the fact that multitudes of sane men, while he lived and since his death, have debated that proposition in all seriousness and found a plentiful food for sober thought in Nietzsche's statement and defense of it. Ibsen also passed out of life in mental darkness, and so did Schumann, but no reasonable critic would seek thereby to deny all intelligibility to "Peer Gynt" or to the piano quintet in E flat.

Again, it is Nordau who chiefly voices the second of the objections noted at the beginning of this chapter, though here many another self-confessed serpent of wisdom follows him. Nietzsche, he says, tore down without building up, and died without having formulated any workable substitute for the Christian morality he denounced. Even to the reader who has got no further into Nietzsche than the preceding chapters of this book, the absurdity of such a charge must be manifest without argument. No man, indeed, ever left a more comprehensive system of ethics, not even Comte or Herbert Spencer, and if it be true that he scattered it through a dozen books and that he occasionally modified it in some of its details, it is equally true that his fundamental principles were always stated with perfect clearness and that they remained substantially unchanged from first to last. But even supposing that he had died before he had arranged his ideas in a connected and coherent form, and that it had remained for his disciples to deduce and group his final conclusions, and to rid the whole of inconsistency—even then it would have been possible to study those conclusions seriously and to accept them for what they were worth. Nordau lays it down as an axiom that a man cannot be a reformer unless he proposes some ready-made and perfectly symmetrical scheme of things to take the place of the notions he seeks to overturn, that if he does not do this he is a mere hurler of bricks and shouter of blasphemies. But all of us know that this is not true. Nearly every considerable reform the world knows has been accomplished, not by one man, but by many men working in series. It seldom happens, indeed, that the man who first points out the necessity for change lives long enough to see that change accomplished, or even to define its precise manner and terms. Nietzsche himself was not the first critic of Christian morality, nor did he so far dispose of the question that he left no room for successors. But he made a larger contribution to it than any man had ever made before him, and the ideas he contributed were so acute and so convincing that they must needs be taken into account by every critic who comes after him.

So much for the first two arguments against the prophet of the superman. Both raise immaterial objections and the second makes an allegation that is grotesquely untrue. The other three are founded upon sounder logic, and, when maintained skillfully, afford more reasonable ground for objecting to the Nietzschean system, either as a whole or in part. It would be interesting, perhaps, to attempt a complete review of the literature embodying them, but that would take a great deal more space than is here available, and so we must be content with a glance at a few typical efforts at refutation. One of the most familiar of these appears in the argument that the messianic obligation of self-sacrifice, whatever its cost, has yet yielded the race a large profit—that we are the better for our Christian charity and that we owe it entirely to Christianity. This argument has been best put forward, perhaps, by Bennett Hume, an Englishman. If it were not for Christian charity, says Mr. Hume, there would be no hospitals and asylums for the sick and insane, and in consequence, no concerted and effective effort to make man more healthy and efficient. Therefore, he maintains, it must be admitted that the influence of Christianity, as a moral system, has been for the good of the race. But this argument, in inspection, quickly goes to pieces, and for two reasons. In the first place, it must be obvious that the advantages of preserving the unfit, few of whom ever become wholly fit again, are more than dubious; and in the second place, it must be plain that modern humanitarianism, in so far as it is scientific and unsentimental and hence profitable, is so little a purely Christian idea that the Christian church, even down to our own time, has actually opposed it. No man, indeed, can read Dr. Andrew D. White's great history of the warfare between science and the church without carrying away the conviction that such great boons as the conquest of smallpox and malaria, the development of surgery, the improved treatment of the insane, and the general lowering of the death rate have been brought about, not by the maudlin alms-giving of Christian priests, but by the intelligent meliorism of rebels against a blind faith, ruthless in their ways and means but stupendously successful in their achievement.

Another critic, this time a Frenchman, Alfred Fouillée by name, [62]chooses as his point of attack the Nietzschean doctrine that a struggle is welcome and beneficial to the strong, that intelligent self-seeking, accompanied by a certain willingness to take risks, is the road of progress. A struggle, argues M. Fouillée, always means an expenditure of strength, and strength, when so expended, is further weakened by the opposing

---

[62] Author of "*Nietzsche et l'Immoralisme*" and other books. The argument discussed appears in an article in the *International Monthly* for March, 1901, pp. 134-165.

strength it arouses and stimulates. Darwin is summoned from his tomb to substantiate this argument, but its exponent seems to forget (while actually stating it!) the familiar physiological axiom, so often turned to by Darwin, that strength is one of the effects of use, and the Darwinian corollary that disuse, whether produced by organized protection or in some other way, leads inevitably to weakness and atrophy. In other words, the ideal strong man of M. Fouillée's dream is one who seeks, with great enthusiasm, the readiest possible way of ridding himself of his strength.

Nordau, Violet Paget and various other critics attack Nietzsche from much the same side. That is to say, they endeavor to controvert his criticism of humility and self-sacrifice and to show that the law of natural selection, with its insistence that only the fittest shall survive, is insufficient to insure human progress. Miss Paget, for example, [63]argues that if there were no belief in every man's duty to yield something to his weaker brother the race would soon become a herd of mere wild beasts. She sees humility as a sort of brake or governor, placed upon humanity to keep it from running amuck. A human being is so constituted, she says, that he necessarily looms in his own view as large as all the rest of the world put together. This distortion of values is met with in the consciousness of every individual, and if there were nothing to oppose it, it would lead to a hopeless conflict between exaggerated egos. Humility, says Miss Paget, tempers the conflict, without wholly ending it. A man's inherent tendency to magnify his own importance and to invite death by trying to force that view upon others is held in check by the idea that it is his duty to consider the welfare of those others. The objection to all this is that the picture of humility Miss Paget draws is not at all a picture of self-sacrifice, of something founded upon an unselfish idea of duty, but a picture of highly intelligent egoism. Whatever his pharisaical account of his motives, it must be obvious that her Christian gentleman is merely a man who throws bones to the dogs about him. Between such wise prudence and the immolation of the Beatitudes a wide gulf is fixed. As a matter of fact, that prudence is certainly not opposed by Nietzsche. The higher man of his visions is far from a mere brawler. He is not afraid of an open fight, and he is never held back by fear of hurting his antagonist, but he also understands that there are times for truce and guile. In brief, his self-seeking is conducted, not alone by his fists, but also by his head. He knows when to pounce upon his foes and rivals, but he also knows when to keep them from pouncing upon him. Thus Miss Paget's somewhat elaborate refutation, though it leads to an undoubtedly sound conclusion, by no means disposes of Nietzsche.

---

[63] In the *North American Review* for Dec., 1904.

The other branches of the argument that self-sacrifice is beneficial open an endless field of debate, in which the same set of facts is often susceptible of diametrically opposite interpretations. We have already glanced at the alleged effects of Christian charity upon progress, and observed the enormous difference between sentimental efforts to preserve the unfit and intelligent efforts to make them fit, and we have seen how practical Christianity, whatever its theoretical effects, has had the actual effect of furthering the former and hindering the latter. It is often argued that there is unfairness in thus burdening the creed with the crimes of the church, but how the two are to be separated is never explained. What sounder test of a creed's essential value can we imagine than that of its visible influence upon the men who subscribe to it? And what sounder test of its terms than the statement of its ordained teachers and interpreters, supported by the unanimous approval of all who profess it? We are here dealing, let it be remembered, not with esoteric doctrines, but with practical doctrines—that is to say, with working policies. If the Christian ideal of charity is to be defended as a working policy, then it is certainly fair to examine it at work. And when that is done the reflective observer is almost certain to conclude that it is opposed to true progress, that it acts as a sentimental shield to the unfit without helping them in the slightest to shake off their unfitness. What is more, it stands contrary to that wise forethought which sacrifices one man today that ten may be saved tomorrow. Nothing could be more patent, indeed, than the high cost to humanity of the Christian teaching that it is immoral to seek the truth outside the Word of God, or to take thought of an earthly tomorrow, or to draw distinctions in value between beings who all possess souls of infinite, and therefore of exactly equal preciousness.

But setting aside the doctrine that self-sacrifice is a religious duty, there remains the doctrine that it is a measure of expediency, that when the strong help the weak they also help themselves. Let it be said at once that this second doctrine, provided only it be applied intelligently and without any admixture of sentimentality, is not in opposition to anything in Nietzsche's philosophy. On the contrary, he is at pains to point out the value of exploiting the inefficient masses, and obviously that exploitation is impossible without some concession to their habits and desires, some offer, however fraudulent, of a *quid pro quo*—and unprofitable unless they can be made to yield more than they absorb. For one thing, there is the business of keeping the lower castes in health. They themselves are too ignorant and lazy to manage it, and therefore it must be managed by their betters. When we appropriate money from the public funds to pay for vaccinating a horde of negroes, we do not do it because we have any sympathy for them or because we crave their blessings, but simply because we don't want them to be falling ill of smallpox in our kitchens and stables, to the peril of our own health and the neglect of our necessary drudgery.[3][64] In so far as the negroes have any voice in the matter at all, they protest against vaccination, for they can't understand its theory and so they see only its tyranny, but we vaccinate them nevertheless, and thus increase their mass efficiency in spite of them. It costs something to do the work, but we see a profit in it. Here we have a good example of self-sacrifice based frankly upon expediency, and Nietzsche has nothing to say against it.

But what he does insist upon is that we must beware of mixing sentimentality with the business, that we must keep the idea of expediency clear of any idea of altruism. The trouble with the world, as he describes it, is that such a corruption almost always takes place. That is to say, we too often practise charity, not because it is worth while, but merely because it is pleasant. The Christian ideal, he says, "knows how to enrapture." Starting out from the safe premise, approved by human experience, that it is sometimes a virtue—*i.e.*, a measure of intelligent prudence—to help the weak, we proceed to the illogical conclusion that it is *always* a virtue. Hence our wholesale coddling of the unfit, our enormous expenditure upon vain schemes of amelioration, our vain efforts to combat the laws of nature. We nurse the defective children of the lower classes into some appearance of health, and then turn them out to beget their kind. We parole the pickpocket, launch him upon society with a tract in his hand— and lose our pocket-books next day. We send missionaries to the heathen, build hospitals for them, civilize and educate them—and later on have to fight them. We save a pauper consumptive today, on the ostensible theory that he is more valuable saved than dead—and so open the way for saving his innumerable grandchildren in the future. In brief, our self-sacrifice of expediency seldom remains undefiled. Nine times out of ten a sentimental color quickly overcomes it, and soon or late there is apt to be more sentimentality in it than expediency.

What is worse, this sentimentalism results in attaching a sort of romantic glamour to its objects. Just as the Sunday-school teaching virgin, beginning by trying to save the Chinese laundryman's soul, commonly ends by falling in love with him, so the virtuoso of any other sort of charity commonly ends by endowing its beneficiary with a variety of imaginary virtues. Sympathy, by some subtle alchemy, is converted into a sneaking admiration. "Blessed are the poor in spirit" becomes "Blessed are the poor." This exaltation of inefficiency, it must be manifest, is a dangerous

---

[64] A more extended treatment of this point will be found in "Men *vs.* the Man, " by Robert Rives La Monte and the present author: New York, 1910.

error. There is, in fact, nothing at all honorable about unfitness, considered in the mass. On the contrary, it is invariably a symptom of actual dishonor—of neglect, laziness, ignorance and depravity—if not primarily in the individual himself, then at least in his forebears, whose weakness he carries on. It is highly important that this fact should be kept in mind by the human race, that the essential inferiority of the inefficient should be insisted upon, that the penalties of deliberate slackness should be swift and merciless. But as it is, those penalties are too often reduced to nothing by charity, while the offense they should punish is elevated to a fictitious martyrdom. Thus we have charity converted into an instrument of debauchery. Thus we have it playing the part of an active agent of decay, and so increasing the hazards of life on earth. "We may compare civilized man, " says Sir Ray Lankester, [65]"to a successful rebel against nature, who by every step forward renders himself liable to greater and greater penalties." No need to offer cases in point. Every one of us knows what the Poor Laws of England have accomplished in a hundred years—how they have multiplied misery enormously and created a caste of professional paupers—how they have seduced that caste downward into depths of degradation untouched by any other civilized race in history—and how, by hanging the crushing burden of that caste about the necks of the English people, they have helped to weaken and sicken the whole stock and to imperil the future of the nation.

So much for the utility of self-sacrifice—undeniable, perhaps, so long as a wise and ruthless foresight rules, but immediately questionable when sentimentality enters into the matter. There remains the answer in rebuttal that sentimentality, after all, is native to the soul of man, that we couldn't get rid of it if we tried. Herein, if we look closely, we will observe tracks of an idea that has colored the whole stream of human thought since the dawn of Western philosophy, and is accepted today, as irrefutably true, by all who pound pulpits and wave their arms and call upon their fellow men to repent. It has clogged all ethical inquiry for two thousand years, it has been a premise in a million moral syllogisms, it has survived the assaults of all the iconoclasts that ever lived. It is taught in all our schools today and lies at the bottom of all our laws, prophecies and revelations. It is the foundation and cornerstone, not only of Christianity, but also of every other compound of theology and morality known in the world. And what is this king of all axioms and emperor of all fallacies? Simply the idea that there are rules of "natural morality" engraven indelibly upon the hearts of man—that all men, at all times and everywhere, have ever agreed, do now agree and will agree forevermore, unanimously and without reservation, that certain things are right and certain other things are

---

[65] In "The Kingdom of Man, " London, 1907

wrong, that certain things are nice and certain other things are not nice, that certain things are pleasing to God and certain other things are offensive to God.

In every treatise upon Christian ethics and "natural theology, " so called, you will find these rules of "natural morality" in the first chapter. Thomas Aquinas called them "the eternal law." Even the Greeks and Romans, for all their skepticism in morals, had a sneaking belief in them. Aristotle tried to formulate them and the Latin lawyers constantly assumed their existence. Most of them are held in firm faith today by all save a small minority of the folk of Christendom. The most familiar of them, perhaps, is the rule against murder—the sixth commandment. Another is the rule against the violation of property in goods, wives and cattle—the eighth and tenth commandments. A third is the rule upon which the solidity of the family is based, and with it the solidity of the tribe—the fifth commandment. The theory behind these rules is, not only that they are wise, but that they are innate and sempiternal, that every truly enlightened man recognizes their validity intuitively, and is conscious of sin when he breaks them. To them Christianity added an eleventh commandment, a sort of infinite extension of the fifth, "that ye love one another"(John 13:34)—and in two thousand years it has been converted from a novelty into a universality. That is to say, its point of definite origin has been lost sight of, and it has been moved over into the group of "natural virtues, " of "eternal laws." When Christ first voiced it, in his discourse at the Last Supper, it was so far from general acceptance that he named a belief in it as one of the distinguishing marks of his disciples, but now our moralists tell us that it is in the blood of all of us, and that we couldn't repudiate it if we would. Brotherhood, indeed, is the very soul of Christianity, and the only effort of the pious today is to raise it from a universal theory to a universal fact.

But the truth is, of course, that it is not universal at all, and that nothing in the so-called soul of man prompts him to subscribe to it. We cling to it today, not because it is inherent in us, but simply because it is the moral fashion of our age. When the disciples first heard it put into terms, it probably struck them as a revolutionary novelty, and on some dim tomorrow our descendants may regard it as an archaic absurdity. In brief, rules of morality are wholly temporal and temporary, for the good and sufficient reason that there is no "natural morality" in man—and the sentimental rule that the strong shall give of their strength to the weak is no exception. There have been times in the history of the race when few, if any intelligent men subscribed to it, and there are thousands of intelligent men who refuse to subscribe to it today, and no doubt there will come a time when those who are against it will once more greatly outnumber those who are in favor of it. So with all other "eternal laws." Their eternality exists only in the imagination of those who seek to glorify them. Nietzsche himself spent his best years demonstrating this, and we have seen how he set about the task—how he showed that the "good" of one race and age was the "bad" of some other race and age—how the "natural morality" of the Periclean Greeks, for example, differed diametrically from the "natural morality" of the captive Jews. All history bears him out. Mankind is ever revising and abandoning its "inherent" ideas. We say today that the human mind instinctively revolts against cruel punishments, and yet a moment's reflection recalls the fact that the world is, and always has been peopled by millions to whom cruelty, not only to enemies but to the weak in general, seems and has seemed wholly natural and agreeable. We say that man has an "innate" impulse to be fair and just, and yet it is a commonplace observation that multitudes of men, in the midst of our most civilized societies, have little more sense of justice than so many jackals. Therefore, we may safely set aside the argument that a "natural" instinct for sentimental self-sacrifice stands as an impassable barrier to Nietzsche's dionysian philosophy. There is no such barrier. There is no such instinct. It is an idea merely—an idea powerful and persistent, but still mutable and mortal. Certainly, it is absurd to plead it in proof against the one man who did most to establish its mutability.

We come now to the final argument against Nietzsche—the argument, to wit, that, even admitting his criticism of Christian morality to be well-founded, he offers nothing in place of it that would serve the world as well. The principal spokesman of this objection, perhaps, is Paul Elmer More, who sets it forth at some length in his hostile but very ingenious little study of Nietzsche.[66] Mr. More goes back to Locke to show the growth of the two ideas which stand opposed as Socialism and individualism, Christianity and Nietzscheism today. So long, he says, as man believed in revelation, there was no genuine effort to get at the springs of human action, for every impulse that was ratified by the Scriptures was believed to be natural and moral, and every impulse that went counter to the Scriptures was believed to be sinful, even by those who yielded to it habitually. But when that idea was cleared away, there arose a need for something to take its place, and Locke came forward with his theory that the notion of good was founded upon sensations of pleasure and that of bad upon sensations of pain. There followed Hume, with his elaborate effort to prove that sympathy was a source of pleasure, by reason of its grateful tickling of the sense of virtue, and so the new conception of good finally stood erect, with one foot on frank self-interest and the other on sympathy. Mr. More shows how,

---

[66] "Nietzsche, " Boston, 1912. Reprinted in "The Drift of Romanticism, " pp. 147-190, Boston, 1913.

during the century following, the importance of the second of these factors began to be accentuated, under the influence of Rousseau and his followers, and how, in the end, the first was forgotten almost entirely and there arose a non-Christian sentimentality which was worse, if anything, than the sentimentality of the Beatitudes. In England, France and Germany it colored almost the whole of philosophy, literature and politics. Stray men, true enough, raised their voices against it, but its sweep was irresistible. Its fruits were diverse and memorable—the romantic movement in Germany, humanitarianism in England, the Kantian note in ethics, and, most important of all, Socialism.

That this exaltation of sympathy was imprudent, and that its effects, in our own time, are far from satisfactory, Mr. More is disposed to grant freely. It is perfectly true, as Nietzsche argues, that humanitarianism has been guilty of gross excesses, that there is a "danger that threatens true progress in any system of education and government which makes the advantage of the average rather than the distinguished man its chief object." But Mr. More holds that the danger thus inherent in sympathy is matched by a danger inherent in selfishness, that we are no worse off on one horn of Hume's dual ethic than we should be on the other. Sympathy unbalanced by self-seeking leads us into maudlin futilities and crimes against efficiency; self-seeking unchecked by sympathy would lead us into sheer savagery. If there is any choice between the two, that choice is probably in favor of sympathy, for the reason that it is happily impossible of realization. The most lachrymose of the romantics, in the midst of their sentimentalizing, were yet careful of their own welfare. Many of them, indeed, displayed a quite extraordinary egoism, and there was some justice in Byron's sneer that Sterne, for one, preferred weeping over a dead ass to relieving the want (at cost to himself) of a living mother.

But in urging all this against Nietzsche, Mr. More and the other destructive critics of the superman make a serious error, and that is the error of assuming that Nietzsche hoped to abolish Christian morality completely, that he proposed a unanimous desertion of the idea of sympathy for the idea of intelligent self-seeking. As a matter of fact, he had no such hope and made no such proposal. Nothing was more firmly fixed in his mind, indeed, than the notion that the vast majority of men would cling indefinitely, and perhaps for all time, to some system of morality more or less resembling the Christian morality of today. Not only did he have no expectation of winning that majority from its idols, but he bitterly resented any suggestion that such a result might follow from his work. The whole of his preaching was addressed, not to men in the mass, but to the small minority of exceptional men—not to those who live by obeying, but to those who live by commanding—not to the race as a race, but only to its masters. It would seem to be impossible that any reader of Nietzsche should overlook this important fact, and yet it is constantly overlooked by most of his critics. They proceed to prove, elaborately and, it must be said, quite convincingly, that if his transvaluation of values were made by all men, the world would be no better off than it is today, and perhaps a good deal worse, but all they accomplish thereby is to demolish a hobgoblin of straw. Nietzsche himself sensed the essential value of Hume's dualism. What he sought to do was not to destroy it, but to restore it, and, restoring it, to raise it to a state of active conflict—to dignify self-interest as sympathy has been dignified, and so to put the two in perpetual opposition. He believed that the former was by long odds the safer impulse for the higher castes of men to follow, if only because of its obviously closer kinship to the natural laws which make for progress upward, but by the same token he saw that these higher castes could gain nothing by disturbing the narcotic contentment of the castes lower down. Therefore, he was, to that extent, an actual apologist for the thing he elsewhere so bitterly attacked. Sympathy, self-sacrifice, charity—these ideas lulled and satisfied the chandala, and so he was content to have the chandala hold to them. "Whom do I hate most among the rabble of today? The Socialist who undermines the workingman's instincts, who destroys his satisfaction with his insignificant existence, who makes him envious and teaches him revenge." [67] In brief, Nietzsche dreamed no dream of all mankind converted into a race of supermen: the only vision he saw was one of supermen at the top.

To make an end, his philosophy was wholly aristocratic, in aim as well as in terms. He believed that superior men, by which he meant alert and restless men, were held in chains by the illusions and inertia of the mass— that their impulse to move forward and upward, at whatever cost to those below, was restrained by false notions of duty and responsibility. It was his effort to break down those false notions, to show that the progress of the race was more important than the comfort of the herd, to combat and destroy the lingering spectre of sin—in his own phrase, to make man innocent. But when he said man he always meant the higher man, the man of tomorrow, and not mere men. For the latter he had only contempt: he sneered at their heroes, at their ideals, at their definitions of good and evil. "There are only three ways, " he said, "in which the masses appear to me to deserve a glance: first, as blurred copies of their betters, printed on bad paper and from worn-out plates; secondly, as a necessary opposition; and thirdly, as tools. Further than that I hand them over to statistics—and the

---

[67] "Der Antichrist, " 57.

devil.[68] ... I am writing for a race of men which does not yet exist. I am writing for the lords of the earth."[69]

HOW TO STUDY NIETZSCHE

Through the diligence and enthusiasm of Dr. Oscar Levy, author of "The Revival of Aristocracy, " a German by birth but for some time a resident of London, the whole canon of Nietzsche's writings is now to be had in English translation. So long ago as 1896 a complete edition in eleven volumes was projected, and Dr. Alexander Tille, lecturer on German in the University of Glasgow, and author of *Von Darwin bis Nietzsche, "* was engaged to edit it. But though it started fairly with a volume including "The Case of Wagner" and "The Antichrist, " and four more volumes followed after a year or so, it got no further than that. Ten years later came Dr. Levy. He met with little encouragement when he began, but by dint of unfailing perseverance he finally gathered about him a corps of competent translators, made arrangements with publishers in Great Britain and the United States, and got the work under way. His eighteenth and last volume was published early in 1913.

These translations, in the main, are excellent, and explanatory prefaces and notes are added wherever needed. The contents of the various volumes are as follows:

I. "The Birth of Tragedy, " translated by Wm. A. Haussmann, Ph. D., with a biographical introduction by Frau Förster-Nietzsche, a portrait of Nietzsche, and a facsimile of his manuscript.

II. "Early Greek Philosophy and Other Essays, " translated by Maximilian A. Mügge, Ph. D., author of "Friedrich Nietzsche: His Life and Work." Contents: "The Greek Woman, " "On Music and Words, " "Homer's Contest, " "The Relation of Schopenhauer's Philosophy to a German Culture, " "Philosophy During the Tragic Age of the Greeks, " and "On Truth and Falsity in Their Ultramoral Sense."

III. "On the Future of Our Educational Institutions" and "Homer and Classical Philology, " translated by J. M. Kennedy, author of "The Quintessence of Nietzsche, " with an introduction by the translator.

IV. "Thoughts Out of Season, " I ("David Strauss, the Confessor and the Writer" and "Richard Wagner in Bayreuth"), translated by Anthony M. Ludovici, author of "Nietzsche: His Life and Works, " "Nietzsche and Art, " and "Who is to be Master of the World?" with an introduction by Dr. Levy and a preface by the translator.

---

[68] *"Vom Nutzen und Nachtheil der Historie für das Leben, "* IX.
[69] *"Der Wille zur Macht",* 958

V. "Thoughts Out of Season, " II ("The Use and Abuse of History" and "Schopenhauer as Educator"), translated by Adrian Collins, M. A., with an introduction by the translator.

VI. "Human All-Too Human, " I, translated by Helen Zimmern, with an introduction by J. M. Kennedy.

VII. "Human All-Too Human, " II, translated by Paul V. Cohn, B. A., with an introduction by the translator.

VIII. "The Case of Wagner" (including "Nietzsche *contra* Wagner" and selected aphorisms), translated by A. M. Ludovici, and "We Philologists, " translated by J. M. Kennedy, with prefaces by the translators.

IX. "The Dawn of Day, " translated by J. M. Kennedy, with an introduction by the translator.

X. "The Joyful Wisdom, " translated by Thomas Common, author of "Nietzsche as Critic, Philosopher, Poet and Prophet" (including "Songs of Prince Free-as-a-Bird, " translated by Paul V. Cohn and Maude D. Petre).

XI. "Thus Spake Zarathustra, " translated by Thomas Common, with an introduction by Frau Förster-Nietzsche and explanatory notes by A. M. Ludovici.

XII. "Beyond Good and Evil, " translated by Helen Zimmern, with an introduction by Thomas Common.

XIII. "The Genealogy of Morals, " translated by Horace B. Samuel, M. A., and "People and Countries, " translated by J. M. Kennedy, with an editor's note by Dr. Levy.

XIV. "The Will to Power, " I, translated by A. M. Ludovici, with a preface by the translator.

XV. "The Will to Power, " II, translated by A. M. Ludovici, with a preface by the translator.

XVI. "The Twilight of the Idols" (including "The Antichrist, " "Eternal Recurrence" and explanatory notes to "Thus Spake Zarathustra"), translated by A. M. Ludovici, with a preface by the translator.

XVII. "Ecce Homo, " translated by A. M. Ludovici; various songs, epigrams and dithyrambs, translated by Paul V. Cohn, Herman Scheffauer, Francis Bickley and Dr. G. T. Wrench; and the music of Nietzsche's "Hymn to Life" (words by Lou Salomé), with an introduction by Mr. Ludovici, a note to the poetry by Dr. Levy, and a reproduction of Karl Donndorf's bust of Nietzsche.

XVIII. Index.

The student who would read Nietzsche had better begin with one of the aphoristic books, preferably "The Dawn of Day." From that let him proceed to "Beyond Good and Evil, " "The Genealogy of Morals" and "The

Antichrist." He will then be ready to understand "Thus Spake Zarathustra." Later on he may read "Ecce Homo" and dip into "The Joyful Wisdom, " "Human All-Too Human" and "The Will to Power, " as his fancy suggests. The Wagner pamphlets are of more importance to Wagnerians than to students of Nietzsche's ideas, and the early philological and critical essays have lost much of their interest by the passage of time. Nietzsche's poetry had better be avoided by all who cannot read it in the original German. The English translations are mostly very free and seldom satisfactory.

Of the larger Nietzschean commentaries in English the best is "Friedrich Nietzsche: His Life and Work, " by M. A. Mügge. Appended to it is a bibliography of 850 titles—striking evidence of the attention that Nietzsche's ideas have gained in the world. Other books that will be found useful are "The Quintessence of Nietzsche, " by J. M. Kennedy; "Nietzsche: His Life and Works, " by Anthony M. Ludovici; "The Gospel of Superman, " by Henri Lichtenberger, translated from the French by J. M. Kennedy; "The Philosophy of Nietzsche, " by Georges Chatterton-Hill, and "The Philosophy of Friedrich Nietzsche, " by Grace Neal Dolson, Ph. D., this last a pioneer work of permanent value. Lesser studies are to be found in "Friedrich Nietzsche, " by A. R. Orage; "Nietzsche as Critic, Philosopher, Poet and Prophet, " by Thomas Common; "Friedrich Nietzsche and His New Gospel, " by Emily S. Hamblen, and "Nietzsche, " by Paul Elmer More. Interesting discussions of various Nietzschean ideas are in "The Revival of Aristocracy, " by Dr. Oscar Levy; "Who is to be Master of the World?" by A. M. Ludovici; "On the Tracks of Life, " by Leo G. Sera, translated from the Italian by J. M. Kennedy; "Nietzsche and Art, " by A. M. Ludovici, and "The Mastery of Life, " by G. T. Wrench. Selections from Nietzsche's writings are put together under subject headings in "Nietzsche in Outline and Aphorism, " by A. R. Orage; "Nietzsche: His Maxims, " by J. M. Kennedy, and "The Gist of Nietzsche, " by H. L. Mencken. An elaborate and invaluable summary of all Nietzsche's writings, book by book, is to be found in "What Nietzsche Taught, " by Willard H. Wright. This volume, the fruit of very diligent labor, is admirably concise and well-ordered.

The standard biography of Nietzsche is "*Das Leben Friedrich Nietzsches*" by Frau Förster-Nietzsche, a large work in three volumes. In 1911 Frau Förster-Nietzsche prepared a shorter version and this has since been done into English by A. M. Ludovici, and published in two volumes, under the title of "The Life of Nietzsche." Unluckily, so devoted a sister was not the best person to deal with certain episodes in the life of her brother and hero. The gaps she left and the ameliorations she attempted are filled and corrected in "The Life of Friedrich Nietzsche, " by Daniel Halévy, translated from the French by J. M. Hone, with an extraordinarily brilliant introduction by T. M. Kettle, M. P.

Small but suggestive studies of Nietzsche and his ideas are to be found in "Egoists, " "Mezzotints in Modern Music, " and "The Pathos of Distance, " by James Huneker; "Degeneration, " by Max Nordau; "Affirmations, " by Havelock Ellis; "Aristocracy and Evolution, " by W. H. Mallock; "Heretics" and "Orthodoxy, " by G. K. Chesterton; "Lectures and Essays on Natural Theology, " by William Wallace; "Heralds of Revolt, " by William Barry, D. D.; "Essays in Sociology, " by J. M. Robertson; "The Larger Aspects of Socialism, " by William English Walling; "Three Modern Seers, " by Mrs. Havelock Ellis; "Slaves to Duty, " by J. Badcock; "In Peril of Change, " by C. F. G. Masterman; "Man's Place in the Cosmos, " by A. Seth Pringle Pattison; and "Gospels of Anarchy, " by Vernon Lee (Violet Paget). George Bernard Shaw's variations upon Nietzschean themes are in "The Revolutionist's Handbook, " appended to "Man and Superman." Of magazine articles dealing with the prophet of the superman there has been no end of late. Most of them are worthless, but any bearing the name of Grace Neal Dolson, Thomas Common, Thomas Stockham Baker or Maude D. Petre may be read with profit. One of the best discussions of Nietzsche I have ever encountered was contributed to the *Catholic World* during December, 1905, and January, February, March, May and June, 1906, by Miss Petre. It is to be regretted that these excellent papers, which sought to rescue Nietzsche from the misunderstandings of Christian critics, have not been re-printed in book-form.

THE END

BOOK FOUR.
A BOOK OF BURLESQUES

The present edition includes some epigrams from "A Little Book in C Major, " now out of print. To make room for them several of the smaller sketches in the first edition have been omitted. Nearly the whole contents of the book appeared originally in *The Smart Set*. The references to a Europe not yet devastated by war and an America not yet polluted by Prohibition show that some of the pieces first saw print in far better days than these.

H. L. M.

February 1, 1920.

I.—DEATH
I.—Death. A Philosophical Discussion

The back parlor of any average American home. The blinds are drawn and a single gas-jet burns feebly. A dim suggestion of festivity: strange chairs, the table pushed back, a decanter and glasses. A heavy, suffocating, discordant scent of flowers—roses, carnations, lilies, gardenias. A general stuffiness and mugginess, as if it were raining outside, which it isn't.

A door leads into the front parlor. It is open, and through it the flowers may be seen. They are banked about a long black box with huge nickel handles, resting upon two folding horses. Now and then a man comes into the front room from the street door, his shoes squeaking hideously. Sometimes there is a woman, usually in deep mourning. Each visitor approaches the long black box, looks into it with ill-concealed repugnance, snuffles softly, and then backs of toward the door. A clock on the mantel-piece ticks loudly. From the street come the usual noises—a wagon rattling, the clang of a trolley car's gong, the shrill cry of a child.

In the back parlor six pallbearers sit upon chairs, all of them bolt upright, with their hands on their knees. They are in their Sunday clothes, with stiff white shirts. Their hats are on the floor beside their chairs. Each wears upon his lapel the gilt badge of a fraternal order, with a crêpe rosette. In the gloom they are indistinguishable; all of them talk in the same strained, throaty whisper. Between their

552

remarks they pause, clear their throats, blow their noses, and shuffle in their chairs. They are intensely uncomfortable. Tempo: Adagio lamentoso, with occasionally a rise to andante maesto. So:

FIRST PALLBEARER

Who woulda thought that *he* woulda been the next?

SECOND PALLBEARER

Yes; you never can tell.

THIRD PALLBEARER

(*An oldish voice, oracularly.*) We're here to-day and gone to-morrow.

FOURTH PALLBEARER

I seen him no longer ago than Chewsday. He never looked no better. Nobody would have——

FIFTH PALLBEARER

I seen him Wednesday. We had a glass of beer together in the Huffbrow Kaif. He was laughing and cutting up like he always done.

SIXTH PALLBEARER

You never know who it's gonna hit next. Him and me was pallbearers together for Hen Jackson no more than a month ago, or say five weeks.

FIRST PALLBEARER

Well, a man is lucky if he goes off quick. If I had *my* way I wouldn't want no better way.

SECOND PALLBEARER

My brother John went thataway. He dropped like a stone, settin' there at the supper table. They had to take his knife out of his hand.

THIRD PALLBEARER

I had an uncle to do the same thing, but without the knife. He had what they call appleplexy. It runs in my family.

FOURTH PALLBEARER

They say it's in *his'n*, too.

FIFTH PALLBEARER

But he never looked it.

SIXTH PALLBEARER

No. Nobody woulda thought *he* woulda been the next.

FIRST PALLBEARER

Them are the things you never can tell anything about.

SECOND PALLBEARER

Ain't it true!

THIRD PALLBEARER

We're here to-day and gone to-morrow.

(*A pause. Feet are shuffled. Somewhere a door bangs.*)

FOURTH PALLBEARER

(*Brightly.*) He looks elegant. I hear he never suffered none.

FIFTH PALLBEARER

No; he went too quick. One minute he was alive and the next minute he was dead.

SIXTH PALLBEARER

Think of it: dead so quick!

FIRST PALLBEARER

Gone!

SECOND PALLBEARER

Passed away!

THIRD PALLBEARER

Well, we all have to go *some* time.

FOURTH PALLBEARER

Yes; a man never knows but what his turn'll come next.

FIFTH PALLBEARER

You can't tell nothing by looks. Them sickly fellows generally lives to be old.

SIXTH PALLBEARER

Yes; the doctors say it's the big stout person that goes off the soonest. They say typhord never kills none but the healthy.

FIRST PALLBEARER

So I have heered it said. My wife's youngest brother weighed 240 pounds. He was as strong as a mule. He could lift a sugar-barrel, and then some. Once I seen him drink damn near a whole keg of beer. Yet it finished him in less'n three weeks—and *he* had it mild.

SECOND PALLBEARER

It seems that there's a lot of it this fall.

THIRD PALLBEARER

Yes; I hear of people taken with it every day. Some say it's the water. My brother Sam's oldest is down with it.

FOURTH PALLBEARER

I had it myself once. I was out of my head for four weeks.

FIFTH PALLBEARER

That's a good sign.

SIXTH PALLBEARER

Yes; you don't die as long as you're out of your head.

FIRST PALLBEARER

It seems to me that there is a lot of sickness around this year.

SECOND PALLBEARER

I been to five funerals in six weeks.

THIRD PALLBEARER

I beat you. I been to six in five weeks, not counting this one.

FOURTH PALLBEARER

A body don't hardly know what to think of it scarcely.

FIFTH PALLBEARER

That.rss what *I* always say: you can't tell who'll be next.

SIXTH PALLBEARER

Ain't it true! Just think of *him.*

FIRST PALLBEARER

Yes; nobody woulda picked *him* out.

SECOND PALLBEARER

Nor my brother John, neither.

THIRD PALLBEARER

Well, what *must* be *must* be.

FOURTH PALLBEARER

Yes; it don't do no good to kick. When a man's time comes he's got to go.

FIFTH PALLBEARER

We're lucky if it ain't us.

SIXTH PALLBEARER

So I always say. We ought to be thankful.

FIRST PALLBEARER

That's the way *I* always feel about it.

SECOND PALLBEARER

It wouldn't do *him* no good, no matter *what* we done.

THIRD PALLBEARER

We're here to-day and gone to-morrow.

FOURTH PALLBEARER

But it's hard all the same.

FIFTH PALLBEARER

It's hard on *her*.

SIXTH PALLBEARER

Yes, it is. Why should *he* go?

FIRST PALLBEARER

It's a question nobody ain't ever answered.

SECOND PALLBEARER

Nor never won't.

THIRD PALLBEARER

You're right there. I talked to a preacher about it once, and even *he* couldn't give no answer to it.

FOURTH PALLBEARER

The more you think about it the less you can make it out.

FIFTH PALLBEARER

When I seen him last Wednesday he had no more ideer of it than what you had.

SIXTH PALLBEARER

Well, if I had *my* choice, that's the way I would always want to die.

FIRST PALLBEARER

Yes; that's what *I* say. I am with you there.

SECOND PALLBEARER

Yes; you're right, both of you. It don't do no good to lay sick for months, with doctors' bills eatin' you up, and then have to go anyhow.

THIRD PALLBEARER

No; when a thing has to be done, the best thing to do is to get it done and over with.

FOURTH PALLBEARER

That's just what I said to my wife when I heerd.

FIFTH PALLBEARER

But nobody hardly thought that *he* woulda been the next.

SIXTH PALLBEARER

No; but that's one of them things you can't tell.

FIRST PALLBEARER

You never know *who'll* be the next.

SECOND PALLBEARER

It's lucky you don't.

THIRD PALLBEARER

I guess you're right.

FOURTH PALLBEARER

That's what my grandfather used to say: you never know what is coming.

FIFTH PALLBEARER

Yes; that's the way it goes.

SIXTH PALLBEARER

First one, and then somebody else.

FIRST PALLBEARER

Who it'll be you can't say.

SECOND PALLBEARER

I always say the same: we're here to-day——

THIRD PALLBEARER

(*Cutting in jealousy and humorously.*) And to-morrow we ain't here.

(*A subdued and sinister snicker. It is followed by sudden silence. There is a shuffling of feet in the front room, and whispers. Necks are craned. The pallbearers straighten their backs, hitch their coat collars and pull on their black gloves. The clergyman has arrived. From above comes the sound of weeping.*)

II.—FROM THE PROGRAMME OF A CONCERT

"Ruhm und Ewigkeit" (Fame and Eternity), a symphonic poem in B flat minor, Opus 48, by Johann Sigismund Timotheus Albert Wolfgang Kraus (1872-).

Kraus, like his eminent compatriot, Dr. Richard Strauss, has gone to Friedrich Nietzsche, the laureate of the modern German tone-art, for his inspiration in this gigantic work. His text is to be found in Nietzsche's *Ecce Homo*, which was not published until after the poet's death, but the composition really belongs to *Also sprach Zarathustra*, as a glance will show:

I

Wie lange sitzest du schonauf deinem Missgeschick?Gieb Acht! Du brütest mir nochein Ei, ein Basilisken-Ei, aus deinem langen Jammer aus.

II

Was schleicht Zarathustra entlang dem Berge?—

III

Misstrauisch, geschwürig, düster, ein langer Lauerer, —aber plötzlich, ein Blitz, hell, furchtbar, ein Schlaggen Himmel aus dem Abgrund:—dem Berge selber schüttelt sichdas Eingeweide....

IV

Wo Hass und BlitzstrahlEins ward, ein Fluch, —auf den Bergen haust jetzt Zarathustra's Zorn, eine Wetterwolke schleicht er seines Wegs.

V

Verkrieche sich, wer eine letzte Decke hat!In's Bett mit euch, ihr Zärtlinge!Nun rollen Donner über die Gewölbe, nun zittert, was Gebälk und Mauer ist, nun zucken Blitze und schwefelgelbe Wahrheiten—Zarathustra flucht ...!

For the following faithful and graceful translation the present commentator is indebted to Mr. Louis Untermeyer:

I

How long brood you nowOn thy disaster?Give heed! You hatch me soonAn egg, From your long lamentation out of.

II

Why prowls Zarathustra among the mountains?

III

Distrustful, ulcerated, dismal, A long waiter—But suddenly a flash, Brilliant, fearful. A lightning strokeLeaps to heaven from the abyss:—The mountains shake themselves andTheir intestines....

IV

As hate and lightning-flashAre united, a *curse!*On the mountains rages now Zarathustra's wrath, Like a thunder cloud rolls it on its way.

V

Crawl away, ye who have a roof remaining!To bed with you, ye tenderlings!Now thunder rolls over the great arches, Now tremble the bastions and battlements, Now flashes palpitate and sulphur-yellow truths—Zarathustra swears ...!

The composition is scored for three flutes, one piccolo, one bass piccolo, seven oboes, one English horn, three clarinets in D flat, one clarinet in G flat, one corno de bassetto, three bassoons, one contra-bassoon, eleven horns, three trumpets, eight cornets in B, four trombones, two alto trombones, one viol da gamba, one mandolin, two guitars, one banjo, two tubas, glockenspiel, bell, triangle, fife, bass-drum, cymbals, timpani, celesta, four harps, piano, harmonium, pianola, phonograph, and the usual strings.

At the opening a long B flat is sounded by the cornets, clarinets and bassoons in unison, with soft strokes upon a kettle-drum tuned to G sharp. After eighteen measures of this, *singhiozzando*, the strings enter *pizzicato* with a figure based upon one of the scales of the ancient Persians—B flat, C flat, D, E sharp, G and A flat—which starts high among the first violins, and then proceeds downward, through the second violins, violas and cellos, until it is lost in solemn and indistinct mutterings in the double-basses. Then, the atmosphere of doom having been established, and the conductor having found his place in the score, there is heard the motive of brooding, or as the German commentators call it, the *Quälerei Motiv*:

The opening chord of the eleventh is sounded by six horns, and the chords of the ninth, which follow, are given to the woodwind. The rapid figure in the second measure is for solo violin, heard softly against the sustained interval of the diminished ninth, but the final G natural is snapped out by the whole orchestra *forzando*. There follows a rapid and daring development of the theme, with the flutes and violoncellos leading, first harmonized with chords of the eleventh, then with chords of the thirteenth, and finally with chords of the fifteenth. Meanwhile, the tonality has moved into D minor, then into A flat major, and then into G sharp minor, and the little arpeggio for the solo violin has been augmented to seven, to eleven, and in the end to twenty-three notes. Here the influence of Claude Debussy shows itself; the chords of the ninth proceed by the same chromatic semitones that one finds in the *Chansons de Bilitis*. But Kraus goes much further than Debussy, for the tones of his chords are constantly altered in a strange and extremely beautiful manner, and, as has been noted, he adds the eleventh, thirteenth and fifteenth. At the end of this incomparable passage there is a sudden drop to C major, followed by the first statement of the *Missgeschick Motiv*, or motive of disaster (misfortune, evil destiny, untoward fate):

This graceful and ingratiating theme will give no concern to the student of Ravel and Schoenberg. It is, in fact, a quite elemental succession of intervals of the second, all produced by adding the ninth to the common chord—thus: C, G, C, D, E—with certain enharmonic changes. Its simplicity gives it, at a first hearing, a placid, pastoral aspect, somewhat disconcerting to the literalist, but the discerning will not fail to note the mutterings beneath the surface. It is first sounded by two violas and the viol da gamba, and then drops without change to the bass, where it is repeated *fortissimo* by two bassoons and the contra-bassoon. The tempo then quickens and the two themes so far heard are worked up into a brief but tempestuous fugue. A brief extract will suffice to show its enormously complex nature:

A pedal point on B flat is heard at the end of this fugue, sounded *fortissimo* by all the brass in unison, and then follows a grand pause, twelve and a half measures in length. Then, in the strings, is heard the motive of warning:

Out of this motive comes the harmonic material for much of what remains of the composition. At each repetition of the theme, the chord in the fourth measure is augmented by the addition of another interval, until in the end it includes every tone of the chromatic scale save C sharp. This omission is significant of Kraus' artistry. If C sharp were included the tonality would at once become vague, but without it the dependence of the whole gorgeous edifice upon C major is kept plain. At the end, indeed, the tonic chord of C major is clearly sounded by the wood-wind, against curious triplets, made up of F sharp, A flat and B flat in various combinations, in the strings; and from it a sudden modulation is made to C minor, and then to A flat major. This opens the way for the entrance of the motive of lamentation, or, as the German commentators call it, the *Schreierei Motiv*:

This simple and lovely theme is first sounded, not by any of the usual instruments of the grand orchestra, but by a phonograph in B flat, with the accompaniment of a solitary trombone. When the composition was first played at the Gewandhaus in Leipzig the innovation caused a sensation, and there were loud cries of sacrilege and even proposals of police action. One indignant classicist, in token of his ire, hung a wreath of *Knackwürste* around the neck of the bust of Johann Sebastian Bach in the Thomaskirche, and appended to it a card bearing the legend, *Schweinehund!* But the exquisite beauty of the effect soon won acceptance for the means employed to attain it, and the phonograph has so far made its way with German composers that Prof. Ludwig Grossetrommel, of Göttingen, has even proposed its employment in opera in place of singers.

This motive of lamentation is worked out on a grand scale, and in intimate association with the motives of brooding and of warning. Kraus is not content with the ordinary materials of composition. His creative force is always impelling him to break through the fetters of the diatonic scale, and to find utterance for his ideas in archaic and extremely exotic tonalities. The pentatonic scale is a favorite with him; he employs it as boldly as Wagner did in *Das Rheingold*. But it is not enough, for he proceeds from it into the Dorian mode of the ancient Greeks, and then into the Phrygian, and then into two of the plagal modes. Moreover, he constantly combines both unrelated scales and antagonistic motives, and invests the combinations in astounding orchestral colors, so that the hearer, unaccustomed to such bold experimentations, is quite lost in the maze. Here, for example, is a characteristic passage for solo French horn and bass piccolo:

The dotted half notes for the horn obviously come from the motive of brooding, in augmentation, but the bass piccolo part is new. It soon appears, however, in various fresh aspects, and in the end it enters into the famous quadruple motive of "sulphur-yellow truth"— *schwefelgelbe Wahrheit*, as we shall presently see. Its first combination is with a jaunty figure in A minor, and the two together form what most of the commentators agree upon denominating the Zarathustra motive:

I call this the Zarathustra motive, following the weight of critical opinion, but various influential critics dissent. Thus, Dr. Ferdinand Bierfisch, of the Hochschule für Musik at Dresden, insists that it is the theme of "the elevated mood produced by the spiritual isolation and low barometric pressure of the mountains, " while Prof. B. Moll, of Frankfurt a/M., calls it the motive of prowling. Kraus himself, when asked by Dr. Fritz Bratsche, of the Berlin *Volkszeitung*, shrugged his shoulders and answered in his native Hamburg dialect, "*So gehts im Leben! 'S giebt gar kein Use*"—Such is life; it gives hardly any use (to inquire?). In much the same way Schubert made reply to one who asked the meaning of the opening subject of the slow movement of his C major symphony: "*Halt's Maul, du verfluchter Narr!*"—Don't ask such question, my dear sir!

But whatever the truth, the novelty and originality of the theme cannot be denied, for it is in two distinct keys, D major and A minor, and they preserve their identity whenever it appears. The handling of two such diverse tonalities at one time would present insuperable difficulties to a composer less ingenious than Kraus, but he manages it quite simply by founding his whole harmonic scheme upon the tonic triad of D major, with the seventh and ninth added. He thus achieves a chord which also contains the tonic triad of A minor. The same thing is now done with the dominant triads, and half the battle is won. Moreover, the instrumentation shows the same boldness, for the double theme is first given to three solo violins, and they are muted in a novel and effective manner by stopping their F holes. The directions in the score say *mit Glaserkitt* (that is, with glazier's putty), but the Konzertmeister at the Gewandhaus, Herr F. Dur, substituted ordinary pumpernickel with excellent results. It is, in fact, now commonly used in the German orchestras in place of putty, for it does less injury to the varnish of the violins, and, besides, it is edible after use. It produces a thick, oily, mysterious, far-away effect.

At the start, as I have just said, the double theme of Zarathustra appears in D major and A minor, but there is quick modulation to B flat major and C sharp minor, and then to C major and F sharp minor. Meanwhile the tempo gradually accelerates, and the polyphonic texture is helped out by reminiscences of the themes of brooding and of lamentation. A sudden hush and the motive of warning is heard high in the wood-wind, in C flat major, against a double organ-point—C natural and C sharp—in the lower strings. There follows a cadenza of no less than eighty-four measures for four harps, tympani and a single tuba, and then the motive of waiting is given out by the whole orchestra in unison:

This stately motive is repeated in F major, after which some passage work for the piano and pianola, the former tuned a quarter tone lower than the latter and played by three performers, leads directly into the quadruple theme of the sulphur-yellow truth, mentioned above. It is first given out by two oboes divided, a single English horn, two bassoons in unison, and four trombones in unison. It is an extraordinarily long motive, running to twenty-seven measures on its first appearance; the four opening measures are given on the next page.

With an exception yet to be noted, all of the composer's thematic material is now set forth, and what follows is a stupendous development of it, so complex that no written description could even faintly indicate its character. The quadruple theme of the sulphur-yellow truth is sung almost uninterruptedly, first by the wood-wind, then by the strings and then by the full brass choir, with the glockenspiel and cymbals added. Into it are woven all of the other themes in inextricable whirls and whorls of sound, and in most amazing combinations and permutations of tonalities. Moreover, there is a constantly rising complexity of rhythm, and on one page of the score the time signature is changed no less than eighteen times. Several times it is 5-8 and 7-4; once it is 11-2; in one place the composer, following Koechlin and Erik Satie, abandons bar-lines altogether for half a page of the score. And these diverse rhythms are not always merely successive; sometimes they are heard together. For example, the motive of disaster, augmented to 5-8 time, is sounded clearly by the clarinets against the motive of lamentation in 3-4 time, and through it all one hears the steady beat of the motive of waiting in 4-4!

This gigantic development of materials is carried to a thrilling climax, with the whole orchestra proclaiming the Zarathustra motive *fortissimo*. Then follows a series of arpeggios for the harps, made of the motive of warning, and out of them there gradually steals the tonic triad of D minor, sung by three oboes. This chord constitutes the backbone of all that follows. The three oboes are presently joined by a fourth. Against this curtain of tone the flutes and piccolos repeat the theme of brooding in F major, and then join the oboes in the D minor chord. The horns and bassoons follow with the motive of disaster and then do likewise. Now come the violins with the motive of lamentation, but instead of ending with the D minor tonic triad, they sound a chord of the seventh erected on C sharp as seventh of D minor. Every tone of the scale of D minor is now being sounded, and as instrument after instrument joins in the effect is indescribably sonorous and imposing. Meanwhile, there is a steady *crescendo*, ending after three minutes of truly tremendous music with ten sharp blasts of the double chord. A moment of silence and a single trombone gives out a theme hitherto not heard. It is the theme of tenderness, or, as the German commentators call it, the *Biermad'l Motiv*: Thus:

Again silence. Then a single piccolo plays the closing cadence of the composition:

Ruhm und Ewigkeit presents enormous difficulties to the performers, and taxes the generalship of the most skillful conductor. When it was in preparation at the Gewandhaus the first performance was postponed twelve times in order to extend the rehearsals. It was reported in the German papers at the time that ten members of the orchestra, including the first flutist, Ewald Löwenhals, resigned during the rehearsals, and that the intervention of the King of Saxony was necessary to make them reconsider their resignations. One of the second violins, Hugo Zehndaumen, resorted to stimulants in anticipation of the opening performance, and while on his way to the hall was run over by a taxicab. The conductor was Nikisch. A performance at Munich followed, and on May 1, 1913, the work reached

Berlin. At the public rehearsal there was a riot led by members of the Bach Gesellschaft, and the hall was stormed by the mounted police. Many arrests were made, and five of the rioters were taken to hospital with serious injuries. The work was put into rehearsal by the Boston Symphony Orchestra in 1914. The rehearsals have been proceeding ever since. A piano transcription for sixteen hands has been published.

Kraus was born at Hamburg on January 14, 1872. At the age of three he performed creditably on the zither, cornet and trombone, and by 1877 he had already appeared in concert at Danzig. His family was very poor, and his early years were full of difficulties. It is said that, at the age of nine, he copied the whole score of Wagner's *Ring*, the scores of the nine Beethoven symphonies and the complete works of Mozart. His regular teacher, in those days, was Stadtpfeifer Schmidt, who instructed him in piano and thorough-bass. In 1884, desiring to have lessons in counterpoint from Prof. Kalbsbraten, of Mainz, he walked to that city from Hamburg once a week—a distance for the round trip of 316 miles. In 1887 he went to Berlin and became fourth cornetist of the Philharmonic Orchestra and valet to Dr. Schweinsrippen, the conductor. In Berlin he studied violin and second violin under the Polish virtuoso, Pbyschbrweski, and also had lessons in composition from Wilhelm Geigenheimer, formerly third triangle and assistant librarian at Bayreuth.

His first composition, a march for cornet, violin and piano, was performed on July 18, 1888, at the annual ball of the Arbeiter Liedertafel in Berlin. It attracted little attention, but six months later the young composer made musical Berlin talk about him by producing a composition called *Adenoids*, for twelve tenors, *a cappella*, to words by Otto Julius Bierbaum. This was first heard at an open air concert given in the Tiergarten by the Sozialist Liederkranz. It was soon after repeated by the choir of the Gottesgelehrheitsakademie, and Kraus found himself a famous young man. His string quartet in G sharp minor, first played early in 1889 by the quartet led by Prof. Rudolph Wurst, added to his growing celebrity, and when his first tone poem for orchestra, *Fuchs, Du Hast die Gans Gestohlen*, was done by the Philharmonic in the autumn of 1889, under Dr. Lachschinken, it was hailed with acclaim.

Kraus has since written twelve symphonies (two choral), nine tone-poems, a suite for brass and tympani, a trio for harp, tuba and glockenspiel, ten string quartettes, a serenade for flute and contra-bassoon, four concert overtures, a cornet concerto, and many songs and piano pieces. His best-known work, perhaps, is his symphony in F flat major, in eight movements. But Kraus himself is said to regard this huge work as trivial. His own favorite, according to his biographer, Dr. Linsensuppe, is *Ruhm und Ewigkeit*, though he is also fond of the tone-poem which immediately preceded it, *Rinderbrust und Meerrettig*. He has written a choral for sixty trombones, dedicated to Field Marshal von Hindenburg, and is said to be at work on a military mass for four orchestras, seven brass bands and ten choirs, with the usual soloists and clergy. Among his principal works are *Der Ewigen Wiederkunft* (a ten part fugue for full orchestra), *Biergemütlichkeit*, his*Oberkellner* and *Uebermensch* concert overtures, and his setting (for mixed chorus) of the old German hymn:

Saufst—stirbst!Saufst net—stirbst a!Also, saufst!

Kraus is now a resident of Munich, where he conducts the orchestra at the Löwenbräuhaus. He has been married eight times and is at present the fifth husband of Tilly Heintz, the opera singer. He has been decorated by the Kaiser, by the King of Sweden and by the Sultan of Turkey, and is a member of the German Odd Fellows.

III.—The Wedding. A Stage Direction

The scene is a church in an American city of about half a million population, and the time is about eleven o'clock of a fine morning in early spring. The neighborhood is well-to-do, but not quite fashionable. That is to say, most of the families of the vicinage keep two servants (alas, more or less intermittently!), and eat dinner at half-past six, and about one in every four boasts a colored butler (who attends to the fires, washes windows and helps with the sweeping), and a last year's automobile. The heads of these families are merchandise brokers; jobbers in notions, hardware and drugs; manufacturers of candy, hats, badges, office furniture, blank books, picture frames, wire goods and patent medicines; managers of steamboat lines; district agents of insurance companies; owners of commercial printing offices, and other such business men of substance—and the prosperous lawyers and popular family doctors who keep them out of trouble. In one block live a Congressman and two college professors, one of whom has written an unimportant textbook and got himself into "Who's Who in America." In the block above lives a man who once ran for Mayor of the city, and came near being elected.

The wives of these householders wear good clothes and have a liking for a reasonable gayety, but very few of them can pretend to what is vaguely called social standing, and, to do them justice, not many of them waste any time lamenting it. They have, taking one with another, about three children apiece, and are good mothers. A few of them belong to women's clubs or flirt with the suffragettes, but the majority can get all of the intellectual stimulation they crave in the Ladies' Home Journal and the Saturday Evening Post, with Vogue added for its fashions. Most of them, deep down in their hearts, suspect their husbands of secret frivolity, and about ten per cent. have the proofs, but it is rare for them to make rows about it, and the divorce rate among them is thus very low. Themselves indifferent cooks, they are unable to teach their servants the art, and so the food they set before their husbands and children is often such as would make a Frenchman cut his throat. But they are diligent housewives otherwise; they see to it that the windows are washed, that no one tracks mud into the hall, that the servants do not waste coal, sugar, soap and gas, and that the family buttons are always sewed on. In religion these estimable wives are pious in habit but somewhat nebulous in faith. That is to say, they regard any person who specifically refuses to go to church as a heathen, but they themselves are by no means regular in attendance, and not one in ten of them could tell you whether transubstantiation is a Roman Catholic or a Dunkard doctrine. About two per cent. have dallied more or less gingerly with Christian Science, their average period of belief being one year.

The church we are in is like the neighborhood and its people: well-to-do but not fashionable. It is Protestant in faith and probably Episcopalian. The pews are of thick, yellow-brown oak, severe in pattern and hideous in color. In each there is a long, removable cushion of a dark, purplish, dirty hue, with here and there some of its hair stuffing showing. The stained-glass windows, which were all bought ready-made and depict scenes from the New Testament, commemorate the virtues of departed worthies of the neighborhood, whose names appear, in illegible black letters, in the lower panels. The floor is covered with a carpet of some tough, fibrous material, apparently a sort of grass, and along the center aisle it is much worn. The normal smell of the place is rather less unpleasant than that of most other halls, for on the one day when it is regularly crowded practically all of the persons gathered together have been very recently bathed.

On this fine morning, however, it is full of heavy, mortuary perfumes, for a couple of florist's men have just finished decorating the chancel with flowers and potted palms. Just behind the chancel rail, facing the center aisle, there is a prie-dieu, and to either side of it are great banks of lilies, carnations, gardenias and roses. Three or four feet behind the prie-dieu and completely concealing the high altar, there is a dense jungle of palms. Those in the front rank are authentically growing in pots, but behind them the florist's men have artfully placed some more durable, and hence more profitable, sophistications. Anon the rev. clergyman, emerging from the vestry-room to the right, will pass along the front of this jungle to the prie-dieu, and so, framed in flowers, face the congregation with his saponaceous smile.

The florist's men, having completed their labors, are preparing to depart. The older of the two, a man in the fifties, shows the ease of an experienced hand by taking out a large plug of tobacco and gnawing off a substantial chew. The desire to spit seizing him shortly, he proceeds to gratify it by a trick long practised by gasfitters, musicians, caterer's helpers, piano movers and other such alien invaders of the domestic hearth. That is to say, he hunts for a place where the carpet is loose along the chancel rail, finds it where two lengths join, deftly turns up a flap, spits upon the bare floor, and then lets the flap fall back, finally giving it a pat with the sole of his foot. This done, he and his assistant leave the church to the sexton, who has been sweeping the vestibule, and, after passing the time of day with the two men who are putting up a striped awning from the door to the curb, disappear into a nearby speak-easy, there to wait and refresh themselves until the wedding is over, and it is time to take away their lilies, their carnations and their synthetic palms.

It is now a quarter past eleven, and two flappers of the neighborhood, giggling and arm-in-arm, approach the sexton and inquire of him if they may enter. He asks them if they have tickets and when they say they haven't, he tells them that he ain't got no right to let them in, and don't know nothing about what the rule is going to be. At some weddings, he goes on, hardly nobody ain't allowed in, but then again, sometimes they don't scarcely look at the tickets at all. The two flappers retire abashed, and as the sexton finishes his sweeping, there enters the organist.

The organist is a tall, thin man of melancholy, uræmic aspect, wearing a black slouch hat with a wide brim and a yellow overcoat that barely reaches to his knees. A pupil, in his youth, of a man who had once studied (irregularly and briefly) with Charles-Marie Widor, he acquired thereby the artistic temperament, and with it a vast fondness for malt liquor. His mood this morning is acidulous and depressed, for he spent yesterday evening in a Pilsner ausschank with two former members of the Boston Symphony Orchestra, and it was 3 A. M. before they finally agreed that Johann Sebastian Bach, all things considered, was a greater man than Beethoven, and so parted amicably. Sourness is the precise sensation that wells within him. He feels vinegary; his blood runs cold; he wishes he could immerse himself in bicarbonate of soda. But the call of his art is more potent than the protest of his poisoned and quaking liver, and so he manfully climbs the spiral stairway to his organ-loft.

Once there, he takes off his hat and overcoat, stoops down to blow the dust off the organ keys, throws the electrical switch which sets the bellows going, and then proceeds to take off his shoes. This done, he takes his seat, reaches for the pedals with his stockinged feet, tries an experimental 32-foot CCC, and then wanders gently into a Bach toccata. It is his limbering-up piece: he always plays it as a prelude to a wedding job. It thus goes very smoothly and even brilliantly, but when he comes to the end of it and tackles the ensuing fugue he is quickly in difficulties, and after four or five stumbling repetitions of the subject he hurriedly improvises a crude coda and has done. Peering down into the church to see if his flounderings have had an audience, he sees two old maids enter, the one very tall and thin and the other somewhat brisk and bunchy.

They constitute the vanguard of the nuptial throng, and as they proceed hesitatingly up the center aisle, eager for good seats but afraid to go too far, the organist wipes his palms upon his trousers legs, squares his shoulders, and plunges into the program that he has played at all weddings for fifteen years past. It begins with Mendelssohn's Spring Song, pianissimo. Then comes Rubinstein's Melody in F, with a touch of forte toward the close, and then Nevin's "Oh, That We Two Were Maying" and then the Chopin waltz in A flat, Opus 69, No. 1, and then the Spring Song again, and then a free fantasia upon "The Rosary" and then a Moszkowski mazurka, and then the Dvořák Humoresque (with its heart-rending cry in the middle), and then some vague and turbulent thing (apparently the disjecta membra of another fugue), and then Tschaikowsky's "Autumn, " and then Elgar's "Salut d'Amour, " and then the Spring Song a third time, and then something or other from one of the Peer Gynt suites, and then an hurrah or two from the Hallelujah chorus, and then Chopin again, and Nevin, and Elgar, and—
—

But meanwhile, there is a growing activity below. First comes a closed automobile bearing the six ushers and soon after it another automobile bearing the bridegroom and his best man. The bridegroom and the best man disembark before the side entrance of the church and make their way into the vestry room, where they remove their hats and coats, and proceed to struggle with their cravats and collars before a mirror which hangs on the wall. The room is very dingy. A baize-covered table is in the center of it, and around the table stand six or eight chairs of assorted designs. One wall is completely covered by a bookcase, through the glass doors of which one may discern piles of cheap Bibles, hymn-books and back numbers of the parish magazine. In one corner is a small washstand. The best man takes a flat flask of whiskey from his pocket, looks about him for a glass, finds it on the washstand, rinses it at the tap, fills it with a policeman's drink, and hands it to the bridegroom. The latter downs it at a gulp. Then the best man pours out one for himself.

The ushers, reaching the vestibule of the church, have handed their silk hats to the sexton, and entered the sacred edifice. There was a rehearsal of the wedding last night, but after it was over the bride ordered certain incomprehensible changes in the plan, and the ushers are now completely at sea. All they know clearly is that the relatives of the bride are to be seated on one side and the relatives of the bridegroom on the other. But which side for one and which for the other? They discuss it heatedly for three minutes and then find that they stand three for putting the bride's relatives on the left side and three for putting them on the right side. The debate, though instructive, is interrupted by the sudden entrance of seven women in a group. They are headed by a truculent old battleship, possibly an aunt or something of the sort, who fixes the nearest usher with a knowing, suspicious glance, and motions to him to show her the way.

He offers her his right arm and they start up the center aisle, with the six other women following in irregular order, and the five other ushers scattered among the women. The leading usher is tortured damnably by doubts as to where the party should go. If they are aunts, to which house do they belong, and on which side are the members of that house to be seated? What if they are not aunts, but merely neighbors? Or perhaps an association of former cooks, parlor maids, nurse girls? Or strangers? The sufferings of the usher are relieved by the battleship, who halts majestically about twenty feet from the altar, and motions her followers into a pew to the left. They file in silently and she seats herself next the aisle. All seven settle back and wriggle for room. It is a tight fit.

(Who, in point of fact, are these ladies? Don't ask the question! The ushers never find out. No one ever finds out. They remain a joint mystery for all time. In the end they become a sort of tradition, and years hence, when two of the ushers meet, they will cackle over old dreadnaught and her six cruisers. The bride, grown old and fat, will tell the tale to her daughter, and then to her granddaughter. It will grow more and more strange, marvelous, incredible. Variorum versions will spring up. It will be adapted to other weddings. The dreadnaught will become an apparition, a witch, the Devil in skirts. And as the years pass, the date of the episode will be pushed back. By 2017 it will be dated 1150. By 2475 it will take on a sort of sacred character, and there will be a footnote referring to it in the latest Revised Version of the New Testament.)

It is now a quarter to twelve, and of a sudden the vestibule fills with wedding guests. Nine-tenths of them, perhaps even nineteen-twentieths, are women, and most of them are beyond thirty-five. Scattered among them, hanging on to their skirts, are about a dozen little girls—one of them a youngster of eight or thereabout, with spindle shanks and shining morning face, entranced by her first wedding. Here and there lurks a man. Usually he wears a hurried, unwilling, protesting look. He has been dragged from his office on a busy morning, forced to rush home and get into his cut-away coat, and then marched to the church by his wife. One of these men, much hustled, has forgotten to have his shoes shined. He is intensely conscious of them, and tries to hide them behind his wife's skirt as they walk up the aisle. Accidentally he steps upon it, and gets a look over the shoulder which lifts his diaphragm an inch and turns his liver to water. This man will be courtmartialed when he reaches home, and he knows it. He wishes that some foreign power would invade the United States and burn down all the churches in the country, and that the bride, the bridegroom and all the other persons interested in the present wedding were dead and in hell.

The ushers do their best to seat these wedding guests in some sort of order, but after a few minutes the crowd at the doors becomes so large that they have to give it up, and thereafter all they can do is to hold out their right arms ingratiatingly and trust to luck. One of them steps on a fat woman's skirt, tearing it very badly, and she has to be helped back to the vestibule. There she seeks refuge in a corner, under a stairway leading up to the steeple, and essays to repair the damage with pins produced from various nooks and crevices of her person. Meanwhile the guilty usher stands in front of her, mumbling apologies and trying to look helpful. When she finishes her work and emerges from her improvised dry-dock, he again offers her his arm, but she sweeps past him without noticing him, and proceeds grandly to a seat far forward. She is a cousin to the bride's mother, and will make a report to every branch of the family that all six ushers disgraced the ceremony by appearing at it far gone in liquor.

Fifteen minutes are consumed by such episodes and divertisements. By the time the clock in the steeple strikes twelve the church is well filled. The music of the organist, who has now reached Mendelssohn's Spring Song for the third and last time, is accompanied by a huge buzz of whispers, and there is much craning of necks and long-distance nodding and smiling. Here and there an unusually gorgeous hat is the target of many converging glances, and of as many more or less satirical criticisms. To the damp funeral smell of the flowers at the altar, there has been added the cacodorous scents of forty or fifty different brands of talcum and rice powder. It begins to grow warm in the church, and a number of women open their vanity bags and duck down for stealthy dabs at their noses. Others, more reverent, suffer the agony of augmenting shines. One, a trickster, has concealed powder in her pocket handkerchief, and applies it dexterously while pretending to blow her nose.

The bridegroom in the vestry-room, entering upon the second year (or is it the third?) of his long and ghastly wait, grows increasingly nervous, and when he hears the organist pass from the Spring Song into some more sonorous and stately thing he mistakes it for the wedding march from "Lohengrin, " and is hot for marching upon the altar at once. The best man, an old hand, restrains him gently, and administers another sedative from the bottle. The bridegroom's thoughts turn to gloomy things. He remembers sadly that he will never be able to laugh at benedicts again; that his days of low, rabelaisian wit and care-free scoffing are over; that he is now the very thing he mocked so gaily but yesteryear. Like a drowning man, he passes his whole life in review—not, however, that part which is past, but that part which is to come. Odd fancies throng upon him. He wonders what his honeymoon will cost him, what there will be to drink at the wedding breakfast, what a certain girl in Chicago will say when she hears of his marriage. Will there be any children? He rather hopes not, for all those he knows appear so greasy and noisy, but he decides that he might conceivably compromise on a boy. But how is he going to make sure that it will not be a girl? The thing, as yet, is a medical impossibility—but medicine is making rapid strides. Why not wait until the secret is discovered? This sapient compromise pleases the bridegroom, and he proceeds to a consideration of various problems of finance. And then, of a sudden, the organist swings unmistakably into "Lohengrin" and the best man grabs him by the arm.

There is now great excitement in the church. The bride's mother, two sisters, three brothers and three sisters-in-law have just marched up the center aisle and taken seats in the front pew, and all the women in the place are craning their necks toward the door. The usual electrical delay ensues. There is something the matter with the bride's train, and the two bridesmaids have a deuce of a time fixing it. Meanwhile the bride's father, in tight pantaloons and tighter gloves, fidgets and fumes in the vestibule, the six ushers crowd about him inanely, and the sexton rushes to and fro like a rat in a trap. Finally, all being ready, with the ushers formed two abreast, the sexton pushes a button, a small buzzer sounds in the organ loft, and the organist, as has been said, plunges magnificently into the fanfare of the "Lohengrin" march. Simultaneously the sexton opens the door at the bottom of the main aisle, and the wedding procession gets under weigh.

The bride and her father march first. Their step is so slow (about one beat to two measures) that the father has some difficulty in maintaining his equilibrium, but the bride herself moves steadily and erectly, almost seeming to float. Her face is thickly encrusted with talcum in its various forms, so that she is almost a dead white. She keeps her eyelids lowered modestly, but is still acutely aware of every glance fastened upon her—not in the mass, but every glance individually. For example, she sees clearly, even through her eyelids, the still, cold smile of a girl in Pew 8 R—a girl who once made an unwomanly attempt upon the bridegroom's affections, and was routed and put to flight by superior strategy. And her ears are open, too: she hears every "How sweet!" and "Oh, lovely!" and "Ain't she pale!" from the latitude of the last pew to the very glacis of the altar of God.

While she has thus made her progress up the hymeneal chute, the bridegroom and his best man have emerged from the vestryroom and begun the short march to the prie-dieu. They walk haltingly, clumsily, uncertainly, stealing occasional glances at the advancing bridal party. The bridegroom feels of his lower right-hand waistcoat pocket; the ring is still there. The best man wriggles his cuffs. No one, however, pays any heed to them. They are not even seen, indeed, until the bride and her father reach the open space in front of the altar. There the bride and the bridegroom find themselves standing side by side, but not a word is exchanged between them, nor even a look of recognition. They stand motionless, contemplating the ornate cushion at their feet, until the bride's father and the bridesmaids file to the left of the bride and the ushers, now wholly disorganized and imbecile, drape themselves in an irregular file along the altar rail. Then, the music having died down to a faint murmur and a hush having fallen upon the assemblage, they look up.

Before them, framed by foliage, stands the reverend gentleman of God who will presently link them in indissoluble chains—the estimable rector of the parish. He has got there just in time; it was, indeed, a close shave. But no trace of haste or of anything else of a disturbing character is now visible upon his smooth, glistening, somewhat feverish face. That face is wholly occupied by his official smile, a thing of oil and honey all compact, a balmy, unctuous illumination—the secret of his success in life. Slowly his cheeks puff out, gleaming like soap-bubbles. Slowly he lifts his prayer-book from the prie-dieu and holds it droopingly. Slowly his soft caressing eyes engage it. There is an almost imperceptible stiffening of his frame. His mouth opens with a faint click. He begins to read.

The Ceremony of Marriage has begun.

IV.—The Visionary

"Yes, " said Cheops, helping his guest over a ticklish place, "I daresay this pile of rocks will last. It has cost me a pretty penny, believe me. I made up my mind at the start that it would be built of honest stone, or not at all. No cheap and shoddy brickwork for *me*! Look at Babylon. It's all brick, and it's always tumbling down. My ambassador there tells me that it costs a million a year to keep up the walls alone— mind you, the walls alone! What must it cost to keep up the palace, with all that fancy work!

"Yes, I grant you that brickwork *looks* good. But what of it? So does a cheap cotton night-shirt—you know the gaudy things those Theban peddlers sell to my sand-hogs down on the river bank. But does it *last*? Of course it doesn't. Well, I am putting up this pyramid to *stay* put, and I don't give a damn for its looks. I hear all sorts of funny cracks about it. My barber is a sharp nigger and keeps his ears open: he brings me all the gossip. But I let it go. This is *my* pyramid. I am putting up the money for it, and I have got to be mortared up in it when I die. So I am trying to make a good, substantial job of it, and letting the mere beauty of it go hang.

"Anyhow, there are plenty of uglier things in Egypt. Look at some of those fifth-rate pyramids up the river. When it comes to shape they are pretty much the same as this one, and when it comes to size, they look like warts beside it. And look at the Sphinx. There is something that cost four millions if it cost a copper—and what is it now? A burlesque! A caricature! An architectural cripple! So long as it was *new*, good enough! It was a showy piece of work. People came all the way from Sicyonia and Tyre to gape at it. Everybody said it was one of the sights no one could afford to miss. But by and by a piece began to peel off here and another piece there, and then the nose cracked, and then an ear dropped off, and then one of the eyes began to get mushy and watery looking, and finally it was a mere smudge, a false-face, a scarecrow. My father spent a lot of money trying to fix it up, but what good did it do? By the time he had the nose cobbled the ears were loose again, and so on. In the end he gave it up as a bad job.

"Yes; this pyramid has kept me on the jump, but I'm going to stick to it if it breaks me. Some say I ought to have built it across the river, where the quarries are. Such gabble makes me sick. Do I look like a man who would go looking around for such *child's-play*? I hope not. A one-legged man could have done *that*. Even a Babylonian could have done it. It would have been as easy as milking a cow. What *I* wanted was something that would keep me on the jump—something that would put a strain on me. So I decided to haul the whole business *across* the river—six million tons of rock. And when the engineers said that it couldn't be done, I gave them two days to get out of Egypt, and then tackled it myself. It was something new and hard. It was a job I could get my teeth into.

"Well, I suppose you know what a time I had of it at the start. First I tried a pontoon bridge, but the stones for the bottom course were so heavy that they sank the pontoons, and I lost a couple of hundred niggers before I saw that it couldn't be done. Then I tried a big raft, but in order to get her to float with the stones I had to use such big logs that she was unwieldy, and before I knew what had struck me I had lost six big dressed stones and another hundred niggers. I got the laugh, of course. Every numskull in Egypt wagged his beard over it; I could hear the chatter myself. But I kept quiet and stuck to the problem, and by and by I solved it.

"I suppose you know how I did it. In a general way? Well, the details are simple. First I made a new raft, a good deal lighter than the old one, and then I got a thousand water-tight goat-skins and had them blown up until they were as tight as drums. Then I got together a thousand niggers who were good swimmers, and gave each of them one of the blown-up goat-skins. On each goat-skin there was a leather thong, and on the bottom of the raft, spread over it evenly, there were a thousand hooks. Do you get the idea? Yes; that's it exactly. The niggers dived overboard with the goat-skins, swam under the raft, and tied the thongs to the hooks. And when all of them were tied on, the raft floated like a bladder. You simply *couldn't* sink it.

"Naturally enough, the thing took time, and there were accidents and setbacks. For instance, some of the niggers were so light in weight that they couldn't hold their goat-skins under water long enough to get them under the raft. I had to weight those fellows by having rocks tied around their middles. And when they had fastened their goat-skins and tried to swim back, some of them were carried down by the rocks. I never made any exact count, but I suppose that two or three hundred of them were drowned in that way. Besides, a couple of hundred were drowned because they couldn't hold their breaths long enough to swim under the raft and back. But what of it? I wasn't trying to hoard up niggers, but to make a raft that would float. And I did it.

"Well, once I showed how it could be done, all the wiseacres caught the idea, and after that I put a big gang to work making more rafts, and by and by I had sixteen of them in operation, and was hauling more stone than the masons could set. But I won't go into all that. Here is the pyramid; it speaks for itself. One year more and I'll have the top course laid and begin on the surfacing. I am going to make it plain marble, with no fancy work. I could bring in a gang of Theban stonecutters and have it carved all over with lions' heads and tiger claws and all that sort of gim-crackery, but why waste time and money? This isn't a menagerie, but a pyramid. My idea was to make it the boss pyramid of the world. The king who tries to beat it will have to get up pretty early in the morning.

"But what troubles I have had! Believe me, there has been nothing but trouble, trouble, trouble from the start. I set aside the engineering difficulties. They were hard for the engineers, but easy for me, once I put my mind on them. But the way these niggers have carried on has been something terrible. At the beginning I had only a thousand or two, and they all came from one tribe; so they got along fairly well. During the whole first year I doubt that more than twenty or thirty were killed in fights. But then I began to get fresh batches from up the river, and after that it was nothing but one fight after another. For two weeks running not a stroke of work was done. I really thought, at one time, that I'd have to give up. But finally the army put down the row, and after a couple of hundred of the ringleaders had been thrown into the river peace was restored. But it cost me, first and last, fully three thousand niggers, and set me back at least six months.

"Then came the so-called labor unions, and the strikes, and more trouble. These labor unions were started by a couple of smart, yellow niggers from Chaldea, one of them a sort of lay preacher, a fellow with a lot of gab. Before I got wind of them, they had gone so far it was almost impossible to squelch them. First I tried conciliation, but it didn't work a bit. They made the craziest demands you ever heard of— a holiday every six days, meat every day, no night work and regular houses to live in. Some of them even had the effrontery to ask for money! Think of it! Niggers asking for money! Finally, I had to order out the army again and let some blood. But every time one was knocked over, I had to get another one to take his place, and that meant sending the army up the river, and more expense, and more devilish worry and nuisance.

"In my grandfather's time niggers were honest and faithful workmen. You could take one fresh from the bush, teach him to handle a shovel or pull a rope in a year or so, and after that he was worth almost as much as he could eat. But the nigger of to-day isn't worth a damn. He never does an honest day's work if he can help it, and he is forever wanting something. Take these fellows I have now—mainly young bucks from around the First Cataract. Here are niggers who never saw baker's bread or butcher's meat until my men grabbed them. They lived there in the bush like so many hyenas. They were ten days' march from a lemon. Well, now they get first-class beef twice a week, good bread and all the fish they can catch. They don't have to begin work until broad daylight, and they lay off at dark. There is hardly one of them that hasn't got a psaltery, or a harp, or some other musical instrument. If they want to dress up and make believe they are Egyptians, I give them clothes. If one of them is killed on the work, or by a stray lion, or in a fight, I have him embalmed by my own embalmers and plant him like a man. If one of them breaks a leg or loses an arm or gets too old to work, I turn him loose without complaining, and he is free to go home if he wants to.

"But are they contented? Do they show any gratitude? Not at all. Scarcely a day passes that I don't hear of some fresh soldiering. And, what is worse, they have stirred up some of my own people—the carpenters, stone-cutters, gang bosses and so on. Every now and then my inspectors find some rotten libel cut on a stone—something to the effect that I am overworking them, and knocking them about, and holding them against their will, and generally mistreating them. I haven't the slightest doubt that some of these inscriptions have actually gone into the pyramid: it's impossible to watch every stone. Well, in the years to come, they will be dug out and read by strangers, and I will get a black eye. People will think of Cheops as a heartless old rapscallion— *me*, mind you! Can you beat it?"

V.—The Artist. A Drama Without Words

CHARACTERS:

A GREAT PIANIST

A JANITOR

SIX MUSICAL CRITICS

A MARRIED WOMAN

A VIRGIN

SIXTEEN HUNDRED AND FORTY-THREE OTHER WOMEN

SIX OTHER MEN

PLACE—*A City of the United States.*

TIME—*A December afternoon.*

(*During the action of the play not a word is uttered aloud. All of the speeches of the characters are supposed to be unspoken meditations only.*)

A large, gloomy hall, with many rows of uncushioned, uncomfortable seats, designed, it would seem, by some one misinformed as to the average width of the normal human pelvis. A number of busts of celebrated composers, once white, but now a dirty gray, stand in niches along the walls. At one end of the hall there is a bare, uncarpeted stage, with nothing on it save a grand piano and a chair. It is raining outside, and, as hundreds of people come crowding in, the air is laden with the mingled scents of umbrellas, raincoats, goloshes, cosmetics, perfumery and wet hair.

At eight minutes past four, THE JANITOR, *after smoothing his hair with his hands and putting on a pair of detachable cuffs, emerges from the wings and crosses the stage, his shoes squeaking hideously at each step. Arriving at the piano, he opens it with solemn slowness. The job seems so absurdly trivial, even to so mean an understanding, that he can't refrain from glorifying it with a bit of hocus-pocus. This takes the form of a careful adjustment of a mysterious something within the instrument. He reaches in, pauses a moment as if in doubt, reaches in again, and then permits a faint smile of conscious sapience and efficiency to illuminate his face. All of this accomplished, he tiptoes back to the wings, his shoes again squeaking.*

THE JANITOR

Now all of them people think I'm the professor's tuner. (*The thought gives him such delight that, for the moment, his brain is numbed. Then he proceeds.*) I guess them tuners make pretty good money. I wish I could get the hang of the trick. It *looks* easy. (*By this time he has disappeared in the wings and the stage is again a desert. Two or three women, far back in the hall, start a halfhearted handclapping. It dies out at once. The noise of rustling programs and shuffling feet succeeds it.*)

FOUR HUNDRED OF THE WOMEN

Oh, I do *certainly* hope he plays that lovely *Valse Poupée* as an encore! They say he does it better than Bloomfield-Zeisler.

ONE OF THE CRITICS

I hope the animal doesn't pull any encore numbers that I don't recognize. All of these people will buy the paper to-morrow morning just to find out what they have heard. It's infernally embarrassing to have to ask the manager. The public expects a musical critic to be a sort of walking thematic catalogue. The public is an ass.

THE SIX OTHER MEN

Oh, Lord! What a way to spend an afternoon!

A HUNDRED OF THE WOMEN

I wonder if he's as handsome as Paderewski.

ANOTHER HUNDRED OF THE WOMEN

I wonder if he's as gentlemanly as Josef Hofmann.

STILL ANOTHER HUNDRED WOMEN

I wonder if he's as fascinating as De Pachmann.

YET OTHER HUNDREDS

I wonder if he has dark eyes. You never can tell by those awful photographs in the newspapers.

HALF A DOZEN WOMEN

I wonder if he can really play the piano.

THE CRITIC AFORESAID

What a hell of a wait! These rotten piano-thumping immigrants deserve a hard call-down. But what's the use? The piano manufacturers bring them over here to wallop their pianos—and the piano manufacturers are not afraid to advertise. If you knock them too hard you have a nasty business-office row on your hands.

ONE OF THE MEN

If they allowed smoking, it wouldn't be so bad.

ANOTHER MAN

I wonder if that woman across the aisle——

(THE GREAT PIANIST *bounces upon the stage so suddenly that he is bowing in the center before any one thinks to applaud. He makes three stiff bows. At the second the applause begins, swelling at once to a roar. He steps up to the piano, bows three times more, and then sits down. He hunches his shoulders, reaches for the pedals with his feet, spreads out his hands and waits for the clapper-clawing to cease. He is an undersized, paunchy East German, with hair the color of wet hay, and an extremely pallid complexion. Talcum powder hides the fact that his nose is shiny and somewhat pink. His eyebrows are carefully penciled and there are artificial shadows under his eyes. His face is absolutely expressionless.*)

THE VIRGIN

Oh!

THE MARRIED WOMEN

Oh!

THE OTHER WOMEN

Oh! How dreadfully handsome!

THE VIRGIN

Oh, such eyes, such depth! How he must have suffered! I'd like to hear him play the Prélude in D flat major. It would drive you crazy!

A HUNDRED OTHER WOMEN

I certainly *do* hope he plays some Schumann.

OTHER WOMEN

What beautiful hands! I could kiss them!

(THE GREAT PIANIST, *throwing back his head, strikes the massive opening chords of a Beethoven sonata. There is a sudden hush and each note is heard clearly. The tempo of the first movement, which begins after a grand pause, is* allegro con brio, *and the first subject is given out in a sparkling cascade of sound. But, despite the buoyancy of the music, there is an unmistakable undercurrent of melancholy in the playing. The audience doesn't fail to notice it.*)

THE VIRGIN

Oh, perfect! I could love him! Paderewski played it like a fox trot. What poetry *he* puts into it! I can see a soldier lover marching off to war.

ONE OF THE CRITICS

The ass is dragging it. Doesn't *con brio* mean—well, what the devil *does* it mean? I forget. I must look it up before I write the notice. Somehow, *brio* suggests cheese. Anyhow, Pachmann plays it a damn sight faster. It's safe to say *that*, at all events.

THE MARRIED WOMAN

Oh, I could listen to that sonata all day! The poetry he puts into it—even into the *allegro*! Just think what the *andante* will be! I like music to be sad.

ANOTHER WOMAN

What a sob he gets into it!

MANY OTHER WOMEN

How exquisite!

THE GREAT PIANIST

(*Gathering himself together for the difficult development section.*) That American beer will be the death of me! I wonder what they put in it to give it its gassy taste. And the so-called German beer they sell over here—*du heiliger Herr Jesu!* Even Bremen would be ashamed of it. In München the police would take a hand.

(Aiming for the first and second C's above the staff, he accidentally strikes the C sharps instead and has to transpose three measures to get back into the key. The effect is harrowing, and he gives his audience a swift glance of apprehension.)

TWO HUNDRED AND FIFTY WOMEN

What new beauties he gets out of it!

A MAN

He can tickle the ivories, all right, all right!

A CRITIC

Well, at any rate, he doesn't try to imitate Paderewski.

THE GREAT PIANIST

(Relieved by the non-appearance of the hisses he expected.) Well, it's lucky for me that I'm not in Leipzig to-day! But in Leipzig an artist runs no risks: the beer is pure. The authorities see to that. The worse enemy of technic is biliousness, and biliousness is sure to follow bad beer. *(He gets to the coda at last and takes it at a somewhat livelier pace.)*

THE VIRGIN

How I envy the woman he loves! How it would thrill me to feel his arms about me—to be drawn closer, closer, closer! I would give up the whole world! What are conventions, prejudices, legal forms, morality, after all? Vanities! Love is beyond and above them all—and art is love! I think I must be a pagan.

THE GREAT PIANIST

And the herring! Good God, what herring! These barbarous Americans——

THE VIRGIN

Really, I am quite indecent! I should blush, I suppose. But love is never ashamed—How people misunderstand me!

THE MARRIED WOMAN

I wonder if he's faithful. The chances are against it. I never heard of a man who was. *(An agreeable melancholy overcomes her and she gives herself up to the mood without thought.)*

THE GREAT PIANIST

I wonder whatever became of that girl in Dresden. Every time I think of her, she suggests pleasant thoughts—good beer, a fine band, *Gemütlichkeit*. I must have been in love with her—not much, of course, but just enough to make things pleasant. And not a single letter from her! I suppose she thinks I'm starving to death over here—or tuning pianos. Well, when I get back with the money there'll be a shock for her. A shock—but not a *Pfennig*!

THE MARRIED WOMAN

(*Her emotional coma ended.*) Still, you can hardly blame him. There must be a good deal of temptation for a great artist. All of these frumps here would——

THE VIRGIN

Ah, how dolorous, how exquisite is love! How small the world would seem if——

THE MARRIED WOMAN

Of course you could hardly call such old scarecrows temptations. But still——

(THE GREAT PIANIST *comes to the last measure of the* coda—*a passage of almost Haydnesque clarity and spirit. As he strikes the broad chord of the tonic there comes a roar of applause. He arises, moves a step or two down the stage, and makes a series of low bows, his hands to his heart.*)

THE GREAT PIANIST

(*Bowing.*) I wonder why the American women always wear raincoats to piano recitals. Even when the sun is shining brightly, one sees hundreds of them. What a disagreeable smell they give to the hall. (*More applause and more bows.*) An American audience always smells of rubber and lilies-of-the-valley. How different in London! There an audience always smells of soap. In Paris it reminds you of sachet bags— and *lingerie*.

(*The applause ceases and he returns to the piano.*)

And now comes that *verfluchte adagio*.

(*As he begins to play, a deathlike silence falls upon the hall.*)

ONE OF THE CRITICS

What rotten pedaling!

ANOTHER CRITIC

A touch like a xylophone player, but he knows how to use his feet. That suggests a good line for the notice—"he plays better with his feet than with his hands, " or something like that. I'll have to think it over and polish it up.

ONE OF THE OTHER MEN

Now comes some more of that awful classical stuff.

THE VIRGIN

Suppose he can't speak English? But that wouldn't matter. Nothing matters. Love is beyond and above——

SIX HUNDRED WOMEN

Oh, how beautiful!

THE MARRIED WOMAN

Perfect!

THE DEAN OF THE CRITICS

(*Sinking quickly into the slumber which always overtakes him during the* adagio.) C-c-c-c-c-c-c-c-c-h-h-h-h-h-h-h-h!

THE YOUNGEST CRITIC

There is that old fraud asleep again. And to-morrow he'll print half a column of vapid reminiscence and call it criticism. It's a wonder his paper stands for him. Because he once heard Liszt, he....

THE GREAT PIANIST

That plump girl over there on the left is not so bad. As for the rest, I beg to be excused. The American women have no more shape than so many matches. They are too tall and too thin. I like a nice rubbery armful—like that Dresden girl. Or that harpist in Moscow—the girl with the Pilsner hair. Let me see, what was her name? Oh, Fritzi, to be sure— but her last name? Schmidt? Kraus? Meyer? I'll have to try to think of it, and send her a postcard.

THE MARRIED WOMAN

What delicious flutelike tones!

ONE OF THE WOMEN

If Beethoven could only be here to hear it! He would cry for very joy! Maybe he *does* hear it. Who knows? I believe he does. I am *sure* he does.

(THE GREAT PIANIST *reaches the end of the* adagio, *and there is another burst of applause, which awakens* THE DEAN OF THE CRITICS.)

THE DEAN OF THE CRITICS

Oh, piffle! Compared to Gottschalk, the man is an amateur. Let him go back to the conservatory for a couple of years.

ONE OF THE MEN

(*Looking at his program.*) Next comes the *shirt-so*. I hope it has some tune in it.

THE VIRGIN

The *adagio* is love's agony, but the *scherzo* is love triumphant. What beautiful eyes he has! And how pale he is!

THE GREAT PIANIST

(*Resuming his grim toil.*) Well, there's half of it over. But this *scherzo* is ticklish business. That horrible evening in Prague—will I ever forget it? Those hisses—and the papers next day!

ONE OF THE MEN

Go it, professor! That's the best you've done yet!

ONE OF THE CRITICS

Too fast!

ANOTHER CRITIC

Too slow!

A YOUNG GIRL

My, but ain't the professor just full of talent!

THE GREAT PIANIST

Well, so far no accident. (*He negotiates a difficult passage, and plays it triumphantly, but at some expenditure of cold perspiration.*) What a way for a man to make a living!

THE VIRGIN

What passion he puts into it! His soul is in his finger-tips.

A CRITIC

A human pianola!

THE GREAT PIANIST

This *scherzo* always fetches the women. I can hear them draw long breaths. That plump girl is getting pale. Well, why shouldn't she? I suppose I'm about the best pianist she has ever heard—or ever *will* hear. What people can see in that Hambourg fellow I never could imagine. In Chopin, Schumann, Grieg, you might fairly say he's pretty good. But it takes an *artist* to play Beethoven. (*He rattles on to the end of the* scherzo *and there is more applause. Then he dashes into the*finale.)

THE DEAN OF THE CRITICS

Too loud! Too loud! It sounds like an ash-cart going down an alley. But what can you expect? Piano-playing is a lost art. Paderewski ruined it.

THE GREAT PIANIST

I ought to clear 200, 000 marks by this tournee. If it weren't for those thieving agents and hotelkeepers, I'd make 300, 000. Just think of it—twenty-four marks a day for a room! That's the way these Americans treat a visiting artist! The country is worse than Bulgaria. I was treated better at Bucharest. Well, it won't last forever. As soon as I get enough of their money they'll see me no more. Vienna is the place to settle down. A nice studio at fifty marks a month—and the life of a gentleman. What was the name of that little red-cheeked girl at the café in the Franzjosefstrasse—that girl with the gold tooth and the silk stockings? I'll have to look her up.

THE VIRGIN

What an artist! What a master! What a——

THE MARRIED WOMAN

Has he really suffered, or is it just intuition?

THE GREAT PIANIST

No, marriage is a waste of money. Let the other fellow marry her. (*He approaches the closing measures of the finale.*) And now for a breathing spell and a swallow of beer. American beer! Bah! But it's better than nothing. The Americans drink water. Cattle! Animals! *Ach, München, wie bist du so schön!*

(*As he concludes there is a whirlwind of applause and he is forced to bow again and again. Finally, he is permitted to retire, and the audience prepares to spend the short intermission in whispering, grunting, wriggling, scraping its feet, rustling its programs and gaping at hats. The* SIX MUSICAL CRITICS *and* SIX OTHER MEN, *their lips parched and their eyes staring, gallop for the door. As* THE GREAT

PIANIST *comes from the stage,* THE JANITOR *meets him with a large seidel of beer. He seizes it eagerly and downs it at a gulp.)*

THE JANITOR

My, but them professors can put the stuff away!

VI.—Seeing The World

The scene is the brow of the Hungerberg at Innsbruck. It is the half hour before sunset, and the whole lovely valley of the Inn—still wie die Nacht, tief wie das Meer—begins to glow with mauves and apple greens, apricots and silvery blues. Along the peaks of the great snowy mountains which shut it in, as if from the folly and misery of the world, there are touches of piercing primary colours—red, yellow, violet. Far below, hugging the winding river, lies little Innsbruck, with its checkerboard parks and Christmas garden villas. A battalion of Austrian soldiers, drilling in the Exerzierplatz, appears as an army of grey ants, now barely visible. Somewhere to the left, beyond the broad flank of the Hungerberg, the night train for Venice labours toward the town.

It is a superbly beautiful scene, perhaps the most beautiful in all Europe. It has colour, dignity, repose. The Alps here come down a bit and so increase their spell. They are not the harsh precipices of Switzerland, nor the too charming stage mountains of the Trentino, but rotting billows of clouds and snow, the high flung waves of some titanic but stricken ocean. Now and then comes a faint clank of metal from the funicular railway, but the tracks themselves are hidden among the trees of the lower slopes. The tinkle of an angelus bell (or maybe it is only a sheep bell) is heard from afar. A great bird, an eagle or a falcon, sweeps across the crystal spaces.

Here where we are is a shelf on the mountainside, and the hand of man has converted it into a terrace. To the rear, clinging to the mountain, is an Alpinegasthaus—a bit overdone, perhaps, with its red-framed windows and elaborate fretwork, but still genuinely of the Alps. Along the front of the terrace, protecting sightseers from the sheer drop of a thousand feet, is a stout wooden rail.

A man in an American sack suit, with a bowler hat on his head, lounges against this rail. His elbows rest upon it, his legs are crossed in the fashion of a figure four, and his face is buried in the red book of Herr Baedeker. It is the volume on Southern Germany, and he is

591

reading the list of Munich hotels. Now and then he stops to mark one with a pencil, which he wets at his lips each time. While he is thus engaged, another man comes ambling along the terrace, apparently from the direction of the funicular railway station. He, too, carries a red book. It is Baedeker on Austria-Hungary. After gaping around him a bit, this second man approaches the rail near the other and leans his elbows upon it. Presently he takes a package of chewing gum from his coat pocket, selects two pieces, puts them into his mouth and begins to chew. Then he spits idly into space, idly but homerically, a truly stupendous expectoration, a staggering discharge from the Alps to the first shelf of the Lombard plain! The first man, startled by the report, glances up. Their eyes meet and there is a vague glimmer of recognition.

THE FIRST MAN

American?

THE SECOND MAN

Yes; St. Louis.

THE FIRST MAN

Been over long?

THE SECOND MAN

A couple of months.

THE FIRST MAN

What ship'd you come over in?

THE SECOND MAN

The *Kronprinz Friedrich.*

THE FIRST MAN

Aha, the German line! I guess you found the grub all right.

THE SECOND MAN

Oh, in the main. I have eaten better, but then again, I have eaten worse.

THE FIRST MAN

Well, they charge you enough for it, whether you get it or not. A man could live at the Plaza cheaper.

THE SECOND MAN

I should *say* he could. What boat did *you* come over in?

THE FIRST MAN

The *Maurentic.*

THE SECOND MAN

How is she?

THE FIRST MAN

Oh, so-so.

THE SECOND MAN

I hear the meals on those English ships are nothing to what they used to be.

THE FIRST MAN

That's what everybody tells me. But, as for me, I can't say I found them so bad. I had to send back the potatoes twice and the breakfast bacon once, but they had very good lima beans.

THE SECOND MAN

Isn't that English bacon awful stuff to get down?

THE FIRST MAN

It certainly is: all meat and gristle. I wonder what an Englishman would say if you put him next to a plate of genuine, crisp, *American* bacon.

THE SECOND MAN

I guess he would yell for the police—or choke to death.

THE FIRST MAN

Did you like the German cooking on the *Kronprinz*?

THE SECOND MAN

Well, I did and I didn't. The chicken à la Maryland was very good, but they had it only once. I could eat it every day.

THE FIRST MAN

Why didn't you order it?

THE SECOND MAN

It wasn't on the bill.

THE FIRST MAN

Oh, bill be damned! You might have ordered it anyhow. Make a fuss and you'll get what you want. These foreigners have to be bossed around. They're used to it.

THE SECOND MAN

I guess you're right. There was a fellow near me who set up a holler about his room the minute he saw it—said it was dark and musty and not fit to pen a hog in—and they gave him one twice as large, and the chief steward bowed and scraped to him, and the room stewards danced around him as if he was a duke. And yet I heard later that he was nothing but a Bismarck herring importer from Hoboken.

THE FIRST MAN

Yes, that's the way to get what you want. Did you have any nobility on board?

THE SECOND MAN

Yes, there was a Hungarian baron in the automobile business, and two English sirs. The baron was quite a decent fellow: I had a talk with him in the smoking room one night. He didn't put on any airs at all. You would have thought he was an ordinary man. But the sirs kept to themselves. All they did the whole voyage was to write letters, wear their dress suits and curse the stewards.

THE FIRST MAN

They tell me over here that the best eating is on the French lines.

THE SECOND MAN

Yes, so I hear. But some say, too, that the Scandinavian lines are best, and then again I have heard people boosting the Italian lines.

THE FIRST MAN

I guess each one has its points. They say that you get wine free with meals on the French boats.

THE SECOND MAN

But I hear it's fourth-rate wine.

THE FIRST MAN

Well, you don't have to drink it.

THE SECOND MAN

That's so. But, as for me, I can't stand a Frenchman. I'd rather do without the wine and travel with the Dutch. Paris is dead compared with Berlin.

THE FIRST MAN

So it is. But those Germans are awful sharks. The way they charge in Berlin is enough to make you sick.

THE SECOND MAN

Don't tell *me*. I have been there. No longer ago than last Tuesday—or was it last Monday?—I went into one of those big restaurants on the Unter den Linden and ordered a small steak, French fried potatoes, a piece of pie and a cup of coffee—and what do you think those thieves charged me for it? Three marks fifty. That's eighty-seven and a half cents. Why, a man could have got the same meal at home for a dollar. These Germans are running wild. American money has gone to their heads. They think every American they get hold of is a millionaire.

THE FIRST MAN

The French are worse. I went into a hotel in Paris and paid ten francs a day for a room for myself and wife, and when we left they charged me one franc forty a day extra for sweeping it out and making the bed!

THE SECOND MAN

That's nothing. Here in Innsbruck they charge you half a krone a day *taxes*.

THE FIRST MAN

What! You don't say!

THE SECOND MAN

Sure thing. And if you don't eat breakfast in the hotel they charge you a krone for it anyhow.

THE FIRST MAN

Well, well, what next? But, after all, you can't blame them. We Americans come over here and hand them our pocket-books, and we ought to be glad if we get anything back at all. The way a man has to tip is something fearful.

THE SECOND MAN

Isn't it, though! I stayed in Dresden a week, and when I left there were six grafters lined up with their claws out. First came the port*eer*. Then came——

THE FIRST MAN

How much did you give the port*eer*?

THE SECOND MAN

Five marks.

THE FIRST MAN

You gave him too much. You ought to have given him about three marks, or, say, two marks fifty. How much was your hotel bill?

THE SECOND MAN

Including everything?

THE FIRST MAN

No, just your bill for your room.

THE SECOND MAN

I paid six marks a day.

THE FIRST MAN

Well, that made forty-two marks for the week. Now the way to figure out how much the port*eer* ought to get is easy: a fellow I met in Baden-Baden showed me how to do it. First, you multiply your hotel bill by two, then you divide it by twenty-seven, and then you knock off half a mark. Twice forty-two is eighty-four. Twenty-seven into eighty-four goes about three times, and half from three leaves two and a half. See how easy it is?

THE SECOND MAN

It *looks* easy, anyhow. But you haven't got much time to do all that figuring.

THE FIRST MAN

Well, let the port*eer* wait. The longer he has to wait the more he appreciates you.

THE SECOND MAN

But how about the others?

THE FIRST MAN

It's just as simple. Your chambermaid gets a quarter of a mark for every day you have been in the hotel. But if you stay less than four days she gets a whole mark anyhow. If there are two in the party she gets half a mark a day, but no more than three marks in any one week.

THE SECOND MAN

But suppose there are two chambermaids? In Dresden there was one on day duty and one on night duty. I left at six o'clock in the evening, and so they were both on the job.

THE FIRST MAN

Don't worry. They'd have been on the job anyhow, no matter when you left. But it's just as easy to figure out the tip for two as for one. All you have to do is to add fifty per cent. and then divide it into two halves, and give one to each girl. Or, better still, give it all to one girl and tell her to give half to her pal. If there are three chambermaids, as you sometimes find in the swell hotels, you add another fifty per cent. and then divide by three. And so on.

THE SECOND MAN

I see. But how about the hall porter and the floor waiter?

THE FIRST MAN

Just as easy. The hall porter gets whatever the chambermaid gets, plus twenty-five per cent.—but no more than two marks in any one week. The floor waiter gets thirty pfennigs a day straight, but if you stay only one day he gets half a mark, and if you stay more than a week he gets two marks flat a week after the first week. In some hotels the hall porter don't shine shoes. If he don't he gets just as much as if he does, but then the actual "boots" has to be taken care of. He gets half a mark every two days. Every time you put out an extra pair of shoes he gets fifty per cent. more for that day. If you shine your own shoes, or go without shining them, the "boots" gets half his regular tip, but never less than a mark a week.

THE SECOND MAN

Certainly it seems simple enough. I never knew there was any such system.

THE FIRST MAN

I guess you didn't. Very few do. But it's just because Americans don't know it that these foreign blackmailers shake 'em down. Once you let the port*eer* see that you know the ropes, he'll pass the word on to the others, and you'll be treated like a native.

THE SECOND MAN

I see. But how about the elevator boy? I gave the elevator boy in Dresden two marks and he almost fell on my neck, so I figured that I played the sucker.

THE FIRST MAN

So you did. The rule for elevator boys is still somewhat in the air, because so few of these bum hotels over here have elevators, but you can sort of reason the thing out if you put your mind on it. When you get on a street car in Germany, what tip do you give the conductor?

THE SECOND MAN

Five pfennigs.

THE FIRST MAN.

Naturally. That's the tip fixed by custom. You may almost say it's the unwritten law. If you gave the conductor more, he would hand you change. Well, how I reason it out is this way: If five pfennigs is enough for a car conductor, who may carry you three miles, why shouldn't it be enough for the elevator boy, who may carry you only three stories?

THE SECOND MAN

It seems fair, certainly.

THE FIRST MAN

And it *is* fair. So all you have to do is to keep account of the number of times you go up and down in the elevator, and then give the elevator boy five pfennigs for each trip. Say you come down in the morning, go up in the evening, and average one other round trip a day. That makes twenty-eight trips a week. Five times twenty-eight is one mark forty—and there you are.

THE SECOND MAN

I see. By the way, what hotel are you stopping at?

THE FIRST MAN

The Goldene Esel.

THE SECOND MAN

How is it?

THE FIRST MAN

Oh, so-so. Ask for oatmeal at breakfast and they send to the livery stable for a peck of oats and ask you please to be so kind as to show them how to make it.

THE SECOND MAN

My hotel is even worse. Last night I got into such a sweat under the big German feather bed that I had to throw it off. But when I asked for a single blanket they didn't have any, so I had to wrap up in bath towels.

THE FIRST MAN

Yes, and you used up every one in town. This morning, when I took a bath, the only towel the chambermaid could find wasn't bigger than a wedding invitation. But while she was hunting around I dried off, so no harm was done.

THE SECOND MAN

Well, that's what a man gets for running around in such one-horse countries. In Leipzig they sat a nigger down beside me at the table. In Amsterdam they had cheese for breakfast. In Munich the head waiter had never heard of buckwheat cakes. In Mannheim they charged me ten pfennigs extra for a cake of soap.

THE FIRST MAN

What do you think of the railroad trains over here?

THE SECOND MAN

Rotten. That compartment system is all wrong. If nobody comes into your compartment it's lonesome, and if anybody *does* come in it's too damn sociable. And if you try to stretch out and get some sleep, some ruffian begins singing in the next compartment, or the conductor keeps butting in and jabbering at you.

THE FIRST MAN

But you can say *one* thing for the German trains: they get in on time.

THE SECOND MAN

So they do, but no wonder! They run so slow they can't *help* it. The way I figure it, a German engineer must have a devil of a time holding his engine in. The fact is, he usually can't, and so he has to wait outside every big town until the schedule catches up to him. They say they never have accidents, but is it any more than you expect? Did you ever hear of a mud turtle having an accident?

THE FIRST MAN

Scarcely. As you say, these countries are far behind the times. I saw a fire in Cologne; you would have laughed your head off! It was in a feed store near my hotel, and I got there before the firemen. When they came at last, in their tinpot hats, they got out half a dozen big squirts and rushed into the building with them. Then, when it was out, they put the squirts back into their little express wagon and drove off. Not a line of hose run out, not an engine puffing, not a gong heard, not a soul letting out a whoop! It was more like a Sunday-school picnic than a fire. I guess if these Dutch ever *did* have a civilised blaze, it would scare them to death. But they never have any.

THE SECOND MAN

Well, what can you expect? A country where all the charwomen are men and all the garbage men are women!—

For the moment the two have talked each other out, and so they lounge upon the rail in silence and gaze out over the valley. Anon the gumchewer spits. By now the sun has reached the skyline to the westward and the tops of the ice mountains are in gorgeous conflagration. Scarlets war with golden oranges, and vermilions fade into palpitating pinks. Below, in the valley, the colours begin to fade slowly to a uniform seashell grey. It is a scene of indescribable loveliness; the wild reds of hades splashed riotously upon the cold whites and pale blues of heaven. The night train for Venice, a long line of black coaches, is entering the town. Somewhere below, apparently in the barracks, a sunset gun is fired. After a silence of perhaps two or three minutes, the Americans gather fresh inspiration and resume their conversation.

THE FIRST MAN

I have seen worse scenery.

THE SECOND MAN

Very pretty.

THE FIRST MAN

Yes, sir; it's well worth the money.

THE SECOND MAN

But the Rockies beat it all hollow.

THE FIRST MAN

Oh, of course. They have nothing over here that we can't beat to a whisper. Just consider the Rhine, for instance. The Hudson makes it look like a country creek.

THE SECOND MAN

Yes, you're right. Take away the castles, and not even a German would give a hoot for it. It's not so much what a thing *is* over here as what *reputation* it's got. The whole thing is a matter of press-agenting.

THE FIRST MAN

I agree with you. There's the "beautiful, blue Danube." To me it looks like a sewer. If *it's* blue, then *I'm* green. A man would hesitate to drown himself in such a mud puddle.

THE SECOND MAN

But you hear the bands playing that waltz all your life, and so you spend your good money to come over here to see the river. And when you get back home you don't want to admit that you've been a sucker, so you start touting it from hell to breakfast. And then some other fellow comes over and does the same, and so on and so on.

THE FIRST MAN

Yes, it's all a matter of boosting. Day in and day out you hear about Westminster Abbey. Every English book mentions it; it's in the newspapers almost as much as Jane Addams or Caruso. Well, one day you pack your grip, put on your hat and come over to have a look—and what do you find? A one-horse church full of statues! And every statue crying for sapolio! You expect to see something magnificent and enormous, something to knock your eye out and send you down for the count. What you do see is a second-rate graveyard under roof. And when you examine into it, you find that two-thirds of the graves haven't even got dead men in them! Whenever a prominent Englishman dies, they put up a statue to him in Westminster Abbey—*no matter where he happens to be buried*! I call that clever advertising. That's the way to get the crowd.

THE SECOND MAN

Yes, these foreigners know the game. They have made millions out of it in Paris. Every time you go to see a musical comedy at home, the second act is laid in Paris, and you see a whole stageful of girls wriggling around, and a lot of old sports having the time of their lives. All your life you hear that Paris is something rich and racy, something that makes New York look like Roanoke, Virginia. Well, you fall for the ballyho and come over to have your fling—and then you find that Paris is largely bunk. I spent a whole week in Paris, trying to find something really awful. I hired one of those Jew guides at five dollars a day and told him to go the limit. I said to him: "Don't mind *me*. I am twenty-one years old. Let me have the genuine goods." But the worst he could show me wasn't half as bad as what I have seen in Chicago. Every night I would say to that Jew: "Come on, now Mr. Cohen; let's get away from these tinhorn shows. Lead me to the real stuff." Well, I believe the fellow did his darndest, but he always fell down. I almost felt sorry for him. In the end, when I paid him off, I said to him: "Save up your money, my boy, and come over to the States. Let me know when you land. I'll show you the sights for nothing. This Baracca Class atmosphere is killing you."

THE FIRST MAN

And yet Paris is famous all over the world. No American ever came to Europe without dropping off there to have a look. I once saw the Bal Tabarin crowded with Sunday-school superintendents returning from Jerusalem. And when the sucker gets home he goes around winking and hinting, and so the fake grows. I often think the government ought to take a hand. If the beer is inspected and guaranteed in Germany, why shouldn't the shows be inspected and guaranteed in Paris?

THE SECOND MAN

I guess the trouble is that the Frenchmen themselves never go to their own shows. They don't know what is going on. They see thousands of Americans starting out every night from the Place de l'Opéra and coming back in the morning all boozed up, and so they assume that everything is up to the mark. You'll find the same thing in Washington. No Washingtonian has ever been up to the top of the Washington monument. Once the elevator in the monument was out of commission for two weeks, and yet Washington knew nothing about it. When the news got into the papers at last, it came from Macon, Georgia. Some honeymooner from down there had written home about it, roasting the government.

THE FIRST MAN

Well, me for the good old U. S. A.! These Alps are all right, I guess— but I can't say I like the coffee.

THE SECOND MAN

And it takes too long to get a letter from Jersey City.

THE FIRST MAN

Yes, that reminds me. Just before I started up here this afternoon my wife got the *Ladies' Home Journal* of the month before last. It had been following us around for six weeks, from London to Paris, to Berlin, to Munich, to Vienna, to a dozen other places. Now she's fixed for the night. She won't let up until she's read every word—the advertisements first. And she'll spend all day to-morrow sending off for things; new collar hooks, breakfast foods, complexion soaps and all that sort of junk. Are you married yourself?

THE SECOND MAN

No; not yet.

THE FIRST MAN

Well, then, you don't know how it is. But I guess you play poker.

THE SECOND MAN

Oh, to be sure.

THE FIRST MAN

Well, let's go down into the town and hunt up some quiet barroom and have a civilised evening. This scenery gives me the creeps.

THE SECOND MAN

I'm with you. But where are we going to get any chips?

THE FIRST MAN

Don't worry. I carry a set with me. I made my wife put it in the bottom of my trunk, along with a bottle of real whiskey and a couple of porous plasters. A man can't be too careful when he's away from home——

They start along the terrace toward the station of the funicular railway. The sun has now disappeared behind the great barrier of ice and the colours of the scene are fast softening. All the scarlets and vermilions are gone; a luminous pink bathes the whole picture in its fairy light. The night train for Venice, leaving the town, appears as a long string of blinking lights. A chill breeze comes from the Alpine vastness to westward. The deep silence of an Alpine night settles down. The two Americans continue their talk until they are out of hearing. The breeze interrupts and obfuscates their words, but now and then half a sentence comes clearly.

THE SECOND MAN

Have you seen any American papers lately?

THE FIRST MAN

Nothing But the Paris *Herald*—if you call *that* a paper.

THE SECOND MAN

How are the Giants making out?

THE FIRST MAN

... bad as usual ... rotten ... shake up ...

THE SECOND MAN

... John McGraw ...

THE FIRST MAN

... homesick ... give five dollars for ...

THE SECOND MAN

... whole continent without a single ...

THE FIRST MAN

... glad to get back ... damn tired ...

THE SECOND MAN.

... damn ...!

THE FIRST MAN.

... *damn* ...!

VII.—From the Memoirs of the Devil

January 6.

And yet, and yet—is not all this contumely a part of my punishment? To be reviled by the righteous as the author of all evil; worse still, to be venerated by the wicked as the accomplice, nay, the instigator, of their sins! A harsh, hard fate! But should I not rejoice that I have been vouchsafed the strength to bear it, that the ultimate mercy is mine? Should I not be full of calm, deep delight that I am blessed with the resignation of the Psalmist (II Samuel XV, 26), the sublime grace of the pious Hezekiah (II Kings XX, 19)? If Hezekiah could bear the cruel visitation of his erring upon his sons, why should I, poor worm that I am, repine?

January 8.

All afternoon I watched the damned filing in. With what horror that spectacle must fill every right-thinking man! Sometimes I think that the worst of all penalties of sin is this: that the sinful actually seem to be glad of their sins (Psalms X, 4). I looked long and earnestly into that endless procession of faces. In not one of them did I see any sign of sorrow or repentance. They marched in defiantly, almost proudly. Ever and anon I heard a snicker, sometimes a downright laugh: there was a coarse buffoonery in the ranks. I turned aside at last, unable to bear it longer. Here they will learn what their laughter is worth! (Eccl. II, 2.)

Among them I marked a female, young and fair. How true the words of Solomon: "Favour is deceitful, and beauty is vain!" (Proverbs XXXI, 30.) I could not bring myself to put down upon these pages the whole record of that wicked creature's shameless life. Truly it has been said that "the lips of a strange woman drop as a honeycomb, and her mouth is smoother than oil." (Proverbs V, 3.) One hears of such careers of evil-doing and can scarcely credit them. Can it be that the children of men are so deaf to all the warnings given them, so blind to the vast certainty of their punishment, so ardent in seeking temptation, so lacking in holy fire to resist it? Such thoughts fill me with the utmost distress. Is not the command to a moral life plain enough? Are we not told to "live soberly, righteously, and godly?" (Titus II, 11.) Are we not solemnly warned to avoid the invitation of evil? (Proverbs I, 10.)

January 9.

I have had that strange woman before me and heard her miserable story. It is as I thought. The child of a poor but pious mother, (a widow with six children), she had every advantage of a virtuous, consecrated home. The mother, earning $6 a week, gave 25 cents of it to foreign missions. The daughter, at the tender age of 4, was already a regular attendant at Sabbath-school. The good people of the church took a Christian interest in the family, and one of them, a gentleman of considerable wealth, and an earnest, diligent worker for righteousness, made it his special care to befriend the girl. He took her into his office, treating her almost as one of his own daughters. She served him in the capacity of stenographer, receiving therefor the wage of $7.00 a week, a godsend to that lowly household. How truly, indeed, it has been said: "Verily, there is a reward for the righteous." (Psalms LVIII, 11.)

And now behold how powerful are the snares of evil. (Genesis VI, 12.) There was that devout and saintly man, ripe in good works, a deacon and pillar in the church, a steadfast friend to the needy and erring, a stalwart supporter of his pastor in all forward-looking enterprises, a tower of strength for righteousness in his community, the father of four daughters. And there was that shameless creature, that evil woman, that sinister temptress. With the noisome details I do not concern myself. Suffice it to say that the vile arts of the hussy prevailed over that noble and upright man—that she enticed him, by adroit appeals to his sympathy, into taking her upon automobile rides, into dining with her clandestinely in the private rooms of dubious hotels, and finally into accompanying her upon a despicable, adulterous visit to Atlantic City. And then, seeking to throw upon him the blame for what she chose to call her "wrong, " she held him up to public disgrace and worked her own inexorable damnation by taking her miserable life. Well hath the Preacher warned us against the woman whose "heart is snares and nets, and her hands as bands." (Eccl. VII, 26.) Well do we know the wreck and ruin that such agents of destruction can work upon the innocent and trusting. (Revelations XXI, 8; I Corinthians VI, 18; Job XXXI, 12; Hosea IV, 11: Proverbs VI, 26.)

January 11.

We have resumed our evening services—an hour of quiet communion in the failing light. The attendance, alas, is not as gratifying as it might be, but the brethren who gather are filled with holy zeal. It is inspiring to hear their eloquent confessions of guilt and wrongdoing, their trembling protestations of contrition. Several of them are of long experience and considerable proficiency in public speaking. One was formerly a major in the Salvation Army. Another spent twenty years in the Dunkard ministry, finally retiring to devote himself to lecturing on the New Thought. A third was a Y. M. C. A. secretary in Iowa. A fourth was the first man to lift his voice for sex hygiene west of the Mississippi river.

All these men eventually succumbed to temptation, and hence they are here, but I think that no one who has ever glimpsed their secret and inmost souls (as I have during our hours of humble heart-searching together) will fail to testify to their inherent purity of character. After all, it is not what we do but what we have in our hearts that reveals our true worth. (Joshua XXIV, 14.) As David so beautifully puts it, it is "the imagination of the thoughts." (I Chronicles XXIII, 9.) I love and trust these brethren. They are true and earnest Christians. They loathe the temptation to which they succumbed, and deplore the weakness that made them yield. How the memory at once turns to that lovely passage in the Book of Job: "Wherefore I abhor myself, and repent in dust and ashes." Where is there a more exquisite thought in all Holy Writ?

January 14.

I have had that scarlet woman before me, and invited her to join us in our inspiring evening gatherings. For reply she mocked me. Thus Paul was mocked by the Athenians. Thus the children of Bethel mocked Elisha the Prophet (II Kings II, 23). Thus the sinful show their contempt, not only for righteousness itself, but also for its humblest agents and advocates. Nevertheless, I held my temper before her. I indulged in no vain and worldly recriminations. When she launched into her profane and disgraceful tirade against that good and faithful brother, her benefactor and victim, I held my peace. When she accused him of foully destroying her, I returned her no harsh words. Instead, I merely read aloud to her those inspiring words from Revelation XIV, 10: "And the evil-doer shall be tormented with fire and brimstone in the presence of the holy angels." And then I smiled upon her and bade her begone. Who am I, that I should hold myself above the most miserable of sinners?

January 18.

Again that immoral woman. I had sent her a few Presbyterian tracts: "The Way to Redemption, " "The Story of a Missionary in Polynesia, " "The White Slave, "—inspiring and consecrated writings, all of them—comforting to me in many a bitter hour. When she came in I thought it was to ask me to pray with her. (II Chronicles VII, 14.) But her heart, it appears, is still shut to the words of salvation. She renewed her unseemly denunciation of her benefactor, and sought to overcome me with her weeping. I found myself strangely drawn toward her—almost pitying her. She approached me, her eyes suffused with tears, her red lips parted, her hair flowing about her shoulders. I felt myself drawn to her. I knew and understood the temptation of that great and good man. But by a powerful effort of the will—or, should I say, by a sudden access of grace?—I recovered and pushed her from me. And then, closing my eyes to shut out the image of her, I pronounced those solemn and awful words: "Vengeance is mine, saith the Lord!" The effect was immediate: she emitted a moan and departed. I had resisted her abhorrent blandishments. (Proverbs I, 10.)

January 25.

I love the Book of Job. Where else in the Scriptures is there a more striking picture of the fate that overtakes those who yield to sin? "They meet with darkness in the day-time, and grope in the noon-day as in the night" (Job V, 14). And further on: "They grope in the dark without light, and he maketh them to stagger like a drunken man" (Job XII, 25). I read these beautiful passages over and over again. They comfort me.

January 28.

That shameless person once more. She sends back the tracts I gave her—torn in halves.

February 3.

That American brother, the former Dunkard, thrilled us with his eloquence at to-night's meeting. In all my days I have heard no more affecting plea for right living. In words that almost seemed to be of fire he set forth the duty of all of us to combat sin wherever we find it, and to scourge the sinner until he foregoes his folly.

"It is not sufficient, " he said, "that we keep our own hearts pure: we must also purge the heart of our brother. And if he resist us, let no false sympathy for him stay our hands. We are charged with the care and oversight of his soul. He is in our keeping. Let us seek at first to save him with gentleness, but if he draws back, let us unsheath the sword! We must be deaf to his protests. We must not be deceived by his casuistries. If he clings to his sinning, he must perish."

Cries of "Amen!" arose spontaneously from the little band of consecrated workers. I have never heard a more triumphant call to that Service which is the very heart's blood of righteousness. Who could listen to it, and then stay his hand?

I looked for that scarlet creature. She was not there.

February 7.

I have seen her again. She came, I thought, in all humility. I received her gently, quoting aloud the beautiful words of Paul in Colossians III, 12: "Put on therefore, holy and beloved, bowels of mercies, kindness, humbleness of mind, meekness, long-suffering." And then I addressed her in calm, encouraging tones: "Are you ready, woman, to put away your evil-doing, and forswear your carnalities forevermore? Have you repented of your black and terrible sin? Do you ask for mercy? Have you come in sackcloth and ashes?"

The effect, alas, was not what I planned. Instead of yielding to my entreaty and casting herself down for forgiveness, she yielded to her pride and mocked me! And then, her heart still full of the evils of the flesh, *she tried to tempt me!* She approached me. She lifted up her face to mine. She smiled at me with abominable suggestiveness. She touched me with her garment. She laid her hand upon my arm.... I felt my resolution going from me. I was as one stricken with the palsy. My tongue clave to the roof of my mouth. My hands trembled. I tried to push her from me and could not....

February 10.

In all humility of spirit I set it down. The words burn the paper; the fact haunts me like an evil dream. I yielded to that soulless and abominable creature. *I kissed her....* And then she laughed, making a mock of me in my weakness, burning me with the hot iron of her scorn, piercing my heart with the daggers of her reviling. Laughed, and slapped my face! Laughed, and spat in my eye! Laughed, *and called me a hypocrite!*...

They have taken her away. *Let her taste the fire!* Let her sin receive its meet and inexorable punishment! Let righteousness prevail! Let her go with "the fearful and unbelieving, the abominable and murderers, the white-slave traders and sorcerers." Off with her to that lake "which burneth with fire and brimstone!" (Revelation XXI, 8.)....

Go, Jezebel! Go, Athaliah! Go, Painted One! Thy sins have found thee out.

February 11.

I spoke myself at to-night's meeting—simple words, but I think their message was not lost. We must wage forever the good fight. We must rout the army of sin from its fortresses....

VIII.—Litanies for the Overlooked

I.—*For Americanos*

From scented hotel soap, and from the Boy Scouts; from home cooking, and from pianos with mandolin attachments; from prohibition, and from Odd Fellows' funerals; from Key West cigars, and from cold dinner plates; from transcendentalism, and from the New Freedom; from fat women in straight-front corsets, and from Philadelphia cream cheese; from *The Star-Spangled Banner*, and from the International Sunday-school Lessons; from rubber heels, and from the college spirit; from sulphate of quinine, and from Boston baked beans; from chivalry, and from laparotomy; from the dithyrambs of Herbert Kaufman, and from sport in all its hideous forms; from women with pointed fingernails, and from men with messianic delusions; from the retailers of smutty anecdotes about the Jews, and from the Lake Mohonk Conference; from Congressmen, vice crusaders, and the heresies of Henry Van Dyke; from jokes in the *Ladies' Home Journal*, and from the Revised Statutes of the United States; from Colonial Dames, and from men who boast that they take cold shower-baths every morning; from the Drama League, and from malicious animal magnetism; from ham and eggs, and from the *Weltanschauung* of Kansas; from the theory that a dark cigar is always a strong one, and from the theory that a horse-hair put into a bottle of water will turn into a snake; from campaigns against profanity, and from the Pentateuch; from anti-vivisection, and from women who do not smoke; from wine-openers, and from Methodists; from Armageddon, and from the belief that a bloodhound never makes a mistake; from sarcerdotal moving-pictures, and from virtuous chorus girls; from bungalows, and from cornets in B flat; from canned soups, and from women who leave everything to one's honor; from detachable cuffs, and from *Lohengrin*; from unwilling motherhood, and from canary birds—good Lord, deliver us!

II.—For Hypochondriacs

From adenoids, and from chronic desquamative nephritis; from Shiga's *bacillus*, and from hysterotrachelorrhaphy; from mitral insufficiency, and from Cheyne-Stokes breathing; from the *streptococcus pyogenes*, and from splanchnoptosis; from warts, wens, and the *spirochæte pallida*; from exophthalmic goitre, and from septicopyemia; from poisoning by sewer-gas, and from the *bacillus coli communis*; from anthrax, and from von Recklinghausen's disease; from recurrent paralysis of the laryngeal nerve, and from pityriasis versicolor; from mania-à-potu, and from nephrorrhaphy; from the *leptothrix*, and from colds in the head; from tape-worms, from jiggers and from scurvy; from endocarditis, and from Romberg's masticatory spasm; from hypertrophic stenosis of the pylorus, and from fits; from the *bacillus botulinus*, and from salaam convulsions; from cerebral monoplegia, and from morphinism; from anaphylaxis, and from neuralgia in the eyeball; from dropsy, and from dum-dum fever; from autumnal catarrh, from coryza vasomotoria, from idiosyncratic coryza, from pollen catarrh, from rhinitis sympathetica, from rose cold, from *catarrhus æstivus*, from periodic hyperesthetic rhinitis, from *heuasthma*, from *catarrhe d' été* and from hay-fever—good Lord, deliver us!

III.—For Music Lovers

From all piano-players save Paderewski, Godowski and Mark Hambourg; and from the *William Tell* and *1812* overtures; and from bad imitations of Victor Herbert by Victor Herbert; and from persons who express astonishment that Dr. Karl Muck, being a German, is devoid of all bulge, corporation, paunch or leap-tick; and from the saxophone, the piccolo, the cornet and the bagpipes; and from the theory that America has no folk-music; and from all symphonic poems by English composers; and from the tall, willing, horse-chested, ham-handed, quasi-gifted ladies who stagger to their legs in gloomy drawing rooms after bad dinners and poison the air with Tosti's *Good-bye*; and from the low prehensile, godless laryngologists who prostitute their art to the saving of tenors who are happily threatened with loss of voice; and from clarinet cadenzas more than two inches in length; and from the first two acts of *Il Trovatore*; and from such fluffy, xanthous whiskers as Lohengrins wear; and from sentimental old maids who sink into senility lamenting that Brahms never wrote an opera; and from programme music, with or without notes; and from Swiss bell-ringers, Vincent D'Indy, the Paris Opera, and Elgar's *Salut d'Amour*; and from the doctrine that Massenet was a greater composer than Dvořák; and from Italian bands and *Schnellpostdoppelschraubendampfer* orchestras; and from Raff's *Cavatina* and all of Tschaikowsky except ten per centum; and from prima donna conductors who change their programmes without notice, and so get all the musical critics into a sweat; and from the abandoned hussies who sue tenors for breach of promise; and from all alleged musicians who do not shrivel to the size of five-cent cigars whenever they think of old Josef Haydn—good Lord, deliver us!

IV.—For Hangmen

From clients who delay the exercises by pausing to make long and irrelevant speeches from the scaffold, or to sing depressing Methodist hymns; and from medical examiners who forget their stethoscopes, and clamor for waits while messenger boys are sent for them; and from official witnesses who faint at the last minute, and have to be hauled out by the deputy sheriffs; and from undertakers who keep looking at their watches and hinting obscenely that they have other engagements at 10:30; and from spiritual advisers who crowd up at the last minute and fall through the trap with the condemned—good Lord, deliver us!

V.—For Magazine Editors

From Old Subscribers who write in to say that the current number is the worst magazine printed since the days of the New York *Galaxy*; and from elderly poetesses who have read all the popular text-books of sex hygiene, and believe all the bosh in them about the white slave trade, and so suspect the editor, and even the publisher, of sinister designs; and from stories in which a rising young district attorney gets the dead wood upon a burly political boss named Terrence O'Flaherty, and then falls in love with Mignon, his daughter, and has to let him go; and from stories in which a married lady, just about to sail for Capri with her husband's old *Corpsbruder*, is dissuaded from her purpose by the news that her husband has lost $700, 000 in Wall Street and is on his way home to weep on her shoulder; and from one-act plays in which young Cornelius Van Suydam comes home from The Club at 11:55 P. M. on Christmas Eve, dismisses Dodson, his Man, with the compliments of the season, and draws up his chair before the open fire to dream of his girl, thus preparing the way for the entrance of Maxwell, the starving burglar, and for the scene in which Maxwell's little daughter, Fifi, following him up the fire-escape, pleads with him to give up his evil courses; and from poems about war in which it is argued that thousands of young men are always killed, and that their mothers regret to hear of it; and from essays of a sweet and whimsical character, in which the author refers to himself as "we, " and ends by quoting Bergson, Washington Irving or Agnes Repplier; and from epigrams based on puns, good or bad; and from stories beginning, "It was the autumn of the year 1950"; and from stories embodying quotations from Omar Khayyam, and full of a mellow pessimism; and from stories in which the gay nocturnal life of the Latin Quarter is described by an author living in Dubuque, Iowa; and from stories of thought transference, mental healing and haunted houses; and from newspaper stories in which a cub reporter solves the mystery of the Snodgrass murder and is promoted to dramatic critic on the field, or in which a city editor who smokes a corn-cob pipe falls in love with a sob-sister; and from stories about trained nurses, young dramatists, baseball players, heroic locomotive engineers, settlement workers, clergymen, yeggmen, cowboys, Italians, employés of the Hudson Bay Company and great detectives; and from stories in which the dissolute son of a department store owner tries to seduce a working girl in his father's employ and then goes on the water wagon and marries her as a tribute to her virtue; and from stories in which the members of a yachting party are wrecked on a desert island in the South Pacific, and the niece of the owner of the yacht falls in love with the bo'sun; and from manuscripts accompanied by documents certifying that the incidents and people described are real, though cleverly disguised; and from authors who send in saucy notes when their offerings are returned with insincere thanks; and from lady authors who appear with satirical letters of introduction from the low, raffish rogues who edit rival magazines— good Lord, deliver us!

IX.—Asepsis. A Deduction in Scherzo Form

CHARACTERS:

A CLERGYMAN

A BRIDE

FOUR BRIDESMAIDS

A BRIDEGROOM

A BEST MAN

THE USUAL CROWD

PLACE—*The surgical amphitheatre in a hospital.*

TIME—*Noon of a fair day.*

Seats rising in curved tiers. The operating pit paved with white tiles. The usual operating table has been pushed to one side, and in place of it there is a small glass-topped bedside table. On it, a large roll of aseptic cotton, several pads of gauze, a basin of bichloride, a pair of clinical thermometers in a little glass of alcohol, a dish of green soap, a beaker of two per cent. carbolic acid, and a microscope. In one corner stands a sterilizer, steaming pleasantly like a tea kettle. There are no decorations—no flowers, no white ribbons, no satin cushions. To the left a door leads into the Anesthetic Room. A pungent smell of ether, nitrous oxide, iodine, chlorine, wet laundry and scorched gauze. Temperature: 98.6 degrees Fahr.

THE CLERGYMAN *is discovered standing behind the table in an expectant attitude. He is in the long white coat of a surgeon, with his head wrapped in white gauze and a gauze respirator over his mouth. His chunkiness suggests a fat, middle-aged Episcopal rector, but it is impossible to see either his face or his vestments. He wears rubber gloves of a dirty orange color, evidently much used.* THE BRIDEGROOM *and* THE BEST MAN *have just emerged from the Anesthetic Room and are standing before him. Both are dressed exactly as he is, save that* THE BRIDEGROOM'S *rubber gloves are white. The benches running up the amphitheatre are filled with spectators, chiefly women. They are in dingy oilskins, and most of them also wear respirators.*

After a long and uneasy pause THE BRIDE *comes in from the Anesthetic Room on the arm of her* FATHER, *with* THE FOUR BRIDESMAIDS *following by twos. She is dressed in what appears to be white linen, with a long veil of aseptic gauze. The gauze testifies to its late and careful sterilization by yellowish scorches. There is a white rubber glove upon* THE BRIDE'S *right hand, but that belonging to her left hand has been removed.* HER FATHER *is dressed like* THE BEST MAN. THE FOUR BRIDESMAIDS *are in the garb of surgical nurses, with*

613

their hair completely concealed by turbans of gauze. As THE BRIDE *takes her place before* THE CLERGYMAN, *with* THE BRIDEGROOM *at her right, there is a faint, snuffling murmur among the spectators. It hushes suddenly as* THE CLERGYMAN *clears his throat.*

THE CLERGYMAN

(*In sonorous, booming tones, somewhat muffled by his respirator.*) Dearly beloved, we are gathered here together in the face of this company to join together this man and this woman in holy matrimony, which is commended by God to be honorable among men, and therefore is not to be entered into inadvisedly or carelessly, or without due surgical precautions, but reverently, cleanly, sterilely, soberly, scientifically, and with the nearest practicable approach to bacteriological purity. Into this laudable and non-infectious state these two persons present come now to be joined and quarantined. If any man can show just cause, either clinically or microscopically, why they may not be safely sutured together, let him now come forward with his charts, slides and cultures, or else hereafter forever hold his peace.

(*Several spectators shuffle their feet, and an old maid giggles, but no one comes forward.*)

THE CLERGYMAN

(*To* THE BRIDE *and* BRIDEGROOM): I require and charge both of you, as ye will answer in the dreadful hour of autopsy, when the secrets of all lives shall be disclosed, that if either of you know of any lesion, infection, malaise, congenital defect, hereditary taint or other impediment, why ye may not be lawfully joined together in eugenic matrimony, ye do now confess it. For be ye well assured that if any persons are joined together otherwise than in a state of absolute chemical and bacteriological innocence, their marriage will be septic, unhygienic, pathogenic and toxic, and eugenically null and void.

(THE BRIDEGROOM *hands over a long envelope, from which* THE CLERGYMAN *extracts a paper bearing a large red seal.*)

THE CLERGYMAN

(*Reading*): We, and each of us, having subjected the bearer, John Doe, to a rigid clinical and laboratory examination, in accordance with Form B-3 of the United States Public Health Service, do hereby certify that, to the best of our knowledge and belief, he is free from all disease, taint, defect, deformity or hereditary blemish, saving as noted herein. Temperature *per ora*, 98.6. Pulse, 76, strong. Respiration, 28.5. Wassermann, −2. Hb., 114%. Phthalein, 1st. hr., 46%; 2nd hr., 21%. W.

B. C., 8, 925. Free gastric HCl, 11.5%. No stasis. No lactic acid. Blood pressure, 122/77. No albuminuria. No glycosuria. Lumbar puncture: clear fluid, normal pressure.

Defects Noted. 1. Left heel jerk feeble. 2. Caries in five molars. 3. Slight acne rosacea. 4. Slight inequality of curvature in meridians of right cornea. 5. Nicotine stain on right forefinger, extending to middle of second phalanx.

(*Signed*)

SIGISMUND	KRAUS,	M.D.
WM.	T. ROBERTSON,	M.D.
JAMES SIMPSON, M.D.		

Subscribed and sworn to before me, a Notary Public for the Borough of Manhattan, City of New York, State of New York.

(*Seal*)ABRAHAM LECHETITSKY.

So much for the reading of the minutes. (*To* THE BRIDE): Now for yours, my dear.

(THE BRIDE *hands up a similar envelope, from which* THE CLERGYMAN *extracts a similar document. But instead of reading it aloud, he delicately runs his eye through it in silence.*)

THE CLERGYMAN

(*The reading finished*) Very good. Very creditable. You must see some good oculist about your astigmatism, my dear. Surely you want to avoid glasses. Come to my study on your return and I'll give you the name of a trustworthy man. And now let us proceed with the ceremony of marriage. (*To* THE BRIDEGROOM): John, wilt thou have this woman to be thy wedded wife, to live together in the holy state of eugenic matrimony? Wilt thou love her, comfort her, protect her from all protozoa and bacteria, and keep her in good health; and, forsaking all other, keep thee unto her only, so long as ye both shall live? If so, hold out your tongue.

(THE BRIDEGROOM *holds out his tongue and* THE CLERGYMAN *inspects it critically.*)

THE CLERGYMAN

(*Somewhat dubiously*) Fair. I have seen worse.... Do you smoke?

THE BRIDEGROOM

(*Obviously lying*) Not much.

THE CLERGYMAN

Well, *how* much?

THE BRIDEGROOM

Say ten cigarettes a day.

THE CLERGYMAN

And the stain noted on your right posterior phalanx by the learned medical examiners?

THE BRIDEGROOM

Well, say fifteen.

THE CLERGYMAN

(*Waggishly*) Or twenty to be safe. Better taper off to ten. At all events, make twenty the limit. How about the booze?

THE BRIDEGROOM

(*Virtuously*) Never!

THE CLERGYMAN

What! Never?

THE BRIDEGROOM

Well, never again!

THE CLERGYMAN

So they *all* say. The answer is almost part of the liturgy. But have a care, my dear fellow! The true eugenist eschews the wine cup. In every hundred children of a man who ingests one fluid ounce of alcohol a day, six will be left-handed, twelve will be epileptics and nineteen will suffer from adolescent albuminuria, withdelusions of persecution.... Have you ever had anthrax?

THE BRIDEGROOM

Not yet.

THE CLERGYMAN

Eczema?

THE BRIDEGROOM

No.

THE CLERGYMAN

Pott's disease?

THE BRIDEGROOM

No.

THE CLERGYMAN

Cholelithiasis?

THE BRIDEGROOM

No.

THE CLERGYMAN

Do you have a feeling of distention after meals?

THE BRIDEGROOM

No.

THE CLERGYMAN

Have you a dry, hacking cough?

THE BRIDEGROOM

Not at present.

THE CLERGYMAN

Are you troubled with insomnia?

THE BRIDEGROOM

No.

THE CLERGYMAN

Dyspepsia?

THE BRIDEGROOM

No.

THE CLERGYMAN

Agoraphobia?

THE BRIDEGROOM

No.

THE CLERGYMAN

Do you bolt your food?

THE BRIDEGROOM

No.

THE CLERGYMAN

Have you lightning pains in the legs?

THE BRIDEGROOM

No.

THE CLERGYMAN

Are you a bleeder? Have you hæmophilia?

THE BRIDEGROOM

No.

THE CLERGYMAN

Erthrocythæmia? Nephroptosis? Fibrinous bronchitis? Salpingitis? Pylephlebitis? Answer yes or no.

THE BRIDEGROOM

No. No. No. No. No.

THE CLERGYMAN

Have you ever been refused life insurance? If so, when, by what company or companies, and why?

THE BRIDEGROOM

No.

THE CLERGYMAN

What is a staphylococcus?

THE BRIDEGROOM

No.

THE CLERGYMAN

(*Sternly*) What?

THE BRIDEGROOM

(*Nervously*) Yes.

THE CLERGYMAN

(*Coming to the rescue*) Wilt them have this woman et cetera? Answer yes or no.

THE BRIDEGROOM

I will.

THE CLERGYMAN

(*Turning to* THE BRIDE) Mary, wilt thou have this gentleman to be thy wedded husband, to live together in the holy state of aseptic matrimony? Wilt thou love him, serve him, protect him from all adulterated victuals, and keep him hygienically clothed; and forsaking all others, keep thee only unto him, so long as ye both shall live? If so——

THE BRIDE

(*Instantly and loudly*) I will.

THE CLERGYMAN

Not so fast! First, there is the little ceremony of the clinical thermometers. (*He takes up one of the thermometers.*) Open your mouth, my dear. (*He Inserts the thermometer.*) Now hold it there while you count one hundred and fifty. And you, too. (*To* THE BRIDEGROOM.) I had almost forgotten you. (THE BRIDEGROOM *opens his mouth and the other thermometer is duly planted. While the two are counting,* THE CLERGYMAN *attempts to turn back one of* THE BRIDE'S *eyelids, apparently searching for trachoma, but his rubber gloves impede the operation and so he gives it up. It is now time to read the thermometers.* THE BRIDEGROOM'S *is first removed.*)

THE CLERGYMAN

(*Reading the scale*) Ninety-nine point nine. Considering everything, not so bad. (*Then he removes and reads* THE BRIDE'S.) Ninety-eight point six. Exactly normal. Cool, collected, at ease. The classical self-possession of the party of the second part. And now, my dear, may I ask you to hold out your tongue? (THE BRIDE *does so.*)

THE CLERGYMAN

Perfect.... There; that will do. Put it back.... And now for a few questions—just a few. First, do you use opiates in any form?

THE BRIDE

No.

THE CLERGYMAN

Have you ever had goitre?

THE BRIDE

No.

THE CLERGYMAN

Yellow fever?

THE BRIDE

No.

THE CLERGYMAN

Hæmatomata?

THE BRIDE

No.

THE CLERGYMAN

Siriasis or tachycardia?

THE BRIDE

No.

THE CLERGYMAN

What did your maternal grandfather die of?

THE BRIDE

Of chronic interstitial nephritis.

THE CLERGYMAN

(*Interested*) Ah, our old friend Bright's! A typical case, I take, with the usual polyuria, œdema of the glottis, flame-shaped retinal hemorrhages and cardiac dilatation?

THE BRIDE

Exactly.

THE CLERGYMAN

And terminating, I suppose, with the classical uræmic symptoms—dyspnœa, convulsions, uræmic amaurosis, coma and collapse?

THE BRIDE

Including Cheyne-Stokes breathing.

THE CLERGYMAN

Ah, most interesting! A protean and beautiful malady! But at the moment, of course, we can't discuss it profitably. Perhaps later on.... Your father, I assume, is alive?

THE BRIDE

(*Indicating him*) Yes.

THE CLERGYMAN

Well, then, let us proceed. Who giveth this woman to be married to this man?

THE BRIDE'S FATHER

(*With a touch of stage fright.*) I do.

THE CLERGYMAN

(*Reassuringly*) You are in good health?

THE BRIDE'S FATHER

Yes.

THE CLERGYMAN

No dizziness in the morning?

THE BRIDE'S FATHER

No.

THE CLERGYMAN

No black spots before the eyes?

THE BRIDE'S FATHER

No.

THE CLERGYMAN

No vague pains in the small of the back?

THE BRIDE'S FATHER

No.

THE CLERGYMAN

Gout?

THE BRIDE'S FATHER

No.

THE CLERGYMAN

Chilblains?

THE BRIDE'S FATHER

No.

THE CLERGYMAN

Sciatica?

THE BRIDE'S FATHER

No.

THE CLERGYMAN

Buzzing in the ears?

THE BRIDE'S FATHER

No.

THE CLERGYMAN

Myopia? Angina pectoris?

THE BRIDE'S FATHER

No.

THE CLERGYMAN

Malaria? Marasmus? Chlorosis? Tetanus? Quinsy? Housemaid's knee?

THE BRIDE'S FATHER

No.

THE CLERGYMAN

You had measles, I assume, in your infancy?

THE BRIDE'S FATHER

Yes.

THE CLERGYMAN

Chicken pox? Mumps? Scarlatina? Cholera morbus? Diphtheria?

THE BRIDE'S FATHER

Yes. Yes. No. Yes. No.

THE CLERGYMAN

You are, I assume, a multipara?

THE BRIDE'S FATHER

A what?

THE CLERGYMAN

That is to say, you have had more than one child?

THE BRIDE'S FATHER

No.

THE CLERGYMAN

(*Professionally*) How sad! You will miss her!

THE BRIDE'S FATHER

One job like this is en——

THE CLERGYMAN

(*Interrupting suavely*) But let us proceed. The ceremony must not be lengthened unduly, however interesting. We now approach the benediction.

(*Dipping his gloved hands into the basin of bichloride, he joins the right hands of* THE BRIDE *and* THE BRIDEGROOM.)

THE CLERGYMAN

(*To* THE BRIDEGROOM) Repeat after me: "I, John, take thee, Mary, to be my wedded and aseptic wife, to have and to hold from this day forward, for better, for worse, for richer, for poorer, in sickness, convalescence, relapse and health, to love and to cherish, till death do us part; and thereto I plight thee my troth."

(THE BRIDEGROOM *duly repeats the formula*, THE CLERGYMAN *now looses their hands, and after another dip into the bichloride, joins them together again.*)

THE CLERGYMAN

(*To* THE BRIDE) Repeat after me: "I, Mary, take thee, John, to be my aseptic and eugenic husband, to have and to hold from this day forward, for better, for worse, for richer, for poorer, to love, to cherish and to nurse, till death do us part; and thereto I give thee my troth."

(THE BRIDE *duly promises.* THE BEST MAN *then hands over the ring, which* THE CLERGYMAN *drops into the bichloride. It turns green. He fishes it up again, wipes it dry with a piece of aseptic cotton and presents it to* THE BRIDEGROOM, *who places it upon the third finger of* THE BRIDE'S *left hand. Then* THE CLERGYMAN*goes on with the ceremony,* THE BRIDEGROOM *repeating after him.*)

THE CLERGYMAN

Repeat after me: "With this sterile ring I thee wed, and with all my worldly goods I thee endow."

(THE CLERGYMAN *then joins the hands of* THE BRIDE *and* BRIDEGROOM *once more, and dipping his own right hand into the bichloride, solemnly sprinkles the pair.*)

THE CLERGYMAN

Those whom God hath joined together, let no pathogenic organism put asunder. (*To the assembled company.*) Forasmuch as John and Mary have consented together in aseptic wedlock, and have witnessed the same by the exchange of certificates, and have given and pledged their troth, and have declared the same by giving and receiving an aseptic ring, I pronounce that they are man and wife. In the name of Mendel, of Galton, of Havelock Ellis and of David Starr Jordan. Amen.

(THE BRIDE *and* BRIDEGROOM *now kiss, for the first and last time, after which they gargle with two per cent carbolic and march out of the room, followed by*THE BRIDE'S FATHER *and the spectators.* THE BEST MAN, *before departing after them, hands* THE CLERGYMAN *a ten-dollar gold-piece in a small phial of twenty per cent bichloride.* THE

CLERGYMAN, *after pocketing it, washes his hands with green soap.* THE BRIDESMAIDS *proceed to clean up the room with the remaining bichloride. This done, they and* THE CLERGYMAN *go out. As soon as they are gone, the operating table is pushed back into place by an orderly, a patient is brought in, and a surgeon proceeds to cut off his leg.)*

X.—Tales of the Moral and Pathological

I.—The Rewards of Science

Once upon a time there was a surgeon who spent seven years perfecting an extraordinarily delicate and laborious operation for the cure of a rare and deadly disease. In the process he wore out $400 worth of knives and saws and used up $6, 000 worth of ether, splints, guinea pigs, homeless dogs and bichloride of mercury. His board and lodging during the seven years came to $2, 875. Finally he got a patient and performed the operation. It took eight hours and cost him $17 more than his fee of $20....

One day, two months after the patient was discharged as cured, the surgeon stopped in his rambles to observe a street parade. It was the annual turnout of Good Hope Lodge, No. 72, of the Patriotic Order of American Rosicrucians. The cured patient, marching as Supreme Worthy Archon, wore a lavender baldric, a pea-green sash, an aluminum helmet and scarlet gauntlets, and carried an ormolu sword and the blue polka-dot flag of a rear-admiral....

With a low cry the surgeon jumped down a sewer and was seen no more.

II.—The Incomparable Physician

The eminent physician, Yen Li-Shen, being called in the middle of the night to the bedside of the rich tax-gatherer, Chu Yi-Foy, found his distinguished patient suffering from a spasm of the liver. An examination of the pulse, tongue, toe-nails, and hair-roots revealing the fact that the malady was caused by the presence of a multitude of small worms in the blood, the learned doctor forthwith dispatched his servant to his surgery for a vial of gnats' eyes dissolved in the saliva of men executed by strangling, that being the remedy advised by Li Tan-Kien and other high authorities for the relief of this painful and dangerous condition.

When the servant returned the patient was so far gone that Cheyne-Stokes breathing had already set in, and so the doctor decided to administer the whole contents of the vial—an heroic dose, truly, for it has been immemorially held that even so little as the amount that will cling to the end of a horse hair is sufficient to cure. Alas, in his professional zeal and excitement, the celebrated pathologist permitted his hand to shake like a myrtle leaf in a Spring gale, and so he dropped not only the contents of the vial, but also the vial itself down the œsophagus of his moribund patient.

The accident, however, did not impede the powerful effects of this famous remedy. In ten minutes Chu Yi-Foy was so far recovered that he asked for a plate of rice stewed with plums, and by morning he was able to leave his bed and receive the reports of his spies, informers and extortioners. That day he sent for Dr. Yen and in token of his gratitude, for he was a just and righteous man, settled upon him in due form of law, and upon his heirs and assigns in perpetuity, the whole rents, rates, imposts and taxes, amounting to no less than ten thousand Hangkow taels a year, of two of the streets occupied by money-changers, bird-cage makers and public women in the town of Szu-Loon, and of the related alleys, courts and lanes. And Dr. Yen, with his old age and the old age of his seven sons and thirty-one grandsons now safely provided for, retired from the practise of his art, and devoted himself to a tedious scientific inquiry (long the object of his passionate aspiration) into the precise physiological relation between gravel in the lower lobe of the heart and the bursting of arteries in the arms and legs.

So passed many years, while Dr. Yen pursued his researches and sent his annual reports of progress to the Academy of Medicine at Chan-Si, and Chu Yi-Foy increased his riches and his influence, so that his arm reached out from the mountains to the sea. One day, in his eightieth year, Chu Yi-Foy fell ill again, and, having no confidence in any other physician, sent once more for the learned and now venerable Dr. Yen.

"I have a pain, " he said, "in my left hip, where the stomach dips down over the spleen. A large knob has formed there. A lizard, perhaps, has got into me. Or perhaps a small hedge-hog."

Dr. Yen thereupon made use of the test for lizards and hedge-hogs—to wit, the application of madder dye to the Adam's apple, turning it lemon yellow if any sort of reptile is within, and violet if there is a mammal—but it failed to operate as the books describe. Being thus led to suspect a misplaced and wild-growing bone, perhaps from the vertebral column, the doctor decided to have recourse to surgery, and so, after the proper propitiation of the gods, he administered to his eminent patient a draught of opium water, and having excluded the wailing women of the household from the sick chamber, he cut into the protuberance with a small, sharp knife, and soon had the mysterious object in his hand.... It was the vial of dissolved gnats' eyes—*still full and tightly corked*! Worse, it was *not* the vial of dissolved gnats' eyes, but a vial of common burdock juice—the remedy *for infants griped by their mothers' milk*....

But when the eminent Chu Yi-Foy, emerging from his benign stupor, made a sign that he would gaze upon the cause of his distress, it was a bone that Dr. Yen Li-Shen showed him—an authentic bone, ovoid and evil-looking—and lately the knee cap of one Ho Kwang, brass maker in the street of Szchen-Kiang. Dr. Yen carried this bone in his girdle to keep off the black, blue and yellow plagues. Chu Yi-Foy, looking upon it, wept the soft, grateful tears of an old man.

"This is twice, " he said, "that you, my learned friend, have saved my life. I have hitherto given you, in token of my gratitude, the rents, rates, imposts and taxes, of two streets, and of the related alleys, courts and lanes. I now give you the weight of that bone in diamonds, in rubies, in pearls or in emeralds, as you will. And whichever of the four you choose, I give you the other three also. For is it not said by K'ung Fu-tsze, 'The good physician bestows what the gods merely promise'?"

And Dr. Yen Li-Shen lowered his eyes and bowed. But he was too old in the healing art to blush.

III.—*Neighbours*

Once I lay in hospital a fortnight while an old man died by inches across the hall. Apparently a very painful, as it was plainly a very tedious business. I would hear him breathing heavily for fifteen or twenty minutes, and then he would begin shrieking in agony and yelling for his orderly: "Charlie! Charlie! Charlie!" Now and then a nurse would come into my room and report progress: "The old fellow's kidneys have given up; he can't last the night, " or, "I suppose the next choking spell will fetch him." Thus he fought his titanic fight with the gnawing rats of death, and thus I lay listening, myself quickly recovering from a sanguinary and indecent operation.... Did the shrieks of that old man startle me, worry me, torture me, set my nerves on edge? Not at all. I had my meals to the accompaniment of piteous yells to God, but day by day I ate them more heartily. I lay still in bed and read a book or smoked a cigar. I damned my own twinges and fading malaises. I argued ignorantly with the surgeons. I made polite love to the nurses who happened in. At night I slept soundly, the noise retreating benevolently as I dropped off. And when the old fellow died at last, snarling and begging for mercy with his last breath, the unaccustomed stillness made me feel lonesome and sad, like a child robbed of a tin whistle…. But when a young surgeon came in half an hour later, and, having dined to his content, testified to it by sucking his teeth, cold shudders ran through me from stem to stern.

IV.—From the Chart

Temperature: 99.7. Respiration: rising to 65 and then suddenly suspended. The face is flushed, and the eyes are glazed and half-closed. There is obviously a sub-normal reaction to external stimuli. A fly upon the ear is unnoticed. The auditory nerve is anesthetic. There is a swaying of the whole body and an apparent failure of co-ordination, probably the effect of some disturbance in the semi-circular canals of the ear. The hands tremble and then clutch wildly. The head is inclined forward as if to approach some object on a level with the shoulder. The mouth stands partly open, and the lips are puckered and damp. Of a sudden there is a sound as of a deep and labored inspiration, suggesting the upward curve of Cheyne-Stokes breathing. Then comes silence for 40 seconds, followed by a quick relaxation of the whole body and a sharp gasp….

One of the internes has kissed a nurse.

V.—The Interior Hierarchy

The world awaits that pundit who will study at length the relative respectability of the inward parts of man—his pipes and bellows, his liver and lights. The inquiry will take him far into the twilight zones of psychology. Why is the vermiform appendix so much more virtuous and dignified than its next-door neighbor, the cæcum? Considered physiologically, anatomically, pathologically, surgically, the cæcum is the decenter of the two. It has more cleanly habits; it is more beautiful; it serves a more useful purpose; it brings its owner less often to the doors of death. And yet what would one think of a lady who mentioned her cæcum? But the appendix—ah, the appendix! The appendix is pure, polite, ladylike, even noble. It confers an unmistakable stateliness, a stamp of position, a social consequence upon its possessor. And, by one of the mysteries of viscerology, it confers even *more* stateliness upon its *ex*-possessor!

Alas, what would you! Why is the stomach such a libertine and outlaw in England, and so highly respectable in the United States? No

Englishman of good breeding, save he be far gone in liquor, ever mentions his stomach in the presence of women, clergymen, or the Royal Family. To avoid the necessity—for Englishmen, too, are subject to the colic—he employs various far-fetched euphemisms, among them, the poetical Little Mary. No such squeamishness is known in America. The American discusses his stomach as freely as he discusses his business. More, he regards its name with a degree of respect verging upon reverence—and so he uses it as a euphemism for the whole region from the diaphragm to the pelvic arch. Below his heart he has only a stomach and a vermiform appendix.

In the Englishman that large region is filled entirely by his liver, at least in polite conversation. He never mentions his kidneys save to his medical adviser, but he will tell even a parlor maid that he is feeling liverish. "Sorry, old chap; I'm not up to it. Been seedy for a fortnight. Touch of liver, I dessay. Never felt quite fit since I came Home. Bones full of fever. Damned old liver always kicking up. Awfully sorry, old fellow. Awsk me again. Glad to, pon my word." But never the American! Nay, the American keeps his liver for his secret thoughts. Hobnailed it may be, and the most interesting thing within his frontiers, but he would blush to mention it to a lady.

Myself intensely ignorant of anatomy, and even more so of the punctilio, I yet attempted, one rainy day, a roster of the bodily parts in the order of their respectability. Class I was small and exclusive; when I had put in the heart, the brain, the hair, the eyes and the vermiform appendix, I had exhausted all the candidates. Here were the five aristocrats, of dignity even in their diseases—appendicitis, angina pectoris, aphasia, acute alcoholism, astigmatism: what a row of a's! Here were the dukes, the cardinals, nay, the princes of the blood. Here were the supermembers; the beyond-parts.

In Class II I found a more motley throng, led by the collar-bone on the one hand and the tonsils on the other. And in Class III—but let me present my classification and have done:

CLASS II

Collar-bone

Stomach (American)

Liver (English)

Bronchial tubes

Arms (excluding elbows)

Tonsils

Vocal chords

Ears

Cheeks

Chin

CLASS III

Elbows

Ankles

Aorta

Teeth (if natural)

Shoulders

Windpipe

Lungs

Neck

Jugular vein

CLASS IV

Stomach (English)

Liver (American)

Solar plexus

Hips

Calves

Pleura

Nose

Feet (bare)

Shins

CLASS V

Teeth (if false)

Heels

Toes

Kidneys

Knees

Diaphragm

Thyroid gland

Legs (female)

Scalp

CLASS VI

Thighs

Paunch

Œsophagus

Spleen

Pancreas

Gall-bladder

Cæcum

I made two more classes, VII and VIII, but they entered into anatomical details impossible of discussion in a book designed to be read aloud at the domestic hearth. Perhaps I shall print them in the *Medical Times* at some future time. As my classes stand, they present mysteries enough. Why should the bronchial tubes (Class II) be so much lordlier than the lungs (Class III) to which they lead? And why should the œsophagus (Class VI) be so much *less* lordly than the stomach (Class II in the United States, Class IV in England) to which *it* leads? And yet the fact in each case is known to us all. To have a touch of bronchitis is almost fashionable; to have pneumonia is merely bad luck. The stomach, at least in America, is so respectable that it dignifies even seasickness, but I have never heard of any decent man who ever had any trouble with his œsophagus.

If you wish a short cut to a strange organ's standing, study its diseases. Generally speaking, they are sure indices. Let us imagine a problem: What is the relative respectability of the hair and the scalp, close neighbors, offspring of the same osseous tissue? Turn to baldness and dandruff, and you have your answer. To be bald is no more than a genial jocosity, a harmless foible—but to have dandruff is almost as bad as to have beri-beri. Hence the fact that the hair is in Class I, while the scalp is at the bottom of Class V. So again and again. To break one's collar-bone (Class II) is to be in harmony with the nobility and gentry; to crack one's shin (Class IV) is merely vulgar. And what a difference between having one's tonsils cut out (Class II) and getting a new set of false teeth (Class V)!

Wherefore? Why? To what end? Why is the stomach so much more respectable (even in England) than the spleen; the liver (even in America) than the pancreas; the windpipe than the œsophagus; the pleura than the diaphragm? Why is the collar-bone the undisputed king of the osseous frame? One can understand the supremacy of the heart: it plainly bosses the whole vascular system. But why do the bronchial tubes wag the lungs? Why is the chin superior to the nose? The ankles to the shins? The solar plexus to the gall-bladder?

I am unequal to the penetration of this great ethical, æsthetical and sociological mystery. But in leaving it, let me point to another and antagonistic one: to wit, that which concerns those viscera of the lower animals that we use for food. The kidneys in man are far down the scale—far down in Class V, along with false teeth, the scalp and the female leg. But the kidneys of the beef steer, the calf, the sheep, or whatever animal it is whose kidneys we eat—the kidneys of this creature are close to the borders of Class I. What is it that young Capt. Lionel Basingstoke, M.P., always orders when he drops in at Gatti's on his way from his chambers in the Albany to that flat in Tyburnia where Mrs. Vaughn-Grimsby is waiting for him to rescue her from her *cochon* of a husband? What else but deviled kidneys? Who ever heard of a gallant young English seducer who didn't eat deviled kidneys—not now and then, not only on Sundays and legal holidays, but every day, every evening?

Again, and by way of postscript No. 2, concentrate your mind upon sweetbreads. Sweetbreads are made in Chicago of the pancreases of horned cattle. From Portland to Portland they belong to the first class of refined delicatessen. And yet, on the human plane, the pancreas is in Class VI, along with the cæcum and the paunch. And, contrariwise, there is tripe—"the stomach of the ox or of some other ruminant." The stomach of an American citizen belongs to Class II, and even the stomach of an Englishman is in Class IV, but tripe is far down in Class VIII. And chitterlings—the excised vermiform appendix of the cow. Of all the towns in Christendom, Richmond, Va., is the only one wherein a self-respecting white man would dare to be caught wolfing a chitterling in public.

XI. The Jazz Webster

ACTOR. One handicapped more by a wooden leg than by a wooden head.

ADULTERY. Democracy applied to love.

ALIMONY. The ransom that the happy pay to the devil.

ANTI-VIVISECTIONIST. One who gags at a guinea-pig and swallows a baby.

ARCHBISHOP. A Christian ecclesiastic of a rank superior to that attained by Christ.

ARGUMENT. A means of persuasion. The agents of argumentation under a democracy, in the order of their potency, are (*a*) whiskey, (*b*) beer, (*c*) cigars, (*d*) tears.

AXIOM. Something that everyone believes. When everyone begins to believe anything it ceases to be true. For example, the notion that the homeliest girl in the party is the safest.

BALLOT BOX. The altar of democracy. The cult served upon it is the worship of jackals by jackasses.

BREVITY. The quality that makes cigarettes, speeches, love affairs and ocean voyages bearable.

CELEBRITY. One who is known to many persons he is glad he doesn't know.

CHAUTAUQUA. A place in which persons who are not worth talking to listen to that which is not worth hearing.

CHRISTIAN. One who believes that God notes the fall of a sparrow and is shocked half to death by the fall of a Sunday-school superintendent; one who is willing to serve three Gods, but draws the line at one wife.

CHRISTIAN SCIENCE. The theory that, since the sky rockets following a wallop in the eye are optical delusions, the wallop itself is a delusion and the eye another.

CHURCH. A place in which gentlemen who have never been to Heaven brag about it to persons who will never get there.

CIVILIZATION. A concerted effort to remedy the blunders and check the practical joking of God.

CLERGYMAN. A ticket speculator outside the gates of Heaven.

CONSCIENCE. The inner voice which warns us that someone is looking.

CONFIDENCE. The feeling that makes one believe a man, even when one knows that one would lie in his place.

COURTROOM. A place where Jesus Christ and Judas Iscariot would be equals, with the betting odds in favor of Judas.

CREATOR. A comedian whose audience is afraid to laugh. Three proofs of His humor: democracy, hay fever, any fat woman.

DEMOCRACY. The theory that two thieves will steal less than one, and three less than two, and four less than three, and so on *ad infinitum*; the theory that the common people know what they want, and deserve to get it good and hard.

EPIGRAM. A platitude with vine-leaves in its hair.

EUGENICS. The theory that marriages should be made in the laboratory; the Wassermann test for love.

EVIL. That which one believes of others. It is a sin to believe evil of others, but it is seldom a mistake.

EXPERIENCE. A series of failures. Every failure teaches a man something, to wit, that he will probably fail again next time.

FAME. An embalmer trembling with stage-fright.

FINE. A bribe paid by a rich man to escape the lawful penalty of his crime. In China such bribes are paid to the judge personally; in America they are paid to him as agent for the public. But it makes no difference to the men who pay them—nor to the men who can't pay them.

FIRMNESS. A form of stupidity; proof of an inability to think the same thing out twice.

FRIENDSHIP. A mutual belief in the same fallacies, mountebanks, hobgoblins and imbecilities.

GENTLEMAN. One who never strikes a woman without provocation; one on whose word of honor the betting odds are at least 1 to 2.

HAPPINESS. Peace after effort, the overcoming of difficulties, the feeling of security and well-being. The only really happy folk are married women and single men.

HELL. A place where the Ten Commandments have a police force behind them.

HISTORIAN. An unsuccessful novelist.

HONEYMOON. The time during which the bride believes the bridegroom's word of honor.

HOPE. A pathological belief in the occurrence of the impossible.

HUMANITARIAN. One who would be sincerely sorry to see his neighbor's children devoured by wolves.

HUSBAND. One who played safe and is now played safely. A No. 16 neck in a No. 15½ collar.

HYGIENE. Bacteriology made moral; the theory that the Italian in the ditch should be jailed for spitting on his hands.

IDEALIST. One who, on noticing that a rose smells better than a cabbage, concludes that it will also make better soup.

IMMORALITY. The morality of those who are having a better time. You will never convince the average farmer's mare that the late Maud S. was not dreadfully immoral.

IMMORTALITY. The condition of a dead man who doesn't believe that he is dead.

JEALOUSY. The theory that some other fellow has just as little taste.

JUDGE. An officer appointed to mislead, restrain, hypnotize, cajole, seduce, browbeat, flabbergast and bamboozle a jury in such a manner that it will forget all the facts and give its decision to the best lawyer. The objection to judges is that they are seldom capable of a sound professional judgment of lawyers. The objection to lawyers is that the best are the worst.

JURY. A group of twelve men who, having lied to the judge about their hearing, health and business engagements, have failed to fool him.

LAWYER. One who protects us against robbers by taking away the temptation.

LIAR. (*a*) One who pretends to be very good; (*b*) one who pretends to be very bad.

LOVE. The delusion that one woman differs from another.

LOVE-AT-FIRST-SIGHT. A labor-saving device.

LOVER. An apprentice second husband; victim No. 2 in the larval stage.

MISOGYNIST. A man who hates women as much as women hate one another.

MARTYR. The husband of a woman with the martyr complex.

MORALITY. The theory that every human act must be either right or wrong, and that 99% of them are wrong.

MUSIC-LOVER. One who can tell you offhand how many sharps are in the key of C major.

OPTIMIST. The sort of man who marries his sister's best friend.

OSTEOPATH. One who argues that all human ills are caused by the pressure of hard bone upon soft tissue. The proof of his theory is to be found in the heads of those who believe it.

PASTOR. One employed by the wicked to prove to them by his example that virtue doesn't pay.

PATRIOTISM. A variety of hallucination which, if it seized a bacteriologist in his laboratory, would cause him to report the streptococcus pyogencs to be as large as a Newfoundland dog, as intelligent as Socrates, as beautiful as Mont Blanc and as respectable as a Yale professor.

PENSIONER. A kept patriot.

PLATITUDE. An idea (a) that is admitted to be true by everyone, and (b) that is not true.

POLITICIAN. Any citizen with influence enough to get his old mother a job as charwoman in the City Hall.

POPULARITY. The capacity for listening sympathetically when men boast of their wives and women complain of their husbands.

POSTERITY. The penalty of a faulty technique.

PROGRESS. The process whereby the human race has got rid of whiskers, the vermiform appendix and God.

PROHIBITIONIST. The sort of man one wouldn't care to drink with, even if he drank.

PSYCHOLOGIST. One who sticks pins into babies, and then makes a chart showing the ebb and flow of their yells.

PSYCHOTHERAPY. The theory that the patient will probably get well anyhow, and is certainly a damned fool.

QUACK. A physician who has decided to admit it.

REFORMER. A hangman signing a petition against vivisection.

REMORSE. Regret that one waited so long to do it.

SELF-RESPECT. The secure feeling that no one, as yet, is suspicious.

SOB. A sound made by women, babies, tenors, fashionable clergymen, actors and drunken men.

SOCIALISM. The theory that John Smith is better than his superiors.

SUICIDE. A belated acquiescence in the opinion of one's wife's relatives.

SUNDAY. A day given over by Americans to wishing that they themselves were dead and in Heaven, and that their neighbors were dead and in Hell.

SUNDAY SCHOOL. A prison in which children do penance for the evil conscience of their parents.

SURGEON. One bribed heavily by the patient to take the blame for the family doctor's error in diagnosis.

TEMPTATION. An irresistible force at work on a movable body.

THANKSGIVING DAY. A day devoted by persons with inflammatory rheumatism to thanking a loving Father that it is not hydrophobia.

THEOLOGY. An effort to explain the unknowable by putting it into terms of the not worth knowing.

TOMBSTONE. An ugly reminder of one who has been forgotten.

TRUTH. Something somehow discreditable to someone.

UNIVERSITY. A place for elevating sons above the social rank of their fathers. In the great American universities men are ranked as follows: 1. Seducers; 2. Fullbacks; 3. Booze-fighters; 4. Pitchers and Catchers; 5. Poker players; 6. Scholars; 7. Christians.

VERDICT. The *a priori* opinion of that juror who smokes the worst cigars.

VERS LIBRE. A device for making poetry easier to write and harder to read.

WART. Something that outlasts ten thousand kisses.

WEALTH. Any income that is at least $100 more a year than the income of one's wife's sister's husband.

WEDDING. A device for exciting envy in women and terror in men.

WIFE. One who is sorry she did it, but would undoubtedly do it again.

WIDOWER. One released on parole.

WOMAN. Before marriage, an *agente provocateuse*; after marriage, a *gendarme*.

WOMEN'S CLUB. A place in which the validity of a philosophy is judged by the hat of its prophetess.

YACHT CLUB. An asylum for landsmen who would rather die of drink than be seasick.

XII.—The Old Subject

§ 1.

Men have a much better time of it than women. For one thing, they marry later. For another thing, they die earlier.

§ 2.

The man who marries for love alone is at least honest. But so was Czolgosz.

§ 3.

When a husband's story is believed, he begins to suspect his wife.

§ 4.

In the year 1830 the average American had six children and one wife. How time transvalues all values!

§ 5.

Love begins like a triolet and ends like a college yell.

§ 6.

A man always blames the woman who fools him. In the same way he blames the door he walks into in the dark.

§ 7.

Man's objection to love is that it dies hard; woman's is that when it is dead it stays dead.

§ 8.

Definition of a good mother: one who loves her child almost as much as a little girl loves her doll.

§ 9.

The way to hold a husband is to keep him a little bit jealous. The way to lose him is to keep him a little bit more jealous.

§ 10.

It used to be thought in America that a woman ceased to be a lady the moment her name appeared in a newspaper. It is no longer thought so, but it is still true.

§ 11.

Women have simple tastes. They can get pleasure out of the conversation of children in arms and men in love.

§ 12.

Whenever a husband and wife begin to discuss their marriage they are giving evidence at a coroner's inquest.

§ 13.

How little it takes to make life unbearable!... A pebble in the shoe, a cockroach in the spaghetti, a woman's laugh!

§ 14.

The bride at the altar: "At last! At last!" The bridegroom: "Too late! Too late!"

§ 15.

The best friend a woman can have is the man who has got over loving her. He would rather die than compromise her.

§ 16.

The one breathless passion of every woman is to get some one married. If she's single, it's herself. If she's married, it's the woman her husband would probably marry if she died tomorrow.

§ 17.

Man weeps to think that he will die so soon. Woman, that she was born so long ago.

§ 18.

Woman is at once the serpent, the apple—and the belly-ache.

§ 19.

Cold mutton-stew; a soiled collar; breakfast in dress clothes; a wet house-dog, over-affectionate; the other fellow's tooth-brush; an echo of "Ta-ra-ra-boom-de-ay"; the damp, musty smell of an empty house; stale beer; a mangy fur coat; *Katzenjammer*; false teeth; the criticism of Hamilton Wright Mabie; boiled cabbage; a cocktail *after* dinner; an old cigar butt; ... the kiss of Evelyn after the inauguration of Eleanor.

§ 20.

Whenever a woman begins to talk of anything, she is talking to, of, or at a man.

§ 21.

The worst man hesitates when choosing a mother for his children. And hesitating, he is lost.

§ 22.

Women always excel men in that sort of wisdom which comes from experience. To be a woman is in itself a terrible experience.

§ 23.

No man is ever too old to look at a woman, and no woman is ever too fat to hope that he will look.

§ 24.

Bachelors have consciences. Married men have wives.

§ 25.

Bachelors know more about women than married men. If they did't they'd be married, too.

§ 26.

Man is a natural polygamist. He always has one woman leading him by the nose and another hanging on to his coat-tails.

§ 27.

All women, soon or late, are jealous of their daughters; all men, soon or late, are envious of their sons.

§ 28.

History seems to bear very harshly upon women. One cannot recall more than three famous women who were virtuous. But on turning to famous men the seeming injustice disappears. One would have difficulty finding even two of them who were virtuous.

§ 29.

Husbands never become good; they merely become proficient.

§ 30.

Strike an average between what a woman thinks of her husband a month before she marries him and what she thinks of him a year afterward, and you will have the truth about him in a very handy form.

§ 31.

The worst of marriage is that it makes a woman believe that all men are just as easy to fool.

§ 32.

The great secret of happiness in love is to be glad that the other fellow married her.

§ 33.

A man may be a fool and not know it—but not if he is married.

§ 34.

All men are proud of their own children. Some men carry egoism so far that they are even proud of their own wives.

§ 35.

When you sympathize with a married woman you either make two enemies or gain one wife and one friend.

§ 36.

Women do not like timid men. Cats do not like prudent rats.

§ 37.

He marries best who puts it off until it is too late.

§ 38.

A bachelor is one who wants a wife, but is glad he hasn't got her.

§ 40.

Women usually enjoy annoying their husbands, but not when they annoy them by growing fat.

XIII.—Panoramas of People

I.—Men

Fat, slick, round-faced men, of the sort who haunt barber shops and are always having their shoes shined. Tall, gloomy, Gothic men, with eyebrows that meet over their noses and bunches of black, curly hair in their ears. Men wearing diamond solitaires, fraternal order watchcharms, golden elks' heads with rubies for eyes. Men with thick, loose lips and shifty eyes. Men smoking pale, spotted cigars. Men who do not know what to do with their hands when they talk to women. Honorable, upright, successful men who seduce their stenographers and are kind to their dear old mothers. Men who allow their wives to dress like chorus girls. White-faced, scared-looking, yellow-eyed men who belong to societies for the suppression of vice. Men who boast that they neither drink nor smoke. Men who mop their bald heads with perfumed handkerchiefs. Men with drawn, mottled faces, in the last stages of arterio-sclerosis. Silent, stupid-looking men in thick tweeds who tramp up and down the decks of ocean steamers. Men who peep out of hotel rooms at Swedish chambermaids. Men who go to church on Sunday morning, carrying Oxford Bibles under their arms. Men in dress coats too tight under the arms. Tea-drinking men. Loud, back-slapping men, gabbling endlessly about baseball players. Men who have never heard of Mozart. Tired business men with fat, glittering wives. Men who know what to do when children are sick. Men who believe that any woman who smokes is a prostitute. Yellow, diabetic men. Men whose veins are on the outside of their noses. Now and then a clean, clear-eyed, upstanding man. Once a week or so a man with good shoulders, straight legs and a hard, resolute mouth....

II.—Women

Fat women with flabby, double chins. Moon-faced, pop-eyed women in little flat hats. Women with starchy faces and thin vermilion lips. Man-shy, suspicious women, shrinking into their clothes every time a wet, caressing eye alights upon them. Women soured and robbed of their souls by Christian Endeavor. Women who would probably be members of the Lake Mohonk Conference if they were men. Gray-haired, middle-aged, waddling women, wrecked and unsexed by endless, useless parturition, nursing, worry, sacrifice. Women who look as if they were still innocent yesterday afternoon. Women in shoes that bend their insteps to preposterous semi-circles. Women with green, barbaric bangles in their ears, like the concubines of Arab horse-thieves. Women looking in show-windows, wishing that their husbands were not such poor sticks. Shapeless women lolling in six thousand dollar motorcars. Trig little blondes, stepping like Shetland ponies. Women smelling of musk, ambergris, bergamot. Long-legged, cadaverous, hungry women. Women eager to be kidnapped, betrayed, forced into marriage at the pistol's point. Soft, pulpy, pale women. Women with ginger-colored hair and large, irregular freckles. Silly, chattering, gurgling women. Women showing their ankles to policemen, chauffeurs, street-cleaners. Women with slim-shanked, whining, sticky-fingered children dragging after them. Women marching like grenadiers. Yellow women. Women with red hands. Women with asymmetrical eyes. Women with rococo ears. Stoop-shouldered women. Women with huge hips. Bow-legged women. Appetizing women. Good-looking women....

III.—Babies

Babies smelling of camomile tea, cologne water, wet laundry, dog soap, *Schmierkase*. Babies who appear old, disillusioned and tired of life at six months. Babies that cry "Papa!" to blushing youths of nineteen or twenty at church picnics. Fat babies whose earlobes turn out at an angle of forty-five degrees. Soft, pulpy babies asleep in perambulators, the sun shining straight into their faces. Babies gnawing the tails of synthetic dogs. Babies without necks. Pale, scorbutic babies of the third and fourth generation, damned because their grandfathers and great-grandfathers read Tom Paine. Babies of a bluish tinge, or with vermilion eyes. Babies full of soporifics. Thin, cartilaginous babies that stretch when they are lifted. Warm, damp, miasmatic babies. Affectionate, ingratiating, gurgling babies: the *larvæ* of life insurance solicitors, fashionable doctors, Episcopal rectors, dealers in Mexican mine stock, hand-shakers, Sunday-school superintendents. Hungry babies, absurdly sucking their thumbs. Babies with heads of thick, coarse black hair, seeming to be toupees. Unbaptized babies, dedicated to the devil. Eugenic babies. Babies that crawl out from under tables and are stepped on. Babies with lintels, grains of corn or shoe-buttons up their noses, purple in the face and waiting for the doctor or the embalmer. A few pink, blue-eyed, tight-skinned, clean-looking babies, smiling upon the world....

XIV.—Homeopathics

1.

Scene Infernal.

During a lull in the uproar of Hell two voices were heard.

"My name, " said one, "was Ludwig van Beethoven. I was no ordinary musician. The Archduke Rudolph used to speak to me on the streets of Vienna."

"And mine, " said the other, "was the Archduke Rudolph. I was no ordinary archduke. Ludwig van Beethoven dedicated a trio to me."

2.

The Eternal Democrat.

A Socialist, carrying a red flag, marched through the gates of Heaven.

"To Hell with rank!" he shouted. "All men are equal here."

Just then the late Karl Marx turned a corner and came into view, meditatively stroking his whiskers. At once the Socialist fell upon his knees and touched his forehead to the dust.

"O Master!" he cried. "O Master, Master!"

3.

The School of Honor.

A trembling young reporter stood in the presence of an eminent city editor.

"If I write this story, " said the reporter, "it will rob a woman of her good name."

"If you don't write it, " said the city editor, "I'll give you a kick in the pantaloons."

Next day the young reporter got a raise in salary and the woman swallowed two ounces of permanganate of potassium.

4.

Proposed Plot For a Modern Novel.

Herman was in love with Violet, the wife of Armand, an elderly diabetic. Armand showed three per cent of sugar a day. Herman and Violet, who were Christians, awaited with virtuous patience the termination of Armand's distressing malady.

One day Dr. Frederick M. Allen discovered his cure for diabetes.

5.

Victory.

"I wooed and won her, " said the Man of His Wife.

"I made him run, " said the Hare of the Hound.

XV.—Vers Libre

Kiss me on the other eye;
This one's wearing out.

THE END

BOOK FIVE.
A BOOK OF PREFACES

PREFACE TO THE FOURTH EDITION

This fourth printing of "A Book of Prefaces" offers me temptation, as the third did, to revise the whole book, and particularly the chapters on Conrad, Dreiser and Huneker, all of whom have printed important new books since the text was completed. In addition, Huneker has died. But the changes that I'd make, after all, would be very slight, and so it seems better not to make them at all. From Conrad have come "The Arrow of Gold" and "The Rescue, " not to mention a large number of sumptuous reprints of old magazine articles, evidently put between covers for the sole purpose of entertaining collectors. From Dreiser have come "Free, " "Twelve Men, " "Hey, Rub-a-Dub-Dub" and some chapters of autobiography. From Huneker, before and after his death, have come "Unicorns, " "Bedouins, " "Steeple-Jack, " "Painted Veils" and "Variations." But not one of these books materially modifies the position of its author. "The Arrow of Gold, " I suppose, has puzzled a good many of Conrad's admirers, but certainly "The Rescue" has offered ample proof that his old powers are not diminished. The Dreiser books, like their predecessors that I discuss here, reveal the curious unevenness of the author. Parts of "Free" are hollow and irritating, and nearly all of "Hey, Rub-a-Dub-Dub" is feeble, but in "Twelve Men" there are some chapters that rank with the very best of "The Titan" and "Jennie Gerhardt." The place of Dreiser in our literature is frequently challenged, and often violently, but never successfully. As the years pass his solid dignity as an artist becomes more and more evident. Huneker's last five works changed his position very little. "Bedouins, " "Unicorns" and "Variations" belong mainly to his journalism, but into "Steeple-Jack, " " and above all into "Painted Veils" he put his genuine self. I have discussed all of these books in other places, and paid my small tribute to the man himself, a light burning brightly through a dark night, and snuffed out only at the dawn.

I should add that the prices of Conrad first editions given on page 56 have been greatly exceeded during the past year or two. I should add also that the Comstockian imbecilities described in Chapter IV are still going on, and that the general trend of American legislation and jurisprudence is toward their indefinite continuance.

H. L. M.

Baltimore, January 1, 1922.

I. JOSEPH CONRAD

"Under all his stories there ebbs and flows a kind of tempered melancholy, a sense of seeking and not finding...." I take the words from a little book on Joseph Conrad by Wilson Follett, privately printed, and now, I believe, out of print.[70] They define both the mood of the stories as works of art and their burden and direction as criticisms of life. Like Dreiser, Conrad is forever fascinated by the "immense indifference of things, " the tragic vanity of the blind groping that we call aspiration, the profound meaninglessness of life—fascinated, and left wondering. One looks in vain for an attempt at a solution of the riddle in the whole canon of his work. Dreiser, more than once, seems ready to take refuge behind an indeterminate sort of mysticism, even a facile supernaturalism, but Conrad, from first to last, faces squarely the massive and intolerable fact. His stories are not chronicles of men who conquer fate, nor of men who are unbent and undaunted by fate, but of men who are conquered and undone. Each protagonist is a new Prometheus, with a sardonic ignominy piled upon his helplessness. Each goes down a Greek route to defeat and disaster, leaving nothing behind him save an unanswered question. I can scarcely recall an exception. Kurtz, Lord Jim, Razumov, Nostromo, Captain Whalley, Yanko Goorall, Verloc, Heyst, Gaspar Ruiz, Almayer: one and all they are destroyed and made a mock of by the blind, incomprehensible forces that beset them.

Even in "Youth, " "Typhoon, " and "The Shadow Line, " superficially stories of the indomitable, that same consuming melancholy, that same pressing sense of the irresistible and inexplicable, is always just beneath the surface. Captain Mac Whirr gets the *Nan-Shan* to port at last, but it is a victory that stands quite outside the man himself; he is no more than a marker in the unfathomable game; the elemental forces, fighting one another, almost disregard him; the view of him that we get is one of disdain, almost one of contempt. So, too, in "Youth." A tale of the spirit's triumph, of youth besting destiny? I do not see it so. To me its significance, like that of "The Shadow Line, " is all subjective; it is an aging man's elegy upon the hope and high resolution that the

---

[70] Joseph Conrad: A short study of his intellectual and emotional attitude toward his work and of the chief characteristics of his novels, by Wilson Follett; New York, Doubleday, Page & Co. (1915).

years have blown away, a sentimental reminiscence of what the enigmatical gods have had their jest with, leaving only its gallant memory behind. The whole Conradean system sums itself up in the title of "Victory, " an incomparable piece of irony. Imagine a better label for that tragic record of heroic and yet bootless effort, that matchless picture, in microcosm, of the relentlessly cruel revolutions in the macrocosm!

Mr. Follett, perhaps with too much critical facility, finds the cause of Conrad's unyielding pessimism in the circumstances of his own life—his double exile, first from Poland, and then from the sea. But this is surely stretching the facts to fit an hypothesis. Neither exile, it must be plain, was enforced, nor is either irrevocable. Conrad has been back to Poland, and he is free to return to the ships whenever the spirit moves him. I see no reason for looking in such directions for his view of the world, nor even in the direction of his nationality. We detect certain curious qualities in every Slav simply because he is more given than we are to revealing the qualities that are in all of us. Introspection and self-revelation are his habit; he carries the study of man and fate to a point that seems morbid to westerners; he is forever gabbling about what he finds in his own soul. But in the last analysis his verdicts are the immemorial and almost universal ones. Surely his resignationism is not a Slavic copyright; all human philosophies and religions seem doomed to come to it at last. Once it takes shape as the concept of Nirvana, the desire for nothingness, the will to not-will. Again, it is fatalism in this form or that—Mohammedanism, Agnosticism ... Calvinism! Yet again, it is the "Out, out, brief candle!" of Shakespeare, the "*Eheu fugaces*" of Horace, the "*Vanitas vanitatum; omnia vanitas!*" of the Preacher. Or, to make an end, it is millenarianism, the theory that the world is going to blow up tomorrow, or the day after, or two weeks hence, and that all sweating and striving are thus useless. Search where you will, near or far, in ancient or modern times, and you will never find a first-rate race or an enlightened age, in its moments of highest reflection, that ever gave more than a passing bow to optimism. Even Christianity, starting out as "glad tidings, " has had to take on protective coloration to survive, and today its chief professors moan and blubber like Johann in Herod's rain-barrel. The sanctified are few and far between. The vast majority of us must suffer in hell, just as we suffer on earth. The divine grace, so omnipotent to save, is withheld from us. Why? There, alas, is your insoluble mystery, your riddle of the universe!...

This conviction that human life is a seeking without a finding, that its purpose is impenetrable, that joy and sorrow are alike meaningless, you will see written largely in the work of most great creative artists. It is obviously the final message, if any message is genuinely to be found there, of the nine symphonies of Ludwig van Beethoven, or, at any rate, of the three which show any intellectual content at all. Mark Twain, superficially a humourist and hence an optimist, was haunted by it in secret, as Nietzsche was by the idea of eternal recurrence: it forced itself through his guard in "The Mysterious Stranger" and "What is Man?" In Shakespeare, as Shaw has demonstrated, it amounts to a veritable obsession. And what else is there in Balzac, Goethe, Swift, Molière, Turgenev, Ibsen, Dostoyevsky, Romain Rolland, Anatole France? Or in the Zola of "L'Assomoir, " "Germinal, " "La Débâcle, " the whole Rougon-Macquart series? (The Zola of "Les Quatres Evangiles, " and particularly of "Fécondité, " turned meliorist and idealist, and became ludicrous.) Or in the Hauptmann of "Fuhrmann Henschel, " or in Hardy, or in Sudermann? (I mean, of course, Sudermann the novelist. Sudermann the dramatist is a mere mechanician.)... The younger men in all countries, in so far as they challenge the current sentimentality at all, seem to move irresistibly toward the same disdainful skepticism. Consider the last words of "Riders to the Sea." Or Gorky's "Nachtasyl." Or Frank Norris' "McTeague." Or Stephen Crane's "The Blue Hotel." Or the ironical fables of Dunsany. Or Dreiser's "Jennie Gerhardt." Or George Moore's "Sister Teresa."

Conrad, more than any of the other men I have mentioned, grounds his work firmly upon this sense of cosmic implacability, this confession of unintelligibility. The exact point of the story of Kurtz, in "Heart of Darkness, " is that it is pointless, that Kurtz's death is as meaningless as his life, that the moral of such a sordid tragedy is a wholesale negation of all morals. And this, no less, is the point of the story of Falk, and of that of Almayer, and of that of Jim. Mr. Follett (he must be a forward-looker in his heart!) finds himself, in the end, unable to accept so profound a determinism unadulterated, and so he injects a gratuitous and mythical romanticism into it, and hymns Conrad "as a comrade, one of a company gathered under the ensign of hope for common war on despair." With even greater error, William Lyon Phelps argues that his books "are based on the axiom of the moral law." [71] The one notion is as unsound as the other. Conrad makes war on

---

[71] The Advance of the English Novel. New York, Dodd, Mead & Co., 1916, p. 215.

nothing; he is pre-eminently *not* a moralist. He swings, indeed, as far from revolt and moralizing as is possible, for he does not even criticize God. His undoubted comradeship, his plain kindliness toward the soul he vivisects, is not the fruit of moral certainty, but of moral agnosticism. He neither protests nor punishes; he merely smiles and pities. Like Mark Twain he might well say: "The more I see of men, the more they amuse me—and the more I pity them." He is *simpatico* precisely because of this ironical commiseration, this infinite disillusionment, this sharp understanding of the narrow limits of human volition and responsibility.... I have said that he does not criticize God. One may even imagine him pitying God....

§ 2

But in this pity, I need not add, there is no touch of sentimentality. No man could be less the romantic, blubbering over the sorrows of his own Werthers. No novelist could have smaller likeness to the brummagem emotion-squeezers of the Kipling type, with their playhouse fustian and their naïve ethical cocksureness. The thing that sets off Conrad from these facile fellows, and from the shallow pseudo-realists who so often coalesce with them and become indistinguishable from them, is precisely his quality of irony, and that irony is no more than a proof of the greater maturity of his personal culture, his essential superiority as a civilized man. It is the old difference between a Huxley and a Gladstone, a philosophy that is profound and a philosophy that is merely comfortable, "*Quid est veritas?*" and "Thus saith the Lord!" He brings into the English fiction of the day, not only an artistry that is vastly more fluent and delicate than the general, but also a highly unusual sophistication, a quite extraordinary detachment from all petty rages and puerile certainties. The winds of doctrine, howling all about him, leave him absolutely unmoved. He belongs to no party and has nothing to teach, save only a mystery as old as man. In the midst of the hysterical splutterings and battle-cries of the Kiplings and Chestertons, the booming pedagogics of the Wellses and Shaws, and the smirking at key-holes of the Bennetts and de Morgans, he stands apart and almost alone, observing the sardonic comedy of man with an eye that sees every point and significance of it, but vouchsafing none of that sophomoric indignation, that Hyde Park wisdom, that flabby moralizing which freight and swamp the modern English novel. "At the centre of his web, " says Arthur Symons, "sits an elemental sarcasm discussing human affairs with a calm and cynical ferocity.... He calls up all the dreams and illusions by which men have been destroyed and saved, and lays them mockingly naked.... He shows the bare side of every virtue, the hidden heroism of every vice and crime. He summons before him all the injustices that have come to birth out of ignorance and self-love.... And in all this there is no judgment, only an implacable comprehension, as of one outside nature, to whom joy and sorrow, right and wrong, savagery and civilization, are equal and indifferent...." [72]

Obviously, no Englishman! No need to explain (with something akin to apology) that his name is really not Joseph Conrad at all, but Teodor Josef Konrad Karzeniowski, and that he is a Pole of noble lineage, with a vague touch of the Asiatic in him. The Anglo-Saxon mind, in these later days, becomes increasingly incapable of his whole point of view. Put into plain language, his doctrine can only fill it with wonder and fury. That mind is essentially moral in cut; it is believing, certain, indignant; it is as incapable of skepticism, save as a passing coryza of the spirit, as it is of wit, which is skepticism's daughter. Time was when this was not true, as Congreve, Pope, Wycherley and even Thackeray show, but that time was before the Reform Bill of 1832, the great intellectual levelling, the emancipation of the *chandala*. In these our days the Englishman is an incurable foe of distinction, and being so he must needs take in with his mother's milk the delusions which go with that enmity, and particularly the master delusion that all human problems, in the last analysis, are readily soluble, and that all that is required for their solution is to take counsel freely, to listen to wizards, to count votes, to agree upon legislation. This is the prime and immovable doctrine of the *mobile vulgus* set free; it is the loveliest of all the fruits of its defective powers of observation and reasoning, and above all, of its defective knowledge of demonstrated facts, especially in history. Take away this notion that there is some mysterious infallibility in the sense of the majority, this theory that the consensus of opinion is inspired, and the idea of equality begins to wither; in fact, it ceases to have any intelligibility at all. But the notion is not taken away; it is nourished; it flourishes on its own effluvia. And out of it spring the two rules which give direction to all popular thinking, the first being that no concept in politics or conduct is valid (or more accurately respectable), which rises above the comprehension of the great masses of men, or which violates any of their inherent prejudices or superstitions, and the second being that the articulate individual in

---

[72] Conrad, in the *Forum*, May, 1915.

the mob takes on some of the authority and inspiration of the mob itself, and that he is thus free to set himself up as a soothsayer, so long as he does not venture beyond the aforesaid bounds—in brief, that one man's opinion, provided it observe the current decorum, is as good as any other man's.

Practically, of course, this is simply an invitation to quackery. The man of genuine ideas is hedged in by taboos; the quack finds an audience already agape. The reply to the invitation, in the domain of applied ethics, is the revived and reinforced *Sklavenmoral* that besets all of us of English speech—the huggermugger morality of timorous, whining, unintelligent and unimaginative men—envy turned into law, cowardice sanctified, stupidity made noble, Puritanism. And in the theoretical field there is an even more luxuriant crop of bosh. Mountebanks almost innumerable tell us what we should believe and practice, in politics, religion, philosophy and the arts. England and the United States, between them, house more creeds than all the rest of the world together, and they are more absurd. They rise, they flame, they fall and go out, but always there are new ones, always the latest is worse than the last. What modern civilization save this of ours could have produced Christian Science, or the New Thought, or Billy Sundayism? What other could have yielded up the mawkish bumptiousness of the Uplift? What other could accept gravely the astounding imbecilities of English philanthropy and American law? The native output of fallacy and sentimentality, in fact, is not enough to satisfy the stupendous craving of the mob unleashed; there must needs be a constant importation of the aberrant fancies of other peoples. Let a new messiah leap up with a new message in any part of the world, and at once there is a response from the two great free nations. Once it was Tolstoi with a mouldy asceticism made of catacomb Christianity and senile soul-sickness; again it was Bergson, with a perfumed quasi-philosophy for the boudoirs of the faubourgs; yet again came Rudolf Eucken and Pastor Wagner, with their middle-class beeriness and banality. The list need go no further. It begins with preposterous Indian swamis and yoghis (most of them, to do them justice, diligent Jews from Grand street or the bagnios of Constantinople), and it ends with the fabulous Ibsen of the symbols (no more the real Ibsen than Christ was a prohibitionist), the Ellen Key of the new gyneolatry and the Signorina Montessori of the magical Method. It was a sure instinct that brought Eusapia Palladino to New York. It was the same sure instinct that brought Hall Caine.

I have mentioned Ibsen. A glance at the literature he has spawned in the vulgate is enough to show how much his falser aspects have intrigued the American mind and how little it has reacted to his shining skill as a dramatic craftsman—his one authentic claim upon fame. Read Jennette Lee's "The Ibsen Secret, "[73] perhaps the most successful of all the Ibsen gemaras in English, if you would know the virulence of the national appetite for bogus revelation. And so in all the arts. Whatever is profound and penetrating we stand off from; whatever is facile and shallow, particularly if it reveal a moral or mystical color, we embrace. Ibsen the first-rate dramatist was rejected with indignation precisely because of his merits—his sharp observation, his sardonic realism, his unsentimental logic. But the moment a meretricious and platitudinous ethical purpose began to be read into him—how he protested against it!—he was straightway adopted into our flabby culture. Compare Hauptmann and Brieux, the one a great artist, the other no more than a raucous journalist. Brieux's elaborate proofs that two and two are four have been hailed as epoch-making; one of his worst plays, indeed, has been presented with all the solemn hocus-pocus of a religious rite. But Hauptmann remains almost unknown; even the Nobel Prize did not give him a vogue. Run the roll: Maeterlinck and his languishing supernaturalism, Tagore and his Asiatic wind music, Selma Lagerlöf and her old maid's mooniness, Bernstein, Molnar and company and their out-worn tricks—but I pile up no more names. Consider one fact: the civilization that kissed Maeterlinck on both cheeks, and Tagore perhaps even more intimately, has yet to shake hands with Anatole France....

This bemusement by superficial ideas, this neck-bending to quacks, this endless appetite for sesames and apocalypses, is depressingly visible in our native literature, as it is in our native theology, philosophy and politics. "The British and American mind, " says W. L. George, [74] "has been long honey-combed with moral impulse, at any rate since the Reformation; it is very much what the German mind was up to the middle of the Nineteenth Century." The artist, facing an audience which seems incapable of differentiating between æsthetic and ethical values, tends to become a preacher of sonorous nothings, and the actual moralist-propagandist finds his way into art well greased. No other people in Christendom produces so vast a crop of tin-horn haruspices. We have so many Orison Swett Mardens, Martin Tuppers,

[73] New York and London. G. P. Putnam's Sons, 1907.
[74] The Intelligence of Woman. Boston, Little, Brown & Co., 1916, p. 6-7.

Edwin Markhams, Gerald Stanley Lees, Dr. Frank Cranes and Dr. Sylvanus Stalls that their output is enough to supply the whole planet. We see, too, constantly, how thin is the barrier separating the chief Anglo-Saxon novelists and playwrights from the pasture of the platitudinarian. Jones and Pinero both made their first strikes, not as the artists they undoubtedly are, but as pinchbeck moralists, moaning over the sad fact that girls are seduced. Shaw, a highly dexterous dramaturgist, smothers his dramaturgy in a pifflish iconoclasm that is no more than a disguise for Puritanism. Bennett and Wells, competent novelists, turn easily from the novel to the volume of shoddy philosophizing. Kipling, with "Kim" behind him, becomes a vociferous leader-writer of the *Daily Mail* school, whooping a pothouse patriotism, hurling hysterical objurgations at the foe. Even W. L. George, potentially a novelist of sound consideration, drops his craft for the jehad of the suffragettes. Doyle, Barrie, Caine, Locke, Barker, Mrs. Ward, Beresford, Hewlett, Watson, Quiller-Couch—one and all, high and low, they are tempted by the public demand for sophistry, the ready market for pills. A Henry Bordeaux, in France, is an exception; in England he is the rule. The endless thirst to be soothed with cocksure asseverations, the great mob yearning to be dosed and comforted, is the undoing, over there, of three imaginative talents out of five.

And, in America, of nearly five out of five. Winston Churchill may serve as an example. He is a literary workman of very decent skill; the native critics speak of him with invariable respect; his standing within the craft was shown when he was unanimously chosen first president of the Authors' League of America. Examine his books in order. They proceed steadily from studies of human character and destiny, the proper business of the novelist, to mere outpourings of social and economic panaceas, the proper business of leader writers, chautauquas rabble-rousers and hedge politicians. "The Celebrity" and "Richard Carvel, " within their limits, are works of art; "The Inside of the Cup" is no more than a compendium of paralogy, as silly and smattering as a speech by William Jennings Bryan or a shocker by Jane Addams. Churchill, with the late Jack London to bear him company, may stand for a large class; in its lower ranks are such men as Reginald Wright Kauffman and Will Levington Comfort. Still more typical of the national taste for moral purpose and quack philosophy are the professional optimists and eye-dimmers, with their two grand divisions, the boarding-school romantics and the Christian Endeavor Society sentimentalists. Of the former I give you George Barr McCutcheon, Owen Wister, the late Richard Harding Davis, and a horde of women—most of them now humanely translated to the moving pictures. Of the latter I give you the fair authors of the "glad" books, so gigantically popular, so lavishly praised in the newspapers—with the wraith of the later Howells, the virtuous, kittenish Howells, floating about in the air above them. No other country can parallel this literature, either in its copiousness or in its banality. It is native and peculiar to a civilization which erects the unshakable certainties of the misinformed and quack-ridden into a national way of life....

§ 3

My business, however, is not with the culture of Anglo-Saxondom, but only with Conrad's place therein. That place is isolated and remote; he is neither of it nor quite in it. In the midst of a futile meliorism which deceives the more, the more it soothes, he stands out like some sinister skeleton at the feast, regarding the festivities with a flickering and impenetrable grin. "To read him, " says Arthur Symons, "is to shudder on the edge of a gulf, in a silent darkness." There is no need to be told that he is there almost by accident, that he came in a chance passerby, a bit uncertain of the door. It was not an artistic choice that made him write English instead of French; it was a choice with its roots in considerations far afield. But once made, it concerned him no further. In his first book he was plainly a stranger, and all himself; in his last he is a stranger still—strange in his manner of speech, strange in his view of life, strange, above all, in his glowing and gorgeous artistry, his enthusiasm for beauty *per se*, his absolute detachment from that heresy which would make it no more than a servant to some bald and depressing theory of conduct, some axiom of the uncomprehending. He is, like Dunsany, a pure artist. His work, as he once explained, is not to edify, to console, to improve or to encourage, but simply to get upon paper some shadow of his own eager sense of the wonder and prodigality of life as men live it in the world, and of its unfathomable romance and mystery. "My task, " he went on, "is, by the power of the written word, to make you hear, to make you feel—it is, before all, to make you *see*. That—and no more, and it is everything."... [75]

This detachment from all infra-and-ultra-artistic purpose, this repudiation of the rôle of propagandist, this avowal of what Nietzsche was fond of calling innocence, explains the failure of Conrad to fit into the pigeon-holes so laboriously prepared for him by critics who must shelve and label or be damned. He is too big for any of them, and of a shape too strange. He stands clear, not only of all the schools and

---

[75] In *The New Review*, Dec., 1897.

factions that obtain in latter-day English fiction, but also of the whole stream of English literature since the Restoration. He is as isolated a figure as George Moore, and for much the same reason. Both are exotics, and both, in a very real sense, are public enemies, for both war upon the philosophies that caress the herd. Is Conrad the beyond-Kipling, as the early criticism of him sought to make him? Nonsense! As well speak of Mark Twain as the beyond-Petroleum V. Nasby (as, indeed, was actually done). He is not only a finer artist than Kipling; he is a quite different kind of artist. Kipling, within his limits, shows a talent of a very high order. He is a craftsman of the utmost deftness. He gets his effects with almost perfect assurance. Moreover, there is a poet in him; he knows how to reach the emotions. But once his stories are stripped down to the bare carcass their emptiness becomes immediately apparent. The ideas in them are not the ideas of a reflective and perspicacious man, but simply the ideas of a mob-orator, a mouther of inanities, a bugler, a school-girl. Reduce any of them to a simple proposition, and that proposition, in so far as it is intelligible at all, will be ridiculous. It is precisely here that Conrad leaps immeasurably ahead. His ideas are not only sound; they are acute and unusual. They plough down into the sub-strata of human motive and act. They unearth conditions and considerations that lie concealed from the superficial glance. They get at the primary reactions. In particular and above all, they combat the conception of man as a pet and privy councillor of the gods, working out his own destiny in a sort of vacuum and constantly illumined by infallible revelations of his duty, and expose him as he is in fact: an organism infinitely more sensitive and responsive than other organisms, but still a mere organism in the end, a brother to the wild things and the protozoa, swayed by the same inscrutable fortunes, condemned to the same inchoate errors and irresolutions, and surrounded by the same terror and darkness....

But is the Conrad I here describe simply a new variety of moralist, differing from the general only in the drift of the doctrine he preaches? Surely not. He is no more a moralist than an atheist is a theologian. His attitude toward all moral systems and axioms is that of a skeptic who rejects them unanimously, even including, and perhaps especially including, those to which, in moments of æsthetic detachment, he seems to give a formal and resigned sort of assent. It is this constant falling back upon "I do not know, " this incessant conversion of the easy logic of romance into the harsh and dismaying logic of fact, that explains his failure to succeed as a popular novelist, despite his skill at evoking emotion, his towering artistic passion, his power to tell a thumping tale. He is talked of, he brings forth a mass of punditic criticism, he becomes in a sense the fashion; but it would be absurd to say that he has made the same profound impression upon the great class of normal novel-readers that Arnold Bennett once made, or H. G. Wells, or William de Morgan in his brief day, or even such cheap-jacks as Anthony Hope Hawkins and William J. Locke. His show fascinates, but his philosophy, in the last analysis, is unbearable. And in particular it is unbearable to women. One rarely meets a woman who, stripped of affection, shows any genuine enthusiasm for a Conrad book, or, indeed, any genuine comprehension of it. The feminine mind, which rules in English fiction, both as producer and as consumer, craves inevitably a more confident and comforting view of the world than Conrad has to offer. It seeks, not disillusion, but illusion. It protects itself against the disquieting questioning of life by pretending that all the riddles have been solved, that each new sage answers them afresh, that a few simple principles suffice to dispose of them. Women, one may say, have to subscribe to absurdities in order to account for themselves at all; it is the instinct of self-preservation which sends them to priests, as to other quacks. This is not because they are unintelligent, but rather because they have that sharp and sure sort of intelligence which is instinctive, and which passes under the name of intuition. It teaches them that the taboos which surround them, however absurd at bottom, nevertheless penalize their courage and curiosity with unescapable dudgeon, and so they become partisans of the existing order, and, per corollary, of the existing ethic. They may be menaced by phantoms, but at all events these phantoms really menace them. A woman who reacted otherwise than with distrust to such a book as "Victory" would be as abnormal as a woman who embraced "Jenseits von Gut und Böse" or "The Inestimable Life of the Great Gargantua."

As for Conrad, he retaliates by approaching the sex somewhat gingerly. His women, in the main, are no more than soiled and tattered cards in a game played by the gods. The effort to erect them into the customary "sympathetic" heroines of fiction always breaks down under the drum fire of the plain facts. He sees quite accurately, it seems to me, how vastly the rôle of women has been exaggerated, how little they amount to in the authentic struggle of man. His heroes are moved by avarice, by ambition, by rebellion, by fear, by that "obscure inner necessity" which passes for nobility or the sense of duty—never by that puerile passion which is the mainspring of all masculine acts and aspirations in popular novels and on the stage. If they yield to amour at all, it is only at the urging of some more powerful and characteristic impulse, *e.g.*, a fantastic notion of chivalry, as in the case of Heyst, or the thirst for dominion, as in the case of Kurtz. The one exception is offered by Razumov—and Razumov is Conrad's picture of a flabby fool, of a sentimentalist destroyed by his sentimentality. Dreiser has shown much the same process in Witla and Cowperwood, but he is less free from the conventional obsession than Conrad; he takes a love affair far more naïvely, and hence far more seriously.

I used to wonder why Conrad never tackled a straight-out story of adultery under Christianity, the standard matter of all our more pretentious fiction and drama. I was curious to see what his ethical agnosticism would make of it. The conclusion I came to at first was that his failure marked the limitations of his courage—in brief, that he hesitated to go against the orthodox axioms and assumptions in the department where they were most powerfully maintained. But it seems to me now that his abstinence has not been the fruit of timidity, but of disdain. He has shied at the hypothesis, not at its implications. His whole work, in truth, is a destructive criticism of the prevailing notion that such a story is momentous and worth telling. The current gyneolatry is as far outside his scheme of things as the current program of rewards and punishments, sins and virtues, causes and effects. He not only sees clearly that the destiny and soul of man are not moulded by petty jousts of sex, as the prophets of romantic love would have us believe; he is so impatient of the fallacy that he puts it as far behind him as possible, and sets his conflicts amid scenes that it cannot penetrate, save as a palpable absurdity. Love, in his stories, is either a feeble phosphorescence or a gigantic grotesquerie. In "Heart of Darkness, " perhaps, we get his typical view of it. Over all the frenzy and horror of the tale itself floats the irony of the trusting heart back in Brussels. Here we have his measure of the master sentimentality of them all....

§ 4

As for Conrad the literary craftsman, opposing him for the moment to Conrad the showman of the human comedy, the quality that all who write about him seem chiefly to mark in him is his scorn of conventional form, his tendency to approach his story from two directions at once, his frequent involvement in apparently inextricable snarls of narrative, sub-narrative and sub-sub-narrative. "Lord Jim, " for example, starts out in the third person, presently swings into an exhaustive psychological discussion by the mythical Marlow, then goes into a brisk narrative at second (and sometimes at third) hand, and finally comes to a halt upon an unresolved dissonance, a half-heard chord of the ninth: "And that's the end. He passes away under a cloud, inscrutable at heart, forgotten, unforgiven, and excessively romantic." "Falk" is also a story within a story; this time the narrator is "one who had not spoken before, a man over fifty." In "Amy Foster" romance is filtered through the prosaic soul of a country doctor; it is almost as if a statistician told the tale of Horatius at the bridge. In "Under Western Eyes" the obfuscation is achieved by "a teacher of languages, " endlessly lamenting his lack of the "high gifts of imagination and expression." In "Youth" and "Heart of Darkness" the chronicler and speculator is the shadowy Marlow, a "cloak to goe inbisabell" for Conrad himself. In "Chance" there are two separate stories, imperfectly welded together. Elsewhere there are hesitations, goings back, interpolations, interludes in the Socratic manner. And almost always there is heaviness in the getting under weigh. In "Heart of Darkness" we are on the twentieth page before we see the mouth of the great river, and in "Falk" we are on the twenty-fourth before we get a glimpse of Falk. "Chance" is nearly half done before the drift of the action is clearly apparent. In "Almayer's Folly" we are thrown into the middle of a story, and do not discover its beginning until we come to "An Outcast of the Islands, " a later book. As in structure, so in detail. Conrad pauses to explain, to speculate, to look about. Whole chapters concern themselves with detailed discussions of motives, with exchanges of views, with generalizations abandoned as soon as they are made. Even the author's own story, "A Personal Record" (in the English edition, "Some Reminiscences") starts near the end, and then goes back, halting tortuously, to the beginning.

In the eyes of orthodox criticism, of course, this is a grave fault. The Kipling-Wells style of swift, shouldering, button-holing writing has accustomed readers and critics alike to a straight course and a rapid tempo. Moreover, it has accustomed them to a forthright certainty and directness of statement; they expect an author to account for his characters at once, and on grounds instantly comprehensible. This omniscience is a part of the prodigality of moral theory that I have been discussing. An author who knows just what is the matter with the world may be quite reasonably expected to know just what is the matter with his hero. Neither sort of assurance, I need not say, is to be found in Conrad. He is an inquirer, not a law-giver; an experimentalist, not a doctor. One constantly derives from his stories the notion that he is as much puzzled by his characters as the reader is—that he, too, is feeling his way among shadowy evidences. The discoveries that we make, about Lord Jim, about Nostromo or about Kurtz, come as fortuitously and as unexpectedly as the discoveries we make about the real figures of our world. The picture is built up bit by bit; it is never flashed suddenly and completely as by best-seller calciums; it remains a bit dim at the end. But in that very dimness, so tantalizing and yet so revealing, lies two-thirds of Conrad's art, or his craft, or his trick, or whatever you choose to call it. What he shows us is blurred at the edges, but so is life itself blurred at the edges. We see least clearly precisely what is nearest to us, and is hence most real to us. A man may profess to understand the President of the United States, but he seldom alleges, even to himself, that he understands his own wife.

In the character and in its reactions, in the act and in the motive: always that tremulousness, that groping, that confession of final bewilderment. "He passes away under a cloud, inscrutable at heart...." And the cloud enshrouds the inner man as well as the outer, the secret springs of his being as well as the overt events of his life. "His meanest creatures, " says Arthur Symons, "have in them a touch of honour, of honesty, or of heroism; his heroes have always some error, weakness, or mistake, some sin or crime, to redeem." What is Lord Jim, scoundrel and poltroon or gallant knight? What is Captain MacWhirr, hero or simply ass? What is Falk, beast or idealist? One leaves "Heart of Darkness" in that palpitating confusion which is shot through with intense curiosity. Kurtz is at once the most abominable of rogues and the most fantastic of dreamers. It is impossible to differentiate between his vision and his crimes, though all that we look upon as order in the universe stands between them. In Dreiser's novels there is the same anarchy of valuations, and it is chiefly responsible for the rage he excites in the unintelligent. The essential thing about Cowperwood is that he is two diverse beings at once; a puerile chaser of women and a great artist, a guinea pig and half a god. The essential thing about Carrie Meeber is that she remains innocent in the midst of her contaminations, that the virgin lives on in the kept woman. This is not the art of fiction as it is conventionally practised and understood. It is not explanation, labelling, assurance, moralizing. In the cant of newspaper criticism, it does not "satisfy." But the great artist is never one who satisfies in that feeble sense; he leaves the business to mountebanks who do it better. "My purpose, " said Ibsen, "is not to answer questions; it is to ask them." The spectator must bring something with him beyond the mere faculty of attention. If, coming to Conrad, he cannot, he is at the wrong door.

§ 5

Conrad's predilection for barbarous scenes and the more bald and shocking sort of drama has an obviously autobiographical basis. His own road ran into strange places in the days of his youth. He moved among men who were menaced by all the terrestrial cruelties, and by the almost unchecked rivalry and rapacity of their fellow men, without any appreciable barriers, whether of law, of convention or of sentimentality, to shield them. The struggle for existence, as he saw it, was well nigh as purely physical among human beings as among the carnivora of the jungle. Some of his stories, and among them his very best, are plainly little more than transcripts of his own experience. He himself is the enchanted boy of "Youth"; he is the ship-master of "Heart of Darkness"; he hovers in the background of all the island books and is visibly present in most of the tales of the sea.

And what he got out of that early experience was more than a mere body of reminiscence; it was a scheme of valuations. He came to his writing years with a sailor's disdain for the trifling hazards and emprises of market places and drawing rooms, and it shows itself whenever he sets pen to paper. A conflict, it would seem, can make no impression upon him save it be colossal. When his men combat, not nature, but other men, they carry over into the business the gigantic method of sailors battling with a tempest. "The Secret Agent" and "Under Western Eyes" fill the dull back streets of London and Geneva with pursuits, homicides and dynamitings. "Nostromo" is a long record of treacheries, butcheries and carnalities. "A Point of Honor" is coloured by the senseless, insatiable ferocity of Gobineau's "Renaissance." "Victory" ends with a massacre of all the chief personages, a veritable catastrophe of blood. Whenever he turns from the starker lusts to the pale passions of man under civilization, Conrad fails. "The Return" is a thoroughly infirm piece of writing—a second rate magazine story. One concludes at once that the author himself does not believe in it. "The Inheritors" is worse; it becomes, after the first few pages, a flaccid artificiality, a bore. It is impossible to imagine the chief characters of the Conrad gallery in such scenes. Think of Captain MacWhirr reacting to social tradition, Lord Jim immersed in the class war, Lena Hermann seduced by the fashions, Almayer a candidate for office! As well think of Huckleberry Finn at Harvard, or Tom Jones practising law.

These things do not interest Conrad, chiefly, I suppose, because he does not understand them. His concern, one may say, is with the gross anatomy of passion, not with its histology. He seeks to depict emotion, not in its ultimate attenuation, but in its fundamental innocence and fury. Inevitably, his materials are those of what we call melodrama; he is at one, in the bare substance of his tales, with the manufacturers of the baldest shockers. But with a difference!—a difference, to wit, of approach and comprehension, a difference abysmal and revolutionary. He lifts melodrama to the dignity of an important business, and makes it a means to an end that the mere shock-monger never dreams of. In itself, remember, all this up-roar and blood-letting is not incredible, nor even improbable. The world, for all the pressure of order, is still full of savage and stupendous conflicts, of murders and debaucheries, of crimes indescribable and adventures almost unimaginable. One cannot reasonably ask a novelist to deny them or to gloss over them; all one may demand of him is that, if he make artistic use of them, he render them understandable—that he logically account for them, that he give them plausibility by showing their genesis in intelligible motives and colourable events.

The objection to the conventional melodramatist is that he fails to do this. It is not that his efforts are too florid, but that his causes are too puny. For all his exuberance of fancy, he seldom shows us a downright impossible event; what he does constantly show us is an inadequate and hence unconvincing motive. In a cheap theatre we see a bad actor, imperfectly disguised as a viscount, bind a shrieking young woman to the railroad tracks, with an express train approaching. Why does he do it? The melodramatist offers a double-headed reason, the first part being that the viscount is an amalgam of Satan and Don Juan and the second being that the young woman prefers death to dishonour. Both parts are absurd. Our eyes show us at once that the fellow is far more the floorwalker, the head barber, the Knight of Pythias than either the Satan or the Don Juan, and our experience of life tells us that young women in yellow wigs do not actually rate their virginity so dearly. But women are undoubtedly done to death in this way—not every day, perhaps, but now and then. Men bind them, trains run over them, the newspapers discuss the crime, the pursuit of the felon, the ensuing jousting of the jurisconsults. Why, then? The true answer, when it is forthcoming at all, is always much more complex than the melodramatist's answer. It may be so enormously complex, indeed, as to transcend all the normal laws of cause and effect. It may be an answer made up largely, or even wholly, of the fantastic, the astounding, the unearthly reasons of lunacy. That is the chief, if not the only difference between melodrama and reality. The events of the two may be, and often are identical. It is only in their underlying network of causes that they are dissimilar and incommensurate.

Here, in brief, you have the point of essential distinction between the stories of Conrad, a supreme artist in fiction, and the trashy confections of the literary artisans—*e.g.*, Sienkiewicz, Dumas, Lew Wallace, and their kind. Conrad's materials, at bottom, are almost identical with those of the artisans. He, too, has his chariot races, his castaways, his carnivals of blood in the arena. He, too, takes us through shipwrecks, revolutions, assassinations, gaudy heroisms, abominable treacheries. But always he illuminates the nude and amazing event with shafts of light which reveal not only the last detail of its workings, but also the complex of origins and inducements behind it. Always, he throws about it a probability which, in the end, becomes almost inevitability. His "Nostromo, " for example, in its externals, is a mere tale of South American turmoil; its materials are those of "Soldiers of Fortune." But what a difference in method, in point of approach, in inner content! Davis was content to show the overt act, scarcely accounting for it at all, and then only in terms of conventional romance. Conrad penetrates to the motive concealed in it, the psychological spring and basis of it, the whole fabric of weakness, habit and aberration underlying it. The one achieved an agreeable romance, and an agreeable romance only. The other achieves an extraordinarily brilliant and incisive study of the Latin-American temperament—a full length exposure of the perverse passions and incomprehensible ideals which provoke presumably sane men to pursue one another like wolves, and of the reactions of that incessant pursuit upon the men themselves, and upon their primary ideas, and upon the institutions under which they live. I do not say that Conrad is always exhaustive in his explanations, or that he is accurate. In the first case I know that he often is not, in the second case I do not know whether he is or he isn't. But I do say that, within the scope of his vision, he is wholly convincing; that the men and women he sets into his scene show ineluctably vivid and persuasive personality; that the theories he brings forward to account for their acts are intelligible; that the effects of those acts, upon actors and immediate spectators alike, are such as might be reasonably expected to issue; that the final impression is one of searching and indubitable veracity. One leaves "Nostromo" with a memory as intense and lucid as that of a real experience. The thing is not mere photography. It is interpretative painting at its highest.

In all his stories you will find this same concern with the inextricable movement of phenomena and noumena between event and event, this same curiosity as to first causes and ultimate effects. Sometimes, as in "The Point of Honor" and "The End of the Tether, " he attempts to work out the obscure genesis, in some chance emotion or experience, of an extraordinary series of transactions. At other times, as in "Typhoon, " "Youth, " "Falk" and "The Shadow Line, " his endeavour is to determine the effect of some gigantic and fortuitous event upon the mind and soul of a given man. At yet other times, as in "Almayer's Folly, " "Lord Jim" and "Under Western Eyes, " it is his aim to show how cause and effect are intricately commingled, so that it is difficult to separate motive from consequence, and consequence from motive. But always it is the process of mind rather than the actual act that interests him. Always he is trying to penetrate the actor's mask and interpret the actor's frenzy. It is this concern with the profounder aspects of human nature, this bold grappling with the deeper and more recondite problems of his art, that gives him consideration as a first-rate artist. He differs from the common novelists of his time as a Beethoven differs from a Mendelssohn. Some of them are quite his equals in technical skill, and a few of them, notably Bennett and Wells, often show an actual superiority, but when it comes to that graver business which underlies all mere virtuosity, he is unmistakably the superior of the whole corps of them.

This superiority is only the more vividly revealed by the shop-worn shoddiness of most of his materials. He takes whatever is nearest to hand, out of his own rich experience or out of the common store of romance. He seems to disdain the petty advantages which go with the invention of novel plots, extravagant characters and unprecedented snarls of circumstance. All the classical doings of anarchists are to be found in "The Secret Agent"; one has heard them copiously credited, of late, to so-called Reds. "Youth, " as a story, is no more than an orthodox sea story, and W. Clark Russell contrived better ones. In "Chance" we have a stern father at his immemorial tricks. In "Victory" there are villains worthy of Jack B. Yeats' melodramas of the Spanish Main. In "Nostromo" we encounter the whole stock company of Richard Harding Davis and O. Henry. And in "Under Western Eyes" the protagonist is one who finds his love among the women of his enemies—a situation at the heart of all the military melodramas ever written.

But what Conrad makes of that ancient and fly-blown stuff, that rubbish from the lumber room of the imagination! Consider, for example, "Under Western Eyes, " by no means the best of his stories. The plot is that of "Shenandoah" and "Held by the Enemy"—but how brilliantly it is endowed with a new significance, how penetratingly its remotest currents are followed out, how magnificently it is made to fit into that colossal panorama of Holy Russia! It is always this background, this complex of obscure and baffling influences, this drama under the drama, that Conrad spends his skill upon, and not the obvious commerce of the actual stage. It is not the special effect that he seeks, but the general effect. It is not so much man the individual that interests him, as the shadowy accumulation of traditions, instincts and blind chances which shapes the individual's destiny. Here, true enough, we have a full-length portrait of Razumov, glowing with life. But here, far more importantly, we also have an amazingly meticulous and illuminating study of the Russian character, with all its confused mingling of Western realism and Oriental fogginess, its crazy tendency to go shooting off into the spaces of an incomprehensible metaphysic, its general transcendence of all that we Celts and Saxons and Latins hold to be true of human motive and human act. Russia is a world apart: that is the sum and substance of the tale. In the island stories we have the same elaborate projection of the East, of its fantastic barbarism, of brooding Asia. And in the sea stories we have, perhaps for the first time in English fiction, a vast and adequate picture of the sea, the symbol at once of man's eternal striving and of his eternal impotence. Here, at last, the colossus has found its interpreter. There is in "Typhoon" and "The Nigger of the Narcissus, " and, above all, in "The Mirror of the Sea, " a poetic evocation of the sea's stupendous majesty that is unparalleled outside the ancient sagas. Conrad describes it with a degree of graphic skill that is superb and incomparable. He challenges at once the pictorial vigour of Hugo and the aesthetic sensitiveness of Lafcadio Hearn, and surpasses them both. And beyond this mere dazzling visualization, he gets into his pictures an overwhelming sense of that vast drama of which they are no more than the flat, lifeless representation—of that inexorable and uncompassionate struggle which is life itself. The sea to him is a living thing, an omnipotent and unfathomable thing, almost a god. He sees it as the Eternal Enemy, deceitful in its caresses, sudden in its rages, relentless in its enmities, and forever a mystery.

§ 6

Conrad's first novel, "Almayer's Folly, " was printed in 1895. He tells us in "A Personal Record" that it took him seven years to write it—seven years of pertinacious effort, of trial and error, of learning how to write. He was, at this time thirty-eight years old. Seventeen years before, landing in England to fit himself for the British merchant service, he had made his first acquaintance with the English language. The interval had been spent almost continuously at sea—in the Eastern islands, along the China coast, on the Congo and in the South Atlantic. That he hesitated between French and English is a story often told, but he himself is authority for the statement that it is more symbolical than true. Flaubert, in those days, was his idol, as we know, but the speech of his daily business won, and English literature reaped the greatest of all its usufructs from English sea power. To this day there are marks of his origins in his style. His periods, more than once, have an inept and foreign smack. In fishing for the right phrase one sometimes feels that he finds a French phrase, or even a Polish phrase, and that it loses something by being done into English.

The credit for discovering "Almayer's Folly, " as the publishers say, belongs to Edward Garnett, then a reader for T. Fisher Unwin. The book was brought out modestly and seems to have received little attention. The first edition, it would appear, ran to no more than a thousand copies; at all events, specimens of it are now very hard to find, and collectors pay high prices for them. When "An Outcast of the Islands" followed, a year later, a few alert readers began to take notice of the author, and one of them was Sir (then Mr.) Hugh Clifford, a former Governor of the Federated Malay States and himself the author of several excellent books upon the Malay. Clifford gave Conrad encouragement privately and talked him up in literary circles, but the majority of English critics remained unaware of him. After an interval of two years, during which he struggled between his desire to write and the temptation to return to the sea, he published "The Nigger of the Narcissus."[76] It made a fair success of esteem, but still there was no recognition of the author's true stature. Then followed "Tales of Unrest" and "Lord Jim, " and after them the feeblest of all the Conrad books, "The Inheritors, " written in collaboration with Ford Madox Hueffer. It is easy to see in this collaboration, and no less in the character of the book, an indication of irresolution, and perhaps even of downright loss of hope. But success, in fact, was just around the corner. In 1902 came "Youth, " and straightway Conrad was the lion of literary London. The chorus of approval that greeted it was almost a roar; all sorts of critics and reviewers, from H. G. Wells to W. L. Courtney, and from John Galsworthy to W. Robertson Nicoll, took a hand. Writing home to the *New York Times*, W. L. Alden reported that

[76] Printed in the United States as Children of the Sea, but now restored to its original title.

he had "not heard one dissenting voice in regard to the book, " but that the praise it received "was unanimous, " and that the newspapers and literary weeklies rivalled one another "in their efforts to express their admiration for it."

This benign whooping, however, failed to awaken the enthusiasm of the mass of novel-readers and brought but meagre orders from the circulating libraries. "Typhoon" came upon the heels of "Youth, " but still the sales of the Conrad books continued small and the author remained in very uncomfortable circumstances. Even after four or five years he was still so poor that he was glad to accept a modest pension from the British Civil List. This official recognition of his genius, when it came at last, seems to have impressed the public, characteristically enough, far more than his books themselves had done, and the foundations were thus laid for that wider recognition of his genius which now prevails. But getting him on his legs was slow work, and such friends as Hueffer, Clifford and Galsworthy had to do a lot of arduous log-rolling. Even after the splash made by "Youth" his publishing arrangements seem to have remained somewhat insecure. His first eleven books show six different imprints; it was not until his twelfth that he settled down to a publisher. His American editions tell an even stranger story. The first six of them were brought out by six different publishers; the first eight by no less than seven. But today he has a regular American publisher at last, and in England a complete edition of his works is in progress.

Thanks to the indefatigable efforts of that American publisher (who labours for Gene Stratton-Porter and Gerald Stanley Lee in the same manner) Conrad has been forced upon the public notice in the United States, and it is the fashion among all who pretend to aesthetic consciousness to read him, or, at all events, to talk about him. His books have been brought together in a uniform edition for the newly intellectual, bound in blue leather, like the "complete library sets" of Kipling, O. Henry, Guy de Maupassant and Paul de Kock. The more literary newspapers print his praises; he is hymned by professorial critics as a prophet of virtue; his genius is certificated by such diverse authorities as Hildegarde Hawthorne and Louis Joseph Vance; I myself lately sat on a Conrad Committee, along with Booth Tarkington, David Belasco, Irvin Cobb, Walter Pritchard Eaton and Hamlin Garland— surely an astounding posse of *literati*! Moreover, Conrad himself shows a disposition to reach out for a wider audience. His "Victory, " first published in *Munsey's Magazine*, revealed obvious efforts to be intelligible to the general. A few more turns of the screw and it might have gone into the *Saturday Evening Post*, between serials by Harris Dickson and Rex Beach.

Meanwhile, in the shadow of this painfully growing celebrity as a novelist, Conrad takes on consideration as a bibelot, and the dealers in first editions probably make more profit out of some of his books than ever he has made himself. His manuscripts are cornered, I believe, by an eminent collector of literary curiosities in New York, who seems to have a contract with the novelist to take them as fast as they are produced—perhaps the only arrangement of the sort in literary history. His first editions begin to bring higher premiums than those of any other living author. Considering the fact that the oldest of them is less than twenty-five years old, they probably set new records for the trade. Even the latest in date are eagerly sought, and it is not uncommon to see an English edition of a Conrad book sold at an advance in New York within a month of its publication.

As I hint, however, there is not much reason to believe that this somewhat extravagant fashion is based upon any genuine liking, or any very widespread understanding. The truth is that, for all the adept tub-thumping of publishers, Conrad's sales still fall a good deal behind those of even the most modest of best-seller manufacturers, and that the respect with which his successive volumes are received is accompanied by enthusiasm in a relatively narrow circle only. A clan of Conrad fanatics exists, and surrounding it there is a body of readers who read him because it is the intellectual thing to do, and who talk of him because talking of him is expected. But beyond that he seems to make little impression. When "Victory" was printed in*Munsey's Magazine* it was a failure; no other single novel, indeed, contributed more toward the abandonment of the policy of printing a complete novel in each issue. The other popular magazines show but small inclination for Conrad manuscripts. Some time ago his account of a visit to Poland in war-time was offered on the American market by an English author's agent. At the start a price of $2,500 was put upon it, but after vainly inviting buyers for a couple of months it was finally disposed of to a literary newspaper which seldom spends so much as $2,500, I daresay, for a whole month's supply of copy.

In the United States, at least, novelists are made and unmade, not by critical majorities, but by women, male and female. The art of fiction among us, as Henry James once said, "is almost exclusively feminine." In the books of such a man as William Dean Howells it is difficult to find a single line that is typically and exclusively masculine. One could easily imagine Edith Wharton, or Mrs. Watts, or even Agnes Repplier, writing all of them. When a first-rate novelist emerges from obscurity it is almost always by some fortuitous plucking of the dexter string. "Sister Carrie, " for example, has made a belated commercial success, not because its dignity as a human document is understood, but because it is mistaken for a sad tale of amour, not unrelated to "The Woman Thou Gavest Me" and "Dora Thorne." In Conrad there is no such sweet bait for the fair and sentimental. The sedentary multipara, curled up in her boudoir on a rainy afternoon, finds nothing to her taste in his grim tales. The Conrad philosophy is harsh, unyielding, repellent. The Conrad heroes are nearly all boors and ruffians. Their very love-making has something sinister and abhorrent in it; one cannot imagine them in the moving pictures, played by tailored beauties with long eye-lashes. More, I venture that the censors would object to them, even disguised as floor-walkers. Surely that would be a besotted board which would pass the irregular amours of Lord Jim, the domestic brawls of Almayer, the revolting devil's mass of Kurtz, Falk's disgusting feeding in the Southern Ocean, or the butchery on Heyst's island. Stevenson's "Treasure Island" has been put upon the stage, but "An Outcast of the Islands" would be as impossible there as "Barry Lyndon" or "La Terre." The world fails to breed actors for such rôles, or stage managers to penetrate such travails of the spirit, or audiences for the revelation thereof.

With the Conrad cult, so discreetly nurtured out of a Barabbasian silo, there arises a considerable Conrad literature, most of it quite valueless. Huneker's essay, in "Ivory, Apes and Peacocks, "[77] gets little beyond the obvious; William Lyon Phelps, in "The Advance of the English Novel, " achieves only a meagre judgment; [78] Frederic Taber Cooper tries to estimate such things as "The Secret Agent" and "Under Western Eyes" in terms of the Harvard enlightenment; [79] John Galsworthy wastes himself upon futile comparisons; [80] even Sir Hugh Clifford, for all his quick insight, makes irrelevant objections to

---

[77] New York, Chas. Scribner's Sons, 1915, pp. 1-21.

[78] New York, Dodd, Mead & Co., 1916, pp. 192-217.

[79] Some English Story Tellers: A Book of the Younger Novelists; New York, Henry Holt & Co., 1912, pp. 1-30.

[80] A Disquisition on Conrad, *Fortnightly Review*, April, 1908.

Conrad's principles of Malay psychology.[81] Who cares? Conrad is his own God, and creates his own Malay! The best of the existing studies of Conrad, despite certain sentimentalities arising out of youth and schooling, is in the book of Wilson Follett, before mentioned. The worst is in the official biography by Richard Curle,[82] for which Conrad himself obtained a publisher and upon which his *imprimatur* may be thus assumed to lie. If it does, then its absurdities are nothing new, for we all know what a botch Ibsen made of accounting for himself. But, even so, the assumption stretches the probabilities more than once. Surely it is hard to think of Conrad putting "Lord Jim" below "Chance" and "The Secret Agent" on the ground that it "raises a fierce moral issue." Nothing, indeed, could be worse nonsense—save it be an American critic's doctrine that "Conrad denounces pessimism." "Lord Jim" no more raises a moral issue than "The Titan." It is, if anything, a devastating exposure of a moral issue. Its villain is almost heroic; its hero, judged by his peers, is a scoundrel....

Hugh Walpole, himself a competent novelist, does far better in his little volume, "Joseph Conrad."[83] In its brief space he is unable to examine all of the books in detail, but he at least manages to get through a careful study of Conrad's method, and his professional skill and interest make it valuable.

§ 7

There is a notion that judgments of living artists are impossible. They are bound to be corrupted, we are told, by prejudice, false perspective, mob emotion, error. The question whether this or that man is great or small is one which only posterity can answer. A silly begging of the question, for doesn't posterity also make mistakes? Shakespeare's ghost has seen two or three posterities, beautifully at odds. Even today, it must notice a difference in flitting from London to Berlin. The shade of Milton has been tricked in the same way. So, also, has Johann Sebastian Bach's. It needed a Mendelssohn to rescue it from Coventry—and now Mendelssohn himself, once so shining a light,

---

[81] The Genius of Mr. Joseph Conrad, *North American Review*, June, 1904.

[82] Joseph Conrad: A Study; New York, Doubleday, Page & Co., 1914.

[83] Joseph Conrad; London, Nisbet & Co. (1916).

is condemned to the shadows in his turn. We are not dead yet; we are here, and it is now. Therefore, let us at least venture, guess, opine.

My own conviction, sweeping all those reaches of living fiction that I know, is that Conrad's figure stands out from the field like the Alps from the Piedmont plain. He not only has no masters in the novel; he has scarcely a colourable peer. Perhaps Thomas Hardy and Anatole France—old men both, their work behind them. But who else? James is dead. Meredith is dead. So is George Moore, though he lingers on. So are all the Russians of the first rank; Andrieff, Gorki and their like are light cavalry. In Sudermann, Germany has a writer of short stories of very high calibre, but where is the German novelist to match Conrad? Clara Viebig? Thomas Mann? Gustav Frenssen? Arthur Schnitzler? Surely not! As for the Italians, they are either absurd tear-squeezers or more absurd harlequins. As for the Spaniards and the Scandinavians, they would pass for geniuses only in Suburbia. In America, setting aside an odd volume here and there, one can discern only Dreiser—and of Dreiser's limitations I shall discourse anon. There remains England. England has the best second-raters in the world; nowhere else is the general level of novel writing so high; nowhere else is there a corps of journeyman novelists comparable to Wells, Bennett, Benson, Walpole, Beresford, George, Galsworthy, Hichens, De Morgan, Miss Sinclair, Hewlett and company. They have a prodigious facility; they know how to write; even the least of them is, at all events, a more competent artisan than, say, Dickens, or Bulwer-Lytton, or Sienkiewicz, or Zola. But the literary *grande passion* is simply not in them. They get nowhere with their suave and interminable volumes. Their view of the world and its wonders is narrow and superficial. They are, at bottom, no more than clever mechanicians.

As Galsworthy has said, Conrad lifts himself immeasurably above them all. One might well call him, if the term had not been cheapened into cant, a cosmic artist. His mind works upon a colossal scale; he conjures up the general out of the particular. What he sees and describes in his books is not merely this man's aspiration or that woman's destiny, but the overwhelming sweep and devastation of universal forces, the great central drama that is at the heart of all other dramas, the tragic struggles of the soul of man under the gross stupidity and obscene joking of the gods. "In the novels of Conrad, " says Galsworthy, "nature is first, man is second." But not a mute, a docile second! He may think, as Walpole argues, that "life is too strong, too clever and too remorseless for the sons of men, " but he does not think that they are too weak and poor in spirit to challenge it. It is the challenging that engrosses him, and enchants him, and raises up the magic of his wonder. It is as futile, in the end, as Hamlet's or Faust's—but still a gallant and a gorgeous adventure, a game uproariously worth the playing, an enterprise "inscrutable ... and excessively romantic."...

If you want to get his measure, read "Youth" or "Falk" or "Heart of Darkness, " and then try to read the best of Kipling. I think you will come to some understanding, by that simple experiment, of the difference between an adroit artisan's bag of tricks and the lofty sincerity and passion of a first-rate artist.

II. THEODORE DREISER

§ 1

Out of the desert of American fictioneering, so populous and yet so dreary, Dreiser stands up—a phenomenon unescapably visible, but disconcertingly hard to explain. What forces combined to produce him in the first place, and how has he managed to hold out so long against the prevailing blasts—of disheartening misunderstanding and misrepresentation, of Puritan suspicion and opposition, of artistic isolation, of commercial seduction? There is something downright heroic in the way the man has held his narrow and perilous ground, disdaining all compromise, unmoved by the cheap success that lies so inviting around the corner. He has faced, in his day, almost every form of attack that a serious artist can conceivably encounter, and yet all of them together have scarcely budged him an inch. He still plods along in the laborious, cheerless way he first marked out for himself; he is quite as undaunted by baited praise as by bludgeoning, malignant abuse; his later novels are, if anything, more unyieldingly dreiserian than his earliest. As one who has long sought to entice him in this direction or that, fatuously presuming to instruct him in what would improve him and profit him, I may well bear a reluctant and resigned sort of testimony to his gigantic steadfastness. It is almost as if any change in his manner, any concession to what is usual and esteemed, any amelioration of his blind, relentless exercises of *force majeure*, were a physical impossibility. One feels him at last to be authentically no more than a helpless instrument (or victim) of that inchoate flow of forces which he himself is so fond of depicting as at once the answer to the riddle of life, and a riddle ten times more vexing and accursed.

And his origins, as I say, are quite as mysterious as his motive power. To fit him into the unrolling chart of American, or even of

English fiction is extremely difficult. Save one thinks of H. B. Fuller (whose "With the Procession" and "The Cliff-Dwellers" are still remembered by Huneker, but by whom else?[84] [85]), he seems to have had no fore-runner among us, and for all the discussion of him that goes on, he has few avowed disciples, and none of them gets within miles of him. One catches echoes of him, perhaps, in Willa Sibert Cather, in Mary S. Watts, in David Graham Phillips, in Sherwood Anderson and in Joseph Medill Patterson, but, after all, they are no more than echoes. In Robert Herrick the thing descends to a feeble parody; in imitators further removed to sheer burlesque. All the latter-day American novelists of consideration are vastly more facile than Dreiser in their philosophy, as they are in their style. In the fact, perhaps, lies the measure of their difference. What they lack, great and small, is the gesture of pity, the note of awe, the profound sense of wonder—in a phrase, that "soberness of mind" which William Lyon Phelps sees as the hallmark of Conrad and Hardy, and which even the most stupid cannot escape in Dreiser. The normal American novel, even in its most serious forms, takes colour from the national cocksureness and superficiality. It runs monotonously to ready explanations, a somewhat infantile smugness and hopefulness, a habit of reducing the unknowable to terms of the not worth knowing. What it cannot explain away with ready formulae, as in the later Winston Churchill, it snickers over as scarcely worth explaining at all, as in the later Howells. Such a brave and tragic book as "Ethan Frome" is so rare as to be almost singular, even with Mrs. Wharton. There is, I daresay, not much market for that sort of thing. In the arts, as in the concerns of everyday, the American seeks escape from the insoluble by pretending that it is solved. A comfortable phrase is what he craves beyond all things—and comfortable phrases are surely not to be sought in Dreiser's stock.

I have heard argument that he is a follower of Frank Norris, and two or three facts lend it a specious probability. "McTeague" was

---

84

[85] *Fuller's comparative obscurity is one of the strangest phenomena of American letters. Despite his high achievement, he is seldom discussed, or even mentioned. Back in 1899 he was already so far forgotten that William Archer mistook his name, calling him Henry Y. Puller. Vide Archer's pamphlet, The American Language; New York, 1899.*

printed in 1899; "Sister Carrie" a year later. Moreover, Norris was the first to see the merit of the latter book, and he fought a gallant fight, as literary advisor to Doubleday, Page & Co., against its suppression after it was in type. But this theory runs aground upon two circumstances, the first being that Dreiser did not actually read "McTeague, " nor, indeed, grow aware of Norris, until after "Sister Carrie" was completed, and the other being that his development, once he began to write other books, was along paths far distant from those pursued by Norris himself. Dreiser, in truth, was a bigger man than Norris from the start; it is to the latter's unending honour that he recognized the fact instanter, and yet did all he could to help his rival. It is imaginable, of course, that Norris, living fifteen years longer, might have overtaken Dreiser, and even surpassed him; one finds an arrow pointing that way in "Vandover and the Brute" (not printed until 1914). But it swings sharply around in "The Epic of the Wheat." In the second volume of that incomplete trilogy, "The Pit, " there is an obvious concession to the popular taste in romance; the thing is so frankly written down, indeed, that a play has been made of it, and Broadway has applauded it. And in "The Octopus, " despite some excellent writing, there is a descent to a mysticism so fantastic and preposterous that it quickly passes beyond serious consideration. Norris, in his day, swung even lower—for example, in "A Man's Woman" and in some of his short stories. He was a pioneer, perhaps only half sure of the way he wanted to go, and the evil lures of popular success lay all about him. It is no wonder that he sometimes seemed to lose his direction.

Émile Zola is another literary father whose paternity grows dubious on examination. I once printed an article exposing what seemed to me to be a Zolaesque attitude of mind, and even some trace of the actual Zola manner, in "Jennie Gerhardt"; there came from Dreiser the news that he had never read a line of Zola, and knew nothing about his novels. Not a complete answer, of course; the influence might have been exerted at second hand. But through whom? I confess that I am unable to name a likely medium. The effects of Zola upon Anglo-Saxon fiction have been almost *nil*; his only avowed disciple, George Moore, has long since recanted and reformed; he has scarcely rippled the prevailing romanticism.... Thomas Hardy? Here, I daresay, we strike a better scent. There are many obvious likenesses between "Tess of the D'Urbervilles" and "Jennie Gerhardt" and again between "Jude the Obscure" and "Sister Carrie." All four stories deal penetratingly and poignantly with the essential tragedy of women; all disdain the petty, specious explanations of popular fiction; in each one finds a poetical and melancholy beauty. Moreover, Dreiser himself confesses to an enchanted discovery of Hardy in 1896, three years before "Sister Carrie" was begun. But it is easy to push such a fact too hard, and to search for likenesses and parallels that are really not there. The truth is that Dreiser's points of contact with Hardy might be easily matched by many striking points of difference, and that the fundamental ideas in their novels, despite a common sympathy, are anything but identical. Nor does one apprehend any ponderable result of Dreiser's youthful enthusiasm for Balzac, which antedated his discovery of Hardy by two years. He got from both men a sense of the scope and dignity of the novel; they taught him that a story might be a good one, and yet considerably more than a story; they showed him the essential drama of the commonplace. But that they had more influence in forming his point of view, or even in shaping his technique, than any one of half a dozen other gods of those young days—this I scarcely find. In the structure of his novels, and in their manner of approach to life no less, they call up the work of Dostoyevsky and Turgenev far more than the work of either of these men—but of all the Russians save Tolstoi (as of Flaubert) Dreiser himself tells us that he was ignorant until ten years after "Sister Carrie." In his days of preparation, indeed, his reading was so copious and so disorderly that antagonistic influences must have well-nigh neutralized one another, and so left the curious youngster to work out his own method and his own philosophy. Stevenson went down with Balzac, Poe with Hardy, Dumas *fils* with Tolstoi. There were even months of delight in Sienkiewicz, Lew Wallace and E. P. Roe! The whole repertory of the pedagogues had been fought through in school and college: Dickens, Thackeray, Hawthorne, Washington Irving, Kingsley, Scott. Only Irving and Hawthorne seem to have made deep impressions. "I used to lie under a tree, " says Dreiser, "and read 'Twice Told Tales' by the hour. I thought 'The Alhambra' was a perfect creation, and I still have a lingering affection for it." Add Bret Harte, George Ebers, William Dean Howells, Oliver Wendell Holmes, and you have a literary stew indeed!... But for all its bubbling I see a far more potent influence in the chance discovery of Spencer and Huxley at twenty-three—the year of choosing! Who, indeed, will ever measure the effect of those two giants upon the young men of that era—Spencer with his inordinate meticulousness, his relentless pursuit of facts, his overpowering syllogisms, and Huxley with his devastating agnosticism, his insatiable questionings of the old axioms, above all, his brilliant style? Huxley, it would appear, has been condemned to the scientific hulks, along with bores innumerable and unspeakable; one looks in vain for any appreciation of him in treatises on beautiful letters.[86] And yet the man was a superb artist in works, a master-writer even more than a master-biologist, one of the few truly great stylists that England has produced since the time of Anne. One can easily imagine the effect of two such vigorous and intriguing minds upon a youth groping about for self-understanding and self-expression. They swept him clean, he tells us, of the lingering faith of his boyhood—a mediaeval, Rhenish Catholicism;—more, they filled him with a new and eager curiosity, an intense interest in the life that lay about him, a desire to seek out its hidden workings and underlying causes. A young man set afire by Huxley might perhaps make a very bad novelist, but it is a certainty that he could never make a sentimental and superficial one. There is no need to go further than this single moving adventure to find the genesis of Dreiser's disdain of the current platitudes, his sense of life as a complex biological phenomenon, only dimly comprehended, and his tenacious way of thinking things out, and of holding to what he finds good. Ah, that he had learned from Huxley, not only how to inquire, but also how to report! That he had picked up a talent for that dazzling style, so sweet to the ear, so damnably persuasive, so crystal-clear!

But the more one examines Dreiser, either as writer or as theorist of man, the more his essential isolation becomes apparent. He got a habit of mind from Huxley, but he completely missed Huxley's habit of writing. He got a view of woman from Hardy, but he soon changed it out of all resemblance. He got a certain fine ambition and gusto out of Balzac, but all that was French and characteristic he left behind. So with Zola, Howells, Tolstoi and the rest. The tracing of likenesses quickly becomes rabbinism, almost cabalism. The differences are huge and sprout up in all directions. Nor do I see anything save a flaming up of colonial passion in the current efforts to fit him into a German frame, and make him an agent of Prussian frightfulness in letters. Such childish gabble one looks for in the New York *Times*, and there is where one actually finds it. Even the literary monthlies have stood clear of it; it is important only as material for that treatise upon the patrioteer and his bawling which remains to be written. The name of the man, true

---

[86] For example, in The Cambridge History of English Literature, which runs to fourteen large volumes and a total of nearly 10, 000 pages, Huxley receives but a page and a quarter of notice, and his remarkable mastery of English is barely mentioned in passing. His two debates with Gladstone, in which he did some of the best writing of the century, are not noticed at all.

enough, is obviously Germanic, and he has told us himself, in "A Traveler at Forty, " how he sought out and found the tombs of his ancestors in some little town of the Rhine country. There are more of these genealogical revelations in "A Hoosier Holiday, " but they show a Rhenish strain that was already running thin in boyhood. No one, indeed, who reads a Dreiser novel can fail to see the gap separating the author from these half-forgotten forbears. He shows even less of German influence than of English influence.

There is, as a matter of fact, little in modern German fiction that is intelligibly comparable to "Jennie Gerhardt" and "The Titan, " either as a study of man or as a work of art. The naturalistic movement of the eighties was launched by men whose eyes were upon the theatre, and it is in that field that nine-tenths of its force has been spent. "German naturalism, " says George Madison Priest, quoting Gotthold Klee's "Grunzüge der deutschen Literaturgeschichte" "created a new type only in the drama." [87] True enough, it has also produced occasional novels, and some of them are respectable. Gustav Frenssen's "Jörn Uhl" is a specimen: it has been done into English. Another is Clara Viebig's "Das tägliche Brot, " which Ludwig Lewisohn compares to George Moore's "Esther Waters." Yet another is Thomas Mann's "Buddenbrooks." But it would be absurd to cite these works as evidences of a national quality, and doubly absurd to think of them as inspiring such books as "Jennie Gerhardt" and "The Titan, " which excel them in everything save workmanship. The case of Mann reveals a tendency that is visible in nearly all of his contemporaries. Starting out as an agnostic realist not unlike the Arnold Bennett of "The Old Wives' Tale, " he has gradually taken on a hesitating sort of romanticism, and in one of his later books, "Königliche Hoheit" (in English, "Royal Highness") he ends upon a note of sentimentalism borrowed from Wagner's "Ring." Fräulein Viebig has also succumbed to banal and extra-artistic purposes. Her "Die Wacht am Rhein, " for all its merits in detail, is, at bottom, no more than an eloquent hymn to patriotism—a theme which almost always baffles novelists. As for Frenssen, he is a parson by trade, and carries over into the novel a good deal of the windy moralizing of the pulpit. All of these German naturalists—and they are the only German novelists worth considering—share the weakness of Zola, their *Stammvater*. They, too,

---

[87] *A Brief History of German Literature; New York, Chas. Scribner's Sons, 1909.*

fall into the morass that engulfed "Fécondité, " and make sentimental propaganda.

I go into this matter in detail, not because it is intrinsically of any moment, but because the effort to depict Dreiser as a secret agent of the Wilhelmstrasse, told off to inject subtle doses of *Kultur* into a naïve and pious people, has taken on the proportions of an organized movement. The same critical imbecility which detects naught save a Tom cat in Frank Cowperwood can find naught save an abhorrent foreigner in Cowperwood's creator. The truth is that the trembling patriots of letters, male and female, are simply at their old game of seeing a man under the bed. Dreiser, in fact, is densely ignorant of German literature, as he is of the better part of French literature, and of much of English literature. He did not even read Hauptmann until after "Jennie Gerhardt" had been written, and such typical German moderns as Ludwig Thoma, Otto Julius Bierbaum and Richard Dehmel remain as strange to him as Heliogabalus.

§ 2

In his manner, as opposed to his matter, he is more the Teuton, for he shows all of the racial patience and pertinacity and all of the racial lack of humour. Writing a novel is as solemn a business to him as trimming a beard is to a German barber. He blasts his way through his interminable stories by something not unlike main strength; his writing, one feels, often takes on the character of an actual siege operation, with tunnellings, drum fire, assaults in close order and hand-to-hand fighting. Once, seeking an analogy, I called him the Hindenburg of the novel. If it holds, then "The 'Genius'" is his Poland. The field of action bears the aspect, at the end, of a hostile province meticulously brought under the yoke, with every road and lane explored to its beginning, and every crossroads village laboriously taken, inventoried and policed. Here is the very negation of Gallic lightness and intuition, and of all other forms of impressionism as well. Here is no series of illuminating flashes, but a gradual bathing of the whole scene with white light, so that every detail stands out.

And many of those details, of course, are trivial; even irritating. They do not help the picture; they muddle and obscure it; one wonders impatiently what their meaning is, and what the purpose may be of revealing them with such a precise, portentous air.... Turn to page 703 of "The 'Genius.'" By the time one gets there, one has hewn and hacked one's way through 702 large pages of fine print—97 long chapters, more than 250, 000 words. And yet, at this hurried and impatient point, with the *coda* already begun, Dreiser halts the whole narrative to explain the origin, nature and inner meaning of Christian Science, and to make us privy to a lot of chatty stuff about Mrs. Althea Jones, a professional healer, and to supply us with detailed plans and specifications of the apartment house in which she lives, works her tawdry miracles, and has her being. Here, in sober summary, are the particulars:

1. That the house is "of conventional design."

2. That there is "a spacious areaway" between its two wings.

3. That these wings are "of cream-coloured pressed brick."

4. That the entrance between them is "protected by a handsome wrought-iron door."

5. That to either side of this door is "an electric lamp support of handsome design."

6. That in each of these lamp supports there are "lovely cream-coloured globes, shedding a soft lustre."

7. That inside is "the usual lobby."

8. That in the lobby is "the usual elevator."

9. That in the elevator is the usual "uniformed negro elevator man."

10. That this negro elevator man (name not given) is "indifferent and impertinent."

11. That a telephone switchboard is also in the lobby.

12. That the building is seven stories in height.

In "The Financier" there is the same exasperating rolling up of irrelevant facts. The court proceedings in the trial of Cowperwood are given with all the exactness of a parliamentary report in the London *Times*. The speeches of the opposing counsel are set down nearly in full, and with them the remarks of the judge, and after that the opinion of the Appellate Court on appeal, with the dissenting opinions as a sort of appendix. In "Sister Carrie" the thing is less savagely carried out, but that is not Dreiser's fault, for the manuscript was revised by some anonymous hand, and the printed version is but little more than half the length of the original. In "The Titan" and "Jennie Gerhardt" no such brake upon exuberance is visible; both books are crammed with details that serve no purpose, and are as flat as ditch-water. Even in the two volumes of personal record, "A Traveler at Forty" and "A Hoosier Holiday, " there is the same furious accumulation of trivialities. Consider the former. It is without structure, without selection, without reticence. One arises from it as from a great babbling, half drunken. On the one hand the author fills a long and gloomy chapter with the story of the Borgias, apparently under the impression that it is news, and on the other hand he enters into intimate and inconsequential confidences about all the persons he meets en route, sparing neither the innocent nor the obscure. The children of his English host at Bridgely Level strike him as fantastic little creatures, even as a bit uncanny—and he duly sets it down. He meets an Englishman on a French train who pleases him much, and the two become good friends and see Rome together, but the fellow's wife is "obstreperous" and "haughty in her manner" and so "loud-spoken in her opinions" that she is "really offensive"—and down it goes. He makes an impression on a Mlle. Marcelle in Paris, and she accompanies him from Monte Carlo to Ventimiglia, and there gives him a parting kiss and whispers, "*Avril-Fontainebleau*"—and lo, this sweet one is duly spread upon the minutes. He permits himself to be arrested by a fair privateer in Piccadilly, and goes with her to one of the dens of sin that suffragettes see in their nightmares, and cross-examines her at length regarding her ancestry, her professional ethics and ideals, and her earnings at her dismal craft—and into the book goes a full report of the proceedings. He is entertained by an eminent Dutch jurist in Amsterdam—and upon the pages of the chronicle it appears that the gentleman is "waxy" and "a little pedantic, " and that he is probably the sort of "thin, delicate, well barbered" professor that Ibsen had in mind when he cast about for a husband for the daughter of General Gabler.

Such is the art of writing as Dreiser understands it and practises it—an endless piling up of minutiae, an almost ferocious tracking down of ions, electrons and molecules, an unshakable determination to tell it all. One is amazed by the mole-like diligence of the man, and no less by his exasperating disregard for the ease of his readers. A Dreiser novel, at least of the later canon, cannot be read as other novels are read—on a winter evening or summer afternoon, between meal and meal, travelling from New York to Boston. It demands the attention for almost a week, and uses up the faculties for a month. If, reading "The 'Genius, '" one were to become engrossed in the fabulous manner described in the publishers' advertisements, and so find oneself unable to put it down and go to bed before the end, one would get no sleep for three days and three nights.

Worse, there are no charms of style to mitigate the rigours of these vast steppes and pampas of narration. Joseph Joubert's saying that "words should stand out well from the paper" is quite incomprehensible to Dreiser; he never imitates Flaubert by writing for "*la respiration et l'oreille.*" There is no painful groping for the inevitable word, or for what Walter Pater called "the gipsy phrase"; the common, even the commonplace, coin of speech is good enough. On the first page of "Jennie Gerhardt" one encounters "frank, open countenance, " "diffident manner, " "helpless poor, " "untutored mind, " "honest necessity, " and half a dozen other stand-bys of the second-rate newspaper reporter. In "Sister Carrie" one finds "high noon, " "hurrying throng, " "unassuming restaurant, " "dainty slippers, " "high-strung nature, " and "cool, calculating world"—all on a few pages. Carrie's sister, Minnie Hanson, "gets" the supper. Hanson himself is "wrapped up" in his child. Carrie decides to enter Storm and King's office, "no matter what." In "The Titan" the word "trig" is worked to death; it takes on, toward the end, the character of a banal and preposterous refrain. In the other books one encounters mates for it—words made to do duty in as many senses as the American verb "to fix" or the journalistic "to secure."...

I often wonder if Dreiser gets anything properly describable as pleasure out of this dogged accumulation of threadbare, undistinguished, uninspiring nouns, adjectives, verbs, adverbs, pronouns, participles and conjunctions. To the man with an ear for verbal delicacies—the man who searches painfully for the perfect word, and puts the way of saying a thing above the thing said—there is in writing the constant joy of sudden discovery, of happy accident. A phrase springs up full blown, sweet and caressing. But what joy can there be in rolling up sentences that have no more life and beauty in them, intrinsically, than so many election bulletins? Where is the thrill in the manufacture of such a paragraph as that in which Mrs. Althea Jones' sordid habitat is described with such inexorable particularity? Or in the laborious confection of such stuff as this, from Book I, Chapter IV, of "The 'Genius'"?:

The city of Chicago—who shall portray it! This vast ruck of life that had sprung suddenly into existence upon the dank marshes of a lake shore!

Or this from the epilogue to "The Financier":

There is a certain fish whose scientific name is *Mycteroperca Bonaci*, and whose common name is Black Grouper, which is of considerable value as an afterthought in this connection, and which deserves much to be better known. It is a healthy creature, growing quite regularly to a weight of two hundred and fifty pounds, and living a comfortable, lengthy existence because of its very remarkable ability to adapt itself to conditions....

Or this from his pamphlet, "Life, Art and America":[88]

Alas, alas! for art in America. It has a hard stubby row to hoe.

But I offer no more examples. Every reader of the Dreiser novels must cherish astounding specimens—of awkward, platitudinous marginalia, of whole scenes spoiled by bad writing, of phrases as brackish as so many lumps of sodium hyposulphite. Here and there, as in parts of "The Titan" and again in parts of "A Hoosier Holiday, " an evil conscience seems to haunt him and he gives hard striving to his manner, and more than once there emerges something that is almost graceful. But a backsliding always follows this phosphorescence of reform. "The 'Genius, '" coming after "The Titan, " marks the high tide of his bad writing. There are passages in it so clumsy, so inept, so irritating that they seem almost unbelievable; nothing worse is to be found in the newspapers. Nor is there any compensatory deftness in structure, or solidity of design, to make up for this carelessness in detail. The well-made novel, of course, can be as hollow as the well-made play of Scribe—but let us at least have a beginning, a middle and an end! Such a story as "The 'Genius'" is as gross and shapeless as Brünnhilde. It billows and bulges out like a cloud of smoke, and its internal organization is almost as vague. There are episodes that, with a few chapters added, would make very respectable novels. There are chapters that need but a touch or two to be excellent short stories. The thing rambles, staggers, trips, heaves, pitches, struggles, totters, wavers, halts, turns aside, trembles on the edge of collapse. More than once it seems to be foundering, both in the equine and in the maritime senses. The tale has been heard of a tree so tall that it took two men to see to the top of it. Hereis a novel so brobdingnagian that a single reader can scarcely read his way through it....

§ 3

Of the general ideas which lie at the bottom of all of Dreiser's work it is impossible to be in ignorance, for he has exposed them at length in "A Hoosier Holiday" and summarized them in "Life, Art and America." In their main outlines they are not unlike the fundamental assumptions of Joseph Conrad. Both novelists see human existence as a seeking without a finding; both reject the prevailing interpretations of its

---

[88] *New York, 1917; reprinted from* The Seven Arts *for Feb., 1917.*

meaning and mechanism; both take refuge in "I do not know." Put "A Hoosier Holiday" beside Conrad's "A Personal Record, " and you will come upon parallels from end to end. Or better still, put it beside Hugh Walpole's "Joseph Conrad, " in which the Conradean metaphysic is condensed from the novels even better than Conrad has done it himself: at once you will see how the two novelists, each a worker in the elemental emotions, each a rebel against the current assurance and superficiality, each an alien to his place and time, touch each other in a hundred ways.

"Conrad, " says Walpole, "is of the firm and resolute conviction that life is too strong, too clever and too remorseless for the sons of men." And then, in amplification: "It is as though, from some high window, looking down, he were able to watch some shore, from whose security men were forever launching little cockleshell boats upon a limitless and angry sea.... From his height he can follow their fortunes, their brave struggles, their fortitude to the very end. He admires their courage, the simplicity of their faith, but his irony springs from his knowledge of the inevitable end."...

Substitute the name of Dreiser for that of Conrad, and you will have to change scarcely a word. Perhaps one, to wit, "clever." I suspect that Dreiser, writing so of his own creed, would be tempted to make it "stupid, " or, at all events, "unintelligible." The struggle of man, as he sees it, is more than impotent; it is gratuitous and purposeless. There is, to his eye, no grand ingenuity, no skilful adaptation of means to end, no moral (or even dramatic) plan in the order of the universe. He can get out of it only a sense of profound and inexplicable disorder. The waves which batter the cockleshells change their direction at every instant. Their navigation is a vast adventure, but intolerably fortuitous and inept—a voyage without chart, compass, sun or stars....

So at bottom. But to look into the blackness steadily, of course, is almost beyond the endurance of man. In the very moment that its impenetrability is grasped the imagination begins attacking it with pale beams of false light. All religions, I daresay, are thus projected from the questioning soul of man, and not only all religious, but also all great agnosticisms. Nietzsche, shrinking from the horror of that abyss of negation, revived the Pythagorean concept of *der ewigen Wiederkunft*—a vain and blood-curdling sort of comfort. To it, after a while, he added explanations almost Christian—a whole repertoire of whys and wherefores, aims and goals, aspirations and significances. The late Mark Twain, in an unpublished work, toyed with an equally daring idea: that men are to some unimaginably vast and incomprehensible Being what the unicellular organisms of his body are to man, and so on *ad infinitum*. Dreiser occasionally inclines to much the same hypothesis; he likens the endless reactions going on in the world we know, the myriadal creation, collision and destruction of entities, to the slow accumulation and organization of cells *in utero*. He would make us specks in the insentient embryo of some gigantic Presence whose form is still unimaginable and whose birth must wait for Eons and Eons. Again, he turns to something not easily distinguishable from philosophical idealism, whether out of Berkeley or Fichte it is hard to make out—that is, he would interpret the whole phenomenon of life as no more than an appearance, a nightmare of some unseen sleeper or of men themselves, an "uncanny blur of nothingness"—in Euripides' phrase, "a song sung by an idiot, dancing down the wind." Yet again, he talks vaguely of the intricate polyphony of a cosmic orchestra, cacophonous to our dull ears. Finally, he puts the observed into the ordered, reading a purpose in the displayed event: "life was intended to sting and hurt".... But these are only gropings, and not to be read too critically. From speculations and explanations he always returns, Conrad-like, to the bald fact: to "the spectacle and stress of life." All he can make out clearly is "a vast compulsion which has nothing to do with the individual desires or tastes or impulses of individuals." That compulsion springs "from the settling processes of forces which we do not in the least understand, over which we have no control, and in whose grip we are as grains of dust or sand, blown hither and thither, for what purpose we cannot even suspect." [89] Man is not only doomed to defeat, but denied any glimpse or understanding of his antagonist. Here we come upon an agnosticism that has almost got beyond curiosity. What good would it do us, asks Dreiser, to know? In our ignorance and helplessness, we may at least get a slave's consolation out of cursing the unknown gods. Suppose we saw them striving blindly, too, and pitied them?...

But, as I say, this scepticism is often tempered by guesses at a possibly hidden truth, and the confession that this truth may exist reveals the practical unworkableness of the unconditioned system, at least for Dreiser. Conrad is far more resolute, and it is easy to see why. He is, by birth and training, an aristocrat. He has the gift of emotional detachment. The lures of facile doctrine do not move him. In his irony

---

[89] *Life, Art and America*, p. 5.

there is a disdain which plays about even the ironist himself. Dreiser is a product of far different forces and traditions, and is capable of no such escapement. Struggle as he may, and fume and protest as he may, he can no more shake off the chains of his intellectual and cultural heritage than he can change the shape of his nose. What that heritage is you may find out in detail by reading "A Hoosier Holiday, " or in summary by glancing at the first few pages of "Life, Art and America." Briefly described, it is the burden of a believing mind, a moral attitude, a lingering superstition. One-half of the man's brain, so to speak, wars with the other half. He is intelligent, he is thoughtful, he is a sound artist—but there come moments when a dead hand falls upon him, and he is once more the Indiana peasant, snuffing absurdly over imbecile sentimentalities, giving a grave ear to quackeries, snorting and eye-rolling with the best of them. One generation spans too short a time to free the soul of man. Nietzsche, to the end of his days, remained a Prussian pastor's son, and hence two-thirds a Puritan; he erected his war upon holiness, toward the end, into a sort of holy war. Kipling, the grandson of a Methodist preacher, reveals the tin-pot evangelist with increasing clarity as youth and its ribaldries pass away and he falls back upon his fundamentals. And that other English novelist who springs from the servants' hall—let us not be surprised or blame him if he sometimes writes like a bounder.

The truth about Dreiser is that he is still in the transition stage between Christian Endeavour and civilization, between Warsaw, Indiana and the Socratic grove, between being a good American and being a free man, and so he sometimes vacillates perilously between a moral sentimentalism and a somewhat extravagant revolt. "The 'Genius, '" on the one hand, is almost a tract for rectitude, a Warning to the Young; its motto might be *Scheut die Dirnen*! And on the other hand, it is full of a laborious truculence that can only be explained by imagining the author as heroically determined to prove that he is a plain-spoken fellow and his own man, let the chips fall where they may. So, in spots, in "The Financier" and "The Titan, " both of them far better books. There is an almost moral frenzy to expose and riddle what passes for morality among the stupid. The isolation of irony is never reached; the man is still evangelical; his ideas are still novelties to him; he is as solemnly absurd in some of his floutings of the Code Américain as he is in his respect for Bouguereau, or in his flirtings with the New Thought, or in his naïve belief in the importance of novel-writing. Somewhere or other I have called all this the Greenwich Village complex. It is not genuine artists, serving beauty reverently and proudly, who herd in those cockroached cellars and bawl for art; it is a mob of half-educated yokels and cockneys to whom the very idea of art is still novel, and intoxicating—and more than a little bawdy.

Not that Dreiser actually belongs to this ragamuffin company. Far from it, indeed. There is in him, hidden deep-down, a great instinctive artist, and hence the makings of an aristocrat. In his muddled way, held back by the manacles of his race and time, and his steps made uncertain by a guiding theory which too often eludes his own comprehension, he yet manages to produce works of art of unquestionable beauty and authority, and to interpret life in a manner that is poignant and illuminating. There is vastly more intuition in him than intellectualism; his talent is essentially feminine, as Conrad's is masculine; his ideas always seem to be deduced from his feelings. The view of life that got into "Sister Carrie, " his first book, was not the product of a conscious thinking out of Carrie's problems. It simply got itself there by the force of the artistic passion behind it; its coherent statement had to wait for other and more reflective days. The thing began as a vision, not as a syllogism. Here the name of Franz Schubert inevitably comes up. Schubert was an ignoramus, even in music; he knew less about polyphony, which is the mother of harmony, which is the mother of music, than the average conservatory professor. But nevertheless he had such a vast instinctive sensitiveness to musical values, such a profound and accurate feeling for beauty in tone, that he not only arrived at the truth in tonal relations, but even went beyond what, in his day, was known to be the truth, and so led an advance. Likewise, Giorgione da Castelfranco and Masaccio come to mind: painters of the first rank, but untutored, unsophisticated, uncouth. Dreiser, within his limits, belongs to this sabot-shod company of the elect. One thinks of Conrad, not as artist first, but as savant. There is something of the icy aloofness of the laboratory in him, even when the images he conjures up pulsate with the very glow of life. He is almost as self-conscious as the Beethoven of the last quartets. In Dreiser the thing is more intimate, more disorderly, more a matter of pure feeling. He gets his effects, one might almost say, not by designing them, but by living them.

But whatever the process, the power of the image evoked is not to be gainsaid. It is not only brilliant on the surface, but mysterious and appealing in its depths. One swiftly forgets his intolerable writing, his mirthless, sedulous, repellent manner, in the face of the Athenian tragedy he instils into his seduced and soul-sick servant girls, his barbaric pirates of finances, his conquered and hamstrung supermen, his wives who sit and wait. He has, like Conrad, a sure talent for depicting the spirit in disintegration. Old Gerhardt, in "Jennie Gerhardt, " is alone worth all the *dramatis personae* of popular American fiction since the days of "Rob o' the Bowl"; Howells could no more have created him, in his Rodinesque impudence of outline, than he could have created Tartuffe or Gargantua. Such a novel as "Sister Carrie" stands quite outside the brief traffic of the customary stage. It leaves behind it an unescapable impression of bigness, of epic sweep and dignity. It is not a mere story, not a novel in the customary American meaning of the word; it is at once a psalm of life and a criticism of life—and that criticism loses nothing by the fact that its burden is despair. Here, precisely, is the point of Dreiser's departure from his fellows. He puts into his novels a touch of the eternal *Weltschmerz*. They get below the drama that is of the moment and reveal the greater drama that is without end. They arouse those deep and lasting emotions which grow out of the recognition of elemental and universal tragedy. His aim is not merely to tell a tale; his aim is to show the vast ebb and flow of forces which sway and condition human destiny. One cannot imagine him consenting to Conan Doyle's statement of the purpose of fiction, quoted with characteristic approval by the New York *Times*: "to amuse mankind, to help the sick and the dull and the weary." Nor is his purpose to instruct; if he is a pedagogue it is only incidentally and as a weakness. The thing he seeks to do is to stir, to awaken, to move. One does not arise from such a book as "Sister Carrie" with a smirk of satisfaction; one leaves it infinitely touched.

§ 4

It is, indeed, a truly amazing first book, and one marvels to hear that it was begun lightly. Dreiser in those days (*circa* 1899), had seven or eight years of newspaper work behind him, in Chicago, St. Louis, Toledo, Cleveland, Buffalo, Pittsburgh and New York, and was beginning to feel that reaction of disgust which attacks all newspaper men when the enthusiasm of youth wears out. He had been successful, but he saw how hollow that success was, and how little surety it held out for the future. The theatre was what chiefly lured him; he had written plays in his nonage, and he now proposed to do them on a large scale, and so get some of the easy dollars of Broadway. It was an old friend from Toledo, Arthur Henry, who turned him toward story-writing. The two had met while Henry was city editor of the *Blade*, and

Dreiser a reporter looking for a job. [90] A firm friendship sprang up, and Henry conceived a high opinion of Dreiser's ability, and urged him to try a short story. Dreiser was distrustful of his own skill, but Henry kept at him, and finally, during a holiday the two spent together at Maumee, Ohio, he made the attempt. Henry had the manuscript typewritten and sent it to *Ainslee's Magazine*. A week or so later there came a cheque for $75.

This was in 1898. Dreiser wrote four more stories during the year following, and sold them all. Henry now urged him to attempt a novel, but again his distrust of himself held him back. Henry finally tried a rather unusual argument: he had a novel of his own on the stocks, [91] and he represented that he was in difficulties with it and in need of company. One day, in September, 1899, Dreiser took a sheet of yellow paper and wrote a title at random. That title was "Sister Carrie, " and with no more definite plan than the mere name offered the book began. It went ahead steadily enough until the middle of October, and had come by then to the place where Carrie meets Hurstwood. At that point Dreiser left it in disgust. It seemed pitifully dull and inconsequential, and for two months he put the manuscript away. Then, under renewed urgings by Henry, he resumed the writing, and kept on to the place where Hurstwood steals the money. Here he went aground upon a comparatively simple problem; he couldn't devise a way to manage the robbery. Late in January he gave it up. But the faithful Henry kept urging him, and in March he resumed work, and soon had the story finished. The latter part, despite many distractions, went quickly. Once the manuscript was complete, Henry suggested various cuts, and in all about 40, 000 words came out. The fair copy went to the Harpers. They refused it without ceremony and soon afterward Dreiser carried the manuscript to Doubleday, Page & Co. He left it with Frank Doubleday, and before long there came notice of its acceptance, and, what is more, a contract. But after the story was in type it fell into the hands of the wife of one of the members of the firm, and she conceived so strong a notion of its immorality that she soon convinced her husband and his associates. There followed a series of acrimonious negotiations, with Dreiser holding resolutely to the letter of his contract. It was at this point that Frank Norris entered the combat—bravely but in vain. The pious Barabbases, confronted by their signature, found it impossible to

---

[90] *The episode is related in A Hoosier Holiday.*

[91] *A Princess of Arcady, published in 1900.*

throw up the book entirely, but there was no nomination in the bond regarding either the style of binding or the number of copies to be issued, and so they evaded further dispute by bringing out the book in a very small edition and with modest unstamped covers. Copies of this edition are now eagerly sought by book-collectors, and one in good condition fetches $25 or more in the auction rooms. Even the second edition (1907), bearing the imprint of B. W. Dodge & Co., carries an increasing premium.

The passing years work strange farces. The Harpers, who had refused "Sister Carrie" with a spirit bordering upon indignation in 1900, took over the rights of publication from B. W. Dodge & Co., in 1912, and reissued the book in a new (and extremely hideous) format, with a publisher's note containing smug quotations from the encomiums of the *Fortnightly Review*, the *Athenaeum*, the *Spectator*, the *Academy* and other London critical journals. More, they contrived humorously to push the date of their copyright back to 1900. But this new enthusiasm for artistic freedom did not last long. They had published "Jennie Gerhardt" in 1911 and they did "The Financier" in 1912, but when "The Titan" followed, in 1914, they were seized with qualms, and suppressed the book after it had got into type. In this emergency the English firm of John Lane came to the rescue, only to seek cover itself when the Comstocks attacked "The'Genius,'" two years later…. For his high services to American letters, Walter H. Page, of Doubleday, Page & Co., was made ambassador to England, where "Sister Carrie" is regarded (according to the Harpers), as "the best story, on the whole, that has yet come out of America." A curious series of episodes. Another proof, perhaps, of that cosmic imbecility upon which Dreiser is so fond of discoursing….

But of all this I shall say more later on, when I come to discuss the critical reception of the Dreiser novels, and the efforts made by the New York Society for the Suppression of Vice to stop their sale. The thing to notice here is that the author's difficulties with "Sister Carrie" came within an ace of turning him from novel-writing completely. Stray copies of the suppressed first edition, true enough, fell into the hands of critics who saw the story's value, and during the first year or two of the century it enjoyed a sort of esoteric vogue, and encouragement came from unexpected sources. Moreover, a somewhat bowdlerized English edition, published by William Heinemann in 1901, made a fair success, and even provoked a certain mild controversy. But the author's income from the book remained almost *nil*, and so he was forced to seek a livelihood in other directions. His history during the next ten years belongs to the tragicomedy of letters. For five of them he was a Grub Street hack, turning his hand to any literary job that offered. He wrote short stories for the popular magazines, or special articles, or poems, according as their needs varied. He concocted fabulous tales for the illustrated supplements of the Sunday newspapers. He rewrote the bad stuff of other men. He returned to reporting. He did odd pieces of editing. He tried his hand at one-act plays. He even ventured upon advertisement writing. And all the while, the best that he could get out of his industry was a meagre living.

In 1905, tiring of the uncertainties of this life, he accepted a post on the staff of Street & Smith, the millionaire publishers of cheap magazines, servant-girl romances and dime-novels, and here, in the very slums of letters, he laboured with tongue in cheek until the next year. The tale of his duties will fill, I daresay, a volume or two in the autobiography on which he is said to be working; it is a chronicle full of achieved impossibilities. One of his jobs, for example, was to reduce a whole series of dime-novels, each 60, 000 words in length, to 30, 000 words apiece. He accomplished it by cutting each one into halves, and writing a new ending for the first half and a new beginning for the second, with new titles for both. This doubling of their property aroused the admiration of his employers; they promised him an assured and easy future in the dime-novel business. But he tired of it, despite this revelation of a gift for it, and in 1906 he became managing editor of the *Broadway Magazine*, then struggling into public notice. A year later he transferred his flag to the Butterick Building, and became chief editor of the *Delineator*, the *Designer* and other such gospels for the fair. Here, of course, he was as much out of water as in the dime-novel foundry of Street & Smith, but at all events the pay was good, and there was a certain leisure at the end of the day's work. In 1907, as part of his duties, he organized the National Child Rescue Campaign, which still rages as the *Delineator's* contribution to the Uplift. At about the same time he began "Jennie Gerhardt." It is curious to note that, during these same years, Arnold Bennett was slaving in London as the editor of *Woman*.

Dreiser left the *Delineator* in 1910, and for the next half year or so endeavoured to pump vitality into the *Bohemian Magazine*, in which he had acquired a proprietary interest. But the *Bohemian* soon departed this life, carrying some of his savings with it, and he gave over his enforced leisure to "Jennie Gerhardt, " completing the book in 1911. Its publication by the Harpers during the same year worked his final emancipation from the editorial desk. It was praised, and what is more, it sold, and royalties began to come in. A new edition of "Sister Carrie" followed in 1912, with "The Financier" hard upon its heels. Since then Dreiser has devoted himself wholly to serious work. "The Financier" was put forth as the first volume of "a trilogy of desire"; the second volume, "The Titan, " was published in 1914; the third is yet to come. "The 'Genius'" appeared in 1915; "The Bulwark" is just announced. In 1912, accompanied by Grant Richards, the London publisher, Dreiser made his first trip abroad, visiting England, France, Italy and Germany. His impressions were recorded in "A Traveler at Forty, " published in 1913. In the summer of 1915, accompanied by Franklin Booth, the illustrator, he made an automobile journey to his old haunts in Indiana, and the record is in "A Hoosier Holiday, " published in 1916. His other writings include a volume of "Plays of the Natural and the Supernatural" (1916); "Life, Art and America, " a pamphlet against Puritanism in letters (1917); a dozen or more short stories and novelettes, a few poems, and a three-act drama, "The Hand of the Potter."

Dreiser was born at Terre Haute, Indiana, on August 27, 1871, and, like most of us, is of mongrel blood, with the German, perhaps, predominating. He is a tall man, awkward in movement and nervous in habit; the boon of beauty has been denied him. The history of his youth is set forth in full in "A Hoosier Holiday." It is curious to note that he is a brother to the late Paul Dresser, author of "The Banks of the Wabash" and other popular songs, and that he himself, helping Paul over a hard place, wrote the affecting chorus:

Oh, the moon is fair tonight along the Wabash,

From the fields there comes the breath of new-mown hay;

Through the sycamores the candle lights are gleaming ...

But no doubt you know it.

§ 5

The work of Dreiser, considered as craftsmanship pure and simple, is extremely uneven, and the distance separating his best from his worst is almost infinite. It is difficult to believe that the novelist who wrote certain extraordinarily vivid chapters in "Jennie Gerhardt, " and "A Hoosier Holiday, " and, above all, in "The Titan, " is the same who achieved the unescapable dulness of parts of "The Financier" and the general stupidity and stodginess of "The 'Genius.'" Moreover, the tide of his writing does not rise or fall with any regularity; he neither improves steadily nor grows worse steadily. Only half an eye is needed to see the superiority of "Jennie Gerhardt," as a sheer piece of writing, to "Sister Carrie," but on turning to "The Financier," which followed "Jennie Gerhardt" by an interval of but one year, one observes a falling off which, at its greatest, is almost indistinguishable from a collapse. "Jennie Gerhardt" is suave, persuasive, well-ordered, solid in structure, instinct with life. "The Financier," for all its merits in detail, is loose, tedious, vapid, exasperating. But had any critic, in the autumn of 1912, argued thereby that Dreiser was finished, that he had shot his bolt, his discomfiture would have come swiftly, for "The Titan," which followed in 1914, was almost as well done as "The Financier" had been ill done, and there are parts of it which remain, to this day, the very best writing that Dreiser has ever achieved. But "The 'Genius'"? Ay, in "The 'Genius'" the pendulum swings back again! It is flaccid, elephantine, doltish, coarse, dismal, flatulent, sophomoric, ignorant, unconvincing, wearisome. One pities the jurisconsult who is condemned, by Comstockian clamour, to plough through such a novel. In it there is a sort of humourless *reductio ad absurdum*, not only of the Dreiser manner, but even of certain salient tenets of the Dreiser philosophy. At its best it has a moral flavour. At its worst it is almost maudlin....

The most successful of the Dreiser novels, judged by sales, is "Sister Carrie," and the causes thereof are not far to seek. On the one hand, its suppression in 1900 gave it a whispered fame that was converted into a public celebrity when it was republished in 1907, and on the other hand it shares with "Jennie Gerhardt" the capital advantage of having a young and appealing woman for its chief figure. The sentimentalists thus have a heroine to cry over, and to put into a familiar pigeon-hole; Carrie becomes a sort of Pollyanna. More, it is, at bottom, a tale of love—the one theme of permanent interest to the average American novel-reader, the chief stuffing of all our best-selling romances. True enough, it is vastly more than this—there is in it, for example, the astounding portrait of Hurstwood—, but it seems to me plain that its relative popularity is by no means a test of its relative merit, and that the causes of that popularity must be sought in other directions. Its defect, as a work of art, is a defect of structure. Like Norris' "McTeague" it has a broken back. In the midst of the story of Carrie, Dreiser pauses to tell the story of Hurstwood—a memorably vivid and tragic story, to be sure, but still one that, considering artistic form and organization, does damage to the main business of the book. Its outstanding merit is its simplicity, its unaffected seriousness and fervour, the spirit of youth that is in it. One feels that it was written, not by a novelist conscious of his tricks, but by a novice carried away by his own flaming eagerness, his own high sense of the interest of what he was doing. In this aspect, it is perhaps more typically Dreiserian than any of its successors. And maybe we may seek here for a good deal of its popular appeal, for there is a contagion in naïveté as in enthusiasm, and the simple novel-reader may recognize the kinship of a simple mind in the novelist.

But it is in "Jennie Gerhardt" that Dreiser first shows his true mettle.... "The power to tell the same story in two forms, " said George Moore, "is the sign of the true artist." Here Dreiser sets himself that difficult task, and here he carries it off with almost complete success. Reduce the story to a hundred words, and the same words would also describe "Sister Carrie." Jennie, like Carrie, is a rose grown from turnip-seed. Over each, at the start, hangs poverty, ignorance, the dumb helplessness of the Shudra, and yet in each there is that indescribable something, that element of essential gentleness, that innate inward beauty which levels all barriers of caste, and makes Esther a fit queen for Ahasuerus. Some Frenchman has put it into a phrase: "*Une âme grande dans un petit destin*"—a great soul in a small destiny. Jennie has some touch of that greatness; Dreiser is forever calling her "a big woman"; it is a refrain almost as irritating as the "trig" of "The Titan." Carrie, one feels, is of baser metal; her dignity never rises to anything approaching nobility. But the history of each is the history of the other. Jennie, like Carrie, escapes from the physical miseries of the struggle for existence only to taste the worse miseries of the struggle for happiness. Don't mistake me; we have here no maudlin tales of seduced maidens. Seduction, in truth, is far from tragedy for either Jennie or Carrie. The gain of each, until the actual event has been left behind and obliterated by experiences more salient and poignant, is greater than her loss, and that gain is to the soul as well as to the creature. With the rise from want to security, from fear to ease, comes an awakening of the finer perceptions, a widening of the sympathies, a gradual unfolding of the delicate flower called personality, an increased capacity for loving and living. But with all this, and as a part of it, there comes, too, an increased capacity for suffering—and so in the end, when love slips away and the empty years stretch before, it is the awakened and supersentient woman that pays for the folly of the groping, bewildered girl. The tragedy of Carrie and Jennie, in brief, is not that they are degraded, but that they are lifted up, not that they go to the gutter, but that they escape the gutter and glimpse the stars.

But if the two stories are thus variations upon the same sombre theme, if each starts from the same place and arrives at the same dark goal, if each shows a woman heartened by the same hopes and tortured by the same agonies, there is still a vast difference between them, and that difference is the measure of the author's progress in his craft during the eleven years between 1900 and 1911. "Sister Carrie, " at bottom, is no more than a first sketch, a rough piling up of observations and ideas, disordered and often incoherent. In the midst of the story, as I have said, the author forgets it, and starts off upon another. In "Jennie Gerhardt" there is no such flaccidity of structure, no such vacillation in aim, no such proliferation of episode. Considering that it is by Dreiser, it is extraordinarily adept and intelligent in design; only in "The Titan" has he ever done so well. From beginning to end the narrative flows logically, steadily, congruously. Episodes there are, of course, but they keep their proper place and bulk. It is always Jennie that stands at the centre of the traffic; it is in Jennie's soul that every scene is ultimately played out. Her father and mother; Senator Brander, the god of her first worship; her daughter Vesta, and Lester Kane, the man who makes and mars her—all these are drawn with infinite painstaking, and in every one of them there is the blood of life. But it is Jennie that dominates the drama from curtain to curtain. Not an event is unrelated to her; not a climax fails to make clearer the struggles going on in her mind and heart.

It is in "Jennie Gerhardt" that Dreiser's view of life begins to take on coherence and to show a general tendency. In "Sister Carrie" the thing is still chiefly representation and no more; the image is undoubtedly vivid, but its significance, in the main, is left undisplayed. In "Jennie Gerhardt" this pictorial achievement is reinforced by interpretation; one carries away an impression that something has been said; it is not so much a visual image of Jennie that remains as a sense of the implacable tragedy that engulfs her. The book is full of artistic passion. It lives and glows. It awakens recognition and feeling. Its lucid ideational structure, even more than the artless gusto of "Sister Carrie, " produces a penetrating and powerful effect. Jennie is no mere individual; she is a type of the national character, almost the archetype of the muddled, aspiring, tragic, fate-flogged mass. And the scene in which she is set is brilliantly national too. The Chicago of those great days of feverish money-grabbing and crazy aspiration may well stand as the epitome of America, and it is made clearer here than in any other American novel—clearer than in "The Pit" or "The Cliff-Dwellers"—clearer than in any book by an Easterner—almost as clear as the Paris of Balzac and Zola. Finally, the style of the story is indissolubly wedded to its matter. The narrative, in places, has an almost scriptural solemnity; in its very harshness and baldness there is something subtly meet and fitting. One cannot imagine such a history done in the strained phrases of Meredith or the fugal manner of Henry James. One cannot imagine that stark, stenographic dialogue adorned with the tinsel of pretty words. The thing, to reach the heights it touches, could have been done only in the way it has been done. As it stands, I would not take anything away from it, not even its journalistic banalities, its lack of humour, its incessant returns to C major. A primitive and touching poetry is in it. It is a novel, I am convinced, of the first consideration....

In "The Financier" this poetry is almost absent, and that fact is largely to blame for the book's lack of charm. By the time we see him in "The Titan" Frank Cowperwood has taken on heroic proportions and the romance of great adventure is in him, but in "The Financier" he is still little more than an extra-pertinacious money-grubber, and not unrelated to the average stock broker or corner grocer. True enough, Dreiser says specifically that he is more, that the thing he craves is not money but power—power to force lesser men to execute his commands, power to surround himself with beautiful and splendid things, power to amuse himself with women, power to defy and nullify the laws made for the timorous and unimaginative. But the intent of the author never really gets into his picture. His Cowperwood in this first stage is hard, commonplace, unimaginative. In "The Titan" he flowers out as a blend of revolutionist and voluptuary, a highly civilized Lorenzo the Magnificent, an immoralist who would not hesitate two minutes about seducing a saint, but would turn sick at the thought of harming a child. But in "The Financier" he is still in the larval state, and a repellent sordidness hangs about him.

Moreover, the story of his rise is burdened by two defects which still further corrupt its effect. One lies in the fact that Dreiser is quite unable to get the feel, so to speak, of Philadelphia, just as he is unable to get the feel of New York in "The 'Genius.'" The other is that the style of the writing in the book reduces the dreiserian manner to absurdity, and almost to impossibility. The incredibly lazy, involved and unintelligent description of the trial of Cowperwood I have already mentioned. We get, in this lumbering chronicle, not a cohesive and luminous picture, but a dull, photographic representation of the whole tedious process, beginning with an account of the political obligations of the judge and district attorney, proceeding to a consideration of the habits of mind of each of the twelve jurymen, and ending with a summary of the majority and minority opinions of the court of appeals, and a discussion of the motives, ideals, traditions, prejudices, sympathies and chicaneries behind them, each and severally. When Cowperwood goes into the market, his operations are set forth in their last detail; we are told how many shares he buys, how much he pays for them, what the commission is, what his profit comes to. When he comes into chance contact with a politician, we hear all about that politician, including his family affairs. When he builds and furnishes a house, the chief rooms in it are inventoried with such care that not a chair or a rug or a picture on the wall is overlooked. The endless piling up of such non-essentials cripples and incommodes the story; its drama is too copiously swathed in words to achieve a sting; the Dreiser manner devours and defeats itself.

But none the less the book has compensatory merits. Its character sketches, for all the cloud of words, are lucid and vigorous. Out of that enormous complex of crooked politics and crookeder finance, Cowperwood himself stands out in the round, comprehensible and alive. And all the others, in their lesser measures, are done almost as well—Cowperwood's pale wife, whimpering in her empty house; Aileen Butler, his mistress; his doddering and eternally amazed old father; his old-fashioned, stupid, sentimental mother; Stener, the City Treasurer, a dish-rag in the face of danger; old Edward Malia Butler, that barbarian in a boiled shirt, with his Homeric hatred and his broken heart. Particularly old Butler. The years pass and he must be killed and put away, but not many readers of the book, I take it, will soon forget him. Dreiser is at his best, indeed, when he deals with old men. In their tragic helplessness they stand as symbols of that unfathomable cosmic cruelty which he sees as the motive power of life itself. More, even, than his women, he makes them poignant, vivid, memorable. The picture of old Gerhardt is full of a subtle brightness, though he is always in the background, as cautious and penny-wise as an ancient crow, trotting to his Lutheran church, pathetically ill-used by the world he never understands. Butler is another such, different in externals, but at bottom the same dismayed, questioning, pathetic old man....

In "The Titan" there is a tightening of the screws, a clarifying of the action, an infinite improvement in the manner. The book, in truth, has the air of a new and clearer thinking out of "The Financier," as "Jennie Gerhardt" is a new thinking out of "Sister Carrie." With almost the same materials, the thing is given a new harmony and unity, a new plausibility, a new passion and purpose. In "The Financier" the artistic voluptuary is almost completely overshadowed by the dollar-chaser; in "The Titan" we begin to see clearly that grand battle between artist and man of money, idealist and materialist, spirit and flesh, which is the informing theme of the whole trilogy. The conflict that makes the drama, once chiefly external, now becomes more and more internal; it is played out within the soul of the man himself. The result is a character sketch of the highest colour and brilliance, a superb portrait of a complex and extremely fascinating man. Of all the personages in the Dreiser books, the Cowperwood of "The Titan" is perhaps the most radiantly real. He is accounted for in every detail, and yet, in the end, he is not accounted for at all; there hangs about him, to the last, that baffling mysteriousness which hangs about those we know most intimately. There is in him a complete and indubitable masculinity, as the eternal feminine is in Jennie. His struggle with the inexorable forces that urge him on as with whips, and lure him with false lights, and bring him to disillusion and dismay, is as typical as hers is, and as tragic. In his ultimate disaster, so plainly foreshadowed at the close, there is the clearest of all projections of the ideas that lie at the bottom of all Dreiser's work. Cowperwood, above any of them, is his protagonist.

The story, in its plan, is as transparent as in its burden. It has an austere simplicity in the telling that fits the directness of the thing told. Dreiser, as if to clear decks, throws over all the immemorial baggage of the novelist, making short shrift of "heart interest, " conventional "sympathy, " and even what ordinarily passes for romance. In "Sister Carrie, " as I have pointed out, there is still a sweet dish for the sentimentalists; if they don't like the history of Carrie as a work of art they may still wallow in it as a sad, sad love story. Carrie is appealing, melting; she moves, like Marguerite Gautier, in an atmosphere of romantic depression. And Jennie Gerhardt, in this aspect, is merely Carrie done over—a Carrie more carefully and objectively drawn, perhaps, but still conceivably to be mistaken for a "sympathetic" heroine in a best-seller. A lady eating chocolates might jump from "Laddie" to "Jennie Gerhardt" without knowing that she was jumping ten thousand miles. The tear jugs are there to cry into. Even in "The Financier" there is still a hint of familiar things. The first Mrs. Cowperwood is sorely put upon; old Butler has the markings of an irate father; Cowperwood himself suffers the orthodox injustice and languishes in a cell. But no one, I venture, will ever fall into any such mistake in identity in approaching "The Titan." Not a single appeal to facile sentiment is in it. It proceeds from beginning to end in a forthright, uncompromising, confident manner. It is an almost purely objective account, as devoid of cheap heroics as a death certificate, of a strong man's contest with incontestable powers without and no less incontestable powers within. There is nothing of the conventional outlaw about him; he does not wear a red sash and bellow for liberty; fate wrings from him no melodramatic defiances. In the midst of the battle he views it with a sort of ironical detachment, as if lifted above himself by the sheer aesthetic spectacle. Even in disaster he asks for no quarter, no generosity, no compassion. Up or down, he keeps his zest for the game that is being played, and is sufficient unto himself.

Such a man as this Cowperwood of the Chicago days, described romantically, would be indistinguishable from the wicked earls and seven-foot guardsmen of Ouida, Robert W. Chambers and The Duchess. But described realistically and coldbloodedly, with all that wealth of minute and apparently inconsequential detail which Dreiser piles up so amazingly, he becomes a figure astonishingly vivid, lifelike and engrossing. He fits into no *a priori* theory of conduct or scheme of rewards and punishments; he proves nothing and teaches nothing; the forces which move him are never obvious and frequently unintelligible. But in the end he seems genuinely a man—a man of the sort we see about us in the real world—not a patent and automatic fellow, reacting docilely and according to a formula, but a bundle of complexities and contradictions, a creature oscillating between the light and the shadow—at bottom, for all his typical representation of a race and a civilization, a unique and inexplicable personality. More, he is a man of the first class, an Achilles of his world; and here the achievement of Dreiser is most striking, for he succeeds where all fore-runners failed. It is easy enough to explain how John Smith courted his wife, and even how William Brown fought and died for his country, but it is inordinately difficult to give plausibility to the motives, feelings and processes of mind of a man whose salient character is that they transcend all ordinary experience. Too often, even when made by the highest creative and interpretative talent, the effort has resolved itself into a begging of the question. Shakespeare made Hamlet comprehensible to the groundlings by diluting that half of him which was Shakespeare with a half which was a college sophomore. In the same way he saved Lear by making him, in large part, a tedious and obscene old donkey—the blood brother of any average ancient of any average English tap-room. Tackling Caesar, he was rescued by Brutus' knife. George Bernard Shaw, facing the same difficulty, resolved it by drawing a composite portrait of two or three London actor-managers and half a dozen English politicians. But Dreiser makes no such compromise. He bangs into the difficulties of his problem head on, and if he does not solve it absolutely, he at least makes an extraordinarily close approach to a solution. In "The Financier" a certain incredulity still hangs about Cowperwood; in "The Titan" he suddenly comes unquestionably real. If you want to get the true measure of this feat, put it beside the failure of Frank Norris with Curtis Jadwin in "The Pit."...

"The 'Genius, '" which interrupted the "trilogy of desire, " marks the nadir of Dreiser's accomplishment, as "The Titan" marks its apogee. The plan of it, of course, is simple enough, and it is one that Dreiser, at his best, might have carried out with undoubted success. What he is trying to show, in brief, is the battle that goes on in the soul of every man of active mind between the desire for self-expression and the desire for safety, for public respect, for emotional equanimity. It is, in a sense, the story of Cowperwood told over again, but with an important difference, for Eugene Witla is a much less self-reliant and powerful fellow than Cowperwood, and so he is unable to muster up the vast resolution of spirits that he needs to attain happiness. "The Titan" is the history of a strong man. "The 'Genius'" is the history of a man essentially weak. Eugene Witla can never quite choose his route in life. He goes on sacrificing ease to aspiration and aspiration to ease to the end of the chapter. He vacillates abominably and forever between two irreconcilable desires. Even when, at the close, he sinks into a whining sort of resignation, the proud courage of Cowperwood is not in him; he is always a bit despicable in his pathos.

As I say, a story of simple outlines, and well adapted to the dreiserian pen. But it is spoiled and made a mock of by a donkeyish solemnity of attack which leaves it, on the one hand, diffuse, spineless and shapeless, and on the other hand, a compendium of platitudes. It is as if Dreiser, suddenly discovering himself a sage, put off the high passion of the artist and took to pounding a pulpit. It is almost as if he deliberately essayed upon a burlesque of himself. The book is an endless emission of the obvious, with touches of the scandalous to light up its killing monotony. It runs to 736 pages of small type; its reading is an unbearable weariness to the flesh; in the midst of it one has forgotten the beginning and is unconcerned about the end. Mingled with all the folderol, of course, there is stuff of nobler quality. Certain chapters stick in the memory; whole episodes lift themselves to the fervid luminosity of "Jennie Gerhardt"; there are character sketches that deserve all praise; one often pulls up with a reminder that the thing is the work of a proficient craftsman. But in the main it lumbers and jolts, wabbles and bores. A sort of ponderous imbecility gets into it. Both in its elaborate devices to shake up the pious and its imposing demonstrations of what every one knows, it somehow suggests the advanced thinking of Greenwich Village. I suspect, indeed, that the *vin rouge* was in Dreiser's arteries as he concocted it. He was at the intellectual menopause, and looking back somewhat wistfully and attitudinizingly toward the goatish days that were no more.

But let it go! A novelist capable of "Jennie Gerhardt" has rights, privileges, prerogatives. He may, if he will, go on a spiritual drunk now and then, and empty the stale bilges of his soul. Thackeray, having finished "Vanity Fair" and "Pendennis, " bathed himself in the sheep's milk of "The Newcomes, " and after "The Virginians" he did "The Adventures of Philip." Zola, with "Germinal, " "La Débâcle" and "La Terre" behind him, recreated himself horribly with "Fécondité." Tolstoi, after "Anna Karenina, " wrote "What Is Art?" Ibsen, after "Et Dukkehjem" and "Gengangere, " wrote "Vildanden." The good God himself, after all the magnificence of Kings and Chronicles, turned Dr. Frank Crane and so botched his Writ with Proverbs.... A weakness that we must allow for. Whenever Dreiser, abandoning his fundamental scepticism, yields to the irrepressible human (and perhaps also divine) itch to label, to moralize, to teach, he becomes a bit absurd. Observe "The 'Genius, '" and parts of "A Hoosier Holiday" and of "A Traveler at Forty, " and of "Plays of the Natural and the Supernatural." But in this very absurdity, it seems to me, there is a subtle proof that his fundamental scepticism is sound....

I mention the "Plays of the Natural and the Supernatural." They are ingenious and sometimes extremely effective, but their significance is not great. The two that are "of the natural" are "The Girl in the Coffin" and "Old Ragpicker, " the first a laborious evocation of the gruesome, too long by half, and the other an experiment in photographic realism, with a pair of policemen as its protagonists. All five plays "of the supernatural" follow a single plan. In the foreground, as it were, we see a sordid drama played out on the human plane, and in the background (or in the empyrean above, as you choose) we see the operation of the god-like imbecilities which sway and flay us all. The technical trick is well managed. It would be easy for such four-dimensional pieces to fall into burlesque, but in at least two cases, to wit, in "The Blue Sphere" and "In the Dark, " they go off with an air. Superficially, these plays "of the supernatural" seem to show an abandonment to the wheezy, black bombazine mysticism which crops up toward the end of "The 'Genius.'" But that mysticism, at bottom, is no more than the dreiserian scepticism made visible. "For myself, " says Dreiser somewhere, "I do not know what truth is, what beauty is, what love is, what hope is." And in another place: "I admit a vast compulsion which has nothing to do with the individual desires or tastes or impulses." The jokers behind the arras pull the strings. It is pretty, but what is it all about?... The criticism which deals only with externals sees "Sister Carrie" as no more than a deft adventure into realism. Dreiser is praised, when he is praised at all, for making Carrie so clear, for understanding her so well. But the truth is, of course, that his achievement consists precisely in making patent the impenetrable mystery of her, and of the tangled complex of striving and aspiration of which she is so helplessly a part. It is in this sense that "Sister Carrie" is a profound work. It is not a book of glib explanations, of ready formulae; it is, above all else, a book of wonder....

Of "A Traveler at Forty" I have spoken briefly. It is heavy with the obvious; the most interesting thing in it is the fact that Dreiser had never seen St. Peter's or Piccadilly Circus until he was too old for either reverence or romance. "A Hoosier Holiday" is far more illuminating, despite its platitudinizing. Slow in tempo, discursive, reflective, intimate, the book covers a vast territory, and lingers in pleasant fields. One finds in it an almost complete confession of faith, artistic, religious, even political. And not infrequently that confession takes the form of ingenuous confidences—about the fortunes of the house of Dreiser, the dispersed Dreiser clan, the old neighbours in Indiana, new friends made along the way. In "A Traveler at Forty" Dreiser is surely frank enough in his vivisections; he seldom forgets a vanity or a wart. In "A Hoosier Holiday" he goes even further; he speculates heavily about all his *dramatis personae*, prodding into the motives behind their acts, wondering what they would do in this or that situation, forcing them painfully into laboratory jars. They become, in the end, not unlike characters in a novel; one misses only the neatness of a plot. Strangely enough, the one personage of the chronicle who remains dim throughout is the artist, Franklin Booth, Dreiser's host and companion on the long motor ride from New York to Indiana, and the maker of the book's excellent pictures. One gets a brilliant etching of Booth's father, and scarcely less vivid portraits of Speed, the chauffeur; of various persons encountered on the way, and of friends and relatives dredged up out of the abyss of the past. But of Booth one learns little save that he is a Christian Scientist and a fine figure of a man. There must have been much talk during those two weeks of careening along the high-road, and Booth must have borne some part in it, but what he said is very meagrely reported, and so he is still somewhat vague at the end—a personality sensed but scarcely apprehended.

However, it is Dreiser himself who is the chief character of the story, and who stands out from it most brilliantly. One sees in the man all the special marks of the novelist: his capacity for photographic and relentless observation, his insatiable curiosity, his keen zest in life as a spectacle, his comprehension of and sympathy for the poor striving of humble folks, his endless mulling of insoluble problems, his recurrent Philistinism, his impatience of restraints, his fascinated suspicion of messiahs, his passion for physical beauty, his relish for the gaudy drama of big cities; his incurable Americanism. The panorama that he enrols runs the whole scale of the colours; it is a series of extraordinarily vivid pictures. The sombre gloom of the Pennsylvania hills, with Wilkes-Barre lying among them like a gem; the procession of little country towns, sleepy and a bit hoggish; the flash of Buffalo, Cleveland, Indianapolis; the gargantuan coal-pockets and ore-docks along the Erie shore; the tinsel summer resorts; the lush Indiana farmlands, with their stodgy, bovine people—all of these things are sketched in simply, and yet almost magnificently. I know, indeed, of no book which better describes the American hinterland. Here we have no idle spying by a stranger, but a full-length representation by one who knows the thing he describes intimately, and is himself a part of it. Almost every mile of the road travelled has been Dreiser's own road in life. He knew those unkempt Indiana towns in boyhood; he wandered in the Indiana woods; he came to Toledo, Cleveland, Buffalo as a young man; all the roots of his existence are out there. And so he does his chronicle *con amore*, with many a sentimental dredging up of old memories, old hopes and old dreams.

Save for passages in "The Titan, " "A Hoosier Holiday" marks the high tide of Dreiser's writing—that is, as sheer writing. His old faults are in it, and plentifully. There are empty, brackish phrases enough, God knows—"high noon" among them. But for all that, there is an undeniable glow in it; it shows, in more than one place, an approach to style; the mere wholesaler of words has become, in some sense a connoisseur, even a voluptuary. The picture of Wilkes-Barre girt in by her hills is simply done, and yet there is imagination in it, and touches of brilliance. The sombre beauty of the Pennsylvania mountains is vividly transferred to the page. The towns by the wayside are differentiated, swiftly drawn, made to live. There are excellent sketches of people—a courtly hotelkeeper in some God-forsaken hamlet, his self-respect triumphing over his wallow; a group of babbling Civil War veterans, endlessly mouthing incomprehensible jests; the half-grown beaux and belles of the summer resorts, enchanted and yet a bit staggered by the awakening of sex; Booth *père* and his sinister politics; broken and forgotten men in the Indiana towns; policemen, waitresses, farmers, country characters; Dreiser's own people—the boys and girls of his youth; his brother Paul, the Indiana Schneckenburger and Francis Scott Key; his sisters and brothers; his beaten, hopeless, pious father; his brave and noble mother. The book is dedicated to this mother, now long dead, and in a way it is a memorial to her, a monument to affection. Life bore upon her cruelly; she knew poverty at its lowest ebb and despair at its bitterest; and yet there was in her a touch of fineness that never yielded, a gallant spirit that faced and fought things through. One thinks, somehow, of the mother of Gounod.... Her son has not forgotten her. His book is her epitaph. He enters into her presence with love and with reverence and with something not far from awe....

As for the rest of the Dreiser compositions, I leave them to your curiosity.

§ 6

Dr. William Lyon Phelps, the Lampson professor of English language and literature at Yale, opens his chapter on Mark Twain in his "Essays on Modern Novelists" with a humorous account of the critical imbecility which pursued Mark in his own country down to his last years. The favourite national critics of that era (and it extended to 1895, at the least) were wholly blind to the fact that he was a great artist. They admitted him, somewhat grudgingly, a certain low dexterity as a clown, but that he was an imaginative writer of the first rank, or even of the fifth rank, was something that, in their insanest moments, never so much as occurred to them. Phelps cites, in particular, an ass named Professor Richardson, whose "American Literature," it appears, "is still a standard work" and "a deservedly high authority"—apparently in colleges. In the 1892 edition of this *magnum opus*, Mark is dismissed with less than four lines, and ranked below Irving, Holmes and Lowell—nay, actually below Artemus Ward, Josh Billings and Petroleum V. Nasby! The thing is fabulous, fantastic, *unglaublich*—but nevertheless true. Lacking the "higher artistic or moral purpose of the greater humourists" (*exempli gratia*, Rabelais, Molière, Aristophanes!!), Mark is dismissed by this Professor Balderdash as a hollow buffoon.... But stay! Do not laugh yet! Phelps himself, indignant at the stupidity, now proceeds to credit Mark with a moral purpose!... Turn to "The Mysterious Stranger, " or "What is Man?"...

College professors, alas, never learn anything. The identical gentleman who achieved this discovery about old Mark in 1910, now seeks to dispose of Dreiser in the exact manner of Richardson. That is to say, he essays to finish him by putting him into Coventry, by loftily passing over him. "Do not speak of him, " said Kingsley of Heine; "he was a wicked man!" Search the latest volume of the Phelps revelation, "The Advance of the English Novel, " and you will find that Dreiser is not once mentioned in it. The late O. Henry is hailed as a genius who will have "abiding fame"; Henry Sydnor Harrison is hymned as "more than a clever novelist, " nay, "a valuable ally of the angels" (the right-thinker complex! art as a form of snuffling!), and an obscure Pagliaccio named Charles D. Stewart is brought forward as "the American novelist most worthy to fill the particular vacancy caused by the death of Mark Twain"—but Dreiser is not even listed in the index. And where Phelps leads with his baton of birch most of the other drovers of rah-rah boys follow. I turn, for example, to "An Introduction to American Literature, " by Henry S. Pancoast, A.M., L.H.D., dated 1912. There are kind words for Richard Harding Davis, for Amélie Rives, and even for Will N. Harben, but not a syllable for Dreiser. Again, there is a "A History of American Literature, " by Reuben Post Halleck, A.M., LL.D., dated 1911. Lew Wallace, Marietta Holley, Owen Wister and Augusta Evans Wilson have their hearings, but not Dreiser. Yet again, there is "A History of American Literature Since 1870, " by Prof. Fred Lewis Pattee, [92] instructor in "the English language and literature" somewhere in Pennsylvania. Pattee has praises for Marion Crawford, Margaret Deland and F. Hopkinson Smith, and polite bows for Richard Harding Davis and Robert W. Chambers, but from end to end of his fat tome I am unable to find the slightest mention of Dreiser.

So much for one group of heroes of the new Dunciad. That it includes most of the acknowledged heavyweights of the craft—the Babbitts, Mores, Brownells and so on—goes without saying; as Van Wyck Brooks has pointed out, [93] these magnificoes are austerely above any consideration of the literature that is in being. The other group, more courageous and more honest, proceeds by direct attack; Dreiser is to be disposed of by a moral *attentat*. Its leaders are two more professors, Stuart P. Sherman and H. W. Boynton, and in its ranks march the lady critics of the newspapers, with much shrill, falsetto

---

[92] *New York, The Century Co., 1916.*

[93] *In* The Seven Arts, *May, 1917.*

clamour. Sherman is the only one of them who shows any intelligible reasoning. Boynton, as always, is a mere parroter of conventional phrases, and the objections of the ladies fade imperceptibly into a pious indignation which is indistinguishable from that of the professional suppressors of vice.

What, then, is Sherman's complaint? In brief, that Dreiser is a liar when he calls himself a realist; that he is actually a naturalist, and hence accursed. That "he has evaded the enterprise of representing human conduct, and confined himself to a representation of animal behaviour." That he "imposes his own naturalistic philosophy" upon his characters, making them do what they ought not to do, and think what they ought not to think. That "he has just two things to tell us about Frank Cowperwood: that he has a rapacious appetite for money, and a rapacious appetite for women." That this alleged "theory of animal behaviour" is not only incorrect but downright immoral, and that "when one-half the world attempts to assert it, the other half rises in battle."[94]

Only a glance is needed to show the vacuity of all this *brutum fulmen*. Dreiser, in point of fact, is scarcely more the realist or the naturalist, in any true sense, than H. G. Wells or the later George Moore, nor has he ever announced himself in either the one character or the other—if there be, in fact, any difference between them that any one save a pigeon-holing pedagogue can discern. He is really something quite different, and, in his moments, something far more stately. His aim is not merely to record, but to translate and understand; the thing he exposes is not the empty event and act, but the endless mystery out of which it springs; his pictures have a passionate compassion in them that it is hard to separate from poetry. If this sense of the universal and inexplicable tragedy, if this vision of life as a seeking without a finding, if this adept summoning up of moving images, is mistaken by college professors for the empty, meticulous nastiness of Zola in "Pot-Bouille"—in Nietzsche's phrase, for "the delight to stink"—then surely the folly of college professors, as vast as it seems, has been underestimated. What is the fact? The fact is that Dreiser's attitude of mind, his manner of reaction to the phenomena he represents, the whole of his alleged "naturalistic philosophy, " stems directly, not from Zola, Flaubert, Augier and the younger Dumas, but from the Greeks. In the midst of democratic

---

[94] *The* Nation, *Dec. 2, 1915.*

cocksureness and Christian sentimentalism, of doctrinaire shallowness and professorial smugness, he stands for a point of view which at least has something honest and courageous about it; here, at all events, he is a realist. Let him put a motto to his books, and it might be:

Ιω γενεαι βροτων,

Ὠ ς ὑ μας ἱ σα χαι το μηδεν

Ζὼ σας εναριθμω.

Iô geneai brotôn,

Hôs umas isa chai to mêden

Zôsas enarithmô.

If you protest against that as too harsh for Christians and college professors, right-thinkers and forward-lookers, then you protest against "Oedipus Rex."[95]

As for the animal behaviour prattle of the learned head-master, it reveals, on the one hand, only the academic fondness for seizing upon high-sounding but empty phrases and using them to alarm the populace, and on the other hand, only the academic incapacity for observing facts correctly and reporting them honestly. The truth is, of course, that the behaviour of such men as Cowperwood and Witla and of such women as Carrie and Jennie, as Dreiser describes it, is no more merely animal than the behaviour of such acknowledged and undoubted human beings as Woodrow Wilson and Jane Addams. The whole point of the story of Witla, to take the example which seems to concern the horrified watchmen most, is this: that his life is a bitter conflict between the animal in him and the aspiring soul, between the flesh and the spirit, between what is weak in him and what is strong, between what is base and what is noble. Moreover, the good, in the end, gets its hooks into the bad: as we part from Witla he is actually bathed in the tears of remorse, and resolved to be a correct and godfearing man. And what have we in "The Financier" and "The Titan"? A conflict, in the ego of Cowperwood, between aspiration and ambition, between the passion for beauty and the passion for power. Is either passion animal? To ask the question is to answer it.

I single out Dr. Sherman, not because his pompous syllogisms have any plausibility in fact or logic, but simply because he may well stand

---

[95] 1186-1189. So translated by Floyd Dell: "O ye deathward-going tribes of man, what do your lives mean except that they go to nothingness?"

as archetype of the booming, indignant corrupter of criteria, the moralist turned critic. A glance at his paean to Arnold Bennett[96] at once reveals the true gravamen of his objection to Dreiser. What offends him is not actually Dreiser's shortcoming as an artist, but Dreiser's shortcoming as a Christian and an American. In Bennett's volumes of pseudo-philosophy—e.g., "The Plain Man and His Wife" and "The Feast of St. Friend"—he finds the intellectual victuals that are to his taste. Here we have a sweet commingling of virtuous conformity and complacent optimism, of sonorous platitude and easy certainty—here, in brief, we have the philosophy of the English middle classes—and here, by the same token, we have the sort of guff that the half-educated of our own country can understand. It is the calm, superior num-skullery that was Victorian; it is by Samuel Smiles out of Hannah More. The offence of Dreiser is that he has disdained this revelation and gone back to the Greeks. Lo, he reads poetry into "the appetite for women"—he rejects the Pauline doctrine that all love is below the diaphragm! He thinks of Ulysses, not as a mere heretic and criminal, but as a great artist. He sees the life of man, not as a simple theorem in Calvinism, but as a vast adventure, an enchantment, a mystery. It is no wonder that respectable school-teachers are against him....

The comstockian attack upon "The 'Genius'" seems to have sprung out of the same muddled sense of Dreiser's essential hostility to all that is safe and regular—of the danger in him to that mellowed Methodism which has become the national ethic. The book, in a way, was a direct challenge, for though it came to an end upon a note which even a Methodist might hear as sweet, there were undoubted provocations in detail. Dreiser, in fact, allowed his scorn to make off with his taste—and *es ist nichts fürchterlicher als Einbildungskraft ohne Geschmack.* The Comstocks arose to the bait a bit slowly, but none the less surely. Going through the volume with the terrible industry of a Sunday-school boy dredging up pearls of smut from the Old Testament, they achieved a list of no less than 89 alleged floutings of the code—75 described as lewd and 14 as profane. An inspection of these specifications affords mirth of a rare and lofty variety; nothing could more cruelly expose the inner chambers of the moral mind. When young Witla, fastening his best girl's skate, is so overcome by the carnality of youth that he hugs her, it is set down as lewd. On page 51, having become an art student, he is fired by "a great, warm-tinted nude of Bouguereau"—lewd again.

---

[96] The New York *Evening Post*, Dec. 31, 1915.

On page 70 he begins to draw from the figure, and his instructor cautions him that the female breast is round, not square—more lewdness. On page 151 he kisses a girl on mouth and neck and she cautions him: "Be careful! Mamma may come in"—still more. On page 161, having got rid of mamma, she yields "herself to him gladly, joyously" and he is greatly shocked when she argues that an artist (she is by way of being a singer) had better not marry—lewdness doubly damned. On page 245 he and his bride, being ignorant, neglect the principles laid down by Dr. Sylvanus Stall in his great works on sex hygiene—lewdness most horrible! But there is no need to proceed further. Every kiss, hug and tickle of the chin in the chronicle is laboriously snouted out, empanelled, exhibited. Every hint that Witla is no vestal, that he indulges his unchristian fleshliness, that he burns in the manner of I Corinthians, VII, 9, is uncovered to the moral inquisition.

On the side of profanity there is a less ardent pursuit of evidences, chiefly, I daresay, because their unearthing is less stimulating. (Beside, there is no law prohibiting profanity in books: the whole inquiry here is but so much *lagniappe*.) On page 408, in describing a character called Daniel C. Summerfield, Dreiser says that the fellow is "very much given to swearing, more as a matter of habit than of foul intention, " and then goes on to explain somewhat lamely that "no picture of him would be complete without the interpolation of his various expressions." They turn out to be *God damn* and *Jesus Christ*—three of the latter and five or six of the former. All go down; the pure in heart must be shielded from the knowledge of them. (But what of the immoral French? They call the English *Goddams*.) Also, three plain *damns*, eight *hells*, one *my God*, five *by Gods*, one *go to the devil*, one *God Almighty* and one plain *God*. Altogether, 31 specimens are listed. "The 'Genius'" runs to 350, 000 words. The profanity thus works out to somewhat less than one word in 10, 000.... Alas, the comstockian proboscis, feeling for such offendings, is not as alert as when uncovering more savoury delicacies. On page 191 I find an overlooked *by God*. On page 372 there are *Oh God, God curse her*, and *God strike her dead*. On page 373 there are *Ah God, Oh God* and three other invocations of God. On page 617 there is *God help me*. On page 720 there is *as God is my judge*. On page 723 there is *I'm no damned good*.... But I begin to blush.

When the Comstock Society began proceedings against "The 'Genius, '" a group of English novelists, including Arnold Bennett, H. G. Wells, W. L. George and Hugh Walpole, cabled an indignant caveat.

This bestirred the Author's League of America to activity, and its executive committee issued a minute denouncing the business. Later on a protest of American *literati*was circulated, and more than 400 signed, including such highly respectable authors as Winston Churchill, Percy MacKaye, Booth Tarkington and James Lane Allen, and such critics as Lawrence Gilman, Clayton Hamilton and James Huneker, and the editors of such journals as the *Century*, the *Atlantic Monthly* and the *New Republic*. Among my literary lumber is all the correspondence relating to this protest, not forgetting the letters of those who refused to sign, and some day I hope to publish it, that posterity may not lose the joy of an extremely diverting episode. The case attracted wide attention and was the theme of an extraordinarily violent discussion, but the resultant benefits to Dreiser were more than counterbalanced, I daresay, by the withdrawal of "The 'Genius'" itself.[97]

§ 7

Dreiser, like Mark Twain and Emerson before him, has been far more hospitably greeted in his first stage, now drawing to a close, in England than in his own country. The cause of this, I daresay, lies partly in the fact that "Sister Carrie" was in general circulation over there during the seven years that it remained suppressed on this side. It was during these years that such men as Arnold Bennett, Theodore Watts-Dunton, Frank Harris and H. G. Wells, and such critical journals as the *Spectator*, the *Saturday Review* and the *Athenaeum* became aware of him, and so laid the foundations of a sound appreciation of his subsequent work. Since the beginning of the war, certain English newspapers have echoed the alarmed American discovery that he is a literary agent of the Wilhelmstrasse, but it is to the honour of the

---

[97] Despite the comstockian attack, Dreiser is still fairly well represented on the shelves of American public libraries. A canvas of the libraries of the 25 principal cities shows that but two libraries, those of Providence and New Orleans, bar Dreiser altogether. The effect of alarms from newspaper reviewers is indicated by the scant distribution of The "Genius, " which is barred by 14 of the 25. It should be noted that some of these libraries issue certain of the books only under restrictions. This I know to be the case in Louisville, Los Angeles, Newark and Cleveland. The Newark librarian informs me that Jennie Gerhardt is to be removed altogether, presumably in response to some protest from local Comstocks. In Chicago The "Genius" has been stolen, and on account of the withdrawal of the book the Public Library has been unable to get another copy.

English that this imbecility has got no countenance from reputable authority and has not injured his position.

At home, as I have shown, he is less fortunate. When criticism is not merely an absurd effort to chase him out of court because his ideas are not orthodox, as the Victorians tried to chase out Darwin and Swinburne, and their predecessors pursued Shelley and Byron, it is too often designed to identify him with some branch or other of "radical" poppycock, and so credit him with purposes he has never imagined. Thus Chautauqua pulls and Greenwich Village pushes. In the middle ground there proceeds the pedantic effort to dispose of him by labelling him. One faction maintains that he is a realist; another calls him a naturalist; a third argues that he is really a disguised romanticist. This debate is all sound and fury, signifying nothing, but out of it has come a valuation by Lawrence Gilman[98] which perhaps strikes very close to the truth. He is, says Mr. Gilman, "a sentimental mystic who employs the mimetic gestures of the realist." This judgment is apt in particular and sound in general. No such thing as a pure method is possible in the novel. Plain realism, as in Gorky's "Nachtasyl" and the war stories of Ambrose Bierce, simply wearies us by its vacuity; plain romance, if we ever get beyond our nonage, makes us laugh. It is their artistic combination, as in life itself, that fetches us—the subtle projection of the concrete muddle that is living against the ideal orderliness that we reach out for—the eternal war of experience and aspiration—the contrast between the world as it is and the world as it might be or ought to be. Dreiser describes the thing that he sees, laboriously and relentlessly, but he never forgets the dream that is behind it. "He gives you, " continues Mr. Gilman, "a sense of actuality; but he gives you more than that: out of the vast welter and surge, the plethoric irrelevancies, ... emerges a sense of the infinite sadness and mystery of human life."... [99]

"To see truly, " said Renan, "is to see dimly." Dimness or mystery, call it what you will: it is in all these overgrown and formless, but profoundly moving books. Just what do they mean? Just what is Dreiser driving at? That such questions should be asked is only a proof of the straits to which pedagogy has brought criticism. The answer is simple: he is driving at nothing, he is merely trying to represent what

---

[98] The *North American Review*, Feb., 1916.

[99] Another competent valuation, by Randolph Bourne, is in *The Dial*, June 14, 1917.

he sees and feels. His moving impulse is no flabby yearning to teach, to expound, to make simple; it is that "obscure inner necessity" of which Conrad tells us, the irresistible creative passion of a genuine artist, standing spell-bound before the impenetrable enigma that is life, enamoured by the strange beauty that plays over its sordidness, challenged to a wondering and half-terrified sort of representation of what passes understanding. And *jenseits von Gut und Böse*. "For myself, " says Dreiser, "I do not know what truth is, what beauty is, what love is, what hope is. I do not believe any one absolutely and I do not doubt any one absolutely. I think people are both evil and well-intentioned." The hatching of the Dreiser bugaboo is here; it is the flat rejection of the rubber-stamp formulae that outrages petty minds; not being "good, " he must be "evil"—as William Blake said of Milton, a true poet is always "of the devil's party." But in that very groping toward a light but dimly seen there is a measure, it seems to me, of Dreiser's rank and consideration as an artist. "Now comes the public, " says Hermann Bahr, "and demands that we explain what the poet is trying to say. The answer is this: If we knew exactly he would not be a poet...."

III. JAMES HUNEKER

§ 1

Edgar Allan Poe, I am fond of believing, earned as a critic a good deal of the excess of praise that he gets as a romancer and a poet, and another over-estimated American dithyrambist, Sidney Lanier, wrote the best textbook of prosody in English; [100]but in general the critical writing done in the United States has been of a low order, and most American writers of any genuine distinction, like most American painters and musicians, have had to wait for understanding until it appeared abroad. The case of Emerson is typical. At thirty, he was known in New England as a heretical young clergyman and no more, and his fame threatened to halt at the tea-tables of the Boston Brahmins. It remained for Landor and Carlyle, in a strange land, to discern his higher potentialities, and to encourage him to his real life-work. Mark Twain, as I have hitherto shown, suffered from the same lack of critical perception at home. He was quickly recognized as a funny fellow, true enough, but his actual stature was not even faintly apprehended, and even after "Huckleberry Finn" he was still bracketed

---

[100] The Science of English Verse; New York, Scribner, 1880.

with such laborious farceurs as Artemus Ward. It was Sir Walter Besant, an Englishman, who first ventured to put him on his right shelf, along with Swift, Cervantes and Molière. As for Poe and Whitman, the native recognition of their genius was so greatly conditioned by a characteristic horror of their immorality that it would be absurd to say that their own country understood them. Both were better and more quickly apprehended in France, and it was in France, not in America, that each founded a school. What they had to teach we have since got back at second hand—the tale of mystery, which was Poe's contribution, through Gaboriau and Boisgobey; and *vers libre*, which was Whitman's, through the French *imagistes*.

The cause of this profound and almost unbroken lack of critical insight and enterprise, this puerile Philistinism and distrust of ideas among us, is partly to be found, it seems to me, in the fact that the typical American critic is quite without any adequate cultural equipment for the office he presumes to fill. Dr. John Dewey, in some late remarks upon the American universities, has perhaps shown the cause thereof. The trouble with our educational method, he argues, is that it falls between the two stools of English humanism and German relentlessness—that it produces neither a man who intelligently feels nor a man who thoroughly knows. Criticism, in America, is a function of this half-educated and conceited class; it is not a popular art, but an esoteric one; even in its crassest journalistic manifestations it presumes to a certain academic remoteness from the concerns and carnalities of everyday. In every aspect it shows the defects of its practitioners. The American critic of beautiful letters, in his common incarnation, is no more than a talented sophomore, or, at best, a somewhat absurd professor. He suffers from a palpable lack of solid preparation; he has no background of moving and illuminating experience behind him; his soul has not sufficiently adventured among masterpieces, nor among men. Imagine a Taine or a Sainte-Beuve or a Macaulay—man of the world, veteran of philosophies, "lord of life"— and you imagine his complete antithesis. Even on the side of mere professional knowledge, the primary material of his craft, he always appears incompletely outfitted. The grand sweep and direction of the literary currents elude him; he is eternally on the surface, chasing bits of driftwood. The literature he knows is the fossil literature taught in colleges—worse, in high schools. It must be dead before he is aware of it. And in particular he appears ignorant of what is going forward in other lands. An exotic idea, to penetrate his consciousness, must first become stale, and even then he is apt to purge it of all its remaining validity and significance before adopting it.

This has been true since the earliest days. Emerson himself, though a man of unusual discernment and a diligent drinker from German spigots, nevertheless remained a *dilettante* in both aesthetics and metaphysics to the end of his days, and the incompleteness of his equipment never showed more plainly than in his criticism of books. Lowell, if anything, was even worse; his aesthetic theory, first and last, was nebulous and superficial, and all that remains of his pleasant essays today is their somewhat smoky pleasantness. He was a Charles Dudley Warner in nobler trappings, but still, at bottom, a Charles Dudley Warner. As for Poe, though he was by nature a far more original and penetrating critic than either Emerson or Lowell, he was enormously ignorant of good books, and moreover, he could never quite throw off a congenital vulgarity of taste, so painfully visible in the strutting of his style. The man, for all his grand dreams, had a shoddy soul; he belonged authentically to the era of cuspidors, "females" and Sons of Temperance. His occasional affectation of scholarship has deceived no one. It was no more than Yankee bluster; he constantly referred to books that he had never read. Beside, the typical American critic of those days was not Poe, but his arch-enemy, Rufus Wilmot Griswold, that almost fabulous ass—a Baptist preacher turned taster of the beautiful. Imagine a Baptist valuing Balzac, or Molière, or Shakespeare, or Goethe—or Rabelais!

Coming down to our own time, one finds the same endless amateurishness, so characteristic of everything American, from politics to cookery—the same astounding lack of training and vocation. Consider the solemn ponderosities of the pious old maids, male and female, who write book reviews for the newspapers. Here we have a heavy pretension to culture, a campus cocksureness, a laborious righteousness—but of sound aesthetic understanding, of alertness and hospitality to ideas, not a trace. The normal American book reviewer, indeed, is an elderly virgin, a superstitious bluestocking, an apostle of Vassar *Kultur*; and her customary attitude of mind is one of fascinated horror. (The Hamilton Wright Mabie complex! The "white list" of novels!) William Dean Howells, despite a certain jauntiness and even kittenishness of manner, was spiritually of that company. For all his phosphorescent heresies, he was what the up-lifters call a right-thinker at heart, and soaked in the national tradition. He was easiest intrigued, not by force and originality, but by a sickly, *Ladies' Home Journal* sort of piquancy; it was this that made him see a genius in the Philadelphia

Zola, W. B. Trites, and that led him to hymn an abusive business letter by Frank A. Munsey, author of "The Boy Broker" and "Afloat in a Great City, " as a significant human document. Moreover Howells ran true to type in another way, for he long reigned as the leading Anglo-Saxon authority on the Russian novelists without knowing, so far as I can make out, more than ten words of Russian. In the same manner, we have had enthusiasts for D'Annunzio and Mathilde Serao who knew no Italian, and celebrants of Maeterlinck and Verhaeren whose French was of the finishing school, and Ibsen authorities without a single word of Dano-Norwegian—I met one once who failed to recognize "Et Dukkehjem" as the original title of "A Doll's House, "—and performers upon Hauptmann who could no more read "Die Weber" than they could decipher a tablet of Tiglath-Pileser III.

Here and there, of course, a more competent critic of beautiful letters flings out his banner—for example, John Macy, Ludwig Lewisohn, André Tridon, Francis Hackett, Van Wyck Brooks, Burton Rascoe, E. A. Boyd, Llewellyn Jones, Otto Heller, J. E. Spingarn, Lawrence Gilman, the late J. Percival Pollard. Well-informed, intelligent, wide-eyed men—but only four of them even Americans, and not one of them with a wide audience, or any appreciable influence upon the main stream of American criticism. Pollard's best work is buried in the perfumed pages of *Town Topics*; his book on the Munich wits and dramatists[101] is almost unknown. Heller and Lewisohn make their way slowly; a patriotic wariness, I daresay, mixes itself up with their acceptance. Gilman disperses his talents; he is quite as much musician as critic of the arts. As for Macy, I recently found his "The Spirit of American Literature, "[102] by long odds the soundest, wisest book on its subject, selling for fifty cents on a Fifth avenue remainder counter.

How many remain? A few competent reviewers who are primarily something else—Harvey, Aikin, Untermeyer and company. A few youngsters on the newspapers, struggling against the business office. And then a leap to the Victorians, the crêpe-clad pundits, the bombastic word-mongers of the campus school—H. W. Boynton, W. C. Brownell, Paul Elmer More, William Lyon Phelps, Frederick Taber Cooper *et al.* Here, undoubtedly, we have learning of a sort. More, it appears, once

---

[101] *Masks and Minstrels of New Germany; Boston, John W. Luce & Co., 1911.*

[102] *New York, Doubleday, Page & Co., 1913.*

taught Sanskrit to the adolescent suffragettes of Bryn Mawr—an enterprise as stimulating (and as intelligible) as that of setting off fireworks in a blind asylum. Phelps sits in a chair at Yale. Boynton is a master of arts in English literature, whatever that may mean. Brownell is both L.H.D. and Litt.D., thus surpassing Samuel Johnson by one point, and Hazlitt, Coleridge and Malone by two. But the learning of these august *umbilicarii,* for all its pretensions, is precisely the sterile, foppish sort one looks for in second-rate college professors. The appearance is there, but not the substance. One ingests a horse-doctor's dose of words, but fails to acquire any illumination. Read More on Nietzsche[103] if you want to find out just how stupid criticism can be, and yet show the outward forms of sense. Read Phelps'"The Advance of the English Novel"[104] if you would see a fine art treated as a moral matter, and great works tested by the criteria of a small-town Sunday-school, and all sorts of childish sentimentality whooped up. And plough through Brownell's "Standards, "[105] if you have the patience, and then try to reduce its sonorous platitudes to straight-forward and defensible propositions.

§ 2

Now for the exception. He is, of course, James Gibbons Huneker, the solitary Iokanaan in this tragic aesthetic wilderness, the only critic among us whose vision sweeps the whole field of beauty, and whose reports of what he sees there show any genuine gusto. That gusto of his, I fancy, is two-thirds of his story. It is unquenchable, contagious, inflammatory; he is the only performer in the commissioned troupe who knows how to arouse his audience to anything approaching enthusiasm. The rest, even including Howells, are pedants lecturing to the pure in heart, but Huneker makes a joyous story of it; his exposition, transcending the merely expository, takes on the quality of an adventure hospitably shared. One feels, reading him, that he is charmed by the men and women he writes about, and that their ideas, even when he rejects them, give him an agreeable stimulation. And to the charm that he thus finds and exhibits in others, he adds the very positive charm of his own personality. He seems a man who has found the world fascinating, if perhaps not perfect; a friendly and good-

---

[103] *The Drift of Romanticism; Boston, Houghton Mifflin Co., 1913.*

[104] *New York, Dodd, Mead & Co., 1916.*

[105] *New York, Chas. Scribner's Sons, 1917.*

humoured fellow; no frigid scholiast, but something of an epicure; in brief, the reverse of the customary maker of books about books. Compare his two essays on Ibsen, in "Egoists" and "Iconoclasts," to the general body of American writing upon the great Norwegian. The difference is that between a portrait and a Bertillon photograph, Richard Strauss and Czerny, a wedding and an autopsy. Huneker displays Ibsen, not as a petty mystifier of the women's clubs, but as a literary artist of large skill and exalted passion, and withal a quite human and understandable man. These essays were written at the height of the symbolism madness; in their own way, they even show some reflection of it; but taking them in their entirety, how clearly they stand above the ignorant obscurantism of the prevailing criticism of the time—how immeasurably superior they are, for example, to that favourite hymn-book of the Ibsenites, "The Ibsen Secret" by Jennette Lee! For the causes of this difference one need not seek far. They are to be found in the difference between the bombastic half-knowledge of a school teacher and the discreet and complete knowledge of a man of culture. Huneker is that man of culture. He has reported more of interest and value than any other American critic, living or dead, but the essence of his criticism does not lie so much in what he specifically reports as in the civilized point of view from which he reports it. He is a true cosmopolitan, not only in the actual range of his adventurings, but also and more especially in his attitude of mind. His world is not America, nor Europe, nor Christendom, but the whole universe of beauty. As Jules Simon said of Taine: "*Aucun écrivain de nos jours n'a ... découvert plus d'horizons variés et immenses.*"

Need anything else be said in praise of a critic? And does an extravagance or an error here and there lie validly against the saying of it? I think not. I could be a professor if I would and show you slips enough—certain ponderous nothings in the Ibsen essays, already mentioned; a too easy bemusement at the hands of Shaw; a vacillating over Wagner; a habit of yielding to the hocus-pocus of the mystics, particularly Maeterlinck. On the side of painting, I am told, there are even worse aberrations; I know too little about painting to judge for myself. But the list, made complete, would still not be over-long, and few of its items would be important. Huneker, like the rest of us, has sinned his sins, but his judgments, in the overwhelming main, hold water. He has resisted the lure of all the wild movements of the generation; the tornadoes of doctrine have never knocked him over. Nine times out of ten, in estimating a new man in music or letters, he has come curiously close to the truth at the first attempt. And he has always announced it in good time; his solo has always preceded the chorus. He was, I believe, the first American (not forgetting William Morton Payne and Hjalmar Hjorth Boyesen, the pioneers) to write about Ibsen with any understanding of the artist behind the prophet's mask; he was the first to see the rising star of Nietzsche (this was back in 1888); he was beating a drum for Shaw the critic before ever Shaw the dramatist and mob philosopher was born (*circa*1886-1890); he was writing about Hauptmann and Maeterlinck before they had got well set on their legs in their own countries; his estimate of Sudermann, bearing date of 1905, may stand with scarcely the change of a word today; he did a lot of valiant pioneering for Strindberg, Hervieu, Stirner and Gorki, and later on helped in the pioneering for Conrad; he was in the van of the MacDowell enthusiasts; he fought for the ideas of such painters as Davies, Lawson, Luks, Sloan and Prendergest (Americans all, by the way: an answer to the hollow charge of exotic obsession) at a time when even Manet, Monet and Degas were laughed at; he was among the first to give a hand to Frank Norris, Theodore Dreiser, Stephen Crane and H. B. Fuller. In sum, he gave some semblance of reality in the United States, after other men had tried and failed, to that great but ill-starred revolt against Victorian pedantry, formalism and sentimentality which began in the early 90's. It would be difficult, indeed, to overestimate the practical value to all the arts in America of his intellectual alertness, his catholic hospitality to ideas, his artistic courage, and above all, his powers of persuasion. It was not alone that he saw clearly what was sound and significant; it was that he managed, by the sheer charm of his writings, to make a few others see and understand it. If the United States is in any sort of contact today, however remotely, with what is aesthetically going on in the more civilized countries—if the Puritan tradition, for all its firm entrenchment, has eager and resourceful enemies besetting it—if the pall of Harvard quasiculture, by the Oxford manner out of Calvinism, has been lifted ever so little—there is surely no man who can claim a larger share of credit for preparing the way....

§ 3

Huneker comes out of Philadelphia, that depressing intellectual slum, and his first writing was for the Philadelphia *Evening Bulletin*. He is purely Irish in blood, and is of very respectable ancestry, his maternal grandfather and godfather having been James Gibbons, the Irish poet and patriot, and president of the Fenian Brotherhood in America. Once, in a review of "The Pathos of Distance, " I ventured the guess that there was a German strain in him somewhere, and based it upon the beery melancholy visible in parts of that book. Who but a German sheds tears over the empty bottles of day before yesterday, the Adelaide Neilson of 1877? Who but a German goes into woollen undershirts at 45, and makes his will, and begins to call his wife "Mamma"? The green-sickness of youth is endemic from pole to pole, as much so as measles; but what race save the wicked one is floored by a blue distemper in middle age, with sentimental burblings *a cappella*, hallucinations of lost loves, and an unquenchable lacrymorrhea?... I made out a good case, but I was wrong, and the penalty came swiftly and doubly, for on the one hand the Boston *Transcript* sounded an alarm against both Huneker and me as German spies, and on the other hand Huneker himself proclaimed that, even spiritually, he was less German than Magyar, less "Hun" than Hun. "I am, " he said, "a Celto-Magyar: Pilsner at Donneybrook Fair. Even the German beer and cuisine are not in it with the Austro-Hungarian." Here, I suspect, he meant to say Czech instead of Magyar, for isn't Pilsen in Bohemia? Moreover, turn to the chapter on Prague in "New Cosmopolis, " and you will find out in what highland his heart really is. In this book, indeed, is a vast hymn to all things Czechic—the Pilsen *Urquell*, the muffins stuffed with poppy-seed jam, the spiced chicken liver *en casserole*, the pretty Bohemian girls, the rose and golden glory of Hradschin Hill.... One thinks of other strange infatuations: the Polish Conrad's for England, the Scotch Mackay's for Germany, the Low German Brahms' for Italy. Huneker, I daresay, is the first Celto-Czech—or Celto-Magyar, as you choose. (Maybe the name suggests something. It is not to be debased to *Hoon*-eker, remember, but kept at *Hun*-eker, rhyming initially with *nun* and *gun*.) An unearthly marriage of elements, by all the gods! but there are pretty children of it....

Philadelphia humanely disgorged Huneker in 1878. His father designed him for the law, and he studied the institutes at the Philadelphia Law Academy, but like Schumann, he was spoiled for briefs by the stronger pull of music and the *cacoëthes scribendi*. (Grandpa John Huneker had been a composer of church music, and organist at St. Mary's.) In the year mentioned he set out for Paris to see Liszt; his aim was to make himself a piano virtuoso. His name does not appear on his own exhaustive list of Liszt pupils, but he managed to quaff of the Pierian spring at second-hand, for he had lessons from Theodore Ritter (*né* Bennet), a genuine pupil of the old walrus, and he was also taught by the venerable Georges Mathias, a pupil of Chopin. These days laid the foundations for two subsequent books, the

"Chopin: the Man and His Music" of 1900, and the "Franz Liszt" of 1911. More, they prepared the excavations for all of the others, for Huneker began sending home letters to the Philadelphia *Bulletin* on the pictures that he saw, the books that he read and the music that he heard in Paris, and out of them gradually grew a body of doctrine that was to be developed into full-length criticism on his return to the United States. He stayed in Paris until the middle 80's, and then settled in New York.

All the while his piano studies continued, and in New York he became a pupil of Rafael Joseffy. He even became a teacher himself and was for ten years on the staff of the National Conservatory, and showed himself at all the annual meetings of the Music Teachers' Association. But bit by bit criticism elbowed out music-making, as music-making had elbowed out criticism with Schumann and Berlioz. In 1886 or thereabout he joined the *Musical Courier*; then he went, in succession, to the old *Recorder*, to the *Morning Advertiser*, to the *Sun*, to the *Times*, and finally to the Philadelphia *Press* and the New York *World*. Various weeklies and monthlies have also enlisted him: *Mlle. New York*, the *Atlantic Monthly*, the *Smart Set*, the *North American Review* and *Scribner's*. He has even stooped to *Puck*, vainly trying to make an American *Simplicissimus* of that dull offspring of synagogue and barbershop. He has been, in brief, an extremely busy and not too fastidious journalist, writing first about one of the arts, and then about another, and then about all seven together. But music has been the steadiest of all his loves; his first three books dealt almost wholly with it; of his complete canon more than half have to do with it.

§ 4

His first book, "Mezzotints in Modern Music, " published in 1899, revealed his predilections clearly, and what is more, his critical insight and sagacity. One reads it today without the slightest feeling that it is an old story; some of the chapters, obviously reworkings of articles for the papers, must go back to the middle 90's, and yet the judgments they proclaim scarcely call for the change of a word. The single noticeable weakness is a too easy acquiescence in the empty showiness of Saint-Saëns, a tendency to bow to the celebrated French parlour magician too often. Here, I daresay, is an echo of old Paris days, for Camille was a hero on the Seine in 1880, and there was even talk of pitting him against Wagner. The estimates of other men are judiciously arrived at and persuasively stated. Tschaikowsky is correctly put down as a highly talented but essentially shallow fellow—a blubberer in the regalia of a philosopher. Brahms, then still under attack by Henry T. Finck, of the *Evening Post* (the press-agent of Massenet: ye gods, what Harvard can do, even to a Würtemberger!) is subjected to a long, an intelligent and an extremely friendly analysis; no better has got into English since, despite too much stress on the piano music. And Richard Strauss, yet a nine days' wonder, is described clearly and accurately, and his true stature indicated. The rest of the book is less noteworthy; Huneker says the proper things about Chopin, Liszt and Wagner, and adds a chapter on piano methods, the plain fruit of his late pedagogy. But the three chapters I have mentioned are enough; they fell, in their time, into a desert of stupidity; they set a standard in musical criticism in America that only Huneker himself has ever exceeded.

The most popular of his music books, of course, is the "Chopin" (1900). Next to "Iconoclasts, " it is the best seller of them all. More, it has been done into German, French and Italian, and is chiefly responsible for Huneker's celebrity abroad as the only critic of music that America has ever produced. Superficially, it seems to be a monument of pedantry, a meticulous piling up of learning, but a study of it shows that it is very much more than that. Compare it to Sir George Grove's staggering tome on the Beethoven symphonies if you want to understand the difference between mere scholastic diligence and authentic criticism. The one is simply a top-heavy mass of disorderly facts and worshipping enthusiasm; the other is an analysis that searches out every nook and corner of the subject, and brings it into coherence and intelligibility. The Chopin rhapsodist is always held in check by the sound musician; there is a snouting into dark places as well as a touching up of high lights. I myself am surely no disciple of the Polish tuberose—his sweetness, in fact, gags me, and I turn even to Moszkowski for relief—but I have read and re-read this volume with endless interest, and I find it more bethumbed than any other Huneker book in my library, saving only "Iconoclasts" and "Old Fogy." Here, indeed, Huneker is on his own ground. One often feels, in his discussions of orchestral music, that he only thinks orchestrally, like Schumann, with an effort—that all music, in his mind, gets itself translated into terms of piano music. In dealing with Chopin no such transvaluation of values is necessary; the raw materials are ready for his uses without preparation; he is wholly at home among the black keys and white.

His "Liszt" is a far less noteworthy book. It is, in truth, scarcely a book at all, but merely a collection of notes for a book, some of them considerably elaborated, but others set down in the altogether. One reads it because it is about Liszt, the most fantastic figure that ever came out of Hungary, half devil and half clown; not because there is any conflagration of ideas in it. The chapter that reveals most of Huneker is the appendix on latter-day piano virtuosi, with its estimates of such men as de Pachmann, Rosenthal, Paderewski and Hofmann. Much better stuff is to be found in "Overtones, " "The Pathos of Distance" and "Ivory, Apes and Peacocks"—brilliant, if not always profound studies of Strauss, Wagner, Schoenberg, Moussorgsky, and even Verdi. But if I had my choice of the whole shelf, it would rest, barring the "Chopin, " on "Old Fogy"—the *scherzo* of the Hunekeran symphony, the critic taking a holiday, the Devil's Mass in the tonal sanctuary. In it Huneker is at his very choicest, making high-jinks with his Davidsbund of one, rattling the skeletons in all the musical closets of the world. Here, throwing off his critic's black gown, his lays about him right and left, knocking the reigning idols off their perches; resurrecting the old, old dead and trying to pump the breath into them; lambasting on one page and lauding on the next; lampooning his fellow critics and burlesquing their rubber stamp fustian; extolling Dussek and damning Wagner; swearing mighty oaths by Mozart, and after him, Strauss—not Richard, but Johann! The Old Fogy, of course, is the thinnest of disguises, a mere veil of gossamer for "Editor" Huneker. That Huneker in false whiskers is inimitable, incomparable, almost indescribable. On the one hand, he is a prodigy of learning, a veritable warehouse of musical information, true, half-true and apocryphal; on the other hand, he is a jester who delights in reducing all learning to absurdity. Reading him somehow suggests hearing a Bach mass rescored for two fifes, a tambourine in B, a wind machine, two tenor harps, a contrabass oboe, two banjos, eight tubas and the usual clergy and strings. The substance is there; every note is struck exactly in the middle—but what outlandish tone colours, what strange, unearthly sounds! It is not Bach, however, who first comes to mind when Huneker is at his tricks, but Papa Haydn—the Haydn of the Surprise symphony and the Farewell. There is the same gargantuan gaiety, the same magnificent irreverence. Haydn did more for the symphony than any other man, but he also got more fun out of it than any other man.

"Old Fogy, " of course, is not to be taken seriously: it is frankly a piece of fooling. But all the same a serious idea runs through the book from end to end, and that is the idea that music is getting too subjective to be comfortable. The makers of symphonies tend to forget beauty altogether; their one effort is to put all their own petty trials and tribulations, their empty theories and speculations into cacophony.

Even so far back as Beethoven's day that autobiographical habit had begun. "Beethoven, " says Old Fogy, is "dramatic, powerful, a maker of storms, a subduer of tempests; but his speech is the speech of a self-centred egotist. He is the father of all the modern melomaniacs, who, looking into their own souls, write what they see therein—misery, corruption, slighting selfishness and ugliness." Old Ludwig's groans, of course, we can stand. He was not only a great musician, but also a great man. It is just as interesting to hear him sigh and complain as it would be to hear the private prayers of Julius Caesar. But what of Tschaikowsky, with his childish Slavic whining? What of Liszt, with his cheap playacting, his incurable lasciviousness, his plebeian warts? What of Wagner, with his delight in imbecile fables, his popinjay vanity, his soul of a *Schnorrer*? What of Richard Strauss, with his warmed-over Nietzscheism, his flair for the merely horrible? Old Fogy sweeps them all into his ragbag. If art is to be defined as beauty seen through a temperament, then give us more beauty and cleaner temperaments! Back to the old gods, Mozart and Bach, with a polite bow to Brahms and a sentimental tear for Chopin! Beethoven tried to tell his troubles in his music; Mozart was content to ravish the angels of their harps. And as for Johann Sebastian, "there was more real musical feeling, uplifting and sincerity in the old Thomas-kirche in Leipzig ... than in all your modern symphony and oratorio machine-made concerts put together."

All this is argued, to be sure, in extravagant terms. Wagner is a mere ghoul and impostor: "The Flying Dutchman" is no more than a parody on Weber, and "Parsifal" is "an outrage against religion, morals and music." Daddy Liszt is "the inventor of the Liszt pupil, a bad piano player, a venerable man with a purple nose—a Cyrano de Cognac nose." Tschaikowsky is the Slav gone crazy on vodka. He transformed Hamlet into "a yelling man" and Romeo and Juliet into "two monstrous Cossacks, who gibber and squeak at each other while reading some obscene volume." "His Manfred is a libel on Byron, who was a libel on God." And even Schumann is a vanishing star, a literary man turned composer, a pathological case. But, as I have said, a serious idea runs through all this concerto for slapstick and seltzer siphon, and to me, at least, that idea has a plentiful reasonableness. We are getting too much melodrama, too much vivisection, too much rebellion—and too little music. Turn from Tschaikowsky's Pathétique or from any of his wailing tone-poems to Schubert's C major, or to Mozart's Jupiter, or to Beethoven's *kleine Sinfonie in F dur*: it is like coming out of a *Kaffeeklatsch* into the open air, almost like escaping from a lunatic asylum. The one unmistakable emotion that much of this modern music from the steppes and morgues and *Biertische* engenders is a longing for form, clarity, coherence, a self-respecting tune. The snorts and moans of the pothouse Werthers are as irritating, in the long run, as the bawling of a child, the squeak of a pig under a gate. One yearns unspeakably for a composer who gives out his pair of honest themes, and then develops them with both ears open, and then recapitulates them unashamed, and then hangs a brisk coda to them, and then shuts up.

§ 5

So much for "Old Fogy" and the musical books. They constitute, not only the best body of work that Huneker himself has done, but the best body of musical criticism that any American has done. Musical criticism, in our great Calvinist republic, confines itself almost entirely to transient reviewing, and even when it gets between covers, it keeps its trivial quality. Consider, for example, the published work of Henry Edward Krehbiel, for long the *doyen* of the New York critics. I pick up his latest book, "A Second Book of Operas, "[106] open it at random, and find this:

On January 31, 1893, the Philadelphia singers, aided by the New York Symphony Society, gave a performance of the opera, under the auspices of the Young Men's Hebrew Association, for the benefit of its charities, at the Carnegie Music Hall, New York. Mr. Walter Damrosch was to have conducted, but was detained in Washington by the funeral of Mr. Blaine, and Mr. Hinrichs took his place.

O Doctor *admirabilis, acutus et illuminatissimus*! Needless to say the universities have not overlooked this geyser of buttermilk: he is an honourary A.M. of Yale. His most respectable volume, that on negro folksong, impresses one principally by its incompleteness. It may be praised as a sketch, but surely not as a book. The trouble with Krehbiel, of course, is that he mistakes a newspaper morgue for Parnassus. He has all of the third-rate German's capacity for unearthing facts, but he doesn't know how either to think or to write, and so his criticism is mere pretence and pishposh. W. J. Henderson, of the *Sun*, doesn't carry that handicap. He is as full of learning as Krehbiel, as his books on singing and on the early Italian opera show, but he also wields a slippery and intriguing pen, and he could be hugely entertaining if he would. Instead, he devotes himself to manufacturing primers for the

---

[106] *New York, The Macmillan Co., 1917.*

newly intellectual. I can find little of the charm of his *Sun* articles in his books. Lawrence Gilman? A sound musician but one who of late years has often neglected music for the other arts. Philip H. Goepp? His three volumes on the symphonic repertoire leave twice as much to be said as they say. Carl Van Vechten? A very promising novice, but not yet at full growth. Philip Hale? His gigantic annotations scarcely belong to criticism at all; they are musical talmudism. Beside, they are buried in the program books of the Boston Symphony Orchestra, and might as well be inscribed on the temple walls of Baalbec. As for Upton and other such fellows, they are merely musical chautauquans, and their tedious commentaries have little more value than the literary criticisms in the religious weeklies. One of them, a Harvard *maestro*, has published a book on the orchestra in which, on separate pages, the reader is solemnly presented with pictures of first and second violins!

It seems to me that Huneker stands on a higher level than any of these industrious gentlemen, and that his writings on music are of much more value, despite his divided allegiance among the *beaux arts*. Whatever may be said against him, it must at least be admitted that he knows Chopin, and that he has written the best volumes upon the tuberculous Pole in English. Vladimir de Pachmann, that king of all Chopin players, once bore characteristic testimony to the fact—I think it was in London. The program was heavy with the études and ballades, and Huneker sat in the front row of fanatics. After a storm of applause de Pachmann rose from the piano stool, levelled a bony claw at Huneker, and pronounced his dictum: "*He* knows more than *all* of you." Joseffy seems to have had the same opinion, for he sought the aid of his old pupil in preparing his new edition of Chopin, the first volume of which is all he lived to see in print.... And, beyond all the others, Huneker disdains writing for the kindergarten. There is no stooping in his discourse; he frankly addresses himself to an audience that has gone through the forms, and so he avoids the tediousness of the A B C expositors. He is the only American musical critic, save Van Vechten, who thus assumes invariably that a musical audience exists, and the only one who constantly measures up to its probable interests, supposing it to be there. Such a book as "Old Fogy, " for all its buffoonery, is conceivable only as the work of a sound musician. Its background is one of the utmost sophistication; in the midst of its wildest extravagances there is always a profound knowledge of music on tap, and a profound love of it to boot. Here, perhaps, more than anywhere else, Huneker's delight in the things he deals with is obvious.

It is not a seminary that he keeps, but a sort of club of tone enthusiasts, and membership in it is infinitely charming.

§ 6

This capacity for making the thing described seem important and delightful, this quality of infectious gusto, this father-talent of all the talents that a critic needs, sets off his literary criticism no less than his discourse on music and musicians. Such a book as "Iconoclasts" or "Egoists" is full of useful information, but it is even more full of agreeable adventure. The style is the book, as it is the man. It is arch, staccato, ironical, witty, galloping, playful, polyglot, allusive—sometimes, alas, so allusive as to reduce the Drama Leaguer and women's clubber to wonderment and ire. In writing of plays or of books, as in writing of cities, tone-poems or philosophies, Huneker always assumes that the elements are already well-grounded, that he is dealing with the initiated, that a pause to explain would be an affront. Sad work for the Philistines—but a joy to the elect! All this polyphonic allusiveness, this intricate fuguing of ideas, is not to be confused, remember, with the hollow showiness of the academic soothsayer. It is as natural to the man, as much a part of him as the clanging Latin of Johnson, or, to leap from art to art Huneker-wise, the damnable cross-rhythms of Brahms. He could no more write without his stock company of heretic sages than he could write without his ration of malt. And, on examination, all of them turned out to be real. They are far up dark alleys, but they are there!... And one finds them, at last, to be as pleasant company as the multilingual puns of Nietzsche or Debussy's chords of the second.

As for the origin of that style, it seems to have a complex ancestry. Huneker's first love was Poe, and even today he still casts affectionate glances in that direction, but there is surely nothing of Poe's elephantine labouring in his skipping, *pizzicato* sentences. Then came Carlyle—the Carlyle of "Sartor Resartus"—a god long forgotten. Huneker's mother was a woman of taste; on reading his first scribblings, she gave him Cardinal Newman, and bade him consider the Queen's English. Newman achieved a useful purging; the style that remained was ready for Flaubert. From the author of "L'Education Sentimentale, " I daresay, came the deciding influence, with Nietzsche's staggering brilliance offering suggestions later on. Thus Huneker, as stylist, owes nearly all to France, for Nietzsche, too, learned how to write there, and to the end of his days he always wrote more like a Frenchman than a German. His greatest service to his own country, indeed, was not as anarch, but as teacher of writing. He taught the Germans that their language had a snap in it as well as sighs and gargles—that it was possible to write German and yet not wander in a wood. There are whole pages of Nietzsche that suggest such things, say, as the essay on Maurice Barrès in "Egoists, " with its bold tropes, its rapid gait, its sharp *sforzandos*. And you will find old Friedrich at his tricks from end to end of "Old Fogy."

Of the actual contents of such books as "Egoists" and "Iconoclasts" it is unnecessary to say anything. One no longer reads them for their matter, but for their manner. Every flapper now knows all that is worth knowing about Ibsen, Strindberg, Maeterlinck and Shaw, and a great deal that is not worth knowing. We have disentangled Hauptmann from Sudermann, and, thanks to Dr. Lewisohn, may read all his plays in English. Even Henry Becque has got into the vulgate and is familiar to the Drama League. As for Anatole France, his "Revolt of the Angels" is on the shelves of the Carnegie Libraries, and the Comstocks have let it pass. New gods whoop and rage in Valhalla: Verhaeren, Artzibashef, Przybyszewski. Huneker, alas, seems to drop behind the procession. He writes nothing about these second-hand third-raters. He has come to Wedekind, Schnitzler, Schoenberg, Korngold and Moussorgsky, and he has discharged a few rounds of shrapnel at the Gallo-Asiatic petti-coat philosopher, Henri Bergson, but here he has stopped, as he has stopped at Matisse, Picasso, Epstein and Augustus John in painting. As he says himself, "one must get off somewhere."...

Particularly if one grows weary of criticism—and in Huneker, of late, I detect more than one sign of weariness. Youth is behind him, and with it some of its zest for exploration and combat. "The pathos of distance" is a phrase that haunts him as poignantly as it haunted Nietzsche, its maker. Not so long ago I tried to induce him to write some new Old Fogy sketches, nominating Puccini, Strawinsky, Schoenberg, Korngold, Elgar. He protested that the mood was gone from him forever, that he could not turn the clock back twenty years. His late work in*Puck*, the *Times* and the *Sun*, shows an unaccustomed acquiescence in current valuations. He praises such one-day masterpieces as McFee's "Casuals of the Sea"; he is polite to the gaudy heroines of the opera-house; he gags a bit at Wright's "Modern Painting"; he actually makes a gingery curtsy to Frank Jewett Mather, a Princeton professor.... The pressure in the gauges can't keep up to 250 pounds forever. Man must tire of fighting after awhile, and seek his ease in his inn....

Perhaps the post-bellum transvaluation of all values will bring Huneker to his feet again, and with something of the old glow and gusto in him. And if the new men do not stir up, then assuredly the wrecks of the ancient cities will: the Paris of his youth; Munich, Dresden, Vienna, Brussels, London; above all, Prague. Go to "New Cosmopolis" and you will find where his heart lies, or, if not his heart, then at all events his oesophagus and pylorus.... Here, indeed, the thread of his meditations is a thread of nutriment. However diverted by the fragrance of the Dutch woods, the church bells of Belgium, the music of Stuttgart, the bad pictures of Dublin, the plays of Paris, the musty romance of old Wien, he always comes back anon to such ease as a man may find in his inn. "The stomach of Vienna, " he says, "first interested me, not its soul." And so, after a dutiful genuflexion to St. Stephen's ("Old Steffel, " as the Viennese call it), he proceeds to investigate the paprika-chicken, the *Gulyas*, the *Risi-bisi*, the *Apfelstrudel*, the *Kaiserschmarrn* and the native and authentic *Wienerschnitzel*. And from food to drink—specifically, to the haunts of Pilsner, to "certain semi-sacred houses where the ritual of beer-drinking is observed, " to the shrines at which beer maniacs meet, to "a little old house near a Greek church" where "the best-kept Pilsner in Vienna may be found."

The best-kept Pilsner in Vienna! The phrase enchants like an entrance of the horns. The best caviare in Russia, the worst actor on Broadway, the most virtuous angel in Heaven! Such superlatives are transcendental. And yet, —so rare is perfection in this world!—the news swiftly follows, unexpected, disconcerting, that the best Pilsner in Vienna is far short of the ideal. For some undetermined reason—the influence of the American tourist? the decay of the Austrian national character?—the Vienna *Bierwirte* freeze and paralyze it with too much ice, so that it chills the nerves it should caress, and fills the heart below with heaviness and repining. Avoid Vienna, says Huneker, if you are one who understands and venerates the great Bohemian brew! And if, deluded, you find yourself there, take the first *D-zug* for Prague, that lovely city, for in it you will find the Pilsen *Urquell*, and in the Pilsen *Urquell* you will find the best Pilsner in Christendom—its colour a phosphorescent, translucent, golden yellow, its foam like whipped cream, its temperature exactly and invariably right. Not even at Pilsen itself (which the Bohemians call Plezen) is the emperor of malt liquors more stupendously grateful to the palate. Write it down before you forget: the Pilsen *Urquell*, Prague, Bohemia, 120 miles S. S. E. of Dresden, on the river Moldau (which the natives call the Vitava). Ask for Fräulein Ottilie. Mention the name of Herr Huneker, the American *Schriftsteller*.

Of all the eminent and noble cities between the Alleghenies and the Balkans, Prague seems to be Huneker's favourite. He calls it poetic, precious, delectable, original, dramatic—a long string of adjectives, each argued for with eloquence that is unmistakably sincere. He stands fascinated before the towers and pinnacles of the Hradschin, "a miracle of tender rose and marble white with golden spots of sunshine that would have made Claude Monet envious." He pays his devotions to the Chapel of St. Wenceslaus, "crammed with the bones of buried kings, " or, at any rate, to the shrine of St. John Nepomucane, "composed of nearly two tons of silver." He is charmed by the beauty of the stout, black-haired, red-cheeked Bohemian girls, and hopes that enough of them will emigrate to the United States to improve the fading pulchritude of our own houris. But most of all, he has praises for the Bohemian cuisine, with its incomparable apple tarts, and its dumplings of cream cheese, and for the magnificent, the overpowering, the ineffable Pilsner of Prague. This Pilsner motive runs through the book from cover to cover. In the midst of Dutch tulip-beds, Dublin cobblestones, Madrid sunlight and Atlantic City leg-shows, one hears it insistently, deep down in the orchestra. The cellos weave it into the polyphony, sometimes clearly, sometimes in scarcely recognizable augmentation. It is heard again in the wood-wind; the bassoons grunt it thirstily; it slides around in the violas; it rises to a stately choral in the brass. And chiefly it is in minor. Chiefly it is sounded by one who longs for the Pilsen *Urquell* in a far land, and among a barbarous and teetotaling people, and in an atmosphere as hostile to the recreations of the palate as it is to the recreations of the intellect.

As I say, this Huneker is a foreigner and hence accursed. There is something about him as exotic as a samovar, as essentially un-American as a bashi-bazouk, a nose-ring or a fugue. He is filled to the throttle with strange and unnational heresies. He ranks Beethoven miles above the native gods, and not only Beethoven, but also Bach and Brahms, and not only Bach and Brahms, but also Berlioz, Bizet, Bruch and Bülow and perhaps even Balakirew, Bellini, Balfe, Borodin and Boïeldieu. He regards Budapest as a more civilized city than his native Philadelphia, Stendhal as a greater literary artist than Washington Irving, "Künstler Leben" as better music than "There is Sunlight in My Soul." Irish? I still doubt it, despite the *Stammbaum*. Who ever heard of an Irish epicure, an Irish *flâneur*, or, for that matter, an Irish contrapuntist? The arts of the voluptuous category are unknown west of Cherbourg; one leaves them behind with the French pilot. Even the Czech-Irish hypothesis (or is it Magyar-Irish?) has a smell of the lamp. Perhaps it should be Irish-Czech....

§ 7

There remain the books of stories, "Visionaries" and "Melomaniacs." It is not surprising to hear that both are better liked in France and Germany than in England and the United States. ("Visionaries" has even appeared in Bohemian.) Both are made up of what the Germans call *Kultur-Novellen*—that is, stories dealing, not with the emotions common to all men, but with the clash of ideas among the civilized and godless minority. In some of them, *e.g.*, "Rebels of the Moon, " what one finds is really not a story at all, but a static discussion, half aesthetic and half lunatic. In others, *e.g.*, "Isolde's Mother, " the whole action revolves around an assumption incomprehensible to the general. One can scarcely imagine most of these tales in the magazines. They would puzzle and outrage the readers of Gouverneur Morris and Gertrude Atherton, and the readers of Howells and Mrs. Wharton no less. Their point of view is essentially the aesthetic one; the overwhelming importance of beauty is never in any doubt. And the beauty thus vivisected and fashioned into new designs is never the simple Wordsworthian article, of fleecy clouds and primroses all compact; on the contrary, it is the highly artificial beauty of pigments and tone-colours, of Cézanne landscapes and the second act of "Tristan and Isolde, " of Dunsanyan dragons and Paracelsian mysteries. Here, indeed, Huneker riots in the aesthetic occultism that he loves. Music slides over into diabolism; the Pobloff symphony rends the firmament of Heaven; the ghost of Chopin drives Mychowski to drink; a single drum-beat finishes the estimable consort of the composer of the Tympani symphony. In "The Eighth Deadly Sin" we have a paean to perfume—the only one, so far as I know, in English. In "The Hall of the Missing Footsteps" we behold the reaction of hasheesh upon Chopin's ballade in F major.... Strangely-flavoured, unearthly, perhaps unhealthy stuff. I doubt that it will ever be studied for its style in our new Schools of Literature; a devilish cunning if often there, but it leaves a smack of the pharmacopoeia. However, as George Gissing used to say, "the artist should be free from everything like moral prepossession." This lets in the Antichrist....

Huneker himself seems to esteem these fantastic tales above all his other work. Story-writing, indeed, was his first love, and his Opus 1 a bad imitation of Poe, by name "The Comet, " was done in Philadelphia so long ago as July 4, 1876. (Temperature, 105 degrees Fahrenheit.) One rather marvels that he has never attempted a novel. It would have been as bad, perhaps, as "Love Among the Artists, " but certainly no bore. He might have given George Moore useful help with "Evelyn Innes" and "Sister Teresa": they are about music, but not by a musician. As for me, I see no great talent for fiction *qua* fiction in these two volumes of exotic tales. They are interesting simply because Huneker the story teller so often yields place to Huneker the playboy of the arts. Such things as "Antichrist" and "The Woman Who Loved Chopin" are no more, at bottom, than second-rate anecdotes; it is the filling, the sauce, the embroidery that counts. But what filling! What sauce! What embroidery!... One never sees more of Huneker....

§ 8

He must stand or fall, however, as critic. It is what he has written about other men, not what he has concocted himself, that makes a figure of him, and gives him his unique place in the sterile literature of the republic's second century. He stands for a *Weltanschauung* that is not only un-national, but anti-national; he is the chief of all the curbers and correctors of the American Philistine; in praising the arts he has also criticized a civilization. In the large sense, of course, he has had but small influence. After twenty years of earnest labour, he finds himself almost as alone as a Methodist in Bavaria. The body of native criticism remains as I have described it; an endless piling up of platitudes, an homeric mass of false assumptions and jejune conclusions, an insane madness to reduce beauty to terms of a petty and pornographic morality. One might throw a thousand bricks in any American city without striking a single man who could give an intelligible account of either Hauptmann or Cézanne, or of the reasons for holding Schumann to have been a better composer than Mendelssohn. The boys in our colleges are still taught that Whittier was a great poet and Fennimore Cooper a great novelist. Nine-tenths of our people—perhaps ninety-nine hundredths of our native-born—have yet to see their first good picture, or to hear their first symphony. Our Chamberses and Richard Harding Davises are national figures; our Norrises and Dreisers are scarcely tolerated. Of the two undoubted world figures that we have contributed to letters, one was allowed to die like a stray cat up an alley and the other was mistaken for a cheap buffoon. Criticism, as the average American "intellectual" understands it, is what a Frenchman, a German or a Russian would call donkeyism. In all the arts we still cling to the ideals of the dissenting pulpit, the public cemetery, the electric sign, the bordello parlour.

But for all that, I hang to a somewhat battered optimism, and one of the chief causes of that optimism is the fact that Huneker, after all these years, yet remains unhanged. A picturesque and rakish fellow, a believer in joy and beauty, a disdainer of petty bombast and moralizing, a sworn friend of all honest purpose and earnest striving, he has given his life to a work that must needs bear fruit hereafter. While the college pedagogues of the Brander Matthews type still worshipped the dead bones of Scribe and Sardou, Robertson and Bulwer-Lytton, he preached the new and revolutionary gospel of Ibsen. In the golden age of Rosa Bonheur's "The Horse Fair, " he was expounding the principles of the post-impressionists. In the midst of the Sousa marches he whooped for Richard Strauss. Before the rev. professors had come to Schopenhauer, or even to Spencer, he was hauling ashore the devil-fish, Nietzsche. No stranger poisons have ever passed through the customs than those he has brought in his baggage. No man among us has ever urged more ardently, or with sounder knowledge or greater persuasiveness, that catholicity of taste and sympathy which stands in such direct opposition to the booming certainty and snarling narrowness of Little Bethel.

If he bears a simple label, indeed, it is that of anti-Philistine. And the Philistine he attacks is not so much the vacant and harmless fellow who belongs to the Odd Fellows and recreates himself with *Life* and *Leslie's Weekly* in the barber shop, as that more belligerent and pretentious donkey who presumes to do battle for "honest" thought and a "sound" ethic—the "forward looking" man, the university ignoramus, the conservator of orthodoxy, the rattler of ancient phrases—what Nietzsche called "the Philistine of culture." It is against this fat milch cow of wisdom that Huneker has brandished a spear since first there was a Huneker. He is a sworn foe to "the traps that snare the attention from poor or mediocre workmanship—the traps of sentimentalism, of false feeling, of cheap pathos, of the cheap moral." He is on the trail of those pious mountebanks who "clutter the marketplaces with their booths, mischievous half-art and tubs of tripe and soft soap." Superficially, as I say, he seems to have made little progress in this benign *pogrom*. But under the surface, concealed from a first glance, he has undoubtedly left a mark—faint, perhaps, but still a mark. To be a civilized man in America is measurably less difficult, despite the war, than it used to be, say, in 1890. One may at least speak of "Die Walküre" without being laughed at as a half-wit, and read Stirner without being confused with Castro and Raisuli, and argue that Huxley got the better of Gladstone without being challenged at the polls. I know of no man who pushed in that direction harder than James Huneker.x

IV. PURITANISM AS A LITERARY FORCE

§ 1

"Calvinism, " says Dr. Leon Kellner, in his excellent little history of American literature, [107] "is the natural theology of the disinherited; it never flourished, therefore, anywhere as it did in the barren hills of Scotland and in the wilds of North America." The learned doctor is here speaking of theology in what may be called its narrow technical sense— that is, as a theory of God. Under Calvinism, in the New World as well as in the Old, it became no more than a luxuriant demonology; even God himself was transformed into a superior sort of devil, ever wary and wholly merciless. That primitive demonology still survives in the barbaric doctrines of the Methodists and Baptists, particularly in the South; but it has been ameliorated, even there, by a growing sense of the divine grace, and so the old God of Plymouth Rock, as practically conceived, is now scarcely worse than the average jail warden or Italian padrone. On the ethical side, however, Calvinism is dying a much harder death, and we are still a long way from the enlightenment. Save where Continental influences have measurably corrupted the Puritan idea—*e.g.*, in such cities as New York, San Francisco and New Orleans, —the prevailing American view of the world and its mysteries is still a moral one, and no other human concern gets half the attention that is endlessly lavished upon the problem of conduct, particularly of the other fellow. It needed no official announcement to define the function and office of the republic as that of an international expert in morals, and the mentor and exemplar of the more backward nations. Within, as well as without, the eternal rapping of knuckles and proclaiming of new austerities goes on. The American, save in moments of conscious and swiftly lamented deviltry, casts up all ponderable values, including even the values of beauty, in terms of right and wrong. He is beyond all things else, a judge and a policeman; he believes firmly that there is a mysterious power in law; he supports and embellishes its operation with a fanatical vigilance.

Naturally enough, this moral obsession has given a strong colour to American literature. In truth, it has coloured it so brilliantly that American literature is set off sharply from all other literatures. In none other will you find so wholesale and ecstatic a sacrifice of aesthetic ideas, of all the fine gusto of passion and beauty, to notions of what is

---

[107] American Literature, tr. by Julia Franklin; New York, Doubleday, Page & Co., 1915.

meet, proper and nice. From the books of grisly sermons that were the first American contribution to letters down to that amazing literature of "inspiration" which now flowers so prodigiously, with two literary ex-Presidents among its chief virtuosi, one observes no relaxation of the moral pressure. In the history of every other literature there have been periods of what might be called moral innocence—periods in which a naif *joie de vivre* has broken through all concepts of duty and responsibility, and the wonder and glory of the universe have been hymned with unashamed zest. The age of Shakespeare comes to mind at once: the violence of the Puritan reaction offers a measure of the pendulum's wild swing. But in America no such general rising of the blood has ever been seen. The literature of the nation, even the literature of the enlightened minority, has been under harsh Puritan restraints from the beginning, and despite a few stealthy efforts at revolt—usually quite without artistic value or even common honesty, as in the case of the cheap fiction magazines and that of smutty plays on Broadway, and always very short-lived—it shows not the slightest sign of emancipating itself today. The American, try as he will, can never imagine any work of the imagination as wholly devoid of moral content. It must either tend toward the promotion of virtue, or be suspect and abominable.

If any doubt of this is in your mind, turn to the critical articles in the newspapers and literary weeklies; you will encounter enough proofs in a month's explorations to convince you forever. A novel or a play is judged among us, not by its dignity of conception, its artistic honesty, its perfection of workmanship, but almost entirely by its orthodoxy of doctrine, its platitudinousness, its usefulness as a moral tract. A digest of the reviews of such a book as David Graham Phillips' "Susan Lenox" or of such a play as Ibsen's "Hedda Gabler" would make astounding reading for a Continental European. Not only the childish incompetents who write for the daily press, but also most of our critics of experience and reputation, seem quite unable to estimate a piece of writing as a piece of writing, a work of art as a work of art; they almost inevitably drag in irrelevant gabble as to whether this or that personage in it is respectable, or this or that situation in accordance with the national notions of what is edifying and nice. Fully nine-tenths of the reviews of Dreiser's "The Titan, " without question the best American novel of its year, were devoted chiefly to indignant denunciations of the morals of Frank Cowperwood, its central character. That the man was superbly imagined and magnificently depicted, that he stood out from the book in all the flashing vigour of life, that his creation was an artistic achievement of a very high and difficult order—these facts seem to have made no impression upon the reviewers whatever. They were Puritans writing for Puritans, and all they could see in Cowperwood was an anti-Puritan, and in his creator another. It will remain for Europeans, I daresay, to discover the true stature of "The Titan, " as it remained for Europeans to discover the true stature of "Sister Carrie."

Just how deeply this corrective knife has cut you may find plainly displayed in Dr. Kellner's little book. He sees the throttling influence of an ever alert and bellicose Puritanism, not only in our grand literature, but also in our petit literature, our minor poetry, even in our humour. The Puritan's utter lack of aesthetic sense, his distrust of all romantic emotion, his unmatchable intolerance of opposition, his unbreakable belief in his own bleak and narrow views, his savage cruelty of attack, his lust for relentless and barbarous persecution—these things have put an almost unbearable burden upon the exchange of ideas in the United States, and particularly upon that form of it which involves playing with them for the mere game's sake. On the one hand, the writer who would deal seriously and honestly with the larger problems of life, particularly in the rigidly-partitioned ethical field, is restrained by laws that would have kept a Balzac or a Zola in prison from year's end to year's end; and on the other hand the writer who would proceed against the reigning superstitions by mockery has been silenced by taboos that are quite as stringent, and by an indifference that is even worse. For all our professed delight in and capacity for jocosity, we have produced so far but one genuine wit—Ambrose Bierce—and, save to a small circle, he remains unknown today. Our great humourists, including even Mark Twain, have had to take protective colouration, whether willingly or unwillingly, from the prevailing ethical foliage, and so one finds them levelling their darts, not at the stupidities of the Puritan majority, but at the evidences of lessening stupidity in the anti-Puritan minority. In other words, they have done battle, not against, but *for* Philistinism—and Philistinism is no more than another name for Puritanism. Both wage a ceaseless warfare upon beauty in its every form, from painting to religious ritual, and from the drama to the dance—the first because it holds beauty to be a mean and stupid thing, and the second because it holds beauty to be distracting and corrupting.

Mark Twain, without question, was a great artist; there was in him something of that prodigality of imagination, that aloof engrossment in the human comedy, that penetrating cynicism, which one associates with the great artists of the Renaissance. But his nationality hung around his neck like a millstone; he could never throw off his native

Philistinism. One ploughs through "The Innocents Abroad" and through parts of "A Tramp Abroad" with incredulous amazement. Is such coarse and ignorant clowning to be accepted as humour, as great humour, as the best humour that the most humorous of peoples has produced? Is it really the mark of a smart fellow to lift a peasant's cackle over "Lohengrin"? Is Titian's chromo of Moses in the bullrushes seriously to be regarded as the noblest picture in Europe? Is there nothing in Latin Christianity, after all, save petty grafting, monastic scandals and the worship of the knuckles and shin-bones of dubious saints? May not a civilized man, disbelieving in it, still find himself profoundly moved by its dazzling history, the lingering remnants of its old magnificence, the charm of its gorgeous and melancholy loveliness? In the presence of all beauty of man's creation—in brief, of what we roughly call art, whatever its form—the voice of Mark Twain was the voice of the Philistine. A literary artist of very high rank himself, with instinctive gifts that lifted him, in "Huckleberry Finn" to kinship with Cervantes and Aristophanes, he was yet so far the victim of his nationality that he seems to have had no capacity for distinguishing between the good and the bad in the work of other men of his own craft. The literary criticism that one occasionally finds in his writings is chiefly trivial and ignorant; his private inclination appears to have been toward such romantic sentimentality as entrances school-boys; the thing that interested him in Shakespeare was not the man's colossal genius, but the absurd theory that Bacon wrote his plays. Had he been born in France (the country of his chief abomination!) instead of in a Puritan village of the American hinterland, I venture that he would have conquered the world. But try as he would, being what he was, he could not get rid of the Puritan smugness and cocksureness, the Puritan distrust of new ideas, the Puritan incapacity for seeing beauty as a thing in itself, and the full peer of the true and the good.

It is, indeed, precisely in the works of such men as Mark Twain that one finds the best proofs of the Puritan influence in American letters, for it is there that it is least expected and hence most significant. Our native critics, unanimously Puritans themselves, are anaesthetic to the flavour, but to Dr. Kellner, with his half-European, half-Oriental culture, it is always distinctly perceptible. He senses it, not only in the harsh Calvinistic fables of Hawthorne and the pious gurglings of Longfellow, but also in the poetry of Bryant, the tea-party niceness of Howells, the "maiden-like reserve" of James Lane Allen, and even in the work of Joel Chandler Harris. What! A Southern Puritan? Well, why not? What could be more erroneous than the common assumption that Puritanism is exclusively a Northern, a New England, madness? The truth is that it is as thoroughly national as the kindred belief in the devil, and runs almost unobstructed from Portland to Portland and from the Lakes to the Gulf. It is in the South, indeed, and not in the North, that it takes on its most bellicose and extravagant forms. Between the upper tier of New England and the Potomac river there was not a single prohibition state—but thereafter, alas, they came in huge blocks! And behind that infinitely prosperous Puritanism there is a long and unbroken tradition. Berkeley, the last of the Cavaliers, was kicked out of power in Virginia so long ago as 1650. Lord Baltimore, the Proprietor of Maryland, was brought to terms by the Puritans of the Severn in 1657. The Scotch Covenanter, the most uncompromising and unenlightened of all Puritans, flourished in the Carolinas from the start, and in 1698, or thereabout, he was reinforced from New England. In 1757 a band of Puritans invaded what is now Georgia—and Georgia has been a Puritan barbarism ever since. Even while the early (and half-mythical) Cavaliers were still in nominal control of all these Southern plantations, they clung to the sea-coast. The population that moved down the chain of the Appalachians during the latter part of the eighteenth century, and then swept over them into the Mississippi valley, was composed almost entirely of Puritans—chiefly intransigeants from New England (where Unitarianism was getting on its legs), kirk-crazy Scotch, and that plupious beauty-hating folk, the Scotch-Irish. "In the South today, " said John Fiske a generation ago, "there is more Puritanism surviving than in New England." In that whole region, an area three times as large as France or Germany, there is not a single orchestra capable of playing Beethoven's C minor symphony, or a single painting worth looking at, or a single public building or monument of any genuine distinction, or a single factory devoted to the making of beautiful things, or a single poet, novelist, historian, musician, painter or sculptor whose reputation extends beyond his own country. Between the Mason and Dixon line and the mouth of the Mississippi there is but one opera-house, and that one was built by a Frenchman, and is now, I believe, closed. The only domestic art this huge and opulent empire knows is in the hands of Mexican greasers; its only native music it owes to the despised negro; its only genuine poet was permitted to die up an alley like a stray dog.

§ 2

In studying the anatomy and physiology of American Puritanism, and its effects upon the national literature, one quickly discerns two main streams of influence. On the one hand, there is the influence of the original Puritans—whether of New England or of the South—, who came to the New World with a ready-made philosophy of the utmost clarity, positiveness and inclusiveness of scope, and who attained to such a position of political and intellectual leadership that they were able to force it almost unchanged upon the whole population, and to endow it with such vitality that it successfully resisted alien opposition later on. And on the other hand, one sees a complex of social and economic conditions which worked in countless irresistible ways against the rise of that dionysian spirit, that joyful acquiescence in life, that philosophy of the *Ja-sager*, which offers to Puritanism, today as in times past, its chief and perhaps only effective antagonism. In other words, the American of the days since the Revolution has had Puritanism diligently pressed upon him from without, and at the same time he has led, in the main, a life that has engendered a chronic hospitality to it, or at all events to its salient principles, within.

Dr. Kellner accurately describes the process whereby the aesthetic spirit, and its concomitant spirit of joy, were squeezed out of the original New Englanders, so that no trace of it showed in their literature, or even in their lives, for a century and a half after the first settlements. "Absorption in God, " he says, "seems incompatible with the presentation (*i.e.*, aesthetically) of mankind. The God of the Puritans was in this respect a jealous God who brooked no sort of creative rivalry. The inspired moments of the loftiest souls were filled with the thought of God and His designs; spiritual life was wholly dominated by solicitude regarding salvation, the hereafter, grace; how could such petty concerns as personal experience of a lyric nature, the transports or the pangs of love, find utterance? What did a lyric occurrence like the first call of the cuckoo, elsewhere so welcome, or the first sight of the snowdrop, signify compared with the last Sunday's sermon and the new interpretation of the old riddle of evil in the world? And apart from the fact that everything of a personal nature must have appeared so trivial, all the sources of secular lyric poetry were offensive and impious to Puritan theology.... One thing is an established fact: up to the close of the eighteenth century America had no belletristic literature."

This Puritan bedevilment by the idea of personal sin, this reign of the God-crazy, gave way in later years, as we shall see, to other and somewhat milder forms of pious enthusiasm. At the time of the Revolution, indeed, the importation of French political ideas was accompanied by an importation of French theological ideas, and such men as Franklin and Jefferson dallied with what, in those days at least, was regarded as downright atheism. Even in New England this influence made itself felt; there was a gradual letting down of Calvinism to the softness of Unitarianism, and that change was presently to flower in the vague temporizing of Transcendentalism. But as Puritanism, in the strict sense, declined in virulence and took deceptive new forms, there was a compensating growth of its brother, Philistinism, and by the first quarter of the nineteenth century, the distrust of beauty, and of the joy that is its object, was as firmly established throughout the land as it had ever been in New England. The original Puritans had at least been men of a certain education, and even of a certain austere culture. They were inordinately hostile to beauty in all its forms, but one somehow suspects that much of their hostility was due to a sense of their weakness before it, a realization of its disarming psychical pull. But the American of the new republic was of a different kidney. He was not so much hostile to beauty as devoid of any consciousness of it; he stood as unmoved before its phenomena as a savage before a table of logarithms. What he had set up on this continent, in brief, was a commonwealth of peasants and small traders, a paradise of the third-rate, and its national philosophy, almost wholly unchecked by the more sophisticated and civilized ideas of an aristocracy, was precisely the philosophy that one finds among peasants and small traders at all times and everywhere. The difference between the United States and any other nation did not lie in any essential difference between American peasants and other peasants, but simply in the fact that here, alone, the voice of the peasant was the single voice of the nation—that here, alone, the only way to eminence and public influence was the way of acquiescence in the opinions and prejudices of the untutored and Philistine mob. Jackson was the *Stammvater* of the new statesmen and philosophers; he carried the mob's distrust of good taste even into the field of conduct; he was the first to put the rewards of conformity above the dictates of common decency; he founded a whole hierarchy of Philistine messiahs, the roaring of which still belabours the ear.

Once established, this culture of the intellectually disinherited tended to defend and perpetuate itself. On the one hand, there was no appearance of a challenge from within, for the exigent problems of existence in a country that was yet but half settled and organized left its people with no energy for questioning what at least satisfied their gross needs, and so met the pragmatic test. And on the other hand, there was no critical pressure from without, for the English culture which alone reached over the sea was itself entering upon its Victorian decline, and the influence of the native aristocracy—the degenerating *Junkers* of the great estates and the boorish magnates of the city *bourgeoisie*—was quite without any cultural direction at all. The chief concern of the American people, even above the bread-and-butter question, was politics. They were incessantly hag-ridden by political difficulties, both internal and external, of an inordinate complexity, and these occupied all the leisure they could steal from the sordid work of everyday. More, their new and troubled political ideas tended to absorb all the rancorous certainty of their fading religious ideas, so that devotion to a theory or a candidate became translated into devotion to a revelation, and the game of politics turned itself into a holy war. The custom of connecting purely political doctrines with pietistic concepts of an inflammable nature, then firmly set up by skilful persuaders of the mob, has never quite died out in the United States. There has not been a presidential contest since Jackson's day without its Armageddons, its marching of Christian soldiers, its crosses of gold, its crowns of thorns. The most successful American politicians, beginning with the anti-slavery agitators, have been those most adept at twisting the ancient gauds and shibboleths of Puritanism to partisan uses. Every campaign that we have seen for eighty years has been, on each side, a pursuit of bugaboos, a denunciation of heresies, a snouting up of immoralities.

But it was during the long contest against slavery, beginning with the appearance of William Lloyd Garrison's *Liberator* in 1831 and ending at Appomattox, that this gigantic supernaturalization of politics reached its most astounding heights. In those days, indeed, politics and religion coalesced in a manner not seen in the world since the Middle Ages, and the combined pull of the two was so powerful that none could quite resist it. All men of any ability and ambition turned to political activity for self-expression. It engaged the press to the exclusion of everything else; it conquered the pulpit; it even laid its hand upon industry and trade. Drawing the best imaginative talent into its service—Jefferson and Lincoln may well stand as examples—it left the cultivation of belles lettres, and of all the other arts no less, to women and admittedly second-rate men. And when, breaking through this taboo, some chance first-rate man gave himself over to purely aesthetic expression, his reward was not only neglect, but even a sort of ignominy, as if such enterprises were not fitting for males with hair on their chests. I need not point to Poe and Whitman, both disdained as dreamers and wasters, and both proceeded against with the utmost rigours of outraged Philistinism.

In brief, the literature of that whole period, as Algernon Tassin shows in "The Magazine in America," (New York, Dodd, Mead & Co., 1916) was almost completely disassociated from life as men were then living it. Save one counts in such crude politico-puritan tracts as "Uncle Tom's Cabin, " it is difficult to find a single contemporaneous work that interprets the culture of the time, or even accurately represents it. Later on, it found historians and anatomists, and in one work, at least, to wit, "Huckleberry Finn, " it was studied and projected with the highest art, but no such impulse to make imaginative use of it showed itself contemporaneously, and there was not even the crude sentimentalization of here and now that one finds in the popular novels of today. Fenimore Cooper filled his romances, not with the people about him, but with the Indians beyond the sky-line, and made them half-fabulous to boot. Irving told fairy tales about the forgotten Knickerbockers; Hawthorne turned backward to the Puritans of Plymouth Rock; Longfellow to the Acadians and the prehistoric Indians; Emerson took flight from earth altogether; even Poe sought refuge in a land of fantasy. It was only the frank second-raters—e.g., Whittier and Lowell—who ventured to turn to the life around them, and the banality of the result is a sufficient indication of the crudeness of the current taste, and the mean position assigned to the art of letters. This was pre-eminently the era of the moral tale, the Sunday-school book. Literature was conceived, not as a thing in itself, but merely as a hand-maiden to politics or religion. The great celebrity of Emerson in New England was not the celebrity of a literary artist, but that of a theologian and metaphysician; he was esteemed in much the same way that Jonathan Edwards had been esteemed. Even down to our own time, indeed, his vague and empty philosophizing has been put above his undeniable capacity for graceful utterance, and it remained for Dr. Kellner to consider him purely as a literary artist, and to give him due praise for his skill.

The Civil War brought that era of sterility to an end. As I shall show later on, the shock of it completely reorganized the American scheme of things, and even made certain important changes in the national Puritanism, or, at all events, in its machinery. Whitman, whose career straddled, so to speak, the four years of the war, was the leader—and for a long while, the only trooper—of a double revolt. On the one hand he offered a courageous challenge to the intolerable prudishness and dirty-mindedness of Puritanism, and on the other hand he boldly sought the themes and even the modes of expression of his poetry in the arduous, contentious and highly melodramatic life that lay all about him. Whitman, however, was clearly before his time. His countrymen could see him only as immoralist; save for a pitiful few of them, they were dead to any understanding of his stature as artist, and even unaware that such a category of men existed. He was put down as an invader of the public decencies, a disturber of the public peace; even his eloquent war poems, surely the best of all his work, were insufficient to get him a hearing; the sentimental rubbish of "The Blue and the Gray" and the ecstatic supernaturalism of "The Battle Hymn of the Republic" were far more to the public taste. Where Whitman failed, indeed, all subsequent explorers of the same field have failed with him, and the great war has left no more mark upon American letters than if it had never been fought. Nothing remotely approaching the bulk and beam of Tolstoi's "War and Peace, " or, to descend to a smaller scale, Zola's "The Attack on the Mill, " has come out of it. Its appeal to the national imagination was undoubtedly of the most profound character; it coloured politics for fifty years, and is today a dominating influence in the thought of whole sections of the American people. But in all that stirring up there was no upheaval of artistic consciousness, for the plain reason that there was no artistic consciousness there to heave up, and all we have in the way of Civil War literature is a few conventional melodramas, a few half-forgotten short stories by Ambrose Bierce and Stephen Crane, and a half dozen idiotic popular songs in the manner of Randall's "Maryland, My Maryland."

In the seventies and eighties, with the appearance of such men as Henry James, William Dean Howells, Mark Twain and Bret Harte, a better day seemed to be dawning. Here, after a full century of infantile romanticizing, were four writers who at least deserved respectful consideration as literary artists, and what is more, three of them turned from the conventionalized themes of the past to the teeming and colourful life that lay under their noses. But this promise of better things was soon found to be no more than a promise. Mark Twain, after "The Gilded Age, " slipped back into romanticism tempered by Philistinism, and was presently in the era before the Civil War, and finally in the Middle Ages, and even beyond. Harte, a brilliant technician, had displayed his whole stock when he had displayed his technique: his stories were not even superficially true to the life they presumed to depict; one searched them in vain for an interpretation of it; they were simply idle tales. As for Howells and James, both quickly showed that timorousness and reticence which are the distinguishing marks of the Puritan, even in his most intellectual incarnations. The American scene that they depicted with such meticulous care was chiefly peopled with marionettes. They shrunk, characteristically, from those larger, harsher clashes of will and purpose which one finds in all truly first-rate literature. In particular, they shrunk from any interpretation of life which grounded itself upon an acknowledgment of its inexorable and inexplicable tragedy. In the vast combat of instincts and aspirations about them they saw only a feeble jousting of comedians, unserious and insignificant. Of the great questions that have agitated the minds of men in Howells' time one gets no more than a faint and far-away echo in his novels. His investigations, one may say, are carried on *in vacuo*; his discoveries are not expressed in terms of passion, but in terms of giggles.

In the followers of Howells and James one finds little save an empty imitation of their emptiness, a somewhat puerile parodying of their highly artful but essentially personal technique. To wade through the books of such characteristic American fictioneers as Frances Hodgson Burnett, Mary E. Wilkins Freeman, F. Hopkinson Smith, Alice Brown, James Lane Allen, Winston Churchill, Ellen Glasgow, Gertrude Atherton and Sarah Orne Jewett is to undergo an experience that is almost terrible. The flow of words is completely purged of ideas; in place of them one finds no more than a romantic restatement of all the old platitudes and formulae. To call such an emission of graceful poppycock a literature, of course, is to mouth an absurdity, and yet, if the college professors who write treatises on letters are to be believed, it is the best we have to show. Turn, for example, to "A History of American Literature Since 1870, " by Prof. Fred Lewis Pattee, one of the latest and undoubtedly one of the least unintelligent of these books. In it the gifted pedagogue gives extended notice to no less than six of the nine writers I have mentioned, and upon all of them his verdicts are flattering. He bestows high praises, direct and indirect, upon Mrs. Freeman's "grim and austere" manner, her "repression, " her entire lack of poetical illumination. He compares Miss Jewett to both Howells and Hawthorne, not to mention Mrs. Gaskell—and Addison! He grows enthusiastic over a hollow piece of fine writing by Miss Brown. And he forgets altogether to mention Dreiser, or Sinclair, or Medill Patterson, or Harry Leon Wilson, or George Ade!...

So much for the best. The worst is beyond description. France has her Brieux and her Henry Bordeaux; Germany has her Mühlbach, her stars of the *Gartenlaube*; England contributes Caine, Corelli, Oppenheim and company. But it is in our country alone that banality in letters takes on the proportions of a national movement; it is only here that a work of the imagination is habitually judged by its sheer emptiness of ideas, its fundamental platitudinousness, its correspondence with the imbecility of mob thinking; it is only here that "glad" books run up sales of hundreds of thousands. Richard Harding Davis, with his ideals of a floor-walker; Gene Stratton-Porter, with her snuffling sentimentality; Robert W. Chambers, with his "society" romances for shop-girls; Irvin Cobb, with his laboured, *Ayers' Almanac* jocosity; the authors of the *Saturday Evening Post* school, with their heroic drummers and stockbrokers, their ecstatic celebration of the stupid, the sordid, the ignoble—these, after all, are our typical *literati*. The Puritan fear of ideas is the master of them all. Some of them, in truth, most of them, have undeniable talent; in a more favourable environment not a few of them might be doing sound work. But they see how small the ring is, and they make their tricks small to fit it. Not many of them ever venture a leg outside. The lash of the ringmaster is swift, and it stings damnably....

I say not many; I surely do not mean none at all. As a matter of fact, there have been intermittent rebellions against the prevailing pecksniffery and sentimentality ever since the days of Irving and Hawthorne. Poe led one of them—as critic more than as creative artist. His scathing attacks upon the Gerald Stanley Lees, the Hamilton Wright Mabies and the George E. Woodberrys of his time keep a liveliness and appositeness that the years have not staled; his criticism deserves to be better remembered. Poe sensed the Philistine pull of a Puritan civilization as none had before him, and combated it with his whole artillery of rhetoric. Another rebel, of course, was Whitman; how he came to grief is too well known to need recalling. What is less familiar is the fact that both the *Atlantic Monthly* and the *Century* (first called *Scribner's*) were set up by men in revolt against the reign of mush, as *Putnam's* and the *Dial* had been before them. The salutatory of the *Dial*, dated 1840, stated the case against the national mugginess clearly. The aim of the magazine, it said, was to oppose "that rigour of our conventions of religion and education which is turning us to stone" and to give expression to "new views and the dreams of youth." Alas, for these brave *révoltés*! *Putnam's* succumbed to the circumambient rigours and duly turned to stone, and is now no more. The *Atlantic*, once so heretical, has become as respectable as the New York *Evening Post*. As for the *Dial*, it was until lately the very pope of orthodoxy and jealously guarded the college professors who read it from the pollution of ideas. Only the *Century* has kept the faith unbrokenly. It is, indeed, the one first-class American magazine that has always welcomed newcomers, and that maintains an intelligent contact with the literature that is in being, and that consistently tries to make the best terms possible with the dominant Philistinism. It cannot go the whole way without running into danger; let it be said to the credit of its editors that they have more than once braved that danger.

The tale might be lengthened. Mark Twain, in his day, felt the stirrings of revolt, and not all his Philistinism was sufficient to hold him altogether in check. If you want to find out about the struggle that went on within him, read the biography by Albert Bigelow Paine, or, better still, "The Mysterious Stranger" and "What is Man?" Alive, he had his position to consider; dead, he now speaks out. In the preface to "What is Man?" dated 1905, there is a curious confession of his incapacity for defying the taboos which surrounded him. The studies for the book, he says, were begun "twenty-five or twenty-seven years ago"—the period of "A Tramp Abroad" and "The Prince and the Pauper." It was actually written "seven years ago"—that is, just after "Following the Equator" and "Personal Recollections of Joan of Arc." And why did it lie so long in manuscript, and finally go out stealthily, under a private imprint?[108] Simply because, as Mark frankly confesses, he "dreaded (*and could not bear*) the disapproval of the people around" him. He knew how hard his fight for recognition had been; he knew what direful penalties outraged orthodoxy could inflict; he had in him the somewhat pathetic discretion of a respectable family man. But, dead, he is safely beyond reprisal, and so, after a prudent interval, the faithful Paine begins printing books in which, writing knowingly behind six feet of earth, he could set down his true ideas without fear. Some day, perhaps, we shall have his microbe story, and maybe even his picture of the court of Elizabeth.

A sneer in Prof. Pattee's history, before mentioned, recalls the fact that Hamlin Garland was also a rebel in his day and bawled for the Truth with a capital T. That was in 1893. Two years later the guardians of the national rectitude fell afoul of "Rose of Dutchers' Coolly" and Garland began to think it over; today he devotes himself to the safer enterprise of chasing spooks; his name is conspicuously absent from the Dreiser Protest. Nine years before his brief offending John Hay had set off a discreet bomb in "The Bread-Winners"—anonymously because "my standing would be seriously compromised" by an avowal. Six years later Frank Norris shook up the Phelpses and Mores of the time with "McTeague." Since then there have been assaults timorous and assaults

---

[108] The first edition for public sale did not appear until June, 1917, and in it the preface was suppressed.

head-long—by Bierce, by Dreiser, by Phillips, by Fuller—by Mary MacLanes and by Upton Sinclairs—by ploughboy poets from the Middle West and by jitney geniuses in Greenwich Village—assaults gradually tapering off to a mere sophomoric brashness and deviltry. And all of them like snow-ballings of Verdun. All of them petered out and ineffectual. The normal, the typical American book of today is as fully a remouthing of old husks as the normal book of Griswold's day. The whole atmosphere of our literature, in William James' phrase, is "mawkish and dishwatery." Books are still judged among us, not by their form and organization as works of art, their accuracy and vividness as representations of life, their validity and perspicacity as interpretations of it, but by their conformity to the national prejudices, their accordance with set standards of niceness and propriety. The thing irrevocably demanded is a "sane" book; the ideal is a "clean, " an "inspiring, " a "glad" book.

§ 3

All this may be called the Puritan impulse from within. It is, indeed, but a single manifestation of one of the deepest prejudices of a religious and half-cultured people—the prejudice against beauty as a form of debauchery and corruption—the distrust of all ideas that do not fit readily into certain accepted axioms—the belief in the eternal validity of moral concepts—in brief, the whole mental sluggishness of the lower orders of men. But in addition to this internal resistance, there has been laid upon American letters the heavy hand of a Puritan authority from without, and no examination of the history and present condition of our literature could be of any value which did not take it constantly into account, and work out the means of its influence and operation. That authority, as I shall show, transcends both in power and in alertness the natural reactions of the national mind, and is incomparably more potent in combating ideas. It is supported by a body of law that is unmatched in any other country of Christendom, and it is exercised with a fanatical harshness and vigilance that make escape from its operations well nigh impossible. Some of its effects, both direct and indirect, I shall describe later, but before doing so it may be well to trace its genesis and development.

At bottom, of course, it rests upon the inherent Puritanism of the people; it could not survive a year if they were opposed to the principle visible in it. That deep-seated and uncorrupted Puritanism, that conviction of the pervasiveness of sin, of the supreme importance of moral correctness, of the need of savage and inquisitorial laws, has been a dominating force in American life since the very beginning. There has never been any question before the nation, whether political or economic, religious or military, diplomatic or sociological, which did not resolve itself, soon or late, into a purely moral question. Nor has there ever been any surcease of the spiritual eagerness which lay at the bottom of the original Puritan's moral obsession: the American has been, from the very start, a man genuinely interested in the eternal mysteries, and fearful of missing their correct solution. The frank theocracy of the New England colonies had scarcely succumbed to the libertarianism of a godless Crown before there came the Great Awakening of 1734, with its orgies of homiletics and its restoration of talmudism to the first place among polite sciences. The Revolution, of course, brought a set-back: the colonists faced so urgent a need of unity in politics that they declared a sort of *Treuga Dei* in religion, and that truce, armed though it was, left its imprint upon the First Amendment to the Constitution. But immediately the young Republic emerged from the stresses of adolescence, a missionary army took to the field again, and before long the Asbury revival was paling that of Whitefield, Wesley and Jonathan Edwards, not only in its hortatory violence but also in the length of its lists of slain.

Thereafter, down to the outbreak of the Civil War, the country was rocked again and again by furious attacks upon the devil. On the one hand, this great campaign took a purely theological form, with a hundred new and fantastic creeds as its fruits; on the other hand, it crystallized into the hysterical temperance movement of the 30's and 40's, which penetrated to the very floor of Congress and put "dry" laws upon the statute-books of ten States; and on the third hand, as it were, it established a prudery in speech and thought from which we are yet but half delivered. Such ancient and innocent words as "bitch" and "bastard" disappeared from the American language; Bartlett tells us, indeed, in his "Dictionary of Americanisms, "[109] that even "bull" was softened to "male cow." This was the Golden Age of euphemism, as it was of euphuism; the worst inventions of the English mid-Victorians were adopted and improved. The word "woman" became a term of opprobrium, verging close upon downright libel; legs became the inimitable "limbs"; the stomach began to run from the "bosom" to the pelvic arch; pantaloons faded into "unmentionables"; the newspapers spun their parts of speech into such gossamer webs as "a statutory offence, " "a house of questionable repute" and "an interesting

[109] Second edition; Boston, Little, Brown & Co., 1859, xxvi.

condition." And meanwhile the Good Templars and Sons of Temperance swarmed in the land like a plague of celestial locusts. There was not a hamlet without its uniformed phalanx, its affecting exhibit of reformed drunkards. The Kentucky Legislature succumbed to a travelling recruiting officer, and two-thirds of the members signed the pledge. The National House of Representatives took recess after recess to hear eminent excoriators of the Rum Demon, and more than a dozen of its members forsook their duties to carry the new gospel to the bucolic heathen—the vanguard, one may note in passing, of the innumerable Chautauquan caravan of later years.

Beneath all this bubbling on the surface, of course, ran the deep and swift undercurrent of anti-slavery feeling—a tide of passion which historians now attempt to account for on economic grounds, but which showed no trace of economic origin while it lasted. Its true quality was moral, devout, ecstatic; it culminated, to change the figure, in a supreme discharge of moral electricity, almost fatal to the nation. The crack of that great spark emptied the jar; the American people forgot all about their pledges and pruderies during the four years of Civil War. The Good Templars, indeed, were never heard of again, and with them into memory went many other singular virtuosi of virtue—for example, the Millerites. But almost before the last smoke of battle cleared away, a renaissance of Puritan ardour began, and by the middle of the 70's it was in full flower. Its high points and flashing lighthouses halt the backward-looking eye; the Moody and Sankey uproar, the triumphal entry of the Salvation Army, the recrudescence of the temperance agitation and its culmination in prohibition, the rise of the Young Men's Christian Association and of the Sunday-school, the almost miraculous growth of the Christian Endeavour movement, the beginnings of the vice crusade, the renewed injection of moral conceptions and rages into party politics (the "crime" of 1873!), the furious preaching of baroque Utopias, the invention of muckraking, the mad, glad war of extermination upon the Mormons, the hysteria over the Breckenridge-Pollard case and other like causes, the enormous multiplication of moral and religious associations, the spread of zoöphilia, the attack upon Mammon, the dawn of the uplift, and last but far from least, comstockery.

In comstockery, if I do not err, the new Puritanism gave a sign of its formal departure from the old, and moral endeavour suffered a general overhauling and tightening of the screws. The difference between the two forms is very well represented by the difference between the program of the half-forgotten Good Templars and the program set forth in the Webb Law of 1913, or by that between the somewhat diffident prudery of the 40's and the astoundingly ferocious and uncompromising vice-crusading of today. In brief, a difference between the *re*nunciation and *de*nunciation, asceticism and Mohammedanism, the hair shirt and the flaming sword. The distinguishing mark of the elder Puritanism, at least after it had attained to the stature of a national philosophy, was its appeal to the individual conscience, its exclusive concern with the elect, its strong flavour of self-accusing. Even the rage against slavery was, in large measure, an emotion of the mourners' bench. The thing that worried the more ecstatic Abolitionists was their sneaking sense of responsibility, the fear that they themselves were flouting the fire by letting slavery go on. The thirst to punish the concrete slave-owner, as an end in itself, did not appear until opposition had added exasperation to fervour. In most of the earlier harangues against his practice, indeed, you will find a perfect willingness to grant that slave-owner's good faith, and even to compensate him for his property. But the new Puritanism—or, perhaps more accurately, considering the shades of prefixes, the neo-Puritanism—is a frank harking back to the primitive spirit. The original Puritan of the bleak New England coast was not content to flay his own wayward carcass: full satisfaction did not sit upon him until he had jailed a Quaker. That is to say, the sinner who excited his highest zeal and passion was not so much himself as his neighbour; to borrow a term from psychopathology, he was less the masochist than the sadist. And it is that very peculiarity which sets off his descendant of today from the ameliorated Puritan of the era between the Revolution and the Civil War. The new Puritanism is not ascetic, but militant. Its aim is not to lift up saints but to knock down sinners. Its supreme manifestation is the vice crusade, an armed pursuit of helpless outcasts by the whole military and naval forces of the Republic. Its supreme hero is Comstock Himself, with his pious boast that the sinners he jailed during his astounding career, if gathered into one penitential party, would have filled a train of sixty-one coaches, allowing sixty to the coach.

So much for the general trend and tenor of the movement. At the bottom of it, it is plain, there lies that insistent presentation of the idea of sin, that enchantment by concepts of carnality, which has engaged a certain type of man, to the exclusion of all other notions, since the dawn of history. The remote ancestors of our Puritan-Philistines of today are to be met with in the Old Testament and the New, and their nearer grandfathers clamoured against the snares of the flesh in all the councils of the Early Church. Not only Western Christianity has had to reckon with them: they have brothers today among the Mohammedan Sufi and in obscure Buddhist sects, and they were the chief preachers of the Russian Raskol, or Reformation. "The Ironsides of Cromwell and the Puritans of New England, " says Heard, in his book on the Russian church, "bear a strong resemblance to the Old Believers." But here, in the main, we have asceticism more than Puritanism, as it is now visible; here the sinner combated is chiefly the one within. How are we to account for the wholesale transvaluation of values that came after the Civil War, the transfer of ire from the Old Adam to the happy rascal across the street, the sinister rise of a new Inquisition in the midst of a growing luxury that even the Puritans themselves succumbed to? The answer is to be sought, it seems to me, in the direction of the Golden Calf—in the direction of the fat fields of our Midlands, the full nets of our lakes and coasts, the factory smoke of our cities—even in the direction of Wall Street, that devil's chasm. In brief, Puritanism has become bellicose and tyrannical by becoming rich. The will to power has been aroused to a high flame by an increase in the available draught and fuel, as militarism is engendered and nourished by the presence of men and materials. Wealth, discovering its power, has reached out its long arms to grab the distant and innumerable sinner; it has gone down into its deep pockets to pay for his costly pursuit and flaying; it has created the Puritan *entrepreneur*, the daring and imaginative organizer of Puritanism, the baron of moral endeavour, the invincible prophet of new austerities. And, by the same token, it has issued its letters of marque to the Puritan mercenary, the professional hound of heaven, the moral *Junker*, the Comstock, and out of his skill at his trade there has arisen the whole machinery, so complicated and so effective, of the new Holy Office.

Poverty is a soft pedal upon all branches of human activity, not excepting the spiritual, and even the original Puritans, for all their fire, felt its throttling caress. I think it is Bill Nye who has humorously pictured their arduous life: how they had to dig clams all winter that they would have strength enough to plant corn, and how they had to hoe corn all summer that they would have strength enough to dig clams. That low ebb of fortune worked against the full satisfaction of their zeal in two distinct ways. On the one hand, it kept them but ill-prepared for the cost of offensive enterprise: even their occasional missionarying raids upon the Indians took too much productive energy from their business with the corn and the clams. And on the other hand, it kept a certain restraining humility in their hearts, so that for every Quaker they hanged, they let a dozen go. Poverty, of course, is no discredit, but at all events, it is a subtle criticism. The man oppressed by material wants is not in the best of moods for the more ambitious forms of moral adventure. He not only lacks the means; he is also deficient in the self-assurance, the sense of superiority, the secure and lofty point of departure. If he is haunted by notions of the sinfulness of his neighbours, he is apt to see some of its worst manifestations within himself, and that disquieting discovery will tend to take his thoughts from the other fellow. It is by no arbitrary fiat, indeed, that the brothers of all the expiatory orders are vowed to poverty. History teaches us that wealth, whenever it has come to them by chance, has put an end to their soul-searching. The Puritans of the elder generations, with few exceptions, were poor. Nearly all Americans, down to the Civil War, were poor. And being poor, they subscribed to a *Sklavenmoral*. That is to say, they were spiritually humble. Their eyes were fixed, not upon the abyss below them, but upon the long and rocky road ahead of them. Their moral passion spent most of its force in self-accusing, self-denial and self-scourging. They began by howling their sins from the mourners' bench; they came to their end, many of them, in the supreme immolation of battle.

But out of the War came prosperity, and out of prosperity came a new morality, to wit, the *Herrenmoral*. Many great fortunes were made in the War itself; an uncountable number got started during the two decades following. What is more, this material prosperity was generally dispersed through all classes: it affected the common workman and the remote farmer quite as much as the actual merchant and manufacturer. Its first effect, as we all know, was a universal cockiness, a rise in pretensions, a comforting feeling that the Republic was a success, and with it, its every citizen. This change made itself quickly obvious, and even odious, in all the secular relations of life. The American became a sort of braggart playboy of the western world, enormously sure of himself and ludicrously contemptuous of all other men. And on the ghostly side there appeared the same accession of confidence, the same sure assumption of authority, though at first less self-evidently and offensively. The religion of the American thus began to lose its inward direction; it became less and less a scheme of personal salvation and more and more a scheme of pious derring-do. The revivals of the 70's had all the bounce and fervour of those of half a century before, but the mourners' bench began to lose its standing as their symbol, and in its place appeared the collection basket. Instead of accusing himself, the convert volunteered to track down and bring in the other fellow. His enthusiasm was not for repentance, but for what he began to call service. In brief, the national sense of energy and fitness gradually superimposed itself upon the national Puritanism, and from that marriage sprung a keen *Wille zur Macht*, a lusty will to power.[110] The American Puritan, by now, was not content with the rescue of his own soul; he felt an irresistible impulse to hand salvation on, to disperse and multiply it, to ram it down reluctant throats, to make it free, universal and compulsory. He had the men, he had the guns and he had the money too. All that was needed was organization. The rescue of the unsaved could be converted into a wholesale business, unsentimentally and economically conducted, and with all the usual aids to efficiency, from skilful sales management to seductive advertising, and from rigorous accounting to the diligent shutting off of competition.

Out of that new will to power came many enterprises more or less futile and harmless, with the "institutional" church at their head. Piety was cunningly disguised as basketball, billiards and squash; the sinner was lured to grace with Turkish baths, lectures on foreign travel, and free instructions in stenography, rhetoric and double-entry book-keeping. Religion lost all its old contemplative and esoteric character, and became a frankly worldly enterprise, a thing of balance-sheets and ponderable profits, heavily capitalized and astutely manned. There was no longer any room for the spiritual type of leader, with his white choker and his interminable fourthlies. He was displaced by a brisk gentleman in a "business suit" who looked, talked and thought like a seller of Mexican mine stock. Scheme after scheme for the swift evangelization of the nation was launched, some of them of truly astonishing sweep and daring. They kept pace, step by step, with the mushroom growth of enterprise in the commercial field. The Y. M. C. A. swelled to the proportions of a Standard Oil Company, a United States Steel Corporation. Its huge buildings began to rise in every city; it developed a swarm of specialists in new and fantastic moral and social sciences; it enlisted the same gargantuan talent which managed the railroads, the big banks and the larger national industries. And beside it rose the Young People's Society of Christian Endeavour, the Sunday-school associations and a score of other such grandiose organizations, each with its seductive baits for recruits and money. Even the enterprises that had come down from an elder and less expansive day were pumped up and put on a Wall Street basis: the

---

[110] *Cf.* The Puritan, by Owen Hatteras, *The Smart Set*, July, 1916; and The Puritan's Will to Power, by Randolph S. Bourne, *The Seven Arts*, April, 1917.

American Bible Society, for example, began to give away Bibles by the million instead of by the thousand, and the venerable Tract Society took on the feverish ardour of a daily newspaper, even of a yellow journal. Down into our own day this trustification of pious endeavour has gone on. The Men and Religion Forward Movement proposed to convert the whole country by 12 o'clock noon of such and such a day; the Order of Gideons plans to make every traveller read the Bible (American Revised Version!) whether he will or not; in a score of cities there are committees of opulent devotees who take half-pages in the newspapers, and advertise the Decalogue and the Beatitudes as if they were commodities of trade.

Thus the national energy which created the Beef Trust and the Oil Trust achieved equal marvels in the field of religious organization and by exactly the same methods. One needs be no psychologist to perceive in all this a good deal less actual religious zeal than mere lust for staggering accomplishment, for empty bigness, for the unprecedented and the prodigious. Many of these great religious enterprises, indeed, soon lost all save the faintest flavour of devotion—for example, the Y. M. C. A., which is now no more than a sort of national club system, with its doors open to any one not palpably felonious. (I have drunk cocktails in Y. M. C. A. lamaseries, and helped fallen lamas to bed.) But while the war upon godlessness thus degenerated into a secular sport in one direction, it maintained all its pristine quality, and even took on a new ferocity in another direction. Here it was that the lamp of American Puritanism kept on burning; here, it was, indeed, that the lamp became converted into a huge bonfire, or rather a blast-furnace, with flames mounting to the very heavens, and sinners stacked like cordwood at the hand of an eager black gang. In brief, the new will to power, working in the true Puritan as in the mere religious sportsman, stimulated him to a campaign of repression and punishment perhaps unequalled in the history of the world, and developed an art of militant morality as complex in technique and as rich in professors as the elder art of iniquity.

If we take the passage of the Comstock Postal Act, on March 3, 1873, as a starting point, the legislative stakes of this new Puritan movement sweep upward in a grand curve to the passage of the Mann and Webb Acts, in 1910 and 1913, the first of which ratifies the Seventh Commandment with a salvo of artillery, and the second of which put the overwhelming power of the Federal Government behind the enforcement of the prohibition laws in the so-called "dry" States. The mind at once recalls the salient campaigns of this war of a generation:

751

first the attack upon "vicious" literature, begun by Comstock and the New York Society for the Suppression of Vice, but quickly extending to every city in the land; then the long fight upon the open gambling house, culminating in its practical disappearance; then the recrudesence of prohibition, abandoned at the outbreak of the Civil War, and the attempt to enforce it in a rapidly growing list of States; then the successful onslaught upon the Louisiana lottery, and upon its swarm of rivals and successors; then the gradual stamping-out of horse-racing, until finally but two or three States permitted it, and the consequent attack upon the pool-room; then the rise of a theatre-censorship in most of the large cities, and of a moving picture censorship following it; then the revival of Sabbatarianism, with the Lord's Day Alliance, a Canadian invention, in the van; then the gradual tightening of the laws against sexual irregularity, with the unenforceable New York Adultery Act as a typical product; and lastly, the general ploughing up and emotional discussion of sexual matters, with compulsory instruction in "sex hygiene" as its mildest manifestation and the mediaeval fury of the vice crusade as its worst. Differing widely in their targets, these various Puritan enterprises had one character in common: they were all efforts to combat immorality with the weapons designed for crime. In each of them there was a visible effort to erect the individual's offence against himself into an offence against society. Beneath all of them there was the dubious principle—the very determining principle, indeed, of Puritanism—that it is competent for the community to limit and condition the private acts of its members, and with it the inevitable corollary that there are some members of the community who have a special talent for such legislation, and that their arbitrary fiats are, and of a right ought to be, binding upon all.

§ 4

This is the essential fact of the new Puritanism; its recognition of the moral expert, the professional sinhound, the virtuoso of virtue. Under the original Puritan theocracy, as in Scotland, for example, the chase and punishment of sinners was a purely ecclesiastical function, and during the slow disintegration of the theocracy the only change introduced was the extension of that function to lay helpers, and finally to the whole body of laymen. This change, however, did not materially corrupt the ecclesiastical quality of the enterprise: the leader in the so-called militant field still remained the same man who led in the spiritual field. But with the capitalization of Puritan effort there came a radical overhauling of method. The secular arm, as it were, conquered as it helped. That is to say, the special business of forcing sinners to be good was taken away from the preachers and put into the hands of laymen trained in its technique and mystery, and there it remains. The new Puritanism has created an army of gladiators who are not only distinct from the hierarchy, but who, in many instances, actually command and intimidate the hierarchy. This is conspicuously evident in the case of the Anti-Saloon League, an enormously effective fighting organization, with a large staff of highly accomplished experts in its service. These experts do not wait for ecclesiastical support, nor even ask for it; they force it. The clergyman who presumes to protest against their war upon the saloon, even upon the quite virtuous ground that it is not effective enough, runs a risk of condign and merciless punishment. So plainly is this understood, indeed, that in more than one State the clergy of the Puritan denominations openly take orders from these specialists in excoriation, and court their favour without shame. Here a single moral enterprise, heavily capitalized and carefully officered, has engulfed the entire Puritan movement, and a part has become more than the whole. [111]

In a dozen other directions this tendency to transform a religious business into a purely secular business, with lay backers and lay officers, is plainly visible. The increasing wealth of Puritanism has not only augmented its scope and its daring, but it has also had the effect of attracting clever men, of no particular spiritual enthusiasm, to its service. Moral endeavour, in brief, has become a recognized trade, or rather a profession, and there have appeared men who pretend to a special and enormous knowledge of it, and who show enough truth in their pretension to gain the unlimited support of Puritan capitalists. The vice crusade, to mention one example, has produced a large crop of such self-constituted experts, and some of them are in such demand that they are overwhelmed with engagements. The majority of these men have wholly lost the flavour of sacerdotalism. They are not pastors, but detectives, statisticians and mob orators, and not infrequently their secularity becomes distressingly evident. Their aim, as they say, is to do things. Assuming that "moral sentiment" is behind them, they override all criticism and opposition without argument, and proceed to the business of dispersing prostitutes, of browbeating and terrorizing

---

[111] An instructive account of the organization and methods of the Anti-Saloon League, a thoroughly typical Puritan engine, is to be found in Alcohol and Society, by John Koren; New York, Henry Holt & Co., 1916.

weak officials, and of forcing legislation of their own invention through City Councils and State Legislatures. Their very cocksureness is their chief source of strength. They combat objection with such violence and with such a devastating cynicism that it quickly fades away. The more astute politicians, in the face of so ruthless a fire, commonly profess conversion and join the colours, just as their brethren went over to prohibition in the "dry" States, and the newspapers seldom hold out much longer. The result is that the "investigation" of the social evil becomes an orgy, and that the ensuing "report" of the inevitable "vice commission" is made up of two parts sensational fiction and three parts platitude. Of all the vice commissions that have sat of late in the United States, not one has done its work without the aid of these singularly confident experts, and not one has contributed an original and sagacious idea, nor even an idea of ordinary common sense, to the solution of the problem.

I need not go on piling up examples of this new form of Puritan activity, with its definite departure from a religious foundation and its elaborate development as an everyday business. The impulse behind it I have called a *Wille zur Macht*, a will to power. In terms more homely, it was described by John Fiske as "the disposition to domineer, " and in his usual unerring way, he saw its dependence on the gratuitous assumption of infallibility. But even stronger than the Puritan's belief in his own inspiration is his yearning to make some one jump. In other words, he has an ineradicable liking for cruelty in him: he is a sportsman even before he is a moralist, and very often his blood-lust leads him into lamentable excesses. The various vice crusades afford innumerable cases in point. In one city, if the press dispatches are to be believed, the proscribed women of the Tenderloin were pursued with such ferocity that seven of them were driven to suicide. And in another city, after a campaign of repression so unfortunate in its effects that there were actually protests against it by clergymen elsewhere, a distinguished (and very friendly) connoisseur of such affairs referred to it ingenuously as more fun "than a fleet of aeroplanes." Such disorderly combats with evil, of course, produce no permanent good. It is a commonplace, indeed, that a city is usually in worse condition after it has been "cleaned up" than it was before, and I need not point to New York, Los Angeles and Des Moines for the evidence as to the social evil, and to any large city, East, West, North, South, for the evidence as to the saloon. But the Puritans who finance such enterprises get their thrills, not out of any possible obliteration of vice, but out of the galloping pursuit of the vicious. The new Puritan gives no more serious thought to the rights and feelings of his quarry than the gunner gives to the rights and feelings of his birds. From the beginning of the prohibition campaign, for example, the principle of compensation has been violently opposed, despite its obvious justice, and a complaisant judiciary has ratified the Puritan position. In England and on the Continent that principle is safeguarded by the fundamental laws, and during the early days of the anti-slavery agitation in this country it was accepted as incontrovertible, but if any American statesman were to propose today that it be applied to the license-holder whose lawful franchise has been taken away from him arbitrarily, or to the brewer or distiller whose costly plant has been rendered useless and valueless, he would see the days of his statesmanship brought to a quick and violent close.

But does all this argue a total lack of justice in the American character, or even a lack of common decency? I doubt that it would be well to go so far in accusation. What it does argue is a tendency to put moral considerations above all other considerations, and to define morality in the narrow Puritan sense. The American, in other words, thinks that the sinner has no rights that any one is bound to respect, and he is prone to mistake an unsupported charge of sinning, provided it be made violently enough, for actual proof and confession. What is more, he takes an intense joy in the mere chase: he has the true Puritan taste for an *auto da fé* in him. "I am ag'inst capital punishment, " said Mr. Dooley, "but we won't get rid av it so long as the people enjie it so much." But though he is thus an eager spectator, and may even be lured into taking part in the pursuit, the average American is not disposed to initiate it, nor to pay for it. The larger Puritan enterprises of today are not popular in the sense of originating in the bleachers, but only in the sense of being applauded from the bleachers. The burdens of the fray, both of toil and of expense, are always upon a relatively small number of men. In a State rocked and racked by a war upon the saloon, it was recently shown, for example, that but five per cent. of the members of the Puritan denominations contributed to the war-chest. And yet the Anti-Saloon League of that State was so sure of support from below that it presumed to stand as the spokesman of the whole Christian community, and even ventured to launch excommunications upon contumacious Christians, both lay and clerical, who objected to its methods. Moreover, the great majority of the persons included in the contributing five per cent. gave no more than a few cents a year. The whole support of the League devolved upon a dozen men, all of them rich and all of them Puritans of purest ray serene. These men supported a costly organization for their private entertainment and stimulation. It was their means of recreation, their sporting club. They were willing to spend a lot of money to procure good sport for themselves—*i.e.*, to procure the best crusading talent available—and they were so successful in that endeavour that they enchanted the populace too, and so shook the State.

Naturally enough, this organization of Puritanism upon a business and sporting basis has had a tendency to attract and create a type of "expert" crusader whose determination to give his employers a good show is uncontaminated by any consideration for the public welfare. The result has been a steady increase of scandals, a constant collapse of moral organizations, a frequent unveiling of whited sepulchres. Various observers have sought to direct the public attention to this significant corruption of the new Puritanism. The New York *Sun*, for example, in the course of a protest against the appointment of a vice commission for New York, has denounced the paid agents of private reform organizations as "notoriously corrupt, undependable and dishonest, " and the Rev. Dr. W. S. Rainsford, supporting the charge, has borne testimony out of his own wide experience to their lawlessness, their absurd pretensions to special knowledge, their habit of manufacturing evidence, and their devious methods of shutting off criticism. But so far, at all events, no organized war upon them has been undertaken, and they seem to flourish more luxuriantly year after year. The individual whose common rights are invaded by such persons has little chance of getting justice, and less of getting redress. When he attempts to defend himself he finds that he is opposed, not only by a financial power that is ample for all purposes of the combat and that does not shrink at intimidating juries, prosecuting officers and judges, but also by a shrewdness which shapes the laws to its own uses, and takes full advantage of the miserable cowardice of legislatures. The moral gladiators, in brief, know the game. They come before a legislature with a bill ostensibly designed to cure some great and admitted evil, they procure its enactment by scarcely veiled insinuations that all who stand against it must be apologists for the evil itself, and then they proceed to extend its aims by bold inferences, and to dragoon the courts into ratifying those inferences, and to employ it as a means of persecution, terrorism and blackmail. The history of the Mann Act offers a shining example of this purpose. It was carried through Congress, over the veto of President Taft, who discerned its extravagance, on the plea that it was needed to put down the traffic in prostitutes; it is enforced today against men who are no more engaged in the traffic in prostitutes than you or I. Naturally enough, the effect of this extension of its purposes, against which its author has publicly protested, has been to make it a truly deadly weapon in the hands of professional Puritans and of denouncers of delinquency even less honest. "Blackmailers of both sexes have arisen, " says Mr. Justice McKenna, "using the terrors of the construction now sanctioned by the [Supreme] Court as a help—indeed, the means—for their brigandage. The result is grave and should give us pause."[112]

But that is as far as objection has yet gone; the majority of the learned jurist's colleagues swallowed both the statute and its consequences.[113] There is, indeed, no sign as yet of any organized war upon the alliance between the blackmailing Puritan and the pseudo-Puritan blackmailer. It must wait until a sense of reason and justice shows itself in the American people, strong enough to overcome their prejudice in favour of the moralist on the one hand, and their delight in barbarous pursuits and punishments on the other. I see but faint promise of that change today.

§ 5

I have gone into the anatomy and physiology of militant Puritanism because, so far as I know, the inquiry has not been attempted before, and because a somewhat detailed acquaintance with the forces behind so grotesque a manifestation as comstockery, the particular business of the present essay, is necessary to an understanding of its workings, and of its prosperity, and of its influence upon the arts. Save one turn to England or to the British colonies, it is impossible to find a parallel for the astounding absolutism of Comstock and his imitators in any civilized country. No other nation has laws which oppress the arts so ignorantly and so abominably as ours do, nor has any other nation handed over the enforcement of the statutes which exist to agencies so openly pledged to reduce all aesthetic expression to the service of a stupid and unworkable scheme of rectitude. I have before me as I write a pamphlet in explanation of his aims and principles, prepared by Comstock himself and presented to me by his successor. Its very title is a sufficient statement of the Puritan position: "MORALS, Not Art or Literature."[New York, (1914).] The capitals are in the original. And within, as a sort of general text, the idea is amplified: "It is a question

---

[112] U.S. Rep., vol. 242, No. 7, p. 502.

[113] The majority opinion, written by Mr. Justice Day, is given in U. S. Rep., vol. 242, no. 7, pp. 482-496.

of peace, good order and morals, and not art, literature or science." Here we have a statement of principle that, at all events, is at least quite frank. There is not the slightest effort to beg the question; there is no hypocritical pretension to a desire to purify or safeguard the arts; they are dismissed at once as trivial and degrading. And jury after jury has acquiesced in this; it was old Anthony's boast, in his last days, that his percentage of convictions, in 40 years, had run to 98.5.[114]

Comstockery is thus grounded firmly upon that profound national suspicion of the arts, that truculent and almost unanimous Philistinism, which I have described. It would be absurd to dismiss it as an excrescence, and untypical of the American mind. But it is typical, too, in the manner in which it has gone beyond that mere partiality to the accumulation of a definite power, and made that power irresponsible and almost irresistible. It was Comstock himself, in fact, who invented the process whereby his followers in other fields of moral endeavour have forced laws into the statute books upon the pretence of putting down John Doe, an acknowledged malefactor, and then turned them savagely upon Richard Roe, a peaceable, well-meaning and hitherto law-abiding man. And it was Comstock who first capitalized moral endeavour like baseball or the soap business, and made himself the first of its kept professors, and erected about himself a rampart of legal and financial immunity which rid him of all fear of mistakes and their consequences, and so enabled him to pursue his jehad with all the advantages in his favour. He was, in brief, more than the greatest Puritan gladiator of his time; he was the Copernicus of a quite new art and science, and he devised a technique and handed down a professional ethic that no rival has been able to better.

The whole story is naïvely told in "Anthony Comstock, Fighter,"[115] a work which passed under the approving eye of the old war horse himself and is full of his characteristic pecksniffery.[116] His beginnings,

---

[114] I quote from page 157 of Anthony Comstock, Fighter, the official biography. On page 239 the number of his prosecutions is given as 3, 646, with 2, 682 convictions, which works out to but 73 per cent. He is credited with having destroyed 50 tons of books, 28, 425 pounds of stereotype plates, 16, 900 photographic negatives, and 3, 984, 063 photographs—enough to fill "sixteen freight cars, fifteen loaded with ten tons each, and the other nearly full."

[115] By Charles Gallaudet Trumbull; New York, Fleming H. Revell Co. (1913).

[116] An example: "All the evil men in New York cannot harm a hair of my head, were it not the will of God. If it be His will, what right have I or any one to say aught? I am only a speck, a mite, before God, yet not a hair of my head can be harmed unless it be His will. Oh, to live, to feel, to be—Thy will be done!" (pp. 84-5). Again: "I prayed that, if my bill might not pass, I might go back to New York submissive to God's will, feeling

it appears, were very modest. When he arrived in New York from the Connecticut hinterland, he was a penniless and uneducated clodhopper, just out of the Union army, and his first job was that of a porter in a wholesale dry-goods house. But he had in him several qualities of the traditional Yankee which almost always insure success, and it was not long before he began to make his way. One of these qualities was a talent for bold and ingratiating address; another was a vast appetite for thrusting himself into affairs, a yearning to run things—what the Puritan calls public spirit. The two constituted his fortune. The second brought him into intimate relations with the newly-organized Young Men's Christian Association, and led him to the discovery of a form of moral endeavour that was at once novel and fascinating—the unearthing and denunciation of "immoral" literature. The first, once he had attracted attention thereby, got him the favourable notice, and finally the unlimited support, of the late Morris K. Jesup, one of the earliest and perhaps the greatest of the moral *entrepreneurs* that I have described. Jesup was very rich, and very eager to bring the whole nation up to grace by *force majeure.* He was the banker of at least a dozen grandiose programs of purification in the seventies and eighties. In Comstock he found precisely the sort of field agent that he was looking for, and the two presently constituted the most formidable team of professional reformers that the country had ever seen.

The story of the passage of the Act of Congress of March 3, 1873, [117] under cover of which the Comstock Society still carries on its campaigns of snouting and suppression, is a classical tale of Puritan impudence and chicanery. Comstock, with Jesup and other rich men backing him financially and politically, [118] managed the business. First, a number of spectacular raids were made on the publishers of such pornographic books as "The Memoirs of Fanny Hill" and "Only a Boy." Then the newspapers were filled with inflammatory matter about the wide dispersal of such stuff, and its demoralizing effects upon the youth of the republic. Then a committee of self-advertising clergymen and "Christian millionaires" was organized to launch a definite "movement." And then a direct attack was made upon Congress, and,

---

that it was for the best. I asked for forgiveness and asked that my bill might pass, if possible; but over and above all, that the will of God be done" (p. 6). Nevertheless, Comstock neglected no chance to apply his backstairs pressure to the members of both Houses.

[117] Now, with amendments, sections 211, 212 and 245 of the United States Criminal Code.

[118] *Vide* Anthony Comstock, Fighter, pp. 81, 85, 94.

to the tune of fiery moral indignation, the bill prepared by Comstock himself was forced through both houses. All opposition, if only the opposition of inquiry, was overborne in the usual manner. That is to say, every Congressman who presumed to ask what it was all about, or to point out obvious defects in the bill, was disposed of by the insinuation, or even the direct charge, that he was a covert defender of obscene books, and, by inference, of the carnal recreations described in them. We have grown familiar of late with this process: it was displayed at full length in the passage of the Mann Act, and again when the Webb Act and the Prohibition Amendment were before Congress. In 1873 its effectiveness was helped out by its novelty, and so the Comstock bill was rushed through both houses in the closing days of a busy session, and President Grant accommodatingly signed it.

Once it was upon the books, Comstock made further use of the prevailing uproar to have himself appointed a special agent of the Postoffice Department to enforce it, and with characteristic cunning refused to take any salary. Had his job carried a salary, it would have excited the acquisitiveness of other virtuosi; as it was, he was secure. As for the necessary sinews of war, he knew well that he could get them from Jesup. Within a few weeks, indeed, the latter had perfected a special organization for the enforcement of the new statute, and it still flourishes as the New York Society for the Suppression of Vice; or, as it is better known, the Comstock Society. The new Federal Act, dealing only with the mails, left certain loopholes; they were plugged up by fastening drastic amendments upon the New York Code of Criminal Procedure—amendments forced through the legislature precisely as the Federal Act had been forced through Congress.[119] With these laws in his hands Comstock was ready for his career. It was his part of the arrangement to supply the thrills of the chase; it was Jesup's part to find the money. The partnership kept up until the death of Jesup, in 1908, and after that Comstock readily found new backers. Even his own death, in 1915, did not materially alter a scheme of things which offered such admirable opportunities for the exercise of the Puritan love of spectacular and relentless pursuit, the Puritan delusion of moral grandeur and infallibility, the Puritan will to power.

Ostensibly, as I have said, the new laws were designed to put down the traffic in frankly pornographic books and pictures—a traffic which, of course, found no defenders—but Comstock had so drawn them that their actual sweep was vastly wider, and once he was firmly in the

---

[119] Now sections 1141, 1142 and 1143 of the Penal Laws of New York.

saddle his enterprises scarcely knew limits. Having disposed of "The Confessions of Maria Monk" and "Night Life in Paris, " he turned to Rabelais and the Decameron, and having driven these ancients under the book-counters, he pounced upon Zola, Balzac and Daudet, and having disposed of these too, he began a *pogrom* which, in other hands, eventually brought down such astounding victims as Thomas Hardy's "Jude the Obscure" and Harold Frederic's "The Damnation of Theron Ware." All through the eighties and nineties this ecstatic campaign continued, always increasing in violence and effectiveness. Comstock became a national celebrity; his doings were as copiously reported by the newspapers as those of P. T. Barnum or John L. Sullivan. Imitators sprang up in all the larger cities: there was hardly a public library in the land that did not begin feverishly expurgating its shelves; the publication of fiction, and particularly of foreign fiction, took on the character of an extra hazardous enterprise. Not, of course, that the reign of terror was not challenged, and Comstock himself denounced. So early as 1876 a national organization demanding a reasonable amendment of the postal laws got on its legs; in the late eighties "Citizen" George Francis Train defied the whirlwind by printing the Old Testament as a serial; many indignant victims, acquitted by some chance in the courts, brought suit against Comstock for damages. Moreover, an occasional judge, standing out boldly against the usual intimidation, denounced him from the bench; one of them, Judge Jenkins, accused him specifically of "fraud and lying" and other "dishonest practices."[120] But the spirit of American Puritanism was on his side. His very extravagances at once stimulated and satisfied the national yearning for a hot chase, a good show—and in the complaints of his victims, that the art of letters was being degraded, that the country was made ridiculous, the newspaper-reading populace could see no more than an affectation. The reform organization of 1876 lasted but five years; and then disbanded without having accomplished anything; Train was put on trial for "debauching the young" with an "obscene" serial;[121] juries refused to bring in punitive verdicts against the master showman.

---

[120] U. S. *vs.* Casper, reported in the *Twentieth Century*, Feb. 11, 1892.

[121] The trial court dodged the issue by directing the jury to find the prisoner not guilty on the ground of insanity. The necessary implication, of course, was that the publication complained of was actually obscene. In 1895, one Wise, of Clay Center, Kansas, sent a quotation from the Bible through the mails, and was found guilty of mailing obscene matter. See The Free Press Anthology, compiled by Theodore Schroeder; New York, Truth Seeker Pub. Co., 1909, p. 258.

In carrying on this way of extermination upon all ideas that violated their private notions of virtue and decorum, Comstock and his followers were very greatly aided by the vagueness of the law. It prohibited the use of the mails for transporting all matter of an "obscene, lewd, lascivious ... or filthy" character, but conveniently failed to define these adjectives. As a result, of course, it was possible to bring an accusation against practically *any* publication that aroused the comstockian blood-lust, however innocently, and to subject the persons responsible for it to costly, embarrassing and often dangerous persecution. No man, said Dr. Johnson, would care to go on trial for his life once a week, even if possessed of absolute proofs of his innocence. By the same token, no man wants to be arraigned in a criminal court, and displayed in the sensational newspapers, as a purveyor of indecency, however strong his assurance of innocence. Comstock made use of this fact in an adroit and characteristically unconscionable manner. He held the menace of prosecution over all who presumed to dispute his tyranny, and when he could not prevail by a mere threat, he did not hesitate to begin proceedings, and to carry them forward with the aid of florid proclamations to the newspapers and ill concealed intimidations of judges and juries.

The last-named business succeeded as it always does in this country, where the judiciary is quite as sensitive to the suspicion of sinfulness as the legislative arm. A glance at the decisions handed down during the forty years of Comstock's chief activity shows a truly amazing willingness to accommodate him in his pious enterprises. On the one hand, there was gradually built up a court-made definition of obscenity which eventually embraced almost every conceivable violation of Puritan prudery, and on the other hand the victim's means of defence were steadily restricted and conditioned, until in the end he had scarcely any at all. This is the state of the law today. It is held in the leading cases that anything is obscene which may excite "impure thoughts" in "the minds ... of persons that are susceptible to impure thoughts, "[122] or which "tends to deprave the minds" of any who, because they are "young and inexperienced, " are "open to such influences"[123]—in brief, that anything is obscene that is not fit to be handed to a child just learning to read, or that may imaginably stimulate the lubricity of the most foul-minded. It is held further that words that are perfectly innocent in themselves—"words, abstractly

---

[122] U. S. *vs.* Bennett, 16 Blatchford, 368-9 (1877).
[123] *Idem*, 362; People *vs.* Muller, 96 N. Y., 411; U. S. *vs.* Clark, 38 Fed. Rep. 734.

considered, [that] may be free from vulgarism"—may yet be assumed, by a friendly jury, to be likely to "arouse a libidinous passion ... in the mind of a modest woman." (I quote exactly! The court failed to define "modest woman.")[124] Yet further, it is held that any book is obscene "which is unbecoming, immodest...."[125] Obviously, this last decision throws open the door to endless imbecilities, for its definition merely begs the question, and so makes a reasonable solution ten times harder. It is in such mazes that the Comstocks safely lurk. Almost any printed allusion to sex may be argued against as unbecoming in a moral republic, and once it is unbecoming it is also obscene.

In meeting such attacks the defendant must do his fighting without weapons. He cannot allege in his defence that the offending work was put forth for a legitimate, necessary and decent purpose;[126] he cannot allege that a passage complained of is from a standard work, itself in general circulation;[127] he cannot offer evidence that the person to whom a book or picture was sold or exhibited was not actually depraved by it, or likely to be depraved by it;[128] he cannot rest his defence on its lack of such effect upon the jurymen themselves;[129] he cannot plead that the alleged obscenity, in point of fact, is couched in decent and unobjectionable language;[130] he cannot plead that the same or a similar work has gone unchallenged elsewhere;[131] he cannot argue that the circulation of works of the same class has set up a presumption of toleration, and a tacit limitation of the definition of obscenity.[132] The general character of a book is not a defence of a particular passage, however unimportant; if there is the slightest descent to what is "unbecoming, " the whole may be ruthlessly condemned.[133] Nor is it an admissible defence to argue that the book was not generally circulated, and that the copy in evidence was obtained by an *agent provocateur*,

---

[124] U. S. *vs.* Moore, 129 Fed., 160-1 (1904).

[125] U. S. *vs.* Heywood, judge's charge, Boston, 1877. Quoted in U. S. *vs.* Bennett, 16 Blatchford.

[126] U. S. *vs.* Slenker, 32 Fed. Rep., 693; People *vs.* Muller, 96 N. Y. 408-414; Anti-Vice Motion Picture Co. *vs.* Bell, reported in the *New York Law Journal*, Sept. 22, 1916; Sociological Research Film Corporation *vs.* the City of New York, 83 Misc. 815; Steele *vs.* Bannon, 7 L. R. C. L. Series, 267; U. S. *vs.* Means, 42 Fed. Rep. 605, etc.

[127] U. S. *vs.* Cheseman, 19 Fed. Rep., 597 (1884).

[128] People *vs.* Muller, 96 N. Y., 413.

[129] U. S. *vs.* Bennett, 16 Blatchford, 368-9.

[130] U. S. *vs.* Smith, 45 Fed. Rep. 478.

[131] U. S. *vs.* Bennett, 16 Blatchford, 360-1; People *vs.* Berry, 1 N. Y., Crim. R., 32.

[132] People *vs.* Muller, 32 Hun., 212-215.

[133] U. S. *vs.* Bennett, 16 Blatchford, 361.

and by false representations. [134] Finally, all the decisions deny the defendant the right to introduce any testimony, whether expert or otherwise, that a book is of artistic value and not pornographic, and that its effect upon normal persons is not pernicious. Upon this point the jury is the sole judge, and it cannot be helped to its decision by taking other opinions, or by hearing evidence as to what is the general opinion.

Occasionally, as I have said, a judge has revolted against this intolerable state of the court-and Comstock-made law, and directed a jury to disregard these astounding decisions. [135] In a recent New York case Judge Samuel Seabury actually ruled that "it is no part of the duty of courts to exercise a censorship over literary productions." [136] But in general the judiciary has been curiously complaisant, and more than once a Puritan on the bench has delighted the Comstocks by prosecuting their case for them. [137] With such decisions in their hands and such aid from the other side of the bar, it is no wonder that they enter upon their campaigns with impudence and assurance. All the odds are in their favour from the start. They have statutes deliberately designed to make the defence onerous; they are familiar by long experience with all the tricks and surprises of the game; they are sheltered behind organizations, incorporated without capital and liberally chartered by trembling legislatures, which make reprisals impossible in case of failure; above all, they have perfected the business of playing upon the cowardice and vanity of judges and prosecuting officers. The newspapers, with very few exceptions, give them ready aid. Theoretically, perhaps, many newspaper editors are opposed to comstockery, and sometimes they denounce it with great eloquence,

---

[134] U. S. *vs.* Moore, 16 Fed. Rep., 39; U. S. *vs.* Wright, 38 Fed. Rep., 106; U. S. *vs.* Dorsey, 40 Fed. Rep., 752; U. S. *vs.* Baker, 155 Mass., 287; U. S. *vs.* Grimm, 15 Supreme Court Rep., 472.

[135] Various cases in point are cited in the Brief on Behalf of Plaintiff in Dreiser *vs.* John Lane Co., App. Div. 1st Dept. N. Y., 1917. I cite a few: People *vs.* Eastman, 188 N. Y., 478; U. S. *vs.* Swearingen, 161 U. S., 446; People *vs.* Tylkoff, 212 N. Y., 197; In the matter of Worthington Co., 62 St. Rep. 116-7; St. Hubert Guild *vs.* Quinn, 64 Misc., 336-341. But nearly all such decisions are in New York cases. In the Federal courts the Comstocks usually have their way

[136] St. Hubert Guild *vs.* Quinn, 64 Misc., 339

[137] For example, Judge Chas. L. Benedict, sitting in U. S. *vs.* Bennett, *op. cit.* This is a leading case, and the Comstocks make much of it. Nevertheless, a contemporary newspaper denounces Judge Benedict for his "intense bigotry" and alleges that "the only evidence which he permitted to be given was on the side of the prosecution." (Port Jervis, N. Y., *Evening Gazette*, March 22, 1879.) Moreover, a juror in the case, Alfred A. Valentine, thought it necessary to inform the newspapers that he voted guilty only in obedience to judicial instructions.

but when a good show is offered they are always in favour of the showman[138]—and the Comstocks are showmen of undoubted skill. They know how to make a victim jump and writhe in the ring; they have a talent for finding victims who are prominent enough to arrest attention; they shrewdly capitalize the fact that the pursuer appears more heroic than the prey, and the further fact that the newspaper reader is impatient of artistic pretensions and glad to see an artist made ridiculous. And behind them there is always the steady pressure of Puritan prejudice—the Puritan feeling that "immorality" is the blackest of crimes, and that its practitioner has no rights. It was by making use of these elements that Comstock achieved his prodigies, and it is by making use of them that his heirs and assigns keep up the sport today. Their livelihood depends upon the money they can raise among the righteous, and the amount they can raise depends upon the quality of the entertainment they offer. Hence their adept search for shining marks. Hence, for example, the spectacular raid upon the Art Students' League, on August 2, 1906. Hence the artful turning to their own use of the vogue of such sensational dramatists as Eugène Brieux and George Bernard Shaw, and of such isolated plays as "Trilby" and "Sapho." Hence the barring from the mails of the inflammatory report of the Chicago Vice Commission—a strange, strange case of dog eating dog.

But here we have humour. There is, however, no humour in the case of a serious author who sees his work damaged and perhaps ruined by a malicious and unintelligent attack, and himself held up to public obloquy as one with the vendors of pamphlets of flagellation and filthy "marriage guides." He finds opposing him a flat denial of his decent purpose as an artist, and a stupid and ill-natured logic that baffles sober answer.[139] He finds on his side only the half-hearted support of a publisher whose interest in a single book is limited to his profits from it, and who desires above all things to evade a nuisance and an expense.

---

[138] *Vide* Newspaper Morals, by H. L. Mencken, the *Atlantic Monthly*, March, 1914

[139] As a fair specimen of the sort of reasoning that prevails among the consecrated brethren I offer the following extract from an argument against birth control delivered by the present active head of the New York Society for the Suppression of Vice before the Women's City Club of New York, Nov. 17, 1916:

"Natural and inevitable conditions, over which we can have no control, will assert themselves wherever population becomes too dense. This has been exemplified time after time in the history of the world where over-population has been corrected by manifestations of nature or by war, flood or pestilence.... Belgium may have been regarded as an over-populated country. Is it a coincidence that, during the past two years, the territory of Belgium has been devastated and its population scattered throughout the other countries of the world?"

Not a few publishers, knowing the constant possibility of sudden and arbitrary attack, insert a clause in their contracts whereby an author must secure them against damage from any "immoral" matter in his book. They read and approve the manuscript, they print the book and sell it—but if it is unlucky enough to attract the comstockian lightning, the author has the whole burden to bear, [140] and if they seek safety and economy by yielding, as often happens, he must consent to the mutilation or even the suppression of his work. The result is that a writer in such a situation, is practically beaten before he can offer a defence. The professional book-baiters have laws to their liking, and courts pliant to their exactions; they fill the newspapers with inflammatory charges before the accused gets his day in court; they have the aid of prosecuting officers who fear the political damage of their enmity, and of the enmity of their wealthy and influential backers; above all, they have the command of far more money than any author can hope to muster. Finally, they derive an advantage from two of the most widespread of human weaknesses, the first being envy and the second being fear. When an author is attacked, a good many of his rivals see only a personal benefit in his difficulties, and not a menace to the whole order, and a good many others are afraid to go to his aid because of the danger of bringing down the moralists' rage upon themselves. Both of these weaknesses revealed themselves very amusingly in the Dreiser case, and I hope to detail their operations at some length later on, when I describe that *cause célèbre* in a separate work.

Now add to the unfairness and malignancy of the attack its no less disconcerting arbitrariness and fortuitousness, and the path of the American author is seen to be strewn with formidable entanglements indeed. With the law what it is, he is quite unable to decide *a priori*

---

[140] For example, the printed contract of the John Lane Co., publisher of Dreiser's The "Genius, " contains this provision: "The author hereby guarantees ... that the work ... contains nothing of a scandalous, an immoral or a libelous nature." The contract for the publication of The "Genius" was signed on July 30, 1914. The manuscript had been carefully read by representatives of the publisher, and presumably passed as not scandalous or immoral, inasmuch as the publication of a scandalous or immoral book would have exposed the publisher to prosecution. About 8, 000 copies were sold under this contract. Two years later, in July, 1916, the Society for the Suppression of Vice threatened to begin a prosecution unless the book was withdrawn. It was withdrawn forthwith, and Dreiser was compelled to enter suit for a performance of the contract. The withdrawal, it will be noticed, was not in obedience to a court order, but followed a mere comstockian threat. Yet Dreiser was at once deprived of his royalties, and forced into expensive litigation. Had it not been that eminent counsel volunteered for his defence, his personal means would have been insufficient to have got him even a day in court.

what is permitted by the national delicacy and what is not, nor can he get any light from the recorded campaigns of the moralists. They seem to strike blindly, unintelligently, without any coherent theory or plan. "Trilby" is assaulted by the united comstockery of a dozen cities, and "The Yoke" somehow escapes. "Hagar Revelly" is made the subject of a double prosecution in the State and Federal courts, and "Love's Pilgrimage" and "One Man" go unmolested. The publisher of Przybyszewski's "Homo Sapiens" is forced to withdraw it; the publisher of Artzibashef's "Sanine" follows it with "The Breaking Point." The serious work of a Forel is brought into court as pornography, and the books of Havelock Ellis are barred from the mails; the innumerable volumes on "sex hygiene" by tawdry clergymen and smutty old maids are circulated by the million and without challenge. Frank Harris is deprived of a publisher for his "Oscar Wilde: His Life and Confession" by threats of immediate prosecution; the newspapers meanwhile dedicate thousands of columns to the filthy amusements of Harry Thaw. George Moore's "Memoirs of My Dead Life" are bowdlerized, James Lane Allen's "A Summer in Arcady" is barred from libraries, and a book by D. H. Lawrence is forbidden publication altogether; at the same time half a dozen cheap magazines devoted to sensational sex stories attain to hundreds of thousands of circulation. A serious book by David Graham Phillips, published serially in a popular monthly, is raided the moment it appears between covers; a trashy piece of nastiness by Elinor Glyn goes unmolested. Worse, books are sold for months and even years without protest, and then suddenly attacked; Dreiser's "The 'Genius, '" Kreymborg's "Edna" and Forel's "The Sexual Question" are examples. Still worse, what is held to be unobjectionable in one State is forbidden in another as *contra bonos mores*. [141] Altogether, there is madness, and no method in it. The livelihoods and good names of hard-striving and decent men are at the mercy of the whims of a horde of fanatics and mountebanks, and they have no way of securing themselves against attack, and no redress for their loss when it comes.

---

[141] The chief sufferers from this conflict are the authors of moving pictures. What they face at the hands of imbecile State boards of censorship is described at length by Channing Pollock in an article entitled "Swinging the Censor" in the *Bulletin* of the Authors' League of America for March, 1917.

So beset, it is no wonder that the typical American maker of books becomes a timorous and ineffective fellow, whose work tends inevitably toward a feeble superficiality. Sucking in the Puritan spirit with the very air he breathes, and perhaps burdened inwardly with an inheritance of the actual Puritan stupidity, he is further kept upon the straight path of chemical purity by the very real perils that I have just rehearsed. The result is a literature full of the mawkishness that the late Henry James so often roared against—a literature almost wholly detached from life as men are living it in the world—in George Moore's phrase, a literature still at nurse. It is on the side of sex that the appointed virtuosi of virtue exercise their chief repressions, for it is sex that especially fascinates the lubricious Puritan mind; but the conventual reticence that thus becomes the enforced fashion in one field extends itself to all others. Our fiction, in general, is marked by an artificiality as marked as that of Eighteenth Century poetry or the later Georgian drama. The romance in it runs to set forms and stale situations; the revelation, by such a book as "The Titan, " that there may be a glamour as entrancing in the way of a conqueror of men as in the way of a youth with a maid, remains isolated and exotic. We have no first-rate political or religious novel; we have no first-rate war story; despite all our national engrossment in commercial enterprise, we have few second-rate tales of business. Romance, in American fiction, still means only a somewhat childish amorousness and sentimentality—the love affairs of Paul and Virginia, or the pale adulteries of their elders. And on the side of realism there is an almost equal vacuity and lack of veracity. The action of all the novels of the Howells school goes on within four walls of painted canvas; they begin to shock once they describe an attack of asthma or a steak burning below stairs; they never penetrate beneath the flow of social concealments and urbanities to the passions that actually move men and women to their acts, and the great forces that circumscribe and condition personality. So obvious a piece of reporting as Upton Sinclair's "The Jungle" or Robert Herrick's "Together" makes a sensation; the appearance of a "Jennie Gerhardt" or a "Hagar Revelly" brings forth a growl of astonishment and rage.

In all this dread of free inquiry, this childish skittishness in both writers and public, this dearth of courage and even of curiosity, the influence of comstockery is undoubtedly to be detected. It constitutes a sinister and ever-present menace to all men of ideas; it affrights the publisher and paralyzes the author; no one on the outside can imagine its burden as a practical concern. I am, in moments borrowed from more palatable business, the editor of an American magazine, and I thus know at first hand what the burden is. That magazine is anything but a popular one, in the current sense. It sells at a relatively high price; it contains no pictures or other baits for the childish; it is frankly addressed to a sophisticated minority. I may thus assume reasonably, I believe, that its readers are not sex-curious and itching adolescents, just as my colleague of the *Atlantic Monthly* may assume reasonably that his readers are not Italian immigrants. Nevertheless, as a practical editor, I find that the Comstocks, near and far, are oftener in my mind's eye than my actual patrons. The thing I always have to decide about a manuscript offered for publication, before ever I give any thought to its artistic merit and suitability, is the question whether its publication will be permitted—not even whether it is intrinsically good or evil, moral or immoral, but whether some roving Methodist preacher, self-commissioned to keep watch on letters, will read indecency into it. Not a week passes that I do not decline some sound and honest piece of work for no other reason. I have a long list of such things by American authors, well-devised, well-imagined, well-executed, respectable as human documents and as works of art—but never to be printed in mine or any other American magazine. It includes four or five short stories of the very first rank, and the best one-act play yet done, to my knowledge, by an American. All of these pieces would go into type at once on the Continent; no sane man would think of objecting to them; they are no more obscene, to a normal adult, than his own bare legs. But they simply cannot be printed in the United States, with the law what it is and the courts what they are.

I know many other editors. All of them are in the same boat. Some of them try to get around the difficulty by pecksniffery more or less open—for example, by fastening a moral purpose upon works of art, and hawking them as uplifting.[142] Others, facing the intolerable fact, yield to it with resignation. And if they didn't? Well, if one of them didn't, any professional moralist could go before a police magistrate, get a warrant upon a simple affidavit, raid the office of the offending editor, seize all the magazines in sight, and keep them impounded until after the disposition of the case. Editors cannot afford to take this risk.

---

[142] For example, the magazine which printed David Graham Phillips' Susan Lenox: Her Rise and Fall as a serial prefaced it with a moral encomium by the Rev. Charles H. Parkhurst. Later, when the novel appeared in book form, the Comstocks began an action to have it suppressed, and forced the publisher to bowdlerize it.

Magazines are perishable goods. Even if, after a trial has been had, they are returned, they are worthless save as waste paper. And what may be done with copies found in the actual office of publication may be done too with copies found on news-stands, and not only in one city, but in two, six, a dozen, a hundred. All the costs and burdens of the contest are on the defendant. Let him be acquitted with honour, and invited to dinner by the judge, he has yet lost his property, and the Comstock hiding behind the warrant cannot be made to pay. In this concealment, indeed, lurk many sinister things—not forgetting personal enmity and business rivalry. The actual complainant is seldom uncovered; Comstockery, taking on a semi-judicial character, throws its chartered immunity around the whole process. A hypothetical outrage? By no means. It has been perpetrated, in one American city or another, upon fully half of the magazines of general circulation published today. Its possibility sticks in the consciousness of every editor and publisher like a recurrent glycosuria.[143]

But though the effects of comstockery are thus abominably insane and irritating, the fact is not to be forgotten that, after all, the thing is no more than an effect itself. The fundamental causes of all the grotesque (and often half-fabulous) phenomena flowing out of it are to be sought in the habits of mind of the American people. They are, as I have shown, besotted by moral concepts, a moral engrossment, a delusion of moral infallibility. In their view of the arts they are still unable to shake off the naïve suspicion of the Fathers.[144] A work of the imagination can justify itself, in their sight, only if it show a moral purpose, and that purpose must be obvious and unmistakable. Even in their slow progress toward a revolt against the ancestral Philistinism, they cling to this ethical bemusement: a new gallery of pictures is welcomed as "improving, " to hear Beethoven "makes one better." Any questioning of the moral ideas that prevail—the principal business, it must be plain, of the novelist, the serious dramatist, the professed inquirer into human motives and acts—is received with the utmost hostility. To attempt such an enterprise is to disturb the peace—and the

---

[143] An account of a typical prosecution, arbitrary, unintelligent and disingenuous, is to be found in Sumner and Indecency, by Frank Harris, in *Pearson's Magazine* for June, 1917, p. 556

[144] For further discussions of this point consult Art in America, by Aleister Crowley, *The English Review*, Nov., 1913; Life, Art and America, by Theodore Dreiser, *The Seven Arts*, Feb., 1917; and The American; His Ideas of Beauty, by H. L. Mencken, *The Smart Set*, Sept., 1913.

disturber of the peace, in the national view, quickly passes over into the downright criminal.

These symptoms, it seems to me, are only partly racial, despite the persistent survival of that third-rate English strain which shows itself so ingenuously in the colonial spirit, the sense of inferiority, the frank craving for praise from home. The race, in truth, grows mongrel, and the protest against that mongrelism only serves to drive in the fact. But a mongrel race is necessarily a race still in the stage of reaching out for culture; it has not yet formulated defensible standards; it must needs rest heavily upon the superstitions that go with inferiority. The Reformation brought Scotland among the civilized nations, but it took Scotland a century and a half to live down the Reformation. [145] Dogmatism, conformity, Philistinism, the fear of rebels, the crusading spirit; these are the marks of an upstart people, uncertain of their rank in the world and even of their direction. [146] A cultured European, reading a typical American critical journal, must needs conceive the United States, says H. G. Wells, as "a vain, garrulous and prosperous female of uncertain age and still more uncertain temper, with unfounded pretensions to intellectuality and an ideal of refinement of the most negative description ... the Aunt Errant of Christendom."[In Boon; New York, George H. Doran Co., 1915] There is always that blushful shyness, that timorous uncertainty, broken by sudden rages, sudden enunciations of impeccable doctrine, sudden runnings amuck. Formalism is the hall-mark of the national culture, and sins against the one are sins against the other. The American is school-mastered out of gusto, out of joy, out of innocence. He can never fathom William Blake's notion that "the lust of the goat is also to the glory of God." He must be correct, or, in his own phrase, he must bust.

Via trita est tutissima. The new generation, urged to curiosity and rebellion by its mounting sap, is rigorously restrained, regimented, policed. The ideal is vacuity, guilelessness, imbecility. "We are looking at this particular book, " said Comstock's successor of "The 'Genius, '" "from the standpoint of its harmful effect on female readers of immature mind."[In a letter to Felix Shay, Nov. 24, 1916.] To be curious is to be lewd; to know is to yield to fornication. Here we have the mediaeval doctrine still on its legs: a chance word may arouse "a libidinous passion" in the mind of a "modest" woman. Not only youth must be

---

[145] *Vide* The Cambridge History of English Literature, vol. XI, p. 225.

[146] The point is discussed by H. V. Routh in The Cambridge History of English Literature, vol. XI, p. 290

safeguarded, but also the "female, " the untrustworthy one, the temptress. "Modest, " is a euphemism; it takes laws to keep her "pure." The "locks of chastity" rust in the Cluny Museum; in place of them we have comstockery....

But, as I have said in hymning Huneker, there is yet the munyonic consolation. Time is a great legalizer, even in the field of morals. We have yet no delivery, but we have at least the beginnings of a revolt, or, at all events, of a protest. We have already reached, in Howells, our Hannah More; in Clemens, our Swift; in Henry James, our Horace Walpole; in Woodberry, Robinson *et al.*, our Cowpers, Southeys and Crabbes; perhaps we might even make a composite and call it our Johnson. We are sweating through our Eighteenth Century, our era of sentiment, our spiritual measles. Maybe a new day is not quite so far off as it seems to be, and with it we may get our Hardy, our Conrad, our Swinburne, our Thomas, our Moore, our Meredith and our Synge.

THE END

BOOK SIX.
DAMN! A BOOK OF CALUMNY

I. PATER PATRIÆ

If George Washington were alive today, what a shining mark he would be for the whole camorra of uplifters, forward-lookers and professional patriots! He was the Rockefeller of his time, the richest man in the United States, a promoter of stock companies, a land-grabber, an exploiter of mines and timber. He was a bitter opponent of foreign alliances, and denounced their evils in harsh, specific terms. He had a liking for all forthright and pugnacious men, and a contempt for lawyers, schoolmasters and all other such obscurantists. He was not pious. He drank whisky whenever he felt chilly, and kept a jug of it handy. He knew far more profanity than Scripture, and used and enjoyed it more. He had no belief in the infallible wisdom of the common people, but regarded them as inflammatory dolts, and tried to save the republic from them. He advocated no sure cure for all the sorrows of the world, and doubted that such a panacea existed. He took no interest in the private morals of his neighbors.

Inhabiting These States today, George would be ineligible for any office of honor or profit. The Senate would never dare confirm him; the President would not think of nominating him. He would be on trial in all the yellow journals for belonging to the Invisible Government, the Hell Hounds of Plutocracy, the Money Power, the Interests. The Sherman Act would have him in its toils; he would be under indictment by every grand jury south of the Potomac; the triumphant prohibitionists of his native state would be denouncing him (he had a still at Mount Vernon) as a debaucher of youth, a recruiting officer for insane asylums, a poisoner of the home. The suffragettes would be on his trail, with sentinels posted all along the Accotink road. The initiators and referendors would be bawling for his blood. The young college men of the *Nation* and the *New Republic* would be lecturing him weekly. He would be used to scare children in Kansas and Arkansas. The chautauquas would shiver whenever his name was mentioned....

And what a chance there would be for that ambitious young district attorney who thought to shadow him on his peregrinations—and grab him under the Mann Act!

II. THE REWARD OF THE ARTIST

A man labors and fumes for a whole year to write a symphony in G minor. He puts enormous diligence into it, and much talent, and maybe no little downright genius. It draws his blood and wrings his soul. He dies in it that he may live again.... Nevertheless, its final value, in the open market of the world, is a great deal less than that of a fur overcoat, half a Rolls-Royce automobile, or a handful of authentic hair from the whiskers of Henry Wadsworth Longfellow.

III. THE HEROIC CONSIDERED

For humility and poverty, in themselves, the world has little liking and less respect. In the folk-lore of all races, despite the sentimentalization of abasement for dramatic effect, it is always power and grandeur that count in the end. The whole point of the story of Cinderella, the most widely and constantly charming of all stories, is that the Fairy Prince lifts Cinderella above her cruel sisters and stepmother, and so enables her to lord it over them. The same idea underlies practically all other folk-stories: the essence of each of them is to be found in the ultimate triumph and exaltation of its protagonist. And of the real men and women of history, the most venerated and envied are those whose early humiliations were but preludes to terminal glories; for example, Lincoln, Whittington, Franklin, Columbus, Demosthenes, Frederick the Great, Catherine, Mary of Magdala, Moses. Even the Man of Sorrows, cradled in a manger and done to death between two thieves, is seen, as we part from Him at last, in a situation of stupendous magnificence, with infinite power in His hands. Even the Beatitudes, in the midst of their eloquent counselling of renunciation, give it unimaginable splendor as its reward. The meek shall inherit—what? The whole earth! And the poor in spirit? They shall sit upon the right hand of God!...

IV. THE BURDEN OF HUMOR

What is the origin of the prejudice against humor? Why is it so dangerous, if you would keep the public confidence, to make the public laugh? Is it because humor and sound sense are essentially antagonistic? Has humanity found by experience that the man who sees the fun of life is unfitted to deal sanely with its problems? I think not. No man had more of the comic spirit in him than William Shakespeare, and yet his serious reflections, by the sheer force of their sublime obviousness, have pushed their way into the race's arsenal of immortal platitudes. So, too, with Aesop, and with Balzac, and with Dickens, to come down the scale. All of these men were fundamentally humorists, and yet all of them achieved what the race has come to accept as a penetrating sagacity. Contrariwise, many a haloed pundit has had his occasional guffaw. Lincoln, had there been no Civil War, might have survived in history chiefly as the father of the American smutty story—the only original art-form that America has yet contributed to literature. Huxley, had he not been the greatest intellectual duellist of his age, might have been its greatest satirist. Bismarck, pursuing the gruesome trade of politics, concealed the devastating wit of a Molière; his surviving epigrams are truly stupendous. And Beethoven, after soaring to the heights of tragedy in the first movement of the Fifth Symphony, turned to the sardonic bull-fiddling of the *scherzo*.

No, there is not the slightest disharmony between sense and nonsense, humor and respectability, despite the skittish tendency to assume that there is. But, why, then, that widespread error? What actual fact of life lies behind it, giving it a specious appearance of reasonableness? None other, I am convinced, than the fact that the average man is far too stupid to make a joke. He may *see* a joke and *love* a joke, particularly when it floors and flabbergasts some person he dislikes, but the only way he can himself take part in the priming and pointing of a new one is by acting as its target. In brief, his personal contact with humor tends to fill him with an accumulated sense of disadvantage, of pricked complacency, of sudden and crushing defeat; and so, by an easy psychological process, he is led into the idea that the thing itself is incompatible with true dignity of character and intellect. Hence his deep suspicion of jokers, however adept their thrusts. "What a damned fool!"—this same half-pitying tribute he pays to wit and butt alike. He cannot separate the virtuoso of comedy from his general concept of comedy itself, and that concept is inextricably mingled with memories of foul ambuscades and mortifying hurts. And so it is not often that he is willing to admit any wisdom in a humorist, or to condone frivolity in a sage.

V. THE SAVING GRACE

Let us not burn the universities—yet. After all, the damage they do might be worse.... Suppose Oxford had snared and disemboweled Shakespeare! Suppose Harvard had set its stamp upon Mark Twain!

VI. MORAL INDIGNATION

The loud, preposterous moral crusades that so endlessly rock the republic—against the rum demon, against Sunday baseball, against Sunday moving-pictures, against dancing, against fornication, against the cigarette, against all things sinful and charming—these astounding Methodist jehads offer fat clinical material to the student of mobocracy. In the long run, nearly all of them must succeed, for the mob is eternally virtuous, and the only thing necessary to get it in favor of some new and super-oppressive law is to convince it that that law will be distasteful to the minority that it envies and hates. The poor numskull who is so horribly harrowed by Puritan pulpit-thumpers that he can't go to a ball game on Sunday afternoon without dreaming of hell and the devil all Sunday night is naturally envious of the fellow who can, and being envious of him, he hates him and is eager to destroy his offensive happiness. The farmer who works 18 hours a day and never gets a day off is envious of his farmhand who goes to the crossroads and barrels up on Saturday afternoon; hence the virulence of prohibition among the peasantry. The hard-working householder who, on some bitter evening, glances over the *Saturday Evening Post* for a square and honest look at his wife is envious of those gaudy drummers who go gallivanting about the country with scarlet girls; hence the Mann act. If these deviltries were equally open to all men, and all men were equally capable of appreciating them, their unpopularity would tend to wither.

I often think, indeed, that the prohibitionist tub-thumpers make a tactical mistake in dwelling too much upon the evils and horrors of alcohol, and not enough upon its delights. A few enlarged photographs of first-class bar-rooms, showing the rows of well-fed, well-dressed *bibuli* happily moored to the brass rails, their noses in fragrant mint and hops and their hands reaching out for free rations of olives, pretzels, cloves, pumpernickle, Bismarck herring, anchovies, *schwartenmagen*, wieners, Smithfield ham and dill pickles—such a gallery of contentment would probably do far more execution among the dismal *shudra* than all the current portraits of drunkards' livers. To vote for prohibition in the face of the liver portraits means to vote for the good of the other fellow, for even the oldest bibulomaniac always thinks that he himself will escape. This is an act of altruism almost impossible to the mob-man, whose selfishness is but little corrupted by the imagination that shows itself in his betters. His most austere renunciations represent no more than a matching of the joys of indulgence against the pains of hell; religion, to him, is little more than synthesized fear.... I venture that many a vote for prohibition comes from gentlemen who look longingly through swinging doors—and pass on in propitiation of Satan and their alert consorts, the lake of brimstone and the corrective broomstick....

VII. STABLE-NAMES

Why doesn't some patient drudge of a *privat dozent* compile a dictionary of the stable-names of the great? All show dogs and race horses, as everyone knows, have stable-names. On the list of entries a fast mare may appear as Czarina Ogla Fedorovna, but in the stable she is not that at all, nor even Czarina or Olga, but maybe Lil or Jennie. And a prize bulldog, Champion Zoroaster or Charlemagne XI. on the bench, may be plain Jack or Ponto *en famille*. So with celebrities of the *genus homo*. Huxley's official style and appellation was "The Right Hon. Thomas Henry Huxley, P. C., M. D., Ph. D., LL. D., D. C. L., D. Sc., F. R. S., " and his biographer tells us that he delighted in its rolling grandeur—but to his wife he was always Hal. Shakespeare, to his fellows of his Bankside, was Will, and perhaps Willie to Ann Hathaway. The Kaiser is another Willie: the late Czar so addressed him in their famous exchange of telegrams. The Czar himself was Nicky in those days, and no doubt remains Nicky to his intimates today. Edgar Allan Poe was always Eddie to his wife, and Mark Twain was always Youth to his. P. T. Barnum's stable-name was Taylor, his middle name; Charles Lamb's was Guy; Nietzsche's was Fritz; Whistler's was Jimmie; the late King Edward's was Bertie; Grover Cleveland's was Steve; J. Pierpont Morgan's was Jack; Dr. Wilson's is Tom.

Some given names are surrounded by a whole flotilla of stable-names. Henry, for example, is softened variously into Harry, Hen, Hank, Hal, Henny, Enery, On'ry and Heinie. Which did Ann Boleyn use when she cooed into the suspicious ear of Henry VIII.? To which did Henrik Ibsen answer at the domestic hearth? It is difficult to imagine his wife calling him Henrik: the name is harsh, clumsy, razor-edged. But did she make it Hen or Rik, or neither? What was Bismarck to the Fürstin, and to the mother he so vastly feared? Ottchen? Somehow it seems impossible. What was Grant to his wife? Surely not Ulysses! And

Wolfgang Amadeus Mozart? And Rutherford B. Hayes? Was Robert Browning ever Bob? Was John Wesley ever Jack? Was Emmanuel Swendenborg ever Manny? Was Tadeusz Kosciusko ever Teddy?

A fair field of inquiry invites. Let some laborious assistant professor explore and chart it. There will be more of human nature in his report than in all the novels ever written.

VIII. THE JEWS

The Jews, like the Americans, labor under a philosophical dualism, and in both cases it is a theological heritage. On the one hand there is the idealism that is lovely and uplifting and will get a man into heaven, and on the other hand there is the realism that works. The fact that the Jews cling to both, thus running, as it were, upon two tracks, is what makes them so puzzling, now and then, to the *goyim*. In one aspect they stand for the most savage practicality; in another aspect they are dreamers of an almost fabulous other-worldiness. My own belief is that the essential Jew is the idealist—that his occasional flashing of hyena teeth is no more than a necessary concession to the harsh demands of the struggle for existence. Perhaps, in many cases, it is due to an actual corruption of blood. The Jews come from the Levant, and their women were exposed for many centuries to the admiration of Greek, Arab and Armenian. The shark that a Jew can be at his worst is simply a Greek or Armenian at his best.

As a statement of post-mortem and super-terrestrial fact, the religion that the Jews have foisted upon the world seems to me to be as vast a curse as the influenza that we inherit from the Tatars or the democratic fallacies set afloat by the French Revolution. The one thing that can be said in favor of it is that it is not true, and yet we suffer from it almost as much as if it were true. But with it, encasing it and preserving it, there has come something that is positively valuable—something, indeed, that is beyond all price—and that is Jewish poetry. To compare it to the poetry of any other race is wholly impossible; it stands completely above all the rest; it is as far beyond the next best as German music is beyond French music, or French painting beyond English painting, or the English drama beyond the Italian drama. There are single chapters in the Old Testament that are worth all the poetry ever written in the New World and nine-tenths of that written in the Old. The Jews of those ancient days had imagination, they had dignity, they had ears for sweet sound, they had, above all, the faculty of grandeur. The stupendous music that issued from them has swept their barbaric demonology along with it, setting at naught the collective intelligence of the human species; they embalmed their idiotic taboos and fetishes in undying strains, and so gave them some measure of the same immortality. A race of lawgivers? Bosh! Leviticus is as archaic as the Code of Manu, and the Decalogue is a fossil. A race of seers? Bosh again! The God they saw survives only as a bogey-man, a theory, an uneasy and vexatious ghost. A race of traders and sharpers? Bosh a third time! The Jews are as poor as the Spaniards. But a race of poets, my lords, a race of poets! It is a vision of beauty that has ever haunted them. And it has been their destiny to transmit that vision, enfeebled, perhaps, but still distinct, to other and lesser peoples, that life might be made softer for the sons of men, and the goodness of the Lord God— whoever He may be—might not be forgotten.

IX. THE COMSTOCKIAN PREMISS

It is argued against certain books, by virtuosi of moral alarm, that they depict vice as attractive. This recalls the king who hanged a judge for deciding that an archbishop was a mammal.

X. THE LABIAL INFAMY

After five years of search I have been able to discover but one book in English upon the art of kissing, and that is a very feeble treatise by a savant of York, Pa., Dr. R. McCormick Sturgeon. There may be others, but I have been quite unable to find them. Kissing, for all one hears of it, has not attracted the scientists and literati; one compares its meagre literature with the endless books upon the other phenomena of love, especially divorce and obstetrics. Even Dr. Sturgeon, pioneering bravely, is unable to get beyond a sentimental and trivial view of the thing he vivisects, and so his book is no more than a compendium of mush. His very description of the act of kissing is made up of sonorous gabble about heaving bosoms, red lips, electric sparks and such-like imaginings. What reason have we for believing, as he says, that the lungs are "strongly expanded" during the act? My own casual observation inclines me to hold that the opposite is true, that the lungs are actually collapsed in a pseudo-asthmatic spasm. Again, what is the ground for arguing that the lips are "full, ripe and red?" The real effect of the emotions that accompany kissing is to empty the superficial capillaries and so produce a leaden pallor. As for such salient symptoms as the temperature, the pulse and the rate of respiration, the learned pundit passes them over without a word. Mrs. Elsie Clews Parsons would be a good one to write a sober and accurate treatise upon kissing. Her books upon "The Family" and "Fear and Conventionality" indicate her possession of the right sort of learning. Even better would be a work by Havelock Ellis, say, in three or four volumes. Ellis has devoted his whole life to illuminating the mysteries of sex, and his collection of materials is unsurpassed in the world. Surely there must be an enormous mass of instructive stuff about kissing in his card indexes, letter files, book presses and archives.

Just why the kiss as we know it should have attained to its present popularity in Christendom is probably one of the things past finding out. The Japanese, a very affectionate and sentimental people, do not practise kissing in any form; they regard the act, in fact, with an aversion matching our own aversion to the rubbing of noses. Nor is it in vogue among the Moslems, nor among the Chinese, who countenance it only as between mother and child. Even in parts of Christendom it is girt about by rigid taboos, so that its practise tends to be restricted to a few occasions. Two Frenchmen or Italians, when they meet, kiss each other on both cheeks. One used to see, indeed, many pictures of General Joffre thus bussing the heroes of Verdun; there even appeared in print a story to the effect that one of them objected to the scratching of his moustache. But imagine two Englishmen kissing! Or two Germans! As well imagined the former kissing the latter! Such a display of affection is simply impossible to men of Northern blood; they would die with shame if caught at it. The Englishman, like the American, never kisses if he can help it. He even regards it as bad form to kiss his wife in a railway station, or, in fact, anywhere in sight of a third party. The Latin has no such compunctions. He leaps to the business regardless of place or time; his sole concern is with the lady. Once, in driving from Nice to Monte Carlo along the lower Corniche road, I passed a hundred or so open taxicabs containing man and woman, and fully 75 per cent. of the men had their arms around their companions, and were kissing them. These were not peasants, remember, but well-to-do persons. In England such a scene would have caused a great scandal; in most American States the police would have charged the offenders with drawn revolvers.

The charm of kissing is one of the things I have always wondered at. I do not pretend, of course, that I have never done it; mere politeness forces one to it; there are women who sulk and grow bellicose unless one at least makes the motions of kissing them. But what I mean is that I have never found the act a tenth part as agreeable as poets, the authors of musical comedy librettos, and (on the contrary side) chaperones and the *gendarmerie* make it out. The physical sensation, far from being pleasant, is intensely uncomfortable—the suspension of respiration, indeed, quickly resolves itself into a feeling of suffocation—and the posture necessitated by the approximation of lips and lips is unfailingly a constrained and ungraceful one. Theoretically, a man kisses a woman perpendicularly, with their eyes, those "windows of the soul, " synchronizing exactly. But actually, on account of the incompressibility of the nasal cartilages, he has to incline either his or her head to an angle of at least 60 degrees, and the result is that his right eye gazes insanely at the space between her eyebrows, while his left eye is fixed upon some vague spot behind her. An instantaneous photograph of such a maneuvre, taken at the moment of incidence, would probably turn the stomach of even the most romantic man, and force him, in sheer self-respect, to renounce kissing as he has renounced leap-frog and walking on stilts. Only a woman (for women are quite devoid of aesthetic feeling) could survive so damning a picture.

But the most embarrassing moment, in kissing, does not come during the actual kiss (for at that time the sensation of suffocation drives out all purely psychical feelings), but immediately afterward. What is one to say to the woman then? The occasion obviously demands some sort of remark. One has just received (in theory) a great boon; the silence begins to make itself felt; there stands the fair one, obviously waiting. Is one to thank her? Certainly that would be too transparent a piece of hypocrisy, too flaccid a banality. Is one to tell her that one loves her? Obviously, there is danger in such assurances, and beside, one usually doesn't, and a lie is a lie. Or is one to descend to chatty commonplaces—about the weather, literature, politics, the war? The practical impossibility of solving the problem leads almost inevitably to a blunder far worse than any merely verbal one: one kisses her again, and then again, and so on, and so on. The ultimate result is satiety, repugnance, disgust; even the girl herself gets enough.

XI. A TRUE ASCETIC

Herbert Spencer's objection to swearing, of which so much has been made by moralists, was not an objection to its sinfulness but an objection to its charm. In brief, he feared comfort, satisfaction, joy. The boarding houses in which he dragged out his gray years were as bare and cheerless as so many piano boxes. He avoided all the little vices and dissipations which make human existence bearable: good eating, good drinking, dancing, tobacco, poker, poetry, the theatre, personal adornment, philandering, adultery. He was insanely suspicious of everything that threatened to interfere with his work. Even when that work halted him by the sheer agony of its monotony, and it became necessary for him to find recreation, he sought out some recreation that was as unattractive as possible, in the hope that it would quickly drive him back to work again. Having to choose between methods of locomotion on his holidays, he chose going afoot, the most laborious and least satisfying available. Brought to bay by his human need for a woman, he directed his fancy toward George Eliot, probably the most unappetizing woman of his race and time. Drawn irresistibly to music, he avoided the Fifth Symphony and "Tristan und Isolde, " and joined a crowd of old maids singing part songs around a cottage piano. John Tyndall saw clearly the effect of all this and protested against it, saying, "He'd be a much nicer fellow if he had a good swear now and then"—i. e., if he let go now and then, if he yielded to his healthy human instincts now and then, if he went on some sort of debauch now and then. But what Tyndall overlooked was the fact that the meagreness of his recreations was the very element that attracted Spencer to them. Obsessed by the fear—and it turned out to be well-grounded—that he would not live long enough to complete his work, he regarded all joy as a temptation, a corruption, a sin of scarlet. He was a true ascetic. He could sacrifice all things of the present for one thing of the future, all things real for one thing ideal.

XII. ON LYING

Lying stands on a different plane from all other moral offenses, not because it is intrinsically more heinous or less heinous, but simply because it is the only one that may be accurately measured. Forgetting unwitting error, which has nothing to do with morals, a statement is either true or not true. This is a simple distinction and relatively easy to establish. But when one comes to other derelictions the thing grows more complicated. The line between stealing and not stealing is beautifully vague; whether or not one has crossed it is not determined by the objective act, but by such delicate things as motive and purpose. So again, with assault, sex offenses, and even murder; there may be surrounding circumstances which greatly condition the moral quality of the actual act. But lying is specific, exact, scientific. Its capacity for precise determination, indeed, makes its presence or non-presence the only accurate gauge of other immoral acts. Murder, for example, is nowhere regarded as immoral save it involve some repudiation of a social compact, of a tacit promise to refrain from it—in brief, some deceit, some perfidy, some lie. One may kill freely when the pact is formally broken, as in war. One may kill equally freely when it is broken by the victim, as in an assault by a highwayman. But one may not kill so long as it is not broken, and one may not break it to clear the way. Some form of lie is at the bottom of all other recognized crimes, from seduction to embezzlement. Curiously enough, this master immorality of them all is not prohibited by the Ten Commandments, nor is it penalized, in its pure form, by the code of any civilized nation. Only savages have laws against lying *per se*.

XIII. HISTORY

It is the misfortune of humanity that its history is chiefly written by third-rate men. The first-rate man seldom has any impulse to record and philosophise; his impulse is to act; life, to him, is an adventure, not a syllogism or an autopsy. Thus the writing of history is left to college professors, moralists, theorists, dunder-heads. Few historians, great or small, have shown any capacity for the affairs they presume to describe and interpret. Gibbon was an inglorious failure as a member of Parliament. Thycydides made such a mess of his military (or, rather, naval) command that he was exiled from Athens for twenty years and finally assassinated. Flavius Josephus, serving as governor of Galilee, lost the whole province to the Romans, and had to flee for his life. Momssen, elected to the Prussian Landtag, flirted with the Socialists. How much better we would understand the habits and nature of man if there were more historians like Julius Caesar, or even like Niccolo Machiavelli! Remembering the sharp and devastating character of their rough notes, think what marvelous histories Bismarck, Washington and Frederick the Great might have written! Such men are privy to the facts; the usual historians have to depend on deductions, rumors, guesses. Again, such men know how to tell the truth, however unpleasant; they are wholly free of that puerile moral obsession which marks the professor.... But they so seldom tell it! Well, perhaps some of them have—and their penalty is that they are damned and forgotten.

XIV. THE CURSE OF CIVILIZATION

A civilized man's worst curse is social obligation. The most unpleasant act imaginable is to go to a dinner party. One could get far better food, taking one day with another, at Childs', or even in a Pennsylvania Railroad dining-car; one could find far more amusing society in a bar-room or a bordello, or even at the Y. M. C. A. No hostess in Christendom ever arranged a dinner party of any pretensions without including at least one intensely disagreeable person—a vain and vapid girl, a hideous woman, a follower of baseball, a stock-broker, a veteran of some war or other, a gabbler of politics. And one is enough to do the business.

XV. EUGENICS

The error of the eugenists lies in the assumption that a physically healthy man is the best fitted to survive. This is true of rats and the *pediculae*, but not of the higher animals, *e. g.*, horses, dogs and men. In these higher animals one looks for more subtle qualities, chiefly of the spirit. Imagine estimating philosophers by their chest expansions, their blood pressures, their Wassermann reactions!

The so-called social diseases, over which eugenists raise such a pother, are surely not the worst curses that mankind has to bear. Some of the greatest men in history have had them; whole nations have had them and survived. The truth about them is that, save in relatively rare cases, they do very little damage. The horror in which they are held is chiefly a moral horror, and its roots lie in the assumption that they cannot be contracted without sin. Nothing could be more false. Many great moralists have suffered from them: the gods are always up to such sardonic waggeries.

Moreover, only one of them is actually inheritable, and that one is transmitted relatively seldom. But among psychic characters one finds that practically all are inheritable. For example, stupidity, credulity, avarice, pecksniffery, lack of imagination, hatred of beauty, meanness, poltroonry, petty brutality, smallness of soul.... I here present, of course, the Puritan complex; there flashes up the image of the "good man," that libel on God and the devil. Consider him well. If you had to choose a sire for a first-rate son, would you choose a consumptive Jew with the fires of eternity in his eyes, or an Iowa right-thinker with his hold full of Bibles and breakfast food?

XVI. THE JOCOSE GODS

What humor could be wilder than that of life itself? Franz Schubert, on his deathbed, read the complete works of J. Fenimore Cooper. John Millington Synge wrote "Riders to the Sea" on a second-hand $40 typewriter, and wore a celluloid collar. Richard Wagner made a living, during four lean years, arranging Italian opera arias for the cornet. Herbert Spencer sang bass in a barber-shop quartette and was in love with George Eliot. William Shakespeare was a social pusher and bought him a bogus coat-of-arms. Martin Luther suffered from the jim-jams.

One of the greatest soldiers in Hungarian history was named Hunjadi Janos....

XVII. WAR

Superficially, war seems inordinately cruel and wasteful, and yet it must be plain on reflection that the natural evolutionary process is quite as cruel and even more wasteful. Man's chief efforts in times of peace are devoted to making that process less violent and sanguinary. Civilization, indeed, may be defined as a constructive criticism of nature, and Huxley even called it a conspiracy against nature. Man tries to remedy what must inevitably seem the mistakes and to check what must inevitably seem the wanton cruelty of the Creator. In war man abandons these efforts, and so becomes more jovian. The Greeks never represented the inhabitants of Olympus as succoring and protecting one another, but always as fighting and attempting to destroy one another.

No form of death inflicted by war is one-half so cruel as certain forms of death that are seen in hospitals every day. Besides, these forms of death have the further disadvantage of being inglorious. The average man, dying in bed, not only has to stand the pains and terrors of death; he must also, if he can bring himself to think of it at all, stand the notion that he is ridiculous.... The soldier is at least not laughed at. Even his enemies treat his agonies with respect.

XVIII. MORALIST AND ARTIST

I dredge up the following from an essay on George Bernard Shaw by Robert Blatchford, the English Socialist: "Shaw is something much better than a wit, much better than an artist, much better than a politician or a dramatist; he is a moralist, a teacher of ethics, austere, relentless, fiercely earnest."

What could be more idiotic? Then Cotton Mather was a greater man than Johann Sebastian Bach. Then the average college critic of the arts, with his balderdash about inspiration and moral purpose, is greater than Georg Brandes or Saint-Beuve. Then Éugene Brieux, with his Y. M. C. A. platitudinizing, is greater than Molière, with his ethical agnosticism, his ironical determinism.

This childish respect for moralizing runs through the whole of contemporary criticism—at least in England and America. Blatchford differs from the professorial critics only in the detail that he can actually write. What he says about Shaw has been said, in heavy and suffocating words, by almost all of them. And yet nothing could be more untrue. The moralist, at his best, can never be anything save a sort of journalist. Moral values change too often to have any serious validity or interest; what is a virtue today is a sin tomorrow. But the man who creates a thing of beauty creates something that lasts.

XIX. ACTORS

"In France they call an actor a *m'as-tu-vu*, which, anglicised, means a have-you-seen-me?... The average actor holds the mirror up to nature and sees in it only the reflection of himself." I take the words from a late book on the so-called art of the mime by the editor of a magazine devoted to the stage. The learned author evades plumbing the psychological springs of this astounding and almost invariable vanity, this endless bumptiousness of the *cabotin* in all climes and all ages. His one attempt is banal: "a foolish public makes much of him." With all due respect, Nonsense! The larval actor is full of hot and rancid gases long before a foolish public has had a fair chance to make anything of him at all, and he continues to emit them long after it has tried him, condemned him and bidden him be damned. There is, indeed, little choice in the virulence of their self-respect between a Broadway star who is slobbered over by press agents and fat women, and the poor ham who plays thinking parts in a No. 7 road company. The two are alike charged to the limit; one more ohm, or molecule, and they would burst. Actors begin where militia colonels, Fifth avenue rectors and Chautauqua orators leave off. The most modest of them (barring, perhaps, a few unearthly traitors to the craft) matches the conceit of the solitary pretty girl on a slow ship. In their lofty eminence of pomposity they are challenged only by Anglican bishops and grand opera tenors. I have spoken of the danger they run of bursting. In the case of tenors it must sometimes actually happen; even the least of them swells visibly as he sings, and permanently as he grows older....

But why are actors, in general, such blatant and obnoxious asses, such arrant posturers and wind-bags? Why is it as surprising to find an unassuming and likable fellow among them as to find a Greek without fleas? The answer is quite simple. To reach it one needs but consider the type of young man who normally gets stage-struck. Is he, taking averages, the intelligent, alert, ingenious, ambitious young fellow? Is he the young fellow with ideas in him, and a yearning for hard and difficult work? Is he the diligent reader, the hard student, the eager inquirer? No. He is, in the overwhelming main, the neighborhood fop and beau, the human clothes-horse, the nimble squire of dames. The youths of more active mind, emerging from adolescence, turn to business and the professions; the men that they admire and seek to follow are men of genuine distinction, men who have actually done difficult and valuable things, men who have fought good (if often dishonest) fights and are respected and envied by other men. The stage-struck youth is of a softer and more shallow sort. He seeks, not a chance to test his mettle by hard and useful work, but an easy chance to shine. He craves the regard, not of men, but of women. He is, in brief, a hollow and incompetent creature, a strutter and poseur, a popinjay, a pretty one....

I thus beg the question, but explain the actor. He is this silly youngster grown older, but otherwise unchanged. An initiate of a profession requiring little more information, culture or capacity for ratiocination than that of the lady of joy, and surrounded in his work-shop by men who are as stupid, as vain and as empty as he himself will be in the years to come, he suffers an arrest of development, and the little intelligence that may happen to be in him gets no chance to show itself. The result, in its usual manifestation, is the average bad actor—a man with the cerebrum of a floor-walker and the vanity of a fashionable clergyman. The result, in its highest and holiest form is the actor-manager, with his retinue of press-agents, parasites and worshipping wenches—perhaps the most preposterous and awe-inspiring donkey that civilization has yet produced. To look for sense in a fellow of such equipment and such a history would be like looking for serviettes in a sailors' boarding-house.

By the same token, the relatively greater intelligence of actresses is explained. They are, at their worst, quite as bad as the generality of actors. There are she-stars who are all temperament and balderdash—intellectually speaking, beggars on horseback, servant girls well washed. But no one who knows anything about the stage need be told that it can show a great many more quick-minded and self-respecting women than intelligent men. And why? Simply because its women are recruited, in the main, from a class much above that which furnishes its men. It is, after all, not unnatural for a woman of considerable intelligence to aspire to the stage. It offers her, indeed, one of the most tempting careers that is open to her. She cannot hope to succeed in business, and in the other professions she is an unwelcome and much-scoffed-at intruder, but on the boards she can meet men on an equal footing. It is, therefore, no wonder that women of a relatively superior class often take to the business.... Once they embrace it, their superiority to their male colleagues is quickly manifest. All movements against puerility and imbecility in the drama have originated, not with actors, but with actresses—that is, in so far as they have originated among stage folks at all. The Ibsen pioneers were such women as Helena Modjeska, Agnes Sorma and Janet Achurch; the men all hung back. Ibsen, it would appear, was aware of this superior alertness and took shrewd advantage of it. At all events, his most tempting acting parts are feminine ones.

The girls of the stage demonstrate this tendency against great difficulties. They have to carry a heavy handicap in the enormous number of women who seek the footlights merely to advertise their real profession, but despite all this, anyone who has the slightest acquaintance with stagefolk will testify that, taking one with another, the women have vastly more brains than the men and are appreciably less vain and idiotic. Relatively few actresses of any rank marry actors. They find close communion with the strutting brethren psychologically impossible. Stock-brokers, dramatists and even theatrical managers are greatly to be preferred.

XX. THE CROWD

Gustave Le Bon and his school, in their discussions of the psychology of crowds, have put forward the doctrine that the individual man, cheek by jowl with the multitude, drops down an intellectual peg or two, and so tends to show the mental and emotional reactions of his inferiors. It is thus that they explain the well-known violence and imbecility of crowds. The crowd, as a crowd, performs acts that many of its members, as individuals, would never be guilty of. Its average intelligence is very low; it is inflammatory, vicious, idiotic, almost simian. Crowds, properly worked up by skilful demagogues, are ready to believe anything, and to do anything.

Le Bon, I daresay, is partly right, but also partly wrong. His theory is probably too flattering to the average numskull. He accounts for the extravagance of crowds on the assumption that the numskull, along with the superior man, is knocked out of his wits by suggestion—that he, too, does things in association that he would never think of doing singly. The fact may be accepted, but the reasoning raises a doubt. The numskull runs amuck in a crowd, not because he has been inoculated with new rascality by the mysterious crowd influence, but because his habitual rascality now has its only chance to function safely. In other words, the numskull is vicious, but a poltroon. He refrains from all attempts at lynching *a cappella*, not because it takes suggestion to make him desire to lynch, but because it takes the protection of a crowd to make him brave enough to try it.

What happens when a crowd cuts loose is not quite what Le Bon and his followers describe. The few superior men in it are not straightway reduced to the level of the underlying stoneheads. On the contrary, they usually keep their heads, and often make efforts to combat the crowd action. But the stoneheads are too many for them; the fence is torn down or the blackamoor is lynched. And why? Not because the stoneheads, normally virtuous, are suddenly criminally insane. Nay, but because they are suddenly conscious of the power lying in their numbers—because they suddenly realize that their natural viciousness and insanity may be safely permitted to function.

In other words, the particular swinishness of a crowd is permanently resident in the majority of its members—in all those members, that is, who are naturally ignorant and vicious—perhaps 95 per cent. All studies of mob psychology are defective in that they underestimate this viciousness. They are poisoned by the prevailing delusion that the lower orders of men are angels. This is nonsense. The lower orders of men are incurable rascals, either individually or collectively. Decency, self-restraint, the sense of justice, courage—these virtues belong only to a small minority of men. This minority never runs amuck. Its most distinguishing character, in truth, is its resistance to all running amuck. The third-rate man, though he may wear the false whiskers of a first-rate man, may always be detected by his inability to keep his head in the face of an appeal to his emotions. A whoop strips off his disguise.

XXI. AN AMERICAN PHILOSOPHER

As for William Jennings Bryan, of whom so much piffle, pro and con, has been written, the whole of his political philosophy may be reduced to two propositions, neither of which is true. The first is the proposition that the common people are wise and honest, and the second is the proposition that all persons who refuse to believe it are scoundrels. Take away the two, and all that would remain of Jennings would be a somewhat greasy bald-headed man with his mouth open.

XXII. CLUBS

Men's clubs have but one intelligible purpose: to afford asylum to fellows who haven't any girls. Hence their general gloom, their air of lost causes, their prevailing acrimony. No man would ever enter a club if he had an agreeable woman to talk to. This is particularly true of married men. Those of them that one finds in clubs answer to a general description: they have wives too unattractive to entertain them, and yet too watchful to allow them to seek entertainment elsewhere. The bachelors, in the main, belong to two classes: (a) those who have been unfortunate in amour, and are still too sore to show any new enterprise, and (b) those so lacking in charm that no woman will pay any attention to them. Is it any wonder that the men one thus encounters in clubs are stupid and miserable creatures, and that they find their pleasure in such banal sports as playing cards, drinking highballs, shooting pool, and reading the barber-shop weeklies?... The day a man's mistress is married one always finds him at his club.

XXIII. FIDELIS AD URNUM

Despite the common belief of women to the contrary, fully 95 per cent. of all married men, at least in America, are faithful to their wives. This, however, is not due to virtue, but chiefly to lack of courage. It takes more initiative and daring to start up an extra-legal affair than most men are capable of. They look and they make plans, but that is as far as they get. Another salient cause of connubial rectitude is lack of means. A mistress costs a great deal more than a wife; in the open market of the world she can get more. It is only the rare man who can conceal enough of his income from his wife to pay for a morganatic affair. And most of the men clever enough to do this are too clever to be intrigued.

I have said that 95 per cent. of married men are faithful. I believe the real proportion is nearer 99 per cent. What women mistake for infidelity is usually no more than vanity. Every man likes to be regarded as a devil of a fellow, and particularly by his wife. On the one hand, it diverts her attention from his more genuine shortcomings, and on the other hand it increases her respect for him. Moreover, it gives her a chance to win the sympathy of other women, and so satisfies that craving for martyrdom which is perhaps woman's strongest characteristic. A woman who never has any chance to suspect her husband feels cheated and humiliated. She is in the position of those patriots who are induced to enlist for a war by pictures of cavalry charges, and then find themselves told off to wash the general's underwear.

XXIV. A THEOLOGICAL MYSTERY

The moral order of the world runs aground on hay fever. Of what use is it? Why was it invented? Cancer and hydrophobia, at least, may be defended on the ground that they kill. Killing may have some benign purpose, some esoteric significance, some cosmic use. But hay fever never kills; it merely tortures. No man ever died of it. Is the torture, then, an end in itself? Does it break the pride of strutting, snorting man, and turn his heart to the things of the spirit? Nonsense! A man with hay fever is a natural criminal. He curses the gods, and defies them to kill him. He even curses the devil. Is its use, then, to prepare him for happiness to come—for the vast ease and comfort of convalescence? Nonsense again! The one thing he is sure of, the one thing he never forgets for a moment, is that it will come back again next year.

XXV. THE TEST OF TRUTH

The final test of truth is ridicule. Very few religious dogmas have ever faced it and survived. Huxley laughed the devils out of the Gadarene swine. Dowie's whiskers broke the back of Dowieism. Not the laws of the United States but the mother-in-law joke brought the Mormons to compromise and surrender. Not the horror of it but the absurdity of it killed the doctrine of infant damnation.... But the razor edge of ridicule is turned by the tough hide of truth. How loudly the barber-surgeons laughed at Harvey—and how vainly! What clown ever brought down the house like Galileo? Or Columbus? Or Jenner? Or Lincoln? Or Darwin?... They are laughing at Nietzsche yet....

XXVI. LITERARY INDECENCIES

The low, graceless humor of names! On my shelf of poetry, arranged by the alphabet, Coleridge and J. Gordon Cooglar are next-door neighbors! Mrs. Hemans is beside Laurence Hope! Walt Whitman rubs elbows with Ella Wheeler Wilcox; Robert Browning with Richard Burton; Rossetti with Cale Young Rice; Shelly with Clinton Scollard; Wordsworth with George E. Woodberry; John Keats with Herbert Kaufman!

Ibsen, on the shelf of dramatists, is between Victor Hugo and Jerome K. Jerome. Sudermann follows Harriet Beecher Stowe. Maeterlinck shoulders Percy Mackaye. Shakespeare is between Sardou and Shaw. Euripides and Clyde Fitch! Upton Sinclair and Sophocles! Aeschylus and F. Anstey! D'Annunzio and Richard Harding Davis! Augustus Thomas and Tolstoi!

More alphabetical humor. Gerhart Hauptmann and Robert Hichens; Voltaire and Henry Van Dyke; Flaubert and John Fox, Jr.; Balzac and John Kendrick Bangs; Ostrovsky and E. Phillips Oppenheim; Elinor Glyn and Théophile Gautier; Joseph Conrad and Robert W. Chambers; Zola and Zangwill!...

Midway on my scant shelf of novels, between George Moore and Frank Norris, there is just room enough for the two volumes of "Derringforth, " by Frank A. Munsey.

XXVII. VIRTUOUS VANDALISM

A hearing of Schumann's B flat symphony of late, otherwise a very caressing experience, was corrupted by the thought that music would be much the gainer if musicians could get over their superstitious reverence for the mere text of the musical classics. That reverence, indeed, is already subject to certain limitations; hands have been laid, at one time or another, upon most of the immortal oratorios, and even the awful name of Bach has not dissuaded certain German editors. But it still swathes the standard symphonies like some vast armor of rubber and angel food, and so imagination has to come to the aid of the flutes and fiddles when the band plays Schumann, Mozart, and even parts of Beethoven. One discerns, often quite clearly, what the reverend Master was aiming at, but just as often one fails to hear it in precise tones.

This is particularly true of Schumann, whose deficiency in instrumental cunning has passed into proverb. And in the B flat symphony, his first venture into the epic form, his failures are most numerous. More than once, obviously attempting to roll up tone into a moving climax, he succeeds only in muddling his colors. I remember one place—at the moment I can't recall where it is—where the strings and the brass storm at one another in furious figures. The blast of the brass, as the vaudevillains say, gets across—but the fiddles merely scream absurdly. The whole passage suggests the bleating of sheep in the midst of a vast bellowing of bulls. Schumann overestimated the horsepower of fiddle music so far up the E string—or underestimated the full kick of the trumpets.... Other such soft spots are well known.

Why, then, go on parroting *gaucheries* that Schumann himself, were he alive today, would have long since corrected? Why not call an ecumenical council, appoint a commission to see to such things, and then forget the sacrilege? As a self-elected delegate from heathendom, I nominate Dr. Richard Strauss as chairman. When all is said and done, Strauss probably knows more about writing for orchestra than any other two men that ever lived, not excluding Wagner. Surely no living rival, as Dr. Sunday would say, has anything on him. If, after hearing a new composition by Strauss, one turns to the music, one is invariably surprised to find how simple it is. The performance reveals so many purple moments, so staggering an array of lusciousness, that the ear is bemused into detecting scales and chords that never were on land or sea. What the exploratory eye subsequently discovers, perhaps, is no more than our stout and comfortable old friend, the highly well-born *hausfrau*, Mme. C Dur—with a vine leaf or two of C sharp minor or F major in her hair. The trick lies in the tone-color—in the flabbergasting magic of the orchestration. There are some moments in "Elektra" when sounds come out of the orchestra that tug at the very roots of the hair, sounds so unearthly that they suggest a caroling of dragons or *bierfisch*—and yet they are made by the same old fiddles that play the Kaiser Quartet, and by the same old trombones that the Valkyrie ride like witch's broomsticks, and by the same old flutes that sob and snuffle in Tit'l's Serenade. And in parts of "Feuersnot"—but Roget must be rewritten by Strauss before "Feuersnot" is described. There is one place where the harps, taking a running start from the scrolls of the violins, leap slambang through (or is it into?) the firmament of Heaven. Once, when I heard this passage played at a concert, a woman sitting beside me rolled over like a log, and had to be hauled out by the ushers.

Yes; Strauss is the man to reorchestrate the symphonies of Schumann, particularly the B flat, the Rhenish and the Fourth. I doubt that he could do much with Schubert, for Schubert, though he is dead nearly a hundred years, yet remains curiously modern. The Unfinished symphony is full of exquisite color effects—consider, for example, the rustling figure for the strings in the first movement—and as for the C major, it is so stupendous a debauch of melodic and harmonic beauty that one scarcely notices the colors at all. In its slow movement mere loveliness in music probably says all that will ever be said.... But what of old Ludwig? Har, har; here we begin pulling the whiskers of Baal Himself. Nevertheless, I am vandal enough to wonder, on sad Sunday mornings, what Strauss could do with the first movement of the C minor. More, if Strauss ever does it and lets me hear the result just once, I'll be glad to serve six months in jail with him.... But in Munich, of course! And with a daily visitor's pass for Cousin Pschorr!...

The conservatism which shrinks at such barbarities is the same conservatism which demands that the very typographical errors in the Bible be swallowed without salt, and that has thus made a puerile dream-book of parts of Holy Writ. If you want to see how far this last madness has led Christendom astray, take a look at an article by Abraham Mitrie Rihbany, an intelligent Syrian, in the *Atlantic Monthly* of a couple of years ago. The title of the article is "The Oriental Manner of Speech, " and in it Rihbany shows how much of mere Oriental extravagance of metaphor is to be found in many celebrated passages, and how little of literal significance. This Oriental extravagance, of course, makes for beauty, but as interpreted by pundits of no imagination it surely doesn't make for understanding. What the Western World needs is a Bible in which the idioms of the Aramaic of thousands of years ago are translated into the idioms of today. The man who undertook such a translation, to be sure, would be uproariously denounced, just as Luther and Wycliffe were denounced, but he could well afford to face the storm. The various Revised Versions, including the Modern Speech New Testament of Richard Francis Weymouth, leave much to be desired. They rectify many naif blunders and so make the whole narrative more intelligible, but they still render most of the tropes of the original literally.

These tropes are not the substance of Holy Writ; they are simply its color. In the same way mere tone-color is not the substance of a musical composition. Beethoven's Eighth Symphony is just as great a work, in all its essentials, in a four-hand piano arrangement as in the original score. Every harmonic and melodic idea of the composer is there; one can trace just as clearly the subtle processes of his mind; every step in the working out of the materials is just as plain. True enough, there are orchestral compositions of which this cannot be reasonably said; their color is so much more important than their form that when one takes away the former the latter almost ceases to exist. But I doubt that many competent critics would argue that they belong to the first rank. Form, after all, is the important thing. It is design that counts, not decoration—design and organization. The pillars of a musical masterpiece are like the pillars of the Parthenon; they are almost as beautiful bleached white as they were in all their original hues.

XXVIII. A FOOTNOTE ON THE DUEL OF SEX

If I were a woman I should want to be a blonde, with golden, silky hair, pink cheeks and sky-blue eyes. It would not bother me to think that this color scheme was mistaken by the world for a flaunting badge of stupidity; I would have a better arm in my arsenal than mere intelligence; I would get a husband by easy surrender while the brunettes attempted it vainly by frontal assault.

Men are not easily taken by frontal assault; it is only strategem that can quickly knock them down. To be a blonde, pink, soft and delicate, is to be a strategem. It is to be a ruse, a feint, an ambush. It is to fight under the Red Cross flag. A man sees nothing alert and designing in those pale, crystalline eyes; he sees only something helpless, childish, weak; something that calls to his compassion; something that appeals powerfully to his conceit in his own strength. And so he is taken before he knows that there is a war. He lifts his portcullis in Christian charity—and the enemy is in his citadel.

The brunette can make no such stealthy and sure attack. No matter how subtle her art, she can never hope to quite conceal her intent. Her eyes give her away. They flash and glitter. They have depths. They draw the male gaze into mysterious and sinister recesses. And so the male behind the gaze flies to arms. He may be taken in the end—indeed, he usually is—but he is not taken by surprise; he is not taken without a fight. A brunette has to battle for every inch of her advance. She is confronted by an endless succession of Dead Man's Hills, each equipped with telescopes, semaphores, alarm gongs, wireless. The male sees her clearly through her densest smoke-clouds.... But the blonde captures him under a flag of truce. He regards her tenderly, kindly, almost pityingly, until the moment the gyves are upon his wrists.

It is all an optical matter, a question of color. The pastel shades deceive him; the louder hues send him to his artillery. God help, I say, the red-haired girl! She goes into action with warning pennants flying. The dullest, blindest man can see her a mile away; he can catch the alarming flash of her hair long before he can see the whites, or even the terrible red-browns, of her eyes. She has a long field to cross, heavily under defensive fire, before she can get into rifle range. Her quarry has a chance to throw up redoubts, to dig himself in, to call for reinforcements, to elude her by ignominious flight. She must win, if she is to win at all, by an unparalleled combination of craft and resolution. She must be swift, daring, merciless. Even the brunette of black and penetrating eye has great advantages over her. No wonder she never lets go, once her arms are around her antagonist's neck! No wonder she is, of all women, the hardest to shake off!

All nature works in circles. Causes become effects; effects develop into causes. The red-haired girl's dire need of courage and cunning has augmented her store of those qualities by the law of natural selection. She is, by long odds, the most intelligent and bemusing of women. She shows cunning, foresight, technique, variety. She always fails a dozen times before she succeeds; but she brings to the final business the abominable expertness of a Ludendorff; she has learnt painfully by the process of trial and error. Red-haired girls are intellectual stimulants. They know all the tricks. They are so clever that they have even cast a false glamour of beauty about their worst defect—their harsh and gaudy hair. They give it euphemistic and deceitful names—auburn, bronze, Titian. They overcome by their hellish arts that deep-seated dread of red which is inborn in all of God's creatures. They charm men with what would even alarm bulls.

And the blondes, by following the law of least resistance, have gone in the other direction. The great majority of them—I speak, of course, of natural blondes; not of the immoral wenches who work their atrocities under cover of a synthetic blondeness—are quite as shallow and stupid as they look. One seldom hears a blonde say anything worth hearing; the most they commonly achieve is a specious, baby-like prattling, an infantile artlessness. But let us not blame them for nature's work. Why, after all, be intelligent? It is, at best, no more than a capacity for unhappiness. The blonde not only doesn't miss it; she is even better off without it. What imaginable intelligence could compensate her for the flat blueness of her eyes, the xanthous pallor of her hair, the doll-like pink of her cheeks? What conceivable cunning could do such execution as her stupendous appeal to masculine vanity, sentimentality, egoism?

If I were a woman I should want to be a blonde. My blondeness might be hideous, but it would get me a husband, and it would make him cherish me and love me.

XXIX. ALCOHOL

Envy, as I have said, is at the heart of the messianic delusion, the mania to convert the happy sinner into a "good" man, and so make him miserable. And at the heart of that envy is fear—the fear to sin, to take a chance, to monkey with the buzzsaw. This ineradicable fear is the outstanding mark of the fifth-rate man, at all times and everywhere. It dominates his politics, his theology, his whole thinking. He is a moral fellow because he is afraid to venture over the fence—and he hates the man who is not.

The solemn proofs, so laboriously deduced from life insurance statistics, that the man who uses alcohol, even moderately, dies slightly sooner than the teetotaler—these proofs merely show that this man is one who leads an active and vigorous life, and so faces hazards and uses himself up—in brief, one who lives at high tempo and with full joy, what Nietzsche used to call the *ja-sager*, or yes-sayer. He may, in fact, die slightly sooner than the teetotaler, but he lives infinitely longer. Moreover, his life, humanly speaking, is much more worth while, to himself and to the race. He does the hard and dangerous work of the world, he takes the chances, he makes the experiments. He is the soldier, the artist, the innovator, the lover. All the great works of man have been done by men who thus lived joyously, strenuously, and perhaps a bit dangerously. They have never been concerned about stretching life for two or three more years; they have been concerned about making life engrossing and stimulating and a high adventure while it lasts. Teetotalism is as impossible to such men as any other manifestation of cowardice, and, if it were possible, it would destroy their utility and significance just as certainly.

A man who shrinks from a cocktail before dinner on the ground that it may flabbergast his hormones, and so make him die at 69 years, ten months and five days instead of at 69 years, eleven months and seven days—such a man is as absurd a poltroon as the fellow who shrinks from kissing a woman on the ground that she may floor him with a chair leg. Each flees from a purely theoretical risk. Each is a useless encumberer of the earth, and the sooner dead the better. Each is a discredit to the human race, already discreditable enough, God knows.

Teetotalism does not make for human happiness; it makes for the dull, idiotic happiness of the barnyard. The men who do things in the world, the men worthy of admiration and imitation, are men constitutionally incapable of any such pecksniffian stupidity. Their ideal is not a safe life, but a full life; they do not try to follow the canary bird in a cage, but the eagle in the air. And in particular they do not flee from shadows and bugaboos. The alcohol myth is such a bugaboo. The sort of man it scares is the sort of man whose chief mark is that he is always scared.

No wonder the Rockefellers and their like are hot for saving the workingman from John Barleycorn! Imagine the advantage to them of operating upon a flabby horde of timorous and joyless slaves, afraid of all fun and kicking up, horribly moral, eager only to live as long as possible! What mule-like fidelity and efficiency could be got out of such a rabble! But how many Lincolns would you get out of it, and how many Jacksons, and how many Grants?

XXX. THOUGHTS ON THE VOLUPTUOUS

Why has no publisher ever thought of perfuming his novels? The final refinement of publishing, already bedizened by every other art! Barabbas turned Petronius! For instance, consider the bucolic romances of the hyphenated Mrs. Porter. They have a subtle flavor of new-mown hay and daffodils already; why not add the actual essence, or at all events some safe coal-tar substitute, and so help imagination to spread its wings? For Hall Caine, musk and synthetic bergamot. For Mrs. Glyn and her neighbors on the tiger-skin, the fragrant blood of the red, red rose. For the ruffianish pages of Jack London, the pungent, hospitable smell of a first-class bar-room—that indescribable mingling of Maryland rye, cigar smoke, stale malt liquor, radishes, potato salad and *blutwurst*. For the Dartmoor sagas of the interminable Phillpotts, the warm ammoniacal bouquet of cows, poultry and yokels. For the "Dodo" school, violets and Russian cigarettes. For the venerable Howells, lavender and mignonette. For Zola, Rochefort and wet leather. For Mrs. Humphrey Ward, lilies of the valley. For Marie Corelli, tuberoses and embalming fluid. For Chambers, sachet and lip paint. For——

But I leave you to make your own choices. All I offer is the general idea. It has been tried in the theatre. Well do I remember the first weeks of "Florodora" at the old Casino, with a mannikin in the lobby squirting "La Flor de Florodora" upon all us Florodorans.... I was put on trial for my life when I got home!

XXXI. THE HOLY ESTATE

Marriage is always a man's second choice. It is entered upon, more often than not, as the safest form of intrigue. The caitiff yields quickest; the man who loves danger and adventure holds out longest. Behind it one frequently finds, not that lofty romantic passion which poets hymn, but a mere yearning for peace and security. The abominable hazards of the high seas, the rough humors and pestilences of the forecastle—these drive the timid mariner ashore.... The authentic Cupid, at least in Christendom, was discovered by the late Albert Ludwig Siegmund Neisser in 1879.

XXXII. DICHTUNG UND WAHRHEIT

Deponent, being duly sworn, saith: My taste in poetry is for delicate and fragile things—to be honest, for artificial things. I like a frail but perfectly articulated stanza, a sonnet wrought like ivory, a song full of glowing nouns, verbs, adjectives, adverbs, pronouns, conjunctions, prepositions and participles, but without too much hard sense to it. Poetry, to me, has but two meanings. On the one hand, it is a magical escape from the sordidness of metabolism and the class war, and on the other hand it is a subtle, very difficult and hence very charming art, like writing fugues or mixing mayonnaise. I do not go to poets to be taught anything, or to be heated up to indignation, or to have my conscience blasted out of its torpor, but to be soothed and caressed, to be lulled with sweet sounds, to be wooed into forgetfulness, to be tickled under the metaphysical chin. My favorite poem is Lizette Woodworth Reese's "Tears," which, as a statement of fact, seems to me to be as idiotic as the Book of Revelation. The poetry I regard least is such stuff as that of Robert Browning and Matthew Arnold, which argues and illuminates. I dislike poetry of intellectual content as much as I dislike women of intellectual content—and for the same reason.

XXXIII. WILD SHOTS

If I had the time, and there were no sweeter follies offering, I should like to write an essay on the books that have quite failed of achieving their original purposes, and are yet of respectable use and potency for other purposes. For example, the Book of Revelation. The obvious aim of the learned author of this work was to bring the early Christians into accord by telling them authoritatively what to expect and hope for; its actual effect during eighteen hundred years has been to split them into a multitude of camps, and so set them to denouncing, damning, jailing and murdering one another. Again, consider the autobiography of Benvenuto Cellini. Ben wrote it to prove that he was an honest man, a mirror of all the virtues, an injured innocent; the world, reading it, hails him respectfully as the noblest, the boldest, the gaudiest liar that ever lived. Again, turn to "Gulliver's Travels." The thing was planned by its rev. author as a devastating satire, a terrible piece of cynicism; it survives as a story-book for sucklings. Yet again, there is "Hamlet." Shakespeare wrote it frankly to make money for a theatrical manager; it has lost money for theatrical managers ever since. Yet again, there is Caesar's "De Bello Gallico." Julius composed it to thrill and arouse the Romans; its sole use today is to stupefy and sicken schoolboys. Finally, there is the celebrated book of General F. von Bernhardi. He wrote it to inflame Germany; its effect was to inflame England....

The list might be lengthened almost *ad infinitum.* When a man writes a book he fires a machine gun into a wood. The game he brings down often astonishes him, and sometimes horrifies him. Consider the case of Ibsen.... After my book on Nietzsche I was actually invited to lecture at Princeton.

XXXIV. BEETHOVEN

Romain Rolland's "Beethoven, " one of the cornerstones of his celebrity as a critic, is based upon a thesis that is of almost inconceivable inaccuracy, to wit, the thesis that old Ludwig was an apostle of joy, and that his music reveals his determination to experience and utter it in spite of all the slings and arrows of outrageous fortune. Nothing could be more absurd. Joy, in truth, was precisely the emotion that Beethoven could never conjure up; it simply was not in him. Turn to the *scherzo* of any of his trios, quartets, sonatas or symphonies. A sardonic waggishness is there, and sometimes even a wistful sort of merriment, but joy in the real sense—a kicking up of legs, a light-heartedness, a complete freedom from care—is not to be found. It is in Haydn, it is in Schubert and it is often in Mozart, but it is no more in Beethoven than it is in Tschaikovsky. Even the hymn to joy at the end of the Ninth symphony narrowly escapes being a gruesome parody on the thing itself; a conscious effort is in every note of it; it is almost as lacking in spontaneity as (if it were imaginable at all) a piece of *vers libre* by Augustus Montague Toplady.

Nay; Ludwig was no leaping buck. Nor was it his deafness, nor poverty, nor the crimes of his rascally nephew that pumped joy out of him. The truth is that he lacked it from birth; he was born a Puritan—and though a Puritan may also become a great man (as witness Herbert Spencer and Beelzebub), he can never throw off being a Puritan. Beethoven stemmed from the Low Countries, and the Low Countries, in those days, were full of Puritan refugees; the very name, in its first incarnation, may have been Barebones. If you want to comprehend the authentic man, don't linger over Rolland's fancies but go to his own philosophizings, as garnered in "Beethoven, the Man and the Artist, " by Friedrich Kerst, Englished by Krehbiel. Here you will find a collection of moral banalities that would have delighted Jonathan Edwards—a collection that might well be emblazoned on gilt cards and hung in Sunday schools. He begins with a naif anthropomorphism that is now almost perished from the world; he ends with a solemn repudiation of adultery.... But a great man, my masters, a great man! We have enough biographies of him, and talmuds upon his works. Who will do a full-length psychological study of him?

XXXV. THE TONE ART

The notion that the aim of art is to fix the shifting aspects of nature, that all art is primarily representative—this notion is as unsound as the theory that Friday is an unlucky day, and is dying as hard. One even finds some trace of it in Anatole France, surely a man who should know better. The true function of art is to criticise, embellish and edit nature—particularly to edit it, and so make it coherent and lovely. The artist is a sort of impassioned proof-reader, blue-pencilling the *lapsus calami* of God. The sounds in a Beethoven symphony, even the Pastoral, are infinitely more orderly, varied and beautiful than those of the woods. The worst flute is never as bad as the worst soprano. The best violoncello is immeasurably better than the best tenor.

All first-rate music suffers by the fact that it has to be performed by human beings—that is, that nature must be permitted to corrupt it. The performance one hears in a concert hall or opera house is no more than a baroque parody upon the thing the composer imagined. In an orchestra of eighty men there is inevitably at least one man with a sore thumb, or bad kidneys, or a brutal wife, or *katzenjammer*—and one is enough. Some day the natural clumsiness and imperfection of fingers, lips and larynxes will be overcome by mechanical devices, and we shall have Beethoven and Mozart and Schubert in such wonderful and perfect beauty that it will be almost unbearable. If half as much ingenuity had been lavished upon music machines as has been lavished upon the telephone and the steam engine, we would have had mechanical orchestras long ago. Mechanical pianos are already here. Piano-players, bound to put some value on the tortures of Czerny, affect to laugh at all such contrivances, but that is no more than a pale phosphorescence of an outraged *wille zur macht*. Setting aside half a dozen—perhaps a dozen—great masters of a moribund craft, who will say that the average mechanical piano is not as competent as the average pianist?

When the human performer of music goes the way of the galley-slave, the charm of personality, of course, will be pumped out of the performance of music. But the charm of personality does not help music; it hinders it. It is not a reinforcement to music; it is a rival. When a beautiful singer comes upon the stage, two shows, as it were, go on at once: first the music show, and then the arms, shoulders, neck, nose, ankles, eyes, hips, calves and ruby lips—in brief, the sex-show. The second of these shows, to the majority of persons present, is more interesting than the first—to the men because of the sex interest, and to the women because of the professional or technical interest—and so music is forced into the background. What it becomes, indeed, is no more than a half-heard accompaniment to an imagined anecdote, just as color, line and mass become mere accomplishments to an anecdote in a picture by an English academician, or by a sentimental German of the Boecklin school.

The purified and dephlogisticated music of the future, to be sure, will never appeal to the mob, which will keep on demanding its chance to gloat over gaudy, voluptuous women, and fat, scandalous tenors. The mob, even disregarding its insatiable appetite for the improper, is a natural hero worshiper. It loves, not the beautiful, but the strange, the unprecedented, the astounding; it suffers from an incurable *héliogabalisme*. A soprano who can gargle her way up to G sharp in altissimo interests it almost as much as a contralto who has slept publicly with a grand duke. If it cannot get the tenor who receives $3,000 a night, it will take the tenor who fought the manager with bung-starters last Tuesday. But this is merely saying that the tastes and desires of the mob have nothing to do with music as an art. For its ears, as for its eyes, it demands anecdotes—on the one hand the Suicide symphony, "The Forge in the Forest, " and the general run of Italian opera, and on the other hand such things as "The Angelus, " "Playing Grandpa" and the so-called "Mona Lisa." It cannot imagine art as devoid of moral content, as beauty pure and simple. It always demands something to edify it, or, failing that, to shock it.

These concepts, of the edifying and the shocking, are closer together in the psyche than most persons imagine. The one, in fact, depends upon the other: without some definite notion of the improving it is almost impossible to conjure up an active notion of the improper. All salacious art is addressed, not to the damned, but to the consciously saved; it is Sunday-school superintendents, not bartenders, who chiefly patronize peep-shows, and know the dirty books, and have a high artistic admiration for sopranos of superior gluteal development. The man who has risen above the petty ethical superstitions of Christendom gets little pleasure out of impropriety, for very few ordinary phenomena seem to him to be improper. Thus a Frenchman, viewing the undraped statues which bedizen his native galleries of art, either enjoys them in a purely aesthetic fashion—which is seldom possible save when he is in liquor—or confesses frankly that he doesn't like them at all; whereas the visiting Americano is so powerfully shocked and fascinated by them that one finds him, the same evening, in places where no respectable man ought to go. All art, to this fellow, must have a certain bawdiness, or he cannot abide it. His favorite soprano, in the opera house, is not the fat and middle-aged lady who can actually sing, but the girl with the bare back and translucent drawers. Condescending to the concert hall, he is bored by the posse of enemy aliens in funereal black, and so demands a vocal soloist—that is, a gaudy creature of such advanced corsetting that she can make him forget Bach for a while, and turn his thoughts pleasantly to amorous intrigue.

In all this, of course, there is nothing new. Other and better men have noted the damage that the personal equation does to music, and some of them have even sought ways out. For example, Richard Strauss. His so-called ballet, "Josefs Legend, " produced in Paris just before the war, is an attempt to write an opera without singers. All of the music is in the orchestra; the folks on the stage merely go through a pointless pantomime; their main function is to entertain the eye with shifting colors. Thus, the romantic sentiments of Joseph are announced, not by some eye-rolling tenor, but by the first, second, third, fourth, fifth, sixth, seventh and eighth violins (it is a Strauss score!), with the incidental aid of the wood-wind, the brass, the percussion and the rest of the strings. And the heroine's reply is made, not by a soprano with a cold, but by an honest man playing a flute. The next step will be the substitution of marionettes for actors. The removal of the orchestra to a sort of trench, out of sight of the audience, is already an accomplished fact at Munich. The end, perhaps, will be music purged of its current ptomaines. In brief, music.

XXXVI. ZOOS

I often wonder how much sound and nourishing food is fed to the animals in the zoological gardens of America every week, and try to figure out what the public gets in return for the cost thereof. The annual bill must surely run into millions; one is constantly hearing how much beef a lion downs at a meal, and how many tons of hay an elephant dispatches in a month. And to what end? To the end, principally, that a horde of superintendents and keepers may be kept in easy jobs. To the end, secondarily, that the least intelligent minority of the population may have an idiotic show to gape at on Sunday afternoons, and that the young of the species may be instructed in the methods of amour prevailing among chimpanzees and become privy to the technic employed by jaguars, hyenas and polar bears in ridding themselves of lice.

So far as I can make out, after laborious visits to all the chief zoos of the nation, no other imaginable purpose is served by their existence. One hears constantly, true enough (mainly from the gentlemen they support) that they are educational. But how? Just what sort of instruction do they radiate, and what is its value? I have never been able to find out. The sober truth is that they are no more educational than so many firemen's parades or displays of sky-rockets, and that all they actually offer to the public in return for the taxes wasted upon them is a form of idle and witless amusement, compared to which a visit to a penitentiary, or even to Congress or a state legislature in session, is informing, stimulating and ennobling.

Education your grandmother! Show me a schoolboy who has ever learned anything valuable or important by watching a mangy old lion snoring away in its cage or a family of monkeys fighting for peanuts. To get any useful instruction out of such a spectacle is palpably impossible; not even a college professor is improved by it. The most it can imaginably impart is that the stripes of a certain sort of tiger run one way and the stripes of another sort some other way, that hyenas and polecats smell worse than Greek 'bus boys, that the Latin name of the raccoon (who was unheard of by the Romans) is *Procyon lotor*. For the dissemination of such banal knowledge, absurdly emitted and defectively taken in, the taxpayers of the United States are mulcted in hundreds of thousands of dollars a year. As well make them pay for teaching policemen the theory of least squares, or for instructing roosters in the laying of eggs.

But zoos, it is argued, are of scientific value. They enable learned men to study this or that. Again the facts blast the theory. No scientific discovery of any value whatsoever, even to the animals themselves, has ever come out of a zoo. The zoo scientist is the old woman of zoology, and his alleged wisdom is usually exhibited, not in the groves of actual learning, but in the yellow journals. He is to biology what the late Camille Flammarion was to astronomy, which is to say, its court jester and reductio ad absurdum. When he leaps into public notice with some new pearl of knowledge, it commonly turns out to be no more than the news that Marie Bashkirtseff, the Russian lady walrus, has had her teeth plugged with zinc and is expecting twins. Or that Pishposh, the man-eating alligator, is down with locomotor ataxia. Or that Damon, the grizzly, has just finished his brother Pythias in the tenth round, chewing off his tail, nose and remaining ear.

Science, of course, has its uses for the lower animals. A diligent study of their livers and lights helps to an understanding of the anatomy and physiology, and particularly of the pathology, of man. They are necessary aids in devising and manufacturing many remedial agents, and in testing the virtues of those already devised; out of the mute agonies of a rabbit or a calf may come relief for a baby with diphtheria, or means for an archdeacon to escape the consequences of his youthful follies. Moreover, something valuable is to be got out of a mere study of their habits, instincts and ways of mind—knowledge that, by analogy, may illuminate the parallel doings of the *genus homo*, and so enable us to comprehend the primitive mental processes of Congressmen, morons and the rev. clergy.

But it must be obvious that none of these studies can be made in a zoo. The zoo animals, to begin with, provide no material for the biologist; he can find out no more about their insides than what he discerns from a safe distance and through the bars. He is not allowed to try his germs and specifics upon them; he is not allowed to vivisect them. If he would find out what goes on in the animal body under this condition or that, he must turn from the inhabitants of the zoo to the customary guinea pigs and street dogs, and buy or steal them for himself. Nor does he get any chance for profitable inquiry when zoo animals die (usually of lack of exercise or ignorant doctoring), for their carcasses are not handed to him for autopsy, but at once stuffed with gypsum and excelsior and placed in some museum.

Least of all do zoos produce any new knowledge about animal behavior. Such knowledge must be got, not from animals penned up and tortured, but from animals in a state of nature. A college professor studying the habits of the giraffe, for example, and confining his observations to specimens in zoos, would inevitably come to the conclusion that the giraffe is a sedentary and melancholy beast, standing immovable for hours at a time and employing an Italian to feed him hay and cabbages. As well proceed to a study of the psychology of a juris-consult by first immersing him in Sing Sing, or of a juggler by first cutting off his hands. Knowledge so gained is inaccurate and imbecile knowledge. Not even a college professor, if sober, would give it any faith and credit.

There remains, then, the only true utility of a zoo: it is a childish and pointless show for the unintelligent, in brief, for children, nursemaids, visiting yokels and the generality of the defective. Should the taxpayers be forced to sweat millions for such a purpose? I think not. The sort of man who likes to spend his time watching a cage of monkeys chase one another, or a lion gnaw its tail, or a lizard catch flies, is precisely the sort of man whose mental weakness should be combatted at the public expense, and not fostered. He is a public liability and a public menace, and society should seek to improve him. Instead of that, we spend a lot of money to feed his degrading appetite and further paralyze his mind. It is precisely as if the community provided free champagne for dipsomaniacs, or hired lecturers to convert the army to the doctrines of the Bolsheviki.

Of the abominable cruelties practised in zoos it is unnecessary to make mention. Even assuming that all the keepers are men of delicate natures and ardent zoophiles (which is about as safe as assuming that the keepers of a prison are all sentimentalists, and weep for the sorrows of their charges), it must be plain that the work they do involves an endless war upon the nativeinstincts of the animals, and that they must thus inflict the most abominable tortures every day. What could be a sadder sight than a tiger in a cage, save it be a forest monkey climbing dispairingly up a barked stump, or an eagle chained to its roost? How can man be benefitted and made better by robbing the seal of its arctic ice, the hippopotamus of its soft wallow, the buffalo of its open range, the lion of its kingship, the birds of their air?

I am no sentimentalist, God knows. I am in favor of vivisection unrestrained, so long as the vivisectionist knows what he is about. I advocate clubbing a dog that barks unnecessarily, which all dogs do. I enjoy hangings, particularly of converts to the evangelical faiths. The crunch of a cockroach is music to my ears. But when the day comes to turn the prisoners of the zoo out of their cages, if it is only to lead them to the swifter, kinder knife of the *schochet*, I shall be present and rejoicing, and if any one present thinks to suggest that it would be a good plan to celebrate the day by shooting the whole zoo faculty, I shall have a revolver in my pocket and a sound eye in my head.

XXXVII. ON HEARING MOZART

The only permanent values in the world are truth and beauty, and of these it is probable that truth is lasting only in so far as it is a function and manifestation of beauty—a projection of feeling in terms of idea. The world is a charnel house of dead religions. Where are all the faiths of the middle ages, so complex and yet so precise? But all that was essential in the beauty of the middle ages still lives....

This is the heritage of man, but not of men. The great majority of men are not even aware of it. Their participation in the progress of the world, and even in the history of the world, is infinitely remote and trivial. They live and die, at bottom, as animals live and die. The human race, as a race, is scarcely cognizant of their existence; they haven't even definite number, but stand grouped together as x, the quantity unknown ... and not worth knowing.

XXXVIII. THE ROAD TO DOUBT

The first effect of what used to be called natural philosophy is to fill its devotee with wonder at the marvels of God. This explains why the pursuit of science, so long as it remains superficial, is not incompatible with the most naif sort of religious faith. But the moment the student of the sciences passes this stage of childlike amazement and begins to investigate the inner workings of natural phenomena, he begins to see how ineptly many of them are managed, and so he tends to pass from awe of the Creator to criticism of the Creator, and once he has crossed that bridge he has ceased to be a believer. One finds plenty of neighborhood physicians, amateur botanists, high-school physics teachers and other such quasi-scientists in the pews on Sunday, but one never sees a Huxley there, or a Darwin, or an Ehrlich.

XXXIX. A NEW USE FOR CHURCHES

The argument by design, it may be granted, establishes a reasonable ground for accepting the existence of God. It makes belief, at all events, quite as intelligible as unbelief. But when the theologians take their step from the existence of God to the goodness of God they tread upon much less firm earth. How can one see any proof of that goodness in the senseless and intolerable sufferings of man—his helplessness, the brief and troubled span of his life, the inexplicable disproportion between his deserts and his rewards, the tragedy of his soaring aspiration, the worse tragedy of his dumb questioning? Granting the existence of God, a house dedicated to Him naturally follows. He is all-important; it is fit that man should take some notice of Him. But why praise and flatter Him for His unspeakable cruelties? Why forget so supinely His failures to remedy the easily remediable? Why, indeed, devote the churches exclusively to worship? Why not give them over, now and then, to justifiable indignation meetings?

Perhaps men will incline to this idea later on. It is not inconceivable, indeed, that religion will one day cease to be a poltroonish acquiescence and become a vigorous and insistent criticism. If God can hear a petition, what ground is there for holding that He would not hear a complaint? It might, indeed, please Him to find His creatures grown so self-reliant and reflective. More, it might even help Him to get through His infinitely complex and difficult work. Theology has already moved toward such notions. It has abandoned the primitive doctrine of God's arbitrariness and indifference, and substituted the doctrine that He is willing, and even eager, to hear the desires of His creatures—i. e., their private notions, born of experience, as to what would be best for them. Why assume that those notions would be any the less worth hearing and heeding if they were cast in the form of criticism, and even of denunciation? Why hold that the God who can understand and forgive even treason could not understand and forgive remonstrance?

XL. THE ROOT OF RELIGION

The idea of literal truth crept into religion relatively late: it is the invention of lawyers, priests and cheese-mongers. The idea of mystery long preceded it, and at the heart of that idea of mystery was an idea of beauty—that is, an idea that this or that view of the celestial and infernal process presented a satisfying picture of form, rhythm and organization. Once this view was adopted as satisfying, its professional interpreters and their dupes sought to reinforce it by declaring it true. The same flow of reasoning is familiar on lower planes. The average man does not get pleasure out of an idea because he thinks it is true; he thinks it is true because he gets pleasure out of it.

XLI. FREE WILL

Free will, it appears, is still a Christian dogma. Without it the cruelties of God would strain faith to the breaking-point. But outside the fold it is gradually falling into decay. Such men of science as George W. Crile and Jacques Loeb have dealt it staggering blows, and among laymen of inquiring mind it seems to be giving way to an apologetic sort of determinism—a determinism, one may say, tempered by defective observation. The late Mark Twain, in his secret heart, was such a determinist. In his "What Is Man?" you will find him at his farewells to libertarianism. The vast majority of our acts, he argues, are determined, but there remains a residuum of free choices. Here we stand free of compulsion and face a pair or more of alternatives, and are free to go this way or that.

A pillow for free will to fall upon—but one loaded with disconcerting brickbats. Where the occupants of this last trench of libertarianism err is in their assumption that the pulls of their antagonistic impulses are exactly equal—that the individual is absolutely free to choose which one he will yield to. Such freedom, in practise, is never encountered. When an individual confronts alternatives, it is not alone his volition that chooses between them, but also his environment, his inherited prejudices, his race, his color, his condition of servitude. I may kiss a girl or I may not kiss her, but surely it would be absurd to say that I am, in any true sense, a free agent in the matter. The world has even put my helplessness into a proverb. It says that my decision and act depend upon the time, the place—and even to some extent, upon the girl.

Examples might be multiplied *ad infinitum*. I can scarcely remember performing a wholly voluntary act. My whole life, as I look back upon it, seems to be a long series of inexplicable accidents, not only quite unavoidable, but even quite unintelligible. Its history is the history of the reactions of my personality to my environment, of my behavior before external stimuli. I have been no more responsible for that personality than I have been for that environment. To say that I can change the former by a voluntary effort is as ridiculous as to say that I can modify the curvature of the lenses of my eyes. I know, because I have often tried to change it, and always failed. Nevertheless, it has changed. I am not the same man I was in the last century. But the gratifying improvements so plainly visible are surely not to be credited to me. All of them came from without—or from unplumbable and uncontrollable depths within.

The more the matter is examined the more the residuum of free will shrinks and shrinks, until in the end it is almost impossible to find it. A great many men, of course, looking at themselves, see it as something very large; they slap their chests and call themselves free agents, and demand that God reward them for their virtue. But these fellows are simply idiotic egoists, devoid of a critical sense. They mistake the acts of God for their own acts. Of such sort are the coxcombs who boast about wooing and winning their wives. They are brothers to the fox who boasted that he had made the hounds run....

The throwing overboard of free will is commonly denounced on the ground that it subverts morality and makes of religion a mocking. Such pious objections, of course, are foreign to logic, but nevertheless it may be well to give a glance to this one. It is based upon the fallacious hypothesis that the determinist escapes, or hopes to escape, the consequences of his acts. Nothing could be more untrue. Consequences follow acts just as relentlessly if the latter be involuntary as if they be voluntary. If I rob a bank of my free choice or in response to some unfathomable inner necessity, it is all one; I will go to the same jail. Conscripts in war are killed just as often as volunteers. Men who are tracked down and shanghaied by their wives have just as hard a time of it as men who walk fatuously into the trap by formally proposing.

Even on the ghostly side, determinism does not do much damage to theology. It is no harder to believe that a man will be damned for his involuntary acts than it is to believe that he will be damned for his voluntary acts, for even the supposition that he is wholly free does not dispose of the massive fact that God made him as he is, and that God could have made him a saint if He had so desired. To deny this is to flout omnipotence—a crime at which, as I have often said, I balk. But here I begin to fear that I wade too far into the hot waters of the sacred sciences, and that I had better retire before I lose my hide. This prudent retirement is purely deterministic. I do not ascribe it to my own sagacity; I ascribe it wholly to that singular kindness which fate always shows me. If I were free I'd probably keep on, and then regret it afterward.

XLII. QUID EST VERITAS?

All great religions, in order to escape absurdity, have to admit a dilution of agnosticism. It is only the savage, whether of the African bush or the American gospel tent, who pretends to know the will and intent of God exactly and completely. "For who hath known the mind of the Lord?" asked Paul of the Romans. "How unsearchable are his judgments, and his ways past finding out!" "It is the glory of God, " said Solomon, "to conceal a thing." "Clouds and darkness, " said David, "are around him." "No man, " said the Preacher, "can find out the work of God." ... The difference between religions is a difference in their relative content of agnosticism. The most satisfying and ecstatic faith is almost purely agnostic. It trusts absolutely without professing to know at all.

XLIII. THE DOUBTER'S REWARD

Despite the common delusion to the contrary the philosophy of doubt is far more comforting than that of hope. The doubter escapes the worst penalty of the man of hope; he is never disappointed, and hence never indignant. The inexplicable and irremediable may interest him, but they do not enrage him, or, I may add, fool him. This immunity is worth all the dubious assurances ever foisted upon man. It is pragmatically impregnable.... Moreover, it makes for tolerance and sympathy. The doubter does not hate his opponents; he sympathizes with them. In the end, he may even come to sympathize with God.... The old idea of fatherhood here submerges in a new idea of brotherhood. God, too, is beset by limitations, difficulties, broken hopes. Is it disconcerting to think of Him thus? Well, is it any the less disconcerting to think of Him as able to ease and answer, and yet failing?...

But he that doubteth—*damnatus est*. At once the penalty of doubt—and its proof, excuse and genesis.

XLIV. BEFORE THE ALTAR

A salient objection to the prevailing religious ceremonial lies in the attitudes of abasement that it enforces upon the faithful. A man would be thought a slimy and knavish fellow if he approached any human judge or potentate in the manner provided for approaching the Lord God. It is an etiquette that involves loss of self-respect, and hence it cannot be pleasing to its object, for one cannot think of the Lord God as sacrificing decent feelings to mere vanity. This notion of abasement, like most of the other ideas that are general in the world, is obviously the invention of small and ignoble men. It is the pollution of theology by the *sklavmoral*.

XLV. THE MASK

Ritual is to religion what the music of an opera is to the libretto: ostensibly a means of interpretation, but actually a means of concealment. The Presbyterians made the mistake of keeping the doctrine of infant damnation in plain words. As enlightenment grew in the world, intelligence and prudery revolted against it, and so it had to be abandoned. Had it been set to music it would have survived—uncomprehended, unsuspected and unchallenged.

XLVI. PIA VENEZIANI, POI CRISTIANI

I have spoken of the possibility that God, too, may suffer from a finite intelligence, and so know the bitter sting of disappointment and defeat. Here I yielded something to politeness; the thing is not only possible, but obvious. Like man, God is deceived by appearances and probabilities; He makes calculations that do not work out; He falls into specious assumptions. For example, He assumed that Adam and Eve would obey the law in the Garden. Again, He assumed that the appalling lesson of the Flood would make men better. Yet again, He assumed that men would always put religion in first place among their concerns—that it would be eternally possible to reach and influence them through it. This last assumption was the most erroneous of them all. The truth is that the generality of men have long since ceased to take religion seriously. When we encounter one who still does so, he seems eccentric, almost feeble-minded—or, more commonly, a rogue who has been deluded by his own hypocrisy. Even men who are professionally religious, and who thus have far more incentive to stick to religion than the rest of us, nearly always throw it overboard at the first serious temptation. During the past four years, for example, Christianity has been in combat with patriotism all over Christendom. Which has prevailed? How many gentlemen of God, having to choose between Christ and Patrie, have actually chosen Christ?

XLVII. OFF AGAIN, ON AGAIN

The ostensible object of the Reformation, which lately reached its fourth centenary, was to purge the Church of imbecilities. That object was accomplished; the Church shook them off. But imbecilities make an irresistible appeal to man; he inevitably tries to preserve them by cloaking them with religious sanctions. The result is Protestantism.

XLVIII. THEOLOGY

The notion that theology is a dull subject is one of the strangest delusions of a stupid and uncritical age. The truth is that some of the most engrossing books ever written in the world are full of it. For example, the Gospel according to St. Luke. For example, Nietzsche's "Der Antichrist." For example, Mark Twain's "What Is Man?", St. Augustine's Confessions, Haeckel's "The Riddle of the Universe, " and Huxley's Essays. How, indeed, could a thing be dull that has sent hundreds of thousands of men—the very best and the very worst of the race—to the gallows and the stake, and made and broken dynasties, and inspired the greatest of human hopes and enterprises, and embroiled whole continents in war? No, theology is not a soporific. The reason it so often seems so is that its public exposition has chiefly fallen, in these later days, into the hands of a sect of intellectual castrati, who begin by mistaking it for a sub-department of etiquette, and then proceed to anoint it with butter, rose water and talcum powder. Whenever a first-rate intellect tackles it, as in the case of Huxley, or in that of Leo XIII., it at once takes on all the sinister fascination it had in Luther's day.

XLIX. EXEMPLI GRATIA

Do I let the poor suffer, and consign them, as old Friedrich used to say, to statistics and the devil? Well, so does God.

THE END